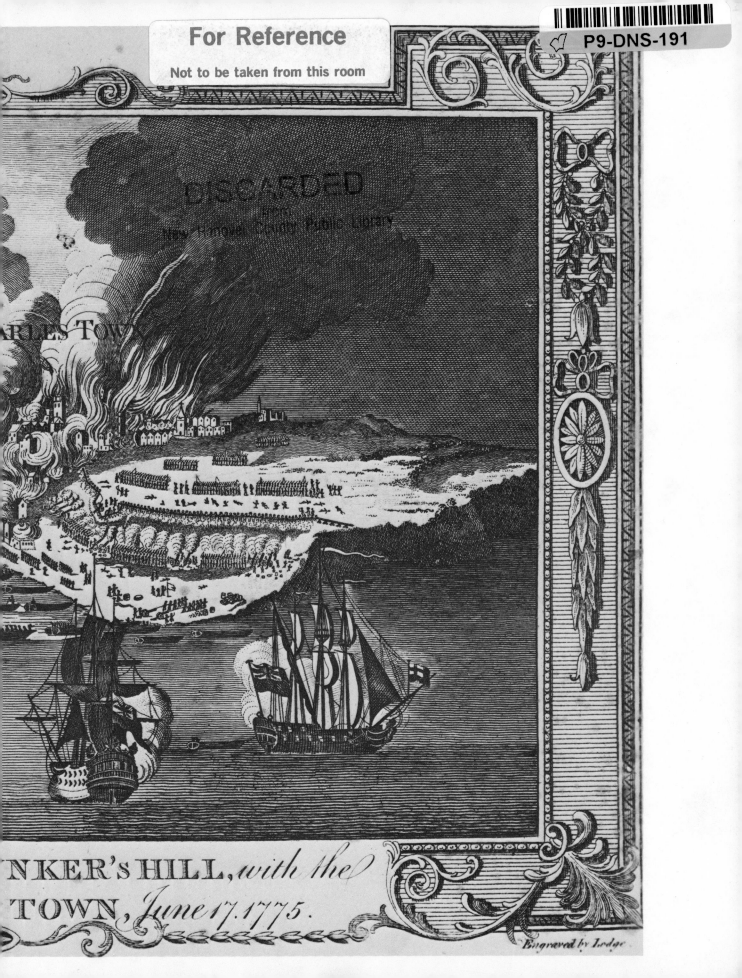

CHARLES TOWN

NKER'S HILL, *with the*
TOWN, *June 17. 1775.*

Engraved by Lodge

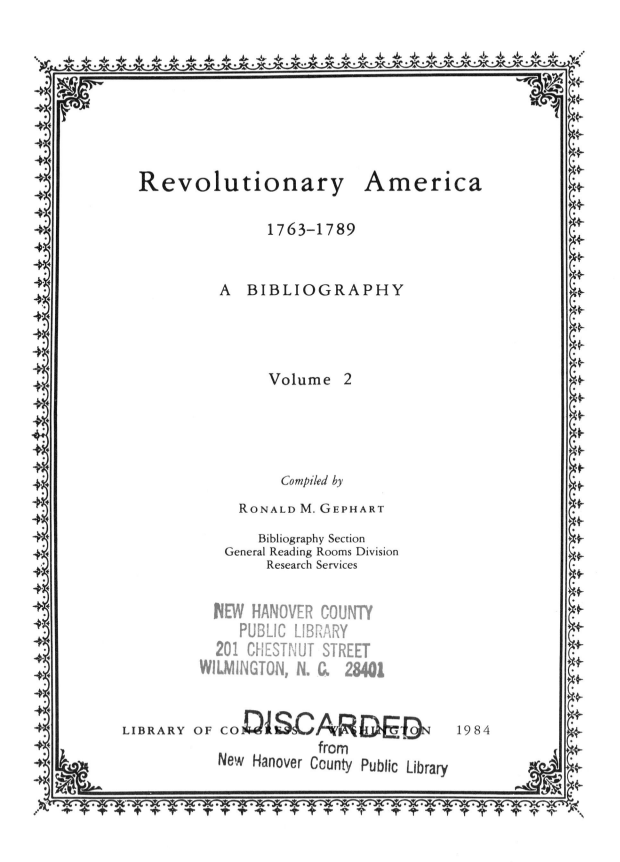

Revolutionary America

1763–1789

A BIBLIOGRAPHY

Volume 2

Compiled by

RONALD M. GEPHART

Bibliography Section
General Reading Rooms Division
Research Services

LIBRARY OF CONGRESS, WASHINGTON   1984

Endpapers:

Front: "View of the Attack on Bunker's Hill, with the Burning of Charles Town, June 17, 1775." Drawn by Mr. Millar. Engraved by [John?] Lodge. From Barnard, *History of England* (London, 1783), p. 687.

Back: "Reddition de L'Armee du Lord Cornwallis." Dessine par le Berbier Peintre du Roi. Grave par Godefroy de l'Academie Imple. et Royale de Vienne &c. a Paris, chez Mr. Godefroy, rue de Francs bourgeois Porte St. Michel; et chez Mr. Ponce, Graveur de Mgr. le Comte. d'Artois, rue Hiacinte. A.P.D.R. [1784?]. From Ponce, *Recueil d'estampes representant . . .* (Paris, 1784?), plate 10.

Library of Congress Cataloging in Publication Data
Gephart, Ronald M.
    Revolutionary America, 1763–1789.

    Includes index.
    Supt. of Docs. no.: 1.12/2:R32/4/763–789
    1. United States—History—Revolution, 1775–1783—
Bibliography—Catalogs.   2. United States—History—
Confederation, 1783–1789—Bibliography—Catalogs.
3. United States—History—Revolution, 1775–1783—Sources
—Bibliography—Catalogs.   4. United States—History—
Confederation, 1783–1789—Sources—Bibliography—Catalogs.
5. United States. Library of Congress—Catalogs.
I. United States. Library of Congress.   II. Title.
Z1238.G43   [E208]   016.9733   80-606802
Volume 1: ISBN 0-8444-0359-8   AACR1
Volume 2: ISBN 0-8444-0379-2

For sale by the Superintendent of Documents, U.S. Government Printing Office
Washington, D.C. 20402

CONTENTS

MAPS, ATLASES, AND GEOGRAPHIC AIDS

CHAPTER TWO: GENERAL STUDIES; REGIONAL, STATE AND LOCAL

HISTORIOGRAPHY

GENERAL INTERPRETATIONS AND HISTORIES

CHAPTER THREE: THE BRITISH EMPIRE AND THE AMERICAN REVOLUTION

Great Britain

CHAPTER FOUR: THE COLONIES ON THE EVE OF INDEPENDENCE: FROM RESISTANCE TO REBELLION

CHAPTER FIVE: THE WEST DURING THE REVOLUTIONARY ERA

CHAPTER SIX: THE WAR FOR INDEPENDENCE, 1775–1783

Entry

CHAPTER SEVEN: THE LOYALISTS IN AMERICA AND IN EXILE

CHAPTER ELEVEN: ECONOMIC, SOCIAL, AND INTELLECTUAL LIFE IN REVOLUTIONARY AMERICA

PREFACE

Since its establishment in 1800 the Library of Congress has become, through purchase, copyright deposit, exchanges, the acquisition of special collections, and the donations of benefactors, the largest repository of Americana in the world. As the Bicentennial of American independence approached, the Library began to plan a publication program that would reveal the breadth of its resources for the study of one of the major events in the American experience. When Congress approved the Library's general plan in 1968, several historians, all specialists in early American history, were added to the staff. Their task was to prepare guides to original sources, bibliographies, facsimile reproductions of historic prints and documents, exhibits, and other special programs. Since then, more than two dozen volumes have been published, among them *Manuscript Sources in the Library of Congress for Research on the American Revolution* (1975), *The American Revolution in Drawings and Prints; a Checklist of 1765–1790 Graphics in the Library of Congress* (1975), and *Maps and Charts of North America and the West Indies, 1750–1789; a Guide to the Collections in the Library of Congress* (1981).

Revolutionary America, 1763–1789; a Bibliography is a guide to the more important printed primary and secondary works in the Library's collections. Compiled over a ten-year period, the bibliography represents a comprehensive review of monographs, doctoral dissertations, collected works, festschriften, pamphlets, and serial publications in both general and special collections. It is intended to serve a wide audience, whether professional historians seeking new fields of inquiry, students examining various aspects of the Revolution for the first time, or librarians, journalists, and other interested readers searching for specific information on a limited topic. Because the Revolution has been variously treated as the culmination of the colonial experience, as the beginning of American national life, and as an event to be compared instructively with other revolutionary movements of the modern era, the selection policy was designed to encompass as many interests, needs, and approaches as space permitted. To introduce the user to the preserva-

tion and publication programs that have served as the bedrock of twentieth-century historiography, the compiler has included, at the end of volume 2, an essay entitled "The Preservation and Publication of Documentary Sources on the Revolution," which contains more than four hundred cross references to the major series of published primary sources listed in the bibliography. When compilation began, it was decided to include only materials published through December 1972. The establishment of a firm cutoff date ensured that the search and annotation procedures would not be interrupted by the continued need to update the files and that the user would have a well-defined starting point for further bibliographic investigation. Moreover, it was felt that the literature produced during the Bicentennial era would be voluminous and discrete enough to merit a separate publication.

Search and Selection Procedures. To be certain that *Revolutionary America* would reflect accurately the Library's holdings, a three-year search of LC catalogs and bibliographies was undertaken, and two thirty-six-thousand-card working files (main entry and subject) were assembled. The compiler and staff members of the Bibliography Section reviewed thousands of trays of cards under appropriate subject headings in the Main Catalog, by classification categories from A to Z in the LC Shelflist, and through a variety of approaches in the special collection catalogs of the Law Library, Local History and Genealogy Reading Room, Geography and Map Division, Rare Book Collection, and Microform Reading Room. Library of Congress card stock was ordered for all potential entries selected. For doctoral dissertations, the staff surveyed and typed nearly two thousand cards for likely entries in Warren F. Kuehl's *Dissertations in History* (entry 520) and *Dissertation Abstracts International* and its antecedents (entry 519). The assembled files were then compared with listings in more than two hundred published bibliographies in the Library's collections, such as the *Writings on American History* (entry 63), that touch on some phase of the American Revolution. Nearly fifteen thousand cards for additional monographs, pamphlets, and especially periodical articles were typed during the process. After the amassed subject file was arranged by call number, a four-year shelf search was undertaken to discover new material not identified in the review of catalogs and bibliographies, to verify the accuracy of the available bibliographic information, and to identify those entries that required annotation. During the process, 910 serials were sampled or searched volume by volume for relevant citations. Final selections were made from well over one hundred thousand separate items reviewed by the compiler and staff. Criteria such as research value, uniqueness of coverage, and historiographical significance were employed in making the selections. As compiled, *Revolutionary America* lists more than twenty thousand titles in 14,810 numbered entries.

Before the search and selection procedure began, certain exceptions were made in the coverage of material. Most of these relate to eighteenth-century publications. Given the large number of contemporary pamphlets, tracts, and broadsides in the Rare Book and Special Collections Division (over seven thousand for the period 1763–89) and the availability of comprehensive guides to eighteenth-century imprints (see entries 358 and 365), only about five hundred pamphlets of advocacy that were important in shaping political and constitutional thought during the Revolution were included. Second, because most early state records have been microfilmed (see entry 616), the bound journals, minutes, and proceedings or the session laws of the colonial and state assemblies, councils, and senates in the collections of the Rare Book and Special Collections Division and the Law Library were also excluded. The same was true of the eighteenth-century newspapers in the Serial and Government Publications Division and the rare book collection. A checklist of eighteenth-century newspapers at the Library of Congress (entry 470) was already available, and most early American newspapers have been widely distributed on either microfilm or microcard (see entry 471).

ARRANGEMENT OF ENTRIES. The arrangement of entries into twelve topico-chronological chapters is relatively straightforward. As the table of contents indicates, a listing of bibliographies, guides to eighteenth-century imprints and manuscript collections, and maps, atlases, and geographical aids serves as a starting point for inquirers. All general studies of the Revolutionary period, whether historiographical or

narrative, are grouped together in chapter 2. Since the writing of purely local history has passed out of fashion in the past half-century, information about Revolutionary events in many regions, counties, and towns can be found only in the local histories that appeared in great number between the Civil War and the First World War. These are arranged by place rather than author under each of the states from Maine to Georgia. Works that focus on Great Britain and the empire during the Revolutionary era, especially the imperial connection between the mother country and the North American and Caribbean colonies, can be found in chapter 3. The first of the chronological chapters, chapter 4 treats pre-Revolutionary events up to the Declaration of Independence. Chapters 6, 9, and 10 continue the sequence, dealing in detail with the War of Independence, the establishment of revolutionary governments in the states, the efforts of the Continental Congress to respond to events during the Confederation period, and the drafting and ratification of the Constitution. Works on the frontier and early developments in the territories of the Old Northwest and the Old Southwest are located in chapter 5, while studies of the Loyalists in the colonies and later in Canada, Great Britain, and the West Indies are in chapter 7. Although many treatments of Revolutionary diplomacy and international relations are linked directly to wartime events or internal politics in Europe and America, they are grouped together with general diplomatic histories in chapter 8. Chapter 11 includes material on nearly all aspects of Revolutionary life and culture, such as commerce and shipping, money and finance, slavery, law and legal institutions, demography, ethnic groups, religion, education, science, medicine, literature, and the fine arts. Chapter 12, which contains one-third of the titles in the bibliography, is a unique listing of works by and about 2,138 participants in the Revolutionary struggle. One of its notable features is a system of cross references in the headnotes to those persons for whom there is a biographical sketch in the *Dictionary of American Biography* (entry 12577), the *Dictionary of National Biography* (entry 12655), or both. The headnotes themselves were compiled primarily to identify the subjects by their geographical locations, occupations, and activities, and to provide terms that would make them more accessible through the index.

Under the topical headings in each chapter, entries are arranged alphabetically by author and title. Exceptions to this format occur in chapters 2 and 12. Because most users searching for regional and local histories would be more likely to know the place names than the names of the authors, the secondary works in chapter 2, "Regional, State, and Local Histories and General Document Collections," are arranged alphabetically by the name of the region, county, parish, or town given in the title. In chapter 12, entries under the name of each individual figure are divided into two categories. Works written by the subject are listed first and are arranged alphabetically by title. Biographical studies about the subject are listed second and are arranged alphabetically by author.

CONSTRUCTION OF ENTRIES AND BIBLIOGRAPHIC STYLE. Entries in the bibliography are constructed according to the general rules established in *Bibliographical Procedures & Style; a Manual for Bibliographers in the Library of Congress* (Washington, 1954), as modified to accord with the 1967 *Anglo-American Cataloging Rules*. The purpose of this bibliographic style is to provide references that can be readily identified in Library of Congress catalogs and, by extension, in the many other institutions throughout the United States where Library of Congress catalog cards are used and where the Library's published catalogs are available. Authors' names are based on the form in which the Library's catalogers have established them. Long titles, particularly in eighteenth-century pamphlet literature, have frequently been shortened by the omission of subtitles or repetitious wording. The form of the publisher's name in imprints follows in general the practices recommended in the 1967 *Anglo-American Cataloging Rules*. In describing pagination, references to preliminary pages numbering fewer than five have been omitted. Call numbers have been included as a further aid to exact identification. Items in the Library's collections that were uncataloged at the time of compilation are indicated by the symbol DLC. Although many reprint notes have been included, no attempt was made to provide comprehensive coverage. The user should refer to the *Guide to Reprints* and other standard bibliographic sources for fuller or more recent information.

Brackets have been used in bibliographic entries to indicate information supplied by catalogers and bibliographers that does not appear on the recto of the title page or in the body of the work. For example, if the author of an anonymous or pseudonymous eighteenth-century pamphlet has been identified, the name, enclosed in brackets, will precede the title. Brackets have also been commonly used around series information or dates of publication not found on the title page. In this bibliography bracketed call numbers indicate that the work cited is no longer available in printed form in the Library's collections but has been replaced by microfilm or microfiche. The Microform Reading Room call number invariably follows such a bracketed classification number. Finally, pagination figures derived from a source such as *Dissertation Abstracts International*, which is known to combine separately paged sections of the work it described, have also been placed in brackets.

ANNOTATIONS. Both bibliographic and descriptive annotations have been written to aid users in determining which works may best meet their needs. Because of the limitations of time and space, annotations were restricted to studies of unquestionable historiographic significance, to representative monographs or articles that provide a broad treatment of a particular subject, to interpretive works that present a unique point of view, and to studies with unclear or misleading titles. Annotations were also supplied to explain how works covering a far broader period are useful for the study of some phase of the Revolution. Slightly more than 40 percent of the entries in chapters 1–11 received annotations ranging in length from a single sentence to several paragraphs. Most often they were restricted to 125 words or less. These annotations and notes were not written as reviews; they are more nearly abstracts intended to reflect the author's own opinion or approach. To avoid the use of extensive quotations, they are in many cases a paraphrase of the author's words. The length of the annotation bears no direct relationship to the importance of the work annotated. The content of well-known studies may be self-evident, while less conspicuous books or articles may require more detailed description to place them in proper relation to the subject or subjects with which they deal.

ACKNOWLEDGMENTS. Throughout the preparation of this bibliography, the compiler benefited from the experience and knowledge of other Library of Congress staff members, especially those in the Shelflisting Section of the Subject Catalog Division, the Rare Book and Special Collections Division, the Law Library, the Geography and Map Division, the Manuscript Division, the Microform Reading Room, and the Loan Division. Within the General Reading Rooms Division itself (formerly the General Reference and Bibliography Division), many members of the staff, who were either permanently or temporarily assigned to the Bibliography Section during the past ten years, contributed various amounts of time to searching, filing, translating, annotating, proofreading, and indexing. They are Donald Baskerville, Edward Cambio, Madlein Csiffary, Judith Farley, Judith Furash, Mary Jane Gibson, James Gilreath, Ted Johnson, Carolyn Larson, Jane Lindley, Anita Nolen, Diana Ramsey, Frances Reynolds, Stanley Rubenstein, Baiba Seefer, and Harry Wrenn. Those who typed, photocopied, and numbered the manuscript are Charlotte Bolton, Cheryl Bowser, Toni Carter, Patricia Garrison, Deborah Jones, Mary McSwain, Nathan Moore, Cheryl Powell, Teena Siggers, Pamela Smith, Richelle Tyson, Kim Wallace, and Joani Ward. The compiler is especially grateful for the contributions of eight others. Robert Land, former chief of the division, guided and supported the project through its early stages. Ellen Hahn, the present chief, and Judith Austin, head of the Bibliography Section, expedited the final production. Richard Andress assisted diligently in the compilation of the original file of thirty-six-thousand working cards. Roy Thomas prepared most of the annotations for chapter 1 and drafted dozens of others for later chapters. Dr. Marguerite Bloxom, in addition to innumerable other tasks, researched the headnotes and arranged the entries for chapter 12. Dr. Marvin Kranz provided counsel on the organization of entries within the subject chapters. And Ruth Freitag, associate chief bibliographer, reviewed and edited every entry with respect to its technical bibliographic details.

RONALD M. GEPHART,
January 1980.

List of Abbreviations

Am Rev	American Revolution Bicentennial Office
Folk	Archive of Folk Song
G&M	Geography and Map Division
LH&G	Local History and Genealogy Room
LL	Law Library
Micro	Microform Reading Room
MRR Alc	Main Reading Room Alcove
Mss	Manuscript Division
P&P	Prints and Photographs Division
Rare Bk. Coll.	Rare Book Collection

List of Serials Cited

Académie de marine, *Paris.* Communications et Mémoires. V2.A34

Académie de marine de Belgique. Communications. V5.A2

Acadiensis. F1036.A16

Agricultural history. S1.A16

Alabama historical quarterly. F321.A17

Alabama lawyer. LL

Alabama review. F321.A2535

Albemarle County Historical Society. Magazine. F232.A3A5

American Academy of Political and Social Science, *Philadelphia.* Annals. H1.A4

American Anthropological Association. Memoirs. GN2.A22

American Antiquarian Society, *Worcester, Mass.* Proceedings. E172.A35

American Antiquarian Society, *Worcester, Mass.* Transactions and collections. E172.A3

American archivist. CD3020.A45

American Bar Association journal. K1.M385

American book collector. Z1007.A47

American Catholic historical researches (title varies). E184.C3A5

American Catholic Historical Society of Philadelphia. Records. E184.C3A4

American Catholic quarterly review. AP2.A332

American collector. Z1007.A475

American ecclesiastical review. BX801.E3

American Economic Association. Publications. HB1.A5

American economic review. HB1.E26

American heritage. E171.A43

American historian. E171.A45

American Historical Association. Annual report. E172.A60

American Historical Association. Papers. E172.A65

American Historical Association. *Pacific Coast Branch.* Proceedings. F851.A5

American historical magazine and Tennessee Historical Society quarterly (title varies). [F431.A53] Micro 38843

American historical register. E171.A56

American historical review. E171.A57

American history illustrated. E171.A574

American Institute of Criminal Law and Criminology. Journal. HV6001.J63

American-Irish Historical Society. Journal. E184.I6A5

American Jewish Archives. E184.J5A37

American Jewish historical quarterly. E184.J5A5

American journal of economics and sociology. H1.A48

American journal of legal history. LL

American journal of numismatics. CJ1.A6

American journal of pharmacy. RS1.A45

American journal of philology. P1.A5

American journal of psychiatry. RC321.A52

American journal of science. Q1.A5

American law review. LL

American law school review. LL

American literature. PS1.A6

American Medical Association. Journal. R15.A48

American Mercury. AP2.A37

American Negro Academy, *Washington, D.C.* Occasional papers. E185.5.A51

American Neptune. V1.A4

American Oxonian. LH1.O8A6

American Pharmaceutical Association. Journal. RS1.A52

American Philosophical Society, *Philadelphia.* Proceedings. Q11.P5

American Philosophical Society, *Philadelphia.* Transactions. Q11.P6

American Philosophical Society, *Philadelphia. Committee of History, Moral Science, and General Literature.* Transactions. E173.A75

American Philosophical Society, *Philadelphia. Library.* Library bulletin. Z881.P49

American pioneer. F516.A53

American political science review. JA1.A6

American quarterly. AP2.A3985

American register; or General repository of history, politics, and science. D301.A5

American register; or, Summary review of history, politics, and literature. Micro 01104 no. 59 AP

American rifleman. SK1.A52

American-Scandinavian review. AP2.A457

American Scenic and Historic Preservation Society. Annual report. E151.A51

American scholar. AP2.A4572

American scientist. LJ85.S502

American sociological review. HM1.A75

American Society Legion of Honor magazine. CR5061.U6A3

American Society of Church History. Papers. BR140.A4

American speech. PE2801.A6

American Statistical Association. Journal. HA1.A6

American Swedish Historical Foundation, *Philadelphia*. Yearbook. E184.S23A685

Americana (title varies). [E171.A53] Micro 52160

Anglican theological review. BR1.A5

Annales de Bretagne. DC611.B841A4

Annales: économies, sociétés, civilisations. AP20.A58

Annals of medical history. R11.A85

Annals of science. Q1.A616

Antiaircraft journal (formerly Journal of the United States Artillery). UF1.J86

Antioch review. AP2.A562

Anuario de estudios americanos. F1401.A587

Architecture. NA1.A77

Archiv für Geschichte von Oberfranken. DD801.B47A8

Archivio storico italiano. DG401.A7

Arkansas historical quarterly. F406.A6

Arlington historical magazine. F232.A4A7

Armor. UE1.C33

Army ordnance. UF1.067

Army quarterly. U1.A85

Army review. U1.A87

Ars typographica. Z119.A78

Art in America. N1.A43

Art quarterly. N1.A64

Association of American Geographers. Annals. G3.A7

Astronomical Society of the Pacific. Publications. QB1.A4

Atlantic monthly. AP2.A8

Augusta historical bulletin. F232.A9A94

Australian journal of politics and history. DU80.A945

Baptist history and heritage. BX6207.A407

Baptist quarterly. BX6201.B5

Barbados Museum and Historical Society, *Bridgetown*. Journal. F2041.B217

Bennington, Vt. Historical Museum and Art Gallery. Publications. F59.B4B6

Bergen County Historical Society, *Hackensack, N.J.* Annual report. F142.B4B4

Berkshire Historical and Scientific Society, *Pittsfield, Mass.* Collections. F72.B5B6

Bermuda historical quarterly. F1636.B55

Bibliographer. Z1007.B572

Bibliographical Society of America. Papers. Z1008.B51P

Biological Society of Washington, *Washington, D.C.* Proceedings. QH1.B4

Birmingham, Eng. University. Historical journal. D1.B37

Blackwood's magazine. AP4.B6

Books at Brown. Z733.P958B6

Boston. Public Library. Bulletin. Z881.B75B

Boston. Public Library. Monthly bulletin (superseded the Bulletin). Z881.B75BM

Boston. Public Library. More books. Z881.B75BR2

Boston. Public Library. Quarterly. Z881.B7535

Boston medical and surgical journal. R11.B7

Boston University law review. LL

Bostonian Society, *Boston*. Proceedings. F73.1.B86

Bostonian Society, *Boston*. Publications. F73.1.B88

Bradford County Historical Society, *Towanda, Pa.* Annual. F157.B7B7

Brethren life and thought. BX7801.B74

Bristol and Gloucestershire Archaeological Society, *Gloucester, Eng.* Transactions. DA670.G4B8

British Academy, *London*. Proceedings. AS122.L5

British Association for American Studies. Bulletin (superseded by Journal of American studies). E172.B72

British medical journal. R31.B93

Brookline Historical Publication Society, *Brookline, Mass.* Publications. F74.B9B8

Brookline Historical Society, *Brookline, Mass.* Proceedings. F74.B9B83

Brookline Historical Society, *Brookline, Mass.* Publications. F74.B9B85

Brown University. *Historical Seminary*. Papers. E173.B87

Bucknell review. AP2.B887

Bucks County Historical Society, *Doylestown, Pa.* Collection of papers. F157.B8B84

Buffalo. University. University of Buffalo studies. AS36.B95

Bulletin historique et scientifique de l'Auvergne. DC611.A941A3

Bulletin of bibliography. Z1007.B94

Bulletin of the history of medicine. R11.B93

Bunker Hill Monument Association. Proceedings. E241.B9B9

Burke newsletter (superseded by Studies in Burke and his time). DA506.B9B86

Burlington magazine for connoisseurs. N1.B95

Burton Historical Collection leaflet. F561.B9

Business history. HF11.B9

Business history review. HF5001.B8262

CLA journal. P1.A1C22

Cahiers d'histoire mondiale. D1.C22

Danvers Historical Society, *Danvers, Mass.* Historical collections. F74.D2D42

Dartmouth alumni magazine. LH1.D3A5

Daughters of the American Revolution magazine. E202.5.A12

Dedham historical register. F74.D3D8

Delaware Historical Society. Papers. F161.D35

Delaware history. F161.D37

Delaware notes. AS36.D35

Detroit Historical Society. Bulletin. F574.D4D4137

Deutsch-amerikanische Geschichtsblätter (title also in English). F550.G3D4

Dialect notes. PE2801.D5

Duke University, Durham, N.C. Trinity College Historical Society. Historical papers. [F251.D83] Micro 9370 F   Reprint call no. F251.D832

Duquesne review. AS30.D8A2

Dutchess County Historical Society. Collections. F127.D8D92

Dutchess County Historical Society. Year book. F127.D8D93

East Tennessee Historical Society, *Knoxville.* Publications. F442.1.E14

Ebony. AP2.E165

Economic development and cultural change. HC10.C453

Economic history review. HC10.E4

Economica. HB1.E5

Edinburgh review. AP4.E3

Eighteenth-century studies. NX452.E54

Emory University quarterly. AS36.E6

Encounter. AP4.E44

English historical review. DA20.E58

Essays in history. D2.E75

Essex antiquarian. F72.E7E4

Essex Institute, *Salem, Mass.* Historical collections. F72.E7E81

Essex Institute, *Salem, Mass.* Proceedings. F72.E7E76

Ethics. BJ1.I6

Ethnohistory. E51.E8

Explorations in entrepreneurial history. HB615.E8

Fergus' historical series. F536.F35

Field artillery journal. UF1.F6

Fighting forces. U1.F5

Filson Club, *Louisville, Ky.* Filson Club publications. F446.F48

Filson Club history quarterly. F446.F484

Firelands pioneer. F497.W5F5

Fitchburg Historical Society, *Fitchburg, Mass.* Proceedings. F74.F5F6

Florida anthropologist. E78.F6F58

Florida historical quarterly. F306.F65

Fort Ticonderoga, N.Y. Museum. Bulletin. E199.F75

Foundations. BX6201.C572

Franco-American review. E183.8.F8F88

Franklin Institute, *Philadelphia.* Journal. T1.F8

Freedom and union. JX1901.F6

Freeman. AP2.F9155

French American review. PS159.F5F74

French historical studies. DC1.F69

French review. PC2001.F75

Friends' Historical Association. Bulletin. BX7635.A1F6

Friends' library. BX7615.F8

Galaxy. AP2.G2

Genealogical magazine. F1.P98

General magazine and historical chronicle. LH1.P3A4

Gentleman's magazine. AP4.G3

Geographical review. G1.G35

Geographical Society of Philadelphia. Bulletin. G3.G34

Georgetown law journal. LL

Georgia. State College, *Atlanta. School of Arts and Sciences.* Publications of the faculty. Z5055.U5G37

Georgia Bar Association. Report. LL

Georgia bar journal. LL

Georgia historical quarterly. F281.G2975

Georgia Historical Society. Collections. F281.G35

Georgia review. AP2.G375

German American annals. E184.G3G3

German-American historical review (title also in German). F550.G3D4

Glasgow Bibliographical Society. Records. Z1008.G53

Gloucester County Historical Society, *Woodbury, N.J.* Publication. F142.G5G6

Government and opposition. JA8.G6

Grafton magazine of history and genealogy. E171.G73

Granada (City). Universidad. Boletín. AP60.G7

Granite monthly. F31.G75

Granite state magazine. F31.G76

Green bag. LL

Groton historical series. F74.G9G76

Gun digest. GV1174.G8

Harper's magazine. AP2.H3

Harvard alumni bulletin. LH1.H3A5

Harvard educational review. L11.H3

Harvard graduates' magazine. LH1.H3G7

Harvard law review. LL

Harvard Library bulletin. Z881.H3403

Hebrew Union College annual. BM11.H4

Herkimer County Historical Society. Papers. F127.H5H5

Hispania. DP1.H5

Hispanic American historical review. F1401.H66

Historian. D1.H22

Historic leaves. F74.S7H6

Historic Nantucket. F72.N2H68

Historical and Philosophical Society of Ohio. Bulletin. F486.H653

Historical and Philosophical Society of Ohio. [Publications (1873–75)] F486.H662

Historical and Philosophical Society of Ohio. Publications (1924+). F486.H663

Historical and Philosophical Society of Ohio. Quarterly publication (superseded by its Publications [1924+]). F486.H676

Historical bulletin. D1.H28

Historical documents from the Old Dominion. E263.V8L6

Historical journal. D1.H33

Historical magazine, and notes and queries. E171.H64

Historical magazine of the Protestant Episcopal Church. BX5800.H5

Historical New Hampshire. F31.H57

Historical review of Berks County. F157.B3H48

Historical Society of Berks County, *Reading, Pa.* Transactions. F157.B3H5

Historical Society of Fairfax County, Virginia. Yearbook. F232.F2H5

Historical Society of Hudson County, N.J. Papers. F142.H8H6

Historical Society of Montgomery County. *Norristown, Pa.* Bulletin. F157.M7H45

Historical Society of Montgomery County, *Norristown, Pa.* Historical sketches. F157.M7H5

Historical Society of Newburgh Bay and the Highlands, *Newburgh, N.Y.* Publication. F127.O8H6

Historical Society of Northwestern Ohio. Quarterly bulletin (now the Northwest Ohio quarterly). F497.A15N6

Historical Society of York County, *York, Pa.* Papers. F157.Y6H62

Historical Society of York County, *York, Pa.* Proceedings and collections. F157.Y6H6

Historical Society of York County, *York, Pa.* Yearbook. F157.Y6H7

Historical studies; Australia and New Zealand. DU80.H5

Historische Vierteljahrschrift. D1.H5

Historische Zeitschrift. D1.H6

Historisk tidsskrift. DL101.H6

History. D1.H816

History; the quarterly journal of the Historical Association. D1.H815

History and theory. D1.H8173

History of American weather. QC857.U6H56

History of education quarterly. L11.H67

History today. D1.H818

Huguenot Society of America. Collections. [E184.H9H63] Micro 38714

Huguenot Society of America. Proceedings. E184.H9H8

Hungarian quarterly. DB901.H83

Huntington Library bulletin. Z733.S24B Z1007.H95

Huntington Library quarterly (supersedes its Bulletin). Z733.S24Q

Hyde Park historical record. F74.H98H95

Hymn. ML1.H92

Illinois. State Historical Library, *Springfield.* Bulletin. F536.I26

Illinois. State Historical Library, *Springfield.* Collections. F536.I25

Illinois. University. Illinois studies in the social sciences. H31.I4

Illinois law review. LL

Illinois State Historical Society. Journal. F536.I18

Illinois State Historical Society. Publication (title varies; Transactions) F536.I34 F536.I2

Imago mundi. GA1.I6

Indiana. University. Indiana University humanities series. AS36.I385

Indiana Historical Society. Lectures. E171.I6

Indiana Historical Society. Publications. F521.I41

Indiana history bulletin. F521.I367

Indiana History Conference, *Indianapolis.* Proceedings. F521.I46

Indiana magazine of history. F521.I52

Indiana quarterly for bookmen. Z1007.I5

Infantry journal. UD1.I6

Institut français de Washington, *Washington, D.C.* Bulletin. E183.8.F8I8

Institute of Jamaica, *Kingston.* Journal. AS73.J21

International Congress on the Enlightenment. Transactions. PQ2105.A2S8
International monthly. AP2.I75
International record of medicine and general practice clinics. R11.M745
International review for social history. HN1.I52
Iowa. University. Studies in sociology, economics, politics, and history. H31.I8
Iowa journal of history. F616.I5
Irish historical studies. DA900.I63
Irish sword. DA914.I7
Iron worker. TS200.I74
Isis. Q1.I7
Italica. PC1068.U618

JEGP; journal of English and Germanic philology. PD1.J7
Jahrbuch für Amerikastudien. E169.1.J33
Jamaican historical review. F1861.J32
James Sprunt studies in history and political science. F251.J28
Jewish quarterly review. DS101.J5
John P. Branch historical papers of Randolph-Macon College. F221.J65
Johns Hopkins alumni magazine. LH1.J7J7
Johns Hopkins Hospital, *Baltimore.* Bulletin (superseded by the Johns Hopkins medical journal). RC31.B2J6
Johns Hopkins University. Studies in historical and political science. H31.J62 E173.J652
Journal of accountancy. HF5601.J7
Journal of American history (1907–35). E171.J86
Journal of American history (formerly the Mississippi Valley historical review). E171.J87
Journal of American studies (supersedes the British Association for American Studies. Bulletin). E151.J6
Journal of British studies. DA20.J6
Journal of Canadian studies. DLC
Journal of chemical education. QD1.J93
Journal of church and state. BV630.A1J6
Journal of comparative legislation and international law. LL
Journal of criminal law, criminology and police science. HV6001.J63
Journal of ecclesiastical history. BR140.J6
Journal of economic and business history. HC10.J6
Journal of economic history. HC10.J64
Journal of educational research. L11.J75
Journal of geography. G1.J87

Journal of inter-American studies. F1401.J68
Journal of interdisciplinary history. D1.J59
Journal of library history. Z671.J67
Journal of Long Island history. F127.L8J75
Journal of medical education. R11.A94
Journal of Mississippi history. F336.J68
Journal of modern history. D1.J6
Journal of Negro education. LC2701.J6
Journal of Negro history. E185.J86
Journal of pediatrics. RJ1.A453
Journal of political economy. HB1.J7
Journal of politics. JA1.J6
Journal of Presbyterian history. BX8905.P7A4
Journal of public law. LL
Journal of religion. BR1.J65
Journal of social history. HN1.J6
Journal of southern history. F206.J68
Journal of the history of ideas. B1.J75
Journal of the history of medicine and allied sciences. R131.A1J6
Journal of the Royal Artillery. UF1.W8
Journal of the West. F591.J65
Journalism quarterly. PN4700.J7

Kentucky Historical Society. Register. F446.K43
Kentucky law journal. LL
Kentucky State Bar Association. Proceedings. LL
Keystone folklore quarterly. GR1.K45
Kingston, Ont. Queen's University. Bulletin of the departments of history and political and economic science. AS42.Q6

Labor history. HD4802.L435
Lackawanna Historical Society, *Scranton.* Publication. F157.L15L24
Lancaster County (Pa.) Historical Society. Journal. F157.L2L5
Land economics. HB1.J65
Law library journal. K12.A9364
Law quarterly review. LL
Lawyer and banker and central law journal. LL
Lebanon County Historical Society, *Lebanon, Pa.* Historical papers and addresses. F157.L4L5
Leeds Philsophical and Literary Society. Proceedings. AS122.L262
Légion d'honneur; honneur et patrie. CR5061.U6A3
Lehigh County Historical Society, *Allentown, Pa.* Proceedings and papers. F157.L5L52
Lexington Historical Society, *Lexington, Mass.* F74.L67L77

Library. Z671.L69

Library chronicle. Z33.P418

Library quarterly. Z671.L713

Literary and Historical Society of Quebec. Historical documents (title varies). F1051.L81

Literary and Historical Society of Quebec. Transactions. F1051.L77

London. University. *Institute of Historical Research.* Bulletin. D1.L65

Long Island forum. F127.L8L73

Long Island Historical Society. Memoirs. F116.L954

Long Island Historical Society. Quarterly. F116.L875

Los Angeles bar bulletin. LL

Louisiana historical quarterly. F366.L79

Louisiana Historical Society, *New Orleans.* F366.L85

Louisiana history. F366.L6238

Louisiana studies. F366.L935

Lutheran church review. BX8001.L2

Lutheran quarterly. BX8001.L617

Lynn Historical Society, *Lynn, Mass.* Register. F74.L98L98

Macalester College, *St. Paul, Minn. Department of History, Literature and Political Science.* Contributions. E173.M12

McGill University, *Montreal.* Publications, series 6: History and economics. H31.M3

Madison quarterly. LH1.M23Q3

Magazine of American history, with notes and queries. E171.M18

Magazine of history, with notes and queries. E171.M23

Magazine of history, with notes and queries. Extra numbers. E173.M24

Magazine of New England history. F1.M18

Maine historical and genealogical recorder. F16.M18

Maine Historical Society. Collections. F16.M33

Manchester Historic Association, *Manchester, N.H.* Collections. F44.M2M3

Manchester Literary and Philosophical Society, *Manchester, Eng.* Memoirs and proceedings. Q41.M2

Manuscripts. Z41.A2A925

Marine Corps gazette. VE7.M4

Marine Historical Association. Publication. E182.M32

Mariner's mirror. VK1.M4

Marxist quarterly. HX1.M18

Maryland historian. E171.M28

Maryland historical magazine. F176.M18

Maryland Historical Society. Fund publications. F176.M37

Maryland Historical Society. [Publications] F176.M34

Maryland State Bar Association. Report. LL

Massachusetts Historical Society, *Boston.* Collections. F61.M41

Massachusetts Historical Society, *Boston.* Proceedings. F61.M38

Massachusetts law quarterly. LL

Massachusetts magazine. F61.M48

Mattatuck Historical Society, *Waterbury, Conn.* Publications. F104.W3M38

Mayflower descendant. F68.M46

Medford historical register. F74.M5M35

Medical arts and sciences. R11.M518

Medical Society of New Jersey. Journal. R15.N515

Medical Society of the State of New York. Transactions. R15.N652

Mennonite quarterly review. BX8101.M4

Methodist history. BX8235.M44

Methodist quarterly review. BX8201.M75

Michigan. *Historical Commission.* Bulletin. F561.M46

Michigan. *Historical Commission.* Michigan historical collections. F561.M47

Michigan. University. *William L. Clements Library.* Bulletin. E172.M53   Z6027.U5M58

Michigan Academy of Science, Arts and Letters. Papers. Q11.M56

Michigan alumnus quarterly review (superseded by the Michigan quarterly review). AP2.M53

Michigan historical publications. F561.M55

Michigan history. F561.M57

Michigan law review. LL

Michigan Political Science Association. Publications. H31.M6

Michigan quarterly review (supersedes the Michigan alumnus quarterly review). AS30.M48

Mid-America. BX1415.I3M5

Midcontinent American studies journal. E169.1.M6215

Middle States Council for the Social Studies. Proceedings (title varies). D16.3.A23

Midwest journal of political science. JA1.M5

Military affairs. E181.M55

Military collector & historian. UC463.M54

Military engineer. TA1.P85

Military medicine (title varies; Military surgeon). RD1.A7

Military review (title varies). Z6723.U35

Military Service Institution of the United States. Journal. U1.M6

Minnesota Historical Society. Annals. F601.M65

Minnesota Historical Society. Collections. F601.M66

Minnesota history. F601.M72

Minnesota law review. LL

Miroir de l'histoire. D1.M6

Miscellaneous Americana. E171.B73

Mississippi Historical Society. Publications. F336.M75

Mississippi Historical Society. Publications. Centenary series. F336.M77

Mississippi law journal. LL

Mississippi Valley Historical Association. Proceedings. F351.M66

Mississippi Valley historical review (now the Journal of American history). E171.J87 Reprint call no. E171.J872

Missouri. University. University of Missouri studies. AS36.M82

Missouri. University. University of Missouri studies. Social science series. H31.M66

Missouri historical review. F461.M59

Missouri Historical Society, *St. Louis.* Bulletin. F461.M6226

Missouri Historical Society, *St. Louis.* Collections. F461.M66

Modern age. AP2.M628

Modern Language Association of America. Publications. PB6.M6

Modern language notes. PB1.M6

Modern language quarterly. PB1.M642

Modern philology. PB1.M7

Monthly military repository. E201.M78 Rare Bk. Coll.

Monthly register, magazine, and review of the United States. AP2.A2M7

Moorsfield antiquarian. E171.M66

Moravian Historical Society, *Nazareth, Pa.* Transactions. BX8553.M7

Music Library Association. Notes. ML27.U5M695

Musical quarterly. ML1.M725

NTM. Zeitschrift für Geschichte der Naturwissenschaften, Technik und Medizin. Q125.N2

Nantucket Historical Association. Proceedings. F72.N2N16

Narragansett historical register. F76.N23

Nassau County historical journal. F127.N2N3

National and English review (title varies; National review). AP4.N25

National Genealogical Society quarterly. CS42.N4

National magazine. E171.N27

Nautical research journal. V1.N27

Navy Records Society. Publications. DA70.A1

Nebraska. University. *Depts. of History and Economics.* Seminary papers. E173.N36

Neptunia. V2.N4

New American church monthly. BX5800.A6

New Brunswick Historical Club. Publications. F144.N5N55

New Brunswick Historical Society. Collections. [F1041.N53] Micro 04070

New-England galaxy. F1.N39

New England historical and genealogical register. F1.N56

New England magazine. AP2.N4

New England quarterly. F1.N62

New England social studies bulletin. H1.N4

New Englander. AP2.N5

New Hampshire Antiquarian Society. Collections. F31.N45

New Hampshire Bar Association. Journal. LL

New Hampshire Bar Association. Proceedings. LL

New Hampshire genealogical record. F33.N54

New Hampshire Historical Society. Collections. F31.N54

New Hampshire Historical Society. Proceedings. F31.N52

New Haven Colony Historical Society, *New Haven.* Journal. F91.N4

New Haven Colony Historical Society, *New Haven.* Papers. F98.N5

New London County Historical Society, *New London, Conn.* Collections. F102.N7N8

New London County Historical Society, *New London, Conn.* Records and papers. F102.N7N7

New Jersey Historical Society. Collections. F131.N62

New Jersey Historical Society. Proceedings (now New Jersey history). F131.N58

New Mexico. University. Sociological series. H31.N5

New York (City). Metropolitan Museum of Art. Bulletin. N610.A4

New York (City). Public Library. Bulletin. Z881.N6B

New York (State). Agricultural Experiment Station, *Ithaca.* Memoir. S95.E325

New York (State). *State Historian.* Annual report. F116.N26

New York (State). State Library, *Albany.* Bulletin. Z1009.N56

New York (State). State Library, *Albany.* History bulletin. Z881.N61BH

Pennsylvania-German. F146.P224

Pennsylvania German Folklore Society. [Yearbook] GR110.P4A35

Pennsylvania-German Society. Proceedings and addresses. F146.P23

Pennsylvania-German Society. Publications (supersedes its Proceedings and addresses). GR110.P4A372

Pennsylvania history. F146.P597

Pennsylvania magazine of history and biography. F146.P65

Perspectives in American history. E171.P47

Philadelphia. Mercantile Library Company. Bulletin. Z881.P543B

Philadelphia medical and physical journal. QH1.P5

Philadelphia medical journal. R11.P5

Philological quarterly. P1.P55

Philosophical review. B1.P5

Philosophy. B1.P55

Picket post. E234.P5

Pittsburgh. Carnegie Institute. *Museum.* Annals. AS36.P7

Pittsburgh. Carnegie Library. Among our books. Z881.P62B

Pocumtuck Valley Memorial Association, *Deerfield, Mass.* History and proceedings. F72.F8P8

Polish-American review. E265.H86

Polish Institute of Arts and Sciences in America, *New York.* Bulletin. AS36.P84

Polish review. DK401.P82

Political science quarterly. H1.P8

Political studies. JA1.P63

Politico. JA18.P65

Population studies. HB881.A1P67

Postal history journal. HE6001.P58

Potter's American monthly. E171.P86

Presbyterian quarterly review. BX8901.P77

Princeton Historical Association, *Princeton, N.J.* Extra publications. F144.P9P9

Princeton theological review. BR1.P6

Princeton University Library chronicle. Z733.P93C5

Prologue. CD3020.P75

Proof. Z1219.P73

Providence magazine. HF1.P8

Psychoanalytic review. BF1.P5

Psychological reports. BF21.P843

Public opinion quarterly. HM261.A1P8

Putnam's monthly magazine. AP2.P97

Quaker history (formerly Friends' Historical Association. Bulletin). BX7635.A1F6

Quarterly journal of economics. HB1.Q3

Quarterly journal of speech. PN4071.Q3

Quarterly review. AP4.Q2

Quarterly review, a survey of Southern Baptist progress. BX6201.Q3

Quebec (City). Université Laval. Revue. AP21.Q4

Queen's quarterly. AP5.Q3

Radford review. LH1.R22R4

Razón y fe; revista hispano-americana de cultura. AP60.R2

Recherches historiques. F1001.R4

Religious magazine and monthly review. BX9801.M7

Renaissance and modern studies. AS121.R4

Researcher. CS42.R4

Review (title varies; Quartermaster review). UC34.Q8

Review of economics and statistics. HA1.R35

Review of politics. JA1.R4

Review of surgery. RD1.Q3

Revista cubana. AP63.R535

Revista de historia. D1.R22

Revista de historia de América. F1401.R44

Revista de Indias. F1401.R442

Révolution française. DC139.R4

Revue canadienne. AP21.R4

Revue d'histoire de l'Amérique française. F1001.R48

Revue d'histoire de la Gaspésie. F1054.G2R4

Revue d'histoire diplomatique. JX3.R3

Revue de Paris. AP20.R27

Revue des deux mondes. AP20.R3

Revue des études historiques. D1.S6

Revue des questions historiques. D1.R5

Revue du dix-huitième siècle. DC131.A2R4

Revue historique. D1.R6

Revue historique de Bordeaux et du département de la Gironde. DC801.B71R4

Revue historique de l'Armée. DC1.R37

Revue historique de la révolution française. DC139.R5

Revue philomathique de Bordeaux et du sud-ouest. AP20.R63

Rhode Island. *Record Commissioner.* Annual report. CD3480.A3

Rhode Island historical magazine (title varies; Newport historical magazine). F76.R35

Rhode Island Historical Society. Collections. F76.R47

Rhode Island Historical Society. Proceedings. F76.R49

Rhode Island Historical Society. Publications. [F76.R51] Micro 39268

Rhode Island historical tracts. F76.R52

Rhode Island history. F76.R472

Rhode Island Jewish historical notes. F90.J5R5

Rhode-Island Medical Society. Transactions. R15.R4

Richmond College historical papers. F221.R53

Richmond County history. F292.R5R52

Rochester Historical Society, *Rochester, N.Y.* Publications. F129.R7R58

Rochester history. F129.R7R59

Roxbury Historical Society, *Roxbury, Mass.* Yearbook. F74.R9R95

Royal Canadian Institute, *Toronto.* Transactions. AS42.C21

Royal Geographical Society of Australasia. *South Australian Branch.* Proceedings. G51.R87

Royal Historical Society, *London.* Transactions. DA20.R9

Royal Irish Academy, *Dublin.* Proceedings. AS122.D81

Royal Society of Canada. Proceedings and transactions. AS42.R6

Royal Society of London. Notes and records. Q41.L835

Royal Statistical Society, *London.* Journal. HA1.R8

Royal United Service Institution, *London.* Journal. U1.R8

Rural sociology. HT401.R8

Russian review. DK1.R82

Rutgers University, *New Brunswick, N.J. Library.* Journal. Z733.R955F

St. John's law review. LL

Salesianum. BX915.S17

Scandinavian economic history review. HC341.A25

Scandinavian studies. PD1505.S6

Scenic and historic America. E151.A55

School review. L11.S55

Schweizer Beiträge zur allgemeinen Geschichte. D6.S37

Science and society. H1.S25

Scientific monthly. Q1.S817

Scotch-Irish Society of America. Proceedings and addresses. [E184.S4S4] Micro 38720

Scots magazine. AP4.S3732

Scottish historical review. DA750.S21

Scribner's magazine. AP2.S4

Scripta mathematica. QA1.S35

Sewanee review. AP2.S5

Shakespeare quarterly. PR2885.S63

Slavic review. D377.A1A5

Smith College studies in history. AS36.S7

Smithsonian. AS30.S6

Smithsonian Institution. Annual report. Q11.S66 Q11.U5

Smithsonian Institution. Smithsonian miscellaneous collections. Q11.S7

Smithsonian journal of history. CB3.S55

Snyder County Historical Society. Bulletin. F157.S5S6

Social education. H62.A1S6

Social research. H1.S53

Social science. H1.S55

Social science quarterly. H1.S65

Social service review. HV1.S6

Social studies. D16.3.S65

Societas. H1.S64

Société des américanistes de Paris. Journal. E51.S68

Société des antiquaires de l'Ouest, *Poitiers.* Mémoires. DC609.1.S7

Société des bibliophiles françois, *Paris.* Mélanges. DC4.S6 1903

Société dunoise: archéologie, histoire, sciences et arts, *Châteaudun.* Bulletins. DC611.D921S6

Société historique de Montréal. Mémoires. F1051.S67

Société historique franco-américaine. Bulletin. E184.F8S58

Société jurassiene d'émulation. Actes. AS322.S623

Society for Army Historical Research, *London.* Journal. DA49.S6

Society for the History of the Germans in Maryland, *Baltimore.* Annual report. F190.G3S6

Society for the Preservation of New England Antiquities, *Boston.* Old-time New England. F1.S68

Society of Architectural Historians. Journal. NA1.A327

Society of Colonial Wars, *Pennsylvania.* Historical publications. E186.3.P41

Society of the Cincinnati. Proceedings. E202.1.A212

Sociology and social research. HM1.S75

Somerset County historical quarterly. F142.S6S6

Sons of the American Revolution. *Kentucky Society.* Year book. E202.3.K57

Sons of the Revolution. *Kentucky Society.* Year book. E202.4.K37

Sons of the Revolution in state of Virginia semi-annual magazine. E202.4.V4

South Atlantic quarterly. AP2.S75

South Carolina Historical Association. Proceedings. F266.S58

South Carolina historical magazine. F266.S55

South Carolina Historical Society. Collections. F266.S71

South Carolina law quarterly. LL

Southeastern geographer. G1.S62

Southern California quarterly. F867.H67

Southern economic journal. HC107.A13A67

Southern History Association. Publications. F206.S73

Southern law review. LL

Southern quarterly. AS30.S658

Southern speech journal. PN4071.S65

Southwest review. AP2.S883

Southwestern historical quarterly. F381.T45

Southwestern social science quarterly (now the Social science quarterly). H1.S65

Speech monographs. PN4077.S6

Sprague's journal of Maine history. F16.S76

Staten Island historian. F127.S7S68

Staten Island Institute of Arts and Sciences. Proceedings. Q11.S9

Studia neophilologica. PB5.S7

Studies. AP4.S78

Studies in Burke and his time. DA506.B9B86

Studies in history and society. D1.S86

Studies on the left. HM1.S85

Studies on Voltaire and the eighteenth century. PQ2105.A2S8

Surveying and mapping. TA501.A6436

Susquehanna University studies. LH1.S78S8

Swedish-American historical bulletin. E184.S23S96

Swedish pioneer historical quarterly. E184.S23S955

Tasks of economic history. HC10.T3

Technology review. T171.M47

Tennessee historical magazine (supersedes the American historical magazine and Tennessee Historical Society quarterly). F431.T28

Tennessee historical quarterly (supersedes the Tennessee historical magazine). F431.T285

Tennessee law review. K24.E5

Texas law review. LL

Texas studies in literature and language. AS30.T4

Thought. AP2.T333

Topsfield Historical Society, *Topsfield, Mass.* Historical collections. F74.T6T6

Toronto. University. University of Toronto studies. History and economics series. H31.T6

Town planning review. NA9000.T6

Tulane law review. K24.U4

Tulane studies in English. PR13.T8

Tyler's quarterly historical and genealogical magazine. F221.T95

Ukrainian quarterly. DK508.A2U66

Ulster County Historical Society, *Kingston, N.Y.* Collections (1860–62). F127.U4U4

Ulster County Historical Society, *Kingston, N.Y.* Collections (1931+). F127.U4U42

Ulster County Historical Society, *Kingston, N.Y.* Proceedings. F127.U4U43

Union County Historical Society, *Elizabeth, N.J.* Proceedings. F142.U5U5

Unitarian review. BX9801.U7

United service. U1.U4

United service magazine. U1.U6

U.S. *Bureau of American Ethnology.* Annual report. E51.U55

U.S. *Bureau of American Ethnology.* Bulletin. E51.U6

U.S. *Bureau of Rolls and Library.* Bulletin. CD3031

U.S. *Dept. of Agriculture.* Miscellaneous publication. S21.A46

U.S. *Dept. of Agriculture.* Yearbook of agriculture. S21.A35

U.S. *Engineer School.* Occasional papers. UG1.U5

U.S. *Library of Congress.* Quarterly journal. Z881.U49A3   Z663.A5

U.S. *Museum of History and Technology.* Contributions. Q11.U6 T7.U627

U.S. *National Archives.* National Archives accessions. CD3023.A318

U.S. *National Museum.* Report. Q11.U5

United States Armed Forces medical journal. RC970.U7

United States Catholic Historical Society. Historical records and studies. E184.C3U5

United States Naval Institute. Proceedings. V1.U8

Universal asylum and Columbian magazine (title varies; Columbian magazine; or, Monthly miscellany). AP2.A2U6 Rare Bk. Coll.

University magazine. AP5.U5

University of California chronicle. LD739

University of Cincinnati law review. LL

University of Kansas City law review. LL

University of Pennsylvania law review and American law register. K25.N69

University of Pennsylvania medical bulletin. R11.U6

University of Pittsburgh law review. K25.N7

University of Toronto quarterly. AP5.U55

Utah Academy of Sciences, Arts and Letters. Proceedings. Q11.U85

CHAPTER TEN

The Making of the Constitution, 1787–1789

Historiography

9307
Barker, Eugene C. Economic interpretation of the Constitution. Texas law review, v. 22, June 1944: 373–391.
LL

9308
Bellot, Hugh Hale. The literature of the last half-century on the constitutional history of the United States. *In* Royal Historical Society, *London*. Transactions. 5th ser., v. 7; 1957. London. p. 159–182.
DA20.R9, 5th s., v. 7

9309
Blinkoff, Maurice. The influence of Charles A. Beard upon American historiography. [Buffalo, 1936] 84 p. (The University of Buffalo studies, v. 12, May 1936)
AS36.B95, v. 12
E175.5.B38

Monographs in history, no. 4.

9310
Brogan, Denis W. The quarrel over Charles Austin Beard and the American Constitution. Economic history review, 2d ser., v. 18, no. 1, 1965: 199–223.
HC10.E4, 2d s., v. 18

9311
Brown, Robert E. Charles Beard and the Constitution, a critical analysis of "An Economic Interpretation of the Constitution." Princeton, Princeton University Press, 1956. 219 p.
JK146.B53B7

Bibliographic footnotes.

A chapter-by-chapter critique of Beard's *Economic Interpretation of the Constitution* in which Brown argues that Beard's evidence does not support his thesis that the framers of the Constitution were motivated by selfish economic interests or that it was foisted undemocratically upon an unsuspecting populace. According to Brown, the delegates to the convention represented a wide spectrum of conflicting interest groups. They were too practical, moreover, to draft an instrument that favored any one segment of society, for they knew that their constituents would not ratify such a document. Since the majority of adult white males were middle-class property owners who could and did vote on matters that concerned them, the small number of votes cast in the ratification process indicates apathy and possibly consent rather than disfranchisement.

9312
Coleman, Peter J. Beard, McDonald, and economic determinism in American historiography: a review article. Business history review, v. 34, spring 1960: 113–121.
HF5001.B8262, v. 34

9313
Commager, Henry S. The Constitution: was it an economic document? American heritage, v. 10, Jan. 1958: 58–61, 100–103.
E171.A43, v. 10

9314
Commager, Henry S. The economic interpretation of the Constitution reconsidered. *In his* The search for a usable past, and other essays in historiography. New York, Knopf, 1967. p. 56–73.
E178.6.C64

9315
Elkins, Stanley M., *and* Eric L. McKitrick. The Founding Fathers: young men of the Revolution. Washington, Service Center for Teachers of History [1962] 28 p. (Service Center for Teachers of History, Publication no. 44)
JK146.E4

"Selected bibliography": p. 28.

An earlier version of the essay appeared in the *Political Science Quarterly*, v. 76, June 1961, p. 181–216.

Beginning with the work of Charles A. Beard, the authors review interpretations of the struggle over the drafting and ratification of the Constitution. Elkins and McKitrick contend that the dispute was not between competing economic groups or those holding differing ideologies or even between some favoring localism and others espousing nationalism. Instead, it was a contest between a lethargic older generation of revolutionists—Anti-Federalists whose careers were launched before 1776 and who remained state-oriented—and an energetic group of younger politicians—Federalists who rose to positions of authority during the Revolution and who identified with the continental war effort and with a national government that would uphold the underlying commitments of their culture: republicanism and capitalism.

9316

Giddens, Paul H.   The views of George Bancroft and Charles A. Beard on the making of the Constitution. Journal of American history, v. 27, July/Sept. 1933: 129–141.   E171.J86, v. 27

9317

Goldman, Eric F.   The origins of Beard's *Economic Interpretation of the Constitution.* Journal of the history of ideas, v. 13, Apr. 1952: 234–249.   B1.J75, v. 13

9318

Hepburn, Charles M.   Charles Beard and the Founding Fathers. 1966. ([573] p.)   Micro AC–1, no. 67–4363

Thesis (Ph.D.)—Stanford University.

Abstracted in *Dissertation Abstracts,* v. 27A, Apr. 1967, p. 3398–3399.

9319

Hofstadter, Richard.   Beard and the Constitution: the history of an idea. American quarterly, v. 2, fall 1950: 195–213.   AP2.A3985, v. 2

9320

Kenyon, Cecilia M.   "An economic interpretation of the Constitution" after fifty years. Centennial review of arts and sciences, v. 7, summer 1963: 327–352.
                                      AS30.M55A18, v. 7

9321

Lynd, Staughton.   Beard, Jefferson, and the tree of liberty. Midcontinent American studies journal, v. 9, spring 1968: 8–22.   E169.1.M6215, v. 9

On Beard's acceptance of Jefferson's economic philosophy and his pessimistic view of history.

9322

Main, Jackson T.   Charles A. Beard and the Constitution: a critical review of Forrest McDonald's *We the People.* With a rebuttal by Forrest McDonald. William and Mary quarterly, 3d ser., v. 17, Jan. 1960: 86–110.
                                      F221.W71, 3d s., v. 17

9323

Radabaugh, Jack S.   Charles A. Beard's economic interpretations of the Constitution: a consensus. Social studies, v. 51, Dec. 1960: 243–250.   D16.3.S65, v. 51

9324

Rein, Adolf.   Die historische Forschung über die Ursprünge der Verfassung der Vereinigten Staaten von Amerika. Historische Zeitschrift, 122. Bd., 2. Heft, 1920: 241–259.   D1.H6, v. 122

9325

Schuyler, Robert L.   Forrest McDonald's critique of the Beard thesis. Journal of southern history, v. 27, Feb. 1961: 73–80.   E206.J68, v. 27

9326

Thomas, Robert E.   A reappraisal of Charles A. Beard's *An Economic Interpretation of the Constitution of the United States.* American historical review, v. 57, Jan. 1952: 370–375.   E171.A57, v. 57

9327

Trask, David F.   Historians, the Constitution and objectivity: a case study. Antioch review, v. 20, spring 1960: 65–78.   AP2.A562, v. 20

9328

Wilkins, Robert P.   Orin G. Libby: his place in the historiography of the Constitution. North Dakota quarterly, v. 37, summer 1969: 5–20.   AS36.N6, v. 37

9329

Williams, William A.   A note on Charles Austin Beard's search for a general theory of causation. American historical review, v. 62, Oct. 1956: 59–80.
                                      E171.A57, v. 62

Considers in part Beard's use of Madison's theory of factions from the 10th *Federalist.*

General Works

9330

Bancroft, George.   History of the formation of the Constitution of the United States of America. New York, D. Appleton, 1885. xxii, 495 p.   JK116.B2 1885

Chronicles the origin and operation of the Confederation government, postwar developments leading to the Constitutional Convention, the deliberations and decisions of the Convention, the ratification process, and the establishment of the new government. Emphasis is given to the contributions of individual leaders, the uniqueness of the American experience, and the evolutionary development of libertarian institutions in the new nation.

9331

Carson, Hampton L., *ed.*   History of the celebration of the one hundredth anniversary of the promulgation of the Constitution of the United States. Philadelphia, Under the direction and by the authority of the commission, by J. B. Lippincott., 1889. 2 v. facsims., plans, plates, ports.   JK166.1889

"These memorial volumes have been prepared by direction of the Constitutional Centennial Commission."—Preface.

Partial contents: v. 1. History of the formation of the Constitution and of the causes which led to its adoption, by J. A. Kasson. Biographies of the members of the federal Convention, by H. L. Carson.—v. 2. Plans for the union of the British colonies of North America, 1643–1776, compiled by F. D. Stone.

9332

Catholic University of America.   The Constitution of the United States; addresses in commemoration of the sesquicentennial of its signing, 17 September 1787.

Washington, 1938. 82 p. (*Its* Publications of the Department of Politics) JK21.C3

Bibliographic footnotes.

Partial contents: The philosophy of the Constitution, by M. I. X. Millar.—The Catholic signers of the Constitution, by E. C. Burnett.—The Catholic contribution to constitutional law, by W. C. Walsh.

9333
Chandler, Julian A. C., *ed.* Genesis and birth of the federal Constitution; addresses and papers in the Marshall-Wythe School of Government and Citizenship of the College of William and Mary. New York, Macmillan Co., 1924. xii, 397 p. JK268.C5

"Authorities" at end of some chapters.

Partial contents: The government of Massachusetts prior to the federal Constitution, by Frank W. Grinnell.—The Continental Congress and the Articles of Confederation, by Henry C. Black.—The Constitution in the making, by Harrington Putnam.—Compromises of the Constitution, by Randolph Harrison.—The fight for ratification, by James B. Scott.

9334
Curtis, George T. Constitutional history of the United States from their Declaration of Independence to the close of the Civil War. v. 1. [1774–88] New York, Harper, 1889. xiii, 774 p. KF4541.C84

A revised edition of the author's *History of the Origin, Formation, and Adoption of the Constitution of the United States; With Notices of Its Principal Framers* (New York, Harper, 1854–58. 2 v. KF4541.C86).

9335
Curtis, George T. The Constitution of the United States, and its history. *In* Winsor, Justin, *ed.* Narrative and critical history of America. v. 7. The United States of North America. pt. 2. Boston, Houghton, Mifflin, 1888. p. [237]–266. ports. E18.W76, v. 7

9336
Dewey, Donald O. James Madison helps Clio interpret the Constitution. American journal of legal history, v. 15, Jan. 1971: 38–55. LL

Madison contended throughout his career that those who interpreted the Constitution had to keep constantly in mind the intentions of those who drew up and ratified the document.

9337
Eriksson, Erik M., *and* David N. Rowe. American constitutional history. New York, W. W. Norton [ᶜ1933] xi, 527 p. JK271.E7

"Selected references" at end of each chapter.

The first 10 chapters (p. 1–238) provide a general treatment of the period through 1789.

9338
Farrand, Max. The federal Constitution and the defects of the Confederation. American political science review, v. 2, Nov. 1908: 532–544. JA1.A6, v. 2

9339
Fisher, Sydney G. The evolution of the Constitution of the United States, showing that it is a development of progressive history and not an isolated document struck off at a given time or an imitation of English or Dutch forms of government. Philadelphia, J. B. Lippincott Co., 1897. 398 p. JK37.F6

9340
Goodman, Paul, *comp.* The American Constitution. New York, Wiley [1970] x, 191 p. (Problems in American history) KF4541.Z9G6

Includes bibliographic references.

A collection of contemporary writings by Alexander Hamilton, James Madison, Patrick Henry, William Grayson, Richard Henry Lee, James Lincoln, Patrick Dollard, Edmund Pendleton, Robert Yates, and Melancthon Smith, together with more recent essays by Lucian W. Pye, Bernard Bailyn, Robert R. Palmer, John P. Roche, Charles A. Beard, Cecilia Kenyon, and Douglass G. Adair.

9341
Hendrick, Burton J. Bulwark of the Republic; a biography of the Constitution. New and rev. ed. Boston, Little, Brown, 1938. x, 489 p. plates, ports. JK31.H4 1938

"The United States becomes a nation": p. 9–99.

9342
Jones, Robert F., *comp.* The formation of the Constitution. New York, Holt, Rinehart and Winston [1971] 136 p. illus. (American problem studies) JK146.J64

Contents: An economic document for an economic end, by C. A. Beard.—An economic interpretation tested and found wanting, by R. E. Thomas.—The Constitution: a result of social and economic interests, by S. Bruchey and E. J. Ferguson.—The influence of geography and paper money, by O. G. Libby.—Capitalism versus agrarianism, by J. T. Main.—An uneasy alliance of defensive aristocrats and restless mechanics, by S. Lynd.—Youth and energy carry the day, by S. M. Elkins and E. McKitrick.—A democratic cure for the "diseases" and "defects" of democracy, by M. Diamond.—A government by and for the majority, by R. E. Brown.—Government-making by consensus, By B. F. Wright.—Government-making by caucus, By J. P. Roche.—Worthy aristocrats versus licentious democrats, by G. Wood.—Guide to further reading (p. 134–136).

9343
Kelly, Alfred H., *and* Winfred A. Harbison. The American Constitution; its origins and development. 4th ed. New York, Norton [1970] xviii, 1211 p. JK31.K4 1970

Bibliography: p. 1103–1149.
First edition published in 1948.

The first six chapters cover the period through the ratification of the Constitution.

9344

King, John A.   The framing of the federal Constitution and the cause leading thereto. An address delivered before the New York Historical Society. New York, Printed for the Society, 1888. 40 p.   JK146.K53

9345

Levy, Leonard W., *comp.*   Essays on the making of the Constitution. New York, Oxford University Press, 1969. xxii, 260 p.   JK146.L47

Bibliography: p. 258–260.

Provides excerpts from the writings of Charles A. Beard, Charles Warren, Andrew C. McLaughlin, Merrill Jensen, Robert E. Brown, Forrest McDonald, Jackson T. Main, E. James Ferguson, John P. Roche, Stanley M. Elkins, and Eric McKitrick.

9346

Lodge, Henry Cabot.   The Constitution and its makers. *In his* The democracy of the Constitution, and other addresses and essays. New York, C. Scribner's Sons, 1915. p. 32–87.   JK21.L58

9347

Long, Breckinridge.   Genesis of the Constitution of the United States of America. New York, Macmillan Co., 1926. 260 p.   JK268.L6
   KF4541.L64

After reviewing the constitutional basis of the colonial governments, the author discusses briefly the Stamp Act Congress, the Continental Congress, the state constitutions, 1776–80, the Articles of Confederation, and the Constitutional Convention.

9348

McMaster, John B.   The framers and the framing of the Constitution. *In his* With the fathers; studies in the history of the United States. New York, D. Appleton, 1896. p. 107–149.   E173.M16

9349

Mitchell, Broadus, *and* Louise P. Mitchell.   A biography of the Constitution of the United States: its origin, formation, adoption [and] interpretation. New York, Oxford University Press, 1964. xvii, 384 p.   JK31.M55 1964

Bibliography: p. [351]

Reviews the actions of the Constitutional Convention, summarizes the ratification controversies in Massachusetts, Virginia, and New York, and discusses the Bill of Rights and other amendments.

9350

Moran, Thomas F.   The formation and development of the Constitution. Philadelphia, Printed for subscribers only by G. Barrie [ᶜ1904] xix, 504 p. facsims., plates, ports. (part col.) (The History of North America, [v.7])   E178.H7, v. 7

Chapters 1–8 (p. 3–226) are devoted to the origin, development, and ratification of the Constitution.

9351

Morey, William C.   The genesis of a written constitution. *In* American Academy of Political and Social Science, *Philadelphia.* Annals, v. 1, Apr. 1891: 529–557.
   H1.A4, v. 1

9352

Murillo Ferrol, Francisco.   Don Diego de Gardoqui y la Constitucion norteamericana. *In* Granada (City). Universidad. Boletin, v. 22, Oct. 1950: 481–499.
   AP60.G7, v. 22

9353

Murphy, William P.   The triumph of nationalism; state sovereignty, the Founding Fathers, and the making of the Constitution. Chicago, Quadrangle Books [1968, ᶜ1967] viii, 434 p.   JK316.M8

Bibliography: p. [419]–422.

Describes political conditions under the Articles of Confederation, the opinions of the delegates to the Convention of 1787 on questions relating to the issue of a national versus a federal government, and the drafting and ratification of the Constitution. The author concludes that the doctrine of state sovereignty has no basis in the national charter as it was originally established.

9354

Nevins, Allan.   The Constitution makers and the public, 1785–1790. An address before the conference of the Public Relations Society of America, Statler Hilton Hotel, November 13, 1962, Boston, Mass. [New York, Foundation for Public Relations Research and Education, 1963] 20 p. (Foundation [for Public Relations Research and Education] lecture, 2d)   JK119.N4

9355

Pole, Jack Richon.   The making of the Constitution. *In* Allen, Harry C., *and* Charles P. Hill, *eds.* British essays in American history, London, E. Arnold [1957] p. 1–21.   E178.6.A37 1957

Concludes that if the Federalists had waited a few years longer, sectional tensions, heightened by opposing attitudes toward the European wars, would have made agreement over the form of the new government impossible.

9356

Prince, Le Baron Bradford.   The Articles of Confederation vs. the Constitution. The progress of nationality among the people and in the government. New York, G. P. Putnam, 1867. 125 p.   JK139.P9

A 19th-century comparison of the strengths and weaknesses of the two documents.

9357

Read, Conyers, *ed.*   The Constitution reconsidered. Edited for the American Historical Association. New York, Columbia University Press, 1938. xviii, 424 p.   JK271.R33

Partial contents: The fundamental law behind the Constitution of the United States, by Charles H. McIlwain.—The theory of balanced government, by Stanley Pargellis.—European doctrines and the Constitution, by R. M. MacIver.—The concepts of democracy and liberty in the eighteenth century, by Gaetano Salvemini.—The appeal to reason and the American Constitution, by Roland Bainton.—The Puritan background of the First Amendment, by William Haller.—Philosophical differences between the Constitution and the Bill of Rights, by Herbert W. Schneider.—Historiography and the Constitution, by Charles A. Beard.

9358
Schuyler, Robert L. The Constitution of the United States; an historical survey of its formation. New York, Macmillan Co. 1923. viii, 211 p.   JK268.S45

An examination of early American experiments in federalism, the Confederation, and the framing, adoption, and launching of the Constitution. Schuyler credits the success of the Constitution to commercial prosperity, patriotism, the silence of the document on selected controversial issues, the support of clergy, lawyers, and teachers, and the lack of public knowledge of the process through which it was constructed.

9359
Scott, James B. The United States of America: a study in international organization. New York, Oxford University Press, 1920. xix, 605 p. (Publications of the Carnegie Endowment for International Peace. Division of International Law)   JK116.S3

Following a brief survey of the idea of union from the Mayflower Compact to the Philadelphia Convention, the author analyzes the nature and provisions of the federal system and draws parallels between the situation confronted by the Founding Fathers in 1787 and by western leaders in 1918. An extended appendix includes texts of various plans of union for the American colonies and states, the Northwest Ordinance of 1787, and documents from which the Constitution evolved.

9360
Smith, James Allen. The spirit of American government. Edited by Cushing Strout. Cambridge, Belknap Press of Harvard University Press, 1965. lxvi, 419 p. (The John Harvard Library)   JK246.S64 1965

Photographic reproduction of the 1911 reprint of the original edition published in New York by Macmillan in 1907. "Works cited by J. Allen Smith": p. 402–406.

9361
Smith, James M., *comp.* The Constitution. New York, Harper & Row [1971] vii, 211 p. (Interpretations of American history)   KF4541.A2S6

Contents: The background of American federalism, by A. C. McLaughlin.—The theory of the mixed or balanced constitution, by C. C. Weston.—Constitutions and rights, by B. Bailyn.—The people as constituent power, by R. R. Palmer.—The progress of constitutional theory between the Declaration of Independence and the meeting of the Philadelphia Convention, by E. S. Corwin.—The transformation of the republican thought, by G. S. Wood.—The Founding Fathers: a case study in democratic politics, by J. P. Roche.—Republicanism and democratic thought in The Federalist, by M. Diamond.—A spacious Republic: from sovereignty to federalism, by D. J. Boorstin.—Selected bibliography (p. 205–211).

9362
Story, Joseph. Commentaries on the Constitution of the United States; with a preliminary review of the constitutional history of the colonies and states, before the adoption of the Constitution. Boston, Hilliard, Gray, 1833. 3 v.   KF4541.S7 1833

Contents: Book 1. History of the colonies.—Book 2. History of the Revolution and the Confederation.—Book 3. The Constitution of the United States.

Reprinted, with a new introduction by Arthur E. Sutherland, in New York by Da Capo Press (1970).

See also Abel P. Upshur's *A Brief Enquiry Into the True Nature and Character of Our Federal Government: Being a Review of Judge Story's Commentaries on the Constitution of the United States* (Petersburg [Va.] Printed by E. and J. C. Ruffin, 1840. 132 p. JK211.S8U6 1840), which has been reprinted in New York by Da Capo Press (1971. KF4541.Z9U6 1971).

9363
Sutherland, Arthur E. Constitutionalism in America; origin and evolution of its fundamental ideas. New York, Blaisdell Pub. Co. [1965] xv, 618 p. (A Blaisdell book in political science)   JK31.S82

Bibliography: p. 563–581.
"Making the American Constitution": p. 132–219.

9364
Thorpe, Francis N. The constitutional history of the United States. v. 1. 1765–1788. Chicago, Callaghan, 1901. xxi, 595 p. maps.   KF4541.T46 1901, v. 1

Reprinted in New York by Da Capo Press (1970).

Focuses largely on the formation of a national government.

9365
Tucker, John R. The Constitution of the United States. A critical discussion of its genesis, development, and interpretation. Edited by Henry St. George Tucker. 2 v.   JK241.T9

Chapters 5 and 6 (p. 178–337) in volume 1 cover American developments to 1789.

9366
Wright, Benjamin F. Consensus and continuity, 1776–1787. Boston, Boston University Press, 1958. 60 p. (Boston University. The Gaspar G. Bacon lectures on the Constitution of the United States)   JK116.W7

Also published in the *Boston University Law Review*, v. 38, winter 1958, p. 1–52.

Argues that the extensive experience of the American colonials with self-government produced a pervasive unity characterized by common habits and institutions, an unusual capacity for compromise, and a sophisticated mastery of representative politics. The federal Constitution is considered as primary evidence of the essential political continuity of the Revolutionary period.

Intellectual and Political Origins of the Constitution

9367

Adair, Douglass G. "Experience must be our only guide": history, democratic theory, and the United States Constitution. *In* Billington, Ray A., *ed.* The reinterpretation of early American history; essays in honor of John Edwin Pomfret. San Marino, Calif., Huntington Library, 1966. p. 129–148. E175.B5

9368

The Anarchiad: a New England poem. Written in concert by David Humphreys, Joel Barlow, John Trumbull, and Dr. Lemuel Hopkins. Now first published in book form. Edited, with notes and appendices, by Luther G. Riggs. New Haven, T. H. Pease, 1861. viii, 120 p.
PS778.H5A6 1861b Rare Bk. Coll.

Reprinted, with an introduction and index by William K. Bottorff, in Gainesville, Fla., by Scholars' Facsimiles & Reprints (1967).

Originally published in the *New-Haven Gazette and in the Connecticut Magazine* in 12 numbers, from October 26, 1786, to September 13, 1787, the mock-epic satire was intended to stir Federalist sentiment.

9369

Anderson, William. The intention of the framers: a note on constitutional interpretation. American political science review, v. 49, June 1955: 340–352.
JA1.A6, v. 49

9370

Bailey, John B. Some sources of American constitutionalism: a study in the history of ideas. 1964. ([246] p.)
Micro AC–1, no. 64–11,695

Thesis (Ph.D.)—University of Georgia.

Abstracted in *Dissertation Abstracts*, v. 27A, Nov. 1966, p. 1313.

Discusses the adaptation of English constitutional thought in America up to 1787.

9371

Baldwin, Henry. A general view of the origin and nature of the Constitution and government of the United States, deduced from the political history and condition of the colonies and states, from 1774 until 1788. And the decisions of the Supreme Court of the United States. Together with opinions in the cases decided at January term, 1837, arising on the restraints on the powers of the states. Philadelphia, Printed by J. C. Clark, 1837. v, 197 p. illus. KF4541.B2 1837

Reprinted in New York by Da Capo Press (1970).

9372

Beatty, Hubert I. Why form a more perfect union? A study of the origins of the Constitutional Convention of 1787. 1962. ([565] p.) Micro AC–1, no. 63–2704

Thesis (Ph.D.)—Stanford University.

Abstracted in *Dissertation Abstracts*, v. 23, Apr. 1963, p. 3874–3875.

9373

Bennett, Walter H. Early American theories of federalism. Journal of politics, v. 4, Aug. 1942: 383–395.
JA1.J6, v. 4

Traces the American development of the concept of a federally organized system of government before the Constitution.

9374

Bourne, Edward G. The use of history made by the framers of the Constitution. *In* American Historical Association. Annual report. 1896. v. 1. Washington, 1897. p. 221–230. E172.A60, 1896, v. 1

9375

Chinard, Gilbert. Polybius and the American Constitution. Journal of the history of ideas, v. 1, Jan. 1940: 38–58. B1.J75, v. 1

On classical influences in the Constitution.

9376

Coleman, George S. The religious background of the federal Constitution. 1933.

Thesis (Ph.D.)—Harvard University.

9377

Cone, Carl B. Richard Price and the Constitution of the United States. American historical review, v. 53, July 1948: 726–747. E171.A57, v. 53

Speculates upon what effect Price's friendship with noted American leaders and the wide reading of his pamphlets may have had upon the content of the U.S. Constitution.

9378

Eidelberg, Paul. The philosophy of the American Constitution; a reinterpretation of the intentions of the Founding Fathers. New York, Free Press [1968] xvi, 339 p. JK31.E4

Bibliography: p. 323–327.

Contends that the Constitution was written to establish a "mixed regime" combining elements of democracy and aristocracy.

9379

Fisher, Louis. The efficiency side of separated powers. Journal of American studies, v. 5, Aug. 1971: 113–131.
E151.J6, v. 5

Studying the views of Adams, Hamilton, Jay, Jefferson, Madison, and Washington on the separation of powers, the author concludes that their experiences in state government and the Continental Congress convinced them that the powers of the executive, legislative, and judicial branches of the federal government needed to be separate and well defined in order to promote greater administrative efficiency and more reliable governmental machinery.

9380
Goodykoontz, Colin B.   The Founding Fathers and Clio. Pacific historical review, v. 23, May 1954: 111–123.
F851.P18, v. 23

In drawing up the Constitution, the Founding Fathers turned to "the experience of mankind" as a check upon the dictates of reason.

9381
Gummere, Richard M.   The classical ancestry of the United States Constitution. American quarterly, v. 14, spring 1962: 3–18.
AP2.A3985, v. 14

9382
Hoffer, Peter C.   The constitutional crisis and the rise of a nationalistic view of history in America, 1786–1788. *In* New York State Historical Association. New York history, v. 52, July 1971: 305–323. illus.
F116.N865, v. 52

While Revolutionary leaders used examples from ancient and modern European history to justify separation from Great Britain, those who drafted the Constitution turned to American experience and practice in their debates.

9383
Hofstadter, Richard.   A constitution against parties: Madisonian pluralism and the anti-party tradition. Government and opposition, v. 4, summer 1969: 345–366.
JA8.G6, v. 4

Madison and the Founding Fathers believed that political parties, in the British sense, were anathema to liberty. They sought to protect liberty under the Constitution by creating a system of legislative checks. Madison felt that majorities would be formed within the Senate and House of Representatives as weak, shifting coalitions united to promote single causes or issues only to dissolve again upon accomplishing their purpose. He never envisioned a system in which political parties themselves would serve as the instruments of pluralistic forces within society.

9384
Holcombe, Arthur N.   Sections, classes, and the federal Constitution. *In* The Gaspar G. Bacon lectures on the Constitution of the United States, 1940–1950 [by] A. N. Holcombe [and others] Boston, Boston University Press, 1953. p. 3–30.
KF4550.A2G3

Contends that the work of the Philadelphia Convention represented a triumph of middle-class interests.

9385
Hume, Edgar E.   The role of the Society of the Cincinnati in the birth of the Constitution of the United States. Pennsylvania history, v. 5, Apr. 1938: 101–107.
F146.P597, v. 5

9386
Isetti, Ronald E.   The Constitution as an experiment: a study of its religious and scientific origins.   1972.
Thesis (Ph.D.)—University of California, Berkeley.

9387
Katz, Stanley N.   The origins of American constitutional thought. *In* Perspectives in American history. v. 3; 1969. [Cambridge] Charles Warren Center for Studies in American History, Harvard University. p. 474–490.
E171.P47, v. 3

A review article.

9388
Keller, Hans G.   Die Quellen der amerikanischen Verfassung. *In* Schweizer Beiträge aur allgemeinen Geschichte. Bd. 16; 1958. Bern. p. 107–141.   D6.S37, v. 16

Examines the basic elements and resources that the delegates in Philadelphia drew upon in creating the federal Constitution.

9389
Keller, Hans G.   Unitarismus und Föderalismus im Werk der amerikanischen verfassunggebenden Versammlung. Zeitschrift für Politik, new ser., v. 5, no. 3, 1958: 214–229.   JA14.Z4, n.s., v. 5

Argues that the Constitution was not an expression of political philosophy but an instrument intended to meet pressing practical needs.

9390
Kelley, Darwin N.   Separation of powers: the American development of separation of powers and the use of this principle in the Constitution of the United States, 1607–1787. 1953. ([285] p.)   Micro AC–1, no. 6443
Thesis (Ph.D.)—Indiana University.
Abstracted in *Dissertation* Abstracts, v. 13, no. 6, 1953, p. 1173.

9391
Lovejoy, Arthur O.   The theory of human nature in the American Constitution and the method of counterpoise. *In his* Reflections on human nature. Baltimore, Johns Hopkins Press [1961] p. [35]–65.
B945.L583R45

Contends that the Founding Fathers, like most reasoning men in the Western World, held that man was motivated primarily by passion, whether arbitrary and unexamined prejudice, vanity, or the pursuit of private economic advantage. Yet, by employing the theory of counterpoise—that desirable results can be achieved by balancing harmful things against one another—they were able to construct a functioning political system.

9392
McDonald, Forrest.   Constitutional aspects of American federalism. *In* Canadian Historical Association. Report. 1964. [Toronto] p. 136–143.   F1001.C26, 1964

9393

McIlwain, Charles H.   The historical background of federal government: some sources of our American federalism. *In* Pound, Roscoe, Charles H. McIlwain, *and* Roy F. Nichols. Federalism as a democratic process; essays. New Brunswick, Rutgers University Press, 1942. (Rutgers University. Publications of the one hundred seventh-fifth anniversary celebration, no. 2) p. 31–48.
JK311.P7

Examines early instances of British federalism and concludes that the ultimate constitutional issue between the colonists and the English Parliament was a purely federal one—whether the mother country and the various dominions truly constituted one state or whether they were a federation of separate dominions under a common king.

9394

McKeon, Richard P.   The development of the concept of property in political philosophy: a study of the background of the Constitution. Ethics, v. 48, Apr. 1938: 297–366.   BJ1.16, v. 48

9395

McLaughlin, Andrew C.   The background of American federalism. American political science review, v. 12, May 1918: 215–240.   JA1.A6, v. 12

9396

McLaughlin, Andrew C.   Democracy and the Constitution. *In* American Antiquarian Society, *Worcester, Mass.* Proceedings, new ser., v. 22, Oct. 1912: 293–320.
E172.A35, n.s., v. 22

9397

McLaughlin, Andrew C.   The foundations of American constitutionalism. New York City, New York University Press, 1932. vii, 176 p. (New York University. Stokes Foundation. Anson G. Phelps lectureship on early American history)   JK268.M25

Stressing the continuity of thought from the early New England covenants and colonial charters to the federal Constitution, the author analyzes such concepts as the social compact, government by consent, the legitimacy of resistance to usurpation, judicial review, and federalism. McLaughlin concludes that the major achievement of the American Revolution was the insistence of the Founding Fathers upon constitutionally limited government.

9398

Marks, Frederick W.   American pride, European prejudice, and the Constitution. Historian, v. 34, Aug. 1972: 579–597.   D1.H22, v. 34

Finds that a major consideration in the replacement of the Articles of Confederation with an invigorated Union lay in the desire of the nationalists to prevent the further humiliation of the newly united states by European powers.

9399

Marks, Frederick W.   The impact of foreign affairs on the United States Constitution, 1783–1788. 1968 ([245] p.)
Micro AC–1, no. 69–2352

Thesis (Ph.D.)—University of Michigan.
Abstracted in *Dissertation Abstracts*, v. 29A, Feb. 1969, p. 2623–2624.

9400

Mirkin, Harris G.   The revolutionary Republic: the right of revolution and the American constitutional system. 1967. ([284] p.)   Micro AC–1, no. 68–2506

Thesis (Ph.D.)—Princeton University.
Abstracted in *Dissertation Abstracts*, v. 28A, Apr. 1968, p. 4231.

After using the doctrine of the right of revolution to justify resistance to Great Britain, the Founding Fathers thwarted an emerging populist interpretation of revolutionary principle by calling the Philadelphia Convention. Through the Constitution they hoped to protect freedom by institutionalizing controlled revolution and by creating a new political system that provided alternatives to revolution.

9401

Morey, William C.   The sources of American federalism. *In* American Academy of Political and Social Science, *Philadelphia.* Annals, v. 6, Sept. 1895: 197–226.
H1.A4, v. 6

9402

Morgan, Howard Wayne.   The Founding Fathers and the middle ages. Mid-America, v. 42, Jan. 1960: 30–43.
BX1415.I3M5, v. 42

Despite their insistence on the didactic value of history, the Founding Fathers confined their reading to studies of Greece and Rome and post-Reformation histories. They viewed the middle ages as a wasteland marked by universal ignorance and barbarity.

9403

Nagel, Paul C.   One nation indivisible; the Union in American thought, 1776–1861. New York, Oxford University Press, 1964. vii, 328 p.   JK311.N2

Bibliographic references included in "Notes" (p. 289–318).

A study of the Union as symbol and myth showing the great range of meaning Americans gave to the concept.

9404

Panagopoulos, Epaminondas P.   Classicism and the framers of the Constitution. 1952.

Thesis (Ph.D.)—University of Chicago.

9405

Ranney, John C.   The bases of American federalism. William and Mary quarterly, 3d ser., v. 3, Jan. 1946: 1–35.
F221.W71, 3d s., v. 3

Discusses those factors in the American colonial experience and the events of 1786–87 that led to union.

9406

Riemer, Neal.   Two conceptions of the genius of American politics. Journal of politics, v. 20, Nov. 1958: 695–717.
JA1.J6, v. 20

In contrast to Daniel Boorstin's assertion in his *Genius of American Politics* that Americans placed a premium upon experience over theory, the author uses the writings of James Madison, 1787–88, to show that the Founding Fathers used *explicit* models derived from past theory to construct the institutions embodied in the Constitution.

9407

Riker, William H.   Dutch and American Federalism. Journal of the history of ideas, v. 18, Oct. 1957: 495–521.
B1.J75, v. 18

Considers the degree to which the framers were influenced in drafting the U.S. Constitution by their perception of Dutch federalism and public law.

9408

Robinson, James A.   Newtonianism and the Constitution. Midwest journal of political science, v. 1, Nov. 1957: 252–266.
JA1.M5, v. 1

Finds little evidence that the Founding Fathers relied on Newtonian analogies as a source of political ideas. The desire for a science of politics, the concept of balanced or mixed government, and the theory of separation of powers all antedate Newton and Newtonianism.

9409

Robinson, James H.   The original and derived features of the Constitution of the United States of America. [n.p.] 1890. 43 p.
JK148.R62

Inaug.-Diss.—Freiburg.
Also published in the *Annals* of the American Academy of Political and Social Science, v. 1, Oct. 1890, p. 203–243.

9410

Schlesinger, Arthur M.   Economic aspects of the movement for the Constitution. *In his* New viewpoints in American history. New York, Macmillan Co., 1922. p. 184–199.
E175.9.S34

"Bibliographic note": p. 198–199.
The strongest motive behind the drive for a more vigorous central government was the desire to recreate conditions under which property, contracts, and investments might be secure and business and commerce might prosper.

9411

Shattuck, Charles E.   The true meaning of the term "liberty" in those clauses in the federal and state constitutions which protect "life, liberty, and property." Harvard law review, v. 4, Mar. 1891: 365–392.
LL

9412

Shirk, Barbara L.   The uses and abuses of Montesquieu's theories in America, 1787–1788. 1972. ([343] p.)
Micro AC–1, no. 73–8107
Thesis (Ph.D.)—University of California, Santa Barbara.
Abstracted in *Dissertation Abstracts International*, v. 33A, Apr. 1973, p. 5661–5662.

9413

Smylie, James H.   American clergymen and the Constitution of the United States of America, 1781–1796. 1958. ([479] p.)
Micro AC–1, no. 73–12,462
Thesis (Ph.D.)—Princeton Theological Seminary.
Abstracts not available in *Dissertation Abstracts International* (see v. 33A, May 1973, p. 6443).

9414

Stanwood, Edward.   A glimpse at 1786. Atlantic monthly, v. 57, June 1886: 777–788.
AP2.A8, v. 57

Finds it to be a critical year in the evolution of sentiment for a truly national government.

9415

Thorpe, Francis N.   The origin of the federal Constitution. Magazine of American history, with notes and queries, v. 18, Aug. 1887: 130–141.
E171.M18, v. 18

Argues that the causes were economic rather than political in character.

9416

Wright, Benjamin F.   The early history of written constitutions in America. *In* Essays in history and political theory in honor of Charles Howard McIlwain. Cambridge, Mass., Harvard University Press, 1936. p. 344–371.
D6.E75

Traces the evolution of constitutional precedents invoked at the Philadelphia Convention.

9417

Wright, Benjamin F.   The origins of the separation of powers in America. Economica, v. 13, May 1933: 169–185.
HB1.E5, v. 13

Concludes that experience and institutional precedent were more important in determining the structure of American government than the writings of Montesquieu and other political theorists.

The Philadelphia Convention

CONTEMPORARY SOURCES AND DOCUMENTS

9418

Conway, Moncure D.   An unpublished draft of a national constitution by Edmund Randolph, found among the papers of George Mason. Scribner's magazine, v. 2, Sept. 1887: 313–320. facsim.
AP2.S4, v. 2

9419

Farrand, Max.   The records of the federal Convention. American historical review, v. 13, Oct. 1907: 44–65.
E171.A57, v. 13

Surveys the surviving records available for a study of the Convention's proceedings.

9420

Hamilton, Alexander.   Some notes by Alexander Hamilton of debates in the federal Convention of 1787. *In*

Massachusetts Historical Society, *Boston*. Proceedings. 2d ser., v. 18; 1903/4. Boston, 1905. p. 348–362.
F61.M38, 2d s., v. 18

Introduction and notes by Worthington C. Ford. A more complete text with a fuller introduction appeared in the *American Historical Review*, v. 10, Oct. 1904, p. 97–109.

9421

Jameson, John Franklin. Studies in the history of the federal Convention of 1787. *In* American Historical Association. Annual report. 1902. v. 1. Washington, 1903. p. 87–167.   E172.A60, 1902, v. 1

———— ———— Offprint. Washington, Govt. Print. Off., 1903. 87–167 p.   JK146.J3

Includes letters by delegates, texts of plans submitted, and journals and debates of the state conventions.

9422

Keller, Charles R., *and* George W. Pierson. A new Madison manuscript relating to the federal Convention of 1787. American historical review, v. 36, Oct. 1930: 17–30.   E171.A57, v. 36

An examination of a copy of Secretary Jackson's *Journal* in Madison's hand indicates that Madison used his copy of the *Journal* to correct and supplement his *Debates*.

9423

Lansing, John. The delegate from New York; or, Proceedings of the federal Convention of 1787, from the notes of John Lansing, Jr. Edited by Joseph Reese Strayer. Princeton, Princeton University Press, 1939. viii, 125 p. port.   JK141 1939L

Reprinted in Port Washington, N.Y., by Kennikat Press (1967).

9424

McHenry, James. Papers of Dr. James McHenry on the federal Convention of 1787. Edited by J. Franklin Jameson. American historical review, v. 11, Apr. 1906: 595–624.   E171.A57, v. 11

———— ———— Offprint. [New York, 1906] 595–624 p.
JK146.M3

9425

McLaughlin, Andrew C., *ed.* Sketch of Charles Pinckney's plan for a constitution, 1787. American historical review, v. 9, July 1904: 735–747.   E171.A57, v. 9

———— ———— Offprint. [New York? 1904] 735–747 p.
LL

A comparison of James Wilson's outline of Pinckney's constitutional plan as presented to the federal Convention on May 29, 1787, with Pinckney's *Observations on the Plan of Government Submitted to the Federal Convention.*

9426

Paterson, William. Papers of William Paterson on the federal Convention, 1787. American historical review, v. 9, Jan. 1904: 310–340.   E171.A57, v. 9

———— ———— Offprint. [New York? 1904] 310–340 p.
JK148.P3

9427

Pierce, William. Notes of Major William Pierce on the federal Convention of 1787. American historical review, v. 3, Jan. 1898: 310–334.   E171.A57, v. 3

9428

Pinckney, Charles. Sketch of Pinckney's plan for a constitution, 1787. American historical review, v. 9, July 1904: 735–747.   E171.A57, v. 9

Accompanied by an introduction and notes.

9429

Prescott, Arthur T., *comp.* Drafting the federal Constitution; a rearrangement of Madison's notes, giving consecutive developments of provisions in the Constitution of the United States, supplemented by documents pertaining to the Philadelphia Convention and to ratification processes, and including insertions by the compiler. University, La., Louisiana State University Press, 1941. xix, 838 p. front.   JK146.P7

Reprinted in New York by Greenwood Press (1968).

9430

Rogow, Arnold A. The federal Convention: Madison and Yates. American historical review, v. 60, Jan. 1955: 323–335.   E171.A57, v. 60

Comparison of Madison's *Notes* and Robert Yates' *Secret Debates.*

9431

Scott, James B. James Madison's notes of debates in the federal Convention of 1787 and their relation to a more perfect society of nations. New York, Oxford University Press, 1918. xviii, 149 p. facsims. (part fold.), port.   JK148.S4

"Bibliography of Madison's notes of debates in the Federal convention of 1787": p. [xvii]–xviii.

Interprets selections from Madison's notes of the proceedings that have an international significance or value.

9432

Solberg, Winton U., *ed.* The federal Convention and the formation of the Union of the American states. Edited, with an introduction by Winton U. Solberg. New York, Liberal Arts Press [1958] cxviii, 409 p. (The American heritage series, no. 19)   JK146.S6

"The federal Convention: Madison's notes of debates": p. [65]–344.
Bibliography: p. cxii–cxvii.

9433

U.S. *Bureau of Rolls and Library.* Documentary history of the Constitution of the United States of America, 1787–1870. Derived from the records, manuscripts, and rolls deposited in the Bureau of Rolls and Library of the

Department of State. Washington, Dept. of State, 1894–1905. 5 v.   JK111.A5

Vols.1–3 were issued as appendixes to the *Bulletin* of the Bureau of Rolls and Library, no. 1–3, 5, 7, and 9, 1893–97 (no. 9 issued 1900). Vols. 4–5 form pts. 1–2 of *Bulletin* no. 11.

Vols. 1–3 were reprinted in 1901 as House Document 529, 59th Congress, 2d session, and issued also in a Bureau edition. In these issues v. 3 has an appendix not in the original edition: "Additional Notes by Madison for the Introduction to His Notes of Debates in the Federal Convention" (p. 796a–796o).

Vol. 3 has a "special index" (p. 797–904).

Contents: v. 1. [pt.] 1, Sept. 1893. The period preceding the convention that framed the Constitution. [pt.] 2, Jan. 1894. The proceedings of the federal Convention.—v. 2. [pt.] 3, May 1894. The Constitution as signed in Convention; proceedings in Congress; ratification. [pt.] 4, Sept. 1894. The amendments.—v. 3. [pt.] 5, Oct. 1897. Madison's notes of the proceedings of the federal Convention.—v. 4. Letters and papers relating to the Constitution, from August 1, 1788, to the death of Madison. Appendix to the entire work. Bibliography.

9434

U.S. *Constitutional Convention, 1787.*   Constitutional chaff. Rejected suggestions of the Constitutional Convention of 1787, with explanatory argument. Compiled by Jane Butzner from the notes of James Madison, Major William Pierce, Dr. James McHenry, Rufus King, and the Honorable Robert Yates. New York, Columbia University Press, 1941. 197 p.

JK141 1941

"The source of the notes from which this book was compiled is, *Documents Illustrative of the Formation of the Union of the American States*, House Document no. 398, 69th Congress, first session."—Preface.

Appendixes: A. What the authors of the Constitution thought about the power of the courts to declare laws unconstitutional.—B. What the authors of the Constitution thought about a limitation on the number of terms for the President.—C. Character sketches of delegates to the Constitutional Convention, by Major William Pierce.—D. The Constitution of the United States.

Reprinted in Port Washington, N.Y., by Kennikat Press (1970).

9435

U.S. *Constitutional Convention, 1787.*   Debate on the suffrage in Congress. From Madison's Journal of the Constitutional Convention, 1787. [Boston, Directors of the Old South Work, 1896] 20 p. (Old South leaflets. [General ser., v. 3] no. 70)   E173.O44, v. 3, no. 70

9436

U.S. *Constitutional Convention, 1787.*   Journal, acts and proceedings of the Convention, assembled at Philadelphia, Monday, May 14, and dissolved Monday, September 17, 1787, which formed the Constitution of the United States. Boston, Printed and published by Thomas B. Wait, 1819. 510 p.   JK141 1819

"Published under the direction of the President of the United States, conformably to a resolution of Congress of March 27, 1818."

9437

U.S. *Constitutional Convention, 1787.*   Notes of debates in the federal Convention of 1787, reported by James Madison. With an introduction by Adrienne Koch. Athens, Ohio University Press [1966] xxiii, 659 p.

JK141 1966

First published in volumes 2 and 3 of *The Papers of James Madison* (Washington, 1840). The 1893 edition by E. H. Scott, the first to be published separately, has been reprinted in Freeport, N.Y., by Books for Libraries Press (1970). The 1920 edition by Gaillard Hunt and James Brown Scott has been reprinted in Westport, Conn., by Greenwood Press (1970).

9438

U.S. *Constitutional Convention, 1787.*   The records of the federal Convention of 1787. Edited by Max Farrand. Rev. ed. New Haven, Yale University Press, 1937. 4 v. facsims.   KF4510.F3 1937

On the title page of v. 4: With a general index by David M. Matteson.

First published in three volumes in 1911.

9439

U.S. *Constitutional Convention, 1787.*   Secret proceedings and debates of the Convention assembled at Philadelphia, in the year 1787, for the purpose of forming the Constitution of the United States of America. From notes taken by the late Robert Yates, Esquire, chief justice of New York, and copied by John Lansing, Jun., Esquire, late chancellor of that state, members of that Convention. Including "The genuine information," laid before the legislature of Maryland, by Luther Martin, Esquire, then attorney-general of that state, and member of the same Convention. Also, other historical documents, relative to the federal compact of the North American Union. Louisville, Ky., A. Mygatt, 1844. xi, 335 p.   JK141 1787b

Biographical sketch of Robert Yates : p. [329]–335.
First published in 1821.

9440

U.S. *Constitutional Convention, 1787.*   To secure these blessings; the great debates of the Constitutional Convention of 1787, arranged according to topics, by Saul K. Padover. New York, Washington Square Press [1962] 464 p. illus., facsims., ports.

KF4510.P3 1962

Reprinted in New York by Kraus Reprint Co. (1970).

9441

U.S. *Library of Congress. Legislative Reference Service.* Documents illustrative of the formation of the union of the American states. Washington, Govt. Print Off., 1927. x, 1115 p. facsims. (69th Congress, 1st session. House. Doc. 398)   JK11 1927

Running title: *Formation of the United States.*

Selected, arranged and indexed by Charles C. Tansill. Reprinted under the title *The Making of the American Republic; the Great Documents, 1774–1789* in New Rochelle, N.Y., by Arlington House (1972. E303.T3 1972).

Contains the texts of major official documents from the declaration and resolves of the First Continental Congress to the Bill of Rights. The bulk of the text is taken up with James Madison's reports of the debates in the federal Convention with the added notes of Robert Yates, Rufus King, William Paterson, Alexander Hamilton, and James McHenry.

9442

Yates, Abraham.   Abraham Yates's history of the movement for the United States Constitution. William and Mary quarterly, 3d ser., v. 20, Apr. 1963: 223–245.
F221.W71, 3d s., v. 20

An Anti-Federalist's view of the steps leading to the Philadelphia Convention that anticipated the Beard-Jensen interpretation of the Confederation period. Introduction and notes by Staughton Lynd.

SECONDARY WORKS

9443

Andrews, William G.   William Samuel Johnson and the making of the Constitution. Bridgeport, Conn., Standard Print [188–?] 36 p.   E302.6.J7A5

9444

Banks, Margaret.   Drafting the American Constitution: attitudes in the Philadelphia Convention towards the British system of government. American journal of legal history, v. 10, Jan. 1966: 15–33.   LL

9445

Barry, William F.   The influence of English political history on the Constitution of the United States, Article III, Section III. 1936.

Thesis (Ph.D.)—Boston College.

9446

Beard, Charles A.   An economic interpretation of the Constitution of the United States. New York, Macmillan Co., 1913. vii, 330 p. map.   JK146.B5 1913

Surveys the economic interests of the delegates to the Constitutional Convention and suggests that these men sought to enhance their own large holdings of "personalty"—public securities, manufacturing, and trade—when they spearheaded the movement for a new government and dominated the ratification process. The federal Constitution, essentially an economic document intended to protect property rights from the whims of the multitude, was opposed by small farmers—holders of "realty"—and debtors, who were either disfranchised or outmaneuvered in the state ratification battles, especially in New York, Massachusetts, New Hampshire, Virginia, and South Carolina.

9447

Bethea, Andrew J.   The contribution of Charles Pinckney to the formation of the American union. Richmond, Va., Garrett & Massie, 1937. vii, 142 p.
E302.6.P54B4

Bibliography: p. 131–135.

9448

Birkby, Robert H.   Politics of accommodation: the origin of the Supremacy Clause. Western political quarterly, v. 19, Mar. 1966: 123–135.   JA1.W4, v. 19

Finds that the supremacy of the Supreme Court resulted from a negotiated compromise between those who sought a veto by the national legislature over the state courts and those who favored construction of the Constitution by state courts.

9449

Boutell, Lewis H.   Roger Sherman in the federal Convention. *In* American Historical Association. Annual report. 1893. Washington, 1894. p. 229–247.
E172.A60, 1893

9450

Bowen, Catherine D.   Miracle at Philadelphia; the story of the Constitutional Convention, May to September, 1787. Boston, Little, Brown [1966] xix, 346 p. illus., ports.   JK146.B75

In a detailed narrative of the proceedings, the author pictures a company of high-minded statesmen who sincerely believed that disaster would ensue if the Convention failed to remedy the ills of the Confederation by creating a better instrument of government. Operating in the hot, sticky, summer atmosphere of Philadelphia, they worked hard at their task under the chairmanship of Washington and compromised when necessary. Bowen provides short character sketches of the delegates and presents a contemporary portrait of America as seen by foreign visitors.

9451

Brown, David W.   The commercial power of Congress, considered in the light of its origin. The origin, development, and contemporary interpretation of the commerce clause of the federal Constitution, from the New Jersey representations, of 1778, to the embargo laws of Jefferson's second administration, in 1809. New York, G. P. Putnam's Sons, 1910. ix, 284 p.   KF4606.B7

Discusses in chapters 1–9 (p. 1–152) the efforts to enlarge the commercial powers of the Continental Congress and the origins of the commercial clause in the federal Constitution.

9452

Brown, Robert E.   Reinterpretation of the formation of the American Constitution. Boston, Boston University Press [1963] 63 p. (The Gaspar G. Bacon lectures on the Constitution of the United States)   JK119.B7

Bibliographic footnotes.

Contends that the Constitution did not represent the interests of a narrow, undemocratic elite but appealed primarily to the middle-class property owners who made up the bulk of the population and who had fought the Revolution to preserve a society based on the natural rights of life, liberty, and property.

9453

Burke, Joseph C.   Max Farrand revisited: a new look at southern sectionalism and slavery in the federal Convention. Duquesne review, v. 12, fall 1967: 1–21.
AS30.D8A2, v. 12

Contends that Farrand misread the records of the federal Convention that he edited between 1911 and 1937 by concluding in his historical writings that western lands rather than slavery was the primary concern of the delegates in Philadelphia.

9454

Chafee, Zechariah.   How human rights got into the Constitution. Boston, Boston University Press, 1952. ix, 81 p. (Boston University. The Gaspar G. Bacon lectures on the Constitution of the United States, 1951)
KF4750.C44

"Table of documents and cases": p. 75–81.

Discusses the declarations and constitutions of the Revolutionary period, the basic English liberties embodied in the colonial charters, and the most important right in the Constitution—the habeas corpus clause.

9455

Chafee, Zechariah.   Three human rights in the Constitution of 1787. Lawrence, University of Kansas Press, 1956. 245 p. illus., ports.
KF4749.C43

Includes bibliographies.

Examines the origins of freedom of debate in Congress, the prohibition against bills of attainder, and freedom of movement in an effort to determine why these rights were so important to the framers of the Constitution.

9456

Chapin, Bradley.   Colonial and Revolutionary origins of the American law of treason. William and Mary quarterly, 3d ser., v. 17, Jan. 1960: 3–21.
F221.W71, 3d s., v. 17

The definition of treason written into the Constitution stems from a 14th-century English statute designed for the protection of a king.

9457

Chidsey, Donald B.   The birth of the Constitution, an informal history. New York, Crown Publishers [1964] 207 p. illus., ports.
JK146.C47

Bibliography: p. 199–204.

9458

Clark, Jonathan.   The hopes and fears of a yesteryear: 1787. 1972. ([300] p.)   Micro AC–1, no. 73–6357

Thesis (Ph.D.)—Yale University.

Abstracted in *Dissertation Abstracts International*, v. 33A, Mar. 1973, p. 5080–5081.

9459

Coleman, Nannie M.   The Constitution and its framers. Rev.—enl.; with special introduction and chapter 16 by Ira C. Tilton. Chicago, Progressive Book Publishers, 1939. xxxii, 666 p. plates, ports.   JK116.C7 1939

First edition published in 1904.

9460

Corwin, Edward S., *and* Jack W. Peltason.   Corwin and Peltason's Understanding the Constitution. 5th ed. New York, Holt, Rinehart and Winston [1970] x, 210 p.   KF4528.C6 1970

Includes bibliographic references.
First edition published in 1958.

A basic explanation of each article of the Constitution, section by section.

9461

Corwin, Edward S.   Franklin and the Constitution. *In* American Philolophical Society, *Philadelphia*. Proceedings, v. 100, Aug. 31, 1956: 283–288.
Q11.P5, v. 100

9462

Crosskey, William W.   Politics and the Constitution in the history of the United States. [Chicago] University of Chicago Press [1953] 2 v. (xi, 1410 p.)   KF4541.C7

Bibliographic references included in "Notes" (v. 2, p. [1253]–1381).

9463

Donahoe, Bernard, *and* Marshall Smelser.   The congressional power to raise armies: the Constitutional and ratifying conventions, 1787–1788. Review of politics, v. 33, Apr. 1971: 202–211.   JA1.R4, v. 33

9464

Donovan, Frank R.   Mr. Madison's Constitution; the story behind the Constitutional Convention. New York, Dodd, Mead [1965] viii, 148 p. illus., facsim., ports.   JK148.D6

9465

Dumbauld, Edward.   The Constitution of the United States. Norman, University of Oklahoma Press [1964] xiii, 502 p. illus., facsim., ports.   JK31.D8

Bibliography: p. 463–485.

Provides a history and interpretation of each article of the Constitution by section and clause.

9466

Farrand, Max.   Compromises of the Constitution. *In* American Historical Association. Annual report. 1903. v. 1. Washington, 1904. p. 73–84.
E172.A60, 1903, v. 1

Reevaluates the order of importance assigned by historians to the various compromises agreed to at the Convention. Also published in the *American Historical Review*, v. 9, Apr. 1904. p. 479–489.

9467

Farrand, Max. The framing of the Constitution of the United States. New Haven, Yale University Press [1936] ix, 281 p. JK146.F3 1936

First published in 1913.

Examines in detail the proceedings of the Convention, including its organization and debates; the importance of the Articles of Confederation as a basis for the new document; the Virginia and New Jersey plans; and the major compromises. The volume is based primarily on Farrand's work as editor of *The Records of the Federal Convention of 1787* (entry 9438).

9468

Farrand, Max. If James Madison had had a sense of humor. Pennsylvania magazine of history and biography, v. 62, Apr. 1938: 130–139. F146.P65, v. 62

Since Madison left the only full record of the convention's debates, Farrand laments Madison's failure to provide insight into the character of his fellow delegates.

9469

Feerick, John T. The electoral college: why it was created. American Bar Association journal, v. 54, Mar. 1968: 249–255. K1.M385, v. 54

Concludes that it was a compromise between those delegates who objected to the legislative election of the president and those who questioned the ability of the people to choose wisely.

9470

Fletcher, George L. Sidelights on the Federal Constitutional Convention. *In* Virginia State Bar Association. Annual report. v. 39; 1927. Richmond. p. 411–425. LL

9471

Garver, Frank H. The attitude of the Constitutional Convention of 1787 toward the West. Pacific historical review, v. 5, Dec. 1936: 349–358. F851.P18, v. 5

9472

Garver, Frank H. The Constitutional Convention as a deliberative assembly. Pacific historical review, v. 13, Dec. 1944: 412–424. F851.P18, v. 13

9473

Garver, Frank H. Leadership in the Constitutional Convention of 1787. Sociology and social research, v. 21, July/Aug. 1937: 544–553. HM1.S75, v. 21

9474

Garver, Frank H. Some misconceptions relative to the Constitutional Convention. Historian, v. 1, winter 1938: 24–32. D1.H22, v. 1

9475

Garver, Frank H. Some propositions rejected by the Constitutional Convention of 1787. Historian, v. 6, spring 1944: 113–127. D1.H22, v. 6

9476

Gerlach, Larry R. Toward "a more perfect Union": Connecticut, the Continental Congress, and the Constitutional Convention. *In* Connecticut Historical Society, *Hartford*. Bulletin, v. 34, July 1969: 65–78. F91.C67, v. 34

9477

Gottlieb, Theodore D. New Jersey's influence in the Constitutional Convention. *In* New Jersey Historical Society. Proceedings, new ser., v. 56, Apr. 1938: 140–148. F131.N58, n.s., v. 56

9478

Holcombe, Arthur N. The role of Washington in the framing of the Constitution. Huntington Library quarterly, v. 19, Aug. 1956: 317–334. Z733.S24Q, v. 19

9479

Ketcham, Earle H. The direct tax clause of the federal Constitution. North Carolina historical review, v. 4, July 1927: 270–284. F251.N892, v. 4

9480

Klett, Guy S. A phase of the religious influence in the formation of our national government. *In* Presbyterian Historical Society. Journal, v. 24, Sept. 1946: 129–134. BX8905.P7A4, v. 24

On Presbyterian influence in the drafting and ratification of the Constitution.

9481

Krug, Mary L., *Sister*. A critical analysis of the sources of information on the Constitutional Convention. 1951. xv, 256 l.

Thesis (Ph.D.)—University of Southern California.

9482

Lander, Ernest M. The South Carolinians at the Philadelphia Convention, 1787. South Carolina historical magazine, v. 57, July 1956: 134–155. F266.S55, v. 57

9483

Lynd, Staughton. The compromise of 1787. Political science quarterly, v. 81, June 1966: 225–250. H1.P8, v. 81

On the three-fifths compromise.

9484

Lyon, Walter Hastings. The Constitution and the men who made it; the story of the Constitutional Convention, 1787. Boston, Houghton Mifflin Co., 1936. xii, 314 p. JK146.L95

"Partial bibliography": p. [305]–306.

9485

McDonald, Forrest. We the people; the economic origins of the Constitution. Chicago, University of Chicago

Press [1958] x, 436 p. (A Publication of the American History Research Center)   JK146.M27

Bibliographic footnotes.

The author's thesis (Ph.D.), *The Economic Interpretation of the Constitution*, was submitted to the University of Texas in 1955.

Rejects the thesis that the framers of the Constitution were a close-knit economic group and contends that they represented a geographic, political, and economic cross section of state officeholders. Investigating the backgrounds of delegates to both the Philadelphia and the state ratifying conventions, the author finds that realty instead of "personalty" formed the major part of their holdings. McDonald argues that there was no simple, clearly defined relationship among the supports of the Constitution, that conflicts between sectional groups and individual interests within each state turned the ratification struggle into 13 separate contests, and that any hypothesis about the economic origins of the Constitution must take into account a multitude of explanatory factors in order to accommodate the available data. Ultimately, the more prosperous states inclined toward an independent status, while those that found it difficult to stand alone favored a strong central government.

9486
McGee, Dorothy H.   Framers of the Constitution. New York, Dodd, Mead [1968] xvii, 394 p. facsim., ports.
                                                              JK146.M279

Bibliography: p. 381–388.

General biographical information about each delegate is arranged by state.

9487
Meigs, William M.   The growth of the Constitution in the federal Convention of 1787; an effort to trace the origin and development of each separate clause from its first suggestion in that body to the form finally approved. Containing also a facsimile of a heretofore unpublished manuscript of the first draft of the instrument made for use in the Committee of Detail. Philadelphia, J. B. Lippincott Co., 1900. 374 p. facsims.   KF4541.M4

9488
Monaghan, Frank.   The Constitution and the radicals of 1787. *In* Wyoming Commemorative Association, *Wilkes-Barre, Pa.* Proceedings. 1938. Wilkes-Barre, Pa. p. 7–15.   E241.W9W85, 1938

9489
Murphy, William P.   State sovereignty and the Founding Fathers. Mississippi law journal, v. 30, Dec. 1958–May 1959: 135–164, 261–292; v. 31, Dec. 1959: 50–82.
                                                                          LL

9490
Nadelmann, Kurt H.   On the origin of the bankruptcy clause. American journal of legal history, v. 1, July 1957: 215–228.   LL

Article 1, section 8, clause 4 of the Constitution.

9491
Noel, Francis Regis.   A history of the bankruptcy clause of the Constitution of the United States of America. [Gettysburg, Gettysburg Compiler Print, 1918] 210 p.
                                                              HG3766.N6

Thesis (Ph.D.)—Catholic University of America, 1918. Bibliography: p. 205–209.

9492
Noel, Francis Regis.   Vestiges of a supreme court among the colonies and under the Articles of Confederation. *In* Columbia Historical Society, *Washington, D.C.* Records. v. 37/38. Washington, 1937. p. 123–143.
                                                        F191.C72, v. 37/38

9493
Nott, Charles C.   The mystery of the Pinckney draught. New York, Century Co., 1908. 334 p.   JK148.P5N7

Attempting to revive the discredited Pinckney plan, the author argues that the lost draft submitted by Pinckney to the Convention on May 29, 1787, was in fact used by the Committee of Detail as the basis for the Constitution.

9494
Obrecht, Everett D.   The influence of Luther Martin in the making of the Constitution of the United States. Maryland historical magazine, v. 27, Sept.–Dec. 1932: 173–190, 280–296.   F176.M18, v. 27

9495
O'Brien, Francis William.   The executive and the separation principle at the Constitutional Convention. Maryland historical magazine, v. 55, Sept. 1960: 201–220.
                                                          F176.M18, v. 55

9496
Ohline, Howard A.   Republicanism and slavery: origins of the three-fifths clause in the United States Constitution. William and Mary quarterly, 3d ser., v. 28, Oct. 1971: 563–584.   F221.W71, 3d s., v. 28

The clause resulted from a compromise between those who favored legislative supremacy and those who regarded the people as sovereign. It was not intended as an endorsement of slavery or a repudiation of Revolutionary ideals.

9497
Powell, John H.   John Dickinson and the Constitution. Pennsylvania magazine of history and biography, v. 60, Jan. 1936: 1–14.   F146.P65, v. 60

9498
Richardson, Hamilton P.   The journal of the federal Convention of 1787 analyzed; the acts and procedings thereof compared; and their precedents cited; in evidence . . . that . . . Congress have general power to provide for the common defense and general welfare of the United States; direct taxes are taxes direct to the several states . . . and the limits of the Union are coextensive with the bounds of America. San Francisco, Murdock Press, 1899. 244 p.   JK146.R52

9499

Roche, John P.   The Founding Fathers: a reform caucus in action. American political science review, v. 55, Dec. 1961: 799–816.   JA1.A6, v. 55

9500

Rossiter, Clinton L.   1787: the grand Convention. New York, Macmillan [1966] 443 p. illus., ports. (The New American history series)   JK146.R68

Bibliography: p. [337]–348.

Using the Convention as his setting, the author discusses the abilities of the framers, explains the intricacies of the proceedings, and appraises the document drafted. Rossiter maintains that skillful, pragmatic politicians created a fundamental law that was the logical culmination of the war and thereby formalized the legacies of independence, republicanism, and union.

9501

Schuyler, Robert L.   Agreement in the federal Convention. Political science quarterly, v. 31, June 1916: 289–299.   H1.P8, v. 31

9502

Simon, Paul L.   The appointing powers of the President. Cithara, v. 3, Nov. 1963: 41–55.   AS36.S2, v. 3

Discusses the debates in the Constitutional Convention and the questions raised during the ratification process in Virginia and North Carolina.

9503

Smith, David G.   The Convention and the Constitution; the political ideas of the Founding Fathers. New York, St. Martin's Press [1965] 120 p. (St. Martin's series in American politics)   JK146.S55

Bibliography: p. [113]–116.

Examines the theories of government and society that influenced the authors of the Constitution, analyzes their intentions and divisions, and assesses the system that they established. Smith emphasizes the delegates' concern about providing for the future and their hardheaded prudence regarding the fundamentals of government.

9504

Teiser, Sidney.   The genesis of the Supreme Court. Virginia law review, v. 25, Feb. 1939: 398–421.   LL

Describes the evolution of the concept of a Supreme Court from the beginning of the Revolutionary period to its embodiment in the Constitution.

9505

Thach, Charles C.   The creation of the presidency, 1775–1789; a study in constitutional history. Baltimore, Johns Hopkins Press, 1922. 182 p. (Johns Hopkins University studies in historical and political science, 40th ser., no. 4)   H31.J6, 40th s., no. 4
                                                       JK511.T52

Published also as thesis (Ph.D.)—Johns Hopkins University, 1922.

Bibliographic footnotes.

Reprinted in New York by Da Capo Press (1969) and reissued, with an introduction by Herbert J. Storing, in Baltimore by Johns Hopkins Press (1969).

Though the separation of powers may have been important to some of the delegates at the Constitutional Convention, most felt that the single executive could more effectively combat both the legislative excesses and the malaise that they had witnessed at the state and congressional levels during the preceding decade. Thach considers James Wilson, who based his plan on the successful New York experience, to be the key advocate of an independent executive.

9506

Thatcher, Harold W.   Comments on American government and on the Constitution by a New Jersey member of the federal Convention [William Livingston] In New Jersey Historical Society. Proceedings, v. 56, Oct. 1938: 285–303.   F131.N58, v. 56

9507

Tucker, John R.   The history of the federal Convention of 1787 and of its work. New Haven, Law Dept. of Yale College, 1887. 54 p.   JK146.T9

9508

Ulmer, S. Sidney.   Charles Pinckney: father of the Constitution? South Carolina law quarterly, v. 10, winter 1958: 225–247.   LL

9509

Ulmer, S. Sidney.   The role of Pierce Butler in the Constitutional Convention. Review of politics, v. 22, July 1960: 361–374.   JA1.R4, v. 22

9510

Ulmer, S. Sidney.   Sub-group formation in the Constitutional Convention. Midwest journal of political science, v. 10, Aug. 1966: 288–303.   JA1.M5, v. 10

9511

U.S. *Library of Congress.*   The Constitution of the United States, together with an account of its travels since September 17, 1787. Compiled by David C. Mearns and Verner W. Clapp. Washington, 1952. 43 p. illus.
                                              JK34.A5 1952

Bibliography: p. 19–20.

9512

Van Doren, Carl C.   The great rehearsal; the story of the making and ratifying of the Constitution of the United States. New York, Viking Press, 1948. xii, 336 p. illus., ports.   JK146.V3 1948a

"Sources and acknowledgments": p. 321–322.

A synthesis that traces the history of the Convention, sketches the character of its participants, and shows how the great compromises were achieved. Van Doren describes the ratification struggles in the states and, in an appendix, reprints important documents.

9513

Warren, Charles.   The making of the Constitution. Boston, Little, Brown, 1928. xii, 832 p.   JK31.W35

"Books containing letters quoted . . . except when specific authorities are cited in the footnotes": p. [807]
Reprinted in New York by Barnes & Noble (1967).

After introducing the delegates, the public, and the press and examining their fears of disunion under the Confederation, Warren provides a day-by-day narrative of events both inside and outside of the Convention, mainly by quoting from contemporary letters and newspaper stories. He also attempts to trace each important clause in the document to its source and explores the controversies over ratification.

9514

Watson, Paul B.   Our Constitution, as adopted by the Constitutional Convention and ratified by the thirteen original states. Cambridge, Mass., University Press, 1946. v, 166 p.   JK146.W3

Taking most of his material from the 1937 edition of Farrand's *Records of the Federal Convention,* the author presents a narrative of the debates on various provisions in the Constitution, giving particular attention to the three most controversial matters: the senate, the President, and commerce.

9515

Wehtje, Myron F.   Rufus King and the formation of the Constitution. Studies in history and society, v. 1, Apr. 1969: 17–31.   D1.S86, v. 1

Studies King's role in support of a strong central government in both the Philadelphia Convention and the Massachusetts ratifying convention.

9516

Whitten, Dolphus.   The state delegations in the Philadelphia Convention of 1787. 1961. ([1323] p.)
Micro AC–1, no. 61–4726

Thesis (Ph.D.)—University of Texas.
Abstracted in *Dissertation Abstracts,* v. 22, Dec. 1961, p. 1970–1971.

9517

Wilson, Fred T.   Our Constitution and its makers. New York, F. H. Revell Co. [ᶜ1937] 585 p. plates, ports.
JK146.W5

Includes brief biographical sketches of the delegates from each state (p. [189]–538).

9518

Winston, Alexander.   A more perfect union [Philadelphia, 1787] History today, v. 16, June 1966: 391–399. illus., ports.   D1.H818, v. 16

The Ratification of the Constitution
GENERAL WORKS

9519

Bell, Whitfield J.   The federal processions of 1788. *In* New York Historical Society. Quarterly, v. 46, Jan. 1962: 5–39. illus., map, ports.   F116.N638, v. 46

Ceremonies marking the ratification of the Constitution in each of the states. Although they were in part Federalist propaganda, the processions had a dramatic impact.

9520

Buckley, John E.   The role of rhetoric in the ratification of the federal Constitution, 1787–88. 1972. ([294] p.)
Micro AC–1, no. 72–32,394

Thesis (Ph.D.)—Northwestern University.
Abstracted in *Dissertation Abstracts International,* v. 33A, Dec. 1972, p. 3052.

9521

Duniway, Clyde A.   French influence on the adoption of the federal Constitution. American historical review, v. 9, Jan. 1904: 304–309.   E171.A57, v. 9

French ministers in America were instructed not to encourage the movement for a strong central government since France preferred to see the United States remain a weak power.

9522

Libby, Orin G.   The geographical distribution of the vote of the thirteen states on the federal Constitution, 1787–8. Madison, Wis., The University, 1894. vii, 116 p. maps (part fold.) (Bulletin of the University of Wisconsin Economics, political science, and history series, v. 1, no. 1)   H31Wy, v. 1
JK148.L64

"Sources for the local geography, 1787–8": p. 95–104.
"Authorities consulted": p. 105.
Reprinted, with an introduction by Robert P. Wilkins, in Grand Forks by the University of North Dakota Press (1969) and in New York by B. Franklin (1969).

Finds that approval of the Constitution followed a regional, economic pattern. More densely settled urban and commercial areas favored ratification, whereas opposition came from interior or sparsely settled districts where noncommercial agriculture predominated. Eastern capitalists and creditors felt that adoption of the Constitution would lead to specie payment for debts, internal taxation, and the enforcement of contractual obligations; hard-pressed rural farmers, on the other hand, sought paper money, tax relief, and debt control measures.

9523

Marks, Frederick W.   Foreign affairs: a winning issue in the campaign for ratification of the United States Constitution. Political science quarterly, v. 86, Sept. 1971: 444–469.   H1.P8, v. 86

The constitutional provisions for a standing army and navy, which would reduce the likelihood of invasion and increase the United States' ability to wage war, proved the key to consensus in many areas.

9524

Nettels, Curtis P.   The American merchant and the Constitution. *In* Colonial Society of Massachusetts, *Boston*. Publications. v. 34. Transactions, 1937/42. Boston, 1943. p. 26–37.   F61.C71, v. 34

Focuses upon Pelatiah Webster, who was representative of a class that supported the Constitution 18 to 1.

9525

Powell, John H.   The grand federal processions [February–July 1788] *In his* General Washington and the jack ass, and other American characters in portrait. South Brunswick [N.J.] T. Yoseloff [1969] p. 191–212.

E178.6.P77

9526

Roll, Charles W.   We, some of the people: apportionment in the thirteen state conventions ratifying the Constitution. Journal of American history, v. 56, June 1969: 21–40.   E171.J87, v. 56

Shows that districting for the state conventions generally favored the cities and commercial centers, especially in the South.

9527

Rutland, Robert A.   The power of prestige: George Washington and the federal Constitution. *In* Innsbruck. Universität. *Amerika-Institut. Americana-Austriaca:* Festschrift des Amerika-Instituts der Universität Innsbruck, anlässlich seines zehnjährigen Bestehens. Hrsg. im Auftrag des Amerika-Instituts von Klaus Lanzinger. Wien, W. Braumüller [1966] (*Its* Beiträge zur Amerikakunde, Bd. 1) p. 116–128.   E151.A57

Assesses Washington's impact upon the ratification struggle.

9528

Wearing, Leo J.   The adoption of the Constitution: an effort to promote national economic independence. 1938.

Thesis (Ph.D.)—University of Wisconsin.

CONTEMPORARY PAMPHLETS, TRACTS, AND OTHER WRITINGS

9529

Borden, Morton, *ed*.   The Antifederalist papers. [East Lansing, Mich.] Michigan State University Press, 1965. xiv, 258 p.   JK116.B6

Bibliography: p. 253–254.

Following a brief introduction on the Anti-Federalist mind, the editor presents 85 letters and essays that appeared mostly in contemporary newspapers in rebuttal to Federalist arguments.

9530

[Dickinson, John]   The letters of Fabius, in 1788, on the federal Constitution; and in 1797 on the present situation of public affairs. From the office of the *Delaware Gazette*, Wilmington, by W. C. Smyth, 1797. 202 p.

JK171.D5 Rare Bk. Coll.

"The first nine letters . . . published in . . . 1788 . . . appeared separately in news-papers; and have never been published together, before the present edition."—Prefatory notice.

9531

Elliot, Jonathan, ed.   The debates in the several state conventions on the adoption of the federal Constitution, as recommended by the general Convention of Philadelphia, 1787. Together with the journal of the federal Convention, Luther Martin's letter, Yates' opinions, Virginia and Kentucky resolutions of '98–'99, and other illustrations of the Constitution. Published under the sanction of Congress. Philadelphia, J. B. Lippincott Co., 1907. 5 v.   JK141 1836f

Vols. 1–4, 2d edition, with considerable additions (date of copyright, 1836). Vol. 5 has title *Debates on the Adoption of the Federal Constitution, in the Convention Held at Philadelphia, in 1787; With a Diary of the Debates of the Congress of the Confederation; as Reported by James Madison . . . Rev. and Newly Arr. by Jonathan Elliot . . . Supplementary to Elliot's Debates* (date of copyright, 1845).

Reprint from the plates of the 1836–45 edition.

The 1888 edition has been reprinted in New York by B. Franklin (1968?).

9532

The Federalist.   The Federalist. Edited with introduction and notes by Jacob E. Cooke. Middletown, Conn., Wesleyan University Press [1961] xxx, 672 p.

JK154 1961b

Other editions have appeared with notes and introductory matter by John C. Hamilton (659 p. 1864), Henry Cabot Lodge (586 p. 1888), Paul Leicester Ford (793 p. 1898), Goldwin Smith (488 p. 1901), Edward G. Bourne (2 v. 1901), Charles W. Pierson (586 p. 1923), W. J. Ashley (456 p. 1929), Edward Mead Earle (618 p. 1938), and Carl Van Doren (2 v. 1945).

9533

The Federalist.   The Federalist: a collection of essays, written in favour of the new Constitution, as agreed upon by the federal Convention, September 17, 1787. New York, Printed and sold by J. and A. M'Lean, no. 41, Hanover-Square, 1788. 2 v.

JK154 1788 Rare Bk. Coll.

First complete edition.

9534

Ford, Paul L., *ed*.   Essays on the Constitution of the United States, published during its discussion by the people, 1787–1788. Brooklyn, N.Y., Historical Print Club, 1892. viii, 424 p.   JK171.F72

Contents: Sullivan, J. The letters of "Cassius."—Winthrop, J. The letters of "Agrippa."—Gerry E. Replies to "A landholder."—Ellsworth, O. Letters of "A landholder."—Williams, W. A letter to "A landholder."—Sherman, R. The letters of "A countryman."—Sherman, R. The letters of "A citizen of New Haven."—Clinton, G. The letters of "Cato."—Hamilton, A. The letters of "Caesar."—Yates, R. The letters of "Sydney."—Brackenridge, H. H. Cursory remarks on the Constitution.—Chase, S. A letter of "Caution."—Carroll, D. A letter of "A friend to the Constitution."—Martin, L. Letters.—Roane, S. A letter of "A plain dealer."—Williamson, H. Remarks on the Constitution.—Pinckney, C. A letter of "A steady and open Republican."—Bibliography.—Index.

Reprinted in New York by B. Franklin (1970).

9535

Ford, Paul L., *ed.* Pamphlets on the Constitution of the United States, published during its discussion by the people, 1787–1788. Edited with notes and a bibliography. Brooklyn, N.Y., 1888. viii, 351 p.   JK171.F71

Contents: Gerry, E. Observations on the new Constitution, and on the federal and state conventions. By a Columbian patriot.—Webster, N. An examination into the leading principles of the federal Constitution. By a citizen of America.—Jay, J. An address to the people of the state of New York, on the subject of the Constitution. By a citizen of New York.—Smith, M. Address to the people of the state of New York. By a plebeian.—Webster, P. The weakness of Brutus exposed; or, Some remarks in vindication of the Constitution. By a citizen of Philadelphia.—Coxe, T. An examination of the Constitution of the United States of America. By an American citizen.—Wilson, J. Speech on the federal Constitution, delivered in Philadelphia.—Dickinson, J. Letters of Fabius on the federal Constitution.—Hanson, A. C. Remarks on the proposed plan of a federal government. By Aristides.—Randolph, E. Letter on the federal Constitution.—Lee, R. H. Observations of the system of government proposed by the late convention. By a federal farmer.—Mason, G. Objections to the federal Constitution.—Iredell, J. Observations on George Mason's *Objections to the Federal Constitution.* By Marcus.—Ramsay, D. An address to the freemen of South Carolina on the federal Constitution. By Civis.—Bibliography of the Constitution, 1787–1788.—Reference list to the history and literature of the Constitution, 1787–88.—Index.

Reprinted in New York by Da Capo Press (1968) and by B. Franklin (1971).

9536

[Hanson, Alexander Contee] Remarks on the proposed plan of a federal government, addressed to the citizens of the United States of America, and particularly to the people of Maryland, by Aristides. Annapolis, Printed by F. Green [1788] 42 p.   JK171.H2 Rare Bk. Coll.
AC901.M5, v. 1153a Rare Bk. Coll.

9537

Hopkinson, Francis. Account of the grand federal procession, Philadelphia, 1788. Edited by Whitfield J. Bell, Jr. Boston, Old South Association [1962] 30 p. (Old South leaflets. [General series], no. 230–231)
E173.O44, no. 230–231
F158.44.H76 1962

9538

[Jackson, Jonathan] Thoughts upon the political situation of the United States of America, in which that of Massachusetts is more particularly considered. With some observations on the Constitution for a federal government. Addressed to the people of the Union. By a native of Boston. Printed at Worcester, Mass., by I. Thomas, 1788. 209 p.   JK171.J13 Rare Bk. Coll.
E303.J13 Rare Bk. Coll.

This work has also been attributed to George Richards Minot.

9539

[Jay, John] An address to the people of the state of New-York, on the subject of the Constitution, agreed upon at Philadelphia, the 17th of September, 1787. New-York, Printed by S. and J. Loudon [1788] 19 p.
AC901.M5, v. 254 Rare Bk. Coll.
JK171.J4 Rare Bk. Coll.

Signed: a citizen of New-York.

9540

Kenyon, Cecelia M., *ed.* The Antifederalists. Indianapolis, Bobbs-Merrill [1966] cxxii, 455 p. (The American heritage series, 38)   JK116.K4

Bibliography: p. cxvii–cxix.

Following an extended introductory essay in which she further develops her thesis that the Anti-Federalists were "men of little faith," the editor provides supporting evidence in the form of 18 Anti-Federalist pamphlets, debates, and newspaper articles, many reprinted for the first time.

9541

Kurtz, Stephen G., *comp.* The Federalists—creators and critics of the Union, 1780–1801. New York, Wiley [1972] 212 p. (Problems in American history)
E303.K8

Bibliography: p. 209–212.

Includes selections from contemporary documents and appraisals by historians.

9542

[Lee, Richard Henry] Observations leading to a fair examination of the system of government, proposed by the late convention; and to several essential and necessary alterations in it. In a number of letters from the Federal Farmer to the Republican. [New York] Printed in the year 1787. 40 p.   JK146.L45 Rare Bk. Coll.

Printed by Thomas Greenleaf.

———— An additional number of letters prom [sic] the Federal Farmer to the Republican; leading to a fair examination of the system of government, proposed by the late convention; to several essential and necessary alterations in it; and calculated to illustrate and support

the principles and positions laid down in the preceding letters. [New York] Printed in the year 1788. [45]–181 p.   JK146.L4 Rare Bk. Coll.
Printed by Thomas Greenleaf.

Paged continuously with his *Observations Leading to a Fair Examination of the System of Government*, and contains letters 6–18.

The *Additional Number of Letters* has been reprinted, together with *Observations on the New Constitution, and on the Federal and State Conventions, by a Columbian Patriot*, in Chicago by Quadrangle Books (1962. [45]–181, 19 p. JK146.L4 1962).

Gordon Wood has recently questioned the attribution of these pamphlets to Lee in his article, "The Authorship of the *Letters from the Federal Farmer*," in the *William and Mary quarterly*, 3d ser., v. 31, Apr. 1974, p. 299–308.

9543

Lewis, John D., *comp.*   Anti-Federalists versus Federalists; selected documents. San Francisco, Chandler Pub. Co. [1967] xi, 423 p. (Chandler publications on political science)   JK155.L4

Bibliography: p. 411–413.

Contents: pt. 1. Minority reports from the Philadelphia Convention.—pt. 2. General defenses of the Constitution.—pt. 3. The debate over ratification: Anti-Federalist arguments.—pt. 4. Defense of the Constitution by *The Federalist*.

84 contemporary letters and essays.

9544

Martin, Luther.   The genuine information, delivered to the legislature of the state of Maryland, relative to the proceedings of the general convention, lately held at Philadelphia; by Luther Martin, Esquire, attorney general of Maryland, and one of the delegates in the said convention. Together with a letter to the Hon. Thomas Deye, speaker of the House of Delegates, an address to the citizens of the United States, and some remarks relative to a standing army, and a bill of rights. Philadelphia, Printed by Eleazer Oswald, 1788. viii, 93 p.
JK171.M3 Rare Bk. Coll.

9545

Observations on the proposed constitution for the United States of America, clearly shewing it to be a complete system of aristocracy and tyranny, and destructive of the rights and liberties of the people.   Printed in the state of New-York, 1788. 126 p.   JK171.O2

"Address and reasons of dissent of the minority of the convention of . . . Pennsylvania," dated Dec. 12, 1787, at Philadelphia, and signed by 21 members: p. 3–30.

"Letter of . . . Edmund Randolph, esq. on the federal Constitution": p. 30–45.

Nine letters on the Constitution, addressed to the people of Pennsylvania and signed Centinel: p. 46–111.

Appendix, Constitution of the United States: p. [112]–126.

"The 'Letters of Centinel' were by Samuel Bryan of Philadelphia, and appeared originally in the *Independent*

Gazetteer of that city."—P. L. Ford, *Pamphlets on the Constitution*, p. 418.

9546

Pinckney, Charles.   Observations on the plan of government submitted to the federal Convention, in Philadelphia, on the 28th of May, 1787. By Mr. Charles Pinckney, delegate from the state of South-Carolina. Delivered at different times in the course of their discussions. New York, Printed by Francis Childs [1787] 27 p.   JK148.P5A4 Rare Bk. Coll.

9547

Randolph, Edmund.   A letter of His Excellency, Edmund Randolph, Esquire, on the federal Constitution. [Richmond, A. Davis, 1787] 16 p.

JK148.R3 Rare Bk. Coll.

9548

Rozwenc, Edwin C., *and* Frederick E. Bauer, *eds.*   Liberty and power in the making of the Constitution. Boston, Heath [ᶜ1963] 76 p. (Basic concepts in history and social science)   JK148.R68

Bibliography: p. 75–76.

Includes excerpts from the writings of Federalists and Anti-Federalists such as Edmund Randolph, Elbridge Gerry, James Madison, Alexander Hamilton, Richard Henry Lee, Melancthon Smith, and George Clinton and appraisals by Charles Beard, Henry Steele Commager, Richard Hofstadter, and Cecelia Kenyon.

9549

[Smith, Melancthon]   An address to the people of the state of New-York: shewing the necessity of making amendments to the Constitution, proposed for the United States, previous to its adoption. By a plebeian. Printed [by Robert Hodge, in New York] in the state of New-York, 1788. 26 p.   JK171.S5 Rare Bk. Coll.

"Postscript [remarks on a pamphlet] entitled 'An address to the people of the state of New-York, on the subject of the new Constitution' [by John Jay]": p.[23]–26.

9550

[Warren, Mercy Otis]   Observations on the new Constitution, and on the fœderal and state conventions. By a Columbian patriot. Boston, Printed; New-York, Reprinted, 1788. 22 p.   JK171.W3 Rare Bk. Coll.

Probably written by Mercy Otis Warren; attributed also to Elbridge Gerry.

9551

Washington, George.   Washington's letters on the Constitution, 1786–88. [Boston, Directors of the Old South Work, 1899] 20 p. (Old South leaflets. [General ser., v. 4] no. 99)   E173.O44, v. 4

9552

[Webster, Noah]   An examination into the leading principles of the federal Constitution proposed by the late Convention held at Philadelphia. With answers to the principal objections that have been raised against the system. By a citizen of America. Philadelphia, Printed and sold by Prichard & Hall, in Market Street, the second door above Laetitia Court, 1787. 55 p.

> AC901.W7, v. 3 Rare Bk. Coll.
> JA36.P8, v. 122 Rare Bk. Coll.
> AC901.H3, v. 51 Rare Bk. Coll.

9553

[Webster, Pelatiah] Remarks on the address of sixteen members of the Assembly of Pennsylvania, to their constituents, dated September 29, 1787. With some strictures on their objections to the Constitution; recommended by the late federal Convention, humbly offered to the public. By a citizen of Philadelphia. Philadelphia, Printed by Eleazer Oswald, at the Coffee-House, 1787. 28 p.   JK148.W4A3 Rare Bk. Coll.

9554

[Webster, Pelatiah] The weakness of Brutus exposed; or, Some remarks in vindication of the Constitution proposed by the late federal Convention against the objections and gloomy fears of that writer. Humbly offered to the public, by a citizen of Philadelphia. Philadelphia, Printed for, and to be had of John Sparhawk, in Market-Street, near the Court-House, 1787. 23 p.

> JK155.W4 1787 Rare Bk. Coll.

A reply to the first of a series of 16 essays appearing in the *New York Journal*, signed Brutus, who is supposed to be Robert Yates. This first essay was copied in the *Pennsylvania Packet*, Oct. 26, 1787.

9555

Wilson, James.   Commentaries on the Constitution of the United States of America, with the Constitution prefixed, in which are unfolded, the principles of free government, and the superior advantages of republicanism demonstrated. By James Wilson and by Thomas M'Kean. The whole extracted from debates, published in Philadelphia by T. Lloyd. London, Printed for J. Debrett, 1792. 147 p.   JK171.W7 Rare Bk. Coll.

9556

Young, Alfred F., *ed*.   The debate over the Constitution, 1787–1789. Chicago, Rand McNally [1965] 55, [1] p. (The Berkeley series in American history)

> KF4541.Z9Y6

Bibliography: p. 55–[56]

Presents a sampling of opinions focused on New York and Virginia using selections from the writings of James Madison, Patrick Henry, Alexander Hamilton, Melancthon Smith, Thomas Jefferson, and Thomas Paine. Issues relating to states' rights, representation, and proposed amendments are highlighted.

THE AUTHORSHIP AND PHILOSOPHY OF THE *FEDERALIST PAPERS*

9557

Adair, Douglass G.   The authorship of the disputed Federalist Papers. William and Mary quarterly, 3d ser., v. 1, Apr.–July 1944: 97–122, 235–264.

> F221.W71, 3d s., v. 1

Contends that the disputed numbers of *The Federalist* claimed by both Hamilton and Madison, numbers 49–58, 62, and 63, were all written by Madison.

9558

Adair, Douglass G.   *The Federalist Papers*, a review article. William and Mary quarterly, 3d ser., v. 22, Jan. 1965: 131–139.   F221.W71, 3d s., v. 22

Discusses four editions of *Publius* issued in 1961: *The Federalist Papers*, selected and edited by Roy P. Fairfield; *The Federalist*, edited with an introduction by Benjamin F. Wright; *The Federalist*, edited with an introduction and notes by Jacob E. Cooke; and *The Federalist Papers*, with an introduction, table of contents, and index of ideas by Clinton Rossiter.

9559

Adair, Douglass G.   The tenth Federalist revisited. William and Mary quarterly, 3d ser., v. 8, Jan. 1951: 48–67.

> F221.W71, 3d s., v. 8

In tracing Madison's famous theory of government as it developed before the Philadelphia Convention, the author shows that Charles Beard not only lifted Madison's doctrine of class struggle out of context but erroneously argued that Madison believed theories were unimportant in politics. Instead, Adair contends that Madison's theory, as purely abstract thought, played a key role in the writing and ratification of the Constitution.

9560

Adair, Douglass G.   "That politics may be reduced to a science": David Hume, James Madison, and the tenth *Federalist*. Huntington Library quarterly, v. 20, Aug. 1957: 343–360.   Z733.S24Q, v. 20

Madison's theory of factions, based in part on his reading of Hume, made obsolete the system of mixed government advocated by Hamilton and Adams at Philadelphia.

9561

Albertini, Mario.   Che cose e' il federalismo. Politico, v. 21, Dec. 1956: 580–597.   JA18, P65, v. 21

Seeks a practical definition of federalism through an analysis of Alexander Hamilton's views on government as expressed at the Philadelphia Convention and in the *Federalist*.

9562

Benson, Mabel G.   A study of the rhetorical characteristics of the *Federalist*. Chicago, 1945. 296 l.   JK155.B4

Thesis (Ph.D.)—University of Chicago.
Bibliography: leaves 277–296.

9563

Bourne, Edward G. The authorship of *The Federalist*.
American historical review, v. 2, Apr. 1897: 443–460.
E171.A57, v. 2

Investigates the disputed authorship of 15 of the papers:
numbers 18–20, 49–58, and 62–63.

9564

Bourne, Edward G. Essays in historical criticism. New
York, C. Scribner's Sons, 1901. xii, 304 p. (Yale
bicentennial publications) E173.B77

Partial contents: The authorship of *The Federalist*.—
Mr. Paul Leicester Ford on the authorship of *The Federalist*.—*The Federalist* abroad.—Madison's studies in the history of federal government.

9565

Brant, Irving. Settling the authorship of *The Federalist*.
American historical review, 67, Oct. 1961: 71–75.
E171.A57, v. 67

Feeling that all other essays have been properly attributed by other scholars, Brant presents evidence indicating that Madison and not Hamilton was the author of numbers 62 and 63.

9566

Cooke, Jacob E. Alexander Hamilton's authorship of the
"Caesar" letters. William and Mary quarterly, 3d ser.,
v. 17, Jan. 1960: 78–85. F221.W71, 3d s., v. 17

Argues against the common assertion that Hamilton
authored the two letters defending the Constitution that
appeared in the New York *Daily Advertiser* on October 1
and 15, 1787.

9567

Crane, Elaine F. Publius in the provinces: where was *The
Federalist* reprinted outside New York City? William
and Mary quarterly, 3d ser., v.21, Oct. 1964: 589–592.
F221.W71, 3d s., v. 21

9568

Diamond, Martin. Democracy and *The Federalist*: a reconsideration of the framer's intent. American political
science review, v. 53, Mar. 1959: 52–68.
JA1.A6, v. 53

9569

Dietze, Gottfried. The Federalist, a classic on federalism
and free government. Baltimore, Johns Hopkins Press
[1960] ix, 378 p. JK155.D5

Bibliography: p. 355–358.

The author's thesis (Ph.D), *The Political Theory of the
Federalist*, was submitted to Princeton University in 1952
(Micro AC-1, no. 10,881).

Surveys the origin and influence of *The Federalist Papers* and analyzes their purpose and their contribution to
political theory. Dietze concludes that Hamilton, Jay, and
Madison were principally interested in federalism as a means
of protecting individual freedoms against the possible tyrannies of democratic majorities in the states, that the major
original contribution of their work lies in the exposition of

judicial review, and that as a treatise on limited government
based on popular rule, *The Federalist* significantly broadened the concept of federalism.

9570

Dietze, Gottfried. Madison's *Federalist*—a treatise for free
government. Georgetown law journal, v. 46, Nov.
1957: 21–51. LL

9571

Ford, Paul L. The authorship of *The Federalist*. American
historical review, v. 2, July 1897: 675–682.
E171.A57, v. 2

In reply to an article by Edward G. Bourne in the
previous issue, Ford contends that Madison probably wrote
numbers 49–51, and Hamilton numbers 52–58 and 62–63.
Bourne's remarks appear on pages 682–687.

9572

Ford, Paul L. A list of editions of "The Federalist."
Brooklyn, N.Y., 1886. 25 p.
Z6456.F4F7 Rare Bk. Coll.

Printed on one side of leaf only.

Reprinted from his *Bibliotheca Hamiltoniana* (New
York, Printed for the author, Knickerbocker Press, 1886),
p. 13–35, with the addition of a title page.

9573

Ketcham, Ralph L. Notes on James Madison's sources for
the tenth Federalist paper. Midwest journal of political
science, v. 1, May 1957: 20–25. JA1.M5, v. 1

9574

Lodge, Henry Cabot. The authorship of the Federalist. *In*
American Antiquarian Society, *Worcester, Mass.* Proceedings, new ser., v. 3, Apr. 1885: 409–420.
E172.A35, n.s., v. 3

9575

Mason, Alpheus T. The Federalist—a split personality.
American historical review, v. 57, Apr. 1952: 635–643.
E171.A57, v. 57

Examines the attitudes and assumptions that Hamilton
and Madison brought to their commentaries on the principles of government.

9576

Ross, Gordon D. The *Federalist* and the "experience" of
small republics. Eighteenth-century studies, v. 5, summer 1972: 559–568. NX452.E54, v. 5

9577

Rotella, Salvatore G. Montesquieu and the *Federalist*: a
research note on *Federalist 47*. Politico, v. 32, Dec.
1967: 825–832. JA18.P65, v. 32

9578

Scanlan, James P. The concept of interest in the Federalist;
a study of the structure of a political theory. Chicago
[Library, Dept. of Photographic Reproduction, University of Chicago] 1956. (135 l.) Micro 5106 JK

Microfilm copy (positive) of typescript.
Thesis (Ph.D.)—University of Chicago.

9579
Scanlan, James P. *The Federalist* and human nature. Review of politics, v. 21, Oct. 1959: 657–677.
JA1.R4, v. 21

9580
Schaedler, Louis C. James Madison, literary craftsman. William and Mary quarterly, 3d ser., v. 3, Oct. 1946: 515–533. F221.W71, 3d s., v. 3
Analyzes Madison's contributions to *The Federalist*.

9581
Smith, Maynard O. Principles of republican government in the *Federalist*. 1953.
Thesis (Ph.D.)—New School for Social Research.

9582
Smith, Maynard O. Reason, passion, and political freedom in *The Federalist*. Journal of politics, v. 22, Aug. 1960: 525–544. JA1.J6, v. 22

9583
Swindler, William F. The letters of Publius. American heritage, v. 12, Oct. 1961: 4–7, 92–97.
F171.A43, v. 12

9584
Weaver, Irvin W. The social philosophy of the *Federalist*. 1953.
Thesis (Ph.D.)—Boston University.

9585
Wright, Benjamin F. *The Federalist* on the nature of political man. Ethics, v. 59, Jan. 1949: 1–31.
BJ1.I6, v. 59

THE ANTI-FEDERALISTS

9586
De Pauw, Linda G. The anticlimax of antifederalism: the abortive second convention movement, 1788–89. Prologue, the journal of the National Archives, v. 2, fall 1970: 98–114. CD3020.P75, v. 2

9587
Gale, Benjamin. Connecticut Anti-Federalism on the eve of the Constitutional Convention; a letter from Benjamin Gale to Erastus Wolcott, February 10, 1787. *In* Connecticut Historical Society, *Hartford*. Bulletin, v. 28, Jan. 1963: 14–21. F91.C67, v. 28
Introduction and notes by Philip H. Jordan.

9588
Heslin, James J. "Amendments are necessary." *In* New York Historical Society. Quarterly, v. 43, Oct. 1959: 425–439. facsim., ports. F116.N638, v. 43

Concerning communication among Virginia and New York Anti-Federalists, especially George Mason and George Clinton.

9589
Kenyon, Cecelia M. Men of little faith: the Anti-Federalists on the nature of representative government. William and Mary quarterly, 3d ser., v. 12, Jan. 1955: 3–43. F221.W71, 3d s., v. 12

Holding the same pessimistic conception of human nature as the Federalists, the Anti-Federalists feared the malignant effects of power from whatever source it might come—the people, corrupt political factions, or the proposed federal government. Their version of the Constitution would have contained more, not fewer, checks and balances. Although they followed democratic principles within the sphere of state government, the Anti-Federalists lacked both the vision and the faith to extend their principles to the nation at large.

9590
Lynd, Staughton. Anti-Federalism in Dutchess County, New York; a study of democracy and class conflict in the Revolutionary era. Chicago, Loyola University Press, 1962. ix, 126 p. F127.D8L9
Bibliography: p. 109–117.

Studies the economic and political interest of opposing forces during three conflicts in Dutchess County—the tenant riots of 1766, the disputes over the confiscation and sale of Loyalist property, 1780–85, and the debate concerning ratification of the federal Constitution. Lynd argues that loyalty on both sides in each struggle derived from access to the ownership of land, that Anti-Federalists in 1788 were united by a common hostility to aristocratic, landholding families, and that middle-class, Anti-Federalist delegates differed from their constituents, who were or feared they might become tenants.

9591
McDonald, Forrest. The Anti-Federalists, 1781–1789. Wisconsin magazine of history, v. 46, spring 1963: 206–214. F576.W7, v. 46

9592
Main, Jackson T. The Antifederalists; critics of the Constitution, 1781–1788. Chapel Hill, Published for the Institute of Early American History and Culture at Williamsburg, Va., by the University of North Carolina Press [1961] xv, 308 p. JK116.M2
"Historiographical and bibliographical essay": p. 293–297.

The author's thesis (Ph.D.), *The Anti-Federalist Party, 1781–1788*, was submitted to the University of Wisconsin in 1948.

Following a survey of politics and society, the impost controversy, and opposition to a central government before 1787, the author concentrates upon Anti-Federalist activity during the Constitutional Convention and the ratification process. Main contends that the dispute over ratification was essentially a disagreement between commercial and noncommercial segments of the population. Federalist ranks included merchants and other urban dwellers, farmers dependent upon the important cities, and those who exported their surplus production. The Anti-Federalists were less concerned with or did not recognize their dependence upon the mercantile community and foreign markets, usually were less wealthy, and lived outside the areas of commerce, often in isolation. They lost the struggle against centralization, he concludes, because they lacked party organization and leadership, had little control over publicity, and devised few plans for strengthening the Confederation.

9593
Mason, Alpheus T. The states rights debate; antifederalism and the Constitution. 2d ed. New York, Oxford University Press, 1972. ix, 210 p.   JK316.M3 1972

Bibliography: p. 207–210.
First edition published in 1964.

Presents three essays and 35 supplementary documents outlining Anti-Federalist arguments from 1774 to 1790.

9594
Rutland, Robert A. The ordeal of the Constitution; the Antifederalists and the ratification struggle of 1787–1788. Norman, University of Oklahoma Press [1966] xiii, 329 p. facsim., ports.   KF4541.R8

Includes bibliographic references.

Analyzes the campaign strategies of the opposing forces, explores the personalities, problems, and hopes of the Anti-Federalists, and explains their defeat. To secure at a second convention amendments that would hamstring the central government, the Anti-Federalists attempted to capitalize upon sectional differences, the fears of selfish provincial leaders, and a real desire to preserve freedom. They were unsuccessful because they lacked effective leadership and could not agree on tactics or the amendments to be proposed.

9595
Smith, Edward P. The movement towards a second constitutional convention in 1788. *In* Jameson, John Franklin, *ed.* Essays in the constitutional history of the United States in the formative period, 1775–1789. Boston, Houghton, Mifflin, 1889. p. [46]–115.
KF4541.A2J3 1889

The author's thesis (Ph.D.), *The Scheme for a Second Federal Convention*, was submitted to Syracuse University in 1888.

THE CONSTITUTION IN THE STATES

1. New Hampshire

9596
Batchellor, Albert S. A brief view of the influences that moved in adoption of the federal Constitution by the state of New Hampshire. *In* New Hampshire Bar Association. Journal. new ser., v. 1; 1900. Concord. p. 136–166.   LL

——— ——— Offprint. Concord, N.H., Rumford Press, 1900. 35 p.   JK161.N4 1900

9597
Eiseman, Nathaniel J. The ratification of the federal Constitution by the state of New Hampshire. Washington, D.C., N. J. Eiseman, ᶜ1938. 118 l. maps.
JK161.N4 1938

Reproduced from typescript.
"Originally submitted in partial fulfillment of the requirements for the degree of master of arts in the Faculty of Political Science, Columbia University, February 1937."
Bibliography: leaves 108–115.

9598
New Hampshire. *Convention, 1788.* Journal of the proceedings of the convention of the state of New Hampshire, which adopted the federal Constitution. 1788. (Copied from the original . . .) [Concord, 1876] 22 p.
JK161.N4 1788

"Biographical notes [of delegates] by the editor": p. [8]–11.

9599
Straus, Lawrence G. Reactions of supporters of the Constitution to the adjournment of the New Hampshire ratification convention, 1788. Historical New Hampshire, v. 23, autumn 1968: 37–50.   F31.H57, v. 23

9600
Walker, Joseph B. Birth of the federal Constitution. A history of the New Hampshire convention for the investigation, discussion, and decision of the federal Constitution: and of the Old North Meeting-House of Concord, in which it was ratified by the ninth state, and thus rendered operative . . . on . . . the 21st of June, 1788. Boston, Cupples & Hurd, 1888. x, 128 p. illus., plans.   JK161.N4 1888

2. Massachusetts

9601
Clason, Augustus W. The convention of Massachusetts [1788] Magazine of American history, with notes and queries, v. 14, Dec. 1885: 529–545.
E171.M18, v. 14

9602
Cushing, William, *jurist.* Justice Cushing's undelivered speech on the federal Constitution. William and Mary quarterly, 3d ser., v. 15, Jan. 1958: 74–92.
F221.W71, 3d s., v. 15

Possibly suppressed by John Hancock, the speech was intended for delivery at the closing session of the Massachusetts ratifying convention. Introduction and notes by William O'Brien.

9603
Harding, Samuel B. The contest over the ratification of the federal Constitution in the state of Massachusetts. New

York, Longmans, Green, 1896. 194 p. (Harvard historical studies, v. 2) JK161.M4 1896
KF4512.M37H37 1896

Appendixes: a. Letter of "Cornelius." b. Letters of "A Republican Federalist." c. Bibliographical note. d. List of authorities cited (p. 180–184).

Reprinted in New York by Da Capo Press (1970. JK161.M4 1970).

Examines conflicts in the convention of 1788. While the aristocratic and commercial elements in the state favored ratification, Harding finds that widespread popular concern over aristocratic control and fear of delegated power generated extensive opposition to the proposed Constitution. He considers in detail the contributions of Samuel Adams and Gov. John Hancock in developing proposed amendments and securing a decision for ratification.

9604
Haynes, George H. The conciliatory proposition in the Massachusetts Convention of 1788. *In* American Antiquarian Society, *Worcester, Mass.* Proceedings, new ser., v. 29, Oct. 1919: 294–311.
E172.A35, n.s., v. 29

To secure ratification of the Constitution, Massachusetts Federalists agreed to recommend the prompt adoption of nine specific amendments.

9605
Holcombe, Arthur N. Massachusetts and the federal Constitution of 1787. *In* Hart, Albert B., *ed.* Commonwealth history of Massachusetts. v. 3. Commonwealth of Massachusetts, 1775–1820. New York, States History Co., 1929. p. 366–406. ports. F64.H32, v. 3

Bibliography: p. 403–406.

9606
Massachusetts. *Convention, 1788.* Debates and proceedings in the convention of the commonwealth of Massachusetts, held in the year 1788, and which finally ratified the Constitution of the United States. Printed by authority of resolves of the legislature, 1856. Boston, W. White, printer to the commonwealth, 1856. vii, 442 p. JK161.M4 1856

Edited by Bradford K. Peirce and Charles Hale.

9607
Massachusetts. *Convention, 1788.* Debates, resolutions and other proceedings, of the convention of the commonwealth of Massachusetts, convened at Boston, on the 9th of January, 1788, and continued until the 7th of February following, for the purpose of assenting to and ratifying the Constitution recommended by the grand federal Convention. Together with the yeas and nays on the decision of the grand question. To which the federal Constitution is prefixed. Boston, Adams and Nourse, 1788. 219 p. JK161.M4 1788 Rare Bk. Coll.

9608
Myers, Denys P. Massachusetts and the first ten amendments to the Constitution. [Washington, U.S. Govt. Print. Off., 1936] 41 p. ([U.S.] 74th Congress, 2d session. Senate. Doc. 181) JK168.M9

"Reference citations": p. 37–41.

9609
Stone, Eben F. [Theophilus] Parsons and the constitutional convention of 1788. *In* Essex Institute, *Salem, Mass.* Historical collections, v. 35, Apr. 1899: 81–102. port. F72.E7E81, v. 35

9610
Warren, Charles. Elbridge Gerry, James Warren, Mercy Warren, and the ratification of the federal Constitution in Massachusetts. *In* Massachusetts Historical Society, *Boston.* Proceedings. v. 64; 1930/32. p. 142–164.
F61.M38, v. 64

3. Rhode Island

9611
Bishop, Hillman M. Why Rhode Island opposed the federal Constitution. Rhode Island history, v. 8, Jan.–Oct. 1949: 1–10, 33–44, 85–95, 115–126.
F76.R472, v. 8

9612
Conley, Patrick T. Rhode Island in disunion, 1787–1790. Rhode Island history, v. 31, fall 1972: 98–115. illus., facsims., ports. F76.R472, v. 31

9613
Newport, *R. I.* Abstracts from the records of Newport relative to the adoption of the Constitution of the United States, 1788–9. Newport historical magazine, v. 4, Oct. 1883: 92–99. F76.R35, v. 4

9614
Rhode Island. *Convention, South Kingstown, 1790.* Theodore Foster's minutes of the convention held at South Kingstown, Rhode Island, in March, 1790, which failed to adopt the Constitution of the United States. Transcribed with annotations and an introduction by Robert C. Cotner, and a foreword by Verner W. Crane. Providence, Printed for the [Rhode Island Historical] Society, 1929, vi, 99 p. port.
JK161.R5 1790

"This edition of the hitherto unprinted minutes of Theodore Foster is the . . . work of a student in the American history seminar in Brown University."

Reprinted in Freeport, N.Y., by Books for Libraries Press (1970).

4. Connecticut

9615
Katz, Judith M. Connecticut newspapers and the Constitution, 1786–1788. *In* Connecticut Historical Society, *Hartford.* Bulletin, v. 30, Apr. 1965: 33–44. map.
F91.C67, v. 30

9616

Rhodes, James E. Connecticut and the federal Constitution. Hartford [1945] 34 p. [Connecticut. State Dept. of Education. Curriculum laboratory bulletin 14]
JK148.R5 1945

Bibliography: p. 33–34.

9617

Steiner, Bernard C. Connecticut's ratification of the federal Constitution. *In* American Antiquarian Society, *Worcester, Mass.* Proceedings, new ser., v. 25, Apr. 1915: 70–127. E172.A35, n.s., v. 25

5. NEW YORK

9618

Aly, Bower. How Hamilton, outvoted 2 to 1, won New York for federal Union. Freedom and Union, v. 12, July/Aug. 1957: 15–22. illus., facsim., ports.
JX1901.F6, v. 12

9619

Brooks, Robin. Alexander Hamilton, Melancton Smith, and the ratification of the Constitution in New York. William and Mary quarterly, 3d ser., v. 24, July 1967: 339–358. F221.W71, 3d s., v. 24

9620

De Pauw, Linda G. The eleventh pillar; New York State and the federal Constitution. Ithaca, N.Y., Published for the American Historical Association [by] Cornell University Press [1966] xvi, 328 p. map.
JK161.N7 1966

Bibliography: p. 304–322.
The author's thesis (Ph.D.), with the same title, was submitted to Johns Hopkins University in 1964.

In her interpretation of the political contest over ratification, the author examines the common desires of the Federalists and Anti-Federalists to augment the power of the central government, the role of moderates in constructing a compromise for ratification, and the rapid disappearance of antifederalism after the adoption of the Bill of Rights. De Pauw concludes that the conflict was over the time and conditions under which the amendments demanded by the Anti-Federalists would be passed rather than the acceptance or rejection of the Constitution itself.

9621

Dyess, George A. M. The conflict over the ratification of the federal Constitution in the state of New York. [New York? 1901] 36 p. JK161.N7 1901

Thesis (Ph.D)—New York University.
Bibliography: p. 34–36.

9622

Franklin, Mitchell. Brutus, the American praetor. Tulane law review, v. 15, Dec. 1940: 16–50. LL

Reconsiders Robert Yates' "Letters of Brutus," which were published in the spring of 1788 during the ratification controversy in New York. A leading Anti-Federalist, Yates questioned the constitutionality of the "judiciary state" established by the doctrine of judicial review.

9623

Lynd, Staughton. Capitalism, democracy and the United States Constitution: the case of New York. Science and society, v. 27, fall 1963: 385–414. H1.S25, v. 27

While the financial crisis of 1779–80 had crystalized the mercantilist, nationalist program of the Federalist leaders, the depression of 1785–86 helped them to forge an alliance with the city's mechanics and artisans who viewed the newly drafted Constitution as a vehicle for sustaining the national economy and preserving their independence from foreign domination.

9624

Miner, Clarence E. The ratification of the federal Constitution by the state of New York. New York, Columbia University, 1921. 135 p. (Studies in history, economics and public law, v. 94, no. 3; whole no. 214)
H31.C7, v. 94
JK161.N7

Published also as thesis (Ph.D.)—Columbia University, 1920.
Bibliography: p. 133–135.
Reprinted in New York by AMS Press (1968).

Describes party conflict in New York, 1783–87; the background, composition, and operation of the Poughkeepsie Convention of 1788; and the issues involved in the contest over ratification.

9625

New York (*State*). *Convention, 1788.* The debates and proceedings of the constitutional convention of the state of New York assembled at Poughkeepsie on the 17th June, 1788. A facsimile reprint of an original copy in the Adriance Memorial Library. Poughkeepsie, N.Y., Vassar Brothers Institute, 1905. 144 p. JK161.N7 1905

Originally published in New York by F. Childs in 1788.

9626

Simpson, Sarah H. J. The federal procession in the city of New York [1788] *In* New York Historical Society. Quarterly bulletin, v. 9, July 1925: 39–57.
F116.N638, v. 9

9627

Spaulding, Ernest Wilder. New York and the federal Constitution. *In* New York State Historical Association. New York history, v. 20, Apr. 1939: 125–132.
F116.N865, v. 20

9628

Spaulding, Ernest Wilder. The ratification of the federal Constitution. *In* New York State Historical Association. History of the state of New York. v. 5. Conquering the wilderness. New York, Columbia University Press, 1934. p. [29]–63. illus., ports. F119.N65, v. 5

Bibliography: p. 61–63.

9629

Stevens, John A.   New York and the federal Constitution. Magazine of American history, with notes and queries, v. 2, July 1878: 385–406.   E171.M18, v. 2

9630

Van Kleek, Baltus B.   The ratification of the Constitution by the state of New York at Poughkeepsie, 1788. *In* Dutchess County Historical Society. Year book. v. 48; 1963. Poughkeepsie. p. 30–41.   F127.D8D93, v. 48

6. NEW JERSEY

9631

New Brunswick Historical Club, *New Brunswick, N.J.*   18 December 1787: Adoption of the Constitution of the United States by New Jersey. Commemorative exercises by the New Brunswick Historical Club . . . 16 December 1887. With an appendix. [New Brunswick, New Brunswick Home News Print, 1887] 47 p. (New Brunswick, N.J., Historical Club. Publications, 1)
Micro 18709 F
F144.N5N55

9632

New Jersey. *Convention, 1787.*   Minutes of the convention of the state of New Jersey, holden at Trenton the 11th day of December 1787. Trenton, Printed by Isaac Collins, Printer to the State, 1788. 31 p.
JK161.N5 1787 Rare Bk. Coll.

Reprinted in the Rutgers University Library *Journal*, v. 23, Dec. 1959, p. 8–32, with introductions by Justice William J. Brennan, "New Jersey's Ratified Copy of the Federal Constitution" (p. 1–3), and Richard P. McCormick, "The Unanimous State" (p. 4–7). An earlier reprint was issued in Trenton by C. L. Traver (1888. 31 p. JK161.N5 1787a).

7. PENNSYLVANIA

9633

Alberts, Robert C.   Business of the highest magnitude; or, Don't put off until tomorrow what you can ram through today. American heritage, v. 22, Feb. 1971: 48–53, 101–103. illus., facsims.   E171.A43, v. 22

On the tactics used by Pennsylvania Federalists on September 28, 1787, to force through the assembly a resolution for the election of delegates to a convention in November to ratify the federal Constitution.

9634

Benton, William A.   Pennsylvania Revolutionary officers and the federal Constitution. Pennsylvania history, v. 31, Oct. 1964: 419–435.   F146.P597, v. 31

Analyzes factors that prompted Pennsylvania officers to become Federalists or Anti-Federalists.

9635

Clason, Augustus W.   The Pennsylvania Convention, 1788 [i.e. 1787] Magazine of American history, with notes and queries, v. 25, Mar. 1891: 215–226.
E171.M18, v. 25

9636

Egle, William H.   The federal Constitution of 1787: sketches of the members of the Pennsylvania Convention. Pennsylvania magazine of history and biography, v. 10, Jan. 1887: 446–460; v. 11, Apr. 1887–Jan. 1888: 69–79, 213–222, 249–275, 499–500.   F146.P65, v. 10–11

9637

Ford, Paul L.   The origin, purpose and result of the Harrisburg Convention of 1788. A study in popular government. Brooklyn, N.Y., 1890. 40 p.   F153.F71

Called by Pennsylvania Anti-Federalists to consider revisions of the federal Constitution.

9638

Groshens, David E.   Men of Montgomery County who aided the ratification of our federal Constitution by the commonwealth of Pennsylvania. *In* Historical Society of Montgomery County (*Pennsylvania*). Bulletin, v. 5, Apr. 1946: 125–134.   F157.M7H45, v 5

9639

Hopkinson, Francis.   Account of the grand federal procession, Philadelphia, 1788. Edited by Whitfield J. Bell, Jr. Boston, Old South Association [1962] 30 p. (Old South leaflets. [General ser.] no. 230–231)
E173.O44, no. 230–231
F158.44.H76 1962

9640

Ireland, Owen S.   The ratification of the federal Constitution in Pennsylvania. 1966. ([295] p.)
Micro AC–1, no. 67–3039

Thesis (Ph.D.)—University of Pittsburgh.
Abstracted in *Dissertation Abstracts*, v. 27A, Mar. 1967, p. 2989–2990.

9641

Nichols, Roy F.   Pennsylvania and the Constitution. *In* Genealogical Society of Pennsylvania. Publications, v. 13; Oct. 1936/Oct. 1937, no. 1/2. [Philadelphia] 1938. p. 11–23.   F146.G32, v. 13

9642

Pennsylvania. *Convention, 1787.*   Minutes of the convention of the commonwealth of Pennsylvania, which commenced at Philadelphia, on Tuesday, the twentieth day of November, one thousand seven hundred and eighty-seven, for the purpose of taking into consideration the Constitution framed by the late fœderal Convention for the United States of America. Philadelphia, Printed by Hall and Sellers, in Market-Street, 1787. 28 p.   JK161.P4 1787 Rare Bk. Coll.

9643

Pennsylvania. Historical Society.   Pennsylvania and the federal Constitution, 1787–1788. Edited by John Bach McMaster and Frederick D. Stone. [Philadelphia] Published for the subscribers by the Historical Society of

Pennsylvania [Lancaster, Inquirer Print. and Pub. Co., Printers] 1888. viii, 803 p. ports.   JK161.P4 1888

"Sketches of the Pennsylvania members of the Federal convention": p. 699–711.

"Sketches of the members of the Pennsylvania convention": p. 712–761.

Reprinted in New York by DaCapo Press (1970).

In an effort to present a more balanced view of the contest over ratification in Pennsylvania than may be found in Elliot's *Debates* (entry 9531), the editors arrange newspaper accounts, editorials, essays, broadsides, the notes of James Wilson, and the reports of Thomas Lloyd in chronological order to show the creation, labor, and conclusions of the state convention that met from November 21 to December 15, 1787, to consider the merits of the "New Plan."

9644

Wayne, Anthony.   The convention notes of Anthony Wayne [1787] Manuscripts, v. 16, winter 1964: 18–25. facsim.   Z41.A2A925, v. 16

Wayne supported the federal Constitution at the Pennsylvania ratifying convention.

9645

Yeates, Jasper.   Jasper Yeates's notes on the Pennsylvania ratifying convention, 1787. William and Mary quarterly, 3d ser., v. 22, Apr. 1965: 301–318.
F221.W71, 3d s., v. 22

Introduction and notes by R. Carter Pittman.

8. DELAWARE

9646

De Valinger, Leon.   How Delaware became the first state. Dover, State of Delaware, Division of Archives and Cultural Affairs, 1970. 34 p. illus.   JK161.D4D4

On Delaware's unanimous ratification of the Constitution, December 7, 1787.

9647

Ryden, George H.   Delaware—the first state in the Union. Wilmington, Del., Delaware Tercentenary Commission, 1938. 33 p.   F168.R94

"Bibliographical note": p. 29–30.

On Delaware's role in securing passage and ratification of the Constitution.

9. MARYLAND

9648

Crowl, Philip A.   Anti-Federalism in Maryland, 1787–1788. William and Mary quarterly, 3d ser., v. 4, Oct. 1947: 446–469   F221.W71, 3d s., v. 4

The struggle over ratification was fundamentally an internecine war among members of a small, wealthy ruling class.

9649

Delaplaine, Edward S.   Thomas Johnson, Maryland and the Constitution. [Baltimore? 1925] 17 p. port.
E302.6.J65D35

9650

Martin, Luther.   Luther Martin's speech to the House of Delegates, 1788. Maryland historical magazine, v. 5, June 1910: 139–150.   F176.M18, v. 5

Contributed by Bernard C. Steiner.

9651

Steiner, Bernard C.   Maryland's adoption of the federal Constitution. American historical review, v. 5, Oct. 1899–Jan. 1900: 22–44, 207–224.   E171.A57, v. 5

10. VIRGINIA

9652

Beveridge, Albert J.   How Virginia came to vote for the U.S. Constitution. Freedom and union, v. 11, Feb. 1956: 16–19; Mar.: 6–10. illus., ports.
JX1901.F6, v. 11

Condensed from the author's *Life of John Marshall.*

9653

Breitlow, John R.   Rhetorical fantasy in the Virginia Convention of 1788. 1972. ([300] p.)
Micro AC–1, no. 73–10,528

Thesis (Ph.D.)—University of Minnesota.

Abstracted in *Dissertation Abstracts International,* v. 33A, Apr. 1973, p. 5864.

An analysis of Federalist and Anti-Federalist speeches as they reflected the ideologies, organization, strategies, and rhetorical practices of the contending parties.

9654

Clason, Augustus W.   The convention of Virginia, 1788. Magazine of American history, with notes and queries, v. 15, June 1886: 566–589.   E171.M18, v. 15

9655

Cook, Roy B.   Western Virginia's contribution to the adoption of the federal Constitution. West Virginia history, v. 13, Jan. 1952: 90–110.   F236.W52, v. 13

9656

Cox, Harold E.   Federalism and anti-Federalism in Virginia—1787: a study of political and economic motivations. 1958. ([216] p.)   Micro AC–1, no. 58–5526

Thesis (Ph.D)—University of Virginia.

Abstracted in *Dissertation Abstracts,* v. 19, Dec. 1958, p. 1352–1353.

9657

Ford, Worthington C., *comp.*   The federal Constitution in Virginia, 1787–1788. *In* Massachusetts Historical Society, *Boston.* Proceedings. 2d ser., v. 17; 1903. Boston. p. 450–510.   F61.M38, 2d s., v. 17

—————— —————— Offprint. Cambridge [Mass.] J. Wilson, 1903. 63 p.   JK161.V8 1903b

Presents approximately 50 letters to and from such leading figures as Edward Carrington, George Mason, James Madison, William Grayson, James McClurg, Thomas Jefferson, Joseph Jones, and the Reverend James Madison.

9658

Grigsby, Hugh B.   The history of the Virginia federal Convention of 1788, with some account of eminent Virginians of that era who were members of the body. With a biographical sketch of the author and illustrative notes. Edited by R. A. Brock. Richmond, Va. [Virginia Historical] Society, 1890–91. 2 v. (Virginia Historical Society. Collections, new ser., v. 9–10)

F230.G85
F221.V82, n.s., v. 9–10

Reprinted in one volume in New York by Da Capo Press (1969).

9659

Schick, James B   The Antifederalist ideology in Virginia, 1787–1788. 1971. ([340] p.)
Micro AC–1, no. 72–12,972

Thesis (Ph.D.)—Indiana University.

Abstracted in *Dissertation Abstracts International*, v. 32A, Apr. 1972, p. 5721–5722.

9660

Talbert, Charles G.   Kentuckians in the Virginia Convention of 1788. *In* Kentucky Historical Society. Register, v. 58, July 1960: 187–193.   F446.K43, v. 58

On their 10 to 3 vote against ratification of the federal Constitution.

9661

Thomas, Robert E.   The Virginia Convention of 1788: a criticism of Beard's *An Economic Interpretation of the Constitution*. Journal of southern history, v. 19, Feb. 1953: 63–72.   F206.J68, v. 19

9662

Virginia. *Convention, 1788.*   Debates and other proceedings of the convention of Virginia, convened at Richmond, on Monday the second day of June, 1788, for the purpose of deliberating on the Constitution recommended by the grand federal Convention. To which is prefixed the federal Constitution. Taken in short hand, by David Robertson of Petersburg. 2d ed. Richmond, Printed at the Enquirer Press, for Ritchie & Worsley and Augustine Davis, 1805. viii, 477 p.
JK161.V8 1788c

First edition published in Petersburg by Hunter and Prentis (1788–89. JK161.V8 1788a Rare Bk. Coll.).

9663

Virginia. *Convention, 1788.*   Journal of the convention of Virginia; held in the city of Richmond, on the first Monday in June, in the year of Our Lord one thousand seven hundred and eighty-eight. Richmond, Printed by T. W. White, 1827. 39 p.
JK161.V8 1788h Rare Bk. Coll.

". . . Convention . . . held . . . for the purpose of a full and free investigation, discussion and decision upon the plan of federal government for the United States, recommended by the late Federal Convention, held in Philadelphia": p. [5]–6.

9664

When Patrick Henry fought the federal Constitution.   Freedom and union, v. 10, June 1955: 6–13. illus., port.   JX1901.F6, v. 10

Excerpts taken from the Virginia debates in volume 3 of Jonathan Elliot's *Debates of the Several State Conventions on the Adoption of the Federal Constitution.*

9665

Willis, Stanley.   George Mason: agrarian-minded constitutionalist, 1787–1788. *In* Essays in history. v. 11; 1965/66. Charlottesville, Va. [1966?] p. 42–62.
D2.E75, v. 11

11. NORTH CAROLINA

9666

Best, James A.   The adoption of the federal Constitution by North Carolina. *In* Duke University, Durham, N.C. Trinity College Historical Society. Historical papers. ser. 5; 1905. Durham. p. 12–30.
[F251.D83, ser. 5]
Micro 9370F

9667

Cheshire, Joseph B., *Bp.*   The personnel of the North Carolina Convention of 1788. *In* Southern History Association. Publications, v. 3, Apr. 1899: 121–129.
F206.S73, v. 3

Presents extracts from the journal of the convention.

9668

Clason, Augustus W.   The convention of North Carolina, 1788. Magazine of American history, with notes and queries, v. 15, Apr. 1886: 352–364.
E171.M18, v. 15

9669

Connor, Henry G.   The convention of 1788–'89 and the federal Constitution—Hillsborough and Fayetteville. [Raleigh, E. M. Uzzell, Printers, 1904] (The North Carolina booklet, v. 4, no. 4)   F251.N86, v. 4

9670

News, letters and documents concerning North Carolina and the federal constitution. *In* Duke University, Durham, N.C. Trinity College Historical Society. Historical papers. ser. 14; 1922. Durham. p. [75]–95.
[F251.D83, ser. 14]
Micro 9370F

Compiled by William K. Boyd.

9671

Newsome, Albert R.   North Carolina's ratification of the federal Constitution. North Carolina historical review, v. 17, Oct. 1940: 287–301.   F251.N892, v. 17

9672

North Carolina. *Convention, 1788.*   Proceedings and debates of the convention of North-Carolina, convened at Hillsborough, on Monday the 21st day of July, 1788, for the purpose of deliberating and determining on the Constitution recommended by the general convention at Philadelphia, the 17th day of September, 1787. To which is prefixed the said Constitution. Edenton, Printed by Hodge & Wills, 1789. 280 p.
                    JK161.N8 1788 Rare Bk. Coll.

9673

A North Carolina citizen on the federal Constitution, 1788.   Edited by Julian Parkes Boyd. North Carolina historical review, v. 16, Jan. 1939: 36–53.
                    F251.N892, v. 16

Casting his essay in the form of a letter to a friend, the unknown author presents one of the best summaries of North Carolina's objections to the Constitution.

9674

Pierson, William W.   The sovereign state of North Carolina, 1787–1789. *In* North Carolina. State Literary and Historical Association. Proceedings and addresses. 1916. Raleigh. 1917. p. 58–69.   F251.N95, 1916

9675

A Plea for federal union, North Carolina, 1788; a reprint of two pamphlets, with an introduction by Hugh T. Lefler. Charlottesville, Tracey W. McGregor Library, University of Virginia, 1947 [i.e. 1948] 79 p.
                    JK161.N8 1948

"Bibliographical note": p. 75–76.

Contents: To the people of the state of North Carolina, by a citizen of North Carolina (James Iredell).—To the people of the district of Edenton, by a citizen and soldier (unidentified).

9676

Pool, William C.   An economic interpretation of the ratification of the federal Constitution in North Carolina. North Carolina historical review, v. 27, Apr.–Oct. 1950: 119–141, 289–313, 437–461.
                    F251.N892, v. 27

The author's thesis (Ph.D.), with the same title, was submitted to the University of Texas in 1949.

9677

Raper, Charles L.   Why North Carolina at first refused to ratify the federal Constitution. *In* American Historical Association. Annual report. 1905. v. 1. Washington, 1906. p. 99–107.   E172.A60, 1905, v. 1

9678

Trenholme, Louise I.   The ratification of the federal Constitution in North Carolina. New York, Columbia University Press, 1932. 282 p. fold. maps. (Studies in history, economics and public law, no. 363)
                    H31.C7, no. 363
                    JK161.N8 1932a

Issued also as thesis (Ph.D.)—Columbia University. Bibliography: p. 250–267.

Reprinted in New York by AMS Press (1967. JK161.N8 1967).

Investigates the struggle between Federalists and Anti-Federalists in the conventions of 1788 and 1789. Ratification failed at first because agrarians, who were concerned mainly with local affairs, outnumbered the commercial group in the east. Tariff and navigation laws passed by the first U.S. Congress, however, convinced a majority of the delegates at the second convention that agricultural and commercial interests were interdependent.

12. SOUTH CAROLINA

9679

Clason, Augustus W.   The South Carolina Convention, 1788. Magazine of American history, with notes and queries, v. 15, Feb. 1886: 153–161.
                    E171.M18, v. 15

9680

Ramsay, David.   David Ramsay on the ratification of the Constitution in South Carolina, 1787–1788. Edited by Robert L. Brunhouse. Journal of Southern history, v. 9, Nov. 1943: 548–555.   F206.J68, v. 9

9681

Rogers, George C.   South Carolina ratifies the federal Constitution. *In* South Carolina Historical Association. Proceedings. 1961. Columbia, S.C., 1962. p. 41–62.   F266.S58, 1961

9682

South Carolina. *Convention, 1788.*   Journal of the convention of South Carolina which ratified the Constitution of the United States, May 23, 1788. Indexed by A. S. Salley, Jr., Secretary of the Historical Commission of South Carolina. Atlanta, Ga., Printed for the Historical Commission of South Carolina by Foote & Davis Co., 1928. 60 p.   JK161.S6 1788a

9683

South Carolina. *General Assembly. House of Representatives.*   Debates which arose in the House of Representatives of South-Carolina, on the Constitution framed for the United States, by a convention of delegates assembled at Philadelphia. Together with such notices of the convention as could be procured. Charleston, Printed by A. E. Miller, 1831. 95 p.
                    JK161.S6 1831 Rare Bk. Coll.

Speeches, etc., in the state convention held at Charleston, 1788: p. 61–86.

The *Debates* were first published in Charleston in 1788 (55 p. JK161.S6 1788 Rare Bk. Coll.).

13. GEORGIA

9684

Bland, Julia M.   Georgia and the federal Constitution. Proceedings of the state constitutional convention, and proceedings of the state legislature with respect to the amendments proposed by the United States Congress on September 25, 1789, March 4, 1794, and December 9, 1803. Washington, U.S. Govt. Print. Off., 1937. v, 38, [1] p. [U.S. Dept. of State. Publication 1078]

JK161.G4 1937d

"List of authorities": p. 37–[39]

9685

Georgia. *Convention, 1787–1788.*   Minutes of the Georgia convention ratifying the federal Constitution. Georgia historical quarterly, v. 10, Sept. 1926: 223–237.

F281.G2975, v. 10

Introduction and notes by E. M. Coulter.

THE BILL OF RIGHTS

9686

Antieau, Chester J., *and others.*   Freedom from federal establishment; formation and early history of the first amendment religion clauses. Milwaukee, Bruce Pub. Co. [1964] xiv, 272 p.   KF4783.A95

Bibliography: p. 249–266.

Attempting to determine the intention of those who proposed and adopted the first amendment, the authors examine such topics as colonial establishment, areas of church-state accommodation during the Confederation period, the ban on religious test oaths by the Philadelphia Convention, and the proposals for religious amendments by the state conventions that ratified the Constitution. They conclude that the amendment's religious guarantees were meant to incorporate existing state standards and practices into the Constitution and to prevent the development of federal persecution or prejudice on the basis of religion.

9687

Barry, William J.   Influence of English political history on the Constitution of the United States with special reference to Amendment VI. 1942.

Thesis (Ph.D.)—Boston College.

9688

Brant, Irving.   The Bill of Rights; its origin and meaning. Indianapolis, Bobbs-Merrill [1965] vi, 567 p.

KF4749.B7

"Bibliographical notes": p. 527–544.

Identifying 24 assertions of positive rights or restraints upon governmental action in the Constitution of 1787 and an additional 39 in subsequent amendments, the author analyzes the intentions of their creators and the implications of the guarantees. In the half of the volume devoted to developments before 1789, Brant emphasizes the contrast between the more constricted view of individual rights under English common law and the direct and more expansive protections included in even the original provisions of the federal Con-

stitution. He concludes that the American statements of rights are clear, the prohibitions on government action explicit, and the commands to preserve specific liberties categorical.

9689

Donoghue, Daniel C.   Federal Constitutional provisions with respect to religion. *In* American Catholic Historical Society of Philadelphia. Records, v. 39, Mar. 1928: 1–26.   E184.C3A4, v. 39

On the origins of the First Amendment.

9690

Dumbauld, Edward.   State precedents for the Bill of Rights. Journal of public law, v. 7, fall 1958: 323–344.

LL

9691

Dumbauld, Edward.   An unusual constitutional claim. American journal of legal history, v. 1, July 1957: 229–233.   LL

Among the rights that the dissenting minority at the Pennsylvania ratifying convention proposed to include among the first 10 amendments was the "liberty to fowl and hunt."

9692

Gaustad, Edwin S.   A disestablished society: origins of the First Amendment. Journal of church and state, v. 11, autumn 1969: 409–425.   BV630.A1J6, v. 11

9693

Henderson, Edith G.   The background of the Seventh Amendment. Harvard law review, v. 80, Dec. 1966: 289–337.   LL

9694

Lasson, Nelson B.   The history and development of the Fourth Amendment to the United States Constitution. Baltimore, Johns Hopkins Press, 1937. 154 p. (The Johns Hopkins University studies in historical and political science, ser. 55, no. 2)   H31.J6, s. 55, no. 2
JK169 4th 1937a

Issued also as thesis (Ph.D.)—Johns Hopkins University.

"Table of cases": p. 145–147.

"Table of statutes": p. 149–150.

Reprinted in New York by Da Capo Press (1970).

Reviews English precedents, with particular attention to the case of John Wilkes (1765) and the use of Writs of Assistance in the colonies and by the Continental Congress. The author considers the specific development of the amendment through an examination of pertinent debates in the state ratifying conventions of 1787–88 and in the first Congress during 1789.

9695

Levy, Leonard W.   Legacy of suppression; freedom of speech and press in early American history. Cambridge,

Mass., Belknap Press of Harvard University Press, 1960. xiv, 353 p.   JC591.L2

Bibliography: p. [321]–339.

Focusing on the period 1776–91, the author concludes that the Revolutionary generation did not intend the First Amendment to serve a broad libertarian theory of freedom of expression. Instead, the framers accepted the common-law tradition of the right of the state to suppress seditious libel. Not until the conflict over the Sedition Act of 1798 was a justification for a more extensive protection of freedom of speech and press devised.

9696

Levy, Leonard W.   Origins of the Fifth Amendment; the right against self-incrimination. New York, Oxford University Press, 1968. xii, 561 p.   LL

Bibliography: p. 520–544.

9697

Mayers, Lewis.   The federal witness' privilege against self-incrimination: constitutional or common-law? American journal of legal history, v. 4, Apr. 1960: 107–141.   LL

Treats, in part, the origins of the Fifth Amendment.

9698

Rutland, Robert A.   The birth of the Bill of Rights, 1776–1791. Chapel Hill, Published for the Institute of Early American History and Culture by the University of North Carolina Press [1955] vi, 243 p.   JK168.R8

Bibliographic footnotes.

Appendixes (p. [231]–235): A. The Virginia Declaration of Rights.—B. The federal Bill of Rights.

The author's thesis (Ph.D.), *The Movement for Bills of Rights, 1776–1791*, was submitted to Vanderbilt University in 1953 (Micro AC–1, no. 6472).

Studies the emergence of bills of rights on both state and federal levels and discusses precedents derived from English common law, colonial charters, legislation, and experience. Rutland argues that possession of a bill of rights became a political tradition among Americans. When the Constitution as drafted failed to meet this need, public opinion forced its supporters to endorse an addition of a Bill of Rights to ensure its ratification.

9699

Schwartz, Bernard, *comp.*   The Bill of Rights: a documentary history. New York, Chelsea House Publishers, 1971. 2 v. (xvii, 1234 p.)   KF4744 1971

Includes bibliographic references.

Contents: v. 1. English antecedents. Colonial charters and laws. Revolutionary declarations and constitutions. Confederation and judicial review. United States Constitution.—v. 2. State ratifying conventions. Federal Bill of Rights: legislative history. Ratification by the states.

9700

Smylie, James H.   Protestant clergy, the First Amendment, and beginnings of a constitutional debate, 1781–91. *In* The Religion of the Republic. Edited by Elwyn A. Smith. Philadelphia, Fortress Press [1971] p. 116–153.   BR515.R44

9701

Thomas, William H.   The federal Bill of Rights. Alabama lawyer, v. 4, Oct. 1943: 419–432.   LL

On the belated ratification of the Bill of Rights by Massachusetts, Connecticut, and Georgia.

9702

U.S. *Constitution. 1st–10th Amendments.*   Amendments proposed to be added to the federal Constitution by the Congress of the United States of America, begun and held at the city of New-York, on Wednesday, the fourth day of March, in the year M,DCC,LXXXIX. Boston, Printed by T. Adams, 1790. 8 p.

KF4744.5.A3 Rare Bk. Coll.

On cover: The Bill of Rights.

9703

Williamson, René de Visme.   Political process or judicial process: the Bill of Rights and the framers of the Constitution. Journal of politics, v. 23, May 1961: 199–211.

JA1.J6, v. 23

Argues that the framers omitted a bill of rights from the Constitution because they were convinced that it would not accomplish the purposes for which it was intended. The real foundation of civil rights, they believed, was political rather than legal.

CHAPTER ELEVEN

Economic, Social, and Intellectual Life in Revolutionary America

The Economy

BUSINESS AND THE ECONOMY

1. GENERAL

9704

Baldwin, Simeon E. American business corporations before 1789. *In* American Historical Association. Annual report. 1902. v. 1. Washington, 1903. p. 253–274.
E172.A60, 1902, v. 1

Also published in the *American Historical Review*, v. 8, Apr. 1903, p. 449–465.

Examines the origin and activities of the six corporations created by colonial assemblies from 1675 to 1772 and those established under the Articles of Confederation and the new state constitutions. Baldwin attributes the small number of charters granted to ill-defined rights of incorporation and a general fear of monopoly.

9705

Baxter, William T. Accounting in colonial America. *In* Littleton, Ananias C., and Basil S. Yamey, *eds.* Studies in the history of accounting. London, Sweet & Maxwell, 1956. p. 272–287. HF5605.L52

9706

Bjork, Gordon C. Stagnation and growth of the American economy, 1784–1792 1963. ([185] p.)
Micro AC–1, no. 64–4489

Thesis (Ph.D.)—University of Washington.
Abstracted in *Dissertation Abstracts*, v. 24, May 1964, p. 4458.

9707

Bruchey, Stuart W. The roots of American economic growth, 1607–1861; an essay in social causation. New York, Harper & Row [1965] xiii, 234 p. HC51.B7

Bibliography: p. 217–[230]

In chapters 1 and 2 (p. 16–73), the author summarizes economic development to 1790.

9708

Callender, Guy S., *ed.* Selections from the economic history of the United States, 1765–1860, with introductory essays. Boston, Ginn [ᶜ1909] xviii, 819 p. fold. map. (Selections and documents in economics) HC106.C2

Reprinted in New York by A. M. Kelley (1965).

Documents pertaining to the period 1765–89 appear in chapters 2–5 (p. 6–238).

9709

Cole, Arthur H. The tempo of mercantile life in colonial America. Business history review, v. 33, autumn 1959: 277–299. HF5001.B8262, v. 33

9710

Davis, Joseph S. Charters for American business corporations in the eighteenth century. *In* American Statistical Association. Quarterly publications, v. 15, Dec. 1916: 426–435. HA1.A6, v. 15

Characterizes by date, source, and general type the 335 charters issued to business corporations in the United States between 1781 and 1800.

9711

Davis, Joseph S. Essays in the earlier history of American corporations. Cambridge, Harvard University Press, 1917. 2 v. (Harvard economic studies, v. 16)
HD2785.D3

The author's dissertation (Ph.D.) was submitted to Harvard University in 1913.

Contents: v. 1. Corporations in the American colonies. William Duer, entrepreneur, 1747–99. The "S.U.M.": the first New Jersey business corporation.—v. 2. Eighteenth century business corporations in the United States. Bibliography (p. 347–395).

Reprinted in New York by Russell & Russell (1965).

In a series of four extended essays the author examines (1) the legal basis and use of the corporate form in colonization and for municipal, business, ecclesiastical, charitable, and educational purposes, (2) the entrepreneurial activities of William Duer (1747–99) of New York, (3) the operations of the Society for Establishing Useful Manufactures in New Jersey, and (4) the nature and practices of some 300 late 18th-century corporations involved in banking, inland navigation, toll bridges, turnpikes, insurance, water supply, and manufacturing. The author concludes that the Revolution broke down psychological barriers and established relationships among men of affairs that made great combinations of American capital practicable for the first time.

9712
Diamond, Sigmund. Values as an obstacle to economic growth: the American colonies. Journal of economic history, v. 27, Dec. 1967: 561–575.
HC10.J64, v. 27

Because transplanted European values hindered economic production, colonial leaders voluntarily granted concessions that weakened the corporate restraints of the first social order. Eventually, position in the new society became largely a function of direct economic activity, not of birth or privilege.

9713
Dorfman, Joseph. The economic mind in American civilization, 1606–1865. v. 1. New York, Viking Press, 1946. xii, 499, xxxi p. HB119.A2D6, v. 1

Bibliographic references included in "Notes" (p. i–xxxi).
Reprinted in New York by A. M. Kelley (1966).

In chapters on the 18th century, the author explores the relationships between politics and economics, especially as they were affected by imperial policies; discusses the role of paper money in disputes with England and between colonies; compares the outlook of Benjamin Franklin, practical businessman, with that of John Woolman, Quaker humanitarian; and explains the methods of financing the Revolution advocated by Americans. The struggles over economic policy derived, according to Dorfman, from rivalries between mercantile groups rather than between socioeconomic classes. Although American economic thought was tempered by humanitarian ideals, it was basically pragmatic and opportunitistic.

9714
East, Robert A. Business enterprise in the American Revolutionary era. New York, Columbia University Press, 1938. 387 p. (Studies in history, economics and public law, no. 439) H31.C7, no. 439
HC105.E24 1938a

Issued also as thesis (Ph.D.)—Columbia University.
Bibliography: p. 330–356.
Reprinted in Gloucester, Mass., by P. Smith (1964) and in New York by AMS Press (1969).

Analyzes changes that took place in business organization, investment, and stock speculation during and after the war. The author also describes the activities of Robert Morris, Jeremiah Wadsworth, and other capitalists, explaining their innovations in business practice during the transition from personally supervised investments to a more highly developed capitalism in which such enterprises as textile factories, land speculation companies, and commercial banks came under impersonal, institutional management.

9715
East, Robert A. The business entrepreneur in a changing colonial economy. 1763–1795. *In* The tasks of economic history; papers presented at the sixth annual meeting of the Economic History Association, Baltimore, Maryland, September 13–14, 1946. [New York] Published for the Economic History Association by New York University Press [1947] (Journal of economic history. Supplement 6; 1946) p. 16–27.
HC10.T3, no. 6, 1946

9716
Eilenstine, Donald L. America and the world economy of the 1780's: a study in mercantile behavior. 1965. ([183] p.) Micro AC–1, no. 65–11,920

Thesis (Ph.D.)—University of Kansas.
Abstracted in *Dissertation Abstracts*, v. 26, Dec. 1965, p. 3099.

9717
Faulkner, Harold U. American economic history. 8th ed. New York, Harper [1960] xxv, 816 p. illus., maps, plates, ports. (Harper's historical series)
HC103.F3 1960

Bibliography: p. 733–788.
Includes two chapters (p. 107–151) on economic causes and aspects of the Revolution.

9718
Hacker, Louis M. The triumph of American capitalism; the development of forces in American history to the end of the nineteenth century. New York, Simon and Schuster, 1940. x, 460 p. HC103.H146

"Authorities cited in the text": p. 439–445.
"The victory of American mercantile capitalism in the Revolution": p. [91]–195.

9719
Handlin, Oscar, *and* Mary F. Handlin. Origins of the American business corporation. Journal of economic and business history, v. 5, May 1945: 1–23.
HC10.J6, v. 5

9720
Mitchell, Broadus, *and* Louise P. Mitchell. American economic history. [Under the editorship of Edgar S. Furniss] Boston, Houghton Mifflin Co. [1947] xi, 928 p. illus., ports., maps. HC103.M67

Includes bibliographies.
Chapters 6–11 (p. 129–250) deal with the Revolutionary period.

9721
Nettels, Curtis P. The emergence of a national economy, 1775–1815. New York. Holt, Rinehart and Winston [1962] xvi, 424 p. illus., maps, ports. (The Economic history of the United States, v. 2) HC103.E25, v. 2

Bibliography: p. 341–380.
For the Revolutionary and Confederation periods, the author examines such topics as shipping and trade, taxation and finance, paper money and banking, and manufacturing and agriculture. The Revolution fostered America's first national economy, one that was then threatened, Nettels

believes, by state measures enacted to overcome a postwar depression. As a consequence, the framers of the Constitution deliberately attempted to create an instrument that would provide stable government and encourage the development of a unified economy.

9722

North, Douglass C., *and* Robert P. Thomas, *comps.* The growth of the American economy to 1860. Columbia, University of South Carolina Press [1968] vii, 251 p. [Documentary history of the United States]
HC103.N63 1968b

Includes 38 documents on imperial regulation of the colonial economy, growth of the factors of production, increases in colonial per capita income, and economic problems of the new nation.

9723

Rezneck, Samuel. The rise and early development of the industrial consciousness in the United States, 1760–1830. Journal of economic and business history, v. 4, Aug. 1932: supplement, 784–811. HC10.J6, v. 4

9724

Rodda, Albert S. A study of the American economic mind from the beginning of the eighteenth century through the American Revolution. 1951. xvi, 486, xxv l.

Thesis (Ph.D.)—Stanford University.

9725

Sachs, William S., *and* Ari A. Hoogenboom. The enterprising colonials; society on the eve of the Revolution. Chicago, Argonaut, 1965. xi, 236 p. illus., facsims., maps. E195.S25

Bibliography: p. 201–221.

Examines colonial society between 1750 and 1775 from the perspective of the American businessman, analyzes the growth of interurban commercial ties and the development of a national economy, and explains how the business community was affected by the economic aspects of British colonial policy.

9726

Taylor, George R. American economic growth before 1840: an exploratory essay. Journal of economic history, v. 24, Dec. 1964: 427–444. HC10.J64, v. 24

9727

Weir, LeRoy M. Contemporary thought on economic aspects of national problems in the United States, 1780–1800. 1943.

Thesis (Ph.D.)—University of Michigan.

9728

Wilhite, Virgle G. Founders of American economic thought and policy. New York, Bookman Associates [1958] 442 p. HB119.A2W5

Bibliography: p. 429–438

Following four introductory chapters on 17th- and 18th-century social and economic doctrines that influenced early American scholars and statesmen, the author turns to an analysis of the economic viewpoints of William Douglass, Hugh Vance, Pelatiah Webster, Tench Coxe, Alexander Hamilton, Benjamin Franklin, John Taylor, and Albert Gallatin.

9729

Wright, Louis B. The dream of prosperity in colonial America. [New York] New York University Press, 1965. 96 p. (Anson G. Phelps lectureship on early American history) E188.W84

Includes bibliographic references.

Contents: Preface.—American cornucopia for all the world.—The lure of fish, furs, wine, and silk.—Cures for all the ills of mankind.—The continuing dream of an economic Utopia.

2. NEW ENGLAND

9730

Daniels, Bruce C. Probate inventories as a source for economic history in 18th century Connecticut. *In* Connecticut Historical Society, *Hartford.* Bulletin, v. 37, Jan. 1972: 1–9. F91.C67, v. 37

9731

Dewey, Davis R. Economic and commercial conditions. *In* Hart, Albert B., *ed.* Commonwealth history of Massachusetts. v. 3. Commonwealth of Massachusetts, 1775–1820. New York, States History Co., 1929. p. 341–365. facsim. F64.H32, v. 3

Bibliography: p. 364–365.

9732

Douglas, Charles H. J. The financial history of Massachusetts, from the organization of the Massachusetts Bay Colony to the American Revolution. [New York] 1892. 148 p. HJ492.D6

Thesis (Ph.D.)—Columbia University.
Bibliography: p. 138–148.
Reprinted in New York by AMS Press (1969).

A second edition was published as v. 1, no. 4 in the Columbia University Studies in History, Economics and Public Law (New York, 1897. [251]–396 p. H31.C7, v. 1).

9733

Flannagan, John H. Trying times: economic depression in New Hampshire, 1781–1789. (Parts I and II). 1972. ([384] p.) Micro AC–1, no. 72–32,819

Thesis (Ph.D.)—Georgetown University.
Abstracted in *Dissertation Abstracts International*, v. 33A, Jan. 1973, p. 3536–3537.

9734

Harlow, Ralph V. Economic conditions in Massachusetts during the American Revolution. *In* Colonial Society of Massachusetts, *Boston.* Publications. v. 20. Transactions, 1917/19. Boston, 1920. p. 163–190.
F61.C71, v. 20

———————— Offprint. Cambridge [Mass.] J. Wilson, 1918. [163]–190 p.   HC107.M4H3

9735

Jones, Alice H.   Wealth estimates for the New England colonies about 1770. Journal of economic history, v. 32, Mar. 1972: 98–127.   HC10.J64, v. 32

9736

Olson, Albert L.   Economic aspects of the migration from Connecticut, particularly in the late eighteenth century. 1934 ([230] p.)   Micro AC–1, no. 60–19, 344

Thesis (Ph.D.)—Yale University.

Abstracted in *Dissertation Abstracts International,* v. 30A, Dec. 1969, p. 2235.

9737

Sachs, William S.   The business outlook in the northern colonies, 1750–1775. 1957. ([330] p.)
                    Micro AC–1, no. 21,821

Thesis (Ph.D.)—Columbia University.

Abstracted in *Dissertation Abstracts,* v. 17, no. 8, 1957, p. 1690–1691.

9738

Saladino, Gaspare J.   The economic revolution in late eighteenth century Connecticut. 1964. ([475] p.)
                    Micro AC–1, no. 64–12,747

Thesis (Ph.D.)—University of Wisconsin.

Abstracted in *Dissertation Abstracts,* v. 25, Dec. 1964, p. 3545.

3. MIDDLE ATLANTIC REGION

9739

Berg, Harry D.   The organization of business in colonial Philadelphia. Pennsylvania history, v. 10, July 1943: 157–177.   F146.P597, v. 10

9740

Brewington, Marion V.   Maritime Philadelphia, 1609–1837. Pennsylvania magazine of history and biography, v. 63, Apr. 1939: 93–117. plates.   F146.P65, v. 63

9741

Cochran, Thomas C.   New York in the Confederation; an economic study. Philadelphia, University of Pennsylvania Press, 1932. ix, 220 p. maps.   F123.C66

Issued also as thesis (Ph.D.)—University of Pennsylvania.

Bibliography: p. 195–212.

Reprinted in Port Washington, N.Y., by I. J. Friedman (1970) and in Clifton, N.J., by A. M. Kelley (1972).

Emphasizing economic measures passed by the Continental Congress and their effect upon New York, the author investigates such topics as paper money, requisitions, the land question, taxation, and the fiscal strategy of Robert Morris. Cochran finds that financial relations between the state government and Congress were more successful than between the state legislature and its constituents. Ultimately,

New York Federalists supported the Constitution not because they wished to strengthen America's trade or diplomatic position, as advocated by the followers of Hamilton and Schuyler, but because security holders hoped to provide for repayment of the public debt, thus bolstering the credit of the new government.

9742

Farris, Sara G.   Wilmington's maritime commerce, 1775–1807. Delaware history, v. 14, Apr. 1970: 22–51.
                    F161.D37, v. 14

Traces the change from a commercial to an industrial economy. After the war, British manufactures threatened to stifle native American industries. The demands by local industrialists for protective tariffs, however, soon turned Wilmington, Delaware's largest community, into a manufacturing town.

9743

Finkel, Charlotte C.   The store account books of Hendrick Schenk, Fishkill Landing, Dutchess County, New York, 1763–1768. *In* Dutchess County Historical Society. Year book. v. 50; 1965. Poughkeepsie. p. 36–49.
                    F127.D8D93, v. 50

Includes a list of all the names which appear in the account books.

9744

Hartman, J. Lee.   Pennsylvania's grand plan of post-Revolutionary internal improvement. Pennsylvania magazine of history and biography, v. 65, Oct. 1941: 439–457.   F146.P65, v. 65

9745

Jones, Alice H.   La fortune privée en Pennsylvanie, New Jersey, Delaware (1774). Annales: économies, sociétés civilisations, v. 24, Mar./Apr. 1969: 235–249.
                    AP20.A58, v. 24

9746

Jones, Alice H.   Wealth estimates for the American middle colonies, 1774. [Chicago, University of Chicago Press, 1970] x, 172 p. illus., maps. (Economic development and cultural change, v. 18, no. 4, pt. 2, July 1970)
                    HC10.C453, v. 18

Bibliography: p. 167–172.

A pilot study of five counties in Pennsylvania, New Jersey, and Delaware that provides estimates not only of total and per capita wealth but also of its composition. Applying contemporary statistical sampling techniques to probate records, the author sheds light on the level and kind of living yielded by the economy on the eve of the Revolution.

9747

Kavenaugh, William K.   An economic history of Suffolk County, New York: 1783–1812. 1966 ([248] p.)
                    Micro AC–1, no. 67–6033

Thesis (Ph.D.)—New York University.

Abstracted in *Dissertation Abstracts,* v. 27A, June 1967, p. 4023–4024.

9748
Mason, Bernard. Entreprenurial activity in New York during the American Revolution. Business history review, v. 40, summer 1966: 190–212.
HF5001.B8262, v. 40

9749
Mishoff, Willard O. Business in Philadelphia during the British occupation, 1777–1778. Pennsylvania magazine of history and biography, v. 61, Apr. 1937: 165–181.
F146.P65, v. 61

9750
Sachs, William S. Interurban correspondents and the development of a national economy before the Revolution; New York as a case study. *In* New York State Historical Association. New York history, v. 36, July 1955: 320–335.
F116.N865, v. 36

Studies the close relations of New York merchants with those of Boston, Newport, and Philadelphia, 1755–75.

9751
Welsh, Peter C. Merchants, millers, and ocean ships: the components of an early American industrial town [Wilmington] Delaware history, v. 7, Sept. 1957: 319–336.
F161.D37, v. 7

4. THE SOUTH

9752
Gould, Clarence P. The economic causes of the rise of Baltimore [ca. 1740–90] *In* Essays in colonial history presented to Charles McLean Andrews by his students. New Haven, Yale University Press, 1931. p. 225–251.
E187.E78

9753
Hilldrup, Robert L. A campaign to promote the prosperity of colonial Virginia. Virginia magazine of history and biography, v. 67, Oct. 1959: 410–428.
F221.V91, v. 67

On the efforts of the Premium Society of London—Royal Society of Arts—and a committee of the House of Burgesses, headed by Charles Carter, to promote economic diversification in Virginia during the early 1760's.

9754
Low, W. A. Merchant and planter relations in post-Revolutionary Virginia, 1783–1789. Virginia magazine of history and biography, v. 61, July 1953: 308–318.
F221.V91, v. 61

9755
Maganzin, Louis. Economic depression in Maryland and Virginia, 1783–1787. 1967. ([294] p.)
Micro AC–1, no. 68–1893

Thesis (Ph.D.)—Georgetown University.
Abstracted in *Dissertation Abstracts*, v. 28A, Feb. 1968, p. 3116.

9756
Morris, Francis G., *and* Phyllis M. Morris. Economic conditions in North Carolina about 1780. North Caro-lina historical review, v. 16, Apr.–July 1939: 107–133, 296–327. maps.
F251.N892, v. 16

Focuses on the ownership of land, slaves, and cattle.

9757
Paul, Charles L. Factors in the economy of colonial Beaufort. North Carolina historical review, v. 44, spring 1967: 111–134. map, plate.
F251.N892, v. 44

9758
Sellers, Leila. Charleston business on the eve of the American Revolution. Chapel Hill, University of North Carolina Press, 1934. xi, 259 p.
HC108.C3S4 1934a

Bibliography: p. [236]–244.
Issued also as thesis (Ph.D.)—Columbia University.
Reprinted in New York by Arno Press (1970).

Describes the influence of geography, class structure, immigration, and slavery upon commercial practices in Charleston. Although the larger mercantile houses tended to support the imperial system, smaller factors or merchants objected strongly to the regulations and enforcement procedures invoked after 1763. A dramatic increase in smuggling, hitherto of negligible importance, and the organization of nonimportation groups marked the onset of the Revolution in Charleston.

9759
Soltow, James H. The economic role of Williamsburg. Williamsburg, Colonial Williamsburg; distributed by the University Press of Virginia, Charlottesville [°1965] xvi, 209 p. (Williamsburg research studies)
HF3163.W65S6

Bibliography: p. 191–202.

Uses the records of the periodic Meetings of Merchants, formally organized in 1769, to analyze the development of commerce in 18th-century Virginia's decentralized agricultural economy. Soltow concludes that the merchants' organization served an important function as a vehicle for the marketing of exportable agricultural commodities and as a clearinghouse for the exchange of credit, paper money, and sterling.

9760
Soltow, James H. The role of Williamsburg in the Virginia economy, 1750–1775. William and Mary quarterly, 3d ser., v. 15, Oct. 1958: 467–482.
F221.W71, 3d s., v. 15

Because of economic decentralization, Virginia merchants used the political center at Williamsburg as a clearinghouse for financial transactions and a market for the important export commodities of the province.

GOVERNMENT REGULATION OF BUSINESS

9761
Baird, E. G. Business regulation in colonial Massachusetts (1620–1780). Dakota law review, v. 3, Feb. 1931: 227–256.
LL

9762

Bittner, Robert B.   The definition of economic independence and the new nation [1781–1789] 1970. ([341] p.)
Micro AC–1, no. 71–2207

Thesis (Ph.D.)—University of Wisconsin.
Abstracted in *Dissertation Abstracts International,* v. 31A, May 1971, p. 5975–5976.

9763

Dowd, Mary J.   The state in the Maryland economy, 1776–1807. Maryland historical magazine, v. 57, June–Sept. 1962: 90–132, 229–258.   F176.M18, v. 57

In the new age of mercantilism launched by the Revolution regulation and promotion went hand in hand.

9764

Fisher, Willard C.   American trade regulations before 1789. *In* American Historical Association. Papers. v. 3, no. 2; 1888. New York, 1889. p. 221–249.
E172.A65, v. 3

9765

Giesecke, Albert A.   American commercial legislation before 1789. [Philadelphia] University of Pennsylvania; New York, D. Appleton, Agents, 1910. 167 p. [Publications of the University of Pennsylvania. Series in political economy and public law]   HF3025.G4

Bibliography: p. 154–163.
Reprinted in New York by B. Franklin (1970).
The author's thesis (Ph.D.), *The American Policy of Commercial Legislation Before 1789,* was submitted to Cornell University in 1908.

Analyzes and explains the background of import and export duties, of bounties, inspection laws, and embargoes, of tonnage duties and port regulations, and of commercial legislation enacted by the states and Confederation. The author concludes that commercial regulation diminished as trade declined during the Revolution, but after the war the now sovereign states found that England's trade policy was enforced against them. They retaliated, Giesecke continues, by encouraging home industries in the northern states and by supporting them with protective legislation.

9766

Handlin, Oscar, *and* Mary F. Handlin.   Commonwealth; a study of the role of government in the American economy: Massachusetts, 1774–1861. Rev. ed. Cambridge, Belknap Press of Harvard University Press, 1969. xvii, 314 p.   HC107.M4H23 1969

Bibliographical references included in "Notes on the sources" (p. 279–293).
First edition published in 1947.

In the section on the transition from royal government to statehood, the authors survey the changes that occurred in the people's view of governmental power and the relation of government to industry. The Handlins conclude that John Adams merely formalized, in the constitution of 1780, ideas then current—commonwealth interests transcend individual interests and government ought to regulate the economic life of the state. Massachusetts early used its authority to inspect products, grant franchises, provide bounties, and authorize tax exemptions.

9767

Handlin, Oscar, *and* Mary F. Handlin.   Revolutionary economic policy in Massachusetts. William and Mary quarterly, 3d ser., v. 4, Jan. 1947: 3–26.
F221.W71, 3d s., v. 4

Finds that the financial policy of Massachusetts from 1774 to 1780 invariably favored the interests of creditors against those of debtors.

9768

Haywood, Clarence Robert.   The influence of mercantilism on social attitudes in the South, 1700–1763. Journal of the history of ideas, v. 20, Oct./Dec. 1959: 577–586.
B1.J75, v. 20

9769

Haywood, Clarence Robert.   Mercantilism: theory and practice in the southern colonies, 1700–1763. 1956.

Thesis (Ph.D.)—University of North Carolina.

9770

Heath, Milton S.   Constructive liberalism; the role of the state in economic development in Georgia to 1860. Cambridge, Harvard University Press, 1954. xiv, 448 p. illus., maps. (Studies in economic history)
HC107.G4H4

"Notes and bibliography": p. [399]–442.

Contends that Georgia began as a planned economy and that a program of constructive social liberalism (group action) prevailed over laissez-faire liberalism (individual initiative) until the Civil War despite the fact that various pressures had modified initial public policy by 1800. Revolutionary egalitarianism removed some restraints in the governance of land, education, welfare, and transportation, according to Heath, but such excesses as the Yazoo affair restored the trend toward humanism and a common sense of social values.

9771

Jensen, Arthur L.   The inspection of exports in colonial Pennsylvania. Pennsylvania magazine of history and biography, v. 78, July 1954: 275–297. col. plate.
F146.P65, v. 78

9772

Johnson, Robert.   Government regulation of business enterprise in Virginia, 1750–1820. 1958. ([441] p.)
Micro AC–1, no. 59–3779

Thesis (Ph.D.)—University of Minnesota.
Abstracted in *Dissertation Abstracts,* v. 20, Oct. 1959, p. 1342–1343.

9773

Jones, Newton B.   Weights, measures, and mercantilism: the inspection of exports in Virginia, 1742–1820. *In* Rutman, Darrett B., *ed.* The Old Dominion; essays for

Thomas Perkins Abernethy. Charlottesville, University Press of Virginia [1964] p. 122–134.   F226.R8

9774
Williams, William A.   The age of mercantilism: an interpretation of the American political economy, 1763–1828. William and Mary quarterly, 3d ser., v. 15, Oct. 1958: 419–437.   F221.W71, 3d s., v. 15

Advances the hypothesis that the central development in American history from the Revolution to the Monroe Doctrine was the maturation of an expansionist American mercantilism.

9775
Zornow, William F.   The Sandy Hook Lighthouse incident of 1787. Journal of economic history, v. 14, summer 1954: 261–266.   HC10.J64, v. 14

On discriminatory trade legislation passed by New York and New Jersey.

TRADE, COMMERCE, AND SHIPPING

1. GENERAL

9776
Bell, Herbert C. F.   Studies in the trade relations of the British West Indies and North America, 1763–1773; 1783–1793. Philadelphia, 1917. [429]–441, 272–287 p.   HF3079.B4

Reprinted from the *English Historical Review*, v. 31, July 1916, p. 429–441, and from the *American Historical Review*, v. 22, Jan. 1917, p. 272–287.
The author's thesis (Ph.D.), *The Adjustment of Trade Relations Between the United States and the West Indies, 1782–1788*, was submitted to the University of Pennsylvania in 1909.

9777
Bradlee, Francis B. C.   Colonial trade and commerce, 1733–1774. *In* Essex Institute, *Salem, Mass.* Historical collections, v. 63, Jan. 1927: 1–29. plates.   F72.E7E81, v. 63

———————— Offprint. Salem, Mass., Essex Institute, 1927. 29 p. plates.   HF3025.B7

9778
Caruthers, J. Wade.   Influence of maritime trade in early American development, 1750–1830. American Neptune, v. 29, July 1969: 199–210.   V1.A4, v. 29

9779
Chaloner, William H.   Hazards of trade with France in time of war. 1776–1783. Business history, v. 6, June 1964: 79–92.   HF11.B9, v. 6

9780
Channing, Edward.   Commerce during the Revolutionary epoch. *In* Massachusetts Historical Society, *Boston.* Proceedings. v. 44; 1910/11. Boston, 1911. p. 364–377.   F61.M38, v. 44

Importation during the war.

9781
[Coxe, Tench]   An enquiry into the principles on which a commercial system for the United States of America should be founded; to which are added some political observations connected with the subject. Read before the Society for Political Enquiries, convened at the house of His Excellency Benjamin Franklin, Esquire, in Philadelphia May 11th, 1787. [Philadelphia] Printed and sold by Robert Aitken, at Pope's Head, in Market Street, 1787. 52 p.   HC105.C87, v. 3 Rare Bk. Coll.
HF345.C6, v. 3 Rare Bk. Coll.

9782
Ford, Worthington C.   Colonial commerce in 1774–1776. *In* Massachusetts Historical Society, *Boston.* Proceedings. v. 59; 1925/26. Boston, 1926. p. 210–235.   F61.M38, v. 59

Letters and papers drawn from the Lee-Cabot manuscripts.

9783
Gillingham, Harrold E.   Marine insurance in Philadelphia, 1721–1800, with a list of brokers and underwriters as shown by old policies and books of record. [Philadelphia, Patterson & White Co., priv. print.] 1933. 133 p. illus., facsims.   HE964.G5 Rare Bk. Coll.

9784
Huntley, Francis C.   Trade of the thirteen colonies with the foreign Caribbean area. 1947.

Thesis (Ph.D.)—University of California, Berkeley.

9785
Jameson, John Franklin, *ed.*   Privateering and piracy in the colonial period: illustrative documents. New York, Macmillan Co., 1923. xxvi, 619 p.   E195.J32

Reprinted in New York by A. M. Kelley (1970).

Intermingles in chronological order documents that illustrate various aspects of the authorized warfare carried on by privateers and the unauthorized activities of pirate vessels between 1638 and 1772. The compiler includes excerpts from 76 journals, declarations, commissions, lists, and other papers relating to the voyages of 11 ships sailing after 1740.

9786
Johnson, Emory R., *and others.*   History of domestic and foreign commerce of the United States. Washington, D.C., Carnegie Institution of Washington, 1915. 2 v. maps (part fold.) (Carnegie Institution of Washington. Publication no. 215A)   HF3021.J6
HC101.C75, no. 1

Contributions to American economic history from the Department of Economics and Sociology of the Carnegie Institution of Washington. [1]
Bibliography: v. 2, p. 352–386.
Partial contents: v. 1, pt. 1. American commerce to 1789, by E. R. Johnson.
Reprinted in New York by B. Franklin (1964).

9787

McClellan, William S. Smuggling in the American colonies at the outbreak of the Revolution, with special reference to the West Indies trade. New York, Printed for the Dept. of Political Science of Williams College by Moffat, Yard, 1912. xx, 105 p. (Williams College. David A. Wells prize essays, no. 3)   E215.1.M13

Introduction, by David Taggart Clark: p. ix–xx.
Bibliography: p. 95–96.

9788

Martin, Gaston. Commercial relations between Nantes and the American colonies during the War for Independence. Journal of economic and business history, v. 4, Aug. 1932: supplement, 812–829.

HC10.J6, v. 4

9789

Middleton, Arthur P. The struggle for the Cape Henry lighthouse, 1721–1791. American Neptune, v. 8, Jan. 1948: 26–36.   V1.A4, v. 8

9790

Mui, Hoh-cheung, *and* Lorna H. Mui. Smuggling and the British tea trade before 1784. American historical review, v. 74, Oct. 1968: 44–73.   E171.A57, v. 74

In two decades after the Seven Years' War a radical change took place in the extent and structure of the illicit trade that in turn significantly modified the legal or fair trade and affected the fortunes of those merchants and companies engaged in it.

9791

Page, Thomas W. The earlier commercial policy of the United States [1776–1815] Journal of political economy, v. 10, Mar. 1902: 161–192.   HB1.J7, v. 10

9792

Paine, Ralph D. The old merchant marine; a chronicle of American ships and sailors. New Haven, Yale University Press [c1919] vii, 214 p. (The Chronicles of America series, 36)   HE745.P3 1919a

Bibliography: p. 201–204.

Includes five brief chapters (p. 1–95) on the 18th century.

9793

Pares, Richard. Yankees and Creoles; the trade between North America and the West Indies before the American Revolution. London, New York, Longmans, Green [1956] vii, 168 p. maps (on lining papers)

HF3074.P3

Bibliographic footnotes.
Reprinted in Hamden, Conn., by Archon Books (1968).

Concentrating upon the mechanics of the trade, the author studies the characteristics of the entrepreneurs and investigates the relationships between prices, outbound and return cargoes, markets, ports, and ships. Pares concludes with an examination of the role of West Indian commerce in the North American economy. He believes that the trade contributed to the formation of capital in the 13 original colonies and promoted transatlantic commerce by facilitating the payment of debts in Europe. After the introduction of the sugar cane economy, merchants from Boston, Newport, New York, and Philadelphia dominated the colonial branch of the trade, which consisted primarily of exchanging provisions, lumber, and horses for molasses, rum, and sugar. See also the author's *War and Trade in the West Indies, 1739–1763* (Oxford, Clarendon Press, 1936. 631 p. F1621.P32).

9794

Setser, Vernon G. The commercial reciprocity policy of the United States, 1774–1829. Philadelphia, University of Pennsylvania Press, 1937. xi, 305 p.   HF1455.S4

Issued also as thesis (Ph.D.)—University of Pennsylvania.
Bibliography: p. 261–280.

In the section on the years before 1789, the author studies diplomatic and legislative policies that were intended to enlarge America's foreign trade at the expense of the established colonial powers. Since the United States had no colonies, it attempted to persuade other nations that commerce ought to be free from restraint, negotiated reciprocal trade agreements where possible, and retaliated in kind against nations that rejected its offers. American policy, the author contends, was one of attack.

Reprinted in New York by Da Capo Press (1969).

9795

Shepherd, James F., *and* Samuel H. Williamson. The coastal trade of the British North American colonies, 1768–1772. Journal of economic history, v. 32, Dec. 1972: 783–810.   HC10.J64, v. 32

9796

Shepherd, James F., *and* Gary M. Walton. Shipping, maritime trade, and the economic development of colonial North America. Cambridge [Eng.] University Press, 1972. ix, 255 p. illus.   HF3025.S717

Bibliography: p. 246–252.

The authors' theses (Ph.D.), *A Balance of Payments for the Thirteen Colonies, 1768–1772* and *A Quantitative Study of American Colonial Shipping*, were submitted to the University of Washington in 1966 (Micro AC–1, no. 67–7677 and 67–2202).

Focusing on overseas trade and improvements in transportation from 1675 to 1775, the authors examine sources for change in the productivity of shipping and distribution and intensively analyze the colonial balance of trade in the period 1768–72. Shepherd and Walton conclude that the growth of capital resources in America resulted basically from domestic savings rather than trade surpluses or capital inflow from Great Britain and that commodity exporting declined in its relative economic importance. They further conclude that because of British civil and military expenditures in the colonies and "invisible" earnings from shipping, the colonial balance of payments deficit was not as critical on the eve of the Revolution as historians have generally implied. An analysis of the methodology employed and tables of the data used are presented in extensive appendixes.

9797
Shepherd, James F., *and* Gary M. Walton. Trade distribution and economic growth in colonial America. Journal of economic history, v. 32, Mar. 1972: 128–145.
HC10.J64, v. 32

9798
Spears, John R. The story of the American merchant marine. New York, Macmillan Co., 1910. vii, 340 p. plates, ports. HE745.S6 1910

Chapters 1–8 (p. 1–149) provide a general treatment of shipping before the advent of steam navigation.

9799
Symonds, Robert W. The export trade of furniture to colonial America. Burlington magazine for connoisseurs, v. 77, Nov. 1940: 152–163. plates.
N1.B95, v. 77

See also the author's "English Furniture and Colonial American Furniture—a Contrast" in v. 78, June 1941, p. 183–187.

9800
Walton, Gary M. New evidence on colonial commerce. Journal of economic history, v. 28, Sept. 1968: 363–389. HC10.J64, v. 28

An analysis of shipping movements, 1768–72, shows that the shuttle route and the specialized trade route, dictated by ownership and regularity, played a much larger role in colonial commerce than the so-called "triangle trade."

9801
Walton, Gary M. Obstacles to technical diffusion in ocean shipping, 1765–1775. Explorations in entrepreneurial history, 2d ser., v. 8, winter 1970/71: 123–140.
HB615.E8, 2d s., v. 8

Explains that the hazards to New World shipping, such as piracy and privateering, impeded the development of larger, unarmed cargo vessels carrying smaller crews.

9802
Walton, Gary M. A quantitative study of American colonial shipping. 1966. ([193] p.)
Micro AC–1, no. 67–2202
Thesis (Ph.D.)—University of Washington.
Abstracted in *Dissertation Abstracts*, v. 27A, Mar. 1967, p. 2712.

Estimates the source of and changes in shipping productivity, 1680–1770. See the summary of the author's dissertation in the *Journal of Economic History*, v. 26, Dec. 1966, p. 595–598.

9803
Walton, Gary M. Sources of productivity change in American colonial shipping, 1675–1775. Economic history review, 2d ser., v. 20, Apr. 1967: 67–78.
HC10.E4, 2d s., v. 20

Finds that the cost of shipping was lowered by improvements in market organization and the decline of such hazardous risks as piracy and privateering. In his article, "A Measure of Productivity Change in American Colonial Shipping" (2d ser., v. 21, Aug. 1968, p. 268–282), Walton shows an overall increase of productivity of 1.35 percent per annum from 1675 to 1775.

9804
Wilkinson, Henry C. Notes on American privateering as recorded in Bermuda, 1760–1781. *In* Essex Institute, *Salem, Mass.* Historical collections, v. 82, Apr. 1946: 174–178. F72.E7E81, v. 82

9805
Willis, Jean L. The trade between North America and the Danish West Indies, 1756–1807, with special reference to St. Croix. 1963. ([384] p.)
Micro AC–1, no. 64–2799
Thesis (Ph.D.)—Columbia University.
Abstracted in *Dissertation Abstracts*, v. 24, Mar. 1964, p. 3724–3725.

2. New England

9806
Albion, Robert G., William A. Baker, *and* Benjamin W. Labaree. New England and the sea. Middletown, Conn., Published for the Marine Historical Association, Mystic Seaport, by Wesleyan University Press [1972] xiv, 299 p. illus., facsims, maps, ports. (The American maritime library, v. 5) HF3151.A65
"The heroic age, 1775–1815": p. 45–96.

9807
Bigelow, Bruce M. The commerce of Rhode Island with the West Indies, before the American Revolution (Parts I and II). 1930. ([452] p.)
Micro AC–1, no. 69–10,041
Thesis (Ph.D.)—Brown University.
Abstracted in *Dissertation Abstracts International*, v. 30A, Oct. 1969, p. 1490–1491.

9808
Bowden, William H. The commerce of Marblehead, 1665–1775. *In* Essex Institute, *Salem, Mass.* Historical collections, v. 68, Apr. 1932: 117–146. F72.E7E81, v. 68

Concludes that Marblehead's role as a trading center of consequence ended with the Revolution.

9809
Commerce of Rhode Island, 1726–1800. Boston, The Society, 1914–15. 2 v. facsims. (part fold.), port. (Massachusetts Historical Society, Boston. Collections, 7th ser., v. 9–10 [whole no. 69–70])
F61.M41, 7th s., v. 9–10

"The letters and papers printed in these volumes formed a part of the commercial correspondence of four generations of a Newport mercantile house. The earlier letters were of the Redwood family. The house of Ayrault of Newport entered about the middle of the eighteenth century as also that of Lopez. To the second half of the century, the firms of Lopez and Champlin contribute the larger part."—Prefatory note, v. 1.

9810
Crawford, Walter F. The commerce of Rhode Island with the southern continental colonies in the eighteenth century. *In* Rhode Island Historical Society. Collections, v. 14, Oct. 1921: 99–110, 124–129. F76.R47, v. 14

9811
Destler, Chester M. Barnabas Deane and the Barnabas Deane & Company. *In* Connecticut Historical Society, *Hartford.* Bulletin, v. 35, Jan. 1970: 7–19.
F91.C67, v. 35

Concentrates on Deane's career as a merchant engaged in wartime trade and his secret partnership with Jeremiah Wadsworth and Nathanael Greene from 1779 to 1785.

9812
Essex Institute, *Salem, Mass.* Early coastwise and foreign shipping of Salem; a record of the entrances and clearances of the port of Salem, 1750–1769. *In its* Historical collections, v. 62, July–Oct. 1926: 193–200, 305–320; v. 63, Jan.–Apr., Oct. 1927: 49–64, 145–160, 349–364; v. 67, July–Oct. 1931: 281–288, 409–424; v. 68, Jan., July–Oct. 1932: 49–64, 241–256, 337–352; v. 69, Jan.–Apr. 1933: 49–64, 155–198. facsims., plates, ports.
F72.E7E81, v. 62–63, 67–69

———— ———— Offprint. Salem, Mass., Essex Institute, 1934. x, 217 p. facsims., plates, ports.
HE767.S3E69

9813
Forbes, John D. The port of Boston, 1783–1815. 1937.

Thesis (Ph.D.)—Harvard University.

9814
Goebel, Dorothy B. The "New England trade" and the French West Indies, 1763–1774: a study in trade policies. William and Mary quarterly, 3d ser., v. 20, July 1963: 331–372. F221.W71, 3 d s., v. 20

Reviews changes in French policy after 1763 that were designed to stimulate trade between the islands and the British continental colonies and, if possible, to bring about alterations in British colonial regulations.

9815
Gray, Thomas, *and* Edward Payne. "State of the Trade," 1763. *In* Colonial Society of Massachusetts, *Boston.* Publications. v. 19. Transactions, 1916/17. Boston, 1918. p. 379–390. F61.C71, v. 19

Prepared by the Society for Encouraging Trade and Commerce for the immediate purpose of preventing renewal of the Molasses Act of 1733. Introduction and notes by Charles M. Andrews.

9816
Hooker, Roland M. The colonial trade of Connecticut. [New Haven] Published for the Tercentenary Commission by the Yale University Press, 1936. 42 p. (Connecticut. Tercentenary Commission. Committee on Historical Publications. [Tercentenary pamphlet series] 50) HF3161.C7H6

9817
Klingaman, David C. The coastwise trade of colonial Massachusetts. *In* Essex Institute, *Salem, Mass.* Historical collections, v. 108, July 1972: 217–234.
E72.E7E81, v. 108

Based on a comparative analysis of the Massachusetts naval lists for 1714–17 and 1761–65.

9818
Labaree, Benjamin W. Patriots and partisans; the merchants of Newburyport, 1764–1815. Cambridge, Harvard University Press, 1962. viii, 242 p. illus. (Harvard historical studies, v. 73) F74.N55L3

"Bibliographical note": p. [221]–231.
The author's thesis (Ph.D.), *Newburyport, Massachusetts, during the American Revolution, 1764–1790*, was submitted to Harvard University in 1957.

In the first section of the work, the author studies in detail merchants who profited from the carrying trade within the empire yet supported both independence and the federal Constitution. Dominating political as well as economic and social life, these men led the protest against British measures that began in 1765 and developed a militant American nationalism that overshadowed their economic ties with England. Losing their fortunes during the war or the depression that followed it, they gave way to a new generation of mercantile leaders who espoused a narrow sectionalism and opposed the War of 1812.

9819
Lawson, Murray G. The routes of Boston's trade, 1752–1765. *In* Colonial Society of Massachusetts, *Boston.* Publications. v. 38. Transactions, 1947/51. Boston, 1959. p. 81–120. F61.C71, v. 38

9820
Martin, Margaret E. Merchants and trade of the Connecticut River valley, 1750–1820. Northampton, Mass., Dept. of History of Smith College [1939] vii, 284 p. illus., map. (Smith College studies in history, v. 24, Oct. 1938/July 1939) HF3151.M36
AS36.S7, v. 24

Thesis (Ph.D.)—Columbia University, 1942.
Bibliography: p. 269–274.

Studies the commerce—mainly an exchange of agricultural surpluses for imported goods—of East Hartford, Hartford, Middletown, and Wethersfield, Conn., as well as Northampton and Springfield, Mass. The author also investigates the business methods of such merchant capitalists as Jeremiah Wadsworth and Silas Deane, who carried on trade primarily with the West Indies, and Jonathan Dwight and Levi Shepard, who depended upon the coasting trade to acquire manufactures. Although the nonimportation agreements of the 1760's and 1770's caused interruptions, Connecticut River trade prospered until the wartime blockade.

Most river merchants, unlike those in the seaports who had strong ties with England, supported the rebel cause. Although postwar depression and fiscal chaos ruined some, nearly all favored the Constitution.

9821

Morison, Samuel E. The commerce of Boston on the eve of the Revolution. *In* American Antiquarian Society, *Worcester, Mass.* Proceedings, new ser., v. 32, Apr. 1922: 24–51. E172.A35, n.s., v. 32

A statistical description of Boston maritime trade, 1768–73, based on lists of entries and clearances in local newspapers and statistics compiled by the Treasury Board and the Boston customs commissioners.

9822

Morison, Samuel E. The maritime history of Massachusetts, 1783–1860. Boston, Houghton, Mifflin Co., 1941. xi, 420 p. facsim., maps, plates, port.
HF3161.M4M6 1941

Bibliography: p. 399–[410]
First published in 1921.

Chapters 2–4 (p. 8–51) cover the colonial background, the Revolution, and the opening of the China trade.

9823

Phillips, James D. The routine trade of Salem under the Confederation Congress, May 1783–October 1789. American Neptune, v. 1, Oct. 1941: 345–351.
V1.A4, v. 1

9824

Phillips, James D. Salem ocean-borne commerce, from the close of the Revolution to the establishment of the Constitution, 1783–1789. *In* Essex Institute, *Salem, Mass.* Historical collections, v. 75, Apr.–Oct. 1939: 135–158, 249–274, 358–381; v. 76, Jan. 1940: 68–88.
F72.E7E81, v. 75–76

Records culled from Salem and other Massachusetts newspapers.

9825

Saltonstall, William G. Ports of Piscataqua; soundings in the maritime history of the Portsmouth, N.H., customs district from the days of Queen Elizabeth and the planting of Strawberry Banke to the times of Abraham Lincoln and the waning of the American clipper. Cambridge, Mass., Harvard Univeristy Press, 1941. xii, 244 p. facsim., maps, plates, ports. F42.P4S3

Bibliography: p. [227]–235.
Reprinted in New York by Russell & Russell (1968).

Focuses upon the 18th century, especially the Revolutionary period.

9826

Tapley, Harriet S. Capt. Samuel Page and his vessels; an account of the shipping industry at New Mills in the eighteenth and early nineteenth centuries. *In* Danvers Historical Society, *Danvers, Mass.* Historical collections. v. 11, 13–18. Danvers, 1923, 1925–30. p. 92–

111; p. 56–63; p. 25–29; p. 37–45; p. 37–50; p. 20–32; p. 97–103. F74.D2D42, v. 11, 13–18

Gives detailed accounts from the records of each vessel.

9827

Trindell, Roger T. The ports of Salem and Greenwich in the eighteenth century. New Jersey history, v. 86, winter 1968: 199–214. map. F131.N58, v. 86

Includes import-export lists from the 1760's for the two New Jersey ports located on the Delaware River south of Philadelphia.

9828

Trumbull, James Hammond. A business firm in the Revolution: Barnabas Deane & Co. Magazine of American history, with notes and queries, v. 12, July 1884: 17–28.
E171.M18, v. 12

Includes original correspondence.

9829

Van Dusen, Albert E. Colonial Connecticut's trade with the West Indies. New England social studies bulletin, v. 13, Mar. 1956: 11–19, 30. H1.N4, v. 13

9830

Van Dusen, Albert E. The trade of Revolutionary Connecticut. 1948. ([433] p.) Micro AC–1, no. 1640

Thesis (Ph.D.)—University of Pennsylvania.
Abstracted in *Microfilm Abstracts*, v. 10, no. 2, 1950, p. 99–100.

9831

Weaver, Glenn. The New England country store of the eighteenth century. New-England galaxy, v. 5, fall 1963: 14–22. illus. F1.N39, v. 5

3. MIDDLE ATLANTIC REGION

9832

Albion, Robert G. New York port in the new Republic, 1783–1793. *In* New York State Historical Association. New York history, v. 21, Oct. 1940: 388–403.
F116.N865, v. 21

9833

Davisson, William I., *and* Lawrence J. Bradley. New York maritime trade: ship voyage patterns, 1715–1765. *In* New York Historical Society. Quarterly, v. 55, Oct. 1971: 309–317. map, port. F116.N638, v. 55

9834

Gillingham, Harrold E. The Philadelphia Windsor chair and its journeyings. Pennsylvania magazine of history and biography, v. 55, Oct. 1931: 301–332. facsims.
F146.P65, v. 55

Includes tables indicating shipments of Windsor and other chairs and furniture from Philadelphia, 1766–97, by vessel, destination, and merchandise.

9835

Hanna, Mary A.   Trade of the Delaware district before the Revolution. Northampton, Mass., Dept. of History of Smith College [1917] [239]–342 p. (Smith College studies in history, v. 2, no. 4)   HF3025.H3

Issued also as thesis (Ph.D.)—Bryn Mawr College.
Bibliography: p. [334]–338.

9836

Harrington, Virginia D.   The New York merchant on the eve of the Revolution. New York, Columbia University Press, 1935. 389 p. (Studies in history, economics and public law, no. 404)   H31.C7, no. 404
HF3163.N7H3 1935a

Issued also as thesis (Ph.D.)—Columbia University.
Bibliography: p. 369–381.
Reprinted in Gloucester, Mass., by P. Smith (1964).

An institutional study of the mercantile profession between 1750 and 1775 that stresses its economic and procedural aspects. The author treats such subjects as the merchant in provincial life, the organization and conduct of business, overseas and colonial trade, and relations with government. While merchants united with radicals in an economic protest against such laws as the Sugar Act that harmed trade, their concern for law and order prevented them from supporting such violent measures as the Stamp Act riots. See also the author's essay, "The Place of the Merchant in New York Colonial Life," in the New York State Historical Association's *New York History*, v. 13, Oct. 1932, p. 366–380.

9837

Hunter, William C.   The commercial policy of New Jersey under the Confederation, 1783–1789. [Princeton? N.J., 1922] 70 p.   HF3161.N5H8 1922

Thesis (Ph.D.)—Princeton University, 1922.
Bibliography: p. 66–70.

9838

Jensen, Arthur L.   The maritime commerce of colonial Philadelphia. Madison, State Historical Society of Wisconsin for the Dept. of History, University of Wisconsin, 1963. viii, 312 p.   F158.4.J4

"Annotated bibliography": p. [298]–307.
The author's thesis (Ph.D.), with the same title, was submitted to the University of Wisconsin in 1954.

After reviewing the nature and growth of Philadelphia's trade with southern Europe, the "wine islands," Great Britain, the West Indies, and American ports, the author assesses the impact of British imperial policy after 1763 on this commerce and the role played by the city's merchants in the Revolutionary movement. Jensen finds that the reforms of 1766 satisfied the merchants' major grievances, which were almost entirely commercial in nature. Thereafter they became unwilling partners of radical leaders who chose commercial coercion to achieve political ends and used an aroused public to force the merchants to support nonimportation measures that injured them financially and were, they felt, unwise tactically.

9839

King, Charles.   History of the New York Chamber of Commerce, with notices of some of its most distinguished members. *In* New York Historical Society. Collections. 2d ser., v. 49. New York, 1849. p. [381]–446.   F116.N62, 2d s., v. 49

Established by New York merchants in 1768.

9840

Martin, Alfred S.   The port of Philadelphia, 1763–1776: a biography. 1941.

Thesis (Ph.D.)—State University of Iowa.

9841

Muller, H. N.   The commercial history of the Lake Champlain-Richelieu River route, 1760–1815. 1969.

Thesis (Ph.D.)—University of Rochester.

9842

New York (*State*). Chamber of Commerce of the State of New York.   Colonial records of the New York Chamber of Commerce, 1768–1784. With historical and biographical sketches, by John Austin Stevens, Jr. New York, J. F. Trow, 1867. 404, 172 p. fold. map, plates, ports.   HF296.N49

Reprinted in New York by B. Franklin (1971).

9843

Pennsylvania (*Colony*).   Indian traders, Mediterranean passes, letters of marque and ships' registers, 1743–1776. *In* Pennsylvania archives. 2d ser., v. 2. Harrisburg, 1876. p. [617]–671.   F146.P41, 2d s., v. 2

9844

Pennsylvania Historical Survey.   Maritime records, port of Philadelphia. Transcription of historical records containing data on the port of Philadelphia and its shipping industry. Harrisburg [1942?] 190 v.   HE554.P5P45

Partial contents: section 1. Port warden's minutes, 1766–1773, 1784–1880. 11 v.—section 3. Arrivals and clearances of vessels, Philadelphia, 1783–1880. 5 v.

9845

Scott, Kenneth.   The Sandy Hook lighthouse. American Neptune, v. 25, Apr. 1965: 123–127. plates.   V1.A4, v. 25

On its financing and construction, 1762–76.

9846

Tolles, Frederick B.   Benjamin Franklin's business mentors: the Philadelphia Quaker merchants. William and Mary quarterly, 3d ser., v. 4, Jan. 1947: 60–69.   F221.W71, 3d s., v. 4

Investigates the Quaker business ethic.

9847

Tolles, Frederick B.   Meeting house and counting house; the Quaker merchants of colonial Philadelphia, 1682–1763. Chapel Hill, Published for the Institute of Early

American History and Culture at Williamsburg, Va., by the University of North Carolina Press, 1948. xiv, 292 p. illus., ports.   BX7649.P5T64

"Bibliographical essay": p. [258]–276.

The author's thesis (Ph.D.), *The Quaker Merchants of Colonial Philadelphia: a Study in Social and Cultural History*, was submitted to Harvard University in 1947.

Adopting a topical approach, the author explores the economic, social, and intellectual activities of Quakers who risked defilement of their ideals by participating in business and community affairs. The "holy experiment" became so secularized and the Quaker merchants so fond of wealth and luxury that, in 1756–58, a thoroughgoing spiritual reformation was mounted within the jurisdiction of the Philadelphia Yearly Meeting, one that lasted through 1777. In that year, local meetings appointed visitation committees to encourage withdrawal as far as possible from worldly influences and a return to plain speech, behavior, and dress.

9848

Walter, Gaines W.   The commerce of colonial Philadelphia. 1933.

Thesis (Ph.D.)—Yale University.

9849

Walzer, John F.   Colonial Philadelphia and its backcountry. *In* Winterthur portfolio. v. 7. Winterthur, Del., 1972. p. 161–173. map.   N9.W52, v. 7

On the trade networks established by Philadelphia merchants in outlying counties in New Jersey, Pennsylvania, Delaware, and the Maryland eastern shore.

9850

White, Philip L., *ed.*   The Beekman mercantile papers, 1746–1799. New York, New-York Historical Society, 1956. 3 v. (vii, 1485 p.) map (on lining papers)   HF3025.W5

Contents: v. 1. Gerard G. Beekman letter book, 1746–1770.—v. 2. James Beekman correspondence, 1750–1799.—v. 3. James Beekman correspondence (cont'd). Gerard W. Beekman's letters to his brother William, 1777–1782. Appendix: Sample invoices of shipments to James Beekman.

4. THE SOUTH

9851

Brown, Vaughan W.   Shipping in the port of Annapolis, 1748–1775. [Annapolis, U.S. Naval Institute, 1965] 36, [36] p. illus., maps, ports. (Sea power monograph no. 1)   HE554.A88B7

"A list of every vessel that cleared customs at Annapolis between 25 June, 1748, and 19 July, 1775, compiled from the Port of Entry records": [35] p. (2d group).

9852

Clark, Malcolm C.   The coastwise and Caribbean trade of the Chesapeake Bay, 1696–1776. 1970. ([326] p.)   Micro AC–1, no. 70–21,297

Thesis (Ph.D.)—Georgetown University.

Abstracted in *Dissertation Abstracts International*, v. 31A, Nov. 1970, p. 2297–2298.

9853

Coakley, Robert Walter.   Virginia commerce during the American Revolution. 1949. 396 l.

Thesis (Ph.D.)—University of Virginia.

9854

Coulter, Calvin B.   The import trade of colonial Virginia. William and Mary quarterly, 3d ser., v. 2, July 1945: 296–314.   F221.W71, 3d s., v. 2

Surveys the more important commodities imported from Europe, the West Indies, and Africa by Virginia merchants.

9855

Coulter, Calvin B.   The Virginia merchant. 1944. ([290] p.)   Micro AC–1, no. 2930

Thesis (Ph.D.)—Princeton University.

Abstracted in *Dissertation Abstracts*, v. 12, no. 3, 1952, p. 286–287.

Traces the Scots trader's contribution to the economic base of 18th-century Virginia.

9856

Crittenden, Charles Christopher.   The commerce of North Carolina, 1763–1789. New Haven, Yale University Press, 1936. x, 196 p. fold. map. (Yale historical publications. Miscellany, 29)   HF3161.N8C7

Bibliography: p. [171]–181.

The author's thesis (Ph.D.), *Transportation and Commerce in North Carolina, 1763–1789*, was submitted to Yale University in 1930.

Summarizes the geographic, political, economic, and fiscal conditions under which trade was carried on and assesses the effects of the Revolution upon North Carolina's commerce. Crittenden reports that the state prospered under the Navigation Acts and concludes that the scattered complaints against British trade regulations did not cause North Carolinians to revolt. Nonimportation agreements were not generally observed until 1774, and most merchants opposed the break with England. While the war threw the state's commerce into disorder, some merchants, including a few Loyalists, profited greatly. Peace brought both prosperity and inflation. To combat emissions of paper money and to enhance their trading position in London, the West Indies, and American ports, North Carolina's business community supported the federal Constitution.

9857

Crittenden, Charles Christopher.   The seacoast in North Carolina history, 1763–1789. North Carolina historical review, v. 7, Oct. 1930: 433–442.   F251.N892, v. 7

9858

Crittenden, Charles Christopher.   Ships and shipping in North Carolina, 1763–1789. North Carolina historical review, v. 8, Jan. 1931: 1–13.   F251.N892, v. 8

9859

Custom house records of the Annapolis district, Maryland, relating to shipping from the ports of Essex County, Mass., 1756–1775. *In* Essex Institute, *Salem, Mass.* Historical collections, v. 45, July 1909: 256–282.

F72.E7E81, v. 45

9860

Dorsey, Rhoda M.   The pattern of Baltimore commerce during the Confederation period. Maryland historical magazine, v. 62, June 1967: 119–134.

F176.M18, v. 62

9861

Gayle, Charles J.   The nature and volume of exports from Charleston, 1724–1774. *In* South Carolina Historical Association. Proceedings. 1937. Columbia, S.C. p. 25–33.

F266.S58, 1937

Includes tables on the annual export of rice, tar, pitch, turpentine, lumber, shingles, staves, and lath.

9862

Giddens, Paul H.   Trade and industry in colonial Maryland, 1753–1769. Journal of economic and business history, v. 4, May 1932: 512–538.   HC10.J6, v. 4

9863

Goldenberg, Joseph A.   Names and numbers: statistical notes on some port records of colonial North Carolina. American Neptune, v. 29, July 1969: 155–166.

V1.A4, v. 29

Treats records for Port Roanoke, 1771–76, and Port Brunswick, 1767–68 and 1774–75.

9864

Gray, Lewis C.   The market surplus problems of colonial tobacco. William and Mary College quarterly, 3d ser., v. 7, Oct. 1927: 231–245; v. 8, Jan. 1928: 1–16.

F221.W71, 2d s., v. 7–8

Also published in *Agricultural History*, v. 2, Jan. 1928, p. 1–34.

9865

Johnson, Johonnot, and Company, *Baltimore.*   The conduct of business in Baltimore, 1783–1785, as seen in the letterbook of Johnson, Johonnot, and Co. Maryland historical magazine, v. 55, Sept. 1960: 230–242.

F176.M18, v. 55

Introduction and notes by Rhoda M. Dorsey.

9866

Klingaman, David C.   The development of the coastwise trade of Virginia in the late colonial period. Virginia magazine of history and biography, v. 77, Jan. 1969: 26–45.   F221.V91, v. 77

9867

Klingaman, David C.   The development of Virginia's coatwise trade and grain trade in the late colonial period. 1967. ([164] p.) Micro AC-1, no. 67–17, 607

Thesis (Ph.D.)—University of Virginia.
Abstracted in *Dissertation Abstracts*, v. 28A, Jan. 1968, p. 2424.

9868

MacMaster, Richard K.   Georgetown and the tobacco trade, 1751–1783. *In* Columbia Historical Society, *Washington, D.C.* Records. 1966/68. Washington [1969] p. 1–33. illus., port.   F191.C72, 1966/68

9869

Malone, Miles S.   Falmouth and the Shenandoah; trade before the Revolution. American historical review, v. 40, July 1935: 693–703. map.   E171.A57, v. 40

The William Allason papers show that the Rappahannock port of Falmouth and the counties of the lower Shenandoah Valley were bound together by commercial ties and indicate the nature of the trade.

9870

Middleton, Arthur P.   The Chesapeake convoy system, 1662–1763. William and Mary quarterly, 3d ser., v. 3, Apr. 1946: 182–207.   F221.W71, 3d s., v. 3

9871

Middleton, Arthur P.   Tobacco Coast; a maritime history of Chesapeake Bay in the colonial era. Edited for the museum by George Carrington Mason. Newport News, Va., Mariners' Museum, 1953. xii, 482 p. illus., charts, maps, port.   F187.C5M5

Bibliography: p. [429]–452.
The author's thesis (Ph.D.) *Along the Tobacco Coast: The Maritime Life of the Chesapeake Colonies, 1688–1763* was submitted to Harvard University in 1947.

A detailed study of the influence of the bay and its related waterways on the development and character of Maryland and Virginia, with particular emphasis on commerce, shipping and defense.

9872

Morris, Thomas, *and* William Brailsford.   Letters of Morris & Brailsford to Thomas Jefferson [1787–88] Edited by Richard Walsh. South Carolina historical magazine, v. 58, July 1957: 129–144.   F266.S55, v. 58

Concerns the efforts of a Charleston firm to promote trade with France through the intercession of Thomas Jefferson, Minister Plenipotentiary to France.

9873

Norton (John) and Sons.   John Norton & Sons, merchants of London and Virginia, being the papers from their counting house for the years 1750 to 1795. Edited by Frances Norton Mason. Richmond, Dietz Press, 1937. 573 p. facsims, plates.   F226.N67

"Biographical appendix": p. 509–520.
Reprinted, with a new introduction by Samuel M. Rosenblatt, in New York by A. M. Kelley (1968).
Compare with the "Norton Correspondence [1767–92] in *Tyler's Quarterly Historical and Genealogical Magazine*, v. 3, Apr. 1922, p. 287–298; v. 4, July 1922, p. 64–

70; and v. 7, Oct. 1925, p. 95–104. For further information on the firm see the two articles by Samuel M. Rosenblatt, "The Significance of Credit in the Tobacco Consignment Trade: a Study of John Norton & Sons, 1768–1775," and Jacob M. Price, "Who Was John Norton? A Note on the Historical Character of Some Eighteenth-Century London Virginia Firms," inthe *William and Mary Quarterly*, 3d ser., v. 19, July 1962, p. 383–399 and 400–407.

9874
Price, Jacob M.   The beginnings of tobacco manufacture in Virginia. Virginia magazine of history and biography, v. 64, Jan. 1956: 3–29.   F221.V91, v. 64

9875
Price, Jacob M.   The economic growth of the Chesapeake and the European market, 1697–1775. Journal of economic history, v. 24, Dec. 1964: 496–511.
                              HC10.J64, v. 24

9876
Price, Jacob M.   The rise of Glasgow in the Chesapeake tobacco trade, 1707–1775. William and Mary quarterly, 3d ser., v. 11, Apr. 1954: 179–199.
                              F221.W71, 3d s., v. 11

The progressivism and efficiency of the Glasgow store system in Maryland and Virginia hindered the development of an indigenous mercantile element just as it retarded the diversification of crops.

9877
Rich, Myra L.   The experimental years: Virginia, 1781–1789. 1966. ([320] p.)   Micro AC–1, no. 66–4924
Thesis (Ph.D.)—Yale University.
Abstracted in *Dissertation Abstracts*, v. 27A, July 1966, p. 155.

Concentrating upon economic thought and commercial policy, the author studies state attempts to regulate trade in the face of disrupted commerce, backward economic institutions, and mounting debt. The success or failure of these local experiments colored Virginians' attitudes toward a stronger central government.

9878
Robert, Joseph C.   The story of tobacco in America. Chapel Hill, University of North Carolina Press [1967] xviii, 296 p. illus.   SB273.R58 1967
"Bibliographical notes": p. 283–296.
First published in New York by A. A. Knopf (1949).
The period to 1789 is treated on pages 3–53.

9879
Rogers, George C.   Aedanus Burke, Nathanael Greene, Anthony Wayne, and the British merchants of Charleston. South Carolina historical magazine, v. 67, Apr. 1966: 75–83. port.   F266.S55, v. 67
Establishes a community of interest among Burke, Greene, and Wayne, and affirms Burke's authorship in 1785 of the anonymous pamphlet entitled, *A Few Salutary Hints, Pointing out the Policy and Consequences of Admitting Brit-*

ish Subjects to Engross our Trade and Become our Citizens. Addressed to Those who Either Risqued or Lost Their all in Bringing About the Revolution.

9880
Rosenblatt, Samuel M.   The house of John Norton and Sons: a study of the consignment method of marketing tobacco from Virginia to England. 1960. ([282] p.)
                              Micro AC–1, no. 60–4254
Thesis (Ph.D.)—Rutgers University.
Abstracted in *Dissertation Abstracts*, v. 21, Mar. 1961, p. 2525–2526.

9881
Rosenblatt, Samuel M.   Merchant-planter relations in the tobacco consignment trade: John Norton and Robert Carter Nicholas. Virginia magazine of history and biography, v. 72, Oct. 1964: 454–470.
                              F221.V91, v. 72

9882
Sargent, Charles W.   Virginia and the West Indies trade, 1740–1765. 1964. ([157] p.)
                              Micro AC–1, no. 65–1123
Thesis (Ph.D.)—University of New Mexico.
Abstracted in *Dissertation Abstracts*, v. 26, Apr. 1966, p. 6007.

9883
Soltow, James H.   Scottish traders in Virginia, 1750–1775. Economic history review, 2d ser., v. 12, Aug. 1959: 83–99.   HC10.E4, 2d s., v. 12

9884
Thomson, Robert P.   The merchant in Virginia, 1700–1775. 1955. ([416] p.)   Micro AC–1, no. 16,217
Thesis (Ph.D.)—University of Wisconsin.
Abstracted in *Dissertation Abstracts*, v. 16, no. 8, 1956, p. 1367–1368.

9885
Thomson, Robert P.   The tobacco export of the Upper James River Naval District, 1773–1775. William and Mary quarterly, 3d ser., v. 18, July 1961: 393–407.
                              F221.W71, 3d s., v. 18

An examination of the district's manifest book, which is summarized in six tables, reveals that the tobacco system had reached a point where a handful of British merchants controlled the bulk of the export trade.

9886
Ver Steeg, Clarence L.   Stacey Hepburn and Company: enterprisers in the American Revolution. South Carolina historical magazine, v. 55, Jan. 1954: 1–5.
                              F266.S55, v. 55

On a firm organized in 1779 by Stacey Hepburn, John Holker, and Robert Morris to trade in South Carolina commodities.

9887

Wychoff, Vertrees J. Tobacco regulation in colonial Maryland. Baltimore, Johns Hopkins Press, 1936. 228 p. (Johns Hopkins University studies in historical and political science. Extra volumes. New ser., no. 22)
H31.J62, n.s., no. 22
HD9137.M3W9

Bibliography: p. 217–226.

5. POSTWAR COMMERCIAL EXPANSION

9888

Bhagat, G. America's first contacts with India, 1784–1785. American Neptune, v. 31, Jan. 1971: 38–48.
V1.A4, v. 31

9889

Bhagat, G. Americans in India, 1784–1860. New York, New York University Press, 1970. xxvii, 195 p. illus.
E183.8.I4B5

Bibliography: p. 143–187.
"Early probings, 1784–1790": p. 3–20.

9890

Bjork, Gordon C. The weaning of the American economy: independence, market changes, and economic development. Journal of economic history, v. 24, Dec. 1964: 541–566.
HC10.J64, v. 24

Focusing upon improvements in foreign commerce during the Confederation period, the author concludes that while there was only a small increase in the value of American exports in the postwar period, the terms of trade had become much more favorable.

9891

Bruchey, Stuart W. Success and failure factors: American merchants in foreign trade in the eighteenth and early nineteenth centuries. Business history review, v. 32, autumn 1958: 272–292.
HF5001.B8262, v. 32

9892

Brunhouse, Robert L. Lascars in Pennsylvania; a sidelight on the China trade [1785–86] Pennsylvania history, v. 7, Jan. 1940: 20–30.
F146.P597, v. 7

Pennsylvania aid to oriental sailors stranded when John O'Donnell's *Pallas* failed to return to China.

9893

Buron, Edmond J. P. Statistics on Franco-American trade, 1778–1806. Journal of economic and business history, v. 4, May 1932: 571–580.
HC10.J6, v. 4

9894

Clark, William B. Postscripts to the voyage of the merchant ship *United States* [1784] Pennsylvania magazine of history and biography, v. 76, July 1952: 294–310.
F146.P65, v. 76

9895

Coughlin, Magdalen. The entrance of the Massachusetts merchant into the Pacific [in the 1780's] *In* Historical Society of Southern California. Quarterly, v. 48, Dec. 1966: 327–352.
F867.H67, v. 48

9896

Crosby, Alfred W. The beginnings of trade between the United States and Russia. American Neptune, v. 21, July 1961: 207–215.
V1.A4, v. 21

Concerned with the development of direct trade with Russia beginning with the arrival in St. Petersburg of the first vessel from Boston, under Capt. Daniel McNeil, in 1783.

9897

Cross, Francis E. Nootka Sound: winter, 1788–89. American Neptune, v. 15, July 1955: 205–213.
V1.A4, v. 15

Sailing from Boston, the first America flag vessels to enter the Pacific Ocean, the *Columbia* and the *Washington*, wintered at Friendly Cove, Nootka Sound.

9898

Dorsey, Rhoda M. The resumption of Anglo-American trade in New England, 1783–1794. 1956. ([422] p.)
Micro AC–1, no. 17,849

Thesis (Ph.D.)—University of Minnesota.
Abstracted in *Dissertation Abstracts*, v. 16, no. 10, 1956, p. 1891.

9899

Duvall, Rezin F. Philadelphia's maritime commerce with the British Empire, 1783–1789. 1960. ([516] p.)
Micro AC–1, no. 60–3643

Thesis (Ph.D.)—University of Pennsylvania.
Abstracted in *Dissertation Abstracts*, v. 21, Oct. 1960, p. 861–862.

9900

Furber, Holden. The beginnings of American trade with India, 1784–1812. New England quarterly, v. 11, June 1938: 235–265.
F1.N62, v. 11

9901

Godechot, Jacques L. Les relations économiques entre la France et les États-Unis de 1778 à 1789. *In* French historical studies, v. 1, no. 1; 1958. Raleigh, N.C. p. 26–39.
DC1.F69, v. 1

9902

Kohlmeier, Albert L. The commerce between the United States and the Netherlands, 1783–1789. *In* Indiana. University. Studies in American history, inscribed to James Albert Woodburn . . . by his former students. Bloomington, 1926. (Indiana University studies, v. 12, no. 66/68) p. [1]–47.
E173.I56

The author's thesis (Ph.D.), *The Commercial Relations Between the United States and the Netherlands and Dutch West Indies, 1783–1789*, was submitted to Harvard University in 1916.

Contrary to the older view that British merchants regained almost complete control of American trade after the Revolution, Kohlmeier demonstrates that the amount of commerce between the United States and the United Netherlands was much larger than supposed and that it contributed significantly to the economic reconstruction of the United States during the Critical period.

9903
Lowes, Marvin M.   Les premières relations commerciales entre Bordeaux et les États-Unis d'Amérique (1775–1789). Revue historique de Bordeaux, v. 20, Sept./Oct. 1927: 214–226; v. 21, Jan./Feb.–May/June 1928: 31–39, 75–90, 128–140.   DC801.B71R4, v. 20–21

9904
McCoy, Samuel D.   The port of New York (1783–1789); lost island of sailing ships. *In* New York State Historical Association. New York history, v. 17, Oct. 1936: 379–390. facsim., plates.   F116.N865, v. 17

9905
Phillips, James D.   East India voyages of Salem vessels before 1800. *In* Essex Institute, *Salem, Mass.* Historical collections, v. 79, Apr.–Oct. 1943: 117–132, 222–245, 331–365.   F72.E7E81, v. 79

———— ———— Offprint. [Salem? 1943] 75 p.
HE767.S3P5

Gives information on the sailing of 27 vessels between 1784 and 1789.

9906
Phillips, James D.   Salem and the Indies; the story of the great commercial era of the city. Boston, Houghton Mifflin Co., 1947. xx, 468 p. illus., plan (on lining paper), ports.   HF3163.S33P54

Bibliography: p. 430–438.

Chapters 1–14 (p. 1–221) are concerned primarily with the period before 1800.

9907
Rasch, Aage.   American trade in the Baltic, 1783–1807. Scandinavian economic history review, v. 13, no. 1, 1965: 31–64.   HC341.A25, v. 13

9908
Saul, Norman E.   The beginnings of American-Russian trade, 1763–1766. William and Mary quarterly, 3d ser., v. 26, Oct. 1969: 596–600.   F221.W71, 3d s., v. 26

9909
Sée, Henri E., *ed.*   Commerce between France and the United States, 1783–1784. American historical review, v. 31, Apr. 1926: 732–752.   E171.A57, v. 31

Reproduces, in French, documents from the papers of the Chamber of Commerce of Nantes reflecting plans by the French government and merchants to exploit the new commercial markets in the United States.

9910
Snyder, James W.   American trade in eastern seas; a brief survey of its early years, 1783–1815. Americana, v. 32, Oct. 1938: 621–638.   E171.A53, v. 32

9911
Snyder, James W.   The early American China trade: a maritime history of its establishment, 1783–1815. 1939.

Thesis (Ph.D.)—New York University.

9912
Snyder, James W.   Spices, silks, and teas—cargoes of the old China trade. Americana, v. 36, Jan. 1942: 7–26. illus., facsim., map.   E171.A53, v. 36

9913
Stover, John F.   French-American trade during the Confederation, 1781–1789. North Carolina historical review, v. 35, Oct. 1958: 399–414.   F251.N892, v. 35

9914
United States (*Ship*).   Log and journal of the ship *United States* on a voyage to China in 1784. Pennsylvania magazine of history and biography, v. 55, July 1931: 225–258. plates.   F146.P65, v. 55

Introduction and notes by Samuel W. Woodhouse.

9915
Ver Steeg, Clarence L.   Financing and outfitting the first United States ship to China. Pacific historical review, v. 22, Feb. 1953: 1–12.   F851.P18, v. 22

On the *Empress of China*, sent to Canton in 1784 by Robert Morris, Daniel Parker, John Holker, and William Duer.

9916
Winter, Pieter Jan van.   Het aandeel van den Amsterdamschen handel aan den opbouw van het Amerikaansche gemeenebest. 's-Gravenhage, M. Nijhoff, 1927. xxxvi, 240 p.   HJ247.W55 1927

Proefschrift—Leyden.
"Bibliographie": p. [xxvii]–xxxvi

Concerns financial and commercial relations between the United States and the Netherlands during the Confederation period.

9917
Woodhouse, Samuel W.   The voyage of the *Empress of China*. Pennsylvania magazine of history and biography, v. 63, Jan. 1939: 24–36. plates.
F146.P65, v. 63

Includes excerpts from a Chinese paper receipt book kept by F. Molineaux, Capt. John Green's clerk.

9918
Woolfolk, George R.   Rival urban communications schemes for the possession of the northwest trade, 1783–1800. Mid-America, v. 38, Oct. 1956: 214–232.
BX1415.13M5, v. 38

9919
Zook, George F.   Proposals for new commercial treaty between France and the United States, 1778–1793. South Atlantic quarterly, v. 8, July 1909: 267–283.
AP2.S75, v. 8

6. Domestic Transport and Travel

9920

Barton, Thomas. The beginnings of artificial roads in Pennsylvania. *In* Lancaster County (Pa.) Historical Society. Papers, v. 23, June 1919: 99–107.

F157.L2L5, v. 23

Reprint from the *Pennsylvania Gazette* of February 20, 1772, of an article by the Rev. Thomas Barton, signed "Clericus," entitled "Observations on the Improvement of Public Roads, Occasioned by a Petition to Assembly for a Turnpike-Road from Philadelphia to Wrights-Ferry on Susquehanna." A letter from the author to Thomas Penn, dated April 28, 1773, is appended.

9921

Crittenden, Charles Christopher. Inland navigation in North Carolina, 1763–1789. North Carolina historical review, v. 8, Apr. 1931: 145–154. F251.N892, v. 8

9922

Crittenden, Charles Christopher. Means of communication in North Carolina, 1763–1789. North Carolina historical review, v. 8, Oct. 1931: 373–383.

F251.N892, v. 8

9923

Crittenden, Charles Christopher. Overland travel and transportation in North Carolina, 1763–1789. North Carolina historical review, v. 8, July 1931: 239–257.

F251.N892, v. 8

9924

Dunbar, Seymour. A history of travel in America, showing the development of travel and transportation from the crude methods of the canoe and the dog-sled to the highly organized railway systems of the present, together with a narrative of the human experiences and changing social conditions that accompanied this economic conquest of the continent. Indianapolis, Bobbs-Merrill Co. [c1915] 4 v. (li, 1529 p.) illus., facsims., maps, col. plates. HE203.D77

Bibliography: v. 4, p. [1445]–1481.

Reprinted in New York by Greenwood Press (1968).

The first volume focuses on the period before 1800.

9925

Durrenberger, Joseph A. Turnpikes; a study of the toll road movement in the Middle Atlantic states and Maryland. Cos Cob, Conn., J. E. Edwards, 1968. 188 p.

HE356.A12D8 1968

Reprint of the author's thesis (Ph.D.)—Columbia University, 1931.

Bibliography: p. 166–181.

In the first two chapters (p. 9–44), the author discusses early modes of inland transportation and the demands for better roads that followed the Revolution.

9926

Lane, Wheaton J. From Indian trail to iron horse; travel and transportation in New Jersey, 1620–1860. Intro-

duction by Thomas J. Wertenbaker. Princeton, Princeton University Press, 1939. xviii, 437 p. facsims., maps (part fold.), plates. [The Princeton history of New Jersey] HE213.N5L3

"This volume is the outgrowth of a doctoral thesis written . . . several years ago."—p. xiii.

Bibliography: p. [421]–425.

In chapters 1–6 (p. 13–139) the author discusses Indian trails and colonial highways; water transportation by sloop, flatboat, and raft; land transportation by wagon and horse; taverns, inns, and roadside services; and economic reconstruction following the Revolution.

9927

Lane, Wheaton J. Water transportation in colonial New Jersey. *In* New Jersey Historical Society. Proceedings, v. 53, Apr. 1953: 77–89. F131.N58, v. 53

9928

[Mitchell, Isabel S.] Roads and road-making in colonial Connecticut. [New Haven] Published for the Tercentenary Commission by the Yale University Press, 1933. 32 p. fold. map. TE24.C8M5

9929

O'Brien, Michael J. Some pre-Revolutionary ferrymen of Staten Island. Daniel O'Brien and Darby Doyle were the first to establish regular ferry systems. *In* American Irish Historical Society. Journal. v. 15, July 1916: 385–396. E184.I6A5, v. 15

9930

Powell, Richard P. Transportation and travel in colonial New Jersey. *In* New Jersey Historical Society. Proceedings, 4th ser., v. 16, July 1931: 284–310.

F131.N58, 4th s., v. 16

9931

Roach, George W. Colonial highways in the upper Hudson Valley. *In* New York State Historical Association. New York history, v. 40, Apr. 1959: 93–116.

F116.N865, v. 40

9932

Shumway, George, *and* Howard C. Frey. Conestoga wagon, 1750–1850; freight carrier for 100 years of America's westward expansion. 3d ed. [York, Pa.] G. Shumway [1968] xii, 281 p. illus., facsims., maps (part fold.) TS2010.S5 1968

Includes bibliographies.

First edition published in 1964.

Details the design, construction, and mechanical operation of the Conestoga. More than 100 illustrations feature extant wagons, complete specifications, horse and wagon accessories, maps, and documents.

9933

Truett, Randle B. Trade and travel around the southern Appalachians before 1830. Chapel Hill, University of North Carolina Press, 1935. xii, 192 p. map, plates.

HE208.T7

Bibliography: p. [160]–181.

Focuses on the area from Georgia to Louisiana.

9934

Usher, Abbott P.　Colonial business and transportation. *In* Hart, Albert B., *ed.* Commonwealth history of Massachusetts. v. 2. Province of Massachusetts, 1689–1775. New York, States History Co., 1928. p. 386–418. illus.
F64.H32, v. 2

Bibliography: p. 417–418.

9935

Waitley, Douglas.　Roads of destiny; the trails that shaped a nation. Washington, R. B. Luce [1970] 319 p. maps.
E161.5.W34

Bibliography: 314–319.

Recounts the adventures of famous men along 22 important colonial roads. In his section on the King's Highway (Yorktown to Boston) during the war, the author discusses Sam Adams' use of the trail, the battle along the Concord fork, Washington's dependence upon the road for supplies during the Siege of Boston, and his tactical use of the highway during the New Jersey campaign of 1777.

9936

Walzer, John F.　Transportation in the Philadelphia trading area, 1740–1775. 1968. ([351] p.)
Micro AC–1, no. 68–7139

Thesis (Ph.D.)—University of Wisconsin.

Abstracted in *Dissertation Abstracts*, v. 29A, July 1968, p. 202.

9937

Watson, Alan D.　Regulation and administration of roads and bridges in colonial eastern North Carolina. North Carolina historical review, v. 45, autumn 1968: 399–417. maps.
F251.N892, v. 45

MANUFACTURING AND THE EXTRACTIVE INDUSTRIES

1. GENERAL

9938

Bishop, John Leander.　A history of American manufacturers from 1608 to 1860 . . . comprising annals of the industry of the United States in machinery, manufacturers, and useful arts, with a notice of the important inventions, tariffs, and the results of each decennial census. 3d ed., rev. and enl. Philadelphia, E. Young, 1868. 3 v. ports.
TS23.B72

The first issue of volume 1 appeared in 1861. In 1862 Bishop entrusted the charge of the work to Edwin T. Freedley, by whom it was completed, with the aid of Edward Young.

Reprinted, with an introduction by Louis M. Hacker, in New York by A. M. Kelley (1966).

Volume 1 traces in considerable detail the development of principal and secondary industries from their origins to 1790. The author concludes that the British controls on colonial manufacturing and trade retarded the growth of American business enterprise and compelled the colonists to declare their independence.

9939

Clark, Victor S.　History of manufactures in the United States. v. 1. 1607–1860. Washington, D.C., Carnegie Institution of Washington, 1916. xii, 675 p. illus., maps, plates.
HD9725.C5, v. 1

Bibliography: p. 624–650.

The first nine chapters deal with various facets of colonial manufacturing: the European background, British policy, colonial legislation, natural resources, transportation, markets, currency and prices, capital and labor, technology and organization, and contemporary accounts of domestic industries. In chapter 10 Clark discusses the political propaganda promoting nonimportation and home manufactures during the Revolution.

9940

Nichols, Jeanette P.　Colonial industries of New Jersey—1618–1815. Americana, v. 24, July 1930: 299–342.
E171.A53, v. 24

9941

Tilley, Nannie M.　Industries of colonial Granville County. North Carolina historical review, v. 8, Oct. 1936: 273–289.
F251.N892, v. 8

9942

Weiss, Harry B., *and* Grace M. Weiss.　Forgotten mills of early New Jersey: oil, plaster, bark, indigo, fanning, tilt, rolling and slitting mills, nail and screw making. Trenton, New Jersey Agricultural Society, 1960. 94 p. illus., facsims.
T22.N5W4

Bibliography: p. 90–91.

2. WHALING AND FISHING

9943

Alden, Dauril.　Yankee sperm whalers in Brazilian waters, and the decline of the Portuguese whale fishery (1773–1801). Americas, v. 20, Jan. 1964: 267–288.
E11.A4, v. 20

Emphasizes the importance of the whaling industry in the economic life of New England.

9944

Dodge, Stanley D.　The geography of the codfishing industry in colonial New England. *In* Geographical Society of Philadelphia. Bulletin, v. 25, Jan. 1927: 43–50. map.
G3.G34, v. 25

9945

Dow, George F.　Whale ships and whaling, a pictorial history of whaling during three centuries, with an account of the whale fishery in colonial New England. Introduction by Frank Wood. Salem, Mass., Marine Research Society, 1925. xi, 446 p. illus., facsims., plates. (Marine Research Society, Salem Mass. Publication no. 10)
SH381.D6

9946

Graham, Gerald S. The migrations of the Nantucket whale fishery: an episode in British colonial policy. New England quarterly, v. 8, June 1935: 179–202.

F1.N62, v. 8

Britain's determination after the Revolution to enforce the navigation laws with regard to foreign whale oil proved a severe hardship for New England whalers.

9947

McFarland, Raymond. A history of the New England fisheries. [Philadelphia] University of Pennsylvania, 1911. 457 p. maps. [Publications of the University of Pennsylvania series in political economy and public law] SH221.M3

Bibliography: p. 338–363.

Contains two brief chapters (p. 102–128) on the period 1763–83.

9948

Stackpole, Edouard A. The sea-hunters; the New England whalemen during two centuries, 1635–1835. Philadelphia, Lippincott [1953] 510 p. illus., facsims., map, plates, port. SH381.S76

Bibliographic references included in "Notes" (p. 475–497).

9949

Stackpole, Edouard A. Whales & destiny; the rivalry between America, France, and Britain for control of the southern whale fishery, 1785–1825. [Amherst] University of Massachusetts Press [c1972] xii, 427 p. illus., facsims., map, ports. SH383.S7

Focuses on Nantucket's contribution to the survival of the American whale fleet between the Revolution and the War of 1812, especially the parts played by Francis and William Rotch and the Quaker merchants of the island. The Nantucketers not only established a French-supported colony at Dunkirk in 1786 but commanded half the ships in the London whaling fleet of that year and played an important role in opening Australia to settlement.

9950

Starbuck, Alexander. History of the American whale fishery from its earliest inception to the year 1876. Waltham, Mass., 1878. 768 p. plates. SH381.S79

The period to 1789 is covered on pages 1–90.

3. HEMP, PAPER, AND TEXTILES

9951

Bagnall, William R. The textile industries of the United States, including sketches and notices of cotton, woolen, silk, and linen manufacturers in the colonial period. v. 1. 1639–1810. Cambridge [Mass.] Riverside Press, 1893. xxii, 613 p. ports. TS1323.B14, v. 1

No more published.

Reprinted, with an index prepared by Thomas W. Leavitt, in New York by A. M. Kelley (1971).

9952

Cole, Arthur H. The American wool manufacture. Cambridge, Harvard University Press, 1926. 2 v. illus., plates, ports. HD9895.C6

Bibliography: v. 2, p. 303–314.

Reprinted in New York by Harper & Row (1969).

The first four chapters in volume 1 (p. 3–71) deal with woolen manufacturing during the colonial and Revolutionary periods.

9953

Hamer, Marguerite B. The foundation and failure of the silk industry in provincial Georgia. North Carolina historical review, v. 12, Apr. 1935: 125–148.

F251.N892, v. 12

9954

Herndon, George Melvin. Hemp in colonial Virginia. Agricultural history, v. 37, Apr. 1963: 86–93. illus.

S1.A16, v. 37

9955

Herndon, George Melvin. The story of hemp in colonial Virginia. 1959. ([208] p.) Micro AC–1, no. 59–4229

Thesis (Ph.D.)—University of Virginia.

Abstracted in *Dissertation Abstracts*, v. 20, Oct. 1959, p. 1341–1342.

9956

Herndon, George Melvin. A war-inspired industry: the manufacture of hemp in Virginia during the Revolution. Virginia magazine of history and biography, v. 74, July 1966: 301–311. F221.V91, v. 74

9957

Leonard, Eugenie A. Paper as a critical commodity during the American Revolution. Pennsylvania magazine of history and biography, v. 74, Oct. 1950: 488–499.

F146.P65, v. 74

9958

Little, Frances. Early American textiles. New York, Century Co. [c1931] xvi, 267 p. facsims., plates. (Century library of American antiques) NK8812.L5

Bibliography: p. 249–253.

9959

Maxson, John W. Papermaking in America: from art to industry, 1690 to 1860. *In* U.S. *Library of Congress.* Quarterly journal, Apr. 1968: 116–129. illus., facsims., ports. Z881.U49A3

9960

Montgomery, Florence M. "Fortunes to be acquired"—textiles in 18th-century Rhode Island. Rhode Island history, v. 31, spring/summer 1972: 52–63. illus., facsims. F76.R472, v. 31

9961

Rockefeller, George C. Early paper making in Trenton; some account of the Potts and Reynolds mill, 1777–1785. In New Jersey Historical Society. Proceedings, v. 71, Jan. 1953: 24–32. F131.N58, v. 71

9962

Seitz, May A. The history of the Hoffman paper mills in Maryland. [Baltimore, Printed by the Holliday Press, 1946] 63 p. plates. TS1096.H6

Bibliography: p. 63.

Established by William Hoffman (1740–1811) who had emigrated from Germany in 1768.

9963

Weeks, Lyman H. A history of paper-manufacturing in the United States, 1690–1916. New York, Lockwood Trade Journal Co., 1916. xv, 352 p. illus., ports. TS1095.U6W4

Reprinted in New York by B. Franklin (1969).

Devotes five chapters (p. 1–103) to the papermills and paper products of the 18th century.

9964

Weiss, Harry B., and Grace M. Ziegler. The early fulling mills of New Jersey. Trenton, New Jersey Agricultural Society, 1957. 79 p. illus. TS1324.N5W4

Bibliography: p. 74–76.

9965

Willcox, Joseph. The Willcox paper mill (Ivy Mills), 1729–1866. In American Catholic Historical Society of Philadelphia. Records, v. 8, Mar. 1897: 28–85. E184.C3A4, v. 8

Established by Thomas Willcox in Concord, Pa., in 1729, the mill manufactured the paper used for the paper money of the colonies from Massachusetts to South Carolina as well as for Continental currency.

4. MINING AND METAL PRODUCTION

9966

Abbott, Collamer M. Colonial copper mines. William and Mary quarterly, 3d ser., v. 27, Apr. 1970: 295–309. F221.W71, 3d s., v. 27

9967

Beck, Herbert H. Elizabeth Furnace plantation. In Lancaster County Historical Society. Journal, v. 69, winter 1965: 25–41. F157.L2L5, v. 69

On the charcoal iron furnace plantation constructed and operated by Henry William Stiegel and sold later to Robert Coleman.

9968

Bining, Arthur C. The iron plantations of early Pennsylvania. Pennsylvania magazine of history and biography, v. 57, Apr. 1933: 117–137. F146.P65, v. 57

9969

Bining, Arthur C. Pennsylvania iron manufacture in the eighteenth century. Harrisburg, 1938. 227 p. illus., map, ports. (Publications of Pennsylvania Historical Commission, v. 4) TS303.B5
F146.P27, v. 4

Reprinted in New York by A. M. Kelley (1970).

Discusses the establishment of the industry, the technique of iron manufacture, improvements and inventions, the workers, the ironmasters, relations with England, and the progress of the iron industry.

9970

Boyer, Charles S. Early forges & furnaces in New Jersey. Philadelphia, University of Pennsylvania Press, 1931. xv, 287 p. illus., maps, plates. TS303.B6

Bibliography: p. 267–276.

9971

Bruce, Kathleen. Virginia iron manufacture in the slave era. New York, Century Co. [c1930] xiii, 482 p. illus., facsim., fold. map, plates, port. TS303.B88

"A doctoral dissertation [Radcliffe College, 1924]."—Preface.

Bibliography: p. 431–451.

Reprinted in New York by A. M. Kelley (1968. HD9517.V52B7 1968).

9972

Cappon, Lester J. Iron-making—a forgotten industry of North Carolina. North Carolina historical review, v. 9, Oct. 1932: 331–348. F251.N892, v. 9

9973

Doerflinger, Thomas M. Hibernia furnace during the Revolution. New Jersey history, v. 90, summer 1972: 97–114. illus., maps, ports. F131.N58, v. 90

Sheds light on northern New Jersey's iron industry, its relationship to Continental military needs, and the wartime business dealings of William Alexander, Lord Stirling.

9974

Hecht, Arthur. Lead production in Virginia during the seventeenth and eighteenth centuries. West Virginia history, v. 25, Apr. 1964: 173–183. F236.W52, v. 25

9975

Hermelin, Samuel G., friherre. Report about the mines in the United States of America, 1783. Swedish-American historical bulletin, v. 4, Feb. 1931: 7–54; June: 13–33. E184.S23S96, v. 4

Hermelin was a commercial investigator for the Swedish government.

9976

Johnson, Keach D. The establishment of the Baltimore Company: a case study of the American iron industry in the eighteenth century. 1949.

Thesis (Ph.D.)—State University of Iowa.

9977

Miller, Robert L., *and* Harold L. Peterson. Rappahannock Forge: its history and products. Military collector & historian, v. 4, Dec. 1952: 81–84. illus.
UC463.M54, v. 4

On the iron works owned by James Hunter.

9978

National Society of the Colonial Dames of America. *Pennsylvania.* Forges and furnaces in the province of Pennsylvania. Prepared by the Committee on Historical Research. Philadelphia, Printed for the Society, 1914. vii, 204 p. plates. (Publications of the Pennsylvania Society of the Colonial Dames of America, v. 3)
E186.4.P33, v. 3
F152.N27

9979

Neu, Irene D. The iron plantations of colonial New York. *In* New York State Historical Association. New York history, v. 33, Jan. 1952: 3–24. F116.N865, v. 33

Concludes that the availability of a large supply of domestic iron in New York was a contributing factor to the success of the war.

9980

Pearse, John B. A concise history of the iron manufacture of the American colonies up to the Revolution, and of Pennsylvania until the present time. Philadelphia, Allen, Lane & Scott, 1876. 282 p. illus., fold. map.
TN704.U5P3

Reprinted in New York by B. Franklin (1970).

9981

Robbins, Michael W. The Principio Company: ironmaking in colonial Maryland, 1720–1781. 1972. ([398] p.) Micro AC–1, no. 72–25,063

Thesis (Ph.D.)—George Washington University.
Abstracted in *Dissertation Abstracts International*, v. 33A, Oct. 1972, p. 1659.

5. SHIPS, SHIPBUILDING, AND NAVAL STORES

9982

Briggs, Lloyd V. History of shipbuilding on North River, Plymouth County, Massachusetts, with genealogies of the shipbuilders, and accounts of the industries upon its tributaries, 1640 to 1872. Boston, Coburn Bros., Printers, 1889. xv, 420 p. illus., facsims., maps, plates, ports.
F72.P7B8

Reprinted in New York by Research Reprints (1970).

9983

Chandler, Charles L. Early shipbuilding in Pennsylvania, 1683–1812; the tenth anniversary Brackett lecture before Princeton University. [Philadelphia, Colonial Press] 1932. 43 p. VM24.P4C45 1932

9984

Chapelle, Howard I. The history of American sailing ships. With drawings by the author, and George C. Wales and Henry Rusk. New York, W. W. Norton, 1935. xvii, 400 p. illus., plans, plates. VM23.C53 1935a

"Authorities and acknowledgments": p. xv–xvii.

After a preliminary chapter on early American ships and shipbuilding, Chapelle treats the history of each type of vessel topically: naval craft, privateers and slavers, revenue cutters, schooners, merchant craft, and sailing yachts.

9985

Crowther, Simeon J. The shipbuilding industry and the economic development of the Delaware Valley, 1681–1776. 1970 ([247] p.) Micro AC–1, no. 71–7796

Thesis (Ph.D.)—University of Pennsylvania.
Abstracted in *Dissertation Abstracts International*, v. 31A, Apr. 1971, p. 5010.

9986

Fairburn, William A. Merchant sail. Center Lovell, Me., Fairburn Marine Educational Foundation [1945–55] 6 v. (xix, 4179 p.) chart. HE745.F3

Vols. 4–6 were arranged and edited by Ethel M. Ritchie.
Partial contents: v. 1. Early days of exploration and the influence of shipbuilding in the development of the American colonies; the merchant marine during the Revolution; the challenging period between the wars with Britain; raids of the Barbary states on the commerce of the young Republic and the establishment of the U.S. Navy.—v. 5. United States wood shipbuilders and shipbuilding centers during the days of the young Republic and throughout the nineteenth century, with the production of sailing vessels, including packets, clippers, and down easters.—v. 6. Appendixes; index of vessels; general index.

9987

Fitch, Winchester. American pioneers of steam navigation. Magazine of history, with notes and queries, v. 4, Dec. 1906: 326–343. E171.M23, v. 4

William Henry, James Rumsey, John Fitch, and Nicholas Roosevelt.

9988

Goldenberg, Joseph A. The shipbuilding industry in colonial America. 1969. ([417] p.)
Micro AC–1, no. 70–12,061

Thesis (Ph.D.)—University of North Carolina.
Abstracted in *Dissertation Abstracts International*, v. 31A, July 1970, p. 338–339.

Focuses on the northern colonies in the 18th century.

9989

Haldane-Robertson, Langton. Some Philadelphia ships condemned at Jamaica during the Revolution. American Neptune, v. 2, July 1942: 203–208.
V1.A4, v. 2

9990

Herndon, George Melvin. Naval stores in colonial Georgia [1755–75] Georgia historical quarterly, v. 52, Dec. 1968: 426–433. F281.G2975, v. 52

9991

Kelso, William M. Shipbuilding in Virginia, 1763–1774. *In* Columbia Historical Society, *Washington, D.C.* Records. 1971/72. Washington [1973] p. 1–13. illus.
F191.C72, 1971/72

9992

Leach, MacEdward. Notes on American shipping based on records of the Court of the Vice-Admiralty of Jamaica, 1776–1812. American Neptune, v. 20, Jan. 1960: 44–48.
V1.A4, v. 20

9993

McCusker, John J. Colonial tonnage measurement [1740–75]: five Philadelphia merchant ships as a sample. Journal of economic history, v. 27, Mar. 1967: 82–91.
HC10.J64, v. 27

See also the comment by Gary M. Walton in the journal for September on pages 392–397.

9994

McCusker, John J. Sources of investment capital in the colonial Philadelphia shipping industry [1725–75] Journal of economic history, v. 32, Mar. 1972: 146–157.
HC10.J64, v. 32

9995

Morse, Sidney G. The ship *Lord Dartmouth*: American-built merchantman of Revolutionary days. American Neptune, v. 4, July 1944: 207–216.   V1.A4, v. 4

On the construction and subsequent legal battles over the vessel.

9996

Preble, George H. Early ship-building in Massachusetts. New-England historical and genealogical register, v. 23, Jan. 1869: 38–41; v. 25, Jan.–Apr., Oct. 1871: 15–21, 124–130, 362–369; v. 26, Jan., July 1872: 21–29, 271–283.   F1.N56, v. 23, 25–26

———— ———— Offprint. [Boston, 1869–72] 50 p.
VM24.M4P8

Includes a list of armed vessels built or fitted out in Massachusetts, 1776–83.

9997

Renninger, Warren D. Government policy in aid of American shipbuilding; an historical study of the legislation affecting shipbuilding from earliest colonial times to the present. Philadelphia, 1911. iv, 68 p.   HE745.R3

Thesis (Ph.D.)—University of Pennsylvania, 1911.
Bibliography: p. 63–68.
"Policy before 1789": p. 2–21.

9998

Robinson, John, *and* George F. Dow. The sailing ships of New England, 1607–1907. Salem, Mass., Marine Research Society, 1922. 66 p. illus., plates (part col.) (Marine Research Society, Salem, Mass. Publication no. 1)   VM23.R6

Following a discussion of the development of colonial shipping and the use of nautical instruments, the compilers present nearly 200 pictures of 18th- and 19th-century ships taken mostly from contemporary paintings. More than 200 additional plates were published in 1924 as a second series under the same title (51 p. Marine Research Society, Salem, Mass. Publication no. 5. VM23.R62). This volume is devoted largely to the clipper ships of the 19th century.

9999

Ship registers for the port of Philadelphia [Sept. 18, 1761–Mar. 16, 1776] Pennsylvania magazine of history and biography, v. 27, July–Oct. 1903: 346–370, 482–498; v. 28, Jan.–Oct. 1904: 84–100, 218–235, 346–374, 470–507.   F146.P65, v. 27–28

Transcribed from records, whose coverage begins in 1726, in the possession of the Historical Society of Pennsylvania. The registers give the date, vessel, master, owners, tonnage, and place of construction.

10000

Snow, Sinclair. Naval stores in colonial Virginia. Virginia magazine of history and biography, v. 72, Jan. 1964: 75–93.   F221.V91, v. 72

10001

Williams, Milo R. Sailing vessels of the eighteenth century. *In* United States Naval Institute. Proceedings, v. 62, Jan. 1936: 9–27. illus.   V1.U8, v. 62

6. OTHER INDUSTRIES

10002

Braddock-Rogers, Kenneth. Saltworks of New Jersey during the American Revolution. Journal of chemical education, v. 15, Dec. 1938: 586–592. map.
QD1.J93, v. 15

10003

Eavenson, Howard N. The first century and a quarter of American coal industry. Pittsburgh, Pa., Priv. print. [Baltimore, Waverly Press] 1942. xiv, 701 p. illus., maps (part fold.)   TN805.A5E2

Bibliography: p. [619]–664.
"Coal in the Revolutionary War": p. 44–59.

10004

Haynes, William. American chemical industry. v. 1. Background and beginnings. New York, Van Nostrand [1954] lxxvii, 512 p. ports.   TP23.H37, v. 1

"Book titles": p. 445–461.

In part 1, The Colonial Background, 1608–1790 (p. 1–101), the author includes chapters on the political economy of the colonies; forest products; logwood, indigo, and other dyes; chemical pioneering; industry in the colonies; and colonial chemistry.

10005

Hood, Graham. Bonnin and Morris of Philadelphia; the first American porcelain factory, 1770–1772. Chapel Hill, Published for the Institute of Early American

History and Culture at Williamsburg, Va., by the University of North Carolina Press [1972] xiii, 78 p. illus. (An Institute book on the arts and material culture in early America)   NK4210.B66H66

Includes bibliographic references.

10006

Hopkins, Thomas. Journal of Thomas Hopkins of the Friendship Salt Company, New Jersey, 1780. Pennsylvania magazine of history and biography, v. 42, Jan. 1918: 46–61.   F146.P65, v. 42

A day-by-day account of activities at the salt works.

10007

Moss, Roger W. Master builders: a history of the colonial Philadelphia building trades [1682–1790] 1972. ([255] p.)   Micro AC–1, no. 72–32,008

Thesis (Ph.D.)—University of Delaware.

Abstracted in *Dissertation Abstracts International*, v. 33A, Dec. 1972, p. 2841.

10008

Payne, Lloyd. The miller in eighteenth-century Virginia; an account of mills & the craft of milling, as well as a description of the windmill near the palace in Williamsburg. Williamsburg, Colonial Williamsburg, 1958. 32 p. illus., map. (Williamsburg craft series)   TS2135.U62V56

Bibliography: p. 32.

10009

Roberts, William I. American potash manufacture before the American Revolution. *In* American Philosophical Society, *Philadelphia*. Proceedings, v. 116, Oct. 1972: 383–395. illus.   Q11.P5, v. 116

10010

Thompson, James W. A history of livestock raising in the United States, 1607–1860. [Washington] United States Dept. of Agriculture [1942] viii, 182 p. (U.S. [Bureau of Agricultural Economics] Agricultural history series, no. 5)   HD1751.A9145, no. 5

"Literature cited by James Westfall Thompson": p. 147–177.

"Selected references on the history of livestock raising in the United States to 1860, published since the Thompson manuscript was completed": p. 178–182.

10011

Tunnell, James M. The salt business in early Sussex County. Delaware history, v. 4, Mar. 1950: 48–59.   F161.D37, v. 4

10012

Warren, William L. Prefabrication in colonial Connecticut. *In* Connecticut Historical Society, *Hartford*. Bulletin, v. 25, Apr. 1960: 36–48. facsims.   F91.C67, v. 25

On an attempt by the Connecticut firm of Trumbull, Fitch, and Trumbull in 1764 to precut and ship to the West

Indies a house designed and built for Dr. William Bryant of London.

10013

Weiss, Harry B., *and* Robert J. Sim. The early grist and flouring mills of New Jersey. Trenton, New Jersey Agricultural Society, 1956. 135 p. illus.   TS2135.N4W4

Bibliography: p. 129–132.

10014

Weiss, Harry B., *and* Grace M. Weiss. Early tanning and currying in New Jersey. Trenton, New Jersey Agricultural Society, 1959. 74 p. illus.   TS956.N5W4

Bibliographic footnotes.

10015

Welsh, Peter C. The Brandywine Mills: a chronicle of an industry, 1762–1816. Delaware history, v. 7, Mar. 1956: 17–36. plate.   F161.D37, v. 7

10016

Wittlinger, Carlton O. The small arms industry of Lancaster County, 1710–1840. Pennsylvania history, v. 24, Apr. 1957: 121–136. illus.   F146.P597, v. 24

MONEY AND FINANCE

1. General

10017

Baldwin, Benjamin R. Debts owed by Americans to British creditors, 1763–1802. 1932.

Thesis (Ph.D.)—Indiana University.

10018

Bolles, Albert S. The financial history of the United States, from 1774 to 1789: embracing the period of the American Revolution. 4th ed. New York, D. Appleton, 1896. xii, 371 p.   HJ241.B712

First published in 1879.
Reprinted in New York by A. M. Kelley (1969).

Concerned largely with the issuance of paper money, taxation, loans, the performance of the Treasury Board, and the financial administration of Robert Morris.

10019

Bullock, Charles J. Essays on the monetary history of the United States. New York, Macmillan Co., 1900. x, 292 p. (The Citizen's library of economics, politics, and sociology)   HG508.B8

Bibliography: p. 275–288.
Contents: 1. Three centuries of cheap money in the United States.—2. Paper currency of North Carolina [1712–88]—3. Paper currency of New Hampshire [1709–88]
Reprinted in New York by Greenwood Press (1969).

10020

Bullock, Charles J. The finances of the United States from 1775 to 1789, with special reference to the budget. Madison, Wis., The University, 1895. viii, 117–273 p.

(Bulletin of the University of Wisconsin. Economics, political science, and history ser., v. 1, no. 2)
H31.W6
HJ247.B9

Special bibliography at head of chapters.
"General bibliography": p. 266–273.

10021

Bullock, Charles J.   Historical sketch of the finances and financial policy of Massachusetts from 1780 to 1905. New York, For the American Economic Association, by the Macmillan Co. [ᶜ1907] 144 p. (American Economic Association. Publications, 3d ser., v. 8, no. 2)
HB1.A5, 3d s., v.8
HJ491.B9

"List of books consulted in the preparation of this essay": p. 142–144.
"The Revolutionary debt (1780–1794)": p. 7–22.

10022

Davis, Andrew M.   Currency and banking in the province of the Massachusetts-Bay. New York, Published for the American Economic Association by the Macmillan Co. [ᶜ1901] 2 v. facsims., plates. (Publications of the American Economic Association, 3d ser., v. 1, no. 4; v. 2, no. 2)
HB1.A5
HG513.M4D29

Contents: pt. 1. Currency.—pt. 2. Banking.
Reprinted in New York by A. M. Kelley (1970).

Centering his study on the conflict between the governor and the assembly over the chronic currency problem, the author deals in the first volume with provincial bills and coinage, depreciation, adjustment of debts, inflation, and the emissions of neighboring governments in Rhode Island, Connecticut, and New Hampshire. Davis examines English and colonial banking practices in the second volume, taking as his principal topic the Land Bank of 1740 and the 30 years of litigation that followed its closure. He concludes that the currency question contributed significantly to the demand for independence and concurs with John Adams's view that the bank dispute had an even greater political effect in Massachusetts than the Stamp Act crisis.

10023

Gould, Clarence P.   Money and transportation in Maryland, 1720–1765. Baltimore, Johns Hopkins Press, 1915. 176 p. (Johns Hopkins University studies in historical and political science, 33d ser., no. 1)
H31.J6, 33d s., no. 1
HG513.M3G7

Focuses on the monetary system as the chief integrating force promoting trade. In successive chapters Gould discusses coinage, bills of exchange, tobacco as currency, paper money, and barter and concludes with a survey of roads, waterways, ferries, and the postal service as modes of transportation or communication that also encouraged economic intercourse.

10024

Gwyn, Julian.   Money lending in New England: the case of Admiral Sir Peter Warren and his heirs, 1739–1805. New England quarterly, v. 44, Mar. 1971: 117–134.
F1.N62, v. 44

Concludes that the war hardly affected the Warren interests, offering yet another indication of its conservative economic impact.

10025

Higgins, William Robert.   A financial history of the American Revolution in South Carolina. 1970. ([313] p.)
Micro AC–1, no. 71–10,383

Thesis (Ph.D.)—Duke University.
Abstracted in *Dissertation Abstracts International*, v. 31A, Apr. 1971, p. 5319.

Discusses the three methods adopted by the state legislature to finance the war effort—fiat money, direct and indirect taxes, and private loans—and the problems faced in retiring the debt.

10026

Kaminski, John P.   Paper politics: the northern state loan-offices during the Confederation, 1783–1790. 1972. ([310] p.)
Micro AC–1, no. 72–15,361

Thesis (Ph.D.)—University of Wisconsin.
Abstracted in *Dissertation Abstracts International*, v. 32A, June 1972, p. 6895.

Investigates the efforts of pro-paper money forces in Rhode Island, New York, New Jersey, and Pennsylvania to ease the economic burden of debtors, redeem state debts, and assume national securities owned by their citizens.

10027

Sterns, Worthy P.   The international indebtedness of the United States in 1789. Journal of political economy, v. 6, Dec. 1897: 27–53.
HB1.J7, v. 6

A review of obligations incurred from the beginning of the 18th century leads the author to a tentative total indebtedness of $82,500,000.

10028

Sumner, William G.   The financier and the finances of the American Revolution. New York, Dodd, Mead, 1891. 2 v.
HJ247.S8

List of authorities: v. 2, p. [307]–318.
Reprinted in New York by A. M. Kelley (1968) and B. Franklin (1970).

Reviews the financial history of the Confederation period by studying the public service and personal affairs of Robert Morris. The author examines the early treasury system, taxation, commerce, coinage, paper currency, and European loans as well as the establishment of the Bank of Pennsylvania and the Bank of North America. Sumner considers each topic from the perspective of the several elective and appointive positions that Morris held in the Pennsylvania and Confederation governments, especially that of Superintendent of Finance from 1781 to 1784. He also summarizes Morris's post-Revolutionary enterprises, concluding with his eventual bankruptcy and imprisonment.

2. BANKING

10029

[Barton, William]   Observations on the nature and use of paper-credit; and the peculiar advantages to be derived from it, in North-America: from which are inferred the means of establishing and supporting it, including proposals for founding a national bank. Philadelphia, Printed and sold by R. Aitken, 1781. 40 p.

AC901.W7, v. 3 Rare Bk. Coll.

10030

Bayles, William Harrison, *and* Frank Allaben.   The first bank in New York City. Journal of American history, with notes and queries, v. 15, July/Sept. 1921: 259–292.

E171.J86, v. 15

In their last installment of a history of banks and banking in colonial New York, the authors review the events surrounding the establishment of the Bank of New York in 1784.

10031

Bradbury, Miles L.   Legal privilege and the Bank of North America. Pennsylvania magazine of history and biography, v. 96, Apr. 1972: 139–166. F146.P65, v. 96

10032

Domett, Henry W.   A history of the Bank of New York, 1784–1884. Compiled from official records and other sources at the request of the directors. 3d ed. [Cambridge, Mass., Riverside Press, 1902] xv, 139 p. facsims., ports.   HG2613.N54B3 1902

Reprinted in New York by Greenwood Press (1969). First edition published in 1884.

The first three chapters (p. 1–35) deal with the period 1780–91.

10033

Fenstermaker, Joseph Van.   The statistics of American commercial banking, 1782–1818. Journal of economic history, v. 25, Sept. 1965: 400–413.

HC10.J64, v. 25

10034

Gras, Norman S. B.   The Massachusetts First National Bank of Boston, 1784–1934. Cambridge, Mass., Harvard University Press, 1937. xxiv, 768 p. facsims., plates, ports. (Harvard studies in business history, 4)

HG2613.B74F54

Contents: pt. 1. General introduction.—pt. 2. Documents illustrating the history of the Massachusetts bank, 1784–1865.—pt. 3. Statistics illustrating the history of the Massachusetts bank, 1784–1865.

Chapters 1–4 (p. 3–66) treat the period up to 1792. Other references to the bank during the Confederation period are scattered throughout.

10035

Hammond, Bray.   Banks and politics in America, from the Revolution to the Civil War. Princeton, Princeton University Press, 1957. xi, 771 p.   HG2472.H3

Bibliography: p. 747–760.

Follows the struggle between the farmer and business entrepreneur for dominance in American culture as the conflict affected the course of politics from 1694 to 1865. Hammond describes the origins and early histories of the Pennsylvania Bank, the Bank of North America, and the first banks in New York, Boston, and Baltimore and emphasizes the influence of Alexander Hamilton upon these institutions as well as upon the drafting and interpretation of the monetary clauses of the Constitution.

10036

James, Frank Cyril.   The Bank of North America and the financial history of Philadelphia. Pennsylvania magazine of history and biography, v. 64, Jan. 1940: 56–87.

F146.P65, v. 64

A description of the records of the Bank of North America, by A. J. McClurkin, follows on pages 88–96.

10037

Lewis, Lawrence.   A history of the Bank of North America. Philadelphia, J. B. Lippincott, 1882. 153 p. facsims., ports.   HG2613.P54B3

Includes four chapters (p. 13–74) on financial conditions, 1780–89, and the establishment of the bank.

10038

Morgan, Howard Wayne.   The origins and establishment of the First Bank of the United States [1781–91] Business history review, v. 30, Dec. 1956: 472–492.

HF5001.B8262, v. 30

10039

Rappaport, George D.   The sources and early development of the hostility to banks in early American thought [1781–87] 1970. ([268] p.)

Micro AC–1, no. 71–15,421

Thesis (Ph.D.)—New York University.

Abstracted in *Dissertation Abstracts International*, v. 31A, June 1971, p. 6527–6528.

10040

Thayer, Theodore G.   The land bank system in the American colonies. Journal of economic history, v. 13, spring 1953: 145–159.   HC10.J64, v. 13

3. COINAGE AND CURRENCY

10041

Adler, Simon L.   Money and money units in the American colonies. *In* Rochester Historical Society, *Rochester, N.Y.* Publications. v. 8. Rochester, 1929. p. 143–173.

F129.F7R58, v. 8

10042

Behrens, Kathryn L.   Paper money in Maryland, 1727–1789. Baltimore, Johns Hopkins Press, 1923. 98 p.

(Johns Hopkins University studies in historical and political science, ser. 41, no. 1) H31.J6, s. 41, no. 1
HG513.M3B4

Published also as thesis (Ph.D.)—Johns Hopkins University.

Bibliography: p. 95–96.

In tracing the history of paper money emissions, the author devotes primary attention to the Paper Currency Act of 1733 and the paper money issues of the Revolutionary period. Brehrens finds that the assembly generally maintained a sound policy regarding paper emissions, except for the period 1777–81 when inadequate security resulted in severe depreciation. She also reveals that the currency question was a significant issue in the contest over ratification of the federal Constitution.

10043
Breck, Samuel. Historical sketch of Continental paper money. *In* American Philosophical Society, *Philadelphia. Committee of History, Moral Science, and General Literature.* Transactions. v. 3; 1843. Philadelphia, Carey and Hart. p. [1]–40. E173.A75, v. 3

Reprinted separately in Philadelphia by J.C. Clark; reprinted by A. C. Kline (1863. 33 p. HG516.B7 Rare Bk. Coll.). Also reprinted under the title, "The Paper Money of the American Revolution," in the *Journal of American History*, v. 20, Apr. 1926, p. 121–159.

10044
Breckinridge, Sophonisba P. Legal tender; a study in English and American monetary history. Chicago, University of Chicago Press, 1903. xvii, 181 p. ([Chicago. University] The decennial publications. 2d ser., v. 7)
HG363.B8

Bibliography: p. 175–177.

Reprinted in New York by Greenwood Press (1969).

Includes three chapters (p. 49–85) on legal tender in the colonies, under the Confederation government, and in the Constitution.

10045
Brock, Leslie V. The currency of the American colonies, 1700–1764: a study in colonial finance and imperial relations. 1941.

Thesis (Ph.D.)—University of Michigan.

10046
Carothers, Neil. Fractional money; a history of the small coins and fractional paper currency of the United States. New York, J. Wiley, 1930. xiii, 372 p. [Wiley social science series] HG501.C3 1916

Thesis (Ph.D.)—Princeton University, 1916.
Bibliography: p. 359–362.
Reprinted in New York by A. M. Kelley (1967).

In chapters 3–5 (p. 17–56) the author considers coinage during the colonial and Revolutionary periods.

10047
Carroll, Charles. A letter from Charles Carroll, senior, to the reader. With his petition to the General Assembly of Maryland; his speech in support of it; and, the resolution of the House of Delegates thereon. Annapolis, Printed by F. Green, 1779. 16 p.
HG506.C3 Rare Bk. Coll.
AC901.H3, v. 34 Rare Bk. Coll.

Relates to the issue of paper money.

10048
Del Mar, Alexander. The history of money in America from the earliest times to the establishment of the Constitution. New York, Cambridge Encyclopedia Co., 1899. xxiv, 121 p. HG508.D4

Bibliography: p. [xi]–xxiv.
Reprinted in New York by B. Franklin (1969).
"Continental money": p. 93–116.

10049
Douglas, Damon G. The original mint of the New Jersey coppers [1786–89] *In* New Jersey Historical Society. Proceedings, v. 69, July 1951: 223–234.
F131.N58, v. 69

10050
Ernst, Joseph A. Colonial currency: a modest inquiry into the uses of the easy chair and the meaning of the colonial system of freely floating international exchange. Explorations in entrepreneurial history, 2d ser., v. 6, winter 1969: 187–197. HB615.E8, 2d s., v. 6

A critique of M. L. Burstein's "Colonial Currency and Contemporary Monetary Theory: A Review Article," 2d ser., v. 3, spring/summer 1966, p. 220–223.

10051
Felt, Joseph B. An historical account of Massachusetts currency. Boston, Printed by Perkins & Marvin, 1839. 259 p. plates. HG513.M4F5

Reprinted in New York by B. Franklin (1968).

Information on the period 1763–89 appears on pages 150–207.

10052
Fries, Adelaide L. North Carolina certificates of the Revolutionary War period. North Carolina historical review, v. 9, July 1932: 229–241. F251.N892, v. 9

10053
[Hart, Adolphus M] History of the issues of paper-money in the American colonies, anterior to the Revolution, explanatory of the historical chart of the paper money of that period. St. Louis, Union, Print, 1851. 20 p.
HG515.H2 Rare Bk. Coll.

10054
Hickcox, John H. A history of the bills of credit or paper money issued by New York, from 1709 to 1789: with a

description of the bills, and catalogue of the various issues. Albany, N.Y., J. H. Hickcox, 1866. 103 p. illus.   HG513.N5H5

Reprinted in New York by B. Franklin (1969).

10055
Hiden, Martha W. The money of colonial Virginia. Virginia magazine of history and biography, v. 51, Jan. 1943: 36–54. plate.   F221.V91, v. 51

10056
Jellison, Richard M. Paper currency in colonial South Carolina: a reappraisal. South Carolina historical magazine, v. 62, July 1961: 134–148.   F266.S55, v. 62

10057
Jellison, Richard M. Paper currency in colonial South Carolina, 1703–1764. 1952. ([304] p.)   Micro AC–1, no. 5320

Thesis (Ph.D.)—Indiana University.
Abstracted in *Dissertation Abstracts*, v. 13, no. 4, 1953, p. 545.

10058
Kemmerer, Donald L. A history of paper money in colonial New Jersey, 1668–1775. *In* New Jersey Historical Society. Proceedings, v. 74, Apr. 1956: 107–144.   F131.N58, v. 74

10059
McKay, George L. Early American currency; some notes on the development of paper money in the New England colonies, with 36 reproductions of engraved & typographic specimens. New York, The Typophiles, 1944. xxiv, 85 p. facsims. (Typophile chap books, 10)   HG515.M3

"Principal works consulted": p. [77]–78.

10060
Newman, Eric P. Coinage for colonial Virginia. New York, American Numismatic Society, 1956. 57 p. illus. (Numismatic notes and monographs, no. 135)   CJ1848.V5N4

Bibliographic footnotes.

10061
Newman, Eric P. The Continental dollar of 1776 meets its maker. Numismatist, v. 72, Aug. 1959: 914–926. facsims.   CJ1.N8, v. 72

Concludes that the previously unidentified diemaker for the 1776 Continental currency coinage was Elisha Gallaudet of New York.

10062
Newman, Eric P. The early paper money of America. [Racine, Wis., Whitman Pub. Co., 1967] 360 p. facsims.   HG591.N45

Includes bibliographies.
"An illustrated historical, statistical and descriptive compilation of data relating to American paper currency from its inception in 1686 to its transformation by virtue of the ratification in 1789 of the Constitution of the United States, encompassing over 500 issues of the individual American colonies (1690–1776), the united colonies (1775–1777), the United States of America (1777–1785), the individual American states (1776–1788), banks, cities, counties, factories, and individuals (1686–1789). Supplemented by current market values of generally available bills as ascertained by Ben M. Douglas and Richard Picker."

Besides treating emissions in each of the thirteen colonies, the author provides appendixes that contain information on changes in the value of colonial and state shillings in relation to the Spanish dollar between 1740 and 1783, depreciation of currency during the Revolution, and wartime counterfeits.

10063
Newman, Eric P. Nature printing on colonial and Continental currency. Numismatist, v. 77, Feb.–May 1964: 147–154, 299–305, 457–465, 613–623. facsims.   CJ1.N8, v. 77

Analyzes leaf prints on colonial and Continental currency and concludes that they were a closely guarded invention of Benjamin Franklin designed to discourage counterfeiters.

10064
Norton, William B. Paper currency in Massachusetts during the Revolution. New England quarterly, v. 7, Mar. 1934: 43–69.   F1.N62, v. 7

10065
Ogg, Frederic A. Paper money in the New England colonies. New England magazine, new ser., v. 29, Feb. 1904: 772–782.   AP2.N4, n.s., v. 29

10066
Phillips, Henry. Historical sketches of the paper currency of the American colonies, prior to the adoption of the federal Constitution. Roxbury, Mass., W.E. Woodward, 1865–66. 2 v.   HG515.P5

Vol. 2 has title: *Continental Paper Money; Historical Sketches of American Paper Currency*, 2d ser.
Contents: 1st ser. Pennsylvania. New Jersey. Rhode Island, by Elisha R. Potter. Virginia. Vermont.—2d ser. Continental paper money.
Reprinted in one volume in New York by B. Franklin (1969) and in Clifton, N.J. by A. M. Kelley (1972).

10067
Potter, Elisha R., *and* Sidney S. Rider. Some account of the bills of credit or paper money of Rhode Island, from the first issue in 1710, to the final issue, 1786. Providence, S.S. Rider, 1880. xii, 229 p. facsims. (Rhode Island historical tracts, no. 8)   F76.R52, no. 8

10068
Raymond, Wayte, *ed*. The standard paper money catalogue; early colonial notes, state issues, continental currency; United States notes and fractional currency;

bills of the Confederacy and southern states; notes of cities and towns. Giving the average valuations among collectors and dealers for the notes usually obtainable, with many illustrations. Compiled and published by Wayte Raymond, Inc. New York [1940] 106 p. facsims. HG591.R35

Subsequent editions of the catalog were issued in two separate parts. The 1955 edition of part 1 provides lists of known issues of colonial and Continental currency. It also includes illustrations of 20 vignettes or decorative seals found on bills issued by the Continental Congress.

10069
Sumner, William G. The coin shilling of Massachusetts Bay. Yale review, v. 7, Nov. 1898–Feb. 1899: 247–264, 405–420. AP2.Y2, v. 7

———— ———— Offprint. [New Haven, 1899?] [247]–280 p. CJ1848.M4S8

10070
Waxberg, Miriam R. Money in Morris County, 1763–1782, as indicated by mortgage records. *In* New Jersey Historical Society. Proceedings, v. 53, Jan. 1935: 20–26. F131.N58, v. 53

10071
Weiss, Roger W. The issue of paper money in the American colonies, 1720–1774. Journal of economic history, v. 30, Dec. 1970: 770–784. HC10.J64, v. 30

Includes tables that give commodity price indexes in England and the American colonies, indexes of exchange rates with London, and nominal and real values of colonial paper money issues.

10072
Yoder, Paton W. Paper currency in colonial Pennsylvania. 1941.

Thesis (Ph.D.)—Indiana University.

4. Counterfeiting

10073
Gillingham, Harrold E. Counterfeiting in colonial Pennsylvania. New York, American Numismatic Society, 1939. 52 p. facsims. (Numismatic notes and monographs, no. 86) HG336.U5G5

10074
Glaser, Lynn. Counterfeiting in America; the history of an American way to wealth. [New York] C. N. Potter; distributed by Crown Publishers [1967, ℅1968] 274 p. illus., facsims., ports. HG336.U5G55

Bibliographic references included in "Notes" (p. 263–271).

In the first three chapters (p. 11–61) the author briefly surveys colonial and Revolutionary counterfeiting.

10075
Newman, Eric P. Counterfeit Continental currency goes to war. Numismatist, v. 70, Jan.–Feb. 1957: 5–16, 137–147. facsim. CJ1.N8, v. 70

In an effort to undermine public confidence in the stability of the Confederation government, the British government prepared and distributed counterfeit Continental currency.

10076
Reed, John F. "Tis death to counterfeit;" numismatics as a branch of autograph collecting. Manuscripts, v. 20, summer 1968: 13–17. facsims. Z41.A2A925, v. 20

Concerns the 11 issues of paper money, totaling $241,552,780 emitted by the Continental Congress from 1775 to 1779.

10077
Scott, Kenneth. Counterfeiting in colonial America. With a foreword by U. E. Baughman. New York, Oxford University Press, 1957. xii, 283 p. plates. HG336.U5S35

Bibliography: p. [265]–266.

Tells the story of men and women who produced bogus coins and bills for their own enrichment and of British attempts during the Revolution to use the same methods to undermine Continental currency. Counterfeiting increased steadily during the pre-Revolutionary period; authorities invalidated and recalled several emissions that had been duplicated widely, usually by organized gangs operating in each colony. Although most counterfeiters committed other crimes as well, some were otherwise respectable citizens.

10078
Scott, Kenneth. Counterfeiting in colonial Connecticut. New York, American Numismatic Society, 1957. 243 p. facsims., map. (Numismatic notes and monographs, no. 140) HG336.U52C66

Bibliographic footnotes.

10079
Scott, Kenneth. Counterfeiting in colonial Maryland [1638–1775] Maryland historical magazine, v. 51, June 1956: 81–100. F176.M18, v. 51

10080
Scott, Kenneth. Counterfeiting in colonial New Hampshire [1685–1774] Historical New Hampshire, v. 13, Dec. 1957: 3–38. facsims., port. F31.H57, v. 13

10081
Scott, Kenneth. Counterfeiting in colonial New Jersey [1748–76] *In* New Jersey Historical Society. Proceedings, v. 75, July 1957: 170–179. F131.N58, v. 75

10082
Scott, Kenneth. Counterfeiting in colonial New York. New York, American Numismatic Society, 1953. 222 p. plates. (Numismatic notes and monographs, no. 127) HG336.U5N4

Bibliographic footnotes.

10083

Scott, Kenneth.   Counterfeiting in colonial North Carolina [1714–76] North Carolina historical review, v. 34, Oct. 1957: 467–482.   F251.N892, v. 34

10084

Scott, Kenneth.   Counterfeiting in colonial Pennsylvania. New York, American Numismatic Society, 1955. xi, 168 p. illus., map. (Numismatic notes and monographs, no. 132)   HG513.P3S4

Bibliographic footnotes.

10085

Scott, Kenneth.   Counterfeiting in colonial Rhode Island. Providence, Rhode Island Historical Society, 1960. 74 p. illus.   HG336.U52R46

10086

Scott, Kenneth.   Counterfeiting in colonial Virginia. Virginia magazine of history and biography, v. 61, Jan. 1953: 3–33.   F221.V91, v. 61

10087

Scott, Kenneth.   Counterfeiting in New York during the Revolution. *In* New York Historical Society. Quarterly, v. 42, July 1958: 221–259. illus., facsim., ports.   F116.N638, v. 42

10088

Scott, Kenneth.   The Middlesex counterfeiters [1772–73] *In* New Jersey Historical Society. Proceedings, v. 70, Oct. 1952: 246–149.   F131.N58, v. 70

10089

Smits, Edward J.   Long Island's Revolutionary counterfeiting plot. Journal of Long Island history, v. 2, spring 1962: 16–25.   F127.L8J75, v. 2

On a counterfeiting operation conducted in 1776 by Henry Dawkins, Issac Young, and Issac Ketcham of Huntington.

5. LOTTERIES

10090

Anderson, Samuel K.   Public lotteries in colonial New York. *In* New York Historical Society. Quarterly, v. 56, Apr. 1972: 133–146. facsims.   F116.N638, v. 56

10091

Ezell, John S.   Fortune's merry wheel, the lottery in America. Cambridge, Harvard University Press, 1960. viii, 331 p. facsims.   HG126.E9

"Bibliographical essay": p. [285]–298.

Includes three chapters (p. 12–78) on the use of lotteries during the colonial and Revolutionary periods.

10092

Ezell, John S.   The lottery in colonial America. William and Mary quarterly, 3d ser., v.5, Apr. 1948: 185–200.   F221.W71, 3d s., v. 5

Describes governmental and private use of lotteries to finance public projects—including a revolution.

10093

Ezell, John S.   When Massachusetts played the lottery. New England quarterly, v. 22, Sept. 1949: 316–335.   F1.N62, v. 22

10094

Gillingham, Harrold E.   Lotteries in Philadelphia prior to 1776. Pennsylvania history, v. 5, Apr. 1938: 77–100.   F146.P597, v. 5

10095

Nordell, Philip G.   Lotteries in Princeton's history. Princeton University Library chronicle, v. 15, autumn 1953: 16–37. facsims., plates.   Z733.P93C5, v. 15

On the five lotteries, 1749–74, used to help finance the College of New Jersey.

10096

Nordell, Philip G.   Vermont's early lotteries. Vermont history, v. 35, Jan. 1967: 35–71.   F46.V55, v. 35

On 42 authorized lotteries, 1779–1804.

10097

Reed, Doris M.   Continental lottery, 1776. Indiana quarterly for bookmen, v. 3, July 1947: 51–63.   Z1007.I5, v. 3

10098

Ross, Adam F.   The history of lotteries in New York. Magazine of history, with notes and queries, v. 5, Feb.–June 1907: 94–100, 143–152, 217–222, 259–266, 319–325.   E171.M23, v. 5

Includes two sections dealing with lotteries in colonial and Revolutionary New York.

10099

Stiness, John H.   A century of lotteries in Rhode Island. 1744–1844. Providence, R.I., S. S. Rider, 1896. xi, [1], 123 p. illus., facsims. (part fold.) (Rhode Island historical tracts, 2d ser., no. 3)   F76.R52, 2d s., no. 3
HG6133.R4S7

"Authorities used in writing this tract": p. [xii]

10100

Wilmerding, Lucius.   The United States lottery [1776–82] *In* New York Historical Society. Quarterly, v. 47, Jan. 1963: 5–39. facsims., ports.   F116.N638, v. 47

6. PRICES AND INFLATION

10101

Bezanson, Anne.   Inflation and controls, Pennsylvania, 1774–1779. *In* The tasks of economic history; papers presented at the eighth annual meeting of the Economic History Association, Cambridge, Massachusetts, September 10–11, 1948. [New York] Published for the Economic History Association by New York University Press [1949] (Journal of economic history. Supplement 8, 1948) p. 1–20.   HC10.T3, no. 8, 1948

10102
Bezanson, Anne.   Prices and inflation during the American Revolution; Pennsylvania, 1770–1790, by Anne Bezanson, assisted by Blanch Daley, Marjorie C. Denison [and] Miriam Hussey. Philadelphia, University of Pennsylvania Press, 1951. xvi, 362 p. (Industrial Research Dept., Wharton School of Finance and Commerce, University of Pennsylvania. Research studies, 35)   HC107.P4B4

Bibliography: p. 347–351.

"The data in this final volume in the pre-Civil War commodity price history studies for the area of Philadelphia . . . complement . . . two previous publications which cover the years 1720 to 1775 and 1784–1861."

Provides a continuous record of prices during the Revolutionary period and discusses business behavior in the face of wartime inflation and postwar recession and recovery. Despite the difficulties presented by the simultaneous circulation of two, and often three, currencies and the instability of the ratio between paper and specie, Bezanson presents monthly indexes of wholesale prices of 15 domestic and imported commodities ranging from beef to wheat and less complete series for 10 others, including bread, rice, tobacco, and Madeira wine. She concludes that monetary influences were dominant factors in the extravagant rise in prices, although shortages of goods and increased costs also played a role in creating and maintaining the inflationary spiral.

10103
Bezanson, Anne, Robert D. Gray, *and* Miriam Hussey.   Prices in colonial Pennsylvania. Philadelphia, University of Pennsylvania Press, 1935. xix, 445 p. (Industrial Research Department, Wharton School of Finance and Commerce, University of Pennsylvania, Philadelphia. Research studies, 26)   HB235.U6B4

Bibliography: p. 434–438.

Analyzes wholesale prices of 22 commodities in Philadelphia for the period 1720–75. The data, drawn from newspapers and merchants' private records, reveal a strong upward trend in the prices of colonial staples but stability for the prices of British imports, thus indicating the source of capital accumulation in colonial Philadelphia. Graphs of the monthly and annual relative prices for each commodity are provided for the entire period using the monthly averages of 1741–45 as the base. Complete tables of average monthly prices for each year are included in an extensive tabular appendix.

10104
Cole, Arthur H.   Wholesale commodity prices in the United States, 1700–1861. Published under the auspices of the International Scientific Committee on Price History. Cambridge, Mass., Harvard University, 1938. xxiii, 187 p. illus. (part fold.)   HB235.U6C56

——— ——— Statistical supplement: actual wholesale prices of various commodities. Published under the auspices of the International Scientific Committee on

Price History. Cambridge, Mass., Harvard University Press, 1938. x, 359 p.   HB235.U6C56 Suppl.
"Wholesale prices of individual commodities at various cities, monthly, 1700–1861."

10105
Cometti, Elizabeth.   Inflation in Revolutionary Maryland. William and Mary quarterly, 3d ser., v. 8, Apr. 1951: 228–234.   F221.W71, 3d s., v. 8

Indicates the inflationary rise in some foodstuffs, commodities, and wages, as high as 3,900 percent, from 1777 to 1780.

10106
Crandall, Ruth.   Wholesale commodity prices in Boston during the eighteenth century. Review of economic statistics, v. 16, June 1934: 117–128.
HA1.R35, v. 16

Additional statistical tables of the prices of molasses, sperm candles, New England rum, flour, cotton, Bohea tea, cocoa, coffee, Jamaica codfish, bar iron, Russia duck, and potash appeared in the September issue, p. 178–183.

10107
Davis, Andrew M.   The limitation of prices in Massachusetts, 1776–1779. *In* Colonial Society of Massachusetts, *Boston.* Publications. v. 10. Transactions, 1904/6. Boston, 1907. p. 119–134.   F61.C71, v. 10

10108
Grafton, Joseph.   Auction sales in Salem, of shipping and merchandise, during the Revolution. *In* Essex Institute, *Salem, Mass.* Historical collections, v. 49, Apr. 1913: 97–124.   F72.E7E81, v. 49

Records of auction sales that indicate the fluctuating prices, 1776–80, for a wide variety of merchandise.

10109
Lobdell, Jared C.   Some evidence of price inflation on Long Island, 1770–1782, from the papers of Richard Jackson, Jr. Journal of Long Island history, v. 8, summer/fall 1968: 39–43.   F127.L8J75, v. 8

10110
Mitchell, Broadus.   Inflation: revolution and its aftermath. Current history, v. 24, May 1953: 257–263.
D410.C82, v. 24

On the depreciation of currency during the Confederation period.

10111
Scott, Kenneth.   Price control in New England during the Revolution. New England quarterly, v. 19, Dec. 1946: 453–473.   F1.N62, v. 19

10112
Stoker, Herman M.   Wholesale prices at New York City, 1720 to 1800. *In* Wholesale prices for 213 years, 1720 to 1932. Ithaca, 1932. ([New York] Agricultural Experiment Station, Ithaca. Memoir 142) p. 201–222.
S95.E325, no. 142

10113

Taylor, George R. Wholesale commodity prices at Charleston, South Carolina, 1732–1791. Journal of economic and business history, v. 4, Feb. 1932: 356–377.   HC10.J6, v. 4

7. PUBLIC FINANCE

10114

Armentrout, Mary T. A political study of Virginia finance, 1781–1789. 1934.

Thesis (Ph.D.)—University of Virginia.

10115

Baldwin, Simeon E. The New Haven Convention of 1778. *In* New Haven Colony Historical Society, *New Haven*. Papers. v. 3. New Haven, 1882. p. 33–62.
                                                    F98.N5, v. 3

One of a series of financial conferences called by Congress and the interested states between 1776 and 1781 for the purpose of strengthening the public credit. New Hampshire, Massachusetts, Rhode Island, Connecticut, New York, New Jersey, and Pennsylvania were represented at the New Haven Convention that began on January 15th.

10116

Bates, Whitney K. The assumption of state debts, 1783–1793. 1952.

Thesis (Ph.D.)—University of Wisconsin.

10117

Bronson, Henry. A historical account of Connecticut currency, Continental money, and the finances of the Revolution. [New Haven, Printed for the Society, 1865] 192 p. (New Haven Colony Historical Society, New Haven. Papers, v. 1, [pt. 2])   F98.N5, v. 1

10118

Coleman, Edward M. New England Convention, December 25, 1776 to January 2, 1777: an illustration of early American particularism. Historian, v. 4, autumn 1941: 43–55.   D1.H22, v. 4

On an attempt to stabilize New England currency.

10119

Davis, Andrew M. Emergent treasury-supply in Massachusetts in early days. *In* American Antiquarian Society, *Worcester, Mass.* Proceedings, new ser., v. 17, Apr. 1905: 32–68.   E172.A60, n.s., v. 17

Traces through 1780 attempts to supply a denominational currency based solely upon government credit.

10120

Dewey, Davis R. Finance and paper money, 1692–1775. *In* Hart, Albert B., *ed.* Commonwealth history of Massachusetts. v. 2. Province of Massachusetts, 1689–1775. New York, States History Co., 1928. p. 192–221. facsims.   F64.H32, v. 2

Bibliography: p. 220–221.

10121

Dodd, William E. The effect of the adoption of the constitution upon the finances of Virginia. Virginia magazine of history and biography, v. 10, Apr. 1903: 360–370.   F221.V91, v. 10

Virginia finances, 1776–90.

10122

Dupuy, Herbert. A history of some loans made to the United States during the Revolution. Pennsylvania magazine of history and biography, v. 31, Oct. 1907: 486–490.   F146.P65, v. 31

Loans made by a William T. Smith, West Indian merchant, in 1778 and 1779 were not repaid by the U.S. government for 72 years.

10123

Ferguson, Elmer James. Currency finance: an interpretation of colonial monetary practices. William and Mary quarterly, 3d ser., v. 10, Apr. 1953: 153–180.
                                        F221.W71, 3d s., v. 10

Contends that advocates of "sound money" have cast provincial monetary policies in a bad light. Efforts to establish a medium of exchange, create a system of agricultural credit, and provide local governments with the means of incurring and discharging responsibilities were handled with discretion in most colonies.

10124

Ferguson, Elmer James. The power of the purse; a history of American public finance, 1776–1790. Chapel Hill, Published for the Institute of Early American History and Culture at Williamsburg, Va., by the University of North Carolina Press [1961] xvi, 358 p.   HJ247.F4

Bibliography: p. 344–347.

The author's thesis (Ph.D.), *Revenue Power and the Movement for National Government, 1780–1790*, was submitted to the University of Wisconsin in 1951.

To preserve what they considered to be the essential element of their sovereignty, the states had denied the Continental Congress the right to tax in the Articles of Confederation. The pivotal issue during the period, therefore, was the manner in which the large domestic and foreign debt incurred in prosecuting the Revolutionary War would be paid. Because several colonies had successfully managed fiat money, agrarian interests generally favored similar expedients. Mercantile capitalists and their allies, on the other hand, demanded a uniform currency and a debt funded by Congress. After reviewing the various fiscal expedients to which Congress and the states resorted, the author shows how the nationalists, led by Robert Morris, finally achieved their goal in 1790 when Congress, exercising powers granted under the new Constitution, enacted Alexander Hamilton's funding program. For an analysis of Ferguson's thesis, see Stuart W. Bruchey's "The Forces Behind the Constitution; a Critical Review of the Framework of E. James Ferguson's *The Power of the Purse*" in the *William and Mary Quarterly*, 3d ser., v. 19, July 1962, p. 429–434. A rebuttal by Ferguson appears on p. 434–438.

10125
Ferguson, Elmer James. Public finance and the origins of southern sectionalism. Journal of southern history, v. 28, Nov. 1962: 450–461.   F206.J68, v. 28

Most of the issues that gave rise to sectional tensions in the 19th century—tariff, states rights, slavery—had their origins in the Confederation period and the reaction of the South to new federal policies.

10126
Ferguson, Elmer James. State assumption of the federal debt during the Confederation. Mississippi Valley historical review, v. 38, Dec. 1951: 403–424.
        E171.J87, v. 38

An enlarged view of Confederation finances is not just one of Congress struggling to pay debts and being thwarted by the states. Most of the states made earnest efforts to pay federal debts as well as their own.

10127
Fuhlbruegge, Edward A. An abstract of New Jersey finances during the American Revolution. 1936.

Thesis (Ph.D.)—New York University.

10128
Fuhlbruegge, Edward A. New Jersey finances during the American Revolution. *In* New Jersey Historical Society. Proceedings, v. 55, July 1937: 167–190.
        F131.N58, v. 55

10129
Greene, George W. Finances of the Revolution. Atlantic monthly, v. 14, Nov. 1864: 581–603. AP2.A8, v. 14

10130
Harlow, Ralph V. Aspects of Revolutionary finance, 1775–1783. American historical review, v. 35, Oct. 1929: 46–68.   E171.A57, v. 35

Analyzes the paper-money policies of the states and of the Continental Congress.

10131
Higgins, William Robert. The South Carolina Revolutionary debt and its holders, 1776–1780. South Carolina historical magazine, v. 72, Jan. 1971: 15–29.
        F266.S55, v. 72

10132
M'Connel, Matthew. An essay on the domestic debts of the United States of America. Giving an account of the various kinds of public securities, and generally in what manner the debts arose: with the provision made and proposed for payment of the interest and principal thereof by fœderal measures, and. of those adopted by individual states. To which is subjoined, A statement of the foreign debt, as set forth by the United States in Congress assembled, in their address and recommendations of the 18th of April, 1783. Philadelphia, Printed and sold by Robert Aitken, at Pope's Head in Market Street, 1787. 90 p.   HJ8105 1787 Rare Bk. Coll.

10133
McMaster, John B. Liberty loans of the Revolution. *In* Pennsylvania. University. University lectures. v. 6 1918/19. Philadelphia, 1919. p. 233–256.   AC1.P4, v. 6

Concerns the problems faced by the Continental Congress in financing the war.

10134
Marcuse, William. Local public finance in colonial Connecticut. 1956. ([341] p.)   Micro AC–1, no. 16,906

Thesis (Ph.D.)—Columbia University.
Abstracted in *Dissertation Abstracts*, v. 16, no. 7, 1956, p. 1224.

10135
Morrill, James R. The practice and politics of fiat finance; North Carolina in the Confederation, 1783–1789. Chapel Hill, University of North Carolina Press [1969] 240 p.   HJ612.M6

Bibliography: p. [223]–228.
The author's thesis (Ph.D.), *North Carolina Public Finance, 1783–1789: The Problems of Minimal Government in an Under-Developed Land*, was submitted to the University of North Carolina in 1967 (Micro AC–1, no. 68–2215).

Analyzes the state's financial policies as well as state-federal financial relations. The author concludes that an uncertain postwar economy resulting from an excessive dependence upon the sale of raw materials produced a specie drain that made fiat finance in debt redemption and currency emission unavoidable. North Carolina antifederalism was both a cause and a result of the state's decisions to issue fiat currency to pay the men of the Continental Line and to absorb that portion of the national debt held by its citizens.

10136
Powell, Fred W., *comp.* Control of federal expenditures; a documentary history, 1775–1894. Washington, D.C., Brookings Institution, 1939. x, 928 p.   HJ7531.P6

Includes, on p. 3–42, proceedings, resolutions, orders, and ordinances from the *Journals* of the Continental Congress relating to the management and disbursement of public funds from 1775 to 1787.

10137
Ratchford, Benjamin U. American state debts. Durham, N.C., Duke University Press, 1941. xviii, 629 p. (Duke University publications)   HJ8223.R36

"Selected bibliography": p. 603–622.
Reprinted in New York by AMS Press (1966).

Colonial and Revolutionary debts are treated on pages [9]–51.

10138
Rich, Myra L. Speculations on the significance of debt; Virginia, 1781–1789. Virginia magazine of history and biography, v. 76, July 1968: 301–317.
        F221.V91, v. 76

10139

Richmond, John W. Rhode Island repudiation; or, The history of the Revolutionary debt of Rhode Island. 2d ed. Providence, Sayles, Miller & Simons, Printers, 1855. xvi, 208 p. fold. forms.　　HJ8447.R4 1855

With this is bound the author's *Rhode Island Repudiation of Her Registered State Debt.*

First edition published in 1848 under title: *History of the Registered State Debt of Rhode-Island.*

Richmond's account stems from his attempts in the 1840's to gather up Revolutionary certificates, all of which had been previously paid, in hopes of redeeming them with interest compounded since the war. The state government rejected his claims.

10140

Rodney, Richard S. Colonial finances in Delaware. Wilmington, Del., Wilmington Trust Co., 1928. 68 p. illus., facsims.　　HJ352.R6

"References notes": p. 67–68.

"Trustees of loan offices [1723–97]": p. 65–66.

10141

Schuckers, Jacob W. A brief account of the finances and paper money of the Revolutionary War. Philadelphia, J. Campbell, 1874. 128 p. illus.　　HJ247.S3

10142

[Swan, James] National arithmetick; or, Observations on the finances of the commonwealth of Massachusetts: with some hints respecting financiering and future taxation in this state: tending to render the publick contributions more easy to the people. By a late member of the General court. Boston, Printed by Adams and Nourse, in Court-Street [1786] viii, 91 p.
HJ492.S9, v. 3 Rare Bk. Coll.
AC901.M5, v. 935 Rare Bk. Coll.

10143

Tailby, Donald G. Foreign interest remittances by the United States, 1785–1787: a story of malfeasance. Business history review, v. 41, summer 1967: 161–176.
HF5001.B8262, v. 41

10144

U.S. *Register of the Treasury.* History of the currency of the country and of the loans of the United States from the earliest period to June 30, 1896. Prepared by William F. De Knight. Washington, Govt. Print. Off., 1897. 238 p. (Treasury Dept. Doc. no. 1943)
HG501.A3 1897

Information on the Revolutionary period appears on p. 11–32.

10145

U.S. *Treasury Dept.* The national loans of the United States, from July 4, 1776, to June 30, 1880. By Rafael A. Bayley. (2d ed.) As prepared for the tenth census of the United States. Washington, Govt. Print. Off., 1882. 197 p.　　HJ8101.A3 1881a

Reprinted in New York by B. Franklin (1970).

Discusses the loans negotiated with France, Spain, and Holland between 1776 and 1788 (p,. 5–22) and provides tables of issues and redemptions (p. 99–103).

10146

Weissbuch, Ted N. A chapter in Vermont's Revolutionary War finance. Vermont history, new ser., v. 29, Jan. 1961: 3–12. facsim.　　F46.V55, n.s., v. 29

8. TAXATION

10147

Army supplies in the Revolution [1782–83] Virginia magazine of history and biography, v. 4, Apr. 1897: 387–400.　　F221.V91, v. 4

Correspondence of public officials relating to the problem of raising tax revenue to defray the military expenses of the state.

10148

Becker, Robert A. The politics of taxation in America, 1763–1783. 1971. ([444] p.)
Micro AC–1, no. 71–25,178

Thesis(Ph.D.)—University of Wisconsin.

Abstracted in *Dissertation Abstracts International*, v. 32A, Dec. 1971, p. 3193.

Compares pre- and post-1775 tax systems to measure the direction of change.

10149

Cumberland Co., *Pa.* State and supply transcripts of the county of Cumberland for the years 1778, 1779, 1780, 1781, 1782, and 1785. Edited by William Henry Egle. [Harrisburg] W. S. Ray, State Printer of Pennsylvania, 1898. x, 782 p. (Pennsylvania archives, 3d ser., v. 20)
F146.P41, 3d s., v. 20
F157.C8C83

10150

Hill, William. Colonial tariffs. Quarterly journal of economics, v. 7, Oct. 1892: 78–100.　　HB1.Q3, v. 7

Concludes that colonial duties were based on European precedent and had no observable influence on tariff legislation after 1789.

10151

Jones, Frederick R. History of taxation in Connecticut 1636–1776. Baltimore, Johns-Hopkins Press, 1896. 70 p. (Johns Hopkins University studies in historical and political science, 14th ser., no. 8)
H31.J6, 14th s., no. 8
HJ2397.A3J6

10152

Kay, Marvin L. M. The payment of provincial and local taxes in North Carolina, 1748–1771. William and Mary quarterly, 3d ser., v. 26, Apr. 1969: 218–240.
F221.W71, 3d s., v. 26

10153

Kay, Marvin L. M. Provincial taxes in North Carolina during the administration of Dobbs and Tryon [1748–71] North Carolina historical review, v. 42, autumn 1965: 440–453. F251.N892, v. 42

10154

Kinnaman, John A. The internal revenues of colonial Maryland. 1955. ([600] p.) Micro AC–1, no. 12,835

Thesis (Ph.D.)—Indiana University.

Abstracted in *Dissertation Abstracts*, v. 15, no. 8, 1955, p. 1382.

10155

A List of taxable articles in the city of Williamsburg taken by Robert Nicolson for the year 1783 under the Revenue Act. William and Mary College quarterly historical magazine, v. 23, Oct. 1914: 133–142. F221.W71, v. 23

Includes free males above the age of 21, tithable slaves, slaves under 16 years of age, horses, cattle, wheels, and licensed ordinaries.

10156

Mason, David H. A short tariff history of the United States. 1783 to 1789. With a preliminary view. Chicago, C. H. Kerr, 1896. 167 p. (Unity library, no. 59) HF1753.M4

First published in 1884.

10157

Neely, Frederick T. The development of Virginia taxation: 1775 to 1860. 1956. ([511] p.) Micro AC–1, no. 17,623

Thesis (Ph.D.)—University of Virginia.

Abstracted in *Dissertation Abstracts*, v. 17, no. 2, 1957, p. 260–261.

10158

Paine, Thomas. Six new letters of Thomas Paine; being pieces on the five per cent duty, addressed to the citizens of Rhode Island, here first reprinted from the *Providence Gazette and Country Journal* of 1782 and 1783. With an introduction and notes by Harry H. Clark. Madison, University of Wisconsin Press, 1939. xxxii, 63 p. HF1754.P18 1782a

10159

Parker, Coralie. The history of taxation in North Carolina during the colonial period, 1663–1776. New York, Columbia University Press, 1928. x, 178 p. HJ2425.A2P3 1928

Issued also as thesis (Ph.D.)—Columbia University. Bibliography: p. 161–166.

10160

Reams, Louise A. Taxation in Virginia during the Revolution. *In* Richmond College historical papers. v. 2, no. 1; 1917. Richmond. p. 43–73. F221.R53, v. 2

10161

Robinson, Maurice H. A history of taxation in New Hampshire. New York, For the American Economic Association by the Macmillan Co. [1903] vi, 226 p. (American Economic Association. Publications. 3d ser., v. 3) HB1.A5, 3d s., v. 3 HJ2421.A2R6

Bibliography: p. [223]–224.

10162

Seligman, Edwin R. A. The income tax in the American colonies and states. Political science quarterly, v. 10, June 1895: 221–247. H1.P8, v. 10

Notes that the "faculty" or profits and gains tax of the colonial period was not a direct income tax but simply an addendum to the early land tax.

10163

Urdahl, Thomas K. The fee system in the United States. *In* Wisconsin Academy of Sciences, Arts and Letters. Transactions. v. 12, pt. 1; 1898. Madison. p. [49]–242. AS36.W7, v. 12

Includes a chapter on taxation systems during the colonial and Revolutionary periods on p. 96–122. Reprinted, with an introduction, in Madison by the Democrat Print. Co. (1898. xii, [49]–242 p. HJ5321.U8).

10164

Wood, Frederick A. History of taxation in Vermont. New York, Columbia College, 1894. 128 p. (Studies in history, economics and public law, v. 4, no. 3) H31.C7, v. 4, no. 3 HJ2437.A2W7

"Bibliography": p. 126–128.
Reprinted in New York by AMS Press (1968).

10165

Zornow, William F. Georgia tariff policies, 1775 to 1789. Georgia historical quarterly, v. 38, Mar. 1954: 1–10. F281.G2975, v. 38

10166

Zornow, William F. Massachusetts tariff policies, 1775–1789. *In* Essex Institute, *Salem, Mass.* Historical collections, v. 90, Apr. 1954: 194–215. F72.E7E81, v. 90

10167

Zornow, William F. New Hampshire tariff policies, 1775 to 1789. Social studies, v. 45, Nov. 1954: 252–256. D16.3.S65, v. 45

10168

Zornow, William F. New York tariff policies, 1775–1789. *In* New York State Historical Association. New York history, v. 37, Jan 1956: 40–63. F116.N865, v. 37

10169

Zornow, William F. North Carolina tariff policies, 1775–1789. North Carolina historical review, v. 32, Apr. 1955: 151–164. F251.N892, v. 32

10170

Zornow, William F.   The tariff policies of Virginia, 1775–1789. Virginia magazine of history and biography, v. 62, July 1954: 306–318.   F221.V91, v. 62

AGRICULTURE AND LANDHOLDING

1. GENERAL

10171

American husbandry.   Containing an account of the soil, climate, production and agriculture of the British colonies in North-America and the West-Indies; with observations on the advantages and disadvantages of settling in them, compared with Great Britain and Ireland. By an American. London, J. Bew, 1775. 2 v.
          S441.A5 Rare Bk. Coll.

A new edition, edited by Harry J. Carman, was published in New York by Columbia University Press (1939).

Authorship not definitely established; evidence indicates that the author was either John Mitchell or Arthur Yound (see Carman's introduction to the 1939 edition).

10172

Bean, Walton E.   War and the British colonial farmer: a re-evaluation in the light of new statistical records. Pacific historical review, v. 11, Dec. 1942: 439–448.
          F851.P18, v. 11

10173

Bidwell, Percy W., *and* John I. Falconer.   History of agriculture in the northern United States 1620–1860. Washington, Carnegie Institution of Washington, 1925. xii, 512 p. illus., maps, plates. (Carnegie Institution of Washington. Publication no. 358)   S441.B5
          HC101.C75, no. 5

Contributions to American economic history, [5].
"Classified and critical bibliography": p. 454–473.
"Alphabetical index of authors": p. 474–492.
Reprinted in New York by P. Smith (1941).

An encyclopedic description of land, labor, and the techniques of agricultural production. For the 18th century the authors pay particular attention to pioneer farming as a means of capital accumulation, the internal, coastal, and foreign trade in agricultural products, and the evolution from a liberal land policy to one of reckless prodigality after 1780.

10174

Bridgman, Richard.   Jefferson's farmer before Jefferson. American quarterly, v. 14, winter 1962: 567–577.
          AP2.A3985, v. 14

Despite the celebration of the agrarian myth by Jefferson, Crèvecoeur, Freneau, and others following the Revolution, the author reports that more detached observers found the common American farmer to be lazy, slovenly, and debauched.

10175

Brown, Wallace.   The American farmer during the Revolution: rebel or Loyalist? Agricultural history, v. 42, Oct. 1968: 327–338.   S1.A16, v. 42

10176

Edwards, Everett E.   American agriculture—the first 300 years. *In* U.S. Dept. of Agriculture. Farmers in a changing world. [Washington] U.S. Govt. Print. Off., 1940. (*Its* Yearbook of agriculture, 1940) p. 171–276.
          S21.A35, 1940

10177

Eighteenth-century agriculture, a symposium.   Sponsored by the Accokeek Foundation, the Smithsonian Institution, [and] the Agricultural History Society. Edited by John T. Schlebecker. [Berkeley, Calif.] 1969. 214 p. (Agricultural history, v. 43, Jan. 1969)
          S1.A16, v. 43

Partial contents: Plant hybridization and plant breeding in eighteenth-century American agriculture, by Conway Zirkle.—The tobacco staple and the planter's problems: technology, labor, and crops, by Aubrey C. Land.—The small farmer in eighteenth-century Virginia politics, by D. Alan Williams.—The American Revolution and American agriculture, by Merrill Jensen.—Farm and garden: landscape architecture and horticulture in eighteenth-century America, by T. L. Senn.—Horticulture in eighteenth-century America, by Frank Horsfall, Jr.

10178

Eisinger, Chester E.   The farmer in the eighteenth century almanac. Agricultural history, v. 28, July 1954: 107–112.   S1.A16, v. 28

10179

Eisinger, Chester E.   The freehold concept in eighteenth-century American letters. William and Mary quarterly, 3d ser., v. 4, Jan. 1947: 42–59.
          F221.W71, 3d s., v. 4

Analyzes the body of ideas that make up the Jeffersonian myth.

10180

Eisinger, Chester E.   The influence of natural rights and physiocratic doctrines on American agrarian thought during the Revolutionary period. Agricultural history, v. 21, Jan. 1947: 13–23.   S1.A16, v. 21

10181

Eisinger, Chester E.   Land and loyalty: literary expressions of agrarian nationalism in the seventeenth and eighteenth centuries. American literature, v. 21, May 1949: 160–178.   PS1.A6, v. 21

10182

Ford, Amelia C.   Colonial precedents of our national land system as it existed in 1800. [Madison] University of Wisconsin, 1910. 157 p. (Bulletin of the University of Wisconsin, no. 352. History series, v. 2, no. 2)
          H31.W62

Thesis (Ph.D.)—University of Wisconsin.
Bibliography: p. 147–157.

Discusses the development of the rectangular principle in colonial surveys, the township method of survey, the origin of the 640-acre section, the rectangular principle in early national legislation, revenue policies regarding land, land bounties, and squatters' and preemption rights.

10183
Freund, Rudolf.   John Adams and Thomas Jefferson on the nature of landholding in America. Land economics, v. 24, May 1948: 107–119.   HB1.J65, v. 24

10184
Harris, Marshall D.   Origin of the land tenure system in the United States. Ames, Iowa State College Press [1953] xiv, 445 p. maps.   HD194.H3
Bibliography: p. 413–423.
Reprinted in Westport, Conn., by Greenwood Press (1970).

In his survey of the evolution of the land tenure structure through which American colonists dealt with the acquisition, transfer, and control of land before 1800, the author emphasizes the influence of English common law, pertinent differences in practices among the royal, proprietary, and corporate colonies, and adjustments made during the Revolutionary period. Harris concludes that Americans forged a new land system inhibited only slightly by old tenure institutions and based on the concept of land as a commodity to be acquired, utilized, and sold for profit.

10185
Hirsch, Arthur H.   French influence on American agriculture in the colonial period with special reference to southern provinces. Agricultural history, v. 4, Jan. 1930: 1–9.   S1.A16, v. 4

10186
Klingaman, David C.   Food surpluses and deficits in the American colonies, 1768–1772. Journal of economic history, v. 31, Sept. 1971: 553–569.
HC10.J64, v. 31

10187
Loehr, Rodney C.   The influence of English agriculture upon American agriculture, 1775–1825. 1938.
Thesis (Ph.D.)—University of Minnesota.

10188
Loehr, Rodney C.   Self-sufficiency on the farm. Agricultural history, v. 26, Apr. 1952: 37–42.
S1.A16, v. 26
Argues that the 18th-century farmer was not self-sufficient, but engaged in commercial agriculture.

10189
McDonald, Angus H.   Early American soil conservationists. [Washington, U.S. Govt. Print. Off., 1944] 63 p.

illus., ports. (U.S. Dept. of Agriculture. Miscellaneous publication no. 449)   S21.A46, no. 449
S623.M298
"Literature cited": p. 61–63.
Considers the work of Jared Eliot (1685–1763), Samuel Deane (1733–1814), Solomon Drowne (1753–1834), and John Taylor (1753–1824), among others.

10190
Sachs, William S.   Agricultural conditions in the northern colonies before the Revolution. Journal of economic history, v. 13, summer 1953: 274–290.
HC10.J64, v. 13

10191
Sakolski, Aaron M.   The great American land bubble; the amazing story of land-grabbing, speculations, and booms from colonial days to the present time. New York, Harper, 1932. xii, 373 p. illus., facsims., maps, plates, ports.   HD191.S3
Reprinted in New York by Johnson Reprint Co. (1966).
"Pre-Revolutionary precedents": p. 1–28.
"The post-Revolutionary wild land mania": p. 29–53.

10192
Schumacher, Max G.   The Northern farmer and his markets during the late colonial period. 1948. 194 l. fold. map.
Thesis (Ph.D.)—University of California.

10193
Scoville, Warren C.   Did colonial farmers "waste" our land? Southern economic journal, v. 20, Oct. 1953: 178–181.   HC107.A13A67, v. 20

10194
Shine, Mary L.   Ideas of the founders of the American nation on landed property. 1922.
Thesis (Ph.D.)—University of Wisconsin.

10195
Wilson, Mary T.   Americans learn to grow the Irish potato [1685–1796] New England quarterly, v. 32, Sept. 1959: 333–350.   F1.N62, v. 32

2. NEW ENGLAND

10196
Day, Clarence A.   A history of Maine agriculture, 1604–1860. Orono, Me., Printed at the University Press, 1954. ix, 318 p. port. (Maine. University. Bulletin, v. 56, no. 11. University of Maine studies, 2d ser., no. 68)   S451.M2D3
Bibliography: p. [299]–304.

10197
Jackson, Eric P.   Early uses of land in Rhode Island. *In* Geographical Society of Philadelphia. Bulletin, v. 24, Apr. 1926: 69–87. illus.   G3.G34, v. 24

10198

Lockridge, Kenneth A.   Land, population and the evolution of New England society, 1630–1790. Past and present, no. 39, Apr. 1968: 62–80.   D1.P37, no. 39

3. MIDDLE ATLANTIC REGION

10199

Fletcher, Stevenson W.   Pennsylvania agriculture and country life. [v. 1] 1640–1840. Harrisburg, Pennsylvania Historical and Museum Commission, 1950. xiv, 605 p. illus., maps, ports.   S451.P4F55, v. 1

"Bibliographical notes": p. 542–587.

A social and economic review of rural life that treats such topics as buildings and equipment, labor, soil fertility, crops, livestock, horticulture, transportation, marketing, profit and loss, industries associated with agriculture, the farm home, food and clothing, family life, social customs in the home and community, and the rural school and church.

10200

Hedrick, Ulysses P.   A history of agriculture in the state of New York. [Albany] Printed for the New York State Agricultural Society, 1933. xiii, 462 p. illus., maps, plates, ports.   S451.N56H4

"Books helpful to the author": p. 445–450.
Reprinted in New York by Hill and Wang (1966).
"The agricultural legacy of the colony": p. 64–83.

10201

Landis, Ira D.   Mennonite agriculture in colonial Lancaster County, Pennsylvania: the first intensive agriculture in America. Mennonite quarterly review, v. 19, Oct. 1945: 254–272.   BX8101.M4, v. 19

10202

Lemon, James T.   The agricultural practices of national groups in eighteenth-century southeastern Pennsylvania. Geographical review, v. 56, Oct. 1966: 467–496. maps.   G1.G35, v. 56

10203

McCormick, Richard P.   The Royal Society, the grape, and New Jersey. In New Jersey Historical Society. Proceedings, v. 81, Apr. 1963: 75–84.   F131.N58, v. 81

On the society's effort to stimulate wine production in the colonies.

10204

Miller, Frederic K.   The farmer at work in colonial Pennsylvania. Pennsylvania history, v. 3, Apr. 1936: 115–123.   F146.P597, v. 3

10205

Reubens, Beatrice G.   Pre-emptive rights in the disposition of a confiscated estate: Philipsburgh Manor, New York. William and Mary quarterly, 3d ser., v. 22, July 1965: 435–456.   F221.W71, 3d s., v. 22

Under New York's confiscation law of 1779 the patriotic tenants of convicted Loyalists were permitted, through preemption, to buy their own farms at fair market value.

10206

Tilton, James.   James Tilton's notes on the agriculture of Delaware in 1788. Edited by R. O. Bausman and J. A. Munroe. Agricultural history, v. 20, July 1946: 176–187.   S1.A16, v. 20

10207

Wilkinson, Norman B.   Land policy and speculation in Pennsylvania, 1779–1800. 1958. ([375] p.)
        Micro AC–1, no. 58–3382

Thesis (Ph.D.)—University of Pennsylvania.
Abstracted in Dissertation Abstracts, v. 19, Oct. 1958, p. 793–794.

10208

Woodward, Carl R.   Agricultural legislation in colonial New Jersey. Agricultural history, v. 3, Jan. 1929: 15–28.   S1.A16, v. 3

10209

Woodward, Carl R.   The development of agriculture in New Jersey, 1640–1880, a monographic study in agricultural history. New Brunswick, N.J., New Jersey Agricultural Experiment Station, Rutgers University, 1927. 321 p. illus., facsims., ports.   S451.N55W6

Bibliography: p. 294–314.

10210

Wright, James.   Hemp and hop growing in Lancaster County in 1775. In Lancaster County (Pa.) Historical Society. Papers, v. 9, May/June 1905: 285–296.
        F157.L2L5, v. 9

Contemporary views.

10211

Yoshpe, Harry B.   The DeLancey estate; did the Revolution democratize landholding in New York? In New York State Historical Association. New York history, v. 17, Apr. 1936: 167–179. map.   F116.N865, v. 17

4. THE SOUTH

10212

Ballagh, James C.   Introduction to southern economic history—the land system. In American Historical Association. Annual report. 1897. Washington, 1898. p. 99–129.   E172.A60, 1897

Compares the exploitative land system of the South in the 18th century with that of the North.

10213

Bliss, Willard F.   The rise of tenancy in Virginia. Virginia magazine of history and biography, v. 58, Oct. 1950: 427–441.   F221.V91, v. 58

10214

Bonner, James C.   A history of Georgia agriculture, 1732–1860. Athens, University of Georgia Press [1964] viii, 242 p.   S451.G3B6

Bibliography: p. 233–236.

Surveying developments to the end of the 18th century in the first three chapters, the author concludes that independence significantly affected the character of Georgia agriculture. The termination of the imperial bounty ended the production of indigo silk, and the particularly large public domain established in the new state generated a speculative interest in land that remained the central theme of Georgia history for the next half century.

10215
Bonner, James C.   The open range livestock industry of colonial Georgia. Georgia review, v. 17, 1963: 85–92.
AP2.G375, v. 17

10216
[Bordley, John Beale]   A summary view of the courses of crops, in the husbandry of England & Maryland; with a comparison of their products; and a system of improved courses, proposed for farms in America. Philadelphia, Printed by C. Cist, 1784. 22 p.
S603.B72 Rare Bk. Coll.
AC901.H3, v. 39 Rare Bk. Coll.

10217
Cabell, Nathaniel F.   Some fragments of an intended report on the post-Revolutionary history of agriculture in Virginia. William and Mary College quarterly historical magazine, v. 26, Jan. 1918: 145–168.
F221.W71, v. 26

With notes by Earl G. Swem.

10218
Cathey, Cornelius O.   Agricultural developments in North Carolina, 1783–1860. Chapel Hill, University of North Carolina Press, 1956. 229 p. (The James Sprunt studies in history and political science, v. 38)
F251.J28, v. 38
S451.N8C3

Bibliography: p. [207]–220.

In the early chapters the author treats agricultural trends during the Confederation period.

10219
Coon, David L.   The development of market agriculture in South Carolina, 1670–1785. 1972. ([396] p.)
Micro AC–1, no. 73–17,163

Thesis (Ph.D.)—University of Illinois at Urbana-Champaign.

Abstracted in *Dissertation Abstracts International*, v. 34A, Aug. 1973, p. 697–698.

10220
Craven, Avery O.   Soil exhaustion as a factor in the agricultural history of Virginia and Maryland, 1606–1860. Urbana, University of Illinois [ᶜ1926] 179 p. (University of Illinois studies in the social sciences, v. 13, no. 1)
H31.I4, v. 13, no. 1
S451.V8C7

Bibliography: p. 165–172.
Reprinted in Gloucester, Mass., by P. Smith (1965).

In a detailed study of agricultural practices, the author finds that scarcity of labor and lack of capital produced a destructive land-use system during the 17th and 18th centuries that threw the burden of production on the soil. The restrictive Navigation Acts and the high cost of the tobacco consignment trade magnified the effects and contributed to a drop in land prices, a decline in the tobacco trade, the impoverishment of the small farmer, and a general westward migration in search of better land. Craven concludes that prosperity was not restored until such large planters as George Washington founded agricultural societies, experimented with fertilizers and plows, and introduced new crops and methods of cultivation.

10221
Doar, David.   Rice and rice planting in the South Carolina low country. Charleston, S.C., Charleston Museum, 1936. 70 p. illus., plates (part fold.) (Contributions from the Charleston museum, 8)
SB191.R5D57

Contents: Rice and rice planting in South Carolina low country, by David Doar.—The last days of rice planting, by T. D. Ravenel.—The true story of how the Madagascar gold seed rice was introduced into South Carolina, by A. S. Salley.—Bibliography of the rice industry in South Carolina, by A. S. Salley (p. 54–68).

10222
Dunbar, Gary S.   Colonial Carolina cowpens. Agricultural history, v. 35, July 1961: 125–130. map.
S1.A16, v. 35

More than a mere enclosure, the South Carolina "cowpen" was like the headquarters for a "ranch" operation where the owner commonly held title to the cowpen land on which the dwellings, outbuildings, and animal enclosures sat, but not to the savannas or cane swamps over which the cattle ranged.

10223
The Equine F F Vs, a study of the evidence for the English horses imported into Virginia before the Revolution.   Virginia magazine of history and biography, v. 35, Oct. 1927: 329–370. plates, ports.
F221.V91, v. 35

10224
Franklin, W. Neil.   Agriculture in colonial North Carolina. North Carolina historical review, v. 3, Oct. 1926: 539–574.
F251.N892, v. 3

10225
Gray, Lewis C.   History of agriculture in the southern United States to 1860. By Lewis Cecil Gray, assisted by Esther Katherine Thompson, with an introductory note by Henry Charles Taylor. Washington, Carnegie Institution of Washington, 1933. 2 v. (xix, 1086 p.) illus., maps. [Carnegie Institution of Washington, Publication no. 430]
S445.G8
HC101.C75, no. 7
AS32.A5, no. 430

Bibliography: v. 2, p. [943]–1016.
Reprinted in Gloucester, Mass., by P. Smith (1958).

A detailed survey of social, economic, institutional, and sectional aspects of southern agriculture. Focusing on the evolution of the plantation system, which he sees as an outgrowth of European capitalism and the English efforts to establish agricultural and commercial colonies, the author deals with such topics as the land system, methods of cultivation, grain and other crops, livestock husbandry, the tobacco industry and trade, marketing, and plantation management. Gray devotes the first volume to the colonial period and the first four chapters of volume 2 to the years 1775–95.

10226
Klingaman, David C.   The significance of grain in the development of the tobacco colonies. Journal of economic history, v. 29, June 1969: 268–278.   HC10.J64, v. 29

Argues that the production and export of grain, and not tobacco, was responsible for the revitalization of the Virginia economy in the late colonial period.

10227
Laing, Wesley N.   Cattle in early Virginia. 1954. ([273] p.)
Micro AC–1, no. 9652

Thesis (Ph.D.)—University of Virginia.
Abstracted in *Dissertation Abstracts*, v. 14, no. 10, 1954, p. 1687.

The growth of cattle raising in early Virginia and its relation to the plantation economy and westward expansion.

10228
Land, Aubrey C., *comp.*   Bases of the plantation society. Columbia, University of South Carolina Press [1969] vi, 242 p. (Documentary history of the United States) HN9.A13L35 1969

Includes bibliographies.

Arranges selected documents under broad headings related to land, labor, husbandry, enterprise, capital, and the social milieu essential to production.

10229
Land, Aubrey C.   Economic behavior in a planting society: the eighteenth-century Chesapeake. Journal of southern history, v. 33, Nov. 1967: 469–485.
F206.J68, v. 33

10230
Low, W. A.   The farmer in post-Revolutionary Virginia, 1783–1789. Agricultural history, v. 25, July 1951: 122–127.   S1.A16, v. 25

10231
Merrens, Harry Roy.   Colonial North Carolina in the eighteenth century; a study in historical geography. Chapel Hill, University of North Carolina Press [1964] ix, 293 p. charts, maps.   F257.M4

Bibliography: p. [266]–288.

Emphasizing the ecological impact of fire and man upon the land, the author studies changes in population, utilization of forests, commercial farming, and trade during the years 1750–75. He finds that a large-scale influx of migrants and other factors, such as economic and cultural variables among settlers, were the basic causes of change in the colony's geography.

10232
Potter, David M.   The rise of the plantation system in Georgia. Georgia historical quarterly, v. 16, June 1932: 114–135.   F281.G2975, v. 16

10233
Range, Willard.   The agricultural revolution in royal Georgia, 1752–1775. Agricultural history, v. 21, Oct. 1947: 250–255.   S1.A16, v. 21

10234
Seiler, William H.   Land processioning in colonial Virginia. William and Mary quarterly, 3d ser., v. 6, July 1949: 416–436.   F221.W71, 3d s., v. 6

As an established feature of the colony's land policy, the parish vestries, under the direction of the county courts, assumed the duty of determining property lines—a practice that was not discontinued until the disestablishment of the Church of England in Virginia in 1785.

10235
Sharrer, G. Terry.   Indigo in Carolina, 1671–1796. South Carolina historical magazine, v. 72, Apr. 1971: 94–103.   F266.S55, v. 72

10236
Shryock, Richard H.   British versus German traditions in colonial agriculture. Mississippi Valley historical review, v. 26, June 1939: 39–54.   E171.J87, v. 26

Suggests that southern agricultural practices—the money crop, the plantation system, and slavery—were determined more by cultural rather than environmental imperatives.

10237
Stoney, Samuel G.   Plantations of the Carolina low country. Edited by Albert Simons & Samuel Lapham, Jr., with an introduction by John Mead Howells. Charleston, S.C., Carolina Art Association, 1938. 243 p. illus., maps (on lining papers), plans, plates.   F270.S76 NA7235.S6S8 1938

Bibliography: p. 242–243.

10238
Tschan, Francis J.   The Virginia planter: some aspects of the economic history of Virginia, 1700–1775. 1916. xxxix, 428 l.

Thesis (Ph.D.)—University of Chicago.

LABOR AND THE LABORING CLASSES

1. GENERAL

10239
Carpenters' Company of the City and County of Philadelphia.   The rules of work of the Carpenters'

Company of the City and County of Philadelphia, 1786, with the original copper plate illustrations. Annotated, with an introduction by Charles E. Peterson. Princeton, Pyne Press, 1971. xxiii, xv, 47 p. plates.
TH5608.C25 1971a

First published in 1786 under the title *Articles of the Carpenters Company of Philadelphia: And Their Rules for Measuring and Valuing House-Carpenters Work.*

10240

Crowley, John E. Industry, frugality, and community: the persuasion of work in early America [1700–1770] 1970. ([333] p.)   Micro AC–1, no. 72–28,952

Thesis (Ph.D.)—Johns Hopkins University.
Abstracted in *Dissertation Abstracts International,* v. 33A, Nov. 1972, p. 2263–2264.

Feels that a study of the values surrounding the work ethic provides an understanding of the colonists' view of the relationship between self and society.

10241

Jernegan, Marcus W. Laboring and dependent classes in colonial America, 1607–1783; studies of the economic, educational, and social significance of slaves, servants, apprentices, and poor folk. Chicago, Ill., University of Chicago Press [ᶜ1931]. xiii, 256 p. (Social service monographs, no. 17)   E88.J57

"Bibliographical note": p. 211–212.
Reprinted in New York by Ungar (1960).

Focusing on conditions in New England and the southern colonies, the author presents essays on the economic and social aspects of Negro slavery and indentured servitude, on the education of poor children and apprentices, and on types of public poor relief systems.

10242

Johnson, Whittington B. Negro laboring classes in early America, 1750–1820. 1970. ([275] p.)
Micro AC–1, no. 71–13,073

Thesis (Ph.D.)—University of Georgia.

Abstracted in *Dissertation Abstracts International,* v. 31A, May 1971, p. 5986.

10243

McKee, Samuel. Labor in colonial New York, 1664–1776. New York, Columbia University Press, 1935. 193 p. (Studies in history, economics and public law, no. 410)
H31.C7, no. 410
HD8083.N7M3 1935a

Issued also as thesis (Ph.D.)—Columbia University.
Bibliography: p. 180–187.
Reprinted in Port Washington, N.Y., by I. J. Friedman (1965).

An institutional study of the four modes of labor—free, apprenticed, indentured, and enslaved.

10244

Morris, Richard B. Criminal conspiracy and early labor combinations in New York. Political science quarterly, v. 52, Mar. 1937: 51–85.   H1.P8, v. 52

Examines several instances of labor combinations and the collective actions of worker and producer groups during the colonial and Revolutionary periods.

10245

Morris, Richard B. Government and labor in early America. New York, Columbia University Press, 1946. xvi, 557 p.   HD8068.M65

Bibliographic footnotes.
Reprinted in New York by Octagon Books (1965).

Concentrating upon the legal and social status of free laborers, apprentices, and indentured servants, the author examines the relationships between labor and government, including the British imperial administration, Continental Congress, and county, parish, and town officials. Morris investigates such topics as the regulation of wages and prices during the Revolution, collective action by workers, child labor, absenteeism, labor practices of military authorities, and the sources, working conditions, and discipline of bound labor.

10246

Morris, Richard B. Labor and mercantilism in the Revolutionary era. *In* The era of the American Revolution; studies inscribed to Evarts Boutell Greene. Edited by Richard B. Morris. New York, Columbia University Press, 1939. p. 76–139.   E203.E74

Examines the climate of economic opinion and practice during the Revolution to determine the reasons for the introduction of systems of wage and price controls.

10247

Smith, Robert A. The technologies and working conditions of colonial free laborers [1620–1776] 1950. ([228] p.)   Micro AC–1, no. 1669

Thesis (Ph.D.)—University of Illinois.
Abstracted in *Microfilm Abstracts,* v. 10, no. 2, 1950, p. 95–97.

10248

U.S. *Bureau of Labor Statistics.* History of wages in the United States from colonial times to 1928. October 1929. Washington, U.S. Govt. Print. Off., 1929. vi, 527 p. (Bulletin of the United States Bureau of Labor Statistics, no. 499. Wages and hours of labor series)
HD8051.A62, no. 499
HD4973.A45 1928

Part 1 was prepared by Estelle M. Stewart: pt. 2 was prepared under the direction of J. C. Bowen, of the Bureau of Labor Statistics.
Issued also as House doc. 49, 71st Congress, 1st session.
"List of published sources": p. 140–142.
Contents: Introduction.—From colonial times to 1840.—From 1840 to 1928.—Appendixes.
Reprinted in Detroit by the Gale Research Co. (1966).

2. INDENTURED SERVANTS

10249

Ballagh, James C.   White servitude in the colony of Virginia: a study of the system of indentured labor in the American colonies. Baltimore, Johns Hopkins Press, 1895. 99 p. (Johns Hopkins University studies in historical and political science, 13th ser., no. 6–7)

H31.J6, 13th s., no. 6–7
HD4875.U5B2

Bibliography: p. [96]–99.
Reprinted in New York by B. Franklin (1969).

Includes a brief discussion on the institution's rapid decline between 1750 and 1789 when the growth of Negro slavery persuaded the legislature to make white servitude a voluntary condition for adults, to reduce the years of service for bastard children of servant women, and to give children the rights of apprentices.

10250

Geiser, Karl F.   Redemptioners and indentured servants in the colony and commonwealth of Pennsylvania. New Haven, Conn., Tuttle, Morehouse & Taylor Co. [1901] 128 p.   F160.R3G3

Supplement to the *Yale Review*, v. 10, Aug. 1901.
Bibliography: p. 120–125.

10251

Haar, Charles M.   White indentured servants in colonial New York. Americana, v. 34, July 1940: 370–392.

E171.A53, v. 34

10252

Herrick, Cheesman A.   White servitude in Pennsylvania; indentured and redemption labor in colony and commonwealth. Philadelphia, J. J. McVey, 1926. ix, 330 p. facsims.   F160.R3H4

"The subject matter of this book was presented in its original form as a thesis at the University of Pennsylvania in 1899."—Preface.
"Sources": p. 309–326.
Reprinted in New York by Negro Universities Press (1969) and in Freeport, N.Y., by Books for Libraries Press (1970).

An institutional study in which the author investigates such topics as the demand for servants in relation to the need for settlers; the sentiment against Negro slavery; transportation from England and Germany in exchange for service; the sale, distribution, and discipline of servants; and their use as soldiers in colonial wars. While importation of servants ceased during the Revolution, it resumed during the Confederation period with an added emphasis upon the element of apprenticeship.

10253

Hoyt, William D.   The white servants at "Northampton," 1772–74. Maryland historical magazine, v. 33, June 1938: 126–133.   F176.M18, v. 33

A discussion of the origins, occupations, and physical characteristics of 85 white male servants on the plantation Northampton in Baltimore County.

10254

McCormac, Eugene I.   White servitude in Maryland, 1634–1820. Baltimore, Johns Hopkins Press, 1904. 112 p. (Johns Hopkins University studies in historical and political science, 22d ser., no. 3–4)

H31.J6, 22 s., no. 3–4
HD4875.U5M2
E175.J65, 22 s., no. 3–4

Summarizes information on the use of the seven-year indenture to promote immigration, the varying treatment of servants, the superiority of indentured labor over that of slaves and freemen, the constant problem of runaways, and the increased number of convicts sent to Maryland after 1750. The Revolution interrupted the movement of servants to Maryland, and British laws forbidding emigration to the United States all but ended the practice.

10255

Miller, William.   The effects of the American Revolution on indentured servitude. Pennsylvania history, v. 7, July 1940: 131–141.   F146.P597, v. 7

The war disrupted but did not dissolve the system.

10256

Smith, Abbot E.   Colonists in bondage; white servitude and convict labor in America, 1607–1776. Chapel Hill, Published for the Institute of Early American History and Culture at Williamsburg, Va., by the University of North Carolina Press, 1947. viii, 435 p.

HD4875.U5S5

"Bibliographical note": p. 397–417.
Reprinted in Gloucester, Mass., by P. Smith (1965).

Although Smith concentrates upon the institutional development of indentured servitude in the 17th and early 18th centuries, there are references to the period after 1750 in chapters on Scotch migration, convict transportation, and the purchase, legal status, and treatment of redemptioners. He concludes that the system was generally a sound one, for not only did it provide a workable method of supplying cheap labor but, in the end, perhaps one in five completed his indenture and became a landholder or an artisan.

10257

Smith, Warren B.   White servitude in colonial South Carolina. Columbia, University of South Carolina Press, 1961. ix, 151 p. facsims., map.   HD4875.U5S53

Bibliography: p. 140–143.

Offers excerpts from 18th-century statutes and indentures as well as statistical tables on servitude in support of the thesis that South Carolinians wanted servants in addition to slaves and that indentured whites when freed became a major factor in the growth of the colony.

10258

Sollers, Basil.   Transported convict laborers in Maryland during the colonial period. Maryland historical magazine, v. 2, Mar. 1907: 17–47.   F176.M18, v.2

10259

Towner, Lawrence W.   The indentures of Boston's poor apprentices: 1734–1805. *In* Colonial Society of Massachusetts, *Boston*. Publications. v. 43. Transactions, 1956/63. Boston, 1966. p. 417–468.   F61.C71, v. 43

"Table of indentures": p. 435–467.

SLAVERY AND THE SLAVE TRADE

1. GENERAL

10260

Aptheker, Herbert.   American Negro slave revolts, by Herbert Aptheker. New York, Columbia University Press, 1943. 409 p. (Studies in history, economics and public law, no. 501)   H31.C7, no. 501

Issued also as thesis (Ph.D.)—Columbia University. Bibliography: p. 375–405.

The author provides scattered references to the Revolutionary period in his analysis of slave resistance and rebellion from the 17th century to the Civil War.

10261

Brackett, Jeffery R.   The status of the slave, 1775–1789. *In* Jameson, John Franklin, *ed.* Essays in the constitutional history of the United States in the formative period, 1775–1789. Boston, Houghton, Mifflin, 1889. p. [263]–311.   KF4541.A2J3 1889

10262

Bergman, Peter M.   The chronological history of the Negro in America. New York, Harper & Row [1969] 698 p.   E185.B46

"Bibliography of bibliographies": p. 617–624.

The period 1763–89 is summarized on p. 42–68.

10263

Carnathan, Wiley J.   American Negro slavery during the Revolutionary era, 1760–1793. 1949. 425 l.

Thesis (Ph.D.)—University of Texas.

10264

Catterall, Helen H. T., *ed.*   Judicial cases concerning American slavery and the Negro. Washington, D.C., Carnegie Institution of Washington, 1926–37. 5 v. [Carnegie Institution of Washington. Publication no. 374. Papers of the Division of Historical Research]   [E441.C35] Micro 35236

"The index has been prepared by Mr. David M. Matteson."—Preface, v. 1.

Vols. 4–5, "with additions by James J. Hayden."

"Under each state, the cases are set in chronological order, cases in the federal courts arising in that state being incorporated in the placed where their dates would bring them. The compilation has been brought to a close, in each state, at the end of the year 1875."—Preface, v. 1.

Contents: 1. Cases from the courts of England, Virginia, West Virginia, and Kentucky.—2. Cases from the courts of North Carolina, South Carolina, and Tennessee.—

3. Cases from the courts of Georgia, Florida, Alabama, Mississippi, and Louisiana.—4. Cases from the courts of New England, the middle states, and the District of Columbia.—5. Cases from the courts of states north of the Ohio and west of the Mississippi rivers, Canada and Jamaica.

Reprinted in New York by Negro Universities Press (1968. KF4545.S5C3 1968b).

10265

Eighteenth century slaves as advertised by their masters.   Journal of Negro history, v. 1, Apr. 1916: 163–216.   E185.J86, v. 1

Taken from Boston, Philadelphia, Maryland, and South Carolina newspapers.

10266

Jernegan, Marcus W.   Slavery and conversion in the American colonies. American historical review, v. 21, Apr. 1916: 504–527.   E171.A57, v. 21

Although there was less opposition on the part of the masters towards both conversion and baptism from 1724 to 1776, figures indicate that there was no very great increase in the proportionate number of slaves Christianized.

10267

Mecklin, John M.   The evolution of the slave status in American democracy [1619–1789] Journal of Negro history, v. 2, Apr. 1917: 105–125.   E185.J86, v. 2

10268

Moore, Wilbert E.   Slave law and the social structure. Journal of Negro history, v. 26, Apr. 1941: 171–202.   E185.J86, v. 26

10269

Phillips, Ulrich B.   American Negro slavery; a survey of the supply, employment, and control of Negro labor as determined by the plantation régime. New York, D. Appleton, 1918. xi, 529 p.   E441.P549

Bibliographic footnotes.

Besides a brief chapter on the effects of the Revolution upon slavery, there are scattered references to the institution during the late colonial and Confederation periods in chapters on such topics as plantation life, town slaves, and free Negroes.

10270

Read, Allen W.   Speech defects and mannerisms among slaves and servants in colonial America. Quarterly journal of speech, v. 24, Oct. 1938: 397–401.   PN4071.Q3, v. 24

Based on newspaper advertisements for runaways.

10271

Read, Allen W.   The speech of Negroes in colonial America. Journal of Negro history, v. 24, July 1939: 247–258.   E185.J86, v. 24

Based on newspaper descriptions of runaway slaves.

10272

Robinson, Donald L. Slavery in the structure of American politics, 1765–1820. New York, Harcourt Brace Jovanovich [1970, ᶜ1971] xii, 564 p. (The Founding of the American Republic) E446.R63

Includes bibliographic references.

In the early chapters the author examines the place of slavery in Revolutionary ideology, its part in the arguments over the Articles of Confederation, and its influence upon debates concerning representation and federal powers during the Philadelphia Convention. Robinson concludes that most American statesmen did not intend to apply libertarian doctrines to blacks; they knew that slavery was not disappearing where it was strongest and, believing the institution to be ungovernable, tried to ignore white racism in an effort to minimize sectional differences.

10273

Wax, Darold D. The Negro in early America. Social studies, v. 60, Mar. 1969: 109–119. D16.3.S65, v. 60

A historiographical appraisal.

2. NEW ENGLAND

10274

Johnston, William D. Slavery in Rhode Island, 1755–1776. *In* Rhode Island Historical Society. Publications. new ser., v. 2; 1893/94. Providence, 1894. p. [113]–164.
[F76.R51, v. 2]
Micro 39268

——— ——— Detached copy. E445.R4J6

10275

Logan, Gwendolyn E. The slave in Connecticut during the American Revolution. *In* Connecticut Historical Society, *Hartford*. Bulletin, v. 30, July 1965: 73–80.
F91.C67, v. 30

10276

Mitchell, Mary H. Slavery in Connecticut and especially in New Haven. *In* New Haven Colony Historical Society, *New Haven*. Papers. v. 10, New Haven, 1951. p. 286–312. F98.N5, v. 10

10277

Moore, George H. Notes on the history of slavery in Massachusetts. New-York, D. Appleton, 1866. 256 p.
E445.M4M8

Reprinted in New York by Negro Universities Press (1968).

Uses lengthy quotations from petitions, diaries, letters, and legal documents to trace the growth of the institution in the 17th century and the development of an antislavery movement in the 18th. The lawsuits brought by slaves that resulted in emancipation in 1783 were followed by attempts to rid the state of freedmen.

10278

Steiner, Bernard C. History of slavery in Connecticut. Baltimore, Johns Hopkins Press, 1893. 84 p. (Johns Hopkins University studies in historical and political science, 11th ser., no. 9–10)
H31.J6, 11th s., no. 9–10
E445.C7S8

Bibliographic footnotes.

A study of colonial and state laws, testimony and decisions in court cases, and various resolutions and petitions from the years before the Civil War. Slavery was generally accepted in Connecticut until 1774, when Revolutionary ideology prompted an amelioration of the institution. Gradual, free-will emancipation culminated in formal abolition in 1848.

3. MIDDLE ATLANTIC REGION

10279

Connolly, James C. Slavery in colonial New Jersey and the causes operating against its extension. *In* New Jersey Historical Society. Proceedings, new ser., v. 14, Apr. 1929: 181–202. F131.N58, n.s., v. 14

10280

Cooley, Henry S. A study of slavery in New Jersey. Baltimore, Johns Hopkins Press, 1896. 60 p. (Johns Hopkins University studies in historical and political science, 14th ser., no. 9/10) H31.J6, 14th s., no. 9/10
E445.N54C7

Bibliography: p. 59–60.

10281

Earl, Robert. Slavery in the colony and state of New York. *In* Herkimer County Historical Society. Papers. v. 1; 1896/98. Herkimer, N.Y., 1899. p. 103–114.
F127.H5H5, v. 1

10282

Ireland, Ralph R. Slavery on Long Island; a study of economic motivation. Journal of Long Island history, v. 6, spring 1966: 1–12. F127.L8J75, v. 6

10283

McManus, Edgar J. A history of Negro slavery in New York. Foreword by Richard B. Morris. [Syracuse, N.Y.] Syracuse University Press [1966] xi, 219 p.
E445.N56M3

"Bibliographical note": p. 201–212.

The author's thesis (Ph.D.), *Negro Slavery in New York*, was submitted to Columbia University in 1959 (Micro AC–1, no. 59–4077).

Investigates such topics as the slave trade, the profitability of slavery, discipline, conspiracies, and abolition. Importation of Negroes from Africa was greatest between 1750 and 1770, but the supply dwindled, and internal trade became dominant at the New York market. Most slaveholders were small entrepreneurs who found ownership of skilled Negroes more profitable than hiring whites. While Revolutionary ideals fueled the antislavery movement among the upper class, laborers favored abolition in order to eliminate the slave as a competitor.

10284

Morgan, Edwin V.   Slavery in New York; the status of the slave under the English colonial government. *In* American Historical Association. Papers, v. 5, Oct. 1891: 3–16.   E172.A65, v. 5

10285

Moss, Simeon F.   The persistence of slavery and involuntary servitude in a free state (1685–1866). Journal of Negro history, v. 35, July 1950: 289–314.
   E185.J86, v. 35

Although slavery in New Jersey was a dying institution by the mid-18th century, the movement for abolition was a long and tedious one.

10286

Northrup, Ansel Judd.   Slavery in New York, a historical sketch. Albany, University of the State of New York, 1900. [243]–313 p. (New York (State). State Library, Albany. History bulletin no. 4)
   Z881.N61BH, no. 4

10287

Olson, Edwin.   The slave code in colonial New York. Journal of Negro history, v. 29, Apr. 1944: 147–165.
   E185.J86, v. 29

10288

Strange, Charles A.   One hundred years of Negro slavery. New Rochelle [New York], 1698–1799. Westchester historian, v. 44, winter 1968: 3–8.
   F127.W5W594, v. 44

10289

Turner, Edward R.   Slavery in Pennsylvania. Baltimore, Lord Baltimore Press, 1911. 88 p.   E445.P3T9

Thesis (Ph.D.)—Johns Hopkins University, 1910. Bibliographic footnotes.

Arranging his work topically, Turner includes scattered references to slavery at the time of the Revolution.

10290

Wax, Darold D.   The demand for slave labor in colonial Pennsylvania. Pennsylvania history, v. 34, Oct. 1967: 331–345.   F146.P597, v. 34

10291

Williams, Oscar R.   Blacks and colonial legislation in the middle colonies. 1969.

Thesis (Ph.D.)—Ohio State University.

4. The South

10292

Ballagh, James C.   A history of slavery in Virginia. Baltimore, Johns Hopkins Press, 1902. viii, 160 p. (Johns Hopkins University studies in historical and political science. Extra volume, 24)   H31.J62, v. 24
   E445.V8B18

Bibliography: p. 149–154.

Using a topical approach, the author includes occasional references to the Revolutionary era in chapters on the slave trade, legal and social status of Negroes, and manumission.

10293

Bassett, John S.   Slavery and servitude in the colony of North Carolina. Baltimore, Johns Hopkins Press, 1896. 86 p. (Johns Hopkins University studies in historical and political science, 14th ser., no. 4–5)
   H31.J6, 14th s., no. 4–5
   E445.N8B3

"Authorities used": p. [5]

Concentrating upon the 18th century, the author studies such topics as legal codes, religion, social life, runaways, insurrections, manumission practices, free Negroes, Indian slavery, and white servitude.

10294

Brackett, Jeffrey R.   The Negro in Maryland; a study of the institution of slavery. Baltimore, N. Murray, Publication Agent, Johns Hopkins University, 1889. 268 p. (Johns Hopkins University studies in historical and political science, extra v. 6)   H31.J62, v. 6
   E445.M3B7

Reprinted in New York by Negro Universities Press (1969) and in Freeport, N.Y., by Books for Libraries Press (1969).

Surveying legislation enacted between 1639 and the Civil War, the author supplies information about the legal status of Indian slaves, white indentured servants, and black slaves as well as manumissions and free Negroes. Brackett makes infrequent references to the Revolutionary period, but laws passed before 1763 remained in effect during the war.

10295

Clark, Ernest J.   Aspects of the North Carolina slave code, 1715–1860. North Carolina historical review, v. 39, winter 1962: 148–164.   F251.N892, v. 39

10296

Corry, John P.   Racial elements in colonial Georgia. Georgia historical quarterly, v. 20, Mar. 1936: 30–40.
   F281.G2975, v. 20

10297

Duncan, John D.   Servitude and slavery in colonial South Carolina, 1670–1776. 1972. ([878] p.)
   Micro AC–1, no. 72–20,766

Thesis (Ph.D.)—Emory University.
Abstracted in *Dissertation Abstracts International*, v. 33A, July 1972, p. 249.

10298

Flanders, Ralph B.   Plantation slavery in Georgia. Chapel Hill, University of North Carolina Press, 1933. x, 326 p. illus., maps, plates.   E445.G3F62

Bibliography: p. 301–318.
Reprinted in Cos Cob, Conn., by J. E. Edwards (1967).

10299

Guild, June P.   Black laws of Virginia; a summary of the legislative acts of Virginia concerning Negroes from earliest times to the present. Richmond, Va., Whittet & Shepperson, 1936. 249 p.   E185.93.V8G9

Reprinted in New York by Negro Universities Press (1969).

Lists 59 laws, that were passed during the Revolutionary period, affecting the status of Negroes.

10300

Hast, Adele.   The legal status of the Negro in Virginia, 1705–1765. Journal of Negro history, v. 54, July 1969: 217–239.   E185.J86, v. 54

10301

Higgins, William Robert.   The geographical origins of Negro slaves in colonial South Carolina. South Atlantic quarterly, v. 70, winter 1971: 34–47.   AP2.S75, v. 70

10302

Jernegan, Marcus W.   Slavery and the beginnings of industrialism in the American colonies. American historical review, v. 25, Jan. 1920: 220–240.   E171.A57, v. 25

The industrial training the Negro slave artisan received before the Revolution made the self-sufficiency of the southern states possible during and after the war.

10303

Johnston, James H.   Race relations in Virginia & miscegenation in the South, 1776–1860. Foreword by Winthrop Jordan. Amherst, University of Massachusetts Press, 1970. xii, 362 p.   E185.93.V8J6

Bibliography: p. [340]–356.

The author's thesis (Ph.D.), with the same title, was submitted to the University of Chicago in 1937.

10304

Klein, Herbert S.   Slavery in the Americas; a comparative study of Virginia and Cuba. [Chicago] University of Chicago Press [1967] xi, 270 p.   HT1076.K55

Bibliographic footnotes.

Compares the nature and effects of the systems of slavery in Latin, Catholic, and feudal Cuba with that in Anglo-Saxon, Protestant, and capitalistic Virginia. The author finds that, under the more traditional institutions of slavery in Cuba, the crown and the church significantly limited the power of the owner over his slaves, and the class system offered considerable social mobility for Negroes and mulattoes who were released or escaped from slavery. In contrast, Klein contends that the Virginia system had a uniquely dehumanizing effect on its victims.

10305

McColley, Robert.   Slavery and Jeffersonian Virginia. Urbana, University of Illinois Press, 1964. 227 p. maps.   E445.V8M12

Bibliography: p. 200–208.

The author's thesis (Ph.D.), *Gentlemen and Slavery in Jefferson's Virginia*, was submitted to the University of California, Berkeley, in 1960.

Analyzing the conditions of slavery and the attitudes and influence of slaveholders between the Revolution and the War of 1812, the author indicates that progress toward emancipation was arrested during the 1780's as slavery was defended with increasing vigor. McColley finds little evidence that slavery was declining or that the institution had become economically unprofitable in post-Revolutionary Virginia.

10306

McColley, Robert.   Slavery in Jefferson's Virginia. Journal of the Central Mississippi Valley American Studies Association, v. 1, spring 1960: 23–31.
          E169.1.M6215, v. 1

10307

McCrady, Edward.   Slavery in the province of South Carolina (1670–1770). *In* American Historical Association. Annual report. 1895. Washington, 1896. p. 629–673.
          E172.A60, 1895

10308

Mullin, Gerald W.   Flight and rebellion; slave resistance in eighteenth-century Virginia. New York, Oxford University Press, 1972. xii, 219 p. illus.   E445.V8M8

Bibliography: p. 205–213.

The author's thesis (Ph.D.), *Patterns of Slave Behavior in Eighteenth-Century Virginia*, was submitted to the University of California, Berkeley, in 1968 (Micro AC–1, no. 68–13,940).

Drawing heavily upon letters, diaries, notebooks, and fugitive slave advertisements of white Virginians, the author investigates the characteristics and behavior of three groups of black slaves whose patterns of resistance varied. Recently arrived bondsmen knowing little English, possessing few work skills, and laboring on back country lands ran away and formed communal bands on the frontier. Acculturated Africans and American-born Negroes, who spoke English and worked on the main plantation usually as servants or artisans, most often became truants and thieves. The third group, consisting of articulate, relatively independent slaves who frequently hired their own time, sought individual fulfillment before 1775 within the black communities of urban centers like Williamsburg. Encouraged by Lord Dunmore's emancipation and inspired by Revolutionary ideology, they later attempted to overthrow the slave system in such plots as Gabriel Prosser's rebellion in 1800.

10309

Padgett, James A.   The status of slaves in colonial North Carolina. Journal of Negro history, v. 14, July 1929: 300–327.   E185.J86, v. 14

10310

Sheeler, John Reuben.   The Negro on the Virginia frontier. Journal of Negro history, v. 43, Oct. 1958: 279–297.
          E185.J86, v. 43

10311

Snell, William R.   Indian slavery in colonial South Carolina, 1671–1795. 1972. ([257] p.)

Micro AC–1, no. 73–19,561

Thesis (Ph.D.)—University of Alabama.
Abstracted in *Dissertation Abstracts International*, v. 34A, Aug. 1973, p. 713.

10312

Wax, Darold D.   Georgia and the Negro before the American Revolution. Georgia historical quarterly, v. 51, Mar. 1967: 63–77.   F281.G2975, v. 51

10313

Weeks, Stephen B.   Southern Quakers and slavery: a study in institutional history. Baltimore, Johns Hopkins Press, 1896. xiv, 400 p. fold. map. (Johns Hopkins University studies in historical and political science. Extra volume 15)   H31.J62, v. 15
                                                                E441.W4

Bibliography: p. [345]–362.
Reprinted in New York by Bergman Publishers (1968).

In his survey of the settlement, development, and decline of Quaker communities in Virginia and the Carolinas from 1660 to the Civil War, Weeks includes sections on Quaker pacifism, abolitionism, and westward migration during the Revolutionary period.

10314

West, Gerald M.   The status of the Negro in Virginia during the colonial period. New York, W. R. Jenkins [1889?] 76 p.   E445.V8W5

Thesis (Ph.D.)—Columbia College, 1890.
Bibliographic footnotes.

5. THE SLAVE TRADE

a. Contemporary Sources

10315

[Benezet, Anthony]   A short account of that part of Africa inhabited by the Negroes; with respect to the fertility of the country; the good disposition of many of the natives, and the manner by which the slave trade is carried on. Extracted from several authors, in order to shew the iniquity of that trade, and the falsity of the arguments usually advanced in its vindication. Philadelphia, 1762. 56 p.   HT1321.B4 1762 Rare Bk. Coll.

10316

Benezet, Anthony.   Some historical account of Guinea, its situation, produce and the the general disposition of its inhabitants. With an inquiry into the rise and progress of the slave-trade, its nature and lamentable effects. Also a re-publication of the sentiments of several authors of note, on this interesting subject; particularly an extract of a treatise, by Granville Sharp. Philadelphia, Printed by J. Crukshank, 1771. 144, 53, [6] p.
                    HT1331.B4 1771 Rare Bk. Coll.

10317

Champlin, Robert.   A Rhode Island slaver; trade book of the sloop *Adventure*, 1773–1774, from original manuscript in the library of George L. Shepley, with notes and introduction by Prof. Verner W. Crane. Providence, Shepley Library, 1922. 10 p.
                              HT1331.A5 1773

"The Trade book for the owners of the sloop Adventure is an account book kept by the master, Robert Champlin."—Preface.

10318

[Day, Thomas]   A letter from ********, in London, to his friend in America, on the subject of the slave-trade; together with some extracts, from approved authors of matters of fact, confirming the principles contained in said letter. New-York, Printed by S. Loudon, 1784. 28 p.   E446.D28 Rare Bk. Coll.

Also published at Philadelphia in 1784 under title *Fragment of an Original Letter on the Slavery of the Negroes*, with a statement that it was written in 1776 by Thomas Day.

10319

Donnan, Elizabeth, *ed.*   Documents illustrative of the history of the slave trade to America. Washington, D.C., Carnegie Institution of Washington, 1930–35. 4 v. fold. map. (Carnegie Institution of Washington. Publication no. 409)   E441.D68
                                    AS32.A5, no. 409

Contents: 1. 1441–1700.—2. The eighteenth century.—3. New England and the middle colonies.—4. The border colonies and the southern colonies.
Reprinted in New York by Octagon Books (1965).

In volume 2 the author presents a 62-page summary of developments in the 18th century and reprints 294 contemporary documents—petitions, memorials, indentures, and business records—39 of which are dated between 1763 and 1789. In similar fashion in v. 3, Donnan provides copies of 370 manuscripts related to the slave trade in New England and the middle colonies, including 160 from the Revolutionary period; in volume 4 she offers more than 440 transcripts for Maryland and the southern colonies, including 227 from the years 1763–1789.

10320

Swan, James.   A dissuasion to Great-Britain and the Colonies, from the slave trade to Africa. Shewing the contradiction this trade bears, both to laws divine and provincial; the disadvantages arising from it, and advantages from abolishing it, both to Europe and Africa, particularly to Britain and the plantations. Also shewing how to put this trade to Africa on a just and lawful footing. Boston, Printed by E. Russell [1772] 70 p.
                              HT991.S7 1772 Rare Bk. Coll.

10321

Terry, Roderick.   Some old papers relating to the Newport slave trade. *In* Newport Historical Society. Bulletin, no. 62, July 1927: 10–34.   F89.N5N615, no. 62

Chiefly progress reports from Captain William Einglish of the brigantine *Ann* to its owners, Jacob Rodriguez Rivera and Aaron Lopez, on a voyage made in 1772–74.

b. Secondary Works

10322

Blake, William O.   The history of slavery and the slave trade, ancient and modern. The forms of slavery that prevailed in ancient nations, particularly in Greece and Rome. The African slave trade and the political history of slavery in the United States. Columbus, Ohio, Published and sold exclusively by subscription by J. & H. Miller, 1857. 832 p. illus., plates.   HT861.B55

Reprinted in Miami, Fla., by Mnemosyne Pub. Co. (1969) and in two volumes in New York by Haskell House Publishers (1969).

10323

Deane, Charles.   The connection of Massachusetts with slavery and the slave-trade. *In* American Antiquarian Society, *Worcester, Mass.* Proceedings, new ser., v. 4, Oct. 1886: 191–222.   E172.A35, n.s., v. 4

——————— Offprint. Worcester, Mass., Printed by C. Hamilton, 1886. 34 p.   E445.M4D28

10324

Donnan, Elizabeth.   The New England slave trade after the Revolution. New England quarterly, v. 3, Apr. 1930: 251–278.   F1.N62, v. 3

10325

Donnan, Elizabeth.   The slave trade into South Carolina before the Revolution. American historical review, v. 33, July 1928: 804–828.   E171.A57, v. 33

Despite the rapid increase in the labor supply from 1730 to 1774, little economic advantage derived from the slave trade by the 1770's.

10326

Du Bois, William Edward Burghardt.   The suppression of the African slave-trade to the United States of America, 1638–1870. New York, Longmans, Green, 1896. xi, 335 p. (Harvard historical studies, v. 1)   E441.D81

Appendixes: A. A chronological conspectus of colonial and state legislation restricting the African slave-trade, 1641–1787.—B. A chronological conspectus of state, national, and international legislation, 1788–1871.—C. Typical cases of vessels engaged in the American slave-trade, 1619–1864.—D. Bibliography (p. [299]–325).

Reprinted in New York by Russell & Russell (1965) and by Dover Publications (1970).

In the section on the 18th century the author surveys the legislation restricting trade that was enacted by individual mainland colonies, describes the influence of the Revolution upon laws of the states, and examines the debates over suppression in the Constitutional Convention. While legal actions taken against the slave trade before 1774 tended to reflect local conditions, Du Bois finds that a national sentiment against the slave trade arose with the onset of the war and cites five principal reasons: the institution conflicted with Revolutionary ideals, fear of slave insurrections was increasing, commercial intercourse with British traders was being discouraged, slavery had failed economically in the northern states, and the American slave markets were overstocked, with low prices making slave merchants less powerful.

10327

Higgins, William Robert.   Charles Town merchants and factors dealing in the external Negro trade, 1735–1775. South Carolina historical magazine, v. 65, Oct. 1964: 205–217.   F266.S55, v. 65

Lists of merchants and factors receiving cargoes of slaves.

10328

Mason, George C.   The African slave trade in colonial times. American historical record, v. 1, July–Aug. 1872: 311–319, 338–345.   E171.P86, v. 1

10329

Leconfield, Hugh Archibald Wyndham, *Baron*.   The Atlantic and slavery, a report in the study group series of the Royal Institute of International Affairs. London, Oxford University Press, 1935. viii, 310 p. maps (part fold.) (Problems of imperial trusteeship. [2])   HT867.L44

Tracing the migration of native peoples on both sides of the Atlantic through the end of the 18th century, the author devotes four chapters to the changing relationships among Europeans, Indians, and Negroes along the southern coast of North America.

10330

Pope-Hennessy, James.   Sins of the fathers; a study of the Atlantic slave traders, 1441–1807. New York, Knopf, 1968. xiv, 286, x p. illus., maps, ports.   HT985.P6 1968

Bibliography: p. 281–286.

A selective narrative of the trade between the West African coast and the European colonies in the New World. The author concentrates on the British involvement and the effects of the trade on those who conducted or otherwise participated in it.

10331

Riddell, William R.   Pre-Revolutionary Pennsylvania and the slave trade. Pennsylvania magazine of history and biography, v. 52, Jan. 1928: 1–28.   F146.P65, v. 52

10332

Sheridan, Richard B.   Africa and the Carribbean in the Atlantic slave trade [1627–1775] American historical review, v. 77, Feb. 1972: 15–35. illus.   E171.A57, v. 77

Indicates that the conditions of slavery became less harsh in the decade or two preceding the Revolution.

10333
Wax, Darold D. Negro import duties in colonial Virginia; a study of British commercial policy and local public policy. Virginia magazine of history and biography, v. 79, Jan. 1971: 29–44.   F221.V91, v. 79

10334
Wax, Darold D. Negro imports into Pennsylvania, 1720–1766. Pennsylvania history, v. 32, July 1965: 254–287.   F146.P597, v. 32

10335
Wax, Darold D. Negro resistance to the early American slave trade. Journal of Negro history, v. 51, Jan. 1966: 1–15.   E185.J86, v. 51

Gives examples of Negro opposition to bondage from their capture in Africa through every stage of the slave trade.

10336
Wax, Darold D. The Negro slave trade in colonial Pennsylvania. 1962. ([418] p.) Micro AC–1, no. 63–3147

Thesis (Ph.D.)—University of Washington.
Abstracted in *Dissertation Abstracts*, v. 24, July 1963, p. 272.

Finds that the slave trade fell into three distinct phases, the last decade of heavy traffic being 1759–69. The assembly formally outlawed the Negro trade in 1788 and strengthened the legislation regarding abolition.

10337
Wax, Darold D. Quaker merchants and the slave trade in colonial Pennsylvania. Pennsylvania magazine of history and biography, v. 86, Apr. 1962: 143–159.   F146.P65, v. 86

6. PERCEPTIONS OF SLAVERY

10338
Aptheker, Herbert. The Quakers and Negro slavery. Journal of Negro history, v. 25, July 1940: 331–362.   E185.J86, v. 25

10339
Cantor, Milton. The image of the Negro in colonial literature. New England quarterly, v. 36, Dec. 1963: 452–477.   F1.N62, v. 36

Natural rights theorists insisted upon the political equality of Negroes, while biological and economic determinists attempted to demonstrate that blacks were basically inferior.

10340
Carroll, Kenneth L. Maryland Quakers and slavery [1650–1800] Maryland historical magazine, v. 45, Sept. 1950: 215–225.   F176.M18, v. 45

10341
Clifton, Denzil T. Anglicanism and Negro slavery in colonial America. Historical magazine of the Protestant Episcopal church, v. 39, Mar. 1970: 29–70.   BX5800.H5, v. 39

10342
Crane, Verner W. Benjamin Franklin on slavery and American liberties. Pennsylvania magazine of history and biography, v. 62, Jan. 1938: 1–11.   F146.P65, v. 62

Crane cites internal and external evidence to show that Franklin wrote "A Conversation Between an Englishman, a Scotchman, and an American, on the Subject of Slavery," which appeared in the London *Public Advertiser* in 1770 under the signature "N. N." The essay focuses on the contradiction between American slaveholding and demands for personal liberties.

10343
Crawford, Charles. Observations upon Negro-slavery. Philadelphia, Printed by J. Crukshank, 1784. 24 p.   E446.C89 Rare Bk. Coll.

10344
Degler, Carl N. Slavery and the genesis of American race prejudice. Comparative studies in society and history, v. 2, Oct. 1959: 49–66.   H1.C73, v. 2

10345
De Jong, Gerald F. The Dutch Reformed church and Negro slavery in colonial America. Church history, v. 40, Dec. 1941: 423–436.   BR140.A45, v. 40

10346
Drake, Thomas E. Quakers and slavery in America. New Haven, Yale University Press, 1950. viii, 245 p. (Yale historical publications. Miscellany 51)   E441.D75

"Bibliographical note": p. [201]–236.
Reprinted in Gloucester, Mass., by P. Smith (1965).

Includes chapters on the emancipation of Quaker-owned slaves, on the Friends' leadership of antislavery forces during the Confederation period, and on the debates in the Constitutional Convention. With the revival of the slave trade after the war, the Society of Friends lobbied unsuccessfully to obtain national antislavery legislation but achieved victories at the state level, from Pennsylvania to Maine.

10347
Greene, John C. American debate on the Negro's place in nature, 1780–1815. Journal of the history of ideas, v. 15, June 1954: 384–396.   B1.J75, v. 15

10348
Jordan, Winthrop D. American chiaroscuro: the status and definition of mulattoes in the British colonies. William and Mary quarterly, 3d ser., v. 19, Apr. 1962: 183–200.   F221.W71, 3d s., v. 19

Because the presence of mulattoes blurred the essential distinction between slaves and free men, provincials classified the mulatto as a Negro, thus denying that intermixture had occurred at all.

10349
Jordan, Winthrop D., *comp.* The Negro versus equality, 1762–1826. Chicago, Rand McNally [1969] 59 p. (The Berkeley series in American history)   E185.J68

Bibliography: p. 59.

Supports his general view—that the Revolution raised for the first time the question of racial equality—with selections from the writings of Anthony Benezet, John Allen, Samuel Hopkins, and others.

10350
Jordan, Winthrop D.   White over black: American attitudes toward the Negro, 1550–1812. Chapel Hill, Published for the Institute of Early American History and Culture at Williamsburg, Va., by the University of North Carolina Press [1968] xx, 651 p. map.
E185.J69

Bibliography: p. 610–614.

The author's thesis (Ph.D.), *White Over Black: the Attitudes of the American Colonists Toward the Negro, to 1784*, was submitted to Brown University in 1960 (Micro AC–1, no. 62–5752).

In chapters on the Revolutionary and Confederation periods, Jordan traces the growth of antislavery sentiment among Quakers, summarizes arguments in favor of slavery, and explores the development of a sectionalism based mainly on the geographical distribution of Negroes in America. He finds that in the 1750's the colonists began an orgy of self-examination that intensified with the onset of the imperial crisis and the formulation of a Revolutionary ideology. White Americans not only questioned the moral justification of slavery for the first time but faced a seemingly irreconcilable dilemma—an intellectual commitment to equality led them to condemn slavery, yet the institution was based upon their own perception of unalterable physiological differences between the races.

10351
Kates, Don B.   Abolition, deportation, integration: attitudes toward slavery in the early Republic. Journal of Negro history, v. 53, Jan. 1968: 33–47.
E185.J86, v. 53

10352
Klingberg, Frank J.   Anglican humanitarianism in colonial New York. Philadelphia, Church Historical Society [c1940] x, 295 p. [(Church Historical Society, Philadelphia] Publication no. 11)   BV2500.A6K55

Contents: book 1. Introduction. Leading ideas in the annual S.P.G. sermons, particularly with reference to native peoples. The noble savage as seen by the S.P.G. missionary. Sir William Johnson and the S.P.G. The S.P.G. program for Negroes in colonial New York. Conclusion.—book 2. Three notable annual S.P.G. sermons: Foreword. A plea for humanitarianism for the Negro in the institution of slavery, February 16, 1710–11, by William Fleetwood. An argument for the Christianization of whites, Negroes, and Indians as sound imperial policy, February 20, 1740–41, by Thomas Secker. A statement of British manifest destiny, involving aborigines protection and ultimate Negro freedom, February 21, 1766, by William Warburton.—book 3. A select bibliography (p. [251]–265).—book 4. General index.

Reprinted in Freeport, N.Y., by Books for Libraries Press (1971).

10353
Livermore, George.   An historical research respecting the opinions of the founders of the Republic on Negroes as slaves, as citizens, and as soldiers. 4th ed. Boston, A. Williams, 1863. xviii, 184 p.   E185.L79

Reprinted in New York by B. Franklin (1968); with a new preface by Benjamin Quarles, by Arno Press (1969); and by A. M. Kelley (1970).

First published in the *Proceedings* of the Massachusetts Historical Society, v. 6, 1862/63 (Boston, 1863), p. 86–248.

Presents evidence of antislavery opinions expressed in the Declaration of Independence, the Articles of Confederation, and the federal Constitution and by the state conventions ratifying the Constitution. Livermore then turns to contemporary opinion on the use of Negroes as soldiers by both American and British forces during the Revolutionary War.

10354
Mellon, Matthew T.   Early American views on Negro slavery, from the letters and papers of the founders of the Republic. Boston, Meador Pub. Co., 1934. 161 p.
E446.M47

Bibliography: p. 11–13.

Reprinted, with an introduction by Richard B. Morris, in New York by Bergman Publishers (1969).

The views considered are those of Franklin, Washington, Adams, Jefferson, and Madison.

10355
Ruchames, Louis.   The sources of racial thought in colonial America. Journal of Negro history, v. 52, Oct. 1967: 251–272.   E185.J86, v. 52

10356
Ruchames, Louis, *comp*.   Racial thought in America; a documentary history. v. 1. From the Puritans to Abraham Lincoln. [Amherst] University of Massachusetts Press, 1969. xiii, 514 p.   E185.R89, v. 1

In a section entitled "The Revolutionary Age, 1760–1800" (p. 135–236), the compiler presents excerpts from the writings of 19 contemporary authors.

10357
Travelers' impressions of slavery in America from 1750 to 1800.   Journal of Negro history, v. 1, Oct. 1916: 399–435.   E185.J86, v. 1

Some of the extracts are in French.

10358
Wax, Darold D.   The image of the Negro in the *Maryland Gazette*, 1745–75. Journalism quarterly, v. 46, spring 1969: 73–80, 86.   PN4700.J7, v. 46

10359
Woolman, John.   Some considerations on the keeping of Negroes. Recommended to the professors of Christianity of every denomination. Philadelphia, Printed and sold by James Chattin, in Church-Alley, 1754. 24 p.
HT871.W6 Rare Bk. Coll.

Bound with his *Considerations on Keeping Negroes*, part second (Philadelphia, Printed by B. Franklin and D. Hall, 1762. 52 p.).

10360
Wright, Marion T.   The Quakers as social workers among Negroes in New Jersey from 1763 to 1804. *In* Friends' Historical Association. Bulletin, v. 30, autumn 1941: 79–88.   BX7635.A1F6, v. 30

7. THE ANTISLAVERY MOVEMENT

a. Contemporary Sources

10361
Benezet, Anthony.   A caution to Great Britain and her colonies, in a short representation of the calamitous state of the enslaved Negroes in the British dominions. A new ed. Philadelphia printed, London, Reprinted and sold by J. Phillips, 1784. 46 p.
                    E446.B446 Rare Bk. Coll.
                    AC901.M5, v. 247 Rare Bk. Coll.

First published in 1767.
Reprinted in *Views of American Slavery* (New York, Arno Press, 1969. 138 p.), which includes John Wesley's *Thoughts Upon Slavery*.

10362
Bustill, Cyrus.   Cyrus Bustill addresses the blacks of Philadelphia [1787] William and Mary quarterly, 3d ser., v. 29, Jan. 1972: 99–108.   F221.W71, 3d s., v. 29

Expressing a passive Christianity in his talk, Bustill, a free Negro who was active in the Free Africa Society, counseled that only through complete submission to God's will, which included obedience to masters, would slaves become free.

10363
[Cooper, David]   A mite cast into the treasury; or, Observations on slavekeeping. Philadelphia, Printed 1772. 24 p.   E446.C72 Rare Bk. Coll.

In his "Quaker Bibliographical Notes," published in the *Bulletin* of the Friends' Historical Association, v. 26, autumn 1937, p. 45–48, Henry J. Cadbury attributes authorship to Cooper, while Sabin and Evans attribute the address to Anthony Benezet. The same is true of *A Serious Address*.

10364
[Cooper, David]   A serious address to the rulers of America, on the inconsistency of their conduct respecting slavery: forming a contrast between the encroachments of England on American liberty, and American injustice in tolerating slavery. Trenton, printed; London, Reprinted by J. Phillips, 1783. 24 p.
                    E446.C74 Rare Bk. Coll.

Signed: A farmer. February 1783.

10365
Cushing, John D.   The Cushing Court and the abolition of slavery in Massachusetts: more notes on the "Quock

Walker Case." American journal of legal history, v. 5, Apr. 1961: 118–144.   LL

10366
[Hopkins, Samuel]   A dialogue, concerning the slavery of the Africans; shewing it to be the duty and interest of the American Colonies to emancipate all their African slaves: with an address to the owners of such slaves. Dedicated to the honorable the Continental Congress. Norwich, Printed and sold by Judah P. Spooner, 1776. 63 p.   E446.H76 Rare Bk. Coll.

Arno Press has reprinted a 1785 edition of this work (New York, 1970), together with Samuel Sewall's *The Selling of Joseph*.

10367
Hopkins, Samuel.   Timely articles on slavery. Boston, Congregational Board of Publications, 1854. vi, [549]–624 p.   E446.H79

Extracted from his *Works*, v. 2 (Boston, 1854).
Contents: Preface.—A dialogue concerning the slavery of the Africans, showing it to be the duty and interest of the American colonies to emancipate all the African slaves. With an address to the owners of such slaves. 1776.—A discourse upon the slave trade and the slavery of the Africans. Delivered before the Providence Society for Abolishing the Slave Trade . . . May 17, 1793.—The slave trade and slavery. 1787.
Reprinted in Miami, Fla., by Mnemosyne Pub. (1969).

10368
Parsons, Theodore.   A forensic dispute on the legality of enslaving the Africans, held at the public commencement in Cambridge, New-England, July 21st, 1773. Boston, Printed by J. Boyle, for T. Leverett, 1773. 48 p.
                    E446.P27 Rare Bk. Coll.

A debate between Parsons and Eliphalet Pearson.

10369
Pennsylvania Society for Promoting the Abolition of Slavery.   The constitution of the Pennsylvania Society, for Promoting the Abolition of Slavery, and the relief of free Negroes, unlawfully held in bondage. Begun in the year 1774, and enlarged on the twenty-third of April, 1787. To which are added, the acts of the General Assembly of Pennsylvania, for the gradual abolition of slavery. Philadelphia, Printed by F. Bailey, 1788. 29 p.   E446.P41 Rare Bk Coll.

10370
Pennsylvania Society for Promoting the Abolition of Slavery.   An historical memoir of the Pennsylvania Society, for Promoting the Abolition of Slavery; the relief of free Negroes unlawfully held in bondage, and for improving the condition of the African race. Compiled from the minutes of the society and other official documents, by Edward Needles, and published by authority of the society. Philadelphia, Merrihew and Thompson, Printers, 1848. 116 p.   E446.P416

Reprinted in New York by Arno Press (1969).

Includes excerpts from the society's constitution of 1775 as well as minutes for the years 1775 and, following a wartime recess, 1784–89.

10371

[Providence Society for Abolishing the Slave-Trade] Constitution of a society for abolishing the slave-trade. With several acts of the legislatures of the states of Massachusetts, Connecticut and Rhode Island, for that purpose. Providence, Printed by J. Carter, 1789. 19 p.   E446.P96 Rare Bk. Coll.

10372

[Rush, Benjamin] An address to the inhabitants of the British settlements in America, upon slave-keeping. The 2d ed. To which are added observations on a pamphlet, entitled, "Slavery not forbidden by Scripture; or, A defence of the West-India planters." By a Pennsylvanian. Philadelphia, Printed by J. Dunlap, 1773. 28, 54 p.   E446.R96 Rare Bk. Coll.

Reprinted in New York by Arno Press (1969).

b. Secondary Works

10373

Annunziata, Frank.   Three theories on anti-slavery in colonial American literature. Social studies, v. 60, Oct. 1969: 250–257.   D16.3.S65, v. 60

On the views of Samuel Sewall, John Woolman, and Benjamin Franklin.

10374

Bellot, Leland J.   Evangelicals and the defense of slavery in Britain's old colonial empire. Journal of southern history, v. 37, Feb. 1971: 19–40.   F206.J68, v. 37

Contends that the automatic association between evangelicalism and the antislavery movement in the 18th century is unwarranted. Bellot uses the writings of James Habersham and William Knox to show that the principles of evangelical Christianity were often used to justify slavery and to provide the slaveholder with necessary moral sanctions.

10375

Carroll, Kenneth L.   Religious influences on the manumission of slaves in Caroline, Dorchester, and Talbot counties. Maryland historical magazine, v. 56, June 1961: 176–197.   F176.M18, v. 56

Focuses on the three denominations that took official action on the matter of slaveholding—the Quakers, Nicholites, and Methodists.

10376

Davis, David B.   New sidelights on early antislavery radicalism. William and Mary quarterly, 3d ser., v. 28, Oct. 1971: 585–594.   F221.W71, 3d s., v. 28

Shows that the radical views of an obscure Scotsman, George Wallace, were used liberally by Anthony Benezet in his own writings.

10377

Donnan, Elizabeth.   Agitation against the slave trade in Rhode Island, 1784–1790. *In* Persecution and liberty; essays in honor of George Lincoln Burr. New York, Century Co. [c1931] p. 473–482.   D6.P4

10378

Dumond, Dwight L.   Antislavery; the crusade for freedom in America. Ann Arbor, University of Michigan Press [1961] x, 422 p. illus., facsims., maps, ports.
                    E441.D84

Bibliographic references included in "Notes" (p. [373]–413).

Concentrating upon the period before 1850, the author details the activities of numerous workers, both white and black, in the movement from its 18th-century origins to the Civil War. Since the peculiar institution was absolutely contrary to American political, social, and religious ideals, its survival after the Revolution indicates to Dumond that local communities mocked the natural rights doctrine of the Declaration just as they did the social precepts of Christianity.

10379

Fisher, Miles M.   Friends of Humanity: a Quaker antislavery influence. Church history, v. 4, Sept. 1935: 187–202.   BR140.A45, v. 4

10380

Freehling, William W.   The Founding Fathers and slavery. American historical review, v. 77, Feb. 1972: 81–93.
                    E171.A57, v. 77

Defending the antislavery reputation of the Founding Fathers against recent historical criticism, Freehling points to the crucial first steps taken by Jefferson and his generation that permanently crippled slavery and created the conditions for its ultimate abolition.

10381

Greene, Lorenzo J.   Slave-holding New England and its awakening. Journal of Negro history, v. 13, Oct. 1928: 492–533.   E185.J86, v. 13

On the movement to abolish slavery during the colonial period.

10382

Hunt, Gaillard.   William Thornton and Negro colonization. *In* American Antiquarian Society, *Worcester, Mass.* Proceedings, new ser., v. 30, Apr. 1920: 32–61.
                    E172.A35, n.s., v. 30

Deals in part with Thornton's plans in the late 1780's to transport free American Negroes to Sierra Leone where a black commonwealth would be established.

10383

Kraus, Michael.   Slavery reform in the eighteenth century: an aspect of transatlantic intellectual co-operation. Pennsylvania magazine of history and biography, v. 60, Jan. 1936: 53–66.   F146.P65, v. 60

10384
Locke, Mary S.   Anti-slavery in America from the intro-
duction of African slaves to the prohibition of the slave
trade (1619–1808). Boston, Ginn, 1901. xv, 255 p.
(Radcliffe College monographs, no. 11)   [E446.L81]
Micro 8150E

Bibliography: p. [199]–231.
Reprinted in Gloucester, Mass., by P. Smith (1965.
E446.L81 1965).

Following a survey of the moral and religious movement—especially among the Quakers—against the peculiar
institution, the author investigates such topics as the impact
of Revolutionary philosophy and politics upon slavery, the
growth of abolition societies after 1783, attempts at gradual
emancipation, the development of an antislavery literature,
the Constitution and the slave trade, and slavery in the
territories.

10385
MacEacheren, Elaine.   Emancipation of slavery in Mas-
sachusetts: a reexamination, 1770–1790. Journal of
Negro history, v. 55, Oct. 1970: 289–306.
E185.J86, v. 55

Focusing on individual cases of manumission in Boston,
the author argues that by making the status of slave property
uncertain, the Massachusetts Constitution of 1780 may have
had more to do with the withering away of slavery in the
state than did the decisions in the Walker-Jennison cases.

10386
McManus, Edgar J.   Antislavery legislation in New York.
Journal of Negro history, v. 46, Oct. 1961: 207–216.
E185.J86, v. 46

10387
MacMaster, Richard K.   Anti-slavery and the American
Revolution: a crack in the liberty bell. History today,
v. 21, Oct. 1971: 715–723. illus., facsim., ports.
D1.H818, v. 21

Argues that the Revolution retarded the antislavery
cause.

10388
MacMaster, Richard K.   Liberty or property? The
Methodists petition for emancipation in Virginia, 1785.
Methodist history, v. 10, Oct. 1971: 44–55.
BX8235.M44, v. 10

10389
Matthews, Albert.   Notes on the proposed abolition of
slavery in Virginia in 1785. *In* Colonial Society of Massachusetts, *Boston.* Publications. v. 6. Transactions,
1899/1900. Boston, 1904. p. 370–380. F61.C71, v. 6

10390
O'Brien, William.   Did the Jennison Case [1781] outlaw
slavery in Massachusetts? William and Mary quarterly,
3d ser., v. 17, Apr. 1960: 219–241.
F221.W71, 3d s., v. 17

10391
Scarborough, Ruth.   The opposition to slavery in Georgia
prior to 1860. Nashville, Tenn., George Peabody College for Teachers, 1933. xviii, 257 p. (Contributions to
education of George Peabody College for Teachers,
no. 97)   E445.G3S25

Thesis (Ph.D.)—George Peabody College for
Teachers, 1932.
Bibliography: p. 252–257.
Reprinted in New York by Negro Universities Press
(1968).

Includes a chapter on the slave system after 1763 as well
as occasional references to the Revolutionary period in chapters on manumission and the slave trade.

10392
Seeber, Edward D.   Anti-slavery opinion in France during
the second half of the eighteenth century. Baltimore,
Md., Johns Hopkins Press, 1937. 238 p. (The Johns
Hopkins studies in Romance literatures and languages.
Extra volume 10)   HT1176.S4 1937
PC13.J62, v. 10

Issued also as thesis (Ph.D.)—Johns Hopkins Uni-
versity.
Bibliography: p. 201–229.
Reprinted in New York by Greenwood Press (1969).
"From the American Revolution to the French Revolu-
tion: slavery and liberty in the United States": p. 117–125.

10393
Spector, Robert M.   The Quock Walker cases (1781–1783):
slavery, its abolition, and Negro citizenship in early
Massachusetts. Journal of Negro history, v. 53, Jan.
1968: 12–32.   E185.J86, v. 53

10394
Turner, Edward R.   The abolition of slavery in Pennsylvania. Pennsylvania magazine of history and biography,
v. 36, Apr. 1912: 129–142.   F146.P65, v. 36

10395
Turner, Edward R.   The first abolition society in the
United States. Pennsylvania magazine of history and
biography, v. 36, Jan. 1912: 93–110. facsims.
F146.P65, v. 36

———— Offprint. [Philadelphia] Printed by J. B.
Lippincott Co. [1912?] 93–110 p. facsims.   E446.T9

On the work of the Pennsylvania Society for Promoting
the Abolition of Slavery, first organized in Philadelphia in
1775, reorganized in 1784, and incorporated in 1787.

10396
Washburn, Emory.   The extinction of slavery in Massachusetts. *In* Massachusetts Historical Society, *Boston.* Collections. 4th ser., v. 4. Boston, 1858. p. 333–
346.   F61.M41, 4th s., v. 4

On the Quock Walker and related cases in 1781.

10397

Zilversmit, Arthur. The first emancipation; the abolition of slavery in the North. Chicago, University of Chicago Press [1967] x, 262 p.   E446.Z5

"Bibliography essay": p. [245]–250.

After a brief survey of the origins, characteristics, and profitability of the slave system in the North, the author shows how the intellectual ferment of the Revolutionary period contributed to the political success of the antislavery movement. Despite its economic viability, slavery simply proved to be incompatible with the religious beliefs and humanitarian principles of nonslaveholders who felt the system to be detrimental to their interests and to the interests of the community. Ultimately, the idealism of the abolitionists prevailed over the economic interests of the slaveholding minority as provisions that either outlawed slavery or provided for gradual abolition were adopted in all the states between 1777 and 1804.

10398

Zilversmit, Arthur. Quok Walker, Mumbet, and the abolition of slavery in Massachusetts. William and Mary quarterly, 3d ser., v. 25, Oct. 1968: 614–624.
F221.W71, 3d s., v. 25

Law and Politics

LAW AND LEGAL INSTITUTIONS

1. GENERAL

10399

Association of American Law Schools. Select essays in Anglo-American legal history, by various authors, compiled and edited by a committee of the Association of American Law Schools. Boston, Little, Brown, 1907–9. 3 v.   LL

Committee: E. Freund, W. E. Mikell, J. H. Wigmore, chairman.

Reprinted in Frankfurt a.M. by Sauer u. Auvermann (1968).

10400

Aumann, Francis R. The changing American legal system: some selected phases. Columbus [Ohio State University Press] 1940. x, 281 p. [Ohio. State University. Contributions in history and political science, no. 16]
KF352.A77 1940

Bibliography: p. [237]–269.

Contents: the period of colonial legal beginnings, 1608–1776.—The formative period of American law, 1776–1865.—The period of maturity of American law, 1865–1900, and recent trends, 1900–1935.

Reprinted in New York by Da Capo Press (1969).

10401

[Austin, Benjamin] Observations on the pernicious practice of the law. As published occasionally in the *Independent Chronicle*, in the year 1786, and republished at the request of a number of respectable citizens. With an address never before published. Corrected and amended. By Honestus [*pseud.*] With remarks on the rights of jury as judges of law and evidence. Boston, Printed by True & Weston, 1819. 60 p.
KF384.A9 1819

10402

Chester, Alden, *ed.* Legal and judicial history of New York. New York, National Americana Society, 1911. 3 v. plates, ports.   KFN5078.C47

"The text of the first volume was almost wholly written by Mr. Lyman Horace Weeks . . . Mr. Weeks has also contributed all the local monographs in the third volume except such as have been signed by others."—Preface.

On title page of v. 2: *Constitutional History of New York State From the Colonial Period to the Present Time*, by J. Hampden Dougherty.

10403

Chitwood, Oliver P. Justice in colonial Virginia. Baltimore, Johns Hopkins Press, 1905. 123 p. (Johns Hopkins University studies in historical and political science, 23d ser., no. 7–8)   H31.J6, 23d s., no. 7–8
JK93.V7C5

"Manuscripts": 1 p. following p. 123.
Reprinted in New York by Da Capo Press (1971).

Describing the origin, history, and growth of the Virginia colonial judiciary, the author concludes that the structure of the superior and inferior courts after 1682 was aristocratic. At the same time, Chitwood finds that the judges were men of considerable ability and popular influence who often sat in the Council and House of Burgesses and who, in their opposition to the actions of the royal governors, prevented the colony from becoming closely dependent upon the crown.

10404

Chumbley, George L. Colonial justice in Virginia; the development of a judicial system, typical laws and cases of the period. Richmond, Dietz Press, 1938. 174 p.
KFV2478.C45

"Sources consulted": p. [159]–161.

10405

Cushing, John D. The judiciary and public opinion in Revolutionary Massachusetts. *In* Billias, George A., *ed.* Law and authority in colonial America; selected essays. Barre, Mass., Barre Publishers [1965] p. 168–186.   KF361.A2B5

"Footnotes": p. 183–186.

10406

Davis, William T. History of the judiciary of Massachusetts, including the Plymouth and Massachusetts colonies, the province of the Massachusetts Bay, and the commonwealth. [Boston] Boston Book Co., 1900. xxiv, 446 p.   KFM2478.D3

10407

Eastman, Frank M. Courts and lawyers of Pennsylvania; a history, 1623–1923. New York, American Historical

Society, 1922. 3 v. (878 p.) fronts., illus. (facsim.), ports. KF354.P4E3

Information on the Revolutionary period appears in all three volumes.

10408
Flaherty, David H., *comp.* Essays in the history of early American law. Chapel Hill, Published for the Institute of Early American History and Culture of Williamsburg, Va., by the University of North Carolina Press [1969] x, 534 p. KF361.A2F5

Bibliographic footnotes.

Partial contents: An introduction to early American legal history, by D. H. Flaherty.—Law and colonial society, by G. L. Haskins.—Colonial courts and the common law, by Z. Chafee, Jr.—The courts and the law in colonial New York, by J. Goebel, Jr.—Administrative control of the courts of the American plantations, by J. H. Smith.—The influence of colonial conditions as illustrated in the Connecticut intestacy law, by C. M. Andrews.—"Law enforcement in colonial New York"; an introduction, by J. Goebel, Jr.—The rise of the New York bar: the legal career of William Livingston, by M. M. Klein.—Legalism versus Revolutionary doctrine in New England, by R. B. Morris.—The process of outlawry in New York; a study of the selective reception of English law, by M. D. Howe.—Thomas Jefferson and Blackstone's *Commentaries*, by J. S. Waterman.

10409
Goebel, Julius. The courts and the law in colonial New York. *In* New York State Historical Association. History of the state of New York. v. 3. Whig and Tory. New York, Columbia University Press, 1933. p. [1]–43. illus., facsim. F119.N65, v. 3

Bibliography: p. 43.

10410
Grinnell, Frank W. The bench and bar in colony and province, 1630–1776. *In* Hart, Albert B., *ed.* Commonwealth history of Massachusetts. v. 2 Province of Massachusetts, 1689–1775. New York, States History Co., 1928. p. 156–191. ports. F64.H32, v. 2

Bibliography: p. 190–191.

10411
History of the bench and bar of New York. Edited by Honorable David McAdam [and others] v. 1. [New York] New York History Co., 1897. 524 p. illus., ports. F118.H63, v. 1

Partial contents: Redfield, A. A. English colonial polity and judicial administration, 1664–1776.—Truax, C. H. Judicial organization and legal administration from 1776 to the constitution of 1846.—Biographical.

10412
Johnson, Herbert A. Civil procedure in John Jay's New York. American journal of legal history, v. 11, Jan. 1967: 69–80. LL

10413
Kammen, Michael G. Colonial court records and the study of early American history; a bibliographical review. American historical review, v. 70, Apr. 1965: 732–739. E171.A57, v. 70

The recent publication of colonial court records is forcing a new recognition of the importance and character of early American law and court practice.

10414
Keasbey, Edward Q. The courts and lawyers of New Jersey 1661–1912. New York, Lewis Historical Pub. Co., 1912. 3 v. plates, ports. KF354.N4K4

Vol. 3: Biographical.

Information on the Revolutionary period is scattered throughout.

10415
Levy, Leonard W., *and* Lawrence H. Leder. "Exotic fruit": the right against compulsory self-incrimination in colonial New York. William and Mary quarterly, 3d ser., v. 20, Jan. 1963: 3–32. F221.W71, 3d s., v. 20

10416
Morris, Richard B. Studies in the history of American law, with special reference to the seventeenth and eighteenth centuries. New York, Columbia University Press, 1930. 285 p. (Studies in history, economics and public law, no. 316) H31.C7, no. 316
KF361.M67 1930b

Published also as thesis (Ph.D.)—Columbia University.

"A bibliographical essay": p. 259–273.

Reprinted in Philadelphia by the J. M. Mitchell Co. (1959 ['1958]).

Through an examination of laws governing the distribution and alienation of land, the rights of women, and the responsibility for tortious acts, the author considers whether early American law was indigenous or a direct transfer of English common law. Morris finds that during the 17th century the colonists tended to be flexible in adapting English principles to their own particular needs, depending upon the circumstances in which they found themselves. The tightening of imperial bonds and mercantile restrictions in the 18th century, however, led to a revival of the common law tradition as colonial lawyers found the "rights of Englishmen" a more substantive defense than the "rights of man" in their efforts to curb parliamentary excesses.

10417
Pittman, Robert Carter. The colonial and constitutional history of the privilege against self-incrimination in America. Virginia law review, v. 21, May 1935: 763–789. LL

10418
Rackow, Felix. The right to counsel: English and American precedents. William and Mary quarterly, 3d ser., v. 11, Jan. 1954: 3–27. F221.W71, 3d s., v. 11

The right of the accused to the assistance of counsel in making his defense was a recognized right during the colonial period. It did not mean, however, that the court would assign counsel if the defendent had none of his own. Before 1789, assignment was permitted in Massachusetts for treason cases and in South Carolina for capital offenses; only in Pennsylvania was it granted for all crimes.

10419

Sams, Conway W., *and* Elihu S. Riley. The bench and bar of Maryland; a history, 1634 to 1901. Chicago, Lewis Pub. Co., 1901. 2 v. (678 p.) illus., ports. LL

The first volume includes four chapters (p. 103–240) on the Revolutionary period.

10420

Wagner, D. O. Some antecedents of the American doctrine of judicial review. Political science quarterly, v. 40, Dec. 1925: 561–593. H1.P8, v. 40

Seeks in the controversial literature generated by the Townshend Acts, 1767–70, the constitutional arguments employed against the authority of Parliament that might explain why Americans opposed legislative authority both at home and abroad.

10421

Washburn, Emory. Sketches of the judicial history of Massachusetts from 1630 to the Revolution in 1775. Boston, C. C. Little and J. Brown, 1840. 407 p. F67.W31

10422

Wright, Benjamin F. American interpretations of natural law; a study in the history of political thought. Cambridge, Mass., Harvard University Press, 1931. 360 p. (Harvard political studies) JA84.U5W67

Reprinted in New York by Russell & Russell (1962).

Chapters 4–6 (p. 62–148) treat the Revolutionary period.

10423

Younger, Richard D. Grand juries and the American Revolution. Virginia magazine of history and biography, v. 63, July 1955: 257–268. F221.V91, v. 63

2. THE INFLUENCE OF ENGLISH LAW

10424

Aumann, Francis R. The influence of English and civil law principles upon the American legal system during the critical post-Revolutionary period. University of Cincinnati law review, v. 12, June 1938: 289–317. LL

10425

Blackstone, *Sir* William. Commentaries on the laws of England. In four books. Re-printed from the British copy, page for page with the last edition. America, Printed for the subscribers, by Robert Bell, at the late Union Library, in Third-Street, Philadelphia, 1771–72. 4 v. LL

10426

Bliss, William H. English influence on common law development in colonial Pennsylvania. 1959. ([194] p.) Micro AC–1, no. 59–6541

Thesis (Ph.D.)—University of Pittsburgh.
Abstracted in *Dissertation Abstracts*, v. 20, Feb. 1960, p. 3266–3267.

10427

Brown, Elizabeth G. British statutes in American law, 1776–1836. In consultation with William Wirt Blume. Foreword by Allen F. Smith. Ann Arbor, University of Michigan Law School, 1964. xii, 377 p. (Michigan legal studies) KF366.B7

Determines the degree to which British statutory law was utilized in each of the new states and the western territories.

10428

Cooley, Rita W. Predecessors of the federal attorney general: the attorney general in England and the American colonies. American journal of legal history, v. 2, Oct. 1958: 304–312. LL

10429

Franklin, Robert J. The Americanization of the English common law, 1776–1835. 1972. ([420] p.) Micro AC–1, no. 72–11,921

Thesis (Ph.D.)—University of Southern California.
Abstracted in *Dissertation Abstracts International*, v. 32A, Apr. 1971, p. 5710–5711.

10430

Horowitz, Morton J. The emergence of an instrumental conception of American law, 1780–1820. *In* Law in American history. [Cambridge, Mass.] Charles Warren Center for Studies in American History, Harvard University [1971] (Perspectives in American history, v. 5) p. [285]–326. E171.P47, v. 5 1971

During the 18th century, according to Horowitz, the common law was regarded as an eternal set of principles derived from nature and embodied in custom. By the early 19th century, however, common-law judges began consciously to use the law to encourage innovation and to promote socially desirable change.

10431

Reinsch, Paul S. English common law in the early American colonies. Madison, Wis., 1899. 64 p. (Bulletin of the University of Wisconsin, no. 31. Economics, political science, and history series, v. 2, no. 4, p. 393–456) H31.W6., v. 2, no. 4

Thesis (Ph.D.)—Wisconsin University, 1898.
"Bibliography of sources and authorities": p. 60–64.

3. THE COURTS

a. Contemporary Sources

10432

Conductor Generalis; or, The office, duty and authority of justices of the peace, high-sheriffs, under-sheriffs, coroners, constables, gaolers, jury-men, and overseers of the poor. As also the office of clerks of assize, and of the peace, &c. Compiled chiefly from Burns's *Justice*, and the several other books on those subjects, as far as they extend and can be adapted to these American colonies. By James Parker, one of His Majesty's justices of the peace for Middlesex County, in New-Jersey. The whole alphabetically digested under the several titles; with a table directing to the ready finding out the proper matter under those titles. To which is added, A treatise on the law of descents in fee-simple: by William Blackstone. Woodbridge, in New-Jersey, Printed and sold by J. Parker; sold also by J. Holt, near the Exchange, in New York, 1764. xvi, 590 p.   LL

10433

Davis, James, *of North Carolina*. The office and authority of a justice of peace. And also, the duty of sheriffs, coroners, constables, church wardens, overseers of roads, and other officers. Together with precedents of warrants, judgments, executions, and other legal process . . . To which is added an appendix . . . Collected from the common and statute laws of England, and the acts of assembly of this province, and adapted to our constitution and practice. By J. Davis . . . one of His Majesty's justices of the peace for the county of Craven. Newbern, Printed by J. Davis, 1774. 404 p.   LL

10434

Stokes, Anthony. Directions for holding court in colonial Georgia. Edited by Erwin C. Surrency. American journal of legal history, v. 2, Oct. 1958: 321–355.   LL

A reprint of Stokes' *Directions for the Officers of His Majesty's General Court and Sessions of Oyer and Terminer, and General Gaol Delivery, of the Province of Georgia* (Savannah, Printed by J. Johnston, 1771) from the only known copy in the Harvard Law School Library. The author, then chief justice of the colony, laid out in detail the duties of officials in opening and closing court and in serving certain writs.

10435

Vallette, Elie. The deputy commissary's guide within the province of Maryland, together with plan and sufficient directions for testators to form, and executors to perform their wills and testaments; for administrators to compleat their administrations, and for every person any way concerned in deceased person's estates, to proceed therein with safety to themselves and others. By Elie Vallette, Register of the Prerogative Office of the said province. Annapolis, Printed by A. C. Green, 1774. 248, [11] p. plates.   LL

"Appendix: containing precedents of letters, bonds, writs, and other instruments occasionally issuing out of the Prerogative Court, together with a select and approved form for drawing of wills and codicils . . . also the tables, for the reduction of sterling money into common currency": p. [161]–248.

10436

Virginia (*Colony*). *General Court*. Reports of cases determined in the General Court of Virginia. From 1730, to 1740; and from 1768, to 1772. By Thomas Jefferson. Charlottesville, F. Carr, 1829. viii, 145 p.   LL

"Reports of cases from 1730 to 1740, from manuscript notes left by Sir John Randolph, Edward Barradall, and Mr. Hopkins; and also cases from 1768 to 1772, reported by Jefferson himself."—Charles C. Soule, *The Lawyer's Reference Manual* (Boston, 1884).

10437

The Young clerk's magazine; or, English law-repository: containing, a variety of the most useful precedents of articles of agreement, bonds, bills, recognizances, releases, letters and warrants of attorney, awards, bills of sale, gifts, grants, leases, assignments, mortgages, surrenders, jointures, covenants, copartnerships, charter-parties, letters of licence, compositions, conveyances, partitions, wills, and all other instruments that relate to publick business. With necessary directions for making distresses for rent, &c. as the law between landlord and tenant now stands. To which is added, the doctrine of fines and recoveries, and their forms. Together with those of common writs, affidavits, memorials for registering deeds, &c. in Middlesex; as also a choice collection of declarations in the King's Bench and Common Pleas. 5th ed., rev. and corr. London Printed; Philadelphia, Reprinted by J. Dunlap and J. Crukshank, in Market-Street, 1774. 303 p.   LL

10438

The Young clerk's vade mecum; or, Compleat law-tutor. Being a useful collection of a great variety of the most approved precedents in the law, and adapted to almost every transaction in life wherein an attention to legal forms is indispensably necessary. And consisting chiefly of bonds, special conditions, letters of attorney . . . To which is added, a collection of English precedents, relating to the office of a justice of peace. Belfast Printed, New-York, Re-printed by H. Gaine, in Hanover-Square, 1776. 236, iv, 86, [6] p.   LL

b. Secondary Works

10439

Chafee, Zechariah. Colonial courts and the common law. *In* Massachusetts Historical Society, *Boston*. Proceedings. v. 68; 1944–1947. Boston, 1952. p. 132–159.

F61.M38, v. 68

10440

Conley, Patrick T. Rhode Island's paper money issue and *Trevett* v. *Weeden* (1786). Rhode Island history, v. 30, summer 1971: 94–108. facsims., ports.

F76.R472, v. 30

Shows that the decision of the Rhode Island Superior Court in *Trevett* v. *Weeden* was not an authentic or technical precedent in the development of judicial review, and that it did not prevent implementation of the paper money program. Instead, the significance of the case lies in the strong presentation of the doctrine of judicial review made by defense counsel, James Mitchell Varnum. His views were published and advertised for sale in Philadelphia in April and May 1787 as delegates were gathering for the Constitutional Convention.

10441
Corbitt, David L. Judicial districts of North Carolina, 1746–1934. North Carolina historical review, v. 12, Jan. 1935: 45–61. F251.N892, v. 12

Gives the districts, locations of the courthouses, and dates of court meetings for 1762–64, 1767, 1773, 1776, and 1777–90.

10442
Crumrine, Boyd. The county court for the district of West Augusta, Virginia, held at Augusta Town, near Washington, Pennsylvania, 1776–1777 . . . With an account of the county courts for Ohio, Yohogania, and Monongalia counties, Virginia, held 1777–1780. [Washington, Pa.] Printed by the Observer job rooms, for the Washington County Historical Society, 1905, 46 p. fold. maps, plate. F157.W3C86

A history of the boundary controversy between Pennsylvania and Virginia.

10443
Curtis, George M. The Virginia courts during the Revolution. 1970. ([296] p.) Micro AC–1, no. 70–24,740

Thesis (Ph.D.)—University of Wisconsin.
Abstracted in *Dissertation Abstracts International*, v. 31A, May 1971, p. 5979.

10444
Dressler, John B. The shaping of the American judiciary: ideas and institutions in the early Republic. 1971. ([329] p.) Micro AC–1, no. 72–15,085

Thesis (Ph.D.)—University of Washington.
Abstracted in *Dissertation Abstracts International*, v. 32A, May 1972, p. 6335.

Analyzes popular dissatisfaction with lawyers, courts, and the judicial process in the late 18th century.

10445
Durfee, Thomas. Gleanings from the judicial history of Rhode Island. Providence, S. S. Rider, 1883. 164 p. (Rhode Island historical tracts, [1st ser.], no. 18) F76.R52, 1st s., no. 18

10446
Ferguson, Isabel. County court in Virginia, 1700–1830. North Carolina historical review, v. 8, Jan. 1931: 14–40. F251.N892, v. 8

10447
Field, Richard S. The provincial courts of New Jersey, with sketches of the bench and bar. New York, Published for the Society, by Bartlett & Welford, 1849. xi, 311 p. (Collections of the New Jersey Historical Society, v. 3) F131.N62, v. 3
KF361.F5

10448
Goodman, Leonard S. Mandamus in the colonies: the rise of the superintending power of the American courts. American journal of legal history, v. 1, Oct. 1957: 308–335; v. 2, Jan.–Apr. 1958: 1–34, 129–147. LL

10449
Guffey, Alexander S. The first courts in western Pennsylvania. Western Pennsylvania historical magazine, v. 7, July 1924: 145–177. F146.W52, v. 7

Refers to the first county courts held west of the Allegheny Mountains in present day Westmoreland County, 1773–82.

10450
Johnson, Herbert A. George Harison's protest: new light on Forsey versus Cunningham [1763–65] *In* New York State Historical Association. New York history, v. 50, Jan. 1969: 61–82. F116.N865, v. 50

A significant case affecting the right to trial by jury. Harison's instrument of protest provides the only known description of legal procedure in a New York colonial court.

10451
Lloyd, William H. The courts of Pennsylvania in the eighteenth century prior to the Revolution. University of Pennsylvania law review and American law register, v. 56, Jan. 1908: 28–51. K25.N69, v. 56

10452
Lloyd, William H. The early courts of Pennsylvania. Boston, Boston Book Co., 1910. vii, 287 p. (University of Pennsylvania Law School series, no. 2) JK93.P4L8

10453
Morris, Richard B. Judicial supremacy and the inferior courts in the American colonies. Political science quarterly, v. 55, Sept. 1940: 429–434. H1.P8, v. 55

10454
Rankin, Hugh F. The General Court of colonial Virginia, its jurisdiction and personnel. Virginia magazine of history and biography, v. 70, Apr. 1962: 142–153. F221.V91, v. 70

10455
Reed, Henry Clay, *and* Joseph A. Palermo. Justices of the peace in early Delaware. Delaware history, v. 14, Oct. 1971: 223–237. F161.D37, v. 14

10456
Schmidhauser, John R. "States rights" and the origins of the Supreme Court's power as arbiter in federal-state relations [1782–89] Wayne law review, v. 4, spring 1958: 101–114. LL

10457
Scott, Austin. Holmes vs. Walton: the New Jersey precedent. A chapter in the history of judicial power and unconstitutional legislation. American historical review, v. 4, Apr. 1899: 456–469. E171.A57, v. 4

An early case of judicial review involving a New Jersey law of 1778 forbidding trade with the enemy that was held unconstitutional because it specified trial by a jury of only six men.

10458
Scott, Henry W. The courts of the state of New York; their history, development and jurisdiction; embracing a complete history of all the courts and tribunals of justice, both colonial and state, established from the first settlement of Manhattan Island and including the status and jurisdiction of all the courts of the state as now constituted. New York, Wilson Publishing Co., 1909. 506 p. JK3481.S4

10459
Setaro, Franklyn C. The Surrogate's Court of New York: its historical antecedents [1623–1846] New York law forum, v. 2, July 1956: 283–304. LL

10460
Singleton, Marvin K. New light on the chancery side of Virginia's evolution to statehood. Journal of American studies, v. 2, Oct. 1968: 149–160. E151.J6, v. 2

On the development of equity jurisdiction in the colony and the establishment of a High Court of Equity by the new state government in 1777.

10461
Surrency, Erwin C. The courts in the American colonies. American journal of legal history, v. 11, July–Oct. 1967: 253–276, 347–376. LL

10462
Van Ness, James S. The Maryland courts in the American Revolution: a case study. 1968. ([369] p.)
Micro AC–1, no. 68–16,667

Thesis (Ph.D.)—University of Maryland.
Abstracted in *Dissertation Abstracts*, v. 29A, Nov. 1968, p. 1503–1504.

There were no surprising innovations or fundamental alterations in the courts or the judicial process as a result of the Revolution.

4. CRIMINAL LAW

10463
Chandler, Peleg W. American criminal trials. Boston. T. H. Carter, 1844. 2 v. ports. KF220.C5 1844

Partial contents: v. 1. The crew of the *Pitt* packet. The Boston Massacre. Appendix.—v. 2. Bathsheba Spooner and others. Colonel Henley. Major André. Joshua H. Smith. The Rhode Island judges. Appendix: Trial of Mrs. Spooner and others. Major André. Notes.
Reprinted in Freeport, N.Y., by Books for Libraries Press (1970).

10464
Gipson, Lawrence H. The criminal codes of Connecticut. *In* American Institute of Criminal Law and Criminology. Journal, v. 6, July 1915: 177–189.
HV6001.J63, v. 6

10465
Gipson, Lawrence H. The criminal codes of Pennsylvania [1650–1786] *In* American Institute of Criminal Law and Criminology. Journal, v. 6, Sept. 1915: 323–344.
LL

Includes a comparison of the application of the codes of Connecticut and Pennsylvania.

10466
Goebel, Julius, *and* Thomas Raymond Naughton. Law enforcement in colonial New York: a study in criminal procedure (1664–1776). New York, Commonwealth Fund, 1944. xxxix, 867 p. (Publications of the Foundation for Research in Legal History, Columbia University School of Law) KFN6155.G6 1944
"Sources": p. [765]–770.

In a detailed and technical study of legal practice and procedure, the authors seek to determine the extent to which English common law had become part of the colony's legal system before the Revolution. Goebel and Naughton consider the reception article in the constitution of 1777 to be the culmination of a process begun in 1683 when the adoption of a new judicature law established within the colony the practices and forms of the English central courts. Thereafter, a competent bar and bench, using English manuals and precedents, began to shape common law to fit the needs of a new society. They conclude that the formative period of criminal law was virtually completed by 1776, thus rejecting the notion that American mastery of common law was a post-Revolutionary development dependent upon the genius of a few great jurists.

10467
Guba, Emil F. The trial and execution of Nathan Quibbey. Historic Nantucket, v. 15, Oct. 1967: 12–16.
F72.N2H68, v. 15

For the murder of fellow Nantucket Indians aboard the *Sally* in 1767.

10468
Nelson, William E. Emerging notions of modern criminal law in the Revolutionary era: an historical perspective. New York University law review, v. 42, May 1967: 450–482. LL

10469
Rankin, Hugh F. Criminal trial proceedings in the General Court of colonial Virginia. Virginia magazine of history and biography, v. 72, Jan. 1964: 50–74.
F221.V91, v. 72

10470
Rankin, Hugh F. Criminal trial proceedings in the General Court of colonial Virginia. Williamsburg, Va., Colonial Williamsburg; distributed by the University Press of Virginia, Charlottesville ['1965] ix, 240 p. (Williamsburg research studies) KFV2979.R3

Bibliographic footnotes.

10471

Scott, Arthur P.   Criminal law in colonial Virginia. Chicago, University of Chicago Press [ᶜ1930] ix, 335 p.
KFV2961.S36

Bibliography: p. 324–329.
The author's thesis (Ph.D.), *History of the Criminal Law in Virginia During the Colonial Period*, was submitted to the University of Chicago in 1916 (KFV2961.S37 1916).

5. OTHER ASPECTS OF THE LAW

10472

Cantor, Milton.   The writ of habeas corpus: early American origins and development. *In* Freedom and reform; essays in honor of Henry Steele Commager. Edited by Harold M. Hyman and Leonard W. Levy. New York, Harper & Row [1967] p. 55–77.   E183.F72

10473

Carpenter, Allen H.   Habeas corpus in the colonies. American historical review, v. 8, Oct. 1902: 18–27.
E171.A57, v. 8

With the exception of South Carolina, which reenacted the English statute, colonial rights with regard to the writ of habeas corpus were protected by English common law. Most colonies did not pass formal habeas corpus acts until after the Revolution.

10474

Carpenter, Allen H.   Naturalization in England and the American colonies. American historical review, v. 9, Jan. 1904: 288–303.   E171.A57, v. 9

Although they varied from colony to colony, the same methods of naturalization were employed in America as in England: letters of denization were issued, and general laws and private acts were passed.

10475

Chapin, Bradley.   The American law of treason, Revolutionary and early national origins. Seattle, University of Washington Press [1964] viii, 172 p. (University of Washington publications in history)   KF9392.Z9C5
Bibliography: p. 153–164.
The author's thesis (Ph.D.), *The Law of Treason During the American Revolution, 1765–1783*, was submitted to Cornell University in 1951.

After briefly sketching English and colonial precedents, the author considers both substantive and procedural aspects of the laws of treason from their use against Tories in the newly independent states to their application by John Marshall in the trial of Aaron Burr. Chapin concludes that the British legacy, especially the statute of Edward III, was more influential in the construction of the laws than were American attempts to make innovative changes. He also contends that actions taken to protect life and political freedom during the period were moderate in their results, producing binding precedents that firmly limited the use of treason law and thus precluded later attempts to bring charges for partisan political purposes.

10476

Cometti, Elizabeth.   Morals and the American Revolution. South Atlantic quarterly, v. 46, Jan. 1947: 62–71.
AP2.S75, v. 46

On restrictive measures designed to curb moral laxity.

10477

Dillion, John B.   Oddities of colonial legislation in America, as applied to the public lands, primitive education, religion, morals, Indians, etc., etc., with authentic records of the origin and growth of pioneer settlements, embracing also a condensed history of the states and territories, with a summary of the territorial expansion, civil progress and development of the nation. Indianapolis, R. Douglass, 1879. 784 p. ports.   E189.D57
JK54.D5

Edited, with a memoir of the author, by Ben. Douglass.

10478

Farnam, Henry W.   Chapters in the history of social legislation in the United States to 1860. Edited by Clive Day; with an introductory note by Victor S. Clark. Washington, Carnegie Institution of Washington, 1938. xx, 496 p. (Contributions to American economic history)   KF352.F3
HC101.C75, no. 8

Carnegie Institution of Washington. Publication no. 488.
Bibliography: p. [271]–322.
"Slave codes, Southern states": p. [325]–414.
"Slave codes, Northern states": p. [415]–474.

Treats such topics as land tenure, labor policy, fair trade, the public food supply, laws regulating the relation of debtor and creditor, educational policy, and legislation regarding slavery.

10479

Flaherty, David H.   Law and the enforcement of morals in early America. *In* Law in American history. [Cambridge, Mass.] Charles Warren Center for Studies in American History, Harvard University [1971] (Perspectives in American history, v. 5) p. [201]–253.
E171.P47, v. 5 1971

Early attempts to use the law to enforce morality failed. By the end of the Revolutionary period, according to the author, the aim of criminal law had consciously become the protection of property and the preservation of social order.

10480

Fowler, William C.   Local law in Massachusetts, historically considered. New-England historical and genealogical register, v. 25, July–Oct. 1871: 274–284, 345–351; v. 26, Jan., July 1872: 55–60, 284–293.
F1.N56, v. 25–26

10481

Franklin, Frank G.   The legislative history of naturalization in the United States, 1776–1795. *In* American

Historical Association. Annual report. 1901. v. 1. Washington, 1902. p. 299–317.

E172.A60, 1901, v. 1

10482

Franklin, Frank G.   The legislative history of naturalization in the United States, from the Revolutionary War to 1861. Chicago, University of Chicago Press, 1906. ix, 308 p.   JK1814.F84

Bibliography: p. 301–305.

Also issued as thesis (Ph.D.)—University of Chicago, 1900.

Reprinted in New York by Arno Press (1969) and A. M. Kelley (1971).

"The Revolutionary period": p. 1–18.

"The Convention of 1787": p. 19–32.

10483

Gardiner, Asa B.   Martial law during the Revolution. Magazine of American history, with notes and queries, v. 1, Dec. 1877: 705–719.   E171.M18, v. 1

10484

McMaster, John B.   Old standards of public morals. American historical review, v. 11, Apr. 1906: 515–528.

E171.A57, v. 11

Finds the standards of public morality that prevailed during the Revolutionary and early national periods woefully deficient.

10485

Maier, Pauline.   Popular uprisings and civil authority in eighteenth-century America. William and Mary quarterly, 3d ser., v. 27, Jan. 1970: 3–35.

F221.W71, 3d s., v. 27

Because it was viewed as a necessary check against government, popular tumult was tolerated, even condoned, in colonial America. After the Revolution, however, the fear of institutionalized power was eroded as popular uprisings came to be seen as an insult to legitimate authority and a threat to stability.

10486

Nelson, Harold L.   Seditious libel in colonial America. American journal of legal history, v. 3, Apr. 1959: 160–172.   LL

10487

Parkes, Henry B.   Morals and law enforcement in colonial New England. New England quarterly, v. 5, July 1932: 431–452.   F1.N62, v. 5

Contends that standards of morality were unusually high and that the laws were quite humane.

10488

Reeves, Jesse S.   The influence of the law of nature upon international law in the United States. American journal of international law, v. 3, July 1909: 547–561.

JX1.A6, v. 3

Considers the effect that the writings of European legal theorists regarding the law of nations had upon the Revolutionary generation.

10489

Reppy, Alison.   The spectre of attainder in New York [1683–1788] St. John's law review, v. 23, Nov. 1948: 1–67.   LL

10490

Setaro, Franklyn C.   The formative era of American admiralty law [1629–1789] New York law forum, v. 5, Jan. 1959: 9–44.   LL

10491

Surrency, Erwin C.   Revision of colonial laws. American journal of legal history, v. 9, July 1965: 189–202.

LL

10492

Teeter, Dwight L.   The printer [Eleazer Oswald] and the chief justice [Thomas McKean]: seditious libel in 1782–83. Journalism quarterly, v. 45, summer 1968: 235–242, 260.   PN4700.J7, v. 45

10493

Trent, William P.   The case of Josiah Philips. American historical review, v. 1, Apr. 1896: 444–454.

E171.A57, v. 1

The use of the bill of attainder against Josiah Philips, a laborer of Lynnhaven Parish, Va., who led an insurrection in the counties of Princess Anne and Norfolk, 1775–78.

6. Lawyers and Legal Training

10494

Alderman, Ernest H.   The North Carolina colonial bar. *In* The James Sprunt historical publications. v. 13, no. 1. Chapel Hill, The University, 1913. p. [3]–31.

F251.J28, v. 13, no. 1

10495

Bedwell, Cyril E. A.   American Middle Templars. American historical review, v. 25, July 1920: 680–689.

E171.A57, v. 25

A list, with introduction, of prominent American lawyers who studied at the Middle Temple, 115 of whom were admitted to the Inns of Court from 1760 to the close of the Revolution.

10496

Binney, Horace.   The leaders of the old bar of Philadelphia. Pennsylvania magazine of history and biography, v. 14, Apr.–Oct. 1890: 1–27, 143–159, 223–252.

F146.P65, v. 14

Sketches of William Lewis, Edward Tilghman, and Jared Ingersoll.

10497

Blackard, W. R. Requirements for admission to the bar in Revolutionary America. Tennessee law review, v. 15, Feb. 1938: 116–127. LL

10498

Chroust, Anton H. The dilemma of the American lawyer in the post-Revolutionary era. Notre Dame lawyer, v. 35, Dec. 1959: 48–76. LL

10499

Chroust, Anton H. The rise of the legal profession in America. Norman, University of Oklahoma Press [1965] 2 v. KF361.C47

Bibliographic footnotes.
Contents: v. 1. The colonial experience.—v. 2. The Revolution and the post-Revolutionary experience.

In his survey of the practice of law to 1840, the author contends that the Revolution interrupted a general improvement in the competence and status of lawyers in America. Many of the most accomplished members of the colonial bar were driven out of the profession because of their loyalties to the crown; the economic depression that followed the Revolution cast lawyers in the role of oppressors of the debtor class; and the use of English common law and precedent came to be viewed as a scheme to perpetuate a monopolistic legal class. Nonetheless, lawyers attained such prominence in the ranks of public leadership in the half century after the Revolution that Chroust considers that period to be the golden age of the American legal profession.

10500

Eaton, Clement. A mirror of the southern colonial lawyer: the fee books of Patrick Henry, Thomas Jefferson, and Waightstill Avery. William and Mary quarterly, 3d ser., v. 8, Oct. 1951: 520–534. F221.W71, 3d s., v. 8

A study of the fee books, casebooks, and journals of such diverse men offers insight into the practice of law in pre-Revolutionary Virginia and North Carolina.

10501

Gawalt, Gerard W. Massachusetts lawyers: a historical analysis of the process of professionalization, 1760–1840. 1969. ([327] p.) Micro AC–1, no. 70–197

Thesis (Ph.D.)—Clark University.
Abstracted in *Dissertation Abstracts International*, v. 30A, Jan. 1970, p. 2925.

10502

Gawalt, Gerard W. Sources of anti-lawyer sentiment in Massachusetts, 1740–1840. American journal of legal history, v. 14, Oct. 1970: 283–307. LL

Traces the development of a lawyer class, based on education, kinship, and economic status, that came to dominate the most lucrative and prestigious political and judicial positions after the Revolution.

10503

Hamilton, Joseph G. de Roulhac. Southern members of the Inns of Court. North Carolina historical review, v. 10, Oct. 1933: 273–286. F251.N892, v. 10

Lists names and dates of admission by colony.

10504

Hamlin, Paul M. Legal education in colonial New York. New York, New York University, Law Quarterly Review, 1939. xxv, 262 p. facsims., plates, ports. LC1142.N4H3

Thesis (Ph.D.)—Columbia University, 1942.
Facsimile of the "Catalogue of library of John Chambers in his handwriting about 1760" appears on lining-papers.
Reprinted in New York by Da Capo Press (1970. KFN5078.H3 1970).

10505

McKirdy, Charles R. A bar divided: the lawyers of Massachusetts and the American Revolution. American journal of legal history, v. 16, July 1972: 205–214. LL

10506

McKirdy, Charles R. Lawyers in crisis: the Massachusetts legal profession, 1760–1790. 1969. ([279] p.) Micro AC–1, no. 70–117

Thesis (Ph.D.)—Northwestern University.
Abstracted in *Dissertation Abstracts International*, v. 30A, Jan. 1970, p. 2945.

10507

Park, Orville A., *comp.* A history of Georgia in the eighteenth century, as recorded in the reports of the Georgia Bar Association. *In* Georgia Bar Association. Report. 1921. Macon. p. 154–296. LL

——— ——— Reprint. [Macon? Ga., 1921] 143 p. F290.P23

Episodes in the legal history of the colony and state.

10508

Smith, Alan M. Virginia lawyers, 1680–1776: the birth of an American profession. 1967. ([432] p.) Micro AC–1, no. 68–6578

Thesis (Ph.D.)—Johns Hopkins University.
Abstracted in *Dissertation Abstracts*, v. 28A, May 1968, p. 4584–4585.

10509

Suffolk Co., Mass. Bar. Record-book of the Suffolk Bar [1770–1805] *In* Massachusetts Historical Society, *Boston*. Proceedings. v. 19; 1881/82. Boston, 1882. p. 141–179. F61.M38, v. 19

Introduction and notes by George Dexter.
An offprint, with a slightly different title, was published in Cambridge by J. Wilson (1882. 40 p. LL).

10510
Surrency, Erwin C. The lawyer and the Revolution. American journal of legal history, v. 8, Apr. 1964: 125–135. LL

10511
Warren, Charles. A history of the American bar. Boston, Little, Brown, 1911. xii, 586 p. KF352.W3 1911

Contains bibliographies.
Reprinted in New York by H. Fertig (1966 [i.e. 1967]).

The first nine chapters (p. [1]–208) are devoted to the development of the American legal profession to 1789.

10512
Warren, Charles. History of the Harvard Law School and of early legal conditions in America. New York, Lewis Pub. Co., 1908. 3 v. facsims., plates, ports. LC1161.H5W3

Includes bibliographies.
Reprinted in New York by Da Capo Press (1970. KF292.H34W3).

POLITICAL THOUGHT AND PRACTICES

1. The Philosophical and Constitutional Framework of Politics

10513
Adams, Willi P. Das gleichheitspostulat in der amerikanischen Revolution. Historische Zeitschrift, Bd. 212, Feb. 1971: 59–99. D1.H6, v. 212

Discusses several possible reasons why the principle of equality became so important in the political rhetoric of the Revolution.

10514
Antieau, Chester J. Natural rights and the Founding Fathers—the Virginians. Washington and Lee law review, v. 17, spring 1960: 43–79. LL

10515
Arieli, Yehoshua. Individualism and nationalism in American ideology. Cambridge, Mass., Harvard University Press, 1964. xiii, 442 p. (A Publication of the Center for the Study of the History of Liberty in America, Harvard University) HM136.A7

Bibliographic references included in "Notes" (p. [351]–436).

Includes two chapters (p. 49–90) on the breakdown of allegiance to Great Britain and the emergence of a continental American consciousness.

10516
Bell, Robert, comp. Illuminations for legislators, and for sentimentalists. [Philadelphia] Printed and sold by R. Bell, in Third-Street, 1784. 52 p.
JA38.B4 Rare Bk. Coll.
AC901.W7, v. 73 Rare Bk. Coll.

Added title page: Bell's Memorial on the Free Sale of Books: To Which are Added, Sentiments on What is Freedom and What is Slavery, by a Farmer [i.e., John Dickinson]

Contents: 1. Sentiments on what is freedom, and what is slavery, by a farmer.—2. Sentiments on liberty, exhibited in observations on the Revolution of America, by Abbé Raynal.—Sentiments on government, law, arbitrary power, liberty, and social institutions, by J. J. Rousseau.—Sentiments on government, and on the English constitution, by J. L. de Lolme.

10517
Boelte, Hans H. Government; eine Untersuchung zur amerikanischen Herrschaftsweise in der Revolutionszeit: James Otis, Thomas Paine, James Madison. [Köln-Sülz, Druck: A. Bothmann, Dissertationsdruck, 1966?] xii, 297 p. JA84.U5B57

Inaug.-Diss.—Munich.
Bibliography: p. 285–297.

10518
Carpenter, William S. The separation of powers in the eighteenth century. American political science review, v. 22, Feb. 1928: 32–44. JA1.A6, v. 22

10519
Cattelain, Fernand. Étude sur l'influence de Montesquieu dans les constitutions américaines. Besançon, Impr. Millot frères, 1927. 140 p. fold. facsims. JC179.M8C3

Thèse—Université de Besançon.
"Quelques indications bibliographiques": p. [135]–140.

10520
Corwin, Edward S. The "higher law" background of American constitutional law. Harvard law review, v. 42, Dec. 1928–Jan. 1929: 149–185, 365–409. LL

Reissued in Ithaca, N.Y., by Great Seal Books (1955. 89 p. KF4541.Z9C6).

10521
Corwin, Edward S. The progress of constitutional theory between the Declaration of Independence and the meeting of the Philadelphia Convention. American historical review, v. 30, Apr. 1925: 511–536.
E171.A57, v. 30

Finds that the bias in favor of local autonomy was significantly altered by a growing comprehension of judicial review and the notion of a higher law.

10522
Dion, Léon. Natural law and manifest destiny in the era of the American Revolution. Canadian journal of economics and political science, v. 23, May 1957: 227–247. H1.C3, v. 23

10523
Dunbar, Louise B. A study of "monarchical" tendencies in the United States, from 1776 to 1801. Urbana, Uni-

versity of Illinois [ᶜ1923] 164 p. (University of Illinois studies in the social sciences, v. 10, no. 1)

H31.I4, v. 10, no. 1
E210.D87

Issued also as thesis (Ph.D.)—University of Illinois.
Bibliography: p. 135–149.

Reprinted in Urbana by the University of Illinois (1970) and in New York by the Johnson Reprint Corp. (1970).

Following a review of the colonial attitude towards kingship after 1765, the author examines several plans, including those advanced by the comte de Broglie to Silas Deane in Paris, by the Irish-born American officer Col. Lewis Nicola, and by others during the framing of the Constitution. Dunbar concludes that Americans who favored monarchy generally kept silent, that partisan accusations about Federalists being monarchists had little foundation, and that Americans were essentially antimonarchical.

10524

Farnell, Robert S.   Positive valuations of politics and government in the thought of five American Founding Fathers: Thomas Jefferson, John Adams, James Madison, Alexander Hamilton, and George Washington. 1970. ([238] p.)   Micro AC–1, no. 71–1053

Thesis (Ph.D.)—Cornell University.

Abstracted in *Dissertation Abstracts International*, v. 31A, Mar. 1971, p. 4853.

10525

Gilbert, Felix.   The eighteenth-century background. *In* Nelson, William H., *ed.* Theory and practice in American politics. [Chicago] Published for William Marsh Rice University by University of Chicago Press [1964] p. 1–12.   E183.T45

"Note on sources": p. 12.

10526

Gillen, Jerome J.   Political thought in Revolutionary New York, 1763–1789. 1972. ([269] p.)

Micro AC–1, no. 72–25,876

Thesis (Ph.D.)—Lehigh University.

Abstracted in *Dissertation Abstracts International*, v. 33A, Oct. 1972, p. 1641.

10527

Hans, Nicholas A.   Franklin, Jefferson, and the English radicals at the end of the eighteenth century. *In* American Philosophical Society, *Philadelphia*. Proceedings, v. 98, Dec. 23, 1954: 406–426.   Q11.P5, v. 98

10528

Hartz, Louis.   American political thought and the American Revolution. American political science review, v. 46, June 1952: 321–342.   JA1.A6, v. 46

10529

Hartz, Louis.   The liberal tradition in America; an interpretation of American political thought since the Revolution. New York, Harcourt, Brace [1955] ix, 329 p.

E175.9.H37

Bibliographic references included in "Notes" (p. 313–320).

Analyzes the American social and political order to explain the uniqueness of the national experience. The author concludes that the absence of a feudal past was the key factor in determining the nature of America's political tradition. Born free, with no *ancien régime* to overthrow and no class struggle to divide it, the United States has been a monolithic liberal society throughout its history. The patriots of 1776 fought to conserve a Lockean system of natural rights, popular sovereignty, and limited government rather than to gain new liberties. Instead of experiencing a period of reaction or restoration after the Revolution, they formalized their common and tested values in an enduring constitution.

10530

Hewitt, Mary C.   The political philosophy of the American Revolution. 1901.

Thesis (Ph.D.)—Yale University.

10531

Houlette, William D.   Political philosophy of the American Revolutionary era. Journal of American history, v. 29, July/Sept. 1935: 123–135.   E171.J86, v. 29

10532

Jacobson, Norman.   Political science and political education. American political science review, v. 57, Sept. 1963: 561–569.   JA1.A6, v. 57

Discusses the two varieties of political thought competing for allegiance at the time of the Revolution—the individualistic, intuitive, and idealistic views of Rousseau and Paine that found their expression in the Declaration of Independence and Articles of Confederation and the orderly, rationalistic, and materialistic concerns of Hamilton and Madison embodied in the Constitution.

10533

Lewis, Ewart K.   The contribution of medieval thought to the American political tradition. American political science review, v. 50, June 1956: 462–474.

JA1.A6, v. 50

Studies the alterations in major political concepts from medieval thought to the body of systematic theory employed by the Founding Fathers.

10534

McLaughlin, Andrew C.   Social compact and constitutional construction. American historical review, v. 5, Apr. 1900: 467–490.   E171.A57, v. 5

Argues that the compact theory of government popularized during the Revolutionary period influenced political philosophy in subsequent periods of American history.

10535

Mason, Alpheus T., *and* Richard H. Leach.   In quest of freedom; American political thought and practice. Englewood Cliffs, N.J., Prentice-Hall, 1959. viii, 568 p.

JK31.M35

Bibliographic footnotes.

The authors treat the period through the endorsement of the Constitution in chapters 1–6 (p. 1–166).

10536

Miller, Helen D. Hill. The case for liberty. Chapel Hill, University of North Carolina Press [1965] xvi, 254 p. illus., facsims., ports.   KF4749.M5

"Notes on sources": p. 228–250.

Examines the events surrounding nine cases of conflict over individual rights—the right to bear arms, 1676; freedom of the press, 1735; search and seizure, 1761; the right to a jury, 1764; freedom from extortion, 1770; freedom of religion, 1771; quartering of troops, 1771; due process of law, 1773; and trial in the vicinage, 1773. The author emphasizes the political aspects of each case and suggests that colonial experiences were more important than English precedents or political theories in shaping the guarantees of individual rights provided in the constitutions of the new states and nation.

10537

Miller, Ralph N. American nationalism as a theory of nature. William and Mary quarterly, 3d ser., v. 12, Jan 1955: 74–95.   F221.W71, 3d s., v. 12

Attempting to remove the stigma of inferiority placed upon America by European writers, such early historians as Mercy Warren, David Ramsay, and Jedidiah Morse wrote of a nation created in accord with natural principles. It would endure if the qualities demonstrated by Americans—simplicity, learning, initiative, character, and love of liberty—continued to predominate.

10538

Moran, Thomas F. The rise and development of the bicameral system in America. Baltimore, Johns Hopkins Press, 1895. 54 p. (Johns Hopkins University studies in historical and political science, 13th ser., no. 5)   H31.J6, 13th s., no. 5
                    JK1027.M7

Traces the evolution of the bicameral system in the New England, middle, and southern colonies and under the federal Constitution.

10539

Morgan, Edmund S., *ed.* Puritan political ideas, 1558–1794. Indianapolis, Bobbs-Merrill [°1965] liii, 404 p. (The American heritage series, 33)   JA84.U5M7

"Collateral reading": p. xlix–lii.

Presents 22 selected essays, tracts, and sermons by Puritan spokesmen in England and America concluding with works by Abraham Williams, 1762, Samuel Langdon, 1775, and Ezra Stiles, 1794.

10540

Noveck, Simon. The democratic idea in the United States, 1774–1801. 1955. ([440] p.)
                    Micro AC–1, no. 12,459

Thesis (Ph.D.)—Columbia University.
Abstracted in *Dissertation Abstracts*, v. 15, no. 8, 1955, p. 1430.

10541

Patterson, Caleb Perry. The evolution of constitutionalism. Minnesota law review, v. 32, Apr. 1948: 427–457.
                    LL

Includes, on p. 446–457, a discussion of the doctrine of limited government in America, 1761–87.

10542

Sandler, S. Gerald. Lockean ideas in Jefferson's *Bill for Establishing Religious Freedom*. Journal of the history of ideas, v. 21, Jan./Mar. 1960: 110–116.
                    B1.J75, v. 21

10543

Savelle, Max. American political ideas and the American Revolution. *In* Australian and New Zealand American Studies Association. Pacific circle; proceedings of the second biennial conference of the Australian and New Zealand American Studies Association. [Edited by Norman Harper. St. Lucia, Brisbane] University of Queensland Press [1968] (American studies down under, 1) p. 37–53.   E169.1.A975

10544

Savelle, Max. Nationalism and other loyalties in the American Revolution. American historical review, v. 67, July 1962: 901–923.   E171.A57, v. 67

Even though it was accentuated by the war years, the transition in the minds of Americans from the image of the British empire-nation of the colonial era to the image of a genuine, integral American nation took many years.

10545

Schouler, James. Constitutional studies, state and federal. New York, Dodd, Mead, 1897. xii, 332 p.   JK34.S4

Bibliographic footnotes.
Reprinted in New York by Da Capo Press (1971).

In a survey of American political ideology, the author first considers early colonial charters, Revolutionary bills of rights, and the first state constitutions. In part 2 he focuses on early attempts at colonial union, the Articles of Confederation, and the theoretical structure of the government established under the Constitution. A third part is devoted to a comparison of state constitutions adopted after 1789.

10546

Selby, John E. A concept of liberty. 1955. ([208] p.)
                    Micro AC–1, no. 13,188

Thesis (Ph.D.)—Brown University.
Abstracted in *Dissertation Abstracts*, v. 15, no. 8, 1955, p. 1384–1385.

The liberties that Americans demanded of Great Britain and sought to protect under the federal Constitution derived in part from their knowledge and interpretation of history.

10547

Smith, James M. The transformation of republican thought, 1763–1787. *In* Indiana Historical Society. Lectures. 1969/70. Indianapolis, 1970. p. [22]–60.

E171.I6, 1969/70

Reflects on the efforts of political leaders before, during, and after the war to strike a proper balance between power and liberty in their evaluation and reconstruction of governmental institutions. Having debated extensively difficult questions concerning representation, sovereignty, the separation of powers, a written constitution, and the relationship between central and local governments, Americans established a democratic form of republican rule that limited simple majoritarianism in an effort to preserve individual liberty while at the same time creating a strong central government and a federal union of states that derived their power from a sovereign people.

10548

Tate, Thaddeus W. The social contract in America, 1774–1787: revolution theory as a conservative instrument. William and Mary quarterly, 3d ser., v. 22, July 1965: 375–391. F221.W71, 3d s., v 22

Somewhat vague in their understanding of the details of the contract theory, American revolutionaries made particular use of two precepts—the right of revolution and the origin of government in consent—to achieve separation from Great Britain and to provide a constitutional basis for new governments. The procedures that they developed for drafting, ratifying, and amending constitutions proved to be their most enduring contribution to a continuing tradition. Beyond that, however, few were willing to go.

10549

Tate, Thaddeus W. The theory of the social contract in the American Revolution, 1776–1787. 1960. ([300] p.)

Micro AC–1, no. 62–5764

Thesis (Ph.D.)—Brown University.
Abstracted in *Dissertation Abstracts*, v. 23, Nov. 1962, p. 1677–1678.

10550

Wise, Floy S. The growth of political democracy in the states, 1776–1828. 1945.

Thesis (Ph.D.)—University of Texas.

10551

Wood, Gordon S. The creation of the American Republic, 1776–1787. Chapel Hill, Published for the Institute of Early American History and Culture at Williamsburg, Va., by the University of North Carolina Press [1969] xiv, 653 p. JA84.U5W6

Includes bibliographic references.
The author's thesis (Ph.D.), *The Creation of an American Polity in the Revolutionary Era*, was submitted to Harvard University in 1964.

Dividing the book into six parts, the author surveys Whig political ideology before the Revolution, reviews constitution-making in the states, traces the growth of democratic thought, describes the excesses of the Confederation period, compares the ideas of the federal Constitution with the Whig views of 1776, and assesses the Revolutionary achievement. Wood contends that Americans formulated not just new modes of government but also political theories based upon new assumptions. The stability of government no longer rested upon the embodiment in constitutions of the basic social forces, such as classes or estates; instead, a kinetic view of politics replaced the static ideal. Experience gained under the state constitutions taught that society consisted of competing interest groups; the purpose of government, therefore, was to insure that no one group or individual gained ascendency. From the Declaration to the Constitution the definition of "liberty" gradually changed from the old Whig notion of the people's right to share in government to the modern idea that "liberty" depended upon the protection of individual rights from encroachment by dominant forces within society, including government.

10552

Wright, Benjamin F., *ed.* A source book of American political theory. New York, Macmillan Co., 1929. xi, 644 p. JA84.U5W7

Partial contents: Constitutional protest and revolution (p. 41–115).—State constitution making during the Revolution (p. 116–173).—The framing and ratification of the federal Constitution (p. 174–276).

2. THE FRANCHISE, ELECTIONS, AND REPRESENTATION

10553

Bassett, John S. Suffrage in the state of North Carolina (1776–1861). In American Historical Association. Annual report. 1895. Washington, 1896. p. 269–285.

E172.A60, 1895

10554

Bishop, Cortlandt F. History of elections in the American colonies. New York, Columbia College, 1893. v, 297 p. (Studies in history, economics and public law, v. 3, no. 1) H31.C7, v. 3, no. 1

JK97.A3B61

"Authorities quoted": p. [289]–295.
Reprinted in New York by B. Franklin (1968) and AMS Press (1970).

Dividing the work between general and local elections, the author offers in the first part a colony-by-colony history of general elections, analyzes their management, and describes the qualifications of electors. In part 2 he examines town, parish, and municipal elections.

10555

Chandler, Julian A. C. The history of suffrage in Virginia. Baltimore, Johns Hopkins Press, 1901. 76 p. (Johns Hopkins University studies in historical and political science, 19th ser., no. 6/7). H31.J6, 19th s., no. 6/7

JK1936.V8C5

10556

Chandler, Julian A. C. Representation in Virginia. Baltimore, Johns Hopkins Press, 1896. 83 p. (Johns Hop-

kins University studies in historical and political science, 14th ser., 6–7)   JK3968.C5
H31.J6, 14th s., no. 6–7

In a survey of the systems of representation employed in Virginia from 1607 to 1891, the author briefly describes provisions of the constitution of 1776 and the conflict over reapportionment that followed the Revolution.

10557
Chute, Marchette G.   The first liberty; a history of the right to vote in America, 1619–1850. New York, Dutton, 1969. xii, 371 p.   JK1846.C54

Includes bibliographic references.

10558
Cohen, Joel A.   Democracy in Revolutionary Rhode Island: a statistical analysis. Rhode Island history, v. 29, winter/spring 1970: 3–16. facsims., ports.
F76.R472, v. 29

With well over 70 percent of the state's adult males qualified to vote, Rhode Islanders elected town councilmen and assembly representatives who were in either the wealthy or very wealthy categories in their respective towns, thus making the state an upper class, not a middle class democracy.

10559
Daniels, Bruce C.   Deference and rotation of selectmen's offices in 18th-century Connecticut. *In* Connecticut Historical Society, *Hartford.* Bulletin, v. 37, July 1972: 92–96.   F91.C67, v. 37

10560
Dinkin, Robert J.   Elections in colonial Connecticut. *In* Connecticut Historical Society, *Hartford.* Bulletin, v. 37, Jan. 1972: 17–20.   F91.C67, v. 37

10561
Franklin, W. Neil.   Some aspects of representation in the American colonies. North Carolina historical review, v. 6, Jan. 1929: 38–66.   F251.N892, v. 6

10562
Jameson, John Franklin.   Did the fathers vote? New England magazine, new ser., v. 1, Jan. 1890: 484–490.
AP2.N4, n.s., v. 1

Using Massachusetts statistics for 1776–89, Jameson indicates that few white males qualified to vote and even fewer bothered to do so.

10563
Leonard, Joan de Lourdes, *Sister.*   Elections in colonial Pennsylvania. William and Mary quarterly, 3d ser., v. 11, July 1954: 385–401.   F221.W71, 3d s., v. 11

10564
McKinley, Albert E.   The suffrage franchise in the thirteen English colonies in America. Philadelphia, For the University; Boston, Ginn, agents, 1905. v, 518 p. (Publica-

tions of the University of Pennsylvania. Series in history, no. 2)   JK96.A3M2
E172.P4, no. 2

Reprinted in New York by B. Franklin (1969).

Describes parliamentary suffrage in 17th-century England and examines the development of the elective franchise in each of the 13 colonies from the creation of its first legislature to the Revolution. Although a natural adherence to familiar practices and the determined efforts of British authorities made English precedents common in all the colonies, the evolution from a freeman suffrage to a more restrictive freehold suffrage was due as much to the increasing awareness of differing interests between property holders and non-property holders. McKinley suggests that the total of potential voters in the individual colonies varied from one-sixth to one-fiftieth of their populations.

10565
Olbrich, Emil.   The development of sentiment on Negro suffrage to 1860. [Madison, Wis.] University of Wisconsin, 1912. 135 p. (Bulletin of the University of Wisconsin, no. 477. History series, v. 3, no. 1)
H31.W62, v. 3, no. 1
JK1923.O55

Originally presented as the author's thesis (M.A.)—University of Wisconsin, 1906.

Reprinted in New York by Negro Universities Press (1969) and in Freeport, N.Y., by Books for Libraries Press (1971).

"Colonial practice and Revolutionary principles, to 1790": p. 7–20.

10566
Phillips, Hubert.   The development of a residential qualification for representatives in colonial legislatures. Cincinnati, Printed for the author by the Abingdon Press [ᶜ1921] 256 p.   JK81.P5 1921a

Published also as thesis (Ph.D.)—Columbia University, 1921.

Bibliography: p. 248–256.

Surveying 17th-century developments in each of the 13 colonies, the author provides numerous examples of the application of precedent during the 18th century and in some cases the adoption of colonial forms in the new state constitutions.

10567
Pole, Jack R.   Political representation in England and the origins of the American Republic. Berkeley, University of California Press [1971, ᶜ1966] xvii, 606 p. maps.
JK54.P6 1971

Bibliography: p. [565]–581.

In a comparative study of the theory and practice of political representation in England and America from the 17th to the early 19th centuries, the author surveys the concept of representation in the works of Harrington, Sidney, and Locke; analyzes the assertion of legislative power and constitution-making in colonial and Revolutionary Massachusetts, Pennsylvania, and Virginia; and studies the beginnings of majority rule and the evolution of political individualism. Pole concludes that the American Revolution was the fulfillment of the Whig tradition of the supremacy and fiduciary authority of the legislature and that the war was fought to inaugurate sweeping advances toward more democratic government. He contends that the foundation of majority rule during the Revolutionary era was made possible by the emergence of the individual as the basic unit of political representation.

10568

Pole, Jack R.   The reform of suffrage and representation in New Jersey, 1774–1844. 1953. ([303] p.)

Micro AC–1, no. 6829

Thesis (Ph.D.)—Princeton University.
Abstracted in *Dissertation Abstracts*, v. 14, no. 2, 1954, p. 348.

10569

Pole, Jack R.   Representation and authority in Virginia from the Revolution to reform. Journal of southern history, v. 24, Feb. 1958: 16–50.   F206.J68, v. 24

Compares the proportion of votes cast to the total number of free adult white males eligible to vote in elections from 1776 to 1860.

10570

Pole, Jack R.   Suffrage and representation in Maryland from 1776 to 1810: a statistical note and some reflections. Journal of southern history, v. 24, May 1958: 218–225.   F206.J68, v. 24

10571

Pole, Jack R.   Suffrage and representation in Massachusetts: a statistical note. William and Mary quarterly, 3d ser., v. 14, Oct. 1957: 560–592.

F221.W71, 3d s., v. 14

"Election statistics for Massachusetts, Connecticut, and New Hampshire, 1780–1860": p. 580–592.

Finds that under the Massachusetts Constitution of 1780 there was little to prevent any adult male from exercising the suffrage franchise.

10572

Pole, Jack R.   Suffrage reform and the American Revolution in New Jersey. *In* New Jersey Historical Society. Proceedings, v. 74, July 1956: 173–194.

F131.N58, v. 74

Discusses the effect upon suffrage of the reforms embodied in the state constitution of 1776.

10573

Steiner, Bernard C.   Citizenship and suffrage in Maryland. Baltimore, Md., Cushing, 1895. 95 p.   JK1936.M3S8

Considers colonial and Revolutionary practices in the first portion of the work.

10574

Thorpe, James A.   Colonial suffrage in Massachusetts; an essay review. *In* Essex Institute, *Salem, Mass.* Historical collections, v. 106. July 1970: 169–181.

F72.E7E81, v. 106

10575

Williamson, Chilton.   American suffrage and Sir William Blackstone. Political science quarterly, v. 68, Dec. 1953: 552–557.   H1.P8, v. 68

Concludes that Blackstone's ideas were introduced in America just in time to be rejected by reformers.

10576

Williamson, Chilton.   American suffrage; from property to democracy, 1760–1860. Princeton, Princeton University Press, 1960. x, 306 p.   JK1846.W5

Includes bibliographic references in footnotes.

Traces the evolution of legal requirements for voting in each colony and state and describes arguments for and against each major innovation. The author contends that the changes made during the Revolutionary era were the most important of any before the Civil War; they committed the nation to the ultimate qualification—humanity—in place of the earlier standards of property ownership and payment of taxes. Contrary to the Turner thesis, Williamson finds that stimulus for the democratization of the suffrage laws came from the states along the eastern seaboard rather than from the new states of the West.

10577

Wood, Gordon S.   Representation in the American Revolution. Charlottesville, Published for the Jamestown Foundation of the Commonwealth of Virginia by the University Press of Virginia [1969] 66 p. (Jamestown essays on representation)   JK54.W66

Bibliographic footnotes.

The Revolutionary generation became increasingly aware after 1776 that politics was no longer a contest between rulers and ruled or between institutionalized classes of society. As a result, older theories of mixed government and virtual representation gave way to radically new concepts of representation that were soon embodied in the federal Constitution—the concepts that all branches of government are responsible to the people for the use and exercise of their power and that it is the function of government to represent and to mediate among competing interest groups seeking to control the sources of power within society.

Society, Religion, and Culture

GENERAL STUDIES

1. GENERAL

10578

Abbott, Edward.   Revolutionary times: sketches of our country, its people, and their ways one hundred years ago. Boston, Roberts Bros., 1876. 208 p.   E163.A13

"Sources": p. 199–204.

10579

Adair, Douglass G. Fame and the Founding Fathers. *In* Conference on Early American History, *19th, Moravian College, 1966.* Fame and the Founding Fathers; papers and comments. Edited by Edmund P. Willis. Bethlehem, Pa., Moravian College [1967] p. 27–50.
E310.C74 1966aa

The Revolution proved a catalyst in transforming the lifetime ambitions of some of the revolutionaries.

10580

Adams, James T. Provincial society, 1690–1763. New York, Macmillan Co., 1927. xvii, 374 p. facsim., plates, ports. (A History of American life, v. 3)
E169.1.H67, v. 3
E195.A22

"Critical essay on authorities": p. 324–356.

Examining the religious, cultural, social, economic, and commercial sides of colonial life, the author concludes that while the colonists as immigrants were the product of European influences, the colonial-born Revolutionary generation had developed a distinctly American character.

10581

Andrews, Charles M. Colonial folkways; a chronicle of American life in the reign of the Georges. New Haven, Yale University Press, 1919. x, 255 p. plates, port. (The Chronicles of America series, v. 9) E173.C55, v. 9
E162.A57

"Bibliographical note": p. 239–243.

Covers topics such as architecture, home furnishings, clothing, recreation, intellectual life, labor, travel, and religion.

10582

Berthoff, Rowland T. An unsettled people; social order and disorder in American history. New York, Harper & Row [1971] xvi, 528 p. illus., maps. HN57.B47

Includes bibliographic references.

The author considers the Revolution to be a major point of transition between two of three periods in American social history which he defines as the first American society, 1607–1775, the society of individuals, 1775–1875, and the reconstituted society, 1875–1945. Arguing that colonial society was hierarchical with stable institutions based on ancient, accepted values, Berthoff contends that the accelerated economic progress, pervasive individualism, and heightened mobility that followed the Revolution led eventually to the disintegration of the conservative order. In considering the Revolution itself, Berthoff concludes that by 1775 the independence of American society was long-established and unchallenged. The issue that precipitated the war was whether the relationship of the provincial legislatures to Parliament would continue to be one of virtual equality or whether the legislatures would be reduced to a state of subservience.

10583

Bohman, George V. The colonial period. *In* Speech Association of America. A history and criticism of American public address. v. 1. William Norwood Brigance, editor. New York, McGraw-Hill, 1943. p. 3–54.
PS400.S66, v. 1

10584

Bridenbaugh, Carl. Cities in revolt; urban life in America, 1743–1776. New York, Knopf, 1955. xiii, 433, xxi p. illus., facsims., map, ports. E162.B85

"Bibliographical note": p. 427–[434]

A wide-ranging treatment of the spectacular physical, economic, social, and cultural growth of five major cities—Boston, Newport, New York, Philadelphia, and Charleston. In his sequel to *Cities in the Wilderness: The First Century of Urban Life in America, 1625–1742,* 2d ed. (New York, Knopf, 1955), the author contends that the cities were a locus for people, leadership, and events. These three elements interacted to express in concrete fashion the sense of American nationality that had been evident since 1764. The Revolution, he concludes, was the culmination of a deeper, more subtle change that embraced the entire colonial experience. The cities revolted against the past and, in the spirit of the Enlightenment, entered modern times.

10585

Browne, Ray B. Superstitions used as propaganda in the American Revolution. New York folklore quarterly, v. 17, autumn 1961: 202–211. GR1.N473, v. 17

10586

Chinard, Gilbert. Eighteenth century theories on America as a human habitat. *In* American Philosophical Society, *Philadelphia.* Proceedings, v. 91, Aug. 1947: 27–57.
Q11.P5, v. 91

10587

Colonial America from the first settlements to the close of the American Revolution, by the editors of the *Album of American History.* New York, Scribner [1971, ᶜ1944] ix, 449 p. illus. E188.A34 1971

Originally published as: *Album of American History,* v. 1.

Contains black-and-white reproductions of contemporary illustrations and photographs of surviving buildings, implements, and other objects from the 18th century.

10588

Greene, Evarts B. The Revolutionary generation, 1763–1790. New York, Macmillan Co., 1943. xvii, 487 p. illus., facsims., maps, plates, ports. (A History of American life, v. 4) E169.1.H67, v. 4
E302.1.G82

"Critical essay on authorities": p. 424–456.

Tracing the development of American economic, social, and cultural institutions during three phases of the Revolutionary era, the author treats nearly 700 topics as diverse as transatlantic trade, status of women and Negroes, practice of law and medicine, reading tastes, and American linguistic emancipation from English forms. Before 1775, strong bonds linked the English colonies with Europe, but the war encouraged the emergence of an American nationalism that, after 1783, threatened to break most of these ties.

10589

Griffith, Ernest S. History of American city government. [v. 1] The colonial period. New York, Oxford University Press, 1938. 464 p.   JS309.G7, v. 1

Includes bibliographies.

Reprinted in New York by Da Capo Press (1972. JS309.G72).

Studies the charters, powers, privileges, jurisdictions, functions, finances, and constituencies of all municipal corporations and selected unincorporated towns. In assessing the quality of colonial city government, Griffith determines that only in smaller communities, where religious factors were strong, or in municipalities that benefited from the stimulus of a Franklin did a spirit of public service evolve that was divorced from social status, and that on the eve of the Revolution only New York enjoyed a truly representative government.

10590

Hay, Robert P. The Liberty Tree: a symbol for American patriots [1777–1876] Quarterly journal of speech, v. 55, Dec. 1969: 414–424.   PN4071.Q3, v. 55

10591

Hofstadter, Richard. America at 1750; a social portrait. New York, Knopf, 1971. xvi, 293, xiii p.
            HN57.H545

Includes bibliographic references.

Published posthumously, the work was intended to be the first section of a three-volume history of American political culture from 1750 to the present. The author attributes considerable importance to conflict and stress inherent in white servitude and slavery, the Great Awakening, and the class system, yet he finds that American society in the mid-18th century was pluralistic, unified, prosperous, and characterized by significant upward mobility.

10592

Jameson, John Franklin. The American Revolution considered as a social movement. Princeton, Princeton University Press, 1926. 157 p.   E209.J33

Contents: The Revolution and the status of persons.—The Revolution and the land.—Industry and commerce.—Thought and feeling.

Reprinted in New York by P. Smith (1950. 100 p.).

In a series of four lectures delivered during the sesquicentennial of independence, Jameson argued that the Revolution was a major watershed in the development of social and economic democracy in America. Changes that tended "in the direction of a leveling democracy" were produced by the broadening of the franchise, the discontinuance of feudal holdovers such as quit-rents, the abolition of primogeniture and entail, the confiscation and distribution of Tory estates among small landholders, the disestablishment of the Anglican church and the separation of church and state, the abolition of slavery in some of the states, and the decline of artificial class distinctions. Ultimately, the less privileged—the small farmer, laborer, and debtor—were the inheritors of the Revolutionary legacy. In his article, "The American Revolution Considered as a Social Movement; A Re-evaluation," *American Historical Review*, v. 60, Oct. 1954, p. 1–12, Frederick B. Tolles contends that Jameson, in constructing his conceptual model, posited too abrupt a set of social changes.

10593

Jones, Howard M. America and French culture, 1750–1848. Chapel Hill, University of North Carolina Press, 1927. xvi, 615 p. illus.   E183.8.F8J7

Bibliography: p. 573–602.

Concerned primarily with the influence of French culture upon American letters, the author examines a number of subjects, including population movements, language, manners, the arts, education, religion, and politics.

10594

Jones, Howard M. O strange new world; American culture: the formative years. New York, Viking Press [1964] xiv, 464 p. illus., facsim.   E169.1.J644 1964

"Reference notes": p. 397–449.

Summarizes contemporary European and American attitudes toward North American civilization from the discovery to 1800. Jones comments on such topics as the Spanish influence upon New World culture; Renaissance styles in architecture, arts, and manners; the impact of Greco-Roman traditions upon early American culture; and the effect of the sheer vastness of the continent upon the American character. In the concluding chapters he discusses American efforts following the disruption of revolution to create a native culture independent of British influence.

10595

Korn, Harold. The oratory of the American Revolution. 1914.

Thesis (Ph.D.)—New York University.

10596

Kraus, Michael. The Atlantic civilization: eighteenth-century origins. Ithaca, Cornell University Press, 1949. xi, 334 p.   CB411.K7

Bibliographic footnotes. Bibliography: p. 315–325.

Reprinted in New York by Russell & Russell (1961).

Surveys the cultural interchange between America and Europe, stressing the reciprocal nature of influences in the fields of communication, books and learning, the arts, humanitarianism, science, medicine, religion, utopian political thought, and nationalism. Although the American Revolution accelerated the forces of nationalism, Kraus believes that American federalism mitigated this tendency by providing an impetus toward world organization.

10597

Kraus, Michael. Intercolonial aspects of American culture on the eve of the Revolution, with special reference to

the northern towns. New York, Columbia University Press, 1928. 251 p. (Studies in history, economics and public law, no. 302)   H31.C7, no. 302
E163.K9

Published also as thesis (Ph.D.)—Columbia University, 1928.
"Lists of authorities": p. 227–244.
Reprinted in New York by Octagon Books (1964).

Stressing developments that contributed to a growing sense of community, especially in Boston, New York, and Philadelphia, the author investigates cultural exchanges between colonies in ten fields: business, law, medicine, religion, printing, literature, the arts, recreation, education, and science.

10598
Kulikoff, Allan.   The progress of inequality in Revolutionary Boston. William and Mary quarterly, 3d ser., v. 28, July 1971: 375–412.   F221.W71, 3d s., v. 28

Finds a rapid advance in social inequality between 1771 and 1790. By the end of the Confederation period wealth was less evenly distributed, the proportion held by the poor and middle classes declined, and the growth of poverty became a major problem. As the division between the rich and poor by wealth, status, and segregated living patterns grew sharper, a class system based primarily on economic lines developed.

10599
Land, Aubrey C.   Economic base and social structure: the northern Chesapeake in the eighteenth century. Journal of economic history, v. 25, Dec. 1965: 639–654.
HC10.J64, v. 25

10600
Lemon, James T., *and* Gary B. Nash.   The distribution of wealth in eighteenth-century America: a century of changes in Chester County, Pennsylvania, 1693–1802. Journal of social history, v. 2, fall 1968: 1–24.
HN1.J6, v. 2

10601
Main, Jackson T.   The results of the American Revolution reconsidered. Historian, v. 31, Aug. 1969: 539–554.
D1.H22, v. 31

Briefly examines economic, social, cultural, political and ideological changes brought about by the Revolution.

10602
Matthews, Albert.   Brother Jonathan. *In* Colonial Society of Massachusetts, *Boston*. Publications. v. 7. Transactions, 1900/1902. Boston, 1905. p. 94–125.
F61.C71, v. 7

On the origins of the term, applied to Americans collectively during the Revolution and after. Comments by other members of the society are included. For further explication, see Matthews' "Brother Jonathan Once More," in v. 32 of the Society's *Publications* (Transactions, 1933/37. Boston, 1937), p. 374–386.

10603
Miller, Samuel.   A brief retrospect of the eighteenth century. Part first; in two volumes: containing a sketch of the revolutions and improvements in science, arts, and literature, during that period. New-York, Printed by T. and J. Swords, no. 160 Pearl-Street, 1803. 2 v.
AZ351.M5

Reprinted in New York by B. Franklin (1970).

A New York Presbyterian minister and member of the American Philosophical Society, Miller prepared in the early years of the 19th century two volumes of an intended eight-volume review of American and European accomplishments in mechanical and chemical philosophy, natural history, medicine, geography, mathematics, navigation, agriculture, mechanical and fine arts, philosophy, literature, history, biography, and poetry during the 18th century. The portion of Miller's work on American literary history has been reprinted, with an introduction and notes by Lyman H. Butterfield, in the *William and Mary Quarterly*, 3d ser., v. 10, Oct. 1953, p. 579–627. See also "A Landmark in American Intellectual History: Samuel Miller's *A Brief Retrospect of the Eighteenth Century*," by Gilbert Chinard, in the *Princeton University Library Chronicle*, v. 14, winter 1953, p. 55–71.

10604
Moller, Herbert.   Sex composition and correlated culture patterns of colonial America. William and Mary quarterly, 3d ser., v. 2, Apr. 1945: 113–153.
F221.W71, 3d s., v. 2

Computes the numerical proportion of men and women by colony and state and assesses the social consequences of continued imbalance.

10605
Nye, Russel B.   The cultural life of the new Nation, 1776–1830. New York, Harper [1960] xii, 324 p. illus., plates, ports. (The New American Nation series)
E169.1.N9

Bibliography: p. 295–310.

Concerned with the burgeoning cultural nationalism spawned by the Revolution, the author traces the development of distinctively American ideas and institutions in religion, science, education, literature, music, architecture, and art. Nye contends that the American Enlightenment, with its belief in scientific rationalism, unlimited progress, and the perfectibility of man, was less conservative than its European counterpart and that the romantic concepts that began to emerge in the new nation at the end of the 18th century were more constructive, democratic, and individualistic than were those in Europe.

10606
Padover, Saul K.   The world of the Founding Fathers. Social research, v. 25, summer 1958: 191–214.
H1.S53, v. 25

10607

Rourke, Constance M.   The roots of American culture and other essays. Edited, with a preface, by Van Wyck Brooks. New York, Harcourt, Brace [1942] xii, 305 p.
E169.1.R78

Reprinted in Port Washington, N.Y., by Kennikat Press (1965).

Eight essays exploring the origin and nature of American esthetic traditions. The opening selection focuses on the late 18th-century concern for the utility of art. Additional topics examined are early theater and music, Shaker culture, folklore, and the traditions that underlay Negro literature.

10608

Savelle, Max.   Seeds of liberty; the genesis of the American mind. Seattle, University of Washington Press, 1965 [ᶜ1948] xvii, 618 p. illus., facsims., fold. map, music, ports.
E169.1.S27 1965

"Chapter nine . . . entitled 'Of music, and of America singing,' was written by Cyclone Covey."
Includes bibliographic references.

Offering a general cultural history of the 13 colonies between 1740 and 1760, the author treats developments in political, economic, and social thought, religion, philosophy, science, literature, and the arts. In a final chapter on patriotism, Savelle contends that the transition from British to provincial to American loyalty symbolized the emergence of a distinct culture whose keynote was liberty.

10609

Schlesinger, Arthur M.   The birth of the nation; a portrait of the American people on the eve of independence. With an introduction by Arthur M. Schlesinger, Jr. New York, Knopf, 1968. viii, 258, xi p.
E162.S3 1968

Bibliography: p. 253–258.

Reflecting the author's mature thinking about colonial society, these posthumously published essays contain impressions of the family, religion, amusements, labor, education, and urban as well as rural lifestyles. Schlesinger depicts an open, mobile, tolerant, middle-class society, where economic opportunity and material progress were everyday realities for most individuals. Since Americans sought to preserve this way of life, the Revolution was a conservative movement aimed only at safeguarding old liberties.

10610

Schlesinger, Arthur M.   Liberty tree: a genealogy. New England quarterly, v. 25, Dec. 1952: 435–458.
F1.N62, v. 25

Traces the origins of the Tree of Liberty emblem to the pine-tree shilling (1652) and indicates its relationship to the Liberty Pole.

10611

Schouler, James.   Americans of 1776. New York, Dodd, Mead, 1906. xiii, 317 p.
E163.S37

Presents 20 lectures on various aspects of Revolutionary society, including births, marriages, and deaths; philanthropy and disease; dress and diet; crime and punishment; and literature, libraries, and the press.

10612

Scudder, Horace E.   Men and manners in America one hundred years ago. New York, Scribner, Armstrong, 1876. 320 p. plates. (Sanssouci series)
E163.S43

A compilation of excerpts from letters, memoirs, and other contemporary sources depicting life in America, especially in New England and the middle colonies, during the Revolution.

10613

Smith, Helen E.   Colonial days & ways as gathered from family papers. With decorations by T. Guernsey Moore. New York, Century Co., 1900. viii, 376 p. illus.
E162.S64

Reprinted in New York by F. Ungar (1966).

10614

Vaughan, Alden T., comp.   America before the Revolution, 1725–1775. Englewood Cliffs, N.J., Prentice-Hall [1967] vi, 185 p. (A Spectrum book, S–169)
E187.V3

Includes 40 contemporary descriptions of various aspects of colonial society and culture at midcentury.

10615

Wertenbaker, Thomas J.   The golden age of colonial culture. [2d ed., rev.] New York, New York University Press [1949] 171 p. (New York University. Stokes Foundation. Anson G. Phelps lectureship on early American history)
E162.W48 1949

Bibliographic footnotes.
First edition published in 1942.

In lectures on six centers of culture—Boston, New York, Philadelphia, Annapolis, Williamsburg, and Charleston—Wertenbaker surveys developments in 18th-century American architecture, education, literature, the arts, and political philosophy. Because the colonists adapted English models to American conditions, intellectual modes and art forms of the pre-Revolutionary period embodied an element of sameness not present in the homespun culture of the early settlements.

10616

Wish, Harvey.   Society and thought in America. v. 1. A social and intellectual history of the American people through 1865. New York, Longmans, Green, 1950. xii, 612 p. illus., facsims., plates, ports.
E169.1.W65, v. 1

"Select bibliography": p. 577–597.
"The Revolutionary era of Hancock and Jefferson (1763–1789)": p. 184–222.

10617

Wood, Gordon S., comp.   The rising glory of America, 1760–1820. New York, G. Braziller [1971] xii, 403 p. illus. (The American culture, 2)
E164.W65 1971

Bibliography: p. [401]–403.

A collection of broadsides, speeches, and essays selected to illustrate the American transition from a group of disparate colonies whose cultural focus was London to an expansive nation turned inward in a search for identity. Twenty-one authors from Samuel Hopkins to Charles Jared Ingersoll reflect contemporary thought in the fields of religion, art, ethics and morality, medicine, printing, painting, and the theater.

10618
Wright, Louis B.   The cultural life of the American colonies, 1607–1763. New York, Harper [1957] xiv, 292 p. illus., map, ports. (The New American Nation series)
E162.W89

Bibliographic references: p. 253–274.

After analyzing agrarian and mercantile society and leadership, the effect of the work ethic on colonial development, and the role played by non-English groups, the author surveys trends, especially in the southern colonies, in religion, education, science, literature, and the arts.

2. NEW ENGLAND

10619
Bridenbaugh, Carl.   The New England town: a way of life. *In* American Antiquarian Society, *Worcester, Mass.* Proceedings, new ser., v. 56, Apr. 1946: 19–48.
E172.A35, n.s., v. 56

Focuses upon the rural town between 1740 and 1776.

10620
Cook, Edward M.   Social behavior and changing values in Dedham, Massachusetts, 1700 to 1775. William and Mary quarterly, 3d ser., v. 27, Oct. 1970: 546–580.
F221.W71, 3d s., v. 27

10621
Curnick, Arthur R.   Social life in the Revolutionary period. *In* Hart, Albert B., *ed.* Commonwealth history of Massachusetts. v. 3. Commonwealth of Massachusetts, 1775–1820. New York, States History Co., 1929. p. 280–305. illus.
F64.H32, v. 3

Bibliography: p. 304–305.

10622
Loughrey, Mary E.   France and Rhode Island, 1686–1800. New York, King's Crown Press, 1944. vii, 186 p.
F90.F7L6 1944a

Issued also as thesis (Ph.D.)—Columbia University.
Bibliography: p. [161]–174.

Focuses on the cordial relations and interest in French culture that grew out of the presence of French military forces in Rhode Island during the intercolonial wars and the American Revolution.

10623
Lovett, Robert W.   A parish weathers war and dissension: the precinct of Salem and Beverly, 1753–1813. *In* Essex

Institute, *Salem, Mass.* Historical collections, v. 99, Apr. 1963: 88–116.
F72.E7E81, v. 99

10624
Scudder, Horace E.   Life in Boston in the Revolutionary period. *In* Winsor, Justin, *ed.* The memorial history of Boston, including Suffolk County, Massachusetts, 1630–1880. v. 3. The Revolutionary period; the last hundred years, pt. 1. Boston, J. R. Osgood, 1881. p. [149]–188. illus.
F73.3.W77, v. 3

"Supplementary notes by the editor": p. 175–188.

10625
Weeden, William B.   Economic and social history of New England, 1620–1789. Boston, Houghton, Mifflin, 1890. 2 v. (xvi, 964 p.)
F7.W38

Reprinted in New York by Hillary House Publishers (1963).

In a detailed, chronological account of New England's social and economic history, the author considers such diverse topics as Indian trade, land management, the development of commerce and manufactures, education, religious life, manners and morals, indentured servitude, the slave trade, finance, and currency problems. He concludes that economic forces were fundamental in molding the character of New England's people and in shaping her institutions.

10626
Wilson, Arthur E.   Weybosset Bridge in Providence Plantations, 1700–1790, being an account of a quest for liberty, with portraits of many saints and sinners, and a special study of the Rev'd Joseph Snow, Jun'r. Boston, Pilgrim Press [1947] xi, 275 p. map (on lining papers)
BR555.R4W5

Bibliography: p. 261–267.

A detailed view, augmented by long excerpts from letters and other contemporary sources, of religious life in Providence, R. I., and of relations between the commercial section of the city and the agricultural settlement on the opposite side of the river, which were connected by a bridge at Weybosset Point.

3. MIDDLE ATLANTIC REGION

10627
Bell, Whitfield J.   Some aspects of the social history of Pennsylvania, 1760–1790. Pennsylvania magazine of history and biography, v. 62, July 1938: 281–308.
F146.P65, v. 62

10628
Bridenbaugh, Carl, *and* Jessica Bridenbaugh.   Rebels and gentlemen; Philadelphia in the age of Franklin. New York, Reynal & Hitchcock [1942] xvii, 393 p. maps, plates, ports.
F158.4.B6

"Bibliographical note": p. 373–379.

Illustrates the impact of the Enlightenment upon 400 Philadelphia teachers, philosophers, scientists, doctors, artists, and craftsmen by describing their accomplishments between 1740 and 1776. In opposition to conservative gentlemen, who accepted cultural and social conventions directly from England, the rebel middle class combined European intellectual currents with native elements to produce a distinctive American culture that made Philadelphia the first broadly democratic society of the modern world.

10629
Fisher, Darlene E. Social life in Philadelphia during the British occupation. Pennsylvania history, v. 37, July 1970: 237–260. F146.P597, v. 37

10630
Heale, M. J. Humanitarianism in the early Republic: the moral reformers of New York, 1776–1825. Journal of American studies, v. 2, Oct. 1968: 161–175.
E151.J6, v. 2

10631
Klein, Milton M. The cultural tyros of colonial New York. South Atlantic quarterly, v. 66, spring 1967: 218–232.
AP2.S75, v. 66

On the belated cultural development of the province.

10632
Lemon, James T. Urbanization and the development of eighteenth-century southeastern Pennsylvania and adjacent Delaware. William and Mary quarterly, 3d ser., v. 24, Oct. 1967: 501–542.
F221.W71, 3d s., v. 24

10633
Malone, Frank D. Latter days of pre-Revolutionary Charlotteburg. In New Jersey Historical Society. Proceedings, v. 80, July 1962: 181–194. map.
F131.N58, v. 80

On the "Great Charlotteburg Furnace Tract."

10634
Monaghan, Frank. The results of the Revolution. In New York State Historical Association. History of the state of New York. v. 4. The new state. New York, Columbia University Press, 1934. p. [321]–362. illus., plate. F119.N65, v. 4

Bibliography: p. 360–362.

10635
Monaghan, Frank, *and* Marvin Lowenthal. This was New York, the nation's capital in 1789. Garden City, N.Y., Doubleday, Doran, 1943. xi, 308 p. facsims., plates, port. F128.44.M86

Bibliography: p. 289–291.
Reprinted in Freeport, N.Y., by Books for Libraries Press (1970).

10636
Pomerantz, Sidney I. New York, an American city, 1783–1803; a study of urban life. New York, Columbia University Press, 1938. 531 p. illus., map. (Studies in history, economics and public law, no. 442)
F128.44.P752

Issued also as thesis (Ph.D.)—Columbia University.
Bibliography: p. 505–519.
Reprinted in Port Washington, N.Y., by I. J. Friedman (1965).

Provides a wealth of detailed information about such topics as politics and government, economic growth, municipal and social services, financial administration, cultural progress, and recreational opportunities. An astonishing revival of trade made New York the country's leading entrepôt by 1800, while a growing population brought new problems of police and fire protection, health and sanitation, and poor relief. To solve them, the city developed a more sophisticated system of municipal finance and organization.

10637
Read, Allen W. Bilingualism in the middle colonies, 1725–1775. American speech, v. 12, Apr. 1937: 93–99.
PE2801.A6, v. 12

10638
Rosewater, Victor. The Liberty bell, its history and significance. New York, D. Appleton, 1926. 246 p. plates. E221.R8

Bibliography: p. 227–233.

10639
Shearer, Augustus H. The church, the school and the press. In New York State Historical Association. History of the state of New York. v. 3. Whig and Tory. New York, Columbia University Press, 1933. p. [45]–90. illus. F119.N65, v. 3

Bibliography: p. 88–90.

10640
Stone, Frederick D. Philadelphia society one hundred years ago, or the reign of Continental money. Pennsylvania magazine of history and biography, v. 3, no. 4, 1879: 361–394. F146.P65, v. 3

10641
Stoudt, John B. The liberty bells of Pennsylvania. Norristown, Pa., 1930. xvi, 204 p. illus., plates. (Pennsylvania-German Society. Proceedings and addresses, v. 37, pt. 2) F146.P23, v. 37

A historical discussion of the Liberty Bell at Independence Hall and similar bells in the counties surrounding Philadelphia. Stoudt maintains that the Liberty Bell cracked, not while tolling for the funeral of Chief Justice John Marshall in 1835, but during the celebration of Washington's birthday in 1846.

10642
Weiss, Harry B. Life in early New Jersey. Princeton, N.J., Van Nostrand, 1964. xi, 169 p. illus., facsims., col. maps (on lining papers) (The New Jersey historical series, v. 26) F134.W4

"Bibliographical notes": p. 154–162.

A general description of aspects of home life, commerce, transportation, medicine, and recreation. Conditions

and customs of the 18th century receive principal consideration.

10643
Wertenbaker, Thomas J. The founding of American civi-
lization: the middle colonies. New York, C. Scribner's
Sons, 1938. xiii, 367 p. illus., plan, plates.
E169.1.W37

Includes bibliographic footnotes.
Reprinted in New York by Cooper Square Publishers
(1963. F106.W48).

Giving major emphasis to architecture and religion, the
author describes the transit of European cultures to New
York, New Jersey, and Pennsylvania, the creation of a distinctly American society under the influence of a new environment, and the interaction of many different national
groups of settlers. Wertenbaker concludes that because of
the heterodox character of their population, the diversity of
their economic life, and the isolation of many of their ethnic
groups from their homelands, the middle colonies provide a
particularly useful perspective from which to observe the
early development of American civilization.

4. The South

10644
Barker, Charles A. Maryland before the Revolution: soci-
ety and thought. American historical review, v. 46,
Oct. 1940: 1–20.   E171.A57, v. 46

Concludes that the secular and critical moods of the
Enlightenment bound into one intellectual whole the legalism, liberalism, skepticism, and literary values of the cul-
tured classes.

10645
Bowes, Frederick P. The culture of early Charleston.
Chapel Hill, University of North Carolina Press, 1942.
ix, 156 p.   F279.C4B6

Bibliography: p. [137]–145.
The author's thesis (Ph.D.), *The Intellectual Life of
Early Charleston*, was submitted to Princeton University in
1941.

Describes the social, intellectual, and religious life of the
city's 18th-century aristocracy and assesses the group's response to the Revolution. The author concludes that despite
their exceptional prosperity under British rule and unusually
strong cultural ties with England, the Charleston aristocrats
were nearly unanimous in support of independence. Their
intellectual temper did not permit them to accept the interference and inferior status imposed by British policies
after 1765. Bowes adds that the vigorous, cosmopolitan
mentality that characterized the Charleston elite before the
war was replaced by a rigid, almost feudal attitude in the
years that followed.

10646
Coleman, Kenneth. Social life in Georgia in the 1780's.
Georgia review, v. 9, summer 1955: 217–228.
AP2.G375, v. 9

Stresses the growth of social democracy.

10647
Davis, Harold E. A social history of Georgia, 1733–1776.
1972. ([493] p.)   Micro AC–1, no. 72–25,935
Thesis (Ph.D.)—Emory University.
Abstracted in *Dissertation Abstracts International*,
v. 33A, Oct. 1972, p. 1634.

10648
Goodwin, Maud W. The colonial cavalier; or, southern
life before the Revolution. New York, Lovell, Coryell,
1894. 304 p. illus., plates.   F212.G64

"List of authorities": p. 315–316.

10649
Jones, George F. Colonial Georgia's second language
[German] Georgia review, v. 31, spring 1967: 87–99.
AP2.G375, v. 31

10650
Lilly, Samuel A. The culture of Revolutionary Charleston.
1972. ([248] p.)   Micro AC–1, no. 72–29,448
Thesis (Ph.D.)—Miami University.
Abstracted in *Dissertation Abstracts International*,
v. 33A, Nov. 1972, p. 2293–2294.

10651
Noël Hume, Ivor. 1775; another part of the field. New
York, Knopf, 1966. xxviii, 465, xii p. illus., maps (part
fold.)   E263.V8N6

Bibliography: p. [461]–465.

A month-by-month survey of everyday life as reported
by contemporary Virginia newspapers during the year 1775.
The author correlates the details of local history and custom,
such as Indian troubles and horse racing, with the rise of
Revolutionary agitation against Governor Dunmore.

10652
Osborne, Joseph A. Williamsburg in colonial times; incidents in the lives of the English colonists in Virginia
during the 17th and 18th centuries, as revealed in old
documents and files of the Virginia Gazette. Richmond,
Va., Dietz Press, 1935. xxii, 166 p. plates.
F234.W707

Reprinted in Port Washington, N.Y., by the Kennikat
Press (1972).

10653
Raper, Charles L. Social life in colonial North Carolina.
[Raleigh, E. M. Uzzell, Printers, 1903] 23 p. (North
Carolina booklet, v. 3, Sept. 1903)   F251.N86, v. 3

10654
Reps, John W. Tidewater towns: city planning in colonial
Virginia and Maryland. Williamsburg, Va., Colonial
Williamsburg Foundation; distributed by the Universi-
ty Press of Virginia, Charlottesville [1972] xii, 345 p.
illus. (Williamsburg architectural studies)
HT167.5.V8R46

Bibliography: p. 321–328.

Places the development of 17th- and 18th-century towns, including Richmond and Baltimore, in the tradition of city planning that began in medieval England. The 17th- century towns were planned in groups as a part of great settlement schemes, whereas 18th-century cities were planned individually as the need arose. With the exception of Annapolis, Williamsburg, and Washington, authorities in Maryland and Virginia followed the grid system adopted by officials in other English colonies, despite geographical handicaps endemic to a tidewater setting. Unlike Europe, America had no professional city planners; thus, innovations were the work of a few talented amateurs. The author provides 206 illustrations showing original or early plans and contemporary views of the towns discussed.

10655

Reps, John W.   Town planning in colonial Georgia. Town planning review, v. 30, Jan. 1959: 273–285. illus.
NA9000.T6, v. 30

10656

Rogers, George C.   Charleston in the age of the Pinckneys. Norman, University of Oklahoma Press [1969] xv, 187 p. (The centers of civilization series)
F279.C457R6

"Bibliographical note": p. 170–173.

Surveys the economic, political, intellectual, and cultural life in 18th- and early 19th-century Charleston, an expanding commercial town characterized by fluidity and opportunity. The city exhibited perhaps its greatest influence in 1788 when South Carolina ratified the federal Constitution only because Charleston's merchant elite, symbolized by the Pinckney family, generally approved it. Rogers suggests several reasons for Charleston's decline following the cessation of the slave trade in 1808.

10657

Sirmans, Marion Eugene.   Charleston two hundred years ago. Emory University quarterly, v. 19, fall 1963: 129–136.
AS36.E6, v. 19

Characterizes the society of pre-Revolutionary Charleston as one devoted wholeheartedly to amusement.

10658

Stanard, Mary M. P. N.   Colonial Virginia, its people and customs. Philadelphia, J. B. Lippincott Co., 1917. 375 p. facsims., plates, ports.
F229.S776

Reprinted in Detroit by the Singing Tree Press (1970).

10659

Wertenbaker, Thomas J.   The old South; the founding of American civilization. New York, C. Scribner's Sons, 1942. xiv, 364 p. illus., plates.
F212.W5

Bibliographic footnotes.

Reprinted in New York by Cooper Square Publishers (1936).

Focusing on social, economic, and intellectual life, the author analyzes the origins and colonial development of the regional culture of Maryland, Virginia, and the Carolinas. Wertenbaker identifies agriculture and slavery as the uni-

fying forces which made the South a distinct section, but his central theme is the great diversity within the area. He concludes that no American region was more complex in its composition of ethnic groups, economic interests, agricultural practices, and religious organizations.

THE FABRIC OF REVOLUTIONARY SOCIETY

1. SOCIAL STRUCTURE

10660

Brobeck, Stephen J.   Changes in the composition and structure of Philadelphia elite groups, 1756–1790. 1972. ([413] p.)
Micro AC–1, no. 73–13,380

Thesis (Ph.D.)—University of Pennsylvania.

Abstracted in *Dissertation Abstracts International*, v. 33A, June 1973, p. 6832.

10661

Brown, Robert E.   Economic democracy before the Constitution. American quarterly, v. 7, fall 1955: 257–274.
AP2.A3985, v. 7

Cites various observers from the period 1750–90 to show that American society was fundamentally egalitarian, lacking sharp distinctions between upper and lower classes.

10662

Cook, Edward M.   Local leadership and the typology of New England towns, 1700–1785. Political science quarterly, v. 86, Dec. 1971: 586–608.   H1.P8, v. 86

A study of the relationship between town politics and the behavior of provincial elites in 39 Massachusetts, Rhode Island, and Connecticut towns.

10663

Dinkin, Robert J.   Seating the meeting house in early Massachusetts. New England quarterly, v. 43, Sept. 1970: 450–464.   F1.N62, v. 43

People attending the meeting house were assigned specific seats according to their status in the community.

10664

Grant, Charles S.   Democracy in the Connecticut frontier town of Kent. New York, Columbia University Press, 1961. xii, 227 p. illus. (Columbia studies in the social sciences, no. 601)   F104.K3G7
H31.C7, no. 601

Bibliography: p. [216]–220.

The author's thesis (Ph.D.), *A History of Kent, 1738–1796: Democracy on Connecticut's Frontier*, was submitted to Columbia University in 1957 (Micro AC–1, no. 22,049).

Studies the economic, political, and social mobility of all known male residents, including transients. Most of Kent's settlers were proprietors who tilled their own land but looked to speculation as the best means of increasing their wealth. Untroubled by absentee landlords and conflict between economic classes, almost all participated in local politics; half could vote in provincial elections, while others soon held enough property to qualify. Entry into the highest positions of leadership was restricted, however, since custom dictated that incumbents, if competent, be reelected. Anxious to retain its high level of self-government, Kent followed the general assembly into revolution without a recorded dissent. While the first and second generations enjoyed nearly complete democracy, the more numerous third inherited smaller shares of land after the war, experienced poverty more frequently, and left town in greater numbers.

10665

Greenberg, Michael S.   Gentlemen slaveholders: the social outlook of the Virginia planter class. 1972. ([253] p.)
Micro AC–1, no. 73–4749

Thesis (Ph.D.)—Rutgers University.
Abstracted in *Dissertation Abstracts International*, v. 33A, Feb. 1973, p. 4303.

10666

Harris, P. M. G.   The social origins of American leaders: the demographic foundations. *In* Perspectives in American history. v. 3; 1969. [Cambridge] Charles Warren Center for Studies in American History, Harvard University. p. 159–344.
E171.P47, v. 3

In analyzing fluctuations in various forms of opportunity throughout American history, the author considers the question of whether or not the Revolution generated a different type of social structure. See also the author's article, "A Further Note on the Statistics of Historical Change," in v. 6, p. 423–433.

10667

Henretta, James A.   Economic development and social structure in colonial Boston. William and Mary quarterly, 3d ser., v. 22, Jan. 1965: 75–92.
F221.W71, 3d s., v. 22

An analysis of the tax lists for 1687 and 1771 indicates that Boston was transformed during the intervening years from a land-based society to a maritime center.

10668

Jacobson, Norman.   Class and ideology in the American Revolution. *In* Bendix, Reinhard, and Seymour M. Lipset, eds. Class, status, and power; a reader in social stratification. Glencoe, Ill., Free Press [1953] p. 547–554.
HT605.B4

Notes appear on p. 707–709.

Discusses the transition from a society dominated by an aristocracy of wealth to one led by an aristocracy of achievement.

10669

Main, Jackson T.   The distribution of property in post-Revolutionary Virginia. Mississippi Valley historical review, v. 41, Sept. 1954: 241–258.   E171.J87, v. 41

Ascertains that the center of livestock, slave density, and large estates had passed westward into the piedmont, leaving behind an area of greater economic inequalities and decreasing wealth.

10670

Main, Jackson T.   The one hundred. William and Mary quarterly, 3d ser., v. 11, July 1954: 354–384. maps.
F221.W71, 3d s., v. 11

Appendix and "notes": p. 367–384.

Analyzes the holdings—land, slaves, horses, and cattle—of the 100 wealthiest men in Virginia in the 1780's.

10671

Main, Jackson T.   The social structure of Revolutionary America. Princeton, N.J., Princeton University Press, 1965. viii, 330 p.   HN57.M265

Includes bibliographic references.

Examining estate inventories, tax lists, newspapers, and travel accounts, the author studies social and economic classes from 1763 to 1788. Although colonists were not particularly class conscious, older farming regions and larger towns were marked by a fairly stable upper class of merchants, lawyers, shopkeepers, and large landowners—about 20 percent of the population—and a mainly servile lower class approximately the same size. The bulging middle class consisted largely of self-employed property holders, mostly artisans and farmers. While the contrast between extremes was great—nearly half the property was held by 10 percent of the white population—a high degree of social mobility permitted advancement for all but slaves. The increasingly commercial character of colonial society produced a trend toward greater inequality just before the Revolution, but the war caused at least a temporary reversal, due in part to the growing political power of farmers and artisans, the removal of wealthy Loyalists, and a degree of social levelling.

10672

Mrozek, Donald J.   Problems of social history and patterns of inheritance in pre-Revolutionary New Jersey, 1751–1770. *In* Rutgers University, *New Brunswick, N.J. Library.* Journal, v. 36, Dec. 1972: 1–19.
Z733.R955F, v. 36

10673

Nash, Gary B.   Class and society in early America. Englewood Cliffs, N.J., Prentice-Hall [1970] x, 205 p. illus. (Interdisciplinary approaches to history series)
HN57.N33

Bibliography: p. 195–200.

Focusing on conflicting views of early American social structure, the author provides selections from land, tax, census, and probate records as well as excerpts from the writings of Cadwallader Colden, Michel-Guillaume Jean de Crèvecoeur, James Truslow Adams, Bernard Barber, Norman H. Dawes, Jackson T. Main, Aubrey C. Land, James A. Henretta, Kenneth Lockridge, and James T. Lemon.

10674

Oaks, Robert F.   Big wheels in Philadelphia: Du Simitiere's list of carriage owners. Pennsylvania magazine of history and biography, v. 95, July 1971: 351–362.
F146.P65, v. 95

Since there were only 84 carriage owners in 1772 in a city of more than 20,000, the author evaluates the carriage as a status symbol and provides an analytical list of owners.

10675

Powers, Ramon S.   Wealth and poverty: economic base, social structure, and attitudes in pre-Revolutionary Pennsylvania, New Jersey and Delaware. 1971. ([389] p.)   Micro AC–1, no. 71-27,194

Thesis (Ph.D.)—University of Kansas.

Abstracted in *Dissertation Abstracts International*, v. 32A, Oct. 1971, p. 2040.

10676

Schlesinger, Arthur M.   The aristocracy in colonial America. *In* Massachusetts Historical Society, *Boston*. Proceedings. v. 74; 1962. Boston, 1963. p. 3–21.
F61.M38, v. 74

10677

Walsh, Evelyn M.   Effects of the Revolution upon the town of Boston: social, economic, and cultural. (Volumes I and II). 1964. ([641] p.)   Micro AC–1, no. 65–2255

Thesis (Ph.D.)—Brown University.

Abstracted in *Dissertation Abstracts*, v. 25, Feb. 1965, p. 4679.

Shows the remarkable degree of continuity in the social leadership of Boston between the colonial and Federalist periods despite rapid economic and cultural expansion.

10678

Wilkenfeld, Bruce M.   The New York City Common Council, 1689–1800. *In* New York State Historical Association. New York history, v. 52, July 1971: 249–273. illus.   F116.N865, v. 52

Examines several hundred members by occupation, tenure, family background, and religion to determine political patterns in colonial New York and the effects of the Revolution.

10679

Willingham, William F.   Windham, Connecticut: profile of a Revolutionary community, 1755–1818. 1972. ([369] p.)   Micro AC–1, no. 72–32,614

Thesis (Ph.D.)—Northwestern University.

Abstracted in *Dissertation Abstracts International*, v. 32A, Oct. 1971, p. 2040.

2. FAMILY PATTERNS

10680

Calhoun, Arthur W.   A social history of the American family from colonial times to the present. Cleveland, A. H. Clark Co., 1917–19. 3 v.   HQ535.C2

Bibliography: v. 1, p. 337–348; v. 2, p. [377]–390; v. 3, p. [333]–358.

Reprinted in one volume in New York by Barnes & Noble (1945).

Tracing the evolution of family institutions, the author deals in the first volume with courtship and marriage, the position and status of women and children in the family, the nature of family life, and pathological aspects of sex and marriage in all three regions of the original colonies as well as in French settlements in the West. In the second volume Calhoun extends the discussion to the period from independence to the Civil War.

10681

The Colonial American family; collected essays.   New York, Arno Press, 1972. 1 v. (various pagings) (Family in America)   HQ535.C6 1972

Includes bibliographic references.

Contents: An essay on marriage [first published 1788]—Elizabeth in her holy retirement, by C. Mather [first published 1710]—The school of good manners, by E. Moody [first published 1775]—An appeal to the public, by B. Trumbull [first published 1788]—The well-ordered family, by B. Wadsworth [first published 1712]—Educational directory, by E. Weed [first published 1803?]

10682

Caley, Percy B.   Child life in colonial western Pennsylvania. Western Pennsylvania historical magazine, v. 9, Jan.–Oct. 1926: 33–49, 104–121, 188–201, 256–275.
F146.W52, v. 9

———— ———— Offprint. [Pittsburgh, 1926] 68 p.
F152.C24

10683

Demos, John.   Families in colonial Bristol, Rhode Island [1680–1780]: an exercise in historical demography. William and Mary quarterly, 3d ser., v. 25, Jan. 1968: 40–57.   F221.W71, 3d s., v. 25

10684

Earle, Alice M.   Child life in colonial days. New York, Macmillan Co., 1899. xxi, 418 p. illus., facsims, plates, ports.   E162.E13

Provides information on the care of babies, education, discipline, religious training, recreational activities, and dress of children in the 18th century and includes lengthy excerpts from letters, diaries, and other contemporary sources.

10685

Earle, Alice M.   Home and child life in colonial days. Edited by Shirley Glubok. Special photography by Alfred Tamarin. [New York] Macmillan [1969] 357 p. illus., ports.   E162.E183

The editor provides modern photographs of 18th-century buildings, material objects, paintings, and drawings that illustrate the text—an abridged version of Alice Earle's *Home Life in Colonial Days* and *Child Life in Colonial Days*.

10686

Earle, Alice M.   Home life in colonial days. New York, Macmillan Co., 1898. xvi, 470 p. illus., plates.
E162.E18

Besides describing and explaining the use of a wide variety of material objects found in 18th-century homes, the author provides information on handicrafts, occupations, travel, Sabbath-day activities, and gardens.

10687

Ellet, Elizabeth F. L.   Domestic history of the American Revolution. New York, Baker and Scribner, 1850. 308 p.   E208.E45

Reprinted in Philadelphia by J. B. Lippincott (1876. E208.E46).

Provides illustrative anecdotes about personal wartime experiences.

10688

Fleming, Sandford.   Children & Puritanism; the place of children in the life and thought of New England churches, 1620–1847. New Haven, Yale University Press, 1933. xii, 236 p. (Yale studies in religious education, [8])   BV1467.F5 1933

"The results of this study were presented to the faculty of the Yale Graduate school in partial fulfilment of the requirements for the degree of doctor of philosophy [1929]"—Acknowledgment.

Reprinted in New York by Arno Press (1969).

A study of religious appeals to children under 17 years of age within the Congregational church and their responses, especially during periods of evangelical fervor. The author finds that children throughout the 17th and 18th centuries were viewed as small adults who were the "heirs of hell" and therefore fit subjects for weighty theological disquisitions on sinfulness, depravity, and imminent death. Children often tried to live up to their parents' expectations by making rigorous examinations of soul and practicing extreme forms of self-abasement and denial. Fleming concludes that the emotional devastation produced by this approach was finally relieved under the 19th-century impact of Horace Bushnell's doctrine of Christian nurture.

10689

Greven, Philip J.   The average size of families and households in the province of Massachusetts in 1764 and in the United States in 1790: an overview. *In* Laslett, Peter. Household and family in past time. Cambridge [Eng.] University Press, 1972. p. [545]–560. (A Publication of the Cambridge Group for the History of Population and Social Structure)   HQ515.L38

10690

Greven, Philip J.   Four generations: population, land, and family in colonial Andover, Massachusetts. Ithaca, N.Y., Cornell University Press, 1970. xvi, 329 p. illus., fold. map.   F74.A6G7

Bibliography: p. [295]–315.

The author's thesis (Ph.D.), *Four Generations: a Study of Family Structure, Inheritance, and Mobility in Andover, Massachusetts, 1630–1750*, was submitted to Harvard University in 1965.

Investigates the demographic and economic influences upon family life between 1650 and 1800. Although the town's population increased throughout the period, the rate of growth decreased in a cyclical pattern. As the population-land ratio became less favorable, economic decline set in during the Revolutionary era. Family ties loosened, and the agrarian society of Andover acquired characteristics heretofore associated with industrialization: sons matured sooner, became economically independent earlier, married younger, inherited less, left town more frequently, and died sooner than their forefathers.

10691

Kiefer, Monica M.   Early American childhood in the Middle Atlantic area. Pennsylvania magazine of history and biography, v. 68, Jan. 1944: 3–37.   F146.P65, v. 68

10692

Lantz, Herman R., *and others*.   Pre-industrial patterns in the colonial family in America: a content analysis of colonial magazines [1741–94] American sociological review, v. 33, June 1968: 413–426.   HM1.A75, v. 33

Suggests that some of the characteristics of the modern family, such as freedom of choice in mate selection, romantic love, and parental permissiveness, were also present in the 18th century and were not necessarily products of industrialization and urbanization.

10693

Lotka, Alfred J.   The size of American families in the eighteenth century. *In* American Statistical Association. Journal, v. 22, June 1927: 154–170.   HA1.A6, v. 22

10694

Meehan, Thomas R.   "Not made out of levity": evolution of divorce in early Pennsylvania. Pennsylvania magazine of history and biography, v. 92, Oct. 1968: 441–464.   F146.P65, v. 92

10695

Morgan, Edmund S.   Virginians at home; family life in the eighteenth century. Williamsburg, Va., Colonial Williamsburg [1952] ix, 99 p. facsims., ports. (Williamsburg in America series, 2)   P234.W7W7, v. 2

"A note on the sources": p. [95]–96.

Contents: Growing up.—Getting married.—Servants and slaves.—Houses and holidays.

10696

Rogers, Albert A.   Family life in 18th century Virginia. 1939. 330 l.

Thesis (Ph.D.)—University of Virginia.

10697

Rothman, David J.   A note on the study of the colonial family. William and Mary quarterly, 3d ser., v. 23, Oct. 1966: 627–634.   F221.W71, 3d s., v. 23

10698

Schlesinger, Arthur M.   Patriotism names the baby. New England quarterly, v. 14, Dec. 1941: 611–618.

F1.N62, v. 14

Finds that the tendency to name children after contemporary heroes was an indication of growing patriotic sentiment.

10699

Spaletta, Matteo. Divorce in colonial New York [1655–1787] *In* New York Historical Society. Quarterly, v. 39, Oct. 1955: 422–440. F116.N638, v. 39

10700

Stevenson, Noel C. Marital rights in the colonial period. New England historical and genealogical register, v. 109, Apr. 1955: 84–90. F1.N56, v. 109

10701

Wells, Robert V. A demographic analysis of some middle colony Quaker families of the eighteenth century. 1969. ([169] p.) Micro AC–1, no. 70–14,249

Thesis (Ph.D.)—Princeton University.

Abstracted in *Dissertation Abstracts International*, v. 31A, Aug. 1970, p. 721.

Attempts to determine what demographic changes may have taken place as a result of the Revolution.

10702

Wells, Robert V. Family size and fertility control in eighteenth-century America: a study of Quaker families. Population studies, v. 25, Mar. 1971: 73–82. HB881.A1P67, v. 25

By deliberately limiting the size of their families, Quakers achieved a birthrate that was not matched by the general population until well into the 19th century.

10703

Wells, Robert V. Quaker marriage patterns in a colonial perspective. William and Mary quarterly, 3d ser., v. 29, July 1972: 415–442. F221.W71, 3d s., v. 29

Examines the patterns of marriage among 276 Quaker families in the middle colonies, considers the possible existence of distinct marriage patterns in all colonies, and explores the effect these patterns may have had on family size before 1800.

3. The Role of Women

10704

Bartlett, Helen R. Eighteenth century Georgia women. [College Park, Md., 1939] 135 l. F289.B27

Thesis (Ph.D.)—University of Maryland, 1939.
Typescript (carbon copy).
Bibliography: leaves [130]–135.

10705

Benson, Mary S. Women in eighteenth-century America; a study of opinion and social usage. New York, Columbia University Press, 1935. 343 p. (Studies in history, economics and public law, no. 405)
H31.C7, no. 405
HQ1416.B4 1935a

Issued also as thesis (Ph.D.)—Columbia University. "Bibliographical essay": p. 317–333.
Reprinted in Port Washington, N.Y., by Kennikat Press (1966).

After examining European influence upon American opinion, the author surveys contemporary attitudes expressed—mainly by men—in letters, diaries, travel journals, statutes, and literary works. Writers at the turn of the century emphasized the religious nature of American women, but by midcentury Franklin and others turned their attention to the woman's role in marriage and education. The idealism of the Revolution led to slight gains in the legal and economic status of women as well as a distinct improvement in educational opportunity; instruction for women, however, stressed "accomplishments" of little practical or intellectual value.

10706

Blumenthal, Walter H. Brides from Bridewell; female felons sent to colonial America. Rutland, Vt., C. E. Tuttle Co., 1962. 139 p. illus., plate. HQ1416.B55

Bibliographic references included in "Notes" (p. 131–139).

10707

Bruce, Kathleen. Massachusetts women of the Revolution, 1761–1789. *In* Hart, Albert B., *ed.* Commonwealth history of Massachusetts, 1775–1820. v. 3. New York, States History Co., 1929. p. 306–340. ports. F64.H32, v. 3

Bibliography: p. 337–340.

10708

Campbell, Amelia D. Women of New York state in the Revolution. *In* New York State Historical Association. Quarterly journal, v. 3, July 1922: 155–168. F116.N865, v. 3

10709

Cometti, Elizabeth. Women in the American Revolution. New England quarterly, v. 20, Sept. 1947: 329–346. F1.N62, v. 20

10710

Dexter, Elisabeth W. A. Colonial women of affairs; women in business and the professions in America before 1776. 2d ed., rev. Boston, Houghton Mifflin Co., 1931. xxi, 223 p. facsims., plates, ports. E195.D522

"References": p. [195–202]

The first edition, published in 1924, was based on the author's thesis (Ph.D.), of the same title, which she submitted to Clark University in 1923.

Reprinted in New York by A. M. Kelley (1972).

Offers long quotations from contemporary letters, diaries, and newspapers that relate to women who worked as tavernkeepers, merchants, dressmakers, nurses, teachers, authors, religious leaders, actresses, and printers, or who were landed proprietors.

10711

Drinker, Sophie H.   Votes for women in 18th-century New Jersey. *In* New Jersey Historical Society. Proceedings, v. 80, Jan. 1962: 31–45.   F131.N58, v. 80

The *femme sole*, the woman without a husband, whether spinster or widow, had legal rights approaching those of her male contemporaries and therefore fell into the category of potential voters.

10712

Earle, Alice M.   Colonial dames and good wives. Boston, Houghton, Mifflin, 1895. 315 p.   E162.E15

Reprinted in New York by F. Ungar (1962).

Offers excerpts from letters, diaries, and other contemporary material along with information on marriage, women of affairs, 18th-century manners, and women's patriotic societies formed during the Revolution.

10713

James, Janet W.   Changing ideas about women in the United States, 1776–1825. 1954.

Thesis (Ph.D.)—Radcliffe College.

10714

Lutz, Alma.   Early American women historians. *In* Boston. Public Library. Quarterly, v. 8, Apr. 1956: 85–99.   Z881.B7535, v. 8

Hannah Adams, Mercy Otis Warren, Emma Willard, and Elizabeth Lummis Ellet are among those discussed.

10715

Manges, Frances M.   Women shopkeepers, tavernkeepers, and artisans in colonial Philadelphia. 1958. ([153] p.)   Micro AC–1, no. 58–1854

Thesis (Ph.D.)—University of Pennsylvania.
Abstracted in *Dissertation Abstracts*, v. 19, Aug. 1958, p. 310–311.

10716

Marlow, Holt C.   The ideology of the woman's movement, 1750–1850. 1966. ([374] p.)   Micro AC–1, no. 66–5328

Thesis (Ph.D.)—University of Oklahoma.
Abstracted in *Dissertation Abstracts*, v. 26, May 1966, p. 6677–6678.

A conservative social philosophy that celebrated the natural inferiority of women permeated 18th-century America. The early woman's movement of the 1790's denied innatism and adopted environmentalism.

10717

Oldham, Ellen M.   Early women printers of America. *In* Boston. Public Library. Quarterly, v. 10, Jan.–July 1958: 6–26, 78–92, 141–153.   Z881.B7535, v. 10

Among them are Sarah Goddard, Anne Greene, Clementina Rind, Margaret Draper (Loyalist), Mary Crouch, and Mary Goddard.

10718

Parker, *Mrs*. Alton B.   The mothers of New York. *In* New York State Historical Association. History of the state of New York. v. 4. The new state. New York, Columbia University Press, 1934. p. [283]–319. illus.   F119.N65, v. 4

Bibliography: p. 318–319.

10719

Spruill, Julia C.   Southern housewives before the Revolution. North Carolina historical review, v. 13, Jan. 1936: 25–46.   F251.N892, v. 13

10720

Spruill, Julia C.   Women's life and work in the southern colonies. Chapel Hill, University of North Carolina Press, 1938. viii, 426 p. facsims., plates.   HQ1416.S65

Bibliography: p. 367–394.
Reprinted in New York by Russell & Russell (1969).

In the first half of the work the author describes in detail the education, marriage, and domestic activities of women of wealth whose lifestyle is most frequently reflected in surviving accounts. The second half is devoted to the participation of women in public affairs outside the home as ministers, politicians, or as breadwinners in a variety of occupations—lawyers, clerks, storekeepers, gunsmiths, pewterers, printers, upholsterers, and jailers. In concluding chapters on crime and punishment and women under the law, Spruill points to the often cruel treatment meted out to women bearing bastard children and demonstrates the inferior legal status in which women were placed.

10721

Woody, Thomas.   A history of women's education in the United States. New York, Science Press, 1929. 2 v. illus., facsims., plates, ports. (Science and education, v. 4, book 1–2)   LC1752.W6

Bibliography: v. 2, p. 481–589.
Reprinted in New York by Octagon Books (1966).

4. DEMOGRAPHY

a. General

10722

American Council of Learned Societies Devoted to Humanistic Studies. *Committee on Linguistic and National Stocks in the Population of the United States.*   Report. *In* American Historical Association. Annual report. 1931. v. 1. Washington, 1932. p. 103–441.   E172.A60, 1931, v. 1

Bibliography: p. 325–359.
Contents: Report of Committee on Linguistic and National Stocks in the Population of the United States.—Annex A. National stocks in the population of the United States as indicated by surnames in the census of 1790, by Howard F. Barker.—Annex B. The minor stocks in the American population of 1790, by Marcus L. Hansen.—Annex C. The population of the American outlying regions in 1790, by Marcus L. Hansen.

———— ———— Offprint. Washington, U.S. Govt. Print. Off., 1932. 103–441 p.   E184.A1A6

Reprinted in Baltimore by the Genealogical Pub. Co. under the title *Surnames in the United States Census of 1790; an Analysis of National Origins of the Population* (1969).

10723

Bolton, Charles K., *comp.*   Marriage notices 1785–1794 for the whole United States. Salem, E. Putnam, 1900. 139 p.   CS68.B7

Copied from the *Massachusetts Centinel* and the *Columbian Centinel*.

Reprinted in Baltimore by the Genealogical Pub. Co. (1965).

10724

Cassedy, James H.   Demography in early America; beginnings of the statistical mind, 1600–1800. Cambridge, Harvard University Press, 1969. 357 p.   HA37.U55C35

Bibliography: p. [311]–338.

Concentrating on the use of quantitative data in public health and medicine, the author traces the development of statistical methods as evidenced in political and economic pamphlets, newspapers, almanacs, and sermons. In a chapter on the Revolution, the author quotes passages in which Americans used demographic arguments—e.g., the growth of colonial population entitled Americans to political equality within the empire—to justify opposition to imperial measures and, once the war began, to bolster morale.

10725

Cuthbertson, John.   Register of marriages and baptisms performed by Rev. John Cuthbertson, Covenanter minister, 1751–1791, with index to locations and persons visited, by S. Helen Fields. Washington, D.C. [Lancaster, Pa., Lancaster Press Inc.] 1934. xv, 301 p. facsims.   CS68.C7

Largely quotations from Cuthbertson's diary arranged chronologically and geographically by the states that he visited, from Massachusetts to Maryland.

10726

Dexter, Franklin B.   Estimates of population in the American colonies [1620–1790] *In* American Antiquarian Society, *Worcester, Mass.* Proceedings, new ser., v. 5, Oct. 1887: 22–50. illus.   E172.A35, n.s., v. 5

An early attempt to marshal statistical data for historical use.

10727

Greene, Evarts B., *and* Virginia D. Harrington.   American population before the federal census of 1790. New York, Columbia University Press, 1932. xxii, 228 p.   HB3505.G7

Bibliography: p. [xi]–xii.
Reprinted in Gloucester, Mass., by P. Smith (1966).

Presents statistics on five political-geographic levels. For the thirteen original colonies as a whole, for regions like New England, the Illinois country, Kentucky, and Tennessee, and for individual states, the compilers arrange in chronological order sometimes conflicting estimates derived from contemporary and later sources. In 1775, for instance, there were 2,418,000 people in the colonies according to an estimate found in the George Clinton papers, while J. D. B. DeBow reckoned the number at 2,803,000. The sections on Indians in the northern and southern departments contain similar data on the various tribes. At the county and town levels, the compilers provide information, much of it in tabular form, on numbers of inhabitants, families, whites and blacks, males and females, children, freemen, those able to bear arms, militiamen, taxables, tithables, Quakers, and strangers.

10728

Potter, J.   The growth of population in America, 1700–1860. *In* Glass, David V., *and* David E. C. Eversley, *eds.* Population in history; essays in historical demography. London, E. Arnold [1965] p. 631–688.   HB881.G59 1965a

10729

Rosenwaike, Ira.   An estimate and analysis of the Jewish population of the United States in 1790. *In* American Jewish Historical Society. Publication, v. 50, Sept. 1960: 23–35.   E184.J5A5, v. 50

Finds that Jews formed only 0.04 percent of the total population and numbered between 1,300 and 1,500.

10730

Sutherland, Stella H.   Colonial statistics. Explorations in entrepreneurial history, 2d ser., v. 5, fall 1967: 58–107.   HB615.E8, 2d s., v. 5

Discussed the nature of colonial recordkeeping and the availability of statistical data for the period 1607–1789. While Sutherland supplies some raw data in the course of her essay, she also suggests sources likely to reveal information on such topics as population, agricultural production, and trade. The article serves as an interpretive introduction to the colonial section of *Historical Statistics of the United States* (entry 207), published by the U.S. Bureau of the Census.

10731

Sutherland, Stella H. Population distribution in colonial America. New York, Columbia University Press, 1936. xxxii, 353 p. fold. maps.   HB1965.S84

Bibliography: p. [xvii]–xxxii.
Reprinted in New York by AMS Press (1966).

The author's thesis (Ph.D.), with the same title, was submitted to the University of Illinois in 1931.

Considers the geographic, economic, and ethnic factors that influenced immigration and settlement patterns in each of the 13 colonies. Drawing upon census returns, tax lists, and land grant records, the author shows that there were few significant concentrations of people outside the coastal cities as the lure of cheap land encouraged dispersal to the west. In 1775 there were an estimated 2,507,180 persons in the colonies, almost equally divided between North and South. By 1790 the number had increased to 3,699,525. Sutherland illustrates the distribution of population in 1775 by including three large maps in which each dot represents 50 inhabitants. She also includes in an appendix over 50 pages of population tables and import-export statistics.

10732
U.S. *Bureau of the Census.* Heads of families at the first census of the United States taken in the year 1790. Washington, Govt. Print. Off., 1907–8. 12 v. fold. maps. E302.5.U57
HA201 1790.C

Roster of heads of families in 1790, so far as can be shown from records of the Census Office. The returns for Delaware, Georgia, Kentucky, New Jersey, Tennessee, and Virginia were destroyed by fire in 1814. As the federal census schedules of the state of Virginia for 1790 are missing, the lists of the state enumerations made in 1782, 1783, 1784, and 1785, while not complete, have been substituted.

Contents: Maine.—New Hampshire.—Vermont.—Massachusetts.—Rhode Island.—Connecticut.—New York.—Pennsylvania.—Maryland.—Virginia.—North Carolina.—South Carolina.

b. New England

(1) GENERAL

10733
Smith, Daniel S. The demographic history of colonial New England [to 1790] Journal of economic history, v. 32, Mar. 1972: 165–183. HC10.J64, v. 32

(2) MAINE

10734
Lebanon, *Me.* Vital records of Lebanon, Maine, to the year 1892. Editor, George Walter Chamberlain. [Boston] Under authority of the Maine Historical Society, 1922–23. 3 v. F29.L4L4

Contents: v. 1. Births.—v. 2. Marriages.—v. 3. Deaths.

10735
Patterson, William D., *ed.* The probate records of Lincoln County, Maine. 1760 to 1800. Portland, Me., Printed for the Society, 1895. 12, xxi, 368, 53 p. F27.L7P2

10736
U.S. *Bureau of the Census.* Heads of familes at the first census of the United States, taken in the year 1790. Maine. Washington, Govt. Print. Off., 1908. [Spartanburg, S.C., Reprint Co., 1963] 105 p. map (on lining papers) F24.U5

Also reprinted in Baltimore by the Genealogical Pub. Co. (1966).

(3) NEW HAMPSHIRE

10737
Hammond, Otis G., *comp.* Vital records from the *New Hampshire Gazette,* 1765–1800. Genealogical quarterly magazine, [3d] ser., v. 4, Apr. 1903, Jan. 1904: 16–20, 289–296; v. 5, July 1904: 57–64; [4th ser.] v. 1, Apr.–June, Sept. 1905–Mar. 1906: 15–21, 61–64, 93–96, 191–194, 223–226, 237–241, 267–268, 295–298, 327–333, 362–365; v. 2, Jan.–Apr./Dec. 1907: 37–44, 83–86. F1.P98, 3d s., v. 4–5; 4th s., v. 1–2

10738
New Hampshire. *State Planning and Development Commission.* Population of New Hampshire. Pt. 1. Basic data on growth and distribution since the time of settlement, 1623–1940. [Prepared by Sydnor Hodges, statistician] Concord, 1946. 20 p. maps.
HB3525.N4A5, pt. 1

Census figures from 1767, 1773, 1775, 1783, 1786, and 1790 are arranged by county and town.

10739
U.S. *Bureau of the Census.* Heads of families at the first census of the United States, taken in the year 1790: New Hampshire. Washington, Govt. Print. Off., 1907. [Spartanburg, S.C., Reprint Co., 1964] 146 p. map (on lining papers) F38.A57

Also reprinted in Baltimore by the Genealogical Pub. Co. (1966).

(4) VERMONT

10740
U.S. *Bureau of the Census.* Heads of families at the first census of the United States, taken in the year 1790: Vermont. Washington, Govt. Print. Off., 1907. [Spartanburg, S.C., Reprint Co., 1963] 95 p. map (on lining papers) F52.U5

Also reprinted in Baltimore by the Genealogical Pub. Co. (1966).

(5) MASSACHUSETTS

10741
Bailey, Frederic W., *comp.* Early Massachusetts marriages prior to 1800. New Haven, Conn., Bureau of American Ancestry [1897–1914] 3 v. F63.B15

Contents: 1st book. As found on the official records of Worcester County, 1897.—2d book. As found on the official records of Plymouth County, 1900.—3d book. As found on ancient court records of the counties of Middlesex, Hampshire, Berkshire and Bristol, 1914.

Reprinted, with the addition of Plymouth County marriages from 1692 to 1746, in Baltimore by the Genealogical Pub. Co. (1968).

Arranged by town. Most of the marriages fall within the Revolutionary period.

10742
Blake, Francis E. Worcester County, Massachusetts, warnings, 1737–1788. Worcester, Mass., F. P. Rice, 1899. 101 p. (Systematic history fund [publications, no. 1]) F72.W9B6

Lists, under names of towns, of those "warned" under an act of 1692–93. This act provided that "strangers entertained in any town for the space of three months, and not 'warned out,' and their names returned to the Court of quarter sessions, would be considered as inhabitants of such towns. . . . Towns issuing warnings . . . were relieved from liability of their support . . . if they proved to be improvident."

10743

Boston. *Assessing Dept.* Assessors' "taking books" of the town of Boston, 1780. *In* Bostonian Society, *Boston.* Publications. v. 9. Boston, 1912. p. [9]–59. facsim.
F73.1.B88, v. 9

The lists contain the names, polls, and occupations of over 2,000 white males. An index of names appears on p. 137-148.

10744

Boston. First Church. The records of the First Church in Boston, 1630–1868. Edited by Richard D. Pierce. Boston, The Society, 1961. 3 v. facsims. (part fold.), plates, ports. (Publications of the Colonial Society of Massachusetts. v. 39–41. Collections) F61.C71, v. 39–41

Includes lists of admissions to membership, church votes, marriages, and baptisms.

10745

Boston. Old South Church. An historical catalogue of the Old South Church (Third Church) Boston. Boston, Printed for private distribution, 1883. x, 370 p. facsims., ports. F73.62.O4B7

Preface signed: Hamilton Andrews Hill, George Frederick Bigelow.

Partial contents: pt. 1. List of pastors. List of deacons. List of members. List of members under the baptismal covennant, 1669–1818.—pt. 2. Alphabetical list of members. Alphabetical list of members under the baptismal covenant.

10746

Chickering, Jesse. A statistical view of the population of Massachusetts, from 1765 to 1840. Boston, C. C. Little and J. Brown, 1846. 160 p. HA436.C5

Includes figures from the 1765 and 1790 censuses for each county and town.

10747

Codman, Ogden. Index of obituaries in Boston newspapers, 1704–1800; Boston Athenaeum. Boston, G. K. Hall, 1968. 3 v. F73.25.C6

On spine, v. 1–3: 1704–1795; on title page, v. 2–3, 1704–1795.

A facsimile of the original manuscript in the Boston Athenaeum.

Contents: v. 1. Deaths within Boston.—v. 2–3. Deaths outside Boston.

10748

Dow, George F., *comp.* Record of deaths in Topsfield, 1685–1800, compiled from the town and church records and returns made to the county court. *In* Topsfield Historical Society, *Topsfield, Mass.* Historical collections. v. 3; 1897. Topsfield. p. 101–153.
F74.T6T6, v. 3

10749

Essex Institute, *Salem, Mass.* [Vital records of the towns of Massachusetts] Salem, Mass., Essex Institute, 1903–34. 55 v.

Each volume is separately classified. The series provides, for the occupants of 35 Massachusetts towns, marriage, birth, and death dates gleaned from town records, newspapers, family Bibles, cemetery inscriptions, etc., from the 17th century to 1849. Similar data for the residents of other towns have been published by the New England Historic and Genealogical Society, the Topsfield Historical Society, the "Systematic History Fund" under the direction of Franklin P. Rice, the Society of Mayflower Descendants, individual towns, and private persons. The vital records of over 200 Massachusetts towns have been issued to date; nearly all are uniform in format, style, and binding. For a complete account see "A List of the Massachusetts Published Vital Records," by Kenneth R. Brown, in the National Genealogical Society's *Quarterly*, v. 45, Sept. 1957, p. 137-143.

10750

Norton, Susan L. Population growth in colonial America: a study of Ipswich, Massachusetts [1640–1790] Population studies, v. 25, Nov. 1971: 433–452.
HB881.A1P67, v. 25

10751

[Plymouth, Mass. First Church] Plymouth church records, 1620–1859. [Boston, The Society, 1920–23] 2 v. facsims., plates, ports. [Publications of the Colonial Society of Massachusetts. v. 22–23. Collections]
F61.C71, v. 22–23

The original records are in three volumes: 1620–1732, 1732–1799, 1799–1859.

Bibliographies: [v. 1] p. lv–lxii.

10752

A Short census of Massachusetts—1779. National Genealogical Society quarterly, v. 49, Mar.–Sept. 1961: 14–20, 96–100, 137–141; v. 50, Mar., Dec. 1962: 26–28, 207–214; v. 51, Mar. 1963: 44–48.
CS42.N4, v. 49–51

A list of the names of 3,380 persons who presented Continental bank notes to the Massachusetts loan office, established by a congressional resolution of January 2, 1799, calling in the paper money issues of 1777 and 1778. The county of residence and the amount of money deposited is also recorded. Introduction and notes by William H. Dumont.

10753

Subscription list [of Bostonians] for a map of the "four New England states," 1784. *In* Bostonian Society, *Boston.* Publications. v. 9. Boston, 1929. p. [127]–134. plates.
F73.1.B88, v. 9

10754

Topsfield, *Mass.* Congregational Church. Baptismal records of the church in Topsfield. Communicated by Geo. Frs. Dow. *In* Topsfield Historical Society, *Tops-*

field, Mass. Historical collections. v. 1–2; 1895–96. Appendix. Topsfield, The Society. 42 p; 19 p.

F74.T6T6, v. 1–2

10755

U.S. *Bureau of the Census.* Heads of families at the first census of the United States, taken in the year 1790: Massachusetts. Washington, Govt. Print. Off., 1908. [Spartanburg, S.C., Reprint Co., 1964] 363 p. map (on lining papers) F63.U5

Also reprinted in Baltimore by the Genealogical Pub. Co. (1966. F69.U52 1966).

10756

Vinovskis, Maris A. Mortality rates and trends in Massachusetts before 1860. Journal of economic history, v. 32, Mar. 1972: 184–213. HC10.J64, v. 30

10757

Weston, *Mass.* Town of Weston. The tax lists, 1757–1827. Boston, A. Mudge, Printers, 1897. v. 438 p. fold. plan. F74.W74W62

Preface signed: Mary Frances Peirce.

10758

Worcester, *Mass.* Inscriptions from the old burial grounds in Worcester, Massachusetts, from 1727 to 1859, with biographical and historical notes. Worcester, Mass., Worcester Society of Antiquity, 1878. 160 p. plans. (Worcester Historical Society. Proceedings, v. 1, no. 4) F74.W9W85, v. 1

10759

Worcester, *Mass.* Worcester births, marriages, and deaths [1714–1848] Compiled by Franklin P. Rice. Worcester, Mass., Worcester Society of Antiquity, 1894. 527 p. (Worcester Historical Society. Collections, v. 12)

F74.W9W85, v. 12
F74.W9W88

10760

Worcester, *Mass.* Worcester tax list, 1789. *In* Worcester Historical Society, *Worcester, Mass.* Collections. v. 16. Proceedings. no. 54; 1899. Worcester, 1900. p. 373–388. facsim. F74.W9W85, v. 16

(6) RHODE ISLAND

10761

Arnold, James N. Vital record of Rhode Island. 1636–1850. First series. Births, marriages, and deaths. A family register for the people. Providence, R.I., Narragansett Historical Pub. Co., 1891–1912. 21 v.

F78.A75

Contents: v. 1. Kent County.—v. 2–3. Providence County.—v. 4. Newport County.—v. 5. Washington County.—v. 6. Bristol County.—v. 7. Friends and ministers.—v. 8. Episcopal and Congregational.—v. 9. Seekonk (including East Providence), Pawtucket, and Newman Congregational Church.—v. 10. Town and church.—v. 11. Church records.—v. 12. Revolutionary rolls and newspapers. Deaths, *Providence Journal*, A to R.—v. 13. Deaths, *Providence Journal*, S to Z. *Providence Gazette*, A to J, 1762–1830.—v. 14. *Providence Gazette*—Deaths, K to Z. Marriages, A, B, C, 1762–1825.—v. 15. *Providence Gazette*—Marriages, D to Z. *United States Chronicle*—Deaths, A to Z.—v. 16. *United States Chronicle*—Marriages; *American Journal, Impartial Observer,* and *Providence Journal*—Marriages and deaths; *Providence Semiweekly Journal*—Marriages.—v. 17. *Providence Phenix, Providence Patriot,* and *Columbian Phenix*—Marriages, A to R.—v. 18. *Providence Phenix, Providence Patriot,* and *Columbian Phenix*—Marriages, S to Z; deaths, A to M.—v. 19. *Providence Phenix, Providence Patriot,* and *Columbian Phenix*—Deaths, N. to Z; *Rhode Island American*—Marriages, A to G.—v. 20. *Rhode Island American*—Marriages, H to Z; deaths, A and B.—v. 21. *Rhode Island American*—Deaths, C to S.

10762

Miller, William D. Dr. Joseph Torrey and his record book of marriages. Providence, Rhode Island Historical Society, 1925. 24 p. facsims. F89.S7M5

"A record of the names &c of the persons joyned together in marriage by Joseph Torrey pastor of the Chts. of Christ in South Kingstown . . ." 1736–1783.

10763

Newport, *R.I.* The occupants of the houses in Newport, R.I., during the Revolution. Newport historical magazine, v. 2, July 1881: 41–45. F76.R35, v. 2

10764

Providence. *City Registrar.* Alphabetical index of the births, marriages and deaths, recorded in Providence from 1636 to 1850 inclusive, by Edwin M. Snow. Providence, S. S. Rider, 1879. ix, 599 p. F89.P9P86, v. 1

10765

Rhode Island (*Colony*). *General Assembly.* Census of the inhabitants of the colony of Rhode Island and Providence Plantations, 1774. Arr. by John R. Bartlett. With index by E. E. Brownell. Baltimore, Genealogical Pub. Co., 1969. v, 238, 120 p. F78.A59 1969

Reprint of the 1858 ed. (Providence, Knowles, Anthony, State Printers. HA612.A4 1774). The index, p. 1–120 (2d group), was first published in 1954. Arranged by county, town, and family.

10766

U.S. *Bureau of the Census.* Heads of families at the first census of the United States, taken in the year 1790: Rhode Island. Washington, Govt. Print. Off., 1908. [Spartanburg, S.C., Reprint Co., 1963] 71 p. map (on lining papers) F83.U5

Also reprinted in Baltimore by the Genealogical Pub. Co. (1966).

(7) CONNECTICUT

10767

Bailey, Frederic W., *ed.* Early Connecticut marriages as found on ancient church records prior to 1800. New

Haven, Conn., Bureau of American Ancestry [1896–1906] 7 v.   F93.B15

From records of Congregational churches, with a few Episcopal church records in book 7.

Most of the volumes contain lists of errata which include all preceding volumes.

Reprinted in one volume with additions, corrections, and introduction by Donald L. Jacobus, and with integrated errata, in Baltimore by the Genealogical Pub. Co. (1968).

10768

Canterbury, Conn. Congregational Church. Records of the Congregational church in Canterbury, Connecticut, 1711–1844, published jointly by the Connecticut Historical Society and the Society of Mayflower Descendants in the State of Connecticut. Hartford [Press of Finlay Bros.] 1932. xii, 217 p. port. F104.C18C2

Introduction signed: Albert C. Bates.

10769

Connecticut (*Colony*). *General Assembly.* An account of the number of inhabitants in the colony of Connecticut, January 1, 1774: together with an account of the number of inhabitants, taken January 1, 1756. Published by order of the General Assembly. Hartford, Printed by E. Watson, near the Great Bridge, 1774. 9 l.

HA281 1774 Rare Bk. Coll.

10770

Deep River, *Conn.* Vital records of Saybrook, 1647–1834. Hartford, Connecticut Historical Society and the Connecticut Society of the Order of the Founders and Patriots of America, 1952 [c1948] 197 p. (Vital records of Connecticut. Series 1: Towns, v. 9. seventh town)

F104.D3D42

10771

Dimock, Susan W., *comp.* Births, baptisms, marriages and deaths, from the records of the town and churches in Mansfield, Connecticut, 1703–1850. New York, Baker & Taylor Co., 1898. vi, 475 p.   F104.M2D5

10772

East Granby, *Conn.* Congregational Church. Records of the Congregational church in Turkey Hills, now the town of East Granby, Connecticut, 1776–1858; published by Albert Carlos Bates. Hartford, 1907. 158 p. (Turkey Hills series, no. 3)   F104.E1E13

10773

New Haven. Vital records of New Haven, 1649–1850. Hartford, Connecticut Society of the Order of the Founders and Patriots of America, 1917–24. 2 v. (Vital records of Connecticut. Series 1: Towns, v. 4, pt. 1–2)

F104.N6N66

10774

Norwich, *Conn.* Vital records of Norwich, 1659–1848. Hartford, Society of Colonial Wars in the State of Connecticut, 1913. 2 v. (Vital records of Connecticut. Series 1: Towns, v. 2, pt. 1–2)   F104.N93N68

10775

Olson, Albert L. Agricultural economy and the population in eighteenth-century Connecticut. [New Haven] Published for the Tercentenary Commission by the Yale University Press, 1935. 31 p. map. (Connecticut. Tercentenary Commission. Committee on Historical Publications. [Tercentenary pamphlet series] 40)

S451.C704

"Bibliographical note": p. 31.

10776

Prichard, Katherine A., *comp.* Ancient burying-grounds of the town of Waterbury, Connecticut, together with other records of church and town. [Waterbury] Mattatuck Historical Society, 1917. 338 p. (Publications of the Mattatuck Historical Society, v. 2)

F104.W3M38, v. 2

Includes a list of tax-paying inhabitants, 1730–83.

10777

Simsbury, *Conn.* Simsbury, Connecticut, births, marriages, and deaths, transcribed from the town records, and published by Albert C. Bates. Hartford [Case, Lockwood & Brainard Co.] 1898. 345 p. facsim.

F104.S6S6

10778

Suffield, Conn. First Congregational Church. Records of the Congregational church in Suffield, Conn. (except church votes), 1710–1836. Hartford, Connecticut Historical Society, 1941. 224 p. (Vital records of Connecticut. Series 2: Churches, v. 7. Fifth town)

F104.S9S955

10779

Turkey Hills Parish, *Conn.* Records of the society or parish of Turkey Hills, now the town of East Granby, Connecticut, 1737–1791. Published by Albert Carlos Bates. Hartford, 1901. 78 p. (Turkey Hills series, no. 1)

F104.E1T8

10780

U.S. *Bureau of the Census.* Heads of families at the first census of the United States, taken in the year 1790: Connecticut. Washington, Govt. Print. Off., 1908. [Spartanburg, S.C., Reprint Co., 1964] 227 p. map (on lining papers)   F93.U5

Also reprinted in Baltimore by the Genealogical Pub. Co. (1966. F99.U5 1966).

10781

Welles, Edwin S. Newington, Conn., inhabitants, 1776. Putnam's historical magazine, new ser., v. 7, May, July, Sept., Nov./Dec. 1899: 145–148, 205–206, 233, 294–297; [3d] ser., v. 1, Apr. 1900: 28–36.

F1.P98, n.s., v. 7; [3d] s., v. 1

10782

Willard, Josiah. A census of Newington, Connecticut, taken according to households in 1776. Edited by Edwin Stanley Welles. Hartford, F. B. Hartranft, 1909. 41 p.   F104.N75W6

10783

Windham, Conn. First Church. Records of the Congregational church in Windham, Conn. (except church votes), 1700–1851. Hartford, Connecticut Historical Society and the Society of Mayflower Descendants in the State of Connecticut, 1943. vi, 153 p. (Connecticut vital records, 8) F104.W65W5

10784

Woodruff, George C. A genealogical register of the inhabitants of the town of Litchfield, Conn., from the settlement of the town, A.D. 1720, to the year 1800. [Hartford, Conn.] Case, Lockwood & Brainard Co., 1900. 267 p. F104.L7W6

c. Middle Atlantic Region

(1) NEW YORK

10785

Blank, John. The census of 1781. Nassau County historical journal, v. 13, Oct. 1951–Jan. 1952: 1–9, 39–52. F127.N2N3, v. 13

Presents statistical information from a census of parts of Queens (now Nassau) County taken by Capt. Daniel Youngs at the order of Loyalist Gen. Oliver De Lancey. In addition to the numbers of white and black men, women, children, horses, cattle, sheep, hogs, and carts per family unit, the lists also include the amount of wheat, rye, corn, oats, and timber available.

10786

Moriarty, John H. Directory information material (printed) for New York City residents, 1626–1786; a bibliographic study. In New York (City). Public Library. Bulletin, v. 46, Oct. 1942: 807–864. Z881.N6B, v. 46

Offprint. New York, New York Public Library, 1942. 60 p. Z1318.N5M6

Describes 356 sources of information on the inhabitants of colonial New York City. The compilations are arranged according to 19 subject categories, including political parties, taxpayers, ship passengers, military units, churches, institutions, ethnic groups, courts, and several occupations. An annotation for each work provides an estimate of the names it contains, an explanation of its arrangement, and the inclusive dates of its entries.

10787

New Hackensack, N.Y. Reformed Dutch Church. The records of the Reformed Dutch church of New Hackensack, Dutchess County, New York. Edited by Maria Bockée Carpenter Tower. [Poughkeepsie, N.Y., 1932] xv, 333 p. plate. (Collections of the Dutchess County Historical Society, v. 5) F127.D8D92, v. 5

10788

New Windsor residents of Revolutionary and pre-Revolutionary days. In Historical Society of Newburgh Bay and the Highlands, Newburgh, N.Y. Publication. no. 26. Newburgh, 1931. p. 23–26. F127.O8H6, no. 26

Includes the names of hundreds of patients listed in the day book (1764–84) of Dr. Charles Clinton, Jr.

10789

New York (City). French church du Saint Esprit. Registers of the births, marriages, and deaths, of the "Église françoise à la Nouvelle York," from 1688 to 1804. Edited by the Rev. Alfred V. Wittmeyer. New York, 1886. lxxxviii, 431, xlii p. fold. facsim., plates. (Collections of the Huguenot Society of America, v. 1) [E184.H9H63, v.1]
Micro 38714

10790

New York (City). Roll of freemen of New York City, 1675–1866. In New York Historical Society. Collections. 1885. Publication fund series, [v. 18] New York, 1886. p. [37]–443. F116.N63, 1885

"Appendix to roll of freemen, 1695–1774": p. [445]–561.

The names of those admitted as freemen from 1763 to 1789 appear on pages 200–286.

10791

New York (Colony). New York marriages previous to 1784. Baltimore, Genealogical Pub. Co., 1968. ix, 618 p. facsim. F118.N485

Orginally published as Names of Persons for Whom Marriage Licenses Were Issued by the Secretary of the Province of New York, Previous to 1784 (Albany, Weed, Parsons, 1860); with the addition of Supplementary List of Marriage Licenses (Albany, University of the State of New York, 1898), issued as New York State Library History Bulletin no. 1; "New York Marriage Licenses," from the New York Genealogical and Biographical Record, v. 46, July–Oct. 1915, and v. 47, Jan.–July 1916; "New York Marriage Licenses, 1639–1706," by Kenneth Scott, from the New York Genealogical and Biographical Record, v. 98, Jan.–Apr. 1967; and the hitherto unpublished Index to New York Marriage Licenses, 1639–1706, by Kenneth Scott.

10792

New York (County). Surrogate's Court. Abstracts of wills on file in the Surrogate's Office, City of New York. [New York, Printed for the Society, 1893–1913] 17 v. facsims. (New York Historical Society. Collections, 1892–1908. Publication fund series, [v. 25–41]) F116.N63, v. 25–41

Vols. 15–16 having imprints dated respectively 1907, 1908, 1909 were actually issued in 1913.

Vols. 1–11, Publication Fund Series; v. 12–17, The John Watts de Peyster Publication Fund Series.

Vols. 1–9 and 11 copied and edited by William S. Pelletreau; v. 10 copied by the Reverend John Keller.

Vols. 3–9, 13–15 include letters of administration.

Wills covering the entire colony of New York were recorded with the Prerogative Court, and later with the Court of Probates under the first constitution of the state. A portion of the files are in the office of the clerk of the Court of Appeals in Albany, while others, chiefly those relating to

Westchester and counties further south, were transferred by legislative act in 1797 to the Surrogate's Office of New York County.

Contents: 1. 1665–1707.—2. 1708–1729.—3. 1730–1744.—4. 1744–1753.—5. 1754–1760.—6. 1760–1766.—7. June 6, 1766–November 29, 1771.—8. 1771–1776.—9. Jan. 7, 1777–Feb. 7, 1783.—10. Oct. 23, 1780–Nov. 5, 1782.—11. Abstracts of unrecorded wills prior to 1790 [i.e. 1800]—12. June 17, 1782–Sept. 11, 1784.—13. Sept. 3, 1784–June 12, 1786.—14. June 12, 1786–Feb. 13, 1796.—15. Feb. 15, 1796–Jan. 14, 1801.—16.–17. Corrections [of] Abstracts of wills, v. 1–9, 11.

10793

New York Genealogical and Biographical Society. Collections of the New-York Genealogical and Biographical Society. v. 1–8. New York, Printed for the Society, 1890–1928. 8 v. in 9. illus., col. coats of arms, facsims., ports.   F116.N36 LH&G

Partial contents: v. 1. Marriages from 1639 to 1801 in the Reformed Dutch Church, New York.—v. 3. Baptisms from 1731 to 1800 in the Reformed Dutch Church, New York.—v. 4. Records of the Dutch Reformed Church of Port Richmond, S.I.: baptisms from 1696 to 1772. United Brethren Congregation, commonly called Moravian Church, S.I., births and baptisms: 1749 to 1853; marriages: 1764 to 1863; deaths and burials: 1758 to 1828. St. Andrew's Church, Richmond, S.I., births and baptisms from 1752 to 1795, marriages from 1754 to 1808. Edited by T. A. Wright.—v. 5. Minisink Valley Reformed Dutch Church records [1716 to 1830. Edited by R. W. Vosburgh]—v. 7. Wawarsing Reformed Dutch Church records, edited by R. W. Vosburgh.—v. 8. The Presbyterian Church records, Newtown (now Elmhurst) L.I., N.Y. The Reformed Dutch Church records and the Presbyterian Church records at Smithfield, Pa. Clove Dutch Reformed Church records of Clove Valley, Wantage, N.J.

10794

Pelletreau, William S., *ed.* Early wills of Westchester County, New York, from 1664 to 1784. A careful abstract of all wills (nearly 800) recorded in New York surrogate's office and at White Plain's, N.Y., from 1664 to 1784. New York, F. P. Harper, 1898. xii, 488 p. plate, port.   F127.W5P3

10795

Poucher, John Wilson, *and* Helen W. Reynolds, *comps.* Old gravestones of Dutchess County, New York; nineteen thousand inscriptions. Poughkeepsie, N.Y., 1924. xi, 401 p. illus., plates. (Collections of the Dutchess County Historical Society, v. 2)   F127.D8D92, v. 2

10796

Poucher, John Wilson, *and* Bryon J. Terwilliger, *eds.* Old gravestones of Ulster County, New York; twenty-two thousand inscriptions. [Kingston, N.Y., Ulster County Historical Society] 1931. xii, 407 p. illus. (Collections of the Ulster County Historical Society, v. 1)   F127.U4U42, v. 1

———— ———— Index [by] Ruth P. Heidgerd. New Paltz, N.Y., 1958. 28 l.   F127.U4U42, v. 1 Index

10797

Reynolds, Helen W., *ed.* Notices of marriages and deaths, about 4,000 in number, published in newspapers printed at Poughkeepsie, New York, 1778–1825. [Poughkeepsie, N.Y., Printed by F. B. Howard, 1930] xii, 140 p. (Collections of the Dutchess County Historical Society, v. 4)   F127.D8D92, v. 4
F127.D8R41

10798

Rosenwaike, Ira. Population history of New York City. [Syracuse, N.Y.] Syracuse University Press, 1972. xvii, 224 p. map.   HB3527.N7R66

Bibliography: p. 207–216.

The colonial and Revolutionary periods are treated in chapters 1 and 2 (p. 1–32).

10799

Stryker-Rodda, Kenn, *comp.* Genealogical gleanings from account books of Elias Pelletreau of Southampton, Long Island [1759–1805] Journal of Long Island history, v. 5, winter 1965: 27–47; spring: 28–46.
F127.L8J75, v. 5

An alphabetical list of persons from the Southampton area whose names appeared in the account books of a local metalsmith. The information provided includes names, variations in their spelling, earliest and latest dates of entry, and methods of payment.

10800

U.S. *Bureau of the Census.* Heads of families at the first census of the United States, taken in the year 1790: New York. Washington, Govt. Print. Off., 1908. [Spartanburg, S.C., Reprint Co., 1964] 308 p. map (on lining papers)   F118.U5

Also reprinted in Baltimore by the Genealogical Pub. Co. (1966. F123.U5 1966).

10801

Williams, Joshua. Southampton calls a new pastor. Long Island forum, v. 34, Oct. 1971: 214–222.
F127.L8L73, v. 34

Comprises the journal of the Rev. Joshua Williams, pastor of the Southampton Presbyterian Church, which is devoted largely to vital statistics, 1784–89. Introduction and notes by James M. Aldrich.

(2) NEW JERSEY

10802

Ellis, William A. Census of Morris Township, Morris County, N.J., 1771–2. *In* New Jersey Historical Society. Proceedings, v. 63, Jan. 1944: 24–36.
F131.N58, v. 63

10803

Nelson, William, *ed.* Marriage records, 1665–1800. Paterson, N.J., Press Print. and Pub. Co., 1900. xii, cxxvi, 678 p. facsims. (Documents relating to the colonial history of the state of New Jersey, v. 22)

F131.D63, v. 22
F133.N42

Archives of the state of New Jersey, 1st ser., v. 22.

The marriage records of the Hackensack and Schraalenburg churches are reprinted from volume 1 of the *Collections* of the Holland Society of New York.

Contents: The early marriage laws of New Jersey, by William Nelson.—Index to marriage bonds and records in the office of the Secretary of State at Trenton.—Marriage records of the following churches and county clerks: Hackensack Reformed (Dutch) Church, 1695–1800. Schraalenburgh Reformed (Dutch) Church, 1724–1801. Paramus Reformed (Dutch) Church, 1799–1801. Bergen County, 1795–1800. Bergen Reformed (Dutch) Church, 1664–1801. Essex County, 1795–1801. Lyons Farms Baptist Church, 1795–1800. Second River Reformed (Dutch) Church, 1730–1774, 1794–1800. Christ Church, New Brunswick, 1758–1778. New Brunswick Reformed (Dutch) Church, 1794–1799. Middlesex County, 1795–1800. Piscataway, Seventh Day Baptist Church, 1745–1776. Scotch Plains Baptist Church, 1758–1761. Chesterfield (Burlington County) Friends' Monthly Meeting, 1686–1800.

Reprinted in Baltimore by the Genealogical Pub. Co. (1967).

10804

New Jersey. *Dept. of State.* Compendium of censuses, 1726–1905, together with the tabulated returns of 1905. Trenton, N.J., J. L. Murphy Pub. Co., Printers, 1906. 41, 71 p. HA522.1726C

Statistics from enumerations made before 1790 are included in a series of folded tables (p. 11–41, 1st group) printed on one side of the leaf only.

10805

New Jersey Historical Society. Calendar of New Jersey wills, administrations, etc. v. 1–9; 1670/1730–1796/1800. Newark, N.J., 1901–44. 9 v.

F13.D63, v. 23, 30, 32–38
F133.N52

At head of title: Documents relating to the colonial, Revolutionary, and post-Revolutionary history of the state of New Jersey (v. 1–4, Documents relating to the colonial history of the state of New Jersey; v. 5, Documents relating to the colonial and Revolutionary history of the state of New Jersey), first series, v. 23, 30, 32–38.

Half title, v. 1–9: *Archives of the State of New Jersey* (on spine: *New Jersey Archives*), first series, v. 23, 30, 32–38.

Title varies slightly.

Editors: v. 1, William Nelson.—v. 2–5, A. Van D. Honeyman.—v. 6–9, E. T. Hutchinson.

Contents: v. 1. 1670–1730.—v. 2. 1730–1750.—v. 3. 1751–1760.—v. 4. 1761–1770.—v. 5. 1771–1780.—v. 6. 1781–1785.—v. 7. 1786–1790.—v. 8. 1791–1795.—v. 9. 1796–1800.

10806

Stryker-Rodda, Kenn. Revolutionary census of New Jersey; an index, based on ratables, of the inhabitants of New Jersey during the period of the American Revolution. Cottonport, Polyanthos, 1972. xi, 248, 13 p. facsim. F133.S77

Presents three separate alphabetical compilations of surnames found in tax lists dated 1773–74, 1778–80, and 1784–86. For each Christian name under a particular family name, the compiler indicates the counties in which the person was taxed, thus providing an entree to the manuscript tax rate lists, which are available on microfilm at the Division of Archives and History in Trenton, N.J.

10807

Vecoli, Rudolph J. The people of New Jersey. Princeton, N.J., Van Nostrand, 1965. xv, 299 p. illus. (The New Jersey historical series. Supplementary volume)

HB3525.N5V4

"Bibliographical note": p. 283–290.

Discusses in chapters 1 and 2 (p. 1–65) the composition of New Jersey's population during the colonial and Revolutionary periods.

(3) PENNSYLVANIA

10808

Berks Co., *Pa.* Proprietary and state tax lists of the county of Berks, for the years 1767, 1768, 1779, 1780, 1781, 1784, 1785. Edited by William Henry Egle. [Harrisburg] W. S. Ray, State Printer of Pennsylvania, 1898. xii, 814 p. (Pennsylvania archives, 3d ser., v. 18)

F146.P41, 3d s., v. 18
F157.B3B32

10809

Bucks Co., *Pa.* Proprietary and other tax lists of the county of Bucks for the years 1779, 1781, 1782, 1783, 1784, 1785, 1786. Edited by William Henry Egle. [Harrisburg] W. S. Ray, State Printer of Pennsylvania, 1897. xiv, 820 p. (Pennsylvania archives, 3d ser., v. 13)

F146.P41, 3d s., v. 13
F157.B8B82

10810

Chester Co., *Pa.* Proprietary tax lists of the county of Chester. Edited by William Henry Egle. [Harrisburg] W. S. Ray, State Printer of Pennsylvania, 1897. 2 v. col. plates, fold. maps. (Pennsylvania archives, 3d ser., v. 11–12)

F146.P41, 3d s., v. 11–12
F157.C4C28

Contents: [v. 1] 1765–1769, 1771.—[v. 2] 1774, 1779–1781, 1785.

10811

Dunaway, Wayland F. Pennsylvania as an early distributing center of population. Pennsylvania magazine of history and biography, v. 55, Apr. 1931: 134–169.

F146.P65, v. 55

Bibliography: p. 164–169.

10812

Easton, Pa. First Reformed Church. Some of the first settlers of "the forks of the Delaware" and their descendants; being a translation from the German of the record books of the First Reformed Church of Easton, Penna., from 1760 to 1852. Translated and published by the Rev. Henry Martyn Kieffer. Easton, Pa., 1902. vii, 404 p. illus., facsims., plates, ports.   F159.E15E2

10813

Egle, William H., *ed.* Names of foreigners who took the oath of allegiance to the province and state of Pennsylvania, 1727–1775, with the foreign arrivals, 1786–1808. Harrisburg, E. K. Meyers, State Printer, 1892. 788 p. (Pennsylvania archives, 2d ser., v. 17)

F146.P41, 2d s., v. 17
F148.E3

Reprinted in Baltimore by the Genealogical Pub. Co. (1967).

10814

Egle, William H., *ed.* Returns of taxables for the counties of Bedford (1773 to 1784), Huntingdon (1788), Westmoreland (1783, 1786), Fayette (1785, 1786), Allegheny (1791), Washington (1786). And census of Bedford (1784) and Westmoreland (1783). [Harrisburg] W. S. Ray, State Printer, 1898. xii, 782 p. (Pennsylvania archives, 3d ser., v. 22)   F146.P41, 3d s., v. 22
F153.E373

10815

Gilbert, Russell W. Pennsylvania German wills. [Allentown, Pa., 1950] 139 p. (Pennsylvania German Folkore Society. [Yearbook], v. 15)   GR110.P4A35, v. 15

The author arranges generous excerpts from Pennsylvania German wills according to such varied categories as the rights and privileges of widows, gifts to sons, implements, produce, and animals.

10816

Hildeburn, Charles S. R. An index to the obituary notices published in the "Pennsylvania Gazette," from 1728–1791. Pennsylvania magazine of history and biography, v. 10, Oct. 1886: 334–349.   F146.P65, v. 10

10817

Jordan, John W. Moravian immigration to Pennsylvania, 1734–1765. Pennsylvania magazine of history and biography, v. 33, Apr. 1909: 228–248.

F146.P65, v. 33

Mostly lists of names.

10818

Lancaster Co., *Pa.* Proprietary and state tax lists of the county of Lancaster. For the years 1771, 1772, 1773, 1779, and 1782. Edited by William Henry Egle. [Harrisburg] W. S. Ray, State Printer of Pennsylvania, 1898. vii, 898 p. (Pennsylvania archives, 3d ser., v. 17)

F146.P41, 3d s., v. 17
F157.L2L3

10819

List of taxable inhabitants in the town and county of Westmoreland, (Wyoming, Penn'a,) State of Connecticut, 1776–1780. *In* Wyoming Historical and Geological Society, *Wilkes-Barre, Pa.* Proceedings and collections. v. 5; 1900. Wilkes-Barre. p. [205]–242.

F157.W9W94, v. 5

10820

Marshall, William. Wm. Marshall's register of births and baptisms in the Scotch Church of Philadelphia from the year 1767 to the year 1801. *In* Presbyterian Historical Society. Journal, v. 5, Dec. 1909: 188–197; June 1910: 274–300.   BX8905.P7A4, v. 5

Introduction and notes by John McAllister, Jr.

10821

Northampton Co., *Pa.* Proprietary, supply, and state tax lists of the counties of Northampton and Northumberland for the years 1772 to 1787. Edited by William Henry Egle. [Harrisburg] W. S. Ray, State Printer of Pennsylvania, 1898. xii, 805 p. (Pennsylvania archives, 3d ser., v. 19)   F146.P41, 3d s., v. 19
F157.N7N73

10822

Pennsylvania (*Colony*). *Provincial Secretary's Office.* Names of persons for whom marriage licences were issued in the province of Pennsylvania previous to 1790. *In* Pennsylvania archives. 2d ser., v. 2. Harrisburg, 1876. p. [3]–344.   F146.P41, 2d s., v. 2

Reprinted in Baltimore by the Genealogical Pub. Co. (1968).

After the separation from Great Britain marriage licenses were issued by the Supreme Executive Council.

10823

Pennsylvania marriage licenses, 1784–86. *In* Pennsylvania archives. 6th ser., v. 6. Harrisburg, 1907. p. 283–310.

F146.P41, 6th s., v. 6
F159.E3E32

10824

Philadelphia. Proprietary, supply, and state tax lists of the city and county of Philadelphia. Edited by William Henry Egle. [Harrisburg] W. S. Ray, State Printer of Pennsylvania, 1897. 3 v. (Pennsylvania archives, 3d ser., v. 14–16)   F146.P41, 3d s., v. 14–16
F158.44.P24

Contents: [v. 1] 1769, 1774, 1779.—[v. 2] 1779–1781.—[v. 3] 1781–1783.

10825

Philadelphia. *Mayor.* Record of indentures of individuals bound out as apprentices, servants, etc., and of German and other redemptioners in the office of the mayor of the city of Philadelphia, October 3, 1771, to October 5, 1773. Copied under the direction of the Publication Committee of the Pennsylvania-German Society from the original volume in possession of the American Philosophical Society. *In* Pennsylvania-German Society. Proceedings and addresses. v. 16; 1905. [Lancaster, Pa.] 1907. 325 p. (5th group) F146.P23, v. 16

See also the "Record of Servants and Apprentices Bound and Assigned Before Hon. John Gibson, Mayor of Philadelphia, December 5th, 1772–May 21, 1773," in the *Pennsylvania Magazine of History and Biography*, v. 33, Oct. 1909, p. 475–491, and v. 34, Jan.–Apr. 1910, p. 99–121, 213–228. The information in this list, which was taken from a record book in the Manuscript Department of the Pennsylvania Historical Society, differs from that given by the Pennsylvania-German Society.

10826

Record of Pennsylvania marriages, prior to 1810. Harrisburg, L. S. Hart, State Printer, 1880–90. 2 v. plates. (Pennsylvania archives, 2d ser., v. 8–9)
  F146.P41, 2d s., v. 8–9
  F158.25.R4

Vol. 2 has imprint: E. K. Meyers, State Printer, 1890.

Marriages recorded by the registrar general together with marriage records of churches of Philadelphia and vicinity.
"List of Officers of the colonies on the Delaware and the province of Pennsylvania, 1614–1776": v. 2, p. [621]–818.

10827

Schumacher, Daniel. Daniel Schumacher's baptismal register [1754–1773] Translated with an introduction by Frederick S. Weiser. *In* Pennsylvania-German Society. Publications. v. 1. Allentown, Pa., 1968. p. [185]–407.
  GR110.P4A372, v. 1

Reflects the pastoral activities of a Lutheran clergyman in Berks and Lehigh counties in Pennsylvania.

10828

Scott, Kenneth. Genealogical data from the *Pennsylvania Chronicle*, 1767–1774. Washington, National Genealogical Society, 1971. 170 p. ([National Genealogical Society] Special publication, no. 37)
  CS42.N43, no. 37

10829

U.S. *Bureau of the Census.* Heads of families at the first census of the United States, taken in the year 1790. Pennsylvania. Washington, Govt. Print. Off., 1908. [Spartanburg, S.C., Reprint Co., 1963] 426 p. map (on lining papers) [Pennsylvania heritage series, no. 1]
  F146.P4375, no. 1

Also reprinted in Baltimore by the Genealogical Pub. Co. (1966. F153.U5 1966).

10830

York Co., *Pa.* Returns of taxables of the county of York, for the years 1779, 1780, 1781, 1782, and 1783. Edited by William Henry Egle. [Harrisburg] W. S. Ray, State Printer of Pennsylvania, 1898. viii, 820 p. (Pennsylvania archives, 3d ser., v. 21) F146.P41, 3d s., v. 21
  F157.Y6Y63

(4) DELAWARE

10831

Delaware. *Public Archives Commission.* Calendar of Kent County, Delaware, probate records, 1680–1800. Compiled by Leon de Valinger, Jr., state archivist. Dover, Public Archives Commission, State of Delaware, 1944. 558, 133 p. facsim. F172.K3A53

10832

Delaware. *Public Archives Commission.* Calendar of Sussex County, Delaware, probate records, 1680–1800. Compiled by Leon de Valinger, Jr., state archivist. Dover, 1964. 310, 87 p. F172.S8D4

10833

National Society of the Colonial Dames of America. *Delaware.* A calendar of Delaware wills, New Castle County, 1682–1800. New York, F. H. Hitchcock [ᶜ1911] 218 p. F172.N5N2
  Micro 8829 F

Reprinted in Baltimore by the Genealogical Pub. Co. (1969).

10834

Turner, Charles H. B., *comp.* Some records of Sussex County, Delaware. Philadelphia, Allen, Lane & Scott, 1909. 387 p. plates, ports. F172.S8T7

A collection of vital records taken from civil, judicial, ecclesiastical, vestry, and miscellaneous sources.

10835

Wilmington, Del. Holy Trinity Church. The records of Holy Trinity (Old Swedes) Church, Wilmington, Del., from 1697 to 1773. Translated from the original Swedish by Horace Burr, with an abstract of the English records from 1773 to 1810. [Wilmington] Historical Society of Delaware, 1890. 772 p. front. (Historical Society of Delaware. Papers, 9) F161.D35, no. 9
  F174.W7W73

——— Catalogue and errata of the records of Holy Trinity (Old Swedes) Church as translated by Horace Burr. Published by the Historical Society of Delaware, 1919. Wilmington, Del., Press of C. L. Story Co. [1919] 166 p. ([Historical Society of Delaware. Papers], 9–A) F161.D35, no. 9a

d. The South

(1) MARYLAND

10836

Burns, Annie W., *comp.* Maryland inventories and accounts. Annapolis, Md., 1938. 5 v. F180.B465

On cover: Maryland colonial statistics and indices. Cover dated 1936.
Typescript.
Index only.
Contents: 1. [Early records]— 2. [1700 to 1718]—[3] 1718 to 1745.—[4] 1745 to 1762.—[5] 1762 to 1777.

10837

Burns, Annie W., *comp*. Maryland marriage records. Annapolis, Md., 1938–39. 39 v.   F180.B47

Reproduced from typescript.

On cover: Maryland colonial statistics and indices.

10838

Burns, Annie W., *comp*. Marriage records, Baltimore City Court House, Baltimore, Maryland, 1777–1799. Baltimore, Md. [1940?]   F189.B1B546

Typescript.

Records wanting for December 1778; January–March 1779; January–October 1780; November–December 1786; January–October 1787.

10839

Burns, Annie W., *comp*. Maryland records of deaths, 1718–1777. [pt.1–2] Annapolis, Md., 1936. 2 v.   F180.B48

Reproduced from typescript.

On cover: Maryland colonial statistics and indices.

10840

Burns, Annie W. Maryland will book, number 24–[38] Contains wills from all Maryland counties [1744–72] Annapolis, Md., 1937–38. 15 v.   F180.B485

Mimeographed and typewritten.

On cover: Maryland colonial statistics and indices.

No more issued.

——— ——— Index. Annapolis, Md. 1938–39. 11 v.   F180.B485 Index

Typescript.

10841

Harford County 1783 Maryland tax list from the collection of the Maryland Historical Society. Philadelphia, Historic Publications, 1970. 163, 163a p.   F187.H2A56 1970

Opposite pages numbered in duplicate.

Photo-offset of the handwritten tax list originally in the collection of J. Thomas Scharf, commissioner of the Maryland Land Office.

10842

Maryland. *Commissioners of the Tax (Baltimore Co.)*. Maryland tax list, 1783: Baltimore County. Philadelphia, Historic Publications [1970] 165, 164a p.   F187.B2A53

Opposite pages numbered in duplicate.

"From the collection of the Maryland Historical Society."

Reproduction from manuscript of the incomplete assessment list, which was returned by the assessors appointed under the Maryland law of 1782 entitled *An Act to Raise the Supplies for the Year Seventeen Hundred and Eighty Three*.

10843

Residents of Baltimore before 1776. Maryland historical magazine, v. 42, Mar. 1947: 41–45.   F176.M18, v. 42

The few surviving lists of residents given here are the best available directory of early Baltimoreans before the official census of 1775.

10844

U.S. *Bureau of the Census*. Heads of families at the first census of the United States, taken in the year 1790: Maryland. Washington, Govt. Print. Off., 1907. [Spartanburg, S.C., Reprint Co., 1964] 189 p. map (on lining papers)   F185.U5

Also reprinted in Baltimore by the Genealogical Pub. Co. (1965).

(2) VIRGINIA

10845

Fothergill, Augusta B. M., *and* John M. Naugle. Virginia tax payers, 1782–87, other than those published by the United States Census Bureau. [Richmond? Va.] 1940. 142 p.   F225.F6

Reproduced from typescript.

Fayette and Lincoln counties of the present Kentucky have been included, but the lists for Jefferson County are omitted.

Reprinted in Baltimore by the Genealogical Pub. Co. (1967).

10846

Gilliam, Sara K. Virginia's people. A study of the growth and distribution of the population of Virginia from 1607 to 1943. [Richmond, Division of Purchase and Print.] 1944. 132 p. illus., maps. (Virginia. State Planning Board. Population study report no. 4)   HB3525.V8A3, no. 4

Bibliographic footnotes.

A companion report by Joseph B. Gittler is entitled *Virginia's People; a Cultural Panorama* ([Richmond, Division of Purchase and Print.] 1944. 125 p. HB3525.V8A3, no. 5).

10847

Lunenburg Co., *Va*. Sunlight on the southside; lists of tithes, Lunenburg County, Virginia, 1748–1783. With an introduction by Landon C. Bell. Philadelphia, Penna, G. S. Ferguson Co., 1931. 503 p. fold. facsims., fold. map.   F232.L9L92

10848

A Short census of Virginia—1779. National Genalogical Society quarterly, v. 46, Dec. 1958: 163–211.   CS42.N4, v. 46

On January 2, 1779, Congress passed a resolution calling in paper money issues for 1777 and 1778. Each state established a loan office where the names of persons presenting Continental bank notes were recorded along with their county and the amount of money deposited. The list of 4,658 presenters from Virginia is reproduced, with an introduction and notes by William H. Dumont, from a manuscript volume entitled "Register of Bills, Va. Continental Loan Office," now in the National Archives.

10849
U.S. *Bureau of the Census.*   Heads of families at the first census of the United States, taken in the year 1790: records of the state enumerations, 1782 to 1785, Virginia. Washington, Govt. Print. Off., 1908. [Spartanburg, S.C., Reprint Co., 1961] 189 p. map (on lining paper) (Virginia heritage series no. 1)   F225.U6

Also reprinted in Baltimore by the Genealogical Pub. Co. (1970. 189 p. F230.U5 1970).

The returns of the United States census for 1790 for the state of Virginia were destroyed by fire in 1814. In their place, the Bureau of the Census published the records of state enumerations for the years 1782–85, which cover only 39 of the 80 counties, and the tax lists of Greenbrier County from 1783 to 1786 from the originals in the Virginia State Library. In 1940 Augusta B. M. Fothergill and John M. Naugle compiled a list of *Virginia Tax Payers, 1782–87; Other Than Those Published by the United States Census Bureau* ([Richmond? Va.] 142 p. F225.F6) that has been reprinted in Baltimore by the Genealogical Pub. Co. (1966 [i.e. 1967]).

10850
Wulfeck, Dorothy F.   Marriages of some Virginia residents, 1607–1800. Series I. Naugatuck, Conn., 1961–67. 7 v.   F225.W8

Includes bibliographies.

(3) NORTH CAROLINA

10851
[Burgwin, John]   North-Carolina. A table of the number of taxables in this province from the year 1748 inclusive, with the taxes laid for each year, and an account of the sums that should arise by the sinking tax yearly to the year 1770. [n.p., 1770? Boston, 1936] facsim.: 2 fold. tables. [Photostat Americana, 2d ser., no. 21]
HJ2425.A3B8 Rare Bk. Coll.

One of 15 copies from the original in the Massachusetts Historical Society, November, 1936.

Reprinted in *Some Eighteenth Century Tracts Concerning North Carolina* (entry 2250), with introduction and notes by William K. Boyd.

10852
Clemens, William M., *ed.*   North and South Carolina marriage records, from the earliest colonial days to the Civil War. New York, E. P. Dutton [c1927] x, 295 p.
F253.C62

10853
Fries, Adelaide L., *ed.*   Records of the Moravians in North Carolina. v. 1–5. 1752–1792. Raleigh, Edwards & Broughton Print. Co., 1922–41. 5 v. illus. (Publications of the North Carolina Historical Commission)
F265.M8F82, v. 1–5

Vol. 5 has imprint: Raleigh, North Carolina Historical Commission.

Contents: v. 1. 1752–1771.—v. 2. 1772–1775.—v. 3. 1776–1779.—v. 4. 1780–1783.—v. 5. 1784–1792.

10854
North Carolina. *Secretary of State.*   North Carolina wills and inventories copied from original and recorded will and inventories in the office of the secretary of state by J. Bryan Grimes, secretary of state. Published under the authority of the Trustees of the Public Libraries. Raleigh, Edwards & Broughton Print. Co., Printers, 1912. 587 p.   F253.N87

See also the supplement to Grimes' list prepared by Fred A. Olds, entitled *An Abstract of North Carolina Wills From About 1760 to About 1800* (Oxford, N.C., Priv. print. by "The Orphan's Friend," 1925. 326 p. F253.N862), which has been reprinted in Baltimore by the Genealogical Pub. Co. (1965).

10855
North Carolina. *State Dept. of Archives and History.*   State census of North Carolina, 1784–1787, from records in the North Carolina Department of Archives and History, Raleigh, N.C. Transcribed and indexed by Alvaretta Kenan Register. 2d ed., rev. [Norfolk, Va., 1971] 240 p.   F258.N92 1971

First edition published in 1969.

10856
Olds, Fred A., *comp.*   An abstract of North Carolina wills from about 1760 to about 1800. Supplementing Grimes' *Abstract of North Carolina Wills, 1663 to 1760.* Oxford, N.C., Priv. print. by "The Orphan's friend," 1925. 326 p.   F253.N862

Reprinted in Baltimore by the Genealogical Pub. Co. (1965).

Further supplementary material may be found in William Perry Johnson's *Index to North Carolina Wills, 1663–1900* (Raleigh, N.C. [1963]+ F262.A15J6).

10857
U.S. *Bureau of the Census.*   Heads of families at the first census of the United States, taken in the year 1790: North Carolina. Baltimore, Genealogical Pub. Co., 1966. 292 p.   F258.U9 1966

"Originally published: Washington, Government Printing Office, 1908."

Also reprinted in Spartanburg, S.C., by the Reprint Co. (1961).

(4) SOUTH CAROLINA

10858
Bridenbaugh, Carl.   Charlestonians at Newport, 1767–1775. South Carolina historical and genealogical magazine, v. 41, Apr. 1940: 43–47.   F266.S55, v. 41

Names from the *Newport Mercury* of southern planters who summered in Rhode Island.

10859

Hayne, Isaac.   Records kept by Colonel Isaac Hayne [1755–81] South Carolina historical and genealogical magazine, v. 10, July–Oct. 1909: 145–170, 220–233; v. 11, Jan.–July 1910: 27–38, 92–106, 160–170; v. 12, Jan. 1911: 14–23.   F266.S55, v. 10–12

Consists chiefly of births, deaths, and marriages taken from local newspapers or from Colonel Hayne's personal knowledge.

10860

Jervey, Elizabeth H., *comp.*   Death notices from the *Gazette of the State of South Carolina*, Charleston, S.C. [1777–88] South Carolina historical and genealogical magazine, v. 50, July–Oct. 1949: 127–130, 204–208; v. 51, Jan.–July 1950: 24–28, 97–102, 164–169.   F266.S55, v. 50–51

10861

Petty, Julian J.   The growth and distribution of population in South Carolina. Prepared for South Carolina State Planning Board. Columbia, S.C., State Council for Defense, Industrial Development Committee, 1943. 233 p. maps (part fold.) (South Carolina. State Planning Board. Bulletin no. 11)   HC107.S7A36, no.11

Bibliography: p. 209–213.

"Population growth and distribution before 1790": p. [13]–58.

10862

Salley, Alexander S., *comp. and ed.*   Death notices in the *South-Carolina Gazette*, 1732–1775. From the files in the library of the Charleston Library Society, Charleston, S.C. Columbia, S.C., Printed for the Historical Commission of South Carolina by the State Co., 1917. 42 p.   F268.S15

These listings have been supplemented by Mabel L. Webber's "Death Notices from *The South Carolina and American General Gazette*, and Its Continuation *The Royal Gazette*, May 1766–June 1782," which appeared in the *South Carolina Historical and Genealogical Magazine*, v. 16, Jan.–Oct. 1915, p. 34–38, 86–92, 129–133, 184–185, and v. 17, Jan.–Oct. 1916, p. 46–50, 87–93, 121–128, 147–166.

Both sets of notices have been reprinted together in Charleston by the South Carolina Archives Dept. (1954. 42, 39 p. F268.S15 1954).

10863

Salley, Alexander S., *comp. and ed.*   Marriage notices in the *South-Carolina and American General Gazette* from May 30, 1766, to February 28, 1781, and in its successor the *Royal Gazette* (1781–1782). From the files in the library of the Charleston Library Society, Charleston, S.C. Columbia, S.C., Printed for the Historical Commission of South Carolina by the State Co., 1914. 52 p.   F268.S175

10864

Salley, Alexander S., *comp. and ed.*   Marriage notices in the *South Carolina Gazette; and Country Journal* (1765–1775) and in the *Charlestown Gazette* (1778–1780). From the files in the library of the Charleston Library Society, Charleston, S.C. Columbia, S.C., 1904. 44 p.   F268.S17

10865

Salley, Alexander S., *comp. and ed.*   Marriage notices in the *South-Carolina Gazette* and its successors. (1732–1801.) From the files in the library of the Charleston Library Society, Charleston, S.C. Albany, J. Munsell's Sons, 1902. 174 p.   F268.S16

Reprinted in Baltimore by the Genealogical Pub. Co. (1965).

10866

U.S. *Bureau of the Census.*   Heads of families at the first census of the United States, taken in the year 1790: South Carolina. Washington, Govt. Print. Off. 1908. [Spartanburg, S.C., Reprint Co., 1960] 150 p. (South Carolina heritage series, no. 6)   F266.S53, no. 6

Also reprinted in Baltimore by the Genealogical Pub. Co. (1966. F273.U5 1966).

10867

Webber, Mabel L., *comp.*   Marriage and death notices from the *South Carolina Weekly Gazette* [Feb. 1783–Apr. 1789] South Carolina historical and genealogical magazine, v. 18, Jan.–Oct. 1917: 37–41, 85–90, 143–148, 184–189; v. 19, Jan.–Oct. 1918: 77–79, 105–113, 136–145, 170–180; v. 20, Jan.–Oct. 1919: 50–56, 142–146, 213–219, 260–263; v. 21, Jan. 1920: 24–29.   F266.S55, v. 18–21

(5) GEORGIA

10868

Bishop, William A., *comp.*   Marriages and deaths in Georgia colony, 1763–1800. Genealogical quarterly magazine, [3d] ser., v. 4, July 1903–Jan. 1904: 153–157, 161–168, 297–304; v. 5, Apr. 1904, Jan. 1905: 16–32, 160–166; [4th ser.] v. 1, July 1905: 145–154.   F1.P98, 3d s., v. 4–5; 4th s., v. 1

Taken from the *Georgia Gazette*.

10869

Warren, Mary B.   Marriages and deaths, 1763 to 1820; abstracted from extant Georgia newspapers. Danielsville, Ga., Printed by Heritage Papers [1968] [vi], 155 p. illus.   F285.W3

Bibliography: p. [v]

5. IMMIGRANT AND ETHNIC GROUPS
a. General

10870

Bean, Robert Bennett.   The peopling of Virginia. Boston, Chapman & Grimes [c1938] viii, 302 p. ports.   F229.B43

Bibliography: p. 263–264.

Includes brief histories of Virginia's counties with tables showing the national origins of the inhabitants at various periods.

10871

Bolton, Ethel S., *comp.* Immigrants to New England, 1700–1775. Salem, Mass., Essex Institute, 1931. 235 p.
F7.B74

Reprinted from the *Historical Collections* of the Essex Institute, v. 63–67.

An alphabetical list of names with brief biographical information and bibliographic citations.

10872

Conner, Robert D. W. Race elements in the white population of North Carolina. [Raleigh, N.C.] The College, 1920. 115 p. (North Carolina State Normal & Industrial College. Historical publications, no. 1) F265.F6C75

Bibliography: p. [113]–115.

Reprinted in Spartanburg, S.C., by the Reprint Co. (1971).

Includes chapters on the English, Highland Scotch, Scotch-Irish, and Germans in North Carolina.

10873

Crary, Catherine S. The humble immigrant and the American dream: some case histories, 1746–1776. Mississippi Valley historical review, v. 46, June 1959: 46–66.
E171.J87, v. 46

Examines the careers of 30 obscure immigrants who found ample opportunities for economic and social advancement.

10874

Giuseppi, Montague S., *ed.* Naturalizations of foreign Protestants in the American and West Indian colonies (pursuant to Statute 13 George II, c. 7). Baltimore, Genealogical Pub. Co., 1964. xix, 195 p.
E184.A1G52 1964

Originally published in 1921 as v. 24 of the *Publications* of the Huguenot Society of London.

Lists all of the notices of naturalization, the majority being from Pennsylvania, sent from the colonies to the Board of Trade, 1740–72.

10875

Hansen, Marcus L. The Atlantic migration, 1607–1860; a history of the continuing settlement of the United States. Edited with a foreword by Arthur M. Schlesinger. Cambridge, Mass., Harvard University Press, 1940. xvii, 391 p. plates. JV6451.H3

"Bibliography and notes": p. [309]–371.

Studying the subject from the perspective of Europe and viewing the North Atlantic region as a single population basin, the author examines the causes and processes of European migration to America. In the brief section on the Revolutionary period, Hansen indicates that the rate of the movement to America increased significantly after 1763, was

especially high in 1770–73 and again in 1784–85, but declined sharply in 1786.

10876

Heaton, Herbert. The industrial immigrant in the United States, 1783–1812. *In* American Philosophical Society, *Philadelphia.* Proceedings, v. 95, Oct. 1951: 519–527.
Q11.P5, v. 95

10877

Hindle, Brooke. American culture and the migrations of the Revolutionary era. *In* Dickinson College, *Carlisle, Pa.* "John and Mary's College." [Westwood, N.J.] Revell [1956] (The Boyd Lee Spahr lectures in Americana, 1951–1956) p. 107–131. LD1663.A53

Contends that, in cultural matters, the immigrants of the Revolutionary era more than made up for the losses caused by Loyalist emigrations.

10878

Hoyt, Edward A. Naturalization under the American colonies: signs of a new community. Political science quarterly, v. 67, June 1952: 248–266. H1.P8, v. 67

10879

Livingston, William S. Emigration as a theoretical doctrine during the American Revolution. Journal of politics, v. 19, Nov. 1957: 591–615. JA1.J6, v. 19

Examining the causes and nature of emigration during the period, the author finds that the Revolutionary generation was only partly sympathetic to the "doctrine of emigration"—the right of the citizen to withdraw his consent to the social contract and leave the community, thus abandoning his loyalty and obligation to it.

10880

Newsome, Albert R., *ed.* Records of emigrants from England and Scotland to North Carolina, 1774–1775. North Carolina historical review, v. 11, Jan.–Apr. 1934: 39–54, 129–143. F251.N892, v. 11

10881

Pennsylvania (*Colony*). *Supreme Court.* Persons naturalized in the province of Pennsylvania [1740–1773] *In* Pennsylvania archives. 2d ser., v. 2. Harrisburg, 1876. p. [345]–486. F146.P41, 2d s., v. 2

Reprinted in Baltimore by the Genealogical Pub. Co. (1967).

10882

Proper, Emberson E. Colonial immigration laws: a study of the regulation of immigration by the English colonies in America. New York, Columbia University Press, 1900. 91 p. (Studies in history, economics and public law, v. 12, no. 2) H31.C7, v. 12, no. 2

Reprinted in New York by AMS Press (1967. KF4819.3.P76 1967).

Focuses on the attempts of colonial governments to encourage, regulate, and restrict immigration, the attitude of the British ministry toward provincial regulation, and the distribution of non-English nationalities in the colonies.

10883

Revill, Janie, *comp.* A compilation of the original lists of Protestant immigrants to South Carolina, 1763–1773. Columbia, S.C., State Co., 1939. 163 p.

F252.5.R49

Reprinted in Baltimore by the Genealogical Pub. Co. (1968).

10884

Risch, Erna. Immigrant aid societies before 1820. Pennsylvania magazine of history and biography, v. 60, Jan. 1936: 15–33. F146.P65, v. 60

10885

Rupp, Israel Daniel. A collection of upwards of thirty thousand names of German, Swiss, Dutch, French, and other immigrants in Pennsylvania from 1727 to 1776 . . . Reprint of the second rev. and enl. ed. with an added index. Baltimore, Genealogical Pub. Co., 1965. viii, 583 p. F152.R9614 1965

First edition published in 1856 under title: *A Collection of Thirty Thousand Names.*

Editorial matter in English and German.

"Index by Ernst Wecken": p. 497–581.

See also the mimeographed *Index to the Names of 30,000 Immigrants . . . Supplementing the I. Daniel Rupp Ship Load Volume* ([Pennington Gap, Va., ᶜ1935] 232 p. F152.R963), by M. V. Koger.

10886

Start, Cora. Naturalization in the English colonies in America. *In* American Historical Association. Annual report. 1893. Washington, 1894. p. 317–328.

E172.A60, 1893

10887

Wittke, Carl F. We who built America; the saga of the immigrant. [Rev. ed. Cleveland] Press of Case Western Reserve University [ᶜ1967] xviii, 550 p.

JV6455.W55 1967

Includes bibliographic references.

First edition published in 1939.

Summarizes in the first six chapters (p. 3–98) patterns of immigration to 1790.

b. Afro-American

10888

Aptheker, Herbert. The Negro in the American Revolution. *In his* Essays in the history of the American Negro. New York, International Publishers [1945] p. [71]–110. E185.A6

10889

Bardolph, Richard. Social origins of distinguished Negroes, 1770–1865. Journal of Negro history, v. 40, July 1955: 211–249. E185.J86, v. 40

10890

Bennett, Lerone. Before the Mayflower; a history of black America. 4th ed. Chicago, Johnson Pub. Co., 1969. 461 p. illus., map, ports. E185.B4 1969

Bibliography: p. [440]–453.

First edition published in 1962.

A general account that includes a chapter on the exploits of Negroes during the Revolution.

10891

Bennett, Lerone. The Negro in the American Revolution. Ebony, v. 17, Nov. 1961: 89–92, 94, 96, 98, 100. illus., ports. AP2.E165, v. 17

10892

Bergman, Peter M., *and* Jean McCarroll, *comps.* The Negro in the Continental Congress. New York, Bergman [1969] 153 p. facsim. (The Negro in the Congressional Record, v. 1) E185.B47

Extracts taken from the *Journals of the Continental Congress, 1774–1789* (Washington, Govt. Print. Off., 1904–37. 34 v.).

10893

Everett, Donald E. Free persons of color in colonial Louisiana. Louisiana history, v. 7, winter 1966: 21–50.

F366.L6238, v. 7

10894

Franklin, John H. From slavery to freedom; a history of Negro Americans. 3d ed [rev. and enl.] New York, Knopf, 1967. xxii, 686, xliii p. illus., ports.

E185.F825 1967

"Bibliographical notes": p. [653]–686.

First edition published in 1947.

Contains chapters on the 17th- and 18th-century origins of slavery, the growth of the institution in Latin America, and the activities of Negroes during the American Revolution.

10895

Greene, Lorenzo J. The Negro in colonial New England, 1620–1776. New York, Columbia University Press, 1942. 404 p. (Studies in history, economics and public law, no. 494) H31.C7, no. 494

Issued also as thesis (Ph.D.)—Columbia University.

Bibliography: p. 361–384.

Reprinted in Port Washington, N.Y., by Kennikat Press (1966).

Organizes the book around such topics as population, legal status, occupations, the family, religion, and free Negroes. Estimating that there were just over 16,000 blacks in New England during the Revolutionary era, the author finds that Negroes were not merely household servants, but that they participated in every aspect of economic life, from agriculture to whaling, and even manned slave ships and privateers.

10896

Jacobs, Donald M.   A history of the Boston Negro from the Revolution to the Civil War. 1968. ([408] p.)
Micro AC–1, no. 68–18,097

Thesis (Ph.D.)—Boston University.

Abstracted in *Dissertation Abstracts*, v. 29A, Jan. 1969, p. 2182.

The period before 1789 is treated on pages 1–39.

10897

Klingberg, Frank J.   The African immigrant in colonial Pennsylvania and Delaware. Historical magazine of the Protestant Episcopal Church, v. 11, June 1942: 126–153.
BX5800.H5, v. 11

10898

Klingberg, Frank J.   An appraisal of the Negro in colonial South Carolina, a study in Americanization. Washington, D.C., Associated Publishers, 1941. xii, 180 p.
E185.93.S7K6

Bibliographic footnotes.

Traces almost exclusively the development of Negro religious life with particular attention to the activities of the Society for the Propagation of the Gospel in Foreign Parts and the growth of Negro churches.

10899

Pinchbeck, Raymond B.   The Virginia Negro artisan and tradesman. Richmond, Va., William Byrd Press, 1926. 146 p. (Publications of the University of Virginia. Phelps-Stokes fellowship papers, no. 7)
E185.93.V8P6

Bibliography: p. 133–137.

10900

Porter, Dorothy B., *comp.*   Early Negro writing, 1760–1837. Boston, Beacon Press [ᶜ1971] xiii, 658 p. port.
PS508.N3P6

Includes bibliographic references.

Contains only seven works from the Revolutionary period, among them a slave petition to the representatives of Thompson, Mass., the life and confession of Johnson Green, a narrative of the sufferings of Briton Hammon, an elegiac poem by Phillis Wheatley, and two addresses and a broadside by Jupiter Hammon.

10901

Reynolds, Helen W.   The Negro in Dutchess County in the eighteenth century. *In* Dutchess County Historical Society. Year book. v. 26; 1941. Poughkeepsie. p. 89–100.
F127.D8D93, v. 26

10902

Russell, John H.   The free Negro in Virginia, 1619–1865. Baltimore, Johns Hopkins Press, 1913. 194 p. (Johns Hopkins University studies in historical and political science, 31st ser., no. 3)
E185.93.V8R9
H31.J6, 31st s., no. 3

Published also as thesis (Ph.D.)—Johns Hopkins University, 1913.

Bibliography: p. 178–186.

Reprinted in New York by Dover Publications (1969) and by Negro Universities Press (1969).

Following a discussion of the origin of the free Negro class, the author considers manumission practices and the social as well as the legal status of free blacks. Most were freed by their owners under the voluntary manumission law of 1782, itself a product of the Revolution.

10903

Stavisky, Leonard P.   Negro craftsmanship in early America. American historical review, v. 54, Jan. 1949: 315–325.
E171.A57, v. 54

Although skilled Negroes pursued nearly every trade or craft, Stavisky finds that white prejudice, original inexperience, and a lack of opportunity for improvement limited the development of Negro craftsmanship in the years before and after independence. An earlier version of the article appeared in the *Journal of Negro History*, v. 32, Oct. 1947, p. 417–429.

10904

Tate, Thaddeus W.   The Negro in eighteenth-century Williamsburg. Williamsburg, Va., Colonial Williamsburg; distributed by the University Press of Virginia, Charlottesville [ᶜ1965] xiv, 256 p. (Williamsburg research studies)
F234.W7T3

Bibliography: p. [237]–246.

Reproduced from typescript.

A printed edition was published in 1972 (141 p. E234.W7T3 1972).

Reports on such topics as the growth of slavery in the 18th century, patterns of slave ownership, the work of the Negro in Williamsburg, the slave market, and Negro social life, religion, education, and legal status.

10905

Turner, Edward R.   The Negro in Pennsylvania, slavery—servitude—freedom, 1639–1861. Washington, American Historical Association, 1911. xii, 314 p. (Prize essays of the American Historical Association, 1910)
E185.93.P41T9

Bibliography: p. 255–294.

Reprinted in New York by the Negro Universities Press (1969) and Arno Press (1969).

10906

Wesley, Charles H.   In freedom's footsteps, from the African background to the Civil War. New York, Publishers Co. [1968] xii, 307 p. illus., facsims., ports. (International library of Negro life and history)
E185.W45

Bibliography: p. [271]–290.

A general overview of the Negro's role in the Revolution appears in chapters 6 and 7 (p. 81–110).

10907

Williams, George W.   History of the Negro race in America from 1619 to 1880. Negroes as slaves, as soldiers, and as citizens; together with a preliminary consideration of the unity of the human family, an historical sketch of Africa, and an account of the Negro governments of Sierra Leone and Liberia. v. 1. 1619 to 1800. New York, G. P. Putnam's Sons, 1883. xix, 481 p. front.   E185.W7, v. 1

Bibliographic footnotes.
Reprinted in New York by Arno Press (1968).
"The Negro During the Revolution": p. 324–441.

10908

Woodson, Carter G.   The education of the Negro prior to 1861; a history of the education of the colored people of the United States from the beginning of slavery to the Civil War. New York, G. P. Putnam's Sons, 1915. v, 454 p.   LC2741.W7

Bibliography: p. 399–434.
Reprinted in New York by Arno Press (1968).

10909

Woodson, Carter G.   The history of the Negro church. 2d ed. Washington, D.C., Associated Publishers [1945] xi, 322 p. illus., ports.   BR563.N4W6 1945

Includes three chapters (p. 1–70) on early missionaries and the Negro, the effects of the Great Awakening and the Revolution, and the work of pioneer Negro preachers.

10910

Wright, James M.   The free Negro in Maryland, 1634–1860. New York, Columbia University, 1921. 362 p. (Studies in history, economics and public law, v. 97, no. 3; whole no. 222)   H31.C7, v. 97
                                                     E185.W95

Bibliography: p. 348–362.
Reprinted in New York by Octagon Books (1971).

c. English

10911

Campbell, Mildred L.   English emigration on the eve of the American Revolution. American historical review, v. 61, Oct. 1955: 1–20.   E171.A57, v. 61

Analyzes customs officials' reports on 12,000 emigrants who left the British Isles for America, 1773–76.

10912

Dunaway, Wayland F.   The English settlers in colonial Pennsylvania. Pennsylvania magazine of history and biography, v. 52, Oct. 1928: 317–341.
                                                     F146.P65, v. 52

10913

Fothergill, Gerald.   Emigrants from England [1773–76] New England historical and genealogical register, v. 62, July–Oct. 1908: 242–253, 320–332; v. 63, Jan.–Oct. 1909: 16–31, 134–146, 234–244, 342–355; v. 64, Jan.–

Oct. 1910: 18–25, 106–115, 214–227, 314–326; v. 65, Jan.–July 1911: 20–35, 116–132, 232–251.
                                                     F1.N56, v. 62–65

An offprint of this article (Boston, New England Historic Genealogical Society, 1913. 206 p. E187.5.E53) has been reprinted in Baltimore by the Genealogical Pub. Co. (1964. E187.5.F69).

The list of 6,000 names, transcribed by Fothergill from treasury records in the Public Record Office, also includes the age, occupation, place of origin, ship sailed on, destination, and New World status of each emigrant.

10914

Mellor, George R.   Emigration from the British Isles to the New World, 1765–1775. History, new ser., v. 40, Feb./June 1955: 68–83.   D1.H815, n.s., v. 40

10915

Read, Allen W.   The assimilation of the speech of British immigrants in colonial America. Journal of English and Germanic philology, v. 37, Jan. 1938: 70–79.
                                                     PD1.J7, v. 37

Uses 18th-century newspaper advertisements to show that American English had a consistency of its own, similar to dialects in the region around London.

d. German

10916

Bittinger, Lucy F.   The Germans in colonial times. Philadelphia, J. B. Lippincott Co., 1901. 314 p. map.
                                                     E184.G3B4

"List of works consulted": p. 300–305.
Reprinted in New York by Russell & Russell (1968).

10917

Bittinger, Lucy F.   German religious life in colonial times. J. B. Lippincott Co., 1906. 145 p.   BR563.G3B6

"The German churches during the Revolution": p. 107–133.

10918

Bittinger, Lucy F.   The Pennsylvania Germans. New England magazine, new ser., v. 26, May–July 1902: 366–384, 498–512, 617–624.   AP2.N4, n.s., v. 26

10919

Bressler, Leo A.   Agriculture among the Germans in Pennsylvania during the eighteenth century. Pennsylvania history, v. 22, Apr. 1955: 103–133.
                                                     F146.P597, v. 22

10920

Chambers, Theodore F.   The early Germans of New Jersey: their history, churches and genealogies. [Dover, N.J., Dover Print. Co., 1895] xiii, 667 p. fold. map, plans, plates, ports.   F145.G3C4

Reprinted in Baltimore, with a new foreword by Kenn Stryker-Rodda, by the Genealogical Pub. Co. (1969).

10921

Cunz, Dieter.   The Maryland Germans, a history. Princeton, Princeton University Press, 1948. xi, 476 p. illus., ports.   F190.G3C8

Bibliography: p. 439–449.

Reprinted in Port Washington, N.Y., by Kennikat Press (1972).

In the section on immigration before 1789, the author tells of German settlement at Frederick and Hagerstown in western Maryland and, later, in Baltimore city and county; of the spirit that led Marylanders to form all-German military units during the Revolution; and of the experiences of Hessian prisoners, some of whom stayed in the area after the war.

10922

Diffenderffer, Frank R.   The German immigration into Pennsylvania through the port of Philadelphia, 1700 to 1775. Part II. The redemptioners. Prepared at the request of the Pennsylvania-German Society. Lancaster, Pa., 1900. ix, 330 p. illus., facsims., plates, ports.
                                                            F152.D55

Also published as pt. 7 of Pennsylvania: the German Influence in its Settlement and Development in the *Proceedings and Addresses*, v. 10, 1899 (F146.P23, v. 10), of the Pennsylvania-German Society.

10923

Dorpalen, Andreas.   The political influence of the German element in colonial America. Pennsylvania history, v. 6, July–Oct. 1939: 147–158, 221–239.   F146.P597, v. 6

10924

Eshleman, Henry Frank.   Historic background and annals of the Swiss and German pioneer settlers of southeastern Pennsylvania, and of their remote ancestors, from the middle of the dark ages, down to the time of the Revolutionary War; . . . with particular reference to the German-Swiss Mennonites or Anabaptists, the Amish and other nonresistant sects. Lancaster, Pa., 1917. 386 p.   F160.S9E8

Reprinted in Baltimore by the Genealogical Pub. Co. (1969).

10925

Faust, Albert B.   The German element in the United States with special reference to its political, moral, social, and educational influence. Boston, Houghton Mifflin Co., 1909. 2 v. facsims., maps, plates, ports.   E184.G3F3

Bibliography: v. 2, p. [477]–562.

Reprinted in New York by Arno Press (1969).

Starting with the Palatine immigration of the early 18th century, Faust traces the history of German settlement, especially in Pennsylvania, New Jersey, Maryland, Virginia, and the Carolinas; describes the role of Germans in defending the frontier from Maine to Georgia against Indian attack; and follows the movement of Germans into Kentucky, Tennessee, and the Ohio Valley. In a chapter on the Revolution, he recounts the exploits of Germans who supported the rebel cause and defends the conduct of Hessian mercenaries, whose services were sold to the British by tyrannical rulers.

10926

Gagliardo, John G.   Germans and agriculture in colonial Pennsylvania. Pennsylvania magazine of history and biography, v. 83, Apr. 1959: 192–218.
                                                        F146.P65, v. 83

10927

Jantz, Harold S.   German thought and literature in New England, 1620–1820. Journal of English and German philology, v. 41, Jan. 1941: 1–45.   PD1.J7, v. 41

10928

Jordan, John W.   Moravian immigration to Pennsylvania, 1734–1767, with some of the transport vessels. *In* Moravian Historical Society, *Nazareth, Pa.* Transactions. v. 5, pt. 2. Bethlehem, Pa., 1896. p. 51–90.
                                                        E184.M8M8, v. 2
                                                        BX8553.M7, v. 2

10929

Knauss, James O.   Social conditions among the Pennsylvania Germans in the eighteenth century, as revealed in German newspapers published in America. [Lancaster, Pa., New Era Print. Co., ʻ1922] x, 217 p.
                                                            F160.G3K6

Thesis (Ph.D.)—Cornell University, 1918.

Bibliography: p. 212–217.

"Table of German-American newspapers of the eighteenth century": p. 169–211.

First published as part 30 of Pennsylvania: the German Influence in its Settlement and Development in the *Proceedings and Addresses*, v. 29, 1918 (F146.P23, v. 29), of the Pennsylvania-German Society.

10930

Krebs, Friedrich.   Emigrants from the Palatinate to the American colonies in the 18th century. Edited, with an introduction by Milton Rubincam. Norristown, Pennsylvania German Society, 1953. 32 p. map. ([Pennsylvania-German Society] Special study, no. 1)
                                                            F160.P2K7

Bibliographic references included in "Note" (p. 32).

10931

Kuhns, Levi Oscar.   The German and Swiss settlements of colonial Pennsylvania: a study of the so-called Pennsylvania Dutch. New York, H. Holt, 1901. v. 268 p.
                                                            F160.G3K9

Bibliography: p. 247–257.

Reprinted in New York by AMS Press and in Ann Arbor by Gryphon Books (1971).

10932

Miller, Daniel.   Early German American newspapers. *In* Pennsylvania-German Society. Proceedings and addresses. v. 19; 1908. [Lancaster, Pa.] 1910. 107 p. (3d group) illus., facsims., port.   F146.P23, v. 19

Pt. 22 of Pennsylvania: the German Influence in its Settlement and Development.

10933
Nead, Daniel W.   The Pennsylvania-German in the settlement of Maryland. Part XXV. of a narrative and critical history prepared at the request of the Pennsylvania-German Society. Lancaster, Pa. [Press of the New Era Print. Co.] 1914. xii, 304 p. illus., facsims., maps, plates, ports.   F190.G3N3

Bibliography: p. xi–xii.
Also published in the *Proceedings and Addresses*, v. 22, 1911 (F146.P23, v. 22), of the Pennsylvania-German Society.
Includes five chapters (p. [176]–271) on the period 1763–83 and the role of Maryland troops in the war.

10934
Pollak, Otto.   German immigrant problems in eighteenth century Pennsylvania as reflected in trouble advertisements. American sociological review, v. 8, Dec. 1943: 674–684.   HM1.A75, v. 8

Analyzes two German-language newspapers for information concerning the stresses of adjustment to American conditions.

10935
Rosenberger, Homer T.   Migrations of the Pennsylvania Germans to western Pennsylvania. Western Pennsylvania historical magazine, v. 53, Oct. 1970: 319–335; v. 54, Jan. 1971: 58–76.   F146.W52, v. 53–54

10936
Rothermund, Dietmar.   The German problem of colonial Pennsylvania. Pennsylvania magazine of history and biography, v. 84, Jan. 1960: 3–21.   F146.P65, v. 84

10937
Rush, Benjamin.   An account of the manners of the German inhabitants of Pennsylvania, written in 1789. Notes added by Prof. I. Daniel Rupp. Philadelphia, S. P. Town, 1875. 72 p. ports.   F160.G3R8

10938
Schantz, Franklin J. F.   The domestic life and characteristics of the Pennsylvania-German pioneer. Part VI. of a narrative and critical history prepared at the request of the Pennsylvania-German Society. *In* Pennsylvania-German Society. Proceedings and addresses. v. 10; 1899. [Lancaster, Pa.] 1900. 97 p. (2d group) illus., col. facsim., plates (part col.)   F146.P23, v. 10

10939
Schuricht, Herrmann.   History of the German element in Virginia. Baltimore, T. Kroh, Printers, 1898–1900. 2 v. in 1. port.   F235.G3S3

Issued as appendixes to the annual reports of the Society for the History of the Germans in Maryland: v. 1 with the 11th–12th reports for 1897–98, and v. 2 with the 13th–14th reports for 1899–1900.

Chapters 8 and 9 (p. 112–153) in volume 1 are concerned with German participants in the Revolution.

10940
Shelley, Donald A.   The fraktur-writings or illuminated manuscripts of the Pennsylvania Germans. [Allentown, Pa., 1961] viii, 375 p. illus., facsims. (part col.) (Pennsylvania German Folklore Society. [Yearbook], v. 23)
          GR110.P4A35, v. 23
          ND3035.P4S5

Bibliography: p. 187–219.
Appendix (p. 179–186): A. Fraktur illuminators.—B. Fraktur printing centers.—C. Fraktur printers.

10941
Stoffler, E. Ernest.   Mysticism in German devotional literature of colonial Pennsylvania. [Allentown, Pa., 1950] xii, 173 p. (Pennsylvania German Folklore Society. [Yearbook], v. 14)   GR110.P4A35, v. 14

"Selected bibliography of secondary sources": p. 165–173.

10942
Stoudt, John J.   The German press in Pennsylvania and the American Revolution. Pennsylvania magazine of history and biography, v. 59, Jan. 1935: 74–90.
          F146.P65, v. 59

Contends that the major outlet for German liberal sentiment during the Revolution was *Der Wöchentliche Philadelphische Staatsbote*, published by Henry (Heinrich) Miller.

10943
Stoudt, John J., *ed.*   Pennsylvania German poetry, 1685–1830. [Allentown? Pa., 1956] cvi, 287 p. illus. (Pennsylvania German Folklore Society. [Yearbook], v. 20)
          GR110.P4A35, v. 20

Includes bibliographies.

Following an extensive introduction, the editor reprints the verse of more than 100 writers.

10944
Strassburger, Ralph B.   Pennsylvania German pioneers; a publication of the original lists of arrivals in the port of Philadelphia from 1727 to 1808. Edited by William John Hinke. Norristown, Penn., Pennsylvania German Society, 1934. 3 v. facsims., maps, plates, ports. (Pennsylvania German Society. Proceedings, v. 42–44)
          F146.P23, v. 42–44
          F160.G3S8

Reprinted in Baltimore by the Genealogical Pub. Co. (1966).

10945
Voigt, Gilbert P.   Cultural contributions of German settlers to South Carolina. South Carolina historical magazine, v. 53, Oct. 1952: 183–189.   F266.S55, v. 53

10946

Wayland, John W.   The German element of the Shenandoah Valley of Virginia. Charlottesville, Va., The author, 1907. xi, 272 p.   F232.S5W3

Thesis (Ph.D.)—University of Virginia.
Bibliography: p. 237–272.
———— Index. Charlottesville, Va., 1908. 273–312 p.
F232.S5W3 Index

10947

Wayland, John W.   The Germans of the [Shenandoah] Valley. Virginia magazine of history and biography, v. 9, Apr. 1902: 337–352; v. 10, July–Oct. 1902: 33–48, 113–130.   F221.V91, v. 9–10

10948

Weaver, Glenn.   Benjamin Franklin and the Pennsylvania Germans. William and Mary quarterly, 3d ser., v. 14, Oct. 1957: 536–559.   F221.W71, 3d s., v. 14

Discusses the "Americanization" of disparate German groups in Pennsylvania during Franklin's lifetime.

10949

Wust, Klaus G.   The Virginia Germans. Charlottesville, University Press of Virginia [1969] xii, 310 p. maps.
F235.G3W8

Bibliographic references included in "Notes" (p. [235]–285).

e. Irish

10950

Campbell, John H.   History of the Friendly Sons of St. Patrick and of the Hibernian Society for the Relief of Emigrants from Ireland. March 17, 1771–March 17, 1892. Philadelphia, Hibernian Society, 1892. 570 p. facsims., col. plate, ports.   F158.9.I6S65

"Lists of works written by members of the Hibernian Society": p. 24–26.

The years 1771–90 are covered on pages 33–148.

10951

Donovan, George F.   The pre-Revolutionary Irish in Massachusetts, 1620–1775. [Menasha, Wis., G. Banta Pub. Co., ᶜ1932] 158 p.   F75.I6D8

Thesis (Ph.D.)—St. Louis University, 1931.
Bibliography: p. [140]—153.

In 1770 the Irish numbered 2,198 out of a total population of 120,070 studied in this survey.

1095⁻

Doyle, Richard D.   The pre-Revolutionary Irish in New York (1643–1775). 1932. ([287] p.)
Micro AC–1, no. 169

Thesis (Ph.D.)—St. Louis University.
Abstracted in *Microfilm Abstracts*, v. 2, no. 2, 1939, p. 63–64.

10953

Edwards, Owen D.   The American image of Ireland: a study of its early phases. *In* Perspectives in American history. v. 4; 1970. [Cambridge] Charles Warren Center for Studies in American History, Harvard University. p. 199–282.   E171.P47, v. 4

"Ireland's uses for the Revolutionary generation of Americans": p. 199–241.

10954

O'Brien, Michael J.   A hidden phase of American history; Ireland's part in America's struggle for liberty. Illustrated by portraits from the Emmet collection, facsimiles of documents in English archives, reproduced by Anna Frances Levins. New York, Dodd, Mead, 1919. 533 p. facsims., ports.   E269.I6O232

Appendix: "Officers of the American Army and Navy of the Revolution of Irish birth or descent": p. 393–441; "Non-commissioned officers and enlisted men, named Burke, Connolly, Connor, Doherty, Kelly, Murphy, McCarthy, O'Brien, O'Neill, Reilly, Ryan, and Sullivan, in the American Army and Navy of the Revolution": p. 443–526.

Reprinted in Freeport, N.Y., by Books for Libraries Press (1971).

10955

O'Brien, Michael J.   [Immigration, land, probate, administration, baptismal, marriage, burial, trade, military and other records of the Irish in America in the seventeenth and eighteenth century] *In* American Irish Historical Society. Journal. v. 12–14; 1912/13–1914/15. New York, 1913–15. p. 129–190; p. 171–236; p. [163]–279.   E184.I6A5, v. 12–14

10956

O'Brien, Michael J.   Irish mariners in New England. *In* American Irish Historical Society. Journal. v. 17. New York, 1918. p. 149–190.   E184.I6A5, v. 17

10957

O'Brien, Michael J.   Irish pioneers in New Hampshire. *In* American Irish Historical Society. Journal. v. 25. New York, 1926. p. 62–89.   E184.I6A5, v. 25

10958

O'Brien, Michael J.   Land grants to Irish settlers in the colony and state of Virginia, extracted mainly from the records of the Land Office at Richmond. *In* American Irish Historical Society. Journal. v. 24. New York, 1925. p. 87–124.   E184.I6A5, v. 24

10959

Purcell, Richard J.   Irish builders of colonial Rhode Island. Studies, v. 24, June 1935: 289–300.   AP4.S78, v. 24

10960

Purcell, Richard J.   Irish colonists in colonial Maryland. Studies, v. 23, June 1934: 279–294.   AP4.S78, v. 23

10961

Purcell, Richard J. Irish contribution to colonial New York. Studies, v. 29, Dec. 1940: 591–604; v. 30, Mar. 1941: 107–120.   AP4.S78, v. 29–30

f. Italian

10962

Capponi, Guido. Italy and Italians in early American periodicals (1741–1830). 1958. ([467] p.)
Micro AC–1, no. 58–1891

Thesis (Ph.D.)—University of Wisconsin.
Abstracted in *Dissertation Abstracts*, v. 18, June 1958, p. 2136–2137.

10963

Giannota, Rosario O. Contribution of Italians to the development of American culture during the eighteenth century. 1942.

Thesis (Ph.D.)—St. John's University.

10964

Marraro, Howard R. Italian culture in eighteenth-century American magazines. Italica, v. 22, Mar. 1945: 21–31.
PC1068.U6I8, v. 22

See also his article on "The Teaching of Italian in America in the Eighteenth Century," in the *Modern Language Journal*, v. 25, Nov. 1940, p. 120–125.

10965

Marraro, Howard R. Italo-Americans in Pennsylvania in the eighteenth century. Pennsylvania history, v. 7, July 1940: 159–166.   F146.P597, v. 7

g. Jewish

10966

Chyet, Stanley F. The political rights of the Jews in the United States, 1776–1840. American Jewish archives, v. 9, Apr. 1958: 14–75.   E184.J5A37, v. 9

Although the Revolution established full rights for Jews on the federal level, Chyet shows that they continued to labor under political disabilities in many of the individual states.

10967

Coleman, Edward D. Plays of Jewish interest on the American stage, 1752–1821. *In* American Jewish Historical Society. Publications. no. 33. New York, 1934. p. 171–198.   E184.J5A5, no. 33

10968

Elzas, Barnett A. The Jews of South Carolina from the earliest times to the present day. Philadelphia, Press of J. B. Lippincott Co., 1905. 352 p. plates, ports.
F280.J5E52

Bibliography: p. 295–305.
Reprinted in Spartanburg, S.C., by the Reprint Co. (1972).

Chapters 2–7 cover the years 1750–1800 and provide sketches of Moses Lindo and Francis and Joseph Dalvador.

10969

Freund, Miriam K. Jewish merchants in colonial America; their achievements and their contributions to the development of America. New York, Behrman's Jewish Book House, 1939. 127 p.   E184.J5F68

Thesis (Ph.D.)—New York University, 1936
Published also without thesis note (E184.J5F67).
Bibliography: p. [109]–117; "References": p. 118–127.

10970

Friedenwald, Herbert. Jews mentioned in the journal of the Continental Congress. *In* American Jewish Historical Society. Publications. no. 1; 1892. New York, 1893. p. 65–89.   E184.J5A5, no. 1

10971

Friedman, Lee M. Early American Jews. Cambridge, Mass., Harvard University Press, 1934. xii, 238 p. facsims., plate, port.   E184.J5F7

Contents: pt. 1. Jews in Massachusetts.—pt. 2. The coming of Jews to New York.—pt. 3. Jews in other American lands.—Notes.—Appendices.—Bibliography (p. [211]–219).

Reprints lengthy excerpts from letters, wills, and other contemporary papers and presents information on Jews in Massachusetts and New York, including Judah Monis, the first instructor of Hebrew at Harvard, and Haym Salomon, who raised large sums of money for the Revolutionary cause.

10972

Goodman, Abram V. American overture; Jewish rights in colonial times. Philadelphia, Jewish Pub. Society of America, 5707–1947. xiv, 265 p. map, plates, ports.
E184.J5G65

Bibliography: p. 229–251.
The author's thesis (Ph.D.), with the same title, was submitted to the University of Texas in 1949.

10973

Gutstein, Morris A. The story of the Jews of Newport; two and a half centuries of Judaism, 1658–1908. Introduction by David De Sola Pool. New York, Bloch Pub. Co., 1936. 393 p. facsims., plans, plates, ports.
F89.N5G9

"Selected bibliography": p. 383–384.

10974

Heller, Bernard. The role of Jews in the American Revolution. Michigan alumnus quarterly review, v. 61, summer 1955: 302–312. port.   AP2.M53, v. 61

10975

Hershkowitz, Leo, *comp.* Wills of early New York Jews, 1704–1799. With a foreword by Isidore S. Meyer. New York, American Jewish Historical Society, 1967. xvi, 229 p. facsims. (Studies in American Jewish History, no. 4)   F128.25.H58

Bibliography: p. 216–220.

The 41 wills were first published in the *American Jewish Historical Quarterly*, v. 55, Mar. 1966, p. 319–363; v. 56, Sept.–Dec. 1966, p. 62–122, 163–207.

10976

Hollander, Jacob H. The civil status of the Jews in Maryland, 1634–1776. *In* American Jewish Historical Society. Publications. v. 2; 1893. [Baltimore] 1894. p. 33–44.　　　　　　　　　　E184.J5A5, v. 2

10977

Hühner, Leon. Jews in America in colonial and Revolutionary times. A memorial volume. New York, Gertz Bros., 1959. 242 p.　　　　　E184.J5H82

Bibliographic footnotes.

Articles which originally appeared in the *Publications* of the American Jewish Historical Society.

10978

Hühner, Leon. Jews in connection with the colleges of the thirteen original states prior to 1800. *In* American Jewish Historical Society. Publications. no. 19. New York, 1910. p. 101–124.　　　　E184.J5A5, no. 19

10979

Hühner, Leon. Jews in the legal and medical professions in America prior to 1800. *In* American Jewish Historical Society. Publications. no. 22. New York, 1914. p. 147–165.　　　　　　　　E184.J5A5, no. 22

10980

Hühner, Leon. Jews interested in privateering in America during the eighteenth century. *In* American Jewish Historical Society. Publications. no. 23. New York, 1915. p. 163–176.　　　　E184.J5A5, no. 23

10981

Hühner, Leon. The Jews of Georgia from the outbreak of the American Revolution to the close of the 18th century. *In* American Jewish Historical Society. Publications. no. 17. New York, 1909. p. 89–108.

　　　　　　　　　　　　E184.J5A5, no. 17

———— ———— Offprint. [Baltimore? 1909] 89–108 p.

　　　　　　　　　　　　　　F295.J5H9

10982

Hühner, Leon. The Jews of New England (other than Rhode Island) prior to 1800. *In* American Jewish Historical Society. Publications. no. 11. New York, 1903. p. 75–99.　　　　　　E184.J5A5, v. 11

10983

Hühner, Leon. The Jews of South Carolina from the earliest settlement, to the end of the American Revolution. *In* American Jewish Historical Society. Publications. no. 12. New York, 1904. p. [39]–61.

　　　　　　　　　　　　E184.J5A5, no. 12

———— ———— Offprint. Baltimore, Friedenwald Co. [1904] [39]–61 p.　　　　　　F280.J5H9

"Some Additional Notes on the History of the Jews of South Carolina" appears in no. 19 (New York, 1910), p. 151–156.

10984

Hühner, Leon. The Jews of Virginia from the earliest times to the close of the eighteenth century. *In* American Jewish Historical Society. Publications. no. 20. New York, 1911. p. 85–105.　　　E184.J5A5, no. 20

10985

Jacobson, Jacob M. Jewish merchants of Newport in pre-Revolutionary days. Rhode Island Jewish historical notes, v. 5, Nov. 1970: 332–381.　　F90.J5R5, v. 5

Includes in a bibliography of sources for Rhode Island Jewish materials a calendar of Aaron Lopez's commercial letters, 1755–82. The author also provides a list of Jewish commercial advertisements in the Newport *Mercury*, 1761–76.

10986

Karp, Abraham J., *comp.* The Jewish experience in America; selected studies from the publications of the American Jewish Historical Society. Edited with an introduction by Abraham J. Karp. Waltham, Mass., American Jewish Historical Society [1969] 5 v. illus., facsims., ports.　　　　　　　　E184.J5K17

Includes bibliographies.

Contents: v. 1. The colonial period.—v. 2. In the early Republic.—v. 3. The emerging community.—v. 4. The era of immigration.—v. 5. At home in America.

Volume 1 includes over a dozen essays on the Revolution.

10987

Kohler, Max J. Phases of Jewish life in New York before 1800. *In* American Jewish Historical Society. Publications. v. 2–3; 1893–94. [Baltimore] 1894–95. p. 77–100; p. 73–86.　　　　　　E184.J5A5, v. 2–3

10988

Lamm, Hans. The so-called "Letter of a German Jew to the President of the Congress of the United States of America" of 1783. *In* American Jewish Historical Society. Publications. no. 37. New York, 1947. p. 171–184.

　　　　　　　　　　　　E184.J5A5, no. 37

Gives the text of the letter and speculates on its authorship.

10989

Lebeson, Anita L. Jews in the War of the Revolution. *In her* Jewish pioneers in America, 1492–1848. New York, Brentano's [ᶜ1931] p. 205–241. facsim.　E184.J5L56

10990

A Letter from a German Jew to the president of the American Continental Congress. *In* Deutsch-amerikanische Geschichtsblätter. v. 27/28; 1927/28. Chicago, University of Chicago Press, 1928. p. 185–194.

　　　　　　　　　　　　F550.G3D4, v. 27/28

Text of a pamphlet published in Frankfurt and Leipzig in 1787 and edited by Moses Mendelssohn, which draws the attention of the Confederation government to the sad plight of the German Jews. Introduction by Edwin H. Zeydel.

10991
Lyons, Jacques J.   The Lyons Collection. v. 2. Transcripts and summaries of the manuscripts embraced in the collection, as well as the most important material selected from the note books and scrap books of the late Rev. J. J. Lyons. [Baltimore] The Society, 1920. xx, 618, 10 p. facsims., plates, ports. (Publications of the American Jewish Historical Society, no. 27)
E184.J5A5, no. 27

Contains transcripts from miscellaneous manuscripts, pamphlets, newspapers, and secondary works relating to Jews in America during the 18th and early 19th centuries.

10992
Marcus, Jacob R.   American Jewry: documents; eighteenth century; primarily hitherto unpublished manuscripts. Cincinnati, Hebrew Union College Press, 1959. xix, 492 p. (Publications of the American Jewish Archives, no. 3)   E184.J5M2

A collection of 196 documents that reflect personal, religious, communal, and commercial aspects of Jewish life in America during the last half of the 18th century.

10993
Marcus, Jacob R.   The colonial American Jew, 1492–1776. Detroit, Wayne State University Press, 1970. 3 v. (xxiv, 1650 p.) illus., ports.   E184.J5M215 1970

Includes bibliographic references.

Using a topical approach, the author presents information on the economic activities, legal and political status, religious practices, social welfare concerns, and educational endeavors of Jews in British North America and the West Indies. In the section on the Jew in the larger American community, Marcus discusses acculturation and deculturation as well as the motivation of those who became patriots or Loyalists.

10994
Marcus, Jacob R.   Early American Jewry. Philadelphia, Jewish Publication Society of America, 1951–53. 2 v. illus., facsim., ports.   E184.J5M22

Bibliographic references at end of each volume.
Contents: v. 1. The Jews of New York, New England, and Canada, 1649–1794.—v. 2. The Jews of Pennsylvania and the South, 1655–1790.

A general account that includes extensive quotations from business letters, frequently addressed to members of a merchant's own family, thus providing insight into the feelings as well as the commercial activities of Jews in the 18th century.

10995
Marcus, Jacob R.   Light on early Connecticut Jewry. American Jewish archives, v. 1, Jan. 1949: 3–52. illus., facsims.   E184.J5A37, v. 1

Includes selections from the wartime correspondence of Aaron Lopez (p. 38–52).

10996
Morris, Richard B.   Civil liberties and the Jewish tradition in early America. *In* American Jewish Historical Society. Publication, v. 46, Sept. 1956: 20–39.
E184.J5A5, v. 46

Finds that when Jews gained equal protection of the laws other minorities profited.

10997
Oppenheim, Samuel.   The Jews and Masonry in the United States before 1810. *In* American Jewish Historical Society. Publications. no. 19. New York, 1910. p. 1–94.
E184.J5A5, no. 19

———— ———— Offprint. [New York?] ᶜ1910. 94 p.
HS521.O7

10998
Simonhoff, Harry.   Jewish notables in America, 1776–1865; links of an endless chain. Foreword by David de Sola Pool. New York, Greenberg [1956] xiv, 402 p. illus.   E184.J5S53

Bibliography: p. 386–391.

Includes biographical sketches of more than two dozen Jews from the Revolutionary era from Francis Salvador to Gov. David Emanuel.

10999
Wolf, Edwin, *and* Maxwell Whiteman.   The history of the Jews of Philadelphia from colonial times to the age of Jackson. Philadelphia, Jewish Publication Society of America, 1957 [ᶜ1956] xv, 534 p. illus., facsims., plates, ports. (The Jacob R. Schiff library of Jewish contributions to American democracy)   F158.9.J5W86

Originally written as a series of weekly articles which appeared in the Philadelphia *Jewish Exponent* during 1954–55.

Bibliographic footnotes.

Chapters 3–9 (p. 36–186) pertain to the Revolutionary period.

h. Scotch-Irish

11000
[Chambers, George]   A tribute to the principles, virtues, habits, and public usefulness of the Irish and Scotch early settlers of Pennsylvania. By a descendant. Chambersburg, Pa., M. A. Foltz, Printer, 1871. 172 p.
F160.S4C46

First edition published in 1856.

11001
Dickson, R. J.   Ulster emigration to colonial America, 1718–1775. London, Routledge & K. Paul [1966] xiv, 320 p. map. (Ulster-Scot historical series, no. 1)
E184.S4D47

Bibliography: p. 298–311.

Describes the background and phases of Irish-Presbyterian emigration to America and details the activities and attitudes of agents, promoters, and officials in Ulster. Appendixes contain extensive data on ships, emigrants, and ports. The author finds that economic opportunity in America, not religious persecution in Ulster, was the principal stimulus for emigration.

11002
Dunaway, Wayland F.   The Scotch-Irish of colonial Pennsylvania. Chapel Hill, University of North Carolina Press, 1944. 273 p.   F160.S4D8

Bibliography: p. 233–257.

Summarizing the Ulster background, the author concentrates upon the details of Scotch-Irish settlement in various sections of Pennsylvania and in neighboring colonies as well as upon the political, economic, social, and religious life of the group. Dunaway also provides information on the activities of individuals who served with distinction during the American Revolution and in Pennsylvania military units composed mainly of Scotch-Irishmen.

11003
Ford, Henry J.   The Scotch-Irish in America. Princeton, N.J., Princeton University Press, 1915. viii, 607 p.
                                                          E184.S4F9

Appendixes: A. Ireland at the time of the plantation.—B. The Scottish undertakers.—C. The making of the Ulster Scot, by James Heron.—D. Statement of frontier grievances.—E. Galloway's account of the American revolt.—F. The Mecklenburg resolves.

"List of authorities consulted": p. 593–596.

Reprinted in Hamden, Conn., by Archon Books (1966) and in New York by Arno Press (1969).

Reviews the 17th- and 18th-century migration of Scots to Ireland and America, describes their settlements in Pennsylvania, New England, New York, and New Jersey, and traces the development of the Presbyterian Church in America. Ford also surveys the spread of popular education and discusses the roles assigned the Scotch-Irish in the American Revolution by contemporaries and historians.

11004
Glasgow, Maude.   The Scotch-Irish in northern Ireland and in the American colonies. New York, G. P. Putnam's Sons, 1936. 345 p.   DA910.G5

"The Scotch-Irish in America and the Revolutionary War": p. 253–341.

11005
Green, Edward R. R.   The Scotch-Irish and the coming of the Revolution in North Carolina. Irish historical studies, v. 7, Sept. 1950: 77–86.   DA900.I63, v. 7

11006
Green, Edward R. R.   Scotch-Irish emigration, an imperial problem. Western Pennsylvania historical magazine, v. 35, Dec. 1952: 193–209.   F146.W52, v. 35

11007
Klett, Guy S.   The Scotch-Irish in Pennsylvania. Gettysburg, Pennsylvania Historical Association, 1948. 46 p. (Pennsylvania history studies, no. 3)   F160.S4K55

Bibliography: p. 44–46.

11008
Klett, Guy S.   The Scotch-Irish Presbyterians pioneering along the Susquehanna River [ca. 1728–75] Pennsylvania history, v. 20, Apr. 1953: 165–179.
                                            F146.P597, v. 20

11009
Leyburn, James G.   The Scotch-Irish: a social history. Chapel Hill, University of North Carolina Press [1962] xix, 377 p. maps.   E184.S4L5

Bibliography: p. [354]–372.

Following a survey of conditions that led to the 17th-century migration of Scots to the English plantation in Ireland, the author examines the motivations, patterns of settlement, and social institutions of more than 200,000 Ulstermen who came to America between 1717 and 1775. The Scotch-Irish settled mainly in Virginia's Shenandoah Valley, the Carolina Piedmont, and southeastern Pennsylvania. In this back country, they battled Indians for land as their ancestors had fought Irishmen, built their community life around the Presbyterian church, and entered colonial politics, most becoming ardent supporters of the Revolution.

11010
Moody, Theodore W.   The Ulster Scots in colonial and Revolutionary America. Studies, v. 34, Mar.–June 1945: 89–94, 211–221.   AP4.S78, v. 34

11011
Northampton County (Pa.) Historical and Genealogical Society.   The Scotch-Irish of Northampton County, Pennsylvania. [Easton, Pa., J. S. Correll, Printer] 1926. 594 p. coat of arms, facsims., maps, plates, port. [*Its* Publications, v. 1]   F157.N7N85, v. 1

Contains the unpublished manuscripts and a reprint of the published writings of Dr. John Cunningham Clyde, together with other original documents and records.
——— Index to The Scotch-Irish of Northampton County. By Preston A. Laury. Easton, Pa., 1939. 81 p. [*Its* Publications, v. 1, Supplement]
                                  F157.N7N85, v. 1 Index

11012
Shepardson, Francis W.   A study of some of the Scotch-Irish settlements in the American colonies. 1892.

Thesis (Ph.D.)—Yale University.

11013
Stephenson, Jean.   Scotch-Irish migration to South Carolina, 1772. (Rev. William Martin and his five shiploads of settlers.) [Washington, 1971] 137 p.   F280.S4S8

Includes bibliographic references.

11014

Tallmadge, William H.   The Scotch-Irish and the British traditional ballad in America. New York folklore quarterly, v. 24, Dec. 1968: 261–274.

GR1.N473, v. 24

Contends that the Scotch-Irish were primarily responsible for the transmission of British balladry to America in the 18th century.

i. Scottish

11015

Cameron, Viola R.   Emigrants from Scotland to America, 1774–1775. Copied from a loose bundle of Treasury papers in the Public Record Office, London, England. [New York?] ᶜ1930. 117 l.   E187.5.C18 1930

Reprinted in Baltimore by the Southern Book Co. (1959) and the Genealogical Pub. Co. (1965).

11016

Cummings, Hubertis M.   Scots breed and Susquehanna. [Pittsburgh] University of Pittsburgh Press [ᶜ1964] x, 404 p. (Presbyterian Historical Society publications, 6)

F160.S4C8

Bibliography: p. [383]–387.

Information on the years 1763–89 appears throughout.

11017

Fingerhut, Eugene R.   From Scots to Americans: Ryegate's immigrants in the 1770's. Vermont history, v. 35, autumn 1967: 186–207.   F46.V55, v. 35

11018

Graham, Ian C. G.   Colonists from Scotland: emigration to North America, 1707–1783. Ithaca, N.Y., Published for the American Historical Association [by] Cornell University Press [1956] x, 213 p. map.   E184.S3G7

Bibliography: p. 191–206.

Reprinted in Port Washington, N.Y., by Kennikat Press (1972).

The author's thesis (Ph.D.), *Scottish Emigration to North America, 1707–1783*, was submitted to the University of Illinois in 1955 (Micro AC–1, no. 13,484).

Differentiating between Scots who came to America directly from Scotland and Scotch-Irish who emigrated first to Ulster and then to America, the author reviews conditions in Scotland that forced some 25,000 to leave between 1763 and 1775 and investigates problems encountered by Scots during the American Revolution, when most remained loyal to the crown. North Carolina, with its settlement of about 15,000, and Virginia were centers of Loyalist activity among Scots. King's Mountain, the author points out, was mainly a battle between Highlanders and rebel Scotch-Irishmen.

11019

MacLean, John P.   An historical account of the settlements of Scotch Highlanders in America prior to the peace of 1783; together with notices of Highland regiments and biographical sketches. Cleveland, Helman-Taylor Co., 1900. 459 p. illus., port.   E184.S3M2

Reprinted in Baltimore by the Genealogical Pub. Co. (1968).

11020

Meyer, Duane G.   The Highland Scots of North Carolina, 1732–1776. Chapel Hill, University of North Carolina Press [1961] viii, 218 p. maps.   F265.S3M4 1961

Bibliography: p. [194]–204.

The author's thesis (Ph.D.), *The Scottish Highlanders in North Carolina, 1733–1776*, was submitted to the state University of Iowa in 1956 (Micro AC–1, no. 16,125).

A condensed version of the author's work was published under the same title by the Carolina Charter Tercentenary Commission (Raleigh, N.C., 1963. 75 p. F265.S3M42).

Explores the motivation of 12,000 or more emigrants to North Carolina, many of whom became Loyalists during the American Revolution even though their forebears in Scotland had been Jacobite rebels in 1745. Meyer concludes that they supported George III because of a fear of reprisal, the liberal land grants offered them, the leadership of a number of retired British officers living near them, and, finally, because Highlanders in Scotland now looked with favor upon the crown.

11021

Pryde, George S.   Scottish colonization in the province of New York. *In* New York State Historical Association. New York history, v. 16, Apr. 1935: 138–157.

F116.N865, v. 16

11022

Whyte, Donald.   A dictionary of Scottish emigrants to the U.S.A. Baltimore, Md., Magna Carta Book Co., 1972. xiii, 504 p.   E184.S3W49

Bibliography: p. 467–472.

Includes the names of 6,471 immigrants, most of whom arrived in America during the 18th century.

j. Others

11023

Browning, Charles H.   Welsh settlement of Pennsylvania. Philadelphia, W. J. Campbell, 1912. 631 p. maps, plates.   F160.W4B8

Reprinted in Baltimore by the Genealogical Pub. Co. (1967).

11024

Dunaway, Wayland F.   The French racial strain in colonial Pennsylvania. Pennsylvania magazine of history and biography, v. 53, Oct. 1929: 322–342.

F146.P65, v. 53

11025

Faust, Albert B.   Lists of Swiss emigrants in the eighteenth century to the American colonies. Washington, D.C., National Genealogical Society, 1920–25. 2 v. facsims.

E184.S9F2

Vol. 2 compiled and edited by Albert Bernhardt Faust and Gaius Marcus Brumbaugh.

Contents: 1. Zurich, 1734–1744, from the archives of Switzerland.—2. From the state archives of Bern [1706–95] and Basel, Switzerland [1734–94]

Reprinted in one volume in Baltimore by the Genealogical Pub. Co. (1968).

11026
Faust, Albert B.   Swiss emigration to the American colonies in the eighteenth century. American historical review, v. 22, Oct. 1916: 21–44.   E171.A57, v. 22

11027
Hamilton, Kenneth G.   Salem in Wachovia: an example of Moravian colonizing genius. *In* Moravian Historical Society, *Nazareth, Pa.* Transactions. v. 21; 1966. Nazareth. p. 53–75.   BX8553.M7, v. 21
E184.M8M8, v. 21

About the older portion of Winston-Salem, North Carolina, established in 1766.

11028
Hirsch, Arthur H.   The Huguenots of colonial South Carolina. Durham, N.C., Duke University Press, 1928. xv, 338 p. facsims., maps, plan, ports. (Duke University publications)   F280.H8H6

Bibliography: p. 265–282.

11029
Kenney, Alice P.   The Albany Dutch: Loyalists and patriots. *In* New York State Historical Association. New York history, v. 42, Oct. 1961: 331–350.
F116.N865, v. 42

Divisions created among the Dutch by the Revolution shattered their unity as a religious and linguistic group.

11030
Ledet, Wilton P.   Acadian exiles in Pennsylvania. Pennsylvania history, v. 9, Apr. 1942: 118–128.
F146.P597, v. 9

11031
Schelbert, Leo.   Eighteenth century migration of Swiss Mennonites to America. Mennonite quarterly review, v. 42, July/Oct. 1968: 163–183, 285–300. plan.
BX8101.M4, v. 42

11032
Struble, George G.   The French in Pennsylvania prior to 1800. French review, v. 26, Oct. 1953: 50–58.
PC2001.F75, v. 26

6. Social Problems

a. Crime and Penology

11033
Andrews, William.   Old-time punishments. Hull, W. Andrews, 1890. x, 251 p. illus.   HV8532.G8A6

Reprinted in Detroit by Singing Tree Press (1970).

Emphasizing 18th-century applications, the author describes a variety of criminal punishments employed in England and America, ranging from the ducking-stool and public whippings to various forms of capital punishment.

11034
Barnes, Harry E.   The evolution of penology in Pennsylvania; a study in American social history. Indianapolis, Bobbs-Merrill Co. [ᶜ1927] 414 p. plans, plates.
HV9475.P4B3

Bibliographic footnotes.
Reprinted in Montclair, N.J., by Patterson Smith (1968).

Includes three chapters (p. 9–180) on the period to 1835.

11035
Caldwell, Robert G.   The penitentiary movement in Delaware, 1776 to 1829. [Newark? Del.] viii, 268 l. plan.
HV9475.D3C3

Reproduced from typescript.
Bibliography: leaves 260–268.

11036
Earle, Alice M.   Curious punishments of bygone days. Chicago, H. S. Stone, 1896. vii, 148 p. plates.
HV8532.U5E3

Reprinted in Detroit by Singing Tree Press (1968) and in Rutland, Vt., by C. E. Tuttle Co. (1972).

Briefly reviews the use of such devices as bilboes, ducking stools, stocks, pillories, whipping posts, branks, and gags. Earle also discusses branding and maiming, military punishments, and public penance.

11037
Fitzroy, Herbert W. K.   The punishment of crime in provincial Pennsylvania. Pennsylvania magazine of history and biography, v. 60, July 1936: 242–269.
F146.P65, v. 60

11038
Gibson, George H.   "Stop, thief!" Constitution and minutes of the Friends to Justice, 1786–1794. Delaware history, v. 11, Oct. 1964: 91–110. plate.
F161.D37, v. 11

On a society formed in Wilmington, Del., for mutual protection against the lawless.

11039
Gipson, Lawrence H.   Crime and its punishment in provincial Pennsylvania: a phase of the social history of the commonwealth. Pennsylvania history, v. 2, Jan. 1935: 3–16.   F146.P597, v. 2

11040
Lewis, Orlando F.   The development of American prisons and prison customs, 1776–1845, with special reference to early institutions in the state of New York. [Albany?] Prison Association of New York [1922] 350 p.
HV9466.L4

Bibliography: p. 347–350.
Reprinted, with a new introduction by Donald H. Goff, in Montclair, N.J., by Patterson Smith (1967).

Includes scattered references to the Revolutionary period.

b. Debt and Debtors

11041
Coleman, Peter J. The insolvent debtor in Rhode Island, 1745–1828. William and Mary quarterly, 3d ser., v. 22, July 1965: 413–434.   F221.W71, 3d s., v. 22

Rhode Island was the only colony to devise a system of relief that survived the Revolution. Despite the moratorium on insolvency petitions during the war, an average of fewer than five a year were submitted during the so-called Critical period—a sharp contrast with the next decade.

11042
Feer, Robert A. Imprisonment for debt in Massachusetts before 1800. Mississippi Valley historical review, v. 48, Sept. 1961: 252–269.   E171.J87, v. 48

Altered significantly by legislation and practice, the Massachusetts system of imprisonment for debt had lost most of its oppressive features by the end of the 18th century—a trend that was accelerated by the Revolution.

11043
Plummer, Wilbur C. Consumer credit in colonial Philadelphia. Pennsylvania magazine of history and biography, v. 66, Oct. 1942: 385–409.   F146.P65, v. 66

The widespread use of credit created a chain of debt that extended from the farmer on the frontier to the British merchant capitalist.

11044
Shaiman, S. Laurence. The history of imprisonment for debt and insolvency laws in Pennsylvania as they evolved from the common law. American journal of legal history, v. 4, July 1960: 205–225.   LL

11045
Taylor, Horace Braughn. Creditor v. debtor; a study of the statutory, administrative, and procedural aspects of debt recovery in colonial North Carolina. 1972. ([234] p.)   Micro AC–1, no. 72–24,850

Thesis (Ph.D.)—University of North Carolina.
Abstracted in *Dissertation Abstracts International*, v. 33A, Oct. 1972, p. 1624–1625.

11046
Thompson, Tommy R. Marylanders, personal indebtedness, and the American Revolution. 1972. ([239] p.)   Micro AC–1, no. 73–13,641

Thesis (Ph.D.)—University of Maryland.
Abstracted in *Dissertation Abstracts International*, v. 33A, June 1973, p. 6822.

c. Poverty and Poor Laws

11047
Capen, Edward W. The historical development of the poor law of Connecticut. New York, Columbia University Press, 1905. 520 p. (Studies in history, economics, and public law, v. 22)   H31.C7, v. 22
HV98.C8C3

Published also as thesis (Ph.D.)—Columbia University, 1904.
Bibliography: p. 467–472.
Reprinted in New York by AMS Press (1968).
"Late colonial period, 1713–1784": p. 59–96.

11048
Clark, William B. The sea captains club. Pennsylvania magazine of history and biography, v. 81, Jan. 1957: 39–68.   F146.P65, v. 81

On the Society for the Relief of Poor and Distressed Masters of Ships, their Widows and Children, that flourished in Philadelphia, 1765–1801.

11049
Creech, Margaret. Three centuries of poor law administration; a study of legislation in Rhode Island. Introductory note by Edith Abbott. Chicago, Ill., University of Chicago Press [1936] xxii, 331 p. (Social service monographs, no. 24)   KFR349.C7 1936

Reprinted in College Park, Md., by McGrath Pub. Co. (1969).
The author's thesis (Ph.D.), with the same title, was submitted to the University of Chicago in 1935 (HV75.R43C7 1935).
"The colonial period": p. [1]–107.
"Select documents relating to the history of poor relief in the colonial period and the late eighteenth century": p. 264–283.

11050
D'Agostino, Lorenzo. The history of public welfare in Vermont. Washington, Catholic University of America Press, 1948. viii, 387 p.   HV98.V5D3

Thesis (Ph.D.)—Catholic University of America.
Bibliography: p. [351]–359.

References to legislation and practice during the period 1763–89 are scattered throughout.

11051
Deutsch, Albert. The sick poor in colonial times. American historical review, v. 46, Apr. 1941: 560–579.   E171.A57, v. 46

The welfare level generally depended upon the extent of need, the resources available to meet it, and the degree of social consciousness in the community. The shift in emphasis from governmental responsibility to private enterprise in social welfare was already evident at the time of the Revolution.

11052
Heffner, William C. History of poor relief legislation Pennsylvania, 1682–1913. Cleona, Pa., Holzapfel Pub. [ᶜ1913] 302 p.   [HV98.P4H4]
Micro 19478 HV

Thesis (Ph.D.)—University of Pennsylvania, 1911.

Includes two chapters (p. 66–118) on legislation 1736–98 and one (p. 119–134) on revenue 1682–1798.

11053

Hunter, Robert J. The activities of the American Philosophical Society in the early history of the Philadelphia Almshouse (the Philadelphia General Hospital). *In* American Philosophical Society, *Philadelphia*. Proceedings, v. 71, no. 6, 1932: 309–319. illus., facsims., plates. Q11.P5, v. 71

11054

Jernegan, Marcus W. The development of poor relief in colonial New England. Social service review, v. 5, June 1931: 175–198. HV1.S6, v. 5

11055

Jernegan, Marcus W. The development of poor relief in colonial Virginia. Social service review, v. 3, Mar. 1929: 1–18. HV1.S6, v. 3

11056

Kelso, Robert W. The history of public poor relief in Massachusetts, 1620–1920. Boston, Houghton Mifflin Co., 1922. 200 p. HV98.M39K4

Reprinted in Montclair, N.J., by Patterson Smith (1969).

References to the Revolutionary period are scattered throughout.

11057

Mackey, Howard. The operation of the English old poor law in colonial Virginia. Virginia magazine of history and biography, v. 73, Jan. 1965: 29–40. F221.V91, v. 73

Tailored to local conditions by the House of Burgesses, the parochial system of poor relief used by Virginians was based upon English law.

11058

Mackey, Howard. Social welfare in colonial Virginia: the importance of the English old poor law. Historical magazine of the Protestant Episcopal church, v. 36, Dec. 1967: 357–382. BX5800.H5, v. 36

Includes a table of parish tithes, 1665–1786, which indicates the amount allotted to the poor law.

11059

Mappen, Marc A. The paupers of Somerset County, 1760–1800. *In* Rutgers University, *New Brunswick, N.J. Library*. Journal, v. 33, June 1970: 33–45. Z733.R955F, v. 33

Examines the lives of 71 paupers from Franklin and Hillsborough in Somerset County and finds that they were part of a growing but nonmobile depressed class cut off from family support in an area where the amount of arable land was sharply reduced.

11060

Mohl, Raymond A. Poverty in early America, a reappraisal; the case of eighteenth-century New York City. *In* New York State Historical Association. New York history, v. 50, Jan. 1969: 5–27. illus., port. F116.N865, v. 50

11061

Parkhurst, Eleanor. Poor relief in a Massachusetts village [Chelmsford] in the eighteenth century. Social service review, v. 11, Sept. 1937: 446–464. HV1.S6, v. 11

11062

Rothman, David J. The discovery of the asylum; social order and disorder in the new Republic. Boston, Little, Brown [1971] xx, 376 p. illus., ports. HV91.R73

"Bibliographic note": p. [299]–312.

In an introductory section on 18th-century methods of caring for the poor and punishing lawbreakers, the author emphasizes the fact that neither poverty nor crime was defined as a critical social problem. Charity and correction were not administered through institutions that isolated or confined the needy and deviant. Poor relief was the responsibility of the town, county, or parish, and simple retribution was the community's response to criminal acts.

11063

Schneider, David M. The history of public welfare in New York State. [v. 1] 1609–1866. Chicago, Ill., University of Chicago Press [1938] xvii, 395 p. illus., facsims., plates, ports. (Social service monographs) HV98.N7S3, v. 1

"Bibliographical references" at end of most of the chapters.

Reprinted in Montclair, N.J., by Patterson Smith (1969).

Poor-relief administration, according to the author, became completely secularized during the Revolutionary period. The responsibility for local relief functions passed entirely from the hands of ecclesiastical officials, churchwardens, and vestrymen into the hands of purely civil authorities—the overseers of the poor.

11064

Schneider, David M. The patchwork of relief in provincial New York, 1664–1775. Social service review, v. 12, Sept. 1938: 464–494. HV1.S6, v. 12

11065

Wisner, Elizabeth. The Puritan background of the New England poor laws. Social service review, v. 19, Sept. 1945: 381–390. HV1.S6, v. 19

d. Mental Illness

11066

Blackmon, Dora M. E. The care of the mentally ill in America, 1604–1812, in the thirteen original colonies. 1964. ([226] p.) Micro AC–1, no. 65–5408

Thesis (Ph.D.)—University of Washington.
Abstracted in *Dissertation Abstracts*, v. 25, June 1965, p. 7216.

11067

Cochrane, Hortense S.   Early treatment of the mentally ill in Georgia. Georgia historical quarterly, v. 32, June 1948: 105–118.   F281.G2975, v. 32

11068

Dain, Norman.   Disordered minds; the first century of Eastern State Hospital in Williamsburg, Va., 1766–1866. Williamsburg, Va., Colonial Williamsburg Foundation; distributed by the University Press of Virginia, Charlottesville [1971] xiii, 207 p. illus., geneal. table, map, port. (Williamsburg in America series, 8)   F234.W7W7, v. 8

Includes bibliographic references.

In the brief section on the Revolutionary era, the author provides detailed information about the founding of the first hospital in the colonies operated entirely by the state and devoted solely to the care of the mentally ill. Although 47 patients were admitted to the asylum after its opening in 1773, financial difficulties brought on by wartime inflation and the removal of the state capital and the commissary to Richmond in 1782 forced the institution to close. Reopened four years later, the hospital admitted 36 patients before 1790.

11069

Deutsch, Albert.   The mentally ill in America; a history of their care and treatment from colonial times. 2d ed., rev. and enl. New York, Columbia University Press, 1949. xx, 555 p. illus., ports.   RC443.D4 1949

Bibliography: p. [520]–537.

The first five chapters (p. 1–87) are concerned with the treatment of the mentally ill during the 17th and 18th centuries.

11070

Deutsch, Albert.   Public provision for the mentally ill in colonial America. Social service review, v. 10, Dec. 1936: 606–622.   HV1.S6, v. 10

11071

Harris, Collier C.   "For persons of insane and disordered minds": the treatment of mental deficiency in colonial Virginia. Virginia cavalcade, v. 21, summer 1971: 34–41. illus., ports.   F221.V74, v. 21

RELIGION IN REVOLUTIONARY AMERICA

1. GENERAL WORKS

11072

Ahlstrom, Sydney E.   A religious history of the American people. New Haven, Yale University Press, 1972. xvi, 1158 p.   BR515.A4 1972

Bibliography: p. 1097–1128.
"The century of awakening and revolution": p. [261]–384.

11073

Alexander, Jon A.   "The disturbance of the spring": the attitude of selected American clergy toward the use of violence against British authority, 1763–1776. 1971. ([296] p.)   Micro AC–1, no. 71–19,944

Thesis (Ph.D.)—Temple University.
Abstracted in *Dissertation Abstracts International*, v. 32A, Aug. 1971, p. 867–868.

11074

Armstrong, Maurice W.   The English dissenting deputies and the American colonists. Journal of Presbyterian history, v. 40, Mar.–Sept. 1962: 24–37, 75–91, 144–159.   BX8905.P7A4, v. 40

On the close communication between religious "radicals" in England and American colonists, 1740–76. An earlier version of this article appeared in *Church History*, v. 29, Sept. 1960, p. 298–320.

11075

Bailyn, Bernard.   Religion and revolution: three biographical studies. *In* Perspectives in American history. v. 4; 1970. [Cambridge] Charles Warren Center for Studies in American History, Harvard University. p. 85–169.   E171.P47, v. 4

Appendix A, Jonathan Mayhew's memorandum of August 25, 1765 (p. 140–143); Appendix B, Stephen Johnson's *New London Gazette* articles, September 6–November 1, 1765 (p. 144–169).

Explores the complex role of religion in the coming of the Revolution through the lives and writings of Andrew Eliot, an enthusiastic libertarian, Stephen Johnson, a New Divinity Calvinist, and Jonathan Mayhew, a theological liberal.

11076

Balch, Thomas.   Calvinism and American independence. Philadelphia, Allen, Lane and Scott, 1909. 18 p.   E269.P9B1

Originally printed in the *Presbyterian Quarterly Review* for July 1876.

11077

Bassett, John S.   Development of the popular churches after the Revolution. *In* Massachusetts Historical Society, *Boston*. Proceedings. v. 48; 1914/15. Boston, 1915. p. 254–268.   F61.M38, v. 48

11078

Bridenbaugh, Carl.   Church and state in America, 1689–1775. *In* American Philosophical Society, *Philadelphia*. Proceedings, v. 105, Dec. 15, 1961: 521–524.   Q11.P5, v. 105

11079

Brock, Peter.   Pacifism in the United States, from the colonial era to the First World War. Princeton, N.J., Princeton University Press, 1968. xii, 1005 p. [*His* A History of pacifism, v. 2]   JX1944.B75

Bibliography: p. 949–983.

"Part One: Pacifism in colonial America and the American Revolution": p. [19]–329.

Part one consists of a study on such religious groups as the Quakers, Moravians, Mennonites, and Dunkers, whose members refused military service on the basis of their objection to war. The author points to the many personal tragedies that resulted from a strict adherence to the dictates of conscience as well as the practical compromises and doctrinal inconsistencies that permitted participation in government in the form of voting, taxpaying, and even officeholding. Brock concludes that the more assertive pacifism and urban presence of the Quakers made them the principal targets of persecution and charges of Toryism directed at pacifists during the Revolution.

11080
Brugler, Charles E.   The influence of the clergy in the Revolution. Magazine of history, with notes and queries, v. 22, June 1916: 235–240; v. 23, July–Aug. 1916: 16–21, 80–87.   E171.M23, v. 22–23

11081
Carroll, Peter N., *comp*.   Religion and the coming of the American Revolution. Waltham, Mass., Ginn-Blaisdell [1970] xvi, 157 p. (Primary sources in American history)   E209.C36

Briefly examines the religious background of the imperial controversy and presents selections from the sermons and writings of Jonathan Edwards, Samuel Davies, Jonathan Mayhew, William Livingston, Richard Bland, Ezra Stiles, Joseph Emerson, Charles Chauncy, Thomas Bradbury Chandler, William Smith, Joseph Perry, Samuel Langdon, David Jones, and Samuel West.

11082
Cecil, Robert.   "Pulpit incendiaries" in the American colonies. History today, v. 16, Nov. 1966: 773–780.   D1.H818, v. 16

11083
Clebsch, William A.   A new historiography of American religion. Historical magazine of the Protestant Episcopal church, v. 32, Sept. 1963: 225–257.   BX5800.H5, v. 32

11084
Cobb, Sanford H.   The rise of religious liberty in America; a history. New York, Macmillan Co., 1902. xx, 541 p.   BR515.C6

"Authorities": p. xvii–xx.
Reprinted in New York by Cooper Square Publishers (1968) and Johnson Reprint Corp. (1970. BR516.C66 1970).

Concerned with the development of civil law to 1800 relating to liberty of conscience and worship.

11085
Cousins, Norman, *ed*.   "In God we trust"; the religious beliefs and ideas of the American Founding Fathers. New York, Harper [1958] viii, 464 p.   E302.5.C67

"Guide to further reading and research": p. 445–454.

Presents excerpts from the works of Franklin, Washington, the Adamses, Jefferson, Madison, Hamilton, Jay, and Paine that reflect their attitudes toward religion.

11086
Gifford, Frank D.   The influence of the clergy on American politics from 1763 to 1776. Historical magazine of the Protestant Episcopal church, v. 10, June 1941: 104–123.   BX5800.H5, v. 10

11087
Greene, Evarts B.   Religion and the state; the making and testing of an American tradition. New York, New York University Press [ᶜ1941] 172 p. (Anson G. Phelps lectureship on early American history, New York University, Stokes Foundation)   BR516.G67

Bibliographic footnotes.

After tracing the Old World traditions in the relationship between church and state and reviewing the liberalizing factors in the American colonial experience, Greene shows in his fourth essay that the early state constitutions left many points at which the government could interfere in religious matters.

11088
Hanley, Thomas O.   Colonial Protestantism and the rise of democracy. American ecclesiastical review, v. 141, July 1959: 24–32.   BX801.E3, v. 141

11089
Headley, Joel T.   The chaplains and clergy of the Revolution. New York, C. Scribner, 1864. 402 p.
          E206.H33 Rare Bk. Coll.

Explores the religious dimension of the Revolution and contends that the systematic influence of the clergy was a significant factor in the achievement of independence.

11090
Heimert, Alan E.   Religion and the American mind, from the Great Awakening to the Revolution. Cambridge, Harvard University Press, 1966. x, 668 p.
          BR520.H4

Bibliographic references included in "Sources" & "Notes" (p. 564–639).

Reviewing colonial religious literature from 1740, the author reverses the role historians ordinarily assign Jonathan Edwards and his Calvinist heirs and emphasizes the revolutionary potential of their thought. The supporters of evangelical enthusiasm—New Light Congregationalists, Baptists, and New Side Presbyterians—were not retrogrades but providers of a radical, perhaps democratic, social and political ideology that inspired and gave impetus to American nationalism. Heimert also reconsiders the contribution of their doctrinal opponents, including such liberal or rationalist divines as Jonathan Mayhew and Charles Chauncy, who opposed the Awakening. He contends that these Old Light Congregationalists and Old Side Presbyterians were politically and socially conservative and that their leaders became reluctant rebels. Three extended essay reviews of Heimert's work are William G. McLoughlin's "The American Revolution as a Religious Revival: 'The Millennium in One Country,' " which appeared in the *New England Quarterly*, v. 40, Mar. 1967, p. 99–110, Charles W. Akers' " 'New Light' on the American Revolution," in the New York Historical Society *Quarterly*, v. 51, July 1967, p. 283–291, and Sidney E. Mead's "Through and Beyond the Lines," in the *Journal of Religion*, v. 48, July 1968, p. 274–288.

11091

Hoskins, John P.   German influence on religious life and thought in America during the colonial period. Princeton theological review, v. 5, Jan.–Apr. 1907: 49–79, 210–241.   BR1.P6, v. 5

11092

Humphrey, Edward F.   Nationalism and religion in America, 1774–1789. Boston, Chipman Law Pub. Co., 1924. viii, 536 p.   BR520.H75

Bibliography: p. [517]–532.
Reprinted in New York by Russell & Russell (1965 [i.e. 1966]).

Documents the contribution of various religious groups to American independence, the formation of an American church within each denomination, and the evolution of church-state relationships through the ratification of the Constitution. Humphrey provides extensive quotes from printed sources for each of several denominations, among them Protestant Episcopal, Congregational, Presbyterian, Methodist, Dutch and German Reformed, Roman Catholic, Baptist, Lutheran, Moravian, Quaker, and Unitarian.

11093

Joyce, Lester D.   Church and clergy in the American Revolution; a study in group behavior. New York, Exposition Press [1966] 224 p.   BR520.J6

Bibliography: p. [216]–224.

Postulates that representative clergymen during the Revolution, like all men, were motivated primarily by the desire to perpetuate the survival of their respective group attachments, whether it be Congregationalist or Baptist, instead of the urge to uphold "divine law."

11094

Kerr, Harry P.   Politics and religion in colonial fast and Thanksgiving sermons, 1763–1783. Quarterly journal of speech, v. 46, Dec. 1960: 372–382.
                                              PN4071.Q3, v. 46

11095

Latourette, Kenneth S.   The contribution of the religion of the colonial period to the ideals and life of the United States. Americas, v. 14, Apr. 1958: 340–355.
                                                    E11.A4, v. 14

Comments by Sidney E. Mead appear on pages 356–360.

11096

Lauer, Paul E.   Church and state in New England. Baltimore, Johns Hopkins Press, 1892. 106 p. (Johns Hopkins University studies in historical and political science, 10th ser., no. 2/3)   H31.J6, 10th s., no. 2/3
                                                              F7.L37

Bibliographic footnotes.
"Development of religious liberty in the eighteenth century to 1787": p. 66–94.

11097

McLoughlin, William G.   Issac Backus and the separation of church and state in America. American historical review, v. 73, June 1968: 1392–1413.
                                              E171.A57, v. 73

Relates the contributions of Roger Williams, Thomas Jefferson, James Madison, and Isaac Backus to the development of the American tradition of church and state and finds that Backus represents most adequately the evangelical view of separationism.

11098

Mead, Sidney E.   American Protestantism during the Revolutionary epoch. Church history, v. 22, Dec. 1953: 279–297.   BR140.A45, v. 22

11099

Mead, Sidney E.   Denominationalism: the shape of Protestantism in America. Church history, v. 23, Dec. 1954: 291–320.   BR140.A45, v. 23

Discusses the important elements, ideas, or practices that gave denominations their distinctive character between the Revolution and the Civil War.

11100

Mead, Sidney E.   From coercion to persuasion: another look at the rise of religious liberty and the emergence of denominationalism. Church history, v. 25, Dec. 1956: 317–337.   BR140.A45, v. 25

11101

Mead, Sidney E.   The lively experiment: the shaping of Christianity in America. New York, Harper & Row [1963] xiii, 220 p.   BR515.M43
"Notes": p. 192–195.
"American Protestantism during the Revolutionary epoch": p. 38–54.

11102

Miller, Perry.   The contribution of the Protestant churches to religious liberty in colonial America. Church history, v. 4, Mar. 1935: 57–66.   BR140.A45, v. 4

11103

Miller, Perry.   From the covenant to the revival. *In* Smith, James W., *and* Albert Leland Jamison, *eds*. Religion in American life. v. 1. The shaping of American religion. Princeton, N.J., Princeton University Press, 1961. (Princeton studies in American civilization, no. 5) p. 322–368.   BR515.S6, v. 1

Analyzes sermons and public proclamations from the period and concludes that despite its rationalistic facade the Revolution was preached to the masses as an act of religious regeneration.

11104

[Moore, Frank] *ed.* The patriot preachers of the American Revolution. With biographical sketches. 1766–1783. [New York] Printed for the subscribers, 1860. 368 p.
E297.M68

Reprints 13 sermons delivered between 1766 and 1783 by such noted divines as Samuel Langdon, David Tappan, and George Duffield, in which the clergymen attacked such contemporary social and political evils as dancing and Toryism.

11105

Moore, LeRoy. Religious liberty: Roger Williams and the Revolutionary era. Church history, v. 34, Mar. 1965: 57–76.
BR140.A45, v. 34

On the use of Williams as a symbol to promote religious reform.

11106

Niebuhr, Helmut Richard. The social sources of denominationalism. New York, H. Holt [°1929] viii, 304 p.
BR115.S6N5

"Notes": p. 285–295.

An analysis of the social, racial, economic, political, and sectional factors shaping the character of Christian denominations in America. For the Revolutionary period, the author examines the political and class functions of the churches, giving particular attention to the Anglicans, Baptists, and Methodists. He concludes that the liberating doctrines of the Revolution exercised a greater influence on the Baptists and Methodists than any of the other American sects.

11107

Pears, Thomas C. The story of the Aitken Bible. *In* Presbyterian Historical Society. Journal, v. 18, June 1939: 225–241.
BX8905.P7A4, v. 18

11108

The Religious history of New England; King's Chapel lectures. Cambridge, Harvard University Press, 1917. v, 356 p.
BR530.R4

Contents: The Congregationalists, by J. W. Platner.—The revolt against the standing order, by W. W. Fenn.—The Baptists, by G. E. Hodges.—The Methodists, by W. E. Huntington.—The Universalists, by J. C. Adams.—The Swedenborgians, by W. L. Worcester.

11109

Root, Robert W. The religious ideas of some major early writers of America. 1959. ([1001] p.)
Micro AC–1, no. 60–383

Thesis (Ph.D.)—Syracuse University.
Abstracted in *Dissertation Abstracts*, v. 20, May 1960, p. 4378.

Focuses for the 18th century upon Jonathan Edwards, John Woolman, Benjamin Franklin, Thomas Paine, Thomas Jefferson, Philip Freneau, Alexander Hamilton, John Adams, and Timothy Dwight.

11110

Shea, Daniel B. Spiritual autobiography in early America. Princeton, N.J., Princeton University Press, 1968. xvi, 280 p.
BR520.S5

Includes bibliographic references.

Analyzes 20 narratives written before 1800 mostly by Puritans and Quakers, among them David Ferris, Nathan Cole, Jonathan Edwards, Samuel Hopkins, and Benjamin Franklin.

11111

Shewmaker, William O. The training of the Protestant ministry in the United States of America, before the establishment of the theological seminaries. *In* American Society of Church History. Papers. 2d ser., v. 6. New York, 1921. p. 71–202.
BR140.A4, 2d s., v. 6

11112

Smith, Hilrie Shelton, Robert T. Handy, *and* Lefferts A. Loetscher. American Christianity; an historical interpretation with representative documents. v. 1. 1607–1820. New York, C. Scribner's Sons [1960] xv, 615 p. illus., ports.
BR514.S55, v. 1

Includes bibliographies.

"Freedom and renewal, 1765–1820": p. 419–602.

Approximately two-thirds of the text consists of documents.

11113

Smith, Hilrie Shelton. Changing conceptions of original sin; a study in American theology since 1750. New York, Scribner, 1955. xi, 242 p.
BT720.S5

Bibliographic footnotes.

In the first three chapters (p. 1–59), Smith discusses the Puritan doctrine of original sin, the impact of John Taylor, and the spread of Taylorism through the work of Samuel Webster and Charles Chauncy.

11114

Smith, James W., *and* Albert Leland Johnson, *eds.* Religion in American life. Princeton, N.J., Princeton University Press, 1961. 3 v. in 4. illus., plans. (Princeton studies in American civilization, no. 5)
BR515.S6

Partial contents: v. 1. Catholicism in the United States, by Henry J. Browne. Judaism in the United States, by Oscar Handlin. Religions on the Christian perimeter, by A. Leland Jamison. Theology in America: a historical survey, by Sydney E. Ahlstrom. From the covenant to the revival, by Perry Miller. Religion and science in American philosophy, by James Ward Smith.—v. 2. Religion and education in America, by Will Herberg. Religion and law in America, by Wilbur G. Katz. Religious poetry in the United States, by Richard P. Blackmur. Religious music in America, by

Leonard Ellinwood. Religious expression in American architecture, by Donald Drew Egbert.

11115

Smith, Timothy L.   Congregation, state, and denomination: the forming of the American religious structure. William and Mary quarterly, 3d ser., v. 25, Apr. 1968: 155–176.   F221.W71, 3d s., v. 25

11116

Sprague, William B.   Annals of the American pulpit; or, Commemorative notices of distinguished American clergymen of various denominations, from the early settlement of the country to the close of the year eighteen hundred and fifty-five. With historical introductions. New York, R. Carter, 1857–[69] 9 v. ports.   BR569.S7

The volumes for each denomination were also issued separately with special title pages.

Contents: v. 1–2. Trinitarian Congregational. 1857.— v. 3–4. Presbyterian. 1859.—v. 5. Episcopalian. 1859.—v. 6. Baptist. 1860.—v. 7. Methodist. [1860]—v. 8. Unitarian Congregational. 1865.—v. 9. Lutheran. Reformed Dutch. Associate. Associate Reform. Reformed Presbyterian. 1869.

Reprinted in New York by Arno Press (1969).

A compilation of biographical sketches, some contributed by churches in which the ministers served, arranged within each volume by date of ordination.

11117

Stokes, Anson P.   Church and state in the United States. Introduction by Ralph Henry Gabriel. New York, Harper [1950] 3 v. illus., facsims., ports.   BR516.S85

"Critical and classified selected bibliography": v. 3, p. 769–836.

In the chapters on the colonial and Revolutionary periods in volume 1, the author provides information on leaders in the movement for religious freedom, including Isaac Backus, Samuel Livermore, and John Carroll; summarizes developments in the struggles against the established church in Virginia, North Carolina, New York, Connecticut, and Massachusetts; and reprints excerpts from contemporary documents illustrating thought on the subject before 1789. A one-volume condensation by Leo Pfeffer appeared in 1964 (New York, Harper & Row. 660 p.)

11118

Sweet, William W.   Makers of Christianity: from John Cotton to Lyman Abbott. New York, H. Holt [1937] viii, 351 p. (Makers of Christianity, [v. 3])   BR145.M23, v. 3

"Selected bibliography": p. 335–343.

Includes biographical sketches of religious leaders of the Great Awakening—such Revolutionary figures as John Witherspoon, Francis Asbury, and Isaac Backus and frontier missionaries and pioneers, like John Taylor, Peter Cartwright, John Eliot, and David Brainerd.

11119

Sweet, William W.   Natural religion and religious liberty in America. Journal of religion, v. 25, Jan. 1945: 45–55.   BR1.J65, v. 25

11120

Sweet, William W.   Religion in colonial America. New York, C. Scribner's Sons, 1942. xiii, 367 p.   BR520.S88

"Selected bibliography": p. 341–356.

Reprinted in New York by Cooper Square Publishers (1965).

Recounts the development from colonization to the Great Awakening of several denominations, among them the Episcopalians, Congregationalists, Baptists, Quakers, Roman Catholics, Presbyterians, German and Dutch Reformed, and Lutherans. By the time of the Revolution, Sweet points out, the battle for religious freedom and separation of church and state had almost been won; the inclusion of these principles in the state and national constitutions merely ratified colonial experience.

11121

Sweet, William W.   Religion in the development of American culture, 1765–1840. New York, C. Scribner's Sons, 1952. xiv, 338 p.   BR520.S882

Bibliography: p. 315–332.

Reprinted in Gloucester, Mass., by P. Smith (1963).

In this the second volume of his history of religion in America, the author stresses the impact of organized religion upon the westward movement of American civilization. He surveys the attitudes of each denomination toward the Revolution, including those that were pacifist, and outlines the organizational adjustments required of each after independence.

11122

Sweet, William W.   The story of religion in America. [2d rev. ed.] New York, Harper [1950] ix, 492 p.   BR515.S82 1950

First edition (1930) has title: *The Story of Religions in America*.

Bibliography: p. 453–472.

Includes two chapters (p. 172–204) on the War of Independence and the nationalization of the American churches.

11123

Thornton, John W., *ed*.   The pulpit of the American Revolution; or, The political sermons of the period of 1776. With a historical introduction, notes, and illustrations. By John Wingate Thornton. Boston, Gould and Lincoln, 1860. 537 p. plates, port.   E297.T51

Reprint of nine sermons, 1750–83, including original title pages.

Contents: Thornton, J. W. Historical introduction.— Discourses: 1. Mayhew, J. Sermon of Jan. 30, 1750.—2. Chauncy, C. Thanksgiving sermon on the repeal of the Stamp Act, 1766.—3. Cooke, S. Election sermon, 1770.—4. Gordon, W. Thanksgiving sermon, 1774.—5. Langdon, S. Election sermon at Watertown, 1775.—6. West, S. Election sermon, 1776.—7. Payson, P. Election sermon, 1778.—8. Howard, S. Election sermon, 1780.—9. Stiles, E. Election sermon, 1783.

Reprinted in New York by B. Franklin (1970) and Da Capo Press (1970).

11124

Trent, William P. The period of constitution-making in the American churches. *In* Jameson, John Franklin, *ed.* Essays in the constitutional history of the United States in the formative period, 1775–1789. Boston, Houghton, Mifflin, 1889. p. [186]–262. KF4541.A2J3 1889

11125

Van Tyne, Claude H. Influence of the clergy, and of religious and sectarian forces, on the American Revolution. American historical review, v. 19, Oct. 1913: 44–64.
E171.A57, v. 19

——— ——— Offprint. [New York, 1913] 44–64 p.
E210.V28

Rates religious bigotry, sectarian antipathy, and the influence of the Calvinistic clergy among the most important causes of the Revolution.

11126

Williams, Ray S. The American national covenant: 1730–1800. 1965. ([166] p.) Micro AC–11, no. 66–5461

Thesis (Ph.D.)—Florida State University.

Abstracted in *Dissertation Abstracts*, v. 26, June 1966, p. 7302.

Originating in Massachusetts Puritan theology, the concept of a national covenant—a contract between God and the community—was mentioned most frequently in election day sermons. Although the number of references decreased toward the end of the century, ministers continued to link the well-being of the country to a pervasive spirituality.

2. REGIONAL ACCOUNTS

a. New England

11127

Adams, Charles F. Some phases of sexual morality and church discipline in colonial New England. *In* Massachusetts Historical Society, *Boston*. Proceedings. 2d ser., v. 6; 1890/91. Boston, 1891. p. 477–516.
F61.M38, 2d s., v. 6

11128

Baldwin, Alice M. The clergy of Connecticut in Revolutionary days. [New Haven] Published for the Tercentenary Commission by the Yale University Press, 1936. 31 p. (Connecticut. Tercentenary Commission. Committee on Historical Publications. [Tercentenary pamphlet series] 56) F99.B26

"Bibliographical note": p. 31.

11129

Baldwin, Alice M. The New England clergy and the American Revolution. Durham, N.C., Duke University Press, 1928. xiii, 222 p. (Duke University Publications) E210.B18

Bibliography: p. 190–209.

Reprinted in New York by F. Ungar Pub. Co. (1958).

The author's thesis (Ph.D.), *The Influence of the New England Clergy Upon the Constitutional Doctrine of the American Revolution*, was submitted to the University of Chicago in 1926.

Attempts to demonstrate that the teachings of Congregational, Presbyterian, and other nonconformist ministers provide an unbroken line of descent from 17th-century political philosophy to the ideology of the Declaration of Independence and the state constitutions. Basic to nonconformist thought was a belief in the contractual nature of man's relationship to God and to government. Several related principles—natural rights, social contract, right of resistance, and a government bounded by law—were reiterated from pulpits over the years, becoming part of New England's intellectual baggage and naturally dominating pre-Revolutionary ideology.

11130

Bumsted, John M. Orthodoxy in Massachusetts: the ecclesiastical history of Freetown, 1683–1776. New England quarterly, v. 43, June 1970: 274–284.
F1.N62, v. 43

11131

Bumsted, John M. The pilgrims' progress: the ecclesiastical history of the Old Colony, 1620–1775 (Volumes I and II). 1965. ([485] p.)
Micro AC–1, no. 65–13,635

Thesis (Ph.D.)—Brown University.

Abstracted in *Dissertation Abstracts*, v. 26, Dec. 1965, p. 3274–3275.

Investigates the dynamics of local institutions in the three-county area of southeastern Massachusetts and finds that the basic divisive issues in the standing churches were neither doctrinal nor tied to major religious currents like the Great Awakening; instead, they revolved around unique local problems that remained important through the colonial period.

11132

Child, Frank S. The colonial parson of New England; a picture. New York, Baker & Taylor Co. [ᶜ1896] 226 p.
BR520.C49

Reprinted in Ann Arbor, Mich., by Gryphon Books (1971).

Offers chapters on the minister in a number of roles, including those of farmer, scholar, and politician.

11133

Cole, Franklin P. They preached liberty; an anthology of timely quotations from New England ministers of the American Revolution on the subject of liberty: its sources, nature, obligations, types, and blessings, with an introductory essay and biographical sketches. New York, F. H. Revell Co. [ᶜ1941] 174 p. plates, ports.
E210.C6

Bibliographic footnotes.

Taken mostly from election sermons, 1750–85.

11134

Counts, Martha L. The political views of the eighteenth century New England clergy expressed in their election sermons. 1956. ([290] p.) Micro AC–1, no. 16,894

Thesis (Ph.D.)—Columbia University.

Abstracted in *Dissertation Abstracts*, v. 16, no. 7, 1956, p. 1245.

11135

Cushing, John D. Notes on disestablishment in Massachusetts, 1780–1833. William and Mary quarterly, 3d ser., v. 26, Apr. 1969: 169–190.

F221.W71, 3d s., v. 26

11136

De Jong, Peter Y. The covenant idea in New England theology, 1620–1847. Grand Rapids, Mich., W. B. Eerdmans Pub. Co., 1945. 264 p. BX7250.D4

Bibliography: p. 251–259.

11137

Foster, Frank H. A genetic history of the New England theology. Chicago, University of Chicago Press, 1907. xv, 568 p. BX7250.F7

Bibliographical footnotes.

Reprinted in New York by Russell & Russell (1963).

Surveys the origin, growth, and decline of New England theology in three principal divisions: the evangelical theology of Jonathan Edwards, the work of such contemporaries as Samuel Hopkins, and the controversies of the 19th century.

11138

Goddard, Delano A. The pulpit, press, and literature of the Revolution. *In* Winsor, Justin, *ed.* The memorial history of Boston, including Suffolk County, Massachusetts, 1630–1880. v. 3. The Revolutionary period; the last hundred years, pt. 1. Boston, J. R. Osgood, 1881. p. [119]–148. illus. F73.3.W77, v. 3

11139

Greene, Maria Louise. The development of religious liberty in Connecticut. Boston, Houghton, Mifflin, 1905. xiii, 552 p. BR555.C8G7

Bibliography: p. [514]–543.

Reprinted in Freeport, N.Y., by Books for Libraries Press (1970) and in New York by Da Capo Press (1970).

Based in part on the author's thesis (Ph.D.), *Church and State in Connecticut to 1818*, submitted to Yale University in 1895.

Traces the history of church-state relations from the 17th-century Puritan migrations to the drafting of a new state constitution in 1818. In the chapter on the Revolutionary era, the author tells of the rise of religious toleration after the Great Awakening that led to the overthrow of the Saybrook Platform in 1784. The revised civil laws of that year omitted for the first time all mention of the platform, a document that set forth the basic tenets of the established Congregational church.

11140

Haroutunian, Joseph. Piety versus moralism; the passing of the New England theology. New York, H. Holt [ᶜ1932] xxv, 329 p. (Studies in religion and culture. American religion series, 4) BX7250.H3 1932

Issued also as thesis (Ph.D.)—Columbia University. Bibliography: p. 307–322.

Reprinted in Hamden, Conn., by Archon Books (1964).

Traces from 1750 to 1850 the decline of Calvinistic piety and its God-centered scheme of salvation and the rise of religious liberalism concerned primarily with the furthering of human happiness.

11141

Hill, Hamilton A. History of the Old South Church (Third Church), Boston, 1669–1884. v. 2. Boston, Houghton, Mifflin, 1890. viii, 688 p. illus., plates, ports. F73.62.O4H6, v. 2

Includes four chapters on the Revolutionary period.

11142

Kinney, Charles B. Church & state; the struggle for separation in New Hampshire, 1630–1900. New York, Teachers College, Columbia University, 1955. vii, 198 p. (Teachers College studies in education) BR555.N4K5

Bibliography: p. 179–186.

"The Revolutionary era—movement toward toleration": p. 83–118.

11143

Markwyn, Daniel W. The Christian state and public order in Revolutionary Massachusetts, 1770–1780. 1970. ([327] p.) Micro AC–1, no. 71–13,811

Thesis (Ph.D.)—Cornell University.

Abstracted in *Dissertation Abstracts International*, v. 31A, June 1971, p. 6520–6521.

By focusing on the proposal that nonsectarian religion be publicly supported in Massachusetts, the author explores a wide range of contemporary theories involving the place of man and religion in society.

11144

Meyer, Jacob C. Church and state in Massachusetts from 1740 to 1833, a chapter in the history of the development of individual freedom. Cleveland, Western Reserve University Press, 1930. viii, 276 p. BR555.M4M4

Published under the Francis G. Butler fund for the publication of research in American history.

Reprinted in New York by Russell & Russell (1968).

The author's thesis (Ph.D.), with the same title, was submitted to Harvard University in 1924.

After sifting through the political and doctrinal controversies that divided New Light or Separate Congregationalists, Old Light Congregationalists, Baptists, Anglicans, and Quakers, the author shows that the Baptists, in view of their increased numbers following the Great

Awakening, presented the greatest challenge to the established Congregational church. The Revolution seemed to present a favorable opportunity for all dissenting groups to join the Baptists in their demand for religious liberty, but the need for wartime political loyalty and the Congregationalists' enthusiastic support of the Revolutionary cause left them solidly entrenched, thus delaying disestablishment for nearly two generations.

11145
Minnick, Wayne C.   The New England execution sermon, 1639–1800. Speech monographs, v. 35, Mar. 1968: 77–89.   PN4077.S6, v. 35

After examining 67 printed texts written by 49 different clergymen, Minnick concludes that the New England clergy used the occasion to reinforce prevailing attitudes and mores.

11146
Odiorne, James C.   A complete list of the ministers of Boston of all denominations, from 1630 to 1842. New England historical and genealogical register, v. 1, Apr.–Oct. 1847: 134–136, 240–243, 318–322.
F1.N56, v. 1

11147
Sexton, John E.   Massachusetts' religious policy with the Indians under Governor Bernard, 1760–1769. Catholic historical review, v. 24, Oct. 1938: 310–328.
BX1404.C3, v. 24

11148
Tapley, Harriet S.   St. Peter's Church in Salem before the Revolution. *In* Essex Institute, *Salem, Mass.* Historical collections, v. 80, July–Oct. 1944: 229–260, 334–367. facsims., plates, ports.   F72.E7E81, v. 80

An appendix appeared in v. 81, Jan. 1945, p. 66–82.

11149
Walker, Williston.   The Sandemanians of New England. *In* American Historical Association. Annual report. 1901. v. 1. Washington, 1902. p. 131–162.
E172.A60, 1901, v. 1

Leader of the Glasite movement in Scotland, Robert Sandeman (1718–1771), author of the influential *Letters on Theron and Aspasio* (Edinburgh, 1757), emigrated to New England in 1764, establishing churches in Danbury, Portsmouth, Boston, and Taunton.

11150
Weaver, Glenn.   Anglican-Congregationalist tensions in pre-Revolutionary Connecticut. Historical magazine of the Protestant Episcopal church, v. 26, Sept. 1957: 269–285.   BX5800.H5, v. 26

11151
Weis, Frederick L.   The colonial clergy and the colonial churches of New England. Lancaster, Mass., 1936. 280 p. illus., ports. [Publications of the Society of the Descendants of the Colonial Clergy, 2]   BR520.W4

Bibliography: p. 12–14.

Presents alphabetically biographical information about 2,064 clergymen—1,586 Congregationalists, 217 Baptists, 127 Episcopalians, 64 Separatists, 51 Presbyterians, and 19 from five other denominations—and lists chronologically the clergy of 1,001 churches from Abington, Mass., to York, Me.

11152
Williamson, William D.   Condition of the religious denominations of Maine at the close of the Revolution. *In* Maine Historical Society. Collections. v. 7. Bath, 1876. p. [217]–229.   F16.M33, v. 7

11153
Winslow, Ola E.   Meetinghouse Hill, 1630–1783. New York, Macmillan, 1952. 344 p. illus.   BR530.W5

A social history of New England churches in which the author indicates how such everyday activities and procedures as the selection of psalms to be sung and disputes over the minister's salary shaped democratic attitudes and influenced patterns of group action. In the section on the Revolutionary era, Winslow stresses the growing power of the laity and provides brief quotations from sermons and other contemporary sources to illustrate the close relationship that developed between religion and politics.

b. Middle Atlantic Region

11154
Bergendoff, Conrad J. I.   The Swedish church on the Delaware. Church history, v. 7, Sept. 1938: 215–230.
BR140.A45, v. 7

11155
Cody, Edward J.   Church and state in the middle colonies, 1689–1763. 1970.

Thesis (Ph.D.)—Lehigh University.

11156
Corwin, Charles E.   Incidents of Reformed church life in New York City during the Revolutionary War. *In* Presbyterian Historical Society. Journal, v. 9, Dec. 1918: 355–367.   BX8905.P7A4, v. 9

11157
Ferguson, John De Lancey.   The relations of the state to religion in New York and New Jersey during the colonial period. [New Brunswick] Published by the College, 1912. 104 p. (Rutgers College Publications)
AS36.R8

"Select bibliography": p. 99–104.

11158
Gibbons, Herbert A.   Old Pine Street Church, Philadelphia, in the Revolutionary War. *In* Presbyterian Historical Society. Journal, v. 3, June 1905: 71–78. plate.   BX8905.P7A4, v. 3

11159

Good, James I. History of the Reformed church in the United States. 1725–1792. Reading, Pa., D. Miller, 1899. vii, 701 p. plates. BX9565.G7

11160

Hanley, Thomas O. The state and dissenters in the Revolution. Maryland historical magazine, v. 58, Dec. 1963: 325–332. F176.M18, v. 58

On the establishment of the right of religious dissent in Maryland.

11161

Jamison, Wallace N. Religion in New Jersey: a brief history. Princeton, N.J., Van Nostrand, 1964. xiii, 183 p. illus., maps (on lining papers) (The New Jersey historical series, v. 13) BR555.N5J3

"Bibliographical note": p. 164–170.
"Diversity takes root (1702–1776)": p. 30–56.
"Revolution and religion (1776–1835)": p. 57–84.

11162

Jefferys, Charles P. B. The provincial and Revolutionary history of St. Peter's Church, Philadelphia, 1753–1783. Pennsylvania magazine of history and biography, v. 47, Oct. 1923: 328–356; v. 48, Jan.–Oct. 1924: 39–65, 181–192, 251–269, 354–371. F146.P65, v. 47–48

11163

New York (*State*). *State Historian.* Ecclesiastical records, state of New York. Published by the state under the supervision of Hugh Hastings, State Historian. Albany, J. B. Lyon, State Printer, 1901–16. 7 v. facsims., plates (part fold.), ports. BR555.N7A3
F120.N45

"All documents arranged under the heads of the respective governors, and in chronological order."
Collected and edited by the Rev. E. T. Corwin.
Vol. 7, Index, prepared by the Rev. E. T. Corwin under the auspices of the State Historian, James A. Holden.
Vol. 7 has imprint: Albany, The University of the State of New York, 1916.

Volume 6 contains reprints of letters, committee reports, legislative acts, and other material dated between 1761 and 1800 relating mainly to the Dutch Reformed and Anglican or Episcopal churches. Most correspondence was exchanged between the church in New York and the Classis of Amsterdam and concerns the activities of the clergy, education, and church administration.

11164

Osgood, Herbert L., *ed.* The Society of Dissenters founded at New York in 1769. American historical review, v. 6, Apr. 1901: 498–507. E171.A57, v. 6

Minutes of various meetings held in February and March 1769 by leading members of the Presbyterian and Baptist churches of New York City in which they organized to protest and enlarge their rights in a colony dominated by the Anglican church.

11165

Pratt, John W. Religion, politics, and diversity; the church-state theme in New York history. Ithaca, N.Y., Cornell University Press [1967] xi, 327 p.
BR555.N7P7

"Bibliographical note": p. 317–319.

Includes three chapters (p. 49–116) on the 18th-century experience, the constitution of 1777, and the Revolutionary settlement.

11166

Rightmyer, Nelson W. Churches under enemy occupation, Philadelphia, 1777–8. Church history, v. 14, Mar. 1945: 33–60. BR140.A45, v. 14

Discusses the impact on all denominations.

11167

Schuyler, Hamilton. A history of St. Michael's Church, Trenton: in the diocese of New Jersey, from its foundation in the year of Our Lord 1703 to 1926. Princeton, Princeton University Press, 1926. xxiii, 459 p. illus., facsim., maps (part fold.), plates, ports.
BX5980.T7M5
F144.T7S4

Bibliography: p. 445–450.

Includes eight chapters (p. 54–132) that deal in part with the Revolutionary years.

11168

Slosser, Gaius J. A chapter from the religious history of western Pennsylvania. *In* Presbyterian Historical Society. Journal, v. 16, Sept. 1934: 97–125.
BX8905.P7A4, v. 16

Includes a list, by denomination, of churches founded in western Pennsylvania prior to 1800.

11169

Stillé, Charles J. Religious tests in provincial Pennsylvania. Pennsylvania magazine of history and biography, v. 9, Jan. 1886: 365–406. F146.P65, v. 9

11170

Wall, Alexander J. The controversy in the Dutch church in New York concerning preaching in English, 1754–1768. *In* New York Historical Society. Quarterly bulletin, v. 12, July 1928: 39–58. facsims., port.
F116.N638, v. 12

11171

Walsh, James G. Some religious discussions in Philadelphia just after the Revolution. *In* American Catholic Historical Society of Philadelphia. Records, v. 17, Mar. 1906: 33–43. E184.C3A4, v. 17

On conversations among clergymen of several faiths, held mostly in the home of Benjamin Franklin, as reported by a young Spanish priest, Don Antonio José Ruiz.

11172

Waterston, Elizabeth. Churches in Delaware during the Revolution, with a brief account of their settlement and growth. Wilmington, Del., Historical Society of Delaware, 1925. ix, 117 p. plates.   BR555.D4W3

Presented as a master's thesis, University of Chicago. Bibliography: p. 94–106.

11173

Weis, Frederick L. The colonial clergy of the middle colonies, New York, New Jersey, and Pennsylvania, 1628–1776. *In* American Antiquarian Society, *Worcester, Mass.* Proceedings. v. 66, pt. 2. Worcester, 1957. p. [167]–351.   E172.A35, v. 66

11174

Weis, Frederick L. The colonial churches and the colonial clergy of the middle and southern colonies, 1607–1776. Lancaster, Mass., 1938. 140 p. front. [Publications of the Society of the Descendants of the Colonial Clergy, 3]   BR520.W38

Lists chronologically the service of 2,826 clergymen—1,136 Episcopalians, 462 Presbyterians, 391 Baptists, 279 Reformed, 180 Moravians, 151 Lutherans, 113 Congregationalists, 110 Roman Catholics, 110 Mennonites, 24 Methodists, and 14 from six other sects—according to the geographical location of 1,956 churches, whether in a town, parish, or county.

c. The South

11175

Allen, Ethan. The Garrison church; sketches of the history of St. Thomas' Parish, Garrison Forest, Baltimore County, Maryland, 1742–1852. Edited by Rev. Hobart Smith. New York, J. Pott, 1898. x, 193 p. illus., facsims., plates, ports.   F187.B2A4

11176

Baker, Gloria B. Dissenters in colonial North Carolina. 1970. ([227] p.)   Micro AC–1, no. 71–11,668

Thesis (Ph.D.)—University of North Carolina.
Abstracted in *Dissertation Abstracts International,* v. 31A, May 1971, p. 5966.

11177

Caldwell, James R. The churches of Granville County, North Carolina, in the eighteenth century. *In* Sitterson, Joseph C., *ed.* Studies in southern history [in memory of Albert Ray Newsome, 1894–1951, by his former students at the University of North Carolina] Chapel Hill, University of North Carolina Press, 1957. (The James Sprunt studies in history and political science, v. 39) p. 1–22.   F251.J28, v. 39

11178

Conkin, Paul. The church establishment in North Carolina, 1765–1776. North Carolina historical review, v. 32, Jan. 1955: 1–30.   F251.N892, v. 32

11179

Daniel, Marjorie L. Anglicans and dissenters in Georgia, 1758–1777. Church history, v. 7, Sept. 1938: 247–262.   BR140.A45, v. 7

11180

The French Protestants of Abbeville District, S.C., 1761–1765. *In* South Carolina Historical Society. Collections. v. 2. Charleston, 1858. p. [75]–103.   F266.S71, v. 2

Introduction by W. Noel Sainsbury.

On the transactions that led to the settlement of a colony of French Protestants at New Bordeaux in 1764.

11181

Gambrall, Theodore C. Church life in colonial Maryland. Baltimore, G. Lycett, 1885. 309 [6] p.   F184.G18

"Authorities used": p. 308–309.

11182

German Protestants in South Carolina in 1788. A petition for the incorporation of their churches. South Carolina historical and genealogical magazine, v. 47, Oct. 1946: 195–204.   S266.S55, v. 47

Contributed by Paul Quattlebaum.

11183

Gundersen, Joan R. The Anglican ministry in Virginia, 1723–1776: a study of social class. 1972 ([336] p.)   Micro AC–1, no. 72–26,805

Thesis (Ph.D.)—University of Notre Dame.
Abstracted in *Dissertation Abstracts International,* v. 33A, Oct. 1972, p. 1643.

11184

Hanley, Thomas O. The American Revolution and religion; Maryland 1770–1800. Washington, Catholic University of America Press [1971] 260 p.   BR555.M3H28

Bibliography: p. 249–256.

Considers the effects of Maryland's constitution upon church-state relations, the growth of the Episcopal, Methodist, Reformed, and Catholic churches, and Christian social concerns—care of the poor, emancipation of slaves, and education. Hanley contends that a period of religious vitality followed the Revolution and that it occurred because the constitution of 1776 disestablished the Anglican church and, more important, because a spiritual awakening inspired Marylanders to create a Christian state.

11185

Hanley, Thomas O. The impact of the American Revolution on religion in Maryland, 1776–1800. 1961.

Thesis (Ph.D.)—Georgetown University.

11186

Hood, Fred J. Revolution and religious liberty: the conservation of the theocratic concept in Virginia. Church history, v. 40, June 1971: 170–181.   BR140.A45, v. 40

Contends that conservative Protestants, such as Virginia's Presbyterians, considered religious liberty to be a religious dogma compatible with established religion and that this belief persisted despite the legal separation of church and state.

11187
James, Charles F. Documentary history of the struggle for religious liberty in Virginia. Lynchburg, Va., J. P. Bell Co., 1900. 272 p. BR555.V8J3

Reprinted in New York by Da Capo Press (1971).

Relying primarily on memorials and other petitions found in the journals of the Virginia assembly, the author attempts to prove that the Baptists were the first and only denomination to seek independence from Great Britain, persist in the demand for disestablishment, and oppose the Constitution on the grounds that it did not provide sufficient security for religious liberty.

11188
Lohrenz, Otto. The Virginia clergy and the American Revolution, 1774–1799. 1970. ([436] p.)
Micro AC–1, no. 70–25,370

Thesis (Ph.D.)—University of Kansas.
Abstracted in *Dissertation Abstracts International*, v. 31A, Dec. 1970, p. 2849–2850.

11189
Long, Ronald W. Religious revivalism in the Carolinas and Georgia, 1740–1805. 1968. ([257] p.)
Micro AC–1, no. 69–9501

Thesis (Ph.D.)—University of Georgia.
Abstracted in *Dissertation Abstracts*, v. 29A, June 1969, p. 4430.

11190
Miller, Wallace E. Relations of church and state in Georgia, 1732–1775. 1937.

Thesis (Ph.D.)—Northwestern University.

11191
Quinlivan, Mary E. Ideological controversy over religious establishment in Revolutionary Virginia. 1971. ([215] p.) Micro AC–1, no. 71–29,009
Thesis (Ph.D.)—University of Wisconsin.
Abstracted in *Dissertation Abstracts International*, v. 32A, Jan. 1972, p. 3932.

Examines agitation for the separation of church and state and arguments favoring the use of religion as an instrument for maintaining order in secular society, especially the proposal for a multiple religious establishment supported by taxes predesignated by the citizen.

11192
Rhodes, Daniel D. The struggle for religious liberty in Virginia, 1740–1802. 1951.

Thesis (Ph.D.)—Duke University.

11193
Russell, William T., *Bp*. Maryland; the land of sanctuary. A history of religious toleration in Maryland from the first settlement until the American Revolution. Baltimore, J. H. Furst Co., 1907. xxxviii, 621 p. ports.
F184.R96

Bibliography: p. xix–xxxviii.

In the section on the 18th century, Russell compares the performance and the moral integrity of the Anglican and Catholic clergy, and tells of Charles Carroll's service to the Revolutionary cause.

11194
Sappington, Roger E. North Carolina and the non-resistant sects during the American War of Independence. Quaker history, v. 60, spring 1971: 29–47.
BX7635.A1F6, v. 60

11195
Stephens, Alonzo T. An account of the attempts at establishing a religious hegemony in colonial North Carolina, 1663–1773. 1956. ([299] p.)
Micro AC–1, no. 15,118

Thesis (Ph.D.)—University of Pittsburgh.
Abstracted in *Dissertation Abstracts*, v. 16, no. 1, 1956, p. 112.

11196
Stillé, Charles J. Religious liberty in Virginia, and Patrick Henry. *In* American Historical Assocation. Papers. v. 3, no. 1; 1887. New York, 1888. p. 205–211.
E172.A65, v. 3

Relates to article 16 of the Virginia Declaration of Rights adopted by the convention of delegates in June 1776.

11197
Stokes, Durward T. The clergy of the Carolinas and the American Revolution. 1968. ([352] p.)
Micro AC–1, no. 69–1684

Thesis (Ph.D.)—University of North Carolina.
Abstracted in *Dissertation Abstracts*, v. 29A, Jan. 1969, p. 2199.

The ministers of all denominations, save the Methodists, Quakers, United Brethren, and North Carolina Anglicans, were active promoters of revolution.

11198
Strickland, Reba C. Religion and the state in Georgia in the eighteenth century. New York, Columbia University Press, 1939. 211 p. (Studies in history, economics and public law, no. 460) H31.C7, no. 460
BR555.G4S8, 1939 a

Issued also as thesis (Ph.D.)—Columbia University.
Bibliography: p. 187–197.

Founded by proprietors who encouraged the immigration of Protestant dissenters, Georgia early adopted a policy of toleration toward all except Catholics. Although the Church of England was established in 1758, it remained a feeble institution without sufficient clergy to serve its parishes. Moreover, the government granted glebes to Lutherans and Congregationalists as well as Anglicans, and dissenters were often elected vestrymen. Such policies promoted a harmony that preluded the spread of the Great Awakening into Georgia. With the coming of the Revolution, Strickland shows, most older Anglicans, especially those born in England, remained loyal, while their children joined Baptists and other dissenters in enthusiastic support of separation from England.

11199

Virginia. State Library, *Richmond. Archives Division.* Separation of church and state in Virginia; a study in the development of the Revolution. Richmond, D. Bottom, Supt. of Public Print., 1910. 164 p.
BR555.V8A55

Published also in the sixth *Annual Report* (Richmond, 1909. Z733.V64, 6th) of the Virginia State Library.

Reprinted in New York by Da Capo Press (1971. F230.A36 1971).

Concentrating upon the years 1748–87, the author, H. J. Eckenrode, analyzes the disputes over salary payments known as the Parson's Cause, reviews the activities of the established Anglican church, and differentiates between law-abiding dissenters—Presbyterians and Methodists—and radical Baptists. He also discusses Virginia's bill of rights and describes the successful struggle during the Confederation period against taxes levied to support religion and against the incorporation of the Protestant Episcopal church. While the separation of church and state caused innumerable difficulties for clergymen and legislators, Eckenrode doubts that the mass of common people were much affected. Evangelical denominations prospered, moreover, in the absence of an established church.

11200

Voigt, Gilbert P. Religious conditions among German-speaking settlers in South Carolina, 1732–1774. South Carolina historical magazine, v. 56, Apr. 1955: 59–66.
F266.S55, v. 56

11201

Weeks, Stephen B. Church and state in North Carolina. Baltimore, Johns Hopkins Press, 1893. 65 p. (Johns Hopkins University studies in historical and political science, 11th ser., 5/6) H31.J6, 11th s., no. 5/6
JS315.M8W4

"Bibliographical note": p. 65.

Discusses church-state relations under the proprietary and royal governments and the establishment of freedom of worship in 1776.

11202

Weis, Frederick L. The colonial clergy of Maryland, Delaware, and Georgia. Lancaster, Mass., 1950. 104 p. front. (Publications of the Society of the Descendants of the Colonial Clergy, 5) BR520.W43

Presents in six lists biographical information about 587 clergymen—421 who served in Maryland, 127 in Delaware, and 39 in Georgia—and the location, denomination, and

date of establishment of 322 churches—217 in Maryland, 81 in Delaware, and 24 in Georgia.

11203

Weis, Frederick L. The colonial clergy of Virginia, North Carolina, and South Carolina. Boston, 1955. vii, 100 p. (Publications of the Society of the Descendants of the Colonial Clergy, 7) BR569.W42

Arranging the entries in three separate alphabetic lists, the compiler supplies biographical information on 648 Virginians, including 489 Episcopalians and 86 Baptists; 155 North Carolinians, including 51 Baptists, 42 Episcopalians, 24 Moravians, and 19 Presbyterians; and 276 South Carolinians, including 127 Episcopalians, 59 Presbyterians, and 51 Baptists. Weis reports clergymen of all denominations who were "regularly ordained, installed, or settled over" Christian churches before July 4, 1776. He also names the Quaker meetings founded in the three colonies before that date.

11204

Werline, Albert W. Problems of church and state in Maryland during the seventeenth and eighteenth centuries. South Lancaster, Mass., College Press [1948] ix, 236 p.
BR555.M3W4

Bibliography: p. 212–223.

The author's thesis (Ph.D.), with the same title, was submitted to Columbia University in 1947.

Surveys Anglican church history during the institution's ascendency in the state from 1692 to 1776, notes the effects of the Revolution upon the Protestant Episcopal church, and examines the failure of Maryland legislators to provide financial support for churches in accordance with the new state constitution.

11205

Zipperer, Manfred. Thomas Jefferson's "Act for establishing religious freedom in Virginia" vom 16. Januar 1786; ein verfassungsgeschichtlicher und rechtsvergleichender Beitrag zum Staatskirchenrecht. [Erlangen, Offsetdruck-Fotodruck J. Hogl, 1967] xxi, 282 p.
LL

Inaug.–Diss.—Universität Erlangen-Nürnberg, Erlangen.

Bibliography: p. [i]–xix.

3. DENOMINATIONAL ACCOUNTS

a. Anglicans

(1) GENERAL

11206

Babcock, Mary K. Difficulties and dangers of pre-Revolutionary ordinations. Historical magazine of the Protestant Episcopal church, v. 12, Sept. 1943: 225–241.
BX5800.H5, v. 12

11207

Beardsley, William A. The episcopate of Bishop Seabury. Historical magazine of the Protestant Episcopal church, v. 3, Sept. 1934: 210–225. BX5800.H5, v. 3

11208

Brydon, George MacLaren. New light on the origins of the method of electing bishops adopted by the American Episcopal church [1786] Historical magazine of the Protestant Episcopal church, v. 19, Sept, 1950: 202–213. BX5800.H5, v. 19

11209

Chorley, Edward Clowes. The election and consecration. Historical magazine of the Protestant Episcopal church, v. 3, Sept. 1934: 146–191. BX5800.H5, v. 3

Concerns negotiations with the Church of England over the consecration of Samuel Seabury, the first bishop of the American Episcopal church, 1782–85. Additional letters relating to the Seabury consecration appear in v. 3, Dec. 1934, p. 234–261.

11210

Chorley, Edward Clowes. The general [Episcopal] conventions of 1785, 1786 and 1789. Historical magazine of the Protestant Episcopal church, v. 4, Dec. 1935: 246–266. BX5800.H5, v. 4

11211

Fothergill, Gerald. A list of emigrant ministers to America, 1690–1811. London, E. Stock, 1904. 65 p. CS61.F6

Reprinted in Baltimore by the Genealogical Pub. Co. (1965).

11212

Gerlach, Don R. Champions of an American episcopate: Thomas Secker of Canterbury and Samuel Johnson of Connecticut. Historical magazine of the Protestant Episcopal church, v. 41, Dec. 1972: 381–414. BX5800.H5, v. 41

11213

Hooker, Richard J. The Anglican church and the American Revolution. Chicago, 1943. vi, 378 l. BX5881.H6

Thesis (Ph.D.)—University of Chicago.
Bibliography: leaves 360–378.

Reviews the background of the church in America to 1763; provides a detailed analysis of the controversy over an American episcopate, especially in New York and Pennsylvania; and treats briefly the activities of Anglicans in the New England, middle, and southern colonies during the war.

11214

Klingberg, Frank J. The expansion of the Anglican church in the eighteenth century. Historical magazine of the Protestant Episcopal church, v. 16, Sept. 1947: 292–301. BX5800.H5, v. 16

11215

Lamb, George W. Clergymen licensed to the American colonies by the bishops of London, 1745–1781. Historical magazine of the Protestant Episcopal church, v. 13, June 1944: 128–143. BX5800.H5, v. 13

11216

Libby, Robert M. G. Anglican-Lutheran ecumenism in early American history. Historical magazine of the Protestant Episcopal Church, v. 36, Sept. 1967: 211–231. BX5800.H5, v. 36

11217

Loveland, Clara O. The critical years; the reconstitution of the Anglican church in the United States of America: 1780–1789. Greenwich, Conn., Seabury Press, 1956. vi, 311 p. BX5881.L6

"Catalogue of correspondence": p. [289]–293.
Bibliography: p. [294]–306.

Describes the post-Revolutionary problems of ecclesiastical authority, the disputes over conflicting plans of organization, the threats of schism, and the emergence of the General Convention as the legislative body. As a result of the reorganization controversy, the Protestant Episcopal church differed from the English church in three ways: Americans accepted the separation of church and state, bishops had no secular power, and laymen were represented at every level of church government.

11218

Manross, William W. A history of the American Episcopal church. [3d ed., rev.] New York, Morehouse-Gorham, 1959. xiv, 420 p. BX5880.M35 1959

Bibliography: p. 377–392.

Chapters 8 and 9 (p. 154–201) treat the struggle for the episcopate, the war, and post-Revolutionary reorganization.

11219

Manross, William W. Interstate meetings and general conventions of 1784, 1785, 1786, and 1787. Historical magazine of the Protestant Episcopal church, v. 8, Sept. 1939: 257–280. BX5800.H5, v. 8

11220

Mills, Frederick V. Anglican expansion in colonial America, 1761–1775. Historical magazine of the Protestant Episcopal church, v. 39, Sept. 1970: 315–324. BX5800.H5, v. 39

11221

Mills, Frederick V. Mitre without sceptre: an eighteenth century ecclesiastical revolution. Church history, v. 39, Sept. 1970: 365–371. BR140.A45, v. 39

On the effects of the disestablishment of the Anglican church in America and the election of the first bishop.

11222

Monk, Robert C. Unity and diversity among eighteenth century colonial Anglicans and Methodists. Historical magazine of the Protestant Episcopal church, v. 38, Mar. 1969: 51–69. BX5800.H5, v. 38

11223

Painter, Borden W. The Anglican vestry in colonial America. 1965. ([266] p.) Micro AC–1, no. 65–15,095

Thesis (Ph.D.)—Yale University.

Abstracted in *Dissertation Abstracts*, v. 26, May 1966, p. 6661.

11224

Pennington, Edgar L. Some observations regarding the colonial clergy. Historical magazine of the Protestant Episcopal church, v. 10, Mar 1941: 45–56.

BX5800.H5, v. 10

11225

Pennington, Edgar L. Colonial [Anglican] clergy conventions. Historical magazine of the Protestant Episcopal church, v. 8, Sept. 1939: 178–218. BX5800.H5, v. 8

11226

Perry, William S., *Bp., ed.* Historical collections relating to the American colonial church. New York, AMS Press [1969] 5 v. in 4. BX5881.P42

Reprint of the 1870–78 ed.

Includes bibliographic references.

Contents: v. 1. Virginia.—v. 2. Pennsylvania.—v. 3. Massachusetts.—v. 4. Maryland.—v. 5. Delaware.

Reprints extracts from correspondence, reports, and other records of the Anglican church in America. Transcribed in England from the originals, the documents date mainly from the 18th century and are arranged in chronological order to 1785.

11227

Perry, William S., *Bp.* The history of the American Episcopal church, 1587–1883. v. 1. The planting and growth of the American colonial church, 1587–1783. Boston, J. R. Osgood, 1885. xx, 665 p. illus., facsims., maps, ports. 4BX 1602

Bibliographic footnotes.

11228

A Registry of ordinations by Bishop Seabury and Bishop Jarvis of Connecticut. Historical magazine of the Protestant Episcopal church, v. 13, Mar. 1944: 44–71.

BX5800.H5, v. 13

Introduction and notes by William A. Beardsley.

11229

Salomon, Richard G. British legislation and American episcopacy. Historical magazine of the Protestant Episcopal church, v. 20, Sept. 1951: 278–293.

BX5800.H5, v. 20

Traces the history of the British act which made possible the consecration of bishops White, Provoost, and Madison, and thus the continuation of English episcopal succession in America.

11230

Stowe, Walter H., *and others.* The clergy of the Episcopal church in 1785. Historical magazine of the Protestant Episcopal church, v. 20, Sept. 1951: 243–277.

BX5800.H5, v. 20

Following Stowe's introductory essay, "The Critical Period in the History of the American Episcopal Church, 1776–1789," there are alphabetical lists (and in some cases biographical sketches) of the clergy in each of the existing states, Vermont, and Florida.

11231

Stowe, Walter H. The state of diocesan conventions of the war and post-war periods. Historical magazine of the Protestant Episcopal church, v. 8, Sept. 1939: 220–256. BX5800.H5, v. 8

11232

Stowe, Walter H. A study in conscience: some aspects of the relations of the clergy to the state. Historical magazine of the Protestant Episcopal church, v. 19, Dec. 1950: 301–323. BX5800.H5, v. 19

On the problems encountered during the Revolutionary War by the Anglican clergy who were bound at their ordination by a special oath of allegiance to the king.

11233

Sweet, William W. The role of the Anglicans in the American Revolution. Huntington Library quarterly, v. 11, Nov. 1947: 51–70. Z733.S24Q, v. 11

11234

Woolverton, John F. Histories of the Episcopal church in America: a survey and evaluation. Historical magazine of the Protestant Episcopal church, v. 34, Mar. 1965: 59–78. BX5800.H5, v. 34

(2) NEW ENGLAND

11235

Beardsley, Eben Edwards. The history of the Episcopal church in Connecticut, from the settlement of the colony to the death of Bishop Seabury. New York, Hurd and Houghton, 1866. xxix, 470 p. front.

BX5917.C8B4 1866, v. 1

Bibliography: p. [453]–455.

The period from the attacks on the Society for the Propagation of the Gospel in 1763–64 to the first consecration in America of an Episcopal bishop in 1792 are treated in chapters 17–31 (p. 223–431).

11236

Burr, Nelson R. The story of the diocese of Connecticut, a new branch of the vine. [Hartford, Church Missions Pub. Co., ᶜ1962] xvi, 568 p. illus., facsims., plates, ports. BX5918.C7B8

Bibliography: p. 477–533.

The first 11 chapters (p. 3–154) are concerned with the establishment of the Episcopal church in a Puritan state during the colonial and Revolutionary periods.

11237

Hawks, Francis L., *and* William S. Perry, *Bp., eds.* Documentary history of the Protestant Episcopal church in the United States of America. Containing numerous hitherto unpublished documents concerning the church in Connecticut. New-York, J. Pott, 1863–64. 2 v.

BX5917.C8H3

Facsimile issued in Hartford by Historiographer (1959. 2 v. in 1. BX5917.C8H32).

Mainly correspondence, arranged in chronological order from 1705 to 1789, relating to the missionary activities of the Venerable Society for the Propagation of the Gospel in Foreign Parts.

11238

Kinloch, Hector C. L. M.   Anglican clergy in Connecticut, 1701–1785. 1960.

Thesis (Ph.D.)—Yale University.

11239

Mampoteng, Charles.   The New England Anglican clergy in the American Revolution. Historical magazine of the Protestant Episcopal church, v. 9, Dec. 1940: 267–304.

BX5800.H5, v. 9

11240

Steiner, Bruce E.   New England Anglicanism: a genteel faith? William and Mary quarterly, 3d ser., v. 27, Jan. 1970: 122–135.   F221.W71, 3d s., v. 27

Anglicanism in New England had its greatest numerical strength in farm communities and rural villages, making it predominantly a lower class movement.

(3) MIDDLE ATLANTIC REGION

11241

Burr, Nelson R.   The Anglican church in New Jersey. Philadelphia, Church Historical Society [1954] xvi, 768 p. maps. (Church Historical Society (U.S.) Publication no. 40)   BX5917.N55B8

Bibliography: p. [657]–700.

"Historical sketches of colonial churches": p. [487]–575.

"Biographical sketches of colonial clergymen": p. [577]–654.

A comprehensive treatment of Anglicanism and other religious movements in New Jersey from the mission of George Keith in 1702 to the establishment of the American Protestant Episcopal church in 1789.

11242

Burr, Nelson R.   The critical period of the Episcopal church in New Jersey. Historical magazine of the Protestant Episcopal church, v. 29, June 1960: 139–144.

BX5800.H5, v. 29

11243

Burr, Nelson R.   The Episcopal church and the Dutch in colonial New York and New Jersey, 1664–1784. Historical magazine of the Protestant Episcopal church, v. 19, Mar. 1950: 90–111.   BX5800.H5, v. 19

11244

Dix, Morgan, *ed.*   A history of the parish of Trinity Church in the city of New York. pt. 1. To the close of the rectorship of Dr. Inglis, A.D. 1783. Compiled by order of the Corporation. New York, G. P. Putnam's Sons., 1898. xvi, 506 p. illus., facsims., plates, ports.

BX5980.N5T7, v. 1

"Lists of works referred to": p. 490–498.

Part 1 includes five chapters (p. 307–450) on the period 1764–83; the second volume (New York, G. P. Putnam's Sons, 1901) contains twelve chapters (p. 1–140) on the years 1783–92.

11245

Klingberg, Frank J.   The Anglican minority in colonial Pennsylvania, with particular reference to the Indian. Pennsylvania magazine of history and biography, v. 65, July 1941: 276–299.   F146.P65, v. 65

Examines the work of the Society for the Propagation of the Gospel along the frontier.

11246

Pennington, Edgar L.   The Anglican clergy of Pennsylvania in the American Revolution. Pennsylvania magazine of history and biography, v. 63, Oct. 1939: 401–431.

F146.P65, v. 63

11247

Poughkeepsie, N.Y. Christ Church.   The records of Christ Church, Poughkeepsie, New York. Edited by Helen Wilkinson Reynolds. Poughkeepsie, F. B. Howard 1911–[19?] 2 v. illus., map, plates, ports.

F129.P9P75

Contents: [v. 1. History] 1755–1910.—v. 2. Parish register, 1766–1916.

11248

Rightmyer, Nelson W.   The Anglican church in Delaware. Philadelphia, Church Historical Society [1947] xiv, 217 p. map (Church Historical Society (U.S.) Publication 23)   BX5917.D4R5

Includes bibliographies.

"Through revolution to independence": p. 167–184.

11249

Seabury, Samuel.   The Seabury minutes of the New York clergy conventions of 1766 and 1767. Historical magazine of the Protestant Episcopal church, v. 10, June 1941: 124–162.   BX5800.H5, v. 10

Introduction and notes by Walter Herbert Stowe.

(4) THE SOUTH

11250

Beaufort, S.C. St. Helena's Parish.   Minutes of the vestry of St. Helena's Parish, South Carolina, 1726–1812. Edited by A. S. Salley, Jr. Columbia, S.C., Printed for the Historical Commission of South Carolina by the State Co., 1919. 296 p. facsim.   F279.B3B36

11251

Bell, Landon C.   Cumberland Parish, Lunenburg County, Virginia, 1746–1816. Vestry book, 1746–1816. Richmond, Va., William Byrd Press [ᶜ1930] 633 p. fold. map, port. F234.C94B43

11252
Blissland Parish, *Va*. The vestry book of Blisland (Blissland) Parish, New Kent and James City counties, Virginia, 1721–1786. Transcribed and edited by C. G. Chamberlayne. Published by the Library Board. Richmond, Division of Purchase and Print., 1935. lxii, 277 p. facsims. (part fold.), fold. map, plates. F232.B55B5

11253
Bristol Parish, *Va*. The vestry book and register of Bristol Parish, Virginia, 1720–1789. Transcribed and published by C. G. Chamberlayne. Richmond, Va. [W. E. Jones, Printer] 1898. vii, 419 p. F232.B8B8

11254
Bryan, C. Braxton. The church in Virginia during the Revolutionary period. *In* Goodwin, William A. R., *ed.* History of the Theological Seminary in Virginia and its historical background. Centennial ed. v. 1. New York, E. S. Gorham, 1923. p. 31–68. BV4070.A46G7 1923, v. 1

11255
Brydon, George MacLaren. The clergy of the established church in Virginia and the Revolution. Virginia magazine of history and biography, v. 41, Jan.–Oct. 1933: 11–23, 123–143, 231–243, 297–309. F221.V91, v. 41

————Offprint. [Richmond? 1933] 11–23, 123–143, 231–243, 297–309 p. BX5917.V8B7

A partial list of the Anglican clergy at the time of the Revolution, with a brief sketch of each.

11256
Brydon, George MacLaren. Early days of the diocese of Virginia. Historical magazine of the Protestant Episcopal church, v. 4, Mar. 1935: 27–46. BX5800.H5, v. 4

Bears largely on the work of the Episcopal conventions during the Confederation period.

11257
Brydon, George MacLaren. A list of clergy of the Protestant Episcopal church ordained after the American Revolution who served in Virginia between 1785 and 1814, and a list of Virginia parishes and their rectors for the same period. William and Mary College quarterly historical magazine, 2d ser., v. 19, Oct. 1939: 397–434. F221.W71, 2d s., v. 19

11258
Brydon, George MacLaren. New light upon the history of the church in colonial Virginia. Historical magazine of the Protestant Episcopal Church, v. 10, June 1941: 69–103. BX5800.H5, v. 10

———— ———— Offprint. Richmond, Va., Virginia Diocesan Library [1941] 34 p. BX5917.V8B73

11259
Brydon, George MacLaren. Revision of the prayer book by an American civil legislature. Historical magazine of the Protestant Episcopal church, v. 19, June 1950: 133–138. BX5800.H5, v. 19

On the adoption of an ordinance by the Virginia Convention on July 5, 1776, deleting from the established prayer book references to the king and royal family.

11260
Brydon, George MacLaren. Virginia's mother church and the political conditions under which it grew. Richmond, Virginia Historical Society, 1947–52. 2 v. port. BX5917.V8B77

Vol. 2 has imprint: Philadelphia, Church Historical Society.
Includes bibliographies.
Contents: [v. 1] An interpretation of the records of the colony of Virginia and of the Anglican church of that colony, 1607–1727.—v. 2. The story of the Anglican church and the development of religion in Virginia, 1727–1814.

For the Revolutionary period, the author offers an account of the Parsons' Cause, the tenure of commissaries William Robinson, James Horrocks, and John Camm, the disestablishment of the church, and the fate of the clergy during the war. Of the 105 Anglican clergymen in Virginia in 1776, most became rebels, 19 disappeared from the church's records in 1777 when the legal salary terminated, five took the oath to the rebel government but later accepted British authority in the wake of American military reverses, and 15 remained loyal, including most of the theological faculty of William and Mary College. For the next 40 years, the Episcopal church had to rely upon other denominational schools to train its clergy.

11261
Dalcho, Frederick. An historical account of the Protestant Episcopal church, in South-Carolina, from the first settlement of the province, to the War of the Revolution; with notices of the present state of the church in each parish: and some account of the early civil history of Carolina, never before published. Charleston, Published by E. Thayer, at his theological bookstore, Broad Street, Arch'd. E. Miller, Printer, 120 Broad-street, 1820. vii, 613 p. BX5917.S6D2
F272.D13

Reprinted in New York by Arno Press (1972).

11262
Ervin, Spencer. The Anglican church in North Carolina. Historical magazine of the Protestant Episcopal church, v. 25, June 1956: 102–161. BX5800.H5, v. 25

11263
Ervin, Spencer. The established church of colonial Maryland. Historical magazine of the Protestant Episcopal church, v. 24, Sept. 1955: 232–292.
BX5800.H5, v. 24

11264

Ervin, Spencer. The establishment, government, and functioning of the church in colonial Virginia. Historical magazine of the Protestant Episcopal church, v. 26, Mar. 1957: 65–110.   BX5800.H5, v. 26

11265

Goodwin, Edward L. The colonial church in Virginia, with biographical sketches of the first six bishops of the diocese of Virginia, and other historical papers, together with brief biographical sketches of the colonial clergy of Virginia. With a foreword by the Rt. Rev. William Cabell Brown and introduction by the Rev. G. MacLaren Brydon. Milwaukee, Morehouse Pub. Co. [c1927] xxiv, 342 p. plates, ports.   BX5917.V8G6

Bibliography: p. [343]

A posthumously published compilation of material relating to the work of the Anglican clergy in Virginia between 1607 and 1785.

11266

Hartdagen, Gerald E. The Anglican vestry in colonial Maryland: organizational structure and problems. Historical magazine of the Protestant Episcopal church, v. 38, Dec. 1969: 349–360. plate. BX5800.H5, v. 38

11267

Hartdagen, Gerald E. Vestry and clergy in the Anglican church of colonial Maryland. Historical magazine of the Protestant Episcopal church, v. 37, Dec. 1968: 371–396.   BX5800.H5, v. 37

11268

Hawks, Francis L. Contributions to the ecclesiastical history of the United States. New York, Harper, 1836–39 [c1835–39] 2 v.   BX5880.H3

Vol. 2 has imprint: New York, J. S. Taylor.

Contents: v. 1. A narrative of events connected with the rise and progress of the Protestant Episcopal church in Virginia.—v. 2. A narrative of the events connected with the rise and progress of the Protestant Episcopal church in Maryland.

A microfilm copy has been issued in Ann Arbor, Mich., by University Microfilms as part of the American Culture Series (Micro 01291, reel 258, no. 1 E).

11269

Kingston, Va. (Parish). The vestry book of Kingston Parish, Mathews County, Virginia (until May 1, 1791, Gloucester County), 1679–1796. Transcribed, annotated, and indexed by C. G. Chamberlayne. Richmond, Va., Old Dominion Press, 1929. xvi, 161 p. facsims.   F232.K54K5

11270

Lemmon, Sarah M. The genesis of the Protestant Episcopal diocese of North Carolina, 1701–1823. North Carolina historical magazine, v. 28, Oct. 1951: 426–462.   F251.N892, v. 28

11271

Lynnhaven Parish, *Princess Anne Co., Va.* The colonial vestry book of Lynnhaven Parish, Princess Anne County, Virginia, 1723–1786. Transcribed and edited by George Carrington Mason. Newport News, Va., G. C. Mason, 1949. xxvii, 134 p. illus., map.   F232.P87L9

11272

Malone, Henry T. The Episcopal church in Georgia, 1733–1957. Atlanta, Protestant Episcopal Church in the Diocese of Atlanta [1960] xiv, 334 p. illus., plates.   BX5917.G4M3

"The Anglican church in colonial Georgia": p. [1]–49.

11273

Malone, Michael T. Sketches of the Anglican clergy who served in North Carolina during the period, 1765–1776. Historical magazine of the Protestant Episcopal church, v. 39, June, Dec. 1970: 137–161, 399–438.   BX5800.H5, v. 39

11274

Meade, William, Bp. Old churches, ministers, and families of Virginia. Philadelphia, J. B. Lippincott, 1857. 2 v. plates.   F225.M48

Micro 8973 F

Reprinted, together with *Wise's Digested Index and Genealogical Guide to Bishop Meade's Old Churches, Ministers, and Families of Virginia, Embracing 6,900 Personal Names,* compiled by Jennings C. Wise (Richmond, Va., Printed for subscribers, 1910. 114 p. F225.M494), in Baltimore by the Genealogical Pub Co. (1966).

An index to Meade compiled by J. M. Toner was issued in 1898 as a supplement to volume 2 of the *Publications* of the Southern History Association.

11275

Middleton, Arthur P. The colonial Virginia parish. Historical magazine of the Protestant Episcopal church, v. 40, Dec. 1970: 431–446.   BX5800.H5, v. 40

11276

Middleton, Arthur P. The colonial Virginia parson. William and Mary quarterly, 3d ser., v. 26, July 1969: 425–440.   F221.W71, 3d s., v. 26

11277

Petsworth Parish, *Va.* The vestry book of Petsworth Parish, Gloucester County, Virginia, 1677–1793. Transcribed, annotated, and indexed by C. G. Chamberlayne; published by the Library Board. Richmond, Division of Purchase and Print., 1933. xv, 429 p. facsims., fold. map.   F232.P45P4

11278

Prince Frederick Parish, *S.C.* The register book for the parish, Prince Frederick, Winyaw, Ann: Dom. 1713. Published by the National Society of the Colonial Dames of America. Baltimore, Williams & Wilkins Co., 1916. ix, 246 p. plan, plates.   F277.P95P9

Foreword signed: Elizabeth W. Allston Pringle.
Covers the period 1713–78.

11279
Rightmyer, Nelson W.   The Anglican church in Maryland: factors contributory to the American Revolution. Church history, v. 19, Sept. 1950: 187–198.
BR140.A45, v. 19

11280
Rightmyer, Nelson W.   The character of the Anglican clergy of colonial Maryland. Maryland historical magazine, v. 44, Dec. 1949: 229–250.   F176.M18, v. 44

11281
Rightmyer, Nelson W.   Maryland's established church. Baltimore, Church Historical Society for the diocese of Maryland, 1956. 239 p. [Church Historical Society (U.S.) Publication no. 45]   BX5917.M3R5

Bibliography: p. 225–231.
"Biographical sketches of the colonial clergy of Maryland's Established Church": p. [153]–221.
"Revolution and reconstruction": p. 113–132.

11282
Ruffin, Beverley.   Augusta Parish, Virginia, 1738–1780. Verona, Va., McClure Press [1970] vii, 71 p.
BX5917.V8R8

Bibliography: p. 56–58.

11283
St. Paul's Parish, *Hanover Co., Va.*   The vestry book of St. Paul's Parish, Hanover County, Virginia, 1706–1786. Transcribed and edited by C. G. Chamberlayne. Published by the Library Board. Richmond, Division of Purchase and Printing, 1940. xx, 672 p. facsims., fold. map.   BX5980.S3A3

11284
St. Peter's Parish, *New Kent Co., Va.*   The vestry book and register of St. Peter's Parish, New Kent and James City counties, Virginia, 1684–1786. Transcribed and edited by C. G. Chamberlayne; published by the Library Board. Richmond, Division of Purchase and Print., 1937. xxvi, 840 p. facsims., fold. map, plates.
F232.N3S4

11285
St. Stephen's Parish, *S.C.*   Minutes of the vestry of St. Stephen's Parish, South Carolina [1756–1802] Edited by Anne Allston Porcher. South Carolina historical and genealogical magazine, v. 45, July–Oct. 1944: 157–171, 217–221; v. 46, Jan 1945: 40–48.   F266.S55, v. 45–46

11286
Seiler, William H.   The Anglican parish in tidewater Virginia, 1607–1776. 1948.

Thesis (Ph.D.)—State University of Iowa.

11287
Stokes, Durward T.   Different concepts of government expressed in the sermons of two eighteenth century clergymen. Historical magazine of the Protestant Episcopal church, v. 40, Mar. 1971: 81–94.
BX5800.H5, v. 40

Concerns two North Carolinians—George Micklejohn, a Loyalist, and Adam Boyd, a proponent of republicanism.

11288
Stratton Major Parish, *Va.*   The vestry book of Stratton Major Parish, King and Queen County, Virginia, 1729–1783. Transcribed, annotated, and indexed by C. G. Chamberlayne; published by the Library Board. Richmond, Division of Purchase and Print., 1931. xxi, 257 p. facsims.   F232.K4S7

11289
Upper Parish, *Nansemond Co., Va.*   The vestry book of the Upper Parish, Nansemond County, Virginia, 1743–1793. Published by the Library Board of Virginia, Wilmer L. Hall, editor. Richmond, Commonwealth of Virginia Division of Purchase and Print., 1949 [i.e. 1950] lxxiv, 328 p.   F232.N2U6

b. Congregationalists

11290
Foster, Stephen.   A Connecticut separate church: strict Congregationalism in Cornwall, 1780–1809. New England quarterly, v. 39, Sept. 1966: 309–333.
F1.N62, v. 39

11291
Gambrell, Mary L.   Ministerial training in eighteenth-century New England. New York, Columbia University Press, 1937. 169 p. (Studies in history, economics and public law, no. 428)   H31.C7, no. 428
BV4033.G3 1937a

Issued also as thesis (Ph.D.)—Columbia University.
Bibliography: p. 148–159.
Reprinted in New York by AMS Press (1967).

Studies changes in the theory and practice of clerical education among Trinitarian Congregationalists from the Great Awakening of 1740 to the founding of Andover Theological Seminary in 1808. During the last half of the 18th century, young men were trained at college—Yale, Dartmouth, and Williams—or in "schools of the prophets," an arrangement whereby parish clergymen took students into their homes for instruction according to a general plan. Dissatisfaction with irregularities inherent in this dual system led to the development of professional seminaries.

11292
Hooker, Richard J.   The Mayhew controversy. Church history, v. 5, Sept. 1936: 239–255.   BR140.A45, v. 5

Concerns anti-Episcopal agitation among New England Congregationalists, 1763–65.

11293

Oberholzer, Emil. Delinquent saints; disciplinary action in the early Congregational churches of Massachusetts. New York, Columbia University Press, 1956, [ᶜ1955] x, 379 p. (Columbia studies in the social sciences, no. 590) H31.C7, no. 590

Bibliography: p. [337]–371.

Reprinted in New York by AMS Press (1968. BX7148.M402).

The author's thesis (Ph.D.), *Saints in Sin: a Study of the Disciplinary Action of the Congregational Churches of Massachusetts in the Colonial and Early National Periods*, was submitted to Columbia University in 1954 (Micro AC–1, no. 8748).

Basing his study on church records from more than 80 towns, the author provides examples of such sins committed as adultery, heresy, and bearing false witness and describes efforts of church officials to investigate alleged transgressions, obtain confessions, and punish offenders. Church discipline began to suffer after the Great Awakening, and the American Revolution so weakened traditions that apathy towards religious authority became apparent. Except for those involving absenteeism, the number of cases receiving attention from clergymen generally decreased, although the shift in emphasis from temperance to abstinence brought more complaints about alcoholism after 1770.

11294

Record of the transactions of the annual convention of [Congregational] ministers in the province of New Hampshire, 1747 to 1788. *In* New Hampshire Historical Society. Collections. v. 9. Concord, 1889. p. 1–67. F31.N54, v. 7

11295

Walsh, James P. The pure church: in eighteenth century Connecticut. 1967. ([293] p.) Micro AC–1, no. 67–14,104

Thesis (Ph.D.)—Columbia University.

Abstracted in *Dissertation Abstracts*, v. 28A, Nov. 1967, p. 1747.

c. Presbyterians

11296

Altfather, Alton B. Early Presbyterianism in Virginia. *In* Presbyterian Historical Society. Journal, v. 13, June 1929: 267–281. BX8905.P7A4, v. 13

11297

Anthony, Robert W. Schenectady, 1769–1775, as shown by the unpublished account book of the First Presbyterian Church. *In* New York State Historical Association. New York history, v. 13, Oct. 1932: 381–389. F116.N865, v. 13

On the building of the church with descriptions of the town.

11298

Baird, Charles W. Civil status of the Presbyterians in the province of New York. Magazine of American history, with notes and queries, v. 3, Oct. 1879: 593–628. E171.M18, v. 3

The effort to separate civil and church authority was realized in the Revolution.

11299

Baldwin, Alice M. Sowers of sedition: the political theories of some of the New Light Presbyterian clergy of Virginia and North Carolina. William and Mary quarterly, 3d ser., v. 5, Jan. 1948: 52–76. F221.W71, 3d s., v. 5

Basing their political convictions on the Bible rather than on natural law, southern clergymen popularized the doctrines upon which the Revolution would be fought by teaching that a God-given covenant between a ruler and his people could be abrogated in the face of tyranny.

11300

Boothbay, Me. Presbyterian Church. Sessional records of the Presbyterian church of Booth Bay, Maine, 1767–1778. Introductory note by Rev. Thomas C. Pears, Jr. *In* Presbyterian Historical Society. Journal, v. 16, Mar.–Dec. 1935: 203–240, 243–288, 308–336, 337–355. BX8905.P7A4, v. 16

11301

Breed, William P. Presbyterians and the Revolution. Philadelphia, Presbyterian Board of Publication [ᶜ1876] 205 p. E269.P9B8

11302

Brown, Katharine L. The role of Presbyterian dissent in colonial and Revolutionary Virginia, 1740–1785. 1969. ([437] p.) Micro AC–1, no. 60–13,488

Thesis (Ph.D.)—Johns Hopkins University.

Abstracted in *Dissertation Abstracts International*, v. 30A, Aug. 1969, p. 648.

11303

Funk, Henry D. The influence of the Presbyterian church in early American history. *In* Presbyterian Historical Society. Journal, v. 12, Apr. 1924: 26–63; Apr.–Oct. 1925: 152–189, 193–224; Apr. 1926: 281–316. BX8905.P7A4, v. 12

11304

Gillett, Ezra H. History of the Presbyterian church in the United States of America. Philadelphia, Presbyterian Publication Committee [1864] 2 v. BX8935.G5

Several chapters touch upon the state of the church during the Revolutionary period.

11305

Graham, James R. The planting of the Presbyterian church in northern Virginia, prior to the organization of Winchester presbytery, December 4, 1794. Winchester, Va., G. Norton Pub. Co., 1904. 168 p. BX8947.V8G7

11306

Hodge, Charles. The constitutional history of the Presbyterian church in the United States of America. Philadelphia, W. S. Martien, 1839–40. 2 v.

BX8936.H6 1839

Contents: pt. 1. 1705 to 1741.—pt. 2. 1741 to 1788. Reissued in one volume by the Presbyterian Board of Publication (Philadelphia [1851]).

11307

Hopkins, Samuel M. The period from the War of the Revolution to the adoption of the "Presbyterian form of government" (1786). *In* A Short history of American Presbyterianism from its foundations to the reunion of 1869. Philadelphia, Presbyterian Board of Publication and Sabbath-School Work, 1903. p. 65–142.

BX8935.S5

11308

Howe, George. History of the Presbyterian church in South Carolina. v. 1. Prepared by order of the Synod of South Carolina. Columbia, Duffie & Chapman, 1870. 709 p. BX8947.S6H8, v. 1

Reprinted in Columbia, S.C., by the Synod of South Carolina (1965. BX8947.S6H82).

Includes 18 chapters (p. 305–563) on the period 1760–90.

11309

Ingram, George H. The Presbytery of New Brunswick in the struggle for American independence. *In* Presbyterian Historical Society. Journal, v. 9, June 1917: 49–64. BX8905.P7A4, v. 9

11310

Klett, Guy S. Presbyterians in colonial Pennsylvania. Philadelphia, University of Pennsylvania Press, 1937. xi, 297 p. maps. BX8947.P4K5

"Bibliographical notes": p. 267–286.

Focusing on the distribution of settlers and the establishment and development of local congregations and presbyteries, the author analyzes the religious, social, and political influence of the Presbyterians on the frontier from 1720 to the eve of the Revolution. Klett concludes that in the absence of effective civil authority the sessions and presbyteries were significant institutions of social organization and control.

11311

Klett, Guy S. Some aspects of the Presbyterian church on the American colonial frontier [1706–1776] *In* Presbyterian Historical Society. Journal, v. 19, Sept. 1940: 110–126. BX8905.P7A4, v. 19

11312

Knapp, Shepherd. A history of the Brick Presbyterian Church in the city of New York. New York, Trustees of the Brick Presbyterian Church, 1909. xxii, 566 p. facsims., plans, plates, ports. F128.62.B8K6

Bibliography: p. [495]–510.

Chapters 2–5 (p. 17–72) deal with the period 1765–83.

11313

Kramer, Leonard J. Muskets in the pulpit, 1776–1783. *In* Presbyterian Historical Society. Journal, v. 31, Dec. 1953: 229–244; v. 32, Mar. 1954: 37–51.

BX8905.P7A4, v. 31–32

On the arguments of the Presbyterian clergy in support of Revolution, their agitation for the separation of church and state and their services as chaplains.

11314

Kramer, Leonard J. Presbyterians approach the American Revolution. *In* Presbyterian Historical Society. Journal, v. 31, June–Sept. 1953: 71–86, 167–180.

BX8905.P7A4, v. 31

11315

McKinney, William W. Early Pittsburgh Presbyterianism; tracing the development of the Presbyterian church, United States of America, in Pittsburgh, Pennsylvania, from 1758–1839. Pittsburgh, Pa., Gibson Press, 1938. 345 p. map, plates, ports. BX8949.P55M3 1936

Thesis (Ph.D)—University of Pittsburgh, 1936. Bibliography: p. 323–335.

Also published serially under the title "The Early Development of the Presbyterian Church in the United States of America in Pittsburgh" in the *Journal* of the Presbyterian Historical Society, v. 17, Mar./June–Sept./Dec. 1937, p. 207–295, 299–390, and v. 18, Mar./Sept. 1938, p. 3–136.

11316

McKinney, William W. The establishment of the Presbyterian church in Pittsburgh [1761–87] Western Pennsylvania historical magazine, v. 18, Sept. 1935: 177–188. F146.W52, v. 18

11317

Miller, Guy H. A contracting community: American Presbyterians, social conflict, and higher education, 1730–1820 (Volumes I and II). 1970 ([562] p.)

Micro AC–1, no. 71–15,239

Thesis (Ph.D.)—University of Michigan. Abstracted in *Dissertation Abstracts International*, v. 31A, June 1971, p. 6523.

Studies Presbyterian institutions of higher learning in order to detect changes in the denomination's attitude toward social conflict. Convinced that society ideally is an organic unit whose citizens must be taught to subordinate individual desire to the common good, Presbyterians looked upon Princeton and six schools established during the Revolutionary period—the antecedents of modern Dickinson College, Hampden-Sydney College, Transylvania College, Washington and Jefferson College, Washington and Lee University, and the University of North Carolina—as instruments of social reform and regeneration. Ultimately, however, the radical implications of the Revolution compelled Presbyterians to accept the inevitability of social discord in American society.

11318

Pears, Thomas C. Presbyterian expansion across the Alleghenies; a tale of vision and courage. *In* Presbyterian Historical Society. Journal, v. 29, Sept. 1951: 127–144. BX8905.P7A4, v. 29

11319

Pears, Thomas C. Presbyterians and American freedom. *In* Presbyterian Historical Society. Journal, v. 29, June 1951: 77–95. BX8905.P7A4, v. 29

On Presbyterian contributions to the Revolutionary movement.

11320

Posey, Walter B. The Presbyterian church in the Old Southwest, 1778–1838. Richmond, John Knox Press, 1952. 192 p. map (on lining papers) BX8941.P65

Bibliographic references included in "Notes" (p. [139]–185).

11321

Presbyterian Church in the U.S.A. The constitution of the Presbyterian church, in the United States of America. Containing, the confession of faith, the catechisms, the government and discipline, and the directory for the worship of God. Ratified and adopted by the synod of New-York and Philadelphia, held at Philadelphia, May the 16th, 1788, and continued by adjournments, until the 28th of the same month. Wilmington, Printed and sold by Bonsal and Niles, 1801. iv, 407 p.
BX8955.A3 1801 Rare Bk. Coll.

11322

Presbyterian Church in the U.S.A. Records of the Presbyterian church in the United States of America; embracing the minutes of the General Presbytery and General Synod, 1706–1788, together with an index. Philadelphia, Presbyterian Board of Publication and Sabbath-School Work, 1904. 582 p. BX8952.P73

Reprinted in New York by Arno Press (1969).

11323

Presbyterian Church in the U.S.A. *Presbyteries. New York.* Minutes of the presbytery of New York, 1775–1776. *In* New York State Historical Association. Quarterly journal, v. 1, Oct. 1919–Oct. 1920: 22–43, 48–49, 109–111, 178–188, 244–258. F116.N865, v. 1

Introduction and notes by Dixon Ryan Fox.

11324

Reports upon the early history of Presbyterian churches. *In* Presbyterian Historical Society. Journal, v. 2, June–Dec. 1904: 221–228, 310–315, 332–339; v. 3, Mar.–June 1905: 33–37, 86–95; v. 4, June, Dec. 1907: 62–64, 162–164. BX8905.P7A4, v. 2–4

Includes contemporary sketches of churches and congregations in Pennsylvania towns such as Neshaminy, Tinicum, Great Valley, Charleston, Fairfield, and Greenwich.

11325

Scott, Robert F. Colonial Presbyterianism in the valley of Virginia. *In* Presbyterian Historical Society. Journal, v. 35, June–Sept. 1957: 71–92, 171–192.
BX8905.P7A4, v. 35

11326

Sengel, William R. Rebellion in the meeting house. Virginia cavalcade, v. 14, summer 1964: 34–39. illus., port.
F221.V74, v. 14

A British traveler, Nicholas Cresswell, characterized Alexandria's Presbyterians as "liberty mad."

11327

Sharpless, Isaac. Presbyterian and Quaker in colonial Pennsylvania. *In* Presbyterian Historical Society. Journal, v. 3, Mar. 1906: 201–218. BX8905.P7A4, v. 3

11328

Slosser, Gaius J., *ed.* They seek a country; the American Presbyterians, some aspects. New York, Macmillan, 1955. xvi, 330 p. illus., ports. BX8935.S55

Bibliography: p. 322–324.

Partial contents: Beginnings in the North, by William W. McKinney.—Beginnings in the South, by Ernest T. Thompson.—The United Presbyterian church, by John H. Gerstner, Jr.—The Reformed Presbyterian church in America, by David M. Carson.—The founding of educational institutions, by William W. Sweet.—Service in founding and preserving the nation, by H. Gordon Harold.

11329

Smith, Elwyn A. The Presbyterian ministry in American culture, a study in changing concepts, 1700–1900. Philadelphia, Published for the Presbyterian Historical Society by Westminster Press [1962] 269 p. (Presbyterian Historical Society. Studies in Presbyterian history)
BX8936.S4

"Bibliographical comment": p. 256–264.

11330

Smylie, James H. Presbyterian clergy and problems of "dominion" in the Revolutionary generation. Journal of Presbyterian history, v. 48, fall 1970: 161–175.
BX8905.P7A4, v. 48

11331

Stokes, Durward T. The Presbyterian clergy in South Carolina and the American Revolution. South Carolina historical magazine, v. 71, Oct. 1970: 270–282.
F266.S55, v. 71

11332

Sweet, William W., *ed.* The Presbyterians, 1783–1840, a collection of source materials. New York, Harper, 1936. xii, 939 p. illus., maps. (*His* Religion on the American frontier, v. 2) BX8935.S75

Bibliography: p. 888–917.

Reprinted in New York by Cooper Square Publishers (1964).

"American Presbyterianism at the close of the Revolution": p. 3–20.

11333

Thompson, Ernest T. Presbyterians in the South. v. 1. 1607–1861. Richmond, John Knox Press [ᶜ1963] 629 p. map (on lining papers)　　　BX8941.T5, v. 1

Bibliography: p. [597]–608.

11334

Trinterud, Leonard J. The forming of an American tradition, a re-examination of colonial Presbyterianism. Philadelphia, Westminster Press [1949] 352 p.
　　　BX8936.T7

Bibliography: p. [309]–320.

Reprinted in Freeport, N.Y., by Books for Libraries Press (1970).

Traces the doctrinal and organizational disputes between the controlling Scotch-Irish group and the New Side revivalists within the Presbyterian church. The Great Awakening brought into the church a large number of laity who sympathized with the Log College party, led by the Tennents, and their influence became central for the next 40 years. Trinterud discusses the contributions of the church to the Revolution, its social and missionary activities, and its resistance to the threat of Anglican establishment. He concludes that despite a conservative reaction in the early 19th century, the founding of the General Assembly in 1788 marked the success of the revivalists—who emphasized practical piety—in transforming colonial Presbyterianism into a distinctly American institution.

11335

Trinterud, Leonard J. The New England contribution to colonial American Presbyterianism. Church history, v. 17, Mar. 1948: 32–43.　　　BR140.A45, v. 17

11336

Trinterud, Leonard J. Presbyterianism in colonial New England. *In* Presbyterian Historical Society. Journal, v. 27, Mar. 1949: 1–20.　　　BX8905.P7A4, v. 27

11337

Vass, Lachlan C. History of the Presbyterian church in New Bern, N.C., with a resumé of early ecclesiastical affairs in eastern North Carolina, and a sketch of the early days of New Bern, N.C. Richmond, Va., Whittet & Shepperson, Printers, 1886. 196 p. illus., plan, plates, ports.　　　F264.N5V3
　　　BX9211.N43V3

11338

Willtown, S.C. Willtown Presbyterian Church. Records of the Willtown Presbyterian Church [1753–1841] South Carolina historical magazine, v. 62, Jan.–July 1961: 33–50, 107–112, 172–181.　　　F266.S55, v. 62

d. Baptists

11339

Backus, Isaac. A history of New-England, with particular reference to the denomination of Christians called Baptists . . . Collected from the most authentic records and writings, both ancient and modern. By Isaac Backus, pastor of the First Baptist Church in Mid[d]leborough. Boston, Printed by E. Draper at his Print.-Off. in Newbury-Street; and sold by P. Freeman, in Union-Street, 1777–96. 3 v.
　　　BX6239.B3 1777 Rare Bk. Coll.

Title and imprint vary: v. 2: *A Church History of New-England . . . Extending From 1690, to 1784. Including a Concise View of the American War, and of the Conduct of the Baptists Therein, With the Present State of Their Churches* (Providence, Printed by J. Carter, and sold by P. Freeman, in Union-Street, Boston, 1784); v. 3: *A Church History of New-England, Extending From 1783 to 1796. Containing an Account of the Religious Affairs of the Country, and of the Oppressions Therein on Religious Accounts; With a Particular History of the Baptist Churches in the Five States of New-England* (Boston, Printed by Manning & Loring, Sold by S. Hall, No. 53, Cornhill, and by Manning & Loring, in Spring Lane, 1796).

Appended to v. 1 are three tracts by Backus: *Policy, as Well as Honesty* (1779); *Government and Liberty Described* (1778); and *The Substance of an Address to an Assembly in Bridgewater* (1779).

A second edition, with notes by David Weston, was published in Newton, Mass., by the Backus Historical Society (1871. 2 v.) and has been reprinted in one volume in New York by Arno Press (1969).

11340

Benedict, David. A general history of the Baptist denomination in America, and other parts of the world. Boston, Printed by Lincoln & Edmands, no. 53, Cornhill, for the author, 1813. 2 v.　　　BX6231.B4 1813

Reprinted in Freeport, N.Y., by Books for Libraries Press (1971).

11341

Cathcart, William. The Baptist and the American Revolution. Published for the author. Philadelphia, S. A. George, 1876. 118 p. illus., plates, port.
　　　E269.B2C3

Bibliography: p. 117–118.

11342

Howell, Robert B. C. The early Baptists of Virginia. Philadelphia, Bible and Publication Society [1876?] 246 p.
　　　BX6248.V8H7 1876

11343

Little, Lewis P. Imprisoned preachers and religious liberty in Virginia, a narrative drawn largely from the official records of Virginia counties, unpublished manuscripts, letters, and other original sources. Lynchburg, Va., J. P. Bell Co., 1938. xix, 534 p. illus., facsims., map.
　　　BX6248.V8L5

On the persecution of Baptists in Virginia during the decade 1760–70.

11344

McLoughlin, William G. The Balkcom Case (1782) and the pietistic theory of separation of church and state. William and Mary quarterly, 3d ser., v. 24, Apr. 1967: 267–283.   F221.W71, 3d s., v. 24

A significant test case in the Baptists' fight for disestablishment in Massachusetts.

11345

McLoughlin, William G. The first Calvinistic Baptist association in New England, 1754?–1767. Church history, v. 36, Dec. 1967: 410–418.   BR140.A45, v. 36

11346

McLoughlin, William G. Massive civil disobedience as a Baptist tactic in 1773. American quarterly, v. 21, winter 1969: 710–727.   AP2.A3985, v. 21

11347

McLoughlin, William G. Mob violence against dissent in Revolutionary Massachusetts. Foundations, v. 14, Oct./Dec. 1971: 294–317.   BX6201.C572, v. 14

Concerns mob attacks on Baptist meetings in Pepperell in 1778 and Hingham in 1782.

11348

McLoughlin, William G. New England dissent, 1630–1833; the Baptists and the separation of church and state. Cambridge, Mass., Harvard University Press, 1971. 2 v. (xxiii, 1324 p.)   BX6239.M25

"Bibliographical essay": p. 1285–1294.

An exhaustive study of the struggle for toleration and religious liberty that includes sections or chapters on such topics as the Separatist and Separate-Baptist movements from 1740 to 1777, the controversies over the founding of Rhode Island College (Brown University) and the Warren Baptist Association, the exemption of Massachusetts Baptists from civil taxation under Certificate laws, the Baptists and the Massachusetts Constitution of 1780, and the events surrounding disestablishment in Vermont, New Hampshire, Connecticut, and finally Massachusetts. Baptists resorted to civil disobedience in 1773–74 against the Congregational majority in Massachusetts, protesting unfair administration of the exemption statutes but inadvertently contributing to a dilemma they would face in 1776. They regarded the crown as their best ally against the Congregationalists, yet as dissenters they had a high regard for civil liberties. Loyalists courted them and a few remained neutral, but most Baptist clergymen and laymen eventually supported the Revolutionary cause with enthusiasm.

11349

Maring, Norman H. Baptists in New Jersey; a study in transition. Valley Forge [Pa.] Judson Press [1964] 379 p. illus., map, ports.   BX6248.N5M3

"Bibliographical note": p. 369–370.
"Revivals and revolution": p. 44–77.

11350

Monroe, James L. Baptists in the period of the American Revolution. Quarterly review, v. 14, Apr./June 1954: 46–55.   BX6201.Q3, v. 14

11351

Paschal, George W. History of North Carolina Baptists. v. 1. 1663–1805. Raleigh, General Board, North Carolina Baptist State Convention, 1930. ix, 572 p. illus., map.   BX6248.N8P3

Bibliographic footnotes.
"The Baptists in the Revolution": p. [446]–[473]

11352

Primitive Baptists. *North Carolina. Kehukee Primitive Baptist Association.* Minutes of the Kehukey Association (Baptist) [1769–77], with letter of Joel Battle Fort, and with introduction and notes by Kemp Plummer Battle. [Chapel Hill, N.C.] The University, 1904. 32 p. (The James Sprunt historical monographs, no. 5)
                  F251.J28, no. 5
                  BX6384.N62K4

11353

Ryland, Garnett. The Baptists of Virginia, 1699–1926. Richmond, Virginia Baptist Board of Missions and Education, 1955. 372 p. map (on lining papers)

"Sources": p. 345–353.

Includes five chapters (p. [9]–121) on the period 1743–87.

11354

Semple, Robert B. A history of the rise and progress of the Baptists in Virginia. Richmond, Published by the author, John O'Lynch, Printer, 1810. vii, 446 p.
                  BX6248.V8S4

An edition revised and extended by George W. Beale (Richmond, Va., Pitt and Dickinson, 1894. 536 p.) has been reprinted, with a preface by Joe M. King, in Cottonport, La., by Polyanthos (1972).

11355

Shurden, Walter B. The development of Baptist associations in America, 1707–1814. Baptist history and heritage, v. 4, Jan. 1969: 31–39.   BX6207.A407, v. 4

11356

Stokes, Durward T. The Baptist and Methodist clergy in South Carolina and the American Revolution. South Carolina historical magazine, v. 73, Apr. 1972: 87–96.
                  F266.S55, v. 73

11357

Taylor, James B. Virginia Baptist ministers. With an introduction, by Rev. J. B. Jeter. New York, Sheldon, 1860. 2 v.   BX6248.V8T3, ser. 1–2 1860

First published in 1837, in one volume, under the title *Lives of Virginia Baptist Ministers.* This edition, varying only in imprint from the third edition, published in 1859, contains in the "first series" a revised version of most of the original sketches, and in the "second series," new material.

11358
Thom, William T. The struggle for religous freedom in Virginia: the Baptists. Baltimore, Johns Hopkins Press, 1900. 96 p. fold. map. (Johns Hopkins University studies in historical and political science. Ser. 18, no. 10/12)   H31.J6, s. 18, no. 10/12

Bibliography: p. 94–96.

11359
Townsend, Leah. South Carolina Baptists, 1670–1805. Florence, S.C., Florence Print. Co., 1935. 391 p. fold. map.   BX6248.S6T6

Bibliography: p. 306–325.
The author's thesis (Ph.D.), *Baptists in South Carolina,* was submitted to the University of South Carolina in 1926.

Divides the state into four parts—Charleston, the low country, the Peedee and the back country—and recounts the founding and development of Baptist churches and associations in each section. In separate chapters on the post-Revolutionary revival and the significance of the Baptist movement in South Carolina, Townsend reports that out of a total population of 249,073 in 1790 there were 67 churches, with 91 ministers, ordained preachers, or itinerants, and 3,878 communicants representing a membership of about 19,000 persons.

11360
Wroth, L. Kinvin. The Rev. Nathaniel Green and the tax assessors; passive resistance in eighteenth-century Massachusetts. New-England galaxy, v. 9, fall 1967: 15–21. illus.   F1.N39, v. 9

On Green's successful suit against Worcester County tax assessors in 1769, establishing the principle that Baptist ministers enjoyed the same freedom from local taxation as the "settled" clergy of Massachusetts.

e. Methodists

11361
Armour, Robert A. The opposition to the Methodist church in eighteenth-century Virginia. 1968. ([163] p.)   Micro AC-1, no. 69–3438

Thesis (Ph.D.)—University of Georgia.
Abstracted in *Dissertation Abstracts,* v. 29A, Feb. 1969, p. 2783.

11362
Atkinson, John. The beginnings of the Wesleyan movement in America and the establishment therein of Methodism. New York, Hunt & Eaton, 1896. x, 458 p.   BX8235.A8

Focuses on the missionary activities of Richard Boardman and Joseph Pilmore and culminates with the Philadelphia Conference of 1773.

11363
Baker, Frank. American Methodism: beginnings and ends. Methodist history, v. 6, Apr. 1968: 3–15.   BX8235.M44, v. 6

On the more important goals of early Methodism—piety, evangelism, warmhearted worship, fellowship, discipline, lay leadership, and community service.

11364
Baker, Frank. The beginnings of American Methodism. Methodist history, v. 2, Oct. 1963: 1–15.   BX8235.M44, v. 2

11365
Baker, Frank. Early American Methodism: a key document. Methodist history, v. 3, Jan. 1965: 3–15.   BX8235.M44, v. 3

Includes the text of a letter, dated April 11, 1768, from Thomas Taylor, an English clergyman visiting New York, to John Wesley. Baker contends that the letter finally compelled Wesley to launch an organized crusade to recruit men and money for America.

11366
Bangs, Nathan. A history of the Methodist Episcopal church. v. 1. From the year 1766 to the year 1792. New-York, Published by T. Mason and G. Lane, for the Methodist Episcopal church, 1838. 371 p. illus.   BX8235.B35, 1838, v. 1

11367
Barclay, Wade C. Early American Methodism, 1769–1844. New York, Board of Missions and Church Extension of the Methodist Church, 1949–50. 2 v. maps. (History of Methodist missions, pt. 1)   BV2550.B33, v. 1–2

"References and notes": v. 1, p. [359]–407; v. 2, p. [461]–511. Bibliography: v. 2, p. 515–539.
Contents: v. 1. Missionary motivation and expansion.—v. 2. To reform the nation.

After reviewing the Wesleyan heritage, the author examines in volume 1 British missionary activities in America, the Great Awakening, the missionary work of Thomas Coke, and American missions to Nova Scotia and Canada. In volume 2 Barclay adopts a topical approach and makes scattered references to the 18th century in sections on Methodist clergy, church organization, and practices and beliefs as well as on the social concerns of the church—attitudes toward slavery, Sunday school for the poor, and the services of the circuit riders. Excerpts from contemporary sources are included in both volumes.

11368
Bennett, William W. Memorials of Methodism in Virginia, from its introduction into the state, in the year 1772, to the year 1829. Richmond, 1871. 741 p. port.   BX8248.V8B4

11369
Dawson, Henry B. The early Methodists and the American Revolution. Historical magazine, v. 10, Dec. 1866: 361–368.   E171.H64, v. 10

11370
Grissom, William L. History of Methodism in North Carolina, from 1772 to the present time. v. 1. From the

introduction of Methodism in North Carolina to the year 1805. Nashville, Tenn., Pub. House of the M. E. Church, South, Smith & Lamar, Agents, 1905. xviii, 373 p. fold. map, plates, ports.   BX8248.N8G8, v. 1

11371
Harvey, Marvin E.   The Wesleyan movement and the American Revolution. 1962. ([409] p.)
Micro AC–1, no. 63–3118

Thesis (Ph.D.)—University of Washington.
Abstracted in *Dissertation Abstracts*, v. 24, July 1963, 266–267.

11372
Hedges, John W., *comp.*   Crowned victors; the memoirs of over four hundred Methodist preachers, including the first two hundred and fifty who died on this continent. Baltimore, Methodist Episcopal Book Depository, 1878. xxiii, 630 p.   BX8491.H4

Includes some biographical information on 69 clergymen admitted to the ministry before 1790.

11373
The History of American Methodism.   Editorial Board: Emory Stevens Bucke, general editor [and others] New York, Abingdon Press [1964] 3 v. illus., facsims., ports.
BX8235.H5

Includes bibliographies.

Volume 1 includes chapters on Methodism in colonial America (p. 74–144), by J. Manning Potts and Arthur B. Moss; Methodism and the Revolution (p. 145–184), by Coen G. Pierson; and the formation of the Methodist Episcopal church (p. 185–232), by Norman W. Spellmann.

11374
Hughes, Nathaniel C.   The Methodist Christmas Conference: Baltimore, December 24, 1784–January 2, 1785. Maryland historical magazine, v. 54, Sept. 1959: 272–292.   F176.M18, v. 54

11375
Lednum, John.   A history of the rise of Methodism in America. Containing sketches of Methodist itinerant preachers, from 1736 to 1785. Also, a short account of many hundreds of the first race of lay members, male and female, from New York to South Carolina. Together with an account of many of the first societies and chapels. Philadelphia, 1862. xxiv, 434 p. plates, port.   BX8236.L4 1862

First published in 1859.

11376
May, James W.   From revival movement to denomination: a re-examination of the beginnings of American Methodism [1765–1808] 1962. ([378] p.)
Micro AC–1, no. 65–7379

Thesis (Ph.D.)—Columbia University.
Abstracted in *Dissertation Abstracts*, v. 26, Dec. 1965, p. 3283–3284.

11377
Moats, Francis I.   The rise of Methodism in the Middle West. Mississippi Valley historical review, v. 15, June 1928: 69–88.   E171.J87, v. 15

Offers some information on early Methodist activities from the establishment of the first class in New York City in 1766.

11378
Smith, Warren Thomas.   Attempts at Methodist and Moravian union [1785–86] Methodist history, v. 8, Jan. 1970: 36–48.   BX8235.M44, v. 8

11379
Smith, Warren Thomas.   The Christmas conference. Methodist history, v. 6, July 1968: 3–27.
BX8235.M44, v. 6

Concerns the conference held in Baltimore Dec. 24, 1784–Jan. 2, 1785, that established the Methodist Episcopal Church in America.

11380
Sweet, William W.   Men of zeal; the romance of American Methodist beginnings. New York, Abingdon Press [ᶜ1935] 208 p. [Drew lectureship in biography]
BX8236.S85

Bibliography: p. 203–208.

An appraisal of the principal leaders of the early Methodist movement and the founders of the Methodist Episcopal church.

11381
Sweet, William W.   Methodism in American history. Revision of 1953. Nashville, Abingdon Press [1954] 472 p. illus., facsims., plates, ports.   BX8235.S9 1953

Bibliography: p. 436–451.
First edition published in 1933.

In the first third of the work the author discusses the effect of Wesleyism on the religious climate of 18th-century America and the spread of Methodism along the eastern seaboard from the arrival of the first preachers in 1769 to the establishment of the Methodist Episcopal church in 1784. He also considers the work of Francis Asbury and Richard Wright as well as the controversy created by John Wesley's Toryism and the publication in 1775 of his *Calm Address*. Sweet includes some introductory material and documents relating to the period in *The Methodists, a Collection of Source Materials* (New York, Cooper Square Publishers, 1964. 800 p. BX8235.S92 1964), the fourth volume in his series Religion on the American Frontier, 1783–1840.

11382
Sweet, William W.   New light on the relations of early American Methodism to the Anglican clergy in Virginia and North Carolina. Historical magazine of the Protestant Episcopal church, v. 22, Mar. 1953: 69–90.
BX5800.H5, v. 22

Includes the texts of eight letters by such clergymen as Devereux Jarratt, Caleb Pedicord, and Charles Pettigrew, dated 1782–92, from the Dromgoole and Pettigrew papers at the University of North Carolina.

11383
Sweet, William W.   Virginia Methodism, a history. Richmond, Whittet & Shepperson [1955] xvii, 427 p. illus., maps (on lining papers)   BX8248.V8S9

Bibliographic footnotes.

The first six chapters (p. 1–141) cover the period to 1800.

11384
Vickers, John A.   Coke and Asbury: a comparison of bishops. Methodist history, v. 11, Oct. 1972: 42–51.
BX8235.M44, v. 11

11385
Wakeley, Joseph B.   Lost chapters recovered from the early history of American Methodism. With a memoir of the author by Rev. William E. Ketcham. New York, W. B. Ketcham [1889] viii, 635 p. illus., facsim., plates, ports.   BX8236.W3 1889

First published in 1858.

On the Methodist Episcopal church in New York City and especially the founding of the John Street Methodist Church.

f. Society of Friends (Quakers)

11386
Anscombe, Francis C.   I have called you Friends; the story of Quakerism in North Carolina. Boston, Christopher Pub. House [1959] 407 p. illus., plan, ports.
BX7648.N8A6

Bibliography: p. 381–386.

11387
Applegarth, Albert C.   Quakers in Pennsylvania. Baltimore, Johns Hopkins Press, 1892. 84 p. (Johns Hopkins University studies in historical and political science, 10th ser., no. 8–9)   H31.J6, 10th s., no. 8–9
F153.A66

Discusses Quaker laws and customs, 1682–1776, and the attitude of the sect toward Indians and slavery.

11388
Archer, Adair P.   The Quaker's attitude towards the Revolution. William and Mary College historical quarterly magazine, 2d ser., v. 1, July 1921: 167–182.
F221.W71, 2d s., v. 1

11389
Bauman, Richard.   For the reputation of truth; politics, religion, and conflict among the Pennsylvania Quakers, 1750–1800. Baltimore, Johns Hopkins Press [1971] xviii, 258 p.   BX7648.P4B38 1971

Bibliography: p. 249–254.

The author's thesis (Ph.D.), *For the Reputation of Truth: Quaker Political Behavior in Pennsylvania, 1750–*

1800, was submitted to the University of Pennsylvania in 1968 (Micro AC–1, no. 69–5607).

Combining the methods of anthropology and history, the author identifies three modes of adjustment employed by the Friends to reconcile the conflict between their religious tenets and their participation in politics following the Great Refusal of 1756. Such reformers as Anthony Benezet withdrew from worldly affairs and attempted to reestablish the religious purity of the Society—an act that Bauman regards as political in itself. Politicians like Thomas Mifflin, on the other hand, reached a worldly compromise and subordinated piety to the acquisition of power. A third group, whom Bauman calls *politiques*, pursued political ends outside of formal government while attempting to maintain their ideals, thus creating tension between their secular and religious roles. Eventually, most *politiques*, like James Pemberton, joined the reformers in movements for social betterment, beginning with the abolition of the slave trade.

11390
Bowden, James.   The history of the Society of Friends in America. New York, Arno Press, 1972. 2 v. in 1. illus., facsims., maps (part fold.) (Religion in America, ser. 2)
BX7635.B6 1972

Reprint of the 1850–54 ed.
"Difficulties of Friends during the War of American Independence": p. 295–349.

11391
Brock, Peter.   Pioneers of the peaceable kingdom. Princeton, N.J., Princeton University Press [1970, ʿ1968] xvi, 383 p.   BX7635.B76

Bibliography: p. 359–373.

Consists of chapters relating to the Society of Friends taken from the author's more extensive book, *Pacifism in the United States* (entry 11079).
"Quakers in the American Revolution": p. 141–216.

11392
Cadbury, Henry J.   Intercolonial solidarity of American Quakerism. Pennsylvania magazine of history and biography, v. 60, Oct. 1936: 362–374.
F146.P65, v. 60

Quaker unity was essential for the survival of the sect during the Revolution.

11393
Carroll, Kenneth L.   Joseph Nichols and the Nicholites of Caroline County, Maryland. Maryland historical magazine, v. 45, Mar. 1950: 47–61. F176.M18, v. 45

11394
Carroll, Kenneth L.   More about the Nicholites. Maryland historical magazine, v. 46, Dec. 1951: 278–289.
F176.M18, v. 46

11395
Carroll, Kenneth L.   The Nicholites become Quakers: an example of unity in disunion. *In* Friends Historical Association. Bulletin, v. 47, spring 1958: 3–19.
BX7635.A1F6, v. 47

11396

Carroll, Kenneth L. The Nicholites of North Carolina [1775–1800] North Carolina historical review, v. 31, Oct. 1954: 453–462.   F251.N892, v. 31

Founded by Joseph Nichols (c. 1730–c. 1774), the sect was often called the New Quakers.

11397

Carroll, Kenneth L. Quakerism on the Eastern Shore. [Baltimore] Maryland Historical Society [1970] xi, 328 p. illus.   BX7649.E3C3

Bibliography: p. 287–292.

Includes four chapters (p. 59–144) on Quaker life in the 18th century.

11398

A Collection of memorials concerning divers deceased ministers and others of the people called Quakers, in Pennsylvania, New-Jersey, and parts adjacent, from nearly the first settlement thereof to the year 1787. With some of the last expressions and exhortations of many of them. Philadelphia, Printed by Crukshank, 1787. vii, 439 p.   BX7791.C6 Rare Bk Coll.

11399

Forbes, Susan M. "As many candles lighted": the New Garden Monthly Meeting, 1718–1774. 1972. ([175] p.)   Micro AC–1, no. 73–13,401

Thesis (Ph.D.)—University of Pennsylvania.
Abstracted in *Dissertation Abstracts International,* v. 33A, June 1973, p. 6837–6838.

11400

Frost, Jerry W. The Quaker family in colonial America: a social history of the Society of Friends. 1968. ([533] p.)   Micro AC–1, no. 68–17,894

Thesis (Ph.D.)—University of Wisconsin.
Abstracted in *Dissertation Abstracts,* v. 29A, June 1969, p. 4403.

11401

[Gilpin, Thomas] *ed.* Exiles in Virginia: with observations on the conduct of the Society of Friends during the Revolutionary War, comprising the official papers of the government relating to that period. 1777–1778. Philadelphia, Published for the subscribers [C. Sherman, Printer] 1848. 302 p. fold. facsims.   E269.F8G4

By order of the Pennsylvania council, 20 prisoners, 17 of them Quakers, were removed to Virginia on suspicion of being "disaffected or dangerous to the United States."
"Journal and transactions of the exiles, citizens of Philadelphia, sent to Winchester, Virginia, from 2d September, 1777, to 30 April, 1778": p. [65]–233.

11402

Given, Lois V. Burlington County Friends in the American Revolution. *In* New Jersey Historical Society. Proceedings, v. 69, July 1951: 196–211.   F131.N58, v. 69

11403

Grubb, Israel. Quakerism and home life: an eighteenth century study. *In* Children of light, in honor of Rufus M. Jones. Edited by Howard H. Brinton. New York, Macmillan Co., 1938. p. [277]–303.   BX7615.C53

11404

Hershberger, Guy F. Pacifism and the state in colonial Pennsylvania. Church history, v. 8, Mar. 1939: 54–74.   BR140.A45, v. 8

On the dilemmas faced by Quaker pacifists.

11405

James, Sydney V. The impact of the American Revolution on Quakers' ideas about their sect. William and Mary quarterly, 3d ser., v. 19, July 1962: 360–382.   F221.W71, 3d s., v. 19

11406

James, Sydney V. A people among peoples; Quaker benevolence in eighteenth-century America. Cambridge, Harvard University Press, 1963. xv, 405 p.   BX7747.J3

Bibliographic references included in "Sources" and "Notes" (p. 337-397).

Concentrating upon the period between 1750 and the end of the Revolutionary War, the author traces the changes in the Friends' attitudes—from a condescending neighborliness to a genuine humanitarian concern for the welfare of non-Quakers—in several broad areas, including Indian relations, pacifism, and the condition of Negroes. After their fall from public power, Quakers, especially the wealthy who wished to maintain their preeminent position, turned increasingly to philanthropy. With the onset of war, Friends responded to attacks upon their pacifism by doing good and by rededicating their society to pious living, thus offering Americans a reservoir of spiritual, rather than military, strength.

11407

James, Sydney V. Quaker "charity" before the American Revolution. *In* Friends' Historical Association. Bulletin, v. 50, autumn 1961: 82–95. BX7635.A1F6, v. 50

11408

Jones, Rufus M. The Quakers in the American colonies, by Rufus M. Jones, assisted by Issac Sharpless and Amelia M. Gummere. London, Macmillan, 1911. xxxii, 603 p. fold. maps.   E184.F89J7

Reprinted in New York by Russell & Russell (1962).

Traces the expansion of the group between 1656 and 1780, especially in Pennsylvania, New York, and New Jersey during the early 18th century. The authors include a chapter on the problems of Friends who refused to support either side during the Revolution.

11409

Kobrin, David R. The saving remnant: intellectual sources of change and decline in colonial Quakerism, 1690–1810. 1968. ([350] p.)   Micro AC–1, no. 69–5637

Thesis (Ph.D.)—University of Pennsylvania. Abstracted in *Dissertation Abstracts*, v. 29A, Apr. 1969, p. 3558.

11410
Marietta, Jack D. Ecclesiastical discipline in the Society of Friends (in Pennsylvania), 1682–1776. 1968. ([221] p.)
Micro AC–1, no. 69–9223

Thesis (Ph.D.)—Stanford University.
Abstracted in *Dissertation Abstracts*, v. 29A, May 1969, p. 3956.

11411
Mekeel, Arthur J. Free Quaker movement in New England during the American Revolution. *In* Friends Historical Association. Bulletin, v. 27, autumn 1938: 72–82.
BX7635.A1F6, v. 27

11412
Mekeel, Arthur J. New England Quakers and military service in the American Revolution. *In* Children of light, in honor of Rufus M. Jones. Edited by Howard H. Brinton. New York, Macmillan Co., 1938. p. [241]–265.
BX7615.C53

11413
Mekeel, Arthur J. The Society of Friends and the American Revolution. 1940.

Thesis (Ph.D.)—Harvard University.

11414
New York Quakers in the American Revolution. *In* Friends' Historical Association. Bulletin, v. 29, spring 1940: 47–55.
BX7635.A1F6, v. 29

Consists of a report by New York Quakers to Irish historian John Gough on their experiences during the Revolution. Introduction and notes by Arthur J. Mekeel.

11415
Radbill, Kenneth A. Socioeconomic background of non-pacifist Quakers during the American Revolution. 1971. ([149] p.)
Micro AC–1, no. 71–28,659

Thesis (Ph.D.)—University of Arizona.
Abstracted in *Dissertation Abstracts International*, v. 32A, Nov. 1971, p. 2616.

11416
Sharpless, Isaac. The Quakers in the Revolution. Haverford ed. Philadelphia, T. S. Leach [c1900] 299 p. plates, ports. (*His* A history of Quaker government in Pennsylvania, v. 2)
F152.S53, v. 2

First published in 1899.

Presenting extensive quotations from their letters, the author recounts the activities between 1754 and 1780 of those who were friends of liberty but opposed to war. The Quakers supported such early resistance measures as the nonimportation agreements, but they broke with the Revolutionaries over independence and declared their neutrality. Sharpless appends an account of the Free Quakers—those who were ostracized because they took up arms—and describes Quaker opposition to slavery in the late 18th century.

11417
Thorne, Dorothy G. North Carolina Friends and the Revolution. North Carolina historical review, v. 38, July 1961: 323–340.
F251.N892, v. 38

11418
Tolles, Frederick B. Quakers and the Atlantic culture. New York, Macmillan, 1960. xiii, 160 p.
BX7631.2.T6

Bibliographic references included in "Notes" (p. 135–156).

In seven essays on Quaker contributions to Western civilization in the 17th and 18th centuries, the author discusses in turn Quaker attitudes toward politics, capitalism, science, and the arts and concludes with two chapters on Philadelphia Quakers and the Great Awakening and Quaker culture in early Pennsylvania.

11419
Wetherill, Charles. Free Quakers in the Revolution. American monthly magazine. v. 5, Nov. 1894: 409–429.
E202.5.A12, v. 5

11420
Woody, Thomas. Quaker education in the colony and state of New Jersey; a source book. Philadelphia, Published by the author, University of Pennsylvania, 1923. xii, 408 p. illus., facsims., map.
LA331.W6

Bibliography: p. 378–391.
Reprinted in New York by Arno Press (1969).

g. Roman Catholics

11421
Baisnée, Jules A. France and the establishment of the American Catholic hierarchy; the myth of French interference (1783–1784). Baltimore, Johns Hopkins Press, 1934. ix, 182 p. port.
BX1406.B3

Bibliography: p. 181–182.

Transcriptions of the documents on which the study is based are given at the end of chapters 2–5. Chapter 6 is devoted to historiographical analysis of the works of six church historians who have previously dealt with the topic. An extended review of Baisnée's work, by Maurice Casenave, appeared in *Revue d'histoire diplomatique*, 48. année, oct./déc. 1934, p. 477–498, and 49. année, jan./mars 1935, p. 67–84.

11422
Baisnée, Jules A. The myth of the "French scheme for the enslavement of American Catholics" (1783–1784). Catholic historical review, v. 19, Jan. 1934: 437–459.
BX1404.C3, v. 19

Refutes earlier views that the French government and hierarchy interfered in the negotiations that led to the appointment of John Carroll as Prefect-Apostolic of the American missions on June 9, 1784.

11423

Blied, Benjamin J. Catholic aspects of the American Revolution. Salesianum, v. 4, Apr. 1949: 49–58.

BX915.S17, v. 44

11424

Carthy, Mary Peter, *Mother*. English influences on early American Catholicism. Washington, Catholic University of America Press, 1959. viii, 147 p. (Catholic University of America. Studies in American church history, v. 44)

BX1406.C26

Thesis—Catholic University of America.

Bibliographic footnotes.

Chapter 2 (p. 26–57), "Genesis of an American Catholic Tradition [1774–90]," largely concerns the early career of John Carroll.

11425

Curran, Francis X. Catholics in colonial law. Chicago, Loyola University Press [1963] vii, 129 p.

KF4869.C2C8

"Collections of documents": p. 127–129.

Includes selections from 16 documents (p. 109–125), mostly excerpts from early state constitutions, that indicate the legal status of Catholics during the Revolutionary period.

11426

Documents relative to the adjustment of the Roman Catholic organization in the United States to the conditions of national independence, 1783–1789. American historical review, v. 15, July 1910: 800–829.

E171.A57, v. 15

Introduction and notes by Carl R. Fish.

11427

Durkin, Joseph T. Catholic training for Maryland Catholics, 1773–1786. *In* United States Catholic Historical Society. Historical records and studies. v. 32. New York, 1941. p. 70–82. E184.C3U5, v. 32

Includes the texts of letters written by Monica, Elizabeth, and Theresa Hagan of Maryland, who were then nuns in various communities in Europe.

11428

Ellis, John T. Catholics in colonial America. American ecclesiastical review, v. 136, Jan.–May 1957: 11–27, 100–119, 184–196, 265–274, 304–321.

BX801.E3, v. 136

11429

Ellis, John T. Catholics in colonial America. Baltimore, Helicon [1965] 486 p. (Benedictine studies, v. 8)

BX1406.2.E39

Bibliographic footnotes.

In his account of Spanish, French, and English missions to the territory that later became the United States, the author includes chapters on the Revolutionary generation and on the first American bishop, John Carroll.

11430

Ellis, John T., *ed.* Documents of American Catholic history. [2d ed] Milwaukee, Bruce Pub. Co. [1962] xxii, 667 p. BX1405.E4 1962

Includes bibliographic references.

First edition published in 1956.

For the Revolutionary period, the compiler presents 20 documents ranging from Ferdinand Farmer's rejection of the plan for an American bishop to the proposal for the establishment of the first Catholic college at George Town, Md.

11431

Fish, Carl R., *comp.* Documents relative to the adjustment of the Roman Catholic organization in the United States to the conditions of national independence, 1783–1789. American historical review, v. 15, July 1910: 800–829.

E171.A57, v. 15

———— ———— Offprint. [New York, 1910] [799]–829 p. BX1402.F5

The documents, in Italian and French, are taken from "the archives of the Propaganda at Rome."

11432

Griffin, Martin I. J. The anti-Catholic spirit of the Revolution. American Catholic historical researches, v. 6, Oct. 1889: 146–178. E184.C3A5, v. 6

11433

Griffin, Martin I. J. Catholics and the American Revolution. Ridley Park, Pa., The author, 1907–11. 3 v. illus., facsims., port. E269.C3G8

Vols. 2–3 published in Philadelphia.

No more published?

A potpourri that includes information on anti-Catholicism, especially in connection with the Quebec Act; American Catholics and Canadian Loyalists; Catholic officers of the American army; religious liberty; and the activities of the French clergy. Most of the material appeared earlier in the pages of the *American Catholic Historical Researches*, edited and published by Griffin (E184.C3A5).

11434

Hughes, Thomas A. History of the Society of Jesus in North America, colonial and federal. London, New York, Longmans, Green, 1907–17. 3 v. in 4. facsims., maps (part fold.) BX3707.H8

"Register and notices of the sources": v. 1, p. [1]–45. "Abbreviations and titles of works quoted": v. 2, pt. xix–xxv.

Contents: 1. Text. From the first colonization till 1645. Documents: v. 1, pt. 1, no. 1–140 (1605–1838). v. 1, pt. 2, no. 141–224 (1605–1838).—2. Text. From 1645 till 1773.

11435

Lord, Robert H., John E. Sexton, *and* Edward T. Harrington. History of the archdiocese of Boston in the various stages of its development, 1604 to 1943. v. 1. 1604–1825. New York, Sheed & Ward, 1944. xix, 812 p. illus., facsim., map, plates, ports.

BX1417.B6L6, v. 1

Bibliographic footnotes.

Includes six chapters (p. 220–411) on the Catholic question in Massachusetts, 1760–75, the toleration of Catholicism during the first years of the Revolution, tentative movements toward freedom of religion during the Confederation period, and the foundation of the first Catholic church in Boston.

11436
McAvoy, Thomas T.　A history of the Catholic church in the United States. Notre Dame [Ind.] University of Notre Dame Press [1969] v, 504 p.　BX1406.2.M23

Bibliography: p. 469–483.
"The return of toleration, 1774–1789": p. 33–60.

11437
McEniry, Blanche M., *Sister*.　The Catholic church in colonial Pennsylvania. Pennsylvania history, v. 3, Oct. 1936: 240–258.　F146.P597, v. 3

11438
McEniry, Blanche M., *Sister*.　The Catholic church in Pennsylvania, 1775–1808. Pennsylvania history, v. 4, Jan. 1937: 32–46.　F146.P597, v. 4

11439
Madden, Richard C.　Catholics in colonial South Carolina. *In* American Catholic Historical Society of Philadelphia. Records, v. 73, Mar./June 1962: 10–44.　E184.C3A4, v. 73

Focuses largely upon the Revolutionary period.

11440
Marraro, Howard R.　Rome and the Catholic church in eighteenth-century American magazines. Catholic historical review, v. 32, July 1946: 157–189.　BX1404.C3, v. 32

11441
Maynard, Theodore.　The Catholics in the Revolution. American mercury, v. 28, Mar. 1933: 352–359.　AP2.A37, v. 28

11442
Merrill, William S.　Catholic authorship in the American colonies before 1784. Catholic historical review, v. 3, Oct. 1917: 308–325.　BX1404.C3, v. 3

———— ———— Offprint. [Washington, 1917] 18 p.　Z1229.C3M4
Z1227.M38

11443
Merritt, Edward Percival.　Sketches of the three earliest Roman Catholic priests in Boston [1788] *In* Colonial Society of Massachusetts, *Boston*. Publications. v. 25. Transactions, 1922/24. Boston, 1924. p. 173–229.　F61.C71, v. 25

Claude Florent Bouchard de la Poterie, Louis de Rousselet, and John Thayer.

11444
Metzger, Charles H.　Catholics and the American Revolution; a study in religious climate. Chicago, Loyola University Press, 1962. 306 p. (Jesuit studies; contributions to the arts and sciences by members of the Society of Jesus)　E269.C3M4

Bibliography: p. 281–285.

Despite the fact that the Quebec Act heightened the anti-Catholic prejudice that had prevailed throughout the colonial period, the outbreak of hostilities brought at least a public waning of animosity as the majority of Catholics became supporters of the Revolution and Catholic France came to the aid of the Americans. Those Catholics who did remain loyal to England were more numerous in Pennsylvania, especially among German immigrants, than in Maryland, the two states with the largest Catholic population.

11445
Metzger, Charles H.　Catholics in the period of the American Revolution. *In* American Catholic Historical Society of Philadelphia. Records, v. 59, Sept.–Dec. 1948: 195–219, 295–317.　E184.C3A4, v. 59

11446
Musser, Edgar A.　Old St. Mary's Church, the Jesuit period: 1741–1785. Lancaster, Pa., 1967. [69]–136 p. (Lancaster County Historical Society. Journal, v. 71, spring 1967)　F157.L2L5, v. 71

11447
Nuesse, Celestine J.　The social thought of American Catholics, 1634–1829. Washington, D.C., Catholic University of America Press, 1945. x, 315 p. (The Catholic University of America. Studies in sociology, v. 10)　HN37.C3N8

Thesis (Ph.D)—Catholic University of America, 1944. "Bibliographical notes": p. [287]–304.

Concentrating on more than a dozen prominent Catholic laymen in Maryland and Pennsylvania, the author examines Catholic thinking about human associations and institutions. With the exception of their decided enthusiasm for religious liberty, Catholics were, for the most part, conformist in their attitudes, which were not significantly distinguishable from the mainstream of American thought. They proved to be conservative, middle-class nationalists who supported the Revolution, the Constitution, and the Federalist position in politics.

11448
Parsons, Wilfrid.　Early Catholic publishers of Philadelphia. Catholic historical review, v. 24, July 1938: 141–152.　BX1404.C3, v. 24

11449
Phelan, Thomas P.　Catholic patriotism in Revolutionary days. Catholic historical review, new ser., v. 1, Jan. 1922: 431–440.　BX1404.C3, n.s., v. 1

11450

Phelan, Thomas P.   Catholics in colonial days. New York, P. J. Kenedy [ᶜ1935] xxiii, 292 p. port.   E184.C3P5

Bibliography: p. 281–284.

Reprinted in Ann Arbor, Mich., by Gryphon Books (1971).

11451

A Projected settlement of English-speaking Catholics from Maryland in Spanish Louisiana, 1767, 1768.   American historical review, v. 16, Jan. 1911: 319–327.

E171.A57, v. 16

Introduction and notes by James A. Robertson.

11452

Ray, Mary A., *Sister*.   American opinion of Roman Catholicism in the eighteenth century. New York, Columbia University Press, 1936. 456 p. illus. (Studies in history, economics and public law, no. 416)

H31.C7, no. 416

BX1406.R35 1936a

Issued also as thesis (Ph.D.)—Columbia University. "Bibliographical notes": p. 397–444.

Dividing her study into three parts, the author reviews the English origins of the "no popery" tradition; describes manifestations of that view in colonial literature, education, and religion; and provides examples of religious prejudice during the Revolutionary era. While anti-Catholic sentiment burgeoned during the French and Indian War, it declined after 1763 until the Quebec Act brought forth cries against "popery, France, and arbitrary power." Catholic service in the American army and the alliance with France resulted in a measure of toleration during the War for Independence, but only the constitutions of Pennsylvania, Delaware, and Maryland granted Catholics religious liberty.

11453

Rider, Sidney S.   An inquiry concerning the origin of the clause in the laws of Rhode Island (1719–1783) disfranchising Roman Catholics. Providence, 1889. 72 p. (Rhode Island historical tracts, 2d ser., no. 1)

F76.R52, 2d s., no. 1

11454

Riley, Arthur J.   Catholicism in New England to 1788. Washington, D.C., Catholic University of America, 1936. ix, 479 p. (The Catholic University of America. Studies in American church history, v. 24)

BX1408.R5 1936

Thesis (Ph.D.)—Catholic University of America, 1936. Bibliography: p. 383–451.

Despite Protestant opposition to all aspects of Catholic civilization, especially papal authority, Catholics lived in New England throughout the colonial period. Summarizing anti-Catholic sentiment found in 18th-century diaries, sermons, almanacs, schoolbooks, statutes, and other contemporary sources, the author determines that early criticism of the church centered on theological considerations. During the Revolutionary period, however, pamphleteers used existing anti-Catholicism as a political weapon to increase opposition to such British imperial measures as the Quebec Act.

11455

Schrott, Lambert.   Pioneer German Catholics in the American colonies (1734–1784). New York, United States Catholic Historical Society, 1933. xviii, 139 p. (United States Catholic Historical Society. Monograph series, v. 13 [pt. 1])   BX1407.G4S4 1933

E184.C3U6, v. 13

Bibliographic references included in "Footnotes" p. 111–139).

Evaluates the contribution of German Catholics to the colonial church, especially that of 10 Jesuits headquartered in Pennsylvania whose influence spread from the Potomac to the Hudson.

11456

Shea, John D. G.   A history of the Catholic church within the limits of the United States, from the first attempted colonization to the present time. New York, J. G. Shea, 1886–92. 4 v. illus., facsims., maps, plates, ports.

BX1406.S5 1886

Partial contents: [1] The Catholic church in colonial days. The thirteen colonies, the Ottawa and Illinois country, Louisiana, Florida, Texas, New Mexico, and Arizona. 1521–1763.—[2] Life and times of the Most Rev. John Carroll . . . Embracing the history of the Catholic church in the United States. 1763–1815.

11457

Smyth, Patrick.   The present state of the Catholic mission, conducted by the ex-Jesuits in North-America. Dublin, Printed by P. Byrne, 1788. [Washington, D.C., 1925] facsim. 48 p.   BX1402.S6

Photostat facsimile reproduction (positive) made from an original in the possession of the Rev. Dr. P. J. Guilday, Washington, D.C.

A denunciation of the policy of John Carroll.

h. Lutherans

11458

Bernheim, Gotthardt D.   History of the German settlements and of the Lutheran church in North and South Carolina, from the earliest period of the colonization of the Dutch, German, and Swiss settlers to the close of the first half of the present century. Philadelphia, Lutheran Book Store, 1872. 557 p. port.   F265.G3B5

Reprinted in Spartanburg, S.C., by the Reprint Co. (1972).

11459

De Levie, Dagobert.   Patriotic activity of Calvinistic and Lutheran clergymen during the American Revolution. Lutheran quarterly, v. 8, Nov. 1956: 319–340.

BX8001.L617, v. 8

11460

Fortenbaugh, Robert.   The development of the synodical polity of the Lutheran church in America to 1829. Philadelphia, 1926. 252 p.   BX8041.F6 1926

Thesis (Ph.D.)—University of Pennsylvania, 1926.
Bibliography: p. 231–252.

11461

Glatfelter, Charles H.   The eighteenth century German Lutheran and Reformed clergymen in the Susquehanna Valley. Pennsylvania history, v. 20, Jan. 1953: 57–68.
F146.P597, v. 20

11462

[Helmstaedt Mission Society]   Textbooks for the youth of North Carolina, outlined by a society of Helmstaedt professors. North Carolina historical review, v. 7, Jan. 1930: 79–147. (German tracts concerning the Lutheran Church in North Carolina during the eighteenth century, pt. 1)   F251.N892, v. 7

Translation by Charles A. Krummel of the four *Lehrbücher für die Jugend in Nordcarolina* (Leipzig, S.L. Crusius, 1787–89), with an introduction and notes by William K. Boyd.

11463

Honeyman, John C.   Zion, St. Paul and other early Lutheran churches in central New Jersey. *In* New Jersey Historical Society. Proceedings, 4th ser., v. 9, July–Oct. 1924: 225–273, 347–371; v. 10, Jan., July–Oct. 1925: 41–56, 294–306, 395–409; v. 11, Jan.–Oct. 1926: 57–70, 191–198, 378–396, 532–542; v. 12, Apr.–Oct. 1927: 214–224, 326–335, 462–471; v. 13, Apr.–Oct. 1928: 209–223, 330–347, 433–446; v. 14, Jan., July–Oct. 1929: 55–69, 336–350, 466–475; v. 15, Jan.–Oct. 1930: 95–108, 250–261, 392–401, 503–508; v. 16, Jan.–Apr., Oct. 1931: 34–50, 180–185, 441–451.
F131.N58, 4th s., v. 9–16

11464

Kreider, Harry J.   Lutheranism in colonial New York. New York City, 1942. xviii, 159 p. map.
BX8042.N7K7

Thesis (Ph.D.)—Columbia University, 1942.
"Bibliographical essay": p. 149–158.
Reprinted in New York by Arno Press (1972).

11465

Qualben, Lars P.   The Lutheran church in colonial America. New York, T. Nelson, 1940. x, 320 p. maps.
BX8041.Q3

"Selected bibliography" at end of each chapter.
"Lutherans and the establishment of the American nation": p. 237–271.

11466

Schmauk, Theodore E.   The Lutheran church in Pennsylvania (1638–1800). v. 1. The church prior to the arrival of William Penn in the seventeenth century and prior to the arrival of Henry Melchior Mühlenberg [sic] in the eighteenth century. Illustrated by Julius F. Sachse. *In*

Pennsylvania-German Society. Proceedings and addresses. v. 11; 1900. [Lancaster, Pa.] 1902. viii, 355 p. (2d group) illus., facsims., map, plates, ports.
F146.P23, v. 11

——— A history of the Lutheran church in Pennsylvania (1638–1820), from the original sources. Illustrated by Julius F. Sachse. v. 1. *In* Pennsylvania-German Society. Proceedings and addresses. v. 12; 1901. [Lancaster, Pa.] 1903. xxiii, 357–588 p. (3d group) illus., facsims., maps, plates, ports.   F146.P23, v. 12

Both parts are also designated pt. 9 of Pennsylvania: the German Influence in its Settlement and Development.

11467

Wrangel, Carl Magnus.   Pastor Wrangel's trip to the shore. New Jersey history, v. 87, spring 1969: 5–31. illus., map.   F131.N58, v. 87

As dean or provost of the Swedish Lutheran congregations in America from 1758 to 1768, Wrangel made several trips through the mid-Atlantic region visiting congregations. His diary for October 1764 describes a 10-day, 220-mile trip across New Jersey, from Philadelphia to the Atlantic coast and back. Translated and edited by Carl M. Anderson.

i. Moravians, Dunkers, Mennonites, and Other German Pietist Sects

11468

Bader, P. C.   Extracts from the records of the Moravian congregation at Hebron, Pennsylvania, 1775–1781. Pennsylvania magazine of history and biography, v. 18, Jan. 1895: 449–462.   F146.P65, v. 18

Translations from the German of remnants of Pastor Bader's diary.

11469

Bender, Wilbur J.   Pacifism among the Mennonites, Amish Mennonites and Schwenkfelders of Pennsylvania to 1783. Mennonite quarterly review, v. 1, July 1928: 23–40; Oct.: 21–48.   BX8101.M4, v. 1

11470

Blackwelder, Ruth.   The attitude of the North Carolina Moravians toward the American Revolution. North Carolina historical review, v. 9, Jan. 1932: 1–21.
F251.N892, v. 9

The Brethren remained consistent pacifists throughout the war, but in return for protective legislation cared for the wounded, fed the soldiers, and often paid triple taxes to the states.

11471

Brickenstein, H. A.   Sketch of the early history of Lititz, 1742–75. *In* Moravian Historical Society, *Nazareth, Pa.* Transactions. v. 2. Nazareth, Pa., 1886. p. [341]–374.   E184.M8M8, v. 2
BX8553.M7, v. 2

11472

Brumbaugh, Martin G.   A history of the German Baptist brethren in Europe and America. Mount Morris, Ill.,

Brethren Pub. House, 1899. xxii, 559 p. illus., facsims., plates. BX7815.B8

Includes chapters on colonial leaders and congregations, the two Christopher Sowers, the Ephrata Society, and church doctrine and growth.

11473
Dollin, Norman. The Schwenkfelders in 18th-century America. 1971. ([209] p.)
Micro AC–1, no. 72–01,298
Thesis (Ph.D.)—Columbia University.
Abstracted in *Dissertation Abstracts International*, v. 32A, Dec. 1971, p. 3182.

11474
Durnbaugh, Donald F., comp. The Brethren in colonial America; a source book on the transplantation and development of the Church of the Brethren in the eighteenth century. Elgin, Ill., Brethren Press [1967] 659 p. illus., facsims. BX7816.D8
Bibliographic references included in "Notes" (p. [609]–633).

A collection of letters, wills, and other private papers, interspersed with narrative, dealing with the migration of individuals and groups to America, the establishment of congregations, the relationships among sects, and the important doctrinal and devotional writings of their members. Two chapters on the Revolutionary period illustrate the Brethren's pacifism and conservatism, the response of civil authorities to these convictions, and the tribulations of the Loyalist Christopher Sower II, his family, and his press.

11475
The Ephrata community 120 years ago, as described by an Englishman. With an introduction and notes by F. R. Diffenderffer. *In* Lancaster County (Pa.) Historical Society. Papers, v. 9, Jan. 1905: 127–146.
F157.L2L5, v. 9
Consists of a description written in 1786 by a British officer who visited the community after the war.

11476
Erbe, Hellmuth. Bethlehem, Pa. Eine kommunistische Herrnhuter Kolonie des 18. Jahrhunderts. Stuttgart, Ausland und Heimat Verlags-Aktiengesellschaft, 1929. 190 p. illus., plates, maps, plan. (Schriften des Deutschen Ausland-Instituts, Stuttgart. A: Kulturhistorische Reihe, Bd. 24) F159.B5E65
"Literatur-verzeichnis": p. [185]–190.

11477
Flory, John S. Literary activity of the German Baptist Brethren in the eighteenth century. Elgin, Ill., Brethren Pub. House, 1908. xii, 335 p. BX7816.F6
Thesis (Ph.D.)—University of Virginia, 1907.
Works, either written or printed, by the German Baptists in the eighteenth century: p. 291–[327]
Reviews the origins of the Brethren Church, describes the printing and publishing career of Christopher Sower,

and discusses such Brethren writers as Alexander Mack, Jr., Christopher Sower II, and Peter Leibert.

11478
Frantz, Clair G. The religious teachings of the German almanacs published by the Sauers in colonial Pennsylvania [1738–77] 1955. ([150] p.)
Micro AC–1, no. 55–1561
Thesis (Ph.D.)—Temple University.
Abstracted in *Dissertation Abstracts*, v. 15, no. 12, 1955, p. 2462.

11479
Gollin, Gilliam L. Moravians in two worlds; a study of changing communities. New York, Columbia University Press, 1967. viii, 302 p. BX8568.B4G6
"Selected bibliography": p.[273]—288.

Attempts to identify underlying patterns of social and institutional change in the Moravian communities of Herrnhut, Germany, and Bethlehem, Pa., between 1722 and 1750.

11480
Hamilton, John Taylor. A history of the church known as the Moravian church, or, The Unitas Fratrum, or, The Unity of the Brethren, during the eighteenth and nineteenth centuries. Bethlehem, Pa., Times Pub. Co., Printers, 1900. xi, 631 p. ports. (Transactions of the Moravian Historical Society, v. 6)
BX8553.M7, v. 6
BX8565.H3
Bibliography: p. [v]–viii.

Includes three chapters (p. 238–263) on the church in America and Great Britain during the Revolutionary period. A new edition by the author's son, Kenneth G. Hamilton, has been published under the title *History of the Moravian Church; the Renewed Unitas Fratrum, 1722–1957* ([Bethlehem, Pa., Interprovincial Board of Christian Education, Moravian Church in America, 1967] 723 p. BX8565.H3 1967).

11481
Hofer, J. M. The Georgia Salzburgers. Georgia historical quarterly, v. 18, June 1934: 101–117.
F281.G2975, v. 18

11482
Holder, Edward M. Social life of the early Moravians in North Carolina. North Carolina historical review, v. 11, July 1934: 167–184. F251.N892, v. 11

11483
Holloway, Mark. Heavens on earth; utopian communities in America, 1680–1880. 2d ed. [rev.] New York, Dover Publications [1966] 246 p. illus., map, ports.
HX653.H66 1966
Bibliography: p. 233–239.
First edition published in 1951.

Includes four chapters on the Ephratans and Shakers in the 18th century.

11484
Huebener, Mary A,. Bicentennial history of the Lititz Moravian congregation. *In* Moravian Historical Society, *Nazareth, Pa.* Transactions. v. 14. pts. 3/4. Bethlehem, Pa., 1949. p. 199–271.　　E184.M8M8, v. 14
　　　　　　　　　　　　　　BX8553.M7, v. 14

11485
Kriebel, Howard W. The Schwenkfelders in Pennsylvania, a historical sketch. Illustrated by Julius F. Sachse. Lancaster, Pa. [Press of the New Era Print. Co.] 1904. xii, 246 p. illus., facsims., plates, ports.　F160.S2K9

"Bibliographical notes": p. 183–202.

First published as part 12 of Pennsylvania: the German Influence in its Settlement and Development in the *Proceedings and Addresses,* v. 13, 1902 (F146.P23, v. 13), of the Pennsylvania-German Society, which version was reprinted in New York by AMS Press (1971. 232 p. F160.S2K9 1971).

11486
Lebanon, Pa. Hebron Church. Extracts from the diary of the Moravian pastors of the Hebron Church, Lebanon, 1755–1814. Translated and edited by John W. Heisey. Pennsylvania history, v. 34, Jan. 1967: 44–63.
　　　　　　　　　　　　　　F146.P597, v. 34

11487
Newton, Hester W. The agricultural activities of the Salzburgers in colonial Georgia. Georgia historical quarterly, v. 18, Sept. 1934: 248–263.　F281.G2975, v. 18

11488
Newton, Hester W. The industrial and social influences of the Salzburgers in colonial Georgia. Georgia historical quarterly, v. 18, Dec. 1934: 335–353.
　　　　　　　　　　　　　　F281.G2975, v. 18

11489
Rau, Robert. Sketch of the history of the Moravian congregation at Gnadenhütten on the Mahoning. *In* Moravian Historical Society, *Nazareth, Pa.* Transactions. v. 2. Nazareth, Pa., 1886. p. [397]–414.
　　　　　　　　　　　　　　E184.M8M8, v. 2
　　　　　　　　　　　　　　BX8553.M7, v. 2

11490
Reichel, Levin T. The Moravians in North Carolina. An authentic history. Salem, N.C., O. A. Keehln, 1857. 206 p.　　　　　　　　　F265.M8R3

Reprinted in Baltimore by the Genealogical Pub. Co. (1968).

11491
Reichmann, Felix, *and* Eugene E. Doll, *eds.* Ephrata as seen by contemporaries. [Allentown, Pa., ᶜ1953] xxi, 215 p. illus. (Pennsylvania German Folklore Society. [Yearbook], v. 17)　　　GR110.P4A35, v. 17

Arranges excerpts from contemporary documents chronologically from 1730 to 1790.

11492
Sachse, Julius F. The German sectarians of Pennsylvania, 1708–1800; a critical and legendary history of the Ephrata Cloister and the Dunkers. Philadelphia, Printed for the author, 1899–1900. 2 v. illus., facsims., plates (part col.), ports.　　BX7817.P4S3

Contents: v. 1. 1708–1742.—v. 2. 1742–1800.
Reprinted in New York by AMS Press (1971).

An exhaustive account of life among the mystic Sabbatarians of Lancaster County, Pa., followers of Conrad Beissel and members of the Ephrata community, the monastic "order of the Solitary" whose distinctive creed includes elements drawn from the beliefs of Dunkers (German Baptist Brethren) and Theosophists. The author traces the development of printing among the group; reprints title pages of Bibles amd pamphlets produced on its press, the third in the colony; and provides lengthy quotations from contemporary letters, memoirs, and other documents.

11493
Sappington, Roger E. Dunker beginnings in North Carolina in the eighteenth century. North Carolina historical review, v. 46, summer 1969: 214–238.
　　　　　　　　　　　　　　F251.N892, v. 46

11494
Sappington, Roger E. Two eighteenth century Dunker congregations in North Carolina. North Carolina historical review, v. 47, Apr. 1970: 176–204.
　　　　　　　　　　　　　　F251.N892, v. 47

11495
Sawyer, Edwin A. The religious experience of the colonial American Moravians. Nazareth, Pa., Moravian Historical Society, 1961. 232 p. (Transactions of the Moravian Historical Society, v. 18, pt. 1)　E184.M8M8, v. 18
　　　　　　　　　　　　　　BX8553.M7, v. 18

Thesis (Ph.D.)—Columbia University.
Bibliography: p. 223–227.

11496
Schrag, Felix J. Pietism in colonial America. 1945.

Thesis (Ph.D.)—University of Chicago.

11497
Schrag, Martin M. Influences contributing to an early River Brethren confession of faith. Mennonite quarterly review, v. 38, Oct. 1964: 344–353.
　　　　　　　　　　　　　　BX1801.M4, v. 38

Formed and organized between 1770 and 1788 during the Pennsylvania-German phase of the Great Awakening, the River Brethren's confession of faith was a synthesis of concepts and practices drawn from several historical traditions.

11498
Sessler, Jacob J. Communal pietism among early American Moravians. New York, H. Holt [ᶜ1933] 265 p. facsim., plates, ports, (part col.) (Studies in religion and culture. American religion series, 8)

　　　　　　　　　　　　　　BX8566.S4 1933a

Issued also as thesis (Ph.D.)—Columbia University, 1933.

Bibliography: p. 239–260.

Focuses on the establishment of the General Economy at Bethlehem, Pa., under the leadership of Nicholaus Ludwig von Zinzendorf and August Gottlieb Spangenberg.

11499

Smith, Charles Henry. The Mennonite immigration to Pennsylvania in the eighteenth century. Part xxxiii of a narrative and critical history prepared at the request of the Pennsylvania-German Society. Norristown, Pa. [Norristown Press] 1929. 412 p. illus., facsims., plates, port. (Pennsylvania-German Society. Proceedings and addresses, v. 35, pt. 2)   F146.P23, v. 35

11500

Stolzfus, Grant M. History of the first Amish Mennonite communities in America. Mennonite quarterly review, v. 28, Oct. 1954: 235–262.   BX8101.M4, v. 28

11501

Voight, Gilbert P. Ebenezer, Georgia: an eighteenth-century [Salzburger] utopia. Georgia review, v. 9, summer 1955: 209–215.   AP2.G375, v. 9

11502

Ziegler, Andrew, Isaac Kolb, *and* Christian Funk. A letter from Pennsylvania Mennonites to Holland in 1773. Mennonite quarterly review, v. 3, Oct. 1929: 225–234.   BX8101.M4, v. 3

A response from three Mennonite bishops to four fellow clergymen concerning the sect's communities in America, the reasons for migration, the doctrines and practices of American Mennonites, and the names of bishops and ministers and dates of ordination.

i. Jews

11503

Hühner, Leon. The struggle for religious liberty in North Carolina, with special reference to the Jews. *In* American Jewish Historical Society. Publications. no. 16. New York, 1907. p. 37–71.   E184.J5A5, no. 16

11504

Kohler, Max J. Phases in the history of religious liberty in America, with special reference to the Jews: the Virginia act establishing religious liberty and the emancipation of the Jews of Europe. *In* American Jewish Historical Society. Publications. no. 11. New York, 1903. p. 65–89.   E184.J5A5, no. 11

Links the Virginia Statute for Religious Freedom, adapted in 1786 and widely disseminated in Europe by Thomas Jefferson, with the movement for Jewish emancipation begun in revolutionary France.

11505

New York (City). Congregation Shearith Israel. The earliest extant minute books of the Spanish and Portuguese Congregation Shearith Israel in New York, 1728–1786.

In American Jewish Historical Society. Publications. v. 21. [Baltimore] 1913. p. 1–171. facsims., plates, ports.   E184.J5A5, v. 21

k. Deists and Universalists

11506

Eddy, Richard. Universalism in America. A history. Boston, Universalist Pub. House, 1884–86. 2 v.   BX9933.E3 1884

Contents. 1. 1636–1800.—2. 1801–1886. Bibliography (p. 485–599).

11507

Eliot, Samuel A., *ed.* Heralds of a liberal faith. v. 1. The prophets. Boston, American Unitarian Association, 1910. [43], 282 p.   BX9867.E4, v. 1

Includes biographical sketches of such clergymen as Ebenezer Gay, Charles Chauncy, Jonathan Mayhew, the two Samuel Wests, Henry Cummings, John Lathrop, and Jeremy Belknap.

11508

Koch, Gustav A. Republican religion; the American Revolution and the cult of reason. New York, H. Holt [c1933] xvi, 334 p. illus. (Studies in religion and culture. American religion series, 7)   BL2760.K6 1933a

Issued also as thesis (Ph.D.)—Columbia University. Bibliography: p. 299–328.

Reprinted in New York by Crowell (1968) under the title *Religion of the American Enlightenment.*

Charts the rise, momentary triumph, and decline of Deism in America, 1770–1810, as revealed in the writings of Ethan Allen, Elihu Palmer, Thomas Paine, and others.

11509

Morais, Herbert M. Deism in eighteenth century America. New York, Columbia University Press, 1934. 203 p. (Studies in history, economics and public law, no. 397)   H31.C7, no. 397
      BL2760.M6 1934a

Issued also as thesis (Ph.D.)—Columbia University. "List of authorities": p. 179–193.

Reprinted in New York by Russell & Russell (1960).

Traces the growth of natural religion during the colonial period, summarizes the religious beliefs of the Revolutionary leaders and their attitudes toward Deism, and describes the increased militancy of its advocates in 1763 and especially after 1784, including the trend toward an open, critical examination of Christian revelation. Jefferson's beliefs, the author concludes, were typical of American Deism; he wanted Christians to return to the moral precepts of Christ, uncorrupted by clergy.

11510

Morais, Herbert M. Deism in Revolutionary America (1763–1789). International journal of ethics, v. 42, July 1932: 434–453.   BJ1.I6, v. 42

11511

Taussig, Harold E.   Deism in Philadelphia during the age of Franklin. Pennsylvania history, v. 37, July 1970: 217–236.   F146.P597, v. 37

11512

Wright, Conrad.   The beginnings of Unitarianism in America. Boston, Starr King Press; distributed by Beacon Press [1955] 305 p. maps.   BX9833.W7

"Biographical appendix": p. [281]–291.
"Biographical note": p. [292]–294.

Focusing on the rise of Arminianism within the New England Congregational church during the period 1735 to 1805, the author analyzes the writings of the liberal clergy—most notably Charles Chauncy, Jonathan Mayhew, and Ebenezer Gay—examines the social and economic basis of the Arminian movement, and considers the development of its basic tenets, among them anti-Trinitarianism, supernatural rationalism, the benevolence of God, and the dignity of human nature.

4. REVIVALISM AND THE GREAT AWAKENING

11513

Berk, Stephen E.   The church militant: Timothy Dwight and the rise of American Evangelical Protestantism. 1971. ([510] p.)   Micro AC–1, no. 71–22,004

Thesis (Ph.D.)—University of Iowa.
Abstracted in *Dissertation Abstracts International,* v. 32A, Oct. 1971, p. 2010.

11514

Cowing, Cedric B.   The Great Awakening and the American Revolution: colonial thought in the 18th century. Chicago, Rand McNally [1971] ix, 260 p. (The Rand McNally series on the history of American thought and culture)   BR520.C68

Presents a general synthesis of social history, stressing evangelical religion and its influence upon the major theme of 18th-century America: civil and religious liberty.

11515

Gaustad, Edwin S.   The Great Awakening in New England. New York, Harper [1957] 173 p. maps, plates.   BR520.G2

Bibliographical references included in "Notes" (p. 141–159). Bibliography: p. 160–168.
Reprinted in Gloucester, Mass., by P. Smith (1965).

Describes the wave of piety that swept the colonies between 1740 and 1743, particularly as it affected the Congregationalists of the Connecticut River valley, and examines its influence upon the next generation. The two main lines of New England religious thought in the Revolutionary period—the pietism of Jonathan Edwards and the rationalism of Charles Chauncy—took form during the Awakening.

11516

Gaustad, Edwin S.   The theological effects of the Great Awakening in New England. Mississippi Valley historical review, v. 40, Mar. 1954: 681–706.
                                                   E171.J87, v. 40

Few of the major issues raised by Liberals and Calvinists were ever satisfactorily "settled"; but rationalism gained a strong foothold while religion became "more comfortable, more intelligent, more unnecessary."

11517

Gewehr, Wesley M.   The Great Awakening in Virginia, 1740–1790. Durham, N.C., Duke University Press, 1930. viii, 292 p. maps, ports. (Duke University publications)   BR555.V8G4

Bibliography: p. 263–279.
Reprinted in Gloucester, Mass., by P. Smith (1965).
The author's thesis (Ph.D.), with the same title, was submitted to the University of Chicago in 1922.

Investigates the effects of the revivals that swept the colony's Presbyterian, Baptist, and Methodist churches before and after the Revolution. According to Gewehr, evangelical doctrines produced a democratic feeling among the masses of the people, encouraged the development of self-respect, inculcated ideas of self-government, and promoted the concept of equality. The Awakening also caused disputes that led to the founding of new colleges, introduced the Christian religion among slaves, and broke down class distinctions among whites. A review of this work by George M. Brydon, first published in the *Virginia Magazine of History and Biography*, was issued separately under the title *The Established Church in Virginia and the Revolution* (Richmond, Va., Virginia Diocesan Library, 1930. 19 p. BR555.V8G42).

11518

Goen, C. C.   Revivalism and separatism in New England, 1740–1800; Strict Congregationalists and Separate Baptists in the Great Awakening. New Haven, Yale University Press, 1962. x, 370 p. maps. (Yale publications in religion, 2)   BR520.G6

Revision of a thesis, Yale University.
Bibliography: p. 328–346.
Reprinted in Hamden, Conn., by Archon Books (1969).

Emphasizing the role of pietism as a cause of dissension, the author reviews the theological and ecclesiastical disagreements that split Congregationalists into three groups—conservative Old Lights, moderate New Lights, and extreme Separatists—and follows the development of some 100 Separate congregations from the beginning of their discontent to the assimilation of many within the Baptist fellowship. The author illustrates the process by focusing upon representative churches in each colony and upon such religious leaders as Elisha Paine, an evangelist; Paul Parke, a pastor; Ebenezer Frothingham, an apologist; Nathan Cole, a layman; and Joseph Marshall, a frontiersman. More attention is given to James Davenport and Isaac Backus, who dominated the movement in its earlier and later stages.

11519

Labaree, Leonard W.   The conservative attitude toward the Great Awakening. William and Mary quarterly, 3d ser., v. 1, Oct. 1944: 331–352.   F221.W71, 3d s., v. 1

Traces the reaction to evangelical Christianity by conservative members of all denominations.

11520

Lumpkin, William L. Baptist foundations in the South; tracing through the Separates the influence of the Great Awakening, 1754–1787. Nashville, Broadman Press [1961] ix, 166 p. BX6389.63.L8

Bibliography: p. 163–166.

11521

Maxson, Charles H. The Great Awakening in the middle colonies. Chicago, Ill., University of Chicago Press, 1920. vii, 158 p. BR520.M55 1920a

Thesis (Ph.D.)—University of Chicago, 1915.
Bibliography: p. 152–158.

Concludes that the significant religious and social unity created among the colonies by the Great Awakening prepared the way for the political unity of the Revolution and that the middle colonies were the center of the unifying movement.

11522

Mead, Sidney E. The rise of the evangelical conception of the ministry in America (1607–1850). *In* Niebuhr, Helmut Richard, *and* Daniel D. Williams, *eds.* The ministry in historical perspectives. New York, Harper [1956] p. 207–249. BV660.N48

11523

Morgan, David T. The Great Awakening in North Carolina, 1740–1775: the Baptist phase. North Carolina historical review, v. 45, summer 1968: 264–283.
F251.N892, v. 45

11524

Morgan, David T. The Great Awakening in South Carolina, 1740–1775. South Atlantic quarterly, v. 70, autumn 1971: 595–606. AP2.S75, v. 70

11525

Morgan, David T. The Great Awakening in the Carolinas and Georgia, 1740–1775. 1968. ([288] p.)
Micro AC–1, no. 69–1652

Thesis (Ph.D.)—University of North Carolina.
Abstracted in *Dissertation Abstracts*, v. 29A, Jan. 1969, p. 2189.

11526

Rutman, Darrett B., *comp.* The Great Awakening; event and exegesis. New York, Wiley [1970] viii, 200 p. (Problems in American history) BR250.R88 1970

Includes bibliographic references.

Provides excerpts from the writings of 14 contemporaries and 9 historians, such as Edwin G. Gaustad, Vernon L. Parrington, H. Richard Niebuhr, Alan Heimert, Perry Miller, Richard L. Bushman, Dietmar Rothermund, Leonard J. Trinterud, and J. M. Bumsted.

11527

Sweet, William W. Revivalism in America, its origin, growth and decline. New York, C. Scribner's Sons, 1944. 192 p. BV3773.S8

"Selected bibliography": p. 183–188.
Reprinted in Gloucester, Mass., by P. Smith (1965).

The first five chapters (p. 1–111) provide a general treatment of 18th-century revivalism.

5. THE MISSIONARY IMPULSE

11528

Beaver, Robert Pierce. American missionary motivation before the Revolution. Church history, v. 31, June 1962: 216–226. BR140.A45, v. 31

11529

Beaver, Robert Pierce, *ed.* Pioneers in mission; the early missionary ordination sermons, charges, and instructions [1733–1812] A source book on the rise of American missions to the heathen. Grand Rapids, W. B. Eerdmans Pub. Co. [1966] vi, 291 p. BV2410.B4

Bibliography: p. 279–286.

11530

Bultmann, William A. The S.P.G. and the foreign settler in the American colonies. *In* McCulloch, Samuel C., *ed.* British humanitarianism; essays honoring Frank J. Klingberg. Philadelphia, Church Historical Society [1950] (Church Historical Society (U.S.). Publication 32) p. 51–65. HN15.M2

11531

Goodykoontz, Colin B. Home missions on the American frontier, with particular reference to the American Home Missionary Society. Caldwell, Id., Caxton Printers, 1939. 460 p. BV2765.G62

"This book . . . is the outgrowth of a doctoral dissertation prepared at Harvard University."—Preface.
"Selected bibliography": p. [429]–452.
Reprinted in New York by Octagon Books (1971).

Includes two chapters (p. 63–114) on the organized efforts of 18th-century Protestants to carry religious and educational institutions to the frontier regions.

11532

Goodwin, Mary F. Christianizing and educating the Negro in colonial Virginia. Historical magazine of the Protestant Episcopal Church, v. 1, Sept., 1932: 143–152. BX5800.H5, v. 1

11533

Hirsch, Charles B. The experiences of the S.P.G. in eighteenth century North Carolina. 1954. ([390] p.)
Micro AC–1, no. 7532

Thesis (Ph.D.)—Indiana University.
Abstracted in *Dissertation Abstracts*, v. 14, no. 4, 1954, p. 664–665.

11534

Kellaway, William. The New England Company, 1649–1776; missionary society to the American Indians. New York, Barnes & Noble [1962, ᶜ1961] 303 p. illus.
E98.M6K28 1962

Bibliographic footnotes. "List of manuscript sources": p. 284–287.

Backed for the most part by prosperous London merchants, the company channeled funds from gifts, collections, and property rent to commissioners in New England who paid the salaries of such missionaries as John Eliot, Experience and Zachariah Mayhew, and John Sergeant of Stockbridge. The Revolution did not immediately affect the relationship between the missionaries and the company, but payments were suspended in 1779, and the funds diverted to Canada after the war.

11535

King, Irving H. The S.P.G. in New England, 1701–1784. 1968. ([324] p.) Micro AC–1, no. 68–18,067

Thesis (Ph.D.)—University of Maine.
Abstracted in *Dissertation Abstracts*, v. 29A, Dec. 1968, p. 1835.

11536

Klingberg, Frank J. The S.P.G. program for Negroes in colonial New York. Historical magazine of the Protestant Episcopal church, v. 8, Dec. 1939: 306–371.
BX5800.H5, v. 8

11537

Kohnova, Marie J. The Moravians and their missionaries: a problem in Americanization. Mississippi Valley historical review, v. 19, Dec. 1932: 348–361.
E171.J87, v. 19

The efforts of the missionaries hindered the Americanization of their people, bore little fruit among the Indians, and brought few permanent settlements.

11538

Midwinter, *Sir* Edward C. The Society for the Propagation of the Gospel and the church in the American colonies: New York, New Jersey, Massachusetts. Historical magazine of the Protestant Episcopal church, v. 4, June 1935: 67–115.
BX5800.H5, v. 4

11539

Midwinter, *Sir* Edward C. The S.P.G. missionaries in New Jersey during the Revolutionary War. Historical magazine of the Protestant Episcopal church, v. 9, June 1940: 131–141.
BX5800.H5, v. 9

11540

Miller, Norbert H. Pioneer Capuchin missionaries in the United States (1784–1816). *In* United States Catholic Historical Society. Historical records and studies. v. 21. New York, 1932. p. 170–234.
E184.C3U5, v. 21

11541

Mulvey, Mary D., *Sister*. French Catholic missionaries in the present United States (1604–1791). Washington, D.C., Catholic University of America, 1936. ix, 158 p. (The Catholic University of America. Studies in American church history, v. 23)
BV2770.M8 1936

Thesis (Ph.D.)—Catholic University of America, 1936. Bibliography: p. 127–133.

Using a geographical approach for the years before 1763, the author tells of the work of Jesuit missionaries among Indian tribes in Maine, the Iroquois country, the Old Northwest, the Illinois country, and French Louisiana. Mulvey summarizes, in a chapter on the Revolutionary era, the role of the French clergy in the war.

11542

Newcombe, Alfred W. The appointment and instruction of S.P.G. missionaries. Church history, v. 5, Dec. 1936: 340–358.
BR140.A45, v. 5

11543

O'Neil, Maud. A struggle for religious liberty: an analysis of the work of the S.P.G. in Connecticut. Historical magazine of the Protestant Episcopal church, v. 20, June 1951: 173–189.
BX5800.H5, v. 20

11544

Pascoe, Charles F. Two hundred years of the S.P.G.: an historical account of the Society for the Propagation of the Gospel in Foreign Parts, 1701–1900. London, Published at the Society's office, 1901. 2 v. illus., ports.
BV2500.A6P4 1901

"Published in 1893 under the title of 'A Classified Digest' of the Society's Records . . . After passing through seven editions the book has been carefully revised and nearly 500 pages added."—Preface, p. xii–xiii.
"Missionary roll, S.P.G.": v. 2, p. 849–931ᶜ.
"List of the references": v. 2, p. 1301–1389.

Organizing the books according to geographic mission fields all over the world, the compiler provides in volume 1 information excerpted from the society's records that relates to the work of missionaries in the British colonies of North America.

11545

Pennington, Edgar L. The S.P.G. anniversary sermons, 1702–1783. Historical magazine of the Protestant Episcopal church, v. 20, Mar. 1951: 10–43.
BX5800.H5, v. 20

11546

Pennington, Edgar L. The work of the Bray Associates in Pennsylvania. Pennsylvania magazine of history and biography, v. 48, Jan. 1934: 1–25. F146.P65, v. 48

11547

Schell, Edwin, *comp*. Methodist traveling preachers in America, 1773–1799. Methodist history, new ser., v. 2, Jan. 1964: 51–67. BX8235.M44, n.s., v. 2

A list of 850 clergymen with the dates of their appointments, ordination, location, and termination.

11548

Thompson, Henry P. Into all lands; the history of the Society for the Propagation of the Gospel in Foreign Parts, 1701–1950. With a foreword by the Archbishop of Canterbury. London, S.P.C.K., 1951. xv, 760 p. plates, ports.   BV2500.A6T5

Bibliography: p. 723–735.

In a section on 18th-century America, Thompson reviews the aspirations, problems, and accomplishments of the 309 Anglican clergymen who labored under the society's auspices until support of missionary activity in the United States was withdrawn after the Revolution.

11549

Vassar, Rena L. The aftermath of the Revolution; letters of Anglican clergy in Connecticut, 1781–1785. Historical magazine of the Protestant Episcopal church, v. 41, Dec. 1972: 429–461.   BX5800.H5, v. 41

Includes the correspondence of five S.P.G. missionaries—Ebenezer Dibblee, Bela Hubbard, Richard Mansfield, John Tyler, and Roger Viets—who had remained loyal to the crown. Only Viets chose to leave at the end of the war.

11550

Vibert, Faith. The Society for the Propagation of the Gospel in Foreign Parts: its work for the Negroes in North America before 1783. Journal of Negro history, v. 18, Apr. 1933: 171–212.   E185.J86, v. 18

11551

Walker, Fintan G. Some correspondence of an eighteenth century bishop with his missionaries, 1767–1778. Catholic historical review, v. 27, July 1941: 186–209.
                                         BX1404.C3, v. 27

On the exchange of views between Bishop Joseph Oliver Baird in Quebec and fathers Sebastian Meurin and Pierre Gibault in the Illinois country.

6. CHURCH MUSIC

11552

Benson, Louis F. The American revisions of Watts's "Psalms." *In* Presbyterian Historical Society. Journal, v. 2, June 1903: 18–34.   BX8905.P7A4, v. 2

On the textual revisions by John Mycall (1781), Joel Barlow (1785), and Isaiah Thomas (1786) that altered passages referring to British citizenship and loyalty to the king.

11553

Bultmann, Phyllis W. Everybody sing: the social significance of the eighteenth century hymn. 1950.

Thesis (Ph.D.)—University of California, Los Angeles.

11554

Covey, Cyclone. Religion and music in colonial America. 1949. 335 l.

Thesis (Ph.D.)—Stanford University.

11555

Daniel, Ralph T. The anthem in New England before 1800. Evanston, Northwestern University Press, 1966. xvi, 282 p. facsims., music. (Pi Kappa Lambda studies in American music)   ML2911.D35

"Musical supplement": p. [173]–272.
Bibliography: p. 156–171.

Studying the origins, composers, and evolution of the anthem in the period 1760–1800, Daniel considers over 100 American works and relates them to the English anthems after which they are modeled. He concludes that after 155 years of the complete subservience of music to liturgical function, the anthem marked the introduction of an aesthetic impulse in American church music. Appendixes list all anthems published in New England during the period; 14 compositions are reproduced in full.

11556

David, Hans T. Musical life in the Pennsylvania settlements of the *Unitas Fratrum*. *In* Moravian Historical Society, *Nazareth, Pa.* Transactions. v. 13; pts. 1/2. Bethlehem, Pa. 1942. p. 19–58.   E184.M8M8, v. 13
                                         BX8553.M7, v. 13

11557

Ellinwood, Leonard W. The history of American church music. New York, Morehouse-Gorham Co., 1953. xiv, 274 p. music, plates, ports.   ML200.E4

"Biographies of American church musicians": p. 201–242.
"Notes and bibliography": 243–254.
Reprinted in New York by Da Capo Press (1970).

The section on the colonial and Revolutionary periods contains a brief survey of metrical psalmody, singing schools, early choirs, fuguing tunes, non-Puritan music, 18th-century composers, and the first organs and bells. An appendix includes biographical sketches of 11 composers who were active in the late 18th century.

11558

Foote, Henry W. Three centuries of American hymnody. Cambridge, Mass., Harvard University Press, 1940. x, 418 p. facsim.   ML3111.F6T4

Reprinted in Hamden, Conn., by Archon Books (1968).

The first five chapters (p. 3–186) are devoted to the period before 1800.

11559

Haussmann, William A. German-American hymnology, 1683–1800. Americana Germanica, v. 2, no. 3, 1898: 1–61.   E184.G3G3, v. 2

11560

Henry, Hugh T. Philadelphia choir book of 1787. *In* American Catholic Historical Society of Philadelphia. Record, v. 26, Sept. 1915: 208–223.
                                         E184.C3A4, v. 26

Discusses the content of *A Compilation of the Litanies and Vesper Hymns and Anthems as They Are Sung in the*

Catholic Church: Adapted to the Voice or Organ, published by John Aitken.

11561
McCorkle, Donald M.   The Moravian contribution to American music (1740–1840). *In* Music Library Association. Notes, v. 13, Sept. 1956: 597–603.
ML27.U5M695, v. 13

11562
Macdougall, Hamilton C.   Early New England psalmody; an historical appreciation, 1620–1820. Brattleboro, Stephen Daye Press [ᶜ1940] 179 p. facsims., music.
ML200.3.M23E2

Reprinted in New York by Da Capo Press (1969).

Studies the origin, nature, and development of American sacred music in New England. In his consideration of the Revolutionary period, the author focuses on the work of William Billings and his influence on other composers.

11563
Maurer, Maurer.   Music in Wachovia, 1753–1800. William and Mary quarterly, 3d ser., v. 8, Apr. 1951: 214–227.
F221.W71, 3d s., v. 8

Points to the unique Moravian music of Pennsylvania and North Carolina.

11564
National Society of the Colonial Dames of America. *Pennsylvania*.   Church music and musical life in Pennsylvania in the eighteenth century . . . prepared by the Committee on Historical Research. Philadelphia, Printed for the Society, 1926–47. 3 v. in 4. illus., facsims. (part fold.), ports. (Publications of the Pennsylvania Society of the Colonial Dames of America, 4)
E186.4.P33, no. 4
ML3111.P3N18

Bibliography: v. 1, p. [251]–255; v. 2, p. [273]–278; v. 3, pt. 2, p. [541]–550.
Reprinted in New York by AMS Press (1972).

Primarily a compilation of representative sacred and secular music. The compilers consider numerous Pennsylvania sects individually and provide miscellaneous essays on such subjects as Indian music, English secular music, Francis Hopkinson, and Benjamin Franklin. Part 2 of volume 3 includes essays on Roman Catholic, Episcopal, Jewish, and Welsh music and Lutheran and Reformed Church hymnody.

11565
Satcher, Herbert B.   Music of the Episcopal church in Pennsylvania in the eighteenth century. Historical magazine of the Protestant Episcopal church, v. 18, Dec. 1949: 372–413.
BX5800.H5, v. 18

11566
Smith, Carleton S.   The 1774 psalm book of the Reformed Protestant Dutch Church in New York City. Musical quarterly, 34, Jan. 1948: 84–96. facsims.
ML1.M725, v. 34

11567
Stevenson, Robert M.   Protestant church music in America; a short survey of men and movements from 1564 to the present. New York, W. W. Norton [1966] xiii, 168 p. music, plates.
ML3111.S83

Bibliography: p. 133–151.

Chapters 1–7 (p. 3–73) provide an overview of the period to 1800.

11568
Wienandt, Elwyn A., *and* Robert H. Young.   The anthem in England and America. New York, Free Press [1970] xiii, 495 p. illus., music.
ML3265.W53

Bibliography: p. [460]–470.

In chapters 5 and 6 (p. 169–242) the author discusses the efforts of such men as James Lyon, William Billings, Daniel Bayley, and Andrew Law to establish the anthem in America.

11569
Williams, George W.   Eighteenth-century organists of St. Michael's, Charleston. South Carolina historical magazine, v. 53, July–Oct. 1952: 146–154, 212–222. illus.
F266.S55, v. 53

See also his "Early Organists at St. Philip's, Charleston," in v. 54, Apr. 1953, p. 83–87.

11570
Wolf, Edward C.   Lutheran church music in America during the eighteenth and early nineteenth centuries. 1960. ([473] p.)
Micro AC–1, no. 61–218

Thesis (Ph.D.)—University of Illinois.

Abstracted in *Dissertation Abstracts*, v. 21, Apr. 1961, p. 3118–3119.

11571
Wolf, Edward C.   Music in old Zion, Philadelphia, 1750–1850. Musical quarterly, v. 58, Oct. 1972: 622–652. facsims.
M1.M725, v. 58

7. Church Architecture

11572
Chyet, Stanley F.   A synagogue in Newport. American Jewish archives, v. 16, Apr. 1964: 41–50.
E184.J5A37, v. 16

Designed by Peter Harrison and consecrated in December 1763.

11573
Dorsey, Stephen P.   Early English churches in America, 1607–1807. New York, Oxford University Press, 1952. xvi, 206 p. illus., maps (on lining papers), ports.
NA5207.D6

Bibliography: p. 195–199.

Surveys Episcopal churches in New England, the middle states, Maryland, Virginia, and the Carolinas. Following an essay on architectural developments and a list of all Episcopal churches extant in each region in 1952, Dorsey provides 118 illustrations, with accompanying historical notes, showing interior views, ornaments, and exteriors of 52 selected churches.

11574

Friary, Donald R.   The architecture of the Anglican church in the northern American colonies: a study of religious, social, and cultural expression. 1971. ([1237] p.)

Micro AC–1, no. 71–26,010

Thesis (Ph.D.)—University of Pennsylvania.
Abstracted in *Dissertation Abstracts International*, v. 32A, Oct. 1971, p. 2026.

11575

Kelly, John Frederick.   Early Connecticut meetinghouses; being an account of the church edifices built before 1830, based chiefly upon town and parish records. New York, Columbia University Press, 1948. 2 v. illus., maps, plans.   NA5230.C8K4

An elaborate historical and technical description of the design, construction, and maintenance of 87 meetinghouses extant in 1948. Nearly 700 photographs and measured drawings are included. In an introductory essay, the author defines four phases in the development of architectural style for the meetinghouse and credits the contributions of several master builders, notably Asher Benjamin, Ithiel Town, and David Hoadley.

11576

Mason, George C.   Colonial churches of tidewater Virginia. Richmond, Va., Whittet and Shepperson, 1945. xv, 381 p. 89 plates (incl. maps, plans)

BR555.V8M35

"Based on a study . . . the results of which were first published in the William and Mary quarterly historical magazine (second series), during the years 1938–1943."— Introduction.
Bibliographic footnotes.

11577

Murtagh, William J.   Moravian architecture and town planning; Bethlehem, Pennsylvania, and other eighteenth-century American settlements. Chapel Hill, University of North Carolina Press [1967] viii, 145 p. illus., plans.   NA735.B4M8

Bibliography: p. 135–139.

11578

Rawlings, James S.   Virginia's colonial churches, an architectural guide; together with their surviving books, silver & furnishings. Richmond, Garrett & Massie, 1963. xi, 286 p. col. illus., map (on lining papers)   NA5230.V8R3

Bibliography: p. 271–273.

A technical description of the architectural features of 48 edifices constructed between 1647 and 1776.

11579

Rose, Harold W.   The colonial houses of worship in America; built in the English colonies before the Republic,

1607–1789, and still standing. New York, Hastings House [1964, ᶜ1963] xiv, 574 p. illus., maps.

NA5207.R6

Bibliography: p. 543–550.

Presents photographs of 345 churches, devoting a separate chapter to each of the original states as well as Maine, Vermont, and West Virginia. Rose includes individual maps of the states locating all identified edifices.

11580

Wallace, Philip B.   Colonial churches and meeting houses, Pennsylvania, New Jersey, and Delaware. Measured drawings by William Allen Dunn; introduction by Horace Wells Sellers. New York City, Architectural Book Pub. Co. [ᶜ1931] xii, 291 p. (chiefly illus.)

NA5207.W3

PHILOSOPHY AND THOUGHT

1. GENERAL

11581

Anderson, Paul R., *and* Max H. Fisch.   Philosophy in America from the Puritans to James, with representative selections. New York, D. Appleton-Century Co. [ᶜ1939] xiii, 570 p. illus., facsim. (The Century philosophy series)   B851.A5

"General bibliography": p. [543]–562.
Reprinted in New York by Octagon Books (1969).

For the 18th century, the editors discuss and present representative selections from the works of Jonathan Mayhew, John Woolman, Samuel Johnson, Jonathan Edwards, Cadwallader Colden, Benjamin Franklin, Ethan Allen, Thomas Jefferson, John Taylor, John Adams, Benjamin Rush, and Samuel Stanhope Smith.

11582

Barker, Charles A.   American convictions; cycles of public thought, 1600–1850. Philadelphia, Lippincott [1970] xix, 632 p. illus., ports.   E169.1.B228

Includes bibliographic references.

Contains a narrative survey of intellectual developments in science, religion, and politics during the Enlightenment and Revolutionary period.

11583

Boorstin, Daniel J.   The lost world of Thomas Jefferson. New York, H. Holt [1948] xi, 306 p.   B878.B6

Bibliographic references included in "Notes" (p. [249]– 294).

An analysis of the Jeffersonian world view based on the writings of Jefferson and a kindred circle composed of David Rittenhouse, Benjamin Rush, Joseph Priestley, Charles Willson Peale, Benjamin Barton Smith, and Thomas Paine. Boorstin contends that the American environment was the critical element in Jeffersonian thought—the conquest of the wilderness had produced an outlook that was naturalistic, utilitarian, and activist. At its core, Jeffersonianism harbored an anti-intellectual mistrust of speculative philosophy, placing a premium instead on "constructive" action.

Casting the deity in the role of a Supreme Workman who had created in nature a perfect order, the Jeffersonians saw man as a free, rational being whose task it was to dominate his world and to establish a social system that would protect individual liberties, especially the right of each citizen to make a beneficial adjustment to his environment.

11584
Brasch, Frederick E. The Newtonian epoch in the American colonies (1680–1783). *In* American Antiquarian Society, *Worcester, Mass.* Proceedings, new ser., v. 49, Oct. 1939: 314–332.   E172.A35, n.s., v. 49

11585
Buchanan, John G. The Puritan philosophy of history from Restoration to Revolution. *In* Essex Institute, *Salem, Mass.* Historical collections, v. 104, Oct. 1968: 329–348.   F72.E7E81, v. 104

11586
Buranelli, Vincent. Colonial philosophy. William and Mary quarterly, 3d ser., v. 16, July 1959: 343–362.
F221.W71, 3d s., v. 16

The study of colonial metaphysics, epistemology, psychology, and ethics reveals, as in no other areas, the debt that provincial thinkers like Cadwallader Colden and John Witherspoon owed to earlier Western philosophers.

11587
Burns, Edward M. The philosophy of history of the Founding Fathers. Historian, v. 16, spring 1954: 142–168.   D1.H22, v. 16

11588
Commager, Henry S. America and the eighteenth-century community of learning. *In* American Society for Eighteenth-Century Studies. Irrationalism in the eighteenth century. Edited by Harold E. Pagliaro. Cleveland, Press of Case Western Reserve University, 1972. (Studies in eighteenth-century culture, v. 2) p. 13–31.
CB411.A57

11589
Curti, Merle E. The growth of American thought. 3d ed. New York, Harper & Row [1964] xx, 939 p. illus., facsims., ports.   E169.1.C87 1964

Bibliography: p. 797–900.

In the early chapters of his comprehensive social history of American thought, the author considers the adaptation of the European heritage during the 17th century, the impact of the doctrines and values of the Enlightenment, and the surge of cultural nationalism that accompanied the Revolution. Although Curti feels that the Revolution dealt severe blows to the agencies of intellectual life—schools and colleges, churches, libraries, and the colonial press—he also finds that it did much to popularize freedom of religion, the philosophy of natural rights, Deism, and humanitarianism, and to instill a more democratic conception of culture.

11590
Curti, Merle E. Human nature in American thought: the age of reason and morality, 1750–1860. Political science quarterly, v. 68, Sept. 1953: 354–375.
H1.P8, v. 68

11591
Davis, Richard B. The intellectual golden age in the colonial Chesapeake Bay country [1720–89] Virginia magazine of history and biography, v. 78, Apr. 1970: 131–143.   F221.V91, v. 78

11592
Delmage, Rutherford E. The American idea of progress, 1750–1800. *In* American Philosophical Society, *Philadelphia.* Proceedings, v. 91, Oct. 24, 1947: 307–314.
Q11.P5, v. 91

11593
Delmage, Rutherford E. The theory of the future: a study of the idea of progress in the literature of the American Revolution. 1937. 218 l.

Thesis (Ph.D.)—Cornell University.

11594
Fay, Jay W. American psychology before William James. New Brunswick, N.J., Rutgers University Press, 1939. x, 240 p. (Rutgers University studies in psychology, no. 1)   BF108.U5F3

"Bibliography of primary sources in American psychology before 1890": p. 227–232.
Reprinted in New York by Octagon Books (1966).

In two sections entitled the "American Enlightenment, 1714–1776" (p. 16–49) and the "Scottish Philosophy, 1776–1827" (p. 50–90), the author discusses the writings of Samuel Johnson, Jonathan Edwards, Thomas Clap, J. D. Gros, John Witherspoon, S. Stanhope Smith, Levi Hedge, Frederick Beasley, Benjamin Rush, and Asa Burton.

11595
Fiering, Norman S. President Samuel Johnson and the circle of knowledge. William and Mary quarterly, 3d ser., v. 28, Apr. 1971: 199–236.
F221.W71, 3d s., v. 28

In tracing Johnson's study of the fundamental relationships between the branches of knowledge and their proper philosophical order, the author discovers that by the mid-18th century moral philosophy had become the queen of the sciences.

11596
Foster, William E. Some Rhode Island contributions to the intellectual life of the last century. *In* American Antiquarian Society, *Worcester, Mass.* Proceedings, new ser., v. 8, Apr. 1892: 103–132.
E172.A35, n.s., v. 8

11597
Gummere, Richard M. The American colonial mind and the classical tradition; essays in comparative culture.

Cambridge, Harvard University Press, 1963. xiii, 228 p.   E162.G88

Bibliography and notes: p. [201]–223.

Explores in 11 essays the impact of Greek and Roman ideas on American life and thought between 1607 and 1789. The author finds that the classic tradition was an ever present, almost overpowering companion of such Revolutionary leaders as Franklin, Adams, and Jefferson as well as Loyalists like Jonathan Boucher.

11598

Gummere, Richard M.   The heritage of the classics in colonial North America; an essay on the Greco-Roman tradition. *In* American Philosophical Society, *Philadelphia*. Proceedings, v. 99, Apr. 1955: 68–78.
                    Q11.P5, v. 99

11599

Jones, Adam L.   Early American philosophers. New York, Macmillan Co., 1898. 80 p. (Columbia University contributions to philosophy, psychology and education, v. 2, no. 4)   B21.C75, v. 2, no. 4

Bibliography: p. [79]–80.
Reprinted in New York by F. Ungar Pub. Co. (1958).

This early work surveys briefly the formal philosophical thought of William Brattle, Benjamin Franklin, Cadwallader Colden, and Thomas Clap and then concentrates upon the two major colonial philosophers Samuel Johnson and Jonathan Edwards. Americans were concerned before 1800, Jones surmises, with the more practical aspects of life, and thus only Edwards' *Freedom of the Will* attracted much attention.

11600

Miller, Perry.   The life of the mind in America, from the Revolution to the Civil War. New York, Harcourt, Brace & World [1965] xi, 338 p.   E169.1.M6273

Contains books 1 and 2 and part of book 3 of a work planned for nine books. In his exploration of the contours of the American intellect, the author treats its evangelical basis, the foundations of the legal system, and the development of theoretical and applied science. Miller contends that American writers and thinkers, faced with the challenge of national and self identification, found an explanatory model in the Enlightenment ideal of the sublime—the perfect adaptation of the individual to society and society to nature. Unfinished at the time of Miller's death were extended essays on education, political economy, philosophy, theology, nature and the self, and a prologue on "The Sublime in America."

11601

Muelder, Walter G., Laurence Sears, *and* Anne V. Schlabach, *eds.*   The development of American philosophy; a book of readings. 2d ed. [Boston] Houghton Mifflin [1960] xi, 643 p.   B851.M8 1960

Includes bibliographies.

Contains excerpts (p. 1–107) from the writings of Jonathan Edwards, Samuel Johnson, John Woolman, Benjamin Franklin, Thomas Jefferson, Elihu Palmer, Ethan Allen, Thomas Paine, and John Witherspoon.

11602

Newlin, Claude M.   Philosophy and religion in colonial America. New York, Philosophical Library [1962] ix, 212 p.   BR520.N4

Reprinted in New York by Greenwood Press (1968).

Discusses the philosophic content of works written after 1720 by several New England ministers, especially Jonathan Edwards and Samuel Johnson, but also including Cotton Mather, John Wise, Gilbert Tennent, George Whitefield, Jonathan Mayhew, and others.

11603

Persons, Stow.   American minds; a history of ideas. New York, Holt, Rinehart and Winston [1958] xii, 467 p.
                    B851.P4

"Suggestions for further reading": p. 452–457.
"The mind of the American Enlightenment, 1740–1812": p. [69]–143.

11604

Persons, Stow.   The cyclical theory of history in eighteenth-century America. American quarterly, v. 6, summer 1954: 147–163.   AP2.A3985, v. 6

11605

Petersen, Richard J.   Scottish common sense in America, 1768–1850: an evaluation of its influence. 1963. ([222] p.)   Micro AC–1, no. 64–2225

Thesis (Ph.D.)—American University.
Abstracted in *Dissertation Abstracts*, v. 24, Apr. 1964, p. 4164–4165.

John Witherspoon's assumption of the presidency of Princeton in 1768 marked the formal introduction of the dualistic common sense philosophy into the American colonies.

11606

Riley, Isaac W.   American philosophy, the early schools. New York, Dodd, Mead, 1907. x, 595 p.   B865.R5

Reprinted in New York by Russell & Russell (1958?).

Summarizes the thought and provides brief excerpts from the works of such 18th-century Americans as the idealists Samuel Johnson and Jonathan Edwards; the Deists at Princeton, Yale, Harvard, and King's colleges; the materialists Cadwallader Colden and Benjamin Rush; and the realists John Witherspoon and Samuel Stanhope Smith.

11607

Riley, Issac W.   American thought from Puritanism to pragmatism and beyond. [2d ed.] New York, H. Holt, 1923. x, 438 p.   B851.R5 1923

"Select bibliography: p. 425–432.
Reprinted in New York by Greenwood Press (1969).

Includes five chapters (p. 1–139) on 18th-century philosophers.

11608

Savelle, Max.   Prolegomena to a history of liberalism in eighteenth-century Anglo-America. Bucknell review, v. 9, Dec. 1960: 224–246.   AP2.B887, v. 9

11609

Schneider, Herbert W.   A history of American philosophy. 2d ed. New York, Columbia University Press, 1963. xviii, 590 p.   B851.S4 1963

"Guide to recent literature, compiled with the assistance of Gerald Runkle": p. [525]–581.

First edition published as no. 18 in the Columbia Studies in American culture series (1946. 646 p.)

In the section on the Enlightenment in America, the author surveys the thought of John Wise, Thomas Jefferson, William Bentley, Ethan Allen, Benjamin Rush, and other 18th-century figures, providing excerpts from their writings to illustrate the development of their ideas.

11610

Wright, Louis B.   The classical tradition in colonial Virginia. *In* Bibliographical Society of America. Papers. v. 33; 1939. Portland, Me. p. 85–97.   Z1008.B51P, v. 33

11611

Wright, Louis B.   The first gentlemen of Virginia; intellectual qualities of the early colonial ruling class. San Marino, Calif., Huntington Library, 1940. xi, 373 p. (Huntington Library publications)   F229.W965

Tracing the development of the colony's aristocracy from English patterns, the author reviews the intellectual attainments of the ruling class with emphasis upon the Fitzhugh, Wormeley, Lee, Carter, Beverley, and Byrd families. Wright observes that by the early 18th-century Virginians had already acquired the social and intellectual characteristics that they would display during the Revolutionary era.

11612

Wright, Louis B.   Intellectual history and the colonial South. William and Mary quarterly, 3d ser., v. 16, Apr. 1959: 214–227.   F221.W71, 3d s., v. 16

2. The Enlightenment in Europe and America

11613

Becker, Carl L.   The Heavenly City of the eighteenth century philosophers. New Haven, Yale University Press, 1932. 168 p.   B802.B4

In the Storrs Lectures at Yale University in 1931 the author advanced the proposition that the underlying preconceptions of the Enlightenment were essentially the same, with obvious allowances, as those of the 13th century. The *philosophes* "demolished the Heavenly City of St. Augustine only to rebuild it with more up-to-date material." Rejecting Christian philosophy, Enlightenment thinkers nonetheless retained a naive faith in the authority of nature and reason and a mystical belief in the perfectibility of man. They felt that through the use of their natural faculties they could bring their ideas and conduct, and hence the institutions under which they lived, into harmony with the universal natural order, thus gaining immortality through the memory of posterity. Becker concludes that the *philosophes'* ideology was just as absolutist and doctrinaire as that of the medieval scholastics.

At a symposium held at Colgate University in 1956, 13 scholars presented critiques, commentaries, and reassessments of Becker's work that have been edited by Raymond O. Rockwood and published under the title *Carl Becker's Heavenly City Revisited* (Ithaca, N.Y., Cornell University Press [1958] 227 p. B802.B44R6).

11614

Cassirer, Ernst.   The philosophy of the Enlightenment. Translated by Fritz C. A. Koelln and James P. Pettegrove. Princeton, Princeton University Press, 1951. xiii, 366 p.   B802.C33

Bibliographic footnotes.

Delineates the principal ideas of the continental Enlightenment to explain historically and systematically the substance and point of view of its philosophy. The author contends that Enlightenment thinkers not only ordered, developed, and clarified the content of the philosophical heritage of preceding centuries, but produced a completely original form of philosophical thought. Cassirer sees the movement as a unity dominated by a few fundamental ideas expressed with strict consistency and an exact arrangement and contends that the century of the Enlightenment was neither unhistorical nor antihistorical in spirit.

11615

Clive, John L., *and* Bernard Bailyn.   England's cultural provinces: Scotland and America. William and Mary quarterly, 3d ser., v. 11, Apr. 1954: 200–213.   F211.W71, 3d s., v. 11

Compares the effects of the Enlightenment in Scotland and America.

11616

Gay, Peter.   The Enlightenment, an interpretation. New York, Knopf, 1966–69. 2 v.   B802.G3

Includes bibliographies.

Contents: [v. 1] The rise of modern paganism.—v. 2. The science of freedom.

A comprehensive study conceived as a social history of the environment, philosophy, and program of the *philosophes*. Describing them as a family of cultural critics, religious skeptics, and political reformers, the author examines in the first volume the dialectical interplay between their appeal to antiquity and their tension with Christianity which ultimately ended in triumph of neopagan ideals. In the second, he considers the *philosophes'* appreciation of the accelerated material progress of the 18th century and their contention that progress lay at the base of any program of humanity, toleration, and political reform. In his conclusion, Gay characterizes the American Revolution as the program of the Enlightenment in practice and traces links between the *philosophes* and the Founding Fathers.

11617

Gay, Peter.   The party of humanity; essays in the French Enlightenment. New York, Knopf, 1964 [^c1963] xiii, 289, viii p.   B1925.E5G38

Bibliographic footnotes.

A collection of nine previously published essays on aspects of the Enlightenment, including considerations of Voltaire as the representative *philosophe*, suggestions for a biography of Rousseau, an attempt to find the sources of unity in the French Enlightenment, criticism of Carl Becker's *Heavenly City*, and a final summation in which Gay argues that the *philosophes'* commitment to criticism, humanity, passion, and irreverent humor remains among their most enduring legacies.

11618

Hazard, Paul. European thought in the eighteenth century, from Montesquieu to Lessing. [Translation from the original French by J. Lewis May] New Haven, Yale University Press, 1954. xx, 477 p.   B802.H313

Bibliographic footnotes.

A comprehensive survey tracing the decline of the Christian interpretation of life and the rise of characteristic Enlightenment attitudes toward science, social science, and religion. The author's stated purpose is to detect and bring to light the flaws which were the undoing of 18th-century philosophy.

11619

Kaplan, Lawrence S. The *philosophes* and the American Revolution. Social science, v. 31, Jan. 1956: 31–35.   H1.S55, v. 31

Stresses the influence of the French Enlightenment on the political philosophy of the American revolutionaries.

11620

Koch, Adrienne, *ed.* The American Enlightenment; the shaping of the American experiment and a free society. New York, G. Braziller [ᶜ1965] 669 p.   E183.K65

"Sources": p. 660–667. "For further reading": p.[668]–669.

A selection of 289 letters and autobiographical and other writings of Benjamin Franklin, John Adams, Thomas Jefferson, James Madison, and Alexander Hamilton.

11621

Koch, Adrienne. The contest of democracy and aristocracy in the American Enlightenment. *In* International Congress on the Enlightenment, *1st, Geneva.* Transactions. v. 3. Genève, Institut et musée Voltaire, 1963. (Studies on Voltaire and the eighteenth century, v. 24) p. 999–1018.   PQ2105.A2S8, v. 24

11622

Koch, Adrienne. Power, morals, and the Founding Fathers; essays in the interpretation of the American Enlightenment. Ithaca, N.Y., Great Seal Books [1961] xi, 158 p.   E175.9.K6

Explores the contributions made by Franklin, Jefferson, Hamilton, Adams, and Madison to the American tradition of experimental humanism and contends that their ability to balance power and morals in order to protect individual liberties ensured the success of the early Republic.

11623

Koch, Adrienne. Pragmatic wisdom and the American Enlightenment. William and Mary quarterly, 3d ser., v. 18, July 1961: 313–329.   F221.W71, 3d s., v. 18

The American Enlightenment was characterized by a firm commitment to the humanistic ideal of the whole man and a strong attachment to experimental empiricism as the best guide to attainable human ends.

11624

Kraus, Michael. America and the utopian ideal in the eighteenth century. Mississippi Valley historical review, v. 22, Mar. 1936: 487–504.   E171.J87, v. 22

Deals in part with the effect of the American Revolution upon utopian thought in England and on the Continent.

11625

Kraus, Michael. Eighteenth century humanitarianism: collaboration between Europe and America. Pennsylvania magazine of history and biography, v. 60, July 1936: 270–286.   F146.P65, v. 60

11626

Lucas, Frank L. The art of living; four eighteenth-century minds: Hume, Horace Walpole, Burke, Benjamin Franklin (sequel to *The Search for Good Sense*). London, Cassell [1959] 285 p. illus.   CB411.L8

11627

Martin, Kingsley. French liberal thought in the eighteenth century; a study of political ideas from Bayle to Condorcet. Edited by J. P. Mayer. New York, Harper and Row [1963, ᶜ1962] xxiv, 316 p. (Harper torchbooks; the Academy library)   JA84.F8M3 1963

Reprint of the 3d rev. ed.
First published in 1929.
Bibliography: p. 306–312.

In waging the age-old battle between authoritarianism and liberalism, French thinkers of the 18th century formulated a secular religion that wedded the concepts of progress and democracy, substituted reason and knowledge for faith and grace as the means of salvation, and held that the prospect of improving the conditions of man and society by bringing them into harmony with natural law was an ideal sufficient to coordinate men's purposes and to serve as a criterion of right and wrong.

11628

Schlereth, Thomas J. The cosmopolitan ideal in Enlightenment thought: its form and function in the ideas of Franklin, Hume, and Voltaire, 1694–1790. 1969.

Thesis (Ph.D.)—State University of Iowa.

11629

Spurlin, Paul M. Diderot, Alembert and the *Encyclopédie* in the United States, 1760–1800. *In* International Congress on the Enlightenment, *2d, St. Andrews, Scot., 1967.* Transactions. v. 3. Genève, Institut et Musée Voltaire, 1967. (Studies on Voltaire and the eighteenth century, v. 57) p. 1417–1434.   PQ2105.A2S8, v. 57

11630

Switzer, Richard. America in the *Encyclopédie. In* International Congress on the Enlightenment, *2d, St. Andrews, Scot., 1967.* Transactions. v. 4. Genève, Institut et Musée Voltaire, 1967. (Studies on Voltaire and the eighteenth century, v. 58) p. 1481–1499.

PQ2105.A2S8, v. 58

11631

Wohl, Harold B. Charles Chauncy and the Age of Enlightenment in New England. 1956. ([216] p.)

Micro AC–1, no. 18,565

Thesis (Ph.D.)—State University of Iowa.
Abstracted in *Dissertation Abstracts*, v. 16, no. 10, 1956, p. 1895.

Investigates the conditions that spawned an indigenous enlightened movement among the cultural elite of New England between the Great Awakening and the Revolution by focusing upon the leadership exerted by Charles Chauncy, minister of the First Church of Boston.

EDUCATION

1. GENERAL

11632

Cremin, Lawrence A. American education; the colonial experience, 1607–1783. New York, Harper & Row [1970] xiv, 688 p. LA215.C73 1970

"Bibliographical essay": p. [577]–668.

Believing that the education of man encompasses more than the content of formal programs in schools and colleges, the author broadens his study to include the educational influence of home, church, and community as well as that of the popular instruments of learning: the press, libraries, and voluntary associations. Cremin notes that the colonial experience taught Americans to live in freedom largely because of the differences as well as the distance between London and the colonies; the Revolution then hastened the development of a uniquely American education, since the new government had to educate its citizens in order to ensure the survival of both freedom and virtue.

11633

Greene, Evarts B. Some educational values of the American Revolution. *In* American Philosophical Society, *Philadelphia.* Proceedings, v. 68, no. 3, 1929: 185–194.

Q11.P5, v. 68

The very fact of participation in the Revolution proved educational for professional men from all states.

11634

Hansen, Allen O. Liberalism and American education in the eighteenth century. With an introduction by Edward H. Reisner. New York, Macmillan Co., 1926. xxv, 317 p. LA206.H3

Issued also as thesis (Ph.D.)—Columbia University.
Bibliography: p. 265–296.
Reprinted in New York by Octagon Books (1965).

Describes nine plans for a national system of education in the United States published between 1786 and 1800. Included are the proposals of Benjamin Rush (1786) and Noah Webster (1788) and those submitted by Samuel Knox and Samuel Harrison Smith (1797) in a competition conducted by the American Philosophical Society.

11635

Jernegan, Marcus W. Factors influencing the development of American education before the Revolution. *In* Mississippi Valley Historical Association. Proceedings. v. 5; 1911/12. Cedar Rapids, Iowa, 1912. p. 190–206. F351.M66, v. 5

11636

Klassen, Frank H. Persistence and change in eighteenth century colonial education. History of education quarterly, v. 2, June 1962: 83–99. L11.H67, v. 2

11637

Middlekauff, Robert. A persistent tradition: the classical curriculum in eighteenth-century New England. William and Mary quarterly, 3d ser., v. 18, Jan. 1961: 54–67. F221.W71, 3d s., v. 18

11638

Monroe, Paul. Founding of the American public school system; a history of education in the United States. v 1. From the early settlements to the close of the Civil War period. New York, Macmillan Co., 1940. xiv, 520 p. illus., facsims. LA212.M62, v. 1

Reprinted in New York by Hafner Pub. Co. (1971).

Contains six chapters (p. 34–182) on colonial educational practices. A second volume of supplementary documents, entitled *Readings in the Founding of the American Public School System*, was originally issued on microfilm.

11639

Reinhold, Meyer. Opponents of classical learning in America during the Revolutionary period. *In* American Philosophical Society, *Philadelphia.* Proceedings, v. 112, Aug. 1968: 221–234. Q11.P5, v. 112

11640

Sensabaugh, George F. Milton in early American schools. Huntington Library quarterly, v. 19, Aug. 1956: 353–383. Z733.S24Q, v. 19

11641

Seybolt, Robert F. Apprenticeship & apprenticeship education in colonial New England & New York. New York City, Teachers College, Columbia University, 1917. 121 p. (Teachers College, Columbia University. Contributions to education, no. 85) HD4885.U5S4 LB5.C8, no. 85

Bibliography: p. [115]–121.
Thesis (Ph.D.)—Columbia University, 1917.
Reprinted in New York by Arno Press (1969) and AMS Press (1972).

11642

Seybolt, Robert F. The evening school in colonial America. Urbana, University of Illinois, 1925. 68 p. ([University of Illinois] College of Education. Bureau of Educational Research. Bulletin no. 24) LA206.S4

Bibliographic footnotes.

Reprinted in New York by Arno Press (1971. LC5551.S4 1971).

11643

Seybolt, Robert F. Source studies in American colonial education: the private school. Urbana, University of Illinois, 1925. 109 p. ([University of Illinois] College of Education. Bureau of Educational Research. Bulletin no. 28) LC49.S4

University of Illinois bulletin, v. 23, no. 4.
Bibliographic footnotes.
Reprinted in New York by Arno Press (1971).

A series of essays on the nature of instruction in the private school.

11644

Tyack, David B. Forming the national character: paradox in the educational thought of the Revolutionary generation. Harvard educational review, v. 36, winter 1966: 29–41. L11.H3, v. 36

11645

Wright, Esmond. Education in the American colonies: the impact of Scotland. *In* Essays in Scotch-Irish history. Edited by E. R. R. Green. London, Routledge & K. Paul; New York, Humanities Press [1969] (Ulster-Scot historical series, 2) p. 18–45. E184.S4E8

2. NEW ENGLAND

11646

Butler, Vera M. Education as revealed by New England newspapers prior to 1850. [Philadelphia, Printed by the Majestic Press] 1935. ix, 503 p. facsim. LA205.B8 1935a

Issued also as thesis (Ed.D.)—Temple University.
Bibliography: p. [468]–481.
Reprinted in New York by Arno Press (1969).

Traces the progress of New England colleges, the development of academies, and the rise of common schools through thirteen Massachusetts and nine Connecticut newspapers published between 1704 and 1850.

11647

Cole, Norwood M. The origin and development of town-school education in colonial Massachusetts, 1635–1775. 1957. ([615] p.) Micro AC–1, no. 58–1076

Thesis (Ed.D.)—University of Washington.
Abstracted in *Dissertation Abstracts*, v. 18, Apr. 1958, p. 1328.

11648

Hendrick, Irving G. A reappraisal of colonial New Hampshire's effort in public education. History of education quarterly, v. 6, summer 1966: 43–60. L11.H67, v. 6

11649

Jackson, George L. The development of school support in colonial Massachusetts. New York City, Teachers College, Columbia University, 1909. 95 p. (Teachers College, Columbia University. Contributions to education, no. 25) LA304.J3

"List of references consulted": p. [93]–95.
Published also as thesis (Ph.D.)—Columbia University.
Reprinted in New York by Arno Press (1969) and AMS Press (1972).

11650

Martin, George H. The evolution of the Massachusetts public school system; a historical sketch. New York, D. Appleton, 1894. xx, 284 p. (International education series, v. 29) [LA304.M38] Micro 1654 LA

"Massachusetts schools before the Revolution": p. 44–89.

11651

Martin, George H. Massachusetts schools before the Revolution. New England magazine, new ser., v. 9, Nov. 1893: 356–368. AP2.N4, n.s., v. 9

11652

Middlekauff, Robert. Ancients and axioms: secondary education in eighteenth-century New England. New Haven, Yale University Press, 1963. xiii, 218 p. illus. (Yale historical publications. Miscellany 77) LA222.M53

"Bibliographical note": p. 196–203.
Reprinted in New York by Arno Press (1971).

Focusing on the decline of the grammar school and the emergence of the academy in the post-Revolutionary period, the author examines change and continuity in the Puritan tradition of public support, state supervision, and classical studies for schools. Middlekauff concludes that institutional changes were made in response to new business and commercial needs, but that the pursuit of liberal learning was continued and incorporated into the curriculum of the academy. Though new in form, the academy was improvised from colonial experiences and bound by the custom of public responsibility.

11653

Seybolt, Robert F. The private schools of colonial Boston. Cambridge, Mass., Harvard University Press, 1935. 106 p. LA306.B7S42

"This little study supplements . . . [the author's] 'Public Schools of Colonial Boston.' It is another pioneer attempt to gather together the sources for an account of the intellectual life of the time."—Foreword.

Contents: Private schools of the seventeenth century.—School announcements of the eighteenth century.—Commentary.—Appendix. Supplementary list of teachers.

Reprinted in New York by Arno Press (1969) and in Westport, Conn., by Greenwood Press (1970).

11654

Seybolt, Robert F.   The public schools of colonial Boston, 1635–1775. Cambridge, Harvard University Press, 1935. viii, 101 p. (Harvard documents in the history of education)   LA306.B7S4

Reprinted in New York by Arno Press (1969).

11655

Small, Walter H.   Early New England schools. Boston, Ginn, 1914. ix, 401 p.   LA206.S6

Edited by William Holden Eddy.
Bibliography: p. 397–401.
Reprinted in New York by Arno Press (1969).

In his survey of 17th- and 18th-century institutions and practices, Small finds a general decline in public support for education after the Revolution.

11656

Small, Walter H.   The New England grammar school, 1700–1800. School review, v. 14, Jan. 1906: 42–56.
L11.S55, v. 14

11657

Teaford, Jon C.   The transformation of Massachusetts education, 1670–1780. History of education quarterly, v. 10, fall 1970: 287–307.   L11.H67, v. 10

3. MIDDLE ATLANTIC REGION

11658

Bonar, James A.   Benjamin Rush and the theory and practice of republican education in Pennsylvania. 1965. ([269] p.)   Micro AC–1, no. 65–6876

Thesis (Ph.D.)—Johns Hopkins University.
Abstracted in *Dissertation Abstracts*, v. 26, Oct. 1965, p. 2034–2035.

11659

Burr, Nelson R.   Education in New Jersey, 1630–1871. Princeton, N.J., Princeton University Press, 1942. 355 p. plates, ports. [The Princeton history of New Jersey]   LA331.B8

Bibliography: p. [317]–344.

11660

Kaestle, Carl F.   The origins of an urban school system: New York City, 1750–1850. 1971.

Thesis (Ph.D.)—Harvard University.

11661

MacConnell, John C.   Charity education in colonial Pennsylvania. 1968. ([338] p)   Micro AC–1, no. 69–9296

Thesis (Ph.D.)—Rutgers University.
Abstracted in *Dissertation Abstracts*, v. 29A, June 1969, p. 4300.

11662

Mulhern, James.   A history of secondary education in Pennsylvania. Philadelphia, 1933. xv, 714 p. facsims.
LA355.M8 1933

Issued also as thesis (Ph.D.)—University of Pennsylvania.

Bibliography: p. 611–684.
Reprinted in New York by Arno Press (1969).

11663

Myers, Charles B.   Public secondary schools in Pennsylvania during the American Revolutionary era, 1760–1800. 1968. ([281] p.)   Micro AC–1, no. 68–16,347

Thesis (Ph.D.)—George Peabody College for Teachers.
Abstracted in *Dissertation Abstracts*, v. 29A, Nov. 1968, p. 1498–1499.

11664

Paltsits, Victor H.   New sources in the history of education at Kingston, New York, 1774–1788. *In* New York State Historical Association. Quarterly journal, v. 12, Apr. 1931: 129–140.   F116.N865, v. 12

11665

Tully, Alan.   Literacy levels and educational development in rural Pennsylvania, 1729–1775. Pennsylvania history, v. 39, July 1972: 301–312.   F146.P597, v. 39

11666

Weber, Samuel E.   The charity school movement in colonial Pennsylvania. Philadelphia, Press of G. F. Lasher [preface 1905] 74 p.   LA355.W35

Thesis (Ph.D.)—University of Pennsylvania.
Bibliography: p. 65–74.
Reprinted in New York by Arno Press (1969).

4. THE SOUTH

11667

Bullock, Thomas K.   Schools and schooling in eighteenth century Virginia. 1961. ([252] p.)
Micro AC–1, no. 62–2198

Thesis (Ph.D.)—Duke University.
Abstracted in *Dissertation Abstracts*, v. 22, June 1962, p. 4253.

11668

Easterby, James H.   The South Carolina education bill of 1770. South Carolina historical and genealogical magazine, v. 48, Apr. 1947: 95–111.   F266.S55, v. 48

One of several attempts to establish public schools and colleges in South Carolina. The text of the bill is included.

11669

Hienton, Louise J.   The free school in Prince George's County, 1723–1774. Maryland historical magazine, v. 59, Dec. 1964: 380–391.   F176.M18, v. 59

11670

Jernegan, Marcus W.   The educational development of the southern colonies. School review, v. 27, May–June 1919: 360–376, 405–425.   L11.S55, v. 27

11671

Knight, Edgar W., *ed.* A documentary history of education in the South before 1860. Chapel Hill, University of North Carolina Press [1949–53] 5 v.   LA206.K6

A particularly diverse collection of both unpublished and published materials based on a broad conception of the social and intellectual context of the history of education. The first volume, *European Inheritances*, documents the existence of the common colonial enthusiasm for education for religious and economic reasons. The second, *Toward Educational Independence*, focuses on the expanding interest in native plans for democratic education following the Revolution.

11672

McCaul, Robert L. Education in Georgia during the period of royal government, 1752–1776. Georgia historical quarterly, v. 40, June–Sept. 1956: 103–112, 248–259.   F281.G2975, v. 40

Contents: 1. The financial support of schools and schoolmasters.—2. Public-school masters and private-venture teachers.

11673

McCrady, Edward. Education in South Carolina prior to and during the Revolution. Charleston, S.C., News and Courier Book Presses, 1883. 54 p. [South Carolina Historical Society. Collections. v. 4, no. 5]
F266.S71, v. 4
LA361.M22

11674

Mathews, Alice E. Pre-college education in the southern colonies. 1968. ([401] p.)
Micro AC–1, no. 69–10,348

Thesis (Ph.D.)—University of California, Berkeley.
Abstracted in *Dissertation Abstracts*, v. 29A, June 1969, p. 4433.

Public and governmental support for education greatly increased with the Revolution, as did a republican bias in learning. Writers stressed the need to create a literate citizenry that would safeguard common liberties and to educate the talented for public life.

11675

Tyler, Lyon G. Education in colonial Virginia. William and Mary quarterly historical magazine, v. 5, Apr. 1897: 219–223; v. 6, July–Oct. 1897, Jan. 1898: 1–7, 71–86, 171–187; v. 7, July–Oct. 1898: 1–9, 65–76.
F221.W71, v. 5–7

11676

Umbreit, Allen G. Education in the southern colonies. 1932.

Thesis (Ph.D.)—State University of Iowa.

5. TEACHERS AND TEACHING

11677

Elsbree, Willard S. The American teacher; evolution of a profession in a democracy. New York, American Book Co. [ᶜ1939] ix, 566 p. illus., plates.   LB1775.E57

Includes "Suggested readings."
Reprinted in Westport, Conn., by Greenwood Press (1970).
"The colonial schoolmaster": p. 7–124.

11678

Kaplan, Sidney. The reduction of teachers' salaries in post-Revolutionary Boston. New England quarterly, v. 21, Sept. 1948: 373–379.   F1.N62, v. 21

11679

Linehan, John C., *and* Thomas H. Murray. Irish schoolmasters in the American colonies, 1640–1775, with a continuation of the subject during and after the War of the Revolution. Washington, D.C., American-Irish Historical Society, 1898. 31 p.   E184.I6L6

11680

Pfeiffer, Robert H. The teaching of Hebrew in colonial America. Jewish quarterly review, v. 45, Apr. 1955: 363–373.   DS101.J5, v. 45

11681

Seybolt, Robert F. The public schoolmasters of colonial Boston. [Cambridge, Mass.] Priv. print. at the Harvard University Press, 1939. 31 p.   LA306.B7S39

11682

Seybolt, Robert F. Schoolmasters of colonial Boston [1635–1776] *In* Colonial Society of Massachusetts, *Boston*. Publications. v. 27. Transactions, 1927/30. Boston, 1932. p. 130–156.   F61.C71, v. 27

11683

Seybolt, Robert F. Schoolmasters of colonial Philadelphia. Pennsylvania magazine of history and biography, v. 52, Oct. 1928: 361–371.   F146.P65, v. 52

11684

Straub, Jean S. Teaching in the Friends' Latin School of Philadelphia in the eighteenth century. Pennsylvania magazine of history and biography, v. 91, Oct. 1967: 434–456.   F146.P65, v. 91

11685

Wilbert, Martin I. Some early teachers of chemistry in America. American journal of pharmacy, v. 76, Aug. 1904: 353–364. illus., ports.   RS1.A45, v. 76

11686

A Young man's journal of a hundred years ago. *In* New Haven Colony Historical Society, *New Haven*. Papers. v. 4. New Haven, 1888. p. 193–208.   F98.N5, v. 4

Excerpts from the journal of an unidentified Yale graduate who took up a teaching post at Albany Academy. Edited by Simeon E. Baldwin, the excerpts are dated August 5, 1782, to September 14, 1785.

6. PRIMERS AND TEXTBOOKS

11687

Belok, Michael V. The courtesy tradition and early school-books. History of education quarterly, v. 8, fall 1968: 306–318. L11.H67, v. 8

11688

Ford, Paul L., *ed.* The New-England primer; a history of its origin and developments, with a reprint of the unique copy of the earliest known edition and many fac-simile illustrations and reproductions. New York, Printed for Dodd, Mead, 1897. xi, 354 p. plates. (The Booklovers' library of early American literature)
PE1119.A1N43 Rare Bk. Coll.

Contents: Introduction.—Reprint of the *New England Primer.*—Appendices. Reprint of the *New English Tutor.* Reprint of Rogers' exhortation unto his children. Cotton Mather's plea for catechising. Clarke's *Saying the Catechism.* Reprint of *The Holy Bible in Verse.* Bibliography of the *New England Primer.* Variorum of the *New England Primer.*

11689

Kiefer, Monica M. American children through their books, 1700–1835. Philadelphia, 1948. 248 p. facsims.
PN1009.A1K5 1948a

Thesis (Ph.D.)—University of Pennsylvania.
Bibliography: p. [230]–243.

11690

Littlefield, George E. Early schools and school-books of New England. Boston, Mass., Club of Odd Volumes, 1904. 354 p. illus., facsims., plates.
LA206.L77 Rare Bk. Coll.

Reprinted in New York by Russell & Russell (1965).

11691

Nash, Ray. American writing masters and copybooks; history and bibliography through colonial times. Boston, Colonial Society of Massachusetts, 1959. xiii, 77 p., xxxvi p. of facsims. (Studies in the history of calligraphy, 3) Z43.A2N28

11692

Nietz, John A. Old textbooks: spelling, grammar, reading, arithmetic, geography, American history, civil government, physiology, penmanship, art, music, as taught in the common schools from colonial days to 1900. [Pittsburgh] University of Pittsburgh Press [1961] vii, 364 p. facsims., map, ports. LT23.N5

Bibliographic footnotes.

11693

Pike, Nicholas. A new and complete system of arithmetic, composed for the use of the citizens of the United States. Newbury-port [Mass.] Printed and sold by J. Mycall, 1788. 512 p. illus.
QA101.P65 Rare Bk. Coll.

"Rules for reducing all the coins, from Canada to Georgia; also English, Irish and French coins and Spanish dollars, each to the par of all the others": p. 111–123.

The first mathematical textbook published in the United States.

11694

Smith, Lydia A. H. Three spelling books of American schools, 1740–1800. Harvard Library bulletin, v. 16, Jan. 1968: 72–93. plates. Z881.H3403, v. 16

On Thomas Dilworth's *New Guide to the English Tongue*, William Perry's *Only Sure Guide to the English Tongue*, and Daniel Fenning's *Universal Spelling-Book.*

7. RELIGIOUS EDUCATION

11695

Dunn, William K. What happened to religious education? The decline of religious teaching in the public elementary school, 1776–1861. Baltimore, Johns Hopkins Press, 1958. 346 p. facsim. LC111.D8

A condensation and a reworking, in some parts, of the writer's doctoral dissertation completed at the Johns Hopkins University in 1956. The title of the original work was *The Decline of the Teaching of Religion in the American Public Elementary School in the States Originally the Thirteen Colonies, 1776–1861.*

Bibliography: p. [313]–338.

11696

Garrett, Edwin A. The evolution and early years of the Episcopal Academy in Philadelphia [1749–1816] Historical magazine of the Protestant Episcopal church, v. 21, Dec. 1952: 461–473. BX5800.H5, v. 21

11697

Haller, Mabel. Early Moravian education in Pennsylvania. Nazareth, Pa. Moravian Historical Society, 1953. xiii, 428 p. illus., facsims., map, ports. (Transactions of the Moravian Historical Society, v. 15)
E184.M8M8, v. 15
BX8553.M7, v. 15

Thesis—University of Pennsylvania.
Bibliography: p. 359–397.

11698

Holtz, Adrian A. A study of the moral and religious elements in American secondary education up to 1800. [Menasha, Wis., 1917] 86 p. LC311.H6

Thesis (Ph.D.)—University of Chicago, 1914.
Bibliography: p. [78]–86.

11699

Hunter, Margaret A. Education in Pennsylvania promoted by the Presbyterian church, 1726–1837. Philadelphia, 1937. 170 p. LC580.H8 1937

Thesis (Ed.D.)—Temple University, 1937.
Bibliography: p. 163–170.

11700

Jackson, James C. The religious education of the Negro in South Carolina prior to 1850. Historical magazine of the Protestant Episcopal church, v. 36, Mar. 1967: 35–61. BX5800.H5, v. 36

11701

James, Sydney V. Quaker meetings and education in the eighteenth century. Quaker history, v. 51, autumn 1962: 87–102. BX7635.A1F6, v. 51

11702

Kemp, William W. The support of schools in colonial New York by the Society for the Propagation of the Gospel in Foreign Parts. New York City, Teachers College, Columbia University, 1913. viii, 279 p. facsim. (Teachers College, Columbia University. Contributions to education, no. 56) LA337.K4
LB5.C8

Published also as thesis (Ph.D.)—Columbia University, 1914.
Bibliography: p. 278–279.
Reprinted in New York by Arno Press (1969) and AMS Press (1972).

Describes the founding and general work of the society, its regulations concerning schoolmasters, its role in developing elementary schools in various parts of the colony, and the routine and curriculum of the society's schools.

11703

Livingood, Frederick G. Eighteenth century Reformed church schools. Part xxxv of a narrative and critical history prepared at the request of the Pennsylvania German Society. Norristown, Pa., 1930. xix, 313 p. illus., facsims., plates, ports. LC586.R35L5

Bibliography: p. [299]–313.
First published in the *Proceedings and Addresses*, v. 38, 1927 (F146.P23, v. 38) of the Pennsylvania-German Society.
The author's thesis (Ph.D.), *German Reformed Education in Pennsylvania During the Eighteenth Century*, was submitted to Harvard University in 1925.

11704

Maurer, Charles L. Early Lutheran education in Pennsylvania. Philadelphia, Dorrance [c1932] xii, 294 p. facsims., plates, ports. LC574.M3 1932

A part of "A Narrative and Critical History of the Pennsylvania Germans" (see preface).
Bibliography: p. [272]–284.
First published in the *Proceedings and Addresses*, v. 40, 1929 (F146.P23, v. 40), of the Pennsylvania-German Society.

11705

Pears, Thomas C. Colonial education among Presbyterians. *In* Presbyterian Historical Society. Journal, v. 30, June–Sept. 1952: 115–126, 165–174.
BX8905.P7A4, v. 30

11706

Seybolt, Robert F. The S.P.G. myth: a note on education in colonial New York. Journal of educational research, v. 13, Feb. 1926: 129–137. L11.J75, v. 13

To counter assertions that the majority of English schools in the province of New York, 1700–1776, were organized under the auspices of the Society for the Propagation of the Gospel in Foreign Parts, the author lists the names of 200 "English schools" not supported by the society.

11707

Straub, Jean S. Quaker school life in Philadelphia before 1800. Pennsylvania magazine of history and biography, v. 89, Oct. 1965: 447–458. F146.P65, v. 89

11708

Wells, Guy F. Parish education in colonial Virginia. New York City, Teachers College, Columbia University, 1923. 95 p. (Teachers College, Columbia University. Contributions to education, no. 138) LA379.W4
LB5.C8, no. 138

Bibliography: p. 93–95.
Thesis (Ph.D.)—Columbia University.
Reprinted in New York by Arno Press (1969) and AMS Press (1972).

11709

Woody, Thomas. Early Quaker education in Pennsylvania. New York City, Teachers College, Columbia University, 1920. 287 p. map. (Teachers College, Columbia University. Contributions to education, no. 105)
LA355.W66
LB5.C8, no. 105

Published also as thesis (Ph.D.)—Columbia University, 1918.
Bibliography: p. 272–282.
Reprinted in New York by Arno Press (1969) and AMS Press (1972).

8. HIGHER EDUCATION AND THE COLLEGES

a. General

11710

Brinton, Howard H. The Quaker contribution to higher education in colonial America. Pennsylvania history, v. 25, July 1958: 234–250. illus. F146.P597, v. 25

11711

Carrell, William D. American college professors, 1750–1800. History of education quarterly, v. 8, fall 1968: 289–305. L11.H67, v. 8

11712

Carrell, William D. Biographical list of American college professors to 1800. History of education quarterly, v. 8, fall 1968: 358–374. L11.H67, v. 8

11713

Carrell, William D. Social, political, and religious involvements of American college professors, 1750–1800. 1968. ([194] p.) Micro AC–1, no. 68–16,341

Thesis (Ph.D.)—George Peabody College for Teachers.

Abstracted in *Dissertation Abstracts*, v. 29A, Nov. 1968, p. 1432.

11714

Casteel, James D. Professors and applied ethics: higher education in a Revolutionary era, 1750–1800. 1964. ([320] p.)   Micro AC–1, no. 65–3560

Thesis (Ph.D.)—George Peabody College for Teachers.

Abstracted in *Dissertation Abstracts*, v. 25, May 1965, p. 6561–6562.

Focuses on five American moral philosophers—Samuel Johnson, William Smith, John Witherspoon, Ezra Stiles, and Samuel Stanhope Smith.

11715

Conner, Robert D. W. The genesis of higher education in North Carolina [1745–89] North Carolina historical review, v. 28, Jan. 1951: 1–14.   F251.N892, v. 28

11716

Demarest, William H. S. A survey of the colonial colleges in the Revolution. American collector, v. 2, Apr. 1926: 245–254.   Z1007.A475, v. 2

11717

Durnin, Richard D. The role of the presidents in the American coilleges of the colonial period. History of education quarterly, v. 1, June 1961: 23–31.
                                                        L11.H67, v. 1

11718

Gummere, Richard M. The schools, colleges and the classics in colonial America. *In* Numismatic and Antiquarian Society of Philadelphia. Proceedings. v. 32; 1928/35. Philadelphia, 1935. p. 178–195.
                                                        CJ15.N7, v. 32

11719

Haddow, Anna. Political science in American colleges and universities, 1636–1900. Edited, with an introduction and concluding chapter, by William Anderson. New York, D. Appleton-Century Co. [c1939] xiv, 308 p. (The Century political science series)   JA88.U6H27

The author's thesis (Ph.D.), *History of the Teaching of Political Science in the Colleges and Universities of the United States, 1636–1916*, was submitted to George Washington University in 1937.

Reprinted in New York by Octagon Books (1969). "The period of independence and federation, 1770–1825": p. [41]–110.

11720

Hangartner, Carl A. Movements to change American college teaching, 1700–1830. 1955. ([394] p.)
                                        Micro AC–1, no. 65–7517

Thesis (Ph.D.)—Yale University.

Abstracted in *Dissertation Abstracts*, v. 28A, May 1968, p. 4459–4460.

Establishes the existence of five movements that altered the traditional teacher-student relationship, ranging from the introduction of the lecture system to the use of the logical synthetic method in teaching almost all subject matter.

11721

Hofstadter, Richard, *and* Walter P. Metzger. The development of academic freedom in the United States. New York, Columbia University Press, 1955. xvi, 527 p.   LA205.H55

Bibliographic footnotes.

Contents: The age of the college, by R. Hofstadter.—The age of the university, by W. P. Metzger.

Includes two chapters (p. 114–208) on higher education and the emergent academic profession in the 18th century.

11722

Humphrey, David C. Colonial colleges and English dissenting academies: a study in transatlantic culture. History of education quarterly, v. 12, summer 1972: 184–197.   L11.H67, v. 12

11723

McAnear, Beverly. College founding in the American colonies, 1745–1775. Mississippi Valley historical review, v. 42, June 1955: 24–44.   E171.J87, v. 42

A new spirit of rationalism and the development of promotional techniques contributed to the firm establishment of seven new colleges, each more easily founded and better planned than its predecessor. Along with three that were opened during the Revolution, these colleges raised the cultural level of the population at large as well as the educational standards of the professions.

11724

McAnear, Beverly. The raising of funds by the colonial colleges. Mississippi Valley historical review, v. 38, Mar. 1952: 591–612.   E171.J87, v. 38

Sudden popular interest in higher education was translated by educational promoters into financial support for new colleges in six colonies that soon emulated Harvard, Yale, and William and Mary.

11725

McAnear, Beverly. The selection of an alma mater by pre-Revolutionary students. Pennsylvania magazine of history and biography, v. 73, Oct. 1949: 429–440.
                                                        F146.P65, v. 73

11726

Masson, Margaret W. The premises and purposes of higher education in American society, 1745–1770. 1971. ([295] p.)   Micro AC–1, no. 72–15,121

Thesis (Ph.D.)—University of Washington.

Abstracted in *Dissertation Abstracts International*, v. 32A, May 1972, p. 6346.

11727

Meriwether, Colyer. Our colonial curriculum, 1607–1776. Washington, D.C., Capital Pub. Co., 1907. 301 p.   LA206.M4

Discusses the content of college courses in ancient languages, theology and philosophy, geography, history, science, mathematics, disputation, and modern languages.

11728

Middleton, Arthur P.   Anglican contributions to higher education in colonial America. Pennsylvania history, v. 25, July 1958: 251–268.   F146.P597, v. 25

11729

Peckham, Howard H.   *Collegia Ante Bellum*: attitudes of college professors and students toward the American Revolution. Pennsylvania magazine of history and biography, v. 95, Jan. 1971: 50–72.   F146.P65, v. 95

Unorganized and indecisive, professors were by and large followers or reluctant joiners, not leaders.

11730

Moore, Herbert G.   Our colonial colleges. Daughters of the American Revolution magazine, v. 82, June–Dec. 1948: 413–418, 513–518, 584–587, 677–681, 741–747, 810–814, 875–880; v. 83, Jan.–Dec. 1949: 8–14, 104–110, 189–195, 277–282, 384–388, 453–459, 567–571, 640–647, 735–742, 807–812, 891–896, 961–965. illus.
E202.5.A12, v. 82–83

Contents: 1. Moravian Seminary and College.—2. The Ursuline Convent.—3. Salem Academy and College.—4. Linden Hall.—5. Harvard University.—6. The College of William and Mary.—7. Yale University.—8. University of Pennsylvania.—9. Princeton University.—10. Columbia University.—11. Washington and Lee University.—12. Brown University.—13. Rutgers University.—14. St. John's College.—15. Dartmouth College.—16. Dickinson College.—17. College of Charleston.—18. Hampden-Sidney College.—19. University of Delaware.

11731

Potter, David.   Debating in the colonial chartered colleges; an historical survey, 1642 to 1900. New York, Teachers College, Columbia University, 1944. xiv, 158 p. (Teachers College, Columbia University. Contributions to education, no. 899)   PN4187.P6
LB5.C8, no. 899

Issued also as thesis (Ph.D.)—Columbia University. Bibliography: p. 149–158.

Discusses the procedure for and the subject matter of syllogistic and forensic disputation and traces the rise of literary and debating societies in the colonial chartered colleges.

11732

Pryde, George S.   The Scottish universities and the colleges of colonial America. Glasgow, Jackson, 1957. 55 p. (Glasgow University publications, new ser., 1)
LA227.P7

Bibliographic footnotes.

Attempts to measure the influence exerted by the five Scottish universities upon the nine colleges established in America before the Revolution.

11733

Sack, Saul   History of higher education in Pennsylvania. Harrisburg, commonwealth of Pennsylvania, Pennsylvania Historical and Museum Commission, 1963. 2 v. (xii, 817 p.) illus., ports.   LA355.S25

Bibliography: v. 2, p. 753–801.

11734

Schneider, Donald O.   Education in colonial American colleges, 1750–1770, and the occupations and political offices of their alumni. 1965. ([254] p.)
Micro AC–1, no. 66–10,705

Thesis (Ph.D.)—George Peabody College for Teachers.

Abstracted in *Dissertation Abstracts*, v. 27A, Nov. 1966, p. 1244.

11735

Sloan, Douglas.   The Scottish Enlightenment and the American college ideal. [New York] Teachers College Press, Columbia University [1971] xi, 298 p. (Teachers College studies in education)   LA226.S58

Contents: The Scottish universities in the Enlightenment.—Log colleges, revivals, and the mother church of Scotland: the Presbyterian academy.—Old Side educator: Francis Alison.—The Scottish Enlightenment comes to Princeton: John Witherspoon.—Education, progress, and polygamy: Samuel Stanhope Smith.—From Nottingham Academy to the Edinburgh of America: Benjamin Rush.—Science, society, and the curriculum: conclusions.—Bibliography (p. [249]–280).—Appendix (p. 281–284): Presbyterian academies.

11736

Smith, Willard W.   The relations of college and state in colonial America. 1950. ([177] p.)
Micro AC–1, no. 1654

Thesis (Ph.D.)—Columbia University.

Abstracted in *Microfilm Abstracts*, v. 10, no. 2, 1950, p. 97–98.

11737

Stoeckel, Althea L.   Politics and administration in the American colonial colleges. 1958. ([176] p.)
Micro AC–1, no. 59–586

Thesis (Ph.D.)—University of Illinois.

Abstracted in *Dissertation Abstracts*, v. 19, Apr. 1959, p. 2595–2596.

11738

Tewksbury, Donald G.   The founding of American colleges and universities before the Civil War, with particular reference to the religious influences bearing upon the college movement. New York City, Teachers College, Columbia University, 1932. x, 254 p. illus., maps. (Teachers College, Columbia University. Contributions to education, no. 543)   LB5.C8, no. 543
LA226.T35 1932a

Issued also as thesis (Ph.D.)—Columbia University.

Bibliography: p. 223–254.

Reprinted in New York by Arno Press (1969).

Of 182 permanent colleges and universities founded before the Civil War, 19 were established before 1790.

11739
Thomson, Robert P.   Colleges in the Revolutionary South; the shaping of a tradition. History of education quarterly, v. 10, winter 1970: 399–412.   L11.H67, v. 10

11740
Walsh, James J.   Education of the founding fathers of the Republic; scholasticism in the colonial colleges; a neglected chapter in the history of American education. New York, Fordham University Press, 1935. xii, 377 p. facsims.   LA226.W3

Reprinted in Freeport, N.Y., by Books for Libraries Press (1970).

Examines the colonial curriculum through the commencement theses and *quaestiones* of Harvard, William and Mary, Yale, the College of New Jersey, King's College, the College of Philadelphia, and the College of Rhode Island. The author finds that scholasticism continued to form the philosophic base of American higher education through the Revolutionary period. Walsh contends that a significant number of the signers of the Declaration of Independence and the Constitution had been trained in this medieval mode of teaching and thought and that their approach to the problems of creating a new nation was shaped by its influence.

b. Harvard

11741
Adams, Henry.   Harvard College, 1786–1787. *In his* Historical essays. New York, C. Scribner's Sons, 1891. p. 80–121.   D7.A21

Based on the student diary of John Quincy Adams.

11742
Chandler, Samuel.   Harvard on the eve of the Revolution. Harvard graduates' magazine, v. 10, Mar.–June 1902: 375–381, 529–535.   LH1.H3G7, v. 10

The diary of a Harvard student, February 10, 1773, to December 9, 1774, with an introduction by Sarah E. Mulliken.

11743
Davis, Andrew M.   The investments of Harvard College, 1776–1790: an episode in the finances of the Revolution. Quarterly journal of economics, v. 20, May 1906: 399–418.   HB1.Q3, v. 20

11744
Dexter, Franklin B.   On some social distinctions at Harvard and Yale, before the Revolution. *In* American Antiquarian Society, *Worcester, Mass.* Proceedings, new ser., v. 9, Oct. 1893: 34–59.
E172.A35, n.s., v. 9

An examination of class lists reveals that students were ranked according to the social position of their fathers or families.

11745
Foster, Francis Apthorp.   The burning of Harvard Hall, 1764, and its consequences. *In* Colonial Society of Massachusetts, *Boston.* Publications. v. 14. Transactions, 1911/13. Boston, 1913. p. 2–43.   F61.C71, v. 14

11746
Lane, William C.   The rebellion of 1766 in Harvard College. *In* Colonial Society of Massachusetts, *Boston.* Publications. v. 10. Transactions, 1904/6. Boston, 1907. p. 33–59.   F61.C71, v. 10

11747
The Laws of Harvard College [1767]   *In* Colonial Society of Massachusetts, *Boston.* Publications. v. 31. Collections. Boston, 1933. p. 347–383.   F61.C71, v. 31

11748
Matthews, Albert.   Tentative lists of temporary students at Harvard College, 1639–1800. *In* Colonial Society of Massachusetts, *Boston.* Publications. v. 17. Transactions, 1913/14. Boston, 1915. p. 271–285.
F61.C71, v. 17

11749
Morison, Samuel E.   Three centuries of Harvard, 1636–1936. Cambridge, Mass., Harvard University Press, 1936. viii, 512 p. map.   LD2151.M65

11750
Peirce, Benjamin.   A history of Harvard University, from its foundation, in the year 1636, to the period of the American Revolution. Cambridge, Brown, Shattuck, 1833. xix, 316, 159 p.   LD2152.P4

11751
Quincy, Josiah.   The history of Harvard University. Cambridge, J. Owen, 1840. 2 v. illus., facsim.
LD2152.Q7 1840

11752
Young, Edward J.   Subjects for master's degree in Harvard College from 1655 to 1791. *In* Massachusetts Historical Society, *Boston.* Proceedings. v. 18; 1880/81. Boston, 1881. p. 119–151.   F61.M38, v. 18

c. William and Mary

11753
Davis, Virginia W.   Phi Beta Kappa, December 5, 1776. Virginia cavalcade, v. 9, autumn 1959: 34–41. illus., ports.   F221.V74, v. 9

A fraternity founded by five students from the College of William and Mary—John Heath, Thomas Smith, Richard Booker, Armistead Smith, and John Jones.

11754
Phi Beta Kappa. *Virginia Alpha, William and Mary College.* Original records of the Phi Beta Kappa Society [1776–81] William and Mary College quarterly historical magazine, v. 4, Apr. 1896: 213–241.
F221.W71, v. 4

11755

Thomson, Robert P. The reform of the College of William and Mary, 1763–1780. *In* American Philosophical Society, *Philadelphia*. Proceedings, v. 115, June 1971: 187–213. Q11.P5, v. 115

11756

Tyler, Lyon G. Early courses and professors at William and Mary College. [n.p., 1904] 13 p. LD6051.W52T8

Also published in the *William and Mary College Quarterly Historical Magazine*, v. 14, Oct. 1905, p. 71–83.

11757

Tyler, Lyon G. A few facts from the records of William and Mary College. *In* American Historical Association. Papers, v. 4, Oct. 1890: 127–141. E172.A65, v. 4

11758

Vanderbilt, Arthur T. An example to emulate. South Atlantic quarterly, v. 52, Jan. 1953: 5–19. AP2.S75, v. 52

On the members of Phi Beta Kappa at the College of William and Mary from its organization in 1776 until the college closed when the British approached Yorktown in 1781.

11759

William and Mary College, *Williamsburg, Va.* Journal of the meetings of the president and masters of William and Mary College [1763–1784] William and Mary College quarterly historical magazine, v. 3, Apr. 1895: 262–265; v. 4, July 1895–Jan. 1896: 43–46, 130–132, 187–192; v. 5, July 1896–Apr. 1897: 15–17, 83–89, 187–189, 224–229; v. 13, July 1904–Apr. 1905: 15–22, 133–137, 148–157, 230–235; v. 14, July 1905, Apr. 1906: 25–31, 242–246; v. 15, July 1906–Apr. 1907: 1–14, 134–142, 164–174, 264–269; v. 16, Oct. 1907: 73–80. F221.W71, v. 3–5, 13–16

11760

William and Mary College, *Williamsburg, Va.* Notes relative to some of the students who attended the College of William and Mary, 1770–1778. William and Mary College quarterly historical magazine, 2d ser., v. 1, Apr. 1921: 116–130. F221.W71, 2d s., v. 1

Compiled from the bursar's books in the college library. Notes on students attending during 1753–70 appear in the preceding issue, Jan. 1921, p. 27–41.

d. Yale

11761

Bainton, Roland H. Yale and the ministry; a history of education for the Christian ministry at Yale from the founding in 1701. New York, Harper [1971] xiii, 297 p. illus., ports. BV4070.Y36B3

Bibliographic references included in "Notes" (p. 269–290).

The 18th century is treated in chapters 1–6 (p. 1–78).

11762

Clap, Thomas. The annals or history of Yale-College, in New-Haven, in the colony of Connecticut, from the first founding thereof, in the year 1700, to the year 1766: with an appendix, containing the present state of the college, the method of instruction and government, with the officers, benefactors, and graduates. New-Haven, Printed for J. Hotchkiss and B. Mecom, 1766. 122 p. LD6335.C5 Rare Bk. Coll.
AC901.M5, v. 754 Rare Bk. Coll.

Catalogus eorum qui . . . ab anno 1702, ab annum 1765, alicujus gradûs laureâ donati sunt: p. [105]–122.

11763

Cohen, Sheldon S. The Parnassus articles. History of education quarterly, v. 5, Sept. 1965: 174–186. L11.H67, v. 5

Discusses the background and effects of a series of articles which appeared under the pen name Parnassus in the *Connecticut Courant* in 1783, attacking the government of Yale College.

11764

Cowie, Alexander. Educational problems at Yale College in the eighteenth century. [New Haven] Published for the Tercentenary Commission by the Yale University Press, 1936. 32 p. (Connecticut. Tercentenary Commission. Committee on Historical Publications. [Tercentenary pamphlet series] 55) LD6335.C65

11765

Daggy, Robert E. Measures for Yalensia: Naphtali Daggett and Yale College, 1766–1778. 1971. ([379] p.) Micro AC–1, no. 71–25,185

Thesis (Ph.D.)—University of Wisconsin.

Abstracted in *Dissertation Abstracts International*, v. 32A, Dec. 1971, p. 3067.

11766

Gabriel, Ralph H. Religion and learning at Yale; the Church of Christ in the college and university, 1757–1957. New Haven, Yale University Press, 1958. x, 271 p. illus., plates. BR561.Y3G2

Bibliographic references included in "Notes" (p. [256]–260).

"The chapel in a Revolutionary age": p. [32]–53.

11767

McKeehan, Louis W. Yale science, the first hundred years, 1701–1801. New York, H. Schuman [1947] ix, 82 p. (Yale University. School of Medicine. [Yale Medical Library] Historical Library. Publication no. 18) LD6335.M3

Bibliographic references in "Notes" (p. 61–77).

11768

Tucker, Louis Leonard. The Church of England and religious liberty at pre-Revolutionary Yale. William and Mary quarterly, 3d ser., v. 17, July 1960: 314–328. F221.W71, 3d s., v. 17

Focuses upon the presidency of Thomas Clap, 1740–66.

e. College of New Jersey (Princeton)

11769

Alexander, Samuel D.   Princeton College during the eighteenth century. New York, A. D. F. Randolph [ᶜ1872] xv, 326 p.   LD4609.A3

11770

Broderick, Francis L.   Pulpit, physics, and politics: the curriculum of the College of New Jersey, 1746–1794. William and Mary quarterly, 3d ser., v. 6, Jan. 1949: 42–68.   F221.W71, 3d s., v. 6

Traces the growing secularization of the Princeton curriculum.

11771

Come, Donald R.   The influence of Princeton on higher education in the South before 1825. William and Mary quarterly, 3d ser., v. 2, Oct. 1945: 359–396.
                                    F221.W71, 3d s., v. 2

11772

Maclean, John.   History of the College of New Jersey, from its origin in 1746 to the commencement of 1854. Philadelphia, J. B. Lippincott, 1877. 2 v.
                                    LD4608.M16

Reprinted in New York by Arno Press (1969).

11773

Princeton University.   An account of the College of New-Jersey. In which are described the methods of government, modes of instruction, manner and expences of living in the same, &c. With a prospect of the college neatly engraved. Published, by order of the trustees, for the information of the public; particularly of the friends and benefactors of the institution, in Europe and America. Woodbridge, in New-Jersey, Printed by James Parker, 1764. 47 p. fold. plate.
                                    LD4609.A2 Rare Bk. Coll.

Probably written by Samuel Finley, president of the college.

11774

Savage, Henry L., *ed.*   Nassau Hall, 1756–1956. Edited for the Committee [on Bicentennial of Nassau Hall] Princeton, N.J., Princeton University, 1956. vii, 188 p. plans, plates.   LD4615.N3S3

Includes bibliographic references.

11775

Wertenbaker, Thomas J.   Princeton, 1746–1896. Princeton, N.J., Princeton University Press, 1946. plan, plates, ports.   LD4609.W4

Bibliographic footnotes.

f. College and Academy of Philadelphia (University of Pennsylvania)

11776

Adams, Thomas R.   The commencement dialogues and odes of the College of Philadelphia. Library chronicle, v. 17, fall 1950: 30–37.   Z733.P418, v. 17

A bibliography of 11 dialogues composed principally by students, 1761–90.

11777

Cheyney, Edward P.   History of the University of Pennsylvania, 1740–1940. Philadelphia, University of Pennsylvania Press, 1940. x, 461 p.   LD4528.C45

"The printed and manuscript material used in the preparation of this volume and all other known references to the history of the University have been listed, and this list will be preserved in the University library in accessible form for the use of subsequent investigators."—Preface.

11778

Haviland, Thomas P.   "Attend! Be firm! Ye fathers of the state." An account of the commencement, College of Philadelphia, May 17, 1775. General magazine and historical chronicle, v. 52, spring 1950: 129–137.
                                    LH1.P3A4, v. 52

11779

Turner, William L.   The college, academy, and charitable school of Philadelphia, 1740–1779. 1952.

Thesis (Ph.D.)—University of Pennsylvania.

11780

Wood, George B.   The history of the University of Pennsylvania, from its origin to the year 1827. *In* Pennsylvania. Historical Society. Memoirs. v. 3, [pt. 1] Philadelphia, 1834. p. [169]–280.   F146.P36, v. 3

g. King's College (Columbia)

11781

Humphrey, David C.   King's College in the city of New York, 1754–1776. 1968. ([669] p.)
                                    Micro AC–1, no. 69–1852

Thesis (Ph.D.)—Northwestern University.
Abstracted in *Dissertation Abstracts*, v. 29A, Feb. 1969, p. 2643.

11782

Thomas, Milton H.   The King's College building, with some notes on its later tenants. *In* New York Historical Society. Quarterly, v. 39, Jan. 1955: 23–61. map, plates, port.   F116.N638, v. 39

h. Rhode Island College (Brown)

11783

Bronson, Walter C.   The history of Brown University, 1764–1914. Providence, The University, 1914, ix, 547 p. illus.   LD638.B7

Bibliography: p. 522–534.
Reprinted in New York by Arno Press (1971).

11784

The College scene in Providence, 1786–1787.   Transcribed and annotated by Noel P. Conlon. Introduction and interpolation by Clarkson A. Collins. Rhode Island history, v. 27, June 1968: 65–71.   F76.R472, v. 27

Concerns an unsigned manuscript couched in pseudo-biblical language that was found among the Carter-Danforth papers at the Rhode Island Historical Society and that alludes to an apparent struggle between Congregationalists and Baptists at Rhode Island College. The principal figures involved were Asher Robbins, Abel Flint, Jonathan Abbot, and Samuel Eddy.

11785

Goodman, Abram V.   Jewish elements in Brown's early history. *In* American Jewish Historical Society. Publications. no. 37. New York, 1947. p. 135–145.
E184.J4A5, no. 37

11786

Guild, Reuben A.   The first commencement of Rhode Island College [1769], and especially the discussion of American independence, which constituted the prominent feature of the commencement exercises. *In* Rhode Island Historical Society. Collections. v. 7. Providence, 1885. p. [265]–298.
F76.R47, v. 7

"Disputatio forensica. James Mitchel Varnum, respondent. William Williams, opponent. 'Whether British America can under her present circumstances consistent with good policy, affect to become an independent state'": p. 281–298.

i. Queen's College (Rutgers)

11787

Demarest, William H. S.   A history of Rutgers College, 1766–1924. New Brunswick, N.J., Rutgers College, 1924. 570 p. plates, ports.   LD4753.D4

Bibliography: p. 551–557.

In the first six chapters (p. 1–167) the author discusses the founding of Queen's College in 1766 by members of the Dutch Reformed Church, the second charter of 1770, the city and college in the Revolution, and developments during the 1780's under President Jacob Hardenbergh.

11788

McCormick, Richard P.   Rutgers: a bicentennial history. New Brunswick, N.J., Rutgers University Press [1966] xiv, 336 p. illus., ports.   LD4753.M25

Includes bibliographic references.

j. Dartmouth

11789

Chapman, George T.   Sketches of the alumni of Dartmouth College, from the first graduation in 1771 to the present time, with a brief history of the institution. Cambridge, Riverside Press, 1867. 520 p.
LD1435.4.C5

11790

Crosby, Nathan.   The first half century of Dartmouth College: being historical collections and personal reminiscences. Hanover, J. B. Parker, 1876. 56 p.
LD1438.C8

11791

Hill, Ralph N.   The historic college. *In his* The College on the hill; a Dartmouth chronicle. Hanover, N.H., Dartmouth Publications [1965, ᶜ1964] p. 21–87.
LD1438.H58 1965

11792

Richardson, Leon B.   History of Dartmouth College. Hanover, N.H., Dartmouth College publications, 1932. 2 v. (854 p.)   LD1438.R5

11793

Smith, Baxter P.   The history of Dartmouth College. Boston, Houghton, Osgood, 1878. vii, 474 p. facsim., plates, ports.   LD1438.S6

k. Dickinson College

11794

Aldridge, Alfred O.   Dickinson College and the "broad bottom" of early education in Pennsylvania. *In* Dickinson College, *Carlisle, Pa. Library.* Early Dickinsoniana. Carlisle, Pa., 1961 [ᶜ1965] (The Boyd Lee Spahr lectures in Americana, 1757–1961) p. 93–114.
LD1662.A53

11795

Edel, William W.   "John and Mary's College" over Susquehanna. *In* Dickinson College, *Carlisle, Pa.* "John and Mary's College." [Westwood, N.J.] Revell [1956] (The Boyd Lee Spahr lectures in Americana, 1951–1956) p. 17–32.   LD1663.A53

11796

Smith, Joseph B.   A frontier experiment with higher education: Dickinson College, 1783–1800. Pennsylvania history, v. 16, Jan. 1949: 1–19. plate. F146.P597, v. 16

l. Newark Academy (University of Delaware)

11797

McAnear, Beverly.   The charter of the Academy of Newark. Delaware history, v. 4, Sept. 1950: 149–156.
F161.D37, v. 4

11798

Morgan, George.   The colonial origin of Newark Academy and of other classical schools from which arose many colleges and universities. *In* Delaware notes. v. 8; 1934. Newark. p. 7–30.   AS36.D35, v. 8

11799

Ryden, George H.   The Newark Academy of Delaware in colonial days. Pennsylvania history, v. 2, Oct. 1935: 205–224.   F146.P597, v. 2

11800

Ryden, George H.   The relation of the Newark Academy of Delaware to the Presbyterian Church and to higher education in the American colonies. *In* Delaware notes. v. 9; 1935. Newark. p. 7–42.   AS36.D35, v. 9

m. Others

11801
Barroll, L. Wethered. Washington College, 1783. Maryland historical magazine, v. 6, June 1911: 164–179.
F176.M18, v. 6

11802
Connely, Willard. Colonial Americans in Oxford and Cambridge. American Oxonian, v. 29, Jan. 1942: 6–17.
LH1.O8A6, v. 29

11803
Easterby, James H. A history of the College of Charleston, founded 1770. [Charleston, S.C.] 1935. 379 p. illus., plates, ports. LD891.C62E3

Bibliography: p. 335.

11804
Gaines, Richard H. Richmond's first academy, projected by M. Quesnay de Beaurepaire, 1786. *In* Virginia Historical Society. Collections. new ser., v. 11. Richmond, 1892. p. [165]–175. F221.V82, n.s., v. 11

———— ———— Detached copy. AS36.R54

11805
Hislop, Codman. The ghost college that came to life [Union College, Schenectady, N.Y.] American heritage, new ser., v. 3, spring 1952: 29–31. illus.
E171.A43, n.s., v. 3

11806
Ingram, George H. Biographies of the alumni of the Log College. *In* Presbyterian Historical Society. Journal, v. 13, Dec. 1928: 175–184; Mar.–Dec. 1929: 217–223, 255–266, 297–319, 356–362; v. 14, Mar. 1930: 1–27.
BX8905.P7A4, v. 13–14.

Biographical sketches of Charles McKnight, James McCrea, William Robinson, John Roan, John Campbell, Hamilton Bell, William Dean, David Alexander, Daniel Lawrence, John Redman, and William Tennent.

11807
Klein, Frederic S. The spiritual and educational background of Franklin College. Pennsylvania history, v. 5, Apr. 1938: 65–76. F146.P597, v. 5

Founded in 1787.

11808
Lefavour, Henry. The proposed college in Hampshire County in 1762. *In* Massachusetts Historical Society, *Boston.* Proceedings. v. 66, 1936/41. Boston, 1942. p. 53–79. F61.M38, v. 66

11809
McCaul, Robert L. Whitefield's Bethesda College project and other attempts to found colonial colleges. Georgia historical quarterly, v. 44, Sept.–Dec. 1960: 263–277, 381–398. F281.G2975, v. 44

Contents: pt. 1. Whitefield's negotiations in England and in Georgia, to August 1766.—pt. 2. Failure of Whitefield's negotiations with Secker and Northington and the aftermath, August 1766–September 1770.

11810
Tilghman, Tench F. The founding of St. John's College, 1784–1789. Maryland historical magazine, v. 44, June 1949: 75–92. F176.M18, v. 44

11811
Wilmington, Del. Academy. The minutes of the Wilmington Academy, 1777–1802. Edited by E. Miriam Lewis. Delaware history, v. 3, Sept. 1949: 182–226. port.
F161.D37, v. 3

SCIENCE

1. General

11812
Bedini, Silvio A. Early American scientific instruments and their makers. Washington, Museum of History and Technology, Smithsonian Institution, 1964. xii, 184 p. illus., facsims., map (on lining papers), ports. (U.S. National Museum. Bulletin 231) Q11.U6, no. 231
Q185.B4

Bibliography: p. 172–176.

11813
Bell, Whitfield J. A box of old bones: a note on the identification of the mastodon, 1766–1806. *In* American Philosophical Society, *Philadelphia.* Proceedings, v. 93, May 1949: 169–177. illus. Q11.P5, v. 93

Also published in the Society's *Library Bulletin* for 1949, p. 169–177.

On the examination and subsequent identification of bones in the collection of Dr. John Morgan of Philadelphia.

11814
Bell, Whitfield J. Science and humanity in Philadelphia, 1775–1790. 1947. ([323] p.)
Micro AC–1, no. 50–2499

Thesis (Ph.D.)—University of Pennsylvania.
Abstracted in *Microfilm Abstracts*, v. 11, no. 3, 1951, p. 645–646.

11815
Bell, Whitfield J. The scientific environment of Philadelphia, 1775–1790. *In* American Philosophical Society, *Philadelphia.* Proceedings, v. 92, Mar. 1948: 6–14.
Q11.P5, v. 92

11816
Bell, Whitfield J. Some American students of "that shining oracle of physic," Dr. William Cullen of Edinburgh, 1755–1766. *In* American Philosophical Society, *Philadelphia.* Proceedings, v. 94, June 1950: 275–281. facsims. Q11.P5, v. 94

Also published in the Society's *Library Bulletin* for 1950, p. 275–281.

Cullen's students included Edmund Dana and Thomas Bulfinch of Massachusetts, Adam Kuhn, John Morgan, and

William Shippen, Jr, of Pennsylvania, Theodorick Bland and Arthur Lee of Virginia, and Charles Drayton and Nicholas and Samuel Eveleigh of South Carolina.

11817
Clark, Harry H.   The influence of science on American ideas, from 1775–1809. *In* Wisconsin Academy of Sciences, Arts and Letters. Transactions. v. 35. Madison, 1943. p. 305–349.   AS36.W7, v. 35

11818
Cohen, I. Bernard.   The beginning of chemical instruction in America: a brief account of the teaching of chemistry at Harvard prior to 1800. *In* Chymia. v. 3. Philadelphia, 1950. p. 17–44.   QD11.C56, v. 3

11819
Cohen, I. Bernard.   Science and the Revolution. Technology review, v. 47, Apr. 1945: 367–368, 374, 376, 378. illus.   T171.M47, v. 47

On the union of government, science, and technology to produce the nation's first "war industry."

11820
Cohen, I. Bernard.   Some early tools of American science; an account of the early scientific instruments and mineralogical and biological collections in Harvard University. With a foreword by Samuel Eliot Morison. Cambridge, Harvard University Press, 1950. xxi, 201 p. illus.   Q127.U6C6

"References and notes": p. [177]–189.
Reprinted in New York by Russell & Russell (1967).

11821
Cope, Thomas D.   The stargazer's stone. Pennsylvania history, v. 6, Oct. 1939: 205–220.   F146.P597, v. 6

Reports on the observatory known as "stargazers' stone" that Charles Mason and Jeremiah Dixon erected 31 miles west of Philadelphia, the best location that they could find for making observations to determine the size and shape of the earth, 1764–68.

11822
Daniels, George H.   Science in American society; a social history. New York, Knopf, 1971. xii, 390, x p.
                                Q127.U6D33

Bibliography: p. [373]–390.

In the first six chapters (p. 3–151) the author outlines scientific developments in America to the end of the 18th century.

11823
Ewing, Galen W.   Early teaching of science at the College of William and Mary in Virginia. Journal of chemical education, v. 15, Jan. 1938: 3–13. illus., ports.
                                QD1.J93, v. 15

11824
Forster, Johann R., *comp*.   A catalogue of the animals of North America. Containing, an enumeration of the known quadrupeds, birds, reptiles, fish, insects, crustaceous and testaceous animals . . . to which are added short directions for collecting, preserving, and transporting, all kinds of natural history curiosities. London, Sold by B. White, 1771. 43 p. front.
                                QL151.F7 Rare Bk. Coll.

11825
Gillingham, Harrold E.   Some early Philadelphia instrument makers. Pennsylvania magazine of history and biography, v. 51, Oct. 1927: 289–308. facsim., plates.
                                F146.P65, v. 51

Among them were James Ham, David Rittenhouse, and Andrew Ellicott.

11826
Goode, George Brown.   The beginnings of natural history in America. *In* Biological Society of Washington, *Washington, D.C.* Proceedings. v. 3; 1884/86. Washington, 1886. p. [35]–105.   QH1.B4, v. 3

———— ———— Offprint. Washington, Printed for the Society, 1886. [35]–105 p.   QH21.U5G6

Also published in the *Report* of the U.S. National Museum which forms pt. 2 of the *Annual Report* of the Smithsonian Institution for 1897 (Washington, 1901), p. 357–406.

11827
Greene, John C.   American science comes of age, 1780–1820. Journal of American history, v. 55, June 1968: 22–41.   E171.J87, v. 55

Explores the period in which Americans terminated their "colonial" dependence upon British and European science for inspiration and ideas, training, books, instruments, and the accouterments of scientific achievement.

11828
Greene, John C.   Some aspects of American astronomy, 1750–1815. Isis, v. 45, Dec. 1954: 339–358.
                                Q1.I7, v. 45

11829
Hedrick, Ulysses P.   A history of horticulture in America to 1860. New York, Oxford University Press, 1950. xiii, 551 p. illus., ports.   SB83.H4

Bibliography: p. 515–523.

In the first part of the work the author assesses the relative importance of native and immigrant plants in the development of horticulture through the Revolution and focuses on the three major pursuits of the period: gardening, fruit growing, and viticulture.

11830
Hindle, Brooke.   The pursuit of science in Revolutionary America, 1735–1789. Chapel Hill, Published for the Institute of Early American History and Culture, Williamsburg, Va., by University of North Carolina Press [1956] xi, 410 p. illus., ports.   Q127.U6H5

"Bibliographical note": p. 387–392.

Chronicles the organization of scientific work in medical societies and colleges and in such institutions as the American Academy and the American Philosophical Society and analyzes the effects of the Revolution upon scientific investigation. Pointing out that the American pursuit of science was consistently dominated by a utilitarian impulse, Hindle concludes that the agitation for political independence in the 1760's stimulated the colonial commitment to science and that the spirit of nationalism that accompanied the Revolution added to the demand for scientific accomplishment as an indicator of cultural maturity.

11831

Hindle, Brooke.   The Quaker background and science in colonial Philadelphia. Isis, v. 46, Sept. 1955: 243–250.
Q1.I7, v. 46

Finds that those on the periphery of the Quaker circle—liberal Quakers, former Quakers, and near-Quakers—were more responsible for the encouragement and advancement of science than those at its center.

11832

Hornberger, Theodore.   Scientific thought in the American colleges, 1638–1800. Austin, University of Texas Press, 1945. 108 p. illus., port.   Q181.H77

"Published as Project no. 67 of the University Research Institute."

Bibliographic references included in "Notes" (p. [98]–103).

Reprinted in New York by Octagon Books (1968).

11833

Jellison, Richard M.   Scientific enquiry in eighteenth century Virginia. Historian, v. 25, May 1963: 292–311.
D1.H22, v. 25

11834

Kilgour, Frederick G.   Science in the American colonies and the early republic, 1664–1845. Cahiers d'histoire mondiale, v. 10, no. 2, 1967: 393–415.
D1.C22, v. 10

11835

Love, John B.   The colonial surveyor in Pennsylvania [1681–1792] 1970. ([297] p.)
Micro AC–1, no. 71–19,253

Thesis (Ph.D.)—University of Pennsylvania.

Abstracted in *Dissertation Abstracts International,* v. 32A, July 1971, p. 338.

11836

Lovell, John H.   The beginnings of American science; the first botanist. New England magazine, new ser., v. 30, Aug. 1904: 753–767.   AP2.N4, n.s., v. 30

On the work of John Bartram and several other 18th-century scientists.

11837

Ludlum, David M.   Early American hurricanes, 1492–1870. Boston, American Meteorological Society [ᶜ1963]

xii, 198 p. charts, maps. (The History of American weather, no. 1)   QC857.U6H56, no. 1

"A bibliography of early American hurricanes to 1870": p. 185–190. Includes other bibliographies.

Contains three chapters (p. 19–76) on 18th-century hurricanes north and south of Hatteras and along the Gulf Coast.

11838

Ludlum, David M.   Early American tornadoes, 1586–1870. Boston, American Meteorological Society, 1970. 219 p. illus., maps. (The history of American weather, [4])   QC857.U6H56, no. 4

Includes bibliographies.

Discusses chronologically all reported tornadoes and accompanying severe storms occurring in New England, the Middle Atlantic area, the South, and the Old Northwest and reviews early American thought on tornadoes. At least 15 were observed during the Revolutionary period.

11839

Ludlum, David M.   Early American winters. [v. 1] 1604–1820. Boston, American Meteorological Society, 1966. xii, 285 p. illus., maps. (The History of American weather, [2])   QC857.U6H56, no. 2, v. 1

Includes bibliographies.

Contains three chapters on winters in the Northeast, South, and Old Northwest during the 18th century and a fourth (p. 88–137) on the winters of the Revolution.

11840

Morse, William N.   Lectures on electricity in colonial times. New England quarterly, v. 7, June 1934: 364–374.   F1.N62, v. 7

11841

Oliver, John W.   History of American technology. New York, Ronald Press Co. [1956] 676 p.   T21.O45

Bibliographic references at end of each chapter.

"Yankee ingenuity: from Jamestown and Plymouth to the American Revolution": p. 1–21.

11842

Overfield, Richard A.   Science in the *Virginia Gazette,* 1736–1780. Emporia, Graduate Division of the Kansas State Teachers College, 1968. 53 p. (The Emporia State research studies, v. 16, no. 3)   Q225.O92

Bibliographic footnotes.

Although essays and notices may be found touching on nearly all fields of scientific investigation, only medicine received thorough and representative coverage.

11843

Rice, Howard C.   The Rittenhouse orrery; Princeton's eighteenth-century planetarium, 1767–1954. A commentary on an exhibition held in the Princeton University Library. Princeton, N.J., Princeton University Library, 1954. xi, 88 p. illus., facsims., plates, ports.
QB70.A1R5

Bibliography: p. 76–81.

An explanation and history of the mechanical model of the solar system built by David Rittenhouse and acquired by the College of New Jersey (Princeton) in 1771.

11844
Smallwood, William M., *and* Mabel S. C. Smallwood. Natural history and the American mind. New York, Columbia University Press, 1941. xiii, 445 p. illus., facsim., plates, port. (Columbia studies in American culture, no. 8)   QH21.U5S5

Bibliography: p. [355]–424.

11845
Smart, Charles E. The makers of surveying instruments in America since 1700. Troy, N.Y., Regal Art Press, 1962–67. 2 v. (xxvi, 282 p.) illus., facsims.
      TA562.S65

Contains brief sketches of more than 300 men and firms engaged in the manufacture of surveyors' instruments.

11846
Stadelman, Bonnie S. S. Flora and fauna versus mice and mold. William and Mary quarterly, 3d ser., v. 28, Oct. 1971: 595–606.   F221.W71, 3d s., v. 28

Indicates the techniques employed by natural historians in collecting and preserving plant and animal specimens shipped across the Atlantic during the 18th century.

11847
Stearns, Raymond P. Science in the British colonies of America. Urbana, University of Illinois Press [1970] xx, 766 p. illus., facsims., ports.   Q127.N6S7

Bibliography: p. 712–717.

A comprehensive study organized around the role of the Royal Society of London as the central institution and force influencing scientific endeavors in British America. In a major section dealing with the emergence of American science (1740–70), the author concludes that a degree of scientific independence was achieved as a part of the general cultural maturation of colonial society, that the scientific communities of the American Philosophical Society and the American Academy of Arts and Sciences were the key factors in this development, and that American research was dominated by utilitarian concerns for applied science. Numerous detailed biographical sketches are integrated into the text, and comprehensive analytical bibliographic notes are included. A checklist of the Colonial Fellows of the Royal Society is provided in an appendix.

11848
Struik, Dirk J. Yankee science in the making. Boston, Little, Brown, 1948. xiii, 430 p.   Q127.U6S8 1948

Bibliography: p. [387]–416.
Reissued in New York by Cameron Associates in 1957 under the title *The Origins of American Science (New England)*.

Following a background chapter on the colonial setting, the author presents a social history of New England science and technology from the Revolution to the Civil War. Struik concludes that the Revolution stimulated the organization of natural science and medicine, the growth of manufacturing, and the development of technology, but he also contends that throughout the late 18th and early 19th centuries there were few connections between theory and practice in scientific work. The study of science was largely limited to the merchants' concern for astronomy, mathematics, and medicine.

11849
Wilson, J. Walter. The first natural history lectures at Brown University, 1786, by Dr. Benjamin Waterhouse. Annals of medical history, 3d ser., v. 4, Sept. 1942: 390–398. illus., facsims.   R11.A85, 3d s., v. 4

11850
Woolf, Harry. The transits of Venus; a study of eighteenth-century science. Princeton, N.J., Princeton University Press, 1959. xiii, 258 p. illus., facsims., maps (part fold.), ports.   QB509.W75

Bibliography: p. 215–251.

On the attempts made in 1761 and 1769 to determine the dimensions of the solar system from calculations derived from transit observations made at different parts of the earth. Although he focuses on the British and French expeditions, the author notes the independent observations made in North American colonies by such private individuals as John Winthrop and Joseph Brown or under the sponsorship of such institutions as the American Philosophical Society and the Library Company of Philadelphia.

2. LEARNED SOCIETIES

11851
American Philosophical Society, *Philadelphia*. The early history of science and learning in America, with especial reference to the work of the American Philosophical Society during the eighteenth and nineteenth centuries. Philadelphia, American Philosophical Society, 1942. 204 p. illus., facsims., maps, ports. (*Its* Proceedings, v. 86, no. 1, Sept. 25, 1942)   Q11.P5, v. 86

Partial contents: Astronomy during the early years of the American Philosophical Society, by Samuel A. Mitchell.—Medicine and the American Philosophical Society, by Francis R. Packard.—Joseph Priestley and the early history of the American Philosophical Society, by Detlev W. Bronk.—The beginnings of vertebrate paleontology in North America, by George G. Simpson.

11852
Bates, Ralph S. Scientific societies in the United States. New York, J. Wiley [1945] vii, 246 p.   Q11.A1B3

"A publication of the Technology Press, Massachusetts Institute of Technology."
Bibliography: p. 193–220.
"Scientific societies in eighteenth century America": p. 1–27.

11853
Bell, Whitfield J. The American Philosophical Society and medicine. Bulletin of the history of medicine, v. 40, Mar./Apr. 1966: 112–123. R11.B93, v. 40

11854
Bell, Whitfield J. Astronomical observatories of the American Philosophical Society, 1769–1843. *In* American Philosophical Society, *Philadelphia.* Proceedings, v. 108, Feb. 1964: 7–14. Q11.P5, v. 108

11855
Bell, Whitfield J. Patriot-improvers: some early Delaware members of the American Philosophical Society. Delaware history, v. 11, Apr. 1965: 195–207. facsim., ports. F161.D37, v. 11

Among the members were William Poole, Nicholas Way, Charles Henry Wharton, and Col. John Jones.

11856
Brasch, Frederick E. The Royal Society of London and its influence upon scientific thought in the American colonies. Scientific monthly, v. 33, Oct.–Nov. 1931: 336–355, 448–469. ports. Q1.S817, v. 33
——— ——— Offprint. [New York, Science Press, 1931] 43 p. ports. Q127.U6B7

11857
Chinard, Gilbert. The American Philosophical Society and the early history of forestry in America. *In* American Philosophical Society, *Philadelphia.* Proceedings, v. 89, July 1945: 444–488. illus., facsims., port. Q11.P5, v. 89

11858
Chinard, Gilbert. The American Philosophical Society and the world of science (1768–1800). *In* American Philosophical Society, *Philadelphia.* Proceedings, v. 87, July 1943: 1–11. facsim. Q11.P5, v. 87

11859
Denny, Margaret. The Royal Society and American scholars. Scientific monthly, v. 65, Nov. 1947: 415–427. Q1.S817, v. 65

On the influence of the Royal Society in America from 1663 to 1800.

11860
Dvoichenko-Markova, Eufrosina M. The American Philosophical Society and early Russian-American relations. *In* American Philosophical Society, *Philadelphia.* Proceedings, v. 94, Dec. 1950: 549–610. illus., ports. Q11.P5, v. 94

11861
Ellsworth, Lucius F. The Philadelphia Society for the Promotion of Agriculture and Agricultural Reform, 1785–1793. Agricultural history, v. 42, July 1968: 189–199. S1.A16, v. 42

11862
Faÿ, Bernard. Learned societies in Europe and America in the eighteenth century. American historical review, v. 37, Jan. 1932: 255–266. E171.A57, v. 37

Finds that while they played a social, moral, and religious role of great importance, they were inferior to the academies of the 17th century. Almost all the major scientific discoveries of the 18th century were made by individuals.

11863
Grimm, Dorothy F. Franklin's scientific institution. Pennsylvania history, v. 23, Oct. 1956: 437–462. plates, ports. F146.P597, v. 23

The Junto and Library Company, 1728–70.

11864
Hindle, Brooke. The rise of the American Philosophical Society, 1766–1787. 1949. ([71] p.) Micro AC–1, no. 3430

Thesis (Ph.D.)—University of Pennsylvania.
Abstracted in *Dissertation Abstracts*, v. 12, no. 2, 1952, p. 178–179.

11865
Lingelbach, William E. The story of "Philosophical Hall." *In* American Philosophical Society, *Philadelphia.* Proceedings, v. 94, June 1950: 185–213. illus., facsims., ports. Q11.P5, v. 94

Also published in the Society's *Library Bulletin* for 1950, p. 185–213.

11866
Murray, Chalmers S. This our land; the story of the Agricultural Society of South Carolina. Illus. by Anna Heyward Taylor. Charleston, Carolina Art Association [1949] 290 p. illus. S111.A558M3

Bibliography: p. 273–275.

Formed on August 21, 1785, through the efforts of Thomas Heyward, Jr.

11867
Read, Allen W. The Philological Society of New York, 1788. American speech, v. 9, Apr. 1934: 131–136. PE2801.A6, v. 9

11868
Rubincam, Milton. History of Benjamin Franklin's Junto Club. *In* Pennsylvania Historical Junto, *Washington, D.C.* Junto selections; essays on the history of Pennsylvania. Washington, D.C., 1946. p. 7–24. F146.P29

11869
Sioussat, St. George L. The *Philosophical Transactions* of the Royal Society in the libraries of William Byrd of Westover, Benjamin Franklin, and the American Philosophical Society. *In* American Philosophical Society, *Philadelphia.* Proceedings, v. 93, May 1949: 99–113. illus., facsims. Q11.P5, v. 93

Also published in the Society's *Library Bulletin* for 1949, p. 99–113.

11870

Stearns, Raymond P. Colonial fellows of the Royal Society of London, 1661–1788. William and Mary quarterly, 3d ser., v. 3, Apr. 1946: 208–268.

F221.W71, 3d s., v. 3

Analysis with brief biographical sketches.

11871

True, Rodney H. The early development of agricultural societies in the United States. *In* American Historical Association. Annual report. 1920. Washington, 1925. p. 293–306. E172.A60, 1920

11872

[True, Rodney H.] Sketch of the history of the Philadelphia Society for Promoting Agriculture. Prepared for the celebration of the 150th anniversary of its foundation. [Philadelphia, Philadelphia Society for Promoting Agriculture, 1935] 52 p. port. S108.P578

List of members, 1785–1935: p. 25–52.

Established on February 11, 1785, at the instigation of John Beale Bordley.

MEDICINE

1. GENERAL

11873

Aldredge, Robert C. Weather observers and observations at Charleston, South Carolina, 1670–1871. *In* Charleston, *S.C.* Year book. 1940. Charleston, 1942. p. [189]–257. plates, ports. JS13.C33, 1940

Discusses in part 18th-century attempts to correlate air temperature with the appearance of yellow fever.

11874

Beck, John B. An historical sketch of the state of American medicine before the Revolution. *In* Medical Society of the State of New York. Transactions. 1840/43. Albany, 1868. p. 277–305. R15.N652, 1840/43

A reprint from the original *Transactions*, which appeared in a limited edition, was published in Albany by J. Munsell (1842. 35 (i.e. 37) p. R152.B4 Rare Bk. Coll.). The second edition, published in Albany by C. Van Benthuysen, Printer (1850. 63 p.), was reprinted, with a foreword by Charles F. Fishback, in Albuquerque, N.M., by Horn & Wallace (1966. 100 p. R152.B4 1966).

11875

Bell, Whitfield J. Medical practice in colonial America. Bulletin of the history of medicine, v. 31, Sept./Oct. 1957: 442–453. R11.B93, v. 31

11876

Bell, Whitfield J. A portrait of the colonial physician. Bulletin of the history of medicine, v. 44, Nov./Dec. 1970: 497–517. R11.B93, v. 44

11877

Cassedy, James H. Meteorology and medicine in colonial America: beginnings of the experimental approach. Journal of the history of medicine and allied sciences, v. 24, Apr. 1969: 193–204. R131.A1J6, v. 24

On studies of the relationship between diseases and the environment, 1720–80.

11878

Caulfield, Ernest. Infant feeding in colonial America. Journal of pediatrics, v. 41, Dec. 1952: 673–687. RJ1.A453, v. 41

11879

Cowen, David L. America's pre-pharmacopoeial literature. Madison, Wis., American Institute of the History of Pharmacy, 1961. 40 p. illus., facsims., ports. RS139.C6

Bibliographic references included in "Notes and references" (p. 34–40).

Discusses the origin and nature of pharmaceutical literature used in America by doctors and laymen between 1720 and 1820.

11880

Donegan, Jane B. Midwifery in America, 1760–1860: a study in medicine and morality. 1972. ([317] p.) Micro AC–1, no. 72–20,325

Thesis (Ph.D.)—Syracuse University.

Abstracted in *Dissertation Abstracts International,* v. 33A, July 1972, p. 248.

11881

Gordon, Maurice B. AEsculapius comes to the colonies; the story of the early days of medicine in the thirteen original colonies. Ventnor, N.J., Ventnor Publishers [1949] xiv, 560 p. illus., facsims., ports. R152.G66

Bibliographic references included in "Major sources and acknowledgments" (p. 512–517).

Reprinted in New York by Argosy-Antiquarian (1969).

For a critical review of this work by Ernest Caulfield, see the *William and Mary Quarterly*, 3d ser., v. 6, Oct. 1949, p. 660–664.

11882

Guerra, Francisco. Medical almanacs of the American colonial period. Journal of the history of medicine and allied sciences, v. 16, July 1961: 234–255. R131.A1J6, v. 16

11883

Heaton, Claude E. Obstetrics in colonial America. Ciba symposia, v. 1, Mar. 1940: 379–388. facsims., ports. R11.C47, v. 1

11884

Jameson, Edwin M. Eighteenth century obstetrics and obstetricians in the United States. Annals of medical history, new ser., v. 10, Sept. 1938: 413–428. facsims. R11.A85, n.s., v. 10

11885
Kett, Joseph F.   The formation of the American medical profession; the role of institutions, 1780–1860. New Haven, Yale University Press, 1968. xi, 217 p.
R151.K47

Bibliography: p. 194–207.
The author's thesis (Ph.D.), *The Regulation of the Medical Profession in America, 1780–1860*, was submitted to Harvard University in 1964.

Although his main focus is the impact of the proprietary medical schools of the early 19th century on the standards and identity of the profession, the author reviews the British and colonial backgrounds and finds that the British profession, despite its rigid structure, never succeeded in controlling the practice of medicine. In the colonies a medical license was primarily a certificate of individual competence and trustworthiness, not evidence of membership in a tightly knit professional group.

11886
King, Lester S.   The medical world of the eighteenth century. [Chicago] University of Chicago Press [1958] xix, 346 p. illus., facsims., ports.
R148.K5

Bibliographic references included in "Notes": p. 327–340.

Discusses aspects of the English medical scene in 10 separate essays that related to guild divisions among physicians and apothecaries, changes in medical ethics and practice, developments in nosology and pathology, and the career of Hermann Boerhaave.

11887
Kraus, Michael.   American and European medicine in the eighteenth century. Bulletin of the history of medicine, v. 8, May 1940: 679–695.
R11.B93, v. 8

11888
Krumbhaar, Edward B.   The early history of anatomy in the United States. Annals of medical history, v. 4, Sept. 1922: 271–286. facsims., ports.
R11.A85, v. 4

11889
Miller, Genevieve.   European influences in colonial medicine. Ciba symposia, v. 8, Jan. 1947: 511–521. illus., facsim., ports.
R11.C47, v. 8

11890
Morais, Herbert M.   Doctors and the American Revolution. NTM, v. 2, no. 6, 1965: 99–120.
Q125.N2, v. 2

11891
Norwood, William F.   The early history of American medical societies. Ciba symposia, v. 9, Dec. 1947: 762–772. illus., facsims., ports.
R11.C47, v. 9

11892
Norwood, William F.   Medicine in the era of the American Revolution. International record of medicine, v. 171, July 1958: 391–407.
R11.M745, v. 171

11893
Packard, Francis R.   History of medicine in the United States. New York, P. B. Hoeber, 1931. 2 v. (xxv, 1323 p.) illus., facsims., plates, ports.
R151.P12 1931

"Pre-Revolutionary medical publications": v. 1, p. [489]–512; Bibliography: v. 2, p. [1241]–1266.
Reprinted in New York by Hafner Pub Co. (1963).

In the first volume the author surveys medical practices of the 17th and 18th centuries in sections dealing with epidemics, mortality, hospitals, legislation, education, and publication. Chapter 8 treats the medical profession in the War for Independence. In the second volume Packard deals with selected topics from the 19th century. Volume 1 first appeared as *The History of Medicine in the United States; a Collection of Facts and Documents Relating to the History of Medical Science in This Country, From the Earliest English Colonization to the Year 1800; With a Supplemental Chapter on the Discovery of Anaesthesia* (Philadelphia, J. B. Lippincott Co., 1901. 542 p. R151.P12).

11894
Packard, Francis R.   Medical societies in this country founded prior to the year 1787. Philadelphia medical journal, v. 5, Jan. 27, 1900: 229–231.
R11.P5, v. 5

11895
Shryock, Richard H.   Eighteenth century medicine in America. *In* American Antiquarian Society, *Worcester, Mass.* Proceedings, new ser., v. 59, Oct. 1949: 275–292.
E172.A35, n.s., v. 59

——— ——— Offprint. Worcester, Mass., The Society, 1950. 20 p.
R152.S5

11896
Shryock, Richard H.   Medicine and society in America, 1660–1860. [New York] New York University Press, 1960. viii, 182 p. (Anson G. Phelps lectureship on early American history)
R148.S45

Bibliographic footnotes.

Examines patterns of health and disease, developments in medical thought and practice, and the growth of early medical schools and societies. Although he terms the contributions of Drs. John Morgan and Benjamin Rush significant and exceptional, the author concludes that the general indifference to scientific investigation among 18th-century practitioners resulted in little new knowledge, with the exception of primitive clinical research in identifying and observing particular diseases. Nevertheless, conscious efforts to improve public hygiene, a rising standard of living, dietary changes, and an extensive use of vaccinations contributed to a gradual improvement in public health during the 18th century.

11897
Stevenson, Isobel.   Medical literature produced during the War of Independence. Ciba symposia, v. 2, July 1940: 520–528. illus., facsims.
R11.C47, v. 2

11898

Stevenson, Isobel.   Political activities of Revolutionary physicians. Ciba symposia, v. 2, July 1940: 512–519. illus., facsims., ports.   R11.C47, v. 2

11899

Thacher, James.   American medical biography; or, Memoirs of eminent physicans who have flourished in America. To which is prefixed a succint history of medical science in the United States, from the first settlement of the country. Boston, Richardson & Lord, 1828. 2 v. ports.   R153.T3

Reprinted in New York by Milford House (1967) and, with a new introduction and a bibliography by Whitfield J. Bell, Jr., by Da Capo Press (1967).

11900

Thomson, Elizabeth H.   The role of physicians in the humane societies of the eighteenth century. Bulletin of the history of medicine, v. 37, Jan./Feb. 1963: 43–51.   F11.B93, v. 37

11901

Toner, Joseph M.   Contributions to the annals of medical progress and medical education in the United States before and during the War of Independence. Washington, Govt. Print. Off., 1874. 118 p.   R151.T67

Reprinted in New York by B. Franklin (1970).

Miscellaneous notes on numerous topics relating to the development of the medical profession in the 18th century. Individual physicians, legislation, schools and societies, epidemics, and activities in particular colonies are among the subjects considered. Surgeons in the Revolution are listed for several of the states.

11902

Twiss, John R.   Medical practice in colonial America. *In* New York Academy of Medicine. Bulletin, v. 36, Aug. 1960: 538–551.   R15.N62, v. 36

2. NEW ENGLAND

11903

Blake, John B.   Public health in the town of Boston, 1630–1822. Cambridge, Harvard University Press, 1959. x, 278 p. illus., maps. (Harvard historical studies, v. 72)   RA447.M4B6

"A note on the sources": p. [259]–267.

The author's thesis (Ph.D.), with the same title, was submitted to Harvard University in 1954.

Examines political, social, and medical theories and practices dealing with town sanitation and the prevention and treatment of epidemic disease, most notably smallpox, which had a dominant influence on attitudes and policies affecting public health in the 18th century. In a chapter on the Revolutionary era, the author discusses organization and training within the medical profession, the employment of physicians in public health administration, popular support for health and sanitation measures, and efforts to curb distemper, camp fever, and other diseases that proliferated under wartime conditions.

11904

Green, Samuel A.   History of medicine in Massachusetts. Boston, A. Williams, 1881. 131 p.   R245.G78

11905

Loring, George B.   The medical profession in Massachusetts during the Revolutionary War. Boston medical and surgical journal, v. 92, June 17–24, 1875: 704–715, 749–751.   R11.B7, v. 92

11906

Parsons, Usher.   Sketches of Rhode Island physicians, deceased prior to 1850. Providence, Knowles, Anthony, Printers, 1859. 64 p.   R319.R43P3

The sketches precede, and serve as an introduction to, the first volume of papers published by the Rhode Island Medical Society, and bear the series title, *Transactions* of the Rhode-Island Medical Society.

11907

Russell, Gurdon W.   Early medicine and early medical men in Connecticut. [Hartford] 1892. 158 p.   R184.R96

Reprinted from the *Proceedings* of the Connecticut Medical Society.

11908

[Thomas, Herbert] *ed.*   The heritage of Connecticut medicine. New Haven [Printed by the Whaples-Bullis Co.] 1942. 233 p. illus., facsim., port.   R184.T5

"Footnotes and bibliography": p. 213–221.

Consists of papers which originally appeared in *The Connecticut State Medical Journal*, including essays on the origin of the Connecticut Medical Society, cases and observations made by the Medical Society of New Haven County, early medical teachers in Connecticut, early medical practice in Hartford County, and early doctors of Windham County.

11909

Viets, Henry R.   A brief history of medicine in Massachusetts. Boston, Houghton Mifflin Co., 1930. x, 194 p. ports.   R245.V5

"References": p. [185]

Includes two chapters (p. 53–118) on 18th-century practices.

11910

Viets, Henry R.   Some features of the history of medicine in Massachusetts during the colonial period (1620–1770). Isis, v. 23, Sept. 1935: 389–405. facsim. (part fold.), ports.   Q1.I7, v. 23

3. MIDDLE ATLANTIC REGION

11911

Carson, Joseph.   A history of the Medical Department of the University of Pennsylvania, from its foundation in 1765. With sketches of the lives of deceased professors. Philadelphia, Lindsay and Blakiston, 1869. 227 p.   R747.P42 1869

11912
Diller, Theodore. Pioneer medicine in western Pennsylvania. With a foreword by J. J. Buchanan, M.D. New York, P. B. Hoeber, 1927. xiv, 230 p. plates, ports.
R313.P4D5

11913
Drinker, Cecil K. Not so long ago; a chronicle of medicine and doctors in colonial Philadelphia. New York, Oxford University Press, 1937. xii, 183 p. facsim., maps, plates, ports. R314.P5D7

Includes extracts from Elizabeth Drinker's journal for the years 1758–1807.

11914
Duffy, John. A history of public health in New York City, 1625–1866. New York, Russell Sage Foundation, 1968. xix, 619 p. illus., maps, ports. RA807.N5N52

Bibliography: p. 591–605.
"From frontier post to settled community [1664–1792]": p. [1]–93.

11915
Gordon, Maurice B. Medicine in colonial New Jersey and adjacent areas. Bulletin of the history of medicine, v. 17, Jan. 1945: 38–60. R11.B93, v. 17

11916
Harris, Jonathan. The rise of medical science in New York, 1720–1820. 1971. ([451] p.)
Micro AC–1, no. 72–24,742

Thesis (Ph.D.)—New York University.
Abstracted in *Dissertation Abstracts International*, v. 33A, Nov. 1972, p. 2286.

11917
Heaton, Claude E. Medicine in New York during the English colonial period, 1664–1775. Bulletin of the history of medicine, v. 17, Jan. 1945: 9–37. facsims., ports.
R11.B93, v. 17

11918
Hunter, Robert J. Benjamin Franklin and the rise of free treatment of the poor by the medical profession of Philadelphia. Bulletin of the history of medicine, v. 31, Mar./Apr. 1957: 137–146. R11.B93, v. 31

11919
Hunter, Robert J. The origin of the Philadelphia General Hospital. Pennsylvania magazine of history and biography, v. 57, Jan. 1933: 32–57. plate, ports.
F146.P65, v. 57

Traces the 18th-century history of the hospital, founded in 1732.

11920
Johnson, Frederick C. Pioneer physicians of Wyoming Valley, 1771–1825. *In* Wyoming Historical and Geological Society, *Wilkes-Barre, Pa.* Proceedings and collections. v. 9; 1905. Wilkes-Barre. p. [47]–106.
F157.W9W94, v. 9

11921
Kieffer, John E. Philadelphia controversy, 1775–1780. Bulletin of the history of medicine, v. 11, Feb. 1942: 148–159. facsim., ports. R11.B93, v. 11

On the struggle between the factions headed by John Morgan and William Shippen, Jr., for control of Philadelphia medicine and the director-generalship of the Army medical service.

11922
Ladenheim, Jules C. "The Doctors' Mob" of 1788. Journal of the history of medicine and allied sciences, v. 5, winter 1950: 23–43. R131.A1J6, v. 5

The indiscriminate acquisition of cadavers for dissection by students and members of the medical profession in New York City provoked a three-day riot in April that led ultimately to the passage of the first practical anatomy laws and licensing regulations in the United States.

11923
McClenahan, Richard L. New Jersey medical history in the colonial period. *In* New Jersey Historical Society. Proceedings, new ser., v. 10, Oct. 1925: 362–374.
F131.N58, n.s., v. 10

11924
Norris, George W. The early history of medicine in Philadelphia. Philadelphia [Collins Print. House] 1886. xii, 232 p. ports. [R314.P5N8]
Micro 22991 R

In the first section Norris presents brief biographical sketches of 18th-century physicians, with particular attention to John Morgan. He then describes epidemics, sanitation, medical societies, publications, and medical schools in the second half of the 18th century.

11925
Packard, Francis R. How London and Edinburgh influenced medicine in Philadelphia in the eighteenth century. Annals of medical history, new ser., v. 4, May 1932: 219–244. R11.A85, n.s., v. 4

11926
Packard, Francis R. The practice of medicine in Philadelphia in the eighteenth century. Annals of medical history, new ser., v. 5, Mar. 1933: 135–150.
R11.A85, n.s., v. 5

11927
Reynolds, Helen W. Physicians and medicine in Dutchess County in the eighteenth century. *In* Dutchess County Historical Society. Year book. v. 26; 1941. Poughkeepsie. p. 78–88. F127.D8D93, v. 26

11928
Shryock, Richard H. A century of medical progress in Philadelphia, 1750–1850. Pennsylvania history, v. 8, Jan. 1941: 7–28. F146.P597, v. 8

11929

Strecker, Edward A.   Reminiscences from the early days of the Pennsylvania hospital. Annals of medical history, new ser., v. 1, July 1929: 429–434.

R11.A85, n.s., v. 1

11930

Walsh, James J.   History of medicine in New York, three centuries of medical progress. New York, National Americana Society, 1919. 5 v. facsims., plates, ports.

R291.W2

The last two volumes are biographical.

11931

Wickes, Stephen.   History of medicine in New Jersey, and of its medical men, from the settlement of the province to A.D. 1800. Newark, N.J., M. R. Dennis, 1879. 449 p.   R283.W63

Following a brief survey of the organization and practice of medicine in the province, the author provides biographical information on approximately 300 New Jersey physicians.

11932

Williams, William H.   The Pennsylvania Hospital, 1751–1801: an internal examination of Anglo-America's first hospital. 1971. ([402] p.)

Micro AC–1, no. 72–14,517

Thesis (Ph.D.)—University of Delaware.
Abstracted in *Dissertation Abstracts International,* v. 32A, May 1972, p. 6360–6361.

4. The South

11933

Blanton, Wyndham B.   Medicine in Virginia in the eighteenth century. Richmond, Garrett & Massie, 1931. x, 449 p. facsims., plans, plates, ports.   R345.B52

Surveys the study and practice of medicine, pharmacy, and dentistry. Among the topical chapters are two dealing with medicine during the Revolution and the treatment and death of George Washington. The author concludes that a distinctly American medicine—evidenced by the development of medical societies, hospitals, and experimental and research literature—had emerged by the end of the century.

An appendix lists Virginia doctors who served in the American army and navy during the War for Independence.

11934

Childs, St. Julien R.   Notes on the history of public health in South Carolina, 1670–1800. *In* South Carolina Historical Association. Proceedings. 1932. Columbia, S.C., 1933.   F266.S58, 1932

11935

Harrell, Laura D.   Colonial medical practice in British West Florida, 1763–1781. Bulletin of the history of medicine, v. 41, Nov./Dec. 1967: 539–558.

R11.B93, v. 41

11936

Jones, Gordon W.   Medical and scientific books in colonial Virginia. Bulletin of the history of medicine, v. 40, Mar./Apr. 1966: 146–157.   R11.B93, v. 40

11937

Karst, Judith W.   Newspaper medicine: a cultural study of the colonial South, 1730–1770. 1971. ([360] p.)

Micro AC–1, no. 72–3888

Thesis (Ph.D.)—Tulane University.
Abstracted in *Dissertation Abstracts International,* v. 32A, Jan. 1972, p. 3895.

11938

Krafka, Joseph.   Medicine in colonial Georgia. Georgia historical quarterly, v. 20, Dec. 1936: 326–344.

F281.G2975, v. 20

11939

Krafka, Joseph.   Notes on medical practice in colonial Georgia. Georgia historical quarterly, v. 23, Dec. 1939: 351–361.   F281.G2975, v. 23

11940

Parramore, Thomas C.   [North Carolina] doctors, Whig and Tory. North Carolina medical journal, v. 29, Feb. 1968: 65–69.   R11.N93, v. 29

11941

Seward, Blanton P.   Pioneer medicine in Virginia. Annals of medical history, new ser., v. 10, Jan.–Mar. 1938: 61–70, 169–187.   R11.A85, n.s., v. 10

11942

Waring, Joseph I.   A history in South Carolina, 1670–1825. With a foreword by Richard H. Shryock. [Charleston?] South Carolina Medical Association [1964] xviii, 407 p. illus., facsims., maps, ports.

R321.W3

Includes bibliographic references.

Focusing on disease, medical practice, and professional activities in Charleston, the author concludes that the city's medical progress ranked with that of Boston, Philadelphia, and New York, and that its practitioners demonstrated an exceptional enthusiasm for scientific research before the Revolution. Waring devotes two chapters to the Revolutionary War and its aftermath and includes, following the narrative, more than 80 biographical sketches together with lists of South Carolina doctors in the Continental Army, local graduates from Edinburgh University, and the names of doctors in the Charleston directories of 1782, 1785, and 1802.

11943

Waring, Joseph I.   Medicine in Charlestown, 1750–1775. Annals of medical history, new ser., v. 7, Jan. 1935: 19–26.   R11.A85, n.s., v. 7

5. Diseases, Treatments, and Cures

11944

Blake, John B. Diseases and medical practice in colonial America. International record of medicine, v. 171, June 1958: 350–363. R11.M745, v. 171

11945

Blake, John B. Smallpox inoculation in colonial Boston. Journal of the history of medicine and allied sciences, v. 8, July 1953: 284–300. R131.A1J6, v. 8

11946

Brendle, Thomas R., *and* Claude W. Unger. Folk medicine of the Pennsylvania Germans; the non-occult cures. Norristown, Pa., Pennsylvania German Society, 1935. 303 p. illus., plates. (Pennsylvania German Society. Proceedings and addresses, v. 45, pt. 2) F146.P23, v. 45

"Bibliography of books containing remedies of the more rational kind": p. [223]–287. "Bibliography of recipes in manuscript": p. [289]–303.

Reprinted in New York by A. M. Kelley (1970).

11947

Caulfield, Ernest. Some common diseases of colonial children. *In* Colonial Society of Massachusetts, *Boston.* Publications. v. 35. Transactions, 1942/46. Boston, 1951. p. 4–65. illus., facsim. F161.C71, v. 35

A chronological treatment by disease—measles, diphtheria, scarlet fever, whooping cough, mumps, chicken pox, and dysentery.

11948

Clarfield, Gerard H. Salem's great inoculation controversy, 1773–1774. *In* Essex Institute, *Salem, Mass.* Historical collections, v. 106, Oct. 1970: 277–296. F72.E81, v. 106

11949

Duffy, John. Epidemics in colonial America. Baton Rouge, Louisiana State University Press [1953] xi, 274 p. facsim., maps, port. RA650.5.D8

Bibliography: p. 249–265.

Reprinted in Port Washington, N.Y., by Kennikat Press (1972).

The author's thesis (Ph.D.), *The History of Epidemics in the American Colonies*, was submitted to the University of California, Los Angeles, in 1946.

Describing major communicable diseases, the author reviews in chronological order their epidemic occurrence and analyzes their impact on social and economic development in the thirteen colonies. Duffy concludes that malaria and dysentery were the afflictions most damaging to colonial productivity, followed by respiratory disorders and smallpox. Because smallpox, like yellow fever, held such terror for colonials, Duffy devotes over a third of his work to an exploration of its effects. He credits 18th-century improvements in American health to a rising standard of living and an expanding native-born population, adding that the medical profession contributed little to this advancement.

11950

Duffy, John. Yellow fever in colonial Charleston. South Carolina historical and genealogical magazine, v. 52, Oct. 1951: 189–197. F266.S55, v. 52

11951

Fitz, Reginald. The treatment for inoculated smallpox in 1764 and how it actually felt. Annals of medical history, 3d ser., v. 4, Mar. 1942: 110–113. facsim. R11.A85, 3d s., v. 4

Based on an anonymous pamphlet of instructions in use in Philadelphia and Boston.

11952

Gill, Harold B. The apothecary in colonial Virginia. Williamsburg, Va., Colonial Williamsburg Foundation; distributed by the University Press of Virginia, Charlottesville [1972] vii, 127 p. illus., plates, ports. (Williamsburg research studies) RS67.U7V53

Bibliography: p. 117–121.

Dealing primarily with the second half of the 18th century, the author examines the education, practices, and materials of the apothecary and briefly discusses the role of the apothecary in the Revolution. In three appendixes Gill describes Revolutionary hospitals in Williamsburg, provides a list of Williamsburg apothecaries, and presents an extended diary account of Virginia diseases, 1745–81, by Dr. John de Sequeyra.

11953

Griffenhagen, George B., *and* James H. Young. Old English patent medicines in America. [Washington, Smithsonian Institution, 1959] 159–183 p. illus., facsims. (Contributions from the Museum of History and Technology, Paper 10) Q11.U6, no. 218, 1959

U.S. National Museum. Bulletin 218.

Bibliographic footnotes.

11954

McKusick, Victor A. Hemophilia in early New England; a follow-up of four kindreds in which hemophilia occurred in the pre-Revolutionary period. Journal of the history of medicine and allied sciences, v. 17, July 1962: 342–365. R131.A1J6, v. 17

11955

Moore, Vivian L. A home doctor of the Revolution. Daughters of the American Revolution magazine, v. 74, Jan. 1940: 12–15. illus., facsim. E202.5.A12, v. 74

Discusses traditional or home remedies for various illnesses that were noted in the diary of one Elkanah Jones,

11956

Parramore, Thomas C. Non-venereal treponematosis in colonial North America. Bulletin of the history of medicine, v. 44, Nov./Dec. 1970: 571–581. R11.B93, v. 44

11957
Ransom, John E. The beginnings of hospitals in the United States. Bulletin of the history of medicine, v. 13, May 1943: 514–539.   R11.B93, v. 13

11958
Rosen, George. Occupational diseases of English seamen during the seventeenth and eighteenth century. Bulletin of the history of medicine, v. 7, July 1939: 751–758.
                    R11.B93, v. 7

11959
Smallpox inoculation in colonial New Jersey; a contemporary account [ca.1750–75] *In* Rutgers University, *New Brunswick, N.J. Library.* Journal, v. 31, Dec. 1967: 21–28.   Z733.R955F, v. 31

Introduction and notes by Larry R. Gerlach.

11960
Wilson, Matthew. Laryngology and otology in colonial times. Annals of medical history, v. 1, Apr. 1917: 86–101.   R11.A85, v. 1

Comprises selections on the above topics made from Wilson's unpublished manuscript, *Multum in Parvo, Being a New Therapeutic—Alphabet or A Pocket-Dictionary, of Medicine, Midwifery, & Surgery*, by the editor, Stanton A. Friedberg.

11961
Wilson, Robert C. Drugs and pharmacy in the life of Georgia, 1733–1959. [Athens, University of Georgia Press, 1959] ix, 443 p. illus.   RS67.U7G4

Bibliography: p. 439–443.

In early chapters the author lists treatments recommended for various diseases and maladies in the 18th century.

11962
Winslow, Charles Edward A. The colonial era and the first years of the Republic (1607–1799)—the pestilence that walketh in darkness. *In* Top, Franklin H., *ed.* The history of American epidemiology. St. Louis, Mosby, 1952. p. 11–51.   RA650.5.T6

6. MEDICAL EDUCATION

11963
Bell, Whitfield J. Medical students and their examiners in eighteenth century America. *In* College of Physicians of Philadelphia. Transactions & studies, 4th ser., v. 21, June 1953: 14–24.   R15.P5, 4th s., v. 21

11964
Bell, Whitfield J. Philadelphia medical students in Europe, 1750–1800. Pennsylvania magazine of history and biography, v. 67, Jan. 1943: 1–29.   F146.P65, v. 67

11965
Corner, George W. Two centuries of medicine; a history of the School of Medicine, University of Pennsylvania. Philadelphia, Lippincott [1965] ix, 363 p. illus., facsims., plans, ports.   R747.P42 1965

"Notes and references": p. 324–346.

Includes three chapters (p. 1–48) on the origins of the school and the pioneering work of Morgan, Shippen, Kuhn, and Rush.

11966
Davis, Nathan S. History of medical education and institutions in the United States, from the first settlement of the British colonies to the year 1850. Chicago, S. C. Griggs, 1851. 228 p.   R745.D27

11967
Gibson, James E. Benjamin Rush's apprenticed students. *In* College of Physicians of Philadelphia. Transactions & studies, 4th ser., v. 14, Dec. 1946: 127–132.
                    R15.P5, 4th s., v. 14

Includes lists of the names of 134 students arranged both alphabetically and geographically.

11968
Miller, Genevieve. Medical apprenticeship in the American colonies. Ciba symposia, v. 8, Jan. 1947: 502–510. illus., facsims., port.   R11.C47, v. 8

11969
Miller, Genevieve. Medical education in the American colonies. Journal of medical education, v. 31, Feb. 1956: 82–94.   R11.A94, v. 31

11970
Miller, Genevieve. Medical schools in the colonies. Ciba symposia, v. 8, Jan. 1947: 522–532. illus., facsim., ports.   R11.C47, v. 8

11971
Moore, Thomas E. The early years of the Harvard Medical School, its founding and curriculum, 1782–1810. Bulletin of the history of medicine, v. 27, Nov./Dec. 1953: 530–561.   R11.B93, v. 27

11972
Norwood, William F. Medical education in the United States before the Civil War. Philadelphia, University of Pennsylvania Press, 1944. xvi, 487 p.   R745.N6

Bibliography: p. 435–462.
Reprinted in New York by Arno Press (1971).

Includes chapters on colonial literature and the practice of physic, early medical legislation and societies, the preceptorship and other methods of instruction, military medicine, and the beginning of formal instruction in such institutions as the College of Philadelphia, 1765; King's College, 1767; William and Mary College, 1779; Harvard College, 1783; and the University of the State of Pennsylvania, 1783.

11973
Olch, Peter D. The Morgan-Shippen controversy: a commentary on the birth of medical education in America. Review of surgery, v. 22, Jan./Feb. 1965: 1–8. facsim., ports.   RD1.Q3, v. 22

11974
Packard, Francis R.   William Cheselden, some of his contemporaries, and their American pupils. Annals of medical history, new ser., v. 9, Nov. 1937: 533–548.
R11.A85, n.s., v. 9

Among Cheselden's American pupils were Thomas Cadwalader (1708–1779) of Philadelphia, James Lloyd (1728–1810) of Boston, and Silvester Gardiner (1707–1786) of Boston.

11975
Postell, William D.   Medical education and medical schools in colonial America. International record of medicine, v. 171, June 1958: 364–370.   R11.M745, v. 171

11976
Stookey, Byron P.   A history of colonial medical education: in the province of New York, with its subsequent development, 1767–1830. Springfield, Ill., Thomas [1962] xix, 286 p. illus., facsims., ports.   R746.N7S7

Bibliographic footnotes.

11977
Thoms, Herbert.   The doctors of Yale College, 1702–1815, and the founding of the medical institution. Hamden, Conn., Shoe String Press, 1960. xxi, 199 p. illus., facsims., ports. (Yale University. School of Medicine. Dept. of the History of Medicine. Publication no. 39)
R747.Y28T45

Bibliography: p. 189–192.

11978
Waite, Frederick C.   Medical degrees conferred in the American colonies and in the United States in the eighteenth century. Annals of medical history, new ser., v. 9, July 1937: 314–320.   R11.A85, n.s., v. 9

ARTS, CRAFTS, AND CRAFTSMEN

1. General

11979
Belknap, Henry W.   Artists and craftsmen of Essex County, Massachusetts. Salem, Mass., Essex Institute, 1927. viii, 127 p. facsims., plates, ports.   N6530.M4B4

"Sources": p. vi.

Provides brief biographical notices for artists and craftsmen from more than 20 occupational groups who flourished from earliest times to about 1860.

11980
Bridenbaugh, Carl.   The colonial craftsman. New York, New York University Press, 1950. xii, 214 p. illus. (New York University. Stokes Foundation. Anson G. Phelps lectureship on early American history)
HD2346.U5B7

Bibliographic references included in "Notes" (p. 182–204).

In six lectures, Bridenbaugh points out the differences between rural artisans, who developed few skills beyond their basic needs, and urban craftsmen, who specialized in such luxury trades as silversmithing and cabinetmaking. He also describes working conditions in the home—the basic industrial unit of the colonial era—and the mechanics' role in politics. During the Revolutionary era, most tradesmen joined the independence movement because of local grievances—indebtedness and lack of political power.

11981
Dow, George F.   The arts & crafts in New England, 1704–1775; gleanings from Boston newspapers relating to painting, engraving, silversmiths, pewterers, clockmakers, furniture, pottery, old houses, costume, trades and occupations, &c. Topsfield, Mass., Wayside Press, 1927. xxxii, 326 p. facsims., plates, ports.
T21.5.N4D6

Reprinted in New York by Da Capo Press (1967).

11982
Dyer, Walter A.   Early American craftsmen . . . Being a series of sketches of the lives of the more important personalities in the early development of the industrial arts in America. New York, Century Co., 1915. xv, 387 p. plates, ports.   NK806.D8

Reprinted in part from various periodicals.
Bibliography: p. 381–382.
Reprinted in New York by B. Franklin (1971).

11983
Forman, Benno M.   Salem tradesmen and craftsmen circa 1762: a contemporary document. *In* Essex Institute, *Salem, Mass.* Historical collections, v. 107, Jan. 1971: 62–81. facsim.   F72.E7E81, v. 107

Based on a document in the institute's collection listing 165 tradesmen and craftsmen of Salem.

11984
Gillingham, Harrold E.   Calico and linen printing in Philadelphia. Pennsylvania magazine of history and biography, v. 52, Apr. 1928: 97–110. facsims., plates.
F146.P65, v. 52

11985
Gottesman, Rita S., *comp.*   The arts and crafts in New York; advertisements and news items from New York City newspapers. [v. 1–2] 1726–1776—1777–1799. New York, Printed for the New York Historical Society, 1938–54. 2 v. illus. (New York Historical Society. Collections, 1936, 1948. The John Watts De Peyster publication fund series, [v. 69, 81])
F116.N63, 1936, 1948

Volume 1, *The Arts and Crafts in New York, 1726–1776*, has been reprinted in New York by Da Capo Press (1970).

11986
Gould, Mary E.   Early American wooden ware & other kitchen utensils. Fully illustrated by the author. [Rev. ed.] Springfield, Mass., Pond-Ekberg Co., [1948, ᶜ1942] xiv, 243 p. illus.   E161.G6 1948

11987

McKay, George L. A register of artists, engravers, book-sellers, book-binders, printers & publishers in New York City, 1633–1820. New York, New York Public Library, 1942. 78 p. plan   Z475.M3

    Reprinted with additions from the *Bulletin* of the New York Public Library, 1939–41.

    "Principal works consulted": p. 4–5.

    For an analysis of the McKay register by occupation and date, see "The Number of Persons and Firms Connected with the Graphic Arts in New York City, 1633–1820," by Harry B. Weiss, v. 50, Oct. 1946, p. 775–786.

11988

Marzio, Peter C. Carpentry in the southern colonies during the eighteenth century with emphasis on Maryland and Virginia. *In* Winterthur portfolio. v. 7. Winterthur, Del., 1972. p. 229–250. illus.   N9.W52, v. 7

11989

Noël Hume, Ivor. James Geddy and sons, colonial craftsmen. Williamsburg, Va., Colonial Williamsburg Foundation [1970] 45 p. illus. (*His* Colonial Williamsburg archaeological series, no. 5)   F234.W7N595

11990

Olton, Charles S. Philadelphia artisans and the American Revolution. 1967. ([416] p.)

    Micro AC–1, no. 67–11,655

    Thesis (Ph.D.)—University of California, Berkeley.

    Abstracted in *Dissertation Abstracts*, v. 28A, Oct. 1967, p. 1376–1377.

    Through effective reorganization of the artisan community itself, tradesmen brought about a major transformation of their economic, political, and social role in Philadelphia.

11991

Ott, Joseph K. Rhode Island housewrights, shipwrights, and related craftsmen. Rhode Island history, v. 31, spring/summer 1972: 64–79. illus., port.

    F76.R472, v. 31

11992

Preservation Society of Newport County. The arts and crafts of Newport, Rhode Island, 1640–1820. [v. 1] By Ralph E. Carpenter, Jr. Newport, 1954. xiii, 218 p. illus., facsims., ports.   NK838.N4P7, v. 1

    Bibliography: p. 211.

    An exhibition catalog that contains brief essays on Newport cabinetmakers and chair craftsmen, limners and engravers, and silversmiths. Over 160 photographs illustrate the work.

11993

Prime, Alfred C., *comp.* The arts & crafts in Philadelphia, Maryland and South Carolina . . . gleanings from newspapers. [Topsfield, Mass.] Walpole Society, 1929. 2 v. facsims., plates, ports.   N6507.P7

    Contents: ser. 1. 1721–1785.—ser. 2. 1786–1800.

    Reprinted in New York by Da Capo Press (1969).

11994

Rawson, Marion N. Handwrought ancestors; the story of early American shops and those who worked therein. [New York] E. P. Dutton [ᶜ1936] 366 p. illus.

    T21.R3

11995

Stoudt, John J. Early Pennsylvania arts and crafts. With a foreword by S. K. Stevens. New York, A. S. Barnes [1964] 364 p. illus., facsims., col. plates, ports.

    NK835.P4S72

    Using more than 300 illustrations, the author considers architecture, furniture, fine arts, crafts, and illumination from 1680 to the opening of the 19th century. He concludes that there is a direct relationship between the personal freedoms of the Penn colony and the creativity and character of the contributions of her artists and craftsmen.

11996

Tunis, Edwin. Colonial craftsmen and the beginnings of American industry. Cleveland, World Pub. Co. [1965] 159 p. illus.   T21.T8

    Describes the working methods employed in nearly 50 crafts and trades.

11997

White, Margaret E. The decorative arts of early New Jersey. Princeton, N.J., Van Nostrand, 1964. xiv, 137 p. illus., facsim., maps (on lining papers) (The New Jersey Historical series, v. 25)   NK835.N45W5

    "Bibliographical note": p. 124–128.

    Giving principal attention to the years 1725–1825, the author discusses arts and crafts dealing with glass, pottery, textiles, silver, clocks and furniture.

11998

Zankowich, Paul. The craftsmen of colonial New York City (parts one to six). 1956. ([614] p.)

    Micro AC–1, no. 16,621

    Thesis (Ph.D.)—New York University.

    Abstracted in *Dissertation Abstracts*, v. 16, no. 8, 1956, p. 1395–1396.

2. CABINETMAKERS

11999

Berkley, Henry J. A register of the cabinet makers and allied trades in Maryland as shown by the newspapers and directories, 1746–1820. Maryland historical magazine, v. 25, Mar. 1930: 1–27.   F176.M18, v. 25

12000

Bjerkoe, Ethel H. The cabinetmakers of America. By Ethel Hall Bjerkoe assisted by John Arthur Bjerkoe. Foreword by Russell Kettell. Garden City, N.Y., Doubleday, 1957. xvii, 252 p. illus., plates.

    NK2406.B55

Bibliography: p. 249–252.

Offers biographical information on 17th-, 18th-, and early 19th-century cabinetmakers taken from directories, newspapers, wills, inventories, town histories, and the like.

12001

Dorman, Charles G.   Delaware cabinetmakers and allied artisans, 1655–1855. Wilmington, Historical Society of Delaware, 1960. [105]–217 p. facsims., plates, ports. (Delaware history, v. 9, Oct. 1960)   F161.D37, v. 9

Lists, with biographical and bibliographical data, the names of such skilled artisans as Caleb Byrnes, Samuel Canby, William Johnston, Henry Troth, and William Warner.

12002

Harlow, Thompson R., *and others*.   Connecticut cabinetmakers [to 1820] *In* Connecticut Historical Society, *Hartford*. Bulletin, v. 32, Oct. 1967: 97–144; v. 33, Jan. 1968: 1–40. illus., facsims.   F91.C67, v. 32–33

A checklist with biographical information.

12003

Noël Hume, Ivor.   Williamsburg cabinetmakers; the archaeological evidence. Williamsburg, Va., Colonial Williamsburg Foundation [1971] 48 p. illus. (*His* Colonial Williamsburg archaeological series, no. 6)
F234.W7N62

Includes bibliographic references.

12004

Ott, Joseph K.   Recent discoveries among Rhode Island cabinetmakers and their work. Rhode Island history, v. 28, winter 1969: 3–25. illus., facsim., ports.
F76.R472, v. 28

Two supplementary essays entitled "More Notes on Rhode Island Cabinetmakers and Their Work" and "Still More Notes on Rhode Island Cabinetmakers and Allied Cabinetmakers and Allied Craftsmen" were published in the same volume in the spring and fall of 1969, p. 49–52 and p. 111–121.

12005

Randall, Richard H.   An eighteenth century partnership. Art quarterly, v. 23, summer 1960: 153–161. plates.
N1.A64, v. 23

On the collaboration of Marblehead cabinetmakers Nathan Bowen and Ebenezer Martin.

3. Clockmakers

12006

Eckhardt, George H.   Pennsylvania clocks and clockmasters; an epic of early American science, industry, and craftsmanship. New York, Devin-Adair Co., 1955. xviii, 229 p. illus., facsims.   NK7492.E4

12007

Hoopes, Penrose R.   Connecticut clockmakers of the eighteenth century. Hartford, Conn., E. V. Mitchell, 1930. 178 p. plates.   TS543.U6H6 Rare Bk. Coll.

Bibliography: p. 171–173.

12008

Stretch, Carolyn W.   Early colonial clockmakers in Philadelphia. Pennsylvania magazine of history and biography, v. 56, July 1932: 225–235. plates.

F146.P65, v. 56

4. Silver and Silversmiths

12009

Avery, Clara L.   Early American silver. New York, Century Co. [ᶜ1930] xliv, 378 p. illus., 63 plates (incl. facsim.) (Century library of American antiques)
NK7112.A8

"Bibliographical note": p. 361–364.
Reprinted in New York by Russell & Russell (1968).

Surveys early American plate by period and locale, describes the silversmiths' methods of work, and reviews briefly the course of development of characteristic objects—beakers, tankards, teapots, and the like.

12010

Bigelow, Francis H.   Historic silver of the colonies and its makers. New York, Macmillan Co., 1917. xxiv, 476 p. illus.   NK7112.B5

Bibliography: p. xxiii–xxiv.

Describes and provides 325 photographs of nearly 50 different types of silver pieces used in the 17th and 18th centuries.

12011

Bohan, Peter J., *and* Philip H. Hammerslough.   Early Connecticut silver, 1700–1840. Middletown, Conn., Wesleyan University Press [1970] xi, 288 p. illus., facsims., ports.   NK7110.B6

Bibliography: p. 279–283.
"Biographical notes on the silversmiths": p. 219–259.

12012

Boston, Museum of Fine Arts.   American silver, 1655–1825, in the Museum of Fine Arts, Boston, by Kathryn C. Buhler. Boston; distributed by New York Graphic Society, Greenwich, Conn. [1972] 2 v. (xx, 708 p.) illus.   NK7112.B577

Bibliography: v. 1, p. xv–xx.

Describes and provides illustrations of representative pieces made by 128 silversmiths, most of them from Massachusetts.

12013

Brix, Maurice.   List of Philadelphia silversmiths and allied artificers from 1682 to 1850. Philadelphia, Priv. print., 1920. vii, 125 p. front.   NK7112.B7

12014

Buhler, Kathryn C., *and* Graham Hood. American silver, Garvan and other collections in the Yale University Art Gallery. New Haven, Published for the Yale University Art Gallery, by the Yale University Press, 1970. 2 v. illus., facsims., plates, ports. NK7112.B79

Bibliography: v. 1, p. xv–xvi.
Contents: v. 1. New England.—v. 2. Middle colonies & the South.

Describes 1,043 individual pieces in the Yale collections and gives information on markings, original owners, dates of acquisition, provenance, previous exhibitions, and other published references to the object discussed. Photoreproductions of most pieces are included.

12015

Burton, E. Milby. South Carolina silversmiths, 1690–1860. Charleston, S.C., Charleston Museum, 1942. xvii, 311 p. illus., facsims., plates, ports. (Contributions from the Charleston museum, 10) NK7112.B8

"Works consulted": p. [291]–302.

12016

Curtis, George M. Early silver of Connecticut and its makers. Meriden, Conn., International Silver Co., 1913. 115 p. illus., plates, ports. NK7112.C8

The author's article, with the same title, appeared in the *Papers* of the New Haven Colony Historical Society, v. 8 (New Haven, Conn., 1914), p. 181–214.

12017

Cutten, George B. The silversmiths of North Carolina. Raleigh, State Dept. of Archives and History, 1948. v, 93 p. illus., facsims. NK7112.C84

Bibliographic footnotes.

12018

Cutten, George B. The silversmiths of Virginia, together with watchmakers and jewelers, from 1694 to 1850. Richmond, Dietz Press, 1952. xxiv, 259 p. illus., facsims., ports. NK7112.C86

Bibliographic references included in "Notes" (p. 221–245).

12019

Gerstell, Vivian S. Silversmiths of Lancaster, Pennsylvania, 1730–1850. [Lancaster] Lancaster County Historical Society, 1972. ix, 145 p. illus. NK7111.G47

Bibliography: p. 143–145.

12020

Harrington, Jessie. Silversmiths of Delaware, 1700–1850, & old church silver in Delaware. [Wilmington?] National Society of Colonial Dames of America in the State of Delaware, 1939. x, 132 p. facsim., plates. NK7112.H26

Bibliography: p. 131–132.
Contains very brief biographical notices of 33 silversmiths with descriptions and illustrations of their work.

12021

Heritage Foundation. The Heritage Foundation Collection of silver; with biographical sketches of New England silversmiths, 1625–1825. [By] Henry N. Flynt and Martha Gandy Fales. Old Deerfield, Mass., 1968. xiv, 391 p. illus., port. NK7105.H45

Bibliography: p. 367–382.
The biographical sketches appear on p. 143–364.

12022

Hindes, Ruthanna. Delaware silversmiths, 1700–1850. Wilmington, Historical Society of Delaware, 1967. [243]–308 p. illus., facsims, plates, ports. (Delaware history, v. 12, Oct. 1967) F161.D37, v. 12

Includes biographical and bibliographical information on such skilled craftsmen as Duncan Beard, Richard Humphreys, John Stow, and Joseph Warner.

12023

Kauffman, Henry J. The colonial silversmith; his techniques & his products. Drawings by Dorothy Briggs. [Camden, N.J.] T. Nelson [1969] 176 p. illus. (part col.) NK7103.K35

Bibliography: p. 173.
Surveys the tools, materials, technology, and products of the silver trade in 18th-century America.

12024

Kovel, Ralph M., *and* Terry H. Kovel. A directory of American silver, pewter, and silver plate. New York, Crown Publishers [1961] 352 p. illus. NK7112.K66

Bibliography: p. [345]–347.

An exhaustive list of the names of thousands of artisans with cross-references to 89 authoritative sources where more extensive information may be found on the makers of early American silver and pewter.

12025

Miller, William D. The silversmiths of Little Rest. Kingston, R.I. [D. B. Updike, Merrymount Press, Boston] 1928. xii, 50 p. illus., facsims., plates. NK7112.M5

Contents: Samuel Casey.—John Waite.—Joseph Perkins.—Nathaniel Helme.—Gideon Casey.—William Waite.

12026

Phillips, John M. American silver. New York, Chanticleer Press [1949] 128 p. illus. (part col.), col. ports. (American crafts series) NK7112.P5 1949

Bibliography: p. 127–128.
"The exuberance of the Rococo, 1750–1785": 89–108.

12027

Pleasants, Jacob Hall, *and* Howard Sill. Maryland silversmiths, 1715–1830, with illustrations of their silver and their marks and with a facsimile of the design book of William Faris. Baltimore, Md. [Printed by the Lord

Baltimore Press] 1930. xiv, 314 p. illus., facsims., plates, ports. NK7112.P6 Rare Bk. Coll.

Reprinted in Harrison, N.Y., by R. A. Greene (1972).

Following short histories of silversmithing in various Maryland locales, the authors present biographies of all known silversmiths and supplementary lists of apprentices, indentured immigrant silversmiths, watch and clock makers, and silversmiths identified by their initials.

12028
Sabine, Julia. Silversmiths of New Jersey, 1623–1800; compiled from books and newspapers. *In* New Jersey Historical Society. Proceedings, v. 61, July 1943: 145–177, 249–271; v. 62, Apr. 1944: 100–105. F131.N58, v. 61–62

12029
Williams, Carl M. Silversmiths of New Jersey, 1700–1825, with some notice of clockmasters who were also silversmiths. Philadelphia, G. S. MacManus Co., 1949. 164 p. illus., port. NK7110.W5

Bibliography: p. 153–157.

5. OTHER METALWORK

12030
Deas, Alston. The early ironwork of Charleston. Introduction by Albert Simons. Columbia, S.C., Bostick & Thornley, 1941. 111 p. illus. NK8212.S6D4

Bibliography: p. 111.

12031
Evans, John J. "I. C. H.," Lancaster pewterer. *In* Lancaster County (Pa.) Historical Society. Papers, v. 35, Dec. 1931: 301–313. plates. F157.L2L5, v. 35

Identified as Johann Christopher Heyne (1715–1781).

12032
Hamilton, Suzanne. The pewter of William Will: a checklist. *In* Winterthur portfolio. v. 7. Winterthur, Del., 1972. p. 129–160. illus. N9.W52, v. 7

Will (1742–1798) migrated from Germany to Philadelphia in the early 1760's.

12033
Kauffman, Henry J. Early American copper, tin, and brass. New York, McBride [1950] 112 p. illus. NK806.K3

Bibliography: p. 112.

On the implements, utensils, fixtures, and decorative items made from these metals in the 18th century.

12034
Kauffman, Henry J. Early American ironware, cast and wrought. Rutland, Vt., C. E. Tuttle Co. [1966] 166 p. illus., facsims. NK8212.A1K3

Includes bibliographies.

An illustrated survey of objects made of iron and the trades that produced them.

12035
Laughlin, Ledlie I. Pewter in America, its makers and their marks. Boston, Houghton Mifflin Co., 1940. 2 v. illus., 78 plates (incl. facsims., ports.) NK8412.L3

Bibliography: v. 2, p. [161]–[192]

Traces the evolution of the principal forms of American pewter and illustrates the development of every important type of vessel whether for household or ecclesiastical use. Chapters are included on the manufacture of pewter in Massachusetts, Rhode Island, the Connecticut Valley, New York City, Albany, Pennsylvania, and the South. The first appendix comprises a checklist of known American pewterers. A new edition, reprinting volumes 1 and 2 and adding a third volume that corrects, supplements, and updates the earlier material, has been issued (Barre, Mass., Barre Publishers, 1969–71. 3 v. NK8412.L33).

12036
Sonn, Albert H. Early American wrought iron. New York, S. Scribner's Sons, 1928. 3 v. illus., facsims., 320 plates. NK8212.A1S6

Bibliography: v. 3, p. 243–244.

Contains drawings and descriptions of latches, bolts, hinges, handles, hasps, gates, railings, balconies, newels, footscrapers, wall anchors, weather vanes, and other hardware.

12037
Wallace, Philip B. Colonial ironwork in old Philadelphia; the craftsmanship of the early days of the Republic. Measured drawings by William Allen Dunn; introduction by Fiske Kimball. New York, Architectural Book Pub. Co. [ᶜ1930] 147 p. (chiefly illus.) NK8212.P4W3

Reprinted, with a new index, in New York by Dover Publications (1970).

Reproduces photographs and measured drawings of gates, fences, and railings throughout the city.

6. POTTERY, GLASS, AND PORCELAIN

12038
Barber, Edwin A. The pottery and porcelain of the United States; an historical review of American ceramic art from the earliest times to the present day. With 223 illustrations. New York, G. P. Putnam's Sons, 1893. xvii, 446 p. illus., ports. NK4005.B23

Reprinted with a new introduction and a bibliography, in Watkins Glen, N.Y., by Century House Americana (1971).

"Potteries of the eighteenth century": p. 59–106.

12039
Bolton, Reginald P. Porcelain, pottery and glass cast away by the soldiery in the War of Independence. *In* New York Historical Society. Quarterly bulletin, v. 13, Oct. 1929: 87–110. illus. F116.N638, v. 13

12040

Gillingham, Harrold E. Pottery, china, and glass making in Philadelphia. Pennsylvania magazine of history and biography, v. 54, Apr. 1930: 97–129. illus.

F146.P65, v. 54

12041

Knittle, Rhea M. Early American glass. New York, Century Co. [c1927] xxiii, 496 p. illus., facsims, plates. (Century library of American antiques) NK5112.K6

Bibliography: p. 449–453.

Reprinted in Garden City, N.Y., by Garden City Pub. Co. (1948).

"The second period, 1737 to 1827": p. [77]–254.

12042

McKearin, George S., *and* Helen McKearin. American glass. 2000 photographs, 1000 drawings by James L. McCreery. New York, Crown Publishers [1948] xvi, 634 p. illus., facsims., plates. NK5112.M26 1948

Bibliography: p. 615–617.

First published in 1941.

"The 18th-century glass houses": p. 78–131.

12043

McKearin, Helen, *and* George S. McKearin. Two hundred years of American blown glass. Garden City, N.Y., Doubleday, 1950. xvi, 382 p. 115 plates (part col.) NK5112.M28

Bibliography: p. 361–366.

Reprinted in New York by Crown Publishers (1966).

Includes two chapters (p. 6–53) on glassmaking to 1800.

12044

Noël Hume, Ivor. Glass in Colonial Williamsburg's archeological collections. Williamsburg, Va., Colonial Williamsburg [1969] 48 p. illus. (*His* Colonial Williamsburg archaeological series, no. 1) NK5111.N6

12045

Noël Hume, Ivor. Pottery and porcelain in Colonial Williamsburg's archaeological collections. Williamsburg, Va., Colonial Williamsburg [c1969] 46 p. 44 illus. (*His* Colonial Williamsburg archaeological series, no. 2) NK3730.W5C65

12046

Ramsay, John. American potters and pottery. [Boston] Hale, Cushman & Flint [c1939] xx, 304 p. illus., plates. NK4005.R3

Bibliography: p. 244–251.

Reprinted in New York by Tudor Pub. Co. (1947).

"Check-list of American potters, 1611–1900": p. 161–243.

12047

Spargo, John. Early American pottery and china. New York, Century Co. [c1926] xviii, 393 p. illus., 64 plates. [Century library of American antiques] NK4006.S7

"Bibliographical notes": p. 373–376.

Reprinted in Garden City, N.Y., by Garden City Pub. Co. (1948).

Includes two chapters (p. 49–120) on 18th-century wares.

12048

Watkins, Lura W. Early New England potters and their wares. Cambridge, Harvard University Press, 1950. x, 291 p. illus., facsims., ports. NK4005.W3

"Check list of New England potters": p. 249–270.

Bibliography: p. 271–276.

A survey of the technical, artistic, and economic aspects of New England red earthenware and stoneware production. The author considers outstanding potters, states, and regions individually and provides 136 illustrations of surviving specimens.

7. Dress and Fashion

12049

Cunnington, Cecil Willett, Phillis E. Cunnington, *and* Charles R. Beard. A dictionary of English costume. With colour frontispiece and 303 line illus. New York, Barnes & Noble [1968, c1960] vi, 281 p. illus., col. port. GT507.C8 1968

12050

Cunnington, Cecil Willett, *and* Phillis E. Cunnington. Handbook of English costume in the eighteenth century. With illustrations by Barbara Phillipson and Phillis Cunnington. Rev. ed. London, Faber and Faber [1972] 453 p. illus. (part col.) GT736.C8 1972b

Bibliography: p. 426–434.

First edition published in 1957.

12051

Earle, Alice M. Costume of colonial times. New York, C. Scribner's Sons, 1894. xiv, 264 p. [GT607.E2] Micro 18606 GT

Contains a brief history of colonial dress and an extensive glossary (p. 43–264) of terms that relate to costumemaking—fabrics, garments, accessories, and the like.

12052

Earle, Alice M. Customs and fashions in old New England. New York, C. Scribner's Sons, 1893. 387 p. F7.E12

Reprinted in Detroit by Singing Tree Press (1968) and in Williamstown, Mass., by Corner House Publishers (1969).

12053

Earle, Alice M. Two centuries of costume in America, MDCXX–MDCCCXX. New York, Macmillan Co., 1903. 2 v. illus., plates, ports. GT605.E2

Reprinted in New York by B. Blom (1968) and Dover Publications (1970), and in Rutland, Vt., by C. E. Tuttle Co. (1971).

Traces the development of individual items of clothing and various kinds of accessories, including caps and hoods, cloaks, the pocket, wigs, beards, armour, and uniforms. The author also describes the dress of the well-to-do during several periods, including the Revolution.

12054
McClellan, Elisabeth. Historic dress in America, 1607–1800; with an introductory chapter on dress in the Spanish and French settlements in Florida and Louisiana. Illustrations in colour, pen and ink, and half-tone by Sophie B. Steel. Together with reproductions from photographs of rare portraits, original garments, etc. Philadelphia, G. W. Jacobs [1904] 407 p. illus., plates (part col.), ports.   GT607.M2 1904

"Authorities consulted": p. [403]–407.
Reprinted in New York, with her *Historic Dress in America, 1800–1870*, first published in 1910, by Tudor Pub. Co. (1937, 1969, under title: *History of American Costume, 1607–1870*) and B. Blom (1969).

A classic work that depicts, in words and more than 130 illustrations, clothing worn in the 18th century by adults and children of several economic levels, ethnic groups, and vocations. The author also provides excerpts from contemporary letters, songs, and poems that describe the dress of the time and a glossary of 17th- and 18th-century terms relating to costume.

12055
Warwick, Edward, Henry C. Pitz, *and* Alexander Wyckoff. Early American dress: the colonial and Revolutionary periods. New York, B. Blom [1965] 428 p. illus., maps. (The History of American dress, v. 2)   GT605.H64, v. 2

Bibliography: p. 389–398.
First published in New York by the Century Co. (1929) under the title *Early American Costume*.

Describes changes in clothing styles for men, women, and children from the European, Virginia, Dutch, and New England backgrounds through the Revolution. Included are sections on the dress of Quakers, frontiersmen, and seamen.

8. FURNITURE AND INTERIOR DESIGN

12056
Burton, E. Milby. Charleston furniture, 1700–1825. Charleston, S.C., Charleston Museum, 1955. 150 p. illus., facsims. (Contributions from the Charleston Museum, 12)   NK2438.C5B8

Bibliography: p. 143–145.
Reprinted in Columbia by the University of South Carolina Press (1970).

Biographical information about Charleston cabinetmakers appears on p. [67]–132.

12057
Cescinsky, Herbert. English furniture of the eighteenth century. London, G. Routledge [1909–11] 3 v. illus., plates.   NK2529.C4

See also his much briefer work prepared in collaboration with George L. Hunter, *English and American Furniture; a Pictorial Handbook of Fine Furniture Made in Great*

Britain and in the American Colonies, Some in the Sixteenth Century, but Principally in the Seventeenth, Eighteenth and Early Nineteenth Centuries (Garden City, N.Y., Garden City, N.Y., Garden City Pub. Co. [ᶜ1929] 311 p. NK2529.C36 1929a).

12058
Clifton, Ronald D. Forms and patterns: room specialization in Maryland, Massachusetts, and Pennsylvania family dwellings, 1725–1834. 1971. ([441] p.)
Micro AC–1, no. 71–25,990

Thesis (Ph.D.)—University of Pennsylvania.
Abstracted in *Dissertation Abstracts International*, v. 32A, Oct. 1971, p. 1733.

Roughly one-third of the material deals with the period 1775–84.

12059
Comstock, Helen. American furniture: seventeenth, eighteenth, and nineteenth century styles. New York, Viking Press [1962] 336 p. illus. (A Studio book)
NK2406.C58

Bibliography: p. 319–324.
"Chippendale, 1775–1790": p. 115–190.

12060
Cornelius, Charles O. Early American furniture. New York, Century Co. [ᶜ1926] xx, 278 p. illus., plates. (Century library of American antiques)   NK2406.C6

"A brief list of books and articles for the study of American furniture": p. 263–266. Bibliography: p. 266–268.
"Stylistic attainment and rococo influence": p. 129–178.

12061
Cummings, Abbott L., *comp.* Rural household inventories establishing the names, uses, and furnishings of rooms in the colonial New England home, 1675–1775. Boston, Society for the Preservation of New England Antiquities, 1964. vii, 306 p. plan, plates, ports.
F7.C94

Reproduces 109 estate inventories recorded in rural towns in Suffolk County, Mass.

12062
Garrett, Wendell D. The furnishings of Newport houses, 1780–1800. Rhode Island history, v. 18, Jan. 1959: 1–19. plates.   F76.R472, v. 18

12063
Goyne, Nancy A. The bureau table in America. *In* Winterthur portfolio. v. 3; 1967. Winterthur, Del. p. 25–36. illus.   N9.W52, v. 3

12064
Henry Francis du Pont Winterthur Museum. American furniture, Queen Anne and Chippendale periods, in the Henry Francis du Pont Winterthur Museum [by] Joseph Downs. Foreword by Henry Francis du Pont.

New York, Macmillan, 1952. 1 v. (various pagings) illus., col. plates.   NK2406.H4 1952

Includes bibliographies.

Composed of an introductory essay, photographs of 10 18th-century interiors, and 401 illustrations of individual pieces from the Winterthur collection.

12065

Hornor, William M.   Blue book, Philadelphia furniture, William Penn to George Washington, with special reference to the Philadelphia-Chippendale school. Philadelphia, 1935. xv, 340 p. illus., facsims., plates.

NK2438.P5H6

On cover: Philadelphia Furniture, 1682–1807.
"Philadelphia craftsmen," 1783 and 1786: p. [317]–326.
"Articles by the author relating to American furniture, the fine arts, and colonial mansions": p. [315]–316.

12066

Kettell, Russell H., ed.   Early American rooms; a consideration of the changes in style between the arrival of the Mayflower and the Civil War in the regions originally settled by the English and the Dutch, with articles by Frederick Lewis Allen [and others] Portland, Me., Southworth-Anthoensen Press, 1936. xvii, 200 p. illus., plans, plates (part col.)   NK2003.K4

Reprinted in New York by Dover (1967).

12067

Kettell, Russell H.   The pine furniture of early New England. Garden City, N.Y., Doubleday, Doran, 1929. xxiii, [618] p. illus., plates.   NK2410.K4

"A short list of books and museums": p. [616]
Reprinted in New York by Dover Publications (1949).

12068

Lockwood, Luke V.   Colonial furniture in America. Vol. 1 and v. 2 complete. Supplementary chapters and one hundred and thirty-six plates of new subjects have been added to this ed., which now includes over a thousand illustrations of representative pieces. 3d ed. New York, Castle Books, 1957 [c1926] xxiv, 398, xx, 354 p. illus.
NK2406.L8 1947

First edition published in New York by C. Scribner's Sons (1901).

12069

Lyon, Irving W.   The colonial furniture of New England; a study of the domestic furniture in use in the seventeenth and eighteenth centuries. New ed. Boston, Houghton Mifflin Co., 1924. xii, 285 p. plates.
NK2406.L9 1924

First edition published in 1891.

12070

Nagel, Charles.   American furniture, 1650–1850; a brief background and an illustrated history. New York, Chanticleer Press [1949] 110 p. illus. (part col.) ports. (American crafts series)   NK2405.N3

Bibliography: p. 110.
"Triumph of the Rococo, 1750–1780": p. 56–73.

12071

Rogers, Meyric R.   American interior design, the traditions and development of domestic design from colonial times to the present. New York, W. W. Norton [1947] 309 p. illus. (part col.)   NK2003.R6

Bibliography: p. 297–302.
"The age of colonial achievement, 1730–1790": p. 53–90.

12072

Roth, Rodris.   Floor coverings in 18th-century America. Washington, Smithsonian Press, 1967. 63 p. illus. (Contributions from the Museum of History and Technology, paper 59)   Q11.U6, no. 250

U.S. National Museum. Bulletin 250.
Bibliographic footnotes.

12073

Sale, Edith D. T.   Interiors of Virginia houses of colonial times, from the beginnings of Virginia to the Revolution. Richmond, Printed by the W. Byrd Press, 1927. xxiii, 503 p. illus., plans, plates.   NA7235.V5S3

12074

Singleton, Esther.   The furniture of our forefathers. With cultural descriptions of plates by Russell Sturgis. New York, Doubleday, Page, 1901. 8 pt. in 2 v. (xi, 664 p.) illus., plates.   NK2406.S58

Each part has special title page.
Reissued in New York by B. Blom (1970. xxvi, 663 p. NK2406.S6 1970).
Contents: pt. 1. Early southern carved oak and walnut of the seventeenth century.—pt. 2. Later southern oak, walnut and early mahogany.—pt. 3. Early New England imported and home-made pieces of the seventeenth century.—pt. 4. Dutch and English periods, New York from 1615 to 1776.—pt. 5. New England from 1700 to 1776, imported and home-made pieces of the eighteenth century.—pt. 6. Chippendale and other great cabinet-makers of the eighteenth century.—pt. 7. Domestic and imported furniture from 1776 to 1830.—pt. 8. Woods, upholstery and styles of the early nineteenth century.

12075

Wadsworth Atheneum, *Hartford*.   Connecticut furniture: seventeenth and eighteenth centuries. Hartford, 1967. xvi, 156 p. illus.   NK2435.C8W3

Bibliography: p. 154–155.
"An exhibition organized by the Wadsworth Atheneum for its one hundred and twenty-fifth anniversary celebration" (Nov. 3–Dec. 17, 1967).
"Sources and development of styles of Connecticut furniture" and catalog notes, by John T. Kirk.

9. GUNS AND GUNSMITHS

12076

Bivins, John.   Longrifles of North Carolina. York, Pa., G. Shumway [1968] xv, 200 p. illus., facsims., maps, ports. (Longrifle series)   TS533.3.N8B5

Bibliography: p. 193–195.

A survey of the gunsmithing craft in the 18th and early 19th centuries.

12077

Butler, David F.   United States firearms: the first century, 1776–1875. [New York] Winchester Press [1971] 249 p. illus.   TS533.2.B87

In the early chapters the author discusses muskets and muzzle-loading rifles and pistols of the Revolutionary period and indicates tests made to determine their efficiency.

12078

Carey, Arthur M.   American firearms makers: when, where, and what they made from the colonial period to the end of the nineteenth century. New York, Crowell [1953] xiii, 146 p. illus.   TS535.C26

Bibliography: p. 145–146.
An alphabetical register.

12079

Dillin, John G. W.   The Kentucky rifle; a study of the origin and development of a purely American type of firearm, together with accurate historical data concerning early colonial gunsmiths, and profusely illustrated with photographic reproduction of their finest work. Washington, D.C., National Rifle Association of America, 1924. viii, 124, [6] p. illus., facsims., plates, ports.   TS535.D5

"Edited by Kendrick Scofield."

12080

Dixon, Norman.   Georgian pistols: the art and craft of the flintlock pistol, 1715–1840. York, Pa., G. Shumway [1972, ᶜ1971] 184 p. illus.   TS537.D58 1972

Includes bibliographic references.

12081

Hayward, John F.   The art of the gunmaker. v. 2. Europe and America, 1660–1830. New York, St. Martin's Press [1964] 379 p. illus., plates (part col.)   TS535.H35, v. 2

Includes bibliographic references.
"The United States of America: 1750–1820": p. 272–282.

12082

Kauffman, Henry J.   Early American gunsmiths, 1650–1850. Harrisburg, Pa., Stackpole Co. [1952] xx, 94 p. illus., map, port.   TS535.K3

An alphabetical register.

12083

Kauffman, Henry J.   The Pennsylvania-Kentucky rifle. Harrisburg, Pa., Stackpole Co. [1969] 376 p. illus., facsims., map, port.   TS535.K33

Bibliography: p. 373–374.

12084

Russell, Carl P.   Guns on the early frontiers; a history of firearms from colonial times through the years of the Western fur trade. Berkeley, University of California Press, 1957. xv, 395 p. illus.   TS520.R85

Bibliography: p. [357]–381.

Concerned with the weapons, powder, ball, and accessories used by the early fur traders and the commercial and political aspects of the gun trade with the Indians.

PRINTERS, NEWSPAPERS, BOOKS, AND LIBRARIES

1. GENERAL

12085

Barrow, Robert M.   Newspaper advertising in colonial America, 1704–1775. 1967. ([298] p.)
        Micro AC–1, no. 67–17,585

Thesis (Ph.D.)—University of Virginia.
Abstracted in *Dissertation Abstracts*, v. 28A, Jan. 1968, p. 2618.

12086

Barrow, William J.   Black writing ink of the colonial period. American archivist, v. 11, Oct. 1948: 291–307.   CD3020.A45, v. 11

Despite much contrary speculation, intensive research demonstrates that iron gall inks were used almost exclusively.

12087

Barthold, Allen J.   French journalists in the United States, 1780–1800. Franco-American review, v. 1, winter 1937: 215–230.   E183.8.F8F88, v. 1

12088

Benjamin, Samuel G. W.   Notable editors between 1776 and 1800: influence of the early American press. Magazine of American history, with notes and queries, v. 17, Feb. 1887: 97–127. facsims., ports.   E171.M18, v. 17

12089

Bibliographical Society of America.   French newspapers in the United States before 1800. Chicago, Ill., University of Chicago Press [1923] 45–147 p. (*Its* Papers, v. 14, pt. 2, 1920)   Z1008.B51P, v. 14

Various authors discuss *Le Courier de L'Amérique* (Philadelphia, 1784), *Courier de Boston* (1789), and other French newspapers published in Boston, New York, Philadelphia, Charleston, and New Orleans in the 1790's.

12090

Botein, Stephen W. Reluctant partisans; the role of printers in 18th-century American politics. 1971.

Thesis (Ph.D.)—Harvard University.

12091

Brigham, Clarence S. Journals and journeymen; a contribution to the history of early American newspapers. Philadelphia, University of Pennsylvania Press, 1950. xiv, 114 p. illus.   PN4858.B7

"The A. S. W. Rosenbach Fellowship in Bibliography."

Reprinted in Westport, Conn., by Greenwood Press (1971).

Impressionistic sketches based on notes taken during the compilation of his *Bibliography of American Newspapers* (entry 452).

12092

Buckingham, Joseph T. Specimens of newspaper literature: with personal memoirs, anecdotes, and reminiscences. Boston, C. C. Little and J. Brown, 1850. 2 v. illus., ports.   PN4808.B8

Reprinted in Freeport, N.Y., by Books for Libraries Press (1971).

Provides sketches of 18th- and early 19th-century newspapers, editors, and printers.

12093

Case, Leland D. Origins of Methodist publishing in America. *In* Bibliographical Society of America. Papers, v. 59, 1st quarter 1965: 12–27. facsims.
                    Z1008.B51P, v. 59

Finds evidence suggesting that John Wesley's followers in America tried to organize their publishing interests under Thomas Rankin as early as 1775, rather than in 1789 as it is commonly believed. Reprinted in *Methodist History*, v. 4, Apr. 1966, p. 29–41.

12094

Cullen, Maurice R. Middle-class democracy and the press in colonial America. Journalism quarterly, v. 46, autumn 1969: 531–535.   PN4700.J7, v. 46

Argues against those who contend that the Revolution was a class struggle and that the colonial press had little effect on the Revolutionary process.

12095

Emery, Edwin. The press and America, an interpretative history of journalism. 2d ed. Englewood Cliffs, N.J., Prentice-Hall, 1962. x, 801 p. illus., facsims., plates, ports. (Prentice-Hall journalism series)
                    PN4855.E6 1962

Reviews in chapters 1–6 (p. 3–124) the development of the colonial and Revolutionary press.

12096

Faÿ, Bernard. Notes on the American press at the end of the eighteenth century. New York, Grolier Club, 1927. 29 p. fold. facsims.   PN4861.F3 Rare Bk. Coll.

12097

Hart, Jim A. The developing views on the news; editorial syndrome, 1500–1800. Foreword by Howard Rusk Long. Carbondale, Southern Illinois University Press [1970] x, 238 p. (New horizons in journalism)
                    PN4858.H3

Bibliography: p. [227]–232.

Traces the evolution of the English-language newspaper editorial through a review of pamphlets, ballads, essays, prefaces, asides, shoulder notes, introductory letters, newssheets, newsletters, and newsbooks. In six chapters on the Revolutionary period the author notes that American printers were instrumental in shaping opinion through the publication of propagandistic political commentaries, but that newspaper editorials in their modern form did not emerge until the 1790's.

12098

Heartman, Charles F. Checklist of printers in the United States from Stephen Daye to the close of the War of Independence, with a list of places in which printing was done. New York City [1915] 53 p. facsim. (Heartman's historical series, no. 9)   Z208.H37

12099

Hudson, Frederic. Journalism in the United States, from 1690 to 1872. New York, Harper, 1873. 789 p.
                    PN4855.H8

Reprinted in New York by Haskell House (1968) and in Grosse Pointe, Mich., by Scholarly Press (1968).

"The Revolutionary press, 1748–1783": p. 103–140.

12100

Kaser, David, *ed.* Books in America's past; essays honoring Rudolph H. Gjelsness. Charlottesville, Published for the Bibliographical Society of the University of Virginia [by] University Press of Virginia [1966] x, 279 p. illus., ports.   Z674.K35

Includes bibliographic references.

Partial contents: David Hall's bookshop and its British sources of supply [by] R. D. Harlan.—French-language printing in the United States, 1711–1825 [by] S. J. Marino.—The first printing press in Canada, 1751–1800 [by] O. B. Bishop.—James Rivington, Tory, printer [by] L. Hewlett.—Engravings in American magazines, 1741–1810 [by] B. M. Lewis.

12101

Kobre, Sidney. The development of the colonial newspaper. Pittsburgh, Pa. [Colonial Press] 1944. xi, 188 p. facsims.   PN4861.K6

Bibliography: p. 182–188.

Also submitted as thesis (Ph.D.)—Columbia University.

"The Revolutionary newspaper (1750–1783)": p. 95–181.

12102

Kobre, Sidney. Foundations of American journalism. [Tallahassee] Florida State Univeristy [ᶜ1958] vi, 362 p. illus., facsims., maps, ports. PN4855.K6

Bibliographic footnotes.

Reprinted in Westport, Conn., by Greenwood Press (1970).

Discusses the colonial and Revolutionary press in chapters 3 and 4 (p. 29–128).

12103

Kobre, Sidney. The Revolutionary colonial press—a social interpretation. Journalism quarterly, v. 20, Sept. 1943: 193–204. PN4700.J7, v. 20

12104

Lewis, Benjamin M. A register of editors, printers, and publishers of American magazines, 1741–1810. New York, New York Public Library, 1957. 40 p. Z6951.L4

12105

McMurtrie, Douglas C. A history of printing in the United States; the story of the introduction of the press and of its history and influence during the pioneer period in each state of the Union. v. 2. Middle & South Atlantic states. New York, R. R. Bowker Co., 1936. xxvi, 462 p. facsims., maps (on lining papers) Z208.M18

Bibliography: p. [401]–462.

Reprinted in New York by B. Franklin (1969).

Paying special attention to printing in colonial Pennsylvania, the author describes the work of Benjamin Franklin, the early German press, the Philadelphia printers during the Revolution, and the spread of printing into western Pennsylvania. McMurtrie also traces the development of printing in New York and eight other states. Although the work was planned in four volumes, only volume 2 was published.

12106

Mott, Frank L. American journalism; a history, 1690–1960. 3d ed. New York Macmillan [1962] xiv, 901 p. illus., facsims., ports. PN4855.M63 1962

Includes bibliographies.

First edition published in 1950.

"The press in the American Revolution, 1765–1783": p. [69]–110.

12107

Oswald, John C. Printing in the Americas. New York, Gregg Pub. Co. [ᶜ1937] xii, 565, xvii–xli p. illus., facsims., maps (on lining papers) Z205.O86

Reprinted in Port Washington, N.Y., by Kennikat Press (1965) and in New York by Hacker Art Books (1968).

Surveys the development of typography and journalism through the 19th century in North, Central, and South America and the West Indies. In the chapters on individual U.S. states, the author presents biographical sketches of early printers.

12108

Pomerantz, Sidney I. Newspaper humor in the War for Independence. Journalism quarterly, v. 21, Dec. 1944: 311–317. PN4700.J7, v. 21

12109

Preston, Paula S. The severed head of Charles I of England: its use as a political stimulus. *In* Winterthur portfolio, v. 6. Winterthur, Del. 1970. p. 1–13. illus., facsims. N9.W52, v. 6

Finds that the recurring use of the head of Charles I as a political symbol in American cartoons, prints, and paintings implied that George III must suffer the fate of Charles I if the individual rights of the colonists were to be preserved.

12110

Thomas, Charles M. The publication of newspapers during the American Revolution. Journalism quarterly, v. 9, Dec. 1932: 358–373. PN4700.J7, v. 9

12111

Thomas, Isaiah. The history of printing in America, with a biography of printers, and an account of newspapers. 2d ed. With the author's corrections and additions, and a catalogue of American publications previous to the Revolution of 1776 [compiled by Samuel F. Haven, Jr.] Albany, N.Y., J. Munsell, Printer, 1874. 2 v. port., plates. (Archaeologia americana. Transactions and collections of the American Antiquarian Society, v. 5–6). Z208.T451

In this edition the account of printing in the Old World is omitted.

Reprinted in New York by B. Franklin (1967). A one-volume edition, edited by Marcus A. McCorison, was published in Barre, Mass., by the Imprint Society (1970). The first edition was published in 1810 in Worcester, Mass.

Arranging the biographies of individual printers by colony, the author also provides lists of booksellers and of newspapers published in the year 1775. William McCulloch, a leading Philadelphia printer, sent Thomas additional information in six letters, especially on early printing in Pennsylvania. The letters were published in the *Proceedings* of the American Antiquarian Society, new ser., v. 31, Apr. 1921, p. 89–247. In 1879, W. F. Draper reprinted at Andover, Mass., James D. Butler's *American Pre-Revolutionary Bibliography* (72–104 p. Z208.T452), a review of Thomas' *History* that first appeared in *Bibliotheca Sacra*, v. 36, Jan. 1879, p. 72–104. Butler pays particular attention to Samuel F. Haven's appendix to the 1874 edition—"Catalogue of Publications in What Is Now the United States, Prior to the Revolution of 1775–6."

12112

Wroth, Lawrence C. The colonial printer. [2d ed., rev. and enl.] Portland, Me., Southworth-Anthoensen Press, 1938. xxiv, 368 p. illus., facsims. Z208.W95 1938 Rare Bk. Coll.

In case.

"Works referred to in notes": p. [331]–347.

Revision of a work first published in 1931, this ed. was reissued in Charlottesville, Va., by Dominion Books (1964).

After surveying the beginning of printing in each of the English colonies, the author studies the materials and tools of the colonial printers and the techniques devised to improve their presses, type, ink, paper, and bookbinding. Wroth also treats the conditions under which the printers worked, providing biographical information about early printers and describing the several products of the colonial press: almanacs, newspapers, magazines, printed sermons, and broadsides.

2. New England

12113

Bates, Albert C.   Some notes of early Connecticut printing. *In* Bibliographical Society of America. Papers, v. 27, pt. 1, 1933: 1–11.   Z1008.B51P, v. 27

12114

Boston Club of Printing House Craftsmen.   A New England keepsake. [Cambridge] Printed under the auspices of the Boston Club of Printing House Craftsmen by ten New England printers [1938] [153] p. illus., facsims., maps, plates, port.   Z208.B74

Contents: Foreword, by Watson M. Gordon.—Greeting to the craftsmen, by D. B. Updike.—Old New England miscellany.—New England's prospect.—The colonial printing press.—Early Rhode Island printing.—Printing in Concord, New Hampshire.—Colonial printing in Cambridge.—Three hundred years of printing in New England.—Early Vermont printers and printing.

12115

Brown, Harry Glenn, *and* Maude O. Brown.   A directory of printing, publishing, bookselling & allied trades in Rhode Island to 1865. New York, New York Public Library, 1958. 211 p.   Z209.R5B7

An alphabetical list of printers, editors, publishers, binders, periodical dealers, and other tradesmen as well as a list of serials published in Rhode Island. The annotations provide each man's business address, the dates he worked there, and information on periodicals he published.

12116

Brown, Ralph A.   New Hampshire editors win the war: a study in Revolutionary press propaganda. New England quarterly, v. 12, Mar. 1939: 35–51.
   F1.N62, v. 12

12117

Goddard, Delano A.   The press and literature of the provincial period, 1692–1770. *In* Winsor, Justin, *ed.* The memorial history of Boston, including Suffolk County, Massachusetts, 1630–1880 . . . v. 2. The provincial period. Boston, J.R. Osgood, 1882. p. [387]–436. illus.
   F73.3.W77, v. 2

12118

Lane, William C.   The printer of the Harvard theses of 1771. *In* Colonial Society of Massachusetts, *Boston.* Publications. v. 26. Transactions, 1924/26. Boston, 1927. p. 1–15.   F61.C71, v. 26

Richard Draper was the printer.

12119

McCorison, Marcus A.   A bibliography of Vermont bibliography and printing. *In* Bibliographical Society of America. Papers, v. 55, 1st quarter 1961: 17–33.
   Z1008.B51P, v. 55

12120

McMurtrie, Douglas C.   The beginnings of printing in New Hampshire. Library, 4th ser., v. 15, Dec. 1934: 340–363. facsims.   Z671.L69, 4th s., v. 15

———————— Offprint. London, Bibliographical Society, 1934. [340]–363 p. facsims.   Z209.N54M2

12121

McMurtrie, Douglas C.   The beginning of printing in Rhode Island. Americana, v. 29, Oct. 1935: 607–629. facsims.   E171.A53, v. 29

——— ——— Offprint. Somerville, N.J., 1935. 607–629 p. facsims.   Z209.R5M18
Bibliography: p. 626–627.

12122

Morse, Jarvis M.   Connecticut newspapers in the eighteenth century. [New Haven] Published for the Tercentenary Commission by the Yale University Press, 1935. 31 p. (Connecticut. Tercentenary Commission. Committee on Historical Publications. [Tercentenary pamphlet series, 36])   PN4897.C8M7

"Bibliographical note": p. 31.

12123

Nichols, Charles L.   Some notes on Isaiah Thomas and his Worcester imprints. *In* American Antiquarian Society, *Worcester, Mass.* Proceedings, new ser., v. 13, Apr. 1900: 429–447.   E172.A35, n.s., v. 13

——— ——— Offprint. Worcester, Mass., Press of C. Hamilton, 1900. 21 p.   B232.T4N5

Finds a total of 325 books, pamphlets, newspapers, and broadsides were printed by or for Thomas from 1775 to 1802.

12124

Providence newspapers before 1800. *In* International Typographical Union of North America. *Union no. 33, Providence.* Printers and printing in Providence, 1762–1907. [Providence, Providence Print. Co., 1907] p. [9]–20. facsims., ports.   Z209.P85P8

12125

Rugg, Harold G.   The Dresden press. [Hanover, N.H., 1920] [19] p. facsims.   Z209.N54R8

Reprinted from the *Dartmouth Alumni Magazine*, May 1920.

On the work of Alden and Judah Padoch Spooner in what is now Hanover, New Hampshire.

12126
Silver, Rollo G. Government printing in Massachusetts, 1751–1801. *In* Virginia University. *Bibliographical Society.* Studies in bibliography; papers. v. 16. Charlottesville, 1963. p. 161–200.   Z1008.V55, v. 16

12127
Smith, James Eugene. One hundred years of Hartford's *Courant*, from colonial times through the Civil War. New Haven, Yale University Press, 1949. 342 p.
PN4899.H35C6

Bibliography: p. [328]–329.
Reprinted in Hamden, Conn., by Archon Books (1970).
The author's thesis (Ph.D.), with nearly the same title, was submitted to Harvard University in 1943.
"Part I: 1764–1783": p. [3]–55.

12128
Spaulding, Ernest Wilder. The *Connecticut Courant*: a representative newspaper in the eighteenth century. New England quarterly, v. 3, July 1930: 443–463.
F1.N62, v. 3

12129
Streeter, Gilbert L. Account of the newspapers and other periodicals published in Salem, from 1768 to 1856. *In* Essex Institute, *Salem, Mass.* Proceedings, v. 1; 1848/56. Salem, 1856. p. 157–186.   F72.E7E76, v. 1
——— ——— Offprint. Salem, W. Ives and G. W. Pease, Printers, 1856. 33 p.   Z6953.S163S

12130
Winship, George P. Newport newspapers in the eighteenth century. Newport, R.I., 1914. 22 p. plates. (Bulletin of the Newport Historical Society, no. 14)
F89.N5N615, no. 14

12131
Wroth. Lawrence C. The first press in Providence; a study in social development. *In* American Antiquarian Society, *Worcester, Mass.* Proceedings, new ser., v. 51, Oct. 1941: 351–383.   E172.A35, n.s., v. 51

Concerns the printing and publishing activities of William Goddard.

3. MIDDLE ATLANTIC REGION

12132
Andrews, J. Cutler. *The Pittsburgh Gazette*—a pioneer newspaper. Western Pennsylvania historical magazine, v. 15, Nov. 1932: 293–307.   F146.W52, v. 15
Established in 1786.

12133
Bridenbaugh, Carl. The press and the book in eighteenth century Philadelphia. Pennsylvania magazine of history and biography, v. 65, Jan. 1941: 1–30.
F146.P65, v. 65

12134
Brown, Ralph A. *The Pennsylvania Ledger*: Tory news sheet. Pennsylvania history, v. 9, July 1942: 161–175.
F146.P597, v. 9

Published in Philadelphia by James Humphreys, Jr., from 1775 to 1778.

12135
Diffenderffer, Frank R. An early newspaper. *In* Lancaster County (Pa.) Historical Society. Papers, v. 11, May 1907: 175–194. illus.   F157.L2L5, v. 11

A summary of news items and advertisements from the *Neue unpartheyische Lancaster Zeitung*, October 25, 1787, to May 19, 1790.

12136
[Engle, J. Linton] *comp.* Benjamin Franklin, founder; the remarkable record of a Philadelphia institution from 1728 to 1915. Philadelphia, Franklin Print. Co., 1915. 53 p. port.   Z232.F8E7
History of the Franklin Printing Company.

12137
Hildeburn, Charles S. R. Sketches of printers and printing in colonial New York. With numerous illustrations. New York, Dodd, Mead [De Vinne Press] 1895. xiv, 189 p. facsims., ports.   Z209.N559H6

Reprinted in Detroit by Gale Research Co. (1969).

Includes information on the life and work of 28 printers who plied their trade in New York between 1760 and 1789.

12138
Hixson, Richard F. The founding of New Jersey's first permanent newspaper. Journalism quarterly, v. 40, spring 1963: 233–235.   PN4700.J7, v. 40

The *New-Jersey Gazette*, 1777–86.

12139
Hoffman, Ronald. The press in mercantile Maryland: a question of utility. Journalism quarterly, v. 46, autumn 1969: 536–544.   PN4700.J7, v. 46

Finds that the press was helpful but in no way essential to the development of Maryland's mercantile community, 1760–85.

12140
Lee, Alfred M. Dunlap and Claypool[e]: printers and news-merchants of the Revolution. Journalism quarterly, v. 11, June 1934: 160–178.   PN4700.J7, v. 11

On John Dunlap and David C. Claypoole, who published the first successful daily newspaper in the United States, *The Pennsylvania Packet and Daily Advertiser*, first printed at Philadelphia on September 21, 1784.

12141
Lerbscher, August, *and* Albert Cavin. Items of interest from the *Neue Unpartheyische Lancaster Zeitung, und Anzeigs-Nachrichten* [Aug. 8, 1787–Mar. 16, 1791] *In* Lancaster County (Pa.) Historical Society. Papers,

v. 34, Jan., May 1930: 1–10, 97–107; v. 35, Feb. 1931: 25–36. F157.L2L5, v. 34–35

12142
Nelson, William. Some New Jersey printers and printing in the eighteenth century. *In* American Antiquarian Society, *Worcester, Mass.* Proceedings, new ser., v. 21, Apr. 1911: 15–56. E172.A35, n.s., v. 21

———— ———— Offprint. Worcester, Mass., The Society, 1911. 44 p. Z209.N55N3

12143
Parker, Peter J. The Philadelphia printer: a study of an eighteenth-century businessman. Business history review, v. 40, spring 1966: 24–46. HF5001.B8262, v. 40

12144
Steirer, William F. Philadelphia newspapers: years of revolution and transition, 1764–1794. 1972. ([450] p.) Micro AC–1, no. 73–1454

Thesis (Ph.D.)—University of Pennsylvania.
Abstracted in *Dissertation Abstracts International,* v. 33A, Jan. 1973, p. 3561.

12145
Stickle, Warren E. State and press in New Jersey during the American Revolution. New Jersey history, v. 86, fall-winter 1968: 158–170, 236–249. F131.N58, v. 86

12146
Stoudt, John J. The German press in Pennsylvania and the American Revolution. Pennsylvania magazine of history and biography, v. 59, Jan. 1935: 74–90. F146.P65, v. 59

Contends that the major outlet for German liberal sentiment during the Revolution was *Der Wöchentliche Philadelphische Staatsbote*, published by Henry (Heinrich) Miller.

12147
Straub, Jean S. Magazines in the Friends Latin School of Philadelphia in the 1770's. Quaker history, v. 55, spring 1966: 38–45. BX7635.A1F6, v. 55

12148
Teeter, Dwight L. A legacy of expression: Philadelphia newspapers and Congress during the War of Independence, 1775–1783. 1966. ([349] p.) Micro AC–1, no. 66–9975

Thesis (Ph.D.)—University of Wisconsin.
Abstracted in *Dissertation Abstracts*, v. 28A, Sept. 1967, p. 1045.

Describes the economic and political control over Philadelphia's English-language newspapers exerted by Congress and the Pennsylvania government and finds that those printers who accepted the goal of independence enjoyed a genuine freedom of expression.

12149
Weiss, Harry B. A graphic summary of the growth of newspapers in New York and other states, 1704–1820. *In* New York (City). Public Library. Bulletin, v. 52, Apr. 1948: 182–196. illus. Z881.N6B, v. 52

Based upon an analysis of Brigham's *History and Bibliography of American Newspapers* (entry 452).

12150
Weiss, Harry B. The printers and publishers of children's books in New York City, 1698–1830. *In* New York (City). Public Library. Bulletin, v. 52, Aug. 1948: 383–391. Z881.N6B, v. 52

Identifies 32 for the 18th century.

12151
Weiss, Harry B. Type founders, copperplate printers, stereotypers in early New York City [1759–1820] *In* New York (City). Public Library. Bulletin, v. 55, Oct. 1951: 471–483. Z881.N6B, v. 55

12152
Weiss, Harry B. The writing masters and ink manufacturers of New York City, 1737–1820. *In* New York (City). Public Library. Bulletin, v. 56, Aug. 1952: 383–394. Z881.N6B, v. 56

12153
Wroth, Lawrence C. Benjamin Franklin: the printer at work. *In his* Typographic heritage, selected essays. [New York] The Typophiles, 1949. (Typophile chap books, 20) p. [91]–134. Z116.W7

An analysis of the printing business.

12154
Wroth, Lawrence C. The first work with American types. *In his* Typographic heritage, selected essays. [New York] The Typophiles, 1949. (Typophile chap books, 20) p. [133]–157. Z116.W7

Story and Humphreys' *Pennsylvania Mercury*, April 7, 1775.

4. THE SOUTH

12155
Black, William P. The *Virginia Gazette*, 1766–1774: beginnings of an indigenous literature. 1971. ([232] p.) Micro AC–1, no. 72–7473

Thesis (Ph.D.)—Duke University.
Abstracted in *Dissertation Abstracts International,* v. 32A, Feb. 1972, p. 4553.

12156
Castles, William H. The *Virginia Gazette*, 1736–1766: its editors, editorial policies and literary content. 1962. ([365] p.) Micro AC–1, no. 63–1623

Thesis (Ph.D.)—University of Tennessee.
Abstracted in *Dissertation Abstracts*, v. 23, Mar. 1963, p. 3350.

12157
Cohen, Hennig.   The South Carolina Gazette, 1732–1775. Columbia, University of South Carolina Press, 1953. xv, 273 p. facsim.   F272.C64

"Based upon a dissertation written at Tulane University" (1951).
Bibliography: p. 250–258.

Reprints excerpts from the *Gazette*, arranging the vignettes in chronological order in an effort to portray the character of southern, especially Charleston, society. Subjects covered include the theater, sports, club life, gardens, artists, musicians, teachers, doctors, architects, engineers, master builders, books, booksellers, poets, and essayists. Besides a historical sketch of the paper and biographical information on its editors, the compiler offers a list of first notices for South Carolina imprints that appeared in the *Gazette*, including those that were products of its own press.

12158
Crittenden, Charles Christopher.   North Carolina newspapers before 1790. Chapel Hill, University of North Carolina Press, 1928. 83 p. (The James Sprunt historical studies, v. 20, no. 1)   F251.J28, v. 20

Identifying 12 separate publications, the author summarizes the facts of their establishment, physical appearance, and circulation; analyzes their news, editorial, and literary content; and provides information on 18th-century manufacturing, travel, education, and other topics described in their advertisements. Crittenden finds that North Carolina's newspapers, from the first issue in 1751, were less original, less profitable, less regularly published, and less influential than their counterparts in Boston, New York, and Philadelphia.

12159
Dargan, Marion.   Crime and the *Virginia Gazette*, 1736–1775. Albuquerque, N.M., University of New Mexico, 1934. 61 p. (The University of New Mexico bulletin. Sociological series, v. 2, no. 1; whole no. 243)
HV6781.D3
H31.N5, v. 2

Bibliography: p. 60–61.

12160
MacLeod, James L.   A catalogue of references to education in the *South Carolina Gazettes*, Charleston, South Carolina, 1731 to 1770, and commentary. 1972. ([240] p.)   Micro AC–1, no. 73–150

Thesis (Ph.D.)—Mississippi State University.
Abstracted in *Dissertation Abstracts International*, v. 33A, Jan. 1973, p. 3338.

12161
McMurtrie, Douglas C.   The beginnings of printing in Virginia. Lexington, Va. [Printed in the Journalism Laboratory of Washington and Lee University] 1935. 48 p. facsims.   Z209.V6M2 Rare Bk. Coll.

Bibliography: p. 43–[44]

12162
McMurtrie, Douglas C.   Pioneer printing in Georgia. Georgia historical quarterly, v. 16, June 1932: 77–113. facsim.   F281.G2975, v. 16

———   ——— Offprint. Savannah, Ga., Priv. print., 1932. 39 p. facsims.   Z209.G3M3

12163
Myers, Robert M.   The Old Dominion looks to London: a study of English literary influences upon *The Virginia Gazette* (1736–1766). Virginia magazine of history and biography, v. 54, July 1946: 195–217.
F221.V91, v. 54

12164
Paschal, George W.   A history of printing in North Carolina; a detailed account of the pioneer printers, 1749–1880, and of the Edwards & Broughton Company, 1871–1946, including a brief account of the connecting period. Raleigh, Edwards & Broughton Co., 1946. xxii, 313 p. illus., facsims.   Z232.E25P3

Bibliography: p. [295]–298.

Summarizes in the first chapter the development of North Carolina printing to 1800 and adds 14 titles to Douglas C. McMurtrie's *Eighteenth Century North Carolina Imprints, 1749–1800* (entry 388).

12165
Powell, William S.   Patrons of the press: subscription book purchases in North Carolina, 1733–1850. North Carolina historical review, v. 39, autumn 1962: 423–499. facsims.   F251.N892, v. 39

Includes an alphabetical list of subscription books and a full index of subscribers.

12166
The *Royal Georgia Gazette*; facsimiles of some unique issues dated at Savannah, Ga., from August 12, 1779, to August 3, 1780, inclusive, preserved in the British Museum, with an introductory note by Douglas C. McMurtrie.   Evanston, Priv. print., 1942. [30] p.
E263.G3R6 P & P

12167
Skaggs, David C.   Editorial policies of the *Maryland Gazette*, 1765–1783. Maryland historical magazine, v. 59, Dec. 1964: 341–349.   F176.M18, v. 59

12168
Thornton, Mary L.   Public printing in North Carolina, 1749–1815. North Carolina historical review, v. 21, July 1944: 181–202.   F251.N892, v. 21

12169
Wallace, Wesley H.   Cultural and social advertising in early North Carolina newspapers [New Bern and Wilmington, 1751–78] North Carolina historical review, v. 33, July 1956: 281–309.   F251.N892, v. 33

12170

Wallace, Wesley H.   Property and trade: main themes of early North Carolina newspaper advertisements [1751–78] North Carolina historical review, v. 32, Oct. 1955: 451–482.   F251.N892, v. 32

12171

Wroth, Lawrence C.   A history of printing in colonial Maryland, 1686–1776. [Baltimore] Typothetae of Baltimore, 1922. xiv, 275 p. facsims.   Z209.M39W9

Presents a series of biographical sketches of early Maryland printers at work, including Jonas Green and his *Maryland Gazette*, Thomas Bacon and his edition of Maryland laws, and William and Mary Goddard of Baltimore. The author recounts their experience in Maryland and other colonies, considers their ability as craftsmen, and assesses their influence upon colonial printing. An appendix contains an annotated bibliography of 392 books, broadsides, and newspapers printed in Maryland during the years 1689–1776, 150 of which were issued during the Revolutionary period.

5. Freedom of the Press as an Issue

12172

Duniway, Clyde A.   The development of freedom of the press in Massachusetts [1628–1827] New York, Longmans, Green, 1906. xv, 202 p. (Harvard historical studies, v. 12)   Z657.D93

"Bibliographical notes": p. 175–186.
The author's thesis (Ph.D.), *The History of Restrictions Upon the Freedom of the Press in Massachusetts*, was submitted to Harvard University in 1897.
Reprinted in New York by B. Franklin (1969).

12173

Leder, Lawrence H.   The role of newspapers in early America "in defense of their own liberties." Huntington Library quarterly, v. 30, Nov. 1966: 1–16.
                    Z733.S24Q, v. 30

12174

Levy, Leonard W.   Did the Zenger case really matter? Freedom of the press in colonial New York. William and Mary quarterly, 3d ser., v. 17, Jan. 1960: 35–50.
                    F221.W71, 3d s., v. 17

12175

Levy, Leonard W., *ed.*   Freedom of the press from Zenger to Jefferson; early American libertarian theories. Indianapolis, Bobbs-Merrill Co. [1966] lxxxiii, 409 p. (The American heritage series, 41)   KF4774.A75L4

Bibliography: p. lxxxi–lxxxiii.

Includes 43 documents concerned with freedom of the press in America from 1731 to 1823.

12176

Schuyler, Livingston R.   The liberty of the press in the American colonies before the Revolutionary War. With particular reference to conditions in the royal colony of New York. New York, T. Whittaker, 1905. vii, 86 p.
                    Z657.S39

Thesis (Ph.D.)—New York University.
Bibliography: p. 79–81.

12177

Teeter, Dwight L.   Press freedom and the public printing: Pennsylvania, 1775–83. Journalism quarterly, v. 45, autumn 1968: 445–451.   PN4700.J7, v. 45

Finds that the general criticism of government continued during the war.

6. Books, Bookmaking, and the Book Trade

12178

Books in Williamsburg.   William and Mary College quarterly historical magazine, v. 15, Oct. 1906: 101–113.   F221.W71, v. 15

A list of books for sale at the printing office of Dixon & Hunter in 1775.

12179

Boyton, Henry W.   Annals of American bookselling, 1638–1850. New York, J. Wiley, 1932. ix, 209 p. facsims., plates.   Z473.B79

"Source books": p. 196–198.

Includes chapters on the booksellers of Boston, New York, and Philadelphia during the Revolution.

12180

Cometti, Elizabeth.   Some early best sellers in piedmont North Carolina [1769–77] Journal of southern history, v. 16, Aug. 1950: 324–337.   F206.J68, v. 16

12181

Dearden, Robert R., Jr., *and* Douglas S. Watson.   An original leaf from the Bible of the Revolution, and an essay concerning it. San Francisco, Calif., Printed by E. & R. Grabhorn for J. Howell, 1930. 34 p. illus., facsims., ports.   BS185.1782.P52 Rare Bk. Coll.

Contents: An original leaf from the Bible of the Revolution.—The Bible of the Revolution, an essay, by R. R. Dearden, Jr., and D. S. Watson.—Facsimile, with typographical transcript, of General Washington's letter regarding the Aitken Bible.—A note on the typography of the period, by E. E. Grabhorn.

12182

Goff, Frederick R.   Rubrication in American books of the eighteenth century. *In* American Antiquarian Society, *Worcester, Mass.* Proceedings, v. 79, Apr. 1969: 29–43. facsims.   E172.A35, v. 79

Of 48,000 American imprints recorded before 1801, only 26 contain rubricated or two-color title pages.

12183

Hatchett, Marion J.   The making of the first American prayer book [1786–90] 1972. ([572] p.)
                    Micro AC–1, no. 73–16,708

Thesis (Th.D.)—General Theological Seminary.
Abstracted in *Dissertation Abstracts International*, v. 34A, July 1973, p. 405–406.

12184

Jones, Howard M.   The importation of French books in Philadelphia, 1750–1800. Modern philology, v. 32, Nov. 1934: 157–177.   PB1.M7, v. 32

12185

Lehmann-Haupt, Hellmut.   The book in America; a history of the making and selling of books in the United States, by Hellmut Lehmann-Haupt in collaboration with Lawrence C. Wroth and Rollo G. Silver. 2d [rev. and enl. American] ed. New York, Bowker, 1951. xiv, 493 p.   Z473.L522 1951

The first U.S. edition, published in 1939, was revised and enlarged in English text from the German original, *Das amerikanische Buchwesen* (Leipzig, K. W. Hiersemann, 1937).

Contents: Book production and distribution from the beginning to the American Revolution, by L. C. Wroth.— Book production and distribution from the American Revolution to the War between the States, by L. C. Wroth and R. G. Silver.—Book production and distribution from 1860 to the present day, by H. Lehmann-Haupt.—Bibliography (p. 422–466).

12186

Lydenberg, Harry M.   The problem of the pre-1776 American Bible. *In* Bibliographical Society of America. Papers, v. 48, 2d quarter 1954: 183–194.
                    Z1008.B51P, v. 48

Investigates the reprinting in Boston of the Thomas Baskett edition of the Bible published in Oxford, England, about midcentury.

12187

Miles, Wyndman D.   Books on chemistry printed in the United States, 1755–1900: a study of their origin. Library chronicle, v. 18, summer 1952: 51–62.
                    Z733.P418, v. 18

12188

Powell, John H.   The books of a new nation; United States government publications, 1774–1814. Philadelphia, University of Pennsylvania Press [1957] 170 p. facsims.
                    Z1223.Z7P65

Includes bibliographic references.

Consists of three lectures, the first two of which deal with early government printing contracts and printers, the publications of the First Continental Congress, the July 5, 1776, printing of the Declaration of Independence, printed issues of the Constitutional Convention of 1787, and certain individual publications, such as Steuben's *Discipline of the Troops.*

12189

Samford, C. Clement, *and* John M. Hemphill.   Bookbinding in colonial Virginia. Williamsburg, Va., Colonial Williamsburg; Distributed by the University Press of Virginia, Charlottesville [ᶜ1966] xxi, 185 p. (Williamsburg research studies)   Z270.U5S3

Bibliography: p. [177]–181.

12190

Spawn, Willman, *and* Carol M. Spawn.   The Aitken shop—identification of an eighteenth-century bindery and its tools. *In* Bibliographical Society of America. Papers, v. 57, 4th quarter 1963: 422–437. plates.
                    Z1008.B51P, v. 57

12191

Stetson, Sarah P.   American garden books transplanted and native, before 1807. William and Mary quarterly, 3d ser., v. 3, July 1946: 343–369.
                    F221.W71, 3d s., v. 3

12192

Tebbel, John W.   A history of book publishing in the United States. v. 1. The creation of an industry, 1630–1865. New York, R. R. Bowker Co. [1972] xvi, 646 p.
                    Z473.T42, v. 1

A 150-page section on the trade during the 18th century summarizes developments within each colony and treats the economic aspects of book publishing in such areas as copyright, bestsellers, censorship, publishing houses, and children's books.

12193

Winterich, John T.   Early American books & printing. Boston, Houghton, Mifflin, 1935. vii, 256 p. illus., facsims., port.   Z208.W79

Reprinted in Ann Arbor, Mich., by Gryphon Books (1971).

A loosely-connected series of essays on significant American books, authors, printers, booksellers, and bibliographers from the early printers of Boston to the rise of the professional author.

12194

Winton, Calhoun.   The colonial South Carolina book trade. *In* Proof; the yearbook of American bibliographical and textual studies. Edited by Joseph Katz. v. 2; 1972. Columbia S.C., University of South Carolina Press. p. 71–87.   Z1219.P73, v. 2

Examines the principal methods of book distribution in South Carolina: the retail bookshop, book auctions or vendues, purchase by subscription, and importation and sale of books from Great Britain and from other colonies by general merchants.

12195

Wright, John.   Early prayer books of America; being a descriptive account of prayer books published in the United States, Mexico and Canada. St. Paul Minn., Priv. print. [Press of Evans & Bissell] 1896. xv, 492 p. illus., facsims., plate.   Z7813.W95

Quoting generously from several 18th-century works, the author describes books published by churches from 1643 through the 19th century, including those used during the Revolutionary period by Episcopal, Dutch Reformed, Jewish, Unitarian, and other congregations. An appendix contains a list of prayer books arranged by year of publication— 17 appeared between 1763 and 1789—and a compilation of those written in various Indian languages.

7. PUBLIC AND PRIVATE LIBRARIES

12196

Burstyn, Harold L. The Salem Philosophical Library; its history and importance for American science. *In* Essex Institute, *Salem, Mass.* Historical collections, v. 96, July 1960: 169–206. F72.E7E81, v. 96

Founded in 1781 by the Reverend Joseph Willard and a group of associates.

12197

Clough, Wilson O. Libraries for liberty. Georgia review, v. 12, summer 1958: 129–141. AP2.G375, v. 12

12198

Edgar, Walter B. The libraries of colonial South Carolina [1670–1776] 1969. ([261] p.)
Micro AC–1, no. 72–12,032

Thesis (Ph.D.)—University of South Carolina.
Abstracted in *Dissertation Abstracts International*, v. 32A, May 1972, p. 6335–6336.

12199

Edgar, Walter B. Notable libraries of colonial South Carolina. South Carolina historical magazine, v. 72, Apr. 1971: 105–110. F266.S55, v. 72

The owners of 153 libraries appraised at least at £50 are listed with brief descriptions and dates of valuation of their collections.

12200

Edgar, Walter B. Some popular books in colonial South Carolina. South Carolina historical magazine, v. 72, July 1971: 174–178. F226.S55, v. 72

An analysis of 438 estate inventories, 1679–1776.

12201

Gray, Austin K. Benjamin Franklin's library (printed, 1936, as "The first American library") a short account of the Library Company of Philadelphia, 1731–1931. With a foreword by Owen Wister. New York, Macmillan Co. [ᶜ1937] xi, 80 p. facsims., plates, ports.
Z733.P551G

"The Loganian library, formed by James Logan, 1699–1751, and incorporated with the Library company, 1792, by Austin K. Gray": p. [71]–80.

12202

Grimm. Dorothy F. A history of the Library Company of Philadelphia, 1731–1835. 1955. ([367] p.)
Micro AC–1, no. 11,410

Thesis (Ph.D.)—University of Pennsylvania.
Abstracted in *Dissertation Abstracts*, v. 15, no. 5, 1955, p. 800–801.

12203

Hatboro, Pa. Union Library Company. A colonial reading list, from the Union Library of Hatboro, Pennsylvania. Edited by Chester T. Hallenbeck. Pennsylvania magazine of history and biography, v. 56, Oct. 1932: 289–340. F146.P65, v. 56

Largely a reproduction of the library's loan book, 1762–74, arranged by borrower, with a bibliography of the 211 works listed in the book.

12204

Houlette, William D. Books of the Virginia dynasty. Library quarterly, v. 24, July 1954: 226–239.
Z671.L713, v. 24

12205

Keep, Austin B. History of the New York Society Library, with an introductory chapter on libraries in colonial New York, 1698–1776. [New York] Printed for the trustees by the De Vinne Press, 1908. xvi, 607 p. illus., facsims., plates, ports. Z733.N74K

"Authorities quoted and cited": p. 565–571.

Chronicles the library's development, 1754–1904, describes its relation to the other five institutional libraries in colonial New York, and presents excerpts from 18th-century library records, some in facsimile. The Revolution prostrated all six libraries: two were destroyed completely while only fragments from the collections of two others survived. The New York Society Library and King's College (Columbia University) Library collections were rebuilt from the handful of volumes found after the war. The introductory chapter was submitted to Columbia University as the author's thesis (Ph.D.) in 1909, issued under the title *The Library in Colonial New York* by the De Vinne Press in the same year, and reprinted in New York by B. Franklin in 1970.

12206

Kraus, Joseph W. Book collections of five colonial college libraries: a subject analysis. 1960. ([312] p.)
Micro AC–1, no. 60–1661

Thesis (Ph.D.)—University of Illinois.
Abstracted in *Dissertation Abstracts*, v. 20, June 1960, p. 4666–4667.

Harvard, the College of William and Mary, Yale, the College of New Jersey (Princeton), and the College of Rhode Island (Brown).

12207

Kraus, Joseph W. The Harvard undergraduate library of 1773. College & research libraries, v. 22, July 1961: 247–252. Z671.C6, v. 22

12208

Lamberton, E. V. Colonial libraries of Pennsylvania. Pennsylvania magazine of history and biography, v. 42, July 1918: 193–234. F146.P65, v. 42

12209

Landis, Charles I. The Juliana Library Company in Lancaster. Pennsylvania magazine of history and biography, v. 43, Jan.–July 1919: 24–52, 163–181, 228–250.
F146.P65, v. 43

Founded in 1759, the library did not survive the Revolution. The author provides a catalog of books belonging to the library.

12210
Lane, William C.   The sojourn of the Harvard Library in Concord, Massachusetts, 1775–1776. *In* Essays offered to Herbert Putnam. Edited by William Warner Bishop and Andrew Keogh. New Haven, Yale University Press, 1929. p. [275]–287.   Z1009.Z3P9

12211
Mood, Fulmer.   The Continental Congress and the plan for a Library of Congress in 1782–1783: an episode in American cultural history. Pennsylvania magazine of history and biography, v. 72, Jan. 1948: 3–24.   F146.P65, v. 72

"Books proposed by Madison's committee": p. 20–24.

12212
Pantle, Alberta.   Early American almanacs in the library of the Long Island Historical Society. *In* Long Island Historical Society. Quarterly, v. 2, Oct. 1940: 99–107.   F116.L875, v. 2

12213
Phillips, James W.   The sources of the original Dickinson College library. *In* Dickinson College, *Carlisle, Pa.* Bulwark of liberty; early years at Dickinson. [New York] Revell [1950] (The Boyd Lee Spahr lectures in Americana, v. 1, 1947–1950) p. 102–114.   LD1663.A5

Consisted in 1787 of 2,706 volumes.

12214
Reinke, Edgar C.   A classical debate of the Charleston, South Carolina, Library Society [1765] *In* Bibliographical Society of America. Papers, v. 61, 2d quarter 1967: 83–99.   Z1008.B51P, v. 61

The society's decision to sharply limit the number of classical texts purchased annually for its library signaled an early reaction to the classical system.

12215
Robinson, Ruth W.   Four community subscription libraries in colonial Pennsylvania: Darby, Hatboro, Lancaster and Newtown, 1743–1790. 1952. ([291] p.)   Micro AC–1, no. 12,159

Thesis (Ph.D.)—University of Pennsylvania.
Abstracted in *Dissertation Abstracts*, v. 15, no. 6, 1955, p. 1077.

12216
Seybolt, Robert F.   Student libraries at Harvard, 1763–1764. *In* Colonial Society of Massachusetts, *Boston.* Publications. v. 28. Transactions, 1930/33. Boston, 1935. p. 449–460.   F61.C71, v. 28

12217
Shera, Jesse H.   The beginnings of systematic bibliography in America, 1642–1799; an exploratory essay. *In* Essays honoring Lawrence C. Wroth. Portland, Me., 1951. p. 263–278.   Z1009.Z3W7

Investigates the bibliographic system that made possible the formation of early libraries.

12218
Shera, Jesse H.   Foundations of the public library; the origins of the public library movement in New England, 1629–1855. Chicago, University of Chicago Press [1949] xv, 308 p. illus., facsims., maps, ports. (The University of Chicago studies in library science)   Z731.S55

"Checklist of circulating library book catalogs, New England, 1765–1860": p. 261–263.
"Selected bibliography": p. 291–295.
Reprinted in Hamden, Conn., by Shoe String Press (1965).

Includes information on the colonial background of circulating (rental) libraries and the development of social libraries from their beginnings in England early in the 18th century to 1790, the midpoint of their growth in New England. Although the Revolution temporarily halted the formation of new social libraries, more were founded during the 1780's than in the entire period before the war.

12219
Shores, Louis.   Origins of the American college library, 1638–1800. Nashville, Tenn., George Peabody College, 1934. xi, 290 p. (George Peabody College for Teachers [Nashville] Contributions to education, no. 134)   Z675.U5S5

Appendixes: 1. Chronological checklist of colonial college library donations.—2. Notable private libraries received by colonial colleges.—3. Colonial college librarians.
Bibliography: p. 273–288.
Reprinted in Hamden, Conn., by Shoe String Press (1966).
The author's thesis (Ph.D.), with the same title, was submitted to George Peabody College for Teachers in 1934.

Contains information on the effect of the Revolution upon the college libraries of Harvard, Yale, Columbia, Pennsylvania, Brown, and Dartmouth.

12220
Smart, George K.   Private libraries in colonial Virginia. American literature, v. 10, Mar. 1938: 24–52.   PS504.A62, v. 10

12221
Spain, Frances L.   Libraries of South Carolina: their origins and early history, 1700–1830. Chicago, 1944. 179 l. maps.   Z732.S72S59 1944a

Thesis–University of Chicago.
Typescript (carbon copy).
Bibliography: leaves 162–172.
Part of the thesis was published under the same title in the *Library Quarterly*, v. 17, Jan. 1947, p. 28–42, and as an offprint ([n.p., 1947] 28–42 p. Z732.S72S6).

12222

Spruill, Julia C.   The southern lady's library, 1700–1776. South Atlantic quarterly, v. 34, Jan. 1935: 23–41.
AP2.S75, v. 34

12223

Watson, Helen R.   The books they left: some "liberies" in Edgecombe County, 1733–1783. North Carolina historical review, v. 48, July 1971: 245–257.
F251.N892, v. 48

12224

Weeks, Stephen B.   Libraries and literature in North Carolina in the eighteenth century. *In* American Historical Association. Annual report. 1895. Washington, 1896. p. 169–267.
E172.A60, 1895

A supplement to his *The Press of North Carolina in the Eighteenth Century.*

12225

Wheeler, Joseph T.   Books owned by Marylanders, 1700–1776. Maryland historical magazine, v. 35, Dec. 1940: 337–353.
F176.M18, v. 35

Includes a subject analysis of 25 of the larger private libraries in the colony.

12226

Wheeler, Joseph T.   Booksellers and circulating libraries in colonial Maryland. Maryland historical magazine, v. 34, June 1939: 111–137.
F176.M18, v. 34

12227

Wheeler, Joseph T.   Reading interests of Maryland planters and merchants, 1700–1776. Maryland historical magazine, v. 37, Mar., Sept. 1942: 26–41, 291–310. facsim.
F176.M18, v. 37

12228

Wheeler, Joseph T.   Reading interests of the professional classes in colonial Maryland, 1700–1776. Maryland historical magazine, v. 36, June–Sept. 1941: 184–201, 281–301.
F176.M18, v. 36

12229

Wolf, Edwin.   The library of Edward Lloyd IV of Wye House. *In* Winterthur portfolio. v. 5. [Winterthur, Del., 1969] p. 87–121.
N9.W52, v. 5

Provides a descriptive inventory of 732 entries from the largest 18th-century Maryland book collection of which a record has survived.

LITERATURE

1. AMERICAN LITERATURE AND LITERARY THEMES

a. General

12230

Aldridge, Alfred O.   The debut of American letters in France. French American review, v. 3, Jan./Mar. 1950: 1–21.
PS159.F5F74, v. 3

On works of Franklin, Dickinson, Rush, and others published in the *Ephémérides du citoyen; or, Bibliothèque raisonnée des sciences morales et politiques* (Paris, 1765–72. monthly).

12231

Almy, Robert F.   The role of the club in American literary history, 1700–1812. 1935. 2 v.

Thesis (Ph.D.)—Harvard University.

12232

Angoff, Charles.   A literary history of the American people. New York, A. A. Knopf, 1931. 2 v.   PS88.A6
Bibliographic footnotes.
Contents: v. 1. From 1607 to the beginning of the Revolutionary period.—v. 2. From 1750 to 1815.

12233

Andrews, William D.   The *Translatio Studii* as a theme in eighteenth-century American writing. 1971. ([223] p.)
Micro AC–1, no. 72–6129

Thesis (Ph.D.)—University of Pennsylvania.
Abstracted in *Dissertation Abstracts International,* v. 32A, Feb. 1972, p. 4552.

Studies the 18th-century belief that the muses of civilization moved inevitably westward from Greece to America by way of western Europe and searches for expressions of that theme in American literature.

12234

Bradford, Robert W.   Journey into nature: American nature writing, 1733–1860. 1957. ([502] p.)
Micro AC–1, no. 20,813

Thesis (Ph.D.)—Syracuse University.
Abstracted in *Dissertation Abstracts,* v. 17, no. 5, 1957, p. 1080–1081.

Among the writers that Bradford feels contributed to the development of nature writing as a genre are John and William Bartram and Saint John de Crèvecoeur.

12235

Cady, Edwin H.   The gentleman in America; a literary study in American culture. [Syracuse, N.Y.] Syracuse University Press [1949] 232 p.   BJ1601.C2
Bibliographic references included in "Notes" (p. [212]–227).

Includes chapters on the concept of the "fine" as opposed to the Christian gentleman in 18th-century literature and examines the devotion of John Adams and Thomas Jefferson to the tradition of gentility.

12236

The Cambridge history of American literature. v. 1. Colonial and Revolutionary literature. Early national literature, pt. 1. Edited by William Peterfield Trent, John Erskine, Stuart P. Sherman [and] Carl Van Doren. New York, Macmillan Co., 1933. xvii, 380 p.
PS88.C3 1933 a, v. 1

First published in 1917.

Partial contents: The historians, 1607–1783, by John S. Bassett.—Philosophers and divines, 1720–1789, by Woodbridge Riley.—Franklin, by Stuart P. Sherman.—Colonial newspapers and magazines, 1704–1775, by Elizabeth C. Cook.—American political writing, 1760–1789, by William MacDonald.—The beginning of verse, 1610–1808, by Samuel M. Tucker.—Travellers and observers, 1763–1846, by Lane Cooper.—The early drama, 1756–1860, by Arthur H. Quinn.

12237

Christadler, Martin.   Der amerikanische Essay, 1720–1820. Heidelberg, C. Winter, 1968. 410 p. (Jahrbuch für Amerikastudien, Heft 25)   PS420.C5

Habilitationsschrift—Tübingen.
Bibliography: p. 393–401.

12238

Christadler, Martin.   Politische Diskussion und literarische Form in der amerikanischen der Revolutionszeit. *In* Jahrbuch für Amerikastudien. Bd. 13; 1968. Heidelberg, C. Winter, p. 13–33.   E169.1.J33, v. 13

12239

Cole, Charles W.   The beginnings of literary nationalism in America, 1775–1800. 1939.

Thesis (Ph.D.)—George Washington University.

12240

Engdahl, Bonnie T.   Paradise in the New World: a study of the image of the garden in the literature of colonial America. 1967. ([400] p.)
               Micro AC–1, no. 67–11,257
Thesis (Ph.D.)—University of California, Los Angeles.
Abstracted in *Dissertation Abstracts*, v. 28A, Sept. 1967, p. 1073.

12241

Harris, John W.   The glorification of American types in American literature from 1775 to 1825. 1928.

Thesis (Ph.D.)—University of North Carolina.

12242

Howard, Leon.   The late eighteenth century: an age of contradictions. *In* Clark, Harry H., *ed*. Transitions in American literary history. Durham, N.C., Duke University Press, 1953 [i.e. 1954] p. 51–89.   PS88.C6

Finds that the Revolutionary period witnessed an inherent conflict between the ideal of peace and the reality of contentiousness, the widespread spirit of the Enlightenment and the lack of clarity in men's philosophical beliefs, and the denial of empiricism and persistently empirical habits of thought. These contradictions, according to Howard, produced a literature that was original and romantic in substance yet imitative and neoclassic in style.

12243

Jones, Arthur E.   Early American literary criticism: a study of American literary opinions and attitudes, 1741 to 1820. 1950.

Thesis (Ph.D.)—Syracuse University.

12244

Jones, Howard M.   American prose style: 1700–1770. Huntington Library bulletin, no. 6, Nov. 1934: 115–151.   Z733.S24B, no. 6

12245

Knapp, Samuel L.   American cultural history, 1607–1829; a facsimile reproduction of *Lectures on American Literature*, 1829. With an introduction and index by Richard Beale Davis and Ben Harris McClary. Gainesville, Scholars' Facsimiles & Reprints, 1961. x, [10] p., facsim.: 300 p.   PS85.K6 1829a

12246

Literary history of the United States.   Editors: Robert E. Spiller [and others] 3d ed., rev. New York, Macmillan, 1963–72. 3 v.   PS88.L522

Bibliography: v. 1, p. 1446–1481.
Contents: [1] History.—[2] Bibliography. Bibliography supplement.—[3] Bibliography supplement II.
"The republic—inquiry and imitation": v. 1, p. [113]–215.

The bibliography volumes are listed separately in chapter 1 (entry no. 236).

12247

Marble, Annie R.   Heralds of American literature; a group of patriot writers of the Revolutionary and national periods. Chicago, University of Chicago Press, 1907. vii, 383 p. facsims., ports.   PS186.M3

"Four of the chapters, in abbreviated form, have been printed in the *New England Magazine*, and one in the *Critic*."—Preface.
Contents: 1. Introductory: Signs of the dawn. The impulse of Franklin.—2. Francis Hopkinson.—3. Philip Freneau: America's first poet.—4. John Trumbull: satirist and scholar.—5. A group of Hartford wits.—6. Joseph Dennie: "the lay preacher."—7. William Dunlap: the beginnings of drama.—8. Charles Brockden Brown.—Bibliography (p. [319]–353).—Index.
Reprinted in Freeport, N.Y., by Books for Libraries Press (1967).

12248

Mortland, Donald E.   A critical study of Hudibrastic satire in America, 1708–1806. 1971. ([296] p.)
               Micro AC–1, no. 72–3419
Thesis (Ph.D.)—University of Oklahoma.
Abstracted in *Dissertation Abstracts International*, v. 32A, Jan. 1972, p. 3959.

12249

Nye, Russel B.   American literary history: 1607–1830. New York, Knopf [1970] vi, 271 p. (Borzoi studies in history)   PS88.N9

Bibliography: p. 257–262.
"Literature and culture in a Revolutionary society, 1730–1790": p. [101]–173.

12250

Nye, Russel B., *and* Norman S. Grabo, *eds*. American thought and writing. v. 2. The Revolution and the early Republic. Boston, Houghton Mifflin Co. [1965] xl, 456 p. (Riverside editions)   PS504.N9, v. 2

A general anthology that contains excerpts from the essays, poetry, and fiction of more than 40 contemporary writers.

12251

Parrington, Vernon L. Main currents in American thought; an interpretation of American literature from the beginnings to 1920. v. 1. The colonial mind, 1620–1800. New York, Harcourt, Brace, 1927. xvii, 413 p.   PS88.P3, v. 1

In dealing with the issues of imperial sovereignty vs. home rule, the author analyzes the writings of such American Tories as Thomas Hutchinson, Daniel Leonard, Jonathan Boucher, Jonathan Odell, and Samuel Peters and such American Whigs as John Dickinson, Samuel Adams, John Trumbull, and Francis Hopkinson. Turning to what he calls the agrarian defeat, 1783–87, Parrington evaluates English and French contributions to American political theory and studies in particular the position of the "English group"—Alexander Hamilton and John Adams—and the "French group"—Thomas Paine and Thomas Jefferson.

12252

Pattee, Fred L. The first century of American literature, 1770–1870. New York, D. Appleton-Century Co., 1935. viii, 613 p.   PS88.P35

Reprinted in New York by Cooper Square Publishers (1966).

Stressing the native origins of American literature, the author first examines the nature and creators of literary works in the new Republic. He concludes that the creation of a distinctly American literature was not possible until independence and that the nation's early literature was dominated by religious polemics, political satire, and newspaper prose.

12253

Reuss, Jeremias D. Alphabetical register of all the authors actually living in Great-Britain, Ireland and in the United Provinces of North-America, with a catalogue of their publications, from the year 1770 to the year 1790. Berlin, Printed for F. Nicolai, 1791. xiv, xi, 459 p.   Z2010.R43

Added t.p. in German: *Das gelehrte England*.

12254

Sheehan, Bernard W. Paradise and the noble savage in Jeffersonian thought. William and Mary quarterly, 3d ser., v. 26, July 1969: 327–359.   F221.W71, 3d s., v. 26

The 18th-century literary image of the Indian as a "noble savage" living in a wilderness paradise provided no conceptual basis for the difficult process of acculturation. The reality of Indian-white relations, therefore, produced little but disappointment and guilt.

12255

Smeall, J. F. S. The date of the Brackenridge-Freneau-Madison "Satires Against the Tories" [1771–72] North Dakota quarterly, v. 30, spring 1962: 36–39.   AS36.N6, v. 30

Composed while the three were students at the College of New Jersey.

12256

Spiller, Robert E., *and* Harold W. Blodgett, *eds*. The roots of national culture, American literature to 1830. Rev. ed. New York, Macmillan Co., 1949. xv, 998 p. (American literature: a period anthology. [Rev. ed. v. 1])   PS504.A62, v. 1

"Notes," containing biographical sketches and bibliographies: p. 893–992.

First edition published in 1933.

A general anthology showing the evolution of early literary forms through the Revolutionary and early national periods.

12257

Stedman, Edmund C., *and* Ellen M. H. Cortissoz, *eds*. A library of American literature from the earliest settlement to the present time. New York, C. L. Webster, 1889–90. 11 v. ports.   PS504.S7 1889

"Short biographies of all authors represented in this work, by Arthur Stedman": v. 11.

"General index": v. 11.

Partial contents: v. 1–2. Early colonial literature, 1607–1764.—v. 3. Literature of the Revolutionary period, 1765–1787.

Reprinted in St. Clair Shores, Mich., by Scholarly Press (1971).

12258

Tyler, Moses Coit. A history of American literature. New York, G. P. Putnam's Sons, 1878. 2 v.   PS185.T8 1878

Contents: 1. First colonial period: 1607–1676.—2. Second colonial period: 1677–1765.

Reprinted in one volume in Ithaca by Cornell University Press (1949. 551 p.).

12259

Tyler, Moses Coit. The literary history of the American Revolution, 1763–1783. New York, G. P. Putnam's Sons, 1897. 2 v.   PS185.T82

Contents: v. 1. 1763–1776.—v. 2. 1776–1783.

Reprinted, with an introduction by Randolph G. Adams, in New York for Facsimile Library by Barnes & Noble (1941) and by B. Franklin (1970).

Surveys the ideas, spiritual moods, passions, and whims expressed in writings of Americans who favored or opposed England. Examining various types of literature, including songs, poetry, and ballads, Tyler studies particular writers because of their influence on public opinion. He considers them mainly as pamphleteers, essayists, sermon writers, and satirists, and only incidentally in their roles as legislators, politicians, ministers, and generals.

b. New England

12260

Bates, William C. Boston writing masters before the Revolution. New England magazine, new ser., v. 19, Dec. 1898: 403–418. facsims., port.

AP2.N4, n.s., v. 19

Provides information about the master and several students of the South Writing School and reproduces from a surviving copybook specimens of their penmanship.

12261

Howard, Leon. The Connecticut Wits. Chicago, Ill., University of Chicago Press [1943] xiii, 453 p.

PS193.H6

"Check list of the writings of the Connecticut wits": p. [411]–426.
"Bibliographical notes": p. [427]–439.

Analyzes the intellectual and cultural forces that shaped the minds and writings of John Trumbull, Timothy Dwight, David Humphreys, and Joel Barlow. The author traces their development and literary output from common experiences at Yale, 1763–78, through extraordinarily divergent interests and careers. Although they failed as writers, Howard concludes, the Wits illuminated many aspects of the provincial, decentralized society they shared and were prophetic of a later, more successful literature.

12262

Parrington, Vernon L., *ed.* The Connecticut Wits. New York, Harcourt, Brace [c1926] lvii, 514 p. (American authors series)

PS548.C8P3

"Selected reading list": p. l–lvii.
Contents: John Trumbull.—Timothy Dwight.—Joel Barlow.—David Humphreys.—Lemuel Hopkins.—Richard Alsop.—Works done in collaboration.

12263

Stimson, Frederic J. Massachusetts literature in the eighteenth century. *In* Hart, Albert B., *ed.* Commonwealth history of Massachusetts. v. 2. Province of Massachusetts, 1689–1775. New York, States History Co., 1928, p. 291–322. illus.

F64.H32, v. 2

Bibliography: p. 319–322.

c. Middle Atlantic Region

12264

Gummere, Richard M. Apollo on Locust Street. Pennsylvania magazine of history and biography, v. 56, Jan. 1932: 68–92.

F146.P65, v. 56

As a cosmopolitan colonial center, Philadelphia made a unique contribution to 18th-century English literature.

12265

Jackson, M. Katherine. Outlines of the literary history of colonial Pennsylvania. Lancaster, Pa., Press of the New Era Print. Co., 1906. vii, 177 p.

PS253.P4J3

Thesis (Ph.D.)—Columbia University, 1906.
Bibliography: p. 164–172.

Contents: Period of colonization—Attempts in polite learning.—Benjamin Franklin.—Pre-Revolutionary poets.—Prosemen of the Revolution.—Later verse and prose writers.

Reprinted in New York by AMS Press (1966).

12266

McCreary, Nancy H. Pennsylvania literature of the colonial period. Pennsylvania magazine of history and biography, v. 52, Oct. 1928: 289–316.

F146.P65, v. 52

12267

Oberholtzer, Ellis P. The literary history of Philadelphia. Philadelphia, G. W. Jacobs [1906] xv, 433 p. illus., facsims., plates, ports.

PS255.P503

Reprinted in Detroit by Gale Research Co. (1969).
"The writers of the Revolution": p. 84–124.

d. The South

12268

Davis, Richard B., *comp.* The colonial Virginia satirist; mid-eighteenth century commentaries on politics, religion, and society. Philadelphia, American Philosophical Society, 1967. 74 p. illus., ports. (Transactions of the American Philosophical Society, new ser., v. 57, pt. 1)

Q11.P6, n.s., v. 57

Discusses two examples of literary exchange in Virginia—the "Dinwiddianae" group of satirical poems, prose glossaries, and quasi-dialectical letters written anonymously between 1754 and 1757 and the satirical essay "The Religion of the Bible and Religion of K[ing] W[illiam] County Compared" written by or under the pseudonym of James Reid in 1769.

12269

Hubbell, Jay B. The South in American literature, 1607–1900. [Durham, N.C.] Duke University Press, 1954. xix, 987 p.

PS261.H78

Bibliography: p. [883]–974.

In a section on the Revolutionary period (p. 87–166), the author surveys the historical and cultural background of the region from Maryland to Georgia and discusses the life and works of 17 men of letters.

12270

Lemay, Joseph A. Leo. Men of letters in colonial Maryland. Knoxville, University of Tennessee Press [1972] xvi, 407 p.

PS266.M3L4

Bibliography, p. 349–387.

The author's thesis (Ph.D.), *The Literary History of Colonial Maryland*, was submitted to the University of Pennsylvania in 1964 (Micro AC–1, no. 65–5778).

Focuses upon the lives and works of 10 authors and poets from Andrew White, 1579?–1656, to Thomas Bacon, 1700?–1768. In a major section the author considers the role of the mid-18th-century literary club and the writings of Bacon's contemporaries: Jonas Green, Dr. Alexander Hamilton, and James Sterling. Lemay concludes that early

American literature in each colony was essentially local in character, focused on a metropolis, and significantly influenced by the personality and writing of a dominant literary figure. For Maryland, Annapolis was the center and Dr. Hamilton the leader.

12271
Wheeler, Joseph T. Literary culture in colonial Maryland, 1700–1776. 1939. vii, 338 l.

Thesis (Ph.D.)—Brown University.

2. THE INFLUENCE OF EUROPEAN LITERATURE

12272
Coleman, Ernest C. The influence of the Addisonian essay in America before 1810. 1936.

Thesis (Ph.D.)—University of Illinois.

12273
Commager, Henry S., *and* Elmo Giordanetti. Was America a mistake? An eighteenth-century controversy. Columbia, University of South Carolina Press [1968, ᶜ1967] 240 p. illus., map.   E169.1.C675 1968

Bibliography: p. [233]–240.

Presents selections from the writings of 10 European men of letters, including the comte de Buffon, Abbé Raynal, and the marquis de Condorcet, on the meaning of America and its value to the Old World.

12274
Howard, Leon. The influence of Milton on colonial American poetry. Huntington Library bulletin, no. 9, Apr. 1936: 63–89.   Z733.S24B, no. 9

12275
Kraus, Michael. Literary relations between Europe and America in the eighteenth century. William and Mary quarterly, 3d ser., v. 1, July 1944: 210–234.
                          F221.W71, 3d s., v.1

Discusses American reliance upon European models of literary expression despite the desire to create a native literature.

12276
Litto, Fredric M. Addison's *Cato* in the colonies. William and Mary quarterly, 3d ser., v. 23, July 1966: 431–449.
                          F221.W71, 3d s., v. 23

Joseph Addison's heroic drama about Cato, the last of the Roman republicans, was widely read and performed in America after its first production in 1713. During the Revolutionary period his name became the symbol for the martyrdom of liberty.

12277
Sibley, Agnes M. Alexander Pope's prestige in America, 1725–1835. New York, King's Crown Press, 1949. xi, 158 p.   PR3634.S5

Issued also as a thesis (Ph.D.), Columbia University.
Appendix I: A. American editions of *An Essay on Man*, 1747–1850.—B. Some American editions of Pope's other works, to 1835.—C. Pope's poetry in English poetical miscellanies known in the colonies.
Appendix II, The sale of Pope's works by booksellers. Bibliographic references included in "Notes" (p. [115]–135).

12278
Willoughby, Edwin E. The reading of Shakespeare in colonial America. *In* Bibliographical Society of America. Papers, v. 31, pt. 1, 1937: 45–56. Z1008.B51P, v. 31

12279
Winans, Robert B. The reading of English novels in eighteenth-century America, 1750–1800. 1972. ([308] p.)
                          Micro AC–1, no. 73–11,789

Thesis (Ph.D.)—New York University.
Abstracted in *Dissertation Abstracts International*, v.33A, May 1973, p. 6330–6331.

3. MAGAZINES AND PERIODICALS

12280
Doyle, Mildred D. Sentimentalism in American periodicals, 1741–1800. 1941.

Thesis (Ph.D.)—New York University.

12281
Free, William J. The Columbian magazine and American literary nationalism. The Hague, Mouton, 1968. 176 p. (Studies in American literature, v. 15)
                          PN4900.C57F7

Bibliographic footnotes.

Studies the character and role of the *Columbian Magazine*, 1786–92, during the early stages of the American transition from a colonial to a national literature. The author concludes that the *Columbian* was the most important American magazine in the 18th century and that it documents the destructive attempt to place American ideals and themes within an outmoded framework of neoclassical forms and genres.

12282
Moore, Jack B. Native elements in American magazine short fiction, 1741–1800. 1963. ([280] p.)
                          Micro AC–1, no. 64–9429

Thesis (Ph.D.)—University of North Carolina.
Abstracted in *Dissertation Abstracts*, v. 25, Mar. 1965, p. 5261.

12283
Mott, Frank L. A history of American magazines. [v. 1] 1741–1850. Cambridge, Harvard University Press, 1938. xviii, 848 p. illus., facsims., plates, ports.
                          PN4877.M63 1938, v.1

Bibliographic footnotes.

Emphasizes the democratic character of early magazines, their role in the economics of literature, and their value as contemporaneous history. In part one (p. 13–116), Mott examines the motives, nature, and problems of the first magazines, 1741–94, describes their contents, and presents sketches of 13 particularly important ones. Among them are Isaiah Thomas' *Royal American Magazine*, 1774–75, which served as a platform for patriot propaganda; Robert Aitken's *Pennsylvania Magazine*, 1775–76, notable for its coverage of the early phases of the war; Thomas' *Worcester Magazine*, 1786–88, one of the major sources for the history of Shays' Rebellion; Noah Webster's entertaining *American Magazine*, 1787–88; and the first truly successful periodicals, the eclectic *Columbian Magazine* and the *American Museum*, which are invaluable sources for the study of society, economics, and politics during the period 1786–92.

12284
Phillips, Annie R.   Expressions of cultural nationalism in early American magazines, 1741–1789. 1953.

Thesis (Ph.D.)—Brown University.

12285
Redden, Mary M., *Sister*.   The Gothic fiction in the American magazines (1765–1800). Washington, D.C., Catholic University of America Press, 1939. ix, 184 p.
PS374.G6R4 1939

Thesis (Ph.D.)—Catholic University of America, 1939. "Chronological list of magazines (1765–1800) on which present study is based": p. 170–173. "General bibliography": p. 174–176. "Gothic fiction in American magazines . . . original sources": p. 177–181.

12286
Richardson, Lyon N.   A history of early American magazines, 1741–1789. New York, T. Nelson, 1931. xi, 414 p.
PN4877.R5

Issued also as thesis (Ph.D.)—Columbia University. "Bibliography of American magazines 1741–1789": p. 362–375.

Reprinted in New York by Octagon Books (1966).

Details the history of the first 37 magazines published in America. Subject matter, literary forms, contributors, editors, publishers, and engravers are discussed.

12287
Sellen, Robert W.   *The American Museum*, 1787–1792, as a forum for ideas of American foreign policy. Pennsylvania magazine of history and biography, v. 93, Apr. 1969: 179–189.
F146.P65, v. 93

The magazine was edited by Mathew Carey.

12288
Smyth, Albert H.   The Philadelphia magazines and their contributors, 1741–1850. Philadelphia, R. M. Lindsay, 1892. 264 p.
PN4899.P48S6

Reprinted in Detroit by Gale Research Co. (1970) and in Freeport, N.Y., by Books for Libraries Press (1970). "The eighteenth century": p. 23–85.

12289
Sylvester, Howard E.   *The American Museum*, a study of prevailing ideas in late eighteenth-century America. 1954. ([378] p.)
Micro AC–1, no. 10,016

Thesis (Ph.D.)—University of Washington. Abstracted in *Dissertation Abstracts*, v. 14, no. 11, 1954, p. 2060.

Published at Philadelphia, 1787–92, under the editorship of Mathew Carey.

12290
Wheeler, Effie J.   Narrative art in the prose fiction of eighteenth-century American magazines. 1942.

Thesis (Ph.D.)—University of Michigan.

12291
White, Maxwell O.   A history of American historical periodicals, to the founding of the *American Historical Review*, 1741–1895. 1946.

Thesis (Ph.D.)—State University of Iowa.

4. NOVELS, SHORTER FICTION, AND FOLKLORE

12292
Coffin, Tristram P.   Uncertain glory; folklore and the American Revolution. Detroit, Folklore Associates, 1971. 270 p. illus., facsims., ports.   GR105.C62

Includes bibliographic references.

Contains examples of the songs, stories, poems, and legends current during the Revolution and explores the origins of such favorites as "Yankee Doodle Dandy."

12293
Dorson, Richard M.   American folklore. [Chicago] University of Chicago Press [1959] ix, 328 p. (The Chicago history of American civilization)   GR105.D65

"Bibliographic notes": p. 282–300. "Colonial folklore": p. 7–38.

12294
Flanagan, John T.   An early novel of the American Revolution. *In* New York State Historical Association. New York history, v. 32, July 1951: 316–322.
F116.N865, v. 32

On Michel René Hilliard d'Auberteuil's *Mis Mac Rae, roman historique* (A Philadelphie, 1784), dealing with the murder of Jane McCrea by Indians.

12295
Kettler, Robert R.   The eighteenth-century American novel: the beginning of a fictional tradition. 1968. ([212] p.)   Micro AC–1, no. 69–7468

Thesis (Ph.D.)—Purdue University. Abstracted in *Dissertation Abstracts*, v. 29A, May 1969, p. 3975–3976.

12296
Osborne, William S.   John Pendleton Kennedy's *Horse Shoe Robinson*: a novel with "the utmost historical accuracy." Maryland historical magazine, v. 59, Sept. 1964: 286–296.   F176.M18, v. 59

First published in 1835, the novel is supposedly based upon the Revolutionary exploits of a South Carolina blacksmith, James Robertson.

12297

Pickering, James H. New York in the Revolution: Cooper's *Wyandotté*. *In* New York State Historical Association. New York history, v. 49, Apr. 1968: 121–141. facsims., ports. F116.N865, v. 49

12298

Vail, Robert W. G. *Adventures of Jonathan Corncob, Loyal American Refugee* (1787), a commentary. *In* Bibliographical Society of America. Papers, v. 50, 2d quarter 1956: 101–114. Z1008.B51P, v. 50

One of five Revolutionary novels written in America before the close of the century.

12299

Willer, William H. Native themes in American short prose fiction, 1770–1835. 1944.

Thesis (Ph.D.)—University of Minnesota.

5. ALMANACS

12300

Greenough, Chester N. New England almanacs, 1766–1775, and the American Revolution. *In* American Antiquarian Society, *Worcester, Mass.* Proceedings, new ser., v. 45, Oct. 1935: 288–316.
F172.A35, n.s., v. 45

Contends that the almanac played an important role in creating sentiment for independence, especially among those who read little else.

12301

Kellogg, Thelma L. Early American social satire before 1800, with especial reference to social satire in the early American almanac. 1929.

Thesis (Ph.D.)—Radcliffe College.

12302

Meyer, Richard E. Colonial values and the development of the American nation as expressed in almanacs, 1700–1790. 1970. ([321] p.) Micro AC–1, no. 70–25,377

Thesis (Ph.D.)—University of Kansas.

Abstracted in *Dissertation Abstracts International*, v. 31A, Dec. 1970, p. 2852.

12303

Miller, Clarence William. Franklin's *Poor Richard Almanacs*: their printing and publication. *In* Virginia. University. *Bibliographical Society.* Studies in bibliography; papers. v. 14. Charlottesville, 1961. p. 97–115. facsims. Z1008.V55, v. 14

12304

Sagendorph, Robb H. America and her almanacs; wit, wisdom, & weather, 1639–1970. [Dublin, N.H., Yankee, 1970] 318 p. illus. (part col.), facsims., maps, ports. AY31.A1S2

Bibliography: p. 311–312.

Includes chapters on Benjamin Franklin and Poor Richard and the Revolutionary period.

12305

Sidwell, Robert T. The colonial American almanacs: a study in noninstitutional education. 1965. ([585] p.)
Micro AC–1, no. 66–6782

Thesis (Ph.D.)—Rutgers University.

Abstracted in *Dissertation Abstracts*, v. 27A, Aug. 1966, p. 377.

12306

Sidwell, Robert T. "Writers, thinkers and fox hunters": educational theory in the almanacs of eighteenth-century colonial America. History of education quarterly, v. 8, fall 1968: 275–288. L11.H67, v. 8

12307

Wechsler, Louis K. New York almanacs, 1694–1793: their significance and influence. 1936.

Thesis (Ph.D.)—Harvard University.

6. POETRY, SONG, AND VERSE

12308

American poems selected and original. v. 1. Litchfield [Conn.] Printed by Collier and Buel [1793] viii, 304, [6] p. PS601.A5, v. 1 Rare Bk. Coll.

A collection of poems by Trumbull, Dwight, Barlow, Humphreys, Freneau, and others, edited by Elihu Hubbard Smith, this volume is regarded as the first general collection of American poetry. A second volume promised by the editor was never published.

12309

[Barney, Samuel E.] Songs of the Revolution [New Haven, Press of Tuttle, Morehouse & Taylor, 1893] 45 p. port. PS314.B3

Includes the lyrics of several poems, songs, and ballads.

12310

Bates, Mary D. Columbia's bards: a study of American verse from 1783 through 1799. 1954. ([421] p.)
Micro AC–1, no. 9805

Thesis (Ph.D.)—Brown University.

Abstracted in *Dissertation Abstracts*, v. 14, no. 12, 1954, p. 2341–2342.

12311

Bigelow, Gordon E. Rhetoric and American poetry of the early national period. Gainesville, University of Florida Press, 1960. 77 p. (University of Florida monographs. Humanities, no. 4) PS314.B5

"Bibliographical note": p. 76–77.

The author's thesis (Ph.D.), *The Dominance of Rhetoric in American Poetry, 1775–1815*, was submitted to Johns Hopkins University in 1950.

12312

Boys, Richard C. The beginnings of the American poetical miscellany, 1714–1800. American literature, v. 17, May 1945: 127–139. PS504.A62, v. 17

12313

The Columbian muse. A selection of American poetry, from various authors of established reputation. New York, Printed by J. Carey, no. 91, Broad-Street, 1794. 224 p.   PS601.C6 1794 Rare Bk. Coll.

Poems by Trumbull, Freneau, Humphreys, Dwight, Barlow, and others.

12314

Girouard, Robert L. The American dream vision, 1722–1829: its origins, forms, and functions. 1971. ([181] p.)
          Micro AC–1, no. 72–8113

Thesis (Ph.D.)—Brown University.
Abstracted in *Dissertation Abstracts International*, v. 32A, Mar. 1972, p. 5132.

An ancient genre, the religious dream vision reappeared in 18th-century America as political apocrypha, for example *The Vision of Columbus* (1787) by Joel Barlow.

12315

Miner, Louie M. Our rude forefathers; American political verse, 1783–1788. Cedar Rapids, Ia., Torch Press, 1937. viii, 274 p.   PS595.H5M5 1937a

Issued also as thesis (Ph.D.)—Columbia University, 1936.
Bibliographic footnotes.

After exploring the origins of American political verse and the British and American literary models on which it was based, the author examines the major issues of the period that evoked such an outpouring of satirical doggerel: foreign affairs, treatment of the Tories, antipathy toward the Cincinnati, popular resentment of the legal profession, agitation over paper money, fear of anarchy, and apprehension over the results of the constitutional movement of 1787–88.

12316

Moore, Frank, *ed.* Songs and ballads of the American Revolution. New York, D. Appleton, 1856. xii, 394 p.
          E295.M83

Reprinted in Port Washington, N.Y., by Kennikat Press (1964) and in New York by the New York Times (1969).

Observing that Revolutionary songwriters were more renowned for their patriotism than for their poetic ability, the compiler reprints the words to more than 90 pieces written during the war, arranging them in chronological order. For the Centennial observances of 1876, Moore edited the *Illustrated Ballad History of the American Revolution, 1765–1783*, which was scheduled to appear in 30 parts, each containing 64 pages. The Library of Congress holds parts 1–6 (p. 1–384), published in New York by Johnson, Wilson (1876. E295.M82).

12317

Newcomb, Lydia B. Songs and ballads of the Revolution. New England magazine, new ser., v. 13, Dec. 1895: 501–513.   AP2.N4, n.s., v. 13

12318

"On Liberty Tree": a Revolutionary poem from South Carolina. Contributed by Jay B. Hubbell. South Carolina historical and genealogical magazine, v. 41, July 1940: 117–122.   F266.S55, v. 41

Appeared in the *South-Carolina Gazette*, September 21, 1769, over the pseudonym Philo Patriae. Hubbell conjectures that the author may have been Alexander Alexander, a schoolmaster.

12319

Otis, William B. American verse, 1625–1807; a history. New York, Moffat, Yard, 1909. xiv, 303 p.
          PS312.O7

Thesis (Ph.D.)—New York University, 1908.
Without thesis note.
Bibliography: p. 277–293.
Reprinted in New York by Haskell House (1966).

12320

The Patriots of North-America: a sketch. With explanatory notes. New-York, Printed in the year 1775. 47 p.
          AC901.M5, v. 730 Rare Bk. Coll.

Printed by James Rivington?
In verse.
Sometimes attributed to Myles Cooper.
Reprinted in New York by W. Abbatt (1914. E173.M24, no. 27) as extra number, no. 27, of *The Magazine of History, With Notes and Queries*.

12321

Patterson, Samuel W. The spirit of the American Revolution, as revealed in the poetry of the period; a study of American patriotic verse from 1760 to 1783. Boston, R. G. Badger [ᶜ1915] 235 p. ports. (Studies in English literature)   PS314.P3 1915

Issued also as author's thesis (Ph.D.)—New York University, 1913.
"Bibliographical": p. 219–226.

12322

Platt, Charles D. Ballads of New Jersey in the Revolution. Morristown, N.J., Jerseyman Print, 1896. vi, 167 p. illus., maps (part fold.)   PS3531.L5B3 1896

"Sources": p. iv.
Reprinted in Port Washington, N.Y., by Kennikat Press (1972).

Fifty ballads are arranged chronologically according to the events or persons to which they relate.

12323

Prescott, Frederick C., *and* John H. Nelson, *eds.* Prose and poetry of the Revolution. The establishment of the nation, 1765–1789. New York, T. Y. Crowell Co. [ᶜ1925] xxiii, 266 p. illus., facsims., port.   PS533.P7

Selections, with biobibliographic notices of the authors.
Reprinted in Port Washington, N.Y., by Kennikat Press (1969).

12324

Smith, Joseph H.   Magazine verse in eighteenth-century America. Sewanee review, v. 34, Jan. 1926: 89–98.
AP2.S5, v. 34

12325

Stoudt, John J.   The poetry of the American Revolution: a preliminary study. *In* Historical Society of Montgomery County (*Pennsylvania*). Bulletin, v. 11, spring 1958: 102–118.
F157.M7H45, v. 11

12326

Trent, William P., *and* Benjamin W. Wells, *eds.*   Colonial prose and poetry. New York, T. Y. Crowell [ᶜ1901] 3 v. ports.
PS531.T7 1901

Selections, with biobibliographic notices of the authors.
Contents: [v. 1] The transplanting of culture, 1607–1650.—[v. 2] The beginnings of Americanism, 1650–1710.—[v. 3] The growth of the national spirit, 1710–1775.
Reprinted in New York by AMS Press (1970).

12327

Werner, Dorothy L.   The idea of union in American verse (1776–1876). Philadelphia, 1932. 180 p.
PS310.P3W4 1931

Thesis (Ph.D.)—University of Pennsylvania, 1931.
Bibliography: p. 94–108.
"Index of poems": p. 108–177.

12328

Williams, Stanley T.   The beginnings of American poetry, 1620–1855. Uppsala, 1951. 148 p. (The Gottesman lectures, 1)
PS303.W45

Bibliographic reference included in "Notes" (p. [124]–148)
Reprinted in New York by Cooper Square Publishers (1970 [i.e. 1971]).
"The poet of the Enlightenment": p. 36–64.

12329

Winslow, Ola E., *comp.*   American broadside verse from imprints of the 17th & 18th centuries. New Haven, Conn., Yale University Press, 1930. xxvi, 224 p.
PS601.W5

Facsimiles of broadsides with letterpress giving the history and description on versos facing the facsimile.

THE FINE ARTS

1. GENERAL

12330

The Arts in America: the colonial period. [By] Louis B. Wright [and others] New York, Scribner [1966] xvi, 368 p. illus. (part col.)
N6507.A7

Contents: From wilderness to Republic: 1607–1787, by L. B. Wright.—Architecture, by G. B. Tatum.—Painting, by J. W. McCoubrey.—The decorative arts, by R. C. Smith.—Bibliography (p. 353–357).

12331

Dunlap, William.   A history of the rise and progress of the arts of design in the United States. New ed., illustrated, edited, with additions, by Frank W. Bayley and Charles E. Goodspeed. Boston, C. E. Goodspeed, 1918. 3 v. facsims., plates (part col.), ports.
N6505.D9 1918

Bibliography: v. 3, p. 346–377.
The first edition of 1834 has been reprinted, with a new introduction by James T. Flexner, in New York by Dover Publications (1969).

Surveys sculpture, painting, engraving, and architecture to 1835. Numerous artists and their work are considered individually, several hundred additional artists not discussed in the text are identified in an addendum to volume 3, and separate chapters are devoted to engraving, miniature painting, and fine arts academies. Approximately 150 portraits are provided in the three volumes, and an autobiography of the author is included in the first volume.

12332

Grabo, Norman S.   The veiled vision: the role of aesthetics in early American intellectual history. William and Mary quarterly, 3d ser., v. 19, Oct. 1962: 493–510.
F221.W71, 3d s., v. 19

12333

Hagen, Oskar F. L.   The birth of the American tradition in art. New York, C. Scribner's Sons, 1940. xvii, 159 p. plates.
ND207.H3

Reprinted in Port Washington, N.Y., by Kennikat Press (1964).

In tracing the conflict between European traditions and native influences in the development of American portrait painting between 1670 and the end of the Revolutionary era, the author concentrates on the careers of John Smibert, Robert Feke, John Singleton Copley, and Benjamin West and includes more than 100 illustrations of their work as well as that of their peers.

12334

Jones, Edward Alfred.   Lost objects of art in America. Art in America, v. 8, Apr.–June 1920: 137–144, 187–192.
N1.A43, v. 8

On the destruction of art objects during the Revolutionary War.

12335

Sherman, Frederic F.   Early Connecticut artists & craftsmen. New York, Priv. print., 1925. xiv, 78 p. map, plates, ports.
N6530.C8S5

Bibliography: p. xiii–xiv.

2. PAINTERS AND PORTRAITS

12336

Allen, Edward B.   Early American wall paintings, 1710–1850. New Haven, Yale University Press, 1926. xiv, 110 p. illus., fold. plates.
ND2606.A5

Reprinted in Watkins Glen, N.Y., by Century House (1969) and in New York by Kennedy Graphics (1971).

12337
Andrews, William L.   An essay on the portraiture of the American Revolutionary War: being an account of a number of the engraved portraits connected therewith, remarkable for their rarity or otherwise interesting. To which is added an appendix containing lists of portraits of Revolutionary characters to be found in various English and American publications of the eighteenth and early part of the nineteenth century. Illustrated with reproductions by the photogravure process of twenty of the original engravings. New York, Printed by Gillis Bros. for the author and sold by Dodd, Mead, 1896. viii, 100 p. plates, ports.   E209.A53 Rare Bk. Coll.

12338
Barker, Virgil.   American painting, history and interpretation. New York, Macmillan, 1950. xxvii, 717 p. illus.   ND205.B29
Bibliographic references included in "Notes" (p. 669–692).
"Colonial culmination—1725 to 1775": p. [77]–193.
"Revolutionary transition—1775 to 1790": p. [195]–233.

12339
Bayley, Frank W.   Five colonial artists of New England: Joseph Badger, Joseph Blackburn, John Singleton Copley, Robert Feke, John Smibert. Boston, Priv. print., 1929. vi, 448 p. ports.   N6536.B3
Bibliography: p. 447–448.
Reproduces over 200 portraits printed by the five artists.

12340
Belknap, Waldron P.   American colonial painting: materials for a history. Cambridge, Mass., Belknap Press of Harvard University Press, 1959. xxi, 377 p. facsims., coat of arms, ports.   ND1311.B39
"Catalogue of prints and paintings": p. 279–322.
Bibliography: p. 337–344.
A collection of notes, essays, and other materials published posthumously as an exposition of the author's research methods and progress. Individual painters and their patrons are considered, with special emphasis upon the Duyckinck, Schuyler, and Beekman families of New York. A major section deals with the author's conclusion that contemporary English mezzotints were prototypes for American portrait painters during the entire colonial period. A catalog of prints and paintings illustrative of this conclusion is included together with plates reproducing each catalog entry.

12341
Bilodeau, Francis W., and Mrs. Thomas H. Tobias.   Art in South Carolina 1670–1970. Decorative arts by E. Milby Burton. [Columbia] South Carolina Tricentennial Commission, 1970. 229 p. illus. (part col.), maps (part col.), ports. (part col.)   N6530.S6B5
Bibliography: p. 210–212.

An exhibition catalog that includes descriptions and reproductions of 99 portraits and maps from the period 1670–1800.

12342
Birch, John J.   Painters of the American Revolution. Americana, v. 32, Oct. 1938: 639–652.   E171.A53, v. 32

12343
Boston. Museum of Fine Arts.   Loan exhibition of one hundred colonial portraits, Museum of Fine Arts, Boston, 19 June–21 September, 1930. [Boston? 1930] [4] p. 100 plates (ports.)   N7593.B65
Preface signed: Philip Hendy.
Of those reproduced, 44 were painted by Copley.

12344
Clement, Clara E.   Early religious painting in America. New England magazine, new ser., v. 11, Dec. 1894: 387–402. illus.   AP2.N4, n.s., v. 11

12345
Colonial Williamsburg, Inc.   They gave us freedom; the American struggle for life, liberty, and the pursuit of happiness, as seen in portraits, sculptures, historical paintings and documents of the period: 1761–1789. [Williamsburg, Va.] Colonial Williamsburg and the College of William & Mary in Virginia [1951] 65 p. illus., facsims., map (on lining papers), ports.   E302.5.C64
"Catalogue of the exhibition [held May–June 1951]": p. 61–65.
Includes 65 portraits of better-known Revolutionary figures.

12346
Craven, Wayne.   Painting in New York City, 1750–1775. In Winterthur Conference on Museum Operation and Connoisseurship, 17th, 1971. American painting to 1776: a reappraisal. Edited by Ian M. G. Quimby. Charlottesville, Published for the Henry Francis du Pont Winterthur Museum [by] the University Press of Virginia [1971] p. [251]–297.   ND207.W5 1971

12347
Early American historic painters. Scenic and historic America, v. 3, Mar. 1931: 10–22. plates, ports.   E151.A55, v. 3
General discussion of the major artists of the Revolution and early Republic with 17 reproductions of their more important works.

12348
Fleming, Edward McClung.   The American image as Indian princess, 1765–1783. In Winterthur portfolio. v. 2; 1965. Winterthur, Del. p. 65–81. illus.   N9.W52, v. 2
Discusses the evolution of the allegorical figure used by both European and American artists to represent "America"

in paintings and cartoons. See also his article, "From Indian Princess to Greek Goddess: the American Image, 1783–1815," in v. 3, 1967 (Winterthur, Del.), p. 37–66.

12349

Flexner, James T.   America's old masters. Rev. [i.e. 2d] ed. New York, Dover Publications [1967] 365 p. illus., ports.   ND207.F55 1967

Contents: "The American Raphael"; Benjamin West.—The low road and the high; John Singleton Copley.—The ingenious Mr. Peale; Charles Willson Peale.—On desperate seas; Gilbert Stuart.—Appendix: Benjamin West's American neo-classicism.—Acknowledgments.—Bibliography (p. 343–352).—Catalogue of illustrations (p. 353–357).

First edition published in 1939.

12350

Flexner, James T.   First flowers of our wilderness. Boston, Houghton Mifflin, 1947. xxi, 367 p. illus., col. plates. (*His* American painting, 1)   ND207.F57

Bibliographic references included in chapter notes (p. 327–341).

Surveys in their social contexts rival traditions in early American art from New England primitive painting in the 17th century through the Dutch-inspired patroon painters to the imported arts of the colonial South. Robert Feke, Benjamin West, and John Singleton Copley receive particular attention. The 162 illustrations that supplement the text, the information given in the catalog of illustrations, and the historic and bibliographic notes in the appendix make the work useful for reference. Continuing his review of American painting in *The Light of Distant Skies, 1760–1835* (New York, Harcourt, Brace [1954] 306 p. ND207.F58), Flexner concentrates in the early chapters on the works of West, Copley, Ralph Earl, Charles Willson Peale, John Trumbull, and Gilbert Stuart. He includes more than 100 illustrations.

12351

Groce, George C.   New York painting before 1800. *In* New York State Historical Association. New York history, v. 19, Jan. 1938: 44–52. ports.
                                       F116.N865, v. 19

Appendix, "New York painters before 1800": p. 52–57.

12352

Kelby, William.   Notes on American artists, 1754–1820, copied from advertisements appearing in the newspapers of the day. To which is added a list of portraits and sculpture in the possession of the New-York Historical Society. New York, New-York Historical Society, 1922. 80 p. ports. (The New-York Historical Society. The John Divine Jones fund series, 5)   N6507.K4

Reprinted in New York by B. Franklin (1970).

12353

Lee, Cuthbert.   Early American portrait painters: the fourteen principal earliest native-born painters. New Haven, Yale University Press, 1929. xii, 350 p. illus., ports.   ND1311.L46

Bibliography: p. [313]–334.

Concerns Gilbert Stuart, John Singleton Copley, Benjamin West, Charles Willson Peale, John Trumbull, Edward Greene Malbone, Robert Feke, Joseph Badger, Ralph Earl, Joseph Wright, Matthew Pratt, James Peale, Mather Brown, and Robert Fulton.

12354

Little, Nina F.   American decorative wall painting, 1700–1850. Sturbridge, Mass., Old Sturbridge Village, in cooperation with Studio Publications, New York City, 1952. xvi, 145 p. illus. (part col.)   ND2606.L58

Bibliography: p. 138–140.

A consideration of landscape paintings found in wooden panels and plaster walls in private homes and public places. Nearly 150 photographs are included.

12355

National Society of the Colonial Dames of America. *Delaware.*   Portraits in Delaware, 1700–1850; a check list. Wilmington, 1951. 176 p. illus., ports.
                                       N7593.N25

Bibliography: p. [169]

Lists and describes 295 portraits, reproduces 36, and provides brief notes on the artists.

12356

Park, Lawrence.   Joseph Blackburn—portrait painter. *In* American Antiquarian Society, *Worcester, Mass.* Proceedings, new ser., v. 32, Oct. 1922: 270–329.
                                       E172.A35, n.s., v. 32

Includes descriptions of 88 of Blackburn's portraits of subjects such as Jefferey Amherst, Theodore Atkinson, Thomas Bulfinch, William Greenleaf, James Otis, Jr., Jonathan Warner, and Benning Wentworth. An offprint, with an expanded title, was issued by the society in 1923 (62 p. ND237.B595P3).

12357

Pennsylvania Academy of the Fine Arts, *Philadelphia.*   Philadelphia painting and printing to 1776; an exhibition in conjunction with the seventeenth annual Winterthur Conference and with the cooperation of the Historical Society of Pennsylvania. Philadelphia [1971] 50 p. illus., ports. (part col.)   N6535.P5P4

Catalog of an exhibition that included 40 portraits painted by artists living in Philadelphia.

12358

Quandt, Eleanor S.   Technical examination of eighteenth-century paintings. *In* Winterthur Conference on Museum Operation and Connoisseurship, *17th, 1971.* American painting to 1776: a reappraisal. Edited by Ian M. G. Quimby. Charlottesville, Published for the Henry Francis du Pont Winterthur Museum [by] the University Press of Virginia [1971] p. [345]–369.
                                       ND207.W5 1971

12359

Richardson, Edgar P.   Painting in America; the story of 450 years. New York, Crowell [1956] xiii, 447 p. plates (part col.) (The Growth of America series)
ND205.R53

Bibliography: p. 417–427.

Includes two chapters (p. 30–84) on the baroque and rococo styles in American painting.

12360

Sherman, Frederic F.   Early American painting. New York, Century Co. [ᶜ1932] xxi, 289 p. plates, ports. [Century library of American antiques]   ND207.S5

Bibliography: p. [275]–280.

Gives brief biographical sketches and representative illustrations from the works of 17th-, 18th-, and early 19th-century portrait, landscape, miniature, historical, religious, and genre painters.

12361

Warren, William L.   Captain Simon Fitch of Lebanon, 1758–1835, portrait painter. *In* Connecticut Historical Society, *Hartford*. Bulletin, v. 26, Oct. 1961: 97–129. facsims., ports.   F91.C67, v. 26

Also includes representations of portraits painted by Reuben Moulthrop, John Trumbull, Richard Jennys, and William Jennys.

12362

Wehle, Harry B.   American miniatures, 1730–1850; one hundred and seventy-three portraits selected with a descriptive account by Harry B. Wehle & a biographical dictionary of the artists by Theodore Bolton. Garden City, N.Y., Garden City Pub. Co., [1937] xxv, 127 p. plates, ports. (part col.)   ND1337.U5W4 1937

"General bibliography of early American miniature painting": p. [115]–118.

Reprinted in New York by Kennedy Galleries (1970).

12363

Wilson, Rufus R.   America's first painters. New England magazine, new ser., v. 26, Mar. 1902: 26–44. illus., ports.   AP2.N4, n.s., v. 26

3. Engravers and the Graphic Arts

12364

Glaser, Lynn, *comp.*.   Engraved America; iconography of America through 1800. Philadelphia, Ancient Orb Press; [distributed by R. V. Boswell, Beverly Hills, Calif., 1970] 76 p. illus., facsims., maps, 221 plates, ports.   E178.5.G55

Includes bibliographic references.

Presenting hundreds of selections from the major sources of engraved material for the Western Hemisphere from the 16th to the 18th century, the compiler includes several Atlantic Neptune charts, views of American cities, and Revolutionary scenes.

12365

Harlow, Thompson R.   Connecticut engravers, 1774–1820 [a checklist] *In* Connecticut Historical Society, *Hartford*. Bulletin, v. 36, Oct. 1971: 97–136. illus., facsims., ports.   F91.C67, v. 36

12366

Hitchings, Sinclair H.   The graphic arts in colonial New England. *In* Winterthur Conference on Museum Operation and Connoisseurship, *16th, 1970*. Prints in and of America to 1850. Edited by John D. Morse. Charlottesville, University Press of Virginia [1970] p. [75]–109. facsims., plates, ports.   NE505.W55 1970

12367

Murrell, William.   A history of American graphic humor. v. 1. 1747–1865. New York, Whitney Museum of American Art, 1933. xviii, 245 p. illus., facsims., plates.   NC1420.M8, v. 1

"A partial list of works consulted or referred to": p. [241]–242.

Reprinted in New York by Cooper Square Publishers (1967. NC1420.M82, v. 1).

Surveys American pictorial satire and provides reproductions of 237 works. Murrell characterizes native humorous drawings before the mid-19th century as essentially descriptive, a kind of graphic reporting. Twenty-two of the satires included illustrate events of the Revolutionary period.

12368

Quimby, Ian M. G.   The Doolittle engravings of the Battle of Lexington and Concord. *In* Winterthur portfolio, v. 4. Winterthur, Del. 1968. p. 83–108. illus., ports.   N9.W52, v. 4

Considers the dispute over the authorship of the original paintings that Amos Doolittle used as the basis for his four engravings of the battles—the best surviving pictorial record of the events of April 19, 1775.

12369

Stauffer, David M.   American engravers upon copper and steel. New York, Grolier Club of the City of New York, 1907. 2 v. plates, ports.   NE505.S8

Contents: pt. 1. Biographical sketches, illustrated. Index to engravings described, with check-list numbers and names of engravers and artists.—pt. 2. Check-list of the works of the earlier engravers.

A supplement to Stauffer, prepared by Mantle Fielding, was published in Philadelphia in 1917 (365 p. NE505.F5). All three volumes have been reprinted in New York by B. Franklin (1964. NE505.S8 1964). "An Artist's Index to Stauffer's 'American Engravers,' " by Thomas H. Gage, appeared in the *Proceedings* of the American Antiquarian Society, new ser., v. 30, Oct. 1920, p. 295–341. An offprint was also issued (Worcester, Mass., The Society, 1921. 49 p. NE505.S8 Index).

4. ARCHITECTURE

a. General

12370

Eberlein, Harold D.   The architecture of colonial America. Boston, Little, Brown, 1915. xiv, 289 p. plates.
NA707.E3

After reviewing the evolution of domestic architecture in New Amsterdam, New England, the middle colonies, and the South, the author discusses both public buildings and churches and examines the materials, textures, and resources available to early American architects. Eberlein concludes that the post-Revolutionary classical revival was formed by the combined influences of the Adam phase of the Georgian mode, the carpenter-designed houses of the late Georgian period, and the postwar attraction to French thought and styles.

12371

The Georgian period; being photographs and measured drawings of colonial work with text, by William Rotch Ware. 1923 ed., with new classifications and indexes. New York City, U.P.C. Book Co. [ᶜ1923] 6 v. illus., plans, 454 plates.   NA707.G3 1923

Vol. 1, Text and indexes; v. 2–6 plates, in portfolios. First published in three volumes, 1898–1902.

12372

Gowans, Alan.   Images of American living; four centuries of architecture and furniture as cultural expression. Philadelphia, Lippincott [1964] xv, 498 p. illus., plans.
NA705.G6

Includes bibliographic references.
"Classical America: the 18th century": p. [113]–239.

12373

Historic American Buildings Survey.   Historic American Buildings Survey; catalog of the measured drawings and photographs of the survey in the Library of Congress, March 1, 1941. [2d ed. Washington, U.S. Govt. Print. Off., 1941] vii, 470 p. illus.   NA707.H45 1941

Reprinted in New York by B. Franklin (1971).
First edition published in 1938 by U.S. National Park Service.

12374

Isham, Norman M.   Early American houses; and, A glossary of colonial architectural terms. New York, Da Capo Press, 1967. 61, 37 p. illus., plans, plates. (Da Capo Press series in architecture and decorative art, v. 10)   NA7206.I7 1967

Reprint of two works published orginally by the Walpole Society in 1928 and 1939.

12375

Isham, Norman M.   A glossary of colonial architectural terms, by Norman Morrison Isham. With a bibliography of books, 1880–1930. The dating of old houses, by Henry C. Mercer. [Watkins Glen, N.Y.] American Life Foundation, 1968. [64] p. illus.   NA707.I68

Isham's *Glossary* was first published in New York by the Walpole Society (1939. 37 p. NA707.I69).

12376

Kimball, Sidney Fiske.   Domestic architecture of the American colonies and of the early Republic. New York, C. Scribner's Sons, 1922. xx, 314 p. illus., plans.
NA707.K45

Bibliographic footnotes.
Reprinted in New York by Dover Publications (1966).

Considers 200 houses in three periods: the 17th century, the 18th century, and 1783–1835. The author concludes that most elements of colonial architecture were derived from England and Europe rather than developing from conditions peculiar to America. With the post-Revolutionary classical revival, however, there occurred a fundamental change in architectural practice—one that gave physical expression to the independence of the new Republic and represented values deeply rooted in American culture.

12377

Lossing, Benson J.   The historic buildings of America. Potter's American monthly, v. 4, Jan.–May 1875: 1–7, 81–87, 161–167, 241–247, 321–327; v. 5, July–Sept., Dec. 1875: 481–489, 561–568, 641–648, 881–887; v. 6, Jan.–Feb., Apr., June 1876: 1–8, 81–88, 241–247, 401–407, v. 7, July–Sept., Nov. 1876: 1–8, 81–88, 161–167, 321–327. illus., ports.   [E171.P86, v. 4–7]
Micro 39031

Contents: Johnson Hall in the Mohawk Valley.—The Maryland State-House.—Christ Church in Alexandria.—The Verplank mansion on the Hudson.—Washington's headquarters at Valley Forge.—Nassau Hall, College of New Jersey, Princeton.—The dwelling-house of General William Hull.—Maynard, the seat of Cornelius Harnett.—The Province House, in Boston—British prisons on land and water.—The Arlington House.—The [Christopher] Billopp House.—The Stratford House, Virginia.—Independence Hall.—Cliveden, the "Chew House," Germantown, by Thompson Westcott.—Harriton, the residence of Charles Thomson.—Faneuil Hall.

12378

Millar, John F.   The architects of the American colonies; or, Vitruvius Americanus. With drawings rendered by Suzanne Carlson. [Barre, Mass.] Barre Publishers, 1968. 205 p. illus.   NA707.M53

Bibliography: p. 196–197.

Brief descriptions, accompanied by drawings, of houses and public buildings attributed to approximately 40 known and unknown architects.

12379

Morrison, Hugh S.   Early American architecture, from the first colonial settlements to the national period. New York, Oxford University Press, 1952. xiv, 619 p. illus., maps, plans.   NA707.M63

Includes bibliographies.

A detailed examination of 17th-century, Georgian, and early national architecture. Primary consideration is given to developments in the different regions of the English colonies, but Spanish, French, and Dutch contributions are also included. Among the topics given special emphasis are the construction of New England colonial homes, Harvard College, Williamsburg, and the Georgian homes of Maryland and Virginia.

12380

Sarles, Frank B., *and* Charles E. Shedd. Colonials and patriots; historic places commemorating our forebears, 1700–1783. Edited by John Porter Bloom and Robert M. Utley. Washington, U.S. Dept. of the Interior, National Park Service, 1964. xvii, 286 p. illus., col. maps. (The National survey of historic sites and buildings, v. 6)   E159.S2

Bibliography: p. 241–242. Bibliographic references included in "Notes" (p. 245–253).

After surveying the historical background, the authors present information on the significance and condition of 182 major historic buildings and sites that relate to 18th-century America, from Independence Hall and Kings Mountain to Old North Church and Gadsby's Tavern.

12381

Tallmadge, Thomas E. The story of architecture in America. New, enl. and rev. ed. New York, W. W. Norton [ᶜ1936] xi, 332 p. plans, plates.   NA705.T3 1936

"The colonial—1630–1800": p. 25–74.

12382

Waterman, Thomas T. The dwellings of colonial America. Chapel Hill, University of North Carolina Press [1950] 312 p. illus., maps (on lining papers), plans.   NA707.W42

Bibliography: p. 291–293.

Presents a general survey of patterns of domestic architecture to 1783 in four regions: the southern colonies, the Delaware Valley and Pennsylvania, the Hudson Valley and eastern New Jersey, and New England. The latter two regions receive less attention because of the author's conviction that greater homogeneity and the absence of academic architecture make it less difficult to characterize developments in these areas. Waterman notes particularly the cross-fertilization of building trends induced by emigrants from other British colonies as well as Huguenot, Swiss, Moravian, Scotch, and Palatine immigration. He includes with the text 272 plans and photographs together with a five-page, double-column glossary of architectural terms.

12383

Weslager, Clinton A. The log cabin in America; from pioneer days to the present. New Brunswick, N.J., Rutgers University Press [1969] xxv, 382 p. illus., maps, ports.   NA7206.W4

Traces the origins of log construction in Europe and its utilization on the American frontier from the Alleghenies westward. In the largest section, Weslager describes the log cabin in the 13 colonies and illustrates methods of construc-

tion used by seaboard settlers. He finds distinctive differences among those built by the Virginia Cavaliers, Carolinians, and Georgians; Pilgrims, Puritans, and Dutchmen; Maryland planters; Swedes and Finns on the Delaware; and Pennsylvania Germans and Scotch-Irish.

b. New England

12384

Cady, John H. The civic and architectural development of Providence, 1636–1950. Providence, Book Shop, 1957. 320 p. illus., maps.   F89.P9C143

Bibliographic footnotes.

Includes three chapters (p. 37–70) on the years 1760–1800.

12385

Cousins, Frank, *and* Phil M. Riley. The colonial architecture of Salem. Boston, Little, Brown, 1919. xxiii, 232 p. 127 plates.   NA735.S3C7

Plates printed on both sides.

12386

Downing, Antoinette, F., *and* Vincent J. Scully. The architectural heritage of Newport, Rhode Island, 1640–1915. 2d ed., rev. New York, C. N. Potter [1967] xvi, 526 p. illus., maps, plans.   NA735.N54D6 1967

Bibliographic references included in "Notes" (p. 471–481).

First edition published in 1952.

Contains two chapters, "Peter Harrison's Era" (p. 78–91) and "Newport in the Revolutionary War" (p. 92–101), that illustrate, with their accompanying plates, late 18th-century developments.

12387

Downing, Antoinette F. Early homes of Rhode Island. Richmond, Va., Garrett and Massie, 1937. xviii, 480 p. illus., plates   F80.D69
   NA7235.R4D6

Bibliography: p. 467–470.

Describes the development of domestic architecture from the medieval forms of the late 17th century to the Greek revival of the early 19th. Included are 209 photographs and 80 drawings.

12388

Howells, John M. The architectural heritage of the Piscataqua; houses and gardens of the Portsmouth district of Maine and New Hampshire. With an introduction by William Lawrence Bottomley. New York, Architectural Book Pub. Co. [ᶜ1937] xxvi, 217 p. illus., map, plans, plates.   F42.P4H6
   NA707.H74

"Books on architecture and the allied crafts used in America prior to 1830": p. xvii–xx.

Composed chiefly of 301 illustrative drawings, maps, plans, photographs, and portraits.

12389

Kelly, John Frederick. The early domestic architecture of Connecticut. New Haven, Yale University Press, 1924. xx, 210 p. illus., plans, 48 plates.   NA7235.C8K42

Reprinted in New York by Dover Publications (1963).

Traces the development of 17th- and 18th-century house construction from the planning stage through the final application of hardware; 192 photographs and 242 measured drawings are included. See also the author's brief synopsis, with the same title, published in New Haven for the Tercentenary Commission by the Yale University Press (1933. 30 p. NA7235.C8K42 1933).

12390

National Society of the Colonial Dames of America. *Connecticut.* Old houses of Connecticut, from material collected by the Committee on Old Houses of the Connecticut Society of the Colonial Dames of America. Edited by Bertha Chadwick Trowbridge, chairman, with the assistance of Charles McLean Andrews. New Haven, Yale University Press, 1923. xxvii, 519 p. illus., plans, col. plate.   F95.N273
NA7235.C8N3

Gives a history and technical description of 64 notable homes constructed between 1639 and 1820.

12391

Perkins, Mary E. Old houses of the antient town of Norwich, 1660–1800. Norwich, Conn. [Press of the Bulletin Co.] 1895. xviii, 621 p. illus., fold. map, plans, plates, ports.   F104.N93P4

c. Middle Atlantic Region

12392

Bennett, George F. Early architecture of Delaware. Introduction and text by Joseph L. Copeland. Wilmington [Del.] Historical Press [ᶜ1932] 213 p. illus. (part col.), maps (on lining papers), plates.   NA730.D3B4

Mostly photographs and drawings of buildings constructed from 1660 to 1840.

12393

Brumbaugh, G. Edwin. Colonial architecture of the Pennsylvania Germans. Lancaster, Pa., Pennsylvania German Society [ᶜ1933] 60 p. 105 plates (incl. facsims.) (Pennsylvania German Society. Proceedings and addresses, v. 41, pt. 2)   F146.P23, v. 41
NA730.P4B7

12394

Cousins, Frank, *and* Phil M. Riley. The colonial architecture of Philadelphia. Boston, Little, Brown, 1920. xix, 248 p. 95 plates.   NA735.P5C6

Plates printed on both sides.

12395

De Lagerberg, Lars. New Jersey architecture, colonial & federal. Springfield, Mass., Priv. print. by W. Whittum, 1956. 1 v. (various pagings, chiefly illus. (part col.)), maps.   NA730.N36D4

Provides an Index of Plates, arranged by county and town, to 551 photographs of New Jersey buildings erected before 1830.

12396

Eberlein, Harold D., *and* Cortlandt V. D. Hubbard. Historic houses and buildings of Delaware. Dover, Del., Public Archives Commission, 1962. 227 p. illus., maps (on lining papers), plans.   NA730.D3E2

Describes nearly 200 buildings constructed in the colonial and early national periods and provides illustrations for most.

12397

Eberlein, Harold D., *and* Cortlandt V. D. Hubbard. Historic houses of the Hudson Valley. New York, Architectural Book Pub. Co. [1942] 207 p. illus., maps (on lining papers), plates.   F127.H8E18

Contains 200 plates that illustrate, for the most part, 18th-century architecture.

12398

Gilchrist, Agnes A. John McComb, Sr. and Jr., in New York, 1784–1799. *In* Society of Architectural Historians. Journal, v. 31, Mar. 1972: 10–21. illus., port.
NA1.A327, v. 31

On the McCombs' involvement in the reconstruction of New York City after the British evacuation.

12399

Glassie, Henry H. Eighteenth-century cultural process in Delaware Valley folk building. *In* Winterthur portfolio. v. 7. Winterthur, Del., 1972. p. 29–57. illus.
N9.W52, v. 7

A study of house and farm plans that help to explain the cultural life of the valley.

12400

Gowans, Alan. Architecture in New Jersey, a record of American civilization. Princeton, N.J., Van Nostrand, 1964. xiii, 161 p. illus., col. maps (on lining papers) (The New Jersey historical series, v. 6)   NA730.N36G6

"Bibliographical note": p. 153–155.

Includes two brief chapters (p. 5–50) on 17th- and 18th-century architectural style.

12401

Greiff, Constance M., Mary W. Gibbons, *and* Elizabeth G. C. Menzies. Princeton architecture; a pictorial history of town and campus. Princeton, N.J., Princeton University Press, 1967. vii, 200 p. illus., map.
F144.P9G7

Bibliography: p. 194–196.

Chapters 1–5 (p. 3–78) cover the period from settlement to the early 19th century.

12402

Kocher, Alfred L.   The early architecture of Lancaster County, Pennsylvania. *In* Lancaster County (Pa.) Historical Society. Papers, v. 24, May 1920: 91–106. illus.
F157.L2L5, v. 24

12403

Lippold, John W.   Early Lancaster architecture. *In* Lancaster County (Pa.) Historical Society. Journal, v. 75, fall 1971: 145–178. illus.   F157.L2L5, v. 75

12404

Miller, George J.   The "Westminster"—story of a colonial house. *In* New Jersey Historical Society. Proceedings, 4th ser., v. 15, Oct. 1930: 465–484.
F131.N58, 4th s., v. 15

On the construction, upkeep, and inhabitants of the "Proprietary House" in Perth Amboy.

12405

Reynold, Helen W.   Dutch houses in the Hudson Valley before 1776. Prepared under the auspices of the Holland Society of New York. New York, Payson and Clarke, 1929. 467 p. fold. map (in pocket), plates.
NA7235.N7H6

Reprinted in New York by Dover Publications (1965).

Describes and provides illustrations for 150 houses in Albany, Ulster, Westchester, and Dutchess counties. A companion volume, Rosalie F. Bailey's *Pre-Revolutionary Dutch Houses and Families in Northern New Jersey and Southern New York* (New York, W. Morrow, 1936. 612 p. F135.B25; NA7235.N7H62), treats an additional 171 houses.

12406

Wallace, Philip B.   Colonial houses. Philadelphia, pre-Revolutionary period. With measured drawings by M. Luther Miller. Introduction by Joseph Hergesheimer. New York City, Architectural Book Pub. Co. [ᶜ1931] [6] p., 248 p. of illus.   NA7238.P5W3

12407

Wickkiser, Carol B.   Trout Hall, Allentown, Pennsylvania. *In* Lehigh County Historical Society, *Allentown, Pa.* Proceedings. v. 26; 1966. Allentown. p. 97–172. illus., fold. facsim., maps.   F157.L5L52, v. 26

Built by James Allen (1742–1778), son of William Allen (1704–1780), chief justice of Pennsylvania. The author includes chapters on the construction of Trout Hall and the Georgian architecture of Philadelphia and environs.

d. The South

12408

Claiborne, Herbert A.   Comments on Virginia brickwork before 1800. [Boston] Walpole Society, 1957. 47, [42] p. illus., plates.   TH301.C55

12409

Coffin, Lewis A., *and* Arthur C. Holden.   Brick architecture of the colonial period in Maryland & Virginia. New York, Architectural Book Pub. Co., 1919. 29 p. illus., plans, 118 plates.   NA707.C6

Bibliography: p. 28–29.

12410

Dill, Alonzo T.   Tryon's palace: a neglected niche of North Carolina history. North Carolina historical review, v. 19, Apr. 1942: 119–167. maps, plates.
F251.N892, v. 19

An architectural history of the combined statehouse and governor's residence built between 1764 and 1770 as North Carolina's first capitol.

12411

Forman, Henry C.   The architecture of the Old South: the medieval style, 1585–1850. Cambridge, Harvard University Press, 1948. 203 p. illus., plates.   NA720.F6

Bibliography: p. [185]–191.
Reprinted in New York by Russell & Russell (1967).

Reviewing in turn the architecture of Virginia, Maryland, Bermuda, the Carolinas, and Georgia, the author finds that medieval or Gothic building methods were dominant to the end of the 17th century, had a strong influence on construction during the Georgian period, and formed a tradition that persisted even into the 19th century. A dozen photographs and nearly 270 pen sketches by the author illustrate the work.

12412

Forman, Henry C.   Early manor and plantation houses of Maryland; an architectural and historical compendium, 1634–1800, with three hundred twenty photographs and one hundred forty-five plans, details and sketches. Introduction by Leicester B. Holland. Easton, Mo., Priv. print. for the author, 1934. 271 p. illus., maps (on lining-papers), plans.   NA7235.M3F6

Arranged by county. A sequel to this work, entitled *Tidewater Maryland Architecture and Garden*, was published in New York by the Architectural Book Pub. Co. ([ᶜ1956] 208 p. NA730.M3F6). Also see his *Old Buildings, Gardens, and Furniture in Tidewater Maryland* (Cambridge, Md., Tidewater Publishers, 1967. 326 p. NA730.M3F58).

12413

Johnston, Frances B.   The early architecture of North Carolina; a pictorial survey. With an architectural history by Thomas Tileston Waterman; foreword by Leicester B. Holland. Chapel Hill, University of North Carolina Press, 1941. xxiii, 290 p. illus., facsims., maps (on lining papers), plates.   NA730.N8J6

Reprinted in 1947.

Includes sections on pioneer dwellings and the development of log and plank construction, the domestic architecture of the tidewater and piedmont regions, and early churches and public buildings.

12414

Kimball, Sidney Fiske.   Jefferson and the public buildings of Virginia. Huntington Library quarterly, v. 12, Feb.–May 1949: 115–120, 303–310. plates.

Z733.S24Q, v.12

Contents: 1. Williamsburg, 1770–1776.—2. Richmond, 1779–1780.

Reviews Jefferson's architectual drawings in the Huntington Library.

12415

Leiding, Harriette K.   Historic houses of South Carolina. Philadelphia, J. B. Lippincott Co., 1921. xvii, 318 p. facsim., map, plates.   F270.L5

12416

Nichols, Frederick D.   The early architecture of Georgia. With a pictorial survey by Frances Benjamin Johnston. Chapel Hill, University of North Carolina Press, 1957. xvi, 292 p. illus., maps.   NA730.G4N5

12417

Simons, Harriet P., *and* Albert Simons.   The William Burrows house of Charleston. *In* Winterthur portfolio. v. 3; 1967. Winterthur, Del. p. 172–203. illus.

N9.W52, v. 3

The authors' article of the same title appeared in the *South Carolina Historical Magazine*, v. 70, July 1969, p. 155–176.

12418

Spruill, Julia C.   Virginia and Carolina homes before the Revolution. North Carolina historical review, v. 12, Oct. 1935: 320–340.   F251.N892, v. 12

12419

Waterman, Thomas T., *and* John A. Barrows.   Domestic colonial architecture of tidewater Virginia. With an introduction by Fiske Kimball. New York, C. Scribner's Sons, 1932. xvii, 191 p. illus., map, plans, plates.

NA7235.V5W3

Reprinted in Chapel Hill by the University of North Carolina Press (1947) and in New York by Da Capo Press (1968) and Dover Publications (1969).

12420

Waterman, Thomas T.   The mansions of Virginia, 1706–1776. Chapel Hill, University of North Carolina Press [1946] 456 p. illus., facsims., plans.   NA7235.V5W5

Bibliography: p. 425–432.

Using more than 350 photographs and drawings, the author illustrates 17th-century and Georgian reflections of English architecture in the tidewater and piedmont regions. The architectural character of each of 40 residences from Greenspring to Monticello is examined in detail. Particular attention is given to the Governor's Palace in Williamsburg.

12421

Whiffen, Marcus.   The public buildings of Williamsburg, colonial capital of Virginia; an architectural history. Williamsburg, Va., Colonial Williamsburg [1958] xv, 269 p. illus., map, plans, ports. (Williamsburg architectural studies, v. 1)   NA735.W5W47, v. 1

Bibliography: p. 235–240.

Documents the history and architecture of the original public buildings—the Governor's Palace, Bruton Parish Church, the Public Hospital, the Powder Magazine, the courthouse of 1770, the Capitol, and William and Mary College—and provides illustrations of original plans, intermediate remodelings, and present-day replicas or restorations. The author traces the influence of Williamsburg architecture on construction throughout Virginia. In the first part of *The Eighteenth-Century Houses of Williamsburg; a Study of Architecture and Building in the Colonial Capital of Virginia* (Williamsburg, Va., Published by Colonial Williamsburg; distributed by Holt, Rinehart, and Winston, New York [1960] 223 p. NA735.W5W47, v. 2), Whiffen discusses building materials, crafts and craftsmen, tools, design, and construction. He then provides a pictorial survey of 32 structures.

12422

Wilson, Everett B.   Maryland's colonial mansions and other early houses. New York, A. S. Barnes [1965] 249 p. (chiefly illus.)   NA7235.M3W5 1965

Bibliography: p. 249.
Arranged by county.

5. LANDSCAPE ARCHITECTURE

12423

American Society of Landscape Architects.   Colonial gardens; the landscape architecture of George Washington's time. Washington, D.C., United States George Washington Bicentennial Commission [1932] vii, 72 p. illus., plans.   SB466.U6A6

"Some references to American colonial gardens": p. 69–72.

12424

Butler, June R.   Floralia; garden paths and by-paths of the eighteenth century. Chapel Hill, University of North Carolina Press [ᶜ1938] xiii, 187 p. illus., facsim., plan, plates (part col.), ports.   SB451.B8

Bibliography: p. [165]–176.

In a review of the art and science of gardening in the 18th century, the author discusses leading horticulturists, contemporary publications, English landscape gardening, and the study of natural history in America.

12425

Favretti, Rudy J., *and* Gordon P. DeWolf.   Colonial gardens. Barre, Mass., Barre Publishers, 1972. 163 p. illus.

SB451.F28

Includes bibliographies.

Lists flowers, herbs, vegetables, shrubs, trees, fruits and nuts cultivated in the colonies before and after 1700 and identifies them by their botanical names, origin, and use.

12426

Garden Club of America. Gardens of colony and state; gardens and gardeners of the American colonies and of the Republic before 1840. Compiled and edited for the Garden Club of America by Alice G. B. Lockwood [New York] Published for the Garden Club of America by C. Scribner's Sons, 1931–34. 2 v. illus., facsims., maps, plans, ports. SB466.U6G3

Bibliography: [v. 1] p. [443]–450; [v. 2] p. [425]–433.

A comprehensive survey with nearly a thousand illustrations of formal gardens in the northern and southern colonies, the Old Northwest, and the Old Southwest.

6. CARVING AND SCULPTURE

12427

Barba, Preston A. Pennsylvania German tombstones; a study in folk art. Drawings by Eleanor Barba. [Allentown? Pa., 1954] v, 232 p. illus. (Pennsylvania German Folklore Society. [Yearbook] v. 18) GR110.P4A35, v. 18

Bibliography: p. 29–30.

Many of the tombstones for which drawings are supplied fall within the Revolutionary period.

12428

Brewington, Marion V. Shipcarvers of North America. Barre, Mass., Barre Pub. Co., 1962. xiv, 173 p. illus. NK9712.B7

Bibliography: p. 147–153.

12429

Craven, Wayne. Sculpture in America. New York, Crowell [1968] xx, 722 p. illus., plates. NB205.C7

Bibliography: p. 675–690.

The first two chapters (p. 1–84) are devoted to the art of colonial wood carvers and stonecutters and the foreign sculptors in Europe and America who received commissions in the late 18th and early 19th centuries.

12430

Forbes, Harriette M. Gravestones of early New England, and the men who made them, 1653–1800. Boston, Houghton Mifflin Co., 1927. 141 p. illus., plates. NB1855.F6

Reprinted in New York by Da Capo Press (1967).

12431

Ludwig, Allan I. Graven images; New England stonecarving and its symbols, 1650–1815. Middletown, Conn., Wesleyan University Press [1966] xxxi, 482 p. illus., maps, plates. NB1856.N4L8

Includes bibliographic references.

Discusses Puritan religious symbolism, traces the evolution of the major styles of stonecarving, and illustrates

22 classes of images in funerary art using 256 plates with multiple photographs. Ludwig concludes that the radical differences between coastal and inland practices indicates a greater persistence of piety in rural ares, and that the evolution of styles was an unconscious one marked by a continuing concern for line, geometric effect, and stylized clarity.

12432

Pinckney, Pauline A. American figureheads and their carvers. New York, W. W. Norton [ᶜ1940] 223 p. illus., facsims., 32 plates. VM308.P5

Bibliography: p. 204–210.
Reprinted in Port Washington, N.Y., by Kennikat Press (1969).

A chronological record of American ship carving.

THE PERFORMING ARTS

1. MUSIC, OPERA, AND DANCE

12433

Britton, Allen P. Music in colonial times. Michigan alumnus quarterly review, v. 55, winter 1949: 162–170. facsims. AP2.M35, v. 55

12434

Chase, Gilbert. America's music, from the Pilgrims to the present. Rev. 2d ed. New York, McGraw-Hill Book Co. [1966] xxi, 759 p. music. ML200.C5 1966

Bibliography: p. 697–726.
First edition published in 1955.

Chapters 2–7 (p. 22–146) treat music of the 18th century.

12435

Covey, Cyclone. Puritanism and music in colonial America. William and Mary quarterly, 3d ser., v. 8, July 1951: 378–388. F221.W71, 3d s., v. 8

Throughout the 17th and 18th centuries Puritanism had a depressant effect on both secular and sacred music. Even William Billings of Boston, the first outstanding Puritan musician, did nothing to further organ or orchestral music and took no part in the opera, concert, or oratorio production of his time.

12436

Daniel, Ralph T. Handel publications in 18th-century America. Musical quarterly, v. 45, Apr. 1949: 168–174. ML1.M725, v. 45

12437

Drummond, Robert R. Early German music in Philadelphia. New York, D. Appleton, 1910. xiv, 88 p. (Americana Germanica, new ser., [v. 9]) ML200.8.P5D8
E168.G3G32, n.s., no. 9

Thesis (Ph.D.)—University of Pennsylvania.
Contents: Introduction—pt. 1. Beginnings before 1750: Hymn music of Germans in Philadelphia; Church music

and the manner of its performance; Secular music.—pt. 2. Period of progress (1750–1783): Music teachers; Music dealers, etc.; Concert music.—pt. 3. Period of greatest development (1783–1800); Alexander Reinagle; Philip Roth and Philip Phile.—Conclusion.—Appendix: List of Reinagle's compositions.

Reprinted in New York by Da Capo Press (1970).

12438

Eberlein, Harold D., *and* Cortlandt V. D. Hubbard.   Music in the early federal era. Pennsylvania magazine of history and biography, v. 69, Apr. 1945: 103–127. plate.
F146.P65, v. 69

12439

Foote, Henry W.   Musical life in Boston in the eighteenth century. *In* American Antiquarian Society, *Worcester, Mass.* Proceedings, new ser., v. 49, Oct. 1939: 293–313.
E172.A35, n.s., v. 49

—————————Offprint. Worcester, Mass. The Society, 1940. 23 p.   ML200.8.B7F6

12440

Gerson, Robert A.   Music in Philadelphia; a history of Philadelphia music, a summary of its current state, and a comprehensive index dictionary. Philadelphia, T. Presser Co., 1940. viii, 422 p. facsims., music, plates, port.   ML200.8.P5G4

Issued also as thesis (Ph.D.)—University of Pennsylvania.

Bibliography: p. 418–422.

Reprinted in Westport, Conn., by Greenwood Press (1970).

Chapters 1 and 2 (p. 1–40) treat the period 1682–1800.

12441

Hood, George.   A history of music in New England: with biographical sketches of reformers and psalmists. Boston, Wilkins, Carter, 1846. 252 p.   ML200.H77

"List of works published before 1800": p. 170–178.

Reprinted in New York by Johnson Reprint Corp. (1970).

Traces the development of psalmody from 1620 to 1800. Individual psalm books, theological issues, musical practices, and prominent leaders are considered.

12442

Howard, John T.   Our American music; a comprehensive history from 1620 to the present. 4th ed. New York, T. Y. Crowell Co. [1965] xxii, 944 p. facsims., music, ports.   ML200.H8 1965

"Bibliography, revised and brought up to date (1964) by Karl Kroeger": p. 769–845.

First edition published in 1931.

"Part one, 1620–1800: Euterpe in the wilderness": p. 3–110.

12443

Kinscella, Hazel G.   Music in colonial Philadelphia, 1664–1776. 1941.

Thesis (Ph.D.)—University of Washington.

12444

Marraro, Howard R.   Italian music and actors in America during the eighteenth century. Italica, v. 23, June 1946: 103–117.   PC1068.U6I8, v. 23

——— ——— Offprint. [n.p., 1946] 103–117 p.
ML200.3.M3

12445

Mates, Julian.   The American musical stage before 1800. New Brunswick, N.J., Rutgers University Press [1962] ix, 331 p. illus., plates, ports.   ML1711.M4

Bibliography: p. 299–313.

The author's thesis (Ph.D.), with the same title, was submitted to Columbia University in 1959 (Micro AC–1, no. 59–3118).

Using *The Archers* (1796), by William Dunlap and Benjamin Carr, as his focal point, Mates examines 18th-century theaters, entertainers and companies, librettists and composers, audiences, and criticism. He concludes that *The Archers*, called an opera in its own time, should be considered the first extant musical comedy written by Americans and performed in America.

12446

Maurer, Hermana, *Sister*.   The musical life of colonial America in the eighteenth century. 1950.

Thesis (Ph.D.)—Ohio State University.

12447

Maurer, Maurer.   The "professor of musick" in colonial America. Musical quarterly, v. 36, Oct. 1950: 511–524. plate.   ML1.M725, v. 36

12448

Maverick, Lewis A.   Yankee Doodle. American Neptune, v. 22, Apr. 1962: 106–135.   V1.A4, v. 22

On the origin of the name and the song.

12449

Milligan, Harold V.   Pioneers in American music. American scholar, v. 3, spring 1934: 224–237.
AP2.A4572, v. 3

Briefly considers the contributions of such composers as Francis Hopkinson, James Lyon, William Billings, Oliver Holden, and Timothy Swan.

12450

Pichierri, Louis.   Music in New Hampshire, 1623–1800. New York, Columbia University Press, 1960. xv, 297 p. illus.   ML200.7.N4P5

Bibliography: p. [271]–281.

The author's thesis (Ph.D.), with the same title, was submitted to Syracuse University in 1956 (Micro AC–1, no. 16,658).

Describes almost all facets of musical life, discussing in turn instruments, religious and secular music, music for public occasions, opera, concert life, teachers, music in the academies, *The Village Harmony*, and music theory. Noting the absence of Puritan restrictions on music and theater in New Hampshire, Pichierri documents the rise of theatrical presentations and musical instruction in the decades before the Revolution. He devotes individual chapters to John Hubbard, Benjamin Dearborn, and Samuel Holyoke.

12451

Redway, Virginia L.   Handel in colonial and post-colonial America (to 1820). Musical quarterly, v. 21, Apr. 1935: 190–207. facsims.   ML1.M725, v. 21

12452

Sonneck, Oscar G. T.   Early concert-life in America (1731–1800). Leipzig, Breitkopf & Härtel, 1907. 338 p.
ML200.3.S6

Bibliographic footnotes.
Reprinted in Wiesbaden by M. Sändig (1969).

Identifies and describes concert programs and series, musical societies, composers, and performers in Charleston and the South, Philadelphia, New York, and Boston and New England. The author finds that the development of public concerts occurred simultaneously in America and in Europe and that American music was provincial but not primitive. Sonneck also contends that the immigration prompted by the end of the War for Independence submerged the colonial musical traditions and made American music more cosmopolitan. While the new immigration brought additional capable musicians to the United States, it also produced a population less supportive of concert music.

12453

Sonneck, Oscar G. T.   Early opera in America. New York, G. Schirmer [1915] viii, 230 p. illus. (part fold.), facsims., ports.   ML1711.S73

Contents: pt. 1. Pre-Revolutionary opera.—pt. 2. Post-Revolutionary opera.
Reprinted in New York by B. Blom (1963).

In surveying the nature and role of opera in 18th-century American theater, Sonneck considers promoters, companies, performers, theaters, and productions. He emphasizes the dominant role of David Douglass in the development of American theater before the Revolution, describes operatic programs in Philadelphia during the federal Convention, and lists all operas known to have been performed in New York and Philadelphia in the years 1787–92.

12454

Spaeth, Sigmund G.   A history of popular music in America. New York, Random House [1948] xv, 729 p.
ML2811.S7

"Additional popular music from Colonial times to the present": p. 587–657. Bibliography: p. 658–662.
"Round our infancy": p. 15–64.

12455

Stoutamire, Albert.   Music of the old South; colony to confederacy. Rutherford, Fairleigh Dickinson University Press [1972] 349 p. illus.   ML200.7.V5S8

Bibliography: p. 326–333.

Chapters 1 and 2 (p. 15–89) are concerned with music in 18th-century Virginia.

12456

U.S. *George Washington Bicentennial Commission.* The music of George Washington's time. [3d ed.] Washington, D.C., United States George Washington Bicentennial Commission [1932] 34 p. illus.   ML200.3.U622

By John Tasker Howard.

12457

White, William C.   A history of military music in America. New York, Exposition Press [1945] 272 p. illus., facsims., ports.   ML1311.W5

"Martial music of the Continental Army": p. 18–32.

12458

Winter, Marian H.   American theatrical dancing from 1750 to 1800. Musical quarterly, v. 24, Jan. 1938: 58–73. facsims.   ML1.M725, v. 24

12459

Zimmerman, Elena I.   American opera librettos, 1767–1825: the manifestation and result of the imitative principle in an American literary form. 1972. ([294] p.)
Micro AC–1, no. 72–21,369

Thesis (Ph.D.)—University of Tennessee.
Abstracted in *Dissertation Abstracts International,* v. 33A, Aug. 1972, p. 737.

Examines the structure and content of early American operas, beginning with *The Disappointment* (1767), to determine why they were artistic failures.

2. DRAMA AND THE STAGE

12460

Bloom, Arthur W.   The emergence of theatrical entertainment in New Haven, Connecticut, during the eighteenth century. *In* New Haven Colony Historical Society, *New Haven.* Journal, v. 17, Dec. 1968: 123–139.   F91.N4, v. 17

12461

Bonawitz, Dorothy M.   The history of the Boston stage from the beginning to 1810. 1936.

Thesis (Ph.D.)—Pennsylvania State University.

12462

Brown, Benjamin W.   "The colonial theatre in New England." Newport, R.I., 1930. 26 p. (Bulletin of the Newport Historical Society, no. 76)   F89.N5N615, no. 76

12463

Brown, Herbert R.   Sensibility in eighteenth-century American drama. American literature, v. 4, 1932: 47–60.   PS1.A6, v. 4

12464

Coad, Oral S.   Stage and players in eighteenth century America. Journal of English and Germanic philology, v. 19, Apr. 1920: 201–223.   PD1.J7, v. 19

12465

Cohen, Hennig.   Shakespeare in Charleston on the eve of the Revolution. Shakespeare quarterly, v. 4, July 1953: 327–330.   PR2885.S63, v. 4

Charleston playbills show that Shakespearean productions constituted 27 percent of the total number of performances given in a city with a varied and generous theatrical fare.

12466

Culp, Ralph B.   Drama-and-theater in the American Revolution. Speech monographs, v. 32, Mar. 1965: 79–86.   PN4077.S6, v. 32

Concludes that of 128 non-Shakespearean plays of English origin performed in the colonies between 1758 and 1776, 88 were clearly propagandistic, and 70 percent of these favored the Whig cause.

12467

Dye, William S.   Pennsylvania versus the theatre. Pennsylvania magazine of history and biography, v. 55, Oct. 1931: 333–372.   F146.P65, v. 55

Traces the 100-year suppression of the theater in Pennsylvania under 17th-century blue laws until their revision in 1794.

12468

Ford, Paul L.   Some notes towards an essay on the beginnings of American dramatic literature, 1606–1789. New York, B. Franklin [1971] 29 p. (Burt Franklin research & source works series, 819. Theater & drama, 22)   PS341.F6 1971

Reprint of the 1893 edition, which was privately printed.

12469

Ford, Paul L.   Washington and the theatre. New-York, Dunlap Society, 1899. 68, 14 p. (Publications of the Dunlap Society. New ser., no. 8)
                                      PN2016.D7, n.s., no. 8

Reprinted in New York by B. Blom (1967) and B. Franklin (1970).

Appendix contains a facsimile reprint of *Darby's Return, a Comic Sketch* by William Dunlap, a performance of which Washington witnessed on November 24, 1789.

12470

Hornblow, Arthur.   A history of the theatre in America from its beginnings to the present time. Philadelphia, J. B. Lippincott Co., 1919. 2 v. facsims., plates, ports.   PN2221.H6

Reprinted in New York by B. Blom (1965).

Theaters of the colonial and Revolutionary periods are treated in volume 1, chapters 1–7 (p. 21–169).

12471

Hughes, Glenn.   A history of the American theatre, 1700–1950. New York, S. French [1951] ix, 562 p. illus., ports.   PN2221.H76

Bibliography: p. 497–514.

"The professional appears: 1750–1775": p. 14–45.

"Struggle and growth: 1775–1800": p. 46–89.

12472

Hyams, Frances I.   A brief history of the American theatre, with especial reference to the eighteenth century, supplemented by collections toward a bibliography before 1800. 1916.

Thesis (Ph.D.)—Radcliffe College.

12473

Ireland, Joseph N.   Records of the New York stage, from 1750 to 1860. New York, T. H. Morrell, 1866–67. 2 v. ports.   PN2277.N5I7

Reprinted in New York by B. Blom (1966) and B. Franklin (1968).

Discusses in volume 1, chapters 1–6 (p. 1–84), New York theaters of the Revolutionary period.

12474

Kussrow, Van C.   On with the show: a study of public arguments in favor of theatre in America during the eighteenth century. 1959. 380 p.

Thesis (Ph.D.)—Indiana University.

12475

Lees, Charles L.   An introductory study of the American people of the eighteenth century through their drama and theatrical history. 1934.

Thesis (Ph.D.)—University of Wisconsin.

12476

Lewis, Stanley T.   The New York theatre: its background and architectural development, 1750–1853. 1953. ([599] p.)   Micro AC–1, no. 59–2310

Thesis (Ph.D.)—Ohio State University.

Abstracted in *Dissertation Abstracts*, v. 20, July 1959, p. 261–262.

12477

McNamara, Brooks.   The American playhouse in the eighteenth century. Cambridge, Mass., Harvard University Press, 1969. xviii, 174 p. illus., map, plates (part col.), ports.   NA6830.M3

Bibliographic references included in "Notes" (p. 157–170).

Studies the evolution of American theater architecture under the influence of English patterns. Selected individual theaters are examined with particular attention given to Benjamin Latrobe's proposed Richmond theater.

12478

McNamara, Brooks.   David Douglass and the beginnings of American theater architecture. *In* Winterthur portfolio. v. 3; 1967. Winterthur, Del. p. 112–135. illus., ports.   N9.W52, v. 3

Illustrates the adaptation of English stagecraft and theater architecture to the American setting through an analysis of the theaters that Douglass (d. 1786) constructed during his career as a manager.

12479

Michael, Mary R.   A history of the professional theatre in Boston from the beginning to 1816. 1941.

Thesis (Ph.D.)—Radcliffe College.

12480

Moody, Richard.   America takes the stage; romanticism in American drama and theatre, 1750–1900. Bloomington, Indiana University Press [1955] viii, 322 p. illus., facsims., music. (Indiana University publications. Humanities series, no. 34)   AS36.I385, no. 34
                                                        PN2226.M6

Bibliography: p. 257–264. "Selected play list": p. 265–307.

12481

Morse, William N.   Contributions to the history of the New England stage in the eighteenth century, with special reference to Boston and Portsmouth. 1936.

Thesis (Ph.D.)—Harvard University.

12482

Nettleton, George H.   Sheridan's introduction to the American stage [1779–87] *In* Modern Language Association of America. Publications, v. 65, Mar. 1950: 163–182.   PB6.M6, v. 65

12483

Odell, George C. D.   Annals of the New York stage. v. 1. [To 1798] New York, Columbia University Press, 1927. xiii, 496 p. facsims., map, plates, ports.
                                                   PN2277.N5O4, v. 1

Reprinted in New York by AMS Press (1970).
Contents: Book 1. Beginnings to 1767.—Book 2. The area of the theatre in John Street, 1767–1798.

12484

Patrick, John M.   Savannah's pioneer theater from its origins to 1810. Athens, University of Georgia Press [1953] viii, 94 p.   PN2277.S44P3

Bibliographic references included in "Notes" (p. 85–89).

12485

Pattee, Fred L.   The British theater in Philadelphia in 1778. American literature, v. 6, Jan. 1935: 381–388.
                                                        PS1.A6, v. 6

See also Thomas C. Pollock's "Notes on Professor Pattee's 'The British Theater in Philadelphia in 1778,' " v. 7, Nov. 1935, p. 310–314.

12486

Philbrick, Norman, *comp.*   Trumpets sounding; propaganda plays of the American Revolution. New York, B. Blom, 1972. 367 p.   E295.P45

Contents: A dialogue, between a southern delegate, and his spouse, on his return from the grand Continental Congress (1774).—The fall of British tyranny; or, American liberty triumphant (1776).—The blockheads; or, The affrighted officers (1776).—The Battle of Brooklyn, a farce of two acts (1776).—The death of General Montgomery, in storming the city of Quebec (1777).—The patriots, a comedy in five acts (1778).—The motley assembly, a farce (1779).—Bibliography (p. 361–367).

12487

[Playbills during Howe's occupation.   Philadelphia, 1778. Philadelphia, Printed by James Humphreys, Junr., 1778] [Boston, 1926] facsims.: 17 broadsides. [Americana series, no. 162]   PN2277.P5P55 1778a Rare Bk. Coll.

One of 10 photostat copies reproduced from the originals in the Library Company of Philadelphia by the Massachusetts Historical Society, May 1926.

12488

Pollock, Thomas C.   The Philadelphia theatre in the eighteenth century, together with the day book of the same period. Philadelphia, University of Pennsylvania Press, 1933. xviii, 445 p. facsim.   PN2277.P5P6

Part I issued also as thesis (Ph.D.)—University of Pennsylvania, 1930.
Bibliography: p. 67.
Reprinted in New York by Greenwood Press (1968).

In the opening section the author briefly reviews the history of the colonial theater, the performances given by military actors during the war, and the development of the new theater after the Revolution. The remainder of the volume is devoted to the day book—a day-by-day statement of every known production, performance, cast, and performer on the Philadelphia stage and all relevant legislation pertaining to the theater. Indexes of plays, players, and playwrights are also provided.

12489

Quinn, Arthur H.   A history of the American drama, from the beginning to the Civil War. 2d ed. New York, F. S. Crofts, 1943. xvi, 530 p.   PS332.Q5 1943

"A list of American plays": p. [423]–497.
Bibliography: p. [393]–421.
First edition published in 1923.

Includes four chapters on drama and the theater during the colonial and Revolutionary periods.

12490

Rankin, Hugh F.   The theater in colonial America. Chapel Hill, University of North Carolina Press [1965] xiii, 239 p. illus.   PN2237.R3

Bibliographic references included in "Notes" (p. 203–223).

The author's thesis (Ph.D.), *The Colonial Theatre: Its History and Operations*, was submitted to the University of North Carolina in 1959 (Micro AC–1, no. 60–4860).

Describes theaters, acting companies, and company tours from the first theater in Williamsburg in 1716 to the last tour of the American Company, 1772–74. The author concludes that the highly derivative American theater was purely an instrument of entertainment and that any cultural gains from its operation were incidental byproducts. Rankin identifies the plays of Shakespeare as the most popular dramatic fare and *The Beggar's Opera* as the leading musical work.

12491

Seilhamer, George O.   History of the American theatre. Philadelphia, Globe Print. House, 1888–91. 3 v.
PN2221.S4

Contents: [v. 1] Before the Revolution [1749–74]—[v. 2] During the Revolution and after [1774–92]—[v. 3] New foundations [1792–97]
Reprinted in New York by Haskell House (1969).

12492

Shockley, Martin S.   The Richmond theatre, 1780–1790. Virginia magazine of history and biography, v. 60, July 1952: 421–436.   F221.V91, v. 60

12493

Shurter, Robert L.   Shakespearean performances in pre-Revolutionary America. South Atlantic quarterly, v. 36, Jan. 1937: 53–58.   AP2.S75, v. 36

12494

Vail, Robert W. G.   The manuscript of a Revolutionary War play from Long Island. *In* New York Historical Society. Quarterly, v. 40, Jan. 1956: 20–27. illus., facsim.   F116.N638, v. 40

On an amateur production by Jabez Peck, *Columbia and Britannia, a Dramatic Piece* (New London, 1787), performed at Clinton Academy in East Hampton in 1786.

12495

Waldo, Lewis P.   The French drama in America in the eighteenth century and its influence on the American drama of that period, 1701–1800. Baltimore, Johns Hopkins Press, 1942. xvii, 269 p. facsims., ports.
PQ538.W3

Thesis (Ph.D.)—University of Michigan, 1940. Bibliography: p. 245–257.

12496

Wemyss, Francis C.   Wemyss' chronology of the American stage, from 1752 to 1852. New-York, W. Taylor [1852] 191 p.   [PN2251.W4]
Micro 01291, reel 204, no. 5E
Reprinted in New York by B. Blom (1968).

12497

Willis, Eola.   The Charleston stage in the XVIII century, with social settings of the time. Columbia, S.C., State Co., 1924. xv, 483 p. plates, ports.   PN2277.C3W5

"Sources of information": p. viii.
Reprinted in New York by B. Blom (1968).

12498

Yalof, Helen R.   British military theatricals in Philadelphia during the Revolutionary War. 1972. ([240]) p.)
Micro AC–1, no. 72–26,624

Thesis (Ph.D)—New York University.
Abstracted in *Dissertation Abstracts International*, v. 33A, Oct. 1972, p. 1880–1881.

ASPECTS OF POPULAR CULTURE

1. EVERYDAY LIFE, MANNERS, AND CUSTOMS

12499

Booth, Sally S.   Hung, strung & potted; a history of eating in colonial America. New York, C. N. Potter; distributed by Crown Publishers [1971] xii, 238 p. illus., facsims., map, ports.   TX645.B66 1971

Bibliography: p. 223–229.

Describes cooking and eating practices in the home. Separate chapters for individual categories of food include unaltered colonial recipes taken from such contemporary publications as *The Compleat Housewife* (1742), published by William Parks, and *The Frugal Housewife* (1772), by Susannah Carter.

12500

The British jewel; or, Complete housewife's best companion . . . and a choice variety of useful family receipts . . . Also, The complete farrier, being the method of buying, selling, managing, &c and of the diseases incident to horses . . . to which is added The royal gardner, or monthly calendar. London, Printed and sold by J. Miller, 1776. 108 p. TX144.B77 1776 Rare Bk. Coll.

12501

Carson, Jane.   Colonial Virginia cookery. Drawings by Ellen Eames. Williamsburg, Va., Colonial Williamsburg; distributed by the University Press of Virginia, Charlottesville [1968] xxxv, 212 p. illus. (Williamsburg research studies)   TX645.C35

Bibliographic footnotes.

Treats such topics as provisions and menus, the contents of the Virginia kitchen, cooking methods, sauces, garnishes and made dishes, and food preservation.

12502

Doten, Dana.   The art of bundling; being an inquiry into the nature & origins of that curious but universal folk-custom, with an exposition of the rise & fall of bundling in the eastern part of N° America. Drawings by Lee Brown Coye. [Weston, Vt.] Countryman Press ['1938] x, 190 p. illus.   GT2651.D67

12503

Edgerton, Samuel Y.   Heat and style: eighteenth-century house warming by stoves. *In* Society of Architectural Historians. Journal, v. 20, Mar. 1961: 20–26. illus.
NA1.A327, v. 20

12504

Flaherty, David H.   Privacy in colonial New England. Charlottesville, University Press of Virginia [1972] xii, 287 p.   JC599.U52A113

Bibliography: p. [253]–273.

The author's thesis (Ph.D.), with the same title, was submitted to Columbia University in 1967 (Micro AC–1, no. 67–14,041).

Examines customs and conditions affecting the individual's privacy in the home, family, and local community as well as in his relationships with the public institutions of colonial society. The author determines that while New Englanders placed a high value on privacy, it rarely became an issue because its availability was so taken for granted.

12505

Funeral processions in Boston from 1770 to 1800. *In* Bostonian Society, Boston. Publications. v. 4. Boston, 1907. p. [123]–149.   F73.1.B88, v. 4

Consists of accounts or programs from contemporary newspapers and handbills relating to funeral ceremonies for the victims of the Boston Massacre (1770), John Hancock (1793), and George Washington (1800).

12506

Greene, Evarts B.   The code of honor in colonial and Revolutionary times, with special reference to New England. *In* Colonial Society of Massachusetts, *Boston.* Publications. v. 26. Transactions, 1924/26. Boston, 1927. p. 367–388.   F61.C71, v. 26

On the practice of dueling.

12507

Holliday, Carl.   The wit and humor of colonial days (1607–1800). Philadelphia, J. B. Lippincott Co., 1912. 319 p.
PS426.H6

Bibliography: p. 309–315.

Reprinted in New York by F. Ungar Pub. Co. (1960) and in Detroit by Gale Research Co. (1970).

12508

Kimball, Marie G.   Some genial old drinking customs. William and Mary quarterly, 3d ser., v. 2, Oct. 1945: 349–358.   F221.W71, 3d s., v.2

A light review of the early American penchant for spirituous beverages.

12509

Landis, Henry K.   Early kitchens of the Pennsylvania Germans. Norristown, Pa., The Society, 1939. 130 p. illus., port. (Pennsylvania German Society. Proceedings and addresses, v. 47, pt. 2)   F146.P23, v. 47

12510

Lemon, James T.   Household consumption in eighteenth-century America and its relationship to production and trade: the situation among farmers in southwestern Pennsylvania. Agricultural history, v. 41, Jan. 1967: 59–70.   S1.A16, v. 41

12511

Love, William De Loss.   The fast and thanksgiving days of New England. Boston, Houghton, Mifflin, 1895. vii, 607 p. facsims. (part fold.)   F15.F3L8

Calendar and bibliography: p. 464–598.
"The American Revolution, 1765–1783": p. 328–346.

12512

Mellick, Andrew D.   The story of an old farm; or, Life in New Jersey in the eighteenth century. With a genealogical appendix. Somerville, N.J., Unionist-Gazette, 1889. xxiv, 743 p. plates.   F142.S6M7

Bibliography: p. [714]–720.

An abridged version, edited by Hubert G. Schmidt, was published by Rutgers University Press in 1948 under the title *Lesser Crossroads* (402 p. F142.S6M715). A further abridgement was published in 1961 under the title *The Old Farm* (Rutgers University Press. 210 p. F142.S6M7 1961).

12513

Phipps, Frances.   Colonial kitchens, their furnishings, and their gardens. Drawings by Katherine Hickish. New York, Hawthorn Books [1972] xxii, 346 p. illus., facsims., maps (on lining papers), plates.
TX653.P48 1972

Bibliography: p. 327–336.

Includes glossaries of common utensils, beverages and brews, and common foods and prepared dishes.

12514

Pillsbury, Richard.   The urban street pattern as a culture indicator: Pennsylvania, 1682–1815. *In* Association of American Geographers. Annals, v. 60, Sept. 1970: 428–446. illus., maps.   G3.A7, v. 60

Early street patterns were determined by cultural rather than economic of physical considerations.

12515

Roth, Rodris.   Tea drinking in 18th-century America: its etiquette and equipage. [Washington, Smithsonian Institution, 1961] 61–91 p. illus., facsims., ports. (Contributions from the Museum of History and Technology, Paper 14)   Q11.U6, no. 225, 1961a
U.S. National Museum. Bulletin 225.
Bibliographic footnotes.

12516

Scott, Kenneth.   Funeral customs in colonial New York. New York folklore quarterly, v. 15, winter 1959: 274–282.   GR1.N473, v. 15

12517

Shively, Charles A.   A history of the conception of death in America, 1650–1860. 1969.

Thesis (Ph.D.)—Harvard University.

12518

Singleton, Esther.   Social New York under the Georges, 1714–1776; houses, streets and country homes, with chapters on fashions, furniture, china, plate, and manners. New York, D. Appleton, 1902. xix, 407 p. illus.   F128.4.S61

Reprinted in New York by B. Blom (1968) and in Port Washington, N.Y., by I. J. Friedman (1969).

12519

Stahlman, William D.   Astrology in colonial America: an extended query. William and Mary quarterly, 3d ser., v. 13, Oct. 1956: 551–563.   F221.W71, 3d s., v. 13

Notes the comparative lack of interest in astrology during the last half of the 18th century.

12520

Stiles, Henry R.   Bundling; its origin, progress and decline in America. Albany, J. Munsell, 1869. 139 p.
GT2651.S7 1869 Rare Bk. Coll.

Republished in New York by the Book Collectors Association (1934. 146 p. GT2651.S7 1934).

Finds that the courting custom originated among the "humbler classes" as a matter of convenience and necessity. Although it came closest to being a universal custom between 1750 and 1780, according to Stiles, the practice apparently ceased about 1800.

12521

Taussig, Charles W.   Rum, romance & rebellion. New York, Minton, Balch, 1928. xiii, 289 p. illus., map, plates.   HD9394.U5T3

Bibliography: p. 255–264.

On the influence of rum in New England colonial life.

12522

Ulmer, S. Sydney.   Some eighteenth century South Carolinians and the duel. South Carolina historical magazine, v. 60, Jan. 1959: 1–9.   F266.S55, v. 60

2. FRATERNAL ORGANIZATIONS AND CLUBS

12523

Faÿ, Bernard.   Revolution and freemasonry, 1680–1800. Boston, Little, Brown, 1935. xiv, 349 p. facsim., plates, ports.   HS416.F35

Bibliography: p. [327]–333.

Traces the origin, development, and influence of freemasonry. The author claims that freemasonry effected a moral and intellectual revolution in the 18th century through which the political revolutions in America and France were prepared and achieved.

12524

Heaton, Ronald E.   Masonic membership of the Founding Fathers. Washington, Masonic Service Association, 1965. xxiii, 164 p. illus., ports.   HS509.H49

Includes bibliography.

Presents biographical information on 241 Revolutionary leaders—general officers of the Continental Army, Washington's aides and military secretaries, and signers of the Articles of Association, Declaration of Independence, Articles of Confederation, and the Constitution—in an attempt to establish their connection with freemasonry. The author contends that 68 were Masons, 26 were of doubtful membership and 147 were not known to be Masons. The work is based on six earlier publications by Heaton, W. Eugene Rice, and William M. Brown.

12525

Morse, Sidney L.   Freemasonry in the American Revolution. Washington, D.C., Masonic Service Association of the United States [ᶜ1924] xiv, 134 p. (Little Masonic library, [no. 12])   HS371.L5, no. 12

12526

Tatsch, Jacob H.   Freemasonry in the thirteen colonies. New York, Macoy Pub. and Masonic Supply Co., 1929. xx, 245 p. ports.   HS521.T3

Bibliography at end of each chapter.

12527

Tyler, Lyon G.   Williamsburg Lodge of Masons. William and Mary college quarterly, v. 1, July 1892: 1–34.
F221.W71, v. 1

Based on the treasurer's accounts, 1773–86.

12528

Whitlock, Marta N.   Voluntary associations in Salem, Massachusetts before 1800. 1972. ([314] p.)
Micro AC–1, no. 72–21,031

Thesis (Ph.D.)—Ohio State University.

Abstracted in *Dissertation Abstracts International*, v. 33A, Aug. 1972, p. 683.

Examines the various kinds (civic, social, marine) and functions (building bridges, founding hospitals, providing entertainment) of clubs and organizations in Salem.

3. PUBLIC SERVICES

12529

Gillingham, Harrold E.   Philadelphia's first fire defences. Pennsylvania magazine of history and biography, v. 56, Oct. 1932: 355–377. plates.   F146.P65, v. 56

Early methods of fire prevention.

12530

Holmes, Oliver W.   Stagecoach and mail from colonial days to 1820. 1956. ([308] p.)
Micro AC–1, no. 17,059

Thesis (Ph.D.)—Columbia University.

Abstracted in *Dissertation Abstracts*, v. 16, no. 8, 1956, p. 1434–1435.

12531

Konwiser, Harry M. Colonial and Revolutionary posts; a history of the American postal systems; colonial and Revolutionary periods. Richmond, Va., Press of the Dietz Print. Co., 1931. ix, 81 p. illus., facsims, ports.
HE6371.K6

Bibliography: p. 73.

12532

Rich, Wesley E. The history of the United States post office to the year 1829. Cambridge, Harvard University Press, 1924. vii, 190 p. (Harvard economic studies, v. 27) HE6371.R5

Thesis (Ph.D.)—Harvard University, 1917.
Bibliography: p. 175–181.

12533

Wainwright, Nicholas B. A Philadelphia story: the Philadelphia Contributionship for the Insurance of Houses from Loss by Fire. Philadelphia, 1952. 260 p. illus. (part col.), facsims., port. HG9780.P55W3

"Deed of settlement": p. 239–260.

In the first three chapters (p. 1–95), the author traces the history of America's oldest fire insurance company from its founding in 1752 to the death in 1817 of treasurer and clerk, Caleb Carmalt.

4. Sport and Recreation

12534

Begnaud, Allen E. Hoofbeats in colonial Maryland. Maryland historical magazine, v. 65, fall 1970: 207–238. facsim., ports. F176.M18, v. 65

On the sport of horse racing.

12535

Carson, Jane. Colonial Virginians at play. Williamsburg, Va., Colonial Williamsburg; Distributed by the University Press of Virginia, Charlottesville [1965] xv, 326 p. illus. (Williamsburg research studies)
GV54.V8C3

Bibliography: p. [300]–313.

Drawing upon lively excerpts from diaries and letters, account books and inventories, newspaper advertisements, and county court records, Carson surveys the home entertainments, sports, and games that made the social isolation of Virginia plantation life endurable.

12536

Davis, Thomas R. Sport and exercise in the lives of selected colonial Americans: Massachusetts and Virginia, 1700–1775. 1970. ([232] p.) Micro AC–1, no. 71–04,030

Thesis (Ph.D.)—University of Maryland.
Abstracted in *Dissertation Abstracts International*, v. 31A, Feb. 1971, p. 3930.

12537

Goodspeed, Charles E. Angling in America; its early history and literature. Boston, Houghton Mifflin Co., 1939. xiii, 380 p. illus., facsims., plates, ports.
SH463.G6 Rare Bk. Coll.

"Check-list of American angling publications related to freshwater angling in the United States 1660–1900 chronologically arranged": p. 345–[365]
"Angling in the eighteenth century": p. 73–91.

12538

Hervey, John. Racing in America: 1665–1865. v. 1. New York, Priv. print., the Jockey Club [1944] xii, 315 p. illus., facsims., col. plan, plates, ports.
SF347.H4, v. 1, Rare Bk. Coll.

Includes four chapters (p. [27]–163) on 18th-century racing in the North and the South.

12539

Sims, Joseph P. The Fishing Company of Fort St. Davids. [Philadelphia?] The Society, 1951. 30 p. illus., map. (Historical publications of the Society of Colonial Wars in the Commonwealth of Pennsylvania, v. 7, no. 4)
E186.3.P41, v. 7, no. 4

A sporting and social club for the Philadelphia elite located at the falls of the Schuykill. The membership list of 1763 is appended.

12540

Weiss, Harry B., *and* Grace M. Weiss. Early sports and pastimes in New Jersey. Trenton, Past Times Press, 1960. vii, 148 p. illus., facsims. GV54.W5W4

Covers a wide diversity of leisure activities from dancing, quilting bees, sea bathing, and cockfighting to fairs, mechanical shows, balloon ascensions, and horseracing.

5. Inns, Resorts, and Taverns

12541

Boyer, Charles S. Old inns and taverns in West Jersey. Camden, N.J., Camden County Historical Society, 1962. 326 p. illus. F134.B6

Includes bibliography.

12542

Bridenbaugh, Carl. Baths and watering places of colonial America. William and Mary quarterly, 3d ser., v. 3, Apr. 1946: 151–181. F221.W71, 3d s., v. 3

Discusses the colonial penchant for "taking the waters" in the years just before the Revolution.

12543

Bridenbaugh, Carl. Colonial Newport as a summer resort. *In* Rhode Island Historical Society. Collections, v. 26, Jan. 1933: 1–23. F76.R47, v. 26

12544

Earle, Alice M. Stage-coach and tavern days. New York, Macmillan Co., 1900. xvi, 449 p. illus., facsims., plates.
E162.E2 1900

Reprinted in Detroit by Singing Tree Press (1968) and in New York by Haskell House (1968) and B. Blom (1969).

Presents vignettes, often illustrated by quotations from contemporary letters and diaries, of leisure and travel in colonial and Revolutionary times, mainly in New England. The author includes information on such topics as the food, drink, and furnishings of taverns, the role of taverns during war, and the horses, vehicles, and drivers used in public transportation.

12545

Harpster, John W.　Eighteenth-century inns and taverns of western Pennsylvania. Western Pennsylvania historical magazine, v. 19, Mar. 1936: 5–16.　F146.W52, v. 19

12546

Holmes, Oliver W.　The colonial taverns of Georgetown. *In* Columbia Historical Society, *Washington, D.C.* Records. v. 51/52; 1951/52. Washington, 1955. p. 1–18.　F191.C72, v. 51–52

12547

Hutchinson, Elmer T.　An Elizabethtown tavern and its ledger. *In* New Jersey Historical Society. Proceedings, 4th ser., v. 14, Oct. 1929: 443–466; v. 15, Jan. 1930: 84–95.　F131.N58, 4th s., v. 14–15

Includes a list of names of persons who had accounts at Graham's Tavern between 1770 and 1790.

12548

Lathrop, Elise L.　Early American inns and taverns. New York, R. M. McBride, 1926. 365 p. illus., facsims., plates.　GT3803.L3

Bibliography: p. 311–315.
Reprinted in New York by B. Blom (1968).

A descriptive account written in the form of a travel guide.

12549

National Society of the Colonial Dames of America. *Connecticut.*　Old inns of Connecticut. Edited by Marion Dickinson Terry. Hartford, Conn., Prospect Press, 1937. 253 p. illus., facsims., maps (on lining papers), plates.　F95.N28

A descriptive account of individual inns, their construction, and their original owners.

12550

Reichel, William C.　The old Moravian Sun Inn, Bethlehem, Penna., 1758. *In* Pennsylvania-German Society. Proceedings and addresses. v. 6; 1895. [Reading, Pa.] 1896. p. 44–75.　F146.P23, v. 6

Focuses on the construction and use of the inn during the Revolutionary period.

12551

Scott, Kenneth.　Colonial innkeepers of New Hampshire. Historical New Hampshire, v. 19, spring 1964: 3–49.　F31.H57, v. 19

Provides a list of innkeepers' names arranged chronologically by the town or parish of residence.

12552

Shelton, F. H.　Springs and spas of old-time Philadelphians. Pennsylvania magazine of history and biography, v. 47, July 1923: 196–237.　F146.P65, v. 47

12553

Yoder, Paton W.　The American inn, 1775–1850: melting pot or stewing kettle? Indiana magazine of history, v. 59, June 1963: 135–151.　F521.I52, v. 59

6. TRAVEL AND TRAVELERS' REPORTS

12554

Adams, Percy G.　Travelers and travel liars, 1660–1800. Berkeley, University of California Press, 1962. x, 292 p. illus.　G100.A44

Bibliographic references in "Notes": p. 239–270.

Surveys authentic travel accounts that contain falsehoods as well as tales of fictitious voyages that were designed to make the public believe them real. In the chapter on the false topography of the Mississippi River valley, for example, the author tells of inaccurate maps that were based upon the bogus reports of "adventurers" like the Baron de Lahontan, whose works were so popular that they were reprinted throughout the 18th century.

12555

The American character: a Frenchman views the new Republic from Philadelphia, 1777. Translated and edited by Durand Echeverria. William and Mary quarterly, 3d ser., v. 16, July 1959: 376–413.　F221.W71, 3d s., v. 16

Reproduces that part of the anonymous manuscript in which the writer describes his trip north from Charleston, gives his impressions of Philadelphia, and comments on the character of American life. Echeverria tentatively assigns authorship to a young French nobleman, Louis de Récicourt de Ganot.

12556

Benedict, William H.　Travel across New Jersey in the eighteenth century and later. *In* New Jersey Historical Society. Proceedings, new ser., v. 7, Apr. 1922: 97–119.　F131.N58, n.s., v. 7

12557

Comstock, Sarah.　Roads to the Revolution, with here and there a byway to colonial days. With many illustrations by the author & others. New York, Macmillan Co., 1928. xii, 455 p. illus.　E159.C73

Bibliography: p. 437–445.

Twenty journeys to scenes of the American Revolution from three centers: Boston, New York, and Philadelphia.

12558

Gleis, Paul G.　Eighteenth century Maryland through the eyes of German travelers. *In* Society for the History of the Germans in Maryland. 28th report; 1953. Baltimore, Md. p. 44–53.   F190.G3S6, 1953

Concentrates upon the writings of Riedesel, Schöpf, and Closen.

12559

Hubbard, Genevieve G.   French travelers in America, 1775–1840: a study of their observations. 1936.

Thesis (Ph.D.)—American University.

12560

Journal of a French traveller in the colonies, 1765. American historical review, v. 26, July 1921: 726–747; v. 27, Oct. 1922: 70–89.   E171.A57, v 26–27

Apparently a Catholic and an agent of the French government, the author toured the colonies from Charleston to New York.

12561

Marshall, Peter J.   Travellers and the colonial scene. *In* British Association for American studies. Bulletin, new ser., no. 7, Dec. 1963: 5–28.   E172.B72, n.s., no. 7

Finds that the growth in the number of travelers after midcentury indicated the increasing unity of American society.

12562

Masterson, James R.   Records of travel in North America, 1700–1776. 1936.

Thesis (Ph.D.)—Harvard University.

12563

Medeiros, Patricia M.   The literature of travel of eighteenth-century America. 1971. ([235] p.)
Micro AC–1, no. 72–1702

Thesis (Ph.D.)—University of Massachusetts.
Abstracted in *Dissertation Abstracts International*, v. 32A, Jan. 1972, p. 3958–3959.

Among the more important writers, the author discusses William Bartram, Jonathan Carver, Dr. Alexander Hamilton, and Philip Fithian.

12564

Mereness, Newton D.   Travels in the American colonies. New York, Macmillan Co., 1916. vi, 693 p.
E162.M57

Partial contents: Minutes from the journal of Mr. Hamburgh's travels in the Michigan and Illinois country, 1763.—Journal of an officer's (Lord Adam Gordon's) travels in America and the West Indies, 1764–1765.—Journal of Captain Harry Gordon's journey from Pittsburg down the Ohio and the Mississippi to New Orleans, Mobile, and Pensacola, 1766.—David Taitt's journal of a journey through the Creek country, 1772.—Dr. John Berkenhout's journal of an excursion from New York to Philadelphia, 1778.—Travel diary of Bishop Reichel, Mrs. Reichel, and their company from Lititz, Pa., to Salem, N.C., 1780.—Extracts from the travel diary of Bishop Reichel, Mrs. Reichel, and Christian Heckewelder from Salem to Lititz, 1780.—Colonel William

Fleming's journal of travels in Kentucky, 1779–1780.—Colonel William Fleming's journal of travels in Kentucky, 1783.

12565

Merrens, Harry Roy.   The physical environment of early America: images and image makers in colonial South Carolina. Geographical review, v. 59, Oct. 1969: 530–556.   G1.G35, v. 59

Examines contemporary descriptions by promoters, officials, travelers, natural historians, and settlers.

12566

Morrison, Alfred J., *ed.*   Travels in Virginia in Revolutionary times. [Lynchburg, Va., J. P. Bell Co., ᶜ1922] 138 p.   F226.M87

"List of travels": p. [137]–138.
Partial contents: Narrative of John F. D. Smyth: 1769–1775.—Anburey, and the Convention army in Virginia: 1779.—The Abbé Robin, one of the chaplains to the French army in America: 1781.—The Marquis of Chastellux, major-general in the French army and member of the French academy: 1782.—Dr. Schoepf, surgeon to the Hessian troops (Ansbach-Bayreuth division): 1783.—Count Castiglioni, chevalier of the Order of St. Stephen, P.M.: 1786.—Missionary journeys of Dr. Coke: 1785–1791.

12567

On the threshold of liberty; journal of a Frenchman's tour of the American colonies in 1777.   Translated from the original manuscript by Edward D. Seeber. Bloomington, Indiana University Press, 1959. x, 172 p. (Indiana University publications. Humanities series, no. 43)
E163.O5

Bibliographic footnotes.

12568

Ryan, Lee W.   French travelers in the southeastern United States, 1775–1800. Bloomington, Ind., Principia Press, 1939. viii, 107 p.   F213.R96

Bibliography: p. 97–101.
The author's thesis (Ph.D.), with the title, *French Travelers in America Between 1775 and 1800 with Special Reference to the Southern States*, was submitted to the University of Virginia in 1934.

French impressions of southern life and customs.

12569

Sherrill, Charles H.   French memories of eighteenth-century America. New York, C. Scribner's Sons, 1915. xii, 335 p. facsim., plates, ports.   E164.S55

Bibliography: p. 329–335.
Reprinted in Freeport, N.Y., by Books for Libraries Press (1971) and in New York by B. Blom (1971).

Summarizing the impressions of more than 70 Frenchmen who visited America between 1775 and 1800, the author treats all aspects of life during the Revolutionary era, including dress, amusements, city living, education and the press, religion, the professions, and commerce.

12570

Solberg, Curtis B.   As others saw us: travelers in America during the age of the American Revolution. 1968. ([351] p.)   Micro AC–1, no. 70–2070

Thesis (Ph.D.)—University of California, Santa Barbara.

Abstracted in *Dissertation Abstracts International,* v. 30A, Apr. 1970, p. 4356.

12571

Tuckerman, Henry T.   America and her commentators. With a critical sketch of travel in the United States. New York, C. Scribner, 1864. viii, 460 p.   E157.T89

Contents: Introduction.—Early discoverers and explorers.—French missionary exploration.—French travellers and writers.—British travellers and writers.—English abuse of America.—Northern European writers.—Italian travellers.—American travellers and writers.

Reprinted in New York by Antiquarian Press (1961) and A. M. Kelly (1970).

CHAPTER TWELVE

Biographies and Personal Primary Sources

Eₙₜᵣᵢₑₛ ꜰᴏʀ ᴛʜᴇ individual figures in this chapter are arranged alphabetically by the name of the subject. Following each biographical headnote, citations are divided into two categories—works written by the subject (arranged alphabetically by title) and works written about the subject (arranged alphabetically by author). Material considered for inclusion in this chapter falls into four major categories: separate monographic or pamphlet publications, doctoral dissertations, articles in historical periodicals, and printed primary sources published either separately or in historical periodicals. Although desirable it would have been difficult, given the magnitude of the task, to prepare and to include citations to biographical information about subjects contained in such multi-volume series as the *Pennsylvania Archives* (119 v. in 120), the *State Records of North Carolina* (26 v.), or the *Parliamentary History of England* (36 v.). Fortunately, bibliographic notices to these and hundreds of other standard sources are provided with the sketches in the *Dictionary of American Biography* and the *Dictionary of National Biography*. Nearly 30 percent of the subject entries in this chapter are also entries in either the *DAB*, the *DNB*, or both. For those who may wish to consult either of these works for supplementary bibliographic information, an asterisk (✻) has been placed after the names of subjects in this chapter whose names appear in the *DAB* and a dagger (†) for those in the *DNB*.

General

12572

Allen, William. The American biographical dictionary: containing an account of the lives, characters, and writings of the most eminent persons deceased in North America from its first settlement. 3d ed. Boston, J. P. Jewett, 1857. ix, 905 p.   [E176.A435]
Micro 33162 E

Originally published with title: *An American Biographical and Historical Dictionary*.

Focuses on 18th-century figures. The names of the subjects are arranged in the index by occupation.

12573

American Historical Company, Inc. *New York*. Colonial and Revolutionary lineages of America; a collection of genealogical studies, completely documented, and appropriately illustrated, bearing upon notable early American lines and their collateral connections. New York, American Historical Co., 1939–67. 25 v. col. coats of arms, facsims., geneal. tables, plates, ports.
CS61.A5

Includes bibliographies.

12574

Biographical directory of the United States executive branch, 1774–1971. Robert Sobel, editor in chief.

Westport, Conn., Greenwood Pub. Co. [1971] x, 491 p.   E176.B575

Includes for the Revolutionary period career biographies on 14 presidents of the Continental Congress and men with wartime experience who later became cabinet members, Vice President, or President. Each sketch provides information on significant events in the subject's life, family and such personal matters as religious affiliation, and reference sources, both primary and secondary. Besides a name index, the compiler includes eight tables in which he arranges data according to presidential administration, branch of military service, highest level of education, place of birth, marital status, and the federal, state, county, or municipal offices held by the subject.

12575

The Cyclopaedia of American biography. New enl. ed. of *Appleton's Cyclopaedia of American Biography*, originally edited by General James Grant Wilson and John Fiske. Revision to 1914 complete under editorial supervision of Hon. Charles Dick and James E. Homans. New York, Press Association Compilers, 1915–31. 12 v. illus., plates, ports.   E176.A665

Vols. 7, 11–12 designated supplementary ed.

Although it has been nearly superseded by the *Dictionary of American Biography* in its treatment of 18th-century figures, it contains certain information not given in the latter, including portraits and facsimiles of signatures.

12576

Dexter, Franklin B.   Biographical sketches of the graduates of Yale College with annals of the college history. New York, H. Holt, 1885–1912. 6 v.   LD6323.D5

Covers graduating classes from 1701 to 1815. Vols. 3 and 4 are concerned with the years 1763–78 and 1778–92.

12577

Dictionary of American biography, published under the auspices of American Council of Learned Societies. New York, C. Scribner's Sons, 1943. 22 v.

E176.D562

Editors: v. 1–3, Allen Johnson.—v. 4–7, Allen Johnson and Dumas Malone.—v. 8–20, Dumas Malone.—v. 21, Harris E. Starr.—v. 22, Robert Livingston Schuyler.

Contents: 1. Abbe–Barrymore.—2. Barsotti–Brazer.—3. Brearly–Chandler.—4. Chanfrau–Cushing.—5. Cushman–Eberle.—6. Echols–Fraser.—7. Fraunces-Grimké.—8. Grinnell–Hibbard.—9. Hibben–Jarvis.—10. Jasper–Larkin.—11. Larned–MacCracken.—12. McCrady–Millington.—13. Mills–Oglesby.—14. Oglethorpe–Platner.—15. Platt–Roberdeau.—16. Robert–Seward.—17. Sewell–Stevenson.—18. Steward–Trowbridge.—19. Troye–Wentworth.—20. Werden–Zunser.—21. Supplement one (to December 31, 1935).—22. Supplement two (to December 31, 1940).

First published in 21 volumes (1928–37) and later reissued on thin paper in 11 volumes (1946).

———Index: volumes 1–20. New York, C. Scribner's Sons, 1943. vi, 613 p.   E176.D562 Index

Contains 14,870 signed articles in 20 volumes and two supplements. Many of the essays, often several thousand words in length, are written by distinguished authorities. The compilers limit the work to persons who lived in America and made a significant contribution to American life; they do not treat British officers who served in North America after 1776. A list of sources accompanies each article. A separate volume provides several indexes for volumes 1–20, including lists of persons describing their lives, birthplaces, schools and colleges attended, occupations, and important topics mentioned in their biographies. The topical index includes citations for the Revolution under a variety of subheadings, from army tactics and ballads to Loyalists and the names of individual states. The essential facts of each biography in the 20 volumes and supplements are also available in a one-volume *Concise Dictionary of American Biography* (New York, C. Scribner's Sons [1964] 1273 p.).

12578

Dictionary of scientific biography.   Charles Coulston Gillispie, editor-in-chief. New York, C. Scribner's Sons [1970] + illus.   Q141.D5

"Published under the auspices of the American Council of Learned Societies."

Includes bibliographies.

Contents: v. 1. Pierre Abailard–L. S. Berg. 2. Hans Berger–Christop Buys Ballot.—v. 3. Pierre Cabanis–Heinrich von Dechen.—v. 4. Richard Dedekind–Firmicus Maternus.—v. 5. Emil Fisher–Gottlieb Haberlandt.—v. 6. Jean Hachette–Joesph Hyrtl.—

Contains biographical essays, with bibliographic notes, on the professional lives of scientists of all periods.

12579

Egbert, Donald D.   Princeton portraits, by Donald Drew Egbert, with the assistance of Diane Martindell Lee. Princeton, Princeton University Press, 1947. vii, 360 p. [72] p. of ports.   N7593.E36

"This volume on the portraits owned by Princeton University was written and published under the auspices of the University Committee on Humanistic Collections in connection with the bicentennial celebration of the University in 1946."

Contains portraits and biographical sketches of Princeton founders, presidents, faculty, trustees, alumni, and friends and benefactors. Among the dozens of notables from the Revolutionary period are John Witherspoon (1723–1794), the sixth president of the College of New Jersey, and Annis Boudinot Stockton (1736–1801), the only woman ever elected to membership in Whig Hall.

12580

Glenn, Thomas A.   Some colonial mansions and those who lived in them, with genealogies of the various families mentioned. v. 1. Philadelphia, H. T. Coates, 1898. 459 p. illus., plates, ports.   E159.G55

No more published; continuation called 2d series.

Contents: Westover.—Morven and the Stocktons.—Cedar Grove.—Bohemia Manor and the Herrmans.—The patroonship of the Van Rensselaers.—Rosewell: The Page family.—The Carters of Virginia.—Clermont and the Livingstons.—The Carrolls of Maryland: Doughoregan Manor.—Graeme Park: Keith and Graeme families.—Brandon on the lower James: The Harrison family.—The Randolphs.

12581

Glenn, Thomas A.   Some colonial mansions and those who lived in them, with genealogies of the various families mentioned. 2d ser. Philadelphia, H. T. Coates, 1900. 503 p. illus., coats of arms, plates, ports.   E159.G56

"Authorities": p. 329.

Contents: Mount Vernon and the Washingtons.—The Bowne house at Flushing, L.I.—Laurel Hill and the Rawle family.—Monticello.—The manor of Philipsborough.—Waynesborough.—Preston at Patuxent.—The Schuylers.—Mount Pleasant and the Macphersons.

12582

Gummere, Richard M.   Seven wise men of colonial America. Cambridge, Harvard University Press, 1967. xi, 114 p.   E187.5.G8

Bibliographic references included in "Notes" (p. 97–108).

Contents: Hugh Jones.—Robert Calef.—Michael Wigglesworth.—Samuel Davies.—Henry Melchoir Muhlenberg.—Benjamin Rush.—Thomas Paine.

12583

Herring, James, *and* James B. Longacre, *eds.* The national portrait gallery of distinguished Americans. Conducted . . . under the superintendence of the American Academy of the Fine Arts. New York, M. Bancroft, 1834–39. 4 v. ports.   E176.H56

Issued in monthly parts.

Includes engravings of contemporary portraits and miniatures for 73 Revolutionary figures, each followed by a biographical sketch.

12584

Hillard, Elias B. The last men of the Revolution; containing a photograph of each from life, accompanied by brief biographical sketches. Edited by Wendell D. Garret. Introduction by Archibald MacLeish. [Barre, Mass.] Barre Publishers, 1968. 116 p. illus., ports.
E206.H54 1968

Reprint of the 1864 edition (Hartford, N. A. & R. A. Moore. 64 p. E206.H54 Rare Bk. Coll.).

Contents: Samuel Downing.—Daniel Waldo.— Lemuel Cook.—Alexander Milliner.—William Hutchings.—Adam Link.—James Barham.

12585

Hunt, Freeman, *ed.* Lives of American merchants. New York, Derby & Jackson, 1858. 2 v. ports.
HF3023.A2H8

Reprinted in New York by A. M. Kelley (1969).

Includes sketches of Nicholas Brown, Stephen Girard, Henry Laurens, Elias Hasket Derby, Samuel Shaw, John Hancock, and Robert Morris.

12586

Jones, Edward Alfred. American members of the Inns of Court, with a foreword by Hon. William H. Taft. London, Saint Catherine Press, 1924. xxx, 250 p.
KF362.J65

Bibliography: p. viii.

Biographical sketches with an historical introduction.

12587

Judson, Levi Carroll. The sages and heroes of the American Revolution. In two parts, including the signers of the Declaration of Independence. Two hundred and forty three of the sages and heroes are presented in due form and many others are named incidentally. Stereotype ed. Philadelphia, The author, 1851. 480 p. facsim., port.   E206.J92

Reprinted in Port Washington, N.Y., By Kennikat Press (1970).

12588

Lawrence, Ruth, *ed.* Colonial families of America. New York, National Americana Society [1928–48] 27 v. col. coats of arms, plates, ports.   CS61.L3

Louis E. De Forest's *American Colonial Families* ([New York] National Coloniana Society, 1930. 142 p.), which includes names that do not appear in Lawrence's work, may be regarded as a supplement.

12589

Lewis, William D., *ed.* Great American lawyers; the lives and influence of judges and lawyers who have acquired permanent national reputation, and have developed the jurisprudence of the United States. A history of the legal profession in America. Philadelphia, J. C. Winston Co., 1907–9. 8 v. ports.   KF367.L45 1907

Reprinted in South Hackensack, N.J., by Rothman Reprints (1971).

Includes, in volumes 1 and 2, lengthy sketches of George Wythe, Patrick Henry, James Wilson, William Paterson, John Jay, Oliver Ellsworth, Alexander Hamilton, Robert R. Livingston, Luther Martin, Theophilus Parsons, Zephaniah Swift, William Tilghman, William Pinkney, John Marshall, and James Kent.

12590

Mackenzie, George N., *ed.* Colonial families of the United States of America, in which is given the history, genealogy and armorial bearings of colonial families who settled in the American colonies from the time of the settlement of Jamestown, 13th May, 1607, to the Battle of Lexington, 19th April, 1775. New York, Grafton Press, 1907–20. 7 v. coats of arms. CS61.M2
Micro 8668 CS

Vols. 2–7 have imprint: Baltimore, Md., Seaforth Press. Vol. 7 edited by Nelson Osgood Rhoades.

Reprinted in Baltimore by the Genealogical Pub. Co. (1966).

12591

The Macmillan dictionary of Canadian biography, by W. Stewart Wallace. 3d ed., rev. and enl. London, Macmillan; New York, St. Martin's, 1963. 822 p.
F1005.D5 1963

Contains compact biographical sketches with bibliographic references. As a source for the Revolutionary period it will eventually be superseded by the more comprehensive coverage of the *Dictionary of Canadian Biography* (Toronto, University of Toronto Press [1966] + F1005.D49). The first volume in this set covers the period 1000–1700 (1966. 755 p.), and the second treats the years 1701–40 (1969. 759 p.).

12592

Rogers, Thomas J. A new American biographical dictionary; or, Remembrancer of the departed heroes, sages and statesmen of America. Confined exclusively to those who have signalized themselves in either capacity, in the Revolutionary War which obtained the independence of their country. 4th ed., with important alterations and additions. Philadelphia, S. F. Bradford, 1829. 400 p.   E206.R74

First edition published in Easton, Pa., in 1813.

Includes more than 150 individual sketches.

12593

Rosenbloom, Joseph R. A biographical dictionary of early American Jews, colonial times through 1800. [Lexington] University of Kentucky Press [1960] xii, 175 p.
E184.J5R63

Bibliography: p. ix–xii.

12594

Sibley's Harvard graduates; biographical sketches of those who attended Harvard College . . . with bibliographical and other notes. v. 1+ 1642/58+ LD2139.S5

Title varies: v. 1–3, 1642/58–1678/89, *Biographical Sketches of Graduates of Harvard University, in Cambridge, Massachusetts.*
Vols. 1–3 by J. L. Sibley; v. 4+ by C. K. Shipton.
Imprint varies: v. 1–3, Cambridge, C. W. Sever, 1873–85.—v. 4, Cambridge, Harvard University Press, 1933.

Arranges the entries by graduating class and provides an index of proper names in each volume. Beginning with the 12th volume, the compiler includes biographies for some Yale men and others who received honorary degrees in 1746 and after from Harvard, but who never attended the college. The 16th volume, containing essays on 199 students in the classes of 1764–67, was published in 1972. Biographies of 60 men who received degrees between 1690 and 1750 appear in Shipton's *New England Life in the 18th Century; Representative Biographies From Sibley's Harvard Graduates* (Cambridge, Belknap Press of Harvard University Press, 1963. 626 p. F3.S5).

12595

Sparks, Jared, *ed.* The library of American biography. Boston, Hillard, Gray, 1834–48. 25 v. illus., facsims., maps, ports.
E176.S81

Vols. 1–15, 2d ser., published in Boston by C. C. Little and J. Brown.
General indexes to 1st and 2d ser. in last volume of each.
Partial contents: Allen, Ethan, by J. Sparks, 1st ser., v. 1.—Arnold, Benedict, by J. Sparks, 1st ser., v. 3.—Boone, Daniel, by J. M. Peck, 2d ser., v. 13.—Brainerd, David, by W. B. O. Peabody, 1st ser., v. 8.—Davie, William R. by F. M. Hubbard, 2d ser., v. 15.—Dwight, Timothy, by W. B. Sprague, 2d ser., v.4.—Edwards, Jonathan, by S. Miller, 1st ser., v. 8.—Ellery, William, by E. T. Channing, 1st ser., v. 6.—Fitch, John, by C. Whittlesey, 2d ser., v. 6.—Greene, Nathanael, by G. W. Greene, 2d ser., v. 10.—Henry, Patrick, by A. H. Everett, 2d ser., v. 1.—Kirkland, Samuel, by S. K. Lothrop, 2d ser., v. 15.—Lèdyard, John, by J. Sparks, 2d ser., v. 14.—Lee, Charles, by J. Sparks, 2d ser., v. 8.—Lincoln, Benjamin, by F. Bowen, 2d ser., v. 13.—Montgomery, Richard, by J. Armstrong, 1st ser., v. 1.—Oglethorpe, James, by W. B. O. Peabody, 2d ser., v. 2.—Otis, James, by F. Bowen, 2d ser., v. 2.—Palfrey, William by J. G. Palfrey, 2d ser., v. 7.—Pinkney, William, by H. Wheaton, 1st ser., v. 6.—Posey, Thomas, by J. Hall, 2d ser., v. 9.—Preble, Edward, by L. Sabine, 2d ser., v. 12.—Pulaski, Count Casimir, by J. Sparks, 2d ser., v. 4.—Putnam, Israel, by W. B. O. Peabody, 1st ser., v. 7:—Reed, Joseph, by H. Reed, 2d ser., v. 8.—Rittenhouse, David, by J. Renwick, 1st ser., v. 7.—

Rumford, Benjamin Thompson, count, by J. Renwick, 2d ser., v. 5.—Stark, John, by E. Everett, 1st ser., v. 1.—Steuben, Baron, by F. Bowen, 1st ser., v. 9.—Stiles, Ezra, by J. L. Kinglsey, 2d ser., v. 6.—Sullivan, John, by W. B. O. Peabody, 2d ser., v. 3.—Ward, Samuel, by W. Gammell, 2d ser., v. 9.—Warren, Joseph, by A. H. Everett, 1st ser., v. 10.—Wayne, Anthony, by J. Armstrong, 1st ser., v. 4.

A reprint of 22 of the 26 lives in the first series of Sparks' *Library of American Biography* appeared under the title *American Biography* (New York, Harper, 1902. 12 v. facsims, ports. E176.S83).

12596

Swiggett, Howard. The forgotten leaders of the Revolution. Garden City, N.Y., Doubleday, 1955. 284 p.
E302.5.S9

Includes bibliographies.

Contains biographical essays on 19 figures, among them Jeremiah Wadsworth, Lewis Littlepage, Edmund Randolph, John Nicholson, Oliver Wolcott, and the Pinckney brothers.

12597

Tansill, Charles C. The secret loves of the Founding Fathers; the romantic side of George Washington, Thomas Jefferson, Benjamin Franklin, Gouverneur Morris [and] Alexander Hamilton. New York Devin-Adair Co. [1964] xviii, 235 p. ports.
E302.5.T3

Bibliography: p. 219–224.

12598

Thorp, Willard, *ed.* The lives of eighteen from Princeton. Princeton, N.J., Princeton University Press, 1946. ix, 356 p. ports.
LD4598.T5

Partial contents: William Paterson, by J. P. Boyd.—Samuel Kirkland, by Willard Thorp.—Benjamin Rush, by J. K. Wallis.—John Witherspoon, by T. J. Wertenbaker.—Samuel Stanhope Smith, by S. H. Monk.—Henry Lee, by P. A. Crowl.—James Madison, by Douglass Adair.

Reprinted in Freeport, N.Y., by Books for Libraries Press (1968).

12599

U.S. *Congress.* Biographical directory of the American Congress, 1774–1971, the Continental Congress, September 5, 1774, to October 21, 1788, and the Congress of the United States, from the First through the Ninety-first Congress, March 4, 1789, to January 3, 1971, inclusive. [Washington] U.S. Govt. Print. Off., 1971. 1972 p. (92d Congress, 1st session. Senate document no. 92–8)
JK1010.A5 1971

Lawrence F. Kennedy, chief compiler.

"A revision of the Dictionary of the United States Congress and the General Government, published in 1859 and again revised in 1869, by Charles Lanman, was followed by subsequent issues such as the Biographical Annals of the Civil Government of the United States in 1876, by Charles Lanman and James Anglim, and the Lanman edition of 1876 as corrected by Joseph M. Morrison in 1887; the Political Register and Congressional Directory of 1878, by Ben: Perley Poore; the Biographical Congressional Directory of 1903, by O. M. Enyart; the Biographical Congressional Directory of 1911, the Biographical Directory of the American Congress of 1927, by Ansel Wold; the 1949 edition by James L. Harrison; and the 1961 edition by Clifford P. Reynolds.''

Contains biographical data on 415 persons elected to the Continental Congress, including information on their education, political careers, and significant accomplishments. Sketches of other Revolutionary figures who may have served in later Congresses are also included.

12600
White's conspectus of American biography; a tabulated record of American history and biography. 2d ed. A rev. and enl. ed. of *A Conspectus of American Biography*. Compiled by the editorial staff of *The National Cyclopaedia of American Biography*. New York, J. T. White, 1937. viii, 455 p.   E176.N2814

Reprinted in St. Clair Shores, Mich., by the Scholarly Press (1972).

A classified index to the *National Cyclopaedia of American Biography* (New York, J. T. White, 1893 +) that contains chronological lists of colonial and state governors, presidents of colleges and scientific institutions, preeminent members of major occupational groups, and Americans in fiction, poetry, and drama. Since the *Cyclopaedia* is not alphabetically arranged, it must be used in conjunction with the *Conspectus* or one of several indexes to the series.

12601
Wilstach, Paul.   Patriots off their pedestals. Indianapolis, Bobbs-Merrill Co. [c1927] 240 p.   E302.5.W74

Contents: The idea.—George Washington.—Benjamin Franklin.—Patrick Henry.—Alexander Hamilton.—John Adams.—Thomas Jefferson.—John Marshall.—James Madison.

Reprinted in Freeport, N.Y., by Books for Libraries Press (1970).

New England
GENERAL

12602
Cutter, William R.   New England families, genealogical and memorial; a record of the achievements of her people in the making of commonwealths and the founding of a nation. New York, Lewis Historical Pub. Co., 1913. 4 v. (v, 2149 p.) ports.   F3.C98

MAINE

12603
Little, George T., *ed.*   Genealogical and family history of the state of Maine. Compiled under the editorial supervision of George Thomas Little, and including among other local contributors Rev. Henry S. Burrage and Albert Roscoe Stubbs. New York, Lewis Historical Pub. Co., 1909. 4 v. (xxix, 2283 p.) illus., plates, ports.   F18.L77

NEW HAMPSHIRE

12604
Bell, Charles H.   The bench and bar of New Hampshire, including biographical notices of deceased judges of the highest court, and lawyers of the province and state, and a list of names of those now living. Houghton, Mifflin, 1894. xv, 795 p.   KF354.N39B4

12605
Stearns, Ezra S., William F. Whitcher, *and* Edward E. Parker, *eds.*   Genealogical and family history of the state of New Hampshire: a record of the achievements of her people in the making of a commonwealth and the founding of a nation. New York, Lewis Pub. Co., 1908. 4 v. (viii, 2067 p.) plates, ports.   F33.S79

VERMONT

12606
Carleton, Hiram, *ed.*   Genealogical and family history of the state of Vermont; a record of the achievements of her people in the making of a commonwealth and the founding of a nation. New York, Lewis Pub. Co., 1903. 2 v. illus., plates, ports.   F48.C28

Traces the 17th- and 18th-century family origins of prominent 19th-century residents.

MASSACHUSETTS

12607
Cutter, William R., *ed.*   Genealogical and personal memoirs relating to the families of Boston and eastern Massachusetts. New York, Lewis Historical Pub. Co., 1908. 4 v. illus., plates, ports.   F63.C99

12608
Cutter, William R., *and* William F. Adams, *eds.*   Genealogical and personal memoirs relating to the families of the state of Massachusetts. New York, Lewis Historical Pub. Co., 1910. 4 v. plates, ports.   F63.C993

12609
Encyclopedia of Massachusetts, biographical—genealogical; compiled with assistance of the following advisory committee: William Richard Cutter [and others] New York, American Historical Society, 1916. 5 v. fronts., plates, ports.   F63.E56

12610
Representative men and old families of southeastern Massachusetts, containing historical sketches of prominent and representative citizens and genealogical records of many of the old families. Chicago, J. H. Beers, 1912. 3 v. (xiv, 1792 p.) illus., plates, ports.   F63.R4

RHODE ISLAND

12611
Representative men and old families of Rhode Island; genealogical records and historical sketches of prominent and representative citizens and of many of the old

families. Chicago, J. H. Beers, 1908. 3 v. (xvi, 2336 p.) ports. F78.R42

12612

Smith, Joseph J., *comp.* Civil and military list of Rhode Island. 1647–1800. A list of all officers elected by the General Assembly from the organization of the legislative government of the colony to 1800. Providence, R.I., Preston and Rounds Co., 1900. vii, 659 p. F78.S65

Supplemented by his *Civil and Military List of Rhode Island, 1800–1850: A List of All Officers Elected by the General Assembly From 1800 to 1850; Also, All Officers in Revolutionary War, Appointed by Continental Congress, and in the Regular Army and Navy From Rhode Island, to 1850, Including . . . All Officers in Privateer Service During Colonial and Revolutionary Wars* (Providence, R.I., Preston and Rounds Co., 1901. 799 p. F78.S66). Each volume contains its own index, but a much more comprehensive and satisfactory one was issued by the compiler in 1907 under the title *New Index to the Civil and Military Lists of Rhode Island . . . Giving Christian and Family Names, Arranged Alphabetically* (Providence, R.I., J. J. Smith, 1907. 182 p. F78.S67).

12613

Updike, Wilkins. Memoirs of the Rhode Island bar. Boston, T. H. Webb, 1842. 311 p. KF354.R48U6

Includes biographical sketches of James Honyman, Augustus Johnson, Oliver Arnold, Henry Marchant, William Channing, Rouse Helme, John Cole, Archibald Campbell, Jacob Campbell, James Varnum, Matthew Robinson, and Robert Lightfoot.

CONNECTICUT

12614

Commemorative biographical record of New Haven County, Connecticut, containing biographical sketches of prominent and representative citizens and of many of the early settled families. Chicago, J. H. Beers, 1902. 2 v. plates, ports. F102.N5C7

Information about Revolutionary figures is scattered throughout.

12615

Commemorative biographical record of Tolland and Windham counties, Connecticut, containing biographical sketches of prominent and representative citizens and of many of the early settled families. Chicago, J. H. Beers, 1903. xiii, 1358 p. ports. [F102.T6C73] Micro 18242 F

12616

Cutter, William R., *ed.* Genealogical and family history of the state of Connecticut; a record of the achievements of her people in the making of a commonwealth and the founding of a nation. New York, Lewis Historical Pub. Co., 1911. 4 v. (2208 p.) plates, ports. F93.C99

12617

Encyclopedia of Connecticut biography, genealogical-memorial; representative citizens. Compiled with the assistance of the following advisory committee: Samuel Hart [and others] Boston, American Historical Society, 1917–[23] 10 v. plates, ports. F93.E56

12618

Perry, Charles E., *ed.* Founders and leaders of Connecticut, 1633–1783. Boston, D. C. Heath [ᶜ1934] xi, 319 p. illus., ports. F93.P38

"Selected bibliography": p. 311–312.

Reprinted in Freeport, N.Y., by Books for Libraries Press (1971).

Includes 30 biographical sketches of Revolutionary figures.

Middle Atlantic Region
NEW YORK

12619

Cutter, William R. Genealogical and family history of central New York; a record of the achievements of her people in the making of a commonwealth and the building of a nation. New York, Lewis Historical Pub. Co., 1912. 3 v. (viii, 1612 p.) illus., ports. F118.C98

12620

Cutter, William R., *ed.* Genealogical and family history of northern New York; a record of the achievements of her people in the making of a commonwealth and the founding of a nation. New York, Lewis Historical Pub. Co., 1910. 3 v. (vii, 1247 p.) illus., plates, ports. F118.C99

Chiefly Jefferson, Lewis, St. Lawrence, Franklin, Clinton, and Essex counties.

12621

Cutter, William R., *ed.* Genealogical and family history of southern New York and the Hudson River valley; a record of the achievements of her people in the making of a commonwealth and the building of a nation. New York, Lewis Historical Pub. Co., 1913. 3 v. (1168, xviii p.) plates, ports. F118.C993

12622

Cutter, William R., *ed.* Genealogical and family history of western New York; a record of the achievements of her people in the making of a commonwealth and the building of a nation. New York, Lewis Historical Pub. Co., 1912. 3 v. (vii, 1517 p.) illus., plates, ports. F118.C992

12623

MacBean, William M. Biographical register of Saint Andrew's Society of the state of New York. v. 1. 1756–1806. New York, Printed for the Society, 1922. 400 p. ports. F130.S4M2, v. 1

12624

Reynolds, Cuyler, *ed.* Hudson-Mohawk genealogical and family memoirs; a record of achievements of the people of the Hudson and Mohawk valleys in New York State, included within the present counties of Albany, Rensselaer, Washington, Saratoga, Montgomery, Fulton, Schenectady, Columbia and Greene. New York, Lewis Historical Pub. Co., 1911. 4 v. ports.   F118.R46

12625

Scoville, Joseph A. The old merchants of New York City, by Walter Barrett. First [–fifth] series. New York, Greenwood Press, 1968. 5 v.   HF3163.N7S32

Reprint of the 1863–69 edition.

Contains miscellaneous biographical sketches.

NEW JERSEY

12626

Cyclopedia of New Jersey biography, compiled under the direction of the American Historical Society. Newark, N.J., Memorial History Co., 1916. 3 v. plates (part col.), ports.   F133.M54

12627

Lee, Francis B., *ed.* Genealogical and memorial history of the state of New Jersey. New York, Lewis Historical Pub. Co., 1910. 4 v. (xviii, 1694 p.) illus., plates, ports.   F133.L47

12628

Lee, Francis B., *ed.* Genealogical and personal memorial of Mercer County, New Jersey. New York, Lewis Pub. Co., 1907. 2 v. (916 p.) illus., plates, ports.   F142.M5L4

Information on Revolutionary figures is scattered throughout.

12629

Memorial cyclopedia of New Jersey. Under the editorial supervision of Mary Depue Ogden. Newark, N.J., Memorial History Co., 1915–17. 3 v. plates (part col.), ports.   F133.M53

Also published, Newark, 1916, under title *Cyclopedia of New Jersey Biography* (F133.C99).

PENNSYLVANIA

12630

Armor, William C. Lives of the governors of Pennsylvania, with the incidental history of the state, from 1609 to 1872. Philadelphia, J. K. Simon, 1872. 528 p. ports.   F148.A74

Includes sketches of Richard and John Penn and the presidents of the Supreme Executive Council, 1777–88: Thomas Wharton, Jr., George Bryan, Joseph Reed, William Moore, John Dickinson, and Benjamin Franklin (p. 169–269).

12631

Binney, Horace. The leaders of the old bar of Philadelphia. Pennsylvania magazine of history and biography, v. 14, Apr.–Oct. 1890: 1–27, 143–159, 223–252. ports.   F146.P65, v. 14

Sketches of William Lewis, Edward Tilghman, and Jared Ingersoll.

12632

Colonial and Revolutionary families of Pennsylvania; genealogical and personal memoirs. v. 1–16. New York, Lewis Historical Pub. Co., 1911–60. 16 v. coats of arms (part col.), facsims., plates, ports.   F148.C72

Vols. 4–16 called new series.

12633

Harris, Alexander. A biographical history of Lancaster County . . . being a history of early settlers and eminent men of the county; has also much other unpublished historical information, chiefly of a local character. Lancaster, Pa., E. Barr, 1872. 638 p.   F157.L2H2

Biographical sketches arranged in alphabetical order.

——— Index: Lancaster County, Pennsylvania, by Alex Harris. [By Hilda Chance. Huntsville, Ark., Century Enterprises, 1968] 27 p.   F157.L2H2 Index

12634

Jordan, John W., *ed.* Colonial families of Philadelphia. New York, Lewis Pub. Co. 1911. 2 v. illus., coats of arms, facsims., plates, ports.   F158.25.J67

Paged continuously.

12635

Jordan, John W., *ed.* Genealogical and personal history of northern Pennsylvania. New York, Lewis Historical Pub. Co., 1913. 3 v. (vii, 1448 p.) illus., ports.   F148.J83

12636

Jordan, John W. Genealogical and personal history of the Allegheny Valley, Pennsylvania. New York, Lewis Historical Pub. Co., 1913. 3 v. (viii, 1162 p.) illus., facsim., ports.   F157.A5J8

12637

Jordon, Wilfred, *ed.* Colonial and Revolutionary families of Philadelphia, genealogical and personal memoirs. v. 1. New York, Lewis Historical Pub. Co., 1933. 460 p. col. coats of arms, plates, ports.   F158.25.J72

No more published?

The South

GENERAL

12638

Armstrong, Zella, *comp.* Notable southern families. Chattanooga, Lookout Pub. Co. [1918–33] 6 v. ports.   CS61.A6

12639

Hardy, Stella P.   Colonial families of the southern states of America; a history and genealogy of colonial families who settled in the colonies prior to the Revolution. New York, T. A. Wright, 1911. xii, 643 p. illus.
CS61.H3

Reprinted, with minor additions, in Baltimore by the Southern Book Co. (1958) and the Genealogical Pub. Co. (1965).

VIRGINIA

12640

Bruce, Philip A.   The Virginia Plutarch. Chapel Hill, University of North Carolina Press, 1929. 2 v. fold. map, plates, ports.   F225.B88

Contents: 1. The colonial and Revolutionary eras.—2. The national era.

Reprinted in New York by Russell & Russell (1971).

Biographical essays on such important Virginia figures as Washington, Henry, Jefferson, Madison, Richard Henry Lee, George Rogers Clark, Daniel Morgan, and John Sevier.

12641

Reddy, Anne W.   West Virginia Revolutionary ancestors whose services were non-military and whose names, therefore, do not appear in Revolutionary indexes of soldiers and sailors. An index from manuscript public claims of the Revolutionary War in the Virginia State Library. [Washington, D.C., Model Print. Co., 1930] 92 p.   F240.R31

"The counties of that part of . . . Virginia which later became West Virginia have been divided . . . so many times . . . that . . . [a] list of the revolutionary name of a county and the names of the counties taken from it is submitted."—p. 9.

Reprinted in Baltimore by the Genealogical Pub. Co. (1963).

12642

Tyler, Lyon G., *ed.*   Encyclopedia of Virginia biography. New York, Lewis Historical Pub. Co., 1915. 5 v. ports.
F225.T97

12643

Warner, Charles W. H.   Road to Revolution; Virginia's rebels from Bacon to Jefferson, 1676–1776. Richmond, Garrett and Massie, 1961. xiii, 171 p. illus., plates, ports.   F229.W275

Bibliography: p. 157–165.

Includes sketches on Landon Carter, Richard Bland, William Small, Francis Fauquier, George Wythe, and Thomas Jefferson (p. 115–140).

NORTH CAROLINA

12644

Ashe, Samuel A., *ed.*   Biographical history of North Carolina from colonial times to the present. v. 1–8. Greensboro, N.C., C. L. Van Noppen, 1905–17. 8 v. ports.
F253.A82

SOUTH CAROLINA

12645

Hennig, Helen K.   Great South Carolinians. v. 1. From colonial days to the Confederate War. Chapel Hill, University of North Carolina Press [1940] xiii, 369 p. illus., maps, ports.   F268.H53, v. 1

Reprinted in Freeport, N.Y., by Books for Libraries Press (1970).

Includes sketches (p. 47–214) of William Bull II, Henry Laurens, Christopher Gadsden, John Rutledge, William Henry Drayton, Thomas Sumter, Francis Marion, Andrew Pickens, Charles Cotesworth Pinckney, and Charles Pinckney.

GEORGIA

12646

Huxford, Folks.   Pioneers of Wiregrass Georgia; a biographical account of some of the early settlers of that portion of Wiregrass Georgia embraced in the original counties of Irwin, Appling, Wayne, Camden, and Glynn. [Homerville? Ga., 1951–71] 6 v. facsims., maps, ports.   F285.H8

Subtitle varies slightly.

12647

Northen, William J. *ed.*   Men of mark in Georgia; a complete and elaborate history of the state from its settlement to the present time, chiefly told in biographies and autobiographies of the most eminent men of each period of Georgia's progress and development. Historical introductory by John Temple Graves, editor. Atlanta, Ga., A. B. Caldwell, 1907–12. 6 v. ports.
[F285.N87]
Micro 22650 F

Great Britain

12648

[Almon, John]   Biographical, literary, and political anecdotes, of several of the most eminent persons of the present age. Never before printed. With an appendix; consisting of original, explanatory, and scarce papers. By the author of *Anecdotes of the Late Earl of Chatham*. London, T. N. Longman, and L. B. Seeley, 1797. 3 v.   DA483.A1A4

"Dr. Benjamin Franklin": v. 2, p. 175–344.

12649

Brougham and Vaux, Henry Peter Brougham, *Baron*. Historical sketches of statesmen who flourished in the time of George III. London, G. Cox, 1845–53. 6 v. in 3.   DA506.A1B73

The 6 vols. are issued as follows: v. 1–2: first series, v. 1–2; v. 3–4: second series, v. 1–2; v. 5–6: third series, v. 1–2.

12650

Brougham and Vaux, Henry Peter Brougham, *Baron*. Lives of men of letters and science who flourished in the time of George III. Paris, A. and W. Galignani, 1845. xiv, 334 p.   CT118.B76

Contents: Voltair.—Rousseau.—Hume.—Robertson.—Black.—Watt.—Priestley.—Cavendish.—Davy.—Simson.

12651

Brougham and Vaux, Henry Peter Brougham, *Baron.* Lives of men of letters of the time of George III. London, R. Griffin, 1855, vi, 438 p. (Works of Henry, Lord Brougham, v. 2)   DA27.B9, v. 2

Contents: Voltaire.—Rousseau.—Note to the lives of Voltaire and Rousseau.—Hume.—Robertson.—Johnson.—Gibbon.—Additional appendix to the life of Voltaire.

12652

Brougham and Vaux, Henry Peter Brougham, *Baron.* Lives of philosophers of the time of George III. London, R. Griffin, 1855. xiii, 492 p. (Works of Henry, Lord Brougham, v. 1)   DA27.B9, v. 1

Contents: Black.—Watt.—Priestley.—Cavendish.—Davy.—Simson.—Adam Smith.—Analytical view of the *Wealth* of Nations.—Lavoisier.—Sir Joseph Banks.—D'Alembert.—Additional appendix to the lives of Adam Smith and Sir Joseph Banks.—Notes to the lives of Cavendish, Watt, and Black.—Note to the life of Simson.

12653

Campbell, John Campbell, *Baron.* Lives of the lord chancellors and keepers of the great seal of England, from the earliest times till the reign of Queen Victoria. 7th ed. New York, Cockcroft, 1878. 10 v. ports. (part col.)   DA28.4.C35 1878

Volume 6 contains biographical information on Robert Henley, 1st Earl Northington (p. 237–286), Charles Pratt, 1st Earl Camden (p. 287–406), Charles Yorke (p. 407–480), and Henry Bathurst, 2d Earl Bathurst (p. 481–520); volume 7 includes the life of Edward Thurlow, 1st Baron Thurlow (p. 1–203).

12654

Cunningham, George G. Lives of eminent and illustrious Englishmen, from Alfred the Great to the latest times. Glasgow, A. Fullarton, 1834–42. 8 v. in 4. ports.   DA28.C8

Vols. 5–8 include 534 biographical sketches of 18th- and early 19th-century figures.

12655

Dictionary of national biography. Edited by Leslie Stephen and Sidney Lee. London, Smith, Elder, 1908–9. 22 v. port.   DA28.D45

A reissue of the *Dictionary of National Biography*, originally planned by George M. Smith, first issued in 66 volumes.

A compilation of signed articles written by 653 specialists. The main work—first issued as v. 1–63; 1885–1900—and the supplement—v. 64–66; 1901—include more than 5,700 entries for noteworthy 18th-century inhabitants of the British Isles and the colonies. While the average biography is one page in length, those for important persons run to ten pages or more. Errata are noted under the name of the subject in *Corrections and Additions to the Dictionary of National Biography, Cumulated from the Bulletin of the Institute of Historical Research Covering the Years 1923–1963* (Boston, G. K. Hall, 1966. 212 p.). Volume 1 of *The Concise Dictionary of National Biography* (London, Oxford University Press [1953]–61. 2 v.) summarizes the entries in the main work and its supplement; the length of each article is reduced by a ratio of 1 to 14.

12656

A Dictionary of the printers and booksellers who were at work in England, Scotland and Ireland from 1726 to 1775; those in England by H. R. Plomer, Scotland by G. H. Bushnell, Ireland by E. R. McC. Dix. [Oxford] Printed for the Bibliographical Society at the Oxford University Press, 1932 (for 1930). xxi, 432 p. (Bibliographical Society, London. Publications)   Z151.D54

Reprinted in London by the Bibliographical Society (1968).

Skeleton professional biographies arranged in alphabetical order in three separate lists. Four geographic indexes provide references to those who worked at various locations in England and Wales other than London, in Scotland other than Edinburgh, in Ireland, and three places abroad. A fifth index of more than 30 circulating libraries in England and Scotland is arranged according to the date of their founding from 1725 to 1780.

12657

Dobrée, Bonamy, *ed.* From Anne to Victoria; essays by various hands. London, Cassell [1937] x, 630 p.   CT781.D6 1937

Reprinted in New York by Books for Libraries Press (1967).

Includes miscellaneous pieces on William Pitt, John Wesley, Samuel Johnson, John Wilkes, Horace Walpole, George Rodney, William Hogarth, Joseph Priestley, and several others.

12658

The Georgian era: memoirs of the most eminent persons, who have flourished in Great Britain, from the accession of George the First to the demise of George the Fourth. London, Vizetelly, Branston, 1832–34. 4 v. ports.   DA483.A1G3

By ——— Clarke (see the British Museum's *General Catalogue of Printed Books*).

Contents: v. 1. The royal family. The pretenders and their adherents. Churchmen. Dissenters. Statesmen.—v. 2. Military and naval commanders. Judges and barristers. Physicians and surgeons.—v.3. Voyagers and travellers. Philosophers and men of science. Authors.—v. 4. Political and rural economists. Painters, sculptors, architects, and engravers. Composers. Vocal, instrumental and dramatic performers.

12659

Haydn, Joseph T.   The book of dignities, containing lists of the official personages of the British Empire . . . from the earliest periods to the present time . . . Remodelled and brought down to 1851 by . . . Joseph Haydn, continued to the present time, with numerous additional lists and an index . . . by Horace Ockerby. 3d ed. London, W. H. Allen, 1894. xxviii, 1170 p.
DA34.H32

Originally founded on Beatson's *Political Index,* published in 1786.

Reprinted in Baltimore by the Genealogical Pub. Co. (1970).

12660

Judd, Gerrit P.   Members of Parliament, 1734–1832. New Haven, Yale University Press, 1955. vii, 389 p. (Yale historical publications. Miscellany 61)   JN672.J8

Includes bibliographic references.

Reprinted in Hamden, Conn., by Archon Books (1972).

Summarizes and compares data on nationality, age, length of service, social status, education, professions, and economic interests for 5,034 men. The major portion of the work is a checklist of members indicating boroughs and years of service. The author concludes that the unreformed House of Commons reflected the basic distribution of power within British society. It was remarkably cohesive, given the similarity in members' family backgrounds, education, and professional occupations, yet at the same time its representation was extremely cosmopolitan in both geographic diversity and economic interest.

12661

Kunitz, Stanley J., *and* Howard Haycraft, *eds.*   British authors before 1800; a biographical dictionary. New York, H. W. Wilson Co., 1952. vi, 584 p. ports. (The Authors series)   PR105.K9

12662

Musgrave, *Sir* William, *comp.*   Obituary prior to 1800 (as far as relates to England, Scotland, and Ireland). Edited by Sir George J. Armytage. London, 1899–1901. 6 v. (The Publications of the Harleian Society, v. 44–49)
CS410.H3, v. 44–49

12663

Namier, *Sir* Lewis B., *and* John Brooke.   The House of Commons, 1754–1790. New York, Published for the History of Parliament Trust by Oxford University Press, 1964. 3 v.   JN672.N2

Includes bibliographies.

Contents: 1. Introductory survey constituencies, appendices.—2. Members, A–J.—3. Members, K–Y.

Summarizes essential information on the lives and parliamentary careers of 1,964 members and the individual histories of 314 constituencies. Brooke's introductory essay treats the kinds, management, and character of these constituencies; the nature of the six general elections of the period and their Parliaments; the economic, social, profes-

sional, and other groupings evident within the House; and the major features of parliamentary development, especially the growth of party.

12664

Nichols, John.   Minor lives; a collection of biographies. Annotated and with an introduction on John Nichols and the antiquarian and anecdotal movements of the late eighteenth century. Edward L. Hart, editor. Cambridge, Mass., Harvard University Press, 1971. xxxii, 367 p. ports.   CT781.N5 1971

A collection of Nichols' contemporary sketches of antiquarians, booksellers, printers, illustrators, designers, scholars, and poets that appeared in such publications as the *Gentleman's Magazine* and are presented here for the light they shed on late 18th-century England.

12665

Valentine, Alan C.   The British establishment, 1760–1784; an eighteenth-century biographical dictionary. Norman, University of Oklahoma Press [1970] 2 v. (xii, 960 p.)   CT781.V3

Presents about 3,000 skeletal biographies of members of the political and social aristocracy—men and women at influential levels of the government, court, army, navy, church, law, trade, finance, and society, and some individuals of lower social rank who, like John Wilkes, entered the establishment through Parliament or a peerage. Nearly half the entries are not to be found in the *Dictionary of National Biography* or Namier and Brooke's *House of Commons.*

12666

Who's who in history.   General editor: C. R. N. Routh. Oxford, Blackwell, 1960+ illus., geneal. tables, maps (on lining papers), ports.   DA28.W618

Contents: v. 1. British Isles, 55 B. C. to 1485, by W. O. Hassall.—v. 2. England, 1485 to 1603, by C. R. N. Routh.—v. 3. England, 1603 to 1714, by C. P. Hill.—v. 4. England, 1714 to 1789, by Geoffrey Treasure.

A compilation of general biographical sketches, averaging one to two pages in length, arranged roughly according to date of birth or by topic. Each volume includes an index of names.

Women

12667

Biddle, Gertrude B. *and* Sarah D. Lowrie, *eds.*   Notable women of Pennsylvania. Committee of 1926, Philadelphia Sesquicentennial Celebration. Philadelphia, University of Pennsylvania Press, 1942. xviii, 307 p.
F148.B5

Provides brief sketches of more than 50 Pennsylvanians who lived during the Revolutionary era.

12668

Donovan, Frank R.   The women in their lives; the distaff side of the Founding Fathers. New York, Dodd, Mead [1966] 339 p. ports.   E302.5.D6

Contents: The mothers of the Founding Fathers.—Several women and Benjamin Franklin.—The unlucky loves of George Washington.—The one woman for John Adams.—The tragic loves of Thomas Jefferson.—Two women and Alexander Hamilton.—The late love of James Madison.—Epilogue.

12669
Egle, William H.   Some Pennsylvania women during the War of the Revolution. Harrisburg, Pa., Harrisburg Pub. Co., 1898. 208 p.   F148.E325

Reprinted under the title *Pennsylvania Women in the American Revolution* in Cottonport, La., by Polyanthos (1972).

12670
Ellet, Elizabeth F. L.   Pioneer women of the West. New York, C. Scribner, 1852. 434 p. front.   F479.E55

A supplement to her *Women of the American Revolution.*

12671
Ellet, Elizabeth F. L.   The women of the American Revolution. 2d ed. New York, Baker and Scribner, 1848–50. 3 v. ports.   E206.E44

Vol. 3: 1st edition.
Reprinted in New York by Haskell House (1969).

Includes biographical information on more than 150 named figures.

12672
Notable American women, 1607–1950; a biographical dictionary. Edward T. James, editor. Janet Wilson James, associate editor. Paul S. Boyer, assistant editor. Cambridge, Mass., Belknap Press of Harvard University Press, 1971. 3 v.   CT3260.N57

Contents: v. 1. A–F.—v. 2. G–O.—v. 3. P–Z.

Modeled after the *Dictionary of American Biography,* these volumes contain 1,359 biographical essays on women whose public work won them distinction in their own right beyond purely local significance. The essays, prepared by 738 contributors, contain bibliographic references and range from 400 words for colonial printer Ann Timothy to 7,000 words for Harriet Beecher Stowe. Of 706 women who appeared in the *DAB,* 179 were, for various reasons, omitted from Notable American Women. In the classified list of selected biographies (v. 3, p. 709–729), the editors arrange the names of subjects under such categories as Authors, Educators, Entrepreneurs, Feminists, Historians, Indian Captives, Missionaries, Social Leaders, and Wives of the Presidents.

Individual Figures (alphabetically arranged)

12673
ABBOT, JOHN (1750?–*ca.* 1840)
England; Georgia. Naturalist.

ALLEN, ELSA G.   John Abbot, pioneer naturalist of Georgia. Georgia historical quarterly, v. 41, June 1957: 143–157.   F281.G2975, v. 41

12674
ABBOTT, BENJAMIN (1732–1796)*
New Jersey. Farmer, Methodist circuit preacher.

———Experience and gospel labors of the Rev. Benjamin Abbott; to which is annexed, a narrative of his life and death, by John Ffirth. New-York, Carlton & Phillips, 1856. 284 p.   BX8495.A3A3 1856

12675
ACHENWALL, GOTTFRIED (1719–1772)
Germany. Professor.

——— Achenwall's observations on North America, 1767. Translated by Joseph G. Rosengarten. Pennsylvania magazine of history and biography, v. 27, Jan. 1903: 1–19.   F146.P65, v. 27

——— ——— Offprint. Philadelphia, 1903. 19 p.   E163.A19

Translation of *Einige Anmerkugen über Nord-Amerika* (Stuttgart, 1769).

12676
ACLAND, *Lady* CHRISTIAN HENRIETTA CAROLINA (1750–1815)† Known as Lady Harriet.
England.

TROUP, FRANCES B.   An English heroine in the American Revolution. New England magazine, new ser., v. 15, Jan. 1897: 585–599.   AP2.N4, n.s., v. 15

12677
ADAMS, ABIGAIL SMITH (1744–1818)*
Massachusetts. Wife of John Adams (1735–1826).

——— The Adams family in Auteuil, 1784–1785; as told in the letters of Abigail Adams. With an introduction and notes by Howard C. Rice, Jr. Boston, Massachusetts Historical Society, 1956. 31 p. illus., map, plates, port.   E322.1.A33

——— Letters of Mrs. Adams, the wife of John Adams. With an introductory memoir by her grandson, Charles Francis Adams. 4th ed., rev. and enl., with an appendix containing the letters addressed by John Q. Adams to his son on the study of the Bible. Boston, Wilkins, Carter, 1848. lxi, 472 p. facsim., port.   E322.1.A32

First edition published in Boston by C. C. Little and J. Brown (1840).

COIT, MARGARET L.   Dearest friends. American heritage, v. 19, Oct. 1968: 8–13, 102–106. illus. (part col.), facsims., col. ports.   E171.A43, v. 19

On the literary relationship between Abigail and John Adams during their many wartime separations.

RICHARDS, LAURA E. H.   Abigail Adams and her times. New York, D. Appleton, 1917. 282 p. plates, ports.
E322.1.R5

Reprinted in Ann Arbor, Mich., by Plutarch Press (1971).

WHITNEY, JANET P.   Abigail Adams. Boston, Little, Brown, 1947. xii, 357 p. maps (on lining papers), plates, ports.
E322.1.W5

Bibliography: p. [343]–348.

Reprinted in Westport, Conn., by Greenwood Press (1970).

12678

ADAMS, AMOS (1728–1775)

Massachusetts. Clergyman, writer.

LAWRENCE, ROBERT M.   The Rev. Amos Adams, A.M. (1728–1775), patriot minister of Roxbury, Massachusetts, and his American ancestry. Boston [S. Ward Co., Printers] 1912. 17 p. plate.
F74.R9L4

12679

ADAMS, HANNAH (1755–1831)*

Massachusetts. Historical writer.

——— A memoir of Miss Hannah Adams, written by herself. With additional notices, by a friend. Boston, Gray and Bowen, 1832. iv, 110 p. port.
PS1004.A37Z5 1832 Rare Bk. Coll.

"Notices in continuation," by Mrs. Hannah F. Lee: p. [45]–110.

TILDEN, OLIVE M.   Hannah Adams. Dedham historical register, v. 7, July 1896: 83–100. port.
F74.D3D8, v. 7

12680

ADAMS, JAMES (1725–1792)

Ireland; Delaware. Printer.

HAWKINS, DOROTHY L.   James Adams, the first printer of Delaware. In Bibliographical Society of America. Papers, v. 28, pt. 1, 1934: 28–63.   Z1008.B51P, v. 28

12681

ADAMS, JOHN (1735–1826)*

Massachusetts. Lawyer, writer, assemblyman, councilor, delegate to the Continental Congress, diplomat.

——— The Adams-Jefferson letters; the complete correspondence between Thomas Jefferson and Abigail and John Adams. Edited by Lester J. Cappon. Chapel Hill, Published for the Institute of Early American History and Culture at Williamsburg, Va., by the University of North Carolina Press [1959] 2 v. (li, 638 p.) illus., ports.
E322.A516

——— Correspondence between John Adams and Prof. John Winthrop [1775–76] In Massachusetts Historical Society, *Boston*. Collections. 5th ser., v. 4. Boston, 1878. p. 287–313.
F61.M41, 5th s., v. 4

———Diary and autobiography. L.H. Butterfield, editor. Leonard C. Faber and Wendell D. Garrett, assistant editors. Cambridge, Belknap Press of Harvard University Press, 1961. 4 v. illus., facsims., maps, ports. (*His* Papers. Series 1: Diaries)
E322.A3

Contents: v. 1. Diary, 1755–1770.—v. 2. Diary, 1771–1781.—v. 3. Diary, 1782–1804. Autobiography to October 1776.—v. 4. Autobiography, 1777–1780.

——— The earliest diary of John Adams; June 1753–April 1754, September 1758–January 1759. L. H. Butterfield, editor. Wendell D. Garrett and Marc Friedlaender, associate editors. Cambridge, Belknap Press of Harvard University Press, 1966. xx, 120 p. illus., ports. (The Adams papers, ser. 1, diaries)
E322.A34

"Diary and autobiography of John Adams, supplement."

——— Familiar letters of John Adams and his wife Abigail Adams, during the Revolution. With a memoir of Mrs. Adams. By Charles Francis Adams. New York, Hurd and Houghton, 1876. xxxii, 424 p. port.   E322.A518

Reprinted in Freeport, N.Y., by Books for Libraries Press (1970).

——— James Otis, Samuel Adams, and John Hancock. John Adams's tributes to these as the three principal movers and agents of the American Revolution. [Boston, Directors of the Old South Work, 1907] 20 p. (Old South leaflets. [General series, v. 8], no. 179)
E173.O44 v. 8

Letters to William Tudor and William Wirt, from volume 10 of his collected works.

——— The John Adams papers. Selected, edited, and interpreted by Frank Donovan. New York, Dodd, Mead [1965] 335 p. facsim., ports. (The Papers of the founding fathers)
E302.A275

——— Legal papers of John Adams. L. Kinvin Wroth and Hiller B. Zobel, editors. Cambridge, Mass., Belknap Press of Harvard University Press, 1965. 3 v. illus., facsims., map, plan, ports. (The Adams papers. Series 3. General correspondence and other papers of the Adams statesmen)
LL

Bibliographic footnotes.

——— Letters of John Adams, addressed to his wife. Edited by his grandson, Charles Francis Adams. Boston, C. C. Little and J. Brown, 1841. 2 v. port.   E302.A29

The letters bear dates from 1774 to 1801.

——— The selected writings of John and John Quincy Adams. Edited and with an introduction by Adrienne Koch and William Peden. New York, A. A. Knopf, 1946. xxxix (i.e. 41), 413, xxix p. ports.   E302.A28

"Bibliographical note: John Adams": p. 219–221.

——— Twenty-six letters, upon interesting subjects, respecting the Revolution of America. Written in Holland, in the year 1780. By His Excellency John Adams, while he was sole minister plenipotentiary from the United States of America, for negociating a peace, and a treaty of commerce with Great-Britain. [London] Printed for the subscribers [1786] 89 p.   E211.A214

Not "published"; hence the New York edition of 1789 bears on its title page: "Never before published."

————— The works of John Adams, second President of the United States: with a life of the author, notes, and illustrations, by his grandson Charles Francis Adams. Boston, Little, Brown, 1850–56 [v. 1, 1856] 10 v. facsims. (part fold.), plates, ports.   E302.A26
Micro 01291, reels 269–270E

Reprinted in Freeport, N.Y., by Books for Libraries Press (1969) and in New York by AMS Press (1971).

ADAMS, CHARLES FRANCIS.   The life of John Adams. Begun by John Quincy Adams. Completed by Charles Francis Adams. Rev. and corr. Philadelphia, J. B. Lippincott, 1871. 2 v.   E322.A52

Reprinted in New York by Haskell House (1968) and in St. Clair Shores, Mich., by Scholarly Press (1971).

ADAMS, JAMES T.   The Adams family. Boston, Little, Brown, 1930. vi, 364 p. illus., plates, ports.
E176.A23

Contents.—Preface.—Prologue.—The first generation: John Adams.—The second generation: John Quincy Adams.—The third generation: Charles Francis Adams.—The fourth generation: John Quincy, Charles Francis, Henry, and Brooks Adams.—Epilogue.

ADAMS FAMILY. Archives.   Adams family correspondence. L. H. Butterfield, editor; Wendell D. Garrett, associate editor; Marjorie E. Sprague, assistant editor. Cambridge, Belknap Press of Harvard University Press, 1963+ illus., charts, facsims., maps, ports. (The Adams papers, ser. 2)   E322.1.A27

Includes bibliographic references.
Contents: v. 1. December 1761–May 1776.—v. 2. June 1776–March 1778. Index.

ALLISON, JOHN M.   Adams and Jefferson: the story of a friendship. Norman, University of Oklahoma Press [1966] 349 p. ports.   E322.A6
Bibliographic footnotes.

BAILYN, BERNARD.   Butterfield's Adams: notes for a sketch. William and Mary quarterly, 3d ser., v. 19, Apr. 1962: 238–256.   F221.W71, 3d s., v. 19

Based upon a close reading of the Diary and Autobiography, edited by Lyman H. Butterfield.

BOSTON. PUBLIC LIBRARY. Adams Collection.   Catalogue of the John Adams Library in the public library of the city of Boston. Boston, The Trustees, 1917. viii, 271 p.
Z881.B752A

The Adams library of 2,756 volumes was presented to the town of Quincy, Mass., in 1822. The library was lodged, after various transfers, in the Boston Public Library in 1894.

Additions to the original collection brought the number of volumes to 3,019.

BOWEN, CATHERINE DRINKER.   John Adams and the American Revolution. Boston, Little, Brown, 1950. xvii, 699 p. illus., map (on lining paper), ports.
E322.B68

Bibliography: p. 646–676.

BREEN, TIMOTHY H.   John Adams' fight against innovation in the New England constitution, 1776. New England quarterly, v. 40, Dec. 1967: 501–520.
F1.N62, v. 40

BUTTERFIELD, LYMAN H.   The papers of the Adams family: some account of their history. In Massachusetts Historical Society, Boston. Proceedings. v. 71; 1953/57. Boston, 1959. p. 328–356.   F61.M38, v. 71

CALKINS, CARLOS G.   The American navy and the opinions of one of its founders, John Adams, 1735–1826. In United States Naval Institute. Proceedings, v. 37, June 1911: 453–483.   V1.U8, v. 37

CARROLL, WARREN H.   John Adams, puritan revolutionist: a study of his part in making the American Revolution, 1764–1776. 1959. ([457] p.)
Micro AC–1, no. 59–2839

Thesis (Ph.D.)—Columbia University.
Abstracted in Dissertation Abstracts, v. 20, Jan. 1960, p. 2767–2768.

CHAMBERLAIN, MELLEN.   John Adams, the statesman of the American Revolution. Address before the Webster Historical Society. Boston, Published by the Society, 1884. 85 p.   E322.C44

CHINARD, GILBERT.   Honest John Adams. Boston, Little, Brown [1964] xii, 359 p.   E322.C47 1964
Bibliographic footnotes.
First edition published in 1933.

CRONIN, JOHN W., and W. HARVEY WISE, Jr.   A bibliography of John Adams and John Quincy Adams. Washington, D.C., Riverford Pub. Co., 1935. 78 p. (Presidential bibliographical series, no. 2)
Z8015.6.C91

Includes 329 references to writings by or about John Adams.

DAUER, MANNING J.   The political economy of John Adams. Political science quarterly, v. 56, Dec. 1941: 545–572.   H1.P8, v. 56

DORFMAN, JOSEPH.   The regal republic of John Adams. Political science quarterly, v. 59, June 1944: 227–247.
H1.P8, v. 59

ELLSWORTH, JOHN W.   John Adams: the American Revolution as a change of heart? Huntington Library quarterly, v. 28, Aug. 1965: 293–300.
Z733.S24Q, v. 28

EVANS, WILLIAM B.   John Adams' opinion of Benjamin Franklin. Pennsylvania magazine of history and biography, v. 92, Apr. 1968: 220–238.   F146.P65, v. 92

FIELDING, HOWARD I.   John Adams: Puritan, deist, humanist. Journal of religion, v. 20, Jan. 1940: 33–46.   BR1.J65, v. 20

GARRETT, WENDELL D.   The papers of the Adams family: a natural resource of history. Historical New Hampshire, v. 21, fall 1966: 28–37.   F31.H57, v. 21

GUMMERE, RICHARD M.   The classical politics of John Adams. *In* Boston. Public Library. Quarterly, v. 9, Oct. 1957: 167–182.   Z881.B7535, v. 9

————John Adams, *Togatus*. Philological quarterly, v. 13, Apr. 1934: 203–210.   P1.P55, v. 13

HANDLER, EDWARD.   America and Europe in the political thought of John Adams. Cambridge, Harvard University Press, 1964. ix, 248 p.   E322.H227

Bibliographic references included in "Notes" (p. 229–242).

HARASZTI, ZOLTÁN.   John Adams & the prophets of progress. Cambridge, Harvard University Press, 1952. viii, 362 p. port., facsims.   E322.H3

Bibliographic references included in "Notes" (p. [303]–352).

Following a three-chapter introduction, the author presents selections from notes written by Adams in the margins of his books as he read them, indicating his response to the ideas of such authors as Bolingbroke, Rousseau, Voltaire, d'Alembert, Condorcet, and Priestley.

————John Adams and Turgot. *In* Boston. Public Library. Quarterly, v. 1, July 1949: 3–32.   Z881.B7535, v. 1

HARBERT, EARL N.   John Adams' private voice: the *Diary* and *Autobiography. In* Tulane studies in English. v. 15; 1967. New Orleans. p. 89–105.   PR13.T8, v. 15

HAYES, FREDERIC H.   John Adams and American sea power. American Neptune, v. 25, Jan 1965: 35–45.   V1.A4, v. 25

HOWE, JOHN R.   The changing political thought of John Adams. Princeton, N.J., Princeton University Press, 1966. xv, 259 p.   E322.H6

"Bibliographical essay": p. [253]–254. Bibliographic footnotes.

The author's thesis (Ph.D.), *The Search for Stability: An Essay in the Social Thought of John Adams*, was submitted to Yale University in 1963.

IACUZZI, ALFRED.   John Adams, scholar. New York, S. F. Vanni (Ragusa) [1952] 306 p.   E322.I15

"Bibliographical note and references": p. 268–296.

KNOLLENBERG, BERNHARD.   The correspondence of John Adams and Horatio Gates [1776–80] *In* Massachusetts

Historical Society, *Boston*. Proceedings. v. 67; 1941/44. Boston, 1945. p. 135–151.   F61.M38, v. 67

———— John Adams, Knox, and Washington. *In* American Antiquarian Society, *Worcester, Mass.* Proceedings, new ser., v. 56, Oct. 1946: 207–238.

E172.A35, n.s., v.56

Includes Adams-Knox correspondence, 1775–81.

KURTZ, STEPHEN G.   The political science of John Adams: a guide to his statecraft. William and Mary quarterly, 3d ser., v. 25, Oct. 1968: 605–613.

F221.W71, 3d s., v. 25

MEAD, EDWIN D.   John Adams, national statesman, 1735–1826. *In* Hart, Albert B., *ed.* Commonwealth history of Massachusetts. v. 3. Commonwealth of Massachusetts, 1775–1820. New York, States History Co., 1929. p. 212–250. illus.   F64.H32, v. 3

Bibliography: p. 249–250.

MEYER, ISIDORE S.   John Adams writes a letter. *In* American Jewish Historical Society. Publications. no. 37. New York, 1947. p. 185–201. facsims.

E184.J5A5, no. 37

Explores the origins of Adams' attitude toward Jews as expressed in a letter to Francis Adrian Van der Kemp, dated February 16, 1809.

MORSE, ANSON D.   The politics of John Adams [1765–1800] American historical review, v. 4, Jan. 1899: 292–312.   E171.A57, v. 4

MORSE, JOHN T.   John Adams. Boston, Houghton, Mifflin, 1885. vi, 337 p. (American statesmen [v. 6])   E176.A53, v. 6

Reprinted in New Rochelle, N.Y., by Arlington House (1970).

PEEK, GEORGE A.   John Adams on the nature of man and government. Michigan alumnus quarterly review, v. 58, autumn 1951: 70–76. port.   AP2.M53, v. 58

RIPEL, BARBARA D.   The political mind of John Adams: a study of the continuity in his thought. 1971. ([283] p.)   Micro AC–1, no. 72–6408

Thesis (Ph.D.)—State University of New York at Stony Brook.

Abstracted in *Dissertation Abstracts International*, v. 32A, Feb. 1972, p. 4537.

RIPLEY, RANDALL B.   Adams, Burke, and eighteenth-century conservatism. Political science quarterly, v. 80, June 1965: 216–235.   H1.P8, v. 80

Often linked because of similarities in temperament, Adams and Burke nonetheless held opposing views on the Enlightenment.

ROBATHAN, DOROTHY M.   John Adams and the classics. New England quarterly, v. 19, Mar. 1946: 91–98.

F1.N62, v. 19

ROSSITER, CLINTON L.   Homage to John Adams. Michigan alumnus quarterly review, v. 64, spring 1958: 228–238.   AP2.M53, v. 64

On his political career and thought.

———The legacy of John Adams. Yale review, new ser., v. 46, June 1957: 528–550.   AP2.Y2, n.s., v. 46

SMITH, PAGE.   John Adams. Garden City, N.Y., Doubleday, 1962. 2 v. (xx, 1170 p.) illus., facsims., ports.   E322.S64

Includes bibliographic references.
Contents: v. 1. 1735–1784.—v. 2. 1784–1826.
Reprinted in Westport, Conn., by Greenwood Press (1969).

THORPE, FRANCIS N.   The political ideas of John Adams. Pennsylvania magazine of history and biography, v. 14, Jan. 1920: 1–46.   F146.P65, v. 14

WALSH, CORREA M.   The political science of John Adams; a study in the theory of mixed government and the bicameral system. New York, G. P. Putnam's Sons, 1915. xii, 374 p.   JK171.A3W3

Reprinted in Freeport, N.Y., by Books for Libraries Press (1969).

12682
ADAMS, JOHN QUINCY (1767–1848)*
Massachusetts. Diplomatic clerk.

——— Life in a New England town: 1787, 1788. Diary of John Quincy Adams, while a student in the office of Theophilus Parsons at Newburyport. Boston, Little, Brown, 1903. 204 p. port.   F74.N55A2

Introduction signed "C. F. A." (i.e., Charles Francis Adams).

First published in the Massachusetts Historical Society *Proceedings*, v. 36, for 1902 (Boston, 1903), p. 291–464.

EAST, ROBERT A.   John Quincy Adams; the critical years: 1785–1794. New York, Bookman Associates [1962] 252 p.   E377.E2

"Bibliographical aids": p. 195–198.

MUSTO, DAVID F.   The youth of John Quincy Adams. *In* American Philosophical Society, *Philadelphia*. Proceedings, v. 113, Aug. 1969: 269–282. facsim.   Q11.P5, v. 113

12683
ADAMS, JOSIAH (1757–1852)
Massachusetts. Revolutionary officer, farmer.

——— Letters written by Josiah Adams of Newbury during service in the Revolution [1775–77] *In* Essex Institute, *Salem, Mass.* Historical collections, v. 77, Apr. 1941: 143–160.   F72.E7E81, v. 77

12684
ADAMS, RICHARD (1726–1800)
Virginia. Landowner, assemblyman.

——— Letters of Richard Adams to Thomas Adams [1771–78] Virginia magazine of history and biography, v. 22, Oct. 1914: 379–395.   F221.V91, v. 22

12685
ADAMS, SAMUEL (1722–1803)*
Massachusetts. Assemblyman, political writer, delegate to the Continental Congress.

——— Adams-Savage correspondence, 1776–1785. *In* Massachusetts Historical Society, *Boston*. Proceedings. v. 43; 1909/10. Boston, 1910. p. 327–336.   F61.M38, v. 43

——— The writings of Samuel Adams. Collected and edited by Harry Alonzo Cushing. New York, G. P. Putnam's Sons, 1904–8. 4 v.   E302.A31

Contents: v. 1. 1764–1769.—v. 2. 1770–1773.—v. 3. 1773–1777.—v. 4. 1778–1802.
Reprinted in New York by Octagon Books (1968).

BEACH, STEWART.   Samuel Adams; the fateful years, 1764–1776. New York, Dodd, Mead [1965] xiv, 329 p. illus., ports.   E302.6.A2B4

Bibliography: p. 313–321.

FALLOWS, SAMUEL, *Bp.*   Samuel Adams, a character sketch. With supplementary essay, by G. Mercer Adam. Together with anecdotes, characteristics, and chronology by L. B. Vaughan and others. Milwaukee, H. G. Campbell Pub. Co., 1903. 178 p. illus., port. (Great Americans of history)   E207.A2F22

Original copyright, 1898.
Bibliography: p. 178.

GOODELL, ABNER C.   The charges against Samuel Adams. *In* Massachusetts Historical Society, *Boston*. Proceedings. v. 20; 1882/83. Boston, 1884. p. 213–226.   F61.M38, v. 20

HARLOW, RALPH V.   Samuel Adams, promoter of the American Revolution; a study in psychology and politics. New York, H. Holt, 1923. x, 363 p.   E302.6.A2H2

The author's article, "A Psychological Study of Samuel Adams," appeared in the *Psychoanalytic Review*, v. 9, no. 4, 1922, p. 418–428.

HOSMER, JAMES K.   Samuel Adams. Boston, Houghton, Mifflin, 1885. xv, 442 p. (American statesmen)   E207.A2H81

The 1898 edition has been reprinted in New York by AMS Press (E302.6.A2H6 1972).

——— Samuel Adams, the man of the town meeting. Baltimore, N. Murray, Publication Agent, Johns Hopkins

1054 / REVOLUTIONARY AMERICA

University, 1884. 60 p. (Johns Hopkins University studies in historical and political science, 2d ser., v. 4)
H31.J6, 2d s., v. 4
E302.6.A2H84

MILLER, JOHN C. Sam Adams; pioneer in propaganda. Boston, Little, Brown, 1936. 437 p. illus., plates, ports.
E302.6.A2M56

Bibliographic footnotes.
Reprinted in Stanford, Calif., by Stanford University Press (1960).
The author's thesis (Ph.D.), with the same title, was submitted to Harvard University in 1939.

SOMERVILLE, JAMES K. Patriot moralist: an intellectual portrait of Samuel Adams. 1965. ([191] p.)
Micro AC–1, no. 66–8032

Thesis (Ph.D.)—Western Reserve University.
Abstracted in *Dissertation Abstracts*, v. 27A, Aug. 1966, p. 446–447.

TOWNSEND, CHARLES R. The thought of Samuel Adams. 1968. ([348] p.) Micro AC–1, no. 68–7136

Thesis (Ph.D.)—University of Wisconsin.
Abstracted in *Dissertation Abstracts*, v. 29A, Aug. 1968, p. 532.

WARREN, CHARLES. Samuel Adams and the Sans Souci Club in 1785. *In* Massachusetts Historical Society, *Boston*. Proceedings. v. 60; 1926/27. Boston, 1927. p. 318–344.
F61.M38, v. 60

WELLS, WILLIAM V. The life and public services of Samuel Adams, being a narrative of his acts and opinions, and of his agency in producing and forwarding the American Revolution. With extracts from his correspondence, state papers, and political essays. Boston, Little, Brown, 1865. 3 v. ports.
E302.6.A2W4

The 1888 edition was reprinted in Freeport, N.Y., by Books for Libraries Press (1969).

WILLIAMS, WILLIAM A. Samuel Adams: Calvinist, mercantilist, revolutionary. Studies on the left, v. 1, winter 1960: 47–57.
HM1.S85, v. 1

WINSTON, ALEXANDER. Firebrand of the Revolution. American heritage, v. 18, Apr. 1967: 60–64, 105–108. illus (part col.), col. port.
E171.A43, V. 18

12686

ADAMS, SAMUEL (1745–1819)
Massachusetts. Revolutionary surgeon, midwife.

HUNTER, THOMAS M. Doctor Samuel Adams: Revolutionary Army surgeon and diarist. United States armed forces medical journal, v. 8, May 1957: 625–643.
RC970.U7, v. 8

SCOTT, KENNETH. The cruise of the whaler *Nightingale* in 1768. American Neptune, v. 23, Jan. 1963: 22–28.
V1.A4, v. 23

Based on a journal kept by Adams, who was ship's doctor on the cruise.

12687

ADAMS, THOMAS (1730–1788)
Virginia. Assemblyman, landowner, delegate to the Continental Congress.

——— Letters of Thomas Adams, 1768–1775. Virginia magazine of history and biography, v. 23, Jan. 1915: 52–65.
F221.V91, v. 23

12688

ADLUM, JOHN (1759–1836)*
Pennsylvania; Maryland. Revolutionary soldier, farmer, winemaker.

——— Memoirs of the life of John Adlum in the Revolutionary War. Edited with an introduction by Howard H. Peckham. Chicago, Published for the William L. Clements Library Associates by the Caxton Club, 1968. vii, 143 p.
E275.A3A3

GAHN, BESSIE W. B. Major John Adlum of Rock Creek. *In* Columbia Historical Society, *Washington, D.C.* Records. v. 39, Washington, 1938. p. 127–139. plates.
F191.C72, v. 39

12689

AGENO, FRANCESCO MARIA (1727–1788)

Genoa *(Republic). Legazione. Gt. Brit.* I casi della guerra per l'indipendenza d'America, narrati dall'ambasciatore della Repubblica di Genova, presso la corte d'Inghilterra, nella sua corrispondenza ufficiale inedita, per Giuseppe Colucci. Genova, Tip. del R. Istituto sordomuti, 1879. 2 v. in 3.
E203.G33

Volume 1, part 1 contains a biographical sketch by the editor of Ageno, ambassador of Genoa at London from 1760 to 1781, and an historical account of the foundation and development of the British colonies in North America. Volume 1, part 2 and volume 2 contain the letters of Ageno, covering the years 1770 and 1774–80.

12690

AIKMAN, LOUISA SUSANNAH WELLS (1755?–1831)
South Carolina; Jamaica.

——— The journal of a voyage from Charlestown, S.C., to London, undertaken during the American Revolution by a daughter of an eminent American Loyalist (Louisa Susannah Wells) in the year 1778, and written from memory only in 1779. New York, Printed for the New York Historical Society, 1906. 121 p. facsim., port. (The New York Historical Society. The John Divine Jones fund series of histories and memoirs, 2)
E278.A2A29

Reprinted in New York by the New York Times (1968).

12691

AITKEN, JAMES (1752–1777)†
Scotland; England. Painter, soldier.

—— The whole of the proceedings upon the trial of James Hill, otherwise James Hind, otherwise John Hind, otherwise James Acksan, commonly called, John the Painter, on Thursday, March the 6th, 1777. At the Assizes, held at the castle at Winchester, for the county of Hants. Before the Right Honourable Sir William Henery Ashurst, Knt. and Sir Beaumont Hotham, Knt. Taken in short hand by William Blanchard. London, Printed for J. Wenman [1777?] 34 p.   LL

CLARK, WILLIAM B.   John the Painter. Pennsylvania magazine of history and biography, v. 63, Jan. 1939: 1–23. plates.   F146.P65, v. 63

Describes the incindiary activities of "John the Painter" in Portsmouth and Bristol. Attempting to aid the American cause by burning warehouses and docks, the deluded Scotsman was hanged for arson in 1777.

KNAPP, MARY E.   John the Painter and Silas Deane. Yale University Library gazette, v. 29, Apr. 1955: 137–147.   Z733.Y17G, v. 29

SENIOR, WILLIAM.   John the Painter. Mariner's mirror, v. 10, Oct. 1924: 355–365.   VK1.M4, v. 10

SYDENHAM, M. J.   Firing His Majesty's dockyard: Jack the Painter and the American mission to France, 1776–1777. History today, v. 16, May 1966: 324–331. illus., ports.   D1.H818, v. 16

12692

ALEXANDER, JOHN (*ca.* 1738–1799)

Ireland; South Carolina. Clergyman, farmer.

PARRAMORE, THOMAS C.   John Alexander, Anglican missionary. North Carolina historical review, v. 43, summer 1966: 305–315.   F251.N892, v. 43

12693

ALEXANDER, ROBERT (1740?–1805)

Maryland; England. Lawyer, delegate to the Continental Congress, Loyalist.

JOHNSON, JANET B.   Robert Alexander, Maryland Loyalist. New York, G. P. Putnam's Sons [1942] xiii, 152 p. fold. facsim.   E278.A3J6

"References": p. 128–148.
Reprinted, with a new introduction and preface by George A. Billias, in Boston by Gregg Press (1972).

THOMPSON, HENRY F.   A Maryland Loyalist. Maryland historical magazine, v. 1, Dec. 1906: 316–323.   F176.M18, v. 1

12694

ALEXANDER, WILLIAM (1726–1783)*† Also called Lord Stirling.

New York; New Jersey. Mathematician, astronomer, merchant, councilor, Revolutionary general.

—— Letters of William Alexander, Lord Stirling [1773–81] from the Ely collection. *In* New Jersey Historical Society. Proceedings, v. 60, July 1942: 171–179.   F131.N58, v. 60

—— Selections from the correspondence of William Alexander, earl of Stirling [1763–81] *In* New Jersey Historical Society. Proceedings, v. 7, no. 3, 1854–no. 4, 1855: 111–116, 136–148.   F131.N58, v. 7

DANFORTH, GEORGE H.   Lord Stirling's Hibernia furnace [1767–79] *In* New Jersey Historical Society. Proceedings, v. 71, July 1953: 174–186. illus.   F131.N58, v. 71

—— The rebel earl. 1955. ([302] p.)   Micro AC–1, no. 12,421

Thesis (Ph.D.)—Columbia University.
Abstracted in *Dissertation Abstracts*, v. 15, no. 7, 1955, p. 1226–1227.

DITMAS, CHARLES A.   The life and service of Major-General William Alexander also called the Earl of Stirling. Brooklyn, N.Y., Printed for the Society [by the Brooklyn Eagle Press] 1920. 15 p. port. (Kings County Historical Society. Contributions to American history, no. 1)   F127.K5K64
                E207.A3D6

Bibliography: p. 15.

DUER, WILLIAM A.   The life of William Alexander, earl of Stirling; major general in the army of the United States, during the Revolution: with selections from his correspondence. New York, Published for the New Jersey Historical Society by Wiley & Putnam, 1847. xv, 272 p. plans, port. (Collections of the New Jersey Historical Society, v. 2)   F131.N62, v. 2
                E207.A3D8

HEATHCOTE, CHARLES W.   General Stirling—devoted patriot. Picket post, no. 44, Apr. 1954: 39–44. port.   E234.P5, no. 44

LONGLEY, R. S.   Lord Stirling: titled Whig of the American Revolution. *In* Royal Society of Canada. Transactions. 3d ser., v. 56, section 2; 1962. Ottawa. p. 11–22.   AS42.R6, 3d s., v. 56

OGDEN, DAVID.   The plea and answer of the Right Hounourable William, Earl of Stirling, and others, proprietors of East New-Jersey, to John Hunt's bill in Chancery. New-York, Printed by J. Holt, 1770. 38, [13] p.   LL

Signed: David Ogden, Cortlandt Skinner, in their own names, and of council for the defendants.

SCHUMACHER, LUDWIG.   Major-General the earl of Stirling; an essay in biography. New York, New Amsterdam Book Co., 1897. 57 p. ports.   E207.A3S3

Bibliography: p. 55–57.

VALENTINE, ALAN C.   Lord Stirling. New York, Oxford University Press, 1969. 299 p. port.   E207.A3V3

Bibliography: p. 282–286.

VOORHEES, OSCAR M. William Alexander, Earl of Stirling. American collector, v. 1, Mar. 1926: 207–216. port.   Z1007.A475, v. 1

12695

ALISON, FRANCIS (1751–1813)

Pennsylvania. Revolutionary surgeon.

RADBILL, SAMUEL X. Francis Alison, Jr.—a surgeon of the Revolution. Bulletin of the history of medicine, v. 9, Mar. 1941: 243–257. facsims.   R11.B93, v. 9

12696

ALLAN, JOHN (1746–1805)*

Scotland; Nova Scotia; Maine. Farmer, merchant, assemblyman, Indian agent, Revolutionary officer.

ALLAN, GEORGE H. Memoir of Colonel John Allan, an officer of the Revolution, born in Edinburgh Castle, Scotland, Jan. 3, 1746. Died in Lubec, Maine, Feb. 7, 1805. Albany, J. Munsell, 1867. 32 p.   E207.A36A4

"Genealogy of the Allan family": p. [25]–32.

—— Sketch of Col. John Allan of Maine. New-England historical and genealogical register, v. 30, July 1876: 353–359.   F1.N56, v. 30

KIDDER, FREDERIC. Military operations in eastern Maine and Nova Scotia during the Revolution. Chiefly compiled from the journals and letters of Col. John Allan, with notes and a memoir of Col. John Allan. Albany, J. Munsell, 1867. x, 336 p. fold. map.   E263.M2K4

"Nova Scotia" refers to what is now New Brunswick.

SPRAGUE, JOHN F. Colonel John Allan. Sprague's journal of Maine history, v. 2, Feb. 1915: 233–257. facsim.   F16.S76, v. 2

12697

ALLARD, ANDREW (d. 1777)

Massachusetts. Revolutionary soldier.

WEHMANN, HOWARD H. Your loving Andrew Allard. Prologue, the journal of the National Archives, v. 2, fall 1970: 90–95. facsims., map.   CD3020.P75, v. 2

12698

ALLASON, WILLIAM (ca. 1720–1800)

Scotland; Virginia. Merchant, planter.

—— The letters of William Allason, merchant, of Falmouth, Virginia [1757–89] In Richmond College historical papers. v. 2, no. 1; 1917. p. 118–175.   F221.R53, v. 2

THOMSON, EDITH E. B. A Scottish merchant in Falmouth in the eighteenth century. Virginia magazine of history and biography, v. 39, Apr.–July 1931: 108–117, 230–238.   F221.V91, v. 39

12699

ALLEN, BENNET (ca. 1737–ca. 1814)†

England; Maryland. Anglican clergyman, Loyalist.

FISHER, JOSEPHINE. Bennet Allen, fighting parson. Maryland historical magazine, v. 38, Dec. 1943: 299–322; v. 39, Mar. 1944: 49–72.   F176.M18, v. 38–39

12700

ALLEN, ETHAN (1738–1789)*

Connecticut; Vermont. Revolutionary officer, political writer.

—— Reason the only oracle of man; or, A compenduous system of natural religion. Alternately adorned with confutations of a variety of doctrines incompatible to it; deduced from the most exalted ideas which we are able to form of the divine and human characters, and from the universe in general. Bennington, state of Vermont, Printed by Haswell & Russell, 1784. 477 p.
                          BL2773.A5 Rare Bk. Coll.

Reprinted, with an introduction by John Pell, in New York by Scholars' Facsimiles & Reprints (1940. xii p., facsim.: 477 p.; 70 p. BL2773.A5 1784a). "The Appendix to Reason," reprinted from the *Historical Magazine*, v. 22, Apr.–June 1873, p. 193–196, 274–282, 330–333, and v. 23, July–Aug., p. 29–32, 76–82, comprises the 70-page addition.

The scarcest of Allen's works; the greater part of the edition was destroyed by fire in the printing office. An abridged edition was published in New York by G. W. & A. I. Matsell in 1836. This was the first publication in the United States that openly attacked the Christian religion.

ANDERSON, GEORGE P. Who Wrote "Ethan Allen's Bible"? New England quarterly, v. 10, Dec. 1937: 685–696.   F1.N62, v. 10

Finds that the text of Allen's *Reason the Only Oracle of Man* was written largely by Dr. Thomas Young (1732–1777).

BENEDICT, ROBERT D. Ethan Allen's use of language. *In* Vermont Historical Society. Proceedings, 1901/2. [Burlington] 1903. p. [65]–86.   F46.V55, 1901/2

Reprinted in the *Magazine of History, With Notes and Queries*, v. 1, Mar. 1905, p. 162–175.

BUCKHAM, JOHN W. The Robin Hood of Vermont, New England quarterly, new ser., v. 25, Sept. 1901: 102–119. illus., facsims., ports.   AP2.N4, n.s., v. 25

CASSARA, ERNEST. Ethan Allen as philosopher. Vermont history, v. 35, autumn 1967: 208–221. F46.V55, v.35

DE PUY, HENRY W. Ethan Allen and the Green-Mountain heroes of '76. With a sketch of the early history of Vermont. Buffalo, Phinney, 1853. 428 p. map, plates.   F52.D4

Ethan Allen's narrative of his captivity: p. 213–278.
Reprinted in Freeport, N.Y., by Books for Libraries Press (1970).

DITSKY, JOHN. The Yankee insolence of Ethan Allen. Canadian review of American studies, v. 1, spring 1970: 32–38.   F1029.5.U6C35, v. 1

DOTEN, DANA. Ethan Allen's "original something." New England quarterly, v. 11, June 1938: 361–366.   F1.N62, v. 11

On unique aspects of Allen's personality.

GOHDES, CLARENCE L. F. Ethan Allen and his *Magnum Opus.* Open court, v. 43, Mar. 1929: 129–151.   AP2.O495, v. 43

HALL HENRY. Ethan Allen, the Robin Hood of Vermont. New York, D. Appleton, 1892. viii, 207 p.   E207.A4H2

HOLBROOK, STEWART H. Ethan Allen. New York, Macmillan Co., 1940. viii, 283 p. map.   E207.A4H6

"Acknowledgments and bibliography": p. 275–278.
An illustrated edition was published in Portland, Ore., by Binford & Mort (1958).

ISHAM, EDWARD S. Ethan Allen; a study in civic authority. *In* Vermont Historical Society. Proceedings. 1898. Burlington, 1899. p. 25–103.   F46.V55, 1898

———— ———— Detached copy.   E207.A4I7

JELLISON, CHARLES A. Ethan Allen: frontier rebel. [Syracuse, N.Y.] Syracuse University Press [1969] viii, 360 p. map.   E207.A4J4

Bibliographic references included in "Notes" (p. 335–350).

MOORE, HUGH. Memoir of Col. Ethan Allen. Plattsburg, N.Y., O. R. Cook, 1834. 252 p.   E207.A4M8

PELL, JOHN. Ethan Allen. Boston, Houghton Mifflin Co., 1929. xii, 331 p. facsims., map, plan, plates, ports.   E207.A4P38
"Bibliography and key to chronology and notes": p. [271]–279.

"Chronology and notes": p. [281]–317.
Reprinted in Freeport, N.Y., by Books for Libraries Press (1972).

————Ethan Allen's literary career. New England quarterly, v. 2, Oct. 1929: 585–602.   F1.N62, v. 2

RIFE, CLARENCE W. Ethan Allen; an interpretation. New England quarterly v. 2, Oct. 1929: 561–584.   F1.N62, v. 2

SCHANTZ, BRADFORD T. Ethan Allen's religious ideas. Journal of religion, v. 18, Apr. 1938: 183–217.   BR1.J65, v. 18

SHAPIRO, DARLINE. Ethan Allen: philosopher-theologian to a generation of American revolutionaries. William and Mary quarterly, 3d ser., v. 21, Apr. 1964: 236–255.   F221.W71, 3d s., v. 21

SPARKS, JARED. The life of Col. Ethan Allen. Burlington [Vt.] C. Goodrich, 1858. [89]–226 p.   E207.A4S7

A reprint of *The Life* published together with Daniel Chipman's *Memoir of Colonel Seth Warner* (Middlebury, 1848).
First published in 1834 in volume 1 of Sparks' *Library of American Biography.*

12701
ALLEN, IRA (1751–1814)*
Connecticut; Vermont. Councilor, land speculator.

———— Allen letters in the possession of the Vermont Historical Society. *In* Vermont Historical Society. Proceedings. 1917/18. [Montpelier] 1920. p. [141]–189.   F46.V55, 1917/18

Public and private correspondence.

CROCKETT, WALTER H. Gen. Ira Allen, of Vermont, and his part in Colchester's history. Genealogical quarterly magazine, [3d] ser., v. 2, Dec. 1900: 255–278.   F1.P98, [3d] s., v. 2

GOODRICH, JOHN E. The founder of the University of Vermont. A centennial oration on the life and public services of General Ira Allen. *In* Vermont. University. Centennial addresses. 1891/92; [pt. 2. Burlington, 1892] 45 p.   LD5633.B4, 1891/92

———— ———— Another copy.   E207.A44G6

Historical Records Survey. *Vermont.* Calendar of Ira Allen papers in the Wilbur Library, University of Vermont. Montpelier, Vt., Historical Records Survey, 1939. 149 p.   CD3559.B8H5
Mimeographed.

THOMPSON, DANIEL P. Life, character, and times of Ira Allen. *In* Vermont Historical Society. Proceedings. 1908/9. [Montpelier, 1909] p. 87–172.   F46.V55, 1908/9

WILBUR, JAMES B. Ira Allen, founder of Vermont, 1751–1814. Boston, Houghton Mifflin Co., 1928. 2 v. facsims., map, plates, ports.   F52.W65
Bibliography: v. 2, p. [527]–531.

12702
ALLEN, JAMES (*ca.* 1742–1778)
Pennsylvania. Lawyer, assemblyman.

———— Diary of James Allen, Esq., of Philadelphia, counsellor-at-law, 1770–1778. Pennsylvania magazine of history and biography, v. 9, July 1885–Jan. 1886: 176–196, 278–296, 424–441.   F146.P65, v. 9

HEYL, JOHN K. Trout Hall and its owner, James Allen, Esq. *In* Lehigh County Historical Society, Allentown, Pa. Proceedings. v. 24; 1962. Allentown, p. [59]–95. illus., ports.   F157.L5L52, v. 24

12703
ALLEN, JOHN (*fl.* 1741–1772)†
England; Massachusetts. Baptist clergyman, orator.

BUMSTED, JOHN M. *and* CHARLES E. CLARK. New England's Tom Paine: John Allen and the spirit of liberty. William and Mary quarterly, 3d ser., v. 21, Oct. 1964: 561–570.   F221.W71, 3d s., v. 21

12704

ALLEN, JOLLEY (1718–1782)

England; Massachusetts. Merchant, Loyalist.

———— An account of part of the sufferings and losses of Jolley Allen, a native of London. *In* Massachusetts Historical Society, *Boston*. Proceedings. v. 16; 1878. Boston, 1879.   F61.M38, v. 16

Introduction and notes by Charles C. Smith.

———— ———— Offprint. With a preface and notes by Mrs. Frances Mary Stoddard. Boston, Rand, Avery, 1883. 52 p.   E278.A4A42

12705

ALLEN, RICHARD, *Bp.* (1760–1831)*

Pennsylvania. Methodist clergyman.

———— The life, experience, and gospel labors of the Rt. Rev. Richard Allen, to which is annexed the rise and progress of the African Methodist Episcopal church in the United States of America. Containing a narrative of the yellow fever in the year of Our Lord 1793. With an address to the people of color in the United States. Written by himself and published by his request. With an introduction by George A. Singleton. New York, Abingdon Press [1960] 93 p. illus.
                    BX8449.A6A3 1960

First published in 1793.

WESLEY, CHARLES H. Richard Allen, apostle of freedom. [2d ed.] Washington, Associated Publishers [ᶜ1969] xii, 383 p. illus.   BX8449.A6W4 1969

Bibliography: p. 280–288.
First edition published in 1935.

12706

ALLEN, SAMUEL (1757–1830)

New Jersey. Landowner, Revolutionary officer.

ALLEN, ETHAN, b. 1832. Adventures of a "minute man" in the American Revolution. Journal of American history, v. 3, Apr./June 1909: 297–310.   E171.J86, v. 3

12707

ALLEN, THOMAS (1743–1810)

Massachusetts. Congregational clergyman, Revolutionary chaplain.

BIRDSALL, RICHARD D. The Reverend Thomas Allen, Jeffersonian Calvinist. New England quarterly, v. 30, June 1957: 147–165.   F1.N62, v. 30

BURNHAM, SAMUEL. Rev. Thomas Allen. Cambridge, Welch, Bigelow, Printers, 1869. 21 p. port.
                    BX7260.A52B8

From the *Congregational Quarterly* for October 1869.

GRINNELL, FRANK W. The influence of Thomas Allen and the "Berkshire Constitutionalists" on the constitutional history of the United States. American Bar Association journal, v. 22, Feb. 1936: 168–174, 210–211.
                    K1.M385, v. 22

PLUNKETT, *Mrs.* H. M. "Fighting Parson Allen." New York genealogical and biographical record, v. 28, Oct. 1897: 185–189; v. 30, Jan.–Apr. 1899: 43–46, 79–83. port.   F116.N28, v. 28, 30

12708

ALLEN, WILLIAM (1704–1780)*

Pennsylvania; England. Merchant, assemblyman, judge, Loyalist.

———— Extracts from Chief Justice William Allen's letter book. Selected and arranged by Lewis Burd Walker. Together with an appendix containing pamphlets in the controversy with Franklin. [Pottsville, Pa., Standard Pub. Co.] 1897. 136 p. port. (The Burd papers [v. 1])
                    F152.A43

Appendix: A protest presented to the House of Assembly, by the subscribers, at the close of the late debate there, concerning the sending Mr. Franklin as an assistant to our agent, at the court of Great-Britain.—Remarks on a late protest against the appointment of Mr. Franklin an agent for this province, signed: B. Franklin.—An answer to Mr. Franklin's remarks on a late protest [by William Smith]

———— William Allen-Benjamin Chew correspondence, 1763–1764. Pennsylvania magazine of history and biography, v. 90, Apr. 1966: 202–226.
                    F146.P65, v. 90

Introduction and notes by David A. Kimball and Miriam Quinn.

COHEN, NORMAN S. William Allen: chief justice of Pennsylvania, 1704–1780. 1966. ([374] p.)
                    Micro AC–1, no. 66–8292

Thesis (Ph.D.)—University of California, Berkeley. Abstracted in *Dissertation Abstracts*, v. 27A, Sept. 1966, p. 723.

KISTLER, RUTH M. William Allen, Pennsylvania Loyalist, 1704–1780. *In* Lehigh County Historical Society, *Allentown, Pa.* Proceedings. 1932. Allentown. p. [45]–102.   F157.L5L52, 1932

A reprint, with minor revisions, appeared in volume 24 (Allentown, 1962), p. 5–58.

———— William Allen, provincial man of affairs. Pennsylvania history, v. 1, July 1934: 165–174.
                    F146.P597, v. 1

PARSONS, WILLIAM T. William Allen as seen by a contemporary [Isaac Norris II] *In* Lehigh County Historical

Society, *Allentown, Pa.* Proceedings. v. 25; 1964. Allentown, p. 161–172.   F157.L5L52, v. 25

ROBERTS, CHARLES R.   William Allen, the founder of Allentown, and his descendants. *In* Lehigh County Historical Society, *Allentown, Pa.* Proceedings and papers. v. 1; 1908. Allentown. p. 22–43. ports.
                        F157.L5L52, v.1

12709

ALLEN, WILLIAM (1751–*ca.* 1833)
    Pennsylvania. Loyalist officer. Son of William Allen (1704–1780).

TREXLER, SCOTT A., *and* LEE A. WALCK.   Rebel and Tory colonel, Lieutenant Colonel William Allen, Jr. Edited by Mildred Rowe Trexler. *In* Lehigh County Historical Society, *Allentown, Pa.* Proceedings. v. 26; 1966. Allentown. p. [9]–84. facsims. (part fold.)
                        F157.L5L52, v. 26

12710

ALLINE, HENRY (1748–1784)*
    Rhode Island; Nova Scotia. Itinerant clergyman.

ARMSTRONG, MAURICE W.   Henry Alline: 1748–1784. Hymn, v. 7, July 1956: 73–78.   ML1.H92, v. 7

On 488 hymns published in his *Hymns and Spiritual Songs* (Boston, 1786).

12711

ALMON, JOHN (1737–1085)†
    England. Printer, publisher, pamphleteer.

——Memoirs of John Almon, bookseller, of Piccadilly. London, 1790. 262 p.   Z325.A5

—— *defendant.*   The trial of John Almon, bookseller, upon an information, filed ex officio, by William De Grey, Esq.; His Majesty's attorney-general, for selling Junius's letter to the K———. Before the Right Hon. William Lord Mansfield, and a special jury of the county of Middlesex, in the Court of King's-Bench, Westminster-Hall, on Saturday the second day of June, 1770. To which is prefixed a copy of the information. London, Printed for J. Miller, 1770. 65 p.   LL

REA, ROBERT R.   Amelia Evans Barry and Gov. Pownall's map: an episode in international biblio-philanthropy. Indiana quarterly for bookmen, v. 5, Jan. 1949: 7–16.
                        Z1007.I5, v. 5

On the efforts of John Almon to sell a new edition of Lewis Evans' map of the middle colonies (1755), updated by Thomas Pownall in the winter of 1775–76, in part for the benefit of Evans' daughter, Amelia, who would share in the profits.

—— Bookseller as historian. Indiana quarterly for bookmen, v. 5, Oct. 1949: 75–95.   Z1007.I5, v. 5

—— John Almon: bookseller to John Wilkes. Indiana quarterly for bookmen, v. 4, Jan. 1948: 20–28.
                        Z1007.I5, v. 4

12712

AMBLER, ELIZA JAQUELIN (*ca.* 1765–*ca.* 1823)
    Virginia.

—— An old Virginia correspondence. Atlantic monthly, v. 84, Oct. 1899: 535–549.   AP2.A8, v. 84

Letters to Mildred Smith, 1780–1823.

12713

AMBLER, MARY CARY (*fl.* 1770)
    Virginia.

—— Diary of M. Ambler, 1770. Virginia magazine of history and biography, v. 45, Apr. 1937: 152–170.
                        F221.V91, v. 45

12714

AMELUNG, JOHN FREDERICK (1741 *or* 2–1798)
    Germany; Maryland. Glassmaker.

DELAPLAINE, EDWARD S.   John Frederick Amelung, Maryland glassmaker. Frederick, Md., Frederick News-Post, 1971. 16 p. illus.   NK5198.A44D4

MILFORD, HARRIET N.   Amelung and his New Bremen glass wares. Maryland historical magazine, v. 47, 1952: 1–10. plate.   F176.M18, v. 47

QUYNN, DOROTHY M.   Johann Friedrich Amelung at New Bremen. Maryland historical magazine, v. 43, Sept. 1948: 155–179. plates.   F176.M18, v. 43

12715

AMES, FISHER (1758–1808)
    Massachusetts. Lawyer, assemblyman.

—— Works of Fisher Ames. With a selection from his speeches and correspondence. Edited by his son, Seth Ames. Boston, Little, Brown, 1854. 2 v. port.
                        E302.A52

Contents: 1. Memoir, by J. T. Kirkland. Letters.—2. Speeches. Political essays. Miscellaneous essays.
Reprinted in New York by Da Capo Press (1969) and B. Franklin (1971).
The work edited by Seth Ames represents a rearrangement of the material in the volume prepared by J. T. Kirkland (Boston, T. B. Wait, 1809. 519 p. E302.A5).

BERNHARD, WINFRED E. A.   Fisher Ames, Federalist and statesman, 1758–1808. Chapel Hill, Published for the Institute of Early American History and Culture at Williamsburg, Va., by the University of North Carolina Press [1965] xiii, 372 p. illus., ports.
                        E302.6.A5B4

"A note on the sources": p. 355–360.
The author's thesis (Ph.D.), *Fisher Ames, Spokesman of Federalism, 1758–1797*, was submitted to Columbia University in 1961 (Micro AC–1, no. 64–9154).

DOUGLASS, ELISHA P.   Fisher Ames, spokesman for New England federalism. *In* American Philosophical Society, *Philadelphia*. Proceedings, v. 103, Oct. 15, 1959: 693–715.   Q11.P5, v. 103

12716

AMES, NATHANIEL (1741–1822)

Massachusetts. Almanac writer, Revolutionary surgeon.

———— Extracts from the Ames diary [1758–90] Dedham historical register, v. 1, Jan.–Oct. 1890: 9–16, 49–52, 111–114, 144–148; v. 2, Jan.–Oct. 1891: 25–28, 59–60, 96–99, 148–150; v. 3, Jan.–Oct. 1892: 20–24, 69–73, 129–133, 184–186; v. 4, Jan.–Oct. 1893: 24–25, 65–68, 100–102, 170–172; v. 5, Jan.–Apr. 1894: 32–33, 66.
F74.D3D8, v 1–5

The diary continues to 1807 in subsequent issues. Contributed by Sarah B. Baker.

BRIGGS, SAMUEL, *comp.* The essays, humor, and poems of Nathaniel Ames, father and son, of Dedham, Massachusetts, from their almanacks, 1726–1775. Cleveland, Ohio [Printed by Short & Forman] 1891. 490 p. illus., facsims. (part fold.), fold. map, plates.
PS703.A6A12

Cover title: *The Almanacks of Nathaniel Ames, 1726–1775.*

Reprinted in Detroit by Singing Tree Press (1969).

WARREN, CHARLES. Jacobin and junto; or, Early American politics as viewed in the diary of Dr. Nathaniel Ames, 1758–1822. Cambridge, Mass., Harvard University Press, 1931. 324 p.   E201.W25

Reprinted in New York by Blom (1968) and AMS Press (1970).

"College, country life, and Revolution": p. [15]–41.

12717

AMHERST, JEFFERY AMHERST, *Baron* (1717–1797)*†

England; Virginia. Military officer, royal governor.

————The journal of Jeffrey Amherst, recording the military career of General Amherst in America from 1758 to 1763. Edited with introduction and notes by J. Clarence Webster. Toronto, Ryerson Press; Chicago, University of Chicago Press [c1931] xxiv, 341 p. facsim., maps, plans, plates, ports. (The Canadian historical studies, a library of historical research)   E199.A52

LONG, JOHN C. Lord Jeffery Amherst, a soldier of the king. New York, Macmillan Co., 1933. xxi, 373 p. facsims., maps, plates, ports.   DA67.1.A5L6

The life of Amherst as revealed in his recently discovered correspondence.
Bibliography: p. 354–357.

MAYO, LAWRENCE S. Jeffery Amherst; a biography. New York, Longmans, Green, 1916. 344 p. plates, ports.
E195.A5

RUSSELL, FRANCIS. "Oh Amherst, brave Amherst . . ." American heritage, v. 12, Dec. 1960: 4–10, 89–94. illus. (part col.), col. port.   E171.A43, v. 12

WHITWORTH, REX. Field-Marshall Lord Amherst: a military enigma. History today, v. 9, Feb. 1959: 132–137. illus., ports.   D1.H818, v. 9

12718

AMORY, KATHARINE GREENE (1731–1777)

Massachusetts; England.

————The journal of Mrs. John Amory (Katharine Greene) 1775–1777, with letters from her father, Rufus Greene, 1759–1777. Edited and arranged from manuscripts and illustrated from portraits in the possession of Mrs. Amory's great-great-granddaughter, Martha C. Codman. Boston, Priv. print., 1923. x, 101 p. facsims., plates, ports.   F69.A52

12719

ANBUREY, THOMAS (*fl.* 1776–1781)

British officer in America.

————Travels through the interior parts of America [1776–1781] In a series of letters. By an officer. London, Printed for W. Lane, 1789. 2 v. illus. (part fold.), facsims., fold. map.   E163.A53 1789

Reprinted in Boston by Houghton Mifflin Co. (1923) and in New York by the New York Times (1969).

Volume 1 has been published under the title *With Burgoyne from Quebec; an Account of the Life at Quebec and of the Famous Battle at Saratoga*, edited, and with an introduction by Sydney Jackman (Toronto, Macmillan of Canada, 1963. 220 p. E233.A6).

BELL, WHITFIELD J. Thomas Anburey's "Travels through America": a note on eighteenth-century plagiarism. *In* Bibliographical Society of America. Papers, v. 37, 1st quarter 1943: 23–36.   Z1008.B51P, v. 37

12720

ANDERSON, ENOCH (1754–1824)

Delaware. Revolutionary officer.

———— Personal recollections of Captain Enoch Anderson, an officer of the Delaware regiments in the Revolutionary War. With notes by Henry Hobart Bellas. Wilmington, Historical Society of Delaware, 1896. 61 p. port. (Historical Society of Delaware. Papers, 16)
F161.D35, no. 16
E275.A5 1896

Reprinted in New York by the New York Times (1971).

Eight letters written in 1819 to his nephew Alexander Anderson.

12721

ANDERSON, JOSEPH (1757–1837)*

Pennsylvania; New Jersey; Delaware. Revolutionary officer, lawyer.

HENLEY, MRS. CHARLES F. The Hon. Joseph Anderson. American historical magazine, v. 3, July 1898: 240–255.
[F431.A53, v. 3]
Micro 38843

McMILLAN, FAY E. A biographical sketch of Joseph Anderson (1757–1837). In East Tennessee Historical Society, Knoxville. Publications. no. 2; 1930. Knoxville, Tenn. p. 81–93. F442.1.E14, no. 2

12722

ANDERSON, JOSEPH HORATIO (d. ca. 1781)
Maryland. Architect.

BEIRNE, ROSAMOND R. Two anomalous Annapolis architects: Joseph Horatio Anderson and Robert Key. Maryland historical magazine, v. 55, Sept. 1960: 183–200. F176.M18, v. 55

12723

ANDERSON, RICHARD CLOUGH (1750–1826)*
Virginia; Kentucky. Revolutionary officer, settler.

ANDERSON, EDWARD L. Soldier and pioneer: a biographical sketch of Lt. Col. Richard C. Anderson of the Continental Army. New York, G. P. Putnam's Sons, 1879. 63 p. facsim. E207.A5A5

12724

ANDRÉ, JOHN (1751–1780)†
Switzerland; England. British officer in America.

CAMPBELL, CHARLES A. Bibliography of Major Andre. Magazine of American history, with notes and queries, v. 8, Jan. 1882: 61–72. E171.M18, v. 8

HENSEL, WILLIAM U. Major John André as a prisoner of war at Lancaster, Pa., 1775–6, with some account of a historic house and family. [Lancaster, Press of the New Era Print Co., 1904?] 34 p. plates. E280.A5H5

Also published under the title "Major John Andre's Residence in Lancaster," in the Papers of the Lancaster County Historical Society, v. 8, Mar. 1904, p. 142–172.

LANDIS, CHARLES I. Major John Andre's German letter [April 10, 1776] In Lancaster County (Pa.) Historical Society. Papers, v. 18, June 1914: 127–155.
F157.L2L5, v. 18

Captured at Fort St. John in 1775, André was held prisoner in Pennsylvania, where he struck up friendships and corresponded with local residents, among them Eberhart Michael of Lancaster.

MURRAY, JOSEPH A. André and Despard at Carlisle. [Carlisle, Pa., 1902] [13] p. (Contributions to the local history of Carlisle, Pa., 4) F159.C2M9
Note by Prof. Chas. F. Himes: p. [11]–13.

PLEASANTS, HENRY. John Andre—spy extraordinary. [Philadelphia?] Printed by order of the Society [1939]

62 p. facsims., maps, ports. (Historical publication of the Society of Colonial Wars in the Commonwealth of Pennsylvania, v. 5, no. 2) E186.3.P41, v. 5
Bibliography: p. 60–62.

SARGENT, WINTHROP. The life and career of Major John André, adjutant-general of the British army in America. New ed., with notes and illustrations; edited by William Abbatt. New York, W. Abbatt, 1902. xiv, 543 p. facsims., fold. map, plates, ports.
E280.A5S33

"Poems and ballads relating to Major André": p. [535]–536.

"Dramas relating to Major André": p. 536.
First edition published in 1861.

TILLOTSON, HARRY S. The beloved spy, the life and loves of Major John André. Caldwell, Idaho, Caxton Printers, 1948. 199 p. illus., ports. E280.A5T55
Bibliography: p. [191]–195.

12725

ANDREWS, JOHN (1743–1822)
Massachusetts. Merchant.

—— Letters of John Andrews, Esq., of Boston, 1772–1776. In Massachusetts Historical Society, Boston. Proceedings. v. 8, 1864/65. Boston, 1866. p. 316–412.
F62.M38, v. 8

—— —— Offprint. Cambridge, Press of J. Wilson, 1866. 100 p. F73.44.A56
Introduction and notes by Winthrop Sargent.

Brief sketch of William Barrell, the author's brother-in-law, to whom the letters are addressed: p. 318–319 (p. 5–6 in offprint).

12726

ANDREWS, JOHN (1746–1813)*
Maryland; Pennsylvania. Episcopal clergyman, professor.

—— The end of a siege; a silent Loyalist becomes a reluctant patriot: a letter from John Andrews to William White, December 14, 1779. Edited by David M. Dean. Pennsylvania history, v. 37, Oct. 1970: 381–386.
F146.P597, v. 37

12727

ANGELL, ISRAEL (1740–1832)*
Rhode Island. Farmer, Revolutionary officer.

—— Diary of Colonel Israel Angell, commanding the Second Rhode Island Continental Regiment during the American Revolution, 1778–1781. Transcribed from the original manuscript, together with a biographical sketch of the author and illustrative notes by Edward Field. Providence, R.I., Preston and Rounds Co., 1899. xvi, 149 p. facsim., fold. map. E263.R4A5
Reprinted in New York by the New York Times (1971).

—— Israel Angell and the West in 1788. Rhode Island history, v. 22, Jan.–Apr. 1963: 1–15, 39–50. maps.
F76.R472, v. 22

A journal of Angell's travels from Rhode Island through western Maryland and the Ohio country from August 4 through October 9. Introduction by Dwight L. Smith.

LOVELL, LOUISE L. Israel Angell, colonel of the 2nd Rhode Island Regiment. [New York] Knickerbocker Press (G. P. Putnam's Sons) 1921. facsims., maps, plan, plates.
E263.R4A6

12728

ANNEMOURS, CHARLES FRANÇOIS ADRIEN LE PAULMIER, *chevalier* D' (*ca.* 1742–*ca.* 1809)
France; Maryland. Diplomat.

THOMPSON, HENRY F. The Chevalier d'Annemours. Maryland historical magazine, v. 1, Sept. 1906: 241–246.
F176.M18, v. 1

12729

ANTES, JOHN HENRY (1736–1820)
Pennsylvania. Innkeeper, frontiersman, Revolutionary officer.

MacMINN, EDWIN. On the frontier with Colonel Antes; or, The struggle for supremacy of the red and white races in Pennsylvania. Camden, N.J., S. Chew, Printers, 1900. 513 p. illus., maps, plates, ports.
F149.M16

RUSSELL, HELEN M. The life and times of Henry Antes. Now and then, v. 14, Oct. 1964: 325–344.
F159.M95N6, v. 14

12730

APPLETON, NATHANIEL WALKER (1755–1795)*
Massachusetts. Physician.

—— Letters of Nathaniel Walker Appleton, 1773–1784. *In* Colonial Society of Massachusetts, *Boston.* Publications. v. 8. Transactions, 1902/4. Boston, 1906. p. 289–324.
F61.C71, v. 8

Presented with commentary by William C. Lane.
Reprinted in Cambridge, with a slightly different title, by J. Wilson (1906. [289]–324 p. E203.A65).

The letters were to his classmate, Eliphalet Pearson.

12731

ARCHER, JOHN (1741–1810)*
Maryland. Physician, Revolutionary officer.

BELL, WHITFIELD J. An eighteenth century American medical manuscript: the clinical notebook of John Archer, M.B., 1768. Library chronicle, v. 22, winter 1956: 1–7. plate.
Z733.P418, v. 22

CORDELL, EUGENE F. A biographical sketch of John Archer, M. B. *In* Johns Hopkins Hospital, *Baltimore.* Bulletin, v. 10, Aug./Sept. 1899: 141–147.
RC31.B2J6, v. 10

12732

ARMSTRONG, JOHN (*ca.* 1717–1795)*
Ireland; Pennsylvania. Surveyor, judge, Revolutionary general, delegate to the Continental Congress.

FLOWER, MILTON E. John Armstrong, first citizen of Carlisle. Carlisle, Pa., Cumberland County Historical Society, 1971. 16 p.
F152.A75F55

Includes bibliographic references.

HEATHCOTE, CHARLES W. General John Armstrong—a capable Pennsylvania officer and colleague of Washington. Picket post, no. 66, Nov. 1959: 4–12. illus.
E234.P5, no. 66

KING, J. W. Colonel John Armstrong. Western Pennsylvania historical magazine, v. 10, July 1927: 129–145.
F146.W52, v. 10

12733

ARNOLD, BENEDICT (1741–1801)* †
Connecticut; England. Merchant, Revolutionary general, British officer in America.

—— Benedict Arnold's treasonable cow letter, dated two weeks before the plot to surrender West Point was exposed by the capture of the British spy, Major Andre; this apparently innocent communication is in code that has never been deciphered. [South Hadley Falls, Mass., Hampshire Paper Co., 193–?] 4 l. illus., facsim.
E236.A745 Rare Bk. Coll.

The letter is from Frederick S. Peck's collection of Americana.

—— The present state of the American rebel army, navy, and finances. Transmitted to the British government in October, 1780. Edited by Paul Leicester Ford. Brooklyn, Historical Print. Club, 1891. 17 p. (Winnowings in American history. Revolutionary narratives, no. 5)
E236.A75

Printed from the original in the Public Record Office.

ARNOLD, ISAAC N. The life of Benedict Arnold; his patriotism and his treason. Chicago, Jansen, McClurg, 1880. 444 p. port.
E278.A7A7

DECKER, MALCOLM. Benedict Arnold, son of the Havens. Tarrytown, N.Y., W. Abbatt, 1932. ix, 534 p. facsim., geneal. tables, maps, plates, ports.
E278.A7D3

"Footnote references": p. 473–497; "Literature consulted": p. 501–511.

FLEXNER, JAMES T. Benedict Arnold: how the traitor was unmasked. American heritage, v. 18, Oct. 1967: 6–15. illus. (part col.), map, ports. (part col.)
E171.A43, v. 18

———— The traitor and the spy: Benedict Arnold and John André. New York, Harcourt, Brace [1953] x, 431 p. illus., ports. E278.A7F5

"Statement on sources": p. 417–419.

HILL, GEORGE C. Benedict Arnold. A biography. Boston, E. O. Libby, 1858. vi, 295 p. plates. (American biography) E278.A7H6

LOMASK, MILTON. Benedict Arnold: the aftermath of treason. American heritage, v. 18, Oct. 1967: 16–17, 84–92. illus., ports. E171.A43, v. 18

MURDOCH, RICHARD K. Benedict Arnold and the owners of the *Charming Nancy.* Pennsylvania magazine of history and biography, v. 84, Jan. 1960: 22–25. F146.P65, v. 84

NICHOLS, CHARLES J. The march of Benedict Arnold through the district of Maine. Sprague's journal of Maine history, v. 11, July/Sept.–Oct./Dec. 1923: 144–150, 195–208; v. 13, Apr./June 1925: 69–78. F16.S76, v. 11, 13

A sympathetic review of Arnold's military career.

PATTERSON, GERARD. Benedict Arnold: a personality profile. American history illustrated, v. 3, Aug. 1968: 12–21. illus., facsims., ports. E171.A574, v. 3

SELLERS, CHARLES C. Benedict Arnold, the proud warrior. New York, Minton, Balch, 1930. 303 p. facsim., plates, ports. E278.A7S46

Bibliography: p. 291–295.

SHERWIN, OSCAR. Benedict Arnold, patriot and traitor. New York, Century Co. [ᶜ1931] x, 395 p. facsim., maps, ports. E278.A7S52

Bibliography: p. 371–381.

STEVENS, JOHN A. Benedict Arnold and his apologist. Magazine of American history, with notes and queries, v. 4, Mar. 1880: 181–191. E171.M18, v. 4

Reviews the conclusions reached by Isaac N. Arnold in his *Life of Benedict Arnold, His Patriotism and Treason* (Chicago, Janson, McClurg, 1880. 447 p.).

SULLIVAN, EDWARD D. Benedict Arnold, military racketeer. New York, Vanguard Press, 1932. xii, 306 p. port. E278.A7S94

Bibliography: p. 303–306.

TAYLOR, JOHN G. Some new light on the later life and last resting place of Benedict Arnold and of his wife, Margaret Shippen. Chelsea, London, G. White, 1931. 86 p. facsims., fold. geneal. tables, plates, ports. E278.A7T24

"Sources": p. 11–14.

TODD, CHARLES B. The real Benedict Arnold. New York, A. S. Barnes, 1903. vi, 235 p. maps, plate, port. E278.A7T6

"List of authorities consulted": p. 235.

WALLACE, WILLARD M. Benedict Arnold: traitorous patriot. *In* Billias, George A., *ed.* George Washington's generals. New York, W. Morrow, 1964. p. 163–192. port. E206.B5

Bibliography: p. 191–192.

———— Traitorous hero; the life and fortunes of Benedict Arnold. New York, Harper [1954] xiii, 394 p. facsims., maps, ports. E278.A7W26

Bibliography: p. 375–383.
Reprinted in Freeport, N.Y., by Books for Libraries Press (1970).

12734

ARNOLD, MARGARET SHIPPEN (1760–1804)
Pennsylvania; England. Loyalist. Wife of Benedict Arnold (1741–1801).

TILLOTSON, HARRY S. The exquisite exile, the life and fortunes of Mrs. Benedict Arnold. Boston, Lothrop, Lee & Shepard Co. [ᶜ1932] 205 p. illus., plates, ports. E278.A72T6

Bibliography: p. 203–205.

WALKER, LEWIS B. Life of Margaret Shippen, wife of Benedict Arnold. Pennsylvania magazine of history and biography, v. 24, Oct. 1900, Jan. 1901: 257–266, 401–429; v. 25, Apr.–Oct. 1901, Jan. 1902: 20–46, 145–190, 289–302, 452–497; v. 26, Apr.–Oct. 1902, Jan. 1903: 71–80, 224–244, 322–334, 464–468. F146.P65, v. 24–26

12735

ASBURY, FRANCIS, *Bp.* (1745–1816)*†
England; Delaware. Itinerant Methodist missionary and bishop.

———— The character and career of Francis Asbury, bishop of the Methodist Episcopal church. Illustrated by numerous selections from his journal, arranged in chronological order. By Rev. Edwin L. Janes. New York, Carlton & Lanahan, 1872. 615 p. port. BX8495.A8A4

———— Francis Asbury in North Carolina; the North Carolina portions of the *Journal* of Francis Asbury (v. 1 and 2 of the Clark ed.). With introductory notes by Grady L. E. Carroll. [Nashville, Tenn., 1965] 300 p. port. BX8495.A8A23 1965

Bibliography: p. 281–284.

———— Journal and letters. Elmer E. Clark, editor-in-chief, J. Manning Potts [and] Jacob S. Payton. London, Epworth Press; Nashville, Abingdon Press [1958] 3 v. illus., facsims., maps, ports. BX8495.A8A25

Bibliography: v. 2, p. [809]–815.
Contents: v. 1. The journal, 1771 to 1793.—v. 2. The journal, 1794 to 1816.—v. 3. The letters.

———— The journal of the Rev. Francis Asbury, bishop of the Methodist Episcopal church, from August 7, 1771, to December 7, 1815. New York, N. Bangs and T. Mason, 1821. 3 v.   BX8495.A8A2 1821

ASBURY, HERBERT.   A Methodist saint; the life of Bishop Asbury. New York, A. A. Knopf, 1927. xiv, 335 p. plates, ports.   BX8495.A8A8

Bibliography: p. [337]–342.

BRADLEY, DAVID H.   Francis Asbury and the development of African churches in America. Methodist history, v. 10, Oct. 1971: 3–29.   BX8235.M44, v. 10

DOUGLASS, DONALD D.   Psychological aspects of the pastoral ministry of Francis Asbury. 1957. (vi, 206 l.)   Micro AC–1, no. 21,545

Thesis (Ph.D.)—Boston University.
Abstracted in *Dissertation Abstracts*, v. 17, July 1957, p. 1613.

DUREN, WILLIAM L.   Francis Asbury, founder of American Methodism and unofficial minister of state. New York, Macmillan Co., 1928. xii, 270 p. facsims., plates, ports.   BX8495.A8D8

Bibliography: p. 265–266.

GODBOLD, ALBEA.   Francis Asbury and his difficulties with John Wesley and Thomas Rankin. Methodist history, v. 3. Apr. 1965: 3–19.   BX8235.M44, v. 3

LEWIS, JAMES.   Francis Asbury, bishop of the Methodist Episcopal church. London, Epworth Press [1927] 227 p. map, plates, ports.   BX8495.A8L4

"Principal sources": p. 10

POTTS, J. MANNING.   Francis Asbury, "the prophet of the long road." William and Mary College quarterly historical magazine, 2d ser., v. 22, Jan. 1942: 39–44. fold. map.   F221.W71, 2d s., v.22

The map shows the routes taken by Asbury during his 79 journeys into Virginia from 1775 to 1816.

RUDOLPH, L. C.   Francis Asbury. Nashville, Abingdon Press [1966] 240 p. ports.   BX8495.A8R8

Bibliography: p. 227–234.

STRICKLAND, WILLIAM P.   The pioneer bishop; or, The life and times of Francis Asbury. With an introduction by Nathan Bangs. New York, Carlton & Porter [1858] 496 p. port.   BX8495.A8S8 1858e

TIPPLE, EZRA S.   Francis Asbury, the prophet of the long road. New York, Methodist Book Concern [ᶜ1916] 333 p. facsims. (part fold.), plates, ports.   BX8495.A8T5

12736
ASHMEAD, JOHN (1738–1818)
Pennsylvania. Shipmaster, Revolutionary naval officer.

CLARK, WILLIAM B.   The John Ashmead story, 1738–1818. Pennsylvania magazine of history and biography, v. 82, Jan. 1958: 3–54.   F146.P65, v. 82

12737
ASKIN, JOHN (1739–1815)
Ireland; New York; Michigan. Indian trader.

———— Fur-trade on the upper lakes, 1778–1815. *In* Wisconsin. State Historical Society. Collections. v. 19; 1910. Madison. p. 234–374. map, plates, ports.   F576.W81, v. 19

Askin's correspondence with fur traders, and other fur trade correspondence and documents.

———— The John Askin papers. Edited by Milo M. Quaife. v. 1. 1747–1795. [Detroit] Detroit Library Commission, 1928. 657 p. (Burton historical records, v. 1)   F574.D4A8, v. 1

BURTON, CLARENCE M.   Detroit biographies: John Askin. Burton historical collection leaflet, v. 3, Mar. 1925: 49–64.   F561.B9, v. 3

12738
ATHERTON, JOSHUA (1737–1809)*
New Hampshire. Lawyer, Loyalist.

[ATHERTON, CHARLES H.]   Memoir of the Hon. Joshua Atherton. Boston, Crosby, Nichols, 1852. 57 p.   E278.A86A8

"Printed, not published."

12739
ATKINSON, ROGER (1725–1784)
England; Virginia. Merchant.

———— Letters of Roger Atkinson, 1769–1776. Edited by A. J. Morrison. Virginia magazine of history and biography, v. 15, Apr. 1908: 345–359.   F221.V91, v. 15

12740
ATLEE, SAMUEL JOHN (1739–1786)
New Jersey; Pennsylvania. Revolutionary officer, assemblyman, delegate to the Continental Congress.

PENNYPACKER, SAMUEL W.   Samuel John Atlee. Pennsylvania magazine of history and biography, v. 2, no. 1, 1878: 74–84.   F146.P65, v. 2

12741
ATTMORE, WILLIAM (*d.* 1800)
Pennsylvania. Merchant.

———— Journal of a tour to North Carolina by William Attmore, 1787. Edited by Lida Tunstall Rodman. Chapel Hill, The University, 1922, 46 p. (The James Sprunt historical publications, v. 17. no 2)   F251.J28, v. 17

12742
ATTUCKS, CRISPUS (*ca.* 1723–1770)*
Massachusetts.

FISHER, J. B.   Who was Crispus Attucks? American historical record, v. 1, Dec. 1872: 531–533.
[E171.P86, v. 1]
Micro 39031

Claims that Attucks was a Natick Indian from Framingham who was employed as a sailor aboard a Nantucket whaler.

QUARLES, BENJAMIN.   Crispus Attucks. American history illustrated, v. 5, Nov. 1970: 38–42. illus., facsim.
E171.A574, v. 5

12743

AUCKLAND, WILLIAM EDEN, *Baron* (1744–1814) †
England. Lawyer, Member of Parliament, diplomat.

——— The journal and correspondence of William, lord of Auckland. With a preface and introduction by . . . the Bishop of Bath and Wells. London, R. Bentley. 1861–62. 4 v. ports.   DA506.A94

BROWN, ALAN S.   William Eden and the American Revolution. 1953. ([214] p.)   Micro AC–1, no. 5643
Thesis (Ph.D.)—University of Michigan.
Abstracted in *Dissertation Abstracts*, v. 13, no. 5, 1953, p. 744.

12744

AULD, JAMES (*d.* 1780)
North Carolina.

——— The journal of James Auld, 1765–1770. *In* Southern History Association. Publications, v. 8, July 1904: 253–268.   F206.S73, v. 8
Introduction and notes by R. T. Bennett.

12745

AVERY, DAVID (1746–1818)
Connecticut. Revolutionary chaplain.

———A chaplain of the American Revolution. From the unpublished diary of the Rev. David Avery, chaplain of Col. John Patterson's regiment [Apr. 22, 1775–Oct. 31, 1777] American monthly magazine, v. 17, Oct. 1900: 342–347; v. 18, Feb.–Mar. 1901: 113–117, 235–240; v. 19, July–Oct. 1901: 20–23, 151–156, 260–262, 375–378.   E202.5.A12, v. 17–19
Treats both the siege of Boston and the Battle of Trenton.

12746

AVERY, WAIGHTSTILL (1741–1821)
Connecticut; North Carolina. Lawyer, Revolutionary officer, assemblyman.

PHIFER, EDWARD W.   Saga of a Burke County family. North Carolina historical review, v. 39, winter 1962: 1–17.   F251.N892, v. 39

12747

BACKUS, ELIJAH (*ca.* 1760–1811)
Connecticut. Student.

——— The journal of Elijah Backus Junior, at Yale College, From Jan. ye first to Dec. 31, 1777. Edited by Ellen D. Larned. Connecticut quarterly, v. 1, Oct./Dec. 1895: 355–361.   F91.C8, v. 1

12748

BACKUS, ISAAC (1724–1806)*
Connecticut; Massachusetts. Separatist and Baptist clergyman, historian.

——— An abridgment of the church history of New-England from 1602 to 1804, containing a view of their principles and practice, declensions and revivals, oppression and liberty. With a concise account of the Baptists in the southern parts of America and a chronological table of the whole. Boston, Printed for the author by E. Lincoln, 1804. 271 p.   BR530.B2 1804

——— An address to the inhabitants of New-England, concerning the present bloody controversy therein. Boston, Printed and sold by S. Hall, State-Street, 1787. 7 p.
BX6217.B3, v. 2, no. 3 Rare Bk. Coll.
No. 3 in a volume lettered Tracts. Isaac Backus. 1770–1805.

——— An appeal to the public for religious liberty, against the oppressions of the present day. Boston, Printed by J. Boyle in Marlborough-Street, 1773. 62 p.
BX6217.B3, v. 2, no. 4 Rare Bk. Coll.
No. 4 in a volume lettered Tracts. Isaac Backus. 1770–1805.

——— Isaac Backus on church, state, and Calvinsim; pamphlets, 1753–1789. Edited by William G. McLoughlin. Cambridge, Mass., Belknap Press of Harvard University Press, 1968. vi, 525 p. (The John Harvard Library)
BX6217.B25
Includes bibliographic references.

BACKMAN, MILTON V.   Isaac Backus: a pioneer champion of religious liberty. 1959. ([411] p.)
Micro AC–1, no. 59–4593
Thesis (Ph.D.)—University of Pennsylvania.
Abstracted in *Dissertation Abstracts*, v. 20, Dec. 1959, p. 2243–2244.

HOVEY, ALVAH.   A memoir of the life and times of the Rev. Isaac Backus. Boston, Gould and Lincoln, 1858. 369 p.   BX6495.B32H6 1858
Reprinted in New York by Da Capo Press (1972).

MCLOUGHLIN, WILLIAM G.   Isaac Backus and the American pietistic tradition. Edited by Oscar Handlin. Boston, Little, Brown [1967] xii, 252 p. (The Library of American biography)   BX6495.B32M28
"A note on the sources": p. [234]–238.

MASTON, THOMAS B. Isaac Backus: pioneer of religious liberty. Rochester, N.Y., American Baptist Historical Society [ᶜ1962] 150 p. BX6495.B32M3

"Abridgment of a doctoral dissertation at Yale University."

Bibliography: p. 124–150.

12749

BACKUS, JAMES (1764–1816)

Connecticut; Ohio. Surveyor, frontiersman.

BACKUS, WILLIAM W. A genealogical memoir of the Backus family, with the private journal of James Backus [1788–91], together with his correspondence bearing on the first settlement of Ohio, at Marietta, in 1788. Also, papers and correspondence of Elijah Backus [1775–81], showing the character and spirit of the times during the Revolutionary period. [Norwich, Conn., Press of The Bulletin Co.] 1889. [385], 9 p. facsim., plates, port. [CS71.B12 1889] Micro 8729 CS

PHILLIPS, JOSEPHINE E. James Backus: citizen of Marietta, 1788–1791. Ohio state archaeological and historical quarterly, v. 45, Apr. 1936: 161–172. F486.O51, v. 45

12750

BACON, ANTHONY (ca. 1717–1786)

England. Shipmaster, merchant, provisions contractor, Member of Parliament.

NAMIER, Sir LEWIS B. Anthony Bacon, M.P., an eighteenth century merchant. Journal of economic and business history, v. 2, Nov. 1929: 20–70. HC10.J6, v. 2

12751

BADGER, JOSEPH (1757–1846)*

Massachusetts. Revolutionary soldier, Congregational clergyman.

——— A memoir of Rev. Joseph Badger; containing an autobiography, and selections from his private journal and correspondence. Hudson, O., Sawyer, Ingersoll, 1851. 185 p. port. F497.W5B24 Rare Bk. Coll.

"Rev. H. N. Day wrote the preface."—Sabin, v. 11, p. 579.

RICE, HARVEY. Rev. Joseph Badger. Magazine of Western history, v. 1, Mar. 1885: 432–443. E171.N27, v. 1

12752

BAILEY, ANNE HENNIS (1742–1825)

England; Virginia. Pioneer, Revolutionary recruiter and messenger.

HALL, GRACE M. Anne Bailey in West Virginia tradition. West Virginia history, v. 17, Oct. 1955: 22–85. F236.W52, v. 17

LEWIS, VIRGIL A. Life and times of Anne Bailey, the pioneer heroine of the Great Kanawha Valley. Charleston, W. Va., Butler Print. Co., 1891. v, 90 p. front. F241.B15

12753

BAILEY, JACOB (1731–1808)*

Massachusetts; Maine; Nova Scotia. Anglican clergyman and missionary, Loyalist.

——— Letter from Rev. Jacob Bailey in 1775, describing the destruction of Falmouth, Me. In Maine Historical Society. Collections. v. 5. Portland, 1857. p. 437–450. F16.M33, v. 5

An editorial footnote terms the account "exceedingly exaggerated."

——— Old Nova Scotia in 1783; fragments of an unpublished history. Acadiensis, v. 2, Jan. 1902: 44–52. plate. F1036.A16, v. 2

Introduction and notes by William O. Raymond.

ALLEN, CHARLES E. Rev. Jacob Bailey, missionary of the Church of England on Kennebec River, 1760–1779; his character and work. In Maine Historical Society. Collections and proceedings. 2d ser., v. 7. Portland, 1896. p. 225–253. F16.M33, 2d s., v. 7

The essay was also published, with an abbreviated title, by the Lincoln County Historical Society (1895. 16 p. F27.K2B27).

BAKER, RAY P. The poetry of Jacob Bailey, Loyalist. New England quarterly, v. 2, Jan. 1929: 58–92. F1.N62, v. 2

BARTLET, WILLIAM S. The frontier missionary: a memoir of the life of the Rev. Jacob Bailey, A.M., missionary at Pownalborough, Maine; Cornwallis and Annapolis, N.S. With illustrations, notes, and an appendix. Boston, Ide and Dutton, 1853. xi, 365 p. illus., facsim., map, ports. F27.K2B28 E278.B15B2

Also published as v. 2 of Collections of the Protestant Episcopal Historical Society (New York, 1853).

Rev. Jacob Bailey. Essex antiquarian, v. 1, May 1897: 69–76. illus., port. F72.E7E4, v. 1

12754

BAKER, REMEMBER (1737–1775)*

Connecticut; Vermont. Settler, military officer.

BAKER, RAY S. Remember Baker. New England quarterly, v. 4, Oct. 1931: 595–628. F1.N62, v. 4

12755

BALCH, STEPHEN BLOOMER (1747–1833)

Maryland; Pennsylvania. Schoolmaster, Presbyterian clergyman.

CLARK, ALLEN C. Rev. Stephen Bloomer Balch, a pioneer preacher of Georgetown. *In* Columbia Historical Society, *Washington, D.C.* Records. v. 15, Washington, 1912. p. 73–95. plates. F191.C72, v. 15

12756

BALDWIN, ABRAHAM (1754–1807)*

Connecticut; Georgia. Revolutionary chaplain, lawyer, assemblyman, educator, delegate to the Continental Congress, delegate to the Constitutional Convention.

—— A sermon for the mutinous troops of the Connecticut Line, 1782. New England quarterly, v. 43, Dec. 1970: 621–631. F1.N62, v. 43

Introduction and notes by Patrick J. Furlong.

BROOKS, ROBERT P. Abraham Baldwin, statesman and educator. Georgia historical quarterly, v. 11, June 1927: 171–178. F281.G2975, v. 11

WHITE, HENRY C. Abraham Baldwin, one of the founders of the Republic, and father of the University of Georgia, the first of American state universities. [Athens, Ga., McGregor Co.] 1926. 6, 196 p. port. E302.6.B17W5

12757

BALDWIN, BETHIAH (1743–1830)

Connecticut. Spinster.

BALDWIN, SIMEON E. A ride across Connecticut before the Revolution. *In* New Haven Colony Historical Society, *New Haven.* Papers. v. 9. New Haven, 1918. p. 161–169. F98.N5, v. 9

Based on the diary of her journey from Norwich to Danbury in September 1770.

12758

BALDWIN, JEDUTHAN (1732–1788)

Massachusetts. Revolutionary officer, engineer.

—— The Revolutionary journal of Col. Jeduthan Baldwin, 1775–1778. Edited, with a memoir and notes, by Thomas Williams Baldwin. Bangor, Printed for the De Burians [by C. H. Glass] 1906. lxiii, 164 p. facsims., plates. [De Burians of Bangor, Maine. Publications, v. 3] E275.B18

Reprinted in New York by the New York Times (1971).

12759

BALDWIN, LOAMMI (1740–1807)*

Massachusetts. Surveyor, civil engineer, Revolutionary officer, assemblyman.

ABBOTT, FREDERICK K. The role of the engineer in internal improvements: the observations of the two Loammi Baldwins, father and son, 1776–1838. 1952. ([254] p.) Micro AC–1, no. 3869

Thesis (Ph.D.)—Columbia University.
Abstracted in *Dissertation Abstracts*, v. 12, no. 4, 1952, p. 542.

12760

BALDWIN, SIMEON (1761–1851)*

Connecticut. Tutor, lawyer.

—— Life and letters of Simeon Baldwin. New Haven, Tuttle, Morehouse & Taylor Co. [1919] vi, 503 p. map, plates, ports. E302.6.B19B2

Includes the texts of his journals as a schoolmaster in Albany and a tutor at Yale during the 1780's.

12761

BALLARD, MARTHA MOORE (1735–1812)

Maine. Midwife.

—— Mrs. Ballard's diary. *In* Nash, Charles E. The history of Augusta; first settlements and early days as a town, including the diary of Mrs. Martha Moore Ballard, 1785 to 1812. Augusta, Me., C. E. Nash, 1904 [i.e. 1961] p. [229]–464. F29.A9N3

12762

BALLENDINE, JOHN (d. 1781)

Virginia. Merchant.

BURTON, ARTHUR G., *and* RICHARD W. STEPHENSON. John Ballendine's eighteenth century map of Virginia. *In* U.S. *Library of Congress.* Quarterly journal, v. 21, July 1964: 172–178. maps. Z881.U49A3, v. 21

CHURCH, RANDOLPH W. John Ballendine: unsuccessful entrepreneur of the eighteenth centry. Virginia cavalcade, v. 8, spring 1959: 39–46. illus., facsims., map. F221.V74, v. 8

12763

BALLIET, STEPHEN (1753–1821)

Pennsylvania. Revolutionary officer.

LAUX, JAMES B. Colonel Stephen Balliet, soldier, patriot, and statesman of the Revolution. pt. 1. His ancestry, youth, and education. Allentown, Pa., Lehigh County Historical Society, 1918. 24 p. F153.L39

No more published?

12764

BANCROFT, EDWARD (1744–1821)*†

Massachusetts; England. Physician, double agent.

—— A narrative of the objects and proceedings of Silas Deane, as commissioner of the united colonies to France; made to the British government in 1776. Edited by Paul Leicester Ford. Brooklyn, Historical Print. Club, 1891. 37 p. (Winnowings in American history. Revolutionary narratives, no. 4)

[E249.B21]
Micro 8133E

MILLER, MARGARET. The spy activities of Doctor Edward Bancroft. Journal of American history, v. 22, Jan./Mar.–Apr./June 1928: 70–77, 157–170.
E171.J86, v. 22

12765

BANDOL, SERAPHIN (*fl.* 1778–1785)
France. Roman Catholic clergyman. French naval chaplain in America.

MENG, JOHN J. Abbé Bandol in America. Catholic historical review, v. 20, July 1934: 135–153.
BX1404.C3, v. 20

12766

BANISTER, JOHN (*ca.* 1745–1807)
Rhode Island.

BAKER, DARIUS. The Newport Banisters. Newport, R.I., 1923. 28 p. (Bulletin of the Newport Historical Society, no. 43)
F89.N5N615, no.43

12767

BANKS, JOHN (*d.* 1784)
Virginia. Provisioner.

BANKS, HENRY. A memorial to the Congress of the U. States, relating to Revolutionary events. Frankfort, Ky., Printed by A. G. Hodges, 1827. 60 p.
E255.B21 Rare Bk. Coll.

A statement of losses sustained during the Revolutionary War, by John Banks, of Richmond, Va., with a claim for compensation.

———— The vindication of John Banks, of Virginia, against foul calumnies published by Judge Johnson, of Charleston, South-Carolina, and Doctor Charles Caldwell, of Lexington, Kentucky. Also, the vindication of General Henry Lee, of Virginia. With sketches and anecdotes of many Revolutionary patriots and heroes. Frankfort [Ky.] The author, 1826. 88 p.
E255.B22 Rare Bk. Coll.

A defense of John Banks, a contractor of supplies for Gen. Nathanael Greene's army, against charges made by William Johnson and Charles Caldwell in their biographies of Greene.

12768

BANNEKER, BENJAMIN (1731–1806)
Maryland. Mathematician, surveyor, almanac publisher.

ALLEN, WILL W., *and* DANIEL A. P. MURRAY. Banneker, the Afro-American astronomer. Washington, D.C., 1921. 80 p. port.
QB36.B22A4

Reprinted in Freeport, N.Y., by the Books for Libraries Press (1971).

BAKER, HENRY E. Benjamin Banneker, the Negro mathematician and astronomer. Journal of Negro history, v. 3, Apr. 1918: 99–118.
E185.J86, v. 3

BEDINI, SILVIO A. The life of Benjamin Banneker. New York, Scribner [1971, ᶜ1972] xvii, 434 p. illus.
QB36.B22B4

Bibliography: p. [377]–406.

CONWAY, MONCURE D. Benjamin Banneker, the Negro astronomer. Atlantic monthly, v. 11, Jan. 1863: 79–84.
AP2.A8, v. 11

LATROBE, JOHN H. B. Memoir of Benjamin Banneker. Baltimore, Printed by J. D. Toy, 1845. 16 p. [Maryland Historical Society. Publications, v. 1, no.5]
F176.M34, v. 1
E185.97.B22

[TYSON, MARTHA E] A sketch of the life of Benjamin Banneker; from notes taken in 1836. [Baltimore] Printed by J. D. Toy [1854] 20 p. [Maryland Historical Society. Publications, v. 3, no.8]
F176.M34, v. 3
QB36.B22T8

12769

BANNING, JEREMIAH (1733–1798)
Maryland. Shipmaster, merchant.

———— Log and will of Jeremiah Banning (1733–1798). [New York] Priv. print. [1932] [72] p.
F185.B23

Facsimile reproduction of the manuscript copy of the autobiography made by Mrs. Emily E. Banning in 1880. "Copyright . . . [by] W. F. Austin."

12770

BANT, WILLIAM (*fl.* 1776)
Massachusetts. Merchant.

———— William Bant; five letters from William Bant to John Hancock, 1776, 1777. *In* Boston. Public Library. Monthly bulletin, v. 7, Oct. 1902: 424–430.
Z881.B75BM, v. 7

12771

BARAZER DE KERMORVAN, GILLES JEAN MARIE ROLLAND (1740–1817)
France. Revolutionary officer, engineer.

BUTTERFIELD, LYMAN H. Franklin, Rush, and the Chevalier Kermorvan: an episode of '76. *In* American Philosophical Society, *Philadelphia. Library.* Library bulletin. 1946. Philadelphia, 1947. p. 33–44.
Z881.P49, 1946

Includes two letters from Kermorvan to Franklin revealing what he thought and saw of the American war.

12772

BARBÉ-MARBOIS, FRANÇOIS, *marquis* DE (1745–1837)
France. Diplomat.

———— Complot d'Arnold et de sir Henry Clinton contre les États-Unis d'Amérique et contre le général Washington. Septembre 1780. Orné de deux portraits et d'une carte. Paris, P. Didot, l'aîné, 1816. xliv, 184 p. plan, ports.   E236.B23 Rare Bk. Coll.

A translation of portions of his narrative appeared in *The American Register; Or, Summary Review of History, Politics and Literature* (Philadelphia, T. Dobson, 1817. Micro 01104 no. 59 AP), v. 2, p. 3–63.

———— Our Revolutionary forefathers; the letters of François, marquis de Barbé-Marbois during his residence in the United States as secretary of the French legation, 1779–1785. Translated and edited with an introduction by Eugene Parker Chase. New York, Duffield, 1929. ix, 225 p. illus., plates, port.   E163.B23

"The journal is written to the Marquis' fiancée at home [Mademoiselle de Montry d'Alleray]"—Publisher's note.
"List of books": p. 34–36.
Reprinted in Freeport, N.Y., by Books for Libraries Press (1969).

LYON, ELIJAH WILSON.   The man who sold Louisiana; the career of Francois Barbé-Marbois. Norman, University of Oklahoma Press, 1942. xix, 240 p. maps, plates, ports.   DC146.B17L9

"Bibliographic note": p. 191–193. "Writings of Barbé-Marbois": p. 194–197.

ROSENTHAL, ALFRED.   The Marbois-Longchamps affair [1784–85] Pennsylvania magazine of history and biography, v. 63, July 1939: 294–301. facsim.
                    F146.P65, v. 63

On an attack upon Marbois, a member of the French diplomatic corps, by the adventurer Charles Julian de Longchamps and its results.

12773
BARBER, DANIEL (1756–1834)
Connecticut. Revolutionary soldier, Anglican clergyman.

———— The history of my own times. Washington City, Printed for the author, by S. C. Ustick, 1827–32. 3 v.
                    E275.B23 Rare Bk. Coll.

———— Rev. D. Barber's account of his service in the army of 1775–6. Historical magazine, v. 7, Mar. 1863: 83–88.
                    E171.H64, v. 7

Excerpts taken from his *History*.

12774
BARBER, FRANCIS (1751–1783)*
New Jersey. Schoolmaster, Revolutionary officer.

McCARTHY, CALLAHAN J.   Lieutenant-Colonel Francis Barber, Elizabethtown patriot and hero. *In* Union County Historical Society, *Elizabeth, N.J.* Proceedings. v. 2; 1923/34. [Elizabeth?] 1934. p. 127–136.
                    F142.U5U5, v. 2

Also published in the *Proceedings* of the New Jersey Historical Society, v. 50, July 1932, p. 273–284.

12775
BARBEU-DUBOURG, JACQUES (1709–1779)
France. Physician, scientist.

———— Calendrier de Philadelphie; ou, Constitutions de sancho Pança et du Bon-homme Richard, en Pensyvanie. [n.p.] 1778. xxx, 6, 118 p.
                    AY831.Z7 1778 Rare Bk. Coll.

Purports to be a translation. Added title page: *Calendrier de Philadelphie pour l'année 1777* (Londres, 1777).
Editions of 1802 and 1823 published under title *Almanach de Philadelphie*.
"Sorte de manuel de morale dans le genre et à l'imitation du 'Bon-homme Richard' de Franklin."—John Grand-Carteret, *Les Almanachs français* (Paris, J. Alisie, 1896).

———— Letters of Barbeu-Dubourg to Franklin [1768–75] *In* Massachusetts Historical Society, *Boston*. Proceedings. v. 56; 1922/23. Boston, 1923. p. 127–156.
                    F61.M38, v. 56

The letters are in French.

———— Petit code de la raison humaine; ou, Exposition succincte de ce que la raison dicte à tous les hommes, pour éclairer leur conduite, & assurer leur bonheur. Londres, Becket & De Hondt Libraires, 1774. 54 p.
                    BJ1087.B3 1774 Rare Bk. Coll.

In a case (26 cm.)

ALDRIDGE, ALFRED O.   Jacques Barbeu-Dubourg, a French disciple of Benjamin Franklin. *In* American Philosophical Society, *Philadelphia*. Proceedings, v. 95, Aug. 1951: 331–392.   Q11.P5, v. 95

12776
BARCLAY, ANDREW (1738–1823)
Scotland; Massachusetts; Nova Scotia. Bookbinder, Loyalist.

FRENCH, HANNAH D.   The amazing career of Andrew Barclay, Scottish bookbinder, of Boston. *In* Virginia. University. *Bibliographical Society*. Studies in bibliography; papers. v. 14. Charlottesville, 1961. p. 145–162.
                    Z1008.V55, v. 14

12777
BARCLAY, THOMAS (1753–1830)*
New York; Nova Scotia. Lawyer, Loyalist officer.

———— Selections from the correspondence of Thomas Barclay, formerly British consul-general at New York. Edited by George Lockhart Rives. New York, Harper, 1894. 429 p. fold. map, port.   E302.1.B24

The selection entitled "Earlier Years" (p.1–42) details Barclay's services to the crown during the war.

12778

BARD, SAMUEL (1742–1821)*

Pennsylvania; New York. Physician, professor.

LANGSTAFF, JOHN B. Doctor Bard of Hyde Park, the famous physician of Revolutionary times, the man who saved Washington's life. Introduction by Nicholas Murray Butler. New York, E. P. Dutton, 1942. 365 p. plates, ports. R154.B18L3

Bibliography: p. 281–295.

McVICKAR, JOHN. A domestic narrative of the life of Samuel Bard, M.D., LL.D., late president of the College of Physicians and Surgeons of the University of the State of New York. New York, Literary Rooms [Columbia College] A. Paul, Printer, 1822. 244 p. port. R154.B18M3

THOMAS, MILTON H. Doctor Samuel Bard. Columbia University quarterly, v. 23, June 1931: 114–130. LH1.C7Q2, v. 23

——— ——— Offprint. [New York, 1931] p. port. CT99.B245T5

12779

BARDELEBEN, HEINRICH VON (1752–1835)

Germany. Hessian officer in America.

——— Tagebuch des Hessischen Offiziers Heinrich von Bardeleben. (29. Februar 1776 bis 22. Juni 1777.) In Deutsch-amerikanische Geschichtsblätter. v. 27/28; 1927/28. Chicago, University of Chicago Press, 1928. p. 7–119. F550.G3D4, v. 27/28

Edited with introduction by Julius Goebel.

12780

BARHAM, CHARLES MIDDLETON, *Baron* (1726–1813)

England. Admiral, Member of Parliament.

——— Letters and papers of Charles, Lord Barham, Admiral of the Red Squadron, 1758–1813. Edited by Sir John Knox Laughton. [London] Printed for the Navy Records Society, 1907–11. 3 v. facsims., fold. map, ports. (Publications of the Navy Records Society, v. 32, 38, 39. The Barham papers, v. 1–3) DA70.A1, v. 32, 38, 39

"Bibliographical note": v. 1, p. lxiv.

Volume 1 contains letters relating to naval engagements in American and West Indian waters.

12781

BARKER, JOHN (1750–1804)

England. British officer in America.

——— The British in Boston, being the diary of Lieutenant John Barker of the King's Own Regiment from November 15, 1774, to May 31, 1776. With notes by Elizabeth Ellery Dana. Cambridge, Harvard University Press, 1924. x, 73 p. facsims., plates, ports. E275.B25

Reprinted in New York by the New York Times (1969). Also published, with introduction and notes by J. C. Dalton, in the *Journal* of the Society for Army Historical Research (London), v. 7, Apr.–July 1928, p. 81–109, 145–174.

12782

BARLOW, JOEL (1754–1812)*

Connecticut. Poet, writer.

——— The prospect of peace. A poetical composition, delivered in Yale-College, at the public examination, of the candidates for the degree of bachelor or arts; July 23, 1778. New-Haven, Printed by Thomas and Samuel Green, 1778. 12 p. AC901.H3, v. 38 Rare Bk. Coll

——— Six letters of Joel Barlow to Oliver Wolcott [1779] Edited by Theodore A Zunder. New England quarterly, v. 2, July 1929: 475–489. F1.N62, v. 2

——— The works of Joel Barlow. With an introduction by William K. Bottorff and Arthur L. Ford. Gainesville, Fla., Scholars' Facsimiles & Reprints, 1970. 2 v. illus. PS704.A1 1970

Contents.—v. 1. Prose.—v. 2. Poetry.
Suggested by Barlow's plan, in manuscript at the Harvard University Library, for a two-volume collection of his works.

ADAMS, MARTIN RAY. Joel Barlow, political romanticist. American literature, v. 9, May 1937: 113–153. PS1.A6, v. 9

BLAU, JOSEPH L. Joel Barlow, enlightened religionist. Journal of the history of ideas, v. 10, June 1949: 430–444. B1.J75, v. 10

CANTOR, MILTON. Joel Barlow, lawyer and legal philosopher [1785–86] American quarterly, v. 10, summer 1958: 167–174. AP2.A3985, v. 10

——— Joel Barlow, Yale undergraduate. New-England galaxy, v. 5, fall 1963: 3–13. illus., ports. F1.N39, v. 5

——— The life of Joel Barlow. 1954. ([496] p.) Micro AC–1, no. 10,783

Thesis (Ph.D.)—Columbia University.
Abstracted in *Dissertation Abstracts*, v. 15, no. 4, 1955, p. 562.

———Trials and loves of a New England poet. New-England galaxy, v. 6, spring 1965: 12–20. illus., ports. F1.N39, v. 6

CHRISTENSEN, MERTON A. Deism in Joel Barlow's early work: heterodox passages in *The Vision of Columbus*. American literature, v. 27, Jan. 1956: 509–520. PS1.A6, v. 27

DORFMAN, JOSEPH. Joel Barlow: trafficker in trade and letters. Political science quarterly, v. 59, Mar. 1944: 83–100. H1.P8, v. 59

FORD, ARTHUR L.   Joel Barlow. New York, Twayne Publishers [1971] 144 p. (Twayne's United States authors series)   PS705.F6

Bibliography: p. 136–141.

SQUIRES, VERNON P.   Joel Barlow—patriot, democrat, and man of letters. *In* University of North Dakota. Quarterly journal, v. 9, July 1919: 299–308.
                                                       AS36.N6, v. 9

TODD, CHARLES B.   Life and letters of Joel Barlow, LL.D., poet, statesman, philosopher, with extracts from his works and hitherto unpublished poems. New York, G. P. Putnam's Sons, 1886. iv, 306 p. fold. facsim., port.   PS705.T6

Bibliography: p. 289–294.
Reprinted in New York by DaCapo Press (1970) and by B. Franklin (1972).

TYLER, MOSES C.   The literary strivings of Mr. Joel Barlow. *In his* Three men of letters. New York, G. P. Putnam's Sons, 1895. p. 129–180.   PS185.T85

WOODRESS, JAMES L.   A Yankee's odyssey; the life of Joel Barlow. Philadelphia, Lippincott [1958] 347 p. illus., ports.   PS705.W6

Bibliographic references included in "Notes" (p. 309–320).
Reprinted in New York by Greenwood Press (1968).

ZUNDER, THEODORE A.   The early days of Joel Barlow, a Connecticut wit, Yale graduate, editor, lawyer and poet, chaplain during the Revolutionary War; his life and works from 1754 to 1787. New Haven, Yale University Press, 1934. x, 320 p. port. (Yale studies in English, v. 84)   PS705.Z8 1934
                                                    PR13.Y3, v. 84

Bibliography: p. [308]–311.
Reprinted in Hamden, Conn., by Archon Books (1969).
The author's thesis (Ph.D.), *Joel Barlow: His Life and Work to 1790*, was submitted to Yale University in 1927.

12783
BARNEY, JOSHUA (1759–1818)*
Maryland. Revolutionary naval officer.

BARNEY, MARY C.   A biographical memoir of the late Commodore Joshua Barney: from autographical notes and journals in possession of his family, and other authentic sources. Boston, Gray and Bowen, 1832. xvi, 328 p. port.   E353.1.B26B2

FOOTNER, HULBERT.   Sailor of fortune; the life and adventures of Commodore Barney, U.S.N. New York, Harper [ᶜ1940] 323 p. illus., maps, plates, ports.
                                                    E353.1.B26F7

"Reference notes": p. 306–316.

PAINE, RALPH D.   Joshua Barney, a forgotten hero of blue water. New York, Century Co. [ᶜ1924] viii, 410 p. facsims., map, plates, ports.   E353.1.B26P2

Reprinted in New York by Books for Libraries Press (1970).

WELLER, MICHAEL I.   Commodore Joshua Barney: the hero of the Battle of Bladensburg. Incidents of his life gleaned from contemporaneous sources. *In* Columbia Historical Society, *Washington, D.C.* Records. v. 14. Washington, 1911. p. 67–183. plates.
                                                       F191.C72, v. 14

12784
BARR, JAMES (1754–1848)
Massachusetts. Revolutionary privateersman.

CURWEN, JAMES B.   Reminiscences of Capt. James Barr of Salem, Mass., together with some incidents of his service in private armed vessels during the Revolution. *In* Essex Institute, *Salem, Mass.* Historical collections, v. 27, July/Sept. 1890: 123–148. ports.
                                                       F72.E7E81, v. 27

12785
BARRÉ, ISAAC (1726–1802)†
Ireland; England. Military officer, Member of Parliament.

BRYANT, DONALD C.   "A scarecrow of violence": Colonel Isaac Barre in the House of Commons. Speech monographs, v. 28, Nov. 1961: 233–249.
                                                       PN4077.S6, v. 28

FOLSOM, GEORGE.   The annual discourse, delivered before the New York Historical Society, on the 20th of December, 1859. Ventnor, Eng., Printed by F. Moor, 1866. 48 p.   DA506.B27F6

On the life of Isaac Barré.

MINER, SIDNEY R.   Colonel Isaac Barré. *In* Wyoming Historical and Geological Society, *Wilkes-Barre, Pa.* Proceedings and collections. v. 6; 1901, Wilkes-Barre. p. [113]–136.   F157.W9W94, v. 6

12786
BARRINGTON, *Hon.* SAMUEL (1727–1800)†
England. Admiral.

——— The Barrington papers, selected from the letters and papers of Admiral the Hon. Samuel Barrington; and edited by D. Bonner-Smith. [London] Printed for the Navy Records Society, 1937–41. 2 v. port. (Publications of the Navy Records Society, v. 77, 81)
                                                       DA70.A1, v. 77, 81

See also "Some Letters of Admiral the Hon. Samuel Barrington [1770–99]" in *Mariner's Mirror*, v. 19, July–Oct. 1933, p. 279–291, 381–403, and v. 20, Jan. 1934, p. 67–84.

12787
BARRINGTON, WILLIAM WILDMAN BARRINGTON, *2d Viscount* (1717–1793)†
England. Member of Parliament, Secretary at War.

———— The Barrington-Bernard correspondence and illustrative matter, 1760–1770, drawn from the "Papers of Sir Francis Bernard" (sometime governor of Massachusetts-Bay). Edited by Edward Channing and Archibald Cary Coolidge. Cambridge, Harvard University, 1912. xxiii, 306 p. (Harvard historical studies, v. 17)   F67.B27

"The letters printed in this volume are drawn from the collection of original documents and transcripts which Jared Sparks brought together."—Introduction.

Reprinted in New York by Da Capo Press (1970).

BARRINGTON, SHUTE, *Bp. of Durham.*   The political life of William Wildman, viscount Barrington. Compiled from original papers by his brother, Shute, Bishop of Durham. London, Printed by W. Bulmer, 1814. 207 p. port.   DA501.B2B2

12788

BARRY, JOHN (1745–1803)*†

Ireland; Pennsylvania. Shipmaster and owner, Revolutionary naval officer.

CLARK, WILLIAM B.   Gallant John Barry, 1745–1803; the story of a naval hero of two wars. New York, Macmillan Co., 1938. xii, 530 p. facsims., fold geneal. table, plates, ports.   E207.B2C5

Bibliography: p. 495–503.

GRIFFIN, MARTIN I. J.   Commodore John Barry. *In* American Historical Association. Annual report. 1895. Washington, 1896. p. 337–365.   E172.A60, 1895

———— Commodore John Barry, "the father of the American navy"; the record of his services for his country. Philadelphia, 1903 [1902] xi, 424 p. facsim., map, plates, port.   E207.B2G8

An earlier version of the author's work was published under the title, "The History of Commodore John Barry, A.D. 1745–1803," in the *Records* of the American Catholic Historical Society of Philadelphia, v. 7, June–Sept. 1896, p. 155–224, 235–282; v. 8, Mar.–Sept. 1897, p. 86–128, 129–194, 257–293, and was also reprinted separately (Philadelphia, 1897. 261 p. E207.B2G82). Twelve letters to Barry not available to Griffin before his revised work appeared were published in the *American Catholic Historical Researches*, v. 21, Apr. 1904, p. 73–85.

GURN, JOSEPH.   Commodore John Barry, father of the American navy. New York, P. J. Kenedy [c1933] x, 318 p. facsim., plates, ports.   E207.B2G92

Bibliography: p. [304]–306.

PURCELL, RICHARD J.   Captain John Barry of the American Revolution. Studies, v. 23, Dec. 1934: 623–633.   AP4.S78, v. 23

U.S. *Continental Congress. Marine Committee.*   Orders of the Continental Marine Committee to Captain John Barry [1778–80] American Catholic historical researches, new ser., v. 6, Oct. 1910: 322–333.   E184.C3A5, n.s., v. 6

12789

BARTLETT, JOSIAH (1729–1795)*

Massachusetts; New Hampshire. Physician, delegate to the Continental Congress, judge.

[ELWYN, ALFRED L.] *comp.*   Letters by Josiah Bartlett, William Whipple, and others, written before and during the Revolution. Philadelphia, Press of H. B. Ashmead, 1889. 71 p.   E203.E52 Rare Bk. Coll.

Letters found among the papers of John Langdon of New Hampshire.

PAGE, ELWIN L.   Josiah Bartlett and the federation. Historical New Hampshire, Oct. 1947: 1–6.   F31.H57, 1947

STEVENS, ALICE B.   Josiah Bartlett. Granite monthly, v. 34, Apr. 1903: 243–261. illus., port.   F31.G75, v. 34

Stray leaves from an autograph collection. Correspondence of Josiah Bartlett of N.H. during the American Revolution. Historical magazine, v. 6, Mar., Aug.–Sept. 1862: 73–78, 239–242, 277–279; v. 7, Feb. 1863: 48–54.   E171.H64, v. 6–7

Letters from William Whipple, John Langdon, and Roger Sherman.

12790

BARTLETT, THOMAS (1745–1805)

Massachusetts. Revolutionary officer, assemblyman.

SCALES, JOHN.   General Thomas Bartlett. *In* New Hampshire Historical Society. Proceedings. v. 5, pt. 2; 1907/12. Concord, 1916. p.131–168.   F31.N52, v. 5

12791

BARTON, JOSEPH (1730?–1788)

New Jersey; Nova Scotia. Assemblyman, Loyalist officer.

McCRACKEN, GEORGE E.   Lieut. Colonel Joseph Barton, Loyalist of Sussex County, New Jersey. *In* New Jersey Historical Society. Proceedings, v. 69, Oct. 1951: 287–324.   F131.N58, v. 69

The author presents further evidence on Barton's court-martial of 1781 in volume 78 of the *Proceedings*, Jan. 1960, p. 33–35.

12792

BARTON, THOMAS (1730–1780)†

Ireland; Pennsylvania. Anglican clergyman, Loyalist.

YOUNG, ARCHIBALD H.   Thomas Barton: a Pennsylvania Loyalist. *In* Ontario Historical Society. Papers and records. v. 30. Toronto, 1934. p. 33–42.   F1056.O58, v. 30

12793

BARTON, WILLIAM (1748–1831)*

Rhode Island. Hatter, Revolutionary officer.

WILLIAMS, CATHERINE R. A. Biography of Revolutionary heroes; containing the life of Brigadier Gen. William Barton, and also, of Captain Stephen Olney. Providence, 1839. 312 p. illus.   E207.B25W7
   E263.R405

12794

BARTON, WILLIAM (1754–1817)

Pennsylvania. Lawyer.

——— Memoirs of the life of David Rittenhouse, LL.D., F.R.S., late president of the American Philosophical Society, &c. interspersed with various notices of many distinguished men. Philadelphia, E. Parker, 1813. 614 p. fold. facsim., port.
   QB36.R4B3 Rare Bk. Coll.

RUBINCAM, MILTON. A memoir of the life of William Barton, A.M. (1754–1817). Pennsylvania history, v. 12, July 1945: 179–193.   F146.B597, v. 12

12795

BARTRAM, JOHN (1699–1777)*

Pennsylvania. Botanist, naturalist, traveler.

——— Diary of a journey through the Carolinas, Georgia, and Florida from July 1, 1765, to April 10, 1766. Annotated by Francis Harper. Philadelphia, American Philosophical Society, 1942. 120 p. maps, facsims., plates, port. (Transactions of the American Philosophical Society, new ser., v. 33, pt. 1)   Q11.P6, n.s., v. 33

"Literature cited": p. 108–111.

———John and William Bartram's America; selections from the writings of the Philadelphia naturalists. Edited with an introduction by Helen Gere Cruickshank. Foreword by B. Bartram Cadbury. New York, Devin-Adair Co., 1957. 418 p. illus. (American naturalists series)   QH31.B23A3

BARTRAM, WILLIAM. Some account of the late Mr. John Bartram, of Pennsylvania. In Philadelphia medical and physical journal. v. 1, pt. 1; 1804. Philadelphia, J. Conrad, 1805. p. [115]–124.   QH1.P5, v. 1

DARLINGTON, WILLIAM. Memorials of John Bartram and Humphry Marshall; with notices of their botanical contemporaries. Philadelphia, Lindsay & Blakiston, 1849. 585 p. illus., facsims., plates.   QK31.B3D3

Reprinted in New York, with a new introduction by Joseph Ewan, by Hafner (1967).
Composed largely of letters of Peter Collinson to John Bartram.

EARNEST, ERNEST P. John and William Bartram, botanists and explorers, 1699–1777, 1739–1823. Philadelphia,

University of Pennsylvania Press, 1940. vi, 187 p. ports. (Pennsylvania lives)   QK31.B3E3

"Bibliographical note": p. 181–182.

EDELSTEIN, JEROME M. America's first native botanists. In U.S. Library of Congress. Quarterly journal of current acquisitions, v. 15, Feb. 1958: 51–59. plate.
   Z881.U49A3, v.15

LOGAN, MARTHA. Letters of Martha Logan to John Bartram, 1760–1763. Edited by Mary Barbot Prior. South Carolina historical magazine, v. 59, Jan. 1958: 38–46.
   F266.S55, v. 59

STORK, WILLIAM. An account of East-Florida, with a journal kept by John Bartram of Philadelphia, botanist to His Majesty for the Floridas; upon a journey from St. Augustine up the river St. John's. London, Sold by W. Nicoll and G. Woodfall [1766] 90, viii, 70 p.
   F314.S88 1766a Rare Bk. Coll.

WEST, FRANCIS D. John Bartram and slavery. South Carolina historical magazine, v. 56, Apr. 1955: 115–119.   F266.S55, v. 56

12796

BARTRAM, MOSES (1732–1809)

Pennsylvania. Apothecary, botanist, Revolutionary soldier.

KLEIN, RANDOLPH S. Moses Bartram. Quaker history, v. 57, spring 1968: 28–34.   BX7635.A1F6, v. 57

12797

BARTRAM, WILLIAM (1739–1823)*

Pennsylvania. Explorer, naturalist.

——— Botanical and zoological drawings, 1756–1788; reproduced from the Fothergill album in the British Museum (Natural History). Edited, with an introduction and commentary, by Joseph Ewan. Philadelphia, American Philosophical Society, 1968. x, 180 p. plates (part col.) (Memoirs of the American Philosophical Society, v. 74)   QH46.B35 1968

Bibliography: p. 168–172.

——— Travels in Georgia and Florida, 1773–74. A report to Dr. John Fothergill. Annotated by Francis Harper. Philadelphia, American Philosophical Society, 1943. 121–242 p. maps, plates, port. (Transactions of the American Philosophical Society, new ser., v. 33, pt. 2)
   Q11.P6, n.s., v. 33

"Literature cited": p. 228–231.

———Travels through North & South Carolina, Georgia, East & West Florida, the Cherokee country, the extensive territories of the Muscogulges, or Creek confederacy, and the country of the Chactaws, containing an account of the soil and natural productions of these regions, together with observations on the manners of the Indians. Philadelphia, Printed by James & Johnson, 1791. xxxiv, 522 p. fold map, plates (part fold.), port. F213.B28 Rare Bk. Coll.

The 1928 edition, edited by Mark Van Doren (New York, Macy-Masius. 414 p. F213.B288) was reissued in 1940 by Facsimile Library with an introduction by John Livingston Lowes. In 1958 Yale University Press published a "Naturalist's edition" (727 p. F213.B2893), with commentary and an annotated index by Francis Harper.

FAGIN, NATHAN BRYLLION. William Bartram, interpreter of the American landscape. Baltimore, Johns Hopkins Press, 1933. ix, 229 p. QK31.B33F32 1933

Bibliography: p. 205–215.

Portions of this work, under the same title, were submitted to Johns Hopkins University in 1931 as the author's thesis (PhD.).

GUMMERE, RICHARD M. William Bartram, a classical scientist. Classical journal, v. 50, Jan 1955: 167–170. PA1.C4, v. 50

HARPER, FRANCIS. Proposals for publishing Bartram's *Travels* [in 1786–87] In American Philosophical Library, *Philadelphia. Library.* Library bulletin. 1945. Philadelphia, 1946. p. 27–38. Z881.P49, 1945

———— William Bartram and the American Revolution. *In* American Philosophical Society, *Philadelphia.* Proceedings, v. 97, Oct. 1953: 571–577. Q11.P5, v. 97

Also published in the Society's *Library Bulletin* for 1953, p. 571–577.

MORRIS, GEORGE S. William Bartram. *In* Cassinia. no. 10; 1906. Philadelphia, 1907. p. 1–9. plate, port. QL671.C3, no. 10

12798

BASS, EDWARD, *Bp.* (1726–1803)*

Massachusetts. Anglican clergyman.

ADDISON, DANIEL D. The life and times of Edward Bass. Boston, Houghton, Mifflin, 1897. viii, 350 p. port. BX5995.B38A5

NORTON, JOHN N. Life of Bishop Bass of Massachusetts. New York, General Protestant Episcopal Sunday School Union and Church Book Society, 1859. 192 p. port. BX5995.B38N6

12799

BASSETT, RICHARD (1745–1815)*

Maryland; Delaware. Lawyer, Revolutionary officer, assemblyman, delegate to the Constitutional Convention.

PATTISON, ROBERT E. The life and character of Richard Bassett. Wilmington, Historical Society of Delaware, 1900. 19 p. port. (Delaware Historical Society. Papers, [no.] 29) F161.D35, no.29
E302.6.B28P3

12800

BATES, ISSACHAR (*b.* 1758)

Massachusetts. Fifer, Revolutionary soldier.

———— The Revolutionary War and Issachar Bates. Old Chatham, N.Y., Shaker Museum Foundation, 1960. [14] p. E275.B26

Taken from a manuscript autobiography in the Museum's library.

12801

BAURMEISTER, CARL LEOPOLD (1734–1803)

Germany. Hessian officer in America.

———— Revolution in America; confidential letters and journals, 1776–1784. Translated and annotated by Bernhard A. Uhlendorf. New Brunswick, N.J., Rutgers University Press, 1957. xiv, 640 p. illus., facsim., maps. E268.B4

Bibliographic footnotes.

UHLENDORF, BERHARD A. America during the Revolution, as seen by a Hessian mercenary. Michigan alumnus quarterly review, v. 43, autumn 1936: 346–355. facsims., port. AP2.M53, v. 43

12802

BAXTER, SIMON (1730–1804)

Connecticut; Nova Scotia. Loyalist officer, farmer.

BAXTER, JOHN B. M. Simon Baxter (the first United Empire Loyalist to settle in New Brunswick), his ancestry and descendants. [St. John] New Brunswick Museum (Historical section), 1943. 46 p. maps, plates, port. F1043.B3

12803

BAYARD, JOHN (1738–1807)*

Maryland; Pennsylvania. Merchant, Revolutionary officer, delegate to the Continental Congress.

WILSON, JAMES G. A memorial of Col. John Bayard. *In* New Jersey Historical Society. Proceedings, 2d ser., v. 5, no. 3, 1878: 139–160. F131.N58, 2d s., v. 5

A more extensive version of this essay was published in the *New York Genealogical Record* for April 1885 and reprinted separately under the title *Colonel John Bayard (1738–1807) and the Bayard Family of America* (New York, Trow's Print. and Bookbinding Co., 1885. 24 p. CS71.B376 1885).

12804

BAYARD, STEPHEN (1744–1815)

Maryland; Pennsylvania. Revolutionary officer, land speculator.

WILEY, RICHARD T. Colonel Stephen Bayard, his wife, and their town. Western Pennsylvania historical magazine, v. 18, Mar. 1935: 7–25. F146.W52, v. 18

12805

BAYLEY, FRYE (1749–1827)

Vermont. Revolutionary officer.

———— An account by Frye Bayley of his early life, and his services in the Revolutionary War, written by another hand. Copied from a manuscript in the possession of the Massachusetts Historical Society. [Newbury, Vt., 1826–30. Boston? 19—] 96 l.   E275.B27A3

Typescript.

Also published as "Colonel Frye Bailey's Reminiscences" in the *Proceedings* of the Vermont Historical Society for 1923/25 (Bellow Falls, Vt., 1926), p. 22–86.

12806

BAYLEY, JACOB (1726–1815)

New Hampshire; Vermont. Landowner, Revolutionary general, judge, assemblyman.

BAYLEY, EDWIN A.   An address commemorative of the life and public services of Brig.-Gen. Jacob Bayley, 1726–1815, a founder of the state of Vermont; a neglected patriot of the Revolution. *In* Vermont Historical Society. Proceedings. 1917/18. [Montpelier] 1920. p. [55]–92.   F46.V55, 1917/18

12807

BEACH, ABRAHAM (1740–1828)

Connecticut; New Jersey. Anglican clergyman.

———— The Reverend Abraham Beach, D.D., 1740–1828. Historical magazine of the Protestant Episcopal church, v. 3, June 1934: 76–95.   BX5800.H5, v. 3

Consists of 15 letters written to the Society for the Propagation of the Gospel from 1768 to 1784. Introduction and notes by Walter H. Stowe.

12808

BEACH, SAMUEL (1752?–1827)

Vermont. Revolutionary officer.

BRONG, KARL S.   Vermont's neglected hero. Vermont quarterly, new ser., v. 19, July 1951: 172–177.   F46.V55, n.s., v. 19

12809

BEALE, ROBERT (*b.* 1759)

Virginia. Revolutionary soldier.

———— Revolutionary experiences of Major Robert Beale. *In* Northern Neck historical magazine. v. 6, no.1; 1956. Montross, Va. p. [505]–506.   F232.N86N6, v. 6

12810

BEAMAN, EZRA (1736–1811)

Massachusetts. Innkeeper, Revolutionary officer.

LOVELL, ALBERT A.   Ezra Beaman. *In* Worcester Historical Society, *Worcester, Mass.* Collections. v. 5. Proceedings. no. 18; 1881. Worcester, 1882. p. 124–144.   F74.W9W85, v. 5

12811

BEATTY, CHARLES (1715?–1772)*

Ireland; Pennsylvania. Presbyterian clergyman and missionary. Father of Charles Clinton Beatty (1756–1777), Erkuries Beatty (1759–1823), John Beatty (1749–1826), and Reading Beatty (1757–1831).

———— The journal of a two months tour [1766]; with a view of promoting religion among the frontier inhabitants of Pennsylvania, and of introducing Christianity among the Indians to the westward of the Alegh-geny mountains. To which are added, remarks on the language and customs of some particular tribes among the Indians, with a brief account of the various attempts that have been made to civilize and convert them, from the first settlement of New England to this day. London, Printed for W. Davenhill, 1768. viii, 110 p.
      E98.M6B3
      AC901.W3, v. 118, no. 1

Reprinted in St. Clair Shores, Mich., by Scholarly Press (1972).

———— Journals of Charles Beatty, 1762–1769. Edited with an introduction by Guy Souilliard Klett. University Park, Pennsylvania State University Press, 1962 [i.e. 1963] xxix, 144 p. illus., port. (Presbyterian Historical Society publications)   BX9225.B458A3 1963

KLETT, GUY S.   Charles Beatty, wilderness churchman. *In* Presbyterian Historical Society. Journal, v. 32, Sept. 1954: 143–158.   BX8905.P7A4, v. 32

12812

BEATTY, CHARLES CLINTON (1756–1777)

Pennsylvania. Revolutionary officer.

———— Beatty letters, 1773–1782. *In* New Jersey Historical Society. Proceedings, v. 80, Oct. 1962: 223–235; v. 81, Jan. 1963: 21–46.   F131.N58, v. 80–81

Also includes letters of John, Reading, and Erkuries Beatty.

12813

BEATTY, ERKURIES (1759–1823)

Pennsylvania. Revolutionary officer.

———— Diary of Major Erkuries Beatty, paymaster of the western army, May 15, 1786, to June 5, 1787. Magazine of American history, with notes and queries, v. 1, Mar.–July 1877: 175–179, 235–243, 309–315, 380–384, 432–438.   E171.M18, v. 1

"From the original MS. in the New York Historical Society."

BEATTY, JOSEPH M., *ed*.   Letters of the four Beatty brothers of the Continental Army, 1774–1794. Pennsylvania magazine of history and biography, v. 44, July 1920: 193–263.   F146.P65, v. 44

Mostly letters of Erkuries to Reading, John, and Charles Clinton Beatty.

WEISS, HARRY B., *and* GRACE M. SIEGLER. Colonel Erkuries Beatty, 1759–1823. Pennsylvania Revolutionary soldier, New Jersey judge, senator, farmer, and prominent citizen of Princeton. Trenton, Past Times Press, 1958. vi, 80 p. illus., facsim., plates, port.
                    F138.B4W4

Bibliography: p. 74–75.

12814
BEATTY, JOHN (1749–1826)*
Pennsylvania; New Jersey. Physician, Revolutionary officer, delegate to the Continental Congress.

ROGERS, FRED B.   General John Beatty (1749–1826): patriot and physician. Bulletin of the history of medicine, v. 32, Jan./Feb. 1958: 39–45. port.   R11.B93, v. 32

Also published in the *Journal* of the Medical Society of New Jersey, v. 55, Nov. 1958, p. 613–617 (R15.N515, v. 55).

12815
BEATTY, READING (1757–1831)
Pennsylvania. Revolutionary surgeon.

Letters from Continental officers to Doctor Reading Beatty, 1781–1788.   Pennsylvania magazine of history and biography, v. 54, Apr. 1930: 155–174.
                    F146.P65, v. 54

12816
BEATTY, WILLIAM (1758–1781)
Maryland. Revolutionary officer.

——— Correspondence of Captain William Beatty of the Maryland Line, 1776–1781. Historical magazine, 2d ser., v. 1, Mar. 1867: 147–150.
                    E171.H64, 2d s., v. 1

——— Journal of Capt. William Beatty, 1776–1781. Maryland historical magazine, v. 3, June 1908: 104–119.
                    F176.M18, v. 3

Published earlier in *The Historical Magazine*, 2d ser., v. 1, Feb. 1867. p. 79–85.

12817
BEAUMAN, SEBASTIAN (1739–1803)
Germany; New York. Revolutionary officer.

FAIRCHILD, MARY C. D., *ed.*   Memoirs of Colonel Sebastian Beauman and his descendants, with selections from his correspondence. [Franklin? Ohio, Editor Pub. Co.] 1900. 137 p. facsim., port.   E207.B37F2

12818
BEAUMARCHAIS, PIERRE AUGUSTIN CARON DE (1732–1799)
France. Playwright, international financier.

——— Correspondance. Paris, A.–G. Nizet, 1969+
                    PQ1956.A8 1969

Edited by Brian N. Morton.
Contents: t. 1. 1745–1772.—t. 2. 1773–1776.—t. 3. 1777.—

——— Observations sur le *Mémoire justificatif* de la cour de Londres. A Londres, à Philadelphie, 1779. 56 p.
                    E249.G34 Rare Bk. Coll.

Concerning the assistance given by France to the Americans; written in response to a *Mémoire justificatif* by Edward Gibbon.

——— Le voeu de toutes les nations, et l'intérêt de toutes les puissances, dans l'abaissement et l'humiliation de la Grande-Bretagne. [Paris? 1778] 74 p.
                    DA507.1778.B4

COX, CYNTHIA.   The real Figaro; the extraordinary career of Caron de Beaumarchais. New York, Boward-McCann [1963, ᶜ1962] ix, 212 p. illus.
                    PQ1956.C6 1963

Bibliography: p. 205–207.

DALSÈME, RENÉ.   Beaumarchais, 1732–1799. Translated by Hannaford Bennett. New York, G. P. Putnam's Sons, 1929. viii, 432 p. ports.   PQ1956.D34
Bibliography: p. 425.

LEMAÎTRE, GEORGES É.   Beaumarchais. New York, A. A. Knopf, 1949. viii, 362, xi p. port.   PQ1956.L4 1949
Bibliography: p. 361–362.

LOMÉNIE, LOUIS LÉONARD DE.   Beaumarchais and his times. Sketches of French society in the eighteenth century from unpublished documents. Translated by Henry S. Edwards. London, Addey, 1856. 4 v. PQ1956.L7

RUSKIN, ARIANE.   Spy for liberty; the adventurous life of Beaumarchais, playwright and secret agent for the American Revolution. [New York] Pantheon Books [1965] 178, [1] p. illus., ports.   PQ1956.R8
Bibliography: p. [179]

12819
BÉCHET, ÉTIENNE NICOLAS MARIE, *SIEUR DE ROCHEFONTAINE* (1755–1814)
France. Engineer, Revolutionary officer.

BUZZAIRD, RALEIGH B.   Washington's last chief engineer: Etienne Bechet, sieur de Rochefontaine. Military engineer, v. 45, Mar./Apr. 1953: 118–122. illus., map.
                    TA1.P85, v. 45

HALL, EDWARD H.   Lieutenant Colonel Stephen Rochefontaine; a biographical sketch of Etienne Nicolas

Marie Bechet, sieur de Rochefontaine, later known as Stephen Rochefontaine, a French engineer . . . in the Continental Army. *In* American Scenic and Historic Preservation Society. Annual report. 26th; 1921. Albany, 1922. p. 245–269. map.   E151.A51, v. 26

His role in the Revolution, particularly at Morristown and Yorktown.

12820

BECKER, JOHN P. (1765–1837)

New York. Farmer, Revolutionary wagoner.

—— The sexagenary; or, Reminiscences of the American Revolution. Albany, W. C. Little and O. Steele, 1833. 203 p.   E275.B39 Rare Bk. Coll.

Edited by S. DeWitt Bloodgood.
The question of authorship is discussed in J. H. Brandow's *Story of Old Saratoga* (1900), p. 180–187.
Another edition was published in Albany by J. Munsell (1866. 234 p. E275.B41).

12821

BECKFORD, WILLIAM (1744–1799)†

Jamaica; England. Planter, historian.

—— A descriptive account of the island of Jamaica; with remarks upon the cultivation of the sugar-cane, throughout the different seasons of the year, and chiefly considered in a picturesque point of view; also observations and reflections upon what would probably be the consequences of an abolition of the slave-trade, and of the emancipation of the slaves. London, Printed for T. and J. Egerton, 1790. 2 v.   F1870.B39
Micro 01291 reel 263, no. 9

CUNDALL, FRANK.   Jamaica worthies: William Beckford, historian. *In* Institute of Jamaica, *Kingston.* Journal, v. 1, Dec. 1893: 349–360.   AS73.J21, v. 1

See also "Some Further Notes on William Beckford, Historian," in volume 2 of the *Journal* for April 1895.

SHERIDAN, RICHARD B..   Planter and historian: the career of William Beckford of Jamaica and England, 1744–1799. Jamaican historical review, v. 4, 1964: 36–59.   F1861.J32, v. 4

12822

BECKLEY, JOHN JAMES (1757–1807)

Virginia. Clerk.

BERKLEY, EDMUND, *and* DOROTHY S. BERKLEY.   "The ablest clerk in the U.S.," John James Beckley. Virginia magazine of history and biography, v. 70, Oct. 1962: 434–446.   F221.V91, v. 70

MARTIN, RAYMOND V.   Eminent Virginian—a study of John Beckley. West Virginia history, v. 11, Oct. 1949/ Jan. 1950: 44–61.   F236.W52, v. 11

12823

BEDEL, TIMOTHY (*ca.* 1733–1787)

New Hampshire. Revolutionary officer, assemblyman.

ALDRICH, EDGAR.   The affair of the Cedars and the service of Colonel Timothy Bedel in the Revolution. *In* New Hampshire Historical Society. Proceedings. v. 3; 1897/99. Concord, 1902. p. 194–231.   F31.N52, v. 3

12824

BEDFORD, GUNNING (1747–1812)*

Pennsylvania; Delware. Lawyer, assemblyman, councilor, delegate to the Continental Congress, delegate to the Constitutional Convention.

CONRAD, HENRY C.   Gunning Bedford, Junior. Wilmington, Historical Society of Delaware, 1900. 13 p. plates, port. (Delaware Historical Society. Papers, 26)   F161.D35, no.26
E302.6.B4B75

NIELDS, JOHN P.   Gunning Bedford, Junior, United States district judge, district of Delaware, 1789–1812. Paper on the life of Gunning Bedford, Junior. [Wilmington, Del., 1907] 26 p.   JK1519.B4N6

12825

BEDFORD, JOHN RUSSELL, *4th Duke of,* (1710–1771)†

England. Diplomat.

—— Correspondence of John, fourth duke of Bedford: selected from the originals at Woburn Abbey. With an introduction, by Lord John Russell. London, Longman, Brown, Green, and Longmans, 1842–46. 3 v.   DA501.B4A2

Letters for the years 1763–70 appear in volume 3, on pages 184–417.

12826

BEDINGER, GEORGE MICHAEL (1756–1843)*

Pennsylvania; Kentucky. Frontiersman, Revolutionary officer.

DANDRIDGE, DANSKE B.   George Michael Bedinger: a Kentucky pioneer. Charlottesville, Va., Michie Co., Printers, 1909. 232 p. port.   F451.B4

TALBERT, CHARLES G.   George Michael Bedinger, 1756–1843. *In* Kentucky Historical Society. Register, v. 65, Jan. 1967: 28–46. plate.   F446.K43, v. 65

12827

BEEKMAN, JAMES (1732–1807)

New York. Merchant.

BAILYN, BERNARD.   The Beekmans of New York: trade, politics, and families; a review article. William and Mary quarterly, 3d ser., v. 14, Oct. 1957: 598–608.   F221.W71, 3d s., v. 14

WHITE, PHILIP L., *ed.* The Beekman mercantile papers, 1746–1799. New York, New-York Historical Society, 1956. 3 v. (vii, 1485 p.) map (on lining papers)

HF3025.W5

Contents: v. 1. Gerard G. Beekman letter book, 1746–1770.—v. 2. James Beekman correspondence, 1750–1799.—v. 3. James Beekman correspondence. Gerard W. Beekman's letters to his brother William, 1777–1782. Appendix: Sample invoices of shipment to James Beekman.

——— The Beekmans of New York in politics and commerce, 1647–1877. With an introduction by Fenwick Beekman. New York, New-York Historical Society under a grant from the Beekman Family Association, 1956. xxxi, 705 p. illus., geneal. table, maps. ports.

CS71.B441 1956

Bibliographic footnotes. "Bibliographical note": p. 656–657.

The author's thesis (Ph.D.), with the same title, was submitted to Columbia University in 1954.

12828

BEELEN-BERTHOLFF, FREDERICK EUGENE FRANÇOIS, *baron* DE (1729–1804)
Belgium; Pennsylvania. Austrian agent in America.

———Die Berichte des ersten Agenten Österreichs in den Vereinigten Staaten von Amerika, Baron de Beelen-Bertholff, an die Regierung der Österreichischen Niederlande in Brüssel, 1784–1789. Hrsg. von Hanns Schlitter. Wien, F. Tempsky, 1891. [255]–890 p. (Fontes rerum austriacarum. Œsterreichische Geschichts-Quellen, 2. Abth., 45. Bd., 2. Hälfte)

E303.B41
DB3.F68

Reports given in the original French.

YOUNG, HENRY J. The Baron de Beelen-Bertholff (1729–1805). [York, Pa., 1939?] 6 p. (Historical Society of York County (*Pennsylvania*). Papers, new ser., no.3)

F157.Y6H62, n.s., no.3

12829

BELKNAP, JEREMY (1744–1798)*
Massachusetts. Congregational clergyman, historian.

——— American biography; or, An historical account of those persons who have been distinguished in America, as adventurers, statesmen, philosophers, divines, warriors, authors, and other remarkable characters. Printed at Boston, by I. Thomas and E. J. Andrews, Faust's Statue, No. 45, Newbury Street, 1794–98. 2 v.

E187.5.B43 Rare Bk. Coll.

The third volume, which Belknap intended to issue, was never published.

——— The Belknap papers. Boston, Published by the Society, 1877–91. 3 v. (Massachusetts Historical Society, Boston. Collections, 5th ser., v. 2–3; 6th ser., v. 4)

F61.M41, 5th s., v. 2–3; 6th s., v. 4

Contents: pt. 1. Correspondence between Jeremy Belknap and Ebenezer Hazard, 1779–88.—pt. 2. Correspondence between Jeremy Belknap and Ebenezer Hazard, 1788–1804. Letters and documents relating to slavery in Massachusetts. Negro petitions for freedom. Brief of Levi Lincoln in the slave trade case tried 1781.—pt. 3. Miscellaneous letters, papers, and documents, 1724–98.

——— Journal of a tour to the White Mountains in July, 1784. Printed from the original manuscript, with a prefatory note by the editor [Charles Deane] Boston, Massachusetts Historical Society, 1876. 21 p. fold. map.

F41.44.B43

From the *Belknap Papers.*

———Journey to Dartmouth in 1774. Edited by Edward C. Lathem from the manuscript journal. Hanover, N.H., Dartmouth Publications [1950] 25 p. map (on lining paper)

F37.B45

COLE, CHARLES W. Jeremy Belknap, pioneer nationalist. New England quarterly, v. 10, Dec. 743–751.

F1.N62, v. 10

HAYCOX, STEPHEN W. Jeremy Belknap and early American nationalism; a study in the political and theological foundations of American liberty. 1971. ([267] p.)

Micro AC–1, no. 71–23,113

Thesis (Ph.D.)—University of Oregon.
Abstracted in *Dissertation Abstracts International,* v. 32A, Sept. 1971, p. 1441.

KAPLAN, SIDNEY. *The History of New Hampshire:* Jeremy Belknap as literary craftsman. William and Mary quarterly, 3d ser., v. 21, Jan. 1964: 18–39.

F221.W71, 3d s., v. 21

KIRSCH, GEORGE B. Jeremy Belknap, a biography. 1972. ([374] p.)

Micro AC–1, no. 72–28,059

Thesis (Ph.D.)—Columbia University.
Abstracted in *Dissertation Abstracts International,* v. 33A, Nov. 1972, p. 2289.

[MARCOU, JANE B.] Life of Jeremy Belknap, D.D., the historian of New Hampshire. With selections from his correspondence and other writings. Collected and arranged by his grand-daughter. New York, Harper, 1847. 253 p. port.

E175.5.B43

MAYO, LAWRENCE S. Jeremy Belknap and Ebenezer Hazard, 1782–84. New England quarterly, v. 2, Apr. 1929: 183–198.

F1.N62, v. 2

SMITH, CHARLES C. Financial embarrassments of the New England ministers in the last century. *In* American Antiquarian Society, *Worcester, Mass.* Proceedings, new ser., v. 7, Oct. 1890: 129–135.

E172.A35, n.s., v. 7

12830

BELLAMY, JOSEPH (1719–1790)*
Connecticut. Theologian, writer.

———The works of the Rev. Joseph Bellamy, D.D., late of Bethlehem, Connecticut. New-York, Published by

Stephen Dodge; Printed by J. Seymour, no. 49, John-Street, 1811–12. 3 v.　　　　BX7117.B5

EGGLESTON, PERCY C. A man of Bethlehem, Joseph Bellamy, D.D., and his divinity school. Printed for the Bethlehem, Connecticut, tercentenary. [New London? Conn., 1908] 18 p.　　　　BX7260.B34E4

12831

BELLEVILLE, NICHOLAS JACQUES EMANUEL DE (1753–1831)

France; New Jersey. Revolutionary surgeon.

ROGERS, FRED B. Dr. Nicholas Belleville (1753–1831): aristocratic physician. In Medical Society of New Jersey. Journal, v. 55, Feb. 1958: 71–77.　　　　R15.N515, v. 55

12832

BENBRIDGE, HENRY (1743–1812)*

Pennsylvania; South Carolina. Portrait artist.

National Portrait Gallery, Washington, D.C. Henry Benbridge (1743–1812): American portrait painter. Robert G. Stewart, curator. Washington, Published for the National Portrait Gallery by the Smithsonian Institute Press, 1971. 93 p. illus., ports. (part col.)　　　　ND1329.B45N3

Bibliography: p. 89–90.
Catalog of an exhibition.

STEWART, ROBERT G. Patriot, Loyalist or neutral—he painted them all. Smithsonian, v. 2, Apr. 1971: 48–53. ports.　　　　AS30.S6, v. 2

12833

BENBURY, THOMAS (1736–1793)

North Carolina. Assemblyman, Revolutionary general.

HAYWOOD, EMILY R. B. Thomas Benbury—a brigadier general of the American Revolution. North Carolina booklet, v. 18, Jan. 1919: 134–142. F251.N86, v. 18

12834

BENEZET, ANTHONY (1713–1784)*†

France; Pennsylvania. Merchant, teacher, reform writer.

—— A short account of the people called Quakers; their rise, religious principles and settlement in America, mostly collected from different authors, for the information of all serious inquirers, particularly foreigners. Philadelphia, Printed by Joseph Crukshank, in Market-Street, between Second and Third Streets, 1780. 27 p.　　　　BX7730.B385 Rare Bk. Coll.
AC901.M5, v. 1153a Rare Bk. Coll.

—— Some observations on the situation, disposition, and character of the Indian natives of this continent. Philadelphia, Printed and sold by J. Crukshank, in Market-Street, 1784. 59 p.　　　　E77.B46 Rare Bk. Coll.

BROOKES, GEORGE S. Friend Anthony Benezet. Philadelphia, University of Pennsylvania Press, 1937. ix, 516 p. facsims., plates, ports.　　　　HV28.B4B7

Letters: p. [207]–472; "Writings of Benezet": p. [473]–500.
Bibliography: p. [177]–203.

BRUNS, ROGER A. Anthony Benezet and the natural rights of the Negro. Pennsylvania magazine of history and biography, v. 96, Jan. 1972: 104–113.　　　　F146.P65, v. 96

—— Anthony Benezet's assertation of Negro equality. Journal of Negro history, v. 56, July 1971: 230–238.　　　　E185.J86, v. 56

CADBURY, HENRY J. Anthony Benezet's library. In Friends' Historical Association. Bulletin, v. 23, autumn 1934: 63–75.　　　　BX7635.A1F6, v. 23

LASHLEY, LEONARD C. Anthony Benezet and his anti-slavery activities. 1939.

Thesis (Ph.D.)—Fordham University.

STRAUB, JEAN S. Anthony Benezet: teacher and abolitionist of the eighteenth century. Quaker history, v. 57, spring 1968: 3–16.　　　　BX7635.A1F6, v. 57

VAUX, ROBERTS. Memoirs of the life of Anthony Benezet. Philadelphia, J. P. Parke, 1817. vii, 136 p. front.　　　　HV28.B4V3

Reprinted in New York by B. Franklin (1969).
A revised edition, entitled Anthony Benezet; From the Original Memoir, with additions by Wilson Armistead, was published in Philadelphia by Lippincott (1859) and has been reprinted in Freeport, N.Y., by Books for Libraries Press (1971).

WOODSON, CARTER G. Anthony Benezet. Journal of Negro history, v. 2, Jan. 1917: 37–50.　　　　E185.J86, v. 2

"Letters of Anthony Benezet," dated 1772–83, appear on pages 83–95.

12835

BENJAMIN, SAMUEL (1753–1824)

Massachusetts; Maine. Revolutionary officer, settler.

—— Brief notice of Lieutenant Samuel Benjamin, an officer of the Revolutionary War, with extracts from a diary kept by him during the war. Washington, Buell & Blanchard, Printers [185–?] 15 p.　　　　E275.B46 Rare Bk. Coll.

BENJAMIN, MARY L., comp. A genealogy of the family of Lieut. Samuel Benjamin . . . including biographical sketches, notes, and diary. [Winthrop? Me.] 1900. 112 p. coat of arms, facsim., ports. CS71.B468 1900

12836

BENNETT, CALEB PREW (1758–1836)*

Pennsylvania; Delaware. Revolutionary officer, ferryboat conductor, shipper.

—— The Delaware Regiment in the Revolution. Narrative of the services of the Delaware Regiment with Captain McKennan during the Revolutionary War, by Major C. P. Bennett, late governor of Delaware, a lieutenant under Captain McKennan. Pennsylvania magazine of history and biography, v. 9, Jan. 1886: 451–462. F146.P65, v. 9

12837
BENTLEY, WILLIAM (1759–1819)*
Massachusetts. Unitarian clergyman, linguist.

—— The diary of William Bentley, D.D., pastor of the East Church, Salem, Massachusetts. v. 1. April, 1784–December, 1792. Salem, Mass., Essex Institute, 1905. xlii, 456 p. port. F74.S1B46, v. 1

Reprinted in Gloucester, Mass., by P. Smith (1962).

BARROW, JULIA P. William Bentley: an extraordinary boarder. *In* Essex Institute, *Salem, Mass*. Historical collections, v. 97, Apr. 1961: 129–150. F72.E7E81, v. 97

SMITH, HULDAH M. Some aspects of William Bentley as art collector and connoisseur. *In* Essex Institute, *Salem, Mass*. Historical collections, v. 97, Apr. 1961: 151–164. F72.E7E81, v. 97

12838
BENTON, JESSE (d. 1790)
North Carolina. Land speculator, lawyer.

CHAMBERS, WILLIAM N. As the twig is bent: the family and the North Carolina years of Thomas Hart Benton, 1752–1801. North Carolina historical review, v. 26, Oct. 1949: 385–416. F251.N892, v. 26

12839
BERNARD, *Sir* FRANCIS, *Bart.* (1712–1779)*†
England; New Jersey; Massachusetts. Lawyer, royal governor.

—— Select letters on the trade and government of America; and the Principles of law and polity, applied to the American colonies. Written by Governor Bernard, at Boston, in the years 1763, 4, 5, 6, 7, and 8. Now first published: to which are added The petition of the assembly of Massachuset's Bay against the governor, his answer thereto, and the order of the King in Council thereon. London, Printed for T. Payne, 1774, vii, 130 p. E211.B51 Rare Bk. Coll.

FIORE, JORDAN D. Francis Bernard, colonial governor. 1950.
Thesis (Ph.D.)—Boston University.

——Governor Bernard for an American nobility. *In* Boston. Public Library. Quarterly, v. 4, July 1952: 125–138. Z881.B7535, v. 4

—— Sir Francis Bernard, colonial governor. New England social studies bulletin, v. 12, Oct. 1954: 13–18. Hl.N4, v. 12

HIGGINS, SOPHIA E. "*Mrs*. Napier Higgins." The Bernards of Abington and Nether Winchendon, a family history. London, New York, Longmans, Green, 1903–4. 4 v. DA306.B4H5

The first two volumes deal extensively with Sir Francis Bernard and the coming of the Revolution in Massachusetts.

PENROSE, CHARLES. New England in the year of grace 1766—and Sir Francis Bernard, his outlook on trade and navigation. A Newcomen address, 1940. [Princeton, Printed at the Princeton University Press, 1940] 28 p. HF3025.P4

SAWTELLE, WILLIAM O. Sir Francis Bernard and his grant of Mount Desert. *In* Colonial Society of Massachusetts, *Boston*. Publications. v. 24. Transactions, 1920/22. Boston, 1923. p. 197–254. map. F61.C71, v. 24

12840
BERRY, SIDNEY (*fl.* 1776)
Revolutionary officer.

—— Letters written by Colonel Sidney Berry to his wife, Katharine De Waldron Beekman, during the Revolution. American monthly magazine, v. 4, Feb. 1894: 173–181. E202.5.A12, v.4

12841
BERTHIER, LOUIS ALEXANDRE, *prince* DE NEUCHÂTEL ET DE WAGRAM (1753–1815)
France. French officer in America.

—— Journal de la campagne de l'Amérique, 10 mai 1780–26 août 1781. Publié d'après le manuscrit inédit de l'Université de Princeton par Gilbert Chinard. *In* Institut français de Washington, *Washington, D.C.* Bulletin. nouv. sér., no. 1; déc. 1951. [Washington] p. 43–120. E183.8.F8I8, n.s., 1951

Excerpts from the journal relating to Rhode Island were published, with introduction and notes by Marshall Morgan, in *Rhode Island History*, v. 24, July 1965, p. 77–88. The full journal, together with the "Sea Campaigns, December 1782–April 1783," appears in v. 1 of Rice and Brown's *The American Campaigns of Rochambeau's Army* (entry 7195), p. 221–282.

MAGGS BROS., *London*. The American War for Independence as related in the unpublished manuscript journals and plans of Alexander Berthier, staff officer to General Comte de Rochambeau during the American campaign. London, Maggs Bros., 1936. xii, 36 p. illus., maps, plans, port. Z6616.B54M2

A descriptive catalog of 37 items in the Berthier collection, then in private hands.

12842

BEVERLEY, ROBERT (*d.* 1800)

Virginia. Lawyer, planter, Loyalist.

—— "A sorrowful spectator of these tumultuous times": Robert Beverley describes the coming of the Revolution. Edited by Robert M. Calhoon. Virginia magazine of history and biography, v. 73, Jan. 1965: 41–55.
F221.V91, v. 73

CALHOON, ROBERT M. "Unhinging former intimacies": Robert Beverley's perception of the pre-Revolutionary controversy, 1761–1775. South Atlantic quarterly, v. 68, spring 1969: 246–261. AP2.S75, v. 68

12843

BIDDLE, CHARLES (1745–1821)

Pennsylvania. Revolutionary soldier and seaman, shipmaster, councilor. Brother of Nicholas Biddle (1750–1778).

—— Autobiography of Charles Biddle, vice-president of the Supreme Executive Council of Pennsylvania. 1745–1821. (Priv. print.) Philadelphia, E. Claxton, 1883. xii, 423 p. F153.B58

Edited by J. S. Biddle.

12844

BIDDLE, CLEMENT (1740–1814)*

Pennsylvania. Merchant, Revolutionary officer, judge.

—— Selections from the correspondence of Colonel Clement Biddle [1778–89] Pennsylvania magazine of history and biography, v. 42, Oct. 1918: 310–343; v. 43, Jan. 1919: 53–76. F146.P65, v. 42–43

12845

BIDDLE, NICHOLAS (1750–1778)*

Pennsylvania. Seaman, explorer, Revolutionary naval commander.

——The letters of Captain Nicholas Biddle [1771–1777] Pennsylvania magazine of history and biography, v. 74, July 1950: 348–405. F146.P65, v. 74

Introduction and notes by William B. Clark.

BIDDLE, EDWARD. Captain Nicholas Biddle (Continental Navy), 1750–1778. *In* United States Naval Institute. Proceedings, v. 43, Sept. 1917: 1993–2003.
V1.U8, v. 43

CLARK, WILLIAM B. Captain Dauntless, the story of Nicholas Biddle of the Continental Navy. [Baton Rouge] Louisiana State University Press, 1949. x, 317 p. illus., maps, ports. E207.B48C6

Bibliography: p. 262–270.

12846

BIDDLE, OWEN (1737–1799)

Pennsylvania. Shipper-importer, Revolutionary provisioner.

BIDDLE, HENRY D. Owen Biddle. Pennsylvania magazine of history and biography, v. 16, Oct. 1892: 299–329. facsims. F146.P65, v. 16

Includes letters written during the war.

12847

BIDDULPH, ROBERT (1761–1814)

England. Contractor, banker.

——Letters of Robert Biddulph, 1779–1783. American historical review, v. 29, Oct. 1923: 87–109.
E171.A57, v. 29

—— —— Offprint. [New York, 1923] 87–109 p. E267.B54

Contemporary observations, written from New York and Charleston, by an agent of a British firm that had contracted to pay the British army in America with foreign gold. Introduction by Violet Biddulph, notes by J. Franklin Jameson.

12848

BIGELOW, TIMOTHY (1739–1790)

Massachusetts. Blacksmith, Revolutionary officer.

HERSEY, CHARLES. Reminiscences of the military life and sufferings of Col. Timothy Bigelow, commander of the Fifteenth Regiment of the Massachusetts Line in the Continental Army, during the War of the Revolution. Worcester, Printed by H. J. Howland, 1860. 24 p.
E207.B58H5

12849

BIGGS, WILLIAM (1755–1827)

—— Narrative of the captivity of William Biggs among the Kickapoo Indians in Illinois in 1788, written by himself. [New York, C. F. Heartman] 1922. 36 p. (Heartman's historical series, no. 37) E87.B6

First published in the *Transactions* of the Illinois State Historical Society for 1902 (Springfield, 1902), p. 202–215.

12850

BILLINGS, WILLIAM (1746–1800)*

Massachusetts. Tanner, singing-master, composer.

BARBOUR, JAMES M. The church music of William Billings. [East Lansing] Michigan State University Press [1960] xvi, 167 p. music. ML410.B588B4

Bibliography: p. 159–163.

FERRIS, WILLIAM R. William Billings, the musical tanner. Keystone folklore quarterly, v. 12, winter 1967: 261–279. GR1.K45, v. 12

LINDSTROM, CARL E. William Billings and his times. Musical quarterly, v. 25, Oct. 1939: 479–497. facsims. ML1.M725, v. 25

MORIN, RAYMOND. William Billings, pioneer in American music. New England quarterly, v. 14, Mar. 1941: 25–33. F1.N62, v. 14

SILVER, ROLLO G. Prologue to copyright in America: 1772. *In* Virginia. University. *Bibliographical Society.* Studies in bibliography; papers. v. 11; 1958. Charlottesville. p. 259–262. Z1008.V55, v. 11

On Billings' petition to the Massachusetts House of Representatives for protection of his *New-England Psalm-Singer.*

12851

BILLOPP, CHRISTOPHER (1737–1827)

New York; New Brunswick. Landowner, Loyalist officer.

DAVIS, WILLIAM T. Colonel Christopher Billopp. *In his* The Conference or Billopp House, Staten Island, New York. [Lancaster, Pa., Science Press Print. Co.] 1926. p. 125–173. port. F127.S7D18

12852

BINGHAM, WILLIAM (1752–1804)*

Pennsylvania. Merchant, shipowner, banker, delegate to the Continental Congress.

ALBERTS, ROBERT C. The golden voyage; the life and times of William Bingham, 1752–1804. Boston, Houghton-Mifflin, 1969. xvii, 570 p. illus., map, port. (part col.) E302.6.B5A4

BROWN, MARGARET L. Mr. and Mrs. William Bingham of Philadelphia, rulers of the republican court. Pennsylvania magazine of history and biography, v. 61, July 1937: 286–324. plate, ports. F146.P65, v. 61

——— William Bingham, agent of the Continental Congress in Martinique. Pennsylvania magazine of history and biography, v. 61, Jan 1937: 54–87. F146.P65, v. 61

——— William Bingham, eighteenth century magnate. Pennsylvania magazine of history and biography, v. 61, Oct. 1937: 387–434. F146.P65, v. 61

BIRON, ARMAND LOUIS DE GONTAUT, *duc* DE LAUZUN, afterwards *duc* DE
See LAUZUN, ARMAND LOUIS GONTAUT, *duc* DE

12853

BLACKSTONE, *Sir* WILLIAM (1723–1780)†

England. Lawyer, professor, Member of Parliament, judge.

——— Commentaries on the laws of England. Oxford, Printed at the Clarendon Press, 1765–69. 4 v. LL

LOCKMILLER, DAVID A. Sir William Blackstone. Chapel Hill, University of North Carolina Press, 1938. xiii, 308 p. illus., facsims., fold. geneal. table, plates, ports. LL

"Selected bibliography": p. [283]–294.

MERSKY, ROY M. A bibliography of articles on Blackstone. American journal of legal history, v. 3, Jan 1959: 78–87. LL

STOURZH, GERALD. William Blackstone, teacher of revolution. *In* Jahrbuch für Amerikastudien. Bd. 15; 1970. Heidelberg, C. Winter, p. 184–200. E169.1.J33, v. 15

Suggests that Blackstone's interpretation of the Glorious Revolution was more important than that of Locke in shaping the thought of American revolutionists.

WARDEN, LEWIS C. The life of Blackstone. Charlottesville, Va., Michie Co., 1938. xiv, 451 p. plates, port. LL

"The works of Blackstone": p. [409]–411. "Chronological table of Sir William Blackstone": p. [413]–414. Bibliography: p. [415]–421.

YALE UNIVERSITY. *School of Law. Library. William Blackstone Collection.* The William Blackstone collection in the Yale Law Library; a bibliographical catalogue, by Catherine Spicer Eller. [New Haven] Published for the Yale Law Library by the Yale University Press, 1938. xvii, 113 p. (Yale Law Library publications, no. 6, June 1938) Z8102.2.Y17

ZEYDEL, WALTER H. Sir William Blackstone and his *Commentaries. In* U.S. *Library of Congress.* Quarterly journal, v. 23, Oct. 1966: 302–312. illus. Z881.U49A3, v. 23

12854

BLAGDEN, *Sir* CHARLES (1748–1820)†

Scotland. Physician.

——— Letters from Sir Charles Blagden to Sir Joseph Banks on American natural history and politics, 1776–1780. *In* New York (City). Public Library. Bulletin, v. 7, Nov. 1903: 407–446. Z881.N6B, v. 7

GETMAN, FREDERICK H. Sir Charles Blagden, F.R.S. Osiris, v. 3, pt. 1, 1937: 69–87. Q1.O7, v. 3

12855

BLAIR, JOHN (1732–1800)*

Virginia. Lawyer, assemblyman, councilor, judge, delegate to the Constitutional Convention.

DRINARD, J. ELLIOTT. John Blair, Jr., 1732–1800. *In* Virginia State Bar Association. Annual report. v. 39; 1927. Richmond. p. 436–449. port. LL

12856

BLANCHARD, CLAUDE (1742–1802?)

France. French officer in America.

——— The journal of Claude Blanchard, commissary of the French auxiliary army sent to the United States during the American Revolution. 1780–1783. Translated from a French manuscript, by William Duane, and edited by Thomas Balch. Albany, J. Munsell, 1876. xvi, 207 p.
E265.B65

Reprinted in New York by the New York Times (1969).

12857

BLAND, RICHARD (1710–1776)*

Virginia. Assemblyman, delegate to the Continental Congress.

DETWEILER, ROBERT C. Richard Bland: conservator of self-government in eighteenth-century Virginia. 1968. ([358] p.) Micro AC–1, no. 69–7041
Thesis (Ph.D.)—University of Washington.
Abstracted in *Dissertation Abstracts*, v. 29A, Apr. 1969, p. 3554–3555.

PATE, JAMES E. Richard Bland's inquiry into the rights of the British colonies. William and Mary College quarterly historical magazine, 2d ser., v. 11, Jan. 1931: 20–28.
F221.W71, 2d s., v. 11

ROSSITER, CLINTON L. Richard Bland: the Whig in America. William and Mary quarterly, 3d ser., v. 10, Jan. 1953: 33–79. F221.W71, 3d s., v. 10

12858

BLAND, THEODORICK (1742–1790)*

Virginia. Physician, planter, Revolutionary officer, delegate to the Continental Congress, assemblyman.

——— The Bland papers: being a selection from the manuscripts of Colonel Theodorick Bland, Jr. . . . To which are prefixed an introduction, and a memoir of Colonel Bland. Edited by Charles Campbell. Petersburg [Va.] Printed by E. & J. Ruffin, 1840–43. 2 v. in 1.
E263.V8B6

——— Selections from the Campbell papers [1778–83] Virginia magazine of history and biography, v. 9, July 1901–Jan. 1902: 59–77, 162–170, 298–306.
F221.V91, v. 9

12859

BLEECKER, ANN ELIZA SCHUYLER (1752–1783)*

New York. Poet.

——— The history of Maria Kittle. In a letter to Miss Ten Eyck. Hartford, Printed by B. Babcock, 1797. 70 p.
E87.K62

——— Posthumous works, in prose and verse. To which is added a collection of essays, prose and poetical by

Margaretta V. Faugeres. New York, Printed by T. and J. Swords, 1793. 375 p. port.
PS708.B3 1793a Rare Bk. Coll.

Reprinted in Upper Saddle River, N.J., by Literature House (1970).

12860

BLISS, DANIEL (1740–1806)

Massachusetts; New Brunswick. Lawyer, Loyalist, British military officer.

TOLMAN, GEORGE. John Jack, the slave, and Daniel Bliss, the Tory. [Concord, Mass.] Concord Antiquarian Society [1902?] 21 p. illus. [Concord Antiquarian Society. Publications, no. 6] F74.C8C83, no. 6

First published in v. 13 of the *Collections* of the Worcester Historical Society (Proceedings. no. 40; 1892. Worcester, Mass., 1893), p. 246–265.

12861

BLODGET, SAMUEL (1724–1807)*

Massachusetts. Soldier, merchant, judge.

BROWNE, GEORGE W. Hon. Samuel Blodget, the pioneer of progress in New England. *In* Manchester Historic Association, *Manchester, N.H.* Collections. v. 1, pt. 2; 1898. Manchester. p. 121–176. port.
F44.M2M3, v. 1

12862

BLODGET, WILLIAM (1754–1809)

Connecticut; Rhode Island. Revolutionary officer.

KIHN, PHYLLIS. William Blodget, map maker, 1754–1809. *In* Connecticut Historical Society, *Hartford.* Bulletin, v. 27, Apr. 1962: 33–50. facsims., maps, ports.
F91.C67, v. 27

12863

BLOUNT, JOHN GRAY (1752–1833)

North Carolina. Merchant, assemblyman, land speculator.

——— The John Gray Blount papers. Edited by Alice Barnwell Keith. Raleigh [N.C.] State Dept. of Archives and History, 1952+ illus., maps (part fold.), ports. (North Carolina. State Dept. of Archives and History. Publications) F285.B5
Contents: v. 1. 1764–1789.

KEITH, ALICE B. John Gray and Thomas Blount, merchants, 1783–1800. North Carolina historical review, v. 25, Apr. 1948: 194–205. F251.N892, v. 25

12864

BLOUNT, WILLIAM (1749–1800)*

North Carolina. Revolutionary officer, assemblyman, delegate to the Continental Congress, delegate to the Constitutional Convention.

GOODPASTURE, ALBERT V. William Blount and the old Southwest Territory. American historical magazine and Tennessee Historical Society quarterly, v. 8, Jan. 1903: 1–13. port.   F431.A53, v. 8

KEITH, ALICE B. Three North Carolina Blount brothers in business and politics, 1783–1812. 1940.

Thesis (Ph.D.)—University of North Carolina.

———— William Blount in North Carolina politics, 1781–1789. *In* Sitterson, Joseph C., *ed.* Studies in Southern history [in memory of Albert Ray Newsome, 1894–1951, by his former students at the University of North Carolina] Chapel Hill, University of North Carolina Press, 1957. (The James Sprunt studies in history and political science, v. 39) p. 47–61.   F251.J28, v. 39

MASTERSON, WILLIAM H. William Blount. Baton Rouge, Louisiana State University Press [1954] viii, 378 p. illus., fold. map, ports. (Southern biography series)
                                   E302.6.B6M3

"Critical essay on authorities": p. [353]–368.
Reprinted in New York by Greenwood Press (1969). The author's thesis (Ph.D.), *Business Man in Politics: the Public Career of William Blount*, was submitted to the University of Pennsylvania in 1950.

WRIGHT, MARCUS J. Some account of the life and services of William Blount, an officer of the Revolutionary army, member of the Continental Congress, and of the convention which framed the Constitution of the United States, also governor of the territory south of the Ohio River, and Senator in Congress U.S. 1783–1797. Together with a full account of his impeachment and trial in Congress, and his expulsion from the U.S. Senate. Washington, E. J. Gray [°1884] 142 p. port.
                                   E302.6.B6W9

12865
BLOXHAM, JAMES (*d.* 1793)
England; Virginia. Farm manager.

ABBOTT, WILBUR C. James Bloxham, farmer. *In* Massachusetts Historical Society, *Boston.* Proceedings. v. 59; 1925/26. Boston, 1926. p. 177–203.
                                   F61.M38, v. 59

A slightly condensed version appears in his *Adventures in Reputation, With an Essay on Some "New" History and Historians* (Cambridge, Mass., Harvard University Press, 1935), p. [149]–172.

12866
BLYTH, BENJAMIN (*b. ca.* 1746)
Massachusetts. Portrait artist.

FOOTE, HENRY W. Benjamin Blyth, of Salem, eighteenth-century artist. *In* Massachusetts Historical Society, *Boston.* Proceedings. v. 71; 1953/57. Boston, 1959. p. 64–107. ports.   F61.M38, v. 71

Includes a note on his brother Samuel (p. 78–80), also a painter, and a descriptive catalog of portraits and engravings attributed to Benjamin Blyth (p. 81–106).

LITTLE, NINA F. The Blyths of Salem: Benjamin, limner in crayons and oil and Samuel, painter and cabinetmaker. *In* Essex Institute, *Salem, Mass.* Historical collections, v. 108, Jan 1972: 49–57. illus., ports.
                                   F72.E7E81. v. 108

12867
BOARDMAN, FRANCIS (*d.* 1792)
Massachusetts. Shipmaster, merchant.

CARY, JOHN H. "A contrary wind at sea and contrary times at home": the sea logs of Francis Boardman [1763–88] *In* Essex Institute, *Salem, Mass.* Historical collections, v. 101, Jan 1965: 3–26.
                                   F72.E7E81, v. 101

12868
BOLLAN, WILLIAM (*ca.* 1705–1782)*
England; Massachusetts. Lawyer, colonial agent.

MEYERSON, JOEL D. The private revolution of William Bollan. New England quarterly, v. 41, Dec. 1968: 536–550.   F1.N62, v. 41

12869
BOND, PHINEAS (1749–1815)
Pennsylvania. Lawyer, Loyalist, diplomat.

———— Letters of Phineas Bond, British consul at Philadelphia, to the Foreign Office of Great Britain, 1787–1794. *In* American Historical Association. Annual report. 1896 (v. 1)–97. Washington, 1897–98. p. 513–659; p. 454–568.   E172.A60, 1896 (v. 1)–97

Part of the reports of the Historical Manuscripts Commission, 1896 and 1897.

NEEL, JOANNE L. Phineas Bond; a study in Anglo-American relations, 1786–1812. Philadelphia, University of Pennsylvania Press [1968] xii, 192 p. port. (Haney Foundation series. Publication no. 4) E183.8.G7N45

Bibliography: p. [177]–183.
The author's thesis (Ph.D.), *His Britannic Majesty's Consul General, Phineas Bond, Esq.,* was submitted to Bryn Mawr College in 1963 (Micro AC–1, no. 64–4545).

12870
BOND, THOMAS (*ca.* 1712–1784)*
Maryland; Pennsylvania. Physician, lecturer.

THOMSON, ELIZABETH H. Thomas Bond, 1713–84: first professor of clinical medicine in the American colonies. Journal of medical education, v. 33, Sept. 1958: 614–624.   R11.A94, v. 33

12871
BOONE, DANIEL (1734–1820)*
North Carolina; Kentucky. Frontiersman, surveyor, Indian fighter, assemblyman.

ALVORD, CLARENCE W. The Daniel Boone myth. *In* Illinois State Historical Society. Journal, v. 19, 1926: 16–30.   F536.I18, v. 19

BAKELESS, JOHN E. Daniel Boone. New York, W. Morrow, 1939. xii, 480 p. facsims., map (on lining-papers), plates, ports.   F454.B724

At head of title: *Master of the Wilderness.*
"Bibliography and notes": p. [423]–465.
Reprinted in Harrisburg, Pa., by the Stackpole Co. (1965).

BOGART, WILLIAM H. Daniel Boone, and the hunters of Kentucky. New York, C. M. Saxton, 1859. 464 p. illus., plates.   F454.B728

First published in 1854.

BRUCE, HENRY ADDINGTON B. Daniel Boone and the Wilderness Road. New York, Macmillan Co., 1910. xiii, 349 p. map, plates, ports.   F454.B732

FISHWICK, MARSHALL W. Daniel Boone and the pattern of the western hero. Filson Club history quarterly, v. 27, Apr. 1953: 119–138.   F446.F484, v. 27

FLINT, TIMOTHY. Biographical memoir of Daniel Boone, the first settler of Kentucky; interspersed with incidents in the early annals of the country. Edited for the modern reader by James K. Folsom. New Haven, College & University Press [1967] 188 p. (The Masterworks of literature series)   F454.B752

First published in Cincinnati by N. & G. Guilford (1833. 267 p. F454.B744 Rare Bk. Coll.).

HAGY, JAMES W. The first attempt to settle Kentucky: Boone in Virginia. Filson Club history quarterly, v. 44, July 1970: 227–234.   F446.F484, v. 44

HARTLEY, CECIL B. Life and times of Colonel Daniel Boone, comprising history of the early settlement of Kentucky. To which is added, Colonel Boone's autobiography complete, as dictated to John Filson, and published in 1784. Philadelphia, G. G. Evans, 1860. 351 p. plates.   F454.B757

HILL, GEORGE C. Daniel Boone, the pioneer of Kentucky, a biography. Philadelphia, J. B. Lippincott, 1866. 262 p. plates.   F454.H6

JILLSON, WILLARD R. The Boone narrative; the story of the origin and discovery coupled with the reproduction in facsimile of a rare item of early Kentuckiana, to which is appended a sketch of Boone and a bibliography of 238 titles. Louisville, Ky., Standard Print. Co., 1932. 16 p., facsim.: 17–31 p., [32]–61 p. illus., facsims., plates.   F454.B7596

The reproduced publication was originally published as *The Adventures of Colonel Daniel Boon, One of the First Settlers at Kentucke: Containing the Wars With the Indians on the Ohio, From 1769 to 1783, and the First Establishment and Progress of the Settlement on That River* (Norwich, Printed by John Trumbull, 1786).
"A new Boone bibliography": p. [47]–61.

——— Land surveys of Daniel Boone [1783–1788]. *In* Kentucky Historical Society. Register, v. 44, Apr. 1946: 86–100. facsim.   F446.K43, v. 44

——— With compass and chain, a brief narration of the activities of Col. Daniel Boone as a land surveyor in Kentucky. Frankfort, Ky., Roberts Print. Co., 1954. 14 p. illus., ports.   F454.B75967

KELLOGG, LOUISE P. The fame of Daniel Boone. *In* Kentucky Historical Society. Register, v. 32, July 1934: 187–198.   F446.K43, v. 32

MAURICE, GEORGE H. On the trail of Daniel Boone in North Carolina. Eagle Springs, N.C., 1955. 19 p. illus., maps.   F454.B769

MINER, WILLIAM H. Daniel Boone; contribution toward a bibliography of writings concerning Daniel Boone. New York, Dibdin Club, 1901. ix, 32 p.   Z8109.M6

Reprinted in New York by B. Franklin (1970).

SPRAKER, ELLA H. A. The Boone family; a genealogical history of the descendants of George and Mary Boone who came to America in 1717; containing many unpublished bits of early Kentucky history. Rutland, Vt., Tuttle Co., 1922. 707 p. illus., facsims., maps, plates, ports.   CS71.B725 1922a

"A biographical sketch of Daniel Boone, the pioneer, by Jesse Procter Crump, one of his descendants": p.[559]–580.

STOUDT, JOHN J. Daniel and Squire Boone—a study in historical symbolism. Pennsylvania history, v. 3, Jan. 1936: 27–40.   F146.P597, v. 3

THWAITES, REUBEN G. Daniel Boone. New York, D. Appleton, 1902. xv, 257 p. facsim., plates, port. (Appleton's life histories)   F454.B83

Reprinted in New York by Books for Libraries Press (1971).

VAN NOPPEN, JOHN J., *and* INA W. VAN NOPPEN. Daniel Boone, backwoodsman; the green woods were his portion. Boone [N.C.] Appalachian Press [1966] xi, 209 p. illus., geneal. table, maps.   F454.B843

Bibliography: p. [200]–206.

WILSON, SAMUEL M. Daniel Boone, 1734–1934. Filson Club history quarterly, v. 8, Oct. 1934: 183–204.   F446.F484, v. 8

12872
BOONE, SQUIRE (1744–1815)
Pennsylvania; Virginia; Kentucky. Frontiersman, assemblyman.

IGLEHEART, TED. Squire Boone, the forgotten man. Filson Club history quarterly, v. 44, Oct. 1970: 356–366.   F446.F484, v. 44

JILLSON, WILLARD R. Squire Boone; a sketch of his life and an appraisement of his influence on the early settlement of Kentucky. Filson Club history quarterly, v. 16, July 1942: 141–171. map. port.   F446.F484, v. 16

An offprint with a slightly different title was issued in Louisville, Ky., by the Standard Print Co. (1942. F454.B75964).

12873

BORDA, JEAN CHARLES DE (1733–1799)

France. Scientist, French naval officer in America.

MASCART, JEAN M. La vie et les travaux du chevalier Jean-Charles de Borda (1733–1799); épisodes de la vie scientifique au XVIIIᵉ siècle. Introduction par M. Emile Picard. Lyon, A. Rey, 1919. 821 p. fold. geneal. table. (Annales de l'Université de Lyon. Nouv. sér. 2. Droit, lettres, fasc. 33)   Q143.B6M3

"Index bibliographique des sources": p. [797]–814.

12874

BORDLEY, JOHN BEALE (1727–1804)*

Maryland. Lawyer, farmer, judge, agriculturalist.

FISCHER, DAVID H. John Beale Bordley, Daniel Boorstin, and the American Enlightenment. Journal of southern history, v. 28, Aug. 1962: 327–342.   F206.J68, v. 28

GAMBRILL, OLIVE M. John Beale Bordley and the early years of the Philadelphia Agricultural Society. Pennsylvania magazine of history and biography, v. 66, Oct. 1942: 410–439.   F146.P65, v. 66

GIBSON, ELIZABETH B. John Beale Bordley. In her Biographical sketches of the Bordley family, of Maryland. Philadelphia, Printed by H. B. Ashmead, 1865. p. 65–158.   CS71.B732 1865

12875

BOSCAWEN, FRANCES EVELYN GLANVILLE (1719–1805)

ASPINALL-OGLANDER, Cecil F. Admiral's widow; being the life and letters of the Hon. Mrs. Edward Boscawen from 1761–1805. London, Hogarth Press, 1942. 205 p. fold. geneal. table, plates, ports.   DA501.B63A82

The author's treatment of the earlier years, 1719–61, was published under the title *Admiral's Wife* (London, New York, Longmans, Green [1940] 298 p. DA501.B63A8 1940).

12876

BOSTWICK, ELISHA (1749–1834)

Connecticut. Revolutionary officer.

——— A Connecticut soldier under Washington: Elisha Bostwick's memoirs of the first years of the Revolution. William and Mary quarterly, 3d ser., v. 6, Jan. 1949: 94–107.   F221.W71, 3d s., v. 6

Introduction and notes by William S. Powell.

12877

BOSWELL, JAMES (1740–1795)†

Scotland; England. Writer, lawyer, biographer.

——— Boswell in extremes, 1776–1778. Edited by Charles McC. Weis and Frederick A. Pottle. New York, McGraw-Hill Book Co. [1970] xxviii, 418 p. illus., map, plates, ports. (The Yale editions of the private papers of James Boswell)   PR3325.A887 1970

——— Boswell: the ominous years, 1774–1776. Edited by Charles Ryskamp and Frederick A. Pottle. New York, McGraw-Hill [1963] xxiv, 427 p. illus., fold. map, geneal. tables, ports. (The Yale editions of the private papers of James Boswell)   PR3325.A95 1963

——— The correspondence and other papers of James Boswell relating to the making of the Life of Johnson. Edited, and with an introduction and notes, by Marshall Waingrow. [Research ed.] New York, McGraw-Hill [1969] lxxxv, 659 p. (*His* Correspondence, v. 2)   PR3325.A94, v. 2

The Yale edition of the private papers of James Boswell. Includes bibliographical references.

——— Letters of James Boswell. Collected and edited by Chauncey Brewster Tinker. Oxford, Clarendon Press, 1924. 2 v. facsim., port.   PR3325.A8T5

Contents: v. 1. 29 July 1758–29 November 1777.—v. 2. 8 January 1778–19 May 1795.

——— Private papers of James Boswell from Malahide Castle; in the collection of Lt.–Colonel Ralph Heyward Isham; prepared for the press by Geoffrey Scott and now first printed. [Mount Vernon, N.Y., W. E. Rudge, Priv. print., 1928–34] 18 v. facsims. (part fold.), col. plates, ports.   PR3325.A16

Each volume has special title page.
Vols. 7–18 edited by Geoffrey Scott and F. A. Pottle.
Contents: 1. Early papers of James Boswell, 1754–1763, with the record of David Boswell's oath, devised, written and witnessed by James Boswell, 29 October 1767.—2. Zelide, a correspondence between James Boswell and Belle de Zuylen. Inviolable plan, to be read over frequently; and other papers.—3. Journal of a tour through the courts of Germany, by James Boswell, 1764.—4. Boswell with Rosseau and Voltaire, 1764.—5. Porzia Sansedoni, love-letters of James Boswell written in Italy, 1765; with other records of his Italian tour.—6. The making of The Life of Johnson as shown in Boswell's first notes, original diaries, and revised drafts; a study of Boswell's biographical method marking the successive steps in the composition.—7–18. The journal of James Boswell, 1765/68–1789/94.

——— ——— Index to the Private papers of James Boswell from Malahide Castle, in the collection of Lt.–Colonel Ralph Heyward Isham, compiled by Frederick A. Pottle, with the assistance of Joseph Foladare, John P. Kirby and others. London, New York, Oxford University Press, 1937. xx, 359 p.   PR3325.A16 Index

BRADY, FRANK. Boswell's political career. New Haven, Yale University Press, 1965. xv, 200 p. (Yale studies in English, v. 155)
PR3325.B7
PR13.Y3, v. 155

"In its original form, this study was [the author's] . . . Yale doctoral dissertation."
Bibliographic footnotes.

12878

BOTETOURT, NORBORNE BERKELEY, *Baron* DE (*ca.* 1718–1770)*
England; Virginia. Member of Parliament, royal governor.

Correspondence relating to Lord Botetourt [1770–71] Tyler's quarterly historical and genealogical magazine, v. 3, Oct. 1922: 106–126.   F221.T95, v. 3

LITTLE, BRYAN D. G. Norborne Berkeley, Gloucestershire magnate. Virginia magazine of history and biography, v. 63, Oct. 1955: 379–409. map, plate, port.
F221.V91, v. 63

YOST, GENEVIEVE. The reconstruction of the library of Norborne Berkeley, baron de Botetourt, governor of Virginia, 1768–1770. *In* Bibliographical Society of America. Papers, v. 36, 2d quarter, 1942: 97–123. facsim.   Z1008.B51P, v. 36

12879

BOUCHER, JONATHAN (1738–1804)*†
England; Maryland. Anglican clergyman, planter, Loyalist.

———— Jonathan Boucher (1738–1804), by himself. Blackwood's magazine, v. 231, Mar. 1932: 315–334.
AP4.B6, v. 231

An autobiographical account covering his life through 1792. Contributed by Marcella W. Thompson.

———— Letters of Rev. Jonathan Boucher [1759–99] Maryland historical magazine, v. 7, Mar.–Dec. 1912: 1–26, 150–165, 286–304, 337–356; v. 8, Mar.–Dec. 1913: 34–50, 168–186, 235–256, 338–352; v. 9, Mar., Sept.–Dec. 1914: 54–67, 232–241, 327–336; v. 10, Mar.–June 1915: 25–37, 114–127.   F176.M18, v. 7–10

Only three of the letters were written after 1789.

———— Letters of Jonathan Boucher to George Washington [1768–98] New-England historical and genealogical register, v. 52, Jan.–Oct. 1898: 57–63, 169–176, 329–336, 457–464; v. 53, July–Oct. 1899: 303–309, 417–426; v. 54, Jan. 1900: 32–38.   F1.N56, v. 52–54

Contributed by Worthington C. Ford.
A collected set of the letters was published in Brooklyn, N.Y., by the Historical Print. Club (1899. 53 p. E312.2.B75).

———— Reminiscences of an American Loyalist, 1738–1789, being the autobiography of the Revd. Jonathan Boucher, rector of Annapolis in Maryland and afterwards vicar of Epsom, Surrey, England. Edited by his grandson Jonathan Bouchier. Boston, Houghton Mifflin Co., 1925. xi, 201 p. facsim., port.   E277.B75

Reprinted in Port Washington, N.Y., by Kennikat Press (1967).

BLAU, JOSEPH L. Jonathan Boucher, Tory. History, no. 4, May 1961: 93–109. facsims., ports.
D1.H816, no. 4

CLARK, MICHAEL D. Jonathan Boucher: the mirror of reaction. Huntington Library quarterly, v. 33, Nov. 1969: 19–32.   Z733.S24Q, v. 33

EVANSON, PHILIP. Jonathan Boucher: the mind of an American Loyalist. Maryland historical magazine, v. 58, June 1963: 123–136.   F176.M18, v. 58

FALL, RALPH E. The Rev. Jonathan Boucher, turbulent Tory (1738–1804). Historical magazine of the Protestant Episcopal church, v. 36, Dec. 1967: 323–356.
BX5800.H5, v. 36

GUMMERE, RICHARD M. Jonathan Boucher, toryissimus. Maryland historical magazine, v. 55, June 1960: 138–145.   F176.M18, v. 55

MARSHALL, R. W. What Jonathan Boucher preached. Virginia magazine of history and biography, v. 46, Jan. 1938: 1–12.   F221.V91, v.46

PATE, JAMES E. Jonathan Boucher, an American Loyalist. Maryland historical magazine, v. 25, Sept. 1930: 305–319.   F176.M18, v. 25

READ, ALLEN W. Boucher's linguistic pastoral of colonial Maryland. *In* Dialect notes. v. 6, pt. 7; 1933. New Haven. p. 353–363.   PE2801.D5, v. 6

WALKER, ROBERT G. Jonathan Boucher: champion of the minority. William and Mary quarterly, 3d ser., v. 2, Jan. 1945: 3–14.   F221.W71, 3d s., v. 2

ZIMMER, ANNE Y., *and* ALFRED H. KELLY. Jonathan Boucher: constitutional conservative. Journal of American history, v. 58, Mar. 1972: 897–922.
E171.J87, v. 58

Argues that Boucher was not a Tory reactionary but an 18th-century constitutional conservative who differed from other American conservatives only in his opinions on the contract theory of government and the right of revolution.

ZIMMER, ANNE Y. Jonathan Boucher: moderate Loyalist and public man. 1966. ([583] p.)
Micro AC–1, no. 67–10,499

Thesis (Ph.D.)—Wayne State University.
Abstracted in *Dissertation Abstracts*, v. 28A, Sept. 1967, p. 831–832.

12880

BOUDINOT, ELIAS (1740–1821)*
New Jersey. Lawyer, assemblyman, delegate to the Continental Congress.

—— Journal or historical recollections of American events during the Revolutionary War. Copied from his own original manuscript. Philadelphia, F. Bourquin, 1894. viii, 97 p. fold. facsim.   E275.B75

Reprinted in New York by the New York Times (1968).

—— The life, public services, addresses and letters of Elias Boudinot, LL.D., President of the Continental Congress. Edited by J.J. Boudinot. Boston, Houghton, Mifflin, 1896. 2 v. ports.   E207.B7B7

Reprinted in New York by Da Capo Press (1971. E302.6.B7A45 1971).

ATTERBURY, W. WALLACE. Elias Boudinot: reminiscences of the American Revolution. In Huguenot Society of America. Proceedings. v. 2; 1891/94. New York, 1894. p. 261–298.   E184.H9H8, v. 2

BOYD, GEORGE A. Elias Boudinot, patriot and statesman, 1740–1821. Princeton, Princeton University Press, 1952. xiii, 321 p. illus., map, ports.   E302.6.B7B6
Bibliography: p. [297]–304.
Reprinted in New York by Greenwood Press (1969).

[Letters to Elias Boudinot, 1774–78] In Miscellaneous Americana. A collection of history, biography and genealogy. Published by William F. Boogher, Washington, D.C. Philadelphia, Press of Dando Print. and Pub. Co.[1895] p. 58-70, 80–92.   E171.B73

First published serially in v. 1 of Boogher's Repository (1883).

12881

BOUGAINVILLE, LOUIS ANTOINE DE, comte (1729–1811)
France. Colonizer, explorer, French naval officer in America.

KERALLAIN, RENÉ PRIGENT DE. Bougainville à l'armée du Cte de Grasse, guerre d'Amérique, 1781–1782. In Société des américanistes de Paris. Journal. nouv. ser., t. 20. Paris, 1928. p. 1–70.   E51.S68, n.s., v. 20

—— Bougainville à l'escadre du c^te d'Estaing, guerre d'Amérique, 1778–1779. Paris, Maisonneuve frères, 1927. 54 p.   E265.K39

LA RONCIÈRE, CHARLES G. M. B. DE. Bougainville. Paris, Nouvelle revue critique [^c1942] 251 p. illus., map, ports. (A la gloire de . . .)   G256.B6L35

"Bibliographie": p. 241–243.

MARTIN-ALLANIC, JEAN É. Bougainville, navigateur et lest découvertes de son temps. Paris, Presses universitaires de France, 1964. 2 v. (xii, 1600 p.)   G256.B6M3
Bibliography: v. 2, p. [1561]–1582.

THIÉRY, MAURICE. Bougainville, soldier and sailor. London, Grayson & Grayson [1932] 291 p. maps, plates, ports.   G256.B6T52

"Translation by Anne Agnew."

12882

BOULTON, MATTHEW (1728–1809)†
England. Engineer, industrialist.

DELIEB, ERIC. Matthew Boulton: master silversmith, 1760–1790. Research collaboration by Michael Roberts. New York, C. N. Potter; distributed by Crown Publishers [1971] 144 p. illus.   NK7198.B66D4 1971
Bibliography: p. 139.

DICKINSON, HENRY W. Matthew Boulton. Cambridge [Eng.] University Press, 1937. xiv, 218 p. illus., map, fold. plan, plates, ports.   TJ140.B6D5
"Memoir of Boulton by Watt": p. [203]–208.

ROBINSON, ERIC. Matthew Boulton and the art of parliamentary lobbying. Historical journal, v. 7, no. 2, 1964: 209–229.   D1.H33, v. 7

12883

BOUQUET, HENRY (1719–1765)*†
England; North America. Military officer.

—— [Calendar of the] Bouquet collection. In Canada. Public Archives. Report. 1889. Ottawa, 1890. 337 p. (3d group)   F1001.C13, 1889

—— The papers of Col. Henry Bouquet. Prepared by Frontier Forts and Trails Survey, Federal Works Agency, Work Projects Administration. Edited by Sylvester K. Stevens and Donald H. Kent. Harrisburg, Department of Public Instruction, Pennsylvania Historical Commission, 1940–43. 20 v. in 24. (Northwestern Pennsylvania historical series)   F152.B76

Mimeographed.
"Transcription of the Bouquet papers from the photostats in the Library of Congress obtained from the British Museum."—Foreword.

DARLINGTON, MARY C. O. History of Colonel Henry Bouquet and the western frontiers of Pennsylvania, 1747–1764. [n.p., ^c1920] 224 p. illus., maps, plans, port.   E83.76.B75

Reprinted in New York by Arno Press (1971).

A collection of various documents including more than 80 pages of letters, dated 1763, that were transcribed from the Bouquet papers in the British Museum.

HUTTON, Sir EDWARD T. H. Colonel Henry Bouquet, 60th Royal Americans. 1756–1765. A biographical sketch. Winchester, Warren, 1911. 40 p. port., fold. maps.   E83.76.B76

Reprinted from The King's Royal Rifle Corps Chronicle.

KENT, DONALD H. Henry Bouquet. American heritage, v. 4, spring 1953: 40–43. illus., col. port.
E171.A43, v. 4

ROBBINS, EDWARD E. Life and services of Colonel Henry Boquet [sic] Western Pennsylvania historical magazine, v. 3, July 1920: 120–139.
F146.W52, v. 3

12884

BOWDOIN, JAMES (1726–1790)*
Massachusetts. Merchant, assemblyman, councilor, governor.

——— The Bowdoin and Temple papers [1756–1800] Boston, Published by the Society, 1897–1907. 2. v. (Massachusetts Historical Society, Boston. Collections, 6th ser., v. 9; 7th ser., v. 6)
F61.M41, 6th s., v. 9; 7th s., v. 6

For references to other Bowdoin and Temple papers in the *Proceedings* of the Society, see the 6th series, v. 9, p. xviii.

———Letters of Bowdoin and Pownall [1769–84] *In* Massachusetts Historical Society, *Boston.* Proceedings. v. 5; 1860/62. Boston, 1862. p. 237–248.
F61.M38, v. 5

WALETT, FRANCIS G. James Bowdoin and the Massachusetts Council. 1948. ([265] p.)
Micro AC–1, no. 72–22,306

Thesis (Ph.D.)—Boston University Graduate School. Abstracted in *Dissertation Abstracts International*, v. 33A, Nov. 1972, p. 2267–2268.

——— James Bowdoin, Massachusetts patriot and statesman. *In* Bostonian Society, *Boston.* Proceedings. 1950. Boston. p. 27–47. facsim., plates, port.
F73.1.B86, 1950

——— James Bowdoin, patriot propagandist. New England quarterly, v. 23, Sept. 1950: 320–338. F1.N62, v. 23

WINTHROP, ROBERT C. Life and services of James Bowdoin. *In his* Washington, Bowdoin, and Franklin, as portrayed in occasional addresses. Boston, Little, Brown, 1876. p. 40–89. fold. facsims. E302.5.W79

12885

BOWEN, ASHLEY (1727–1813)
Massachusetts. Midshipman.

——— Personal diary of Ashley Bowen of Marblehead [1772–74] Massachusetts magazine, v. 2, Apr. 1909: 109–114; v. 3, Oct. 1910: 240–245; v. 5, Jan. 1912: 29–35.
F61.M48, v. 2–3, 5

12886

BOWEN, NATHAN (1697–1776)
Massachusetts. Shopkeeper, landowner.

——— Extracts from interleaved almanacs of Nathan Bowen, Marblehead, 1742–1799. *In* Essex Institute, *Salem, Mass.* Historical collections, v. 91, Apr.–Oct. 1955: 163–190, 266–283, 353–383. F72.E7E81, v. 91

Following the death of Nathan Bowen, the entries were continued by his sons Edward and Ashley, and his grandson, Nathan. See also the "Extracts From Journal Kept by Nathan Bowen and Edward Bowen, From 1757 to 1808" in *The Marblehead Manual* (Marblehead, Mass., Statesman Pub. Co., 1883), p. 5–28, compiled by Samuel Roads.

12887

BOWIE, JOHN (*ca* 1746–1801)
Maryland. Anglican clergyman, Loyalist.

BOWIE, LUCY L. The Reverend John Bowie, Tory. Maryland historical magazine, v. 38, June 1943: 141–160. plate.
F176.M18, v. 38

12888

BOWIE, JOHN (*fl.* 1777–1781)
South Carolina. Revolutionary officer.

New York (City). Public Library. The [John] Bowie papers [1776–80] *In its* Bulletin, v. 4, Mar.–Apr. 1900: 83–92, 116–127.
Z881.N6B, v. 4

12889

BOWLER, METCALF (1726–1789)*
England; Rhode Island. Merchant, assemblyman, judge.

——— Metcalf Bowler as a British spy. *In* Rhode Island Historical Society. Collections, v. 23, Oct. 1930: 101–117.
F76.R47, v. 23

Bowler's letters to Sir Henry Clinton, 1776–79. Introduction and notes by Jane Clark.

12890

BOWLES, WILLIAM AUGUSTUS (1763–1805)*
Maryland; Florida. Indian leader, Loyalist officer.

[BAYNTON, BENJAMIN] Authentic memoirs of William Augustus Bowles, Esquire, ambassador from the united nations of Creeks and Cherokees, to the court of London. London, Printed for R. Faulder, 1791. vi, 79 p.
E90.B7B3 Rare Bk. Coll.

Signed, on p. 79: "An observer of mankind." The author was undoubtedly Benjamin Baynton, captain in the Pennsylvania Loyalists Regiment.

Reprinted in New York by Arno Press (1971. E99.C9B62 1971).

DOUGLASS, ELISHA P. The adventurer Bowles. William and Mary quarterly, 3d ser., v. 6, Jan. 1949: 3–23.
F221.W71, 3d s., v. 6

JONES, EDWARD ALFRED. The real author of the *Authentic Memoirs of William Augustus Bowles*. Maryland historical magazine, v. 18, Dec. 1923: 300–308.

F176.M18, v. 18

Contends that it was Capt. Benjamin Baynton, an American-born Loyalist.

WRIGHT, JAMES L. William Augustus Bowles, director general of the Creek nation. Athens, University of Georgia Press [1967] viii, 211 p. map, port.

E99.C9W7

Bibliography: p. 197–205.

12891

BOYD, ADAM (1738–1803)

Pennsylvania; North Carolina. Presbyterian clergyman, newspaper publisher, Revolutionary officer.

STOKES, DURWARD T. Adam Boyd, publisher, preacher, and patriot. North Carolina historical review, v. 49, winter 1972: 1–21. illus., facsims., port.

F251.N892, v. 49

12892

BOYLE, JOHN (1746–1819)

Massachusetts. Printer, bookseller, Revolutionary officer.

———— Boyle's journal of occurrences in Boston, 1759–1778. New England historical and genealogical register, v. 84, Apr.–Oct. 1930: 142–171, 248–272, 357–382; v. 85, Jan.–Apr. 1931: 5–28, 117–133.

F1.N56, v. 84–85

A record of events kept by Boyle in a bound notebook.

12893

BRACKEN, JOHN (1745–1818)

England; Virginia. Anglican clergyman.

GOODWIN, RUTHERFOORD. The Reverend John Bracken [1745–1818], rector of Bruton Parish and president of William and Mary College in Virginia. Historical magazine of the Protestant Episcopal church, v. 10, Dec. 1941: 354–389. facsims. BX5800.H5, v. 10

12894

BRACKENRIDGE, HUGH HENRY (1748–1816)*

Scotland; Maryland; Pennsylvania. Schoolmaster, dramatist, Revolutionary chaplain, lawyer, assemblyman.

———— The death of General Montgomery, in storming the city of Quebec. A tragedy. With An ode, in honour of the Pennsylvania militia, and the small band of regular Continental troops, who sustained the campaign, in the depth of winter, January, 1777, and repulsed the British forces from the banks of the Delaware. By the author of a dramatic piece, on the Battle of Bunker's-Hill. To which are added, Elegiac pieces, commemorative of distinguished characters. By different gentlemen. Phil-

adelphia, Printed and Sold by R. Bell, in Third-Street, Next Door to St. Paul's Church, 1777. 79 p. front.

E241.Q3B7 Rare Bk. Coll.

———— Gazette publications. Carlisle [Pa.] Printed by Alexander & Phillips, 1806. 348 p.

E310.B79 Rare Bk. Coll.

Partial contents: On the situation of the town of Pittsburgh, and the state of society at that place [1786]—Letters to Messrs. Scull and Hall, first publishers of the "Pittsburg Gazette" [1786]—Speech delivered (1788) in the legislature of Pennsylvania on a motion to instruct the delegates of that state in Congress relative to a proposition to cede to Spain the right of navigation of the Mississippi River.—Narrative of the transactions of the late session of Assembly, so far as they respect the system of confederate government proposed by the general convention of the states at Philadelphia.—Cursory remarks on the federal Constitution.—On the calling a convention [to remodel the constitution of Pennsylvania. Dated May 30, 1789]—Sermon delivered to the American army in the capacity of Chaplin, a few days before the Battle of Brandywine.—The representation and remonstrance of Hard Money; addressed to the people of America [Jan. 29, 1779]—The answer of Continental Currency to *The Representation and Remonstrance of Hard Money*. By Hortensius [March 20, 1779]—An eulogium of the brave men who have fallen in the contest with Great-Britain . . . July 5, 1779 . . . Philadelphia.—Correspondence of the author, as editor of the "United States magazine," with Gen. Charles Lee [1779]—Cincinnatus. A poem.—"The establishment of the United States" [1779]—A "memoir to the American Philosophical Society" [1787]—Fragment of a sermon delivered to a section of the American Army . . . at Morristown, N.J., in 1776.—[Address at Pittsburg on adoption of the federal Constitution by Virginia 1788]—The Battle of Bunkers Hill, a dramatic piece [1775]—The modern chevalier [ca. 1788–89].

———— A Hugh Henry Brackenridge reader, 1770–1815. Edited, with an introduction, by Daniel Marder. [Pittsburgh] University of Pittsburgh Press [1970] x, 407 p.

PS708.B5A6 1970

———— Narrative of a late expedition against the Indians; with an account of the barbarous execution of Col. Crawford; and the wonderful escape of Dr. Knight & John Slover from captivity in 1782. To which is added, A narrative of the captivity & escape of Mrs. Frances Scott, an inhabitant of Washington County, Virginia. Andover [Mass.] Printed by Ames & Parker [1798?] 46 p. E85.B796 Rare Bk. Coll.

The narratives of Knight and Slover (p. [3]–39) were first published in the *Freeman's Journal* (Philadelphia), v. 3, no. 106–109, April 30–May 21, 1783, at the request of Brackenridge, by whom they were prepared for publication. They were issued in pamphlet form the same year in Philadelphia under the title *Narratives of a Late Expedition Against the Indians*. This reprint makes no mention of Brackenridge.

BLANCK, JACOB. Brackenridge's *Death of General Montgomery* (1777). Harvard Library bulletin, v. 7, autumn 1953: 357–361. plate. Z881.H3403, v. 7

CONNER, MARTHA. Hugh Henry Brackenridge, at Princeton University, 1768–1771. Western Pennsylvania historical magazine, v. 10, July 1927: 146–162.
F146.W52, v. 10

HAJEK, VIRGINIA A. The dramatic writings of Hugh Henry Brackenridge. 1971. ([299] p.)
Micro AC–1, no. 71–22,736
Thesis (Ph.D.)—Loyola University of Chicago.
Abstracted in *Dissertation Abstracts International*, v. 32A, Sept. 1971, p. 1473.
Includes a review of drama during the Revolutionary period.

HEARTMAN, CHARLES F. A bibliography of the writings of Hugh Henry Brackenridge prior to 1825. New York City, The compiler, 1917. 37 p. illus., facsims., port. (Heartman's historical series, no. 29)
Z8113.H3 Rare Bk. Coll.
Reprinted in New York by B. Franklin (1968).

MARDER, DANIEL. Hugh Henry Brackenridge. New York, Twayne Publishers [1967] 159 p. (Twayne's United States authors series)   PS708.B5Z6
Bibliography: p. 151-155.

NEWLIN, CLAUDE M. Hugh Henry Brackenridge, writer. Western Pennsylvania historical magazine, v. 10, Oct. 1927: 224–256.   F146.W52, v. 10

—— The life and writings of Hugh Henry Brackenridge. Princeton, Princeton University Press, 1932. vi, 328 p.
PS708.B5Z7
Bibliography: p. [309]–322.
Reprinted in Mamaroneck, N.Y., by P. P. Appel (1971).
The author's thesis (Ph.D.), with the same title, was submitted to Harvard University in 1929.

SMEALL, J. F. S. The evidence that Hugh Brackenridge wrote "The Cornwalliad." *In* Modern Language Association of America. Publications, v. 80, Dec. 1965: 542–548.   PB6.M6, v. 80
A 720-line poem that appeared in his *United States Magazine* in 1779.

12895
BRADFORD, JOHN (1747–1830)*
Virginia; Kentucky. Settler, surveyor, printer, newspaper publisher.

—— John Bradford's historical &c. notes on Kentucky, from *The Western Miscellany*, compiled by G. W. Stipp, in 1827. With an introduction by John Wilson Townsend. San Francisco, Grabhorn Press, 1932. 205 p. fold. map. (Rare American series, no. 3)
F454.B86
E173.R24, no. 3
Originally published in the *Kentucky Gazette* beginning August 25, 1826; published in 1827 in *The Western Miscellany*, a compilation by George W. Stipp, printed in Xenia, Ohio. In the present edition the Stipp text has been compared and checked with that of the *Kentucky Gazette*.

COLEMAN, JOHN WINSTON. John Bradford and the *Kentucky Gazette*. Indiana quarterly for bookmen, v. 4, July 1948: 53–61.   Z1007.I5, v. 4
The author's article, with the same title, also appeared in the *Filson Club Historical Quarterly*, v. 34, Jan. 1960, p. 24–34.

——John Bradford, Esq., pioneer Kentucky printer and historian. Lexington, Ky., Winburn Press, 1950. 24 p.
Z232.B799C6

McMURTRIE, DOUGLAS C. John Bradford, pioneer printer of Kentucky. Springfield, Ill., Priv. print., 1931. 11 p. illus., facsims.   Z232.B799M2

WILSON, SAMUEL M. The *Kentucky Gazette* and John Bradford, its founder. *In* Bibliographical Society of America. Papers, v. 31, pt. 2, 1937: 102–132.
Z1008.B51P, v. 31

12896
BRADFORD, WILLIAM (1722–1791)*
Pennsylvania. Printer, publisher, bookseller, Revolutionary officer.

BULLEN, HENRY L. The Bradford family of printers. American collector, v. 1, Jan.–Feb. 1926: 148–156, 164–170. illus., facsims.   Z1007.A475, v. 1

WALLACE, JOHN W. An old Philadelphian, Colonel William Bradford, the patriot printer of 1776. Sketches of his life. Philadelphia, Sherman, printers, 1884. xiii, 517 p. illus., fold. facsims., maps (part fold.), plates, ports.   E263.P4B7 Rare Bk. Coll.
"List (imperfect) of Bradford's publications between 1741 and 1766": p. 349–362.

12897
BRADSTREET, JOHN (*ca.* 1711–1774)*
Nova Scotia. British military officer.

The claims of Col. John Bradstreet to lands in America. *In* American Antiquarian Society, *Worcester, Mass.* Proceedings, new ser., v. 19, Apr. 1908: 151–181.
E172.A35, n.s., v. 19

12898
BRADY, SAMUEL (1756–1795)
Pennsylvania. Indian fighter, Revolutionary officer.

BRADY, WILLIAM Y., *comp.* Captain Sam Brady, Indian fighter. Washington, Brady Pub. Co. [1950] viii, 184 p. illus.   E85.B8B7

FALL, RALPH E. Captain Samuel Brady (1756–1795), chief of the Rangers, and his kin. West Virginia history, v. 29, Apr. 1968: 203–223.   F236.W52, v. 29

NEFF, GEORGE H. Samuel Brady. *In* Northumberland County (Pa.) Historical Society. Proceedings and addresses. v. 5, Sunbury, 1933. p. 121–148.
F157.N8N7, v. 5

Sketches of the life and Indian adventures of Captain Samuel Brady, a native of Cumberland County, born 1758, a few miles above Northumberland, Pa.   These sketches were originally written in numbers for the Blairsville (Pa.) "Record." New York, Reprinted, W. Abbatt, 1914. 37 p. (The Magazine of history, with notes and queries. Extra number, no. 33, [pt. 2])
E173.M24, no. 33

12899

BRAINERD, JOHN (1720–1781)*
Connecticut; New Jersey. Presbyterian clergyman and missionary.

——— The journal of the Rev. John Brainerd, from January, 1761, to October, 1762. With an introduction by George Macloskie. Toms River, N.J., Printed at the office of the New Jersey Courier, 1880. 25 p. plates.
E98.M6B916 1880

A typewritten transcript was reproduced in Newark, N.J., by the Historical Records Survey (1941).

BRAINERD, THOMAS. The life of John Brainerd, the brother of David Brainerd, and his successor as missionary to the Indians of New Jersey. Philadelphia, Presbyterian Publication Committee [1865] xii, 492 p. plates.
E98.M6.B918

12900

BRAND-HOLLIS, THOMAS (1719?–1804)
England. Member of Parliament.

[DISNEY, JOHN] Memoirs of Thomas Brand-Hollis. London, Printed by T. Gilbert, 1808. vii, 60 p. plates, port.
N8386.B7D5

Includes letters of John and Abigail Adams to Brand-Hollis in 1788–90 on p. 31–40.

ROBBINS, CAROLINE. Thomas Brand Hollis (1719–1804) English admirer of Franklin and intimate of John Adams. *In* American Philosophical Society, *Philadelphia.* Proceedings, v. 97, June 1953: 239–247.
Q11.P5, v. 97

12901

BRANT, JOSEPH, *Mohawk chief* (1742–1807)*
New York. War chief.

BONHAM, MILLEDGE L. The religious side of Joseph Brant. Journal of religion, v. 9, July 1929: 398–418.
BR1.J65, v. 9

——— ——— Offprint. [Chicago, 1929] 398–418 p.
CT99.B8214B6

CHALMERS, HARVEY. Joseph Brant: Mohawk [by] Harvey Chalmers in collaboration with Ethel Brant Mon-

ture. East Lansing, Michigan State University Press [1955] 364 p. illus.
E99.M8B79

CRUIKSHANK, ERNEST A. Joseph Brant in the American Revolution. *In* Royal Canadian Institute, *Toronto.* Transactions. v. 5, pt. 2; 1898. Toronto. p. 243–264.
AS42.C21, v. 5

The author's second paper on Brant, with the same title, appeared in v. 7, pt. 2, 1902 (Toronto), p. 391–407.

[DRAKE, SAMUEL G.] Principal events in the life of the Indian chief Brant. New England historical and genealogical register, v. 2, Oct. 1848: 345–348; v. 3, Jan. 1849: 59–64. port.
F1.N56, v. 2–3

——— ——— Reprint. [Boston? 1849?] 8 p. port.
E90.B8D7

HAMILTON, MILTON W. Joseph Brant—"the most painted Indian." *In* New York State Historical Association. New York history, v. 39, Apr. 1958: 119–132. ports.
F116.N865, v. 39

On his visits to London in 1776 and 1786 and the portraits of him painted by George Romney (1776), Gilbert Stuart (1786), and Ezra Ames (1806).

KELSAY, ISABEL T. Joseph Brant: the legend and the man, a foreword. *In* New York State Historical Association. New York history, v. 40, Oct. 1959: 368–379.
F116.N865, v. 40

SMITH, MARC J. Joseph Brant, Mohawk statesman. 1945. Thesis (Ph.D.)—University of Wisconsin.

WOOD, LOUIS A. The war chief of the Six Nations; a chronicle of Joseph Brant. Toronto, Brook, 1914. xi, 147 p. illus. (part col.), map, port. (Chronicles of Canada series, [v. 16])
E99.M8W87

"Bibliographical note": p. 141–142.

12902

BRANT, MOLLY (1736–1796)
New York. Mohawk matron. Sister of Joseph Brant (1742–1807).

GUNDY, H. PEARSON. Molly Brant—Loyalist. Ontario history, v. 45, summer 1953: 97–108.
F1056.O58, v. 45

JOHNSTON, JEAN. Molly Brant: Mohawk matron. Ontario history, v. 56, June 1964: 103–124.
F1056.O58, v. 56

RIDDELL, WILLIAM R. Was Molly Brant married? *In* Ontario Historical Society. Papers and records. v. 19. Toronto, 1922. p. 147–157.
F1056.O58, v. 19

12903

BRAUD, DENIS (*fl.* 1764–1770)
Louisiana. Printer.

DART, HENRY P. The adventures of Denis Braud, the first printer of Louisiana, 1764–1773. Louisiana historical quarterly, v. 14, July 1931: 349–384.
F366.L79, v. 14

McMURTRIE, DOUGLAS C. The pioneer printer of New Orleans. Chicago, Enycourt Press, 1930. 17 p.
Z232.B82M3

12904
BRAUND, WILLIAM (1695–1774)
England. Merchant.

SUTHERLAND, LUCY S. A London merchant, 1695–1774. London, Oxford University Press, H. Milford, 1933. viii, 164 p. geneal. tables. (Oxford historical series)
HF3510.L8S8

Contents: William Braund, merchant, 1695–1774.—The Portuguese ventures of William Braund.—Marine insurance in the mid-eighteenth century.—William Braund and the East India shipping interest.—Conclusion.—Appendixes.
Reprinted in London by F. Cass (1962).

12905
BRAXTON, CARTER (1736–1797)*
Virginia. Assemblyman, delegate to the Continental Congress.

STEVENS, L. TOMLIN. Carter Braxton: signer of the Declaration of Independence. 1969. ([245] p.)
Micro AC–1, no. 70–6889

Thesis (Ph.D.)—Ohio State University.
Abstracted in Dissertation Abstracts International, v. 30A, Apr. 1970, p. 4389.

12906
BRECKINRIDGE, JOHN (1760–1806)*
Virginia. Assemblyman, lawyer.

HARRISON, LOWELL H. John Breckinridge: Jeffersonian Republican. Introduction by Thomas D. Clark. Louisville, Ky., Filson Club [1969] x, 243 p. illus., facsim., ports. (Filson Club publications; second series, no.2)
E302.6.B84H28

Includes bibliographic references.

——— John Breckinridge, western statesman. Journal of southern history, v. 18, May 1952: 137–151.
F206.J68, v. 18

——— ——— Offprint. [137]–151 p. E302.6.B84H3

——— A young Virginian, John Breckinridge. Virginia magazine of history and biography, v. 71, Jan 1963: 19–34.
F221.V91, v. 71

12907
BRIAND, JEAN OLIVIER, Bp. of Quebec (1715–1794)
France; Canada. Roman Catholic clergyman, bishop.

NEATBY, HILDA M. Jean-Olivier Briand: a "minor Canadien." In Canadian Historical Association. Report. 1963. [Toronto] p. 1–18.
F1001.C26, 1963

WILSON, SAMUEL K. Bishop Briand and the American Revolution. Catholic historical review, v. 19, 1933: 133–147.
BX1414.C3, v. 19

12908
BRIDGE, EBENEZER (1742–1823)
Massachusetts. Revolutionary officer.

GARFIELD, JAMES F. D. Captain Ebenezer Bridge. In Fitchburg Historical Society, Fitchburg, Mass. Proceedings. v. 1; 1892/94. Fitchburg, 1895. p. 175–187.
F74.F5F6, v. 1

12909
BRISOUT DE BARNEVILLE, NICOLAS FRANÇOIS DENIS (1746–1839)
French officer in America.

——— Journal de guerre de Barneville, Mai 1780–Octobre 1781. French American review, v. 3, Oct./Dec. 1950: 217–278. port.
PS159.F5F74, v. 3

Introduction and notes by Gilbert Chinard.

12910
BRISSOT DE WARVILLE, JACQUES PIERRE (1754–1793)
France. Lawyer.

——— Boston in 1788. From "New travels in the United States of America" ... published in Paris in 1791. [Boston, Directors of the Old South Work, 1902] 20 p. (Old South leaflets. [General ser., v. 6] no. 126)
E173.O44, v. 6

——— Brissot de Warville on the Pennsylvania Constitution of 1776. Pennsylvania magazine of history and biography, v. 72, Jan. 1948: 25–43.
F146.P65, v. 72

His "Reflections on the Constitution of Pennsylvania," with introduction and notes by J. Paul Selsam.

——— A critical examination of the marquis de Chatellux's travels, in North America, in a letter addressed to the marquis; principally intended as a refutation of his opinions concerning the Quakers, the Negroes, the people, and mankind. Translated from the French of J. P. Brissot de Warville, with additions and corrections of the author. Philadelphia, Printed by Joseph James, in Chesnut-Street, 1788. 89 p.
E164.B88 Rare Bk. Coll.

——— J.-P. Brissot: Mémoires (1754–1793) publiés avec Étude critique et notes par Cl. Perroud. Paris, A. Picard [1911] 2 v. port. (Mémoires et documents relatifs aux xviiie & xixe siècles, [II–III])
DC146.B85A4 1911

"Bibliographie de Brissot": t. 1, p. [xxix]–li.
Contents: t. 1. 1754–1784.—t. 2. 1784–1793.

——— The life of J. P. Brissot, deputy from Eure and Loire, to the National Convention. Written by himself. Translated from the French. 2d ed. London, Printed for J. Debrett, 1794. 92 p. port.   DC146.B85A5

——— New travels in the United States of America. Performed in 1788. London, J. S. Jordan, 1792. 483 p.
E164.B8917 1792b Rare Bk. Coll.

Reprinted in New York by A. M. Kelly (1970).

Translated by Joel Barlow, this work comprises the first two volumes of Brissot de Warville's three-volume *Nouveau voyage dans les États-Unis*, published in Paris in 1791. A new translation by Mara Soceanu Vamos and Durand Echeverria, edited by the latter, was issued in 1964 by the Belknap Press of the Harvard University Press. A translation of the third volume, entitled *The Commerce of America with Europe . . . Shewing the Importance of the American Revolution to the Interests of France*, was published in London in 1794 and has also been reprinted by A. M. Kelly (New York, 1970).

GIDNEY, LUCY M.   L'influence des États-Unis d'Amérique sur Brissot, Condorcet et Mme Roland. Paris, Rieder, 1930. 176 p.   DC145.G63 1930a

At head of title: Société de l'histoire de la révolution française.

Issued also as the author's inaugural dissertation, Paris. "Bibliographie": p. [155]–162.

12911

BROGLIE, CHARLES FRANÇOIS, *comte* DE (1719–1781)
France. Military officer.

——— Correspondance secrète du comte de Broglie avec Louis XV (1756–1774). Publiée pour la Société de l'histoire de France (Série antérieure à 1789) par Didier Ozanam et Michel Antoine. Paris, C. Klincksieck, 1956–61. 2 t. (Société de l'histoire de France. Publications in octavo. Série antérieure à 1789. 459, 467)
DC135.B76A3

STILLÉ, CHARLES J.   Comte de Broglie, the proposed stadtholder of America. Pennsylvania magazine of history and biography, v. 11, Jan 1888: 369–405.
F146.P65, v. 11

12912

BROGLIE, CHARLES LOUIS VICTOR, *prince* DE (1756–1794)
France. French officer in America.

——— Deux Français aux États-Unis et dans la Nouvelle Espagne en 1782. Journal de voyage du prince de Broglie et Lettres du comte de Ségur. Communiqués avec un avant-propos et des notes par le duc de Broglie. Paris, Imp. Lahure, 1903. 200 (i.e. 205) p. (Société des bibliophiles françois. Mélanges, [2. ptie.] pièce n° 6)
DC4.S6 1903

Last page incorrectly numbered 200.

——— Narrative of the Prince de Broglie, 1782. Translated from the original MS., by E. W. Balch. Magazine of American history, with notes and queries, v. 1, Mar.–June 1877: 180–186, 231–235, 306–309, 374–380.
E171.M18, v. 1

12913

BROKAW, ISAAC (1746–1826)
New Jersey. Clockmaker.

HUTCHINSON, ELMER T.   Isaac Brokaw, Jersey clockmaker. *In* New Jersey Historical Society. Proceedings, v. 72, July 1954: 157–162. plate.   F131.N58, v. 72

12914

BROOKE, FRANCIS TALIAFERRO (1763–1851)*
Virginia. Revolutionary officer, lawyer.

——— A narrative of my life; for my family. Richmond, Printed for the writer [by] Macfarlane & Fergusson, 1849. 90 p.   E275.B86 Rare Bk. Coll.

Includes a narrative of the author's service in Harrison's Regiment of Continental Artillery, 1780–83.

The 1921 edition (43 p. E173.M24, no. 74), published as extra number, no. 74, of *The Magazine of History, With Notes and Queries*, has been reprinted in New York by the New York Times (1971. E275.B86 1971).

12915

BROOKS, JOHN (1752–1825)*
Massachusetts. Physician, Revolutionary officer, assemblyman.

BROOKS, CHARLES.   Memoir of John Brooks, governor of Massachusetts. New England historical and genealogical register, v. 19, July 1865: 193–200. port.
F1.N56, v. 19

——— ——— Offprint. [Boston, 1865] 7 p.
F69.B87

12916

BROOM, JACOB (1752–1810)
Delaware. Surveyor, merchant, assemblyman, delegate to the Constitutional Convention.

CAMPBELL, WILLIAM W.   Life and character of Jacob Broom. Wilmington, Historical Society of Delaware, 1909. 37 p. plates. (Historical Society of Delaware. Papers, 51)   F161.D35, no. 51

12917

BROWN, GAWEN (1719–1801)
England; Massachusetts. Clock and watchmaker, Revolutionary officer.

HANSEN, DAVID.   Gawen Brown, soldier and clockmaker. *In* Society for the Preservation of New England Antiquities, *Boston*. Old-time New England, v. 30, July 1939: 1–9. illus., port.   F1.S68, v. 30

12918
BROWN, GUSTAVUS RICHARD (1747–1804)
Maryland. Physician.

CORDELL, EUGENE F. The doctors Gustavus Brown of lower Maryland. *In* Johns Hopkins Hospital, *Baltimore.* Bulletin, v. 13, Aug./Sept. 1902: 188–192.
RC31.B2J6, v. 13

HOWARD, JOHN T. The doctors Gustavus Brown, father and son, of Charles County, Maryland. Annals of medical history, new ser., v. 9, Sept. 1937: 437–448.
R11.A85, n.s., v. 9

TONER, JOSEPH M. A sketch of the life of Dr. Gustavus Richard Brown of Port Tobacco, Maryland, one of the consulting physicians during the last illness of General Washington at Mount Vernon. Sons of the Revolution in state of Virginia quarterly magazine, v. 2, Jan. 1923: 12–23. E202.4.V4, v. 2
"The Will of Dr. Gustavus Brown of Port Tobacco, Maryland": p. 24–45.

12919
BROWN, JACOB (1736–1785)
Virginia; North Carolina; Tennessee. Settler, Indian trader.

FINK, PAUL M. Jacob Brown of Nolichucky. Tennessee historical quarterly, v. 21, Sept. 1962: 235–250.
F431.T285, v. 21

12920
BROWN, JAMES (1761–1834)
Rhode Island.

——— James Brown's diary (1787–1789). Transcribed and annotated by Clarkson A. Collins. Rhode Island history, v. 6, Oct. 1947: 99–107; v. 7, Jan.–Apr. 1948: 9–11, 51–57. port. F76.R472, v. 6–7

12921
BROWN, JAMES (d. 1782)
Kentucky. Surveyor, settler.

PUSEY, WILLIAM A. Three Kentucky pioneers: James, Patrick, and William Brown. Filson Club history quarterly, v. 4, Oct. 1930: 165–183.
F446.F484, v. 4
——— ——— Offprint. Louisville, Ky., J. P. Morton, 1930. 22p. F450.P97

12922
BROWN, JOHN (ca. 1728–1803)
Virginia. Presbyterian clergyman. Father of John Brown (1757–1837).

STOKES, DURWARD T. The Reverend John Brown and his family. Filson Club history quarterly, v. 44, Jan. 1970: 19–37. F446.F484, v. 44

12923
BROWN, JOHN (1736–1803)*
Rhode Island. Merchant, munitioner, assemblyman, shipowner. Father of James Brown (1761–1834).

——— A colonial merchant to his son: from the unpublished letters of John Brown to his son James (1782–83). Edited by Frank Hail Brown. *In* Rhode Island Historical Society. Collections, v. 34, Apr. 1941: 47–57.
F76.R47, v. 34

12924
BROWN, JOHN (1744–1780)*
Massachusetts. Lawyer, Revolutionary officer, assemblyman, judge.

HOWE, ARCHIBALD M. Colonel John Brown, of Pittsfield, Massachusetts: the brave accuser of Benedict Arnold; an address. Boston, W. B. Clarke Co., 1908. 37 p. E207.B8H5
Roster of Col. John Brown's regiment, 3d Berkshire militia, on pages 26–33.

ROOF, GARRET L. Colonel John Brown, his services in the Revolutionary War, Battle of Stone Arabia. An address. Utica, N.Y., E. H. Roberts, Book and Job Printers, 1884. 24 p. E207.B8R7

12925
BROWN, JOHN (1757–1837)*
Virginia; Kentucky. Revolutionary officer, lawyer, assemblyman, landowner, delegate to the Continental Congress.

SPRAGUE, STUART S. Senator John Brown of Kentucky, 1757–1837, a political biography. 1972. ([333] p.)
Micro AC–1, no. 72–21,544
Thesis (Ph.D.)—New York University.
Abstracted in *Dissertation Abstracts International,* v. 33A, Aug. 1972, p. 710–711.

WARREN, ELIZABETH. John Brown and his influence on Kentucky politics, 1784–1805. 1937.
Thesis (Ph.D.)—Northwestern University.

——— Senator John Brown's role in the Kentucky Spanish conspiracy. Filson Club history quarterly, v. 36, Apr. 1962: 158–176. F446.F484, v. 36

12926
BROWN, JOSEPH (1733–1785)*
Rhode Island. Merchant, iron manufacturer, scientist, architect, assemblyman. Brother of Moses Brown (1738–1836).

CRUMP, STUART F. Joseph Brown, astronomer. Rhode Island history, v. 27, Jan. 1968: 1–12.
F76.R472, v. 27

WILSON, J. WALTER. Joseph Brown, scientist and architect. Rhode Island history, v. 4, July-Oct. 1945: 67–79, 121–128.   F76.R472, v. 4

12927
BROWN, MOSES (1738–1836)*
Rhode Island. Merchant, assemblyman, philanthropist.

———— Moses Brown's "Account of journey to distribute donations 12th month 1775." With an introduction by Mack E. Thompson. Rhode Island history, v. 15, Oct. 1956: 97–121.   F76.R472, v. 15

HAZELTON, ROBERT M. Let freedom ring! A biography of Moses Brown. New York, New Voices Pub. Co. [1957] 262 p. illus., map, port.   F83.B86

HEDGES, JAMES B. The Browns of Providence Plantations. [v. 1] Colonial years. Cambridge, Mass., Harvard University Press, 1952. xviii, 379 p. (Studies in economic history)   HC108.P8H4, v. 1
Bibliographic references included in "Notes" (p. [333]–366).
Reissued, with a second volume covering the 19th century, by Brown University Press in 1968.

JONES, AUGUSTINE. Moses Brown: his life and services. Providence, Rhode Island Print. Co., 1892. 47 p.
                    F83.B87

THOMPSON, MACK. Moses Brown, reluctant reformer. Chapel Hill, Published for the Institute of Early American History and Culture at Williamsburg, Virginia by the University of North Carolina Press [1962] 316 p. facsim., map, plates, port.   F83.B875
"Bibliographical essay": p. [301]–303.
The author's thesis (Ph.D.), *Moses Brown, a Man of Public Responsibility*, was submitted to Brown University in 1955 (Micro AC–1, no. 13,191).

WAX, DAROLD D. The Browns of Providence and the slaving voyage of the Brig *Sally*, 1764–1765. American Neptune, v. 32, July 1972: 171–179.   V1.A4, v. 32

12928
BROWN, MOSES (1742–1804)
Massachusetts. Privateersman, Revolutionary naval officer.

MACLAY, EDGAR S. Moses Brown, Captain U.S.N. New York, Baker and Taylor Co. [1904] 220 p. maps, port.
                    E207.B87M16

SWETT, SAMUEL. Sketches of a few distinguished men of Newbury and Newburyport. no. 1. Capt. Moses Brown, of the United States Navy. Boston, Printed by S. N. Dickinson, 1846. 23 p.   F74.N53S9

12929
BROWN, OLIVER (1753–1846)
Massachusetts. Revolutionary officer.

HAYDEN, HORACE E. A biographical sketch of Captain Oliver Brown, an officer of the Revolutionary army, who commanded the party which destroyed the statue of George the Third, in New York City, July 9, 1776. Priv. print. Wilkes-Barre, Pa. [E. B. Yordy, Printer] 1882. 22 p.   E207.B88H4

12930
BROWN, TARLETON (1757–1846)
South Carolina. Revolutionary officer, farmer.

———— Memoirs of Tarleton Brown, a captain of the Revolutionary army, written by himself. With a preface and notes, by Charles I. Bushnell. New York, Priv. print., 1862. 65 p. ports. [Crumbs for antiquarians, v. 1, no. 4]
                    E203.B97, v. 1
                    E275.B87
Reprinted with condensed notes, in Tarrytown, N.Y., by W. Abbatt. (1942. [3]–36 p. E173.M24, no. 101) as extra number, no. 101, of *The Magazine of History, With Notes and Queries*.
Originally issued in 1843, in the *Charleston Rambler*. Also published in Barnwell, S.C., by the People Press (1894. 28 p. E275.B88).

12931
BROWN, THOMAS (d. 1825)*
Georgia; Florida; South Carolina. Loyalist officer.

———— A Loyalist view of the Drayton-Tennent-Hart mission to the upcountry [1775] Edited by James H. O'Donnell. South Carolina historical magazine, v. 67, Jan. 1966: 15–28.   F266.S55, v. 67

OLSON, GARY D. Loyalists and the American Revolution: Thomas Brown and the South Carolina backcountry, 1775–1776. South Carolina historical magazine, v. 68, Oct. 1967: 201–219; v. 69, Jan. 1968: 44–56.
                    F266.S55, v. 68–69

———— Thomas Brown, Loyalist partisan, and the Revolutionary War in Georgia, 1777–1782. Georgia historical quarterly, v. 54, spring–summer 1970: 1–19, 183–208.
                    F281.G2975, v. 54

12932
BROWN, WILLIAM (1737–1789)
Scotland; Canada. Printer.

AUDET FRANÇOIS J. William Brown (1737–1789); premier imprimeur, journaliste et libraire de Québec, savie et ses oeuvres. *In* Royal Society of Canada. Proceedings and transactions. 3d ser., v. 26, section 2; 1932. Ottawa. p. 97–112.   AS42.R6, 3d s., v. 26

12933
BROWNE, ARTHUR (1699–1773)
Ireland; New Hampshire. Anglican clergyman.

PENNINGTON, EDGAR L. The Reverend Arthur Browne of Rhode Island and New Hampshire. Hartford, Conn., Church Missions Pub. Co., 1938. 20 p. (Soldier and servant, [no. 190]) BX5995.B82P4

ROGERS, MARY C. Glimpses of an old social capital (Portsmouth, New Hampshire) as illustrated by the life of the Reverend Arthur Browne and his circle. Boston, Printed for the subscribers, 1923. xii, 92 p. plates, ports. F44.P8R7

12934

BROWNE, WILLIAM (1737–1802)*
    Massachusetts; Bermuda; England. Lawyer, assemblyman, judge, councilor, Loyalist, governor.

—— Extracts from the letter book of Governor William Browne [1782–88] Bermuda historical quarterly, v. 1, 1st quarter–Oct./Dec. 1944: 11–20, 62–80, 109–127, 169–179; v. 2, Jan./Mar. 1944 [i.e. 1945]: 19–29. F1636.B55, v. 1–2

—— Letters of William Browne, American Loyalist [1778–81] Edited by Sydney W. Jackman. In Essex Institute, *Salem, Mass.* Historical collections, v. 96, Jan. 1960: 1–46. F72.E7E81, v. 96

JACKMAN, SYDNEY W. A Tory's claim to the Wanton estates. Rhode Island history, v. 19, Jan.–July 1960: 1–7, 50–61, 79–88. port. F76.R472, v. 19

—— William Browne, governor [of Bermuda], 1782–1788: a study of his early life in his native Massachusetts. Bermuda historical quarterly, v. 13, spring 1956: 17–24. F1636.B55, v. 13

12935

BRUIN, PETER BRYAN (*ca.* 1754–*ca.* 1827)
    Virginia; Louisiana. Revolutionary officer, planter.

COKER, WILLIAM S. Peter Bryan Bruin of Bath: soldier, judge and frontiersman. West Virginia history, v. 30, July 1969: 579–585. F236.W52, v. 30

12936

BRUSH, CREAN (1725?–1778)
    Ireland; New York. Assemblyman, Loyalist.

SMITH, JANE N. Crean Brush, Loyalist, and his descendants. [n.p.] 1938. 30 p. geneal. tables. E278.B863S5

12937

BRYAN, GEORGE (1731–1791)*
    Ireland; Pennsylvania. Importer, assemblyman, judge.

KONKLE, BURTON A. George Bryan and the constitution of Pennsylvania, 1731–1791. Philadelphia, W. J. Campbell, 1922. 381 p. facsims., maps, plates, ports. F153.K8

12938

BRYAN, JONATHAN (1708–1788)
    Georgia. Planter, councilor.

REDDING, ISABELLA R. Life and times of Jonathan Bryan, 1708–1788. Savannah, Ga., Morning News Print, 1901. 97 p. F286.B915

12939

BRYANT, WILLIAM (1730–1786)
    New York; New Jersey. Physician, Loyalist surgeon.

ROGERS, FRED B. Dr. William Bryant (1730–86): an American physician and antiquary. *In* College of Physicians of Philadelphia. Transactions & studies, 4th ser., v. 37, Oct. 1969: 99–105. illus., port. R15.P5, 4th s., v. 37

12940

BUCHER, JOHN CONRAD (1730–1780)*
    Switzerland; Pennsylvania. Reformed Church clergyman, Revolutionary chaplain.

STAPLETON, AMMON. Rev. John Conrad Bucher: scholar, soldier, and pioneer preacher. Pennsylvania-German, v. 4, July 1903: 291–308. F146.P224, v. 4

12941

BUCKINGHAMSHIRE, JOHN HOBART, *2d Earl of* (1723–1793)†
    England. Member of Parliament, diplomat.

—— The despatches and correspondence of John, second earl of Buckinghamshire, ambassador to the court of Catherine II. of Russia 1762–1765. Edited, with introduction and notes, by Adelaide D'Arcy Collyer. London, New York, Longmans, Green, 1900–1902. 2 v. [Royal Historical Society. Publications. Camden series, 3d ser., v. 2–3] DA20.R91, 3d s., v. 2–3

Vol. 2 published at the offices of the Society.

Gt. Brit. *Historical Manuscripts Commission.* Report on the manuscripts of the marquess of Lothian preserved at Blickling Hall, Norfolk. London, Printed for H.M. Stationery Off., by Mackie, 1905, xviii, 514, x p. [*Its* Report. Unnumbered series] DA25.M2L7

Parliament. Papers by command. Cd. 2319.
Edited by D. B. Collyer.
"Buckinghamshire papers. Part 5. 1742–1793. Viceroyalty of Ireland—American rebellion and other private correspondence": p. 238–440.

12942

BUCKLAND, WILLIAM (1734–1774)
    England; Virginia; Maryland. Carpenter, architect.

BEIRNE, ROSAMOND R. William Buckland, architect of Virginia and Maryland. Maryland historical magazine, v. 41, Sept. 1946: 199–218. port. F176.M18, v. 41

BEIRNE, ROSAMOND R., *and* JOHN H. SCARFF. William Buckland, 1734–1774; architect of Virginia and Maryland. Baltimore, Maryland Historical Society, 1958. xiii, 175 p. map, plans, plates, ports. (Studies in Maryland history, no. 4)   NA737.B76B4

Bibliography included in "Notes" (p. 157–165).

12943

BUELL, ABEL (1742–1822)*

Connecticut. Silversmith, engraver.

WROTH, LAWRENCE C. Abel Buell of Connecticut, silversmith, typefounder & engraver. [2d ed., rev.] Middletown, Wesleyan University Press, 1958. xiv, 102 p. illus., facsims.   NK7198.B8W7 1958

Bibliographic references included in "Notes" (p. 86–96).

First edition published in 1926.

An informative review of Wroth's work, *Abel Buell, the First Type Cutter and Caster in English America* (Mount Vernon, N.Y., Priv. print., 1930. [17] p. NK7198.B8W73), by Leonard L. Mackall, first appeared in *Books*, a section of the Sunday *New York Herald Tribune*, January 15 and 22, 1928.

12944

BÜTTNER, JOHANN CARL (*b.* 1754)

Germany; Pennsylvania. Barber-surgeon, Revolutionary soldier, Hessian surgeon.

—— Narrative of Johann Carl Buettner in the American Revolution. New York, Printed for C. F. Heartman [1915] 69 p. col. port. (Heartman's historical series, no. 1)   E268.B95 Rare Bk. Coll.

Reprinted in New York by B. Blom (1971).

The second edition of the German original was published in Camenz (1828. 137, 126 p. E268.B92 Rare Bk. Coll.) under the title *Büttner der Amerikaner; eine Selbstbiographie*. The appendix, *Chronik der Stadt und des Amts Senftenberg*, is omitted from the present translation.

12945

BUGLASS, CALEB (1738?–1797)

England; Pennsylvania. Bookbinder.

FRENCH, HANNAH D. Caleb Buglass, binder of the proposed Book of Common Prayer, Philadelphia, 1786. *In* Winterthur portfolio. v. 6. Winterthur, Del., 1970. p. 15–32. illus.   N9.W52, v. 6

12946

BULL, JOHN (1731–1824)

Pennsylvania. Farmer, Revolutionary officer, assemblyman.

McGEE, ANITA N. Colonel John Bull (1731–1824). A preliminary study. [San Francisco, Priv. print., 1919] [8] p.   E263.P4B9 Rare Bk. Coll.

12947

BULLARD, SETH (1737–1811)

Massachusetts. Schoolmaster, Revolutionary officer, assemblyman.

DOGGETT, SAMUEL B. Seth Bullard of Walpole, Massachusetts; a soldier of the Revolution and some of his descendants. [Norwood, Mass.] Priv. print. [Plimpton Press] 1930. vi, 53 p. facsims., geneal. tables (part fold.), plates, ports.   E207.B89D65

12948

BULLOCH, ARCHIBALD (1730?–1777)*

South Carolina; Georgia. Planter, lawyer, delegate to the Continental Congress.

[BULLOCH, JOSEPH G. B.] A biographical sketch of Hon. Archibald Bulloch, president of Georgia, 1776–77. [n.p., 190–?] 17 p. ports.   E263.G3B9

12949

BUNCOMBE, EDWARD (1742–1778)

West Indies; North Carolina. Judge, Revolutionary officer.

HAYWOOD, MARSHALL D. Colonel Edward Buncombe, Fifth North Carolina Continental Regiment. His life, military career, and death while a wounded prisoner in Philadelphia during the War of the Revolution. Raleigh [N.C.] Alford, Bynum & Christophers, Printers, 1901. 20 p.   E275.B94

12950

BURBECK, HENRY (1754–1848)

Massachusetts. Revolutionary officer.

GARDINER, ASA B. Henry Burbeck, brevet brigadier-general United States Army—founder of the United States Military Academy. Magazine of American history, with notes and queries, v. 9, Apr. 1883: 251–265.   E171.M18, v. 9

See also the author's illustrated *Memoir of Brevt. Brig.-Genl. Henry Burbeck* (New York, A. S. Barnes, 1883. [24] p. U410.M1B85).

12951

BURD, EDWARD (1751–1833)

Pennsylvania. Revolutionary officer.

—— Selections from letters written by Edward Burd. 1763–1828. Edited by Lewis Burd Walker. [Pottsville, Pa., Standard Pub. Co.] 1899. 253 p. port. (The Burd papers, [v. 3])   F158.3.B94

An additional group of letters, written between 1765 and 1786, were published in the *Pennsylvania Magazine of History and Biography*, v. 42, Jan.–Apr. 1918, p. 62–68, 141–155.

12952

BURD, JAMES (1726–1793)

Scotland; Pennsylvania. Revolutionary officer.

NIXON, LILY L.   James Burd, frontier defender, 1726–1793. Philadelphia, University of Pennsylvania Press, 1941. vii, 198 p. map, port. (Pennsylvania lives)
F152.B96N5

"Bibliographical note": p. 187–189.

WATTS, IRMA A.   Colonel James Burd—defender of the frontier. Pennsylvania magazine of history and biography, v. 50, Jan. 1926: 29–37.   F146.P65, v. 50

12953

BURGH, JAMES (1714–1775)†

England. Political writer, schoolmaster.

——— An account of the first settlement, laws, form of government, and police, of the Cessares, a people of South America: in nine letters, from Mr. Vander Neck, one of the senators of that nation, to his friend in Holland. With notes by the editor [William Burgh] London, Printed for J. Payne, 1764. v, 121 p.
HX811.1764.B8 Rare Bk. Coll.

Depicts a utopian state.

——— Britain's remembrancer. Being some thoughts on the proper improvement of the present juncture. The character of this age and nation. A brief view from history of the effects of the vices which now prevail in Britain, upon the greatest empires and states of former times. Remarkable deliverances this nation has had in the most imminent dangers; with suitable reflections. Some hints showing what is in the power of the several ranks of people, and of every individual in Britain, to do toward securing the state. 7th ed. London, printed; Re-printed by B. Mecom, at the new printing office, in Boston, 1759. 51 p.   DA503.1746.B8 Rare Bk. Coll.

First published in 1746.

——— Crito; or, Essays on various subjects. London, J. Dodsley, 1766–67. 2 v.   PR3333.B4 1766

——— The dignity of human nature; or, A brief account of the certain and established means for attaining the true end of our existence. A new ed. London, Printed for J. Johnson and J. Payne, 1767. 2 v.   BJ1520.B85

Contents: 1. Of prudence. Of knowledge.—2. Of virtue. Of revealed religion.

HANDLIN, OSCAR, *and* MARY F. HANDLIN.   James Burgh and American revolutionary theory. In Massachusetts Historical Society, *Boston.* Proceedings. v. 73; 1961. Boston, 1963. p. 38–57.   F61.M38, v. 73

HAY, CARLA H.   Crusading schoolmaster: James Burgh, 1714–1775. 1972. ([342] p.)
Micro AC–1, no. 72–29,275

Thesis (Ph.D.)—University of Kentucky.
Abstracted in *Dissertation Abstracts International,* v. 33A, Nov. 1972, p. 2286–2287.

12954

BURGOYNE, JOHN (1722–1792)†

England. Member of Parliament, British officer in America, dramatist.

BAKSHIAN, ARAM.   General John Burgoyne. History today, v. 22, July 1972: 470–480. illus., ports.
D1.H818, v. 22

BELCHER, HENRY.   Burgoyne. In New York State Historical Association. Proceedings. v. 12; 1912. Albany, 1913. p. 172–195. plate.   F116.N86, v. 12

BILLIAS, GEORGE A.   John Burgoyne: ambitious general. *In his* George Washington's opponents: British generals and admirals in the American Revolution. New York, Morrow, 1969. p. 142–192. port.   E267.B56

Bibliography: p. 191–192.

DE FONBLANQUE, EDWARD B.   Political and military episodes in the latter half of the eighteenth century. Derived from the life and correspondence of the Right Hon. John Burgoyne, general, statesman, dramatist. London, Macmillan, 1876. xiii, 500 p. facsim., fold. plans, plates, port.   DA67.1.B8D5

Includes bibliographic references.
Reprinted, with a new introduction and preface by George A. Billias, in Boston by Gregg Press (1972).

FOX, DIXON R.   Burgoyne, before and after the Revolution. *In* New York State Historical Association. New York history, v. 10, Apr. 1929: 128–137.
F116.N865, v. 10

HARGREAVES, REGINALD.   Burgoyne and America's destiny. American heritage, v. 7, June 1956: 4–7, 83–85. illus. (part col.)   E171.A43, v. 7

HARGROVE, RICHARD J.   General John Burgoyne, 1722–1777. 1971. ([387 p.)   Micro AC–1, no. 71–24,187

Thesis (Ph.D.)—Duke University.
Abstracted in *Dissertation Abstracts International,* v. 32A, Sept. 1971, p. 1440.

HUDELSTON, FRANCIS J.   Gentleman Johnny Burgoyne; misadventures of an English general in the Revolution. Indianapolis, Bobbs-Merrill Co. [ᶜ1927] 367 p. facsims., maps, plates, ports.   DA67.1.B8H8

"Authorities": p. 340–350.

ORR, GUSS.   General John Burgoyne as an author. 1941. ix, 185 l. illus.

Thesis (Ph.D.)—Louisiana State University.

POTTINGER, DAVID T.   John Burgoyne: politician, dandy, and man of letters. *In* Cambridge Historical Society, *Cambridge, Mass.* Publications. v. 22; 1932/33. Cambridge, 1937. p. 29–45.   F74.C1C469, v. 22

SHIPPEN, EDWARD.   General John Burgoyne. United service, v. 4, May 1881: 561–594.   U1.U4, v. 4

Reprinted in the 3d ser., v. 4, Aug. 1903, p. 123–159.

12955

BURK, JOHN DALY (*ca.* 1775–1808)*

Ireland; Virginia. Historian, playwright.

——— Bunker-Hill; or, The death of General Warren: an historic tragedy. In five acts . . . As played at the theatres in America, for fourteen nights, with unbounded applause. New York, Printed by T. Greenleaf, 1797. 55 p.   PS721.B35B8 1797 Rare Bk. Coll.

Reprinted in Tarrytown, N.Y., by W. Abbatt (1931. 45 p. E173.M24, no. 168) as extra number, no. 168 of *The Magazine of History, With Notes and Queries,* and in New York by B. Franklin (1970. 82 p. PS721.B35B8 1970).

SHULIM, JOSEPH I.   John Daly Burk: Irish revolutionist and American patriot. Philadelphia, American Philosophical Society, 1964. 60 p. (Transactions of the American Philosophical Society, new ser., v. 54, pt. 6)   Q11.P6, n.s., v. 54
E302.6.B87S5

Bibliography: p. 53–57.

WYATT, EDWARD A.   John Daly Burk, patriot, playwright, historian. Charlottesville, Va., Historical Pub. Co., 1936. 32 p. (Southern sketches, 1st ser., no. 7)   F206.S89, 1st s., no. 7
F226.B968

12956

BURKE, EDMUND (1729–1797)†

Ireland; England. Lawyer, Member of Parliament, writer.

——— An account of the European settlements in America. In six parts. I. A short history of the discovery of that part of the world. II. The manners and customs of the original inhabitants. III. Of the Spanish settlements. IV. Of the Portuguese. V. Of the French, Dutch, and Danish. VI. Of the English. London, R. and J. Dodsley, 1757. 2 v. fold. maps.   E143.B94 Rare Bk. Coll.

Probably the joint work of Edmund and William Burke, but usually attributed to the former, who called himself merely the reviser of his kinsman's work.

The second edition, with "improvements," was published in London in 1758 and reprinted in New York by Research Reprints (1970. 2 v. E143.B967 1970). The 1777 edition, published in London by J. Dodsley, has been reprinted in New York by Arno Press (1972. 2 v. in 1. E101.B92 1972).

——— Burke's politics; selected writings and speeches on reform, revolution and war. Edited by Ross J. S. Hoffman & Paul Levack. New York, A. A. Knopf, 1949. xxxvii, 536, x p. port.   DA506.B85 1949

——— Burke's speeches & letters on American affairs. London, J. M. Dent; New York, E. P. Dutton [1931] xiii, 295 p. (Everyman's library. Oratory. [no. 340])   E211.B97
AC1.E8, no. 340

"First published in this edition, 1908."

——— The correspondence of Edmund Burke. Edited by Thomas W. Copeland. Cambridge, University Press; Chicago, University of Chicago Press, 1958+ ports.   DA506.B9A18

Bibliography: v. 1, p. xxiii–[xxvi]
As of 1970, nine of a projected ten volumes had been published.

——— The early life, correspondence and writings of the Rt. Hon. Edmund Burke, LL.D., with a transcript of the minute book of the debating "Club" founded by him in Trinity College, Dublin. By the late Arthur P. I. Samuels. With an introduction and supplementary chapters on Burke's contributions to the Reformer and his part in the Lucas controversy, by the Rt. Hon. Arthur Warren Samuels. Cambridge [Eng.] University Press, 1923. xiv, 418 p. facsims., ports.   DA506.B8 1923

Bibliographic footnotes.

——— Edmund Burke, New York agent, with his letters to the New York Assembly and intimate correspondence with Charles O'Hara, 1761–1776. [By] Ross J. S. Hoffman. Philadelphia, American Philosophical Soceity, 1956. ix, 632 p. facsim., ports. (Memoirs of the American Philosophical Society, v. 41)   DA506.B9A43
Q11.P612, v. 41

Includes bibliographic references.

——— On the American Revolution; selected speeches and letters. Edited by Elliott Robert Barkan. New York, Harper & Row [1966] xxx, 220 p. (American perspectives)   E211.B925 1966

Harper torchbooks. The University library, TB3068M. A second edition, with a new preface, was published in Gloucester, Mass., by P. Smith (1972).

——— Selected writings and speeches. Edited by Peter J. Stanlis. Gloucester, Mass., P. Smith, 1968 [ᶜ1963] xii, 585 p.   DA506.B85 1968

Bibliography: p. [581]–585.

——— Selected writings and speeches on America. Edited, with an introduction by Thomas H. D. Mahoney. Indianapolis, Bobbs-Merrill [1964] xxvii, 296 p. (The Library of liberal arts)   E211.B97 1964a

Bibliography: p. xxiii–xxv.

The speeches of the Right Honourable Edmund Burke, in the House of Commons, and in Westminster-Hall. London, Longman, Hurst, Rees, Orme, and Brown, 1816. 4 v.   DA506.B8 1816

——— The works of . . . Edmund Burke. London, J. C. Nimmo, 1899. 12 v. port.   DA509.B8 1899

Partial contents: v. 1. A vindication of natural society. A short account of a late short administration. Observations on a late publication. Thoughts on the cause of the present discontents.—v. 2. Speech on American taxation. Speeches on arrival at Bristol and at the conclusion of the poll. Speech on moving resolutions for conciliation with America. Letter to the sheriffs of Bristol. Two letters to gentlemen of Bristol.

Speech to the House of Commons, 1780. Speech at Bristol previous to the election, 1780. Speech at Bristol on declining the poll. Speech on Mr. Fox's East India bill.—v. 6. Letter to Sir Charles Bingham. Letter to Hon. C. J. Fox on the American war. Letter to the Marquis of Rockingham. Letter to the Right Hon. E. S. Pery. Two letters to Thomas Burgh. Letters and reflections on the executions of the rioters in 1780. Letters to chairman of the Buckinghamshire meetings. Fragments of a tract relative to the laws against popery in Ireland. Letter to William Smith. Second letter to Sir Hercules Langrishe. Letter to Richard Burke.—v. 7. Fragments and notes of speeches in Parliament. Hints for an essay on the drama. An essay towards an abridgment of the English history.

——— The works of the Right Honorable Edmund Burke. Rev. ed. Boston, Little, Brown, 1865–71. 12 v. port.
DA506.B8 1865

——— The works of the Right Honourable Edmund Burke. With a general introduction by the late Judge Willis, and a preface by F. W. Raffety. London, New York, H. Milford, Oxford University Press [1925–30] 6 v. (The World's classics, 71, 81, 111–114)   DA506.B8 1925

A made-up set of different issues, with date of imprint on verso of each title page.

BARKER, ERNEST, *Sir*.   Burke and Bristol, a study of the relations between Burke and his constituency during the years 1774–1780. Bristol, J. W. Arrowsmith [1931] 131 p.   DA506.B9B27

BISSETT, ROBERT.   The life of Edmund Burke. Comprehending an impartial account of his literary and political efforts, and a sketch of the conduct and character of his most eminent associates, coadjutors, and opponents. 2d ed. London, Printed and published by G. Cawthorn, 1800. 2 v. port.   DA506.B9B6

BREWER, JOHN.   Party and the double cabinet: two facets of Burke's *Thoughts*. Historical journal, v. 14, no. 3, 1971: 479–501.   D1.H33, v. 14

BRYANT, DONALD C.   Edmund Burke: a generation of scholarship and discovery. Journal of British studies, v. 2, Nov. 1962: 91–114.   DA20.J6, v. 2

——— Edmund Burke: new evidence, broader view. Quarterly journal of speech, v. 38, Dec. 1952: 435–445.
PN4071.Q3, v. 38

——— Edmund Burke on oratory. Quarterly journal of speech, v. 19, Feb. 1933: 1–18.   PN4071.Q3, v. 19

See also the author's supplementary article, "Edmund Burke's Opinions of Some Orators of His Day," v. 20, Apr. 1934, p. 241–254.

——— The frustrated opposition: Burke, Barré, and their audiences. *In* Washington University, *St. Louis*. Studies in memory of Frank Martindale Webster, by Robert M. Schmitz [and others] of the Dept. of English, Washington University. Saint Louis, 1951. (*Its* Washington University studies. New Ser.: Language and literature, no. 20) p. [49]–66.   PR14.W4

——— A note on Burke's parliamentary character, 1774. Burke newsletter, v. 5, fall 1963: 236–242.
DA506.B9B86, v. 5

CANAVAN, FRANCIS P.   Burke as a reformer. Burke newsletter, v. 5, spring/summer 1964: 300–311.
DA506.B9B86, v. 5

——— Edmund Burke's conception of the role of reason in politics. Journal of politics, v. 21, Feb. 1959: 60–79.
JA1.J6, v. 21

——— The political reason of Edmund Burke. Durham, N.C., Published for the Lilly Endowment Research Program in Christianity and Politics by the Duke University Press, 1960. xvi, 222 p.   JC176.B83C3

"Selected bibliography": p. [215]–217.

CHAPMAN, GERALD W.   Edmund Burke, the practical imagination. Cambridge, Harvard University Press, 1967. x, 350 p. port.   DA506.B9C5

Bibliography: p. [287]–293.

COBBAN, ALFRED B.   Edmund Burke and the origins of the theory of nationality. *In* Cambridge historical journal. v. 2, no. 1, Cambridge [Eng.] 1926. p. 36–47.
D1.C25, v. 2

CONE, CARL B.   Burke and the nature of politics. [Lexington] University of Kentucky Press [1957–64] 2 v. illus., port.   DA506.B9C54

Bibliographic footnotes.
Contents: [1] The age of the American Revolution.—[2] The age of the French Revolution.

——— Edmund Burke's library. *In* Bibliographical Society of America. Papers, v. 44, 2d quarter 1950: 153–172.
Z1008.B51P, v. 44

——— Pamphlet replies to Burke's *Reflections*. Southwestern social science quarterly, v. 26, June 1945: 22–34.
H1.S65, v.26

COPELAND, THOMAS W.   Boswell's portrait of Burke. *In* The Age of Johnson; essays presented to Chauncey Brewster Tinker. New Haven, Yale University Press, 1949. p. [27]–39.   PR442.T5

——— Burke and Dodsley's *Annual Register*. *In* Modern Language Association of America. Publications, v. 54, Mar. 1939: 223–245.   PB6.M6, v. 54

See also his "Edmund Burke and the Book Reviews in Dodsley's *Annual Register*," v. 57, June 1942, p. 446–468.

——— Our eminent friend Edmund Burke; six essays. New Haven, Yale University Press, 1949. ix, 251 p. illus., port.   DA506.B9C6

Bibliographic footnotes.
Reprinted in Westport, Conn., by Greenwood Press (1970).

COURTNEY, CECIL P.   Montesquieu and Burke. Oxford, Blackwell, 1963. xv, 204 p. (Modern language studies)
DA506.B9C65

Bibliography: p. 185–194.

DAVIDSON, JAMES F. Natural law and international law in Edmund Burke. Review of politics, v. 21, July 1959: 483–494. JA1.R4, v. 21

DEANE, SEAMUS F. Burke and the French philosophes. Studies in Burke and his time, v. 10, winter 1968/69: 1113–1137. DA506.B9B86, v. 10

Edmund, Burke Symposium, *Georgetown University, 1964.* The relevance of Edmund Burke. Edited by Peter J. Stanlis. New York, P. J. Kenedy [1964] 134 p. (A Wisdom and discovery book) LL

Contents: Edmund Burke in the twentieth century, by Peter J. Stanlis.—Edmund Burke and the legal order, by C. P. Ives.—Burke as a reformer, by Francis Canavan.—Burke as a practical politician, by Ross J. S. Hoffman.

Edmund Burke; the Enlightenment and the modern world. Edited by Peter J. Stanlis [and others] Detroit, University of Detroit Press [c1967] xviii, 129 p. DA506.B9E3

Five papers originally presented at a symposium held at the University of Detroit on Nov. 11–12, 1965, under the joint sponsorship of the University of Detroit and the Edmund Burke Memorial Foundation.
Includes bibliographic references.
Contents: Edmund Burke and the American Revolution: the repeal of the Stamp Act, by Thomas H. D. Mahoney.—Burke's crusade against the French Revolution: principles and prejudices, by Robert A. Smith.—Burke and Machiavelli on principles in politics, by Harvey C. Mansfield, Jr.—Edmund Burke and the scientific rationalism of the Enlightenment, by Peter J. Stanlis.—"Meaning" in the history of conflicting interpretations of Burke, by Walter D. Love.

EDMUNDS, PAUL J. The political pamphlets of Edmund Burke. 1959. ([367] p.) Micro AC–1, no. 59–2767
Thesis (Ph.D.)—University of Wisconsin.

Abstracted in *Dissertation Abstracts,* v. 20, Aug. 1959, p. 660–661.

EINAUDI, MARIO. The British background of Burke's political philosophy. Political science quarterly, v. 49, Dec. 1934: 576–598. H1.P8, v. 49

GRAHAM, GEORGE G. Edmund Burke's "developmental consensus." Midwest journal of political science, v. 16, Feb. 1972: 29–45. JA1.M5, v. 16

HIGGINS, PATRICK J. Edmund Burke and the old Whigs. 1940.
Thesis (Ph.D.)—Fordham University.

HOFFMAN, ROSS J. S. Edmund Burke as a practical politician. Burke newsletter, v. 4, winter 1963/64: 266–275. DA506.B9B86, v. 4

——— The Wentworth papers of Burke, Rockingham, and Fitzwilliam. *In* American Philosophical Society, *Philadelphia.* Proceedings, v. 94, Aug. 1950: 352–356. Q11.P5, v. 94

See also in the same issue Thomas W. Copeland's article, "Problems of Burke's Letters," p. 357–360.

HUTCHINS, ROBERT M. The theory of state: Edmund Burke. Review of politics, v. 5, Apr. 1943: 139–155. JA1.R4, v. 5

JANES, REGINA M. Edmund Burke: an essay on a style of thought. 1972.
Thesis (Ph.D.)—Harvard University.

JOHNSON, HELEN A. Reform and revolution in the political theory of Edmund Burke: his interpretations of the English, American, and French revolutions. 1967. ([350] p.) Micro AC–1, no. 68–8705
Thesis (Ph.D.)—Pennsylvania State University.
Abstracted in *Dissertation Abstracts,* v. 29A, July 1968, p. 299.

KIRK, RUSSELL. Edmund Burke; a genius reconsidered. New Rochelle, N.Y., Arlington House [1967] 255 p. (Architects of freedom series) DA506.B9K5
Includes bibliographic references.

KNOX, THOMAS R. Edmund Burke: natural law and history. 1969.
Thesis (Ph.D.)—Yale University.

LAPRADE, WILLIAM T. Edmund Burke: an adventure in reputation. Journal of modern history, v. 32, Dec. 1960: 321–332. D1.J6, v. 32

LEVACK, A. PAUL. Edmund Burke, his friends, and the dawn of Irish Catholic emancipation [1761–1778] Catholic historical review, v. 37, Jan 1952: 385–414. BX1404.C3, v. 37

LOVE, WALTER D. Edmund Burke's historical thought. 1956. v, 306 l.
Thesis (Ph.D.)—University of California, Berkeley.

LUCAS, PAUL. On Edmund Burke's doctrine of prescription; or, An appeal from the new to the old lawyers. Historical journal, v. 11, no. 1, 1968: 35–63. D1.H33, v. 11

MACCUNN, JOHN. The political philosophy of Burke. London, E. Arnold, 1913. vi, 272 p. JC176.B83M3
Reprinted in New York by Russell & Russell (1965).

MACKNIGHT, THOMAS. History of the life and times of Edmund Burke. London, Chapman and Hall, 1858–60. 3 v. facsims. DA506.B9M2

MAGNUS, *Sir* PHILIP M., *Bart.* Edmund Burke, a life. London, J. Murray [1939] xiii, 367 p. illus., facsim., plates, ports. DA506.B9M3
"Select bibliography": p. 351–355.

MAHONEY, THOMAS H. D. Edmund Burke and Ireland. Cambridge, Harvard University Press, 1960. xi, 413 p. illus., port. DA506.B9M32
"A note on sources and a selected bibliography": p. 345–350.

The author's thesis (Ph.D.), with the same title, was submitted to George Washington University in 1944.

———— Edmund Burke and Rome. Catholic historical review, v. 43, Jan. 1958: 401–427.   BX1404.C3, v. 43

———— Edmund Burke, 1729–1797; a portrait and an appraisal. History today, v. 6, Nov. 1956: 727–734. illus., ports.   D1.H818, v. 6

MANSFIELD, HARVEY C.   Statesmanship and party government; a study of Burke and Bolingbroke. Chicago, University of Chicago Press [1965] xii, 281 p.   JN1119.M3

Bibliography: p. 269–271.

Analyzes Burke's advocacy of party government in his *Thoughts on the Present Discontents* (1770).

MAZLISH, BRUCE.   The conservative revolution of Edmund Burke. Review of politics, v. 20, Jan. 1958: 21–33.   JA1.R4, v. 20

MURRAY, ROBERT H.   Edmund Burke, a biography. [London, New York] Oxford University Press, 1931. viii, 423 p. port.   DA506.B9M85

MUSGROVE, EUGENE R.   Historical background of Burke's *Conciliation With America*, with practical suggestions. Boston, Sibley, 1912. 60 p.   E211.B98609

Bibliography: p. 41–42.

PARKIN, CHARLES W.   The moral basis of Burke's political thought, an essay. Cambridge [Eng.] University Press, 1956. viii, 145 p.   JC176.B83P3

Bibliography: p. vii–viii.
Reprinted in New York by Russell & Russell (1968).

PHILLIPS, NEVILLE C.   Edmund Burke and the county movement, 1779–1780. English historical review, v. 76, Apr. 1961: 254–278.   DA20.E58, v. 76

POCOCK, JOHN G. A.   Burke and the ancient constitution—a problem in the history of ideas. Historical journal, v. 3, no. 2, 1960: 125–143.   D1.H33, v. 3

PRIOR, *Sir* JAMES.   A life of Edmund Burke. London, G. Bell, 1891. xxx, 545 p. port. (Bohn's standard library)   DA506.B9P8

First edition published in 1824.
"List of the chief writings of the Right Hon. Edmund Burke": p. xxiii–xxviii.
"Portraits of Burke": p. [xxix]–xxx.

———— Memoir of the life and character of the Right Hon. Edmund Burke, with specimens of his poetry and letters, and an estimate of his genius and talents, compared with those of his great contemporaries. A new ed., rev. and enl. Boston, Ticknor, Reed, and Fields, 1854. 2 v.   DA506.B9P8 1854

Reprinted in New York by B. Franklin (1968).
First published in 1825.

SMITH, GOLDWIN.   Burke on party. American historical review, v. 11, Oct. 1905: 36–41.   E171.A57, v. 11

STANLIS, PETER J.   The basis of Burke's political conservatism. Modern age, v. 5, summer 1961: 263–274.   AP2.M628, v. 5

———— Edmund Burke and the law of nations. American journal of international law, v. 47, July 1953: 397–413.   JX1.A6, v. 47

———— Edmund Burke and the natural law. Ann Arbor, University of Michigan Press [1958] xiii, 311 p.   LL

Bibliography: p. 259–264.

TODD, WILLIAM B.   A bibliography of Edmund Burke. London, Hart-Davis, 1964. 312 p. facsims., port. (Soho bibliographies, 17)   Z8133.23.T6

Bibliography: p. 15–17.

UNDERDOWN, P. T.   Bristol and Burke. Bristol [Eng.] Bristol Branch of the Historical Association, The University [1961] 20, [1] p. illus., facsim. (Local history pamphlets, 2)   DA690.B8H5, no. 2

Bibliography: p. [21].

———— Burke's Bristol friends. *In* Bristol and Gloucestershire Archaeological Society, *Gloucester. Eng.* Transactions. v. 77; 1958. Gloucester, 1959. p. 127–150.   DA670.G4B8, v. 77

Includes sketches of Richard Champion, Joseph Harford, Paul Farr, and John Noble—Burke's "inner cabinet" at Bristol.

———— Edmund Burke, the commissary of his Bristol constituents, 1774–1780. English historical review, v. 73, Apr. 1958: 252–269.   DA20.E58, v. 73

VINCITORIO, GAETANO L.   Edmund Burke's international politics. 1950.

Thesis (Ph.D.)—Fordham University.

WEARE, GEORGE E.   Edmund Burke's connection with Bristol, from 1774 till 1780. Bristol, W. Bennett, 1894. xviii, 174 p. illus., facsim., plates, port.   DA506.B9W3

WECTER, DIXON.   Edmund Burke and his kinsmen, a study of the statesman's financial integrity and private relationships. Boulder, Col., 1939. 113 p. (University of Colorado studies. Series B. Studies in the humanities, v. 1, no. 1)   DA506.B9W33

———— The missing years in Edmund Burke's biography [1750–59] *In* Modern Language Association of America. Publications, v. 53, Dec. 1938: 1102–1125.   PB6.M6, v. 53

WESTON, JOHN C.   Edmund Burke's view of history. Review of politics, v. 23, Apr. 1961: 203–229.   JA1.R4, v. 23

WHITE, HOWARD B.   Edmund Burke on political theory and practices. Social research, v. 17, Mar. 1950: 106–127.   H1.S53, v. 17

WILKINS, BURLEIGH T.   The problem of Burke's political philosophy. Oxford, Clarendon Press, 1967. viii, 262 p.   JC176.B83W5

Bibliography: p. 253–257.

WOOD, NEAL.   Burke on power. Burke newsletter, v. 4, spring/summer 1964: 311–326.   DA506.B8B86, v. 4

12957

BURKE, THOMAS (*ca.* 1747–1783)*

Ireland; North Carolina. Physician, lawyer, assemblyman, delegate to the Continental Congress, governor.

——— Poems, on divers matters, including a few written in praise of the American War for Independence against Great Britain; & also a number concerning a young man's affairs of the heart. Introduction & notes by Richard Walser. Raleigh, N.C., State Dept. of Archives and History, 1961. vii, 69 p.   PS721.B38P6

"All but two of the twenty-three poems exist in manuscript. . . . Seventeen are publish'd here for the first time. . . . An effort has been made to publish this volume in a format and type face of eighteenth-century printing."

DOUGLASS, ELISHA P.   Thomas Burke, disillusioned democrat. North Carolina historical review, v. 26, Apr. 1949: 150–186.   F251.N892, v. 26

[Guide to the microfilm edition of] the Thomas Burke papers in the Southern Historical Collection of the University of North Carolina Library.   James W. Patton, project director; Clyde Edward Pitts, editor. Chapel Hill, 1967. 11 p.   Z6616.B9P5 Mss

HAMILTON, JOSEPH G. DE ROULHAC.   Governor Thomas Burke. North Carolina booklet, v. 6, Oct. 1906: 103–122.   F251.N86, v. 6

SANDERS, JENNINGS B.   Thomas Burke in the Continental Congress. North Carolina historical review, v. 9, Jan. 1932: 22–37.   F251.N892, v. 9

WATTERSON, JOHN S.   Dr. Thomas Burke, a Revolutionary career. 1970. ([401] p.)
Micro AC–1, no. 71–2003

Thesis (Ph.D.)—Northwestern University.
Abstracted in *Dissertation Abstracts International*, v. 31A, Jan. 1971, p. 3489.

——— The ordeal of Governor Burke. North Carolina historical review, v. 48, spring 1971: 95–117. illus., map, ports.   F251.N892, v. 48

12958

BURKE, WILLIAM (1730?–1798)†

England. Lawyer, Member of Parliament.

——— The letters of Valens, (which originally appeared in the *London Evening Post*) with corrections, explana-

tory notes, and a preface, by the author. London, Printed for J. Almon, 1777. xv, 160 p.   E211.B99

Attributed to William Burke, assisted by Richard Burke.

The three Burkes, Edmund, William, and Richard, all appear to have written for the *Evening Post* over the signature of Valens.

An Examination of the commercial principles of the late negotiations between Great Britain and France in MDCCLXI. In which the system of that negotiation with regard to our colonies and commerce is considered. London, Printed for R. & J. Dodsley, 1762. 100 p.   DA507.1762.E9

Attributed to William Burke by Rev. William Hunt in *Dictionary of National Biography.*

12959

BURKE, WILLIAM (1752–1836)

Ireland; Connecticut. British soldier in America, nailor.

——— Memoir of William Burke, a soldier of the Revolution. Reformed from intemperance, and for many years a consistent and devoted Christian. Carefully prepared from a journal kept by himself. Hartford, Case, Tiffany, 1837. 126 p.   CT275.B7853A3

12960

BURNABY, ANDREW (1734?–1812)†

England. Traveler, clergyman.

——— Travels through the middle settlements in North America, in the years 1759 and 1760; with observations upon the state of the colonies. Ed. the 3d; rev., corr., and greatly enl. London, T. Payne, 1798. xix, 209 p. illus., map.   E162.B97 Rare Bk. Coll.

Contents: Preface to the third edition.—Introduction.—Travels.—Appendixes; viz. no. 1. Catalogue of trees, plants, birds, fishes, animals, &c. mentioned in the course of this work; with their common names, and the names given them by Catesby and Linnaeus. no. 2. Tables and statements relating to the commercial situation of the United States, both before and since the American war. no. 3. Anecdotes of the Indians. no. 4. [Anecdotes] of several branches of the Fairfax family, now domiciliated in Virginia. no. 5. Diary of the weather.

Originally published in London in 1775 with a second edition issued in New York the same year, this work was reprinted, with an introduction and notes by Rufus R. Wilson, in New York by A. Wessels Co. (1904), and by A. M. Kelley (1970).

12961

BURNETT, WILLIAM (*d.* 1812?)

Old Northwest. Trader, farmer.

——— Letter book [1786–1807] of William Burnett: early fur trader in the land of four flags. Edited by Wilbur M. Cunningham. [n.p.] Fort Miami Heritage Society of

Michigan [ᶜ1967] xxix, 231 p. illus., facsims., map, port. F566.B92

Bibliographic footnotes.

12962

BURNHAM, JOHN (1749?–1843)

Massachusetts. Revolutionary officer.

——— Recollections of the Revolutionary War, from Bunker Hill to Yorktown. Narrative of Major John Burnham, a Gloucester soldier, who served from May, 1775, to January, 1784. [Gloucester, Printed by Woodbury & Haskell, 1881] 16 p. E275.B96

Reprinted under the title *Personal Recollections of the Revolutionary War, by Major John Burnham, of Gloucester* by W. Abbatt (Tarrytown, N.Y., 1917. 19 p. E173.M24, no. 54) as extra number, no. 54, of *The Magazine of History, With Notes and Queries.*

12963

BURR, AARON (1756–1836)*

New York. Lawyer, Revolutionary officer.

——— Memoirs of Aaron Burr. With miscellaneous selections from his correspondence. By Matthew L. Davis. New York, Harper, 1836–37. 2 v. fold. facsim., ports. E302.6.B9B9

Reprinted in Freeport, N.Y., by Books for Libraries Press (1970) and in New York by Da Capo Press (1971).

ALEXANDER, HOLMES M. Aaron Burr, the proud pretender. New York, Harper, 1937. xii, 390 p. plates, ports. E302.6.B9A3

Bibliography: p. 375–382.

JENKINSON, ISAAC. Aaron Burr, his personal and political relations with Thomas Jefferson and Alexander Hamilton. Richmond, Ind., M. Cullaton, 1902. 389 p. E302.6.B9J5

PARMET, HERBERT S., *and* MARIE B. HECHT. Aaron Burr: portrait of an ambitious man. New York, Macmillan [1967] xii, 399 p. illus., ports. E302.6.B9P25

Bibliography: p. 377–388.

PARTON, JAMES. The life and times of Aaron Burr. Enl. ed., with numerous appendices, containing new and interesting information. Boston, Houghton, Mifflin, 1892. 2 v. ports. E302.6.B9P29

First published in 1858.

SCHACHNER, NATHAN. Aaron Burr, a biography. New York, F. A. Stokes Co., 1937. xii, 565 p. facsims. (part fold.), plates, ports. E302.6.B9S3

Bibliography: p. 547–553.

Some papers of Aaron Burr. *In* American Antiquarian Society, *Worcester, Mass.* Proceedings, new ser., v. 29, Apr. 1919: 43–128. E172.A35, n.s., v. 29

Approximately 90 letters to and from Burr, nearly half of which were written during the war. Introduction and notes by Worthington C. Ford.

TOMPKINS, HAMILTON B. Burr bibliography. A list of books relating to Aaron Burr. Brooklyn, N.Y., Historical Print. Club, 1892. 89 l. Z8136.T62

Reprinted in New York by B. Franklin (1970).

WANDELL, SAMUEL H., *and* MEADE MINNIGERODE. Aaron Burr; a biography compiled from rare, and in many cases unpublished, sources. New York, G. P. Putnam's Sons, 1925. 2 v. facsims., plates, ports. E302.6.B9W2

Bibliography: v. 1, p. xxvii–xxxiv.

Reprinted in St. Clair Shores, Mich., by Scholarly Press (1971).

WANDELL, SAMUEL H. Aaron Burr in literature; books, pamphlets, periodicals, and miscellany relating to Aaron Burr and his leading political contemporaries, with occasional excerpts from publications, bibliographical, critical and historical notes, etc. Introduction by Walter F. McCaleb. London, K. Paul, Trench, Trubner, 1936. xx, 302 p. illus., facsims., ports. (Psyche monographs, no. 6) Z8136.W24

Reprinted in Port Washington, N.Y., by Kennikat Press (1972).

Includes extensive annotations.

12964

BURROUGHS, STEPHEN (1765–1840)

New Hampshire; Massachusetts. School teacher, counterfeiter.

——— Memoirs of Stephen Burroughs. Hanover, N.H., Printed by B. True, 1798. 296 p. CT275.B8A3 1798 Rare Bk. Coll.

Republished in several editions, the latest in New York by Dial Press (1924) under the title *Memoirs of the Notorious Stephen Burroughs of New Hampshire.*

12965

BURROWS, JOHN (1760–1837)

New Jersey; Pennsylvania. Revolutionary soldier, farmer.

——— Autobiographical sketch of the life of Gen. John Burrows of Lycoming Co., Penna. (written in 1837). Pennsylvania magazine of history and biography, v. 34, Oct. 1910: 419–437. F146.P65, v. 34

——— Sketch of the life of Gen. John Burrows, of Lycoming County; furnished by himself at the request of his numerous relatives, and republished by his great grandson, Nathaniel Burrows Bubb. [Williamsport, 1917] 25 p. port. F153.B98

First published in 1837 (F153.B97 Rare Bk. Coll.).

12966

BUSHNELL, DAVID (1740–1826)*
  Connecticut. Inventor, Revolutionary officer.

ABBOT, HENRY L. The beginning of modern submarine warfare, under Captain-Lieutenant David Bushnell, Sappers and Miners, Army of the Revolution. [Willets Point, N.Y.H.] Printed on the Battalion Press, Sergt. Carmichael and Pvt. Beck, Printers, 1881. 34 p. plates. ([U.S.] Engineer School. Professional papers, v. 1, no. 3) UG1.U47, v. 1, no. 3

Reprinted with biographical appendixes and bibliography by Frank Anderson in Hamden, Conn., by Archon Books (1966. 69 p. V858.A72 1881a).

BISHOP, MORRIS. David Bushnell and the American Turtle. *In his* The exotics, being a collection of unique personalities and remarkable characters. New York, American Heritage Press [1969] p. 52–60. illus. CT105.B56

THOMSON, DAVID W. David Bushnell and the first American submarine. *In* United States Naval Institute. Proceedings, v. 68, Feb. 1942: 176–186. V1.U8, v. 68

WAGNER, FREDERICK. Submarine fighter of the American Revolution: the story of David Bushnell. New York, Dodd, Mead [1963] x, 145 p. illus., maps, plates, ports. E207.B92W3

Bibliography: p. 132–141.

12967

BUTE, JOHN STUART, *3d Earl of* (1713–1792)†
  Scotland; England. Advisor, First Lord of Treasury.

BREWER, JOHN. The faces of Lord Bute: a visual contribution to Anglo-American political ideology. *In* Perspectives in American history. v. 6; 1972. [Cambridge] Charles Warren Center for Studies in American History, Harvard University. p. 95–116. ports. E171.P47, v. 6

LOVAT-FRASER, JAMES A. John Stuart, earl of Bute. Cambridge [Eng.] University Press, 1912. 108 p. port. DA506.B95L6

"List of the principal authorities used by the author": p. [104]–105.

12968

BUTLER, LAURENCE (d. 1811)
  Virginia. Revolutionary officer.

——— Letters from Lawrence Butler, of Westmoreland County, Virginia, to Mrs. Anna F. Cradock, Cumley House, near Harborough, Leicestershire, England [1784–93] Virginia magazine of history and biography, v. 40, July–Oct. 1932: 259–267, 362–370; v. 41, Jan.–Apr. 1933: 24–32, 111–116. F221.V91, v. 40–41

Some of the letters were first published under the title, "Early Settlement of the Ohio Valley; Letters from Capt. Laurence Butler to Mrs. Joseph Cradock," in the *Magazine of American History*, v. 1, Jan.–Feb. 1877, p. 40–47, 112–118.

12969

BUTLER, SAMUEL EDWARD (1748–1809)
  Virginia; Georgia. Planter.

——— The diary of Samuel Edward Butler, 1784–1786, and the inventory and appraisement of his estate. Georgia historical quarterly, v. 52, June 1968: 203–220. F281.G2975, v. 52

Introduction and notes by G. Melvin Herndon.

HERNDON, GEORGE MELVIN. Samuel Edward Butler of Virginia goes to Georgia, 1784. Georgia historical quarterly, v. 52, June 1968: 115–131. F281.G2975, v. 52

12970

BUTLER, WALTER (1752?–1781)*
  New York. Loyalist officer.

——— Walter Butler's journal of an expedition along the north shore of Lake Ontario, 1779. Canadian historical review, v. 1, Dec. 1920: 381–391. F1001.C27, v. 1

Introduction and notes by James F. Kenney. The journal was published earlier in the *Transactions* of the Royal Canadian Institute, v. 4, 1892/93 (Toronto, 1895), p. 279–283.

CRUIKSHANK, ERNEST A. Memoir of Captain Walter Butler. *In* Royal Canadian Institute, *Toronto.* Transactions. v. 4; 1892/93. Toronto, 1895. p. 284–298. AS42.C21, v. 4

12971

BUTLER, WILLIAM (1759–1821)*
  Virginia; South Carolina. Revolutionary officer, assemblyman.

[SLIDER, THOMAS P.] Memoirs of General William Butler. Including a brief sketch of his father and brother, who fell in the Revolution, at Cloud's Creek, Lexington District, S.C. Atlanta, Ga., J. P. Harrison, Printers and Binders, 1885. 32 p. E275.B98

12972

BUTLER, ZEBULON (1731–1795)*
  Connecticut; Pennsylvania. Settler, assemblyman, Revolutionary officer.

KRUMBHAAR, ANNA C. Colonel Zebulon Butler and Wyoming Valley. Connecticut magazine, v. 6, Mar./Apr. 1900: 143–152. F91.C8, v. 6

12973

BUXTON, HENRY (1740–1827)
  Massachusetts. Bucklemaker.

BUXTON, BESSIE R.   The day book of Henry Buxton, the buckle maker [1761–1800] *In* Essex Institute, *Salem, Mass.* Historical collections, v. 91, Jan. 1955: 80–91.
F72.E7E81, v. 91

12974
BYLES, MATHER (1707–1788)*
Massachusetts. Congregational clergyman, poet, Loyalist.

EATON, ARTHUR W. H.   The famous Mather Byles, the noted Boston Tory preacher, poet, and wit, 1707–1788. Illustrated with many engravings from original paintings by Copley, the Pelhams and others. Boston, W. A. Butterfield, 1914. x, 258 p. facsims., plan, plates, ports.
BX7260.B95E3
"Doctor Byles's chief published writings": p. 240–246. Reprinted in Freeport, N.Y., by Books for Libraries Press (1971), and in Boston, with a new introduction and preface by George A. Billias, by Gregg Press (1972).

EDMONDS, JOHN H.   An account of the Mather-Byles portraits. *In* American Antiquarian Society, *Worcester, Mass.* Proceedings, v. 33, Oct. 1923: 285–290.
E172.A35, v. 33

TUELL, HARRIET E.   Rev. Mather Byles, parson and punster. Magazine of history, with notes and queries, v. 6, Dec. 1907: 311–317.
E171.M23, v. 6

12975
BYRD, WILLIAM (1728–1777)
Virginia. Planter, councilor, military officer.

HATCH, ALDEN.   The Byrds of Virginia. New York, Holt, Rinehart and Winston [1969] xvi, 535 p. illus., ports.
CS71.B9993 1969
Bibliographic footnotes.

WOLF, EDWIN.   The dispersal of the library of William Byrd of Westover. *In* American Antiquarian Society, *Worcester, Mass.* Proceedings, v. 68, Apr. 1958: 19–106.
E172.A35, v. 68

12976
CABOT, GEORGE (1751 *or* 2–1823)*
Massachusetts. Shipmaster, merchant, assemblyman.

LODGE, HENRY CABOT.   Life and letters of George Cabot. Boston, Little, Brown, 1877. xi, 615 p.
E302.6.C11L8

12977
CADWALADER, JOHN (1742–1786)*
Pennsylvania; Maryland. Merchant, Revolutionary general, assemblyman.

—— Selections from the military papers of General John Cadwalader [1776–1780] Pennsylvania magazine of history and biography, v. 32, Apr. 1908: 149–174.
F146.P65, v. 32

HEATHCOTE, CHARLES W.   General John Cadwalader—a sturdy Pennsylvania military officer and devoted to General Washington. Picket post, no. 70, Nov. 1960: 4–9, 28. port.
E234.P5, no. 70

WAINWRIGHT, NICHOLAS B.   Colonial grandeur in Philadelphia; the house and furniture of General John Cadwalader. Foreword by Henry Francis du Pont. Philadelphia, Historical Society of Pennsylvania, 1964. xii, 169 p. illus., facsims., plans, ports.   F158.37.W3
Includes bibliographic references.

12978
CADWALADER, LAMBERT (1743?–1823)*
New Jersey, Pennsylvania. Merchant, Revolutionary officer, delegate to the Continental Congress.

RAWLE, WILLIAM H.   Col. Lambert Cadwalader, a sketch. Pennsylvania magazine of history and biography, v. 10, Apr. 1886: 1–14. port.   F146.P65, v. 10
Also published separately ([Philadelphia? 1878] 16 p. E302.6.C13R25).

12979
CADWALADER, THOMAS (1708–1779)*
Pennsylvania; New Jersey. Physician, councilor.

DULLES, CHARLES W.   Sketch of the life of Dr. Thomas Cadwalader. Pennsylvania magazine of history and biography, v. 27, July 1903: 262–278.
F146.P65, v. 27

MIDDLETON, WILLIAM S.   Thomas Cadwalader and his essay. Annals of medical history, 3d ser., v. 3, Mar. 1941: 101–113. facsims., port.   R11.A85, 3d s., v. 3
Refers to his *Essay on the West-India Dry-Gripes.*

12980
CALDER, WILLIAM (1735–1802)
Massachusetts. Painter and glazier, Revolutionary officer, engineer.

DURRELL, HAROLD C.   Major William Calder of Charlestown, Massachusetts, 1735–1802. Boston, Mass., Printed by T. Groom, 1933. 31 p. illus., facsims., maps, port.   E207.C26D8

12981
CALDWELL, DAVID (1725–1824)*
New Jersey; North Carolina. Presbyterian clergyman, schoolmaster, farmer, physician.

BROOKS, AUBREY L. David Caldwell and his Log College. North Carolina historical review, v. 28, Oct. 1951: 399–407. F251.N892, v. 28

CARUTHERS, ELI W. A sketch of the life and character of the Rev. David Caldwell, D.D., near sixty years pastor of the churches of Buffalo and Almance. Including two of his sermons; some account of the Regulation, together with the Revolutionary . . . incidents in which he was concerned; and a very brief notice of the ecclesiastical and moral condition of North-Carolina while in its colonial state. Greensborough, N.C., Printed by Swaim and Sherwood, 1842. 302 p. F257.C33

12982

CALDWELL, JAMES (1734–1781)*
New Jersey. Presbyterian clergyman, Revolutionary chaplain.

FOLSOM, JOSEPH F. Manuscript light on Chaplain James Caldwell's death. In New Jersey Historical Society. Proceedings, new ser., v. 1, Jan. 1916: 1–12.
F131.N58, n.s., v. 1

FORD, HARRY P. A Revolutionary hero, James Caldwell. In Presbyterian Historical Society. Journal, v. 6, Sept. 1912: 260–266. BX8905.P7A4, v. 6

KEMPSHALL, EVERARD. "Caldwell and the revolution"; a historical sketch of the First Presbyterian Church of Elizabeth, prior to and during the War of the Revolution. Elizabeth, N.J., Elizabeth Daily Journal, 1880. 45 p. F144.E4K32

MURRAY, NICHOLAS. A memoir of the Rev. James Caldwell, of Elizabethtown. In New Jersey Historical Society. Proceedings, v. 3, no. 2, 1848: 77–89.
F131.N58, v. 3

SWEETSER, KATE D. The "fighting parson" of New Jersey. Daughters of the American Revolution magazine, v. 54, Mar. 1920: 140–145. E202.5.A12, v. 54

12983

CALHOUN, WILLIAM (fl. 1749–1776)
South Carolina. Settler.

——— Journal of William Calhoun. Annotated by A. S. Salley, Jr. In Southern History Association. Publications, v. 8, May 1904: 179–195. F206.S73, v. 8

Accounts and personal notes, dated mostly from 1760 to 1770.

12984

CALK, WILLIAM (1740–1823)
Virginia; Kentucky. Frontiersman, surveyor.

——— The Journal of William Calk, Kentucky pioneer. Mississippi Valley historical review, v. 7, Mar. 1921: 363–377. E171.J87, v. 7

Account of a trip from Virginia to Kentucky in 1775. Lewis H. Kilpatrick provides extensive commentary and notes relating to Calk's life.

12985

CALKINS, MATTHEW (b. ca. 1763)
New York. Revolutionary soldier.

PRIEST, JOSIAH. A true story of the extraordinary feats, adventures and sufferings of Matthew Calkins, Chenango Co., N.Y., in the War of the Revolution—never before published. Also, the deeply interesting story of the captivity of General Patchin, of Schoharie Co., N.Y., when a lad: by Brant and his Indians. Lansingburgh, Printed by W. Harkness, 1840. 38 p.
E275.C15

Imperfect: p. 39–40 wanting.
Reprinted in Tarrytown, N.Y., by W. Abbatt (1920. 24 p. E173.M24, no. 69) as extra number, no. 70 [i.e. 69], of *The Magazine of History, With Notes and Queries.*

12986

CALLAWAY, RICHARD (1722–1780)
Virginia; Kentucky. Frontiersman, Revolutionary officer, assemblyman.

BATE, RICHARD ALEXANDER. Colonel Richard Callaway, 1722–1780. Filson Club history quarterly, v. 29, Jan.–Apr. 1955: 3–20, 166–178. F446.F484, v. 29

——— Colonel Callaway's preparedness. [Henderson? Ky.] Society of Transylvanians [1941] 42 p. illus., coat of arms, plates, port. F454.C2B3

BRYAN, CHARLES W. Richard Callaway, Kentucky pioneer. Filson Club history quarterly, v. 9, Jan. 1935: 35–50. F446.F484, v. 9

See also his "Addenda to Biography of Richard Callaway" in v. 9, Oct. 1935, p. 242–243.

12987

CAMDEN, CHARLES PRATT, *1st Earl Camden* (1714–1794)†
England. Lawyer, Member of Parliament, judge.

EELES, HENRY S. Lord Chancellor Camden and his family. London, P. Allan, 1934. xi, 276 p. illus., geneal. tables, ports. DA506.C3E4

Bibliography: p. 269–270.

12988

CAMERON, *Sir* ALAN (1753–1828)†
Scotland; England. British officer in America.

JOHNSON, WILLIAM T. Alan Cameron, a Scotch Loyalist in the American Revolution. Pennsylvania history, v. 8, Jan. 1941: 29–46. F146.P597, v. 8

12989

CAMPBELL, Sir ARCHIBALD (1739–1791)†

Scotland; Jamaica. Member of Parliament, British officer in America, governor.

HOWE, ARCHIBALD M. Letters and memoranda of Sir Archibald Campbell, prisoner of war, captured in Boston Bay, June 17, 1776. *In* Bostonian Society, *Boston.* Publications. v. 12. Boston, 1915. p. [63]–95. port.
F73.1.B88, v. 12

WALCOTT, CHARLES H. Sir Archibald Campbell of Inverneill; sometime prisoner of war in the jail at Concord, Massachusetts. Boston, Printed for the author by T. Todd [c1899] 62 p. plates, ports. E281.C18

12990

CAMPBELL, ARTHUR (1743–1811)

Virginia. Frontiersman, assemblyman, Revolutionary officer, judge.

HAGY, JAMES W., *and* STANLEY J. FOLMSBEE. Arthur Campbell and the separate state movements in Virginia and North Carolina. *In* East Tennessee Historical Society, *Knoxville.* Publications. no. 42; 1970. Knoxville, Tenn. p. 20–46. F442.1.E14, no. 42

QUINN, HARTWELL L. Colonel Arthur Campbell, 1743–1811: a biography. 1972. ([206] p.)
Micro AC–1, no. 72–34,131

Thesis (Ph.D.)—University of Georgia.
Abstracted in *Dissertation Abstracts International,* v. 33A, Jan. 1973, p. 3555–3556.

12991

CAMPBELL, ISAAC (*ca.* 1724–1834)

Scotland; Maryland. Anglican clergyman.

VIVIAN, JAMES F., *and* JEAN H. VIVIAN. The Reverend Isaac Campbell: an anti-Lockean Whig. Historical magazine of the Protestant Episcopal church, v. 39, Mar. 1970: 71–89. BX5800.H5, v. 39

12992

CAMPBELL, THOMAS (1733–1795)†

Ireland. Clergyman.

———— Dr. Campbell's diary of a visit to England in 1775. Newly edited from the MS. by James L. Clifford. Cambridge [Eng.] University Press, 1947. xv, 147 p. port.
DA620.C25 1947

Bibliographic reference included in "Notes" (p. 109–138).

12993

CAMPBELL, WILLIAM (1745–1781)*

Virginia; Kentucky. Frontiersman, Revolutionary general, assemblyman.

RUSSELL, FRAN. A commentary on the life of General William Campbell. *In* Northern Neck historical magazine. v. 4, no. 1; 1954. Montross, Va. p. 338–350.
F232.N86N6, v. 4

U.S. Congress. *Senate. Committee on the Library.* Monument to memory of William Campbell. Report. [Washington, Govt. Print. Off., 1908] 15 p. (60th Congress, 1st session. Senate. Rept. 557)
E241.K5U5

This account of Campbell's services in the Revolutionary War was submitted by John W. Daniel and ordered printed, April 22, 1908.

12994

CAREY, MATHEW (1760–1839)*†

Ireland; Pennsylvania. Publisher.

BRADSHER, EARL L. Mathew Carey, editor, author and publisher; a study in American literary development. New York [Columbia University Press] 1912. xi, 145 p. (Columbia University studies in English. [Ser. 2, no. 19]) PS727.C3Z6 1912a

Thesis (Ph.D.)—Columbia University, 1911.
Bibliography: p. 136–139.
Reprinted in New York by AMS Press (1966).

CARTER, EDWARD C. Mathew Carey in Ireland, 1760–1784. Catholic historical review, v. 51, Jan. 1966: 503–527. BX1404.C3, v. 51

MAIER, EUGENE F. J. Mathew Carey, publicist and politician (1760–1839). *In* American Catholic Historical Society of Philadelphia. Records, v. 39, June 1928: 71–154. E184.C3A4, v. 39

SILVER, ROLLO G. The costs of Mathew Carey's printing equipment. *In* Virginia. University. *Bibliographical Society.* Studies in bibliography; papers. v. 19. Charlottesville, 1966. p. 85–122. Z1008.V55, v. 19

12995

CARIGAL, HAIM ISAAC (1733–1777)

Palestine; West Indies. Itinerant rabbi.

FRIEDMAN, LEE M. Rabbi Haim Isaac Carigal; his Newport sermon and his Yale portrait. Boston, Priv. print. [D. B. Updike, Merrymount Press] 1940. 43 p., 1 l, facsim., port. BM755.C27F7

"This tells of the publication of the first Jewish sermon to have been both delivered and printed in the United States."—Foreword.
"Authorities": leaf at end.

CARLETON, *Sir* GUY
See DORCHESTER, GUY CARLETON, *Baron*

12996

CARLETON, THOMAS (1735?–1817)

Ireland; Canada. British officer in America, Royal governor.

RAYMOND, WILLIAM O. A sketch of the life and administration of General Thomas Carleton, first governor of New Brunswick. *In* New Brunswick Historical Society. Collections. [v. 2], no. 6. Saint John, N.B., 1905. p. 439–480. plates. [F1041.N53, v. 2, no. 6] Micro 04070

12997

CARLISLE, FREDERICK HOWARD, *5th Earl* (1748–1825)†

England. Commissioner.

Gt. Brit. *Historical Manuscripts Commission.* The manuscripts of the earl of Carlisle, preserved at Castle Howard. London, Printed for H.M. Stationery Off., by Eyre and Spottiswoode, 1897. xl, 835 p. (*Its* Report. 15th, appendix, pt. 6) DA25.M2C3

Parliament. Papers by command. C. 8551.

Edited by R. E. G. Kirk.

Among the public documents are papers and minutes relating to the war and Carlisle's mission to America as a British commissioner. Of the private correspondence the largest group contains the letters of George Selwyn to Carlisle, 1767–90. Additional papers, not calendared here, are described by Eric Robson in the *English Historical Review*, v. 24, May 1951, p. 62–69.

12998

CARMICHAEL, WILLIAM (*d.* 1795)*

Maryland; Europe. Diplomat, delegate to the Continental Congress.

—— Letters of William Carmichael to John Cadwalader, 1777. Edited by Harry Ammon. Maryland historical magazine, v. 44, Mar. 1949: 1–17. F176.M18, v. 44

COE, SAMUEL G. The mission of William Carmichael to Spain. Baltimore, Johns Hopkins Press, 1928. vii, 116 p. (Johns Hopkins University studies in historical and political science, 46th ser., no. 1) H31.J6, 46th s., no. 1 E249.C64

Issued also as thesis (Ph.D.)—Johns Hopkins University, 1926.

Bibliography: p. 113.

STREETER, FLOYD B. The diplomatic career of William Carmichael. Maryland historical magazine, v. 8, June 1913: 119–140. F176.M18, v. 8

12999

CARPENTER, EMANUEL (1702–1780)

Switzerland; Pennsylvania. Assemblyman, judge.

ESHLEMAN, HENRY FRANK. The legislative career of Emanuel Carpenter. *In* Lancaster County (Pa.) Historical Society. Papers, v. 24, Sept. 1920: 153–168. F157.L2L5, v. 24

MAGEE, DAVID F. Emanuel Carpenter, the law giver. *In* Lancaster County (Pa.) Historical Society. Papers, v. 24, Sept. 1920: 144–152. illus. F157.L2L5, v. 24

13000

CARR, PATRICK (*fl.* 1780–1783)

Georgia. Revolutionary officer.

—— Letters of Patrick Carr, terror to British Loyalists, to governors John Martin and Lyman Hall, 1782 and 1783. Georgia historical quarterly, v. 1, Dec. 1917: 337–343. F281.G2975, v. 1

13001

CARRINGTON, EDWARD (1749–1810)

Virginia. Revolutionary officer, delegate to the Continental Congress.

HOPKINS, GARLAND E. Colonel Carrington of Cumberland. With a brief sketch of the Carrington family appended. Winchester, Va., Privately issued, 1942. 101 (i.e. 102) p. (Cumberland County, Virginia, historical monograph, no. 2) F232.C93C8, no. 2

Reproduced from typescript.

Bibliographic references included in "Notes" (p. 66–70).

—— The life of Edward Carrington, a brief sketch. Americana, v. 34, July 1940: 458–474. E171.A53, v. 34

KONIGSBERG, CHARLES. Edward Carrington, 1748–1810, "child of the Revolution": a study of the public man in young America. 1966. ([576] p.) Micro AC–1, no. 66–13,324

Thesis (Ph.D.)—Princeton University.

Abstracted in *Dissertation Abstracts*, v. 27A, Feb. 1967, p. 2573–2574.

13002

CARRINGTON, PAUL (1735–1818)*

Virginia. Lawyer, judge.

RIELY, HENRY C. Paul Carrington. *In* Virginia State Bar Association. Annual report. v. 39; 1927. Richmond. p. 450–464. illus., facsims. LL

An offprint, with an expanded title, was published in Richmond by Richmond Press, Printers (1928. 15 p. illus., facsims. LL).

13003

CARROLL, CHARLES ("Barrister") (1723–1783)

Maryland. Lawyer, assemblyman, delegate to the Continental Congress. Cousin to Charles Carroll of Carrollton (1737–1832).

————— Letters of Charles Carroll, barrister [1755–69] Maryland historical magazine, v. 31, Dec. 1936: 298–332; v. 32, Mar.–June, Dec. 1937: 35–46, 174–190, 348–368; v. 33, June, Dec. 1938: 187–202, 371–388; v. 34, June 1939: 180–189; v. 35, June 1940: 200–207; v. 36, Mar., Sept. 1941: 70–73, 336–344; v. 37, Mar., Dec. 1942: 57–68, 414–419; v. 38, June, Dec. 1943: 181–191, 362–369.   F176.M18, v. 31–38

Introduction and notes by W. Stull Holt.

HOLT, WILLIAM STULL. Charles Carroll, barrister: the man. Maryland historical magazine, v. 31, June 1936: 112–126.   F176.M18, v. 31

13004

CARROLL, CHARLES (of Carrollton) (1737–1832)*

Maryland. Planter, Delegate to the Continental Congress, assemblyman.

————— Correspondence of "First citizen"—Charles Carroll of Carrollton, and "Antilon"—Daniel Dulany, Jr., 1773. With a history of Governor Eden's administration in Maryland. 1769–1776. By Elihu S. Riley. Baltimore, King Bros., State Printers, 1902. xi, 252 p.
F184.C31

————— Extracts from the Carroll papers [1750–74] Maryland historical magazine, v. 10, June–Dec. 1915: 143–159, 218–258, 322–344; v. 11, Mar.–Dec. 1916: 66–73, 175–189, 261–278, 322–348; v. 12, Mar.–Dec. 1917: 21–41, 166–187, 276–296, 347–369; v. 13, Mar.–Sept. 1918: 54–75, 171–179, 249–267; v. 14, June–Dec. 1919: 127–154, 272–293, 358–371; v. 15, Mar.–Sept. 1920: 56–65, 194–201, 274–291; v. 16, Mar. 1921: 29–42.
F176.M18, v. 10–16

————— Journal of Charles Carroll of Carrollton, during his visit to Canada in 1776, as one of the commissioners from Congress; with a memoir and notes by Brantz Mayer. Baltimore, Printed by J. Murphy, 1845. 84 p. [Maryland Historical Society. Publications, v. 1, no. 4]
F176.M34, v. 1, no. 4
E231.C29

The 1876 edition, printed in Baltimore by John Murphy for the Maryland Historical Society, has been reprinted in New York by the New York Times (1969).

————— A lost copy-book of Charles Carroll of Carrollton [1770–74] Maryland historical magazine, v. 32, Sept. 1937: 193–225.   F176.M18, v. 32

Introduction and notes by J. G. D. Paul.

————— Revolutionary correspondence of Charles Carroll of Carrollton with William Carmichael [1776–79] In American Catholic Historical Society. Records, v. 42, Mar. 1931: 1–11.   E184.C3A4, v. 42

Introduction and notes by Elizabeth S. Kite.

————— Unpublished letters of Charles Carroll of Carrollton, and his father, Charles Carroll of Doughoregan. Compiled and edited with a memoir by Thomas Meagher Field. New York, United States Catholic Historical Society, 1902. 250 p. facsim., geneal. table, port. (United States Catholic Historical Society. Monograph series, 1)   E302.6.C3C3
E184.C3U6, v. 1

Baltimore. Museum of Art. Charles Carroll of Carrollton (1737–1832) and his family; an exhibition of portraits, furniture, silver and manuscripts. [Baltimore, Lord Baltimore Press, 1937] 54 p. illus., plates, ports.
N7628.C3B3

FITZGERALD, CHARLES E. Charles Carroll of Carrolltown and the Constitution. 1927.

Thesis (Ph.D.)—Fordham University.

GROVE, WILLIAM J. History of Carrollton Manor, Frederick County, Maryland. Frederick, Md., Market & Bielfeld, 1928. x, 496 p. facsim., plates, ports.
F187.F8G82

Guide to the microfilm of the Charles Carroll papers. From the collection of the Maryland Historical Society. Editor: Thomas O'Brien Hanley. Wilmington, Del., Scholarly Resources [1972] [87] p.
Z6616.C326C37 Mss

GURN, JOSEPH. Charles Carroll of Carrollton, 1737–1832. New York, P. J. Kenedy [ᶜ1932] viii, 312 p. plate, ports.   E302.6.C3G94

Bibliography: p. [299]–303.

HANLEY, THOMAS O. Charles Carroll of Carrollton: the making of a revolutionary gentleman. Washington, Catholic University of America Press, 1970. x, 293 p. geneal. table, port.   E302.6.C3H3

Includes bibliographic references.

————— Young Mr. Carroll and Montesquieu. Maryland historical magazine, v. 62, Dec. 1967: 394–418.
F176.M18, v. 62

HAY, ROBERT P. Charles Carroll and the passing of the Revolutionary generation. Maryland historical magazine, v. 67, spring 1972: 54–62. illus., ports.
F176.M18, v. 67

LEONARD, LEWIS A. Life of Charles Carroll of Carrollton. New York, Moffat, Yard, 1918. 313 p. facsims., plates, ports.   E302.6.C3L5

"Sources": p. 11.

PAUL, PETER J. The social philosophy of Charles Carroll of Carrollton. 1947. 264 l.

Thesis (Ph.D.)—University of Chicago.

ROWLAND, KATE M. The life of Charles Carroll of Carrollton, 1737–1832. With his correspondence and public papers. New York, G. P. Putnam's Sons, 1898. 2 v. coat of arms, geneal. tables, plates, ports.
E302.6.C3R8

Bibliography: v. 1, p. xvii–xviii.
List of "portraits of Charles Carroll of Carrollton": v. 1, p. xix–xx.

SMITH, ELLEN H. Charles Carroll of Carrollton. Cambridge, Mass., Harvard University Press, 1942. x, 340 p. plates, ports.   E302.6.C3S56

Bibliography: p. [313]–324.
Reprinted in New York by Russell & Russell (1971).

13005

CARROLL, DANIEL (1730–1796)*
Maryland. Delegate to the Continental Congress, delegate to the Constitutional Convention. Brother of John Carroll (1735–1815).

GEIGER, MARY V., Sister. Daniel Carroll, a framer of the Constitution. Washington, D.C., Catholic University of America, 1943. x, 210 p. fold. geneal. tables.
E302.6.G33G4

Thesis (Ph.D.)—Catholic University of America, 1943.
Bibliography: p. 191–202.

PURCELL, RICHARD J. Daniel Carroll, framer of the Constitution. In American Catholic Historical Society of Philadelphia. Records, v. 52, June–Sept. 1941: 65–87, 137–160.   E184.C3A4, v. 52

13006

CARROLL, JOHN, Abp. (1735–1815)*
Maryland. Roman Catholic clergyman, church organizer, bishop.

—— An address to the Roman Catholics of the United States of America. By a Catholic clergyman. Annapolis, Printed by F. Green, 1784. 116 p.
E312.63.C3 Rare Bk. Coll.
HG2611.M3T6 Rare Bk. Coll.

In reply to A Letter to the Roman Catholics of the City of Worcester From the Late Chaplain of That Society (i.e., Charles H. Wharton).

[BRENT, DANIEL] Biographical sketch of the Most Rev. John Carroll, first archbishop of Baltimore; with select portions of his writings. Edited by John Carroll Brent. Baltimore, J. Murphy, 1843. 321 p. port.
BX4705.C33B7

Based on "the unfinished manuscript of the late Daniel Brent."

GUILDAY, PETER K. The life and times of John Carroll, archbishop of Baltimore (1735–1815). New York, Encyclopedia Press, 1922. 2 v. illus., maps, plates, ports.
BX4705.C33G8

A one-volume edition has been published in Westminster, Md., by Newman Press (1954).

MELVILLE, ANNABELLE M. John Carroll of Baltimore, founder of the American Catholic hierarchy. New York, Scribner [1955] ix, 338 p. illus., plate.
BX4705.C33M4

Bibliography: p. 289–293.

SHEA, JOHN D. G. Life and times of the Most Rev. John Carroll, bishop and first archbishop of Baltimore. Embracing the history of the Catholic church in the United States, 1763–1815. New York, J. G. Shea, 1888. 695 p. illus., facsims., ports. (A history of the Catholic church within the limits of the United States, [v. 2])
BX4705.C33S5 1888

13007

CARTER, JOHN (1745–1814)*
Pennsylvania; Rhode Island. Printer, newspaper editor.

McCORISON, MARCUS A. The wages of John Carter's journeyman printers, 1771–1779. In American Antiquarian Society, Worcester, Mass. Proceedings, new ser., v. 81, Oct. 1971: 273–303.
E172.A35, n.s., v. 81

WOODS, JOHN C. B. John Carter. In Rhode Island Historical Society. Collections, v. 11, Oct. 1918: 101–107. port.   F76.R47, v. 11

—— —— Offprint. [Providence] 1918.
CS71.C323 1918

13008

CARTER, LANDON (1710–1778)*
Virginia. Planter, assemblyman.

—— The diary of Colonel Landon Carter of Sabine Hall, 1752–1778. Edited, with an introduction, by Jack P. Greene. Charlottesville, Published for the Virginia Historical Society [by] the University Press of Virginia, 1965. 2 v. (xvi, 1204 p.) illus., maps, ports. (Virginia Historical Society [Richmond] Documents, v. 4–5)
F229.C29

The introduction, with a few minor changes and the addition of a brief epilogue, was published separately under the title Landon Carter: An Inquiry Into the Personal Values and Social Imperatives of the Eighteenth-Century Virginia Gentry (Charlottesville, Dominion Books [1967, ©1965] 98 p. F229.C293).

Extracts from the diary for the years 1770 to 1776, edited by Lyon G. Tyler, were first published in the William and Mary College Quarterly Historical Magazine, v. 13, July 1904, Jan.–Apr. 1905: 45–53, 157–164, 219–224; v. 14, Jan. 1905, Jan.–Apr. 1906: 38–44, 181–186, 246–253; v. 15, Jan. 1907: 205–211; v. 16, Jan.–Apr. 1908: 149–156, 257–268; v. 17, July 1908: 9–18; v. 18, July 1909: 37–44; v. 20, Jan. 1912: 173–185; v. 21, Jan. 1913: 172–181.

—— A letter from a gentleman in Virginia, to the merchants of Great Britain, trading to that colony. London, Printed in the year 1754. 36 p.
E229.C3 Rare Bk. Coll.

Usually ascribed to Peyton Randolph. Carter's authorship is affirmed in the manuscript minutes of the House of Burgesses, 1752–55, kept by Carter, in which he stated that "Sometime after the first of these Assemblys [Nov. 1–Dec. 19, 1753] I wrote a Pamphlet by way of letter to the Virginia Merchants setting the affair of the Pistole and the

Argumts in favour of it in a true light this Pamphlet was printed in London and sent in here." See Jack P. Greene's article, "Landon Carter and the Pistole Fee Dispute."

——— "Not to be governed or taxed, but by . . . our representatives"; four essays in opposition to the Stamp Act. Edited by Jack P. Greene. Virginia magazine of history and biography, v. 76, July 1968: 259–300. port.
F221.V91, v. 76

GREENE, JACK P. Landon Carter and the Pistole Fee dispute. William and Mary quarterly, 3d ser., v. 14, Jan. 1957: 66–69. F221.W71, 3d s., v. 14

Guide to the microfilm edition of the Carter family papers, 1659–1797, in the Sabine Hall collection. Paul P. Hoffman, editor; Mary F. Crouch, assistant editor; Lindsay M. Gold, editorial assistant. [Charlottesville] University of Virginia Library [1967] 26 p.
Z5315.C3H6 Mss

WINEMAN, WALTER R. The Landon Carter papers in the University of Virginia Library; a calendar and biographical sketch. Charlottesville, University of Virginia Press, 1962. viii, 99 p. F229.C28W5 1962

The author's thesis (Ph.D.), *Calendar of the Landon Carter Papers in the Sabine Hall Collection and a Biographic Sketch of Colonel Landon Carter,* was submitted to the University of Pittsburgh in 1956 (Micro AC–1, no. 19,650).

13009
CARTER, ROBERT (1728–1804)
Virginia. Planter, councilor.

MAURER, MAURER. A musical family in colonial Virginia. Musical quarterly, v. 34, July 1948: 358–364. plates.
ML1.M725, v. 34

MORTON, LOUIS. Robert Carter of Nomini Hall, a Virginia tobacco planter of the eighteenth century. Williamsburg, Va., Colonial Williamsburg, 1941. xi, 332 p. illus., plates, ports. [Williamsburg restoration historical studies, no. 2] F229.C34M6
"Select bibliography": p. [293]–308.
The author's thesis (Ph.D.), *Robert Carter of Virginia: a Study of a Tobacco Planter of the Eighteenth Century,* was submitted to Duke University in 1938.

ROWLAND, KATE M. Robert Carter of Virginia. Magazine of American history, with notes and queries, v. 30, Sept. 1893: 115–136. E171.M18, v. 30

13010
CARTER, ROBERT WORMELEY (1734–1798)
Virginia. Planter.

——— The daybook of Robert Wormeley Carter of Sabine Hall, 1766. Edited by Louis Morton. Virginia magazine of history and biography, v. 68, July 1960: 301–316.
F221.V91, v. 68

MORTON, LOUIS. Robert Wormeley Carter of Sabine Hall; notes on the life of a Virginia planter. Journal of southern history, v. 12, Aug. 1946: 345–365.
F206.J68, v. 12

13011
CARTWRIGHT, GEORGE (1740–1819)
England; Labrador. Military officer, observer.

——— Captain Cartwright and his Labrador journal. Edited by Charles Wendell Townsend. Boston, D. Estes, 1911. xxxiii, 385 p. fold. chart, plates, ports.
F1136.C33

First published under the title *A Journal of Transactions and Events, During a Residence of Nearly Sixteen Years on the Coast of Labrador* (Newark [Eng.] Allin and Ridge, 1792. 3 v. F1136.C32 Rare Bk. Coll.).

13012
CARTWRIGHT, JOHN (1740–1824)†
England. Naval officer, political reformer.

——— The life and correspondence of Major Cartwright. Edited by his niece, F. D. Cartwright. London, H. Colburn, 1826. 2 v. map, plan, port. DA522.C27A2
"List of Major Cartwright's writings": v. 2, p. 299–301. Reprinted in New York by B. Franklin (1972?).

OSBORNE, JOHN W. John Cartwright. Cambridge [Eng.] University Press, 1972. ix, 174 p. (Conference on British Studies. Biographical series) DA522.C2708
Bibliography: p. 166–168.

13013
CARTWRIGHT, RICHARD (1759–1815)
New York; Canada. Loyalist officer, merchant, judge.

CARTWRIGHT, CONWAY E. Life and letters of the late Hon. Richard Cartwright. Edited by Rev. C. E. Cartwright. Toronto, Belford Bros., 1876. 145 p.
F1058.C32

MACHAR, AGNES M. Two typical United Empire Loyalists and founders of Canada. *In* New York State Historical Association. Proceedings. v. 13; 1913. Albany, 1914. p. 168–188. F116.N86, v. 13
Also treats the life of Col. Joel Stone, founder of Gananoque.

13014
CARVER, JONATHAN (1710–1780)*
Massachusetts; Connecticut; England. Explorer, mapmaker.

——— Travels through the interior parts of North America in the years 1766, 1767, and 1768. London, Printed for the author, sold by J. Walter, 1778. 543 p. plates.
F597.C33 Rare Bk. Coll.

ALVORD, CLARENCE W. Jonathan Carver vindicated. Magazine of history, with notes and queries, v. 16, May 1913: 196–199.   E171.M23, v. 16

Answers the charges leveled by Edward G. Bourne in the *American Historical Review*, v. 11, Jan. 1906, p. 287–302.

BROWNING, WILLIAM. The early history of Jonathan Carver. Wisconsin magazine of history, v. 3, Mar. 1920: 291–305.   F576.W7, v. 3

———— ———— Offprint. [n.p., 1920] 17 p.
                    F597.C433

BOURNE, EDWARD G. The travels of Jonathan Carver. American historical review, v. 11, Jan. 1906: 287–302.
                    E171.A57, v. 11

Finds that Carver's *Travels Through the Interior Parts of North America, in the Years 1766, 1767, and 1768*, first published in 1778, was compiled from other books and reports, probably by its editor, Dr. John Coakley Lettsom.

DURRIE, DANIEL S. Captain Jonathan Carver, and "Carver's grant." *In* Wisconsin. State Historical Society. Report and collections. v. 6; 1869/72. Madison, 1872. p. [220]–270. port.   F576.W81, v. 6

ELLIOTT, T. C. The strange case of Jonathan Carver and the name Oregon. *In* Oregon Historical Society, *Portland*. Quarterly, v. 21, Dec. 1920: 341–368; v. 22, June 1921: 91–115; v. 23, Mar. 1922: 53–69.
                    F871.O47, v. 21–23

FRIDLEY, RUSSELL M. The writings of Jonathan Carver. Minnesota history, v. 34, winter 1954: 154–159. illus., port.   F601.M72, v. 34

GREGORY, JOHN G. Jonathan Carver: his travels in the Northwest in 1766–8. Milwaukee [Press of Houtkamp & Cannon] 1896. 31 p. fold. map, port. [Parkman Club papers, no. 5]   F576.P24, no. 5
                    F597.C438

KELLOGG, LOUISE P. The mission of Jonathan Carver. Wisconsin magazine of history, v. 12, Dec. 1928: 127–145.   F576.W7, v. 12

LEE, JOHN T. A bibliography of Carver's *Travels*. *In* Wisconsin State Historical Society, *Madison*. Proceedings. 1909. Madison, 1910. p. 143–183. facsims., plates.
                    F576.W75, 1909

———— Captain Jonathan Carver: additional data. *In* Wisconsin State Historical Society, *Madison*. Proceedings. 1912. Madison, 1913. p. 87–123. facsim.
                    F576.W75, 1912

———— ———— Offprint. Madison, The Society, 1913. 87–123 p. facsim.   F584.L48

[NEILL, EDWARD D.] Minnesota as a British dominion— explorations of Jonathan Carver. *In* Materials for the future history of Minnesota. St. Paul, Minn., J. R. Brown, Territorial Printer, 1856. (Minnesota Historical Society. Annals, 1856) p. 49–64. port.
                    F601.M65, 1856

Reprinted in the *Collections* of the Minnesota Historical Society, v. 1 (St. Paul, 1872), p. 349–367.

QUAIFE, MILO M. Jonathan Carver and the Carver grant. Mississippi Valley historical review, v. 7, June 1920: 3–25.   E171.J87, v. 7

Discusses Carver's career in America and his disputed ownership of a tract of land more than 10,000 acres in size, in present-day Minnesota and Wisconsin.

13015

CARY, ARCHIBALD (1721–1787)*
Virginia. Planter, assemblyman, industrialist.

BROCK, ROBERT K. Archibald Cary of Ampthill, wheelhorse of the Revolution. Richmond, Va., Garrett and Massie, 1937. xi, 183 p. plates, ports.   F230.C29
Bibliography: p. 176.

13016

CARY, JOHN (*ca.* 1754–1835)
England. Map engraver and seller.

FORDHAM, *Sir* HERBERT G. John Cary, engraver, map, chart and printseller and globe-maker 1754 to 1835; a bibliography with an introduction and biographical notes. Cambridge, University Press, 1925. xxxiv, 139 p. illus., facsim.   Z6028.F71

Largely a catalog, beginning in 1779, of the atlases, maps, plans, itineraries, and other engravings and publications of John Cary and his successors, including plans of naval and military operations during the war.

13017

CASE, STEPHEN (1746–1794)
New York.

Defensive arms vindicated; and the lawfulness of the American war made manifest. To which is added, a short receipt for a continental disease, &c. Dedicated to His Excellency, General Washington. By a moderate Whig. [New-Marlborough?] Printed for the author, 1783. 55 p.   E211.D35 Rare Bk. Coll.

Dedication and preface dated New-Marlborough, June 17, 1782.

Possibly by Stephen Case of Marlborough, N.Y., whose name is written in a contemporary hand, after the words "a moderate Whig," on the title page of a copy in the Huntington Library. See *American Imprints, 1648–1797, in the Huntington Library*.

13018

CASEY, GIDEON (*b. ca.* 1726)
Rhode Island. Silversmith.

SCOTT, KENNETH. Gideon Casey, Rhode Island silversmith and counterfeiter. Rhode Island history, v. 12, Apr. 1953: 50–54.   F76.R472, v. 12

13019
CASEY, SAMUEL (*b.* 1724)
Rhode Island. Silversmith.

MILLER, WILLIAM D. Samuel Casey, silversmith. *In* Rhode Island Historical Society. Collections, v. 21, Jan. 1928: 1–14. illus.   F76.R47, v. 21

SCOTT, KENNETH. Samuel Casey, platero y falsario. Numisma, v. 4, Apr./June 1954: 35–40.
                                          CJ9.N75, v. 4

13020
CASTIGLIONI, LUIGI, *conte* (1757–1832)
Italy. Traveler, observer.

—— Castiglioni's visit to Rhode Island. Rhode Island history, v. 26, Apr. 1967: 53–64.   F76.R472, v. 26
Translated and annotated by Samuel Hough.

—— Viaggio negli Stati Uniti dell'America Settentrionale, fatto negli anni, 1785, 1786, e 1787. Con alcune osservazioni sui vegetabili più utili di quel paese. Milano, Stamperia di G. Marelli, 1790. 2 v. maps, plans, plates.
                                  E164.C35 Rare Bk. Coll.

A German translation by Magnus Peterson of volume 1 appeared as *Luigi Castiglioni's . . . Reise durch die Vereinigten Staaten von Nord-Amerika, in den Jahren 1785, 1786 und 1787*, 1. Theil (Memmingen, A. Seyler, 1793. 495 p.). Volume 2 was never published in German.

MARRARO, HOWARD R. Count Luigi Castiglioni, an early Italian traveller to Virginia (1785–1786). Virginia magazine of history and biography, v. 58, Oct. 1950: 473–491.   F221.V91, v. 58

CASTRIES, ARMAND CHARLES
See CHARLUS, ARMAND CHARLES AUGUSTIN DE LA CROIX DE CASTRIES, *comte* DE

13021
CASWELL, RICHARD (1729–1789)*
Maryland; North Carolina. Surveyor, lawyer, assemblyman, delegate to the Continental Congress, Revolutionary general, governor.

ALEXANDER, CLAYTON B. The public career of Richard Caswell. 1930. 298 p.
Thesis (Ph.D.)—University of North Carolina.

—— Richard Caswell: versatile leader of the Revolution. North Carolina historical review, v. 23, Apr. 1946: 119–141.   F251.N892, v. 23

—— Richard Caswell's military and later public services. North Carolina historical review, v. 23, July 1946: 287–312.   F251.N892, v. 23

—— The training of Richard Caswell. North Carolina historical review, v. 23, Jan. 1946: 13–31.
                                          F251.N892, v. 23

13022
CHALMERS, GEORGE (1742–1825)†
Scotland; Maryland; England. Lawyer, Loyalist, historian, writer.

—— An estimate of the comparative strength of Great-Britain, during the present and four preceding reigns; and of the losses of her trade from every war since the Revolution. New ed., corr., and improved; with a dedication to Dr. James Currie. London, J. Stockdale, 1794. cxliv, 289, [17] p.   HC253.C44
Reprinted in New York by A. M. Kelley (1969). First edition published in 1782.

COCKROFT, GRACE A. The public life of George Chalmers. New York, Columbia University Press, 1939. 233 p. port. (Studies in history, economics and public law, no. 454)   H31.C7, no. 454
Issued also as thesis (Ph.D.)—Columbia University. Bibliography: p. 216–230.

13023
CHAMPE, JOHN (1752–1798)
Virginia. Revolutionary soldier, secret agent.

—— Sergeant Champe's adventure. William and Mary College quarterly historical magazine, 2d ser., v. 18, July 1938: 322–342.   F221.W71, 2d s., v. 18
Champe's own account of his attempt to kidnap Benedict Arnold and return him to American lines. Introduction and notes by Wilbur C. Hall.

JUDY, IDA M. John Champe, the soldier and the man. [Strasburg, Va., Printed by Shenandoah Pub. House] 1940. 68 p. plates, ports.   E263.V8C43

LEE, HENRY. Champe's adventure. New-York, Office of the Rebellion Record, 1864. 48 p. (Reading on the rail, no. 1)   E278.A7L4
An account, by his commanding officer, of Champe's attempt in 1780 to seize Benedict Arnold, taken from the author's *Memoirs of the War in the Southern Department of the United States.*

McGROARTY, WILLIAM B. Sergeant John Champe and certain of his contemporaries. William and Mary College quarterly historical magazine, 2d ser., v. 17, Apr. 1937: 145–175.   F221.W71, 2d s., v. 17

SCHEER, GEORGE F. The sergeant major's strange mission. American heritage, v. 8, Oct. 1957: 26–29, 98. illus., map, ports.   E171.A43, v. 8

VAN WINKLE, DANIEL. Story of John Champe. [n.p., 1926?] 24 p. (The Historical Society of Hudson County. [Papers] no. 21)   F142.H8H6, no. 21

13024
CHAMPION, HENRY (1723–1797)
Connecticut. Revolutionary commissary officer.

DESTLER, CHESTER M.   Colonel Henry Champion, Revolutionary commissary. *In* Connecticut Historical Society, *Hartford*. Bulletin, v. 36, Apr. 1971: 52–64.
F91.C67, v. 36

13025

CHAMPION, RICHARD (1743–1791)†
England. Potter, manufacturer.

————The American correspondence of a Bristol merchant, 1766–1776; letters of Richard Champion. Edited, with an introduction, by G. H. Guttridge. Berkeley, Calif., University of California Press, 1934. viii, 71 p. facsim. (University of California publications in history, v. 22, no. 1)
E173.C15, v. 22
DA506.C47A4

MINCHINTON, WALTER E.   Richard Champion, Nicholas Pocock, and the Carolina trade. South Carolina historical magazine, v. 65, Apr. 1964: 87–97. map.
F266.S55, v. 65

An added "Note" by Minchinton appears in v. 70, Apr. 1969, p. 97–103.

OWEN, HUGH.   Two centuries of ceramic art in Bristol, being a history of the manufacture of "the true porcelain" by Richard Champion; with a biography compiled from private correspondence, journals and family papers; containing unpublished letters of Edmund Burke, Richard and William Burke, the duke of Portland, the marquis of Rockingham and others, with an account of the delft, earthenware and enamel glass works. Illustrated with one hundred and sixty engravings. London, Bell and Daldy, 1873. [15], xxiv, 419 p. illus., facsims., plates, ports.
NK4088.B808

13026

CHANDLER, JOHN (1721–1800)
Massachusetts; Nova Scotia. Landowner, judge, Loyalist.

DAVIS, ANDREW M.   The confiscation of John Chandler's estate. Boston, Houghton, Mifflin, 1903. xiii, 296 p. port.
E278.C4D2

In his article "Lawful Money, 1778 and 1779," which appeared in the *New England Historical and Genealogical Register*, v. 57, Apr. 1903, p. 163–167, and which was reprinted separately in Boston by the Press of D. Clapp (1903. 7 p. HG513.M4D35), Davis contends that local appraisers greatly undervalued Chandler's estate.

13027

CHANDLER, JOSHUA (1728–1787)
Connecticut; Nova Scotia. Lawyer, assemblyman, Loyalist.

LAWSON, HARVEY M.   "My country is wrong"—tragedy of Colonel Joshua Chandler. Connecticut magazine, v. 10, Apr./June 1906: 287–292.
F91.C8, v. 10

13028

CHANDLER, THOMAS BRADBURY (1726–1790)*
Connecticut; New Jersey. Anglican clergyman, Loyalist.

————Documentary history of the American church: six letters of Thomas Bradbury Chandler [1766–71] Historical magazine of the Protestant Episcopal Church, v. 32, Dec. 1963: 371–391.
BX5800.H5, v. 32

Introduction and notes by Robert Richardson.

GAVIN, FRANK S. B.   The Rev. Thomas Bradbury Chandler in the light of his (unpublished) diary, 1775–85. Church history, v. 1, June 1932: 90–106.
BR140.A45, v. 1

HOYT, ALBERT H.   The Rev. Thomas Bradbury Chandler, D.D., 1726–1790. New-England historical and genealogical register, v. 27, July 1873: 227–236. port.
F1.N56, v. 27

MCCULLOCH, SAMUEL C.   Thomas Bradbury Chandler, Anglican humanitarian in colonial New Jersey. *In his* British humanitarianism; essays honoring Frank J. Klingberg. Philadelphia, Church Historical Society [1950] (Church Historical Society (U.S.). Publication 32) p. 100–123.
HN15.M2

————Thomas Bradbury Chandler's *An Appeal to the Public. In* Rutgers University, *New Brunswick, N.J. Library*. Journal, v. 12, Dec. 1948: 19–25.
Z733.R955F, v. 12

13029

CHAPMAN, JONATHAN (1756–1832)
Massachusetts. Privateersman.

———— Autobiography of Captain Jonathan Chapman. *In* Colonial Society of Massachusetts, *Boston*. Publications. v. 11. Transactions, 1906/7. Boston, 1910. p. 208–239.
F61.C71, v. 11

Introduction and notes by John Noble.

13030

CHARLOTTE, *consort of George III* (1744–1818)†
Mecklenburg-Strelitz; England.

DORAN, JOHN.   Charlotte Sophia, wife of George III. *In his* Lives of the queens of England of the house of Hanover. v. 2. New York, A. C. Armstrong, 1880. p. [3]–198.
DA483.A1D7 1880, v. 2

GREENWOOD, ALICE D.   Charlotte Sophia of Mecklenburg-Strelitz, queen of George III. *In her* Lives of the Hanoverian queens of England. v. 2. London, G. Bell, 1911. p. [1]–235.
DA483.A1G7, v. 2

13031

CHARLUS, ARMAND CHARLES AUGUSTIN DE LA CROIX DE CASTRIES, comte DE (1756–1824)
France. French officer in America.

—— Dans l'armee de Lafayette, souvenirs in-édits du Comte de Charlus [1780] Revue de Paris, v. 64, July 1957: 94–110.   AP20.R27, v. 64

13032

CHASE, SAMUEL (1741–1811)*

Maryland. Lawyer, assemblyman, delegate to the Continental Congress.

BEIRNE, FRANCIS F.   Sam Chase, "disturber." Maryland historical magazine, v. 57, June 1962: 78–89.
          F176.M18, v. 57

STRAWER, NEIL.   Samuel Chase and the Annapolis paper war. Maryland historical magazine, v. 57, Sept. 1962: 177–194.   F176.M18, v. 57

13033

CHASE, THOMAS (1703–1779)

England; Maryland. Physician, Anglican clergyman.

BEIRNE, ROSAMOND R.   The Reverend Thomas Chase: pugnacious parson. Maryland historical magazine, v. 59, Mar. 1964: 1–14.   F176.M18, v. 59

13034

CHASTELLUX, FRANÇOIS JEAN DE BEAUVOIR, *chevalier* DE (1734–1788)

France. French officer in America.

—— The burned letter of Chastellux. By Randolph G. Adams. New York [American Society of the French Legion of Honor] 1935. 7 p. facsims. (Franco-American pamphlet series, no. 7)
          E183.8.F8F87, no. 7
          E265.C46

Probably written on June 1, 1781, Chastellux's letter to La Luzerne is pointedly critical of Rochambeau.

—— De la félicité publique; ou, Considérations sur le sort des hommes dans les différentes époques de l'histoire. Amsterdam, M. M. Rey, 1772. 2 v. in 1.
          HN14.C6 1772

A 1774 translation has been reprinted, under the title *An Essay on Public Happiness*, in New York by A. M. Kelley (1969. 2 v. HN14.C613 1969).

—— Discours sur les avantages ou les désavantages qui resultent, pour l'Europe, de la découverte de l'Amérique. Objet du prix proposé par M. l'abbé Raynal. Par M. P***, vice-counsul, à E***. Londres, Prault, 1787. 68 p.   E110.C48

Attributed to Chastellux, the discourse is considered by some critics to be the best of his works. He decides the question in favor of the "advantages."

—— Travels in North-America in the years 1780, 1781, and 1782. Translated from the French by an English gentleman, who resided in America at that period. With notes by the translator. London, G. G. J. and J. Robinson, 1787. 2 v. illus., maps.
          E163.C54 Rare Bk. Coll.

Reprinted in New York by the New York Times (1968).

—— —— New-York, White, Gallaher, & White, 1827. 416 p.   D163.C57
Reprinted in New York by A. M. Kelley (1970).

—— —— A rev. translation with introduction and notes by Howard C. Rice, Jr. Chapel Hill, Published for the Institute of Early American History and Culture at Williamsburg, Va., by the University of North Carolina Press [1963] 2 v. (xxiv, 688 p.) illus., ports., maps.
          E163.C59 1963
"Note on bibliographic and cartographic sources": v. 2, p. 556–561.

CARSON, GEORGE B.   The chevalier de Chastellux, soldier and philosopher. Chicago, 1942. v, 192 l.
          E265.C468

Typescript (carbon copy).
Thesis (Ph.D.)—University of Chicago.
"Unpublished letters, 1780–1788": leaves 141–171.
Bibliography: leaves 172–192.

SICOT, LUCIEN.   Le marquis de Chastellux (1734–1788). Paris, A. Rousseau, 1902. 164 p.   [HB105.C4S6]
          Micro 12567 HB

Thèse—Université de Paris.
Reprinted in New York by B. Franklin (1968).

WHITRIDGE, ARNOLD.   Two aristocrats in Rochambeau's army. Virginia quarterly review, v. 40, winter 1964: 114–128.   AP2.V76, v. 40

Focuses on the careers of the Chevalier de Chastellux and the Duc de Lauzun and especially on their impressions of America.

13035

CHAUNCY, CHARLES (1705–1787)*

Massachusetts. Congregational clergyman.

BERNHARD, HAROLD E.   Charles Chauncy: colonial liberal, 1705–1787. Chicago, 1945. v, 140 l. illus.
          BR520.B39

Thesis (Ph.D.)—University of Chicago.
Typescript (carbon copy).
Bibliography: leaves 133–140.

FORD, PAUL L.   Bibliotheca Chaunciana: a list of the writings of Charles Chauncy. Brooklyn, N.Y., Priv. print., 1884. 35 l. (Elzevir Club series, no. 6)
          Z8164.4.F67 Rare Bk. Coll.

In two parts: (a) a list of Chauncy's writings, chronologically arranged, and (b) pamphlets answered by, in answer to, or about Chauncy.

Reprinted in New York by B. Franklin (1971. 30 p. Z8164.4.F67 1971).

GRIFFIN, EDWARD M.   A biography of Charles Chauncy (1705–1787). 1966. ([353] p.)
          Micro AC–1, no. 67–4354

Thesis (Ph.D.)—Stanford University.

Abstracted in *Dissertation Abstracts*, v. 27A, Apr. 1967, p. 3169–3170.

WOHL, HAROLD B.   Charles Chauncy and the age of Enlightenment in New England. 1956. 211 l.

Micro AC–1, no. 18,565

Thesis (Ph.D.)—State University of Iowa.

Abstracted in *Dissertation Abstracts*, v. 16, no. 10, 1956, p. 1895.

13036

CHESNEY, ALEXANDER (1756–1845)

Ireland; South Carolina; England. Settler, Revolutionary soldier, Loyalist officer.

——— The journal of Alexander Chesney, a South Carolina Loyalist in the Revolution and after. Edited by E. Alfred Jones. With an introduction by Professor Wilbur H. Siebert. [Columbus] Ohio State University [1921] xvi, 166 p. (The Ohio State University studies. Contributions in history and political science, no. 7)

E277.C5

The Ohio State University bulletin, v. 26, no. 4. Bibliography: p. xiii–xiv.

13037

CHESTERFIELD, PHILIP DORMER STANHOPE, *4th Earl of* (1694–1773)†

England. Member of Parliament, writer.

——— The letters of Philip Dormer Stanhope, 4th earl of Chesterfield. Edited, with an introduction, by Bonamy Dobrée. London, Eyre & Spottiswoode; New York City, Viking Press, 1932. 6 v. fold. geneal. table, port.

DA501.C5A32

"Previous important editions": v. 1, p. xvii–xviii; "List of the chief authorities referred to in the Introduction": v. 1, p. 3–4.

Contents: v. 1. Introduction, index, etc.—v. 2. Letters: 1742–1745.—v. 3. Letters: 1745–1748.—v. 4. Letters: 1748–1751.—v. 5. Letters: 1751–1761.—v. 6. Letters: 1761–1773. Appendixes.

——— The letters of the earl of Chesterfield to his son. Edited with an introduction by Charles Strachey, and with notes by Annette Calthrop. New York, G. P. Putnam's Sons, 1925. 2 v.   BJ1671.C52 1925

The text is that of the 11th edition (1800) published from the originals by Mrs. Eugenia Stanhope, with Lord Mahon's addenda, corrections, and some of his notes.

COXON, ROGER.   Chesterfield and his critics. London, G. Routledge, 1925. xii, 328 p.   DA501.C5C6

Includes 11 of Chesterfield's essays, reprinted from the originals, and 27 of his personal letters, hitherto unpublished.

"A short bibliographical note on Chesterfield's letters": p. 291–294.

GULICK, SIDNEY L.   A Chesterfield bibliography to 1800. [Chicago, University of Chicago Press, 1935] 114 p. facsim. (Bibliographical Society of America. Papers, v. 29)   Z1008.B51P, v. 29

"Bibliography: works cited and important editions": p. 99–101.

SHELLABARGER, SAMUEL.   Lord Chesterfield and his world. Boston, Little, Brown, 1951. 456 p. port.

DA501.C5S52

Bibliography: p. [423]–435.

Reprinted in New York by Biblo and Tannen (1971).

13038

CHEW, BENJAMIN (1722–1810)*

Maryland; Pennsylvania. Lawyer, councilor, assemblyman, judge, Loyalist.

KONKLE, BURTON A.   Benjamin Chew, 1722–1810, head of the Pennsylvania judiciary system under colony and commonwealth. Philadelphia, University of Pennsylvania Press, 1932. xix, 316 p. facsims., maps, plates, ports.   F153.C43

TINKCOM, MARGARET B.   Cliveden: the building of a Philadelphia country-seat, 1763–1767. Pennsylvania magazine of history and biography, v. 88, Jan. 1964: 3–36. illus., plates.   F146.P65, v. 88

Chew's country house in Germantown.

13039

CHIPMAN, NATHANIEL (1752–1843)*

Connecticut; Vermont. Revolutionary officer, lawyer, judge.

CHIPMAN, DANIEL.   The life of Hon. Nathaniel Chipman, LL.D., formerly member of the United States Senate, and chief justice of the state of Vermont. With selections from his miscellaneous papers. Boston, C. C. Little and J. Brown, 1846. xii, 402 p.   F49.C54

HONEYWELL, ROY J.   Nathaniel Chipman. New England quarterly, v. 5, July 1932: 555–584.   F1.N62, v. 5

13040

CHIPMAN, WARD (1754–1824)*

Massachusetts; New York; New Brunswick. Lawyer, Loyalist officer.

——— Ward Chipman diary: a Loyalist's return to New England in 1783. Edited by Joseph B. Berry. *In* Essex Institute, *Salem, Mass.* Historical collections, v. 87, July 1951: 211–241. ports.   F72.E7E81, v. 87

GRAY, EDWARD.   Ward Chipman, Loyalist. *In* Massachusetts Historical Society, *Boston.* Proceedings. v. 54; 1920/21. Boston, 1922. p. 331–353. port.   F61.M38, v. 54

13041
CHITTENDEN, THOMAS (1730–1797)*
Connecticut; Vermont. Assemblyman, governor.

CHIPMAN, DANIEL. A memoir of Thomas Chittenden, the first governor of Vermont; with a history of the constitution during his administration. Middlebury [Vt.] Printed for the author, 1849. 222 p.   F53.C54

13042
CHOISEUL-STAINVILLE, ÉTIENNE FRANÇOIS, *duc* DE (1719–1785)
France. Minister of Foreign Affairs.

—— Mémoires de m. le duc de Choiseul . . . écrits par lui-même, et imprimés sons ses yeux, dans son cabinet, à Chanteloup, en 1778. Chanteloup et Paris, Buisson, 1790. 2 v.   DC135.C5A2

DAUBIGNY, EUGÈNE T. Choiseul et la France d'outre-mer après le traité de Paris; étude sur la politique coloniale au XVIIIᵉ siècle, avec un appendice sur les origines de la question de Terre-Neuve. Paris, Hachette, 1892. xvi, 352 p.   JV9816.D23

RAMSEY, JOHN F. Anglo-French relations, 1763–1770; a study of Choiseul's foreign policy. Berkeley, Calif., University of California Press, 1939. vii, 143–263 p. port. (University of California publications in history, v. 17, no. 3)   E173.C15, v. 17
JX1548.Z7G77

Bibliography: p. 239–246.

SOLTAU, ROGER H. The duke de Choiseul; the Lothian essay, 1908. Oxford, B. H. Blackwell, 1909. 176 p.   DC135.C5S6

VERDIER, HENRI. Le Duc de Choiseul (la politique et les plaisirs). Paris, Nouvelles éditions Debresse [1969]. 335 p. (Collection L'Histoire au singulier)   DC135.C5V47

13043
CHOVET, ABRAHAM (1704–1790)*
England; Pennsylvania. Lecturer on anatomy.

MILLER, WILLIAM S. Abraham Chovet. Annals of medical history, v. 8, Dec. 1926: 375–393. illus., facsims., ports.   R11.A85, v. 8

13044
CHURCH, BENJAMIN (1734–1778?)*
Rhode Island; Massachusetts. Physician, poet, assemblyman, Revolutionary surgeon.

—— The times, a poem. Boston, 1765. Tarrytown, N.Y., Reprinted, W. Abbatt, 1922. 20 p. (The Magazine of history with notes and queries. Extra number, no. 84, [pt. 1])   E173.M24, no. 84

NORWOOD, WILLIAM F. The enigma of Dr. Benjamin Church: a high-level scandal in the American colonial army medical service. Medical arts and sciences, v. 10, 2d quarter, 1956: 71–93. illus., facsims., ports.   R11.M518, v. 10

VOSBURGH, MAUDE B. The disloyalty of Dr. Benjamin Church. *In* Cambridge Historical Society, *Cambridge, Mass.* Publications. v. 30; 1944. Cambridge, 1945. p. 48–71.   C74.C1C469, v. 30

13045
CHURCHMAN, GEORGE (1730–1814)
Maryland. Farmer.

—— A Quaker travelling in the wake of war, 1781. New England quarterly, v. 23, Sept. 1950: 396–400.   F1.N62, v. 23

Introduction and notes by Henry J. Cadbury.

13046
CHURCHMAN, JOHN (1705–1775)
Pennsylvania. Itinerant Quaker minister.

—— An account of the gospel labours, and Christian experiences of a faithful minister of Christ, John Churchman, late of Nottingham in Pennsylvania, deceased. To which is added a short memorial of the life and death of a fellow labourer in the church, our valuable friend Joseph White, late of Bucks County. Philadelphia, Printed by Joseph Crukshank, on the north side of Market-Street, between Second and Third-Streets, 1779. vii, 256 p.
BX7795.C55A3 1779 Rare Bk. Coll.

Reprinted in *Friends' Library*, v. 6 (Philadelphia, 1842), p. 176–267.

13047
CILLEY, JOSEPH (1734–1799)*
New Hampshire. Farmer, lawyer, Revolutionary general.

SCALES, JOHN. General Joseph Cilley. Granite state magazine, v. 5, July/Sept.–Oct./Dec. 1908: 177–184, 233–240; v. 6, Oct./Nov. 1903–Jan./Apr., Sept.1904: 73–80, 117–124, 145–160, 281–284; v. 7, Nov. 1911: 89–95.   F31.G76, v. 5–7

Also published separately in Manchester, N.H., by the Standard Book Co. (1921. 59 p. E263.N4C5).

13048
CLAGETT, WYSEMAN (1721–1784)*
England; West Indies; New Hampshire. Lawyer, assemblyman, judge.

ATHERTON, CHARLES H. Memoir of Wyseman Clagett. *In* New Hampshire Historical Society. Collections. v. 3. Concord, 1832. p. 24–39.   F31.N54, v. 3

13049

CLAP, THOMAS (1703–1767)*

Massachusetts; Connecticut. Congregational clergyman, educator.

—— An essay on the nature and foundation of moral virtue and obligation; being a short introduction to the study of ethics; for the use of the students of Yale-College. New-Haven, Printed by B. Mecom, 1765. 66 p.　　　　　　　　BJ1241.C5 Rare Bk. Coll.

TUCKER, LOUIS LEONARD. President Thomas Clap and the rise of Yale College, 1740–1766. Historian, v. 19, Nov. 1956: 66–81.　　　　　D1.H22, v. 19

—— President Thomas Clap of Yale College: another "Founding Father" of American science. Isis, v. 52, Mar. 1961: 55–77.　　　　　　Q1.I7, v. 52

—— Puritan protagonist: President Thomas Clap of Yale College. Chapel Hill, Published for the Institute of Early American History and Culture, Williamsburg, Va., by University of North Carolina Press [1962] xv, 283, p. plate.　　　　　　LD6330 1740.T8

Bibliographical note": p. 271–275.

The author's thesis (Ph.D.), *Thomas Clap, First President of Yale College: a Biography*, was submitted to the University of Washington in 1957 (Micro AC–1, no. 58–1098).

13050

CLARK, ABRAHAM (1726–1794)*

New Jersey. Assemblyman, delegate to the Continental Congress.

HART, ANN C., ed. Abraham Clark; signer of the Declaration of Independence. San Francisco, Calif., Pioneer Press, 1923. xv, 176 p. facsim., plates, port.　　　　　　　　　E302.6.C55H3

13051

CLARK, ALEXANDER (1743–1825)

New Jersey; New Brunswick. Loyalist.

WRIGHT, ESTHER C. Alexander Clark, Loyalist; a contribution to the history of New Brunswick. [Kentville, N.S., Printed by the Kentville Pub. Co., 1940] 81 p. geneal. table.　　　　　　　CS71.C6 1940a

13052

CLARK, GEORGE ROGERS (1752–1818)*

Virginia; Kentucky. Frontiersman, Revolutionary officer.

—— George Rogers Clark papers, 1771–1784. Edited with introduction and notes by James Alton James. Springfield, Ill., Trustees of the Illinois State Historical Library, 1912–26. 2 v. ports. (Collections of the Illinois State Historical Library, v. 8, 19. Virginia series, v. 3–4).　　　　　　　F536.I25, v. 8, 19
　　　　　　　　　　　　　　　E324.C57

Includes bibliographies.

Reprinted in New York by AMS Press (1972. E207.C5A3 1972).

BAKELESS, JOHN E. Background to glory; the life of George Rogers Clark. Philadelphia, Lippincott, 1957. 386 p. illus., port.　　　　　　E207.C5B15

Bibliographic references included in "Notes" (p. 363–376).

BODLEY, TEMPLE. George Rogers Clark and historians. *In* Illinois State Historical Society. Transactions; 1935. Springfield. (Illinois State Historical Library. Publication, no. 42) p. 73–109.　　　F536.I34, 1935

—— George Rogers Clark, his life and public services. Boston, Houghton Mifflin Co., 1926. xix, 425 p. map, port.　　　　　　　　　E207.C5B6

Bibliography: p. [405]–408.

——George Rogers Clark's relief claims. *In* Illinois State Historical Society. Journal, v. 22, July 1936: 103–120.　　　　　　F536.I18, v. 22

ENGLISH, SARA J. George Rogers Clark. *In* Illinois State Historical Society. Journal, v. 20, Jan. 1928: 523–546.　　　　　F536.I18, v. 20

JAMES, JAMES A. An appraisal of the contributions of George Rogers Clark to the history of the West. Mississippi Valley historical review, v. 17, June 1930: 98–115.　　　　　　　　E171.J87, v. 17

Points to Clark's conquest of the Old Northwest, his assistance in the establishment of orderly government in Kentucky and in the Illinois country, and his unequaled knowledge of Indian antiquities.

—— George Rogers Clark—civilian. *In* Indiana History Conference, *Indianapolis*. Proceedings. 1928. Indianapolis, 1929. p. 60–76.　　　F521.I46, 1928

Also published as *Indiana History Bulletin*, v. 6, May 1929, extra number 2.

—— The life of George Rogers Clark. Chicago, Ill., University of Chicago Press [c1928] xiii, 534 p. facsim., maps, plates, ports.　　　　　E207.C5J3

Reprinted in New York by Greenwood Press (1969) and AMS Press (1970), and in St. Clair Shores, Mich., by Scholarly Press (1970).

JILLSON, WILLARD R. A bibliography of George Rogers Clark, general commanding the Virginia military forces in Kentucky and the Old Northwest Territory during the American Revolution. Frankfort, Ky., Perry Pub. Co., 1958. 43 p. illus., map, ports.　　　Z8173.8.J5

KELLOGG, LOUISE P. The early biographers of George Rogers Clark. American historical review, v. 35, Jan. 1930: 295–302.　　　　　E171.A57, v. 35

From Allan B. Magruder to Lyman C. Draper.

—— The recognition of George Rogers Clark. Indiana magazine of history, v. 25, Mar. 1929: 40–46.

　　　　　　　　　　　　　　F521.I52, v. 25

LUTZ, PAUL V.   Fact and myth concerning George Rogers Clark's grant of land at Paducah, Kentucky. *In* Kentucky Historical Society. Register, v. 67, July 1969: 248–253.   F446.K43, v. 67

PALMER, FREDERICK.   Clark of the Ohio; a life of George Rogers Clark. New York, Dodd, Mead, 1929. xv, 482 p. facsims., maps, plates, ports.   E207.C5P18

Bibliography: p. ix–x.

THOMAS, SAMUEL W., *and* EUGENE H. CONNER.   George Rogers Clark [1752–1818], natural scientist and historian. Filson Club history quarterly, v. 41, July 1967: 202–226.   F446.F484, v. 41

13053
CLARK, JOHN *Jr.* (*d.* 1819)

Pennsylvania. Lawyer, Revolutionary officer.

——— Letters from Major John Clark, Jr., to Gen. Washington. Written during the occupation of Philadelphia by the British army. [Philadelphia, Printed for the Society, 1847] 36 p. (Pennsylvania. Historical Society. Bulletin, v. 1, no. 10)   F146.P33

——— Memoir of Major John Clark, of York County, Pennsylvania. Pennsylvania magazine of history and biography, v. 20, Apr. 1896: 77–86. F146.P65, v. 20

Contributed by E. W. Spangler.

13054
CLARK, JONAS (1730–1805)*

Massachusetts. Congregational clergyman.

GILMAN, THEODORE.   The Rev. Jonas Clark, pastor at Lexington, leader in Revolutionary thought. [New York, 1911] 20 p. ([Order of the Founders and Patriots of America. New York Society. Publications], no. 31)   E186.6.N39, no. 31

13055
CLARK, LARDNER (*ca.* 1760–1801)

Pennsylvania; Tennessee. Merchant, tavernkeeper.

PROVINE, WILLIAM A.   Lardner Clark, Nashville's first merchant and foremost citizen. Tennessee historical magazine, v. 3, Mar.–June 1917: 28–50, 115–133.   F431.T28, v. 3

13056
CLARK, WILLIAM (1740–1815)

Massachusetts. Anglican clergyman.

MAMPOTENG, CHARLES.   The Reverend William Clark (1740–1815) S.P.G. missionary in Massachusetts. Historical magazine of the Protestant Episcopal church, v. 16, June 1947: 199–216. port.   BX5800.H5, v. 16

13057
CLARKE, ELIJAH (1733–1799)*

South Carolina; Georgia. Revolutionary general, frontiersman.

HAYS, LOUISE F.   Hero of Hornet's Nest; a biography of Elijah Clark, 1733 to 1799. New York, N.Y., Stratford House, 1946. ix, 395 p. facsim., maps (part fold.), plates, port.   E207.C53H3

Bibliographic references included in "Footnotes" (p. 305–367). Bibliography: p. 369–376.

WILLIAMS, SAMUEL C.   Colonel Elijah Clarke in the Tennessee country. Georgia historical quarterly, v. 25, June 1941: 151–158.   F281.G2975, v. 25

13058
CLARKE, RICHARD (1711–1795)*

Massachusetts; England. Merchant, Loyalist.

——— Documents drawn from the papers of Richard Clarke, 1762–1774. *In* Colonial Society of Massachusetts, *Boston.* Publications. v. 8. Transactions, 1902/4. Boston, 1906. p. 78–90.   F61.C71, v. 8

Introduction and notes by Denison R. Slade.

13059
CLARKSON, MATTHEW (1733–1800)

New York; Pennsylvania. Merchant, surveyor, judge.

HALL, JOHN.   Memoirs of Matthew Clarkson of Philadelphia, 1735–1800, by his great-grandson, John Hall, and of his brother, Gerardus Clarkson, 1737–1790, by his great-grandson, Samuel Clarkson. [Philadelphia, Thomson Print. Co.] 1890. 259 p. plates, ports.   CS71.C612 1890

13060
CLAUS, DANIEL (1727–1787)

Germany; New York. Indian agent, Loyalist.

PARSONS, PHYLLIS V.   The early life of Daniel Claus. Pennsylvania history, v. 29, Oct. 1962: 357–372. ports.   F146.P597, v. 29

13061
CLAY, JOSEPH (1741–1804)*

England; Georgia. Merchant, planter, Revolutionary officer.

——— Letters of Joseph Clay, merchant of Savannah, 1776–1793, and a list of ships and vessels entered at the port of Savannah, for May 1765, 1766, and 1767. [Savannah, Ga., Morning News, Printers, ᶜ1913] 259 p. illus., fold. maps, fold. plates, port. (Georgia Historical Society. Collections, v. 8)   F281.G35, v. 8

13062
CLAYPOOLE, JAMES (1720–1796)

Pennsylvania. Artist, limner.

SELLERS, CHARLES C. James Claypoole—a founder of the art of painting in Pennsylvania. Pennsylvania history, v. 17, Apr. 1950: 106–109. F146.P597, v. 17

13063

CLAYTON, JOHN (1686–1773)*†
England; Virginia. Botanist.

BERKELEY, EDMUND, *and* DOROTHY S. BERKELEY. John Clayton, pioneer of American botany. Chapel Hill, University of North Carolina [1963] ix, 236 p. illus. QK31.C55B4

Bibliography: p. [218]–228.

13064

CLENDINEN, GEORGE (1746–1797)
Ireland; Virginia. Revolutionary officer, assemblyman, land speculator.

STEALEY, JOHN E. George Clendinen and the Great Kanawha Valley frontier: a case study of the frontier development of Virginia. West Virginia history, v. 27, July 1966: 278–295. F236.W52, v. 27

13065

CLERMONT-CRÈVECŒUR, JEAN FRANÇOIS LOUIS, *comte* DE (1752–*ca.* 1824)
France. French officer in America.

ROBERTNIER, LOUIS JEAN BAPTISTE SYLVESTRE. Rhode Island in 1780. *In* Rhode Island Historical Society. Collections, v. 16, July 1923: 65–78. illus. F76.R47, v. 16

The so-called Robertnier journal, from which this extract was taken, was actually written by Clermont-Crèvecoeur (see *The American Campaigns of Rochambeau's Army*, v. 1 (Princeton, N.J., Princeton University Press, 1972), compiled by Howard C. Rice and Anne S. K. Brown, p. 3–5). For the full text of Clermont-Crèvecoeur's journal, entitled "Journal of the War in America During the Years 1780, 1781, 1782, 1783, with some remarks on the Habits and Customs of the Americans; an account of the Battles fought, from the beginning of the War in New England, against the English in those places through which the Army of the Comte de Rochambeau passed; with a description of the remarkable sights between Boston and Williamsburg, capital of Virginia, a territory extending some 300 leagues," see Rice and Brown, p. 15–100 (entry 7195).

13066

CLIFFORD, THOMAS (1722–1793)
Pennsylvania. Merchant.

LARSEN, GRACE H. Profile of a colonial merchant: Thomas Clifford of pre-Revolutionary Philadelphia. 1955. ([461] p.) Micro AC–1, no. 15,635
Thesis (Ph.D.)—Columbia University.
Abstracted in *Dissertation Abstracts*, v. 16, no. 2, 1956, p. 326.

13067

CLINKENBEARD, WILLIAM (*ca.* 1760–1834)
Maryland; Kentucky. Settler.

———— Reverend John D. Shane's interview with pioneer William Clinkenbeard. History quarterly, v. 2, Apr. 1928: 95–128. F446.F484, v. 2
"Copied by Lucien Beckner for publication."

13068

CLINTON, GEORGE (1739–1812)*
New York. Lawyer, delegate to the Continental Congress, Revolutionary general, governor.

CALDWELL, LYNTON K. George Clinton—democratic administrator. *In* New York State Historical Association. New York History, v. 32, Apr. 1951: 134–156. F116.N865, v. 32

Governor George Clinton. Olde Ulster, v. 4, Feb.–Dec. 1908: 33–40, 65–77, 97–105, 129–136, 161–167, 193–197, 225–232, 257–266, 289–296, 321–327, 353–360; v. 5, Jan.–Aug., Dec. 1909: 1–6, 42–48, 65–70, 103–108, 136–142, 167–175, 207–213, 234–238, 366–371; v. 6, May 1910: 137–141. F127.U4O4, v. 4–6

HASBROUCK, GILBERT D. B. Governor George Clinton. *In* New York State Historical Association. Quarterly journal, v. 1, July 1920: 143–164. port. F116.N865, v. 1

JENKS, MAJOR B. George Clinton and New York state politics, 1775 to 1801. 1936.
Thesis (Ph.D.)—Cornell University.

PAGANO, FRANCES B. An historical account of the military and political career of George Clinton, 1739–1812. 1956.
Thesis (Ph.D.)—St. John's University.

PRIME, RALPH E. George Clinton, some of his colonial, Revolutionary and post-Revolutionary services. [New York, 1902] 45 p. port. [Order of the Founders and Patriots of America. New York Society. Publications, no. 3] E186.6.N39, no.3
E302.6.C6P9

SPAULDING, ERNEST WILDER. His Excellency George Clinton, critic of the Constitution. New York, Macmillan Co., 1938. xiii, 325 p. map, plates, ports. E302.6.C6S7

"Bibliographical note": p. 305–309.
Reprinted in Port Washington, N.Y., by I. J. Friedman (1964).

13069

CLINTON, *Sir* HENRY (1730–1795)†
Newfoundland; England. Member of Parliament, British officer in America.

———— Authentic copies of letters between Sir Henry Clinton, K.B., and the commissioners for auditing the public accounts. London, 1793. 41 p.
E267.C64 Rare Bk. Coll.

———— A letter from Lieut. Gen. Sir Henry Clinton, K.B., to the commissioners of public accounts, relative to some observations in their seventh report, which may be judged to imply censure on the late commanders in chief of His Majesty's army in North America. London, Printed for J. Debrett, 1784. 31 p.
E267.C642 Rare Bk. Coll.
AC901.M5, v. 752 Rare Bk. Coll.

———— Observations on Mr. Stedman's *History of the American War*. London, Printed for J. Debrett, 1794. 34 p.
E208.S82 Rare Bk. Coll.

ADAMS, RANDOLPH G. The headquarters papers of the British army in North America during the war of the American Revolution; a brief description of Sir Henry Clinton's papers in the William L. Clements Library. Ann Arbor, William L. Clements Library, 1926. 47 p. facsims., maps, plates, port. (William L. Clements Library—University of Michigan. Bulletin no. 14).
E172.M53, no. 14
E267.A24

AMORY, THOMAS C. Clinton's secret journal. *In* Massachusetts Historical Society, *Boston*. Proceedings. 2d ser., v. 1; 1884/85. Boston, 1885. p. 47–64.
F61.M38, 2d s., v. 1

WILLCOX, WILLIAM B. The excitement of historical research: the psychiatrist, the historian, and General Clinton. Michigan quarterly review, v. 6, spring 1967: 123–129.
AS30.M48, v. 6

————Sir Henry Clinton: paralysis of command. *In* Billias, George A., *ed.* George Washington's opponents: British generals and admirals in the American Revolution. New York, Morrow, 1969. p. 73–102.
E267.B56
Bibliography: p. 101–102.

WYATT, FREDERICK, *and* WILLIAM B. WILLCOX. Sir Henry Clinton: a psychological exploration in history. William and Mary quarterly, 3d ser., v. 16, Jan.1959: 3–26.
F221.W71, 3d s., v. 16

13070
CLINTON, JAMES (1736?–1812)*
New York. Revolutionary general.

CAMPBELL, WILLIAM W. Lecture on the life and military services of General James Clinton. Read before the New-York Historical Society, Feb. 1839. New York, Printed by W. Osborn, 1839. 23 p.
E207.C62C2

13071
CLITHERALL, JAMES (*fl.* 1776)

———— Extracts from the diary of Dr. James Clitherall, 1776. Pennsylvania magazine of history and biography, v. 22, Jan. 1899: 468–474.
F146.P65, v. 22
On his travels from South Carolina to Philadelphia and New York.

13072
CLOSEN, LUDWIG, *Baron* VON (*ca.* 1752–1830)
Germany. French officer in America.

———— Revolutionary journal, 1780–1783. Translated and edited with an introduction by Evelyn M. Acomb. Chapel Hill, Published for the Institute of Early American History and Culture at Williamsburg, Virginia by the University of North Carolina Press [1958] xxxvi, 392 p. illus., map, ports.
E265.C613
"Bibliographical notice": p. [366]–382.

As aide-de-camp to Rochambeau, von Closen kept a detailed record of the movements of the French expeditionary force from its embarkation at Brest in the spring of 1780 until its return to France in the summer of 1783. The section of the journal dealing with the Yorktown campaign and its aftermath appeared earlier, with introduction and notes by Evelyn M. Acomb, in the *William and Mary Quarterly*, 3d ser., v. 10, Apr. 1953, p. 196–236.

BOWEN, CLARENCE W. A French officer with Washington and Rochambeau. Century magazine, v. 73, Feb. 1907: 531–538.
AP2.C4, v. 73

13073
CLOSSY, SAMUEL (1724–1786)
Ireland; New York. Physician, professor.

STOOKEY, BYRON P. Samuel Clossy, A.B., M.D., F.R.C.P. of Ireland—first professor of anatomy, King's College (Columbia), New York. Bulletin of the history of medicine, v. 38, Mar./Apr. 1964: 153–167. facsims.
R11.B93, v. 38

13074
CLOW, CHINA (*d.* 1788?)
Delaware. Loyalist.

TURNER, JOSEPH B. Cheney Clow's rebellion. Wilmington, Historical Society of Delaware, 1912. 16 p. (Historical Society of Delaware. Papers, 58)
F161.D35, no. 58
Cheney, or China, Clow was a Delaware Loyalist who was executed for treason in 1788 or 1789.

13075
CLUNY, ALEXANDER

———— The American traveller; or, Observations on the present state, culture and commerce of the British colonies in America, and the further improvements of which they are capable; with an account of the exports, imports and returns of each colony respectively,—and

of the numbers of British ships and seamen, merchants, traders and manufacturers employed by all collectively: together with the amount of the revenue arising to Great-Britain therefrom. In a series of letters written originally to the Right Honourable the Earl of********* By an old and experienced trader. London, Printed for E. and C. Dilly, 1769. 122 p. illus., fold. map.
E162.C64 Rare Bk. Coll.

Reprinted in Tarrytown, N.Y., by W. Abbatt (1930. 77 p. E173.M24, no. 162) as extra number, no. 162, of *The Magazine of History, With Notes and Queries.*

13076

CLYMER, GEORGE (1739–1813)*

Pennsylvania. Merchant, delegate to the Continental Congress, delegate to the Constitutional Convention.

DICKINSON, WHARTON. George Clymer—the signer. Magazine of American history, with notes and queries, v. 5, Sept. 1880: 196–203. illus., port.
E171.M18, v. 5

———— ———— Detached copy. CS71.C648 1880

MACFARLANE, JAMES R. George Clymer, signer of the Declaration of Independence, framer of the Constitution of the United States and of the state of Pennsylvania, his family and descendants. [Sewickley, Pa., Sewickley Print.-Shop] 1927. 28 p. ports.
CS71.C648 1927

13077

COBB, DAVID (1748–1830)*

Massachusetts. Physician, assemblyman, Revolutionary general, judge.

BAYLIES, FRANCIS. Some remarks on the life and character of Gen. David Cobb. New England historical and genealogical register, v. 18, Jan. 1864: 5–17. port.
F1.N56, v. 18

[COBB, SAMUEL C.] A brief memoir of General David Cobb, of the Revolutionary Army. 8 p. port.
F69.C65

Reprinted from the *Memorials of the Society of the Cincinnati of Massachusetts* (Boston, 1873. E202.1.M38), p. 258–262.

13078

COCHRAN, JOHN (1730–1807)*

Pennsylvania; New Jersey. Physician, Revolutionary medical administrator.

———— Excerpts from the private journal of Doctor John Cochran, Director of Military Hospitals during the Revolution and close friend of Washington and Lafayette [1780–81] Edited by Thornton Chard. *In* New York State Historical Association. New York history, v. 25, July 1944: 360–378.
F116.N865, v. 25

Supplemented by the editor's "Illustrations Pertaining to the Medical Life of Doctor John Cochran," in the *Bulletin of the History of Medicine*, v. 20, June 1946, p. 76–84.

CLARKE, THOMAS WOOD. General John Cochran. New York State journal of medicine, v. 42, Apr. 15, 1942: 798–801.
R11.N74, v. 42

13079

COCHRAN, WILLIAM (*ca.* 1757–1833)

Ireland; New York. Schoolteacher, professor.

———— The memoirs of William Cochran, sometime professor in Columbia College, New York, and in King's College, Windsor, Nova Scotia. Edited by Milton H. Thomas. *In* New York Historical Society. Quarterly, v. 38, Jan. 1954: 55–83. illus., port.
F116.N638, v. 38

13080

COCHRANE, CHARLES (1749–1781)

British officer in America.

———— Memorial of Capt. Charles Cochrane. *In* Massachusetts Historical Society, *Boston*. Proceedings. 2d ser., v. 6; 1890/91. Boston, 1891. p. 433–442.
F61.M38, 2d s., v. 6

Introduction and notes by Mellen Chamberlain.
An offprint, with an extended title, was published in Cambridge by J. Wilson (1981. 13 p. E275.C66).

13081

COCKBURN, *Sir* JAMES, *Bart.* (1723–1809)†

England; St. Eustatius. British officer in America, governor.

———— *defendant.* The trial of Lieutenant Colonel Cockburne, late governor of the island of St. Eustatius, for the loss of the said island, before a court martial held at the Horse Guards, on Monday, May 12th, 1783, and nine subsequent days. London, Printed for Faulder [1783] 71 p.
F2097.C66 Rare Bk. Coll.

13082

COFFIN, *Sir* ISAAC, *Bart.* (1759–1839)*†

Massachusetts; Canada; England. Loyalist, British naval officer in America.

AMORY, THOMAS C. Admiral Sir Isaac Coffin, bart. New York genealogical and biographical record, v. 17, Jan. 1886: 1–23. port.
F116.N28, v. 17

13083

COFFIN, PAUL (1737–1821)

Massachusetts; Maine. Congregational clergyman.

———— Memoir and journals of Rev. Paul Coffin, D.D. [1760–1800] *In* Maine Historical Society. Collections. v. 4. Portland, 1856. p. 235–407.
F16.M33, v. 4

The introductory memoir (p. 239–259) was written by Cyrus Woodman.

13084

COGHLAN, MARGARET MONCRIEFFE (*b.* 1763)
America; Europe.

——— Memoirs of Mrs. Coghlan (daughter of the late Major Moncrieffe), written by herself, and dedicated to the British nation; being interspersed with anecdotes of the late American and present French war, with remarks moral and political. London, J. Lane, 1794. xv, 137 p.
CT275.C666A3 1794 Rare Bk. Coll.

Reprinted, with some additions, in New York by J. Fellows (1795), T. H. Morrell (1864), and the New York Times (1971).

13085

COHEN, JACOB RAPHAEL (*d.* 1811)
Pennsylvania. Rabbi.

——— The record book of the Reverend Jacob Raphael Cohen. Compiled with an introduction by Alan D. Corré, with biographical annotations by Malcolm H. Stern. American Jewish historical quarterly, v. 59, Sept. 1969: 23–82. E184.J5A5, v. 59

Begun in 1776, the record book was continued (to 1843) by other hands after Cohen's death.

13086

COIT, JOSHUA (1758–1798)
Connecticut. Lawyer, assemblyman.

DESTLER, CHESTER M. Joshua Coit, American Federalist, 1758–1798. Middletown, Conn., Wesleyan University Press [1962] xiii, 191 p. illus., ports.
E311.D47

Bibliography: p. [165]–173.

13087

COKE, THOMAS, *Bp.* (1747–1814)*†
Wales; England. Methodist clergyman, missionary, church organizer.

——— Extracts of the journals of the late Rev. Thomas Coke, L.L.D.; comprising several visits to North America and the West-Indies; his tour through a part of Ireland, and his nearly finished voyage to Bombay in the East-Indies: to which is prefixed, a life of the doctor. Dublin, Printed by R. Napper, 1816. 271 p.
E164.C72 Rare Bk. Coll.

——— Extracts of the journals of the Rev. Dr. Coke's five visits to America. London, Printed by G. Paramore; and sold by G. Whitfield, 1793. 195 p.
E164.C71 Rare Bk. Coll.

The second, third, and fifth visits were confined, for the most part, to the West Indies.

CANDLER, WARREN A., *Bp.* Life of Thomas Coke. Nashville, Tenn., Publishing House M.E. Church, South, Lamar & Barton, Agents, 1923. vi, 408 p. port. (Methodist founders' series) BX8495.C6C3

DREW, SAMUEL. The life of the Rev. Thomas Coke, LL.D., including in detail his various travels and extraordinary missionary exertions, in England, Ireland, America, and the West-Indies. London, Printed by T. Cordeux, 1817. xix, 391 p. port. BX8495.C6D7

ETHERIDGE, JOHN W. The life of the Rev. Thomas Coke, D.C.L. London, J. Mason, 1860. viii, 450 p. port.
BX8495.C6E7

SMITH, WARREN THOMAS. Thomas Coke and the West Indies. Methodist history, v. 3, Oct. 1964: 1–11.
BX8235.M44, v. 3

VICKERS, JOHN A. The churchmanship of Thomas Coke. Methodist history, v. 7, July 1969: 15–28.
BX8235.M44, v. 7

———Thomas Coke: apostle of Methodism. Nashville, Abingdon Press [1969] xiv, 394 p. illus., maps (on lining papers), port. (The Wesley Historical Society lecture, no. 30) BX8495.C6V5 1969b

"A list of Coke's publications": p. 375–382. Bibliography: p. 383–387.

13088

COLDEN, CADWALLADER (1688–1776)*†
Scotland; Pennsylvania; New York. Physician, councilor, scientist, philosopher, Loyalist.

———The conduct of Cadwallader Colden, Esq., lieutenant governor of New-York; relating to the judges' commissions,—appeals to the King,—and the stamp-duty. [New York] Printed in the year 1767. 56 p.
AC901.H3, v. 19 Rare Bk. Coll.
AC901.M5, v. 682 Rare Bk. Coll.

A vindication of his conduct, prepared by Colden, and first printed in London in 1767 for distribution among members of the ministry and of Parliament. This New York reprint was issued the same year.

The London edition was reprinted in the *Colden Letter Books* (New York Historical Society. Collections, 1876–77. Publication fund series [v. 9–10]).

——— The history of the Five Indian nations of Canada, which are dependent on the province of New-York in America, and are the barrier between the English and French in that part of the world. To which are added, accounts of the several other nations of Indians in North-America . . . and the treaties which have been lately made with them. London, Printed for T. Osborne, 1747. xvi, 90, iv, 91–283 p. fold. map.
E99.I7C6 Rare Bk. Coll.

——— The letters and papers of Cadwallader Colden. 1711–[1775] New York, Printed for the New York Historical Society, 1918–37. 9 v. illus., fold. map, port. (New York Historical Society. Collections, 1917–23, 1934–

35. The John Watts De Peyster publication fund series [v. 50–56, 67–68])   F116.N63, 1917–23, 1934–35
F122.C67

Contents: v. 1. 1711–1729.—v. 2. 1730–1742.—v. 3. 1743–1747.—v. 4. 1748–1754.—v. 5. 1755–1760.—v. 6. 1761–1764.—v. 7. 1765–1775.—v. 8. Additional letters and papers, 1715–1748.—v. 9. Additional letters and papers, 1749–1775, and some of Colden's writings.

GITIN, LOUIS L.   Cadwallader Colden as scientist and philosopher. *In* New York State Historical Association. New York history, v. 16, Apr. 1935: 169–177.
F116.N865, v. 16

HAMLIN, PAUL M.   "He is gone and peace to his shade": William Smith, historian, posthumously boils Lieutenant Governor Cadwallader Colden in oil. *In* New York Historical Society. Quarterly, v. 36, Apr. 1952: 160–174. ports.   F116.N638, v. 36

HINDLE, BROOKE.   Cadwallader Colden's extension of the Newtonian principles. William and Mary quarterly, 3d ser., v. 13, Oct. 1956: 459–475.
F221.W71, 3d s., v. 13

——— A colonial governor's family: the Coldens of Coldengham. *In* New York Historical Society. Quarterly, v. 45, July 1961: 233–250. illus., ports.
F116.N638, v. 45

HOERMANN, ALFRED R.   A figure of the American Enlightenment: Cadwallader Colden. 1970.

Thesis (Ph.D.)—University of Toronto.
Abstracted in *Dissertation Abstracts International*, v. 32A, Aug. 1971, p. 884.
"To obtain a microfilm copy please order directly from the National Library of Canada at Ottawa."

INGRAHAM, CHARLES A.   A great colonial executive and scholar—Cadwallader Colden. Americana, v. 19, July 1925: 295–314.   E171.A53, v. 19

JARCHO, SAUL.   Biographical and bibliographical notes on Cadwallader Colden. Bulletin of the history of medicine, v. 32, July/Aug. 1958: 322–334.
R11.B93, v. 32

——— Cadwallader Colden as a student of infectious disease. Bulletin of the history of medicine, v. 29, Mar./Apr. 1955: 99–115.   R11.B93, v. 29

KEYS, ALICE M.   Cadwallader Colden; a representative eighteenth century official. New York, Columbia University Press, 1906. xiv, 375 p.   F122.C69

Reprinted in New York by AMS Press (1967).
The author's thesis (Ph.D.), with the same title, was submitted to Columbia University in 1906.

MURPHY, MIRIAM E., *Sister*.   Cadwallader Colden, president of the Council, lieutenant governor of New York, 1760–1775. 1957.

Thesis (Ph.D)—Fordham University.

RAYMOND, ALLAN R.   The political career of Cadwallader Colden. 1971. ([316] p.)
Micro AC–1, no. 72–15,276

Thesis (Ph.D.)—Ohio State University.
Abstracted in *Dissertation Abstracts International*, v. 32A, May 1972, p. 6350.

ROLLAND, SIEGFRIED B.   Cadwallader Colden, colonial political and imperial statesman, 1718–1760. 1952.

Thesis (Ph.D.)—University of Wisconsin.

SHAMMAS, CAROLE.   Cadwallader Colden and the role of the king's prerogative. *In* New York Historical Society. Quarterly, v. 53, Apr. 1969: 103–126. facism., map, ports.   F116.N638, v. 53

13089
COLDEN, CADWALLADER (1722–1797)
New York; Nova Scotia. Landowner, judge, Loyalist. Son of Cadwallader Colden (1688–1776).

BRAGDON, JOSEPH.   Cadwallader Colden, second, an Ulster County Tory. *In* New York State Historical Association. New York history, v. 14, Oct. 1933: 411–421.
F116.N865, v. 14

13090
COLEMAN, ROBERT (1748–1825)
Ireland; Pennsylvania. Ironmaster, Revolutionary officer, assemblyman.

KLEIN, FREDERIC S.   Robert Coleman: from immigrant opportunist to millionaire ironmaster. *In* Dickinson College, *Carlisle, Pa. Library*. Early Dickinsoniana. Carlisle, Pa., 1961 [c1965] (The Boyd Lee Spahr lectures in Americana, 1957–1961) p. 141–166.
LD1662.A53

——— Robert Coleman, millionaire ironmaster. *In* Lancaster County (Pa.) Historical Society. Journal, v. 64, winter 1960: 17–33. illus.   F157.L2L5, v. 64

13091
COLLES, CHRISTOPHER (1738–1816)*
Ireland; New York. Engineer, inventor.

GRIFFIN, LLOYD W.   Christopher Colles and his two American map series. *In* Bibliographical Society of America. Papers, v. 48, 2d quarter 1954: 170–182.
Z1008.B51P, v. 48

13092
COLLIN, NICHOLAS (1746–1831)
Sweden; New Jersey; Pennsylvania. Clergyman, inventor, scientist.

——— The journal and biography of Nicholas Collin, 1746–1831, the journal translated from the original Swedish manuscript, by Amandus Johnson; with an introduction by Frank H. Stewart. Philadelphia, The New

Jersey Society of Pennsylvania, 1936. 368 p. facsims., plates, port. BX8080.C65A3

"The journal, 1770–1786, by Nicholas Collin": p. [203]–296.

"Parish register of names, 1786, by Nicholas Collin": p. [297]–346.

Bibliography: p. [347]–353.

13093

COLLINGWOOD, CUTHBERT COLLINGWOOD, *Baron* (1748–1810)†

England. British seaman in America, naval officer.

MURRAY, GEOFFREY. The life of Admiral Collingwood. London, Hutchinson [1936] 288 p. facsims., plates, ports. DA87.1.C7M8 1936

Bibliography: p. 281.

13094

COLLINS, ISAAC (1746–1817)

New Jersey. Printer, newspaper publisher.

HIXSON, RICHARD F. "Faithful Guardian" of press freedom. *In* New Jersey Historical Society. Proceedings, v. 81, July 1963: 155–163. F131.N58, v. 81

——— Isaac Collins, a Quaker printer in 18th century America. New Brunswick, N.J., Rutgers University Press [1968] xi, 241 p. illus., facsims., port. Z232.C703H5

"A list of Collins imprints": [187]–204.

Includes bibliographical references.

13095

COLLINS, JAMES POTTER (1763–1844?)

North Carolina. Revolutionary soldier.

——— Autobiography of a Revolutionary soldier. *In* Miller, Susan F. E. Sixty years in the Nueces Valley, 1870–1930. San Antonio, Naylor Print. Co. [°1930] p. [215]–374. F391.M65

The autobiography, revised and prepared by John M. Roberts, was first published in Clinton, La., by Feliciana Democrat, Print., in 1859.

13096

COLOMB, PIERRE (1754–ca. 1818)

France. Revolutionary officer.

———Memoirs of a Revolutionary soldier. The Collector, a magazine for autograph and historical collectors, v. 63, Oct.–Dec. 1950: 198–201, 223–225, 247–249; v. 64, Jan. 1951: 2–5. Z41.A2C6, v. 63–64

Introduction and notes by Mary A. Benjamin.

13097

CONDICT, JEMIMA (1754–1779)

New Jersey.

———Jemima Condict, her book; being a transcript of the diary of an Essex County maid during the Revolutionary War. Newark, N.J., Carteret Book Club, 1930. 73 p. facsim., plates. F144.O6C74

The author lived "on the western slope of the 'first mountain' about a mile west of Eagle Rock" (introduction). The diary contains many references to persons and events in Orange, N.J., the nearest town.

13098

CONDORCET, MARIE JEAN ANTOINE NICOLAS CARITAT, *marquis* DE (1743–1794)

France. Philosophe.

——— Correspondance inédite de Condorcet et de Turgot 1770–1779; publiée avec des notes et une introduction d'après les autographes de la collection Minoret et les manuscrits de l'Institut. Paris, Charavay frères, 1883. xxx, 326 p. port. DC146.C69A2

——— The influence of the American Revolution on Europe. Translated and edited by Durand Echeverria. William and Mary quarterly, 3d ser., v. 25, Jan. 1968: 85–108. F221.W71, 3d s., v. 25

With a short introduction by the translator.

13099

CONNOLLY, JOHN (*ca.* 1743–1813)*

Pennsylvania; Canada. Physician, land speculator, Indian negotiator, Loyalist officer.

——— A narrative of the transactions, imprisonment, and sufferings of John Connolly, an American Loyalist, and lieutenant-colonel in His Majesty's service. In which are shewn, the unjustifiable proceedings of Congress, in his treatment and detention. London, Printed in the year 1783. [New York, Reprinted for C. L. Woodward, 1889] 62 p. E278.C7C7

Also published in the *Pennsylvania Magazine of History and Biography*, v. 12, Oct. 1888–Jan. 1889, p. 310–324, 407–420, and v. 13, Apr.–Oct. 1889, p. 61–70, 153–167, 281–291.

BURTON, CLARENCE M. John Connolly, a Tory of the Revolution. *In* American Antiquarian Society, *Worcester, Mass.* Proceedings, new ser., v. 20, Oct. 1909: 70–105. E172.A35, n.s., v. 20

——— ——— Offprint. Worcester, Mass., Davis Press, 1909. 38 p. E278.C7B9

CALEY, PERCY B. The life adventures of Lieutenant-Colonel John Connolly: the story of a Tory. Western Pennsylvania historical magazine, v. 11, Jan.–Oct. 1928: 10–49, 76–111, 144–179, 225–259. F146.W52, v. 11

DIFFENDERFFER, FRANK R. Col. John Connolly: Loyalist. Lancaster, Pa., Reprinted from the New Era, 1903. [109]–142 p. (Lancaster County Historical Society. Papers, v. 7, Mar. 1903) F157.L2L5, v. 7

13100

CONSTABLE, WILLIAM (1752–1803)
New York. Merchant, land speculator.

TAILBY, DONALD G. Chapters from the business career of William Constable: a merchant of post-Revolutionary New York. 1961. ([355] p.)
Micro AC–1, no. 61–4218
Thesis (Ph.D.)—Rutgers University.
Abstracted in *Dissertation Abstracts*, v. 22, Nov. 1961, p. 1454–1455.

13101

CONSTANT, SILAS (1750–1825)
New York. Presbyterian clergyman.

——— The journal of the Reverend Silas Constant, pastor of the Presbyterian church at Yorktown, New York; with some of the records of the church and a list of his marriages, 1784–1825, together with notes on the Nelson, Van Cortlandt, Warren, and some other families mentioned in the journal, by Emily Warren Roebling. Edited by Josiah Granville Leach. Philadelphia, Printed for private circulation by J. B. Lippincott Co., 1903. xv, 561 p. illus., facsim., geneal. table, maps, plates, ports. F129.Y6C7

13102

CONWAY, HENRY SEYMOUR (1719–1795)†
England. Member of Parliament, military officer, secretary of state.

CHAPMAN, EDWARD M. A forgotten friend of America: Henry Seymour Conway. New England magazine, new ser., v. 19, Oct. 1898: 189–201. port.
AP2.N4, n.s., v. 19
DE STEFANO, FRANCIS P. Henry Seymour Conway and the Commons' Cause, 1741–1784. 1972. ([[222] p.)
Micro AC–1, no. 73–1473
Thesis (Ph.D.)—Fordham University.
Abstracted in *Dissertation Abstracts International*, v. 33A, Feb. 1973, p. 4297.

13103

CONYNGHAM, DAVID HAYFIELD (1750–1834)
Pennsylvania. Importer and shipper, Revolutionary soldier.

——— The reminiscences of David Hayfield Conyngham, 1750–1834, a hero of the Revolution, and the head of the Revolutionary house of Conyngham and Nesbitt, Philadelphia, Pa. With an introduction, biographical sketches, and annotations by Rev. Horace Edwin Hayden. Wilkes-Barre, Pa., Printed for the Society, 1904. 113 p. plates, ports. F153.C79
Reprinted from volume 8 of the *Proceedings and Collections* of the Wyoming Historical and Geological Society.

13104

CONYNGHAM, GUSTAVUS (1744?–1819)*
Ireland; Pennsylvania. Revolutionary naval officer.

JONES, CHARLES H. Captain Gustavus Conyngham; a sketch of the services he rendered to the cause of American independence. [Philadelphia] Pennsylvania Society of Sons of the Revolution, 1903. 32 p. plates (part col.), ports. E271.C76
Reprinted in Tarrytown, N.Y., by W. Abbatt (1929. [5]–27 p. E173.M24, no. 155) as extra number, no. 155, of *The Magazine of History, With Notes and Queries.*

NEESER, ROBERT W. Les croisières du capitaine Conyngham. *In* Académie de marine, *Paris*. Communications et mémoires. v. 7. Paris, 1928. p. [327]–357.
V2.A34, v. 7

——— ——— Offprint. Paris, Société d'éditions géographiques, maritimes et coloniales, 1928. [327]–357 p. E271.C767

——— *ed.* Letters and papers relating to the cruises of Gustavus Conyngham, a captain of the Continental Navy, 1777–1779. Edited by Robert Wilden Neeser. New York, Printed for the Naval History Society by the De Vinne Press, 1915. liii, 241 p. facsims., plates, ports. (Publications of the Naval History Society, v. 6)
E271.C77
Reprinted in Port Washington, N.Y., by Kennikat Press (1970).

13105

COOK, EDWARD (1738–1808)
Pennsylvania. Frontiersman, judge.

GUFFEY, ALEXANDER S. Colonel Edward Cook and other historical papers. [Pittsburgh, 1941] 57 p. facsims., plates, port. F149.G8

13106

COOK, THOMAS (1752–1841)
Virginia. Revolutionary officer.

——— Captain Thomas Cook (1752–1841), a soldier of the Revolution. Edited by his great-great-grand nephew William M. Sweeny. [New York? 1909] 13 p.
E275.C77
Statement of services submitted to the Bureau of Pensions.

13107

COOK, NICHOLAS (1717–1782)
Rhode Island. Shipmaster, merchant, governor.

——— Revolutionary correspondence of Governor Nicholas Cooke, 1775–1781. *In* American Antiquarian Society, *Worcester, Mass.* Proceedings, new ser., v. 36, Oct. 1926: 231–353. E172.A35, n.s., v. 36
Introduction and notes by Matt B. Jones.

—— Rhode Island Revolutionary correspondence [1775–78] Historical magazine, 2d ser., v. 8, July 1870: 43–49.
E171.H64, 2d s., v. 8

Communicated by E. M. Stone.

13108
COOKE, SILAS (d. 1792)
Rhode Island. Distiller, merchant, farmer.

—— Silas Cooke—a victim of the Revolution. In Rhode Island Historical Society. Collections, v. 31, Oct. 1938: 108–121.
F76.R47, v. 31

Memoranda, 1776–79, that relate to his sufferings during the British occupation of Newport. Introduction and notes by Susan Stanton Brayton.

13109
COOPER, MYLES (1737–1785)*
England; New York. Anglican clergyman, educator, Loyalist.

MINER, DWIGHT C. Doctor Cooper departs. Columbia Library columns, v. 1, May 1952: 4–11.
Z671.C63, v. 1

VANCE, CLARENCE H. Myles Cooper. Columbia University quarterly, v. 22, Sept. 1930: 261–286. port.
LH1.C7Q2, v. 22

13110
COOPER, SAMUEL (1725–1783)*
Massachusetts. Clergyman.

—— Diary of Samuel Cooper, 1775–1776. American historical review, v. 6, Jan. 1901: 301–341.
E171.A57, v. 6

Introduction and notes by Frederick Tuckerman.

—— Extracts from the letters of Samuel Cooper, 1777–78. Pennsylvania magazine of history and biography, v. 10, Apr. 1886: 33–42.
F146.P65, v. 10

Letters to John Litle; contributed by John W. Jordan.

—— Letters of Samuel Cooper to Thomas Pownall, 1769–1777. American historical review, v. 8, Jan. 1903: 301–330.
E171.A57, v. 8

Introduction and notes by Frederick Tuckerman.

—— A sermon preached before His Excellency John Hancock, Esq; governour, the honourable the Senate, and House of Representatives of the commonwealth of Massachusetts, October 25, 1780. Being the day of the commencement of the constitution, and inauguration of the new government. [Boston] Commonwealth of Massachusetts, Printed by T. and J. Fleet, and J. Gill [1780] 55 p.
F69.C77 Rare Bk. Coll.

BUCHANAN, JOHN G. The pursuit of happiness: a study of the Rev. Dr. Samuel Cooper, 1725–1783. 1971. ([386] p.)
Micro AC–1, no. 72–11,072

Thesis (Ph.D.)—Duke University.
Abstracted in Dissertation Abstracts International, v. 32A, Apr. 1972, p. 5703.

13111
COOPER, WILLIAM (1754–1809)*
Pennsylvania; New York. Frontiersman, land speculator.

—— A guide in the wilderness; or, The history of the first settlement in the western counties of New York, with useful instructions to future settlers. In a series of letters addressed by Judge Cooper, of Coopers-town, to William Sampson, barrister, of New York. Dublin, Printed by Gilbert & Hodges, 1810. [Rochester, N.Y., G. P. Humphrey, 1897] viii, 41 p.
F123.C77

Reprinted in Freeport, N.Y., by Books for Libraries Press (1970).

BUTTERFIELD, LYMAN H. Judge William Cooper (1754–1809); a sketch of his character and accomplishment. In New York State Historical Association. New York history, v. 30, Oct. 1949: 385–408.
F116.N865, v. 30

13112
COPLEY, JOHN SINGLETON (1738–1815)*†
Massachusetts; England. Portrait painter.

—— John Singleton Copley to his wife [1774–75] In Boston. Public Library. Quarterly, v. 12, Apr. 1960: 67–78.
Z881.B7535, v. 12

—— John Singleton Copley's houses on Beacon Hill, Boston. In Society for the Preservation of New England Antiquities, Boston. Old-time New England, v. 25, Jan. 1935: 85–95. facsim., ports.
F1.S68, v.25

Abstracted from the Letters & Papers of John Singleton Copley and Henry Pelham.

—— Letters & papers of John Singleton Copley and Henry Pelham, 1739–1776. [Boston] Massachusetts Historical Society, 1914. xxii, 384 p. facsims., ports. (Massachusetts Historical Society, Boston. Collections, v. 71)
F61.M41, v. 7
ND237.C7A3

Reprinted in New York by Kennedy Graphics (1970) and AMS Press (1972).

AMORY, MARTHA B. G. The domestic and artistic life of John Singleton Copley, R. A. Boston, Houghton, Mifflin, 1882, xii, 478 p. port.
ND237.C7A5

Reprinted in New York by Kennedy Galleries (1969).

FLEXNER, JAMES T. John Singleton Copley. Boston, Houghton Mifflin Co., 1948. xv, 139 p. plates.
ND237.C7F6

A completely revised and enlarged version of the biography of John Singleton Copley originally published as part of the author's America's Old Masters.
Bibliography: p. 117–123.

FOOTE, HENRY W. When was John Singleton Copley born? New England quarterly, v. 10, Mar. 1937: 111–120.   F1.N62, v. 10

JULES, DAVID P. The art historian and the computer; an analysis of Copley's patronage, 1753–1774. Smithsonian journal of history, v. 1, winter 1966–67: 17–30. illus., ports.   CB3.S55, v.1

PARKER, BARBARA N., and ANNE B. WHEELER. John Singleton Copley; American portraits in oil, pastel, and miniature, with biographical sketches. Boston, Mass., Museum of Fine Arts, 1938. ix, 284 p. 130 plates on 65 leaves.   ND237.C7P3

PERKINS, AUGUSTUS T. A sketch of the life and a list of some of the works of John Singleton Copley. Boston, J. R. Osgood, 1873. 144, 29 p.   ND237.C7P4

"Supplementary list of paintings by John Singleton Copley": 29 p. at end.
See also *The Life and Works of John Singleton Copley, Founded on the Work of Augustus Thorndike Perkins* (Boston, Taylor Press, 1915. 285 p. ND237.C7B3), by Frank W. Bayley.

PROWN, JULES D. The art historian and the computer; an analysis of Copley's patronage, 1753–1774. Smithsonian journal of history, v. 1, winter 1967: 17–30. ports.   CB3.S55, v. 1

—— John Singleton Copley. Cambridge, Published for the National Gallery of Art, Washington [by] Harvard University Press, 1966. 2 v. (xxiv, 491 p.) illus., geneal. tables, ports. (The Ailsa Mellon Bruce studies in American art, 1)   ND237.C7P7

Includes bibliographies.
Contents: v. 1. In America, 1738–1774.—v. 2. In England, 1774–1815.

RICHARDSON, EDGAR P. Copley's portrait of Mrs. Roger Morris. I. Copley's New York portraits. *In* Winterthur portfolio. v. 2; 1965. Winterthur, Del. p. 1–13. ports.   N9.W52, v. 2

SIMMONS, RICHARD C. Copley's portrait of Mrs. Roger Morris. II. Mrs. Morris and the Philipse family, American Loyalists. *In* Winterthur portfolio. v. 2; 1965. Winterthur, Del. p. 14–26. ports.   N9.W52, v. 2

13113

CORBIN, MARGARET COCHRAN (1751–*ca.* 1800)
Pennsylvania. Revolutionary fighter.

HALL, EDWARD H. Margaret Corbin, heroine of the Battle of Fort Washington, 16 November 1776. New York, American Scenic and Historic Preservation Society, 1932. 45 [i.e. 47] p. illus.   E263.P4C78

13114

CORIOLIS, JEAN BAPTISTE ELZÉAR, *chevalier* DE (1754–1811)
French officer in America

—— Lettres d'un officier de l'armée de Rochambeau: le chevalier de Coriolis [1782–83] Correspondant, new ser., v. 290, Mar. 25, 1932: 807–828.   AP20.C8, n.s., v. 290

Introduction by Ludovic de Contenson.

13115

CORNELL, SAMUEL (1731–1781)
North Carolina. Merchant, councilor, Loyalist.

New York (City). Public Library. Papers relating to Samuel Cornell, North Carolina Loyalist. *In its* Bulletin, v. 17, June 1913: 443–484.   Z881.N6B, v. 17

—— —— Offprint. New York, 1913. 44 p.   E278.C8N5

13116

CORNPLANTER, *Seneca chief* (1732?–1836)

SNOWDEN, JAMES R. The Cornplanter memorial. An historical sketch of Gy-ant-wa-cha—the Cornplanter, and of the Six Nations of Indians. Harrisburg, Pa., Singerly & Myers, State Printers, 1867. 115 p.   E90.C8S6

13117

CORNSTALK, *Shawnee chief* (1720?–1777)*

Sketch of Cornstalk, 1759–1777. Ohio archaeological and historical quarterly, v. 21, Apr./July 1912: 245–262.   F486.O51, v. 21

"The following sketch of Cornstalk, is from the Draper MSS., Border Forays, 3 D, Chap. XVIII, in the possession of the Wisconsin Historical Society."

13118

CORNWALLIS, CHARLES CORNWALLIS, *1st Marquis* (1738–1805)†
England. Member of Parliament, British officer in America.

——Correspondence of Charles, first Marquis Cornwallis. Edited with notes by Charles Ross. London, J. Murray, 1859. 3 v. fold. maps, fold. geneal. table, port.   DA506.C8A2

GRIFFIN, WILLIAM D. Cornwallis in search of employment [1782–86] Studies in Burke and his time, v. 11, spring 1970: 1543–1554.   DA506.B9B86, v. 11

RANKIN, HUGH F. Charles Lord Cornwallis: study in frustration. *In* Billias, George A., *ed.* George Washington's opponents: British generals and admirals in the American Revolution. New York, Morrow, 1969. p. 193–232. port.   E267.B56

Bibliography: p. 232.

13119

CORNWALLIS, *Sir* WILLIAM (1744–1819)†
England. British admiral.

CORNWALLIS-WEST, GEORGE F. M. The life and letters of Admiral Cornwallis. London, R. Holden, 1927. 527 p. facsim., plates, ports. DA506.C83C6

Gt. Brit. *Historical Manuscripts Commission.* The manuscripts of Cornwallis Wykeham-Martin, of the Hill, Purton, Wilts, esquire. *In its* Report on manuscripts in various collections. v. 6. Dublin, Printed for H. M. Stationery Off., by J. Falconer, 1909. p. [xxix]–xliv, [297]–434. DA25.M2V2, v. 6

A report, by W. Fitzpatrick, on a selection of letters addressed to Captain Cornwallis, 1761–1818.

13120

COSTE, JEAN FRANÇOIS (1741–1819)

French military surgeon in America.

LANE, JOHN E. Jean-François Coste, chief physician of the French expeditionary forces in the American Revolution. Americana, v. 22, Jan. 1928: 51–80. plate, ports. E171.A53, v. 22

———— ————Offprint. [Somerville, N.J., American Historical Society] 1928. 30 p. plate, ports. E265.C83

WAGENER, ANTHONY P. The adaptation of the ancient philosophy of medicine to the New World by Jean-François Coste. Journal of the history of medicine and allied sciences, v. 7, winter 1952: 10–67. R131.A1J6, v. 7

13121

COTTEN, JOHN (1745–1811)

North Carolina; Tennessee. Planter, settler.

———— The Battle of the Bluffs [1781] from the journal of John Cotten. Edited by J. W. L. Matlock. Tennessee historical quarterly, v. 18, Sept. 1959: 252–265. F431.T285, v. 18

FOLMSBEE, STANLEY J. The journal of John Cotten, the "reluctant pioneer"—evidences of its unreliability. Tennessee historical quarterly, v. 28, spring 1969: 84–94. F431.T285, v. 28

MATLOCK, J. W. L. John Cotten: reluctant pioneer. Tennessee historical quarterly, v. 27, fall 1968: 277–286. F431.T285, v. 27

13122

COTTLE, JABEZ (1747–1820)

Massachusetts; Vermont. Farmer, Revolutionary soldier, assemblyman.

———— The life of Elder Jabez Cottle (1747–1820): a spiritual autobiography in verse. New England quarterly, v. 38, Sept. 1965: 375–386. F1.N62, v. 38

Introduction and notes by William G. McLoughlin.

13123

COTTON, JAMES (*b.* 1739)

Massachusetts; North Carolina; England. Planter, assemblyman, Loyalist officer.

McBRIDE, ROBERT M. Portrait of an American Loyalist: James Cotton of Anson County, North Carolina. Nashville, 1954. 64 l. illus. E278.C84M3

Thesis (M.A.)—Stanford University.
Bibliography: leaves 59–64.

13124

COUTTS, THOMAS (1735–1822)†

Scotland; England. Financier.

COLERIDGE, ERNEST H. The life of Thomas Coutts, banker. London, New York, Lane, 1920. 2 v. facsim. plates, ports. DA506.C85C6

13125

COWDIN, THOMAS (1720–1792)

Ireland; Massachusetts. Blacksmith, Revolutionary officer, assemblyman.

HOWARD, ADA L. Captain Thomas Cowdin. *In* Fitchburg Historical Society, *Fitchburg, Mass.* Proceedings. v. 3; 1897/99. Fitchburg, 1902. p. 19–38. ports. F74.F5F6, v. 3

STEARNS, EZRA S. Capt. Thomas Cowdin in the Revolution. *In* Fitchburg Historical Society, *Fitchburg, Mass.* Proceedings. v. 5; 1907/13. Fitchburg, 1914. p. 270–277. F74.F5F6, v. 5

13126

COWPER, BASIL (*d.* 1802)

Georgia. Merchant, Loyalist.

HARDEN, WILLIAM. Basil Cowper's remarkable career in Georgia. Georgia historical quarterly, v. 1, Mar. 1917: 24–35. F281.G2975, v. 1

13127

COX, ISAAC (1716?–1783)

Maryland; Kentucky. Settler.

ADAMS, EVELYN C. The Coxes of Cox's Creek, Kentucky. Filson Club history quarterly, v. 22, Apr. 1948: 75–103. F446.F484, v. 22

13128

COXE, TENCH (1755–1824)*

Pennsylvania. Merchant, delegate to the Continental Congress.

———— A brief examination of Lord Sheffield's observations on the commerce of the United States. In seven numbers. With two supplementary notes on American manufactures. Philadelphia, From the press of M. Carey, 1791. vii, 135 p.   HF3025.S6 Rare Bk. Coll.

COOKE, JACOB E.   Tench Coxe, Tory merchant. Pennsylvania magazine of history and biography, v. 96, Jan. 1972: 48–88.   F146.P65, v. 96

HUTCHESON, HAROLD.   Tench Coxe; a study in American economic development. Baltimore, Johns Hopkins Press, 1938. ix, 227 p. (Johns Hopkins University studies in historical and political science. Extra volumes, new ser., no. 26)   H31.J62, n.s., no. 26
HB119.C64H8
Issued also as thesis (Ph.D.)—Johns Hopkins University.
Bibliography: p. 203–220.
Reprinted in New York by Da Capo Press (1969).

13129
CRAFTS, THOMAS (1740–1799)
Massachusetts. Revolutionary officer.

ROBINS, EDWARD B.   Col. Thomas Crafts, Jr., 1740–1799. In Bostonian Society, Boston. Proceedings. v. 33; 1914. Boston. p. 31–38. port.   F73.1.B86, v. 33

13130
CRAIG, ISAAC (ca. 1742–1826)
Ireland; Pennsylvania. Carpenter, Revolutionary officer.

CRAIG, NEVILLE B.   Sketch of the life and services of Isaac Craig, major in the Fourth (usually called Proctor's) Regiment of Artillery, during the Revolutionary War. Pittsburgh, J. S. Davison, 1854. 70 p.   E275.C88

13131
CRAIGIE, ANDREW (1743–1819)*
Massachusetts. Revolutionary apothecary.

HULBERT, ARCHER B.   Andrew Craigie and the Scioto Associates. In American Antiquarian Society, Worcester, Mass. Proceedings, new ser., v. 23, Oct. 1913: 222–236.   E172.A35, n.s., v. 23
——— ——— Offprint. Worcester, Mass., The Society, 1913. 17 p.   F483.H9

KEBLER, LYMAN F.   Andrew Craigie, the first Apothecary General of the United States. In American Pharmaceutical Association. Journal, v. 17, Jan.–Feb. 1928: 63–74, 167–178. facsim.   RS1.A52, v. 17

PRATT, FREDERICK H.   The Craigies: a footnote to the medical history of the Revolution. In Cambridge Historical Society, Cambridge, Mass. Proceedings. v. 27; 1941. Cambridge, 1942. p. 43–86.
F74.C1C469, v. 27

13132
CRAIK, JAMES (1730–1814)*
Scotland; Virginia. Physician, Revolutionary surgeon and medical administrator.

PATTERSON, ROBERT U.   James Craik, Physician General. Military surgeon, v. 70, Feb. 1932: 152–156.
RD1.A7, v. 70

CRANCH, ELIZABETH
See NORTON, ELIZABETH CRANCH

13133
CRANE, THADDEUS (1729–1803)
New York. Assemblyman, Revolutionary officer.

FULCHER, WILLIAM G.   Colonel Thaddeus Crane. In Westchester County Historical Society. Quarterly bulletin, v. 17, Jan.-Apr. 1941: 1–15, 40–45. facsims.
F127.W5W594, v. 17
Includes the texts of several letters to and from Crane, an officer in the Westchester County militia, 1777–81.

13134
CRANNELL, BARTHOLOMEW (fl. 1744–1787)
New York; Nova Scotia. Loyalist.

REYNOLDS, HELEN W.   Bartholomew Crannell. In Dutchess County Historical Society. Year book. 1922. Poughkeepsie. p. 39–60. maps (part fold.)
F127.D8D93, 1922
Crannell's letter to his sons-in-law, dated November 7, 1785, appears on p. 61–63, while his testimony as a Loyalist claimant appears on p. 64–79.

13135
CRAWFORD, CHARLES (b. 1752)
Antigua; England; Pennsylvania. Poet.

LEARY, LEWIS G.   Charles Crawford: a forgotten poet of early Philadelphia. Pennsylvania magazine of history and biography, v. 83, July 1959: 293–306.
F146.P65, v. 83

13136
CRAWFORD, WILLIAM (1732–1782)*
Virginia; Pennsylvania. Farmer, judge, Revolutionary officer.

ANDERSON, JAMES H.   Colonel William Crawford. In Ohio archaeological and historical publications. v. 6. Columbus, 1898. p. [1]–34. plates, ports.
F486.O51, v. 6

13137
CRESAP, MICHAEL (1742–1775)*
Maryland. Frontiersman, Revolutionary officer.

JACOB, JOHN JEREMIAH.   A biographical sketch of the life of the late Captain Michael Cresap. Cincinnati, Ohio, Re-printed from the Cumberland ed. of 1826, with notes and appendix, for W. Dodge, by J. F. Uhlhorn, Steam Job Printer, 1866. 158 p.   F517.C92

A defense of Captain Cresap, contradicting the statements made by Thomas Jefferson in his *Notes on the State of Virginia* and Joseph Doddridge in his *Notes on the Settlement and Indian Wars of the Western Parts of Virginia and Pennsylvania From 1763 to 1783.*

Reprinted in New York by Arno Press (1971) and, with an introduction by Otis K. Rice, in Parsons, W. Va., by McClain Print. Co. (1971. 48, 158 p. F517.C87J3 1971).

13138

CRESAP, THOMAS (1694–1790)*

England; Maryland. Frontiersman, Indian trader.

BAILEY, KENNETH P.   Thomas Cresap, Maryland frontiersman. Boston, Christopher Pub. House [1944] 322 p. facsim., fold. map, plates.   F184.C84
Bibliography: p. 240–263.

WROTH, LAWRENCE C.   The story of Thomas Cresap, a Maryland pioneer. Maryland historical magazine, v. 9, Mar. 1914: 1–37.   F176.M18, v. 9

13139

CRESSWELL, NICHOLAS (1750–1804)

England. Traveler.

——— The journal of Nicholas Cresswell, 1774–1777. New York, L. MacVeagh, Dial Press, 1924. ix, 287 p. illus., facsim.   E163.C78

Reprinted in Port Washington, N.Y., by Kennikat Press (1968).

An account of his travels from Liverpool to Barbados, Virginia, the Virginia backcountry, New York, and back to London.

13140

CRÈVECŒUR, MICHEL GUILLAUME ST. JEAN DE, *called* SAINT JOHN DE CRÈVECŒUR (1735–1813)*

France; New York. Explorer, mapmaker, farmer, writer, Loyalist.

——— Crevecoeur on the Susquehanna, 1774–1776. Edited, with an introduction, by Henri L. Bourdin and Stanley T. Williams. Yale review, new ser., v. 14, Apr. 1925: 552–584. map.   AP2.Y2, n. s., v. 14

——— Eighteenth-century travels in Pennsylvania & New York. Translated & edited by Percy G. Adams. [Lexington] University of Kentucky Press [1961] xliv, 172 p. illus., ports.   F153.C923

"Translation of selections from Jean de Crèvecoeur's *Voyage dans la haute Pensylvanie et dans l'état de New York.*"

——— Hospitals [during the Revolution]: an unpublished essay by J. Hector St. John de Crevecoeur. Edited by H. L. Bourdin and S. T. Williams. Philological quarterly, v. 5, Apr. 1926: 157–165.   P1.P55, v. 5

——— Journey into northern Pennsylvania and the state of New York. Translated by Clarissa Spencer Bostelmann. Ann Arbor, University of Michigan Press [1964] xviii, 619 p.   F153.C923 1964
First published in three volumes in Paris in 1801.

——— Letters from an American farmer; describing certain provincial situations, manners, and customs . . . and conveying some idea of the late and present interior circumstances of the British colonies of North America. Written for the information of a friend in England. London, Printed for T. Davies, 1782. 318 p. fold. maps.   E163.C82 Rare Bk. Coll.

A reprint based on this edition was issued in Gloucester, Mass., by P. Smith (1968). Available in numerous other editions, such as Everyman's Library no. 640 (London, J. M. Dent; New York, E. P. Dutton [1912] 256 p.), with an introduction and notes by Warren B. Blake.

——— Sketches of eighteenth century America; more "Letters from an American farmer," by St. John de Crèvecoeur. Edited by Henri L. Bourdin, Ralph H. Gabriel and Stanley T. Williams. New Haven, Yale University Press, 1925. 342 p. facsim., port.   E163.C873

Reprinted in New York by B. Blom (1972).
Those portions treating "Farm-Life in the Hudson Valley, 1769–1779" were reprinted in the *Year Book* of the Dutchess County Historical Society, v. 18, 1933, p. 41–57.

ADAMS, PERCY G.   Crèvecoeur—realist or romanticist? French American review, v. 2, July/Sept. 1949: 115–134.   PS159.F5F74, v. 2

——— The historical value of Crèvecoeur's *Voyage dans la haute Pensylvania et dans New York.* American literature, v. 25, May 1953: 152–168.   PS1.A6, v. 25

GABRIEL, RALPH H.   Crèvecoeur, an Orange County paradox. *In* New York State Historical Association. Quarterly journal, v. 12, Jan 1931: 45–55.   F116.N865, v. 12

MITCHELL, JULIA P.   St. Jean de Crèvecoeur. New York, Columbia University Press, 1916. xvi, 362 p. (Columbia University studies in English and comparative literature)   PS737.C5Z8 1916a
Issued also as thesis (Ph.D.)—Columbia University.
"Reprints from Crèvecoeur": p. 346–350.
Reprinted in New York by AMS Press (1966).

PHILBRICK, THOMAS.   St. John de Crèvecoeur. New York, Twayne Publishers [1970] 178 p. (Twayne's United States authors series)   PS737.C5Z85
Bibliography: p. 173–175.

RAPPING, ELAYNE A.   Theory and experience in Crèvecoeur's America. American quarterly, v. 19, winter 1967: 707–718.   AP2.A3985, v. 19

SANBORN, FRANKLIN B. The "American farmer," St. John de Crèvecoeur and his famous "Letters" (1735–1813). Pennsylvania magazine of history and biography, v. 30, July 1906: 257–286.   F146.P65, v. 30

——— The conversion of a Loyalist to a patriot: of a St. John to a St. Jean de Crèvecoeur. *In* Massachusetts Historical Society, *Boston*. Proceedings. v. 50, 1916/17. Boston, 1917. p. 94–109.   F61.M38, v. 50

——— St. John de Crevecoeur, the American farmer (1735–1813). *In* Massachusetts Historical Society, *Boston*. Proceedings. 2d ser., v. 20; 1906/7. Boston, 1907. p. 32–83.   F61.M38, 2d s., v. 20

STONE, ALBERT E. Crèvecoeur's *Letters* and the beginnings of an American literature. Emory University quarterly, v. 18, winter 1962: 197–213.   AS36.E6, v. 18

13141

CROCKETT, JOSEPH (1742–1829)

Virginia; Kentucky. Farmer, Revolutionary officer, surveyor.

PRICE, SAMUEL W. Biographical sketch of Colonel Joseph Crockett. [Louisville, 1909] vii, 85, xv p. plates, ports. (Filson Club publications, no. 24, pt. 2)   TK5243.L4T6   F446.F48, no. 24

13142

CROGHAN, GEORGE (d. 1782)*†

Ireland; Pennsylvania. Frontiersman, Indian negotiator, land speculator.

——— George Croghan's journal of his trip to Detroit in 1767, with his correspondence relating thereto: now published for the first time from the papers of General Thomas Gage in the William L. Clements Library. Edited by Howard H. Peckham. Ann Arbor, University of Michigan Press, 1939. vii, 61 p.   F483.C76

——— George Croghan's journal, 1759–1763, from the original in the Cadwalader collection of the Historical Society of Pennsylvania. Edited by Nicholas B. Wainwright. Pennsylvania magazine of history and biography, v. 71, Oct. 1947: 305–444.   F146.P65, v. 71

——— Letters of Colonel George Croghan. Pennsylvania magazine of history and biography, v. 15, Jan. 1892: 429–439.   F146.P65, v. 15

Letters written to Thomas Wharton of Philadelphia describing affairs in the vicinity of Fort Pitt between 1768 and 1774.

——— The opinions of George Croghan on the American Indian [1773] Pennsylvania magazine of history and biography, v. 71, Apr. 1947: 152–159.   F146.P65, v. 71

Introduction and notes by Nicholas B. Wainwright.

——— A selection of George Croghan's letters and journals relating to tours into the western country—November 16, 1750–November 1765. *In* Thwaites, Reuben G., *ed.* Early western travels, 1748–1846, a series of annotated reprints. v. 1. Cleveland, A. H. Clark Co., 1904. p. [45]–173.   F592.T54, v. 1

CRIST, ROBERT G. George Croghan of Pennsboro. Harrisburg, Pa., Dauphin Deposit Trust Co. [1965] 31 p. illus., maps.   F152.C95C7

Bibliographic references included in "Notes" (p. 29–31).

SWETNAM, GEORGE. Where did George Croghan die? Western Pennsylvania historical magazine, v. 55, Jan. 1972: 55–63.   F146.W52, v. 55

In or near Philadelphia, not at Croghan Hall.

VOLWILER, ALBERT T. George Croghan and the development of central New York, 1763–1800. *In* New York State Historical Association. Quarterly journal, v. 4, Jan. 1923: 21–40. map.   F116.N865, v. 4

——— ——— Offprint. [Albany] 1923. 21–40 p.   F122.V94

——— George Croghan and the westward movement, 1741–1782. Cleveland, H. Clark Co., 1926. 370 p. facsim., maps. (Early Western journals, no. 3)   F152.V942

Published in part in the *Pennsylvania Magazine of History and Biography*, 1922–23.
Bibliography: p. [337]–350.
The author's thesis (Ph.D.), with the same title, was submitted to the University of Pennsylvania in 1922.
Reprinted in New York by AMS Press (1971).

WAINWRIGHT, NICHOLAS B. George Croghan, wilderness diplomat. Chapel Hill, Published for the Institute of Early American History and Culture at Williamsburg by the University of North Carolina Press [1959] viii, 334 p. illus., maps.   F483.C76W3

"Bibliographical essay": p. [311]–316.

13143

CROGHAN, WILLIAM (1752–1822)

Virginia; Kentucky. Revolutionary officer, settler.

THOMAS, SAMUEL W. William Croghan, Sr. [1752–1822], a pioneer Kentucky gentleman. Filson Club history quarterly, v. 43, Jan. 1969: 30–61.   F446.F484, v. 43

13144

CROMOT DUBOURG, MARIE FRANÇOIS JOSEPH MAXIME, *baron* (1756–1836)

France. French officer in America.

——— Diary of a French officer, 1781. Magazine of American history, with notes and queries, v. 4, Mar.–June 1880: 205–214, 293–308, 376–385, 441–449; v. 7, Oct. 1881: 293–295.   E171.M18, v. 4, 7

"From an unpublished Manuscript in the possession of C. Fiske Harris, of Providence, R.I."

13145

CROPPER, JOHN (1755–1821)

Virginia. Revolutionary officer.

WISE, BARTON H. Memoir of General John Cropper of Accomack County, Virginia. *In* Virginia Historical Society. Collections. new ser., v. 11. Richmond, 1892. p. [273]–315.   F221.V832, n.s., v. 11

13146

CROSBY, ENOCH (1750–1835)

Massachusetts; New York. Secret agent, Revolutionary soldier, farmer.

—— Enoch Crosby, secret agent of the neutral ground: his own story. *In* New York State Historical Association. New York history, v. 47, Jan. 1966: 61–73.   F116.N865, v. 47

Introduction and notes by James H. Pickering.

BARNUM, H. L. The spy unmasked; or, Memoirs of Enoch Crosby, alias Harvey Birch, the hero of Mr. Cooper's tale of the neutral ground: being an authentic account of the secret services which he rendered his country during the Revolutionary War. (Taken from his own lips, in short-hand.) Comprising many interesting facts and anecdotes, never before published. New-York, Printed by J. & J. Harper, 1828. 206 p. map, plates, port.   E280.C95B6 Rare Bk. Coll.

Reprinted in Fishkill, N.Y., by the Fishkill Weekly Times (1886. 152 p. E280.C95B7).

In an an article entitled "The Identity of Harvey Birch" (*American Literature*, v. 2, May 1930, p. 111–120), Tremaine McDowell argues that Enoch Crosby was not the prototype for Cooper's fictional frontiersman.

13147

CRUGER, HENRY (1739–1827)*

New York, England. Merchant, Member of Parliament.

—— Diary and memoranda of Henry Cruger: conversations with Edmund Burke and Lord North, 1775. Magazine of American history, with notes and queries, v. 7, Nov. 1881: 358–363.   E171.M18, v. 7

Edited by Henry C. Van Schaack.

CHRISTIE, IAN R. Henry Cruger and the end of Edmund Burke's connection with Bristol. *In* Bristol and Gloucestershire Archaeological Society, *Gloucester, Eng.* Transactions. v. 74; 1955. Gloucester, 1956. p. 153–170.   DA670.G4B8, v. 74

UNDERDOWN, P. T. Henry Cruger and Edmund Burke: colleagues and rivals at the Bristol election of 1774. William and Mary quarterly, 3d ser., v. 15, Jan. 1958: 14–34.   F221.W71, 3d s., v. 15

Compares the campaigns of two opposition politicians—a colonial-born radical and an aristocratic Whig—and finds the American issue played only a minor role.

VAN SCHAACK, HENRY C. Henry Cruger: the colleague of Edmund Burke in the British Parliament. New York, C. B. Richardson, 1859. 67 p.   CT275.C92V2

13148

CUGNET, FRANÇOIS JOSEPH (1720–1789)

Quebec. Lawyer, translator.

LELAND, MARINE E. Francois-Joseph Cugnet (1720–1789). *In* Quebec (City). Université Laval. Revue, v. 16, Sept.–Nov. 1961, Jan., Mar., June 1962: 3–13, 129–139, 205–214, 411–420, 618–629, 929–936; v. 17, Sept.–Oct. 1962, Jan., May 1963: 64–73, 145–155, 445–456, 820–841; v. 18, Dec. 1963, Apr. 1964: 337–360, 717–733; v. 19, Oct. 1964, Mar. 1965: 144–157, 658–671; v. 20, Oct.–Dec. 1965, May–June 1966: 143–150, 267–274, 359–365, 832–844, 923–933; v. 21, Oct., Dec. 1966: 178–191, 378–396.   AP21.Q4, v. 16–21

13149

CUMBERLAND, RICHARD (1732–1811)†

England. Secretary, dramatist.

—— Letters from Richard Cumberland to Roger Pinckney with regard to the provost-marshalship of South Carolina [1764–75] *In* Weston, Plowden C. J., *ed.* Documents connected with the history of South Carolina. Printed for private distribution only. London, 1856. p. 101–154.   F272.W53 Rare Bk. Coll.

13150

CUNNINGHAM, LETITIA

—— The case of the Whigs who loaned their money on the public faith fairly stated. Including a memento for Congress to review their engagements, and to establish the honour and honesty of the United States of America. Philadelphia, Printed by Francis Bailey, in Market-Street, 1783. 51 p.   HG516.C8 Rare Bk. Coll.

13151

CURRIER, JOHN (1726–1806)

Massachusetts. Revolutionary officer.

—— The Revolutionary papers of Capt. John Currier of Amesbury. *In* Essex Institute, *Salem, Mass.* Historical collections, v. 84, July–Oct. 1948: 254–276, 349–366.   F72.E7E81, v. 84

13152

CURWEN, SAMUEL (1715–1802)*

Massachusetts; England. Merchant, judge, Loyalist.

—— The journal and letters of Samuel Curwen, an American in England, from 1775 to 1783; with an appendix of biographical sketches. 4th ed. Boston, Little, Brown, 1864. xxiv, 678 p. port.   E278.C9C93

Reprinted in New York by Da Capo Press (1970). First edition published in New York in 1842.

———— The journal of Samuel Curwen, Loyalist. Edited by Andrew Oliver. Cambridge, Mass., Harvard University Press, for the Essex Institute, Salem, Mass., 1972. 2 v. (xxxiv, 1083 p.) (The Loyalist papers)
E278.C9A34 1972

Includes bibliographic references.

13153

CUSHING, THOMAS (1725–1788)*

Massachusetts. Merchant, assemblyman, delegate to the Continental Congress.

———— Letters of Thomas Cushing, from 1767 to 1775. *In* Massachusetts Historical Society, *Boston*. Collections. 4th ser., v. 4. Boston, 1858. p. 347–366.
F61.M41, 4th s., v. 4

O'DONNELL, JAMES J. Thomas Cushing: a reluctant rebel. 1962. ([260] p.)   Micro AC–1, no. 62–4556

Thesis (Ph.D.)—Boston University.
Abstracted in *Dissertation Abstracts*, v. 23, Oct. 1962, p. 1342–1343.

13154

CUSHING, WILLIAM (1732–1810)

Massachusetts. Lawyer, judge.

CUSHING, JOHN D. A revolutionary conservative: the public life of William Cushing, 1732–1810. 1959. ([356] p.)   Micro AC–1, no. 59–6187

Thesis (Ph.D.)—Clark College.
Abstracted in *Dissertation Abstracts*, v. 20, Jan. 1960, p. 2768.

GRINNEL, FRANK W. William Cushing's judicial career in Massachusetts from 1777 to 1789. Massachusetts law quarterly, v. 43, Mar. 1958: 64–69.   LL

RUGG ARTHUR P. William Cushing, chief justice of the supreme judicial court of Massachusetts. Yale law journal, v. 30, Dec. 1920: 128–144.   K29.A4, v. 30

CUSTIS, ELEANOR CALVERT
See STUART, ELEANOR CALVERT CUSTIS

13155

CUTHBERTSON, JOHN (1718–1791)

Scotland; Pennsylvania. Presbyterian clergyman.

———— Register of marriages and baptisms performed by Rev. John Cuthbertson, covenanter minister, 1751–1791, with index to locations and persons visited, by S. Helen Fields. Washington, D.C. [Lancaster, Pa., Lancaster Press] 1934. xv, 301 p. facsims.   CS68.C7

Largely quotations from Cuthbertson's diary arranged chronologically and geographically by the states that he visited, from Massachusetts to Maryland.

AIKEN, A. S., *and* J. M. ADAIR. A biographical sketch of the Rev. John Cuthbertson, the first Reformed Presbyterian minister in America, from 1751 to 1791. Prepared and published, under the appointment of the United Presbyterian presbytery of Big Spring. Pittsburgh, Stevenson, Foster, 1878. 36 p.
BX9225.C79A6

FISK, WILLIAM L. The diary of John Cuthbertson, missionary to the covenanters of colonial Pennsylvania. Pennsylvania magazine of history and biography, v. 73, Oct. 1949: 441–458.   F146.P65, v. 73

An assessment of Cuthbertson's life in America based upon the diary that he kept from the day of his arrival in 1751 until his death. The diary is in the possession of the Pittsburgh-Xenia Theological Seminary.

13156

CUTLER, MANASSEH (1742–1823)*

Connecticut; Massachusetts. Congregational clergyman, Revolutionary chaplain, botanist, colonizer.

———— New Jersey, Pennsylvania and Ohio, 1787–8. Passages from the journals of Rev. Manasseh Cutler, L.L.D. *In* New Jersey Historical Society. Proceedings, 2d ser., v. 3, no. 2, 1873: 73–96.   F131.N58, 2d s., v. 3

Introduction and notes by Joseph F. Tuttle.

———— New York and Philadelphia in 1787: extracts from the journals of Manasseh Cutler. Pennsylvania magazine of history and biography, v. 12, Apr. 1888: 97–115.   F146.P65, v. 12

BROWN, ROBERT ELLIOTT. Manasseh Cutler and the settlement of Ohio, 1788. Marietta, Ohio, Marietta College Press, 1938. 19 p.   F483.B86

CUTLER, WILLIAM P., *and* JULIA P. CUTLER. Life, journals and correspondence of Rev. Manasseh Cutler, LL.D. Cincinnati, R. Clarke, 1888. 2 v. plates, ports.
F483.C93

"The Scioto purchase [by E. C. Dawes]": v. 1, p. 494–524.
"The Ordinance of 1787, and its history, by Peter Force": v. 2, p. 407–427.

In an article entitled "Manasseh Cutler's Writings: A Note on Editorial Practice" in the *Mississippi Valley Historical Review*, v. 47, June 1960, p. 88–101, Lee N. Newcomer disparages the editorial liberties taken by Cutler's grandchildren who published his *Life, Journals, and Correspondence* with the intention of glamorizing Cutler's role in opening Ohio to settlement and framing the Ordinance of 1787.

PULSIFER, JANICE G. The Cutlers of Hamilton. *In* Essex Institute, *Salem, Mass.* Historical collections, v. 107, Oct. 1971: 335–408. port.   F72.E7E81, v. 107

13157

DABNEY, CHARLES (1745–1829)

Virginia. Planter, Revolutionary officer.

DABNEY, CHARLES W. Colonel Charles Dabney of the Revolution; his services as citizen and soldier. Virginia magazine of history and biography, v. 51, Apr. 1943: 186–199. F221.V91, v. 51

13158

DAGWORTHY, JOHN (1721–1784)
New Jersey; Delaware. Military officer.

MARSHALL, GEORGE W. Memoir of Brigadier-General John Dagworthy of the Revolutionary War. Wilmington, Historical Society of Delaware, 1895. 26 p. (Historical Society of Delaware. Papers, 10) F161.D35, no. 10

13159

DALRYMPLE, ALEXANDER (1737–1808)†
Scotland; England. Hydrographer.

FRY, HOWARD T. Alexander Dalrymple (1737–1808) and the expansion of British trade. With a foreword by R. A. Skelton. [Toronto] Published for the Royal Commonwealth Society, by University of Toronto Press, 1970. xxvii, 330 p. geneal. table, maps, port. (Imperial studies, no. 29) HF3504.5.D35F76

Bibliography: p. 281–318.

JACK-HINTON, COLIN. Alexander Dalrymple and the rediscovery of the islands of Solomon. Mariner's mirror, v. 50, May 1964: 93–114. VK1.M4, v. 50

SPRAY, W. A. Alexander Dalrymple, hydrographer. American Neptune, v. 30, July 1970: 200–216. V1.A4, v. 30

13160

DALTON, TRISTRAM (1738–1817)
Massachusetts. Merchant, assemblyman.

STONE, EBEN F. A sketch of Tristram Dalton. *In* Essex Institute, *Salem, Mass.* Historical collections, v. 25, Jan./Mar. 1888: 1–29. F72.E7E81, v. 25

13161

DAL VERME, FRANCESCO, *conte di Bobbio* (1758–1832)
Italy. Traveler.

———— Seeing American and its great men; the journal and letters of Count Francesco dal Verme, 1783–1784. Translated and edited by Elizabeth Cometti. Charlottesville, University Press of Virginia [1969] xxxiii, 147 p. illus., maps, port. E163.D313 1969

Bibliographic references included in "Notes" (p. [95]–136).

A record of travels that ranged from New Brunswick to the West Indies.

13162

DAMBOURGÉS, FRANÇOIS (1742–1798)
Quebec. Merchant, British officer in America.

[BOIS, LOUIS EDOUARD] Étude historique. Le colonel Dambourgés. 3. éd. Québec, Impr. A. Côté, 1877. 182 p. F1053.D153

First edition published in 1866.

13163

DANA, FRANCIS (1743–1811)*
Massachusetts. Lawyer, councilor, delegate to the Continental Congress, diplomat, judge, delegate to the Constitutional Convention.

CRESSON, WILLIAM P. Francis Dana, a Puritan diplomat at the court of Catherine the Great. New York, L. MacVeagh, Dial Press [ᶜ1930] xv, 397 p. facsims. (part fold.), ports. E302.6.D16C92

Bibliography: p. 387–390.

———— Francis Dana, an early envoy of trade. New England quarterly, v. 3, Oct. 1930: 717–735. F1.N62, v. 3

DANA, HENRY W. L. The Dana saga. *In* Cambridge Historical Society, *Cambridge, Mass.* Publications. v. 26. Proceedings. 1940. Cambridge, 1941. p. 63–123. illus., map. F74.C1C469, v. 26

An offprint, with expanded title and added illustrations, was published in Cambridge, Mass. (1941. 61 p. CS71.D17 1941).

DANA, RICHARD H. Francis Dana. *In* Cambridge Historical Society, *Cambridge, Mass.* Publications. v. 3. Proceedings. 1908. Cambridge. p. 56–78. F74.C1C469, v. 3

Includes excerpts from Dana's correspondence from Paris in the spring of 1780.

13164

DANA, JAMES (1735–1817)
Connecticut. Revolutionary officer.

DANA, ELIZABETH E. Lieutenant James Dana at the Battle of Bunker Hill. *In* Cambridge Historical Society, *Cambridge, Mass.* Publications. v. 5. Proceedings. 1910. Cambridge, 1911. p. 21–32. F74.C1C469, v. 5

13165

DANA, SAMUEL (1740–1798)
Massachusetts; New Hampshire. Clergyman, lawyer.

ATHERTON, CHARLES H. Memoir of the life of the Hon. Samuel Dana. *In* New Hampshire Historical Society. Collections. v. 3. Concord, 1832. p. 9–23. F31.N54, v. 3

13166

DANE, NATHAN (1752–1835)*
Massachusetts. Lawyer, assemblyman, delegate to the Continental Congress.

———— [Letter of Nathan Dane concerning the Ordinance of 1787. Indianapolis? Indiana Historical Society, 1831] 7 p.   E309.D17 Rare Bk. Coll.

No title. At head of p. [1]: Published by order of the Indiana Historical Society.

Reprinted, together with Patrick Henry's secret letter of instruction to George Rogers Clark, as part of Indiana Historical Society *Publications*, v. 1, no. 2 (Indianapolis, Bowen-Merrill Co., 1897. F521.I41, v. 1), p. 67–76.

Dane's letter, dated Beverly, May 12, 1831, is in response to a letter from the corresponding secretary of the Indiana Historical Society asking for an account of the drafting of the Ordinance of 1787.

JOHNSON, ANDREW J.   The life and constitutional thought of Nathan Dane. 1964. ([204] p.)
                            Micro AC–1, no. 64–12,043

Thesis (Ph.D.)—Indiana University.
Abstracted in *Dissertation Abstracts*, v. 25, Mar. 1965, p. 5238–5239.

13167

DANIEL, WALKER (*ca.* 1760–1784)
    Virginia; Kentucky. Assemblyman, lawyer, merchant.

FACKLER, CALVIN M.   Walker Daniel, the founder of Danville, one of Kentucky's almost forgotten pioneers. Filson Club history quarterly, v. 13, July 1939: 134–146.   F446.F484, v. 13

13168

DARRAGH, LYDIA BARRINGTON (1728?–1789)
    Ireland; Pennsylvania. Nurse.

DARRACH, HENRY.   Lydia Darragh, one of the heroines of the Revolution. Philadelphia, The Society, 1916. [379]–403 p. illus. (City History Society of Philadelphia. Publication, no. 13)   F158.1.C58, no. 13

A critical examination of the claim that information was furnished to Washington by Lydia Darragh at Whitemarsh, Pa., in December 1777, regarding an impending attack by the British.

13169

DARTMOUTH, WILLIAM LEGGE, *2d Earl of* (1731–1801)†
    England.   President of Board of Trade, secretary of state.

BARGAR, BRADLEY D.   Lord Dartmouth and the American Revolution. Columbia, University of South Carolina Press, 1965. ix, 219 p. ports.   E210.B25
    Bibliography: p. 199–207.
    The author's thesis (Ph.D.), *The Administration of Lord Dartmouth in the American Department, 1772–1775*, was submitted to the University of Toronto in 1952.
    Traces Dartmouth's activities from his presidency of the Board of Trade (1765–66) through his tenure as secretary of state for the colonies (1772–75) and lord privy seal during the

Revolution. Though he was well liked, well connected, and well intentioned, his impact was limited. Bargar concludes that Dartmouth's firm adherence to the doctrine of parliamentary supremacy prevented a successful conclusion to his negotiations with Franklin and others during the winter of 1774–75.

Gt. Brit. *Historical Manuscripts Commission*.   The manuscripts of the earl of Dartmouth. London, Printed for H.M. Stationery Off., by Eyre and Spottiswoode, 1887–96. 3 v. (*Its* Report. 11th, appendix, pt. 5; 14th, appendix, pt. 10; 15th, appendix, pt. 1)
                                            DA25.M2D3

Parliament. Papers by command. C. 5060–IV, 7883, 8156.
    Vol. 1 prepared by W. O. Hewlett; v. 2, American papers, by B. F. Stevens; v. 3, by W. Page.
    Reprinted, with a new introduction and preface by George A. Billias, in Boston by Gregg Press (1972. DA506.D33G7)
    A supplementary report was issued in its 13th *Report*, appendix, pt. 4, p. 495–506.

DASHWOOD, *Sir* FRANCIS
    See LE DESPENCER, FRANCIS DASHWOOD, *Baron*.

13170

DAVENPORT, FRANKLIN (1755–1832)
    Pennsylvania; New Jersey. Lawyer, Revolutionary officer.

EDES, HENRY H.   Sketch of General Franklin Davenport, 1755–1832. *In* Colonial Society of Massachusetts, *Boston*. Publications. v. 10. Transactions, 1904/6. Boston, 1907. p. 358–365. ports.   F61.C71, v. 10

STEWART, FRANK H.   Gloucester County's most famous citizen, General Franklin Davenport, 1755–1832. Woodbury, N.J., Gloucester County Democrat Print, 1921. 7 p. port.   E207.D23S8

13171

DAVES, JOHN (1748–1804)
    North Carolina. Revolutionary officer, planter.

DAVES, GRAHAM.   A sketch of the military career of Captain John Daves of the North Carolina Continental Line of the army of the Revolution. Baltimore, Press of the Friedenwald Co., 1892. 16 p. port.
                                            E263.N8D23

13172

DAVID, EBENEZER (*ca.* 1752–1778)
    Rhode Island. Revolutionary chaplain.

———— A Rhode Island chaplain in the Revolution; letters of Ebenezer David to Nicholas Brown, 1775–1778. Edited by Jeannette D. Black and William Greene Roelker. Providence, Rhode Island Society of the Cincinnati, 1949. xxxi, 82 p. illus., fold. map.   E275.D25

Includes bibliographic references.
Reprinted in Port Washington, N.Y., by Kennikat Press (1970).

13173

DAVIDSON, JOHN (1735–1832)

Pennsylvania; North Carolina. Blacksmith, landowner, assemblyman, Revolutionary officer.

DAVIDSON, CHALMERS G. Major John Davidson of "Rural Hill," Mecklenburg County, N.C., pioneer, industrialist, planter. Charlotte, N.C., Lassiter Press, 1943. x, 93 p. illus., facsim., plates, port. F258.D25

"Sources": p. 74. Bibliography: p. 87–91.

13174

DAVIDSON, WILLIAM (1740–1790) Originally John Godsman.

Scotland; Canada. Merchant, developer of natural resources.

—— An account of the life of William Davidson, otherwise John Godsman, of Banffshire and Aberdeenshire in Scotland and Miramichi in British North America. Saint John, N.B., 1947. 60 p. geneal. table, maps, plates. (Publications of the New Brunswick Museum. Historical studies, no. 6) F1043.D3

13175

DAVIDSON, WILLIAM LEE (1746–1781)*

North Carolina. Revolutionary general.

DAVIDSON, CHALMERS G. Piedmont partisan; the life and times of Brigadier-General William Lee Davidson. [2d ed.] Davidson, N.C., Davidson College [1968] 190 p. E207.D3D3 1968

Bibliography: p. 176–183.
First edition published in 1951.

GRAHAM, WILLIAM A. General William Lee Davidson. North Carolina booklet, v. 13, July 1913: 11–39. F251.N86, v. 13

13176

DAVIE, WILLIAM RICHARDSON (1756–1820)*

England; North Carolina. Revolutionary officer, lawyer, delegate to the Constitutional Convention.

—— William Richardson Davie: a memoir, by J. G. de Roulhac Hamilton, followed by his letters, with notes by Kemp P. Battle. Chapel Hill [N.C.] The University, 1907. 75 p. (James Sprunt historical monograph no. 7) F251.J28, v. 7 E302.6.D2D2

Memoir: p. 4–23.

CLARK, WALTER. General William Richardson Davie, 1756–1820. Magazine of American history, with notes and queries, v. 28, Dec. 1892: 415–430. E171.M18, v. 28

ROBINSON, BLACKWELL P. William R. Davie. Chapel Hill, University of North Carolina Press [1957] xiii, 495 p. illus., plates, ports. E302.6.D2R6

Bibliography: p. 456–476.

WAGSTAFF, HENRY M. William Richardson Davie and federalism. In North Carolina. State Literary and Historical Association. Proceedings and addresses. 1920/21. Raleigh, 1922. p. [46]–57. F251.N95, 1920/21

13177

DAVIES, PRICE (d. 1793)

England; Virginia. Clergyman.

—— Price Davies, rector of Blisland Parish: two letters, 1763, 1765. Edited by Sir David Evans. Virginia magazine of history and biography, v. 79, Apr. 1971: 153–161. F221.V91, v. 79

Further notes on Davies, by John Melville Jennings, appear on pages 162–166.

13178

DAVIES, THOMAS (1737–1812)

England. Artist, British officer in America.

HUBBARD, ROBERT H. Thomas Davies, gunner and artist. In Royal Society of Canada. Transactions. 4th ser., v. 9; 1971. Ottawa, 1972. p. 327–349. plates. AS42.R6, 4th s., v. 9

Includes 12 of Davies' landscapes or topographical sketches of various Canadian scenes.

13179

DAVIS, CALEB (1738–1797)

Massachusetts. Assemblyman, merchant.

SHATTUCK, FREDERICK C. Caleb Davis and his funeral dinner. In Massachusetts Historical Society, Boston. Proceedings. v. 54; 1920/21. Boston, 1922. p. 215–224. port. F61.M38, v. 54

13180

DAVIS, CATHERINE WENDELL (1742–1805)

Massachusetts.

WENDELL, BARRETT. A gentlewoman of Boston, 1742–1805. In American Antiquarian Society, Worcester, Mass. Proceedings, new ser., v. 29, Oct. 1919: 242–293. E172.A35, n.s., v. 29

13181

DAVIS, JAMES (1721–1785)

North Carolina. Printer.

ELLIOTT, ROBERT N. James Davis and the beginning of the newspaper in North Carolina [1749–65] North Carolina historical review, v. 42, winter 1965: 1–20. facsim. F251.N892, v. 42

WEEKS, STEPHEN B. The pre-Revolutionary printers of North Carolina: Davis, Steuart, and Boyd. North Carolina booklet, v. 15, Oct. 1915: 104–121.
F251.N86, v. 15

13182
DAVIS, JOHN (1745–1816)
Pennsylvania. Physician, Revolutionary surgeon.

MORGAN, MORDECAI. Biographical memoir of Dr. John Davis, late of Chester County, Pennsylvania. Philadelphia, 1828. 15 p. R154.D29M6 Rare Bk. Coll.

13183
DAVIS, JOSHUA (b. 1760)
Seaman.

—— A narrative of Joshua Davis, an American citizen, who was pressed and served on board six ships of the British Navy . . . The whole being an interesting and faithful narrative of the discipline, various practices, and treatment of pressed seamen in the British navy, and containing information that never was before presented to the American people. Boston, Printed by B. True, no. 78, State Street, 1811. 72 p.
E271.D25 Rare Bk. Coll.

13184
DAVIS, SAMUEL (1765–1829)
Massachusetts.

—— Journal of a tour to Connecticut.—Autumn of 1789. *In* Massachusetts Historical Society, *Boston.* Proceedings. v. 11, 1869/70. Boston, 1871. p. 9–32.
F61.M38, v. 11

—— —— Detached copy. F69.D26

13185
DAY, JEREMIAH (1737–1806)
Connecticut. Farmer, philosopher, Congregational clergyman, missionary.

—— A missionary tour to Vermont, 1788; from the manuscript journal of the Reverend Jeremiah Day. *In* Vermont Historical Society. Proceedings, new ser., v. 1, no. 4, 1930: 169–176. F46.V55, n.s., v. 1
Introduction and notes by Clive Day.

13186
DAY, THOMAS (1748–1789)†
England. Writer, reformer.

GIGNILLIAT, GEORGE W. The author of Sandford and Merton; a life of Thomas Day, Esq. New York, Columbia University Press, 1932. 361 p. (Columbia University studies in English and comparative literature)
PR3398.D3G5 1932a
Issued also as thesis (Ph.D.)—Columbia University. Bibliography: p. [351]–356.

13187
DAYTON, ELIAS (1737–1807)*
New Jersey. Revolutionary general.

CORIELL, *Mrs.* ABNER S. Major-General Elias Dayton, 1737–1807. *In* Union County Historical Society, *Elizabeth, N.J.* Proceedings. v. 2; 1923/34. [Elizabeth?] 1934. p. 204–211. F142.U5U5, v. 2

13188
DEAN, STEWART (1748–1836)
Maryland; New York. Revolutionary privateersman, importer.

WILGUS, WILLIAM J. Life of Captain Stewart Dean, a character of the American Revolution. Ascutney, Vt., 1942. 80 (i.e. 92) l. geneal. tables (part fold.), plates, ports. E207.D4W5
Bibliography: leaves 52–58.

13189
DEANE, SILAS (1737–1789)*
Connecticut; France. Lawyer, merchant, assemblyman, delegate to the Continental Congress, diplomat.

—— Correspondence of Silas Deane, delegate to the first and second Congress at Philadelphia, 1774–1776. *In* Connecticut Historical Society. Collections. v. 2. Hartford, 1870. p. [127]–368. F91.C7, v. 2
Includes numerous letters addressed to Deane.

—— The Deane papers; correspondence between Silas Deane, his brothers and their business and political associates, 1771–1795. Hartford, Connecticut Historical Society, 1930. xiv, 277 p. (Connecticut Historical Society. Collections, v. 23) F91.C7, v. 23
Includes the correspondence of Barnabas and Simeon Deane.

—— The Deane papers. 1774–[1790. New York, Printed for the Society, 1887–90] 5 v. port. (New York Historical Society. Collections, 1886–90. Publication fund series, [v. 19–23]) F116.N63, 1886–90
Edited by Charles Isham.
Contents: v. 1. Biographical notice of S. Deane, by Charles Isham. The Deane papers. 1774–1777.—v. 2. 1777–1778.—v. 3. 1778–1779.—v. 4. 1779–1781.—v. 5. 1782–1790. Notices of Deane's death. Appendix of additional papers 1774–1780. Indexes.

ABERNETHY, THOMAS P. Commercial activities of Silas Deane in France. American historical review, v. 39, Apr. 1934: 477–485. E171.A57, v. 39

BOYD, JULIAN P. Silas Deane: death by a kindly teacher of treason? William and Mary quarterly, 3d ser., v. 16, Apr.–Oct. 1959: 165–187, 319–342, 515–550.
F221.W71, 3d s., v. 16
On the "partnership in deceit" between Deane and Edward Bancroft.

CLARK, GEORGE L. Silas Deane, a Connecticut leader in the American Revolution. New York, G. P. Putnam's Sons, 1913. xiii, 287 p. facsim., port. E302.6.D25C5
"Authorities consulted": p. vi–vii.

HAYDEN, RALSTON. The apostasy of Silas Deane. Magazine of history, with notes and queries, v. 16, Mar. 1913: 95–103. E171.M23, v. 16

[INGRAHAM, EDWARD D.] ed. Papers in relation to the case of Silas Deane. Now first published from the original manuscripts. Philadelphia, Printed for the Seventy-Six Society, 1855. 201 p. [Seventy-Six Society, Philadelphia. Publications, no. 1] E203.S49
Contents: Mr. Deane's narrative.—Mr. Deane's memorial [to Congress, dated Aug. 16, 1779]—Proposed report on Mr. Deane's memorial.—Amendment to a motion respecting Mr. Deane.—Charges against Mr. Silas Deane, Mr. Franklin, and Mr. Adams.—Proceedings of Congress with reference to the detention of Mr. Deane, and the recall of Mr. Lee.—Appendix of documents referred to in support of the narrative.—Examination of Mr. Carmichael before Congress [Sept.–Oct. 1778]—Mr. Lee's narrative [dated Paris, Feb. 10, 1779]—Appendix of documents referred to in support of Mr. Lee's letter.

ISHAM, CHARLES. A short account of the life and times of Silas Deane. In American Historical Association. Papers. v. 3, no. 1; 1887. New York, 1888. p. 40–47. E172.A65, v. 3

JAMES, COY H. The Revolutionary career of Silas Deane. 1956. ([295] p.) Micro AC–1, no. 21,065
Thesis (Ph.D.)—Michigan State University.
Abstracted in Dissertation Abstracts, v. 17, no. 7, 1957, p. 1537.

KITE, ELIZABETH S. Silas Deane: diplomatist and patriot scapegoat of the Revolution. Daughters of the American Revolution magazine, v. 60, Sept. 1926: 537–546. facsims., ports. E202.5.A12, v. 60

STILLÉ, CHARLES J. Silas Deane, diplomatist of the Revolution. Pennsylvania magazine of history and biography, v. 18, Oct. 1894: 273–292. F146.P65, v. 18
——— ——— Offprint. [Philadelphia, 1894] 20 p. CT99.D284S8

13190

DEARBORN, HENRY (1751–1829)*
New Hampshire. Physician, Revolutionary officer.

——— Revolutionary war journals of Henry Dearborn, 1775–1783. Edited from the original manuscripts by Lloyd A. Brown and Howard H. Peckham, with a biographical essay by Hermon Dunlap Smith. Chicago, Caxton Club, 1939. xvi, 264 p. facsims. (part fold.), fold. maps, port. E275.D283
"Works consulted": p. [237]–245.
Reprinted in Freeport, N.Y., by Books for Libraries Press (1969) and in New York by Da Capo Press (1971).

Extracts from the journals were published in the Proceedings of the Massachusetts Historical Society for 1886 (Boston, 1888), p. 102–133.

ERNEY, RICHARD A. The public life of Henry Dearborn. 1957. ([397] p.) Micro AC–1, no. 21,604
Thesis (Ph.D.)—Columbia University.
Abstracted in Dissertation Abstracts, v. 17, no. 7, 1957, p. 1448–1449.

13191

DE BERDT, DENNYS (1694?–1770)*
England. Merchant, colonial agent.

——— Letters of Dennys De Berdt, 1757–1770. In Colonial Society of Massachusetts, Boston. Publications. v. 13. Transactions, 1910/11. Boston, 1911. p. 293–461. plate, port. F61.C71, v. 13
Introduction and notes by Albert Matthews.
——— ———Offprint. Cambridge [Mass.] J. Wilson, 1911. [293]–461 p. plate, port. E263.M4D28
Reprinted in Freeport, N.Y., by Books for Libraries Press (1971).

13192

DE BLOIS, STEPHEN (1735–1805)
England; Rhode Island. Merchant, Loyalist.

FOX, FRANK B. Stephen De Blois of Newport. In his Two Huguenot families: De Blois, Lucas. Cambridge, Mass., Priv. print., University Press, 1949 [i.e. 1950] p. 72–92. port. CS71.D287 1950

13193

DE BRAHM, JOHN GERAR WILLIAM (1717–ca. 1799)*
Germany; East Florida; Pennsylvania. Engineer, scientist, mapmaker.

BROWN, RALPH H. The De Brahm charts of the Atlantic Ocean, 1772–1776. Geographical review, v. 28, Jan. 1938: 124–132. maps. G1.G35, v. 28

MORRISON, ALFRED J. John G. De Brahm. South Atlantic quarterly, v. 21, July 1922: 252–258. AP2.S75, v. 21

MOWAT, CHARLES L. That "odd being," De Brahm. Florida historical quarterly, v. 20, Apr. 1942: 323–345. F306.F65, v. 20

DE VORSEY, LOUIS. William Gerard De Brahm: eccentric genius of southeastern geography. Southeastern geographer, v. 10, Apr. 1970: 21–29. facsim. G1.S62, v. 10

13194

DE KRAFFT, JOHN CHARLES PHILIP (1752–1804)
Germany; New York. Hessian officer in America.

———— Journal of Lt. John Charles Philip von Krafft, 1776–1784. *In* New York Historical Society. Collections. 1882. Publication fund series, [v. 15] New York, 1883. p. [1]–202. plans (part fold.) F116.N63, 1882

Reprinted in New York by the New York Times (1968. 202 p. E268.K7 1968).

Edited by Thomas H. Edsall, and translated with the assistance of William F. Goldbeck.

The author, after attempting to obtain an appointment in the American army, entered the British army, serving in two Hessian regiments from 1778 to 1783.

13195

DELANOY, ABRAHAM (1742–1795)

New York; Connecticut. Portrait artist.

SAWITZKY, SUSAN. Abraham Delanoy in New Haven. *In* New York Historical Society. Quarterly, v. 41, Apr. 1957: 193–206. ports. F116.N638, v. 41

13196

DEMING, SARAH WINSLOW (1722–1788)

Massachusetts.

———— Journal of Sarah Winslow Deming, 1775. American monthly magazine, v. 4, Jan. 1894: 45–59. E202.5.A12, v. 4

On her flight from Boston to Providence following the events of April 19th.

13197

DEMPSTER, GEORGE (1732–1818)†

Scotland; England. Lawyer, Member of Parliament.

———— Letters of George Dempster to Sir Adam Fergusson, 1756–1813, with some account of his life. Edited by James Fergusson. London, Macmillan, 1934. xxviii, 364 p. geneal. tables, plates, ports. (Studies in modern history) DA506.D35A4

13198

DENNING, WILLIAM (1737–1830)*

Pennsylvania. Maker of cannon.

EGLE, WILLIAM H. The private soldier of the army of the declaration. An address delivered at the unveiling of the monument erected by the state of Pennsylvania to William Denning, the soldier backsmith of the Revolution. Harrisburg, Pa., Harrisburg Pub. Co., 1890. 13 p. front. (*His* Contributions to Pennsylvania history, [pt. 3]) E263.P4D4
F157.W9E49

STROHM, J. W. The life and history of William Denning, who cast the first wrought-iron cannon for the American army at the outbreak of the Revolutionary War. [Newville, Pa., Times Steam Print] 1890. 37 p. illus. E275.D41

13199

DENNY, EBENEZER (1761–1822)

Pennsylvania. Revolutionary officer.

———— Military journal of Major Ebenezer Denny, an officer in the Revolutionary and Indian wars. With an introductory memoir [by W. H. Denny] Philadelphia, Historical Society of Pennsylvania, 1859. 288 p. plans, ports. E83.79.D4

The journal extends from May 1, 1781, to May 31, 1795.

Also published in *Memoirs* of the Historical Society of Pennsylvania, v. 7 (Philadelphia, 1860).

A selection of letters written by General Josiah Harmar, January 19, 1784—December 27, 1796: p. 209–269.

"Vocabulary of words in use with the Delaware and Shawanee Indians": p. 274–281.

Reprinted in New York by the New York Times (1971).

13200

DE PEYSTER, ARENT SCHUYLER (1736–1822)

New York; Michigan; Canada. British officer, Indian negotiator.

———— Miscellanies, by an officer (Colonel Arent Schuyler De Peyster, B.A.), 1774–1813. Part I. With an appendix, explanatory notes, &c., &c., &c. Original letters of Col. De Peyster, Brig. Gen. Sir John Johnson, Bart., Col. Guy Johnson, and others from 1776 to 1813, never before published. Also discovery of the De Peyster Islands in the Pacific Ocean. Part II. Biographical sketches and historical memoirs, especially public and military, of the De Peyster, Watts, and affiliated families, since their settlement in the present United States, by J. Watts De Peyster. New York, A. E. Chasmer, 1888. 2 v. in 1. illus., maps (part fold.), plates (part col.), ports. F567.D41

Pt. 2 has imprint: New York, C. H. Ludwig.

Reprint, with extensive additions by the editor, of a volume of poems by A. S. De Peyster, first published in Dumfries, Scotland, in 1813. Several of the poems relate to the author's experiences as commandant of the British post at Mackinac Island, Mich.

13201

DERBY, ELIAS HASKET (1739–1799)*

Massachusetts. Merchant, shipowner.

McKEY, RICHARD H. Elias Hasket Derby and the American Revolution. *In* Essex Institute, *Salem, Mass.* Historical collections, v. 97, July 1961: 166–196. F72.E7E81, v. 97

———— Elias Hasket Derby and the founding of the eastern trade. *In* Essex Institute, *Salem, Mass.* Historical collections, v. 98, Jan.–Apr. 1962: 1–25, 65–83. F72.E7E81, v. 98

———— Elias Hasket Derby, merchant of Salem, Massachusetts, 1739–1799. 1961. ([524] p.) Micro AC–1, no. 61–5003

Thesis (Ph.D.)—Clark University.
Abstracted in *Dissertation Abstracts*, v. 22, Feb. 1962, p. 2776–2777.

PEABODY, ROBERT E.   Merchant venturers of old Salem; a history of the commercial voyages of a New England family to the Indies and elsewhere in the XVIII century. Boston, Houghton Mifflin Co., 1912. 168 p. plates, ports.   HF3163.S33P4

13202

DERBY, RICHARD (1712–1783)*
Massachusetts. Shipmaster, merchant.

PHILLIPS, JAMES D.   The life and times of Richard Derby, merchant of Salem, 1712 to 1783. Cambridge, Riverside Press, 1929. 116 p. plates, ports.   F74.S1D36
"Derby wills and land titles": p. [51]–116.
"Works consulted": p. 48–50.
First published in the *Historical Collections* of the Essex Institute, Salem, Massachusetts, v. 65, July–Oct. 1929, p. 243–292, 451–482; v. 66, Jan. 1930, p. 65–96.

13203

DESANDROÜINS, JEAN NICOLAS (1729–1792)
France. French officer in America.

GABRIEL, CHARLES N.   Le maréchal de camp Desandrouins, 1729–1792; guerre du Canada 1756–1760; guerre de l'indépendance américaine 1780–1782. Verdun, Impr. Renvé-Lallemant, 1887. viii, 416 p.   E199.G12

13204

DES BARRES, JOSEPH FREDERICK WALLET (1721–1824)†
England; Canada. Military officer, engineer, surveyor, chartmaker.

———— Utility of Nova Scotia. *In* Morse, William I., *ed.* Acadiensia nova (1598–1779) . . . New and unpublished documents and other data relating to Acadia (Nova Scotia, New Brunswick, Maine, etc.). v. 2. London, B. Quaritch, 1935. p. 105–117. facsim.
F1038.M87, v. 2 Rare Bk. Coll.
His proposal of October 1779 to Richard Cumberland, secretary to the Board of Trade.

EVANS, GERAINT N. D.   Uncommon obdurate; the several public careers of J. F. W. DesBarres. Salem, Mass., Peabody Museum, 1969. ix, 130 p. illus., map, ports.   F1032.D47E86
"Bibliographic essay": p. 101–123.
The author's thesis (Ph.D.), *North American Soldier, Hydrographer, Governor: The Public Careers of J. F. W. DesBarres, 1721–1824*, was submitted to Yale University in 1965 (Micro AC-1, no. 65–12,966).

WEBSTER, JOHN C.   Joseph Frederick Wallet Des Barres and the *Atlantic Neptune*. *In* Royal Society of Canada.

Proceedings and transactions. 3d ser., v. 21, section 2; 1927. Ottawa. p. 21–40.   AS42.R6, 3d s., v. 21

———— The life of Joseph Frederick Wallet Des Barres. Shediac, N.B., Priv. print., 1933. 70 p. plates, col. ports.   F1032.D47

13205

DE SEQUEYRA, JOHN (1712–1795)
England; Virginia. Physician.

SHOSTECK, ROBERT.   Notes on an early Virginia physician. American Jewish archives, v. 23, Nov. 1971: 198–212. plate, port.   E184.J5A37, v. 23

13206

DESHLER, DAVID (1734?–1796)
Pennsylvania. Merchant, Revolutionary provisioner.

KOHL, HELEN W., *and* JOHN Y. KOHL.   Colonel David Deshler, Allentown's first citizen. *In* Lehigh County Historical Society, *Allentown, Pa.* Proceedings, v. 15; 1946. Allentown, p. 9–46. ports.   F157.L5L52, v. 15

13207

DESTOUCHES, CHARLES RENÉ DOMINIQUE GOCHET (1727–1793)
French naval officer in America.

American Art Association, *New York*.   The Destouches papers relative to the American Revolution, comprising letters and documents signed by Destouches, Lafayette, Rochambeau, De Grasse, and seventeen letters signed by La Pérouse and others. New York, [1926] [33] p.   Z999.A48
"Unrestricted public sale . . . December 1, 1926."
Summarizes or gives brief excerpts from 116 letters originally in Destouches' possession.

13208

DEUX-PONTS, GUILLAUME, *comte* DE (1754-1807)
France. French officer in America.

———— My campaigns in America: a journal kept by Count William de Deux-Ponts, 1780–81. Translated from the French manuscript, with an introduction and notes, by Samuel Abbott Green. Boston, J. K. Wiggin & W. P. Lunt, xvi, 176 p.   [E265.D48]
Micro 01291, reel 195, no. 7E
French text followed by English translation.

13209

DEWEES, MARY COBURN (*fl.* 1787/88)

———— Mrs. Mary Dewees's journal from Philadelphia to Kentucky, 1787–1788. Pennsylvania magazine of history and biography, v. 28, Apr. 1904: 182–198.   F146.P65, v. 28

Contributed by Samuel P. Cochran. Two later editions were also published. The *Journal of a Trip From Philadelphia to Lexington in Kentucky, Kept by Mary Coburn Dewees in 1787* (Crawfordville, Ind., R. E. Banta, 1936. 16, iii p. E164.D45 Rare Bk. Coll.) and "Mrs. Mary Dewees's Journal From Philadelphia to Kentucky," in the *Register* of the Kentucky Historical Society, v. 63, July 1965, p. 195–217, contain explanatory notes by R. E. Banta and John L. Blair, respectively.

13210
DEWEES, SAMUEL (*b.* 1760)
Pennsylvania. Revolutionary soldier.

HANNA, JOHN S. A history of the life and services of Captain Samuel Dewees, a native of Pennsylvania, and soldier of the Revolutionary and last wars. Also reminiscences of the Revolutionary struggle . . . and late war with Great Britain. In all of which he was patriotically engaged. The whole written (in part from manuscript in the hand writing of Captain Dewees) and compiled by John Smith Hanna. Baltimore, Printed by R. Neilson, 1844. 360 p. illus., port.   E275.D51

13211
DE WITT, CHARLES (1727–1787)
New York. Miller, assemblyman, Revolutionary officer, delegate to the Continental Congress.

——— Letters of Charles De Witt [1751–86] Olde Ulster, v. 4, June–July, Oct.–Dec. 1908: 184–185, 215–217, 306–309, 334–339, 366–372; v. 5, Jan.–Sept. 1909: 12–15, 48–50, 80–85, 110–119, 146–154, 188–190, 213–216, 239–243, 270–274.   F127.U4O4, v. 4–5

[BRINK, BENJAMIN M.] In memoriam—Colonel Charles De Witt. Olde Ulster, v. 5, July 1909: 193–206. plate.   F127.U4O4, v. 5

13212
DE WITT, SIMEON (1756–1834)*
New York. Surveyor, Revolutionary mapmaker.

RISTOW, WALTER W. Simeon De Witt, pioneer American cartographer. Surveying and mapping, v. 30, June 1970: 239–255. facsim., maps, port.   TA501.A6436, v. 30

13213
DEXTER, SAMUEL (1726–1810)*
Massachusetts. Merchant, assemblyman, councilor.

BOWEN, CLARENCE W. Samuel Dexter, councilor, and his son, Hon. Samuel Dexter, secretary of war, and secretary of the treasury. *In* American Antiquarian Society, *Worcester, Mass.* Proceedings, new ser., v. 35, Apr. 1925: 23–27.   E172.A35, n.s., v. 35

An offprint, entitled *Samuel Dexter of Woodstock, Connecticut*, was published in Worcester by the Society in 1926 (7 p. F104.W9D3).

STAPLES, CARLTON A. Samuel Dexter. Dedham historical register, v. 3, Apr. 1892: 45–60. plates, port.   F74.D3D8, v. 3

——— ——— Offprint. Dedham [Mass.] 1892. 18 p. plates, port.   E302.6.D45S7

13214
DEXTER, SAMUEL (1761–1816)*
Massachusetts. Lawyer. Son of Samuel Dexter (1726–1810).

[SARGENT, LUCIUS M.] Reminiscences of Samuel Dexter. Originally written for the Boston Evening Transcript. By Sigma [pseud.] Boston, H. W. Dutton, 1857. 96 p.   E302.6.D52S2

13215
DEXTER, TIMOTHY (1747–1806)*
Massachusetts. Merchant, speculator.

KNAPP, SAMUEL L. Life of Timothy Dexter; embracing sketches of the eccentric characters that composed his associates. Boston, G. N. Thomson, 1838. 108 p. illus.   F74.N55D48 Rare Bk. Coll.

MARQUAND, JOHN P. Lord Timothy Dexter of Newburyport, Mass^tts, first in the East, first in the West, and the greatest philosopher in the Western world. New York, Milton, Balch, 1925. vi, 378 p. illus.   F74.N55D484

The 1838 edition of Dexter's *A Pickle for the Knowing Ones; or, Plain Truths in a Homespun Dress* is reprinted on pages [327]–378.

——— Timothy Dexter revisited. Illustrated by Philip Kappel. Boston, Little, Brown [1960] 306 p. illus.   F74.N55D4843

13216
DIBBLEE, EBENEZER (*ca.* 1714–1799)
Connecticut. Anglican clergyman.

——— Letters of the Reverend Doctor Ebenezer Dibblee, of Stamford, to the Reverend Doctor Samuel Peters, Loyalist refugee in London, 1784–1793. Historical magazine of the Protestant Episcopal church, v. 1, Mar. 1932: 51–85.   BX5800.H5, v. 1

Introduction and notes by E. Clowes Chorley.

13217
DICKINSON, JOHN (1732–1808)*
Delaware; Pennsylvania. Lawyer, assemblyman, delegate to the Continental Congress, delegate to the Constitutional Convention, governor.

———The political writings of John Dickinson, Esquire, late president of the state of Delaware, and of the commonwealth of Pennsylvania. Wilmington [Del.] Printed and sold by Bonsal and Niles, 1801. 2 v.   E302.D55

——— The writings of John Dickinson. v. 1. Political writings, 1764–1774. Edited at the request of the Historical Society of Pennsylvania, by Paul Leicester Ford. Philadelphia, Historical Society of Pennsylvania, 1895. xxii, 501 p. front. (Memoirs of the Historical Society of Pennsylvania, v. 14) F146.P36, v. 14

Life and writings of John Dickinson, v. 2.
The *Writings* were planned to appear in three volumes.
Reprinted in New York by Da Capo Press (1970).

COLBOURN, HAROLD TREVOR.   The historical perspective of John Dickinson. *In* Dickinson College, *Carlisle, Pa. Library*. Early Dickinsoniana. Carlisle, Pa., 1961 [ᶜ1965] (The Boyd Lee Spahr lectures in Americana, 1957–1961) p. 3–37. LD1662.A53

——— John Dickinson, historical revolutionary. Pennsylvania magazine of history and biography, v. 83, July 1959: 271–292. F146.P65, v. 83

COOK, FRANK G.   John Dickinson. Atlantic monthly, v. 65, Jan. 1890: 70–83. AP2.A8, v. 65

GUMMERE, RICHARD M.   John Dickinson, the classical penman of the Revolution. Classical journal, v. 52, Nov. 1956: 81–88. PA1.C4, v. 52

HOOKER, RICHARD J.   John Dickinson on church and state. American literature, v. 16, May 1944: 82–98. PS1.A6, v. 16

JACOBSON, DAVID L.   John Dickinson and the Revolution in Pennsylvania, 1764–1776. Berkeley, University of California Press, 1965. vi, 151 p. (University of California publications in history, v. 78) E173.C15, v. 78

Bibliography: p. 147–151.
The author's thesis (Ph.D.), *John Dickinson and Joseph Galloway, 1764–1776: A Study in Contrasts*, was submitted to Princeton University in 1959 (Micro AC–1, no. 59–5190).

KNOLLENBERG, BERNHARD.   John Dickinson vs. John Adams, 1774–1776. *In* American Philosophical Society, *Philadelphia*. Proceedings, v. 107, Apr. 15, 1963: 138–144. Q11.P5, v. 107
On their rivalry in the Continental Congress.

MOORE, GEORGE H.   John Dickinson, the author of the Declaration, on taking up arms in 1775. With a facsimile from the original draft. New York, Printed for the author, 1890. 53 p. facsim. E302.6.D5M8

POWELL, JOHN H.   "A certain great fortune and piddling genius." *In* Dickinson College, *Carlisle, Pa. Library*. Early Dickinsoniana. Carlisle, Pa., 1961 [ᶜ1965] (The Boyd Lee Spahr lectures in Americana, 1957–1961) p. 41–72. LD1662.A53

Focuses on Dickinson's role in Congress during the summer of 1775 and defends him against John Adams' well-known charge. Also published in Powell's *General Washington and the Jack Ass, and Other American Characters in Portrait* (South Brunswick [N.J.] T. Yoseloff [1969]), p. 86–118.

——— John Dickinson, penman of the American Revolution. 1938.
Thesis (Ph.D.)—State University of Iowa.

POWER, M. SUSAN.   John Dickinson: freedom, change, and protest. Susquehanna University studies, v. 9, June 1972: 99–121. LH1.S78S8, v. 9

STILLÉ, CHARLES J.   The life and times of John Dickinson. 1732–1808. Prepared at the request of the Historical Society of Pennsylvania. Philadelphia, Historical Society of Pennsylvania, 1891. 437 p. facsim., port. (Memoirs of the Historical Society of Pennsylvania, v. 13) F146.P36, v. 13

Life and writings of John Dickinson, v. 1.
Reprinted in New York by B. Franklin (1969).

TOLLES, FREDERICK B.   John Dickinson and the Quakers. *In* Dickinson College, *Carlisle, Pa.* "John and Mary's College." [Westwood, N.J.] Revell [1956] (The Boyd Lee Spahr lectures in Americana, 1951–1956) p. 67–88. LD1663.A53

13218
DICKINSON, PHILEMON (1739–1809)*
Maryland; Pennsylvania; New Jersey; Delaware. Revolutionary general, assemblyman, delegate to the Continental Congress, councilor.

DICKINSON, WHARTON.   Philemon Dickinson, Major-General, New Jersey militia—Revolutionary service. Magazine of American history, with notes and queries, v. 7, Dec. 1881: 420–427. E171.M18, v. 7

13219
DIGGES, THOMAS ATWOOD (1741–1821)
Maryland. Merchant, novelist.

——— Adventures of Alonso: containing some striking anecdotes of the present prime minister of Portugal—in facsimile. Anonymously printed in London in 1775, and now attributed to Thomas Atwood Digges (1741–1821) of Warburton Manor, Maryland. The first American novel, by Robert H. Elias. Edited by Rev. Thomas J. McMahon, S.T.D. New York, United States Catholic Historical Society, 1943. xxviii, 148, 144 p. (United States Catholic Historical Society. Monograph series, 18) PS737.D35A63 1775a
E184.C3U6, v. 18

Facsimile of the American Antiquarian Society's copy of the original London edition in two volumes, with facsimiles of the title page of the New York Public Library copy and the publisher's advertisements. (p. [131]–144 at end) from the Harvard Library copy. In his introduction, which first appeared in volume 12 (1941) of *American Literature*, Robert Elias bases his ascription of authorship on a penciled note on the title page of the New York Public Library copy attributing the work to a "Mr. Digges of Warburton in Maryland," and on internal evidence. He also provides biographical information about Digges and argues that his was the first novel written by an American citizen.

CLARK, WILLIAM B. In defense of Thomas Digges. Pennsylvania magazine of history and biography, v. 77, Oct. 1953: 381–438. F146.P65, v. 77

PARSONS, LYNN H. The mysterious Mr. Digges. William and Mary quarterly, 3d ser., v. 22, July 1965: 486–492. F221.W71, 3d s., v. 22

13220

DILLWYN, WILLIAM 1743–1824)
New Jersey; England.

—— Diary of William Dillwyn during a visit to Charles Town in 1772. Edited by A. S. Salley. South Carolina historical and genealogical magazine, v. 36, Jan.–Oct. 1935: 1–6, 29–35, 73–78, 107–110. F226.S55, v. 36

13221

DOBBS, ARTHUR (1689–1765)*†
Ireland; North Carolina. Member of Irish Parliament, landowner, royal governor.

CLARKE, DESMOND. Arthur Dobbs, Esquire, 1689–1765; surveyor-general of Ireland, prospector and governor of North Carolina. Chapel Hill, University of North Carolina Press [1957] 232 p. port. F257.C55
Includes bibliographies.

13222

DOCK, CHRISTOPHER (ca. 1698–1771)*
Pennsylvania. Farmer, schoolmaster.

—— The life and works of Christopher Dock, America's pioneer writer on education, with a translation of his works into the English language, by Martin G. Brumbaugh. Philadelphia, J. B. Lippincott Co., 1908. 272 p. facsims., plates. LB575.D65

Contents: Introduction.—Life of Christopher Dock.—The *Schul-Ordnung.*—Translation of the *Schul-Ordnung.*—*Geistliches Magazien;* four numbers.—Translation of the *Geistliches Magazien.*—*Schriften* with translation.—Hymns with translation.
Reprinted in New York by Arno Press (1969).

HUNSICKER, ROBERT G. Christopher Dock, early American school master. *In* Historical Society of Montgomery County (*Pennsylvania*). Bulletin, v. 13, fall 1961: 25–46. F157.M7H45, v. 13

KLASSEN, FRANK H. Christopher Dock: eighteenth century American educator. 1962. ([194] p.)
Micro AC–1, no. 63–3280
Thesis (Ph.D.)—University of Illinois.
Abstracted in *Dissertation Abstracts,* v. 23, May 1963, p. 4209–4210.

LEATHERMAN, QUINTUS. Christopher Dock, Mennonite schoolmaster, 1718–1771. Mennonite quarterly review, v. 16, Jan. 1942: 32–44. BX8101.M4, v. 16

MASSANARI, KARL L. The contribution of Christopher Dock to contemporary Christian teaching. Mennonite quarterly review, v. 25, Apr. 1951: 100–115. BX8191.M4, v. 25

STUDER, GERALD C. Christopher Dock: colonial schoolmaster; the biography and writings of Christopher Dock. Scottsdale, Pa., Herald Press [1967] 445 p. illus., facsims. (part col.), maps, ports. (part col.) LB575.D66S8

Bibliography: p. 412–419.

13223

DÖHLA, JOHANN CONRAD (1750–1820)
Germany. Hessian soldier in America.

—— Amerikanische Feldzüge, 1777–1783. Tagebuch von Johann Conrad Döhla. *In* Deutsch-amerikanische Geschichtsblätter. v. 17; 1917. Chicago, University of Chicago Press [1918] p. [7]–358. F550.G3D4, v. 17

—— The Doehla journal [1781] Translated by Robert J. Tilden. William and Mary College quarterly historical magazine, 2d ser., v. 22, July 1942: 229–274. map. F221.W71, 2d s., v. 22

—— Tagebuch eines Bayreuther Soldaten, des Johann Conrad Döhla aus dem nordamerikanischen Freiheitskrieg von 1777 bis 1783. Mit einem Vorwort von W. Frhr. v. Waldenfels. Bayreuth, Druck von L. Ellwanger vorm. T. Burger, 1913. 214 p. fold. map, plate. E268.D64

Offprint from *Archiv für Geschichte und Altertumskunde von Oberfranken,* Bd. 25, Heft 1–2, 1912–13.

13224

DÖRNBERG, KARL LUDWIG, *freiherr* VON (1749–1819)
Germany. Hessian officer in America.

—— Tagebuchblätter eines hessischen Offiziers aus der Zeit des nordamerikanischen Unabhängigkeitskrieges. Von Gotthold Marseille. Pyritz, Bache'sche Buchdruckerei, 1899–1900. 2 v. in 1. map. E268.D66
Written in 1779–81.
Separate, from *Programm,* Königliches Bismarck-Gymnasium, Pyritz.

13225

DONOP, CARL EMIL KURT von (1740–1777)
Germany. Hessian officer in America.

HUTH, HANS. Letters from a Hessian mercenary. Pennsylvania magazine of history and biography, v. 62, Oct. 1938: 488–501. F146.P65, v. 62

Discusses letters written by Colonel Donop in 1776–77 to his friend the prince of Prussia, later King Friedrich Wilhelm II.

13226

DOOLITTLE, AMOS (1754–1832)*

Connecticut. Engraver, illustrator.

BEARDSLEY, WILLIAM A. An old New Haven engraver and his work: Amos Doolittle. *In* New Haven Colony Historical Society, *New Haven.* Papers. v. 8. New Haven, 1914. p. 132–151.   F98.N5, v. 8

——— ——— Offprint. [New Haven? Conn., 1914?] 23 p.   NE539.D6B4

METCALF, FRANK J. Amos Dolittle, engraver and printer. American collector, v. 4, May 1927: 53–56. facsim., port.   Z1007.A475, v. 4

13227

DORCHESTER, GUY CARLETON, *Baron* (1724–1808)†

England; Quebec. British officer in America, governor.

BENOIT, PIERRE. Lord Dorchester (Guy Carleton). Montréal. Éditions H M H [1961] 203 p. map, port. (Figures canadiennes, 5)   F1032.D68
Bibliography: p. 201.

BRADLEY, ARTHUR G. Lord Dorchester. Toronto, Morang, 1907. x, 327 p. port. (The makers of Canada)   F1032.D69

A new edition, edited by A. L. Burt, was published in London by Oxford University Press in 1926 (F1026.M342, v. 3).

BURT, ALFRED L. Guy Carleton, Lord Dorchester: an estimate. *In* Canadian Historical Association. Report. 1935. Toronto. p. 76–87.   F1001.C26, 1935

——— Guy Carleton, Lord Dorchester, 1724–1808. Rev. version. Ottawa, Canadian Historical Association, 1955. 16 p. (Canadian Historical Association booklets, no. 5)   F1001.C24, no. 5
Bibliographic note on p. [3] of cover.

SMITH, PAUL H. Sir Guy Carleton: soldier-statesman. *In* Billias, George A., *ed.* George Washington's opponents: British generals and admirals in the American Revolution. New York, Morrow, 1969. p. 103–141.   E267.B56
Bibliography: p. 140–141.

WOOD, WILLIAM C. H. The father of British Canada; a chronicle of Carleton. Toronto, Glasgow, Brook, 1916. xi, 239 p. fold. maps, ports. (The chronicles of Canada, [v. 12])   F1032.D7
"Bibliographical note": p. 229–231.

13228

DOTY, JOHN (1745–1841)

New York. Anglican clergyman, Loyalist chaplain.

LYDEKKER, JOHN W. The Reverend John Doty. Historical magazine of the Protestant Episcopal church, v. 7, Sept. 1938: 287–300.   BX5800.H5, v. 7

13229

DOUGLAS, WILLIAM (1743–1777)*

Connecticut. Merchant, Revolutionary officer.

——— Letters written during the Revolutionary War by Colonel William Douglas to his wife covering the period July 19, 1775, to December 5, 1776. *In* New York Historical Society. Quarterly bulletin, v. 12, Jan. 1929: 145–154; v. 13, Apr.–Oct. 1929, Jan. 1930: 37–40, 79–82, 118–122, 157–162; v. 14, Apr. 1930: 38–42.   F116.N638, v. 12–14

13230

DOUGLASS, EPHRAIM (1749?–1833)

Pennsylvania. Revolutionary officer, Indian negotiator.

——— Pittsburg and Uniontown, Pennsylvania, in 1782–83. Letters from Ephraim Douglass to Gen. James Irvine. Pennsylvania magazine of history and biography, v. 1, no. 1, 1877: 44–54.   F146.P65, v. 1

BURTON, CLARENCE M. Ephraim Douglass and his times, a fragment of history, with the journal of George McCully (hitherto unpublished) and various letters of the period. New York, W. Abbatt, 1910. 74 p. port. (The Magazine of history, with notes and queries. Extra number, no. 10)   E173.M24, no. 10

Douglass, with McCully as companion, was sent by the U. S. government as a commissioner to the Indians to carry news of peace with Great Britain at the close of the Revolutionary War. The journey extended from Pittsburgh to Sandusky and Detroit.

Report of Ephraim Douglass to the Secretary of War, 1783: p. [50]–61.

13231

DOVE, DAVID JAMES (1696?–1769)*

England; Pennsylvania. Schoolmaster, pamphleteer.

JACKSON, JOSEPH. A Philadelphia schoolmaster of the eighteenth century. Pennsylvania magazine of history and biography, v. 25, July 1911: 315–332.   F146.P65, v. 25

13232

DOWDESWELL, WILLIAM (1721–1775)†

England. Member of Parliament.

HAMBRICK, HORACE T. William Dowdeswell and the Rockingham Whigs. 1953. ([253] p.)   Micro AC–1, no. 25,023

Thesis (Ph.D.)—University of Kentucky.
Abstracted in *Dissertation Abstracts*, v. 18, Mar. 1958, p. 1022.

13233

DOWNING, SAMUEL (*b.* 1761–*ca.* 1866)

Massachusetts. Revolutionary soldier, farmer.

Life of Samuel Downing, one hundred and four years' old, one of the four soldiers of the Revolution now remaining alive. New York, Press of Wynkoop & Hallenbeck, 1865. 19 p.   E275.D73

13234

DOWNMAN, FRANCIS (ca. 1742–1825)
England. British officer in America.

——— The services of Lieut.-Colonel Francis Downman . . . in France, North America, and the West Indies, between the years 1758 and 1784. Edited by Colonel F. A. Whinyates. Woolwich, Printed at the Royal Artillery Institution, 1898. vi, 132 p. fold. maps, ports.
                    E275.D75
                    Micro 22574 E

13235

DRAKE, JOHN HODGES (ca. 1769–1859)
North Carolina.

——— The Revolutionary War in North Carolina: narrative of John Hodges Drake, of Nash County. In Southern History Association. Publications, v. 4, Jan. 1900: 14–21.   F206.S73, v. 4

On a Tory raid in 1781.

13236

DRAYTON, WILLIAM (1732–1790)*
South Carolina. Lawyer, judge.

MOWAT, CHARLES L. The enigma of William Drayton. Florida historical quarterly, v. 22, July 1943: 3–33.
                    F306.F65, v. 22

13237

DRAYTON, WILLIAM HENRY (1742–1779)*
South Carolina. Assemblyman, councilor, delegate to the Continental Congress, judge.

——— The letters of Freeman, &c. London, Printed in the year 1771. 244 p.   E215.1.D76 Rare Bk. Coll.

The letters were written in South Carolina in 1769 in response to the nonimportation resolutions adopted by the assembly that same year. They are published here in the order in which they appeared in the South Carolina Gazette.
A few letters by Christopher Gadsden, John Mackenzie, and William Wragg are included.

DABNEY, WILLIAM M. Drayton and Laurens in the Continental Congress. South Carolina historical magazine, v. 60, Apr. 1959: 74–82.   F266.S55, v. 60

DABNEY, WILLIAM M., and MARION DARGAN. William Henry Drayton & the American Revolution. Albuquerque, University of New Mexico Press [1962] xiii, 225 p. facsims., ports.   E302.6.D7D3
Bibliography: p. 209–217.
Marion Dargan's thesis (Ph.D.), William Henry Drayton and the Revolution in South Carolina, was submit-

ted to the University of Chicago in 1927 (237 l. E302.6.D7D37).

13238

DRINKER, ELIZABETH SANDWITH (1734–1807)
Pennsylvania.

——— Extracts from the journal of Elizabeth Drinker, from 1759 to 1807, A.D. Edited by Henry D. Biddle. Philadelphia, J. B. Lippincott Co., 1889. 423 p.
                    F158.44.D78

Extracts covering the period from September 25, 1777, to July 4, 1778, were published in the Pennsylvania Magazine of History and Biography, v. 13, Oct. 1889, p. 298–308.

REPPLIER, AGNES. A colonial diary. Atlantic monthly, v. 84, July 1899: 45–52.   AP2.A8, v. 84

13239

DROWNE, SOLOMON (1753–1834)
Rhode Island; Pennsylvania. Revolutionary surgeon.

——— Dr. Solomon Drowne [letters, 1774–76] Pennsylvania magazine of history and biography, v. 48, July 1924: 227–250.   F146.P65, v. 48
Introduction and notes by Harrold E. Gillingham.

———Journal of a cruise in the fall of 1780 in the privatesloop of war, Hope. With "notes," by Henry T. Drowne. New York [Printed by C. L. Moreau] 1872. 27 l. plates, ports.   E271.D78 Rare Bk. Coll.

The "notes" consist of a sketch of the author and a genealogy of the Drowne family. Also published in the Rhode Island Historical Magazine, v. 5, July 1884, p. 1–11.

DROWNE, HENRY RUSSELL. Dr. Solomon Drowne—a surgeon of the Revolution. Military surgeon, v. 86, Mar. 1940: 292–297. illus.   RD1.A7, v. 86

The author's article of the same title appeared in the Bulletin of the Fort Ticonderoga, N.Y., Museum, v. 8, Jan. 1949, p. 110–112.

13240

DUANE, JAMES (1733–1797)*
New York. Lawyer, landholder, delegate to the Continental Congress.

——— The Duane letters [1761–89] In Southern History Association. Publications, v. 7, May–Sept. 1903: 170–185, 247–256, 362–368; v. 8, Jan., Sept. 1904: 53–56, 377–390; v. 9, Nov. 1905: 389–400; v. 10, Sept. 1906: 299–310.   F206.S73, v. 7–10

ALEXANDER, EDWARD P. James Duane, moderate rebel. In New York State Historical Association. New York history, v. 17, Apr. 1936: 123–134. port.
                    F116.N865, v. 17

——— A revolutionary conservative, James Duane of New York. New York, Columbia University Press, 1938.

xviii, 283 p. maps, ports. (New York State Historical Association series, no. 6) E302.6.D8A6

Issued also as thesis (Ph.D.)—Columbia University. Bibliography: p. [237]–256.

JONES, SAMUEL W. Memoir of the Hon. James Duane, judge of the District Court of the United States for New York. *In* The Documentary history of the state of New-York. By E. B. O'Callaghan. v. 4. Albany, C. Van Benthuysen, Public Printer, 1851. p. [1061]–1084. F122.D63, v. 4

———— ———— Detached copies. E207.D8J6
KF363.D8J6

13241

DUBOIS, LEWIS (1744–1824)

New York. Farmer, Revolutionary officer.

POUCHER, JOHN WILSON. Dutchess County men of the Revolutionary period: Colonel Lewis DuBois—Captain Henry DuBois. *In* Dutchess County Historical Society. Year book. v. 20; 1935. Poughkeepsie. p. 71–85. F127.D8D93, v. 20

———— Colonel Lewis DuBois. *In* Ulster County Historical Society, *Kingston, N.Y.* Proceedings. 1935/36. Kingston. p. 15–33. F127.U4U43, 1935/36

13242

DUBOUCHET, DENIS JEAN FLORIMOND LANGLOIS (1752–1826)

France. Revolutionary officer, French officer in America.

BISHOP, MORRIS. A French volunteer. American heritage, v. 17, Aug. 1966: 46–49, 103–108. illus. (part col.) E171.A43, v. 17

13243

DU CALVET, PIERRE (*ca.* 1715–1786)

Canada. Fur trader.

———— The case of Peter Du Calvet, Esq., of Montreal, in the Province of Quebeck. Containing, an account of the long and severe imprisonment he suffered in the said province by the order of General Haldimand, the present governour of the same, without the least offence, or other lawful cause, whatever. London, Printed in the year 1784. xi, 284 p. F1032.D32 Rare Bk. Coll.

Du Calvet was arrested in 1780 on suspicion of disloyalty and held in prison until 1783. Another statement of his case, containing different material, was published as *Appel à la justice de l'État* (Imprimé à Londres, 1784. 320 p. F1032.D79).

RIDDELL, WILLIAM R. Pierre Du Calvet: a Huguenot refugee in early Montreal; his treason and his fate. *In* Ontario Historical Society. Papers and records. v. 22. Toronto, 1925. p. 239–254. F1056.O58, v. 22

SULTE, BENJAMIN. Pierre Ducalvet. *In* Royal Society of Canada. Transactions, 3d ser., v. 13, May 1919: 1–11. AS42.R6, 3d s., v. 13

13244

DUCHÉ, JACOB (1738–1798)*

Pennsylvania; England. Anglican clergyman, Loyalist.

———— Caspipina's letters; containing observations on a variety of subjects, literary, moral, and religious. Written by a gentleman who resided some time in Philadelphia. To which is added, the life and character of Wm. Penn, Esq; original proprietor of Pennsylvania. Bath, Reprinted by R. Cruttwell, and sold by E. and C. Dilly and J. Phillips, London, 1777. 2 v. in 1. AC7.D8 1777 Rare Bk. Coll.

The life of Penn is by Edmund Rack.

Published in 1774 under title: *Observations on a Variety of Subjects, Literary, Moral and Religious.*

———— The Washington-Duché letters. Now printed, for the first time, from the original manuscripts, with an introductory note by Worthington Chauncey Ford. Brooklyn, N.Y., Priv. print., 1890. 38 p. E211.W32
E216.D82

Contents: Introductory note.—Duché to Washington, 5 August, 1775.—Washington to the president of Congress, 16 October, 1777.—Duché to Washington, 8 October, 1777.—Duché to Washington, 1777.—Washington to Francis Hopkinson, 21 November, 1777.—Francis Hopkinson to Duché, 14 November, 1777.—Duché to Washington, 2 April, 1783.—Washington to Duché, 10 August, 1783.

HASTINGS, GEORGE E. Jacob Duché, first chaplain of Congress. South Atlantic quarterly, v. 31, Oct. 1932: 386–400. AP2.S75, v. 31

NEILL, EDWARD D. Rev. Jacob Duché, the first chaplain of Congress. Pennsylvania magazine of history and biography, v. 2, no. 1, 1878: 58–73. F146.P65, v. 2

———— ———— Offprint. [Philadelphia? 1878?] [16] p. E278.D9N3

13245

DUCHÉ, THOMAS SPENCE (1763–1790)

Pennsylvania; England. Portrait artist, engraver.

GEGENHEIMER, ALBERT F. Artist in exile: the story of Thomas Spence Duché. Pennsylvania magazine of history and biography, v. 79, Jan. 1955: 3–26. ports. F146.P65, v. 79

13246

DUDLEY, JOHN (1725–1805)

New Hampshire. Assemblyman, judge.

BURNHAM, EDWARD J. The life and public services of Hon. John Dudley of Raymond. *In* New Hampshire Historical Society. Proceedings. v. 4; 1899/1905. Concord, 1906. p. 239–251. F31.N52, v. 4

13247

DUER, WILLIAM (1747–1799)*

England; New York. Financier, delegate to the Continental Congress.

DAVIS, JOSEPH S.   William Duer, entrepreneur, 1747–99. *In his* Essays in the earlier history of American corporations, v. 1. Cambridge, Harvard University Press, 1917. (Harvard economic studies, v. 16) p. [109]–345.
HD2785.D3, v. 1

JONES, ROBERT F.   The public career of William Duer: rebel, Federalist politician, entrepreneur, and speculator, 1775–1792. 1967. ([327] p.)
Micro AC–1, no. 67–13,599

Thesis (Ph.D.)—University of Notre Dame.

Abstracted in *Dissertation Abstracts*, v. 28A, Nov. 1967, p. 1765–1766.

13248

DUFFIELD, GEORGE (1732–1790)*

Pennsylvania. Presbyterian clergyman, Revolutionary chaplain.

COBLENTZ, DAVID H.   George Duffield, 1732–1790, pulpit patriot. Manuscripts, v. 14, fall 1962: 26–32. facsim.
Z41.A2A925, v. 14

MACKIE, ALEXANDER.   George Duffield, Revolutionary patriot. *In* Presbyterian Historical Society. Journal, v. 33, Mar. 1955: 3–22.
BX8905.P7A4, v. 33

Also published in the *Picket Post*, no. 90, Oct. 1965, p. 4–7, 31–40.

13249

DUFFIELD, SAMUEL (1732–1814)

Pennsylvania. Apothecary, Revolutionary surgeon.

KLEIN, RANDOLPH S.   Dr. Samuel Duffield (1732–1814): member of the first medical class graduated in America. *In* College of Physicians of Philadelphia. Transactions & studies, 4th ser., v. 35, Jan. 1968: 119–125.
R15.P5, 4th s., v. 35

13250

DULANY, ANN (*fl.* 1781–1784)

Maryland. Daughter of Daniel Dulany (1722–1797).

ROWLAND, KATE M.   Maryland women and French officers. Atlantic monthly, v. 66, Nov. 1890: 651–659.
AP2.A8, v. 66

Includes excerpts from her letters, 1781–82.

13251

DULANY, DANIEL (1722–1797)*

Maryland. Lawyer, assemblyman, pamphleteer, Loyalist.

———Extracts from the Dulany papers [1743–85] Maryland historical magazine, v. 14, Dec. 1919: 371–383; v. 16, Mar. 1921: 43–50.
F176.M18, v. 14, 16

LAND, AUBREY C.   The Dulanys of Maryland; a biographical study of Daniel Dulany, the elder (1685–1753) and Daniel Dulany, the younger (1722–1797). Baltimore, Maryland Historical Society, 1955. 390 p. ports. (Studies in Maryland history, no. 3)
F184.D8L3

Bibliographical references included in "Notes" (p. 335–370). "Bibliographical note": p. 371–373.

Reprinted in Baltimore by the Johns Hopkins Press (1968).

13252

DUMAS, MATHIEU, *comte* (1753–1837)

France. Cartographer, French officer in America.

——— Memoirs of his own time; including the Revolution, the empire, and the restoration. Philadelphia, Lea & Blanchard, 1839. 2 v.
DC255.D8A2

The French original is entitled *Souvenirs du lieutenant-général Cte M. Dumas, de 1770 à 1836.*

Chapter 2 (p. 19–80) in the first volume treats Dumas' participation in the American war.

13253

DUNBAR, MOSES (1746–1777)*

Connecticut. Loyalist officer.

PECK, EPAPHRODITUS.   Loyal to the crown; Moses Dunbar, Tory, and his fidelity to church and king—executed for treason. Connecticut magazine, v. 8, no. 1–2, 1903: 129–136, 297–300.
F91.C8, v. 8

13254

DUNBAR, WILLIAM (1749–1810)*

Scotland; Mississippi Valley. Indian trader, planter.

——— Life, letters, and papers of William Dunbar of Elgin, Morayshire, Scotland, and Natchez, Mississippi, pioneer scientist of the southern United States. Compiled and prepared from the original documents for the National Society of Colonial Dames in America, by Mrs. Dunbar Rowland (Eron Rowland). Jackson, Miss., Press of the Mississippi Historical Society, 1930. 410 p. plates, ports.
F341.D89

DeROSIER, ARTHUR H.   Natchez and the formative years of William Dunbar. Journal of Mississippi history, v. 34, Feb. 1972: 29–47.
F336.J68, v. 34

——— William Dunbar: a product of the eighteenth century Scottish renaissance. Journal of Mississippi history, v. 28, Aug. 1966: 185–227.
F336.J68, v. 28

RILEY, FRANKLIN L.   Sir William Dunbar—the pioneer scientist of Mississippi. *In* Mississippi Historical Society. Publications. v. 2; 1899. Oxford. p. 85–111.
F336.M75, v. 2

———— ———— Offprint. [Oxford, Miss., 1899] [85]–111 p.   Q143.D88R6

13255

DUNCAN, HENRY (1735?–1814)

Scotland; England. British naval officer in America.

———— Journals of Henry Duncan, Captain, Royal Navy, 1776–1782. *In* The Naval miscellany. v. 1. [London] Printed for the Navy Records Society, 1902. (Publications of the Navy Records Society, v. 20) p. [105]–219. maps (part fold.)   DA70.A1, v. 20

13256

DUNCAN, JAMES (1725 *or* 6–1817)

Massachusetts. Storekeeper.

PHILLIPS, JAMES D. [James Duncan] *In* Essex Institute, *Salem, Mass.* Historical collections, v. 88, Jan. 1952: 1–18; v. 89, Jan. 1953: 19–56. facsims., plate, port.   F72.E7E81, v. 88–89

Contents: [1] James Duncan of Haverhill: pack-peddler, store-keeper and merchant.—[2] James Duncan and Son: merchants, capitalists, and chain store operators.

13257

DUNLAP, ALEXANDER (1743–1828)

Virginia. Revolutionary soldier.

HERNDON, JOHN G. Colonel Alexander Dunlap (1743–1828); the correction of an identification. Virginia magazine of history and biography, v. 54, Oct. 1946: 321–326.   F221.V91, v. 54

13258

DUNLAP, JOHN (1747–1812)*

Ireland; Pennsylvania. Printer, publisher, Revolutionary officer.

MURPHY, LAWRENCE W. John Dunlap's *Packet* and its competitors [1776–96] Journalism quarterly, v. 28, winter 1951: 58–62.   PN4700.J7, v. 28

13259

DUNMORE, JOHN MURRAY, *4th Earl of* (1732–1809)*†

Scotland; New York; Virginia. Royal governor.

CALEY, PERCY B. Dunmore, colonial governor, New York and Virginia, 1770–1782. 1940.

Thesis (Ph.D.)—University of Pittsburgh.

CURRY, RICHARD O. Lord Dunmore—tool of land jobbers or realistic champion of colonial "rights"? An inquiry. West Virginia history, v. 24, Apr. 1963: 289–295.   F236.W52, v. 24

WRICK, ELIZABETH A. Dunmore—Virginia's last royal governor. West Virginia history, v. 8, Apr. 1947: 237–282.   F236.W52, v. 8

13260

DU PETIT-THOUARS, ARISTIDE AUBERT (1760–1798)

French naval officer in America.

———— Aristide Aubert du Petit-Thouars, héros d'Aboukir, 1760–1798; lettres et documents inédits. Introduction d'Albert Mousset. Paris, Plon [1937] xix, 562 p. fold. geneal. table, plates, ports.   DC146.D77A4 1937

At head of title: Amiral Bergasse du Petit Thouars.

13261

DU PONCEAU, PETER STEPHEN (1760–1844)

France; Pennsylvania. Revolutionary officer, lawyer.

———— The autobiography of Peter Stephen Du Ponceau [1760–83] Pennsylvania magazine of history and biography, v. 63, Apr.–Oct. 1939: 189–227, 311–343, 432–461; v. 64, Jan.–Apr. 1940: 97–120, 243–269.   F146.P65, v. 63–64

Written in a series of letters to Robert Walsh, dated 1836–44. Introduction and notes by James L. Whitehead. Some of the letters were published earlier in v. 40, Apr. 1916, p. 172–186.

TIECK, WILLIAM A. In search of Peter Stephen Du Ponceau. Pennsylvania magazine of history and biography, v. 89, Jan. 1965: 52–78. ports.   F146.P65, v. 89

13262

DUPORTAIL, LOUIS LEBÈGUE DE PRESLE (1743–1802)

France. Engineer, Revolutionary general.

HEATHCOTE, CHARLES W. General Chevalier Louis Lebeque Duportail—devoted to the United States and Washington. Picket post, no. 63, Feb. 1959: 14–21. map, port.   E234.P5, no. 63

KITE, ELIZABETH S. Brigadier-General Louis Lebègue Duportail, commandant of engineers in the Continental Army, 1777–1783. Baltimore, Johns Hopkins Press, 1933. vii, 296 p. facsim., port.   E207.D9K48

———— General Duportail, army engineer, lived as American citizen near camp in Montgomery County. Picket post, no. 17, Apr. 1947: 62–66.   E234.P5, no. 17

13263

DURKEE, JOHN (1728–1782)*

Connecticut. Land agent, assemblyman, Revolutionary officer.

BROWNING, AMOS A. A forgotten son of liberty. *In* New London County Historical Society, *New London, Conn.* Records and papers. v. 3, pt. 2. New London, 1912. p. 257–279.   F102.N7N7, v. 3

13264

DU ROI, AUGUST WILHELM

Hessian officer in America.

————— Journal of Du Roi the elder, lieutenant and adjutant, in the service of the duke of Brunswick, 1776–1778. Translated from the original German manuscript in the Library of Congress, Washington, D.C., by Charlotte S. J. Epping. [Philadelphia] University of Pennsylvania; New York, D. Appleton, agents, 1911. 189 p. illus., facsims. (Americana germanica. [New ser., no. 15])   E268.D96

Also published in the *German American Annals*, v. 13, Jan./Apr.–Sept./Dec. 1911, p. 40–64, 77–128, 131–244.

13265

DUROUSSEAU DE FAYOLLE, PIERRE (1746–1780)
France.

————— Journal d'une campagne en Amérique par Durousseau de Fayolle (1777–1779). *In* Société des antiquaires de l'Ouest, *Poitiers*. Bulletin et mémoires. 2d ser., v. 25; 1901. Poitiers, 1902. p. 1–48.
   DC609.1.S7, 2d s., v. 25

Introduction and notes by L. Segretain.

13266

DU SIMITIÈRE, PIERRE EUGÈNE (1737–1784)*
Switzerland; Pennsylvania. Collector, portrait artist.

HUTH, HANS. Pierre Eugène du Simitière and the beginnings of the American historical museum. Pennsylvania magazine of history and biography, v. 69, Oct. 1945: 315–325.   F146.P65, v. 69

LEVEY, MARTIN. The first American museum of natural history. Isis, v. 42, Apr. 1951: 10–12.   Q1.I7, v. 42

Shows that Du Simitière's collections were advertised for display in 1782, four years before that of Charles Willson Peale, who is customarily given credit for founding the first public museum in the United States.

POTTS, WILLIAM J. Du Simitière, artist, antiquary, and naturalist, projector of the first American museum, with some extracts from his notebook. Pennsylvania magazine of history and biography, v. 13, Oct. 1889: 341–375.   F146.P65, v. 13

SIFTON, PAUL G. Pierre Eugene Du Simitiere (1737–1784): collector in Revolutionary America. 1960. ([623] p.)   Micro AC–1, no. 60–3693

Thesis (Ph.D.)—University of Pennsylvania.
Abstracted in *Dissertation Abstracts*, v. 21, Oct. 1960, p. 868–869.

13267

DWIGHT, TIMOTHY (1752–1817)*
Massachusetts; Connecticut. Congregational clergyman, Revolutionary chaplain, educator, poet.

————— The major poems of Timothy Dwight, 1752–1817, with a dissertation on the history, eloquence, and poetry of the Bible. With an introduction by William J. McTaggart and William K. Bottorff. Gainesville, Fla., Scholars' Facsimiles & Reprints, 1969. xvi, 558 p.
   PS739.A17 1969

Contents: America; or, A poem on the settlement of the British colonies.—The conquest of Canaan.—The triumph of infidelity.—Greenfield Hill.— A dissertation on the history, eloquence, poetry of the Bible.

————— Travels in New England and New York. Edited by Barbara Miller Soloman, with the assistance of Patricia M. King. Cambridge, Mass., Belknap Press of Harvard University Press, 1969. 4 v. facsims., maps (part fold.), port. (The John Harvard Library)   F8.D9952

Includes bibliographic references.

BUCHANAN, LEWIS E. The ethical ideas of Timothy Dwight. *In* Washington State University, *Pullman*. Research studies, v. 13, Sept. 1945: 185–199.
   Q11.W593, v. 13

CUNINGHAM, CHARLES E. Timothy Dwight, 1752–1817, a biography. New York, Macmillan Co., 1942. viii, 403 p. facsims., plates, ports.   LD6330.1795.C8

Bibliography: p. 353–362.

FREIMARCK, VINCENT. Timothy Dwight's *Dissertation* on the Bible. American literature, v. 24, Mar. 1952: 73–77.   PS1.A6, v. 24

Delivered as a commencement address at Yale, Dwight's *Dissertation on the History, Eloquence, and Poetry of the Bible* was published in New Haven in 1772.

LEARY, LEWIS G. The author of *The Triumph of Infidelity*. New England quarterly, v. 20, Sept. 1947: 377–385.
   F1.N62, v. 20

SILVERMAN, KENNETH. Timothey Dwight. New York, Twayne Publishers [1969] 174 p. (Twayne's United States authors series)   PS739.Z5S5

Bibliography: p. 163–167.

STILLINGER, JACK. Dwight's *Triumph of Infidelity* [1788]: text and interpretation. *In* Virginia. University. *Bibliographical Society*. Studies in bibliography; papers. v. 15. Charlottesville, 1962. p. 259–266.
   Z1008.V55, v. 15

Dwight's satirical narrative of 778 lines in which Satan visits America.

TYLER, MOSES C. A great college president and what he wrote. *In his* Three men of letters. New York, G. P. Putnam's Sons, 1895. p. 69–127.   PS185.T85

TYNER, WAYNE C. The theology of Timothy Dwight in historical perspective. 1971 ([278] p.)
   Micro AC–1, no. 71–21,007

Thesis (Ph.D.)—University of North Carolina.
Abstracted in *Dissertation Abstracts International*, v. 32A, Aug. 1971, p. 861.

WHITFORD, KATHRYN, *and* PHILIP WHITFORD. Timothy Dwight's place in eighteenth-century American science. *In* American Philosophical Society, *Philadelphia*. Proceedings, v. 114, Feb. 1970: 60–71.
   Q11.P5, v. 114

13268
DYER, ELIPHALET (1721–1807)*
Connecticut. Lawyer, assemblyman, councilor, judge, delegate to the Continental Congress.

———— The expenses of a Congressman in 1777; political account book of Eliphalet Dyer of Connecticut. Connecticut magazine, v. 10, Jan./Mar. 1906: 28–32.
F91.C8, v. 10
Records furnished by Melvil Dewey. Introduction by Francis T. Miller.

————Remarks on Dr. Gale's letter to J. W., Esq. [Hartford] 1769. 27 p.   F97.G154 Rare Bk. Coll.
Relating to the Susquehanna Company.

GROCE, GEORGE C.   Eliphalet Dyer: Connecticut revolutionist. *In* The Era of the American Revolution; studies inscribed to Evarts Boutell Greene. Edited by Richard B. Morris. New York, Columbia University Press, 1939. p. 290–304.   E203.E74

EARDLEY-WILMOT, JOHN
See WILMOT, JOHN

13269
EARL, RALPH (1751–1801)*
Massachusetts; England; New York. Loyalist, portrait artist.

Connecticut. *Tercentenary Commission.* Connecticut portraits by Ralph Earl, 1751–1801. [New Haven, Yale University Press, 1935] 30 p. illus., ports.
ND237.E18C6
Biographical sketch of artist signed: William Sawitzky.

GOODRICH, LAURENCE B.   Ralph Earl, recorder for an era. [Albany] State University of New York [1967] vii, 96 p. illus., ports. (part col.)   ND237.E18G6
Bibliographic references included in "Notes" (p. 95–96).
Includes reproductions of 41 paintings and portraits.

13270
EASTBURN, JOSEPH (1748–1828)
Pennsylvania. Cabinetmaker, Revolutionary soldier, preacher.

GREEN, ASHBEL.   Memoirs of the Rev. Joseph Eastburn, stated preacher in the Mariner's Church, Philadelphia. Philadelphia, G. W. Mentz, 1828. vi, 208 p. port.
F158.44.E125

13271
EASTON, NICHOLAS (*fl.* 1785–1788)
Rhode Island.

MASON, GEORGE C.   Nicholas Easton *vs.* the city of Newport [1785–86] *In* Rhode Island Historical Society. Collections. v. 7. Providence, 1885. p. [327]–344.
F76.R47, v. 7
On his claim to the ownership of the section known as Easton's Pond, Marsh and Beach.

13272
EBELING, CHRISTOPH DANIEL (1741–1817)
Germany. Historian, librarian.

CANNON, DONALD Q.   Christoph D. Ebeling, a German geographer of America. 1967. ([285] p.)
Micro AC–1, no. 67–13538
Thesis (Ph.D.)—Clark University.
Abstracted in *Dissertation Abstracts*, v. 28A, Nov. 1967, p. 1755.

LANDIS, CHARLES I.   Charles Daniel Ebeling, who from 1793 to 1816 published in Germany a geography and history of the United States in seven volumes. *In* Pennsylvania-German Society. Proceedings and addresses. v. 36; 1925. [Lancaster, Pa.] 1929. p. [13]–27.
F146.P23, v. 36

13273
EDDIS, WILLIAM (1738–1825)*
England; Maryland. Secretary, Loyalist.

———— Letters from America, historical and descriptive; comprising occurrences from 1769 to 1777 inclusive. London, Printed for the author, 1792. [48], 455 p.
F184.E2 1792
A new edition, edited by Aubrey C. Land, has been published in Cambridge by the Belknap Press of Harvard University Press (1969. 237 p. F184.E2 1969).

WILLIAMS, GEORGE H.   William Eddis: what the sources say. Maryland historical magazine, v. 60, June 1965: 121–131.   F176.M18, v. 60

13274
EDDY, JONATHAN (1726–1804)
Massachusetts; Nova Scotia; Maine. Revolutionary officer, assemblyman.

BENT, G. O.   Jonathan Eddy and Grand Manan. Acadiensis, v. 6, July 1906: 165–171.   F1036.A16, v. 6

PORTER, JOSEPH W.   Memoir of Colonel Jonathan Eddy, of Eddington, Maine. Bangor historical magazine, v. 4, Sept. 1888: 41–54.   F16.M21, v. 4

———— Memoir of Col. Jonathan Eddy of Eddington, Me.: with some account of the Eddy family, and of the early settlers on Penobscot River. Augusta [Me.] Sprague, Owen & Nash, Printers, 1877. 72 p.   E275.E21

13275
EDEN, Sir ROBERT (1741–1784)*
England; Maryland. Royal governor.

——— Correspondence of Governor Eden [1769–77] Maryland historical magazine, v. 2, Mar.–Dec. 1907: 1–13, 97–110, 227–244, 293–309.   F176.M18, v. 2

BEIRNE, ROSAMOND R.   Portrait of a colonial governor: Robert Eden. Maryland historical magazine, v. 45, Sept.–Dec. 1950: 153–175, 294–311. plate, port.
      F176.M18, v. 45

STEINER, BERNARD C.   Life and administration of Sir Robert Eden. Baltimore, Johns Hopkins Press, 1898. 142 p. port. (Johns Hopkins University studies in historical and political science, 16th ser., no. 7–9)   F184.E22
      H31.J6, 16th s., no. 7–9

EDEN, WILLIAM
   See AUCKLAND, WILLIAM EDEN, 1st Baron

13276
EDES, BENJAMIN (1732–1803)*
Massachusetts. Newspaper editor, journalist.

SILVER, ROLLO G.   Benjamin Edes, trumpeter of sedition. In Bibliographical Society of America. Papers, v. 47, 3d quarter 1953: 248–268.   Z1001.B51P, v. 47

13277
EDES, PETER (1756–1840)
Massachusetts. Printer. Son of Benjamin Edes (1732–1803).

——— A diary of Peter Edes, the oldest printer in the United States, written during his confinement in Boston, by the British, one hundred and seven days, in the year 1775, immediately after the battle of Bunker Hill. Bangor, S. S. Smith, Printer, 1837. 24 p.
      E281.E23 Rare Bk. Coll.
   "A list of the prisoners taken at the battle of Bunker Hill": p. 24.

BOARDMAN, SAMUEL L., ed.   Peter Edes, pioneer printer in Maine, a biography; his diary while a prisoner by the British at Boston, in 1775, with the journal of John Leach, who was a prisoner at the same time. Bangor, Printed for the De Burians, 1901. ix, 159 p. illus., facsims. (The De Burians. Publications, 1)
      Z232.E22B6

13278
EDWARDS, BRYAN (1743–1800)†
England; West Indies. Assemblyman, historian.

——— Thoughts on the late proceedings of government, respecting the trade of the West India islands with the United States of North America. London, T. Cadell, 1784. vi, 55 p.   HF3074.E3 1784 Rare Bk. Coll.

VENDRYES, HARRY E.   Bryan Edwards, 1743–1800. Jamaican historical review, v. 1, June 1945: 76–82.
      F1861.J32, v. 1

13279
EDWARDS, MORGAN (1722–1795)*
England; Pennsylvania; Delaware. Baptist clergyman and historian, Loyalist.

——— Morgan Edwards' materials towards a history of the Baptists in the province of North Carolina. North Carolina historical review, v. 7, July 1930: 365–391.
      F251.N892, v. 7
   Taken from a notebook compiled in 1771–72 and now in the possession of the American Baptist Historical Society. Introduction and notes by G. W. Paschal.

MOORE, JOHN S.   Morgan Edwards: Baptist statesman. Baptist history and heritage, v. 6, Jan. 1971: 24–33.
      BX6207.A407, v. 6

13280
EGAN, EDMUND (d. 1787)
England; South Carolina. Merchant, brewer.

WALSH, WALTER R.   Edmund Egan: Charleston's rebel brewer. South Carolina historical magazine, v. 56, Oct. 1955: 200–204.   F266.S55, v. 56

13281
ELBERT, SAMUEL (1740–1788)*
South Carolina; Georgia. Merchant, Indian trader, Revolutionary officer, governor.

JONES, CHARLES C.   The life and services of the Honorable Maj. Gen. Samuel Elbert, of Georgia. Cambridge [Mass.] Riverside Press, 1887. 48 p.   E207.E3J7
   Reprinted in New York by W. Abbatt (1911. 37 p. E173.M24, no. 13) as extra number, no. 13, of The Magazine of History, With Notes and Queries.

13282
ELFE, THOMAS (1719–1775)
South Carolina. Cabinet maker.

——— The Thomas Elfe account book, 1768–1775. South Carolina historical and genealogical magazine, v. 35, Jan.–Oct. 1934: 13–24, 58–73, 96–106, 153–165; v. 36, Jan.–Oct. 1935: 7–13, 56–66, 79–88, 122–133; v. 37, Jan.–Oct. 1936: 24–32, 77–83, 111–122, 151–156; v. 38, Jan.–Oct. 1937: 37–42, 54–61, 87–94, 131–136; v. 39, Jan.–Oct. 1938: 36–41, 83–90, 134–142, 160–167; v. 40, Jan.–Oct. 1939: 21–27, 58–63, 81–86, 145–150; v. 41, Jan.–Oct. 1940: 23–29, 61–68, 123–129, 151–156; v. 42, Jan. 1941: 12–19.   F266.S55, v. 35–42
   Introduction and notes by Mabel L. Webber.

13283
ELIOT, ANDREW (1718–1778)
Massachusetts. Congregational clergyman.

———Letters from Andrew Eliot to Thomas Hollis [1766–71] *In* Massachusetts Historical Society, *Boston.* Collections. 4th ser., v. 4. Boston, 1858. p. 398–461.
F61.M41, 4th ser., v. 4

——— Letters of Andrew Eliot [1775–76] *In* Massachusetts Historical Society, *Boston.* Proceedings. v. 16; 1878. Boston, 1879. p. 280–306. F61.M38, v. 16

Introduction and notes by George Dexter.

13284
ELIOT, *Lady* HARRIOT PITT (1758–1786)
Daughter of William Pitt, *1st Earl of Chatham* (1708–1778).

———The letters of Lady Harriot Eliot, 1766–1786. Edited by Cuthbert Headlam. Edinburg, Printed by T. and A. Constable, 1914. xv, 151 p. port. DA512.E4A3

13285
ELLERY, WILLIAM (1727–1820)*
Rhode Island. Lawyer, assemblyman, delegate to the Continental Congress.

——— Diary of the Hon. William Ellery, of Rhode Island—October 20 to November 15, 1777. Pennsylvania magazine of history and biography, v. 11, Oct. 1887: 318–329. F146.P65, v. 11

Records his journeys to and from Congress. The section on his travels through Berks County, Pennsylvania, is reprinted in the *Historical Review of Berks County*, v. 25, spring 1960, p. 59–61, with comments by J. Bennett Nolan.

——— Journal of route and occurrences in a journey to Philadelphia from Dighton, begun Oct. 24th, 1778. Pennsylvania magazine of history and biography, v. 12, July 1888: 190–199. F146.P65, v. 12

——— A letter from William Ellery to Henry Marchant [Nov. 6, 1775] Rhode Island history, v. 24, Apr. 1965: 49–54. F76.R472, v. 24

FOWLER, WILLIAM M. William Ellery: a Rhode Island politico and lord of admiralty. 1971. ([224] p.)
Micro AC–1, no. 71–27,756

Thesis (Ph.D.)—University of Notre Dame.
Abstracted in *Dissertation Abstracts International,* v. 32A, Nov. 1971, p. 2578.

——— William Ellery: an American lord of admiralty. American Neptune, v. 31, Oct. 1971: 235–252.
V1.A4, v. 31

——— William Ellery: making of a Rhode Island politician. Rhode Island history, v. 30, fall 1971: 124–135. illus., facsim. F76.R472, v. 30

FRANKLIN, SUSAN B. William Ellery, signer of the Declaration of Independence. Rhode Island history, v. 12, Oct. 1953: 110–119; v. 13, Jan.–Apr. 1954; 11–17, 44–52. F76.R472, v. 12–13

13286
ELLETSON, ROGER HOPE (*b.* 1727)
Jamaica. Assemblyman, councilor.

——— Roger Hope Elletson's letter book [June 2, 1766–September 27, 1768] Jamaican historical review, v. 1, Dec. 1946: 187–220; Dec. 1948: 310–366; v. 2, Dec. 1949: 51–119; Oct. 1952: 63–113; Dec. 1953: 44–90. illus., facsim. F1861.J32, v. 1–2

Introduction and notes by H. P. Jacobs.

13287
ELLICOTT, ANDREW (1754–1820)*
Pennsylvania; Maryland. Revolutionary officer, surveyor.

ALEXANDER, SALLY K. A sketch of the life of Major Andrew Ellicott. *In* Columbia Historical Society, *Washington, D.C.* Records. v. 2. Washington, 1899. p. [158]–202. F191.C72, v. 2

BARTLETT, GEORGE HUNTER. Andrew and Joseph Ellicott. *In* Buffalo Historical Society. Publications. v. 26. Buffalo, 1922. p. 3–48. illus., map, ports.
F129.B8B88, v. 26

MATHEWS, CATHARINE V. Andrew Ellicott, an astronomer, surveyor, and soldier of a hundred years ago. Grafton magazine of history and genealogy, v. 1, June 1908: 32–42. E171.G73, v. 1

——— Andrew Ellicott, his life and letters. New York, Grafton Press [c1908] x, 256 p. facsims., maps (part fold.), plans, plates, ports. F106.E46

13288
ELLIOT, ANDREW (1728–1797)
Scotland; Pennsylvania; New York. Merchant, Loyalist.

DEVEREUX, EUGENE. Andrew Elliot, lieutenant-governor of the province of New York. Pennsylvania magazine of history and biography, v. 11, July 1887: 129–150. F146.P65, v. 11

13289
ELLIOTT, BARNARD (*d.* 1778)
South Carolina. Revolutionary officer.

——— Bernard [*sic*] Elliott's recruiting journal, 1775. South Carolina historical and genealogical magazine, v. 17, July 1916: 95–100. F266.S55, v. 17

Annotated by Joseph W. Barnwell. Reflects conditions in the state just at the outbreak of the war.

13290
ELLIOTT, MATTHEW (*ca.* 1739–1814)
Ireland; Pennsylvania; Ohio. Indian trader, landowner.

HORSMAN, REGINALD. Matthew Elliott, British Indian agent. Detroit, Wayne State University Press, 1964. xiii, 256 p. map.　　　　　　　　　　E92.E45H6

Includes bibliographic references.

13291

ELLIS, JOHN (1710?–1776)†

England. Royal agent, botanist.

REA, ROBERT R. The King's agent for British West Florida. Alabama review, v. 16, Apr. 1963: 141–153.
　　　　　　　　　　　　　　　　F321.A2535, v. 16

13292

ELLSWORTH, OLIVER (1745–1807)*

Connecticut. Lawyer, assemblyman, delegate to the Continental Congress, judge, delegate to the Constitutional Convention.

BROWN, WILLIAM G. A Continental congressman: Oliver Ellsworth, 1777–1783. American historical review, v. 10, July 1905: 751–781.　　　E171.A57, v. 10

———— ———— Offprint. [New York, 1905] p. 751–781.　　　　　　　　　　E302.6.E4B8

——— The early life of Oliver Ellsworth [to 1777] American historical review, v. 10, Apr. 1905: 534–564.
　　　　　　　　　　　　　　　　E171.A57, v. 10

——— The life of Oliver Ellsworth. New York, Macmillan Co., 1905. ix, 369 p. plates, ports.　[E302.6.E4B82]
　　　　　　　　　　　　　　　　KF8745.E4B7

Reprinted in New York by Da Capo Press (1970).

13293

ELMER, JONATHAN (1727–1807)

Connecticut; New Jersey. Clergyman.

CORY, A. M. Life and times of Rev. Jonathan Elmer. In New Jersey Historical Society. Proceedings, 3d ser., v. 3, Apr.–July 1906: 97–105, 171–179; v. 4, Oct. 1906: 41–49.　　　　　F131.N58, 3d s., v. 3–4

ELPHINSTONE, GEORGE KEITH

See KEITH, GEORGE KEITH ELPHINSTONE, Viscount

13294

ELY, SAMUEL CULLICK (1740–1795)

Connecticut; Vermont; Massachusetts. Clergyman, mercenary.

MOODY, ROBERT E. Samuel Ely: forerunner of Shays. New England quarterly, v. 5, Jan. 1932: 105–134.
　　　　　　　　　　　　　　　　F1.N62, v. 5

13295

EMERSON, WILLIAM (1743–1776)

Massachusetts. Revolutionary chaplain.

——— Diaries and letters of William Emerson, 1743–1776, minister of the church in Concord, chaplain in the Revolutionary army. Arranged by Amelia Forbes Emerson. [n.p., 1972] xi, 150 p. illus.
　　　　　　　　　　　　　　BX7260.E64A3 1972

Bibliography: p. 136–137.

EMERSON, EDWARD W. A chaplain of the Revolution. In Massachusetts Historical Society, Boston. Proceedings. v. 55; 1921/22. Boston, 1923. p. 8–29.
　　　　　　　　　　　　　　　　F61.M38, v. 55

13296

EMERY, NOAH (1725–1788)

New Hampshire. Lawyer, assemblyman.

STEVENS, CHARLES E. Noah Emery of Exeter, member of the provincial congress and clerk of the assembly in New Hampshire in the Revolution. [Worcester, Mass.] Priv. print., 1886. 39 p. facsim.　　E263.N4E5

13297

EQUIANO, OLAUDAH (ca. 1745–1797)

Africa; America; England. Seaman, traveler, abolitionist.

——— The interesting narrative of the life of Olaudah Equiano, or Gustavus Vassa, the African. Written by himself. 8th ed., enl. Norwich, 1794. xxxiv, 360 p. fold. plate, port.　　HT869.E6A3 1794 Rare Bk. Coll.

The first edition (London, 1789) has been reprinted, with a new introduction by Paul Edwards, under the title The Life of Olaudah Equiano; or, Gustavus Vassa the African, 1789 (London, Dawsons of Pall Mall, 1969. 2 v. HT869.E6A3 1969b). Edwards has also published an abridged edition under the title Equiano's Travels (New York, Praeger [1967] 196 p. HT869.E6A3 1967).

13298

ERNST, ANNA CATHARINA ANTES (1726–1816)

Pennsylvania. Moravian missionary.

FRIES, ADELAIDE L. The road to Salem. Chapel Hill, University of North Carolina Press [c1944] x, 316 p. facsims., maps, plates, ports.　　　　F265.M8F83

"The story of Anna Catharina [Ernst] is taken from her autobiography, filed in manuscript in the Salem Moravian archives, elaborated with information gained from diaries and other records kept by leaders of the Moravian Church in Georgia, Pennsylvania, and North Carolina."—Preface.

13299

ERSKINE, MARGARET HANDLEY (1753–1842)

Virginia; Ohio.

——— A captive of the Shawnees, 1779–1784. West Virginia history, v. 23, July 1962: 287–296.　F236.W52, v. 23

Introduction and notes by John H. Moore.

13300
ERSKINE, ROBERT (1735–1780)*

Scotland; New Jersey. Engineer, Revolutionary officer and mapmaker.

HEUSSER, ALBERT H.   George Washington's map maker; a biography of Robert Erskine. Edited with an introduction by Hubert G. Schmidt. New Brunswick, N.J., Rutgers University Press [1966] xix, 268 p. illus., facsims., map (part fold.)   E207.E7H6 1966

Bibliographic footnotes.
First published under the title "The Forgotten General" in *Americana*, v. 20, Oct. 1926, p. 465–518; v. 21, Apr.–July 1927, p. 121–175, 333–383; v. 22, Jan. 1928, p. 1–41, and reissued as a single volume as *The Forgotten General, Robert Erskine, F.R.S. (1735–1780), Geographer and Surveyor General to the Army of the United States* (Paterson, N.J., Benjamin Franklin Press [ᶜ1928] 216 p. E207.E7H6).

13301
ERWIN, JOSEPH (1758–1807)

Ireland; Pennsylvania. Merchant.

——— A Philadelphia merchant in 1768–1791. Pennsylvania magazine of history and biography, v. 19, Oct. 1895: 397–402.   F146.P65, v. 19

An autobiographical sketch. Contributed by Arthur E. Brown.

13302
ESTAING, CHARLES HENRI, *comte d'* (1729–1794)

France. French admiral in America.

CALMON-MAISON, JEAN, J. R.   L'amiral d'Estaing (1729–1794). Paris, Calmann-Lévy, 1910. 513 p. port.   DC137.5.E7C2

MORAN, CHARLES.   D'Estaing, an early exponent of amphibious warfare. Military affairs, v. 9, winter 1945: 314–332.   E181.M55, v. 9

13303
ETTWEIN, JOHN, *Bp.* (1721–1802)*

Germany; Pennsylvania. Moravian clergyman, missionary.

——— Correspondence with Sylvester W. Gardiner and his son John Gardiner of Boston. *In* Moravian Historical Society, *Nazareth, Pa.* Transactions. v. 4, pt. 2. Bethlehem, Pa., 1891. p. 53–69.   E184.M8M8, v. 4   BX8553.M7, v. 4

——— Report of the journey of John Ettwein, David Zeisberger and Gottlob Senseman to Friedenshuetten and their stay there, 1768. Ohio archaeological and historical quarterly, v. 21, Jan. 1912: 32–42.   F486.O51, v. 21

——— Rev. John Ettwein's notes of travel from the north branch of the Susquehanna to the Beaver River, Pennsylvania, 1772. Pennsylvania magazine of history and biography, v. 25, July 1901: 208–219.   F146.P65, v. 25

Contributed by John W. Jordan.

——— Some remarks and annotations concerning the traditions, customs, languages &c of the Indians in North America, from the memoirs of the Reverend David Zeisberger, and other missionaries of the United Brethren. Erminie Wheeler-Voegelin, ed. Ethnohistory, v. 6, winter 1959: 42–69.   E51.E8, v. 6

Addenda appear in the issue for spring 1959, p. 186.

Transcribed from a letter, now in the Library of Congress, that was sent to George Washington on March 28, 1788. Ettwein deals mainly with the Indians of Pennsylvania and Ohio and provides a four-column table of words in English, Maqua, Delaware, and Mahikan.

DE SCHWEINITZ, EDMUND A.   John Ettwein, bishop of the Brethren's church. *In* Moravian Historical Society, *Nazareth, Pa.* Transactions. v. 2. Nazareth, Pa., 1886. p. 247–263.   E184.M8M8, v. 2   BX8553.M7, v. 2

HAMILTON, KENNETH G.   John Ettwein and the Moravian church during the Revolutionary period. Bethlehem, Pa., Times Pub. Co., 1940. 346 p. plates, ports.   BX8593.E8H3

Thesis (Ph.D.)—Columbia University, 1941.
"Reprinted from the Transactions of the Moravian Historical Society, volume XII, parts III and IV."
"A catalogue of the Ettwein papers": p. 298–325. Bibliography included in preface.

WARD, A. GERTRUDE.   John Ettwein and the Moravians in the Revolution. Pennsylvania history, v. 1, Oct. 1934: 191–201.   F146.P597, v. 1

13304
EUSTACE, JOHN SKEY (1760–1805)

New York; Georgia. Revolutionary officer, lawyer.

——— Lettre de M. J. S. Eustace, ci-devant aide-de-camp des majors, généraux Lée & Sullivan, colonel, & adjutant-général de l'état de Géorgie, à Monsieur Joseph Fenwick, consul des États-Unis de l'Amérique à Bordeaux. [Bordeaux, Impr. de Moreau & Delormel, 1792] 15 p.   E275.E9 Rare Bk. Coll.

Dated at end: Bordeaux . . . ce 10 mars 1792.

13305
EVANS, CADWALADER (1716–1773)

Pennsylvania. Physician.

KLEIN, RANDOLPH S.   Dr. Cadwalader Evans (1716–1773): physician and friend of Benjamin Franklin. *In* College of Physicians of Philadelphia. Transactions & studies, 4th ser., v. 35, July 1967: 30–36.   R15.P5, 4th s., v. 35

13306

EVANS, GRIFFITH (1760–1845)

Pennsylvania. Revolutionary soldier.

—— Journal of Griffith Evans, 1784–1785. Pennsylvania magazine of history and biography, v. 65, Apr. 1941: 202–233. F146.P65, v. 65

Kept while Evans served as secretary and storekeeper to the Indian commissioners from Pennsylvania at Fort Stanwix and Fort McIntosh.

13307

EVANS, ISRAEL (1747–1807)

New Hampshire. Revolutionary chaplain.

—— A discourse delivered near York in Virginia, on the memorable occasion of the surrender of the British army to the allied forces of America and France, before the brigade of New-York troops and the division of American light-infantry, under the command of the Marquis de La Fayette. By Israel Evans, A.M., chaplain to the troops of New-Hampshire. Philadelphia, Printed by F. Bailey, 1782. 45 p.

E241.Y6E92 Rare Bk. Coll.

Reprinted in Tarrytown, N.Y., by W. Abbatt (1922. [5]–33 p. E173.M24, no. 82) as extra number, no. 82, of *The Magazine of History, With Notes and Queries.*

THORNE, JOHN C. A monograph of the Rev. Israel Evans, A.M., chaplain in the American army during the entire Revolutionary War, 1775–1783. The second settled minister of Concord, New Hampshire, 1789–1797. [Concord? 1902] 26 p. illus., port. F44.C7T4

Reprinted in New York by W. Abbatt (1907. 32 p. E173.M24, no. 1) as extra number, no. 1, of *The Magazine of History, With Notes and Queries.*

—— Reverend Israel Evans, A.M., chaplain, American army, during the entire Revolutionary War, 1776 to 1783; Concord's second settled minister, 1789 to 1797. Granite monthly, v. 33, Nov. 1902: 284–310. illus., facsims., ports. F31.G75, v. 33

13308

EVANS, NATHANIEL (1742–1767)*

Pennsylvania. Poet, Anglican clergyman.

—— Poems on several occasions, with some other compositions. By Nathaniel Evans, A.M., late missionary (appointed by the Society for Propagating the Gospel) for Gloucester County, in New-Jersey; and chaplain to the lord viscount Kilmorey, of the kingdom of Ireland. Philadelphia, Printed by John Dunlap, in Market-Street, 1772. xxviii, 160, 24 p.

PS744.E6P6 Rare Bk. Coll.

The preface, signed William Smith, contains a brief biographical sketch of the author.

Reprinted in New York by Garrett Press (1970).

MILLIGAN, BURTON A. An early American imitator of Milton. American literature, v. 11, May 1939: 200–206. PS1.A6, v. 11

PENNINGTON, EDGAR L. Nathaniel Evans; a poet of colonial America. Ocala, Fla., Taylor Print. Co., 1935. [34] p. PS744.E6Z8

Bibliography: p. [34]

——Nathaniel Evans, some notes on his ministry. *In* American Antiquarian Society, *Worcester, Mass.* Proceedings, new ser., v. 50, Apr. 1940: 91–97.

E172.A35, n.s., v. 50

13309

EVARTS, SYLVANUS (*b.* 1721?)

Connecticut; Vermont. Surveyor, landowner, Loyalist.

ROBERTS, GWILYM R. An unknown Vermonter: Sylvanus Evarts, Governor Chittenden's Tory brother-in-law. Vermont history, new ser., v. 29, Apr. 1961: 92–100. F46.V55, n.s., v. 29

13310

EVE, SARAH (1749 *or* 50–1774)

Pennsylvania.

—— Extracts from the journal of Miss Sarah Eve, written while living near the city of Philadelphia in 1772–73. Pennsylvania magazine of history and biography, v. 5, no. 1–2, 1881: 19–36, 191–205. F146.P65, v. 5

On social and family affairs. She became engaged to Benjamin Rush but died three weeks before the wedding ceremony.

13311

EVELYN, WILLIAM GLANVILLE (1742–1776)

British officer in America.

—— Memoir and letters of Captain W. Glanville Evelyn, of the 4th Regiment ("King's Own") from North America, 1774–1776. Edited and annotated by G. D. Scull. Oxford, Printed for private circulation by J. Parker, 1879. x, 140 p. ports. E275.E93

Reprinted in New York Times (1971).

13312

EWING, GEORGE (1754–1824)

New Jersey; West Virginia. Revolutionary officer, schoolteacher.

—— The military journal of George Ewing (1754–1824), a soldier of Valley Forge. Yonkers, N.Y., Priv. print. by T. Ewing, 1928. 54 p. facsims., maps.

E275.E95 Rare Bk. Coll.

The journal covers a period from November 11, 1775, to May 21, 1778.

[EWING, THOMAS] *comp.* George Ewing, gentleman, a soldier of Valley Forge. Yonkers, N.Y., Priv. print. by

T. Ewing, 1928. 182 (i.e. 195) p. facsims., maps, plate, ports.   E275.E96

Includes his military journal.

13313

EWING, JOHN (1732–1802)*

Maryland; Pennsylvania. Presbyterian clergyman, educator.

—— Memorandum book of Dr. John Ewing with account of a journey to settle the boundary of Penna., May, 1784. *In* Pennsylvania archives. 6th ser., v. 14. Harrisburg, 1907. p. 1–20.   F146.P41, 6th s., v. 14
F157.B7E9

EWING, LUCY E. L.   Dr. John Ewing and some of his noted connections. Introduction by Josiah H. Penniman. Philadephia, Printed for the author [by] the J. C. Winston Co. [c1930] 139 p. coat of arms, plates, ports.
CS71.E942 1930

13314

EXMOUTH, EDWARD PELLEW, *1st Viscount* (1757–1833)†

England. British naval officer in America.

OSLER, EDWARD.   The life of Admiral Viscount Exmouth. London, Smith, Elder; New York, W. Jackson, 1835. xii, 287 p. plan, plates, port.   DA87.1.E9082

PARKINSON, CYRIL NORTHCOTE.   Edward Pellew, Viscount Exmouth, Admiral of the Red. London, Methuen [1934] viii, 478 p. illus., maps, port.
DA87.1.E9P3

13315

EYRE, JEHU (1738–1781)

New Jersey; Pennsylvania. Shipwright, Revolutionary officer.

KEYSER, PETER D.   Memorials of Col. Jehu Eyre. Pennsylvania magazine of history and biography, v. 3, no. 3–4, 1879: 296–307, 412–425.   F146.P65, v. 3

13316

FAIRFAX, THOMAS FAIRFAX, *6th Baron* (1693–1781)*†

England; Virginia. Planter, Loyalist.

BROWN, STUART E.   Virginia baron; the story of Thomas, 6th Lord Fairfax. [Berryville, Va., Chesapeake Book Co., 1965] ix, 245 p. illus., fold. map, ports.
F232.N86F33

Bibliography: p. 205–212.

13317

FANNING, DAVID (1756?–1825)*

North Carolina; New Brunswick. Indian trader, Loyalist officer.

—— Col. David Fanning's narrative of his exploits and adventures as a Loyalist of North Carolina in the American Revolution, supplying important omissions in the copy published in the United States. With an introduction and notes by A. W. Savary. Toronto, Reprinted from the Canadian Magazine, 1908. 55 p.
E278.F2F25

—— The narrative of Colonel David Fanning (a Tory in the Revolutionary War with Great Britain), giving an account of his adventures in North Carolina, from 1775 to 1783, as written by himself, with an introduction [by John H. Wheeler] and explanatory notes. Richmond, Va., Printed for private distribution only, 1861. xxv, 92 p. (Historical documents relating to the old North state, no. 1)   E278.F2F2 Rare Bk. Coll.

Edited, from a copy of the original manuscript, by T. H. Wynne. Many of the notes are by D. L. Swain.

Reprinted in New York for J. Sabin (1865. 86 p. E278.F2F21).

13318

FANNING, KEZIAH COFFIN (1759–1820)

Massachusetts.

—— Keziah Coffin Fanning's diary [1775–89] Historic Nantucket, v. 1, Oct. 1953: 13–14; Jan. 1954: 5–11; Apr.: 11–18; v. 2, July: 33–37; Oct.: 39–45; Jan. 1955: 35–40; Apr.: 33–40; v. 3, July: 62–65; Oct.: 45–50; Jan. 1956: 38–43; Apr.: 23–27; v. 4, July: 35–39. port.
F72.N2H68, v. 1–4

Edited by Nancy S. Adams.

Issues no. 2–4 of v. 3 are erroneously numbered v. 4.

13319

FANNING, NATHANIEL (1755–1805)*

Connecticut. Revolutionary naval officer, privateersman.

—— Narrative of the adventures of an American Navy officer, who served during part of the American Revolution under the command of Com. John Paul Jones. New York, Printed for the author, 1806. 270 p.
E271.F21 Rare Bk. Coll.

The Naval History Society issued a new edition of Fanning's *Narrative*, edited and annotated by John S. Barnes, in New York (De Vinne Press, 1912. 258 p. E271.F22 Rare Bk. Coll.) as volume 2 of its *Publications*. It has been reprinted in New York by the New York Times (1968).

BROOKS, WALTER F.   Lieutenant Nathaniel Fanning. *In his* History of the Fanning family; a genealogical record to 1900 of the descendants of Edmund Fanning, the emigrant ancestor in America, who settled in Connecticut in 1653. v. 2. Worcester, Mass., Priv. print. for the compiler, 1905. p. 715–738.   [CS71.F213 1905]
Micro 8741 CS

13320

FARIS, WILLIAM (1728–1804)

Pennsylvania; Maryland. Clockmaker, silversmith, innkeeper.

BARR, LOCKWOOD A. William Faris, 1728–1804, silversmith, clock and watch maker of Annapolis, Md. Maryland historical magazine, v. 36, Dec. 1941: 420–439.
F176.M18, v. 36

——— ——— Detached copy. NK7198.F3B35

13321

FARNHAM, RALPH (1756–1861)

New Hampshire; Maine. Farmer, Revolutionary soldier, settler.

CLARENCE, C. W. A biographical sketch of the life of Ralph Farnham, of Acton, Maine; now in the one hundred and fifth year of his age, and the sole survivor of the glorious battle of Bunker Hill. Boston, 1860. 48 p. port.
E275.F22

13322

FARNSWORTH, AMOS (1754–1847)

Massachusetts. Revolutionary soldier.

——— Diary kept during a part of the Revolutionary War by Amos Farnsworth, of Groton [April 1775–May 1779] In Massachusetts Historical Society, Boston. Proceedings. 2d ser., v. 12; 1897/99. Boston, 1899. p. 74–107.
F61.M38, 2d s., v. 12

Introduction and notes by Samuel A. Green.
An offprint with a slightly different title was published in Cambridge by J. Wilson (1898. 36 p. E275.F23).

13323

FARNUM, BENJAMIN (1746–1833)

Massachusetts. Revolutionary officer.

——— Diary of Captain Benjamin Farnum: from Lexington to Valley Forge. Picket post, no. 59, Feb. 1958: 11–15.
E234.P5, no. 59

Comments by Edwin W. Lovejoy.

13324

FARRAGUT, GEORGE (1755–1817)*

Minorca; South Carolina. Mariner, Revolutionary officer.

PAULLIN, CHARLES O. The father of Admiral Farragut. Louisiana historical quarterly, v. 13, Jan. 1930: 37–45.
F366.L79, v. 13

13325

FAUQUIER, FRANCIS (1704?–1768)*†

Virginia. Royal governor.

——— Letters of Governor Francis Fauquier [1766–67] William and Mary College quarterly historical magazine, v. 21, Jan. 1913: 163–171. F221.W71, v. 21

NORKUS, NELLIE. Francis Fauquier, Lieutenant-Governor of Virginia, 1758–1768: a study in colonial problems. 1954. ([664] p.) Micro AC–1, no. 7994
Thesis (Ph.D)—University of Pittsburgh.
Abstracted in Dissertation Abstracts, v. 14, no. 9, 1954, p. 1363.

13326

FAVROT, PIERRE JOSEPH (1749–1824)

Louisiana. French and Spanish officer.

PARKHURST, HELEN. Don Pedro Favrot, a Creole Pepys. Louisiana historical quarterly, v. 28, July 1945: 679–734. F366.L79, v. 28

13327

FAYSSOUX, PETER (1745–1795)*

South Carolina. Physician, Revolutionary surgeon.

DAVIDSON, CHALMERS G. Friend of the people; the life of Dr. Peter Fayssoux of Charleston, South Carolina. Columbia, Medical Association of South Carolina, 1950. vii, 151 p. R154.F42D3
Bibliography: p. 142–151.

13328

FEBIGER, CHRISTIAN (1746–1796)*

Denmark; Massachusetts; Virginia; Pennsylvania. Revolutionary officer.

JOHNSTON, HENRY P. Christian Febiger, colonel of the Virginia Line of the Continental Army. Magazine of American history, with notes and queries, v. 6, Mar. 1881: 188–203. E171.M18, v. 6

13329

FELTMAN, WILLIAM

Pennsylvania. Revolutionary officer.

——— The journal of Lieut. William Feltman, of the First Pennsylvania Regiment, 1781–82. Including the march into Virginia and the siege of Yorktown. Philadelphia, Published for the Historical Society of Pennsylvania, by H. C. Baird, 1853. 48 p. E275.F32
Reprinted in New York by the New York Times (1969). First published in the Collections of the Pennsylvania Historical Society, v. 1, May 1853, p. 303–348.

13330

FENWICK, JOHN CESLAS (ca. 1759–1815)

Maryland; Belgium. Roman Catholic priest.

——— Maryland students in Flanders: letters of John Ceslas Fenwick, O.P., 1784–1789. In American Catholic Historical Society of Philadelphia. Records, v. 74, Sept. 1963: 185–192.　　　　　E184.C3A4, v. 74

Introduction and notes by Richard K. McMaster.

O'DANIEL, VICTOR F.　The Rev. John Ceslas Fenwick, O.P. (1759–1815). Catholic historical review, v. 1, Apr. 1915: 17–29.　　　　　BX1404.C3, v. 1

Includes bibliographic footnotes.

13331

FENWICK, JOSEPH (b. ca. 1769)
　Maryland; France. Merchant.

—— The tobacco trade with France: letters of Joseph Fenwick, consul at Bordeaux, 1787–1795. Maryland historical magazine, v. 60, Mar. 1965: 26–55.
　　　　　F176.M18, v. 60

Introduction and notes by Richard K. McMaster.

13332

FERGUSON, ELIZABETH GRAEME (1737–1801)*
　Pennsylvania. Poet, translator.

Some material for a biography of Mrs. Elizabeth Ferguson, née Graeme.　Pennsylvania magazine of history and biography, v. 39, July–Oct. 1915: 257–321, 385–409; v. 41, Oct. 1917: 385–398.　　F146.P597, v. 39, 41

Miscellaneous letters, 1758–96. Introduction and notes by Simon Gratz.

13333

FERGUSON, PATRICK (1744–1780)†
　Scotland. British officer in America.

FERGUSON, ADAM.　Biographical sketch or memoir of Lieutenant-Colonel Patrick Ferguson, originally intended for the British Encyclopaedia. Edinburgh, Printed by J. Moir, 1817. 35 p.　DA67.1.F47F4

13334

FERGUSON, WILLIAM (d. 1791)
　Pennsylvania. Revolutionary officer.

ALEXANDER, CHARLES B.　Major William Ferguson, member of the American Philosophical Society, officer in the army of the Revolution and in the Army of the United States. New York [Trow Press] 1908. 70 p.
　　　　　E207.F3A3

13335

FERSEN, HANS AXEL VON, grefve (1755–1810)*
　Sweden. French officer in America.

—— Le comte de Fersen et la cour de France. Extraits des papiers du grand maréchal de Suède, comte Jean Axel de Fersen, publiés par son petit-neveu, le baron R. M. de Klinckowström. Paris, Firmin-Didot, 1877–78. 2 v. facsim., port.　　　　　DC137.5.F4A3

—— Diary and correspondence of Count Axel Fersen, grand-marshal of Sweden, relating to the court of France. Translated by Katharine Prescott Wormeley. [Versailles ed.] Boston, Hardy, Pratt, 1902. vii, 355 p. facsim., port.　　　　　DC137.5.F4A4

—— The French Army in the Revolutionary War. Count de Fersen's private letters to his father, 1780–81. Magazine of American history, with notes and queries, v. 25, Jan.–Feb. 1891: 55–70, 156–173.　　E171.M18, v. 25

Translated and edited by Georgine Holmes, with a biographical note on Fersen by George McLaughlin.

—— Letters of de Fersen, aid-de-camp to Rochambeau, written to his father in Sweden, 1780–1782. Magazine of American history, with notes and queries, v. 3, Apr.–July 1879: 300–309, 369–376, 437–448.
　　　　　E171.M18, v. 3

Translated from Le Comte de Fersen (Paris, 1877–78), edited by Baron de Klinckowström.

—— Lettres d'Axel de Fersen à son père, pendant la guerre de l'indépendance d'Amérique. Publiées avec une introduction et des notes par le comte F. U. Wrangel. Paris, Firmin-Didot, 1929. vii, 199 p. port.　　E265.F39

BARTON, HILDOR A.　Count Hans Axel von Fersen: a political biography to 1800. 1962. ([484] p.)
　　　　　Micro AC–1, no. 62–3620

Thesis (Ph.D.)—Princeton University.
Abstracted in Dissertation Abstracts, v. 23, Sept. 1962, p. 1002.

BISHOP, MORRIS.　Axel Fersen in America. In his The exotics, being a collection of unique personalities and remarkable characters. New York, American Heritage Press [1969] p. 100–108. port.　　CT105.B56

GAULOT, PAUL.　A friend of the Queen (Marie Antoinette—Count de Fersen) from the French of Paul Gaulot by Mrs. Cashel Hoey. London, W. Heinemann, 1894. 2 v. ports.　　DC137.5.F4G3

13336

FEW, WILLIAM (1748–1828)*
　Maryland; Georgia. Revolutionary officer, assemblyman, delegate to the Continental Congress, delegate to the Constitutional Convention.

—— Autobiography of Col. William Few of Georgia. Magazine of American history, with notes and queries, v. 7, Nov. 1881: 343–358.　　E171.M18, v. 7

13337

FILSON, JOHN (1753?–1788)*
　Pennsylvania; Kentucky. Frontiersman, historian, mapmaker.

—— John Filson's narrative of his defeat on the Wabash, 1786. Filson Club history quarterly, v. 12, Oct. 1938: 187–199.　　　　　F446.F484, v. 12

Introduction and notes by Leonard C. Helderman.

——— Life and adventures of Colonel Daniel Boon, the first white settler of the state of Kentucky, written by himself; to which is added a narration of his latter life until his death; annexed is an eulogy by Lord Byron. Brooklyn, Printed for C. Wilder, 1823. [New York, Reprinted, 1916] 42 p. port. (Heartman's historical series, no. 17)   F454.B743

The first part of the account, extending to 1782, was written in the form of an autobiography of Boone, "from his own mouth," by John Filson and first published in the appendix to his *Discovery, Settlement, and Present State of Kentucky* (Wilmington, Del., 1784). The continuation of the life of Boone is by "a near relation of the colonel" (a resident of Cincinnati).

Reprinted in Tarrytown, N.Y., by W. Abbatt (1932. [5]–29 p. E173.M24, no. 180) as extra number, no. 180, of *The Magazine of History, With Notes and Queries.*

——— Two westward journeys of John Filson, 1785. Mississippi Valley historical review, v. 9, Mar. 1923: 320–330.   E171.J87, v. 9

Especially interesting for his comments about the Indians of the Wabash Valley and life at Vincennes. Introduction and notes by Beverley W. Bond, Jr.

COLEMAN, JOHN WINSTON. John Filson: early Kentucky historian. *In* Historical and Philosophical Society of Ohio. Bulletin, v. 11, Jan. 1953: 56–66. facsim.   F486.H653, v. 11

——— John Filson, Esq., Kentucky's first historian and cartographer. Lexington, Winburn Press, 1954. 16 p.   E175.5.F43

——— John Filson: Kentucky's first historian. Indiana quarterly for bookmen, v. 4, Oct. 1948: 71–80.   Z1007.I5, v. 4

DUNN, C. FRANK. John Filson and Transylvania Seminary. *In* Kentucky Historical Society. Register, v. 45, Oct. 1947: 324–334.   F446.K43, v. 45

DURRETT, REUBEN T. John Filson, the first historian of Kentucky. An account of his life and writings, principally from original sources. Louisville, Filson Club, 1884. 132 p. facsim., fold. map, port. (Filson Club publications, no. 1)   F451.F52

JILLSON, WILLARD R. Filson's map of Wilmington, Delaware. Filson Club history quarterly, v. 7, Oct. 1933: 209–213.   F446.F484, v. 7

THURSTON, ROGERS C. BALLARD. Filson's history and map of Kentucky. Filson Club history quarterly, v. 8, Jan 1934: 1–38.   F446.F484, v. 8

See also Martin F. Schmidt's "Existing Copies of the 1784 Filson Map" in v. 28, Jan. 1954, p. 55–57.

WALTON, JOHN. John Filson of Kentucke. Lexington, University of Kentucky Press [1956] xiv, 130 p. illus., facsim., fold. map (in pocket), port.   E175.5.F44

Bibliographic footnotes.

13338

FINCK, ANDREW (1751–1820)

New York. Revolutionary officer.

KOETTERITZ, JOHN B. Andrew Finck, major in the Revolutionary wars. *In* Herkimer County Historical Society. Papers. v. 1; 1896/98. Herkimer, N.Y., 1899. p. 59–73.   F127.H5H5, v. 1

——— Andrew Finck, major in the Revolutionary wars. Little Falls, N.Y., Press of Stebbins & Burney, 1906. 171 p.   E207.F49K7

Appendix A. Orderly book of Captain A. Finck of the First N.Y. Regiment at Valley Forge and on the Hudson, 1778.—Appendix B. Muster roll of Captain Andrew Finck's company, of Col. Van Schaick's regiment, 1st New York Line, at Valley Forge, April, 1778.—Appendix C. Genealogical notes relating to the Finck family of Stone Arabia, N.Y.

13339

FINDLEY, JOHN (1722–1772)

Ireland; Pennsylvania; Kentucky. Indian trader, settler.

BECKNER, LUCIEN. John Findley: the first pathfinder of Kentucky. Filson Club history quarterly, v. 43, July 1969: 206–215.   F446.F484, v. 43

First published in the *History Quarterly*, v. 1, Apr. 1927, p. 111–122.

13340

FINDLEY, WILLIAM (1741 *or* 2–1821)*

Ireland; Pennsylvania. Farmer, Revolutionary officer, assemblyman.

EWING, ROBERT M. Life and times of William Findley. Western Pennsylvania historical magazine, v. 2, Oct. 1919: 240–251.   F146.W52, v. 2

SCHRAMM, CALLISTA. William Findley in Pennsylvania politics. Western Pennsylvania historical magazine, v. 20, Mar. 1937: 31–40.   F146.W52, v. 20

13341

FINLAY, HUGH (1732–1801)*

Scotland; Quebec. Councilor, road developer, postal surveyor, explorer.

——— Journal kept by Hugh Finlay, Surveyor of the Post Roads on the continent of North America, during his survey of the post offices between Falmouth and Casco Bay, in the Province of Massachusetts, and Savannah in Georgia; begun the 13th Septr. 1773 and ended 26th June 1774. Brooklyn, F. H. Norton, 1867. xxv, 94 p. illus., maps (part fold.)   E163.F51

Edited by Frank H. Norton.

The journal ends abruptly on the 24th of May, 1774, instead of on the 26th of June, as its title page states.

13342

FISHER, ELIJAH (*b.* 1758)

Massachusetts; Maine. Revolutionary soldier.

——— Elijah Fisher's journal while in the War for Independence, and continued two years after he came to Maine. 1775–1784. Augusta [Me.] Press of Badger & Manley, 1880. 29 p.   E275.F53

Transcribed and edited by William B. Lapham.

Reprinted in New York by W. Abbatt (1909. 76 p. E173.M24, no. 6) as extra number, no. 6, of *The Magazine of History, With Notes and Queries.*

13343

FISHER, HENDRICK (1697–1779)

Germany; New Jersey. Farmer, assemblyman.

DAVIS, T. E.   Hendrick Fisher. *In* New Jersey Historical Society. Proceedings, 3d ser., v. 4, May/Oct. 1907: 129–146.   F131.N58, 3d s., v. 4

13344

FISHER, SAMUEL ROWLAND (1745–1834)

Pennsylvania. Merchant, Loyalist.

——— Journal of Samuel Rowland Fisher, of Philadelphia, 1779–1781. Pennsylvania magazine of history and biography, v. 41, Apr.–Oct. 1917: 145–197, 274–333, 399–457.   F146.P65, v. 41

Contributed by Anna W. Morris.

13345

FISHER, SARAH LOGAN (1750 *or* 51–1796)

Pennsylvania. Loyalist.

——— "A diary of trifling occurrences": Philadelphia, 1776–1778. Pennsylvania magazine of history and biography, v. 82, Oct. 1958: 411–465.
                    F146.P65, v. 82

Introduction and notes by Nicholas B. Wainwright.

13346

FITCH, ELIPHALET (*fl.* 1761–1783)

Massachusetts; Jamaica. Import-export merchant.

PARRY, JOHN H.   Eliphalet Fitch: a Yankee trader in Jamaica during the War of Independence. History, new ser., v. 40, Feb./June 1955: 84–98.
                    D1.H815, n.s., v. 40

13347

FITCH, JABEZ (1737–1812)

Connecticut. Farmer, Revolutionary officer.

——— The diary of Jabez Fitch, Jr. [May 29, 1767–Dec. 31, 1770] Mayflower descendant, v. 27, Oct. 1925: 168–175; v. 28, Apr.–Oct. 1926: 71–74, 128–129, 166–170; v. 30, Oct. 1932: 161–164; v. 31, Jan. 1933: 44–46; v. 32, Oct. 1934: 167–171; v. 33, Jan.–Oct. 1935: 30–33,

73–75, 128–131, 176–179; v. 34, Apr.–Oct. 1937: 63–66, 119–122, 165–167.   F68.M46, v. 27–28, 30–34

13348

FITCH, JOHN (1743–1798)*

Connecticut; Kentucky; Pennsylvania. Metalsmith, Revolutionary officer, surveyor, inventor.

——— The original steam-boat supported; or, A reply to Mr. James Rumsey's pamphlet. Shewing the true priority of John Fitch, and the false datings, &c. of James Rumsey. Philadelphia, Printed by Z. Poulson, Junr., 1788. 34 p.   VM619.F54 Rare Bk. Coll.
                    T7.T25, v. 7 Rare Bk. Coll.

Reprinted in Tarrytown, N.Y., by W. Abbatt (1926. 74 p. E173.M24, no. 122) as extra number, no. 12) of *The Magazine of History, With Notes and Queries,* and in Freeport, N.Y., by Books for Libraries Press (1971. 74 p. VM619.F54 1971).

See also Joseph Barnes' *Remarks on Mr. John Fitch's Reply to Mr. James Rumsey's Pamphlet; by Joseph Barnes, Formerly Assistant, and Now Attorney in Fact to James Rumsey* (Philadelphia, Printed by J. James, Chestnut-Street, 1788. xvi, 16 p. VM619.B26 Rare Bk. Coll.) which was reprinted in Tarrytown, N.Y., by W. Abbatt (1928. 5–33 p. E173.M24, no. 139) as extra number, no. 139, to *The Magazine of History, With Notes and Queries.*

BOYD, THOMAS A.   Poor John Fitch, inventor of the steamboat. New York, G. P. Putnam's Sons [ᶜ1935] 315 p. illus., maps (on lining papers)   VM140.F5B6

Bibliography: p. 303–307.

Reprinted in Freeport, N.Y., by Books for Libraries Press (1971).

HACKENSMITH, C. W.   John Fitch: a pioneer in the development of the steamboat. *In* Kentucky Historical Society. Register, v. 65, July 1967: 187–211.
                    F446.K43, v. 65

PARSONS, MIRA C.   John Fitch, inventor of steamboats. *In* Ohio State Archaeological and Historical Society. Publications. v. 8. Columbus, 1900. p. 397–408. map, plate.   F486.O51, v. 8

The author presents further proof of the validity of Fitch's prior claim in the *Ohio Archaeological and Historical Quarterly,* v.9, Oct. 1900, p. 238–242.

PRAGER, FRANK D.   An early steamboat plan of John Fitch [1785] Pennsylvania magazine of history and biography, v. 79, Jan. 1955: 63–80. plans. F146.P65, v. 79

TURNER, DOUGLAS K.   John Fitch, the inventor of steam navigation. *In* Bucks County Historical Society, *Doylestown, Pa.* Collection of papers. v. 2. Doylestown, 1909. p. 22–34.   F157.B8B84, v. 2

WESTCOTT, THOMPSON.   Life of John Fitch, the inventor of the steam-boat. Philadelphia, J. B. Lippincott, 1878. 428 p. illus.   VM140.F5W5 1878

The first edition was published in 1857.

13349

FITHIAN, PHILIP VICKERS (1747–1776)

New Jersey; Virginia. Teacher, Revolutionary chaplain.

—— Letters to his wife, Elizabeth Beatty Fithian. With a biographical sketch by Frank D. Andrews. Vineland, N.J. [Smith Print. House] 1932. 48 p.   E207.F52F5

—— Philip Vickers Fithian, journal and letters, 1767–1774, student at Princeton College, 1770–72, tutor at Nomini Hall in Virginia, 1773–74. Edited for the Princeton Historical Association by John Rogers Williams. Princeton, N.J., University Library, 1900–34. 2 v. maps (part fold.), plates, ports.   E163.F54

Volume 2 has title: *Philip Vickers Fithian: Journal, 1775–1776, Written on the Virginia-Pennsylvania Frontier and in the Army Around New York*, edited by Robert Greenhalgh Albion and Leonidas Dodson.

Volume 2 has imprint: Princeton, Princeton University Press, 1934.

"Journal, October 26, 1774—March 19, 1775": v. 2, p. [254]–258.

Bibliography: v. 2, p. [259]–261.

Volume 1 was reprinted in Freeport, N.Y., by Books for Libraries Press (1969).

Selections from volume 1 were published, with an introduction and notes by John R. Williams, in the *American Historical Review*, v. 5, Jan. 1900, p. 290–319. Since volume 1 was generally unavailable by the 1940's and sections of the Virginia journal had been omitted from it, Hunter Dickinson Farish prepared the *Journal & Letters of Philip Vickers Fithian, 1773–1774: A Plantation Tutor of the Old Dominion* (Williamsburg, Va., Colonial Williamsburg, 1943. 323 p.) and included several contemporary letters as well as Fithian's catalog of the library of Councilor Robert Carter of Nomini Hall. In 1957 Colonial Williamsburg issued a new edition, illustrated by Fritz Kredel (Williamsburg, Va., 1957. 270 p.).

DAVIDSON, MABEL.   Philip Fithian in Virginia. Virginia magazine of history and biography, v. 49, Jan. 1941: 1–19.   F221.V91, v. 49

PARKER, FRANKLIN.   Philip Vickers Fithian: northern tutor on a southern plantation. Journal of the west, v. 4, Jan. 1965: 56–62.   F591.J65, v.4

13350

FITZGERALD, JOHN (d. 1799)

Ireland; Virginia. Revolutionary officer, merchant.

PURCELL, RICHARD J.   A Catholic Revolutionary soldier and patriot. Thought, v. 8, Dec. 1933: 471–488.   AP2.T333, v. 8

13351

FITZPATRICK, JOHN (ca. 1737–1791)

Ireland; Mississippi Valley. Merchant, trader.

BORN, JOHN D.   John Fitzpatrick of Manchac: a Scottish merchant in the lower Mississippi trade prior to the Revolution. Journal of Mississippi history, v. 32, May 1970: 117–134.   F336.J68, v. 32

13352

FITZSIMONS, THOMAS (1741–1811)*

Ireland; Pennsylvania. Merchant, Revolutionary officer, delegate to the Continental Congress, assemblyman, delegate to the Constitutional Convention.

FARRELL, JAMES A.   Thomas FitzSimons. *In* American Catholic Historical Society of Philadelphia. Records, v. 39, Sept. 1928: 175–224.   E184.C3A4, v. 39

FLANDERS, HENRY.   Thomas Fitzsimmons. Pennsylvania magazine of history and biography, v. 2, no. 3, 1878: 306–314.   F146.P65, v. 2

GRIFFIN, MARTIN I. J.   Thomas Fitz Simons, Pennsylvania's Catholic signer of the Constitution of the United States. American Catholic historical researches, v. 5, Jan. 1888: 2–27.   E184.C3A5, v. 5

—— ——   Offprint. Philadelphia, Press of the American Catholic Historical Researches, 1887. 26 p.   E302.6.F56G8

A revised and extended version of the essay appeared in the *Records* of the Catholic Historical Society of Philadelphia, v. 2, 1886/88 (Philadelphia, 1889), p. 45–111.

13353

FLEMING, JOHN (1735–1791)

Virginia; Kentucky. Surveyor, settler.

COTTERILL, ROBERT S.   John Fleming, pioneer of Fleming County. *In* Kentucky Historical Society. Register, v. 49, July 1951: 193–201.   F446.K43, v. 49

13354

FLEMING, WILLIAM (1729–1795)*

Scotland; Virginia. Military surgeon, landowner, Revolutionary officer, assemblyman, councilor.

HOYT, WILLIAM D.   Colonel William Fleming on the Virginia frontier, 1755–1783. [n.p., 1942] [99]–119, 405–434, 175–210 p.   F229.F58H6

Part of thesis (Ph.D.)—Johns Hopkins University, 1940.

Bibliographic footnotes.

Contents: Colonel William Fleming in Dunmore's War, 1774.—Colonel William Fleming, county lieutenant of Botetourt, 1776–1779.—Colonel William Fleming, commissioner to examine and settle the public accounts in the western country, 1782–1783.

Reprinted from *West Virginia History*, v. 3, Jan. 1942, p. 99–119, and *Americana*, v. 35, July 1941, p. 405–434, and v. 36, Apr. 1942, p. 175–210.

13355

FLEMING, WILLIAM (1736–1824)

Virginia. Lawyer, assemblyman, delegate to the Continental Congress, judge.

MAYS, DAVID J. William Fleming, 1736–1824. *In* Virginia State Bar Association. Annual report. v. 39; 1927. Richmond. p. 426–435. LL

13356

FLEURY, FRANÇOIS LOUIS TEISSEIDRE DE (*b.* 1749?)
France. Revolutionary officer, engineer, French officer in America.

KIMBALL, LEROY E. Fleury in the American Revolution. Légion d'honneur, v. 6, July 1935: 21–32. illus., plan.
CR5061.U6A3, v. 6

——— Offprint. New York [American Society of the French Legion of Honor] 1935. 14 p. illus., plan. (Franco-American pamphlet series, no. 6)
E183.8.F8F87, no.6
E265.K52

13357

FLICK, GERLACH PAUL (1728–1826)
Germany; Pennsylvania. Farmer, Revolutionary officer.

FLICK, ALEXANDER C. Captain Gerlach Paul Flick, Pennsylvania pioneer. Pennsylvania magazine of history and biography, v. 53, July 1929: 230–268. facsim.
F146.P65, v. 53

13358

FLOYD, JAMES JOHN (1750?–1783)
Virginia; Kentucky. Surveyor, settler, Revolutionary officer.

CARTLIDGE, ANNA M. Colonel John Floyd: reluctant adventurer. *In* Kentucky Historical Society. Register, v. 66, Oct 1968: 317–366. F446.K43, v. 66

TAPP, HAMBLETON. Colonel John Floyd, Kentucky pioneer. Filson Club history quarterly, v. 15, Jan 1941: 1–24. F446.F484, v. 15

13359

FLOYD, WILLIAM (1734–1821)*
New York. Delegate to the Continental Congress, Revolutionary officer, assemblyman.

MAXWELL, WILLIAM Q. A portrait of William Floyd, Long Islander. [Setauket, Long Island, N.Y., Privately printed by the] Society for the Preservation of Long Island Antiquities, 1956. 43 p. facsims., ports.
F127.L8M29
Bibliography: p. 43.

——— William Floyd at Western, New York. Manuscripts, v. 9, summer 1957: 171–178. Z41.A2A925, v. 9

13360

FOLEY, ELIJAH (*fl.* 1779)
Virginia; Kentucky. Settler.

——— Reverend John D. Shane's notes on an interview with Elijah Foley of Fayette County. Filson Club history quarterly, v. 11, Oct. 1937: 252–259.
F446.F484, v. 11
Introduction and notes by Lucien Beckner.

13361

FOLSOM, NATHANIEL (1726–1790)*
New Hampshire. Merchant, delegate to the Continental Congress, Revolutionary officer, councilor.

BAKER, HENRY M. Nathaniel Folsom. *In* New Hampshire Historical Society. Proceedings. v. 4; 1899/1905. Concord, 1906. p. 253–267. F31.N52, v. 4

——— ——— Offprint. [Concord? N.H., 1904?] 15 p.
E263.N4F7

BRADLEY, CYRUS P. Memoir of Nathaniel Folsom. *In* New Hampshire Historical Society. Collections. v. 5. Concord, 1837. p. 216–221. F31.N54, v. 5

13362

FOOT, CALEB (1750–1787)
Massachusetts. Revolutionary soldier and privateersman.

——— Reminiscences of the Revolution: prison letters and sea journal [1778–82] of Caleb Foot, compiled by his grandson and namesake, Caleb Foote. *In* Essex Institute, *Salem, Mass.* Historical collections, v. 26, Apr./June 1889: 90–122. F72.E7E81, v. 26

13363

FOOTE, EBENEZER (1756–1829)
New York. Revolutionary officer and provisioner.

FOOTE, KATHERINE A., *ed.* Ebenezer Foote, the founder; being an epistolary light on his time as shed by letters from his files, selected by his great-granddaughter Katherine Adelia Foote. Delhi, N.Y., Delaware Express Co., 1927. 224 p. port. CS71.F688F
F123.F7F6

13364

FORBES, JOHN (*d.* 1783)*
Scotland; East Florida. Anglican clergyman, missionary, councilor, judge.

PENNINGTON, EDGAR L. John Forbes (d. 1783): first Church of England clergyman in East Florida, member of the king's council, judge surrogate of the Court of Admiralty, assistant judge of the common law court, chief justice. Florida Historical Society quarterly, v. 8, Jan. 1930: 164–168. F306.F65, v. 8

13365

FORD, TIMOTHY (1762–1830)
New Jersey; South Carolina. Revolutionary soldier, lawyer.

———— Diary of Timothy Ford, 1785–1786. With notes by Joseph W. Barnwell. South Carolina historical and genealogical magazine, v. 13, July–Oct. 1912: 132–147, 181–204. F266.S55, v. 13

Describes his journey from New York to South Carolina.

13366

FOSTER, JEDEDIAH (1726–1779)

Massachusetts. Lawyer, assemblyman, judge.

GRINNELL, FRANK W. A forgotten patriot, Jedediah Foster of Brookfield. *In* Massachusetts Historical Society, *Boston.* Proceedings. v. 67; 1941/44. Boston, 1945. p. 128–134. F61.M38, v. 67

13367

FOTHERGILL, JOHN (1712–1780)†

Scotland; England. Physician, educator.

———— Advice to Philadelphia Freinds by Dr. John Fothergill and David Barclay, 1775. *In* Friends' Historical Association. Bulletin, v. 3, Feb. 1910: 104–111. BX7635.A1F6, v. 3

Letters to James Pemberton on the need to find common grounds for settling the Anglo-American dispute. Introduction by Isaac Sharpless.

———— Chain of friendship; selected letters of Dr. John Fothergill of London, 1735–1780. With introduction and notes by Betsy C. Corner & Christopher C. Booth. Cambridge, Belknap Press of Harvard University Press, 1971. xxiv, 538 p. illus., facsims., geneal. table, map, ports. R489.F6A4 1971

Bibliography: p. 511–519.

———— England vs. America, 1774. *In* Friends' Historical Society of Philadelphia. Bulletin, v. 5, Apr. 1913: 2–8. BX7635.A1F6, v. 5

A letter of December 22d expressing his views on the American crisis.

CORNER, BETSY C. Dr. John Fothergill and the American colonies. Quaker history, v. 52, autumn 1963: 77–89. BX7635.A1F6, v. 52

CORNER, BETSY C., *and* DOROTHY W. SINGER. Dr. John Fothergill, peacemaker. *In* American Philosophical Society, *Philadelphia.* Proceedings, v. 98, Feb. 1954: 11–22. Q11.P5, v. 98

CORNER, BETSY C. Dr. Fothergill's friendship with Benjamin Franklin. *In* American Philosophical Society, *Philadelphia.* Proceedings, v. 102, Oct. 1958: 413–419. Q11.P5, v. 102

FOX, RICHARD HINGSTON. Dr. John Fothergill and his friends; chapters in eighteenth century life. London, Macmillan, 1919. xxiv, 434 p. plates, ports. R489.F6F7

Bibliographic footnotes.

GUMMERE, AMELIA M. An international chess party. *In* Friends' Historical Society of Philadelphia. Bulletin, v. 1, Oct. 1906: 3–22. port. BX7635.A1F6, v. 1

On the attempts of Fothergill, David Barclay, and Benjamin Franklin to achieve a reconciliation between Great Britain and the American colonies in 1774–75.

13368

FOTHERGILL, SAMUEL (1715–1772)†

England; America. Quaker minister, organizer, and traveler.

———— Memoirs of the life and gospel labours of Samuel Fothergill, with selections from his correspondence. Also an account of the life and travels of his father, John Fothergill; and notices of some of his descendants. By George Crosfield. Liverpool, D. Marples, 1843. vii, 544 p. front. BX7795.F67F6

13369

FOULKE, SAMUEL (1718–1797)

Pennsylvania. Assemblyman.

———— Fragments of a journal kept by Samuel Foulke, of Bucks County, while a member of the colonial assembly of Pennsylvania, 1762-3-4. Pennsylvania magazine of history and biography, v. 5. no. 1, 1881: 60–73. F146.P65, v. 5

Introduction and notes by Howard M. Jenkins.

13370

FOWLE, DANIEL (1715–1787) *

Massachusetts; New Hampshire. Printer, editor.

KIDDER, ROBERT W. The contribution of Daniel Fowle to New Hampshire printing, 1756–1787. 1960. ([521] p.) Micro AC–1, no. 60–1655

Thesis (Ph.D.)—University of Illinois.
Abstracted in *Dissertation Abstracts*, v. 20, June 1960, p. 4666.

13371

FOWLER, JOHN (1756–1840)

Virginia; Kentucky. Revolutionary officer, assemblyman.

FOWLER, ILA E. Captain John Fowler of Virginia and Kentucky, patriot, soldier, pioneer, statesman, land baron and civic leader. Cynthiana, Ky., Hobson Press, 1942. xi, 166 p. plates. E302.6.F6F6

Reproduced from typescript.
Bibliographic footnotes.

13372

FOX, CHARLES JAMES (1749–1806) †

England. Member of Parliament.

———— The beauties of Fox, North, and Burke, selected from their speeches, from the passing of the Quebec

Act, in the year 1774, down to the present time. With a copious index to the whole, and an address to the public. London, Printed for J. Stockdale, 1784. viii, 92, [10] p. ports. E211.F79 Rare Bk. Coll.

—— Memorials and correspondence of Charles James Fox. Edited by Lord John Russell. London, R. Bentley, 1853–57. 4 v. DA506.F7A2

Reprinted in New York by AMS Press (1970).

—— The speeches of the Right Honourable Charles James Fox, in the House of Commons. London, Longman, Hurst, Rees, Orme, and Brown, 1815. 6 v.
DA506.F7A3

Edited by John Wright, with an introductory letter by Lord Erskine.

CHRISTIE, IAN R.   Charles James Fox. History today, v. 8, Feb. 1958: 110–118. illus., ports.   D1.H818, v. 8

DERRY, JOHN W.   Charles James Fox. New York, St. Martin's Press [1972] 454 p. illus.
DA506.F7D47 1972b

Bibliography: p. [445]–446.

FELL, RALPH.   Memoirs of the public life of the late Right Honourable Charles James Fox. London, J. F. Hughes, 1808. 2 v.   DA506.F7F3

HOBHOUSE, CHRISTOPHER.   Fox. With a biographical introduction by Harold Nicolson. [New ed.] London, Constable [1947] xxiv, 271 p.   DA506.F7H6 1947

First edition published in 1947.

LANDOR, WALTER S.   Charles James Fox; a commentary on his life and character. Edited by Stephen Wheeler. New York, G. P. Putnam's Sons, 1907. xxv, 255 p. port.   DA506.F7L2

Originally printed in 1812, but suppressed.

LASCELLES, EDWARD C. P.   The life of Charles James Fox. New York, Oxford University Press, 1936. viii, 345 p. facsim., plates, ports.   DA506.F7L3

"Note on authorities": p. [331]–334.
Reprinted in New York by Octagon Books (1970).

MITCHELL, LESLIE G.   Charles James Fox and the disintegration of the Whig party, 1782–1794. London, Oxford University Press, 1971. x, 318 p. (Oxford historical monographs)   DA506.F7H58

Bibliography: p. [303]–313.

REID, LOREN D.   Charles James Fox: a man for the people. [Columbia] University of Missouri Press [1969] xiv, 475 p. illus.   DA506.F7R38 1969

Bibliography: p. 447–457.
The author's thesis (Ph.D.), *Charles James Fox; a Study of the Effectiveness of an Eighteenth Century Parliamentary Speaker*, was submitted to the University of Iowa in 1932.

—— The education of Charles Fox. Quarterly journal of speech, v. 43, Dec. 1957: 357–364.
PN4071.Q3, v. 43

RUSSELL, JOHN RUSSELL, *1st Earl*. The life and times of Charles James Fox. London, R. Bentley, 1859–66. 3 v. port.   DA506.F7R9

TREVELYAN, *Sir* GEORGE O., *Bart*.   The early history of Charles James Fox. New York, Harper, 1880. viii, 470 p.   DA506.F7T7 1880

Reprinted in New York by AMS Press (1971).

—— George the Third and Charles Fox, the concluding part of The American Revolution. New York, Longmans, Green, 1921–27. 2 v. fold. maps.
DA506.F7T87 1921

First published 1912–14.
Concludes both *The Early History of Charles James Fox* and *The American Revolution*.

WILLIAMS, BASIL.   Charles Fox and the American Revolution. Quarterly review, v. 224, Oct. 1915: 426–443.
AP4.Q2, v. 224

13373
FOX, EBENEZER (1763–1843)
Massachusetts. Revolutionary seaman.

—— The Revolutionary adventures of Ebenezer Fox. Boston, Munroe & Francis, 1838. 238 p. port.
E275.F791 Rare Bk. Coll.
Micro 01291, reel 195, no. 9E

A later edition, *The Adventures of Ebenezer Fox, in the Revolutionary War*, was published in Boston by C. Fox (1848. 246 p. E275.F793).

13374
FOX, JOSEPH (1709?–1779)
Pennsylvania. Assemblyman, barrackmaster.

CRESSON, ANNE H.   Biographical sketch of Joseph Fox, Esq., of Philadelphia. Pennsylvania magazine of history and biography, v. 32, Apr. 1908: 175–199.
F146.P65, v. 32

13375
FOX, JUSTUS (1736–1805)
Germany; Pennsylvania. Printer.

NICHOLS, CHARLES L.   Justus Fox, a German printer of the eighteenth century. *In* American Antiquarian Society, *Worcester, Mass.* Proceedings, new ser., v. 25, Apr. 1915: 55–69.   E172.A35, n.s., v. 25

13376
FRANCEY, THEVENEAU DE
French agent in America.

BIGELOW, JOHN.   Beaumarchais the merchant. Letters of Theveneau de Francey, 1777–1780. New York, C. Scribner, 1870. 16 p.   E249.B375

13377

FRANCIS, *Sir* PHILIP (1740–1818)†

Ireland; England. Clerk, secretary.

——— The Francis letters, by Sir Philip Francis and other members of the family. Edited by Beata Francis and Eliza Keary; with a note on the Junius controversy by C. F. Keary. New York, E. P. Dutton [1901] 2 v. (xi, 699 p.) ports. DA506.F8A2

CROWE, CAROL E. Sir Philip Francis, 1740–1818: a biography. 1971. ([369] p.) Micro AC–1, no. 72–10,941

Thesis (Ph.D.)—University of Georgia. Abstracted in *Dissertation Abstracts International*, v. 32A, Apr. 1972, p. 5704–5705.

PARKES, JOSEPH. Memoirs of Sir Philip Francis K.C.B., with correspondence and journals. Commenced by the late Joseph Parkes, Esq. Completed and edited by Herman Merivale. London, Longmans, Green, 1867. 2 v. facsims., ports. DA506.F8P2

13378

FRANCIS, TURBUTT (1740–1777)

Pennsylvania. Army officer, Indian negotiator, judge.

GOODCHARLES, FREDERIC A. Lieutenant Colonel Turbutt Francis, soldier, statesman, diplomat and land owner. *In* Northumberland County (Pa.) Historical Society. Proceedings and addresses. v. 6. Sunbury, 1934. p. [170]–198. F157.N8N7, v. 6

13379

FRANCISCO, PETER (1760?–1831)

Virginia. Revolutionary soldier.

DANIEL, JAMES R. The giant of Virginia, alias the Hercules of the Revolution. Virginia cavalcade, v. 1, autumn 1951: 36–39. illus., ports. F221.V74, v. 1

HALL, J. K. Peter Francisco—hyperpituitary patriot. Annals of medical history, new ser., v. 8, Sept. 1936: 448–452. R11.A85, n.s., v. 8

PORTER, NANNIE F., *and* CATHERINE F. ALBERTSON. The romantic record of Peter Francisco "a Revolutionary soldier." Staunton, Va., Printed by the McClure Co., 1929. 103 p. illus., plates, port. F230.F81

13380

FRANCKLIN, MICHAEL (1720?–1782)

England; Nova Scotia. Merchant, assemblyman, councilor.

KERR, WILFRED B. The rise of Michael Francklin. Dalhousie review, v. 13, Jan. 1934: 489–495. AP5.D3, v. 13

MacDONALD, JAMES S. Memoir Lieut.-Governor Michael Francklin, 1752–1782. *In* Nova Scotia Historical Society, *Halifax*. Collections. v. 16. Halifax, 1912. p. [7]–40. ports. [F1036.N93, v. 16] Micro 03606

13381

FRANKLIN, BENJAMIN (1706–1790)*

Massachusetts; Pennsylvania. Printer, scientist, author, inventor, statesman, diplomat, delegate to the Continental Congress, delegate to the Constitutional Convention.

——— The autobiography of Benjamin Franklin. Edited by Leonard W. Labaree [and others] New Haven, Yale University Press, 1964. 351 p. col. illus., facsim., col. port. E302.6.F7A2 1964

Bibliography: p. 323–325.

——— The autobiography of Benjamin Franklin; a restoration of a "fair copy" by Max Farrand. Published in coöperation with the Huntington Library, San Marino, Calif. Berkeley, University of California Press, 1949. xxvii, 210 p. E302.6.F7A2 1949

Based upon four source texts: the William Temple Franklin edition (1818), the Bigelow edition (1868), the French translation by Louis Guillaume Le Veillard, and the French translation of the first part published by Buisson (1791).

——— Benjamin Franklin: a biography in his own words. Edited by Thomas Fleming. With an introduction by Whitfield J. Bell, Jr. Joan Paterson Kerr, picture editor. New York, Newsweek; distributed by Harper & Row [1972] 416 p. illus. (The Founding fathers) E302.6.F7A23 1972

Based on v. 1–15 of *The Papers of Benjamin Franklin*. Bibliography: p. 408.

——— Benjamin Franklin and Catherine Ray Greene; their correspondence, 1755–1790. Edited and annotated by William Greene Roelker, Philadelphia, American Philosophical Society, 1949. ix, 147 p. illus., facsims., port. (Memoirs of the American Philosophical Society, v. 26) E302.6.F75A14 Q11.P612, v. 24

——— Benjamin Franklin and the first balloons. *In* American Antiquarian Society, *Worcester, Mass.* Proceedings, new ser., v. 18, Apr. 1907: 259–274. E172.A35, n.s., v. 18

Introduction and notes by Abbott L. Rotch.

Five letters written in 1783 to Sir Joseph Banks, president of the Royal Society, relating to the beginnings of aerial navigation.

———Benjamin Franklin's *Experiments;* a new edition of Franklin's *Experiments and Observation on Electricity*. Edited, with a critical and historical introduction, by I. Bernard Cohen. Cambridge, Mass., Harvard University Press, 1941. xxviii, 453 p. illus., facsim., port. QC516.F85 1941

Includes a reproduction of the title page of the fifth edition (1774).

"The editons of Franklin's book": p. [139]–157. "Bibliographical table": p. 158–161. Bibliographic footnotes.

——— The complete works of Benjamin Franklin; including his private as well as his official and scientific correspondence, and numerous letters and documents now for the first time printed, with many others not included in any former collection, also, the unmutilated and correct version of his autobiography. Compiled and edited by John Bigelow. New York, G. P. Putnam's Sons, 1887–88. 10 v. plates (part fold.), port.

E302.F82 1887 Rare Bk. Coll.

——— Correspondence between Dr. Benjamin Franklin and John Walter, regarding the logographic process of printing [1783–89] *In* American Antiquarian Society, *Worcester, Mass.* Proceedings, new ser., v. 38, Oct. 1928: 349–363. E172.A35, n.s., v. 38

Introduction and notes by George S. Eddy.

——— Educational views of Benjamin Franklin. Edited by Thomas Woody. New York, McGraw-Hill Book Co., 1931. xvi, 270 p. facsim., port. (McGraw-Hill education classics) LB575.F723 1931

Includes bibliographic references.
Reprinted in New York by AMS Press (1971).

——— Franklin's accounts against Massachusetts. *In* Massachusetts Historical Society, *Boston.* Proceedings. v. 56; 1922/23. Boston, 1923. p. 94–120.

F61.M38, v. 56

His legal expenses in the proceedings arising from the Hutchinson-Oliver letters affair. Introduction and notes by Worthington C. Ford.

——— Franklin's *Internal State of America* (1786). William and Mary quarterly, 3d ser., v. 15, Apr. 1958: 214–227.

F221.W71, 3d s., v. 15

Introduction and notes by Verner W. Crane.

——— Franklin's wit & folly: The bagatelles. Richard E. Amacher [editor] New Brunswick, N.J., Rutgers University Press, 1953. xiv, 188 p. port. PS750.B3 1953

Bibliography: p. 177–184.

——— Letters and papers of Benjamin Franklin and Richard Jackson, 1753–1785. Edited and annotated, with an introduction, by Carl Van Doren. Philadelphia, American Philosophical Society, 1947. ix, 222 p. facsims., port. [Memoirs of the American Philosophical Society, v. 24] E302.6.F75A18

Q11.P612, v. 24

——— The letters of Benjamin Franklin & Jane Mecom. Edited with an introduction by Carl Van Doren. [Princeton] Published for the American Philosophical Society by Princeton University Press, 1950. xx, 380 p. facsims., port. (Memoirs of the American Philosophical Society, v. 27) E302.6.F75A185

Q11.P612, v. 27

——— Letters to the press, 1758–1775. Collected and edited by Verner W. Crane. Chapel Hill, Published for the Institute of Early American History and Culture at Williamsburg, Va., by the University of North Carolina Press [1950] lxv, 308 p. E302.6.F75A12

——— The life of Benjamin Franklin, written by himself. Now first edited from original manuscripts and from his printed correspondence and other writings, by John Bigelow. Philadelphia, J. B. Lippincott, 1874. 3 v. port.

E302.6.F7A2 1874

Bibliography: v. 3, p. 491–512.

——— Memoirs of the life and writings of Benjamin Franklin, written by himself to a late period, and continued to the time of his death by his grandson, William Temple Franklin. Comprising the private correspondence and public negocations of Dr. Franklin. And his select political, philosophical, and miscellaneous works, published from the original mss. 2d ed. London, Printed for H. Colburn, 1818–19. 6 v. illus., facsim., fold. map, plates (part fold.), port.

E302.F82 1818a Rare Bk. Coll.

Contents: 1–2. Life.—3–4. Private correspondence.— 5–6. Posthumous and other writings.

——— Papers. Leonard W. Labaree, editor. Whitfield J. Bell, Jr., associate editor. Helen C. Boatfield and Helene H. Fineman, assistant editors. New Haven, Yale University Press, 1959+ illus. (part fold., part col.), facsims., ports. E302.F82 1959

"Sponsored by the American Philosophical Society and Yale University."

Bibliographic footnotes.

Contents: v. 1. January 6, 1706, through December 31, 1734.—v. 2. January 1, 1735, through December 31, 1744.—v. 3. January 1, 1745, through June 30, 1750.—v. 4. July 1, 1750, through June 30, 1753.—v. 5. July 1, 1753, through March 31, 1755.—v. 6. April 1, 1755, through September 30, 1756.—v. 7. October, 1, 1756, through March 31, 1758.—v. 8. April 1, 1758, through December 31, 1759.—v. 9. January 1, 1760, through December 31, 1761.—v. 10. January 1, 1762, through December 31, 1763.—v. 11. January 1 through December 31, 1764.—v. 12. January 1 through December 31, 1765.—v. 13. January 1 through December 31, 1766.—v. 14. January 1 through December 31, 1767.—v. 15. January 1 through December 31, 1768.

——— Political, miscellaneous, and philosophical pieces; arranged under the following heads, and distinguished by initial letters in each leaf: (G.P) General politics; (A.P.T.) American politics before the troubles; (P.P.) Provincial or colony politics; and (M.P.) Miscellaneous and philosophical pieces. Now first collected, with explanatory plates, notes, and an index to the whole. London, Printed for J. Johnson, 1779. xi, 567, [7] p. plates (part fold.), port.

E302.F83 1779 Rare Bk. Coll.

Edited by Benjamin Vaughan.

——— Representative selections, with introduction, bibliography, and notes, by Chester E. Jorgenson and Frank Luther Mott. Rev. ed. New York, Hill and Wang [1962] clxxxix, 544 p. (American century series. American writers) PS745.A3M7 1962

Bibliography: p. cli–clxxxix.

——— Two tracts: Information to those who would remove to America. And, Remarks concerning the savages of North America, by Dr. Benjamin Franklin. London, Printed for John Stockdale, 1784. 39 p. E164.F83 Rare Bk. Coll.

——— Unpublished letters of Franklin to [William] Strahan [1744–83] Atlantic monthly, v. 61, Jan. 1888: 21–36. AP2.A8, v. 61

——— The writings of Benjamin Franklin. Collected and edited, with a life and introduction, by Albert Henry Smyth. New York, Macmillan Co., 1907. 10 v. illus., facsims., plates (part fold.). E302.F82 1907

Contents: v. 1. Introduction and autobiography.—v. 2. 1722–1750.—v. 3. 1750–1759.—v. 4. 1760–1766.—v. 5. 1767–1772.—v. 6. 1773–1776.—v. 7. 1777–1779—v. 8. 1780–1782.—v. 9. 1783–1788. v. 10. 1789–1790.

Reprinted in New York by Haskell House (1970).

——— The works of Benjamin Franklin. Containing several political and historical tracts not included in any former ed., and many letters official and private, not hitherto published; with notes and a life of the author. By Jared Sparks. Boston, Hilliard, Gray, 1836–1840. 10 v. illus., facsims., fold. map, plates (part fold.), port. E302.F82 1836

"List of the author's writings, chronologically arranged": v. 10, p. [449]–463.

Contents: 1. Life of Franklin. Autobiography. Continuation, by Jared Sparks. Appendix.—2. Essays on religious and moral subjects and the economy of life. Bagatelles. Essays on general politics, commerce, and political economy. Supplement.—3–4. Essays and tracts, historical and political, before the American Revolution.—5. Political papers, during and after the American Revolution. Letters and papers on electricity. Appendix.—6. Letters and papers on philosophical subjects.—7–10. Correspondence.

ADAMS, FREDERICK B. Franklin and his press at Passy. Yale University library gazette, v. 30, Apr. 1956: 133–138. Z733.Y17G, v. 30

ABBE, CLEVELAND. Benjamin Franklin as a meteorologist. In American Philosophical Society, Philadelphia. Proceedings, v. 45, May/Sept. 1906: 117–128. Q11.P5, v. 45

ALDRIDGE, ALFRED O. Benjamin Franklin and nature's God. Durham, N.C., Duke University Press, 1967. 279 p. E302.6.F8A45

Bibliographic footnotes.

——— Benjamin Franklin and philosophical necessity. Modern language quarterly, v. 12, Sept. 1951: 292–309. PB1.M642, v. 12

——— Benjamin Franklin and the Pennsylvania Gazette. In American Philosophical Society, Philadelphia. Proceedings, v. 106, Feb. 1962: 77–81. Q11.P5, v. 106

——— Benjamin Franklin and the philosophes. In International Congress on the Enlightenment, 1st, Geneva. Transactions. v. 1. Geneve, Institut et musée Voltaire, 1963. (Studies on Voltaire and the eighteenth century, v. 24) p. 43–65. PQ2105.A2S8, v. 24

——— Benjamin Franklin, philosopher & man. Philadelphia, Lippincott [1965] xii, 438 p. port. E302.6.F8A46

Bibliographic references included in "Notes" (p. 418–427).

——— Form and substance in Franklin's Autobiography. In Essays on American literature in honor of Jay B. Hubbell. Edited by Clarence Gohdes. Durham, N.C., Duke University Press, 1967. p. 47–62. PS121.E8

——— Franklin and his French contemporaries. [New York] New York University Press, 1957. 260 p. E302.6.F8A47

Bibliographic reference included in "Notes" (p. 239–256).

——— Franklin as demographer. Journal of economic history, v. 9, May 1949: 25–44. HC10.J64, v. 9

On his Observations Concerning the Increase of Mankind, Peopling of Countries, etc., first published in 1755.

——— Franklin's deistical Indians. In American Philosophical Society, Philadelphia. Proceedings, v. 94, Aug. 1950: 398–410. Q11.P5, v. 94

On Franklin's Remarks Concerning the Savages of North America (1784).

AMACHER, RICHARD E. Benjamin Franklin. New York, Twayne Publishers [1962] 192 p. (Twayne's United States authors series) PS751.A5

"Selected bibliography": p. 179–187.

American Philosophical Society, Philadelphia. Benjamin Franklin, 1706–1956. Philadelphia, 1956. 283–416 p. illus., facsims., ports. (Its Proceedings, v. 100, Aug. 1956) Q11.P5, v. 100

Partial contents: Franklin and the Constitution, by Edward S. Corwin.—The world of science in the late eighteenth century and today, by Arthur H. Compton.—Franklin on the art of being human, by Robert E. Spiller.—Benjamin Franklin: the diplomat and the journalist, by Maurice Couve de Murville.—The return of Mr. Franklin, by Leonard W. Labaree.—Franklin's message in the twentieth century, by Roy F. Nichols.—Benjamin Franklin and the Philosophical Society in 1956, by William E. Lingelbach.—Catalogue of the Society's exhibition of portraits of Benjamin Franklin, by Charles C. Sellers.—Catalogue of Franklin exhibition in the Library of Congress.

——— Studies on Benjamin Franklin, the two hundred and fiftieth anniversary of his birth, January 17, 1956. Philadelphia, 1955. 359–476 p. illus., facsims., ports. (*Its* Proceedings, v. 99, Dec. 1955) Q11.P5, v. 99

Bibliographic footnotes.

Also published as the Society's *Library Bulletin* for 1955.

Contents: Benjamin Franklin's papers and the American Philosophical Society, by W. E. Lingelbach.—Benjamin Franklin and the German charity schools, by W. J. Bell, Jr.—Benjamin Franklin's Stamp Act cartoon, by E. Wolf, 2d.—Three Franklin-Raspe letters, by R. L. Kahn.—Franklin, Grimm, and J. H. Landolt, by R. L. Kahn.—Benjamin Franklin and Count M. A. Benyowski, by E. Dvoichenko-Markova.—Franklin's type: its study past and present, by C. W. Miller.—Jane Mecom's little picture, by C. C. Sellers.—The Franklin-Volta correspondence: legend or fact? By A. Pace.—The apotheosis of Benjamin Franklin, Paris, 1790–1791, by G. Chinard.

——— *Library.* Calendar of the papers of Benjamin Franklin in the Library of the American Philosophical Society. Edited by I. Minis Hays. Philadelphia, Printed for the American Philosophical Society, 1908. 5 v. (The record of the celebration of the two hundredth anniversary of the birth of Benjamin Franklin, under the auspices of the American Philosophical Society, v. 2–6) E302.F84 1906, v. 2–6

The University of Pennsylvania Library also published a *Calendar of the Papers of Benjamin Franklin in the Library of the University of Pennsylvania. Being the Appendix to the "Calendar of the Papers of Benjamin Franklin in the Library of the American Philosophical Society," Edited by I. Minis Hays* (Philadelphia, University of Pennsylvania, 1908. 399–546 p. E172.P4, no. 3). The papers were first calendared by Arthur C. Boggess and later revised and modified by Mrs. Lightner Witmer.

BACHE, RICHARD. "Cash D^r to Benjamin Franklin." Pennsylvania magazine of history and biography, v. 80, Jan. 1956: 46–73. F146.P65, v. 80

The daybook of Richard Bache, Franklin's son-in-law, who kept a detailed account of transactions made in Franklin's behalf from 1772 to 1792. Introduction and notes by Penrose R. Hoopes.

BACHE, FRANKLIN. Where is Franklin's first chart of the Gulf Stream? *In* American Philosophical Society, *Philadelphia.* Proceedings, v. 76, no. 5, 1936: 731–742. fold. maps. Q11.P5, v. 76

BAENDER, PAUL. The basis of Franklin's duplicative satires. American literature, v. 32, Nov. 1960: 267–279. PS1.A6, v. 32

BECKER, CARL L. Benjamin Franklin, a biographical sketch. Ithaca, N.Y., Cornell University Press [1946] xi, 49 p. E302.6.F8B43

Reproduced from the *Dictionary of American Biography,* v. 6, p. 585–598.

Bibliography: p. [39]–42.

BELL, WHITFIELD J. "All clear sunshine": new letters of Franklin and Mary Stevenson Hewson. *In* American

Philosophical Society, *Philadelphia.* Proceedings, v. 100, Dec. 1956: 521–536. illus. facsims., port. Q11.P5, v. 100

Also published in the Society's *Library Bulletin* for 1956, p. 521–536.

——— Benjamin Franklin and the practice of medicine. *In* Cleveland Medical Library Association. Bulletin, new ser., v. 9, July 1962: 51–62. Z881.C5789, n.s., v. 9

——— Franklin's papers and *The Papers of Benjamin Franklin.* Pennsylvania history, v. 22, Jan. 1955: 1–17. F146.P597, v. 22

BELOFF, MAX. Benjamin Franklin, international statesman. *In* Manchester Literary and Philosophical Society. Memoirs and proceedings. v. 97; 1955/56. Manchester, 1956. p. 13–30. Q41.M2, v. 97

BENSON, ADOLPH B. Benjamin Franklin's contact with Swedes. Swedish pioneer historical quarterly, v. 6, Jan. 1955: 3–17. E184.S23S955, v. 6

BRUCE, WILLIAM C. Benjamin Franklin, self-revealed; a biographical and critical study based mainly on his own writings. 3d ed., rev. New York, G. P. Putnam's Sons [1942] viii, 544, 550 p. E302.6.F8B884

First edition published in two volumes in 1917.

BURLINGAME, ROGER. Benjamin Franklin, envoy extraordinary. New York, Coward-McCann [1967] 255 p. illus., map, ports. E302.6.F8B8938

"Selected bibliography": p. 245–248.

BUSHMAN, RICHARD L. On the uses of psychology: conflict and conciliation in Benjamin Franklin. History and theory, v. 5, no. 3, 1966: 225–240. D1.H8173, v. 5

BUXBAUM, MELVIN H. Benjamin Franklin and the zealous Presbyterians. 1968. 425 l.

Thesis (Ph.D.)—University of Chicago.

——— Franklin looks for a rector: "Poor Richard's" hostility to Presbyterians. Journal of Presbyterian history, v. 48, fall 1970: 176–188. BX8905.P7A4, v. 48

CAREY, LEWIS J. Franklin's economic views. Garden City, N.Y., Doubleday, Doran, 1928. vi, 243 p. (Franklin monographs) E302.6.F8C28 Rare Bk. Coll.

Thesis (Ph.D.)—Notre Dame University, 1929. Bibliography at end of each chapter.

CHINARD, GILBERT. Abbé Lefebvre de la Roche's recollections of Benjamin Franklin. *In* American Philosophical Society, *Philadelphia.* Proceedings, v. 94, June 1950: 214–221. port. Q11.P5, v. 94

Also published in the Society's *Library Bulletin* for 1950, p. 214–221.

——— Benjamin Franklin and the mysterious Madame G———. *In* American Philosophical Society, *Philadelphia. Library.* Library bulletin. 1946. Philadelphia, 1947. p. 49–72. ports. Z881.P49, 1946

Includes extracts from 22 letters to Franklin written by the Comtesse Golowkin.

———— Random notes on two "bagatelles." *In* American Philosophical Society, *Philadelphia*. Proceedings, v. 103, Dec. 1959: 727–760. illus., facsims.
Q11.P5, v. 103

Also published in the Society's *Library Bulletin* for 1959, p. 727–760.

Discusses the surviving texts and the importance of Franklin's *Lettre à Madame Helvetius* and *Les Éphémères*.

CLARK, KENNETH M., *Baron* CLARK. The concept of universal man. Ditchley Park, Eng., Ditchley Foundation [1972?] 19 p. (Ditchley Foundation lecture, 11)
DA10.D56, no. 11

In exploring the meaning of the term, Clark compares Franklin and Thomas Jefferson with other so-called universal men.

CLARK, WILLIAM B. A Franklin postcript to Captain Cook's voyages. *In* American Philosophical Society, *Philadelphia*. Proceedings, v. 98, Dec. 1954: 400–405.
Q11.P5, v. 98

Also published in the Society's *Library Bulletin* for 1954, p. 400–405.

COHEN, I. BERNARD. Benjamin Franklin: his contribution to the American tradition. Indianapolis, Bobbs-Merrill [1953] 320 p. illus. (Makers of the American tradition series) E302.6.F8C67

Bibliography: p. 307–308.

———— Franklin and Newton; an inquiry into speculative Newtonian experimental science and Franklin's work in electricity as an example thereof. Philadelphia, American Philosophical Society, 1956. xxvi, 657 p. illus., ports. (Memoirs of the American Philosophical Society, v. 43)
QC7.C65
Q11.P612, v. 43

Bibliography: p. 603–650.

———— How practical was Benjamin Franklin's science? Pennsylvania magazine of history and biography, v. 69, Oct. 1945: 284–293. F146.P65, v. 69

———— The two hundredth anniversary of Benjamin Franklin's two lightning experiments and the introduction of the lightning rod. *In* American Philosophical Society, *Philadelphia*. Proceedings, v. 96, June 1952: 331–366. illus., facsims., port. Q11.P5, v. 96

CONNER, PAUL W. Poor Richard's politicks; Benjamin Franklin and his new American order. New York, Oxford University Press, 1965. xiv, 285 p.
E302.6.F8C72

Bibliography: p. 263–277.
The author's thesis (Ph.D.), *Benjamin Franklin's Quest for Political Order*, was submitted to Princeton University in 1963.

COPE, THOMAS D. Some contacts of Benjamin Franklin with Mason and Dixon and their work. *In* American

Philosophical Society, *Philadelphia*. Proceedings, v. 95, June 1951: 232–238. Q11.P5, v. 95

Also published in the Society's *Library Bulletin* for 1951, p. 232–238.

CORNER, GEORGE W., *and* WILLARD E. GOODWIN. Benjamin Franklin's bladder stone. Journal of the history of medicine and allied sciences, v. 8, Oct. 1953: 359–377. R131.A1J6, v. 8

A condition that severely hampered Franklin's activities from 1782 until his death.

CRANE, VERNER W. Benjamin Franklin and a rising people. Boston, Little, Brown [1954] x, 219 p. (The Library of American biography) E302.6.F8C77 1954

"A note on the sources": p. [207]–209.

———— Benjamin Franklin, Englishmen and American. Baltimore, Md., Published for Brown University, Providence, R.I., by the Williams & Wilkins Co., 1936. 142 p. (The Colver lectures in Brown University, 1935)
E302.6.F8C78

"Bibliographical note": p. 139–142.

———— Certain writings of Benjamin Franklin on the British Empire and the American colonies. *In* Bibliographical Society of America. Papers, v. 28, pt. 1, 1934: 1–27.
Z1008.B51P, v. 28

————The Club of Honest Whigs: friends of science and liberty. William and Mary quarterly, 3d ser., v. 23, Apr. 1966: 210–233. F221.W71, 3d s., v. 23

Franklin's contacts, during his agency in England, with congenial Whig politicians.

———— Dr. Franklin's plan for America. Michigan alumnus quarterly review, v. 64, summer 1958: 322–333. port.
AP2.M53, v. 64

On Franklin's changing ideas and observations about the place of the colonies within the empire, 1750–75.

———— Franklin's marginalia, and the lost "treatise" on empire. *In* Michigan Academy of Science, Arts and Letters. Papers. v. 42; 1956. Ann Arbor, 1957. p. 163–176. Q11.M56, v. 42

From the marginalia Franklin jotted in his pamphlets between 1765 and 1770, Crane reconstructs Franklin's mature theory of empire which he hoped to present in a treatise that was never published, perhaps never completed.

CURREY, CECIL B. Code number 72/Ben Franklin; patriot or spy? Englewood Cliffs, N.J., Prentice-Hall [1972] viii, 331 p. ports. E302.6.F8C798

Bibliography: p. [323]–331.

———— Road to revolution: Benjamin Franklin in England, 1765–1775. Garden City, N.Y., Anchor Books, 1968. xi, 422 p. illus., map, ports. E302.6.F8C8

Bibliography: p. [396]–410.
The author's thesis (Ph.D.), *Benjamin Franklin and the Radicals, 1765–1775*, was submitted to the University of Kansas in 1965.

For a critique of the key evidence employed by the author, see Paul H. Smith's "Benjamin Franklin: Gunrunner?" in the *Pennsylvania Magazine of History and Biography*, v. 95, Oct. 1971, p. 526–529.

CURTIS PUBLISHING COMPANY. The collection of Franklin imprints in the museum of the Curtis Publishing Company; with a short-title check list of all the books, pamphlets, broadsides, &c., known to have been printed by Benjamin Franklin. Compiled by William J. Campbell. Philadelphia, Curtis Pub. Co., 1918. 333 p. facsims. Z232.F8C9

In 1920, the collection of 791 items was presented to the University of Pennsylvania.

DAVIDSON, EDWARD H. Franklin and [Dr. William] Brown-rigg. American literature, v. 23, Mar. 1951: 38–56. PS1.A6, v. 23

DAVY, FRANCIS X. Benjamin Franklin, satirist: the satire of Franklin and its rhetoric. 1958. ([300] p.) Micro AC–1, no. 58–2530

Thesis (Ph.D.)—Columbia University.
Abstracted in *Dissertation Abstracts*, v. 19, Aug. 1958, p. 317.

DUANE, WILLIAM, *ed.* Letters to Benjamin Franklin from his family and friends, 1751–1790. New York, C. B. Richardson, 1859. 195 p. ports. E302.6.F8D7

Reprinted in Freeport, N.Y., by Books for Libraries Press (1970).

DVOICHENKO-MARKOVA, EUFROSINA M. Benjamin Franklin, the American Philosophical Society, and the Russian Academy of Science. *In* American Philosophical Society, *Philadelphia*. Proceedings, v. 91, Aug. 1947: 250–257. Q11.P5, v. 91

ECHEVERRIA, DURAND. "The Sale of the Hessians." Was Benjamin Franklin the author? *In* American Philosophical Society, *Philadelphia*. Proceedings, v. 98, Dec. 1954: 427–431. Q11.P5, v. 98

Also published in the Society's *Library Bulletin* for 1954, p. 427–431.
Although scholars may continue to ascribe the newsletter to Franklin, evidence shows that the attribution must be made tentatively.

EDDY, GEORGE S. Dr. Benjamin Franklin's library. *In* American Antiquarian Society, *Worcester, Mass.* Proceedings, new ser., v. 34, Oct. 1924: 206–226. E172.A35, n.s., v. 34

———— ———— Offprint. Worcester, Mass., The Society, 1925. 23 p. E302.6.F8E3

———— A ramble through the Mason-Franklin Collection. Yale University Library gazette, v. 10, Apr. 1936: 63–90. facsims., port. Z733.Y17G, v. 10

Describes the extensive collection of Frankliniana assembled by William Smith Mason and given to the Yale University Library.

———— A work book of the printing house of Benjamin Franklin and David Hall, 1759–1766. *In* New York (City). Public Library. Bulletin, v. 34, Aug. 1930: 575–589. facsims. Z881.N6B, v. 34

An offprint with a slightly different title was published in New York by the New York Public Library (1930. 17 p. Z232.F8E2).

EISELEN, MALCOLM R. Franklin's political theories. Garden City, N.Y., Doubleday, Doran, 1928. 101 p. (Franklin monographs) E302.6.F8E36 Rare Bk. Coll.

Bibliography: p. 97–101.

ENGLAND, A. B. Some thematic patterns in Franklin's *Autobiography*. Eighteenth-century studies, v. 5, spring 1972: 421–430. NX452.E54, v. 5

FARRAND, MAX. Benjamin Franklin's memoirs. Huntington Library bulletin, no. 10, Oct. 1936: 49–78. facsims. Z733.S24B, no. 10

———— ———— Offprint. [Cambridge, Mass., Harvard University Press, ᶜ1936] [49]–78 p. facsims. E302.6.F7Z45

Outlines the chronology of composition and reveals the utter confusion surrounding the publication of various editions of Franklin's autobiography.

FAŸ, BERNARD. Bernard Faÿ's Franklin, the apostle of modern times. Boston, Little, Brown, 1929. xvi, 547 p. facsims., maps (part fold.), plates, ports. E302.6.F8F282

The English version was prepared by Bravig Imbs.
Bibliography: p. [517]–533.
The Library also holds a French edition published in Paris by Calmann-Lévy (1930–31. F302.6.F8F275).

———— Bernard Faÿ's The two Franklins: fathers of American democracy. Boston, Little, Brown, 1933. xvi, 397 p. facsims., plates, fold. plan, ports. E302.6.B14F3

"Bibliography and references": p. 363–377.
Reprinted in New York by AMS Press (1969) and in St. Clair Shores, Mich., by Scholarly Press (1971).

On Franklin's influence upon his grandson, Benjamin Franklin Bache (1769–98).

FISHER, SYDNEY G. The true Benjamin Franklin. Philadelphia, J. B. Lippincott Co., 1899. 369 p. facsims., plates, ports. [The True series] E302.6.F8F53

Reissued in 1927 under the title *Benjamin Franklin*.

FLEMING, THOMAS J. The man who dared the lightning; a new look at Benjamin Franklin. New York, Morrow, 1971. x, 532 p. illus., ports. E302.6.F8F57

Bibliography: p. 515–520.

FORD, PAUL L. Franklin bibliography. A list of books written by, or relating to Benjamin Franklin. Brooklyn, N.Y., 1889. lxxi, 467 p. Z8313.F69

Reprinted in New York by B. Franklin (1968).

An annotated list of 1,002 titles classified according to (1) Franklin's own writings: books and pamphlets, periodicals and serials, state papers and treaties, pseudonyms, and doubtful or erroneous attributions; and (2) Frankliniana, followed by a subject index and reference list of Franklin literature, a checklist and chronological index, and a general index.

———— The many-sided Franklin. New York, Century Co., 1899. xx, 516 p. illus., facsims., ports. E302.6.F8F7

Reprinted in Freeport, N.Y., by Books for Libraries Press (1972).

———— Who was the mother of Franklin's son? An historical conundrum, hitherto given up—now partly answered. Brooklyn, N.Y., 1889. 15 p.
E302.6.F8F72 Rare Bk. Coll.

The author does not give the name of the woman in question.
Reprinted in New York by B. Franklin (1971).

Franklin Institute, *Philadelphia.* Meet Dr. Franklin. Philadelphia, Franklin Institute, 1943. vi, 234 p. fold. illus.
E302.6.F8F845

"Series of talks . . . printed individually in the Journal of the Franklin Institute during the past two years."—Foreword.

Bibliographic footnotes.

Contents: Meet Dr. Franklin, by Carl Van Doren.—Benjamin Franklin as a scientist, by R. A. Millikan.—Self-portraiture: the autobiography, by Max Farrand.—Dr. Franklin as the English saw him, by Conyers Read.—Franklin's political journalism in England, by V. W. Crane.—Benjamin Franklin: student of life, by R. E. Spiller.—Molding the Constitution, by G. W. Pepper.—Benjamin Franklin, "philosophical revolutionist," by Bernhard Knollenberg.—Looking westward, by Gilbert Chinard.—Benjamin Franklin: the printer at work, by L. C. Wroth.—Benjamin Franklin: adventures in agriculture, by C. R. Woodward.—Dr. Franklin: friend of the Indians, by J. P. Boyd.—Concluding paper, by Carl Van Doren.

———— Panorama of progress. [Philadelphia, 1956] xxxiv, 188 p. illus., facsims., port. (*Its* Journal, v. 261, Jan. 1956) T1.F8, v. 261

Partial contents: B. Franklin and the scientific societies, by William E. Lingelbach.—Franklin's impetus to education, by Gaylord P. Harnwell.—Franklin, the businessman, first great apostle of free and competitive economy on the American scene, by Marion L. Musante.—Some aspects of Franklin's life in England, by E. N. da C. Andrade.

GALLACHER, STUART A. Franklin's *Way to Wealth*: a florilegium of proverbs and wise sayings. Journal of English and German philology, v. 48, Apr. 1949: 229–251.
PD1.J7, v. 48

GOLLADAY, V. DENNIS. The evolution of Benjamin Franklin's theory of value. Pennsylvania history, v. 37, Jan. 1970: 40–52. F146.P597, v. 37

GRAMPP, WILLIAM D. The political economy of Poor Richard. Journal of political economy, v. 55, Apr. 1947: 132–141. HB1.J7, v. 55

GRANGER, BRUCE I. Benjamin Franklin, an American man of letters. Ithaca, N.Y., Cornell University Press [1964] ix, 264 p. PS751.G7

"Bibliographical note": p. 253–255.

HALE, EDWARD E., *and* EDWARD E. HALE, *Jr.* Franklin in France. From original documents, most of which are now published for the first time. Boston, Roberts Bros., 1887–1888. 2 v. illus., plates, ports. E249.F83

Vol. 2 has subtitle: *The Treaty of Peace and Franklin's Life Till His Return.*
Reprinted in New York by B. Franklin (1969).

HALL, MAX. An amateur detective on the trail of B. Franklin, hoaxer. *In* Massachusetts Historical Society, *Boston.* Proceedings. v. 84; 1972. Boston, 1973. p. 26–43. F61.M38, v. 84

———— Benjamin Franklin & Polly Baker; the history of a literary deception. Chapel Hill, Published for the Institute of Early American History and Culture at Williamsburg, Va., by the University of North Carolina Press [1960] xi, 193 p. facsims., port. PN171.F7B3

The appendix includes the text of the earliest known printing of "The speech of Miss Polly Baker" as issued in the *General Advertiser* in London on April 15, 1747, with the verbal variations found in nine other selected texts.
Bibliography: p. 168–184.

HANS, NICHOLAS A. Franklin, Jefferson, and the English radicals at the end of the eighteenth century. *In* American Philosophical Society, *Philadelphia.* Proceedings, v. 98, Dec. 1954: 406–426. facsims. Q11.P5, v. 98

Also published in the Society's *Library Bulletin* for 1954, p. 406–426.

Considers their relationships before, during, and after the war with such groups as the Deistic Society or Society of 13 and the Society of Constitutional Whigs.

———— UNESCO of the eighteenth century; la Loge des Neuf Soeurs and its venerable master, Benjamin Franklin. *In* American Philosophical Society, *Philadelphia.* Proceedings, v. 97, Oct. 1953: 513–524. facsims.
Q11.P5, v. 97

Also published in the Society's *Library Bulletin* for 1953, p. 513–524.

HAYS, ISAAC MINIS. The chronology of Benjamin Franklin, founder of the American Philosophical Society. 1706–1790. Philadelphia, American Philosophical Society, 1904. 32 p. E302.6.F8H42

"References": p. 31–32.

JACOBS, WILBUR R., *comp.* Benjamin Franklin: statesman-philosopher or materialist? New York, Holt, Rinehart and Winston [1971, °1972] 114 p. illus. (American problem studies) E302.6.F8J33

Bibliography: p. 112–114.

Presents selections from the writings of Carl Van Doren, D. H. Lawrence, Vernon L. Parrington, I. Bernard Cohen, Bernard Knollenberg, David Levin, Charles Augustin Sainte-Beuve, Charles Angoff, Philip Gleason, William Carlos Williams, F. L. Lucas, Esmond Wright, and John W. Ward.

JAMES, ALFRED P. Benjamin Franklin's Ohio Valley lands. *In* American Philosophical Society, *Philadelphia*. Proceedings, v. 98, Aug. 1954: 255–265. facsims., maps. Q11.P5, v. 98

JENKINS, CHARLES F. Franklin returns from France— 1785. *In* American Philosophical Society, *Philadelphia*. Proceedings, v. 92, Dec. 1948: 417–432. Q11.P5, v. 92

JERNEGAN, MARCUS W. Benjamin Franklin's "electrical kite" and lightning rod. New England quarterly, v. 1, Apr. 1928: 180–196. F1.N62, v. 1

JUSSERAND, JEAN A. A. J. Franklin in France. *In* Essays offered to Herbert Putnam. Edited by William Warner Bishop and Andrew Keogh. New Haven, Yale University Press, 1929. p. [226]–247. Z1009.Z3P9

KAHN, ROBERT L. George Forster [1754–1794] and Benjamin Franklin. *In* American Philosophical Society, *Philadelphia*. Proceedings, v. 102, Feb. 1958: 1–6. ports. Q11.P5, v. 102

See also Kahn's brief article, "An Account of a Meeting with Benjamin Franklin at Passy on October 9, 1777: From George Forster's English Journal," in the *William and Mary Quarterly*, 3d ser., v. 12, July 1955, p. 472–474.

—— Some unpublished Raspe-Franklin letters. *In* American Philosophical Society, *Philadelphia*. Proceedings, v. 99, June 1955: 127–132. Q11.P5, v. 99

Franklin corresponded with Rudolf Erich Raspe, whom he had met in Germany, between 1766 and 1780.

KEITER, M. ROBERTA WARF. Benjamin Franklin as an educator. 1957. ([284] p.) Micro AC–1, no. 21,525

Thesis (Ph.D.)—University of Maryland.
Abstracted in *Dissertation Abstracts*, v. 17, no. 7, 1957, p. 1507–1508.
Franklin's contributions to and influence upon education in Philadelphia and throughout the colonies.

KETCHAM, RALPH L. Benjamin Franklin. New York, Washington Square Press [1965] xiv, 226 p. (The Great American thinkers) E302.6.F8K43

Bibliography: p. 213–220.

—— Benjamin Franklin and William Smith: new light on an old Philadelphia quarrel. Pennsylvania magazine of history and biography, v. 88, Apr. 1964: 142–163. F146.P65, v. 88

KORTY, MARGARET B. Benjamin Franklin and eighteenth-century American libraries. Philadelphia, American Philosophical Society, 1965. 83 p. illus., facsims. (Transactions of the American Philosophical Society, new ser., v. 55, pt. 9) Q11.P6, n.s., v. 55 Z731.K6

Revision of author's thesis (M.S. in L.S.)—Catholic University.
Bibliography: p. 76–78.

—— Franklin's world of books. Journal of library history, v. 2, Oct. 1967: 271–328. Z671.J67, v. 2

Contents: 1. The library world of Benjamin Franklin.— 2. Franklin's private world of books.

KUSHEN, BETTY S. Benjamin Franklin and his biographers: a critical study. 1969. ([317] p.) Micro AC–1, no. 70–3081

Thesis (Ph.D.)—New York University.
Abstracted in *Dissertation Abstracts International*, v. 30A, Mar. 1970, p. 3946–3947.

LABAREE, LEONARD W. Benjamin Franklin's British friendships. *In* American Philosophical Society, *Philadelphia*. Proceedings, v. 108, Oct. 1964: 423–428. Q11.P5, v. 108

—— Franklin and the Presbyterians. *In* Presbyterian Historical Society. Journal, v. 35, Dec. 1957: 217–228. BX8905.P7A4, v. 35

—— In search of "B. Franklin." William and Mary quarterly, 3d ser., v. 16, Apr. 1959: 188–197. F221.W71, 3d s., v. 16

On the experiences of an editor of the Franklin *Papers* in search of his manuscripts.

LA LAURENCIE, LIONEL DE. Benjamin Franklin and the claveciniste Brillon de Jouy. Musical quarterly, v. 9, Apr. 1923: 245–259. ML1.M725, v. 9

LAPHAM, RUTH. Benjamin Franklin and the Post Office. 1925.
Thesis (Ph.D.)—Northwestern University.

LEMAY, JOSEPH A. LEO. Benjamin Franklin. *In* Emerson, Everett H., *ed.* Major writers of early American literature. [Madison] University of Wisconsin Press [1972] p. 205–243. PS185.E4

—— Franklin and Kinnersley. Isis, v. 52, Dec. 1961: 575–581. Q1.I7, v. 52

On the degree to which Franklin collaborated with the Rev. Ebenezer Kinnersley (1711–1778) in his electrical experiments.

—— Franklin and the *Autobiography*; an essay on recent scholarship. Eighteenth-century studies, v. 1, Dec. 1967: 185–211. NX452.E54, v. 1

The Life of Benjamin Franklin, including a sketch of the rise and progress of the War of Independence, and of the various negociations at Paris for peace; with the history of his political and other writings. London, Printed for Hunt and Clarke, 1826. 407 p. port. E302.6.F8L6

Attributed by Ford (*Franklin Bibliography*) to Leonard Woods.

LINGELBACH, WILLIAM E. B. Franklin, printer—new source materials. *In* American Philosophical Society, *Philadelphia*. Proceedings, v. 92, May 1948: 79–100. facsims. Q11.P5, v. 92

Also published in the Society's *Library Bulletin* for 1948, p. 79–100.

—— Franklin's *American Instructor*; early Americanism in the art of writing. *In* American Philosophical Society, *Philadelphia*. Proceedings, v. 96, Aug. 1952: 367–387. illus., facsims., ports. Q11.P5, v. 96

Also published in the Society's *Library Bulletin* for 1952, p. 367–387.

LOPEZ, CLAUDE A. Benjamin Franklin, Lafayette, and the *Lafayette*. *In* American Philosophical Society, *Philadelphia*. Proceedings, v. 108, June 1964: 181–223. Q11.P5, v. 108

On Franklin's strenuous efforts, 1779–81, to secure from the French, military supplies for the American army.

—— Mon cher Papa, Franklin and the ladies of Paris. New Haven, Yale University Press, 1966. xv, 404 p. illus., facsims., ports. E302.6.F8L8

"Bibliographical note to Franklin's years in Paris, 1777–1785": p. [341]–356. Bibliographic references included in "Notes" (p. [357]–377).

MCGLINCHEE, CLAIRE. Jonathan Edwards and Benjamin Franklin, antithetical figures. *In* International Congress on the Enlightenment, *2d, St. Andrews, Scot., 1967*. Transactions. v. 2. Genève, Institut et Musée Voltaire, 1967. (Studies on Voltaire and the eighteenth century, v. 56) p. 813–822. PQ2105.A2S8, v. 56

MACLAURIN, LOIS M. Franklin's vocabulary. Garden City, N.Y., Doubleday, Doran, 1928. 163 p. (Franklin monographs) PS751.M27

Bibliography: p. 145–155.
The author's thesis (Ph.D.), with the same title, was submitted to the University of Chicago in 1927.

MCMASTER, JOHN B. Benjamin Franklin as a man of letters. Boston, Houghton, Mifflin, 1887. ix, 293 p. port. (American men of letters) PS751.M3

Reprinted in New York by Arno Press (1970).

—— Franklin in France. Atlantic monthly, v. 60, Sept. 1887: 318–326. AP2.A8, v. 60

MATHEWS, LOIS K. Benjamin Franklin's plans for a colonial union, 1750–1775. American political science review, v. 8, Aug. 1914: 393–412. JA1.A6, v. 8

MEISTER, CHARLES W. Franklin as a proverb stylist. American literature, v. 24, May 1952: 157–166. PS1.A6, v. 24

MEYER, GLADYS E. Free trade in ideas; aspects of American liberalism illustrated in Franklin's Philadelphia career. New York, King's Crown Press, 1941. 108 p. E302.6.F8M56 1941 a

Issued also as thesis (Ph.D.)—Columbia University.
Bibliography: p. [101]–105.

MILES, RICHARD D. The American image of Benjamin Franklin. American quarterly, v. 9, summer 1957: 117–143. AP2.A3985, v. 9

—— The political philosophy of Benjamin Franklin: the beginning of the pragmatic tradition in American political thought. 1949. ([303] p.) Micro AC–1, no. 1206

Thesis (Ph.D.)—University of Michigan.
Abstracted in *Microfilm Abstracts*, v. 9, no. 2, 1949, p. 154–155.

MILLER, CLARENCE WILLIAM. Benjamin Franklin's way to wealth. *In* Bibliographical Society of America. Papers, v. 63, 4th quarter 1969: 231–246. Z1008.B51P, v. 63

MORRIS, RICHARD B. Meet Dr. Franklin. American heritage, v. 23, Dec. 1971: 81–91. illus., col. port. E171.A43, v. 23

MORSE, JOHN T. Benjamin Franklin. Boston, Houghton, Mifflin, 1898. xx, 444 p. facsim., plate, ports. (American statesmen, v. 1) E176.A54, v. 1
E302.6.F8M89

First published in 1889.
Reprinted in New York by AMS Press (1972).

NEWCOMB, ROBERT H. The sources of Benjamin Franklin's sayings of Poor Richard. 1957. ([407]p.) Micro AC–1, no. 23,276

Thesis (Ph.D.)—University of Maryland.
Abstracted in *Dissertation Abstracts*, v. 17, Nov. 1957, p. 2584–2585.

NEWMAN, ERIC P. Franklin making money more plentiful. *In* American Philosophical Society, *Philadelphia*. Proceedings, v. 115, Oct. 1971: 341–349. facsims. Q11.P5, v. 115

On Franklin's involvement in the production of paper money scrip from 1723 to 1789.

NOLAN, JAMES BENNETT. Benjamin Franklin in Scotland and Ireland, 1759 and 1771. Philadelphia, University of Pennsylvania Press, 1938. 229 p. illus., maps, plates, port. E302.6.F8N75 Rare Bk. Coll.

"Notes": p. 211–225.

—— General Benjamin Franklin; the military career of a philosopher. Philadelphia, University of Pennsylvania Press, 1936. vi, 101 p. illus., maps (on lining papers), port. E302.6.F8N77

Bibliography: p. 99–101.

OSWALD, JOHN C. Benjamin Franklin, printer. [Garden City, N.Y.] Doubleday, Page, for the Associated Advertising Clubs of the World, 1917. xv, 244 p. illus., facsims. Z232.F808 Rare Bk. Coll.

Reprinted in Ann Arbor, Mich., by Gryphon Books (1971).

PABÓN Y SUÁREZ DE URBINA, JESÚS. Franklin y Europa, 1776–1785. Madrid, Ediciones Rialp, 1957. 200 p. (Biblioteca del pensamiento acutal, 76)   E302.6.F8P2

"Noticia bibliográfica": p. 183–192.

PACE, ANTONIO. Benjamin Franklin and Italy. Philadelphia, American Philosophical Society, 1958. xi, 450 p. illus., facsim., ports. (Memoirs of the American Philosophical Society, v. 47)   E302.6.F8P23
                                Q11.P612, v. 47

"Bibliography of Italian Frankliniana": p. [413]–439.

——— Benjamin Franklin and Italy since the eighteenth century. In American Philosophical Society, Philadelphia. Proceedings, v. 94, June 1950: 242–250.
                                Q11.P5, v. 94

Also published in the Society's Library Bulletin for 1950, p. 242–250.

PARTON, JAMES. Life and times of Benjamin Franklin. New York, Mason Bros., 1864. 2 v. ports.
                                E302.6.F8P27

Reprinted in New York by Da Capo Press (1971).

PEPPER, WILLIAM. The medical side of Benjamin Franklin. University of Pennsylvania medical bulletin, v. 23, Apr.–June, Sept.–Dec. 1910: 87–105, 151–167, 211–222, 333–358, 431–444, 499–507, 549–585. illus., facsims., ports.   R11.U6, v. 23

Also published separately in Philadelphia by W. J. Campbell (1911. 122 p. E302.6.F83P4) and reprinted in New York by Argosy-Antiquarian (1970. 137 p. R154.F8P5 1970).

PHILBRICK, FRANCIS S. Notes on early editions and editors of Franklin. In American Philosophical Society, Philadelphia. Proceedings, v. 97, Oct. 1953: 525–564.
                                Q11.P5, v. 97

Also published in the Society's Library Bulletin for 1953, p. 525–564.

PITT, ARTHUR S. Franklin and religious sectarianism. 1939.

Thesis (Ph.D.)—Yale University.

——— Franklin and the Quaker movement against slavery. In Friends' Historical Association. Bulletin, v. 32, spring 1943: 13–31.   BX7635.A1F6, v. 32

POLINSKY, GERALD R. Benjamin Franklin: scientist-inventor. 1968. ([401] p.)
                                Micro AC–1, no. 68–14,080

Thesis (Ph.D.)—St. Louis University.
Abstracted in Dissertation Abstracts, v. 29A, Oct. 1968, p. 1197.

POWERS, THOMAS J. Benjamin Franklin and his views and opinions on education. 1965. ([121] p.)
                                Micro AC–1, no. 66–6161

Thesis (Ph.D.)—Michigan State University.
Abstracted in Dissertation Abstracts, v. 27A, Sept. 1966, p. 647.

READ, CONYERS. The English elements in Benjamin Franklin. Pennsylvania magazine of history and biography, v. 64, July 1940: 314–330.   F146.P65, v. 64

RIDDELL, WILLIAM R. Benjamin Franklin and colonial money. Pennsylvania magazine of history and biography, v. 54, Jan. 1930: 52–64.   F146.P65, v. 54

ROELKER, WILLIAM G. The Franklin-Greene correspondence. In American Philosophical Society, Philadelphia. Library. Library bulletin. 1946. Philadelphia, 1947. p. 21–32. facsim., plate.   Z881.P49, 1946

On the friendship between Franklin and Catharine Ray Greene.

ROGERS, JAMES F. The physical Franklin. South Atlantic quarterly, v. 15, Jan. 1916: 18–24.   AP2.S75, v. 15

ROSENGARTEN, JOSEPH G. Franklin's bagatelles. In American Philosophical Society, Philadelphia. Proceedings, v. 40, July 1901: 87–135.   Q11.P5, v. 40

ROSS, EARLE D. Franklin and agriculture. Journal of political economy, v. 37, Feb. 1929: 52–72.
                                HB1.J7, v. 37

ROSSITER, CLINTON L. The political theory of Benjamin Franklin. Pennsylvania magazine of history and biography, v. 76, July 1952: 259–293.   F146.P65, v. 76

SANFORD, CHARLES L., ed. Benjamin Franklin and the American character. Boston, Heath [1955] viii, 102 p. (Problems in American civilization: readings selected by the Dept. of American Studies, Amherst College)
                                E302.6.F8S32

"Suggestions for additional reading": p. [99]–102.

Includes excerpts from the writings of Benjamin Franklin, George Washington, and John Adams as well as Carl Van Doren, Frank Davidson, A. Whitney Griswold, Gladys Meyer, Charles Angoff, D. H. Lawrence, Charles L. Sanford, Stuart P. Sherman, Herbert W. Schneider, and I. Bernard Cohen.

SAVELLE, MAX. Benjamin Franklin and American liberalism. Western humanities review, v. 18, summer 1964: 197–209.   AP2.W426, v. 18

SAYRE, ROBERT F. The worldly Franklin and the provincial critics. Texas studies in literature and language, v. 4, winter 1963: 512–524.   AS30.T4, v. 4

SCHILLER, ANDREW. Franklin as a music critic. New England quarterly, v. 31, Dec. 1958: 505–525.
                                F1.N62, v. 31

SCHNEIDER, HERBERT W. The significance of Benjamin Franklin's moral philosophy. In Columbia University. Dept. of Philosophy. Studies in the history of ideas. v. 2. New York, Columbia University Press, 1925. p. [291]–312.   B21.C7, v. 2

SCHONLAND, BASIL F. J. The work of Benjamin Franklin on thunderstorms and the development of the lightning rod. In Franklin Institute, Philadelphia. Journal, v. 253, May 1952: 375–392.   T1.F8, v. 253

SELLERS, CHARLES C.   Benjamin Franklin in portraiture. New Haven, Yale University Press, 1962. xi, 452 p. illus., ports. (part col.)   N7628.F7S4
Bibliographic footnotes.

——— The Peale portraits of Benjamin Franklin. *In* American Philosophical Society, *Philadelphia*. Proceedings, v. 94, June 1950: 251–257. facsim., port.
          Q11.P5, v. 94
Also published in the Society's *Library Bulletin* for 1950, p. 251–257.

SHELLING, RICHARD I.   Benjamin Franklin and the Dr. Bray Associates. Pennsylvania magazine of history and biography, v. 63, July 1939: 282–293.
          F146.P65, v. 63

STEVENS, HENRY.   Benjamin Franklin's life and writings. A bibliographical essay on the Stevens' collection of books and manuscripts relating to Doctor Franklin. London, Printed by Messrs. Davy, 1881. viii, 40 p. facsim., ports.   Z8313.S84
          Z6616.F8S8
A collection of 3,000 different manuscripts and 300 printed books purchased by Congress in 1882 for the Department of State and subsequently transferred to the Library of Congress.

STOURZH, GERALD.   Benjamin Franklin and American foreign policy. [Chicago] University of Chicago Press [1954] xvii, 335 p.   E249.S88
Bibliographic references included in "Notes" (p. 261–318).
A second edition was published in 1969.

——— Reason and power in Benjamin Franklin's political thought. American political science review, v. 47, Dec. 1953: 1092–1115.   JA1.A6, v. 47

THORPE, FRANCIS N., *ed.*   Benjamin Franklin and the University of Pennsylvania. Washington, Govt. Print. Off., 1893. 450 p. facsim., plates, ports. (U.S. Bureau of Education. Circular of information, 1892, no. 2)
          LD4529.3.T5

TYACK, DAVID B.   Education as artifact: Benjamin Franklin and the instruction of a rising people. History of education quarterly, v. 6, spring 1966: 3–15.
          L11.H67, v. 6

U.S. *Library of Congress. Manuscript Division.*   List of the Benjamin Franklin papers in the Library of Congress. Compiled under the direction of Worthington Chauncey Ford, chief, Division of Manuscripts. Washington, Govt. Print. Off., 1905. 322 p.   Z6616.F83U7
          Z663.34.L5

VAN DOREN, CARL C.   Benjamin Franklin. New York, Viking Press, 1938. xix, 845 p. ports.   E302.6.F8V32
"General bibliography": p. [785]–788.

——— The first American man of letters. Michigan alumnus quarterly review, v. 45, summer 1939: 283–296. facsims., port.   AP2.M35, v. 45

VICTORY, BEATRICE M.   Benjamin Franklin and Germany. [Philadelphia] 1915. 180 p. facsim. (Americana germanica, [new ser., no. 21])   E302.6.F8V6
Thesis (Ph.D.)—University of Pennsylvania, 1913. Bibliography: p. 160–180.

WALDEN, DANIEL.   Benjamin Franklin's Deism: a phase. Historian, v. 26, May 1964: 350–361. D1.H22, v. 26

WARD, JOHN W.   "Who was Benjamin Franklin?" American scholar, v. 32, autumn 1963: 541–553.
          AP2.A4572, v. 32

WECTER, DIXON.   Benjamin Franklin and an Irish "enthusiast." Huntington Library quarterly, v. 4, Jan. 1941: 205–234.   Z733.S24Q, v. 4
Treats Franklin's amicable relations with an Irish parliamentarian, Sir Edward Newenham, especially during the important month of the peace negotiations in Paris, October 1782.

——— Burke, Franklin, and Samuel Petrie. Huntington Library quarterly, v. 3, Apr. 1940: 315–338.
          Z733.S24Q, v. 3
On the correspondence between Franklin and Burke during the war and their relationship with Petrie, an adventurer, stock-jobber, and self-appointed mediator.

WETZEL, WILLIAM A.   Benjamin Franklin as an economist. Baltimore, Johns Hopkins Press, 1895. 58 p. (Johns Hopkins University studies in historical and political science, 13th ser., no. 9)   H31.J6, 13th s., no. 9
          HB119.F8W5
Bibliography: p. [57]–58.

WILLIAMS, DAVID.   More light on Franklin's religious ideas. American historical review, v. 43, July 1938: 803–813.   E171.A57, v. 43

WILLIAMS, HOWELL V.   Benjamin Franklin and the poor laws. Social service review, v. 18, Mar. 1944: 77–91.
          HV1.S6, v. 18

WILLIUS, FREDERICK A., *and* THOMAS E. KEYS.   The medical history of Benjamin Franklin (1706–1790). [n.p., 1942] 12 p.   E302.6.F8W73
"References": p. 12.
Reprinted from the *Proceedings of the Staff Meetings of the Mayo Clinic*, v. 17, June 24–July 1, 1942, p. 391–397, 410–416.

WISE, CLAUDE M.   Benjamin Franklin as a phonetician. Speech monographs, v. 15, no. 1, 1948: 99–120.
          PN4077.S6, v. 15
On Franklin's "Scheme for a New Alphabet and a Reformed Mode of Spelling," first published in his *Political, Miscellaneous, and Philosophical Pieces* (London, Printed for J. Johnson, 1779). See also Kemp Malone's "Benjamin Franklin on Spelling Reform," in *American Speech*, v. 1, Nov. 1925, p. 96–100, and William Angus' "Poor Richard's Alphabet and His Pronunciation," in *Speech Monographs*, v. 2, Oct. 1935, p. 60–70.

WOLF, EDWIN. Benjamin Franklin's *Political, Miscellaneous and Philosophical Pieces*, 1779. Library chronicle, v. 16, summer 1950: 50–63.   Z733.P418, v. 16

——— The reconstruction of Benjamin Franklin's library: an unorthodox jigsaw puzzle. *In* Bibliographical Society of America. Papers, v. 56, 1st quarter 1962: 1–16. plate.   Z1008.B51P, v. 56

WRIGHT, ESMOND, *comp.* Benjamin Franklin; a profile. New York, Hill and Wang [1970] xxvii, 227 p. (American profiles)   E302.6.F8W87

Contents: Introduction. Brief biography of Benjamin Franklin. By E. Wright.—A Puritan on prosperity, by W. Griswold.—Quaker business mentors: the Philadelphia merchants, by F. B. Tolles.—The Junto, by C. Van Doren.—The character of Poor Richard, by J. F. Ross.—The autobiography of Benjamin Franklin, by D. Levin.—The empirical temper of Benjamin Franklin, by I. B. Cohen.—The continentalist, by P. W. Conner.—The Stamp Act crisis, by V. W. Crane.—Setting metes and bounds, by R. B. Morris.—The political theory of Benjamin Franklin, by C. Rossiter.—Reason and power in Benjamin Franklin's political thought, by G. Stourzh.—Bibliographical note (p. 224–225).

——— Benjamin Franklin, a tradesman in the Age of Reason. History today, v. 6, July 1956: 439–447. illus., port.   D1.H818, v. 6

——— Benjamin Franklin and American Independence. London, English Universities Press [1966] vii, 181 p. (Teach yourself history library)   E302.6.F8W88

Bibliography: p. 175–176.

WYKOFF, GEORGE S. Problems concerning Franklin's "A dialogue between Britain, France, Spain, Holland, Saxony, and America." American literature, v. 11, Jan. 1940: 439–448.   PS1.A6, v. 11

ZIMMERMAN, JOHN J. Benjamin Franklin and *The Pennsylvania Chronicle*. Pennsylvania magazine of history and biography, v. 81, Oct. 1957: 351–364.   F146.P65, v. 81

13382

FRANKLIN, DEBORAH READ (*ca.* 1707–1774)
Pennsylvania. Wife of Benjamin Franklin (1706–1790)

HART, CHARLES H. Who was the mother of Franklin's son: an inquiry demonstrating that she was Deborah Read, wife of Benjamin Franklin. Pennsylvania magazine of history and biography, v. 35, July 1911: 308–314.   F146.P65, v. 35

RILEY, EDWARD M. The Deborah Franklin correspondence. *In* American Philosophical Society, *Philadelphia.* Proceedings, v. 95, June 1951: 239–245. facsims., port.   Q11.P5, v. 95

Also published in the Society's *Library Bulletin* for 1951, p. 239–245.

13383

FRANKLIN, JOHN (1749–1831)
Connecticut; Pennsylvania. Settler, Revolutionary officer, assemblyman.

BUGBEE, LEROY E. John Franklin and the wild Yankees. *In* Wyoming Historical and Geological Society, *Wilkes-Barre, Pa.* Proceedings and collections. v. 23; 1970. Wilkes-Barre, 1971. p. 41–71. port.   F157.W9W94, v. 23

Colonel John Franklin. *In* Bradford County Historical Society, *Towanda, Pa.* Annual. no. 3. Towanda, 1909. p. 51–66. port.   F157.B76B7, no. 3

MURRAY, LOUISE W. Col. John Franklin and the last stand of the Connecticut settler. *In* Wyoming Commemorative Association, *Wilkes-Barre, Pa.* Proceedings. 1917. p. 12–57.   E241.W9W85, 1917

13384

FRANKLIN, ROSWELL (*d.* 1791 *or* 2)
Pennsylvania. Frontiersman.

HUBBARD, ROBERT. Historical sketches of Roswell Franklin and family. Dansville, N.Y., Printed by A. Stevens, 1839. 103 p.   F157.W9F85 Rare Bk. Coll.

13385

FRANKLIN, WILLIAM (*ca.* 1730–1813)*
Pennsylvania; New Jersey; England. Lawyer, royal governor, Loyalist.

——— Letters from William Franklin to William Strahan [1757–82] Edited with introduction and notes by Charles H. Hart. Pennsylvania magazine of history and biography, v. 35, Oct. 1911: 415–462. port.   F146.P65, v. 34

——— ——— Offprint. Philadelphia [Printed by J. B. Lippincott Co.] 1911. 48 p.   F137.F82

FENNELLY, CATHERINE M. William Franklin of New Jersey. William and Mary quarterly, 3d ser., v. 6, July 1949: 361–382. plate.   F221.W71, 3d s., v. 6

MARIBOE, WILLIAM H. The life of William Franklin, 1730(1)–1813, "Pro Rege et Patria." 1962. ([622] p.)   Micro AC–1, no. 62–4324

Thesis (Ph.D.)—University of Pennsylvania.
Abstracted in *Dissertation Abstracts*, v. 23, Nov. 1962, p. 1674–1675.

WHITEHEAD, WILLIAM A. A biographical sketch of William Franklin, governor from 1765 to 1776. *In* New Jersey Historical Society. Proceedings, v. 3, no. 3, 1848: 137–159.   F131.N58, v. 3

——— ——— Offprint. [Newark, N.J., Daily Advertiser Off., 1849] 23 p.   F137.F83

13386

FRANKS, DAVID SALISBURY (*ca.* 1740–1793)

Canada; Pennsylvania. Revolutionary officer, diplomat.

KOHLER, MAX J. Colonel David S. Franks. Magazine of history, with notes and queries, v. 4, Aug. 1906: 63–72.
E171.M23, v. 4

ROSENBACH, ABRAHAM S. W. Documents relative to Major David S. Franks while aid-de-camp to General Arnold. *In* American Jewish Historical Society. Publications. v. 5; 1896. [Baltimore] 1897. p. 157–189.
E184.J5A5, v. 5

STRAUS, OSCAR S. New light on the career of Colonel David S. Franks. *In* American Jewish Historical Society. Publications. v. 10; 1902. [Baltimore] p. 101–108.
E184.J5A5, v. 10

ZITT, HERSCH L. David Salisbury Franks, Revolutionary patriot (c. 1740–1793). Pennsylvania history, v. 16, Apr. 1949: 77–95. port.
F146.P597, v. 16

13387

FRANKS, ISAAC (1759–1822)

New York; Massachusetts; Pennsylvania. Forage master, Revolutionary officer.

JASTROW, MORRIS. Documents relating to the career of Colonel Isaac Franks. *In* American Jewish Historical Society. Publications. v. 5; 1896. [Baltimore] 1897. p. 7–34.
E184.J5A5, v. 5

————— ————— Offprint. [Baltimore, Press of the Friedenwald Co., 1896] [7]–34 p. port.
E207.F75J3

13388

FRASER, JOHN (1721–1773)

Scotland; Pennsylvania. Settler, land speculator.

CLARK, HOWARD G. John Fraser, western Pennsylvania frontiersman. Western Pennsylvania historical magazine, v. 38, fall/winter 1955: 83–93; v. 39, spring/summer 1956: 35–43, 109–124.
F146.W52, v. 38–39

13389

FRAZER, MARY WORRELL TAYLOR (*ca.* 1745–1830)

Pennsylvania. Wife of Persifor Frazer (1735 *or* 6–1792).

SLAYMAKER, SAMUEL R. Mrs. Frazer's Philadelphia campaign, 1777–78. *In* Lancaster County (Pa.) Historical Society. Journal, v. 73, fall 1969: 185–209. illus.
F157.L2L5, v. 73

13390

FRAZER, PERSIFOR (1735 *or* 6–1792)*

Pennsylvania. Merchant, iron master, Revolutionary officer, assemblyman.

————— Letters from Ticonderoga, 1776. *In* Fort Ticonderoga, N.Y. Museum. Bulletin, v. 10, Feb. 1961–Jan. 1962: 386–396, 450–459.
E199.F75, v. 10

Written to his wife from July to November.

————— Some extracts from the papers of General Persifor Frazer [1776–1778] Pennsylvania magazine of history and biography, v. 31, Apr.–Oct. 1907: 129–144, 311–319, 447–451.
F146.P65, v. 31

FRAZER, PERSIFOR. General Persifor Frazer, a memoir compiled principally from his own papers by his great grandson Persifor Frazer. Philadelphia, 1907. xiii, 430 p. facsims., map, plates, port.
CS71.F848 1907

13391

FRAZER, WILLIAM (*d.* 1795)

New Jersey. Anglican clergyman and missionary.

————— Rev. William Frazer's three parishes—St. Thomas's, St. Andrew's, and Musconetcong, N.J.—1768–70; copies of letters from Rev. William Frazer to the Rev. Dr. Benton, in Abingdon Street, Westminster, London. Pennsylvania magazine of history and biography, v. 12, July 1888: 212–232.
F146.P65, v. 12

Marriage and baptismal records, p. 222–232. Introduction and notes by Henry Race.

13392

FREEMAN, JAMES (1759–1835)*

Massachusetts. Clergyman.

FOOTE, HENRY W. James Freeman and King's Chapel, 1782–87. A chapter in the early history of the Unitarian movement in New England. Religious magazine and monthly review, v. 49, June 1873: 505–531.
BX9801.M7, v. 49

————— ————— Reprint. Boston, L. C. Bowles, 1873. 29 p.
BX9869.F7F6

13393

FREEMAN, SAMUEL (1743–1831)

Maine. Assemblyman.

FREEMAN, WILLIAM. Samuel Freeman—his life and services. *In* Maine Historical Society. Collections and proceedings. 2d ser., v. 5. Portland, 1894. p. 1–32.
F16.M33, 2d s., v. 5

Also published separately ([Portland? Me., 1893] 32 p. F29.P9F85).

13394

FRENEAU, PHILIP MORIN (1752–1832)*

New Jersey. Poet, pamphleteer, mariner.

————— Father Bombo's pilgrimage. Pennsylvania magazine of history and biography, v. 66, Oct. 1942: 459–478.
F146.P65, v. 66

Reproduces, from a manuscript notebook, the text of Freneau's contribution to a "novel" entitled *Father Bombo's Pilgrimage to Mecca in Arabia*, written with Hugh Henry Brackenridge in 1770 when both men were at Princeton. (Brackenridge's contribution was published in *The Life and Writings of Hugh Henry Brackenridge* (Princeton, Princeton University Press, 1932), by Clause M. Newlin.) Introduction and notes by Lewis Leary.

———— A Freneau sampler. Edited by Philip M. Marsh. New York, Scarecrow Press, 1963. 399 p.   PS755.A5M28

"Selected bibliography": p. 23–26.

———— The manuscript of Philip Freneau's *The British Prison-Ship* [1781] *In* Rutgers University, *New Brunswick, N.J. Library*. Journal, v. 6, Dec. 1942: 1–28. facsims. plate.   Z733.R955F, v. 6

Introduction and notes by Lewis Leary.

———— Poems of Freneau. Edited with a critical introduction by Harry Hayden Clark. New York, Harcourt, Brace [c1929] lxiii, 425 p. (American authors series)
    PS755.A5C6

"Selected reading list": p. lxi–lxiii.
Reprinted in New York by Hafner Pub. Co. (1960).

———— The poems of Philip Freneau, poet of the American Revolution. Edited for the Princeton Historical Association by Fred Lewis Pattee. Princeton, N.J., The University Library, 1902–7. 3 v.   PS755.A2 1902

"Bibliography of the poetry of Philip Freneau": v. 3, p. 407–417.
Reprinted in New York by Russell & Russell (1963).

———— Poems relating to the American Revolution. With an introductory memoir and notes, by Evert A. Duyckinck. New York, W. J. Widdleton, 1865. xxxviii, 288 p. facsim., port.   E295.F87

———— Poems written and published during the American Revolutionary War, and now republished from the original manuscripts; interspersed with translations from the ancients, and other pieces not heretofore in print. 3d ed. Philadelphia, from the press of L. R. Bailey, no. 10, North-Alley, 1809. 2 v. fronts.
    PS755.A2 1809 Rare Bk. Coll.

———— Prose. Selected and edited by Philip M. Marsh. New Brunswick, N.J., Scarecrow Press, 1955. xii, 596 p.
    PS755.A5M3

"Selected bibliography": p. 33–37.

Mostly letters and contributions to periodicals, 48 of which were written between 1779 and 1789.

———— Some account of the capture of the ship "Aurora" New York, M. F. Mansfield & A. Wessels [c1899] 49 p. facsim., ports.   E271.F87

Reprinted in New York by the New York Times (1971).

ADKINS, NELSON F. Philip Freneau and the cosmic enigma; the religious and philosophical speculations of an American poet. New York, New York University Press, 1949. 84 p. (A New York University Press study)
    PS758.A4

Bibliographic footnotes.
Reprinted in New York by Russell & Russell (1971. PS758.A6 1971).

AUSTIN, MARY S. Philip Freneau, the poet of the Revolution; a history of his life and times. Edited by Helen Kearny Vreeland. New York, A. Wessels Co., 1901. x, 285 p. facsim., plates, ports.   PS758.A8

Reprinted in Detroit by Gale Research Co. (1968).

AXELRAD, JACOB. Philip Freneau, champion of democracy. Austin, University of Texas Press [1967] xii, 480 p.
    PS758.A9

Bibliography: p. [437]–459.

BROWN, RUTH W. Classical echoes in the poetry of Philip Freneau. Classical journal, v. 45, Oct. 1949: 29–34.
    PA1.C4, v. 45

DEBOER, KATHRYN B. The rhymes of Philip Freneau: a reflection of eighteenth-century American pronunciation. Speech monographs. v. 33, Mar. 1966: 50–56.
    PN4077.S6, v. 33

FORMAN, SAMUEL E. The political activities of Philip Freneau. Baltimore, Johns Hopkins Press, 1902. 105 p. (Johns Hopkins University studies in historical and political science, ser. 20, no. 9/10)   H31.J6, ser. 20
    PS758.F6

"The publications of Philip Freneau": p. [103]–105.
Reprinted in New York by Arno Press (1970).

HAVILAND, THOMAS P. A measure for the early Freneau's debt to Milton. *In* Modern Language Association of America. Publications, v. 55, Dec. 1940: 1033–1040.
    PB6.M6, v. 55

LEARY, LEWIS G. Philip Freneau. *In* Emerson, Everett H. Major writers of early American literature. [Madison] University of Wisconsin Press [1972] p. 245–271.
    PS185.E4

———— That rascal Freneau; a study in literary failure. [New Brunswick, N.J.] Rutgers University Press [c1941] x, 501 p.   PS758.L4

Issued also as thesis (Ph.D.)—Columbia University.
Bibliography: p. 418–480.
Reprinted in New York by Octagon Books (1964).

LEE, HECTOR H. Philip Freneau as a war propagandist in 1775. *In* Utah Academy of Sciences, Arts and Letters. Proceedings. v. 23; 1945/46. Salt Lake City [1947] p. 73–81.   Q11.U85, v. 23

MARBLE, ANNIE R. Philip Freneau, America's first poet. New England magazine, new ser., v. 29, Dec. 1903: 421–435. illus., facsim., port.   AP2.N4, n.s., v. 29

MARSH, PHILIP M. The Freneau-Hopkinson quarrel. *In* New Jersey Historical Society. Proceedings, v. 74, Oct. 1956: 304–314.   F131.N58, v. 74

———— Philip Freneau and Francis Hopkinson. *In* New Jersey Historical Society. Proceedings, v. 63, July 1945: 141–149.　　　　F131.N58, v. 63

Marshals evidence to show that they may have had a friendly relationship.

———— Philip Freneau and his circle. Pennsylvania magazine of history and biography, v. 63, Jan. 1939: 37–59.
　　　　F146.P65, v. 63

———— Philip Freneau, poet and journalist. Minneapolis, Dillon Press [1968, ᶜ1967] v, 444 p. illus., facsims., ports.　　　　PS758.M3

Bibliography: p. [369]–394.

———— Philip Freneau's fame. *In* New Jersey Historical Society. Proceedings, v. 80, Apr.–July 1962: 75–93, 197–212.　　　　F131.N58, v. 80

An appraisal of Freneau historiography.

PALTSITS, VICTOR H.　A bibliography of the separate & collected works of Philip Freneau, together with an account of his newspapers. New York, Dodd, Mead, 1903. xv, 96 p. facsim.　　　　Z8315.P18

Reprinted in New York by B. Franklin (1968) and in Folcroft, Pa., by the Folcroft Press (1969).

THOMAS, OWEN P.　Philip Freneau; a bibliography of biographical, critical, and historical scholarship. *In* New Jersey Historical Society. Proceedings, v. 75, July 1957: 197–205.　　　　F131.N58, v. 75

Lists 140 titles.

13395

FROELIGH, SOLOMON (1750–1827)

New York; New Jersey. Dutch Reformed clergyman.

KIESSEL, WILLIAM C.　Dr. Solomon Froeligh. *In* New Jersey Historical Society. Proceedings, v. 73, Jan. 1955: 28–40.　　　　F131.N58, v. 73

13396

FULLER, DANIEL (1740–1829)

Massachusetts. Clergyman.

———— The diary of the Revᵈ. Daniel Fuller with his account of his family & other matters. Written at Gloucester, in Massachusetts, circa 1775, & edited by his grandson, Daniel Fuller Appleton. New-York, Imprinted for private distribution at the De Vinne Press, 1894. 49 p. port., plates.　　　　F74.G5F9

13397

FURMAN, MOORE (1728–1808)

New Jersey; Pennsylvania. Merchant, Revolutionary officer, judge.

———— The letters of Moore Furman, deputy quarter-master general of New Jersey in the Revolution. Compiled and edited with genealogical notes by the Historical Research Committee of the New Jersey Society of the

Colonial Dames of America. New York, Published for the Society by F. H. Hitchcock, 1912. xiii, 162 p.
　　　　E263.N5F98

Bibliography: p. 155–156.

The letters cover the period from May 1779 to January 1812.

13398

GADSDEN, CHRISTOPHER (1724–1805)*

South Carolina. Merchant, planter, assemblyman, delegate to the Continental Congress, Revolutionary general.

———— The writings of Christopher Gadsden, 1746–1805. Edited by Richard Walsh. Columbia, University of South Carolina Press, 1966. xxviii, 342 p. illus., facsims., ports.　　　　E302.G14A2 1966

Bibliography: p. 318–329.

METTLER, CECILIA C.　A biographical sketch of Christopher Gadsden. 1938.

Thesis (Ph.D.)—Cornell University.

PORCHER, FREDERICK A.　A memoir of Gen. Christopher Gadsden. Charleston, S.C., Journal of Commerce Job Off., 1878. 11 p. [South Carolina Historical Society. Collections. v. 4, no. 4]　　　　F266.S71, v. 4
　　　　E207.G2P7

POTTS, JAMES L.　Christopher Gadsden and the American Revolution. 1958. ([418] p.)
　　　　Micro AC–1, no. 59–1114

Thesis (Ph.D.)—George Peabody College for Teachers.

Abstracted in *Dissertation Abstracts*, v. 19, May 1959, p. 2932.

RENICK, EDWARD I.　Christopher Gadsden. *In* Southern History Association. Publications, v. 2, July 1898: 242–255.　　　　F206.S73, v. 2

———— ———— Offprint. Harrisburg, Pa., Harrisburg Pub. Co., 1898. [242]–255 p.　　　　E207.G2R5

WALSH, RICHARD.　Christopher Gadsden: radical or conservative revolutionary? South Carolina historical magazine, v. 63, Oct. 1962: 195–203.
　　　　F266.S55, v. 63

———— Christopher Gadsden: the challenge of his diaries. Manuscripts, v. 9, summer 1957: 132–139, 187. facsim.　　　　Z41.A2A925, v. 9

See also "The Gadsden 'Diary' Deciphered," v. 16, spring 1964, p. 17–23.

13399

GAGE, THOMAS (1721–1787)*†

England; Massachusetts. Royal governor, British officer in America.

———— The correspondence of General Thomas Gage. Compiled and edited by Clarence Edwin Carter. New

Haven, Yale University Press, 1931–33. 2 v. (Yale historical publications. Manuscripts and edited texts, 11)
E187.G13

Contents: v. 1. With the Secretaries of State, 1763–1775.—v. 2. With the Secretaries of State, and with the War Office and the Treasury, 1763–1775.
Reprinted in Hamden, Conn., by Archon Books (1969).

—— Some letters and papers of General Thomas Gage [1766–72] *In* The John P. Branch historical papers of Randolph-Macon College. v. 4, no. 2; 1914. Ashland, Va. p. 86–111.
F221.J65, v. 4

Written from New York to the officers in command of Fort de Chartres.

ALDEN, JOHN R. General Gage in America: being principally a history of his role in the American Revolution. Baton Rouge, Louisiana State University Press, 1948. xi, 313 p. map, ports.
E207.G23A6

"Bibliographical note": p. 299–303.
Reprinted in New York by Greenwood Press (1969).

SHY, JOHN W. Thomas Gage: weak link of empire. *In* Billias, George A., ed. George Washington's opponents: British generals and admirals in the American Revolution. New York, Morrow, 1969. p. 3–38. port.
E267.B56

Bibliography: p. 37–38.

13400

GAINE, HUGH (1726 or 7–1807)*

Ireland; New York. Printer, newspaper publisher, bookseller.

—— The journals of Hugh Gaine, printer. Edited by Paul Leicester Ford. New York, Dodd, Mead, 1902. 2 v. facsims. (part fold.), port.
Z232.G2F5

Contents: v. 1. Biography and bibliography.—v. 2. Journals and letters.
Reprinted in New York by Arno Press (1970).

LORENZ, ALFRED L. Hugh Gaine: a colonial printer-editor's odyssey to loyalism. Foreword by Howard Rusk Long. Carbondale, Southern Illinois University Press [1972] xii, 192 p. (New Horizons in journalism)
Z232.G2L6

Bibliography: p. 163–176.
The author's thesis (Ph.D.), *Hugh Gaine: a Colonial Printer-Editor, 1752–1783*, was submitted to Southern Illinois University in 1968 (Micro AC–1, no. 69–1752).

13401

GALE, BENJAMIN (1715–1790)*

New York; Connecticut. Physician, assemblyman.

GROCE, GEORGE C. Benjamin Gale. New England quarterly, v. 10, Dec. 1937: 697–716. F1.N62, v. 10

13402

GALLATIN, ALBERT (1761–1849)*

Switzerland; Pennsylvania. Farmer.

DATER, HENRY M. Albert Gallatin—land speculator. Mississippi Valley historical review, v. 26, June 1939: 21–38.
E171.J87, v. 26

Investigates Gallatin's partnership in a store at George Creek on the Monongahela and his speculation in land along the Ohio in the Kanawha Valley, 1783–85.

13403

GALLATIN, GASPARD GABRIEL, *baron* DE (1758–1838)

Switzerland. French officer in America.

—— Un garde suisse de Louis XVI au service de l'Amérique. Correspondant, t. 324, 10 août, 10 sept. 1931: 321–338, 672–692.
AP20.C8, v. 324

The portion covering Gallatin's stay at Newport was translated by Warrington Dawson and published in the *Franco-American Review*, v. 1, spring 1937, p. 330–340. Gallatin's transcription of the official general staff account of the siege of Yorktown was translated by the French Department of the College of William and Mary and published in Washington, D. C., in 1931 (entry 6721). The manuscript is now in the Library of Congress.

13404

GALLOWAY, GRACE GROWDEN (*d.* 1789)

Pennsylvania. Wife of Joseph Galloway (1731–1803).

—— Diary of Grace Growden Galloway. Pennsylvania magazine of history and biography, v. 55, Jan. 1931: 32–94; v. 58, Apr. 1934: 152–189. port.
F146.P65, v. 55, 58

Introduction and notes by Raymond C. Werner.
Reprinted in New York by the New York Times (1971. E278.G12A3).
Covers the period June 17, 1778–September 30, 1779.

13405

GALLOWAY, JOSEPH (1731–1803)*†

Pennsylvania; England. Lawyer, assemblyman, delegate to the Continental Congress, pamphleteer, Loyalist.

BALDWIN, ERNEST H. Joseph Galloway, the Loyalist politician. Pennsylvania magazine of history and biography, v. 26, July-Oct. 1902, Jan. 1903: 161–191, 289–321, 417–442.
F146.P65, v. 26

—— —— Offprint. Philadelphia, 1902. 113 p.
E278.G14B18

The author's thesis (Ph.D.), *Joseph Galloway: a Biography*, was submitted to Yale University in 1901.

BOYD, JULIAN P. Anglo-American union; Joseph Galloway's plans to preserve the British empire, 1774–1788. Philadelphia, University of Pennsylvania Press, 1941. x, 185 p.
E210.B6

Bibliographic footnotes.
Reprinted in New York by Octagon Books (1970).
Galloway's plans of union—1774, 1779, 1780–81, 1785, and 1788—are reproduced in five appendixes (p. 112–177).

——— Joseph Galloway's plans of union for the British Empire, 1774–1788. Pennsylvania magazine of history and biography, v. 64, Oct. 1940: 492–515.

F146.P65, v. 64

Galloway's letter to Charles Jenkinson (1780?) enclosing plans for a permanent union between Great Britain and America, appears on p. 516–544, with notes by Julian P. Boyd.

CALHOON, ROBERT M. "I have deduced your rights": Joseph Galloway's concept of his role, 1774–1775. Pennsylvania history, v. 35, Oct. 1968: 356–378.

F146.P597, v. 35

FERLING, JOHN E. Joseph Galloway: a reassessment of the motivations of a Pennsylvania Loyalist. Pennsylvania history, v. 39, Apr. 1972: 163–186.

F146.P597, v. 39

———Joseph Galloway and the philosophy of loyalism. 1971. ([362] p.) Micro AC–1, no. 71–26,658
Thesis (Ph.D.)—West Virginia University.
Abstracted in Dissertation Abstracts International, v. 32A, Oct. 1971, p. 2052.

KUNTZLEMAN, OLIVER C. Joseph Galloway, Loyalist. Philadelphia, 1941. 191 p. E278.G14K8
Thesis (Ed.D.)—Temple University, 1941.
Bibliography: p. [175]–184.

Letters to Joseph Galloway from leading Tories in America [1778–79] Historical magazine, v. 5, Sept.–Dec. 1861: 271–273, 295–301, 335–338, 356–364; v. 6, June–Aug. 1862: 177–182, 204–206, 237–239. E171.H64, v. 5–6

Letters from Charles Inglis, Isaac Ogden, John Potts, Abel Evans, and others.

SHUYLER, ROBERT L. Galloway's plans for Anglo-American union. Political science quarterly, v. 57, June 1942: 281–285. H1.P8, v. 57

WERNER, RAYMOND C. Joseph Galloway: his life and times. 1927.

Thesis (Ph.D.)—State University of Iowa.

13406
GALLOWAY, SAMUEL (1720–1785)
Maryland. Merchant, planter.

KELLY, J. REANEY. Tulip Hill, its history and its people. Maryland historical magazine, v. 60, Dec. 1965: 349–403. F176.M18, v. 60

13407
GÁLVEZ, BERNARDO DE GÁLVEZ, conde DE (1746–1786)*
Spain; Louisiana. Governor, Spanish officer in America.

CHURCHILL, CHARLES ROBERT. Don Bernardo de Galvez, governor of the province of Louisiana. Daughters of the American Revolution magazine, v. 58, Oct. 1924: 597–604. map. E202.5.A12, v. 58

CAUGHEY, JOHN W. Bernardo de Gálvez in Louisiana, 1776–1783. Berkeley, Calif., University of California Press, 1934. xii, 290 p. port. (Publications of the University of California at Los Angeles in social sciences, v. 4) F373.G252
Bibliography: p. 259–272.
The author's thesis (Ph.D.), Louisiana Under Spain, 1762–1783, was submitted to the University of California in 1928.

13408
GANNET, CALEB (1745–1818?)
Massachusetts. Clergyman, educator.

——— The diary of Caleb Gannet for the year 1776. William and Mary quarterly, 3d ser., v. 3, Jan. 1946: 117–122.

F221.W71, 3d s., v. 3

Refers in part to the first celebration of American independence in Boston on July 10. Introduction and notes by Maurice W. Armstrong.

13409
GANNETT, DEBORAH SAMPSON (1760–1827)
Massachusetts. Revolutionary soldier.

BISHOP, MORRIS. Private Deborah Sampson, U.S.A. In his The exotics, being a collection of unique personalities and remarkable characters. New York, American Heritage Press [1969] p. 110–118. port. CT105.B56

MANN, HERMAN. The female review; or, Memoirs of an American young lady; whose life and character are peculiarly distinguished—being a Continental soldier, for nearly three years, in the late American war. During which time, she performed the duties of every department, into which she was called, with punctual exactness, fidelity and honor, and preserved her chastity inviolate, by the most artful concealment of her sex. By a citizen of Massachusetts. Dedham [Mass.] Printed by Nathaniel and Benjamin Heaton, for the author, 1797. 258 p. port. E275.G21 Rare Bk. Coll.

An account of the experiences of Deborah Sampson, afterwards Mrs. Benjamin Gannett, who served as a soldier in the Revolutionary Army under the name of Robert Shirtliff.

A later edition, with an introduction and notes by John Adams Vinton, was published in Boston by J. K. Wiggin & W. P. Lunt (1866. 267 p. E275.G22), and reprinted in New York by Arno Press (1972).

NORWOOD, WILLIAM F. Deborah Sampson, alias Robert Shirtliff, fighting female of the Continental Line. Bulletin of the history of medicine, v. 31, Mar./Apr. 1957: 147–161. R11.B93, v. 31

STICKLEY, JULIA W. The records of Deborah Sampson Gannett, woman soldier of the Revolution. Prologue, v. 4, winter 1972: 233–241. facsims., port.
CD3020.P75, v. 4

13410

GANSEVOORT, PETER (1749–1812)*
New York. Revolutionary officer.

KENNEY, ALICE P. The Gansevoorts of Albany; Dutch patricians in the upper Hudson Valley. [Syracuse, N.Y.] Syracuse University Press [1969] xxvi, 322 p. illus., map, ports. (A New York State study)
CS71.G194 1969

Bibliography: p. 299–309.
The author's thesis (Ph.D.), *The Gansevoorts of Albany and Anglo-Dutch Relations in the Upper Hudson Valley, 1664–1790*, was submitted to Columbia University in 1961 (Micro AC–1, no. 61–3445).

———— General Gansevoort's standard of living. *In* New York Historical Society. Quarterly, v. 48, June 1964: 197–219. illus., ports. F116.N638, v. 48

13411

GARDEN, ALEXANDER (1730–1791)*†
South Carolina; England. Physician, botanist, Loyalist.

BERKELEY, EDMUND, *and* DOROTHY S. BERKELEY. Dr. Alexander Garden of Charles Town. Chapel Hill, University of North Carolina Press [1969] xiv, 379 p. illus.
QH31.G32B47

Bibliography: p. 359–370.

DENNY, MARGARET. Linnaeus and his disciple in Carolina: Alexander Garden. Isis, v. 38, Feb. 1948: 161–174.
Q1.I7, v. 38

———— Naming the Gardenia. Scientific monthly, v. 67, July 1948: 17–22. Q1.S817, v. 67

JENKINS, PIERRE G. Alexander Garden, M.D., F.R.S. (1728–1791), colonial physician and naturalist. Annals of medical history, v. 10, June 1928: 149–158. facsims.
R11.A85, v. 10

13412

GARDEN, ALEXANDER (1757–1829)*†
South Carolina. Revolutionary officer, planter, assemblyman.

———— Anecdotes of the American Revolution illustrative of the talents and virtues of the heroes and patriots, who acted the most conspicuous parts therein. Second series. Charleston [S.C.] Printed by A. E. Miller, 1828. ix, 240 p. E296.G22

———— Anecdotes of the Revolutionary War in America, with sketches of character of persons the most distinguished, in the Southern states, for civil and military services. Charleston [S.C.] Printed for the author, by A. E. Miller, 1822. xi, 459 p. E296.G21

Reprinted in Spartanburg, S.C., by the Reprint Co. (1972).

13413

GARDINER, JOHN (1737–1793)*
Massachusetts. Lawyer, assemblyman. Son of Silvester Gardiner.

PACKARD, BERTRAM E. An address made by Bertram E. Packard, before the Kennebec Historical Society, December MCMXXIII, on John Gardiner, Barrister [n.p., 1923] 15 p. (Kennebec Historical Society. Brochures, ser. 1, no. 1) F24.G22
F29.K27K3, ser. 1

———— John Gardiner, barrister. Sprague's journal of Maine history, v. 9, Apr./June 1921: 49–59. port.
F16.S76, v. 9

13414

GARDINER, SILVESTER (1708–1786)*
Rhode Island; Massachusetts; England. Physician, Loyalist.

WEBSTER, HENRY S. Silvester Gardiner. Gardiner, Me., Reporter-Journal Press, 1913. 52 p. (Gardiner, Me., historical series, no. 2) F29.G3W3

Includes 11 Gardiner letters dated 1776–86.

13415

GARDNER, ISAAC (1726–1775)
Massachusetts. Revolutionary officer.

BOLTON, CHARLES K. The first Harvard graduate killed in the Revolution. New England magazine, new ser., v. 12, Mar. 1895: 107–111. illus.
AP2.N4, n.s., v. 12

13416

GARRETT, JOHN (1727–1778)
Connecticut; Pennsylvania. Revolutionary officer.

HAYDEN, HORACE E. Major John Garrett, slain July 3, 1778. A forgotten hero of the massacre of Wyoming, Pennsylvania. Wilkes-Barre, Pa. [E.B. Yordy, Printer] 1895. 24 p. E241.W9H4

Evidence that the Maj. Jonathan Waite Garrett mentioned by the historians of the Wyoming massacre was John Garrett, major of the 24th Connecticut militia.
Roll of officers of the regiment is given.

13417

GARRETTSON, FREEBORN (1752–1827)*
Maryland. Itinerant Methodist clergyman and missionary.

———— The experience and travels of Mr. Freeborn Garrettson, minister of the Methodist-Episcopal church in North America. Philadelphia, Printed by Joseph Cruk-

shank, no. 91, High Street, and sold by John Dickins, no. 182, in Race Street, near Sixth Street, 1791. 252 p.
BX8495.G3A3 Rare Bk. Coll.

BANGS, NATHAN. The life of the Rev. Freeborn Garrettson: compiled from his printed and manuscript journals, and other authentic documents. 4th ed., rev. and corr. New-York, G. Lane & C. B. Tippett, for the Methodist Episcopal Church, 1845. 294 p.
BX8495.G3B3 1845

TIPPLE, EZRA S. Freeborn Garrettson. New York, Eaton & Mains [c1910] 128 p. port. BX8495.G3T5

VESEY, WESLEY J. Freeborn Garrettson: apostle to Nova Scotia. Methodist history, v. 1, July 1963: 27–30.
BX8235.M44, v. 1

13418

GARTH, CHARLES (1734–1784)
England. Colonial agent, Member of Parliament.

——— Garth correspondence [1766–73] South Carolina historical and genealogical magazine, v. 28, Oct. 1927: 226–235; v. 29, Jan.–Oct. 1928: 41–48, 115–132, 212–230, 295–305; v. 30, Jan.–Oct. 1929: 27–49, 105–116, 168–184, 215–235; v. 31, Jan.–Oct. 1930: 46–62, 124–153, 228–255, 283–291; v. 33, Apr.–Oct. 1932: 117–139, 228–244, 262–280. F266.S55, v. 28–31, 33

Introduction and notes by Joseph W. Barnwell.

NAMIER, Sir LEWIS B. Charles Garth and his connexions. English historical review, v. 54, July–Oct. 1939: 443–470, 632–652. DA20.E58, v. 54

13419

GATCH, PHILIP (1751–1834)
Maryland; Virginia; Ohio. Itinerant Methodist clergyman.

——— Sketch of Rev. Philip Gatch. Prepared by Hon. John M'Lean. Cincinnati, Swormstedt & Poe, for the Methodist Episcopal Church, 1854. 190 p.
BX8495.G35A3

Taken from the notes of Gatch's son, George.

CONNOR, ELIZABETH. Methodist trail blazer, Philip Gatch, 1751–1834, his life in Maryland, Virginia and Ohio. Cincinnati, Creative Publishers, 1970. xii, 244 p. illus., maps, port. BX8495.G35C6

Includes bibliographic references.

13420

GATES, HORATIO (1728?–1806)*†
England; Virginia. Military officer, Revolutionary general.

BILLIAS, GEORGE A. Horatio Gates: professional soldier. In his George Washington's generals. New York, W. Morrow, 1964. p. 79–108. port. E206.B5

Bibliography: p. 107–108.

NELSON, PAUL D. Horatio Gates: republican soldier of the American Revolution, 1728–1806. 1970. ([349] p.)
Micro AC–1, no. 70–21,998

Thesis (Ph.D.)—Duke University.
Abstracted in Dissertation Abstracts International, v. 31A, Dec. 1970, p. 2853.

PATTERSON, SAMUEL W. Horatio Gates, defender of American liberties. New York, Columbia University Press, 1941. xiv, 466 p. plates, port. E207.G3P3

Bibliography: p. [429]–446.
For a critical review of Patterson's work, see Robert L. Schuyler's "The Life of General Horatio Gates," in the Political Science Quarterly, v. 56, Dec. 1941, p. 600–607.

STITT, EDWARD W. Horatio Gates. In Fort Ticonderoga, N.Y. Museum. Bulletin, v. 9, winter 1953: 93–115. illus., maps, ports. E199.F75, v. 9

13421

GATES, JOHN (1713–ca. 1789)
Massachusetts.

——— Stow [Massachusetts] and John Gates' diary [1755–89] In Worcester Historical Society, Worcester, Mass. Collections. v. 16. Proceedings. no. 53; 1898. Worcester, 1899. p. 266–280. F74.W9W85, v. 16

13422

GAY, MARTIN (1726–1809)
Massachusetts; Nova Scotia. Loyalist.

WHEELWRIGHT, EDWARD. Three letters written by an American Loyalist and his wife, 1775–1788. In Colonial Society of Massachusetts, Boston. Publications. v. 3. Transactions, 1895/97. Boston, 1900. p. 379–400. illus., port. F61.C71, v. 3

Includes the texts of the letters, written by Martin and Ruth Atkins Gay.

13423

GEORGE III, King of Great Britain (1738–1820)†

——— The correspondence of King George the Third from 1760 to December 1783, printed from the original papers in the Royal Archives at Windsor Castle. Arranged and edited by the Hon. Sir John Fortescue. London, Macmillan, 1927–28. 6 v. DA506.A2A2 1927

Contents: 1. 1760–1767.—2. 1768–June 1773.—3. July 1773–December 1777.—4. 1778–1779.—5. 1780–April 1782.—6. May 1782–December 1783.

Reprinted in London by Cass (1967).
See also Sir Lewis B. Namier's Additions and Corrections to Sir John Fortescue's Edition of the Correspondence of King George the Third (vol. 1) ([Manchester] Manchester University Press, 1937. 86 p. DA506.A2N3).

Based upon his familiarity with George III's correspondence, Fortescue published a collection of seven essays under the general heading "George the Third's Papers" in his Historical and Military Essays (London, Macmillan, 1928),

p. [1]–160, in which he analyzes the early years of the king's reign, then focuses upon several selective problems such as Lord North and the secret service money.

———— The correspondence of King George the Third with Lord North from 1768 to 1783. Edited from the originals at Windsor, with an introduction and notes, by W. Bodham Donne. London, J. Murray, 1867. 2 v.
DA506.A2A2
Running title: *Letters to Lord North.*
Reprinted in New York by Da Capo Press (1971).

———— The later correspondence of George III. Edited by A. Aspinall. v. 1. December 1783 to January 1793. Cambridge [Eng.] University Press, 1962. xlvi, 688 p.
DA506.A2A4, v. 1
Bibliography: p. 655–658.

———— The letters of King George III. Edited by Bonamy Dobrée. London, Cassell [1935] xvi, 293 p. geneal. table, port. DA506.A2A25 1935
"Authorities": p. 275–283.
Reissued in London by Cassell (1968) and in New York by Funk & Wagnalls (1968).

———— Letters from George III to Lord Bute, 1756–1766. Edited with an introduction by Romney Sedgwick. London, Macmillan, 1939. lxviii, 277 p. (Studies in modern history) DA506.A2A27

———— A selection from the papers of King George III preserved in the royal archives at Windsor Castle, embracing the period from the 1st day of November 1781 to the 20th day of December 1783; the whole edited by John Fortescue. Cambridge [Eng.] Printed by W. Lewis at the University Press for the Roxburghe Club, 1927. 2 v. port.
PR1105.R7 1927a Rare Bk. Coll.

AYLING, STANLEY E. George the Third. New York, Knopf, 1972. 510 p. illus. DA506.A2A9 1972
Bibliography: p. [487]–493.

BROOKE, JOHN. King George III. With a foreword by H. R. H. the Prince of Wales. New York, McGraw-Hill [1972] xix, 411 p. illus. (part col.) (American Revolution bicentennial program) DA506.A2B75
Includes bibliographic references.

CHENEVIX TRENCH, CHARLES P. The royal malady. New York, Harcourt, Brace & World [1965, ᶜ1964] x, 224 p. illus., ports. DA510.C43 1965
Bibliography: p. 200–203.

DEAN, GEOFFREY. The royal malady! *In his* The porphyrias; a story of inheritance and environment. 2d ed. Philadelphia, J. B. Lippincott [1971] p. 138–168.
RC632.P6D4 1971b

Regards McAlpine's and Hunter's contention that George III and his ancestors suffered from acute porphyria variegata as at best an unproven hypothesis.

Gt. Brit. *Parliament. House of Commons. Committee to Examine Physicians Who Have Attended His Majesty.* Report from the Committee appointed to examine the physicians who have attended His Majesty, during his illness, touching the present state of His Majesty's health. Ordered to be printed 13th January 1789. 2d ed. London, J. Bell [1789] 132 p.
DA506.A2A5 1789b Rare Bk. Coll.
Imperfect: p. 129–132 wanting.

GUTTMACHER, MANFRED S. America's last king; an interpretation of the madness of George III. New York, C. Scribner's Sons, 1941. xv, 426 p. plates, ports.
DA506.A2G8
Bibliography: p. 405–409.

HOLT, EDWARD. The public and domestic life of His late . . . Majesty, George the Third; comprising the most eventful and important period in the annals of British history. London, Printed for Sherwood, Neely, and Jones, 1820. 2 v. illus., plates (part fold.), ports.
DA506.A2H7

HUISH, ROBERT. The public and private life of His late . . . Majesty, George the Third, embracing its most memorable incidents . . . and tending to illustrate the causes, progress, and effects, of the principal political events of his glorious reign. London, Printed for T. Kelly, 1821. viii, 724 p. plates, ports. DA506.A2H8

LONG, JOHN C. George III; the story of a complex man. Boston, Little, Brown [1961, ᶜ1960] 372 p. illus., plates, ports. DA505.L6
Bibliography: p. [347]–353.

KENNEDY, S. D. The acession and early years of George III. Quarterly review, v. 298, Oct. 1960: 435–442.
AP4.Q2, v. 298

MACALPINE, IDA, *and* RICHARD A. HUNTER. George III and the mad-business. New York, Pantheon Books [1970, ᶜ1969] xv, 407 p. illus., facsims., geneal. tables, port. DA506.A2M28 1970
Includes bibliographic references.
See also their earlier article, "A Clinical Reassessment of the 'Insanity' of George III and Some of its Historical Implications," in the *Bulletin* of the Institute of Historical Research, v. 40, Nov. 1967, p. 166–185.

———— Porphyria and King George III. Scientific American, v. 221, July 1969: 38–46. illus., facsim., port.
T1.S5, v. 221

McKELVEY, JAMES L. Lord Bute and George III: the Leicester House years. 1965 ([317] p.)
Micro AC–1, no. 65–12,131
Thesis (Ph.D.)—Northwestern University.
Abstracted in *Dissertation Abstracts*, v. 26, Dec. 1965, p. 3284.

NAMIER, *Sir* LEWIS B. King George III: a study in personality. History today, v. 3, Sept. 1953: 610–621.
D1.H818, v. 3

Reprinted in his *Crossroads of Power; Essays on Eighteenth-Century England* (New York, Macmillan Co. [1963, ᶜ1962]), p. 124–140.

PORRITT, EDWARD. England's last royal political boss. Century magazine, v. 76, June 1908: 304–310.
AP2.C4, v. 76

PLUMB, JOHN H. George III, 1760–1820. *In his* The first four Georges. London, B. T. Batsford [1956] p. 92–144. plates. DA480.P55

See also his two essays "George III" and "A Conscientious Bull in a China Shop" in his *Men and Places* (London, Cresset Press, 1963. DA480.P56 1963), p. 31–45 and p. 46–53.

——— Our last king. American heritage, v. 11, June 1960: 4–6, 95–101. illus., ports. (part col.)
E171.A43, v. 11

"George III, a Picture Portfolio of a Long and Troubled Reign," illustrated chiefly in color, appears on p. 7–23.

Porphyria—a royal malady; articles published in or commissioned by the *British Medical Journal*. London, British Medical Association [1968] vii, 68 p. illus., facsims., ports. RC632.P6P6

Bibliographic footnotes.
Contents: The "insanity" of King George III: a classic case of porphyria, by Ida Macalpine and Richard Hunter.—Porphyria in the royal houses of Stuart, Hanover, and Prussia: a follow-up study of George III's illness, by Ida Macalpine and Richard Hunter.—Historical implications, by John Brooke.—"The porphyrias," by Abe Goldberg.

RAY, ISAAC. The insanity of King George III. American journal of insanity, v. 12, July 1855: 1–29.
RC321.A52, v. 12

SEDGWICK, ROMNEY. The marriage of George III. History today, v. 10, June 1960: 371–377. illus., ports.
D1.H818, v. 10

VULLIAMY, COLWYN E. Royal George, a study of King George III, his experiment in monarchy, his decline and retirement; with a view of society, politics and historic events during his reign. New York, D. Appleton-Century Co., 1937. 318 p. ports. DA506.A2V8

Bibliography: p. 311–314.

WILLSON, BECKLES. George III, as man, monarch and statesman. London, T. C. & E. C. Jack, 1907. xvi, 622 p. facsims., plates, ports. DA506.A2W8

13424

GEORGE IV, *King of Great Britain* (1762–1830)†

——— The correspondence of George, Prince of Wales, 1770–1812. v. 1. 1770–1789. Edited by A. Aspinall. New York, Oxford University Press [c1963] vii, 528 p. illus., facsims., ports. DA538.A1A3, v. 1

[BENJAMIN, LEWIS S.] The first gentleman of Europe. By Lewis Melville [*pseud.*] London, Hutchinson, 1906. 2 v. illus., plates, ports. DA538.A1B5

"Authorities": v. 2, p. 301–309.

FULFORD, ROGER. George the Fourth. [Rev. and enl. ed.] London, G. Duckworth [1949] 240 p. col. port.
DA537.F8 1949

"List of authorities": p. 231–235.

HIBBERT, CHRISTOPHER. George IV, Prince of Wales, 1762–1811. [London] Longman [1972] xiii, 338 p. illus., fold. geneal. table, ports. DA538.A1H5

Bibliography: p. 311–319.

RICHARDSON, JOANNA. George the Magnificent; a portrait of King George IV. New York, Harcourt, Brace & World [1966] xvii, 410 p. illus., ports.
DA538.A1R53 1966a

London edition is entitled *George IV, a Portrait*. Bibliography: p. 394–404.

STUART, DOROTHY M. Portrait of the Prince Regent. London, Methuen [1953] xi, 240 p. illus., ports.
DA538.A1S8

Includes bibliography: p. 225–226.

13425

GÉRARD DE RAYNEVAL, JOSEPH MATHIAS (1736–1812)

France. Secretary.

——— Corespondance intime de Gérard de Rayneval avec Hennin [1782–83] Franco-American review, v. 1, June 1936: 76–84. E183.8.F8F88, v. 1

Introduction and notes by Bernard Faÿ.

GERMAIN, GEORGE SACKVILLE
See SACKVILLE, GEORGE SACKVILLE GERMAIN, *1st Viscount*

13426

GERRY, ELBRIDGE (1744–1814)*

Massachusetts. Merchant, assemblyman, delegate to the Continental Congress, delegate to the Constitutional Convention.

——— Letters of Elbridge Gerry [1784–1804] New-England historical and genealogical register, v. 49, Oct. 1895: 430–441; v. 50, Jan. 1896: 21–30.
F1.N56, v. 49–50

Contributed by Worthington C. Ford.

An offprint, entitled *Some Letters of Elbridge Gerry of Massachusetts*, was issued in 1896 (Brooklyn, N.Y., Historical Print. Club. 28 p. E310.G37).

Austin, James T.   The life of Elbridge Gerry. With contemporary letters. To the close of the American Revolution. Boston, Wells and Lilly, 1828–29. 2 v. port.
E302.6.G37A9

Reprinted in New York by Da Capo Press (1970).

Billias, George A.   Elbridge Gerry's letter code. Manuscripts, v. 20, fall 1968: 3–13. illus., facsims.
Z41.A2A925, v. 20

In his wartime correspondence Gerry used a code that has yet to be deciphered.

Knight, Russell W.   Fire, smoak & Elbridge Gerry. *In* Essex Institute, *Salem, Mass.* Historical collections, v. 106, Jan. 1970: 32–45.   F72.E7E81, v. 106

On a threatened attack upon Marblehead, Massachusetts, by three British warships, December 1, 1775.

Kramer, Eugene F.   The public career of Elbridge Gerry. 1955. ([205] p.)   Micro AC–1, no. 15,851

Thesis (Ph.D.)—Ohio State University.
Abstracted in *Dissertation Abstracts*, v. 16, no. 5, 1956, p. 950–951.

Morison, Samuel E.   Elbridge Gerry, gentleman-democrat. New England quarterly, v. 2, Jan. 1929: 6–33.   F1.N62, v. 2

13427
GERVAIS, JOHN LEWIS (*d.* 1798)
South Carolina. Merchant, planter, delegate to the Continental Congress.

——— Letters from John Lewis Gervais to Henry Laurens, 1777–1778. Edited by Raymond Starr. South Carolina historical magazine, v. 66, Jan. 1965: 15–37.
F266.S55, v. 66

13428
GIBAULT, PIERRE (1737–1804)*
Quebec; Illinois. Roman Catholic priest and missionary.

——— Letters from the archdiocesan archives at Quebec, 1768–1788. Notes by Lionel St. George Lindsay. *In* American Catholic Historical Society of Philadelphia. Records, v. 20, Dec. 1909: 406–430.
E184.C3A4, v. 20

Mostly letters of Gibault to Bishop Jean-Olivier Briand.

Donnelley, Joseph P.   Pierre Gibault, missionary, 1737–1802. Chicago, Loyola University Press [1971] viii, 199 p.   F597.G42D6

Bibliography: p. 181–193.

Dunn, Jacob P.   Father Gibault: the patriot priest of the Northwest. *In* Illinois State Historical Society. Transactions; 1905. Springfield, 1906. (Illinois State Historical Library. Publication, no. 10) p. 15–34.
F536.I34, 1905

Peyton, Pauline L.   Pierre Gibault, priest and patriot of the Northwest in the eighteenth century. *In* American Catholic Historical Society of Philadelphia. Records. v. 12, Dec. 1901: 452–498.   E184.C3A4, v. 12

Thompson, Joseph J.   Illinois' first citizen—Pierre Gibault. Illinois Catholic historical review, v. 1, July 1918–Apr. 1919: 79–94, 234–248, 380–387, 484–494; v. 2, July, 1919: 85–95.   BX1415.I3M5, v. 1–2

13429
GIBBES, WILLIAM HASELL (1754–1834)*
South Carolina. Lawyer, assemblyman, Revolutionary officer.

——— William Hasell Gibbes' story of his life. Edited by Arney R. Childs. South Carolina historical and genealogical magazine, v. 50, Apr. 1949: 59–67.
F266.S55, v. 50

13430
GIBBON, EDWARD (1737–1794)†
England. Historian, professor.

——— The autobiographies of Edward Gibbon. Printed verbatim from hitherto unpublished mss., with an introduction by the Earl of Sheffield. Edited by John Murray. London, J. Murray, 1896. xiv, 435 p. port.
PR3476.A82

——— Memoirs of my life. Edited from the manuscripts by Georges A. Bonnard. New York, Funk & Wagnalls [1969, c1966] xxxv, 346 p. illus., facsims., port.
PR3476.A82 1969

Bibliography: p. 229. Bibliographic references included in "Editor's notes" (p. 231–340).
First edition published in 1796.

Low, David M.   Edward Gibbon, 1737–1794. London, Chatto & Windus, 1937. xiv, 369 p. facsims., ports.
PR3476.L7

"Works . . . referred to": p. xii–xiii.

Lutnick, Solomon.   Edward Gibbon and the decline of the first British empire: the historian as politician. Studies in Burke and his time, v. 10, winter 1968/69: 1097–1112.   DA506.B9B86, v. 10

13431
GIBSON, JOHN (1740–1822)*
Pennsylvania. Indian negotiator, Revolutionary officer, judge.

Gibson, John B.   General John Gibson. Western Pennsylvania historical magazine, v. 5, Oct. 1922: 298–310.
F146.W52, v. 5

Hanko, Charles W.   The life of John Gibson, soldier, patriot, statesman. Daytona Beach, Fla., College Pub. Co. [c1955] vi, 89 p. [Americans of distinction series]
E302.6.G4H3

Bibliography: 86–89.

13432

GILBERT, THOMAS (1715–1797)

Massachusetts; New Brunswick. Loyalist officer.

CRANE, JOHN C. Col. Thomas Gilbert, the leader of New England Tories. Worcester, Mass., E. V. Newton, 1893. 19 p. plate. E278.G4C89

13433

GILL, JOSEPH LOUIS (1719–1798)

Canada. Trader, chief of Abnakis Indians.

HUDEN, JOHN C. The white chief of the St. Francis Abnakis—some aspects of border warfare, 1690–1790. Vermont history, new ser., v. 24, July–Oct. 1956: 199–210, 337–355. maps. F46.V55, n.s., v. 24

13434

GILLILAND, WILLIAM (1734?–1796)

Ireland; New York. Landowner, settler.

MARTING, ELIZABETH. Footnote to the Revolution: the tribulations of William Gilliland. In New York State Historical Society. Quarterly, v. 30, Oct. 1946: 234–253. map, port. F116.N638, v. 30

PELL, JOHN. The saga of Will Gilliland. In New York State Historical Association. New York history, v. 13, Oct. 1932: 390–403. F116.N865, v. 13

WARDENBURG, MARTHA B. Will Gilliland, pioneer of the valley of Lake Champlain. In Vermont Historical Society. Proceedings, new ser., v. 9, Sept. 1941: 186–197. F46.V55, n.s., v. 9

13435

GILLMORE, GEORGE (1720–1811)

Ireland; New England; Canada. Presbyterian clergyman, Loyalist.

TUCKER, SIDVIN F. The vicissitudes of a Loyalist clergyman. In Royal Society of Canada. Transactions. 3d ser., v. 7, section 2; 1913. Ottawa, 1914. p. 107–116. AS42.R6, 3d s., v. 7

Presented by W. D. Lighthall.

13436

GILLON, ALEXANDER (1741–1794)*

Netherlands; South Carolina. Merchant, Revolutionary naval officer, assemblyman.

—— Letters from Commodore Alexander Gillon in 1778 and 1779. South Carolina historical and genealogical magazine, v. 10, Jan.–July 1909: 3–9, 75–82, 131–135. F266.S55, v. 10

Concerns his mission in France.

SMITH, DANIEL E. HUGER. Commodore Alexander Gillon and the frigate South Carolina. South Carolina historical and genealogical magazine, v. 9, Oct. 1908: 189–219. F266.S55, v. 9

13437

GILMER, GEORGE (1743–1792)

Virginia. Physician, Revolutionary surgeon.

—— Papers, military and political, 1775–1778, of George Gilmer, M.D., of "Pen Park," Albemarle County, Va. In Virginia Historical Society, Richmond. Collections. new ser., v. 6. Richmond, 1887. p. [69]–140. F221.V82, n.s., v. 6

CANBY, COURTLANDT. The commonplace book of Doctor George Gilmer [1775–80] Virginia magazine of history and biography, v. 56, Oct. 1948: 379–407. facsim. F221.V91, v. 56

13438

GILPIN, THOMAS (1728–1778)

Pennsylvania. Inventor, planter.

Memoir of Thomas Gilpin. Pennsylvania magazine of history and biography, v. 49, Oct. 1925: 289–328. plate, port. F146.P65, v. 49

13439

GIRAULT, JEAN (1755–1813)

England; Illinois. Revolutionary officer, translator.

ROBERTS, H. W. Letters of Jean Girault relating to the Illinois country. In Illinois State Historical Society. Journal, v. 18, Oct. 1925: 636–657. F536.I18, v. 18

13440

GIRTY, SIMON (1741–1818)

Old Northwest. Indian interpreter.

BOYD, THOMAS A. Simon Girty, the white savage. New York, Minton, Balch, 1928. 252 p. ports. F517.G516

Bibliography: p. 251–252.

BUTTERFIELD, CONSUL W. History of the Girty's; being a concise account of the Girty brothers—Thomas, Simon, James and George, and of their half-brother John Turner—also of the part taken by them in Lord Dunmore's War, in the western border war of the Revolution, and in the Indian war of 1790–95; with a recital of the principal events in the West during these wars. Cincinnati, R. Clarke, 1890. xiii, 425 p. F517.G52

RANCK, GEORGE W. Girty, the white Indian: a study in early Western history. Magazine of American history, with notes and queries, v. 15, Mar. 1886: 256–277. E171.M18, v. 15

SCOMP, HENRY A. The Girty legends and romances; the darkest chapter of the American border. Magazine of history, with notes and queries, v. 12, Nov. 1910: 243–252; v. 13, May 1911: 219–229.

E171.M23, v. 12–13

13441
GIST, NATHANIEL (1733–*ca.* 1815)
Maryland; Virginia. Indian trader, Revolutionary officer.

WILLIAMS, SAMUEL C. Nathaniel Gist, father of Sequoyah. *In* East Tennessee Historical Society, *Knoxville.* Publications. no. 5; 1933. Knoxville, Tenn. p. 39–54. F442.1.E14, no. 5

13442
GLEN, JAMES (1701–1777)
Scotland; South Carolina. Lawyer, royal governor.

—— Colonial South Carolina: two contemporary descriptions, by James Glen and George Milligen-Johnston. Columbia, University of South Carolina Press, 1951. xxii, 209 p. map. (South Caroliniana; sesquicentennial series, no. 1) F272.G55 1761a

Facsimiles of James Glen's *A Description of South Carolina* (London, 1761) and George Milligen's *A Short Description of the Province of South-Carolina* (London, 1770) from the collections of the University South Caroliniana Society and the South Caroliniana Library.

13443
GLENDINNING, WILLIAM (*b.* 1747)
Scotland; Maryland; Virginia. Methodist preacher.

—— The life of William Glendinning, preacher of the gospel. Written by himself. Philadelphia, Printed for the author at the office of W. W. Woodward, 1795. vi, 154 p. BX8495.G6A3 Rare Bk. Coll.

13444
GLENTWORTH, GEORGE (1735–1792)
Pennsylvania. Revolutionary surgeon.

KLEIN, RANDOLPH S. Dr. George Glentworth (1735–1792): "A Physician Eminent and Useful." *In* College of Physicians of Philadelphia. Transactions & studies, 4th ser., v. 34, Jan. 1967: 117–120. port.

R15.P5, 4th s., v. 34

13445
GLOVER, JOHN (1732–1797)*
Massachusetts. Merchant, Revolutionary general, assemblyman.

BILLIAS, GEORGE A. General John Glover and his Marblehead mariners. New York, Holt [1960] xii, 243 p. illus., maps, ports. E207.G56B5

Bibliographic references included in "Notes" (p. 202–236).

The author's thesis (Ph.D.), *John Glover, Revolutionary War General*, was submitted to Columbia University in 1958 (Micro AC–1, no. 58–2673).

—— Of ships, shoes, and sealing wax: the early career of John Glover. *In* Essex Institute, *Salem, Mass.* Historical collections, v. 92, Oct. 1956: 376–387.

F72.E7E81, v. 92

—— Soldier in a longboat. American heritage, v. 11, Feb. 1960: 56–59, 89–94. illus., (part col.), port.

E171.A43, v. 11

HEATHCOTE, CHARLES W. General John Glover—loyal patriot who aided Washington. Picket post, no. 54, Nov. 1956: 4–9, 38. port. E234.P5, no. 54

SANBORN, NATHAN P. Gen. John Glover and his Marblehead regiment in the Revolutionary War; a paper read before the Marblehead Historical Society. [Marblehead, Mass.] The Society, 1903. 56 p. port.

E263.M4S2

UPHAM, WILLIAM P. The memoir of Gen. John Glover. *In* Essex Institute, *Salem, Mass.* Historical collections, v. 5, Apr.–Aug. 1863: 49–72, 97–130, 159–160. port.

F72.E7E81, v. 5

An offprint with a slightly different title was published in Salem (Printed by C. W. Swasey, 1863. 61 p. E275.G56).

13446
GODDARD, WILLIAM (1740–1817)*
Connecticut; Pennsylvania; Maryland. Printer, newspaper publisher.

—— The partnership; or, The history of the rise and progress of the *Pennsylvania Chronicle*, &c. Wherein the conduct of Joseph Galloway, esq., speaker of the honourable House of Representatives of the province of Pennsylvania, Mr. Thomas Wharton, sen., and their man Benjamin Towne, my late partners, with my own, is properly delineated, and their calumnies against me fully refuted. no. I[–II] Philadelphia, Printed by William Goddard, in Arch-Street, between Front and Second streets, 1770. 72 p.

PN4899.P5P4 Rare Bk. Coll.

MINER, WARD L. William Goddard, newspaperman. Durham, N.C., Duke University Press, 1962. viii, 223 p. PN4874.G49M5

"Note on sources": p. [209]–214.

TERWILLIGER, WILLIAM BIRD. William Goddard's victory for the freedom of the press. Maryland historical magazine, v. 36, June 1941: 139–149.

F176.M18, v. 36

13447
GODFREY, THOMAS (1736–1763)*†
Pennsylvania; North Carolina. Poet, playwright.

CARLSON, CARL LENNART. Thomas Godfrey in England. American literature, v. 7, Nov. 1935: 302–309.
PS504.A62, v. 7

GEGENHEIMER, ALBERT F. Thomas Godfrey: protégé of William Smith. Pennsylvania history, v. 9, Oct. 1942: 233–251; v. 10, Jan. 1943: 26–43.
F146.P597, v. 9–10

GODSMAN, JOHN
See DAVIDSON, WILLIAM (1740–1790)

13448
GOFFE, JOHN (1701–1786)
Massachusetts; New Hampshire. Farmer, military officer, assemblyman.

BROWN, WILLIAM H. Colonel John Goffe, eighteenth century New Hampshire. Manchester, L. A. Cummings Co. [1950] 284 p. illus., map, plans.
F37.G6B7
Bibliography: p. 275–284.

WOODBURY, GORDON. Col. John Goffe. *In* Manchester Historic Association, *Manchester, N.H.* Collections. v. 1, pt. 3, 1899. Manchester, 1900. p. 233–272.
F44.M2M3, v. 1
——— ——— Separate.
F44.L8G6

13449
GOLDSBOROUGH, ROBERT (1733–1788)*
Maryland. Lawyer, assemblyman, delegate to the Continental Congress.

THOMPSON, HENRY F., *and* ANNE S. DANDRIDGE. Hon. Robert Goldsborough, barrister, 1733–1788: member Continental Congress, 1774–1776. Maryland historical magazine, v. 10, June 1915: 100–114.
F176.M18, v. 10

13450
GOLDTHWAIT, JOSEPH (1730–1779)
Massachusetts; Nova Scotia. Military officer, Loyalist.

CARTER, ROBERT GOLDTHWAITE. Joseph Goldthwait, the Barrack Master of Boston. *In* Maine Historical Society. Collections and proceedings. 2d ser., v. 9. Portland, 1898. p. 349–382. F16.M33, 2d s., v. 9

13451
GOLDTHWAIT, THOMAS (1717–1799)
Massachusetts; England. Merchant, Loyalist.

CARTER, ROBERT GOLDTHWAITE. Col. Thomas Goldthwait—was he a Tory? *In* Maine Historical Society. Collections and proceedings. 2d ser., v. 7–8. Portland, 1896–97. p. 23–44, 185–200, 254–274, 362–379; p. 31–53. port. F16.M33, 2d s., v. 7–8

——— ——— Offprint [Portland, 1896] 100 p. plate, port. E263.M2C3

13452
GOMEZ, DANIEL (1695–1780)
New York. Merchant, landowner.

HÜHNER, LEON. Daniel Gomez, a pioneer merchant of early New York. *In* American Jewish Historical Society. Publication, v. 41, Dec. 1951: 107–125.
E184.J5A5, v. 41

13453
GORDON, CHARLES (*ca.* 1725–1786)
Scotland; Maryland. Lawyer, planter, Loyalist.

STIMPSON, HERBERT B. Charles Gordon—Jacobite and Loyalist. South Atlantic quarterly, v. 27, Oct. 1928: 390–404. AP2.S75, v. 27

13454
GORDON, HARRY (*ca.* 1721–1787)
Scotland. British military officer, engineer.

——— Extract from journal of Captain Harry Gordon [1766] *In* Missouri Historical Society, St. Louis. Collections, v. 3, no. 4, 1911: 437–443. F461.M66, v. 3
Reprinted from *The Wilderness Trail* (New York, G. P. Putnam's Sons, 1911. 2 v.), by Charles A. Hanna.

——— Extracts from the journal of Captain Harry Gordon, chief engineer in the Western Department in North America, who was sent from Fort Pitt on the river Ohio, down the said River &c. to Illinois, in 1766. Reprinted from Pownall's "Topographical Description of North America," published, London, 1776. *In* Illinois State Historical Society. Journal, v. 2, July 1909: 55–64. F536.I18, v. 2

13455
GORDON, JAMES (1739–1810)
Ireland; New York. Indian trader, Revolutionary officer, assemblyman.

——— The reminiscences of James Gordon. *In* New York State Historical Association. New York history, v. 17, July–Oct. 1936: 316–333, 423–439. port.
F116.N865, v. 17
With preface and biographical sketch by Josephine Mayer.

13456
GORDON, THOMAS KNOX (1728–1796)
Ireland; South Carolina. Lawyer, judge.

STUBBS, THOMAS H. Thomas Knox Gordon (1728–1796): last royal chief justice of South Carolina. South Carolina law quarterly, v. 5, Dec. 1952: 187–200. LL

13457

GORDON, WILLIAM (1728–1807)*†

England; Massachusetts. Congregational clergyman, historian.

—— Letters of the Reverend William Gordon, historian of the American Revolution, 1770–1799. *In* Massachusetts Historical Society, *Boston.* Proceedings. v. 63; 1929/30. Boston, 1931. p. 302–613.
F61.M38, v. 63

—— The plan of a society for making provision for widows, by annuities for the remainder of life; and for granting annuities to persons after certain ages, with the proper tables for calculating what must be paid by the several members in order to secure the said advantages. Boston, Sold by J. Edwards and J. Fleeming, 1772. vi, 35 p. HG9427.G66 Rare Bk. Coll.
AC901.M5, v. 782 Rare Bk. Coll.

A rare publication on the early history of insurance.

LORING, JAMES S. Our first historian of the American Revolution. Historical magazine, v. 6, Feb. 1862: 41–49. E171.H64, v. 6

13458

GORE, CHRISTOPHER (1758–1827)

Massachusetts. Lawyer.

PINKNEY, HELEN R. Christopher Gore, Federalist of Massachusetts, 1758–1827. Waltham, Mass., Gore Place Society, 1969. 180 p. illus. F69.G652P56
Bibliography: p. 147–148.

13459

GOULD, JONATHAN (1762?–1795)

Massachusetts; Maine. Congregational clergyman.

—— Oratorical afterthoughts on American independence [1786] New England quarterly, v. 8, Sept. 1935: 411–417. F1.N62, v. 8
Introduction and notes by Robert E. Moody.

13460

GRAFTON, AUGUSTUS HENRY FITZROY, *3d Duke of* (1735–1811)†

England. Member of Parliament, First Lord of Treasury.

—— Autobiography and political correspondence of Augustus Henry, third duke of Grafton, K.G., from hitherto unpublished documents in the possession of his family. Edited by Sir William R. Anson. London, J. Murray, 1898. xli, 417 p. ports. DA512.G7A2

13461

GRAHAM, ANDREW (*ca.* 1734–1815)

Canada. Fur trader, naturalist.

—— Andrew Graham's observations on Hudson's Bay, 1767–91. Edited by Glyndwr Williams, with an intro-duction by Richard Glover. London, Hudson's Bay Record Society, 1969. lxxii, 423 p. maps, plates. (Hudson's Bay Record Society. Publications, 27)
F1001.H8, no. 27

13462

GRAHAM, JOSEPH (1759–1836)*

Pennsylvania; North Carolina. Revolutionary officer.

—— General Joseph Graham's narrative of the Revolutionary War in North Carolina, in 1780 and 1781. *In* Murphey, Archibald D. The papers of Archibald D. Murphey. Edited by William Henry Hoyt. v. 2. Raleigh, E. M. Uzzell, State Printers, 1914. p. 212–311.
F258.M975, v. 2

GRAHAM, WILLIAM A. General Joseph Graham and his papers on North Carolina Revolutionary history; with appendix: an epitome of North Carolina's military services in the Revolutionary War and of the laws enacted for raising troops. Raleigh, Edwards & Broughton, 1904. 385 p. illus., fold. map, ports. E263.N8G7

13463

GRAHAM, SAMUEL (1756–1831)

Scotland. British officer in America.

—— An English officer's account of his service in America. Historical magazine, v. 9, Aug.–Nov. 1865: 241–249, 267–274, 301–308, 329–335. E171.H64, v. 9

—— Memoir of General Graham, with notices of the campaigns in which he was engaged from 1779 to 1801. Edited by his son, Colonel James J. Graham. Edinburgh, Priv. print. by R. & R. Clark, 1862. xvii, 318 p. maps, plates, port. DA68.12.G74

13464

GRAHAM, SARAH (1773–1844)

Kentucky. Settler.

—— Rev. John Dabney Shane's interview with Mrs. Sarah Graham of Bath County. Filson Club history quarterly, v. 9, Oct. 1935: 222–241. F446.F484, v. 9
Introduction and notes by Lucien Beckner.

13465

GRANBY, JOHN MANNERS, *Marquis of* (1721–1770)†

England. Military officer, Member of Parliament.

MANNERS, WALTER E. Some account of the military, political, and social life of the Right Hon. John Manners, Marquis of Granby. London, New York, Macmillan, 1899. x, 463 p. illus., fold. maps, plans, plates (part col.), ports. DA67.1.G7M2
"Authorities quoted": p. [v]–vii.

13466

GRANCHAIN, GUILLAUME JACQUES CONSTANT DE LIBERGE (1744–1805)

French naval officer in America.

BOUCLON, ADOLPHE DE. Étude historique sur la marine de Louis XVI. Liberge de Granchain, capitaine des vaisseaux du Roi, major d'escadre, directeur général des ports et arsenaux, géographe astronome, chevalier de Saint-Louis et de l'ordre de Cincinnatus. Évreux, A. Hérissy, 1866. 563 p. port.　　　DC137.5.G7B7

13467

GRANGER, DANIEL (1762–ca. 1848)
Massachusetts. Revolutionary soldier.

——— A boy soldier under Washington: the memoir [1775–1780] of Daniel Granger. Mississippi Valley historical review, v. 16, Mar. 1930: 538–560.　E171.J87, v. 16
Introduction and notes by Milo M. Quaife.

13468

GRANT, ANNE MACVICAR (1755–1838)†
Scotland; New York. Author, poet.

——— Memoirs of an American lady, with sketches of manners and scenes in America as they existed previous to the Revolution. With unpublished letters and a memoir of Mrs. Grant by James Grant Wilson. New York, Dodd, Mead, 1901. 2 v. illus., facsim., maps, plates.　　　E162.G83
Reprinted in Freeport, N.Y., by Books for Libraries Press (1972).
First edition, published in London in 1808, was reprinted in New York by Research Reprints (1970). Other editions have been issued.

13469

GRANT, FRANCIS

——— Journal from New York to Canada, 1767. In New York State Historical Association. New York history, v. 13, Apr.–July 1932: 181–196, 305–322.
F116.N865, v. 13

13470

GRANT, JAMES (1720–1806)†
Scotland; East Florida. Royal governor, British officer in America.

GRANT, ALASTAIR M. General James Grant of Ballindalloch, 1720–1806; being an account of his long services in Flanders, America, and the West Indies, with original letters throwing sidelights on many strange and ancient customs in the Highlands, on early days of road making, and the recruitment and equipment of the first Highland regiments. London [1930] 108 p. illus., maps (part fold.)　　　DA810.G7G7

TUCKER, PHILIP C. Notes on the life of James Grant prior and subsequent to his governorship of East Florida. Florida Historical Society quarterly, v. 8, Oct. 1929: 112–119.　　　F306.F65, v. 8

13471

GRASSE-TILLY, FRANÇOIS JOSEPH PAUL, *marquis* DE (1722–1788)
France. French admiral in America.

ANTIER, JEAN JACQUES. L'amiral de Grasse, héros de l'indépendance américaine. [Paris] Plon [1965] 476 p. illus., geneal. tables, maps, ports.　　　E265.A5
Bibliography: p. 465–467.

——— L'amiral de Grasse, vainqueur à la Chesapeake. Illus. de Philippe Ledoux. Paris, Éditions maritimes et d'outremer [1971] 253 p. illus., maps. (Au large l'aventure)　　　E265.G7A83

CARON, MAX. Admiral de Grasse, one of the great forgotten men. Translation by Dr. Mathilde Masse and the Marquis d'Andelarre. Boston, Four Seas Co. [1924] viii, 253 p. coats of arms, plates, ports.
DC52.G8C33
Originally published as *L'Amiral de Grasse* (Paris, P. Téqui, 1919. 275 p. DC52.G8C3).

LEWIS, CHARLES L. Admiral de Grasse and American independence. Annapolis, United States Naval Institute [1945] xviii, 404 p. illus., maps (on lining papers), plans, plates, ports.　　　E265.L45
"Sources and bibliography": p. 313–328.

McCURDY, GLENN A. The intrepid Frenchman. Iron worker, v. 31, winter 1967: 1–9. illus., map, ports.
TS200.I74, v. 31

MILES, ALFRED H. A great forgotten man. In United States Naval Institute. Proceedings, v. 55, Jan.–Feb. 1929: 1–10, 137–139.　　　V1.U8, v. 55

VIVIER, MAX. DeGrasse: forgotten hero. Légion d'honneur, v. 6, Apr. 1936: 233–243. illus., facsim.
CR5061.U6A3, v. 6

13472

GRATIOT, CHARLES (1752–1817)*
Switzerland; Canada; Illinois. Fur trader.

BARNHART, WARREN L. The letterbooks of Charles Gratiot, fur trader: the nomadic years, 1769–1797. Edited with an historical introduction. 1972. ([551] p.)
Micro AC–1, no. 72–23,896
Thesis (Ph.D.)—St. Louis University.
Abstracted in *Dissertation Abstracts International*, v. 33A, Sept. 1972, p. 1102–1103.

MYER, *Mrs.* MAX W. Charles Gratiot's land claim problems. In Missouri Historical Society. Bulletin, v. 21, Apr. 1965: 237–244.　　　F461.M6226, v. 21

13473

GRATZ, BARNARD (ca. 1736–1801)*
Pennsylvania. Merchant.

BYARS, WILLIAM V., *ed.* B. and M. Gratz, merchants in Philadelphia, 1754–1798; papers of interest to their posterity and the posterity of their associates. Selected and edited by William Vincent Byars. Jefferson City, Mo., Hugh Stephens Print. Co., 1916. 386 p.

HF3023.G7

Byars' descriptive calendar of papers (1756–75) of Barnard and Michael Gratz from several depositories appeared in the *Publications* of the American Jewish Historical Society, no. 23 (New York, 1915), p. 1–23.

NEUMANN, JOSHUA N., *comp.* Some eighteenth century American Jewish letters. *In* American Jewish Historical Society. Publications. no. 34. New York, 1937. p. 75–106. E184.J5A5, no. 34

Presents 11 letters in Yiddish, with translation, written to the Gratz brothers between 1758 and 1771 by Meyer Josephson, Nachman Ben Moshe, and Joseph Simon.

13474

GRAVES, MATTHEW (*d.* 1780)

England; Connecticut. Anglican clergyman.

O'NEIL, MAUD. Matthew Graves, Anglican missionary to the Puritans. *In* McCulloch, Samuel C., *ed.* British humanitarians; essays honoring Frank J. Klingberg. Philadelphia, Church Historical Society [1950] (Church Historical Society (U.S.). Publication 32) p. 124–144. HN15.M2

13475

GRAY, HARRISON (1711?–1794)

Massachusetts; England. Loyalist.

——— Letters of Harrison Gray and Harrison Gray, Jr., of Massachusetts [1760–76] Virginia magazine of history and biography, v. 8, Jan. 1901: 225–236.

F221.V91, v. 8

——— Memoir of Dr. Jonathan Mayhew. *In* Bostonian Society, *Boston.* Proceedings. v. 80; 1961. Boston. p. 26–48. F73.1.B86, v. 80

In his introduction, the editor, Louis Leonard Tucker, argues that Gray's whiggish defense of Mayhew's career and philosophy indicates that Gray would have remained a patriot had his mentor not died prematurely of a "nervous fever" in 1766.

MORISON, SAMUEL E. The property of Harrison Gray, Loyalist. *In* Colonial Society of Massachusetts, *Boston.* Publications. v. 14. Transactions, 1911/13. Boston, 1913. p. 320–350. port. F61.C71, v. 14

13476

GRAY, JOHN (1764–1868)

Virginia; Ohio. Revolutionary soldier.

DALZELL, JAMES M. John Gray, of Mount Vernon; the last soldier of the Revolution. Born near Mount Vernon, Va., January 6, 1764; died at Hiramsburg, Ohio, March 29, 1868. Aged 104 years. Washington, Gibson Bros., Printers, 1868. 64 p. E255.G78

13477

GRAY, WILLIAM (1750–1825)*

Massachusetts. Merchant, shipowner.

GRAY, EDWARD. William Gray, of Salem, merchant; a biographical sketch. Boston, Houghton Mifflin Co., 1914. viii, 124 p. facsim., plates, ports. F69.G76

13478

GRAYDON, ALEXANDER (1752–1818)*

Pennsylvania. Revolutionary officer, author.

——— Memoirs of his own time. With reminiscences of the men and events of the Revolution. Edited by John Stockton Littell. Philadelphia, Lindsay & Blakiston, 1846. xxiv, 504 p. E302.1.G81

First edition, Harrisburg, 1811, appeared under title: *Memoirs of a Life, Chiefly Passed in Pennsylvania* (E302.1.G77 Rare Bk. Coll.).

Reprinted in New York by the New York Times (1969).

SANDERLIN, ROBERT R. Alexander Graydon: the life and literary career of an American patriot. 1968. ([285] p.)

Micro AC–1, no. 69–1672

Thesis (Ph.D.)—University of North Carolina.

Abstracted in *Dissertation Abstracts,* v. 29A, Jan. 1969, p. 2280.

13479

GRAYSON, WILLIAM (1736–1790)*

Virginia. Lawyer, Revolutionary officer, delegate to the Continental Congress.

BRISTOW, WESTON. William Grayson: a study in Virginia biography of the eighteenth century. Richmond College historical papers, v. 2, no. 1; 1917. Richmond. p. [74]–117. F221.R53, v. 2

13480

GREEN, ASHBEL (1762–1848)*

New Jersey. Revolutionary soldier, Presbyterian clergyman.

——— The life of Ashbel Green. Prepared for the press . . . by Joseph H. Jones. New York, R. Carter, 1849. 628 p. port. F158.44.G79

LEWIS, ROBERT E. Ashbel Green, 1762–1848—preacher, educator, editor. *In* Presbyterian Historical Society. Journal, v. 35, Sept. 1957: 141–156.

BX8905.P7A4, v. 35

13481

GREEN, DANIEL (*fl.* 1783)

Pennsylvania; Nova Scotia. Chairmaker, Loyalist.

ARNELL, JACK. Letters from American relatives to a New Brunswick Loyalist (1783 to 1807). Postal history journal, v. 14, Sept. 1970: 28–34. facsims.
HE6001.P58, v. 14

Quotes the text of some of the letters described.

13482
GREEN, ENOCH (1733 *or* 4–1776)

New Jersey. Presbyterian clergyman, Revolutionary chaplain.

ANDREWS, FRANK D. A biographical sketch of Enoch Green, eminent Presbyterian divine of Deerfield, New Jersey . . . With baptisms, marriages, and deaths, 1771–1776, as recorded by Mr. Green. Vineland, N.J. [Smith Print. House] 1933. 20 p.   BX9225.G818A5

13483
GREEN, JACOB (1722–1790)*

Massachusetts; New Jersey. Presbyterian clergyman, physician.

TUTTLE, JOSEPH F. Rev. Jacob Green of Hanover, N.J., as an author, statesman, and patriot. *In* New Jersey Historical Society. Proceedings, 2d ser., v. 12, no. 4, 1893: 191–241.   F131.N58, 2d s., v. 12

13484
GREEN, THOMAS (1735–1812)*

Connecticut. Printer, editor.

BATES, ALBERT C. Thomas Green. *In* New Haven Colony Historical Society, *New Haven*. Papers. v. 8. New Haven, 1914. p. 289–309.   F98.N5, v. 8
——— ——— Offprint. [New Haven, 1914] [289]–309 p.   Z232.G875B
——— The work of Hartford's first printer. *In* Bibliographical essays; a tribute to Wilberforce Eames. [Cambridge, Mass., Printed at the Harvard University Press] 1924. p. [345]–361.   Z1009.B51 Rare Bk. Coll.
——— ——— Offprint. Cambridge [Mass., Printed at the Harvard University Press] 1925. [345]–361 p.   Z232.G875B3

Lists and locates copies of 51 items printed by Thomas Green, 1764–1768.

McMURTRIE, DOUGLAS C. The Green family of printers. Americana, v. 26, July 1932: 364–375.   E171.A53, v. 26
——— ——— Offprint. Somerville, N.J., 1932. 364–375 p.   Z232.G874

13485
GREEN, TIMOTHY (1737–1796)

Connecticut; Vermont. Printer, newspaper editor.

MEDER, MARYLOUISE D. Timothy Green III, Connecticut printer, 1737–1796: his life and his times. 1964. ([417] p.)   Micro AC–1, no. 64–12,646

Thesis (Ph.D.)—University of Michigan.

Abstracted in *Dissertation Abstracts*, v. 25, Jan. 1965, p. 4160–4161.

13486
GREEN, WILLIAM (1754–1835)

England; New York. British officer in America, landowner.

——— The memoranda of William Green, secretary of Vice-Admiral Marriot Arbuthnot in the American Revolution. Edited with introduction and notes by Henry S. Fraser. Providence, R.I., Rhode Island Historical Society, 1924. 73 p. facsim.   E271.G793

Appendix (p. 69–73) consists of "a copy of the despatch sent to Paris by Destouches after the battle with Arbuthnot, March 16, 1781." The memoranda, without the appendix, was also published in the *Collections* of the Rhode Island Historical Society, v. 17, Apr.–Oct. 1924, p. 54–64, 90–104, 126–140; v. 18, July–Oct. 1925, p. 112–128, 154–160.

13487
GREENE, CHRISTOPHER (1737–1781)*

Rhode Island. Assemblyman, Revolutionary officer.

RAYMOND, MARCIUS D. Colonel Christopher Greene. Magazine of history, with notes and queries, v. 23, Sept./Oct. 1916: 138–149.   E171.M23, v. 23

13488
GREENE, NATHANAEL (1742–1786)*

Rhode Island. Assemblyman, Revolutionary general.

——— Francis Marion's correspondence with General Nathaniel Greene [1781–82] *In* Southern History Association. Publications, v. 11, May 1907: 186–207.   F206.S73, v. 11

Of 24 letters, 18 were written by Greene.

——— General Greene's visit to St. Augustine in 1785. Edited by Helen Hornbeck Tanner. Ann Arbor, William L. Clements Library, 1964. 21 p. map, port.   F319.S2G7 Rare Bk. Coll.

Bibliographic footnotes.

——— Letters from Major-General Nathaniel Greene to Brigadier-General Thomas Sumter [1780–83] *In* Charleston, *S.C.* Year book. 1899. Charleston. Appendix, p. [71]–135.   JS13.C33, 1899

——— Letters to General Greene and others [1781–99] South Carolina historical and genealogical magazine, v. 16, July–Oct. 1915: 97–108, 139–150; v. 17, Jan.–Apr. 1916: 3–13, 53–57.   F266.S55, v. 16–17

——— Nathanael Greene's letters to "Friend Sammy" Ward [1771–86] Edited by Clifford P. Monahon and Clarkson A. Collins. Rhode Island history, v. 15, Jan.–Apr.

1956: 1–10, 46–54; v. 16, Apr.–Oct. 1957: 53–57, 79–88, 119–121; v. 17, Jan 1958: 14–21.
F76.R472, v. 15–17

———— The Nathaniel Green letters [1777–80] from the Ely collection. *In* New Jersey Historical Society. Proceedings, v. 61, July 1943: 181–190.   F131.N58, v. 61

———— The Revolutionary correspondence of Nathanael Greene and John Adams [1776–82] Rhode Island history, v. 1, Apr.–July 1942: 45–55, 73–83.
F76.R472, v. 1

Introduction and notes by Bernhard Knollenberg.

———— Thomas Sumter. *In* Southern History Association. Publications, v. 11, Mar. 1907: 81–93.
F206.S73, v. 11

Letters from General Greene to General Sumter, with one from Sumter to Joseph Martin. Greene's letters are dated from January 8, 1781, to January 9, 1782.

———— Washington-Greene correspondence [Jan. 21, 1780–Jan. 24, 1782] New England magazine, new ser., v. 25, Sept. 1901–Feb. 1902: 74–80, 220–227, 354–359, 464–468, 595–608, 732–741; v. 26, Mar.–Aug. 1902: 63–69, 229–233, 321–328, 489–493, 583–587, 698–707. facsims.   AP2.N4, n.s., v. 25–26

American Philosophical Society, *Philadelphia. Library.* Calendar of the correspondence of Major-General Nathanael Greene, Quartermaster-General, U.S.A. In the Library of the American Philosophical Society. Prepared under the direction of the Committee on Historical Manuscripts. *In its* Proceedings, v. 39, Apr./June 1900: 154–344.   Q11.P5, v. 39

Also published in a volume with two other calendars (see no. 708).

CALDWELL, CHARLES.   Memoirs of the life and campaigns of the Hon. Nathaniel Greene, major general in the Army of the United States, and commander of the Southern Department, in the War of the Revolution. Philadelphia, Published by R. Desilver, no. 110 Walnut Street, and T. Desilver, no. 2, Decatur Street; J. Maxwell, Printer, 1819. xxiii, 452 p. fold. facsims., port.
E207.G9C1

GOODRICH, FRANCIS L. D.   Some letters of Nathanael Greene from the years 1775 to 1777. Michigan alumnus quarterly review, v. 58, winter 1952: 109–119. port.
AP2.M35, v. 58

GREENE, FRANCIS V.   General Greene. New York, D. Appleton, 1893. 332 p. maps, fold. plans, port. (Great commanders)   E207.G9G7

Reprinted in New York by Research Reprints (1970) and in Port Washington, N.Y., by Kennikat Press (1970).

GREENE, GEORGE W.   The life of Nathanael Greene, major-general in the army of the Revolution. New York, G. P. Putnam, 1867–71. 3 v. map, plans, port.
E207.G9G74

Vols. 2–3 published by Hurd and Houghton.

Reprinted in Freeport, N.Y., by Books for Libraries Press (1972).

GREENE, MARY A.   General Nathanael Greene. New England magazine, new ser., v. 17, Dec. 1897: 558–570. illus., ports.   AP2.N4, n.s., v. 17

HEATHCOTE, CHARLES W.   General Nathanael Greene. Picket post, no. 43, Jan. 1954: 15–20, 28. port.
E234.P5, no. 43

JAMESON, JOHN FRANKLIN.   The papers of Major-Gen. Nathanael Greene. *In* Rhode Island Historical Society. Publications. new ser., v. 3; 1895. Providence. p. 159–167.   [F76.R51, n.s., v. 3]
Micro 39268

JOHNSON, WILLIAM.   Sketches of the life and correspondence of Nathanael Greene, major general of the armies of the United States, in the War of the Revolution. Charleston [S.C.] Printed for the author, by A. E. Miller, 1822. 2 v. maps (part fold.), plans, port.
E207.G9J5

McKINNEY, FRANCIS F.   The integrity of Nathanael Greene. Rhode Island history, v. 28, spring 1969: 53–60. illus., port.   F76.R472, v. 28

REED, JOSEPH.   Nathanael Greene; a biographical sketch by a contemporary, Joseph Reed. Rhode Island history, v. 16, Apr. 1957: 41–48.   F76.R472, v. 16

Introduction and notes by John F. Roche.

SIMMS, WILLIAM GILMORE, *ed.*   The life of Nathanael Greene, major-general in the army of the Revolution. New York, G. F. Cooledge [1849] 393 p. plates, port.
E207.G9S5

THANE, ELSWYTH.   The fighting Quaker: Nathanael Greene. New York, Hawthorn Books [1972] xvi, 304 p. illus.   E207.G9T46 1972

Bibliography: p. 289–291.

THAYER, THEODORE G.   Nathanael Greene: Revolutionary War strategist. *In* Billias, George A., *ed.* George Washington's generals. New York, W. Morrow, 1964. p. 109–136. port.   E206.B5

Bibliography: p. 136.

———— Nathanael Greene; strategist of the American Revolution. New York, Twayne Publishers, 1960. 500 p. illus.   E207.G9T48

Bibliography: p. 477–486.

13489

GREENE, WILLIAM (1731–1809)*
Rhode Island. Assemblyman, judge, governor.

———— Diary of William Greene, 1778. *In* Massachusetts Historical Society, *Boston.* Proceedings. v. 54; 1920/21. Boston, 1922. p. 84–138.   F61.M38, v. 54

Introduction and notes by Worthington C. Ford.

13490

GREENWOOD, JOHN (1727–1792)†

Massachusetts; England. Portrait artist.

WEITENKAMPF, FRANK. John Greenwood: an American-born artist in eighteenth century Europe, with a list of his etchings and mezzotints. *In* New York (City). Public Library. Bulletin, v. 31, Aug. 1927: 623–634. ports.
Z881.N6B, v. 31

13491

GREENWOOD, JOHN (1760–1819)*

Massachusetts; New York. Revolutionary soldier, dentist.

—— The Revolutionary services of John Greenwood of Boston and New York, 1775–1783. Edited from the original manuscript with notes, by his grandson Isaac J. Greenwood. New York [De Vinne Press] 1922. xxii, 155 p. facsims., plates, ports. E275.G81

13492

GREGORY, WILLIAM (*fl.* 1760–1774)

Scotland. Merchant.

—— A Scotchman's journey in New England in 1771. Edited by Mary G. Powell. New England magazine, new ser., v. 12, May 1895: 343–352.
AP2.N4, n.s., v. 12

13493

GRENVILLE, GEORGE (1712–1770)†

England. Member of Parliament, First Lord of Treasury.

JOHNSON, ALLEN S. The political career of George Grenville, 1712–1770. 1955.

Thesis (Ph.D.)—Duke University.

13494

GRENVILLE, THOMAS (1755–1846)†

England. Member of Parliament, diplomat.

SMITH, JEFFREY H. Thomas Grenville, a political biography. 1970. ([179] p.) Micro AC–1, no. 71–21,426

Thesis (Ph.D.)—St. Louis University.

Abstracted in *Dissertation Abstracts International,* v. 32A, Aug. 1971, p. 898.

13495

GREVILLE, *Hon.* ROBERT FULKE (1751–1824)

England. Member of Parliament, military officer.

—— The diaries of Colonel the Hon. Robert Fulke Greville, equerry to His Majesty King George III. Edited, with notes, by F. McKno Bladon; with a foreword by Frances, countess of Warwick. London, J. Lane [1930] xvii, 377 p. facsims., plates, ports. DA506.G7A2

"The first diary (1781)": p. [1]–73.
"The second diary (1788–89) (His Majesty's first illness)": p. [75]–260.

13496

GREY, ISAAC

Pennsylvania.

—— A serious address to such of the people called Quakers, on the continent of North America, as profess scruples relative to the present government: exhibiting the ancient real testimony of that people, concerning obedience to civil authority. Written before the departure of the British Army from Philadelphia, 1778. By a native of Pennsylvania. To which are added, for the information of all rational enquirers, an appendix, consisting of extracts from *An Essay Concerning Obedience to the Supreme Powers, and the Duty of Subjects in All Revolutions,* published in England soon after the Revolution of 1688. Philadelphia, Printed by R. Bell, next door to St. Paul's Church, Third Street, 1788. 41 p.
E269.F8G68 Rare Bk. Coll.

13497

GRIDLEY, JEREMIAH (1702–1767)*

Massachusetts. Lawyer, assemblyman.

CANDAGE, RUFUS G. Jeremy Gridley. Brookline, Mass., The Society, 1903. 32 p. (Publications of the Brookline Historical Society, [no. 1]) F74.B9B85

13498

GRIDLEY, RICHARD (1711–1796)*

Massachusetts. Civil and military engineer, Revolutionary officer.

HUNTOON, DANIEL T. V. Major-General Richard Gridley. Magazine of history, with notes and queries, v. 7, May-June 1908: 278–283, 336–342; v. 8, July 1908: 29–38. E171.M23, v. 7–8

13499

GRIFFITH, DAVID (1742–1789)

New York; Virginia. Revolutionary chaplain and surgeon, Anglican clergyman.

—— David Griffith's sermon before the Virginia convention, December, 1775. Historical magazine of the Protestant Episcopal church, v. 17, June 1948: 184–199.
BX5800.H5, v. 17

The sermon was entitled *Passive Obedience Considered.* Introduction by G. MacLaren Brydon.

BRYDON, GEORGE MACLAREN. David Griffith (1742–1789), first bishop-elect of Virginia. Historical magazine of the Protestant Episcopal Church, v. 9, Sept. 1940: 192–230. BX5800.H5, v. 9

13500

GRIFFITH, JOHN (1713–1776)

Pennsylvania; England. Quaker minister.

———— A journal of the life, travels, and labours in the work of the ministry, of John Griffith. London, Printed; Philadelphia, Re-printed by J. Crukshank in Market-Street, between Second and Third-Streets, 1780. 426 p.
BX7795.G75A3

13501

GRIFFITHS, DORCAS PRINGLE (*b.* 1720)

Massachusetts; England. Shopkeeper, Loyalist.

HERSEY, FRANK W. C. The misfortunes of Dorcas Griffiths. *In* Colonial Society of Massachusetts, *Boston.* Publications. v. 34. Transactions, 1937/42. Boston, 1943. p. 13–25.
F61.C71, v. 34

13502

GRIFFITHS, THOMAS (*fl.* 1767–68)

————A mission for Mr. Wedgwood. American heritage, v. 21, Aug. 1970: 64–67. col. illus., map.
E171.A43, v. 21

Introduction by Hensleigh C. Wedgwood.

Griffiths' record of his journey in 1767–68 from Charleston, S.C., to Franklin, N.C., to obtain samples of "Cherokee clay" for the famous English potter, Josiah Wedgwood.

13503

GROUT, HILKIAH (1728–1795)

Massachusetts; Vermont. Judge.

OSGOOD, HELEN B. Major Hilkiah Grout of Weathersfield, Vermont. Vermont history, new ser., v. 29, July 1961: 168–175.
F46.V55, n.s., v. 29

13504

GUILLOTIN, JOSEPH IGNACE (1738–1814)

France. Physician.

McDERMOTT, JOHN F. Guillotin thinks of America. Ohio state archaeological and historical quarterly, v. 47, Apr. 1938: 129–158.
F486.O51, v. 47

Includes the texts, in French, of several letters written by Guillotin in 1787–88.

13505

GUNBY, JOHN (1745–1807)

Maryland. Revolutionary officer.

GUNBY, ANDREW A. Colonel John Gunby of the Maryland Line; being some account of his contribution to American liberty. Cincinnati, R. Clarke Co., 1902. v, 136 p. plan, plates.
E263.M3G9

Exonerates Colonel Gunby from blame for the defeat at Hobkirk's Hill and criticizes Nathanael Green's generalship.

13506

GUY, PIERRE (1737 *or* 8–1810)

Canada. Merchant.

NEATBY, HILDA M. Pierre Guy: a Montreal merchant of the eighteenth century. Eighteenth-century studies, v. 5, winter 1971: 224–242.
NX452.E54, v. 5

13507

GWINNETT, BUTTON (1735–1777)*

England; Georgia. Merchant, planter, assemblyman, delegate to the Continental Congress.

CLEMENS, WILLIAM M. Button Gwinnett, man of mystery. Member of the Continental Congress. Signer of the Declaration of Independence. President of the Provincial Council of Georgia. A brief biographical review. Pompton Lakes, N.J., W. M. Clemens, 1921. 13 p.
E302.6.G95C6

JENKINS, CHARLES F. Button Gwinnet, signer of the Declaration of Independence. Garden City, N.Y., Doubleday, Page, 1926. xvi, 291 p. illus., facsims., maps, plates, ports.
E302.6.G95J38

JONES, CHARLES C. Button Gwinnett. Magazine of American history, with notes and queries, v. 12, Nov. 1884: 425–432.
E171.M18, v. 12

ROBERTSON, WILLIAM J. Rare Button Gwinnett. Georgia historical quarterly, v. 30, Dec. 1946: 297–307.
F281.G2975, v. 30

13508

HAAS, JOHN PHILIP DE (1735–1786)

Netherlands; Pennsylvania. Revolutionary officer.

HESS, ABRAM. The life and services of General John Philip de Haas, 1735–1786. [Lebanon, Pa., 1916] 69–124 p. plate, port. ([Lebanon County Historical Society. Historical papers and addresses], v. 7, Feb. 1916)
F157.L4L5, v. 7

13509

HABERSHAM, JAMES (1712 *or* 13–1775)*

England; Georgia. Merchant, planter, councilor, Loyalist.

———— The letters of Hon. James Habersham, 1756–1775. Savannah, Ga., Savannah Morning News Print, 1904. 245, vii p. port. (Georgia Historical Society. Collections, v. 6)
F281.G35, v. 6

ELLEFSON, CLINTON ASHLEY. James Habersham and Georgia loyalism, 1764–1775. Georgia historical quarterly, v. 44, Dec. 1960: 359–380. F281.G2975, v. 44

STEVENS, WILLIAM B. A sketch of the life of James Habersham, president of His Majesty's Council in the province of Georgia. Georgia historical quarterly, v. 3, Dec. 1919: 151–168. F281.G2975, v. 3

13510

HABERSHAM, JOHN (1754–1799)
Georgia. Merchant, Revolutionary officer, delegate to the Continental Congress. Son of James Habersham, (1712 or 13–1775).

——— Habersham's Indian expedition, Georgia—1782. Historical magazine, v. 4, May 1860: 129–131. E171.H64, v. 4

JONES, CHARLES C. Biographical sketch of the Honorable Major John Habersham of Georgia. Cambridge, Priv. print., Riverside Press, 1886. 30 p. port. E263.G3H17

Reprinted in New York by W. Abbatt (1909. [29]–50 p. E173.M24, no. 7) as extra number, no. 7, of *The Magazine of History, With Notes and Queries.*

13511

HABERSHAM, JOSEPH (1751–1815)*
Georgia. Merchant, Revolutionary officer, assemblyman. Son of James Habersham (1712 or 13–1775).

———Some leters of Joseph Habersham [1775–90] Edited by Ulrich B. Phillips. Georgia historical quarterly, v. 10, June 1926: 144–163. F281.G2975, v. 10

MEBANE, JOHN. Joseph Habersham in the Revolutionary War. Georgia historical quarterly, v. 47, Mar. 1963: 76–83. F281.G2975, v. 47

SMITH, WALLACE C. Georgia gentlemen: the Habershams of eighteenth-century Savannah. 1971. ([411] p.) Micro AC–1, no. 72–18,452

Thesis (Ph.D.)—University of North Carolina.
Abstracted in *Dissertation Abstracts International,* v. 32A, June 1972, p. 6909.

13512

HADFIELD, JOSEPH (1759–1851)
England. Merchant.

——— An Englishman in America, 1785, being the diary of Joseph Hadfield. Edited and annotated by Douglas S. Robertson. Toronto, Hunter-Rose Co., 1933. ix, 232 p. port. E164.H24

A record of travels from New York to Quebec, Montreal, and Boston.

13513

HAGER, JONATHAN (1714–1775)
Germany; Maryland. Settler, assemblyman.

MISH, MARY V. Jonathan Hager, founder. [Rev. ed.] Hagerstown, Md., Stouffer Print. Co. [1962] 73 p. illus., geneal. table, plates, ports.
F189.H15H134 1962

First edition published in 1937.

SOLLERS, BASIL. Jonathan Hagar, the founder of Hagerstown. Baltimore, T. Kroh, Printers, 1888. 14 p.
F189.H15H14

First published in the second *Annual Report* of the Society for the History of the Germans in Maryland (Baltimore, 1888), p. [15]–30.

13514

HALDIMAND, *Sir* FREDERICK (1718–1791)†
Switzerland. British officer in America.

AUDET, FRANÇOIS J. Sir Frédéric Haldimand. *In* Royal Society of Canada. Proceedings and transactions. 3d ser., v. 17, section 2; 1923. Ottawa. p. 127–149.
AS42.R6, 3d s., v. 17

DENDY, JOHN O. Frederick Haldimand and the defence of Canada, 1778–1784. 1972. ([265] p.)
Micro AC–1, no. 73–12,998

Thesis (Ph.D.)—Duke University.
Abstracted in *Dissertation Abstracts International,* v. 33A, June 1973, p. 6836.

FRENCH, ALLEN. General Haldimand in Boston. *In* Massachusetts Historical Society, *Boston.* Proceedings. v. 66; 1936–46. Boston, 1942. p. 80–95.
F61.M38, v. 66

LE MOINE, *Sir* JAMES M. Le general sir Frederick Haldimand à Québec, 1778–84. *In* Royal Society of Canada. Proceedings and transactions. v. 6, section 1; 1888. Montreal, 1889. p. 93–110. AS42.R6, v. 6

MCILWRAITH; JEAN N. Sir Frederick Haldimand. Toronto, Morang, 1904. 356 p. port. (The makers of Canada) F1032.H15

A new edition, edited by A. L. Burt, was published in London by Oxford University Press in 1926 (F1026.M342, v. 3).

SKULL, G. D. General Sir Frederick Haldimand in Pennsylvania. Pennsylvania magazine of history and biography, v. 8, no. 3, 1884: 300–309. F146.P65, v. 8

13515

HALE, NATHAN (1755–1776)*
Connecticut. Schoolteacher, Revolutionary officer.

DARROW, JANE. Nathan Hale; a story of loyalties. New York, Century Co. [ᶜ1932] xxi, 239 p. illus.
E280.H2D25

Bibliography: p. 237–239.

JOHNSTON, HENRY P. Nathan Hale, 1776; biography and memorials. Rev. and enl. ed. New Haven, Yale University Press, 1914. x, 296 p. facsim., map, plates.
E280.H2J74

First edition published 1901.
"Hale bibliography": p. [271]–278.

LOSSING, BENSON J. The two spies: Nathan Hale and John André. Illustrated with pen-and-ink sketches by H. Rosa. Anna Seward's monody on Major André. New York, D. Appleton, 1886. ix, 169 p. illus., facsims., ports.
E280.H2L88

PRATT, ANNE S. Nine letters to Nathan Hale. Yale University Library gazette, v. 26, July 1951: 1–21.
Z733.Y17G, v. 26

Printed in full for the first time, the letters supplement the 58 included in Seymour's *Documentary Life.*

SEYMOUR, GEORGE D. Captain Nathan Hale, 1755–1776: Yale College 1773; Major John Palsgrave Wyllys, 1754–1790: Yale College, 1773; friends and Yale classmates, who died in their country's service, one hanged as a spy by the British, the other killed in an Indian ambuscade on the far frontier. A disgressive history now told with many antiquarian excursions, genealogical, architectural, social, and controversial: with an account of some members of a great patrician family, their manorial establishment in Hartford, their custody for generations of the Charter of King Charles the Second, and the story of the hiding thereof. New-Haven, Priv. print. for the author [Tuttle, Morehouse & Taylor Co.] 1933. xxv, 296 p. facsims., plates, ports. E280.H2S512

—— Documentary life of Nathan Hale, comprising all available official and private documents bearing on the life of the patriot, together with an appendix, showing the background of his life. New-Haven, Priv. print. for the author, 1941. xxxiii, 627, [5] p. illus., facsims., plate, ports. E280.H2S516

STUART, ISAAC W. Life of Captain Nathan Hale, the martyr-spy of the American Revolution. 2d ed., enl. and improved. Hartford, F. A. Brown, 1856. 271, 12 p. illus., facsim., plates. E280.H2S94

Hales's diary: p. [226]–250.

13516

HALIFAX, GEORGE MONTAGU, *afterwards* DUNK, *2d Earl of* (1716–1771)†
England. Secretary of State.

BLACKEY, ROBERT A. The political career of George Montagu Dunk, 2nd Earl of Halifax, 1748–1771: a study of an eighteenth century English minister. 1968. ([247] p.) Micro AC–1, no. 70–7389
Thesis (Ph.D.)—New York University.
Abstracted in *Dissertation Abstracts International,* v. 30A, May 1970, p. 4904.

13517

HALL, DAVID (1714–1772)*
Scotland; Pennsylvania. Printer, bookseller.

KANY, ROBERT H. David Hall: printing partner of Benjamin Franklin. 1963. ([317] p.)
Micro AC–1, no. 64–5369
Thesis (Ph.D.)—Pennsylvania State University.
Abstracted in *Dissertation Abstracts,* v. 24, June 1964, p. 5361.

13518

HALL, JACOB (1747–1812)
Pennsylvania; Maryland. Revolutionary surgeon, educator.

PLEASANTS, JACOB HALL. Jacob Hall, surgeon and educator, 1747–1812. Maryland historical magazine, v. 8, Sept. 1913: 217–235. F176.M18, v. 8

13519

HALL, LYMAN (1724–1790)*
Connecticut; Georgia. Clergyman, physician, delegate to the Continental Congress, governor.

HALL, HARRY O. Dr. Lyman Hall, one of the signers of the Declaration of Independence. His ancestry, early life, and services in the cause of American independence. American monthly magazine, v. 22, Apr. 1903: 327–340. illus., plate. E202.5.A12, v. 22
—— —— Detached copy. E263.G3H2

HALL, JAMES W. Lyman Hall, Georgia patriot. Savannah, Pigeonhole Press [1959] xii, 113 p. illus., plate.
E263.G3H23

"Select bibliography": p. [vii]–viii.

JONES, CHARLES C. Dr. Lyman Hall, governor of Georgia, 1783, signer of the Declaration of Independence. Magazine of American history, with notes and queries, v. 25, Jan. 1891: 35–46. E171.M18, v. 25

13520

HALL, PRINCE (1748–1807)
West Indies; Massachusetts. Revolutionary soldier, Methodist clergyman.

—— Documents relating to Negro Masonry in America. Journal of Negro history, v. 21, Oct. 1936: 411–432.
E185.J86, v. 21

Correspondence relating to the establishment of African Lodge no. 459 of the Free and Accepted Masons in Boston in 1787 with Hall as master. Introduction and comments by Harry E. Davis.

13521

HALLOCK, JEREMIAH (1758–1826)

New York; Massachusetts; Connecticut. Congregational clergyman.

YALE, CYRUS. The godly pastor. Life of the Rev. Jeremiah Hallock, of Canton, Conn., to which is added a Sketch of the life of the Rev. Moses Hallock, of Plainfield, Mass. A new ed. of the memoir, rev. by the author, and enl., under his sanction, by the sketch from another hand. New York, Boston, American Tract Society [1854?] 389 p. port.   BX7260.H15Y3

13522

HALLOWELL, HENRY

Massachusetts. Revolutionary soldier.

——— A narrative of Henry Hallowell, of Lynn, respecting the Revolution in 1775, 1776, 1777, 1778, 1779, to January 17, 1780. *In* Sanderson, Howard K. Lynn in the Revolution. v. 1. Boston, W. B. Clarke Co., 1909. p. 149–183. facsim., plate.   F74.L98S2, v. 1

13523

HAMILTON, ALEXANDER (1755–1804)*

Nevis; New York. Writer, Revolutionary officer, lawyer, delegate to the Continental Congress, delegate to the Constitutional Convention.

———Alexander Hamilton and the founding of the nation. Edited by Richard B. Morris. New York, Dial Press, 1957. xxi, 617 p.   E302.H2573

Contains excerpts from Hamilton's correspondence, pamphlets, and reports grouped under a dozen broad subject headings.

——— Alexander Hamilton and Thomas Jefferson; representative selections, with introduction, bibliography, and notes by Frederick C. Prescott. New York, American Book Co. [1934] lxxxi, 422 p. ports. (American writers series)   E.302.H257

"Selected bibliographies": p. lxxiii–lxxix.

——— Alexander Hamilton: selections representing his life, his thought, and his style. Edited with an introduction by Bower Aly. New York, Liberal Arts Press [1957] xxvi, 261 p. (The American heritage series, no. 20)   E302.H25734

Bibliography: p. xxiii–xxvi.

——— Alexander Hamilton's pay book. Edited by E. P. Panagopoulus. Detroit, Wayne State University Press, 1961. xii, 128 p. (Wayne State University studies, no. 10. History)   E302.6.H2A13

Bibliographic footnotes.

Reproduces the random notes that Hamilton made in August 1776 in the pay book of the artillery company of which he was captain. In an earlier article, "Hamilton's Notes in His Pay Book of the New York State Artillery Company," *American Historical Review*, v. 62, Jan. 1957,

p. 310–325, the editor analyzed the notes and found that they revealed Hamilton's scholastic background and his early interest in economics and statesmanship.

——— The basic ideas of Alexander Hamilton, edited by Richard B. Morris. [New York, Pocket Books, 1957, ᶜ1956] xxvii, 451 p. (The Pocket Library, PL–33)   E302.H2574

——— A few of Hamilton's letters, including his description of the great West Indian hurricane of 1772. Edited by Gertrude Atherton. New York, Macmillan Co., 1903. xxi, 227 p. facsim., ports.   E302.H26

——— Industrial and commercial correspondence of Alexander Hamilton, anticipating his report on manufactures. Edited by Arthur Harrison Cole, with a preface by Professor Edwin F. Gay. Published under the auspices of the Business Historical Society. Chicago, A. W. Shaw Co., 1928. xxviii, 334 p. facsim., ports. (Business historical studies, v. 1)   HD9725.H3

Reprinted in New York by A. M. Kelly (1968).

——— The law practice of Alexander Hamilton; documents and commentary. Julius Goebel, Jr., editor. Associate editors: Francis K. Decker, Jr. [and others] New York, Published under the William Nelson Cromwell Foundation by Columbia University Press, 1964–69. 2 v. facsims., maps, plates, port.   KF363.H3G6

Includes bibliographic references.

——— The mind of Alexander Hamilton. Arranged and with an introduction by Saul K. Padover. New York, Harper [1958] 461 p.   E302.H28

——— The official and other papers of the late Major-General Alexander Hamilton, compiled chiefly from the originals in the possession of Mrs. Hamilton. v. 1. New York, Wiley & Putnam, 1842. 496 p.   E203.H22

Composed by Francis L. Hawks.
No more published.

———Papers. Harold C. Syrett, editor; Jacob E. Cooke, associate editor. New York, Columbia University Press, 1961+ illus., ports., maps.   E302.H247

Partial contents: v. 1. 1768–1778.—v. 2. 1779–1781.—v. 3. 1782–1786.—v. 4. Jan. 1787—May 1788.—v. 5. June 1788–Nov. 1789.— v. 6. Dec. 1789–Aug. 1790.

——— The works of Alexander Hamilton. Edited by Henry Cabot Lodge. New York, G. P. Putnam's Sons, 1904. 12 v. ports.   E302.H24

"Bibliography of the *Federalist*": v. 11, p. xxxi–xi.
First edition published in 1885–86 in nine volumes.
Reprinted in New York by Haskell House Publishers (1971).

——— The works of Alexander Hamilton; containing his correspondence, and his political and official writings, exclusive of *The Federalist*, civil and military. Published from the original manuscripts deposited in the Department of State, by order of the Joint Library Committee of Congress. Edited by John C. Hamilton. New-York, J. F. Trow, Printer, 1850–51. 7 v. port.   E302.H22

Partial contents: v. 1. Correspondence. 1769–1789.— v. 2. [Miscellanies, 1774–1789; A full vindication; The farmer refuted; Quebec Bill; Resolutions in Congress; Letters from Phocion; New-York Legislature, etc.]—v. 6. Correspondence 1795–1804; 1777; 1791. Letters of H. G. 1789. *Address to Public Creditors*. 1790. *Vindication of Funding System*. 1791.

ADAIR, DOUGLASS G., *and* MARTIN HARVEY.   Was Alexander Hamilton a Christian statesman? William and Mary quarterly, 3d ser., v. 12, Apr. 1955: 308–329.
F221.W71, 3d s., v. 12

ALY, BOWER.   The rhetoric of Alexander Hamilton. New York, Columbia University Press, 1941. x, 226 p.
E302.6.H2A4

"Selected bibliography": p. [199]–213.
Reprinted in New York by Russell & Russell (1965).

BEIN, ALEX.   Die Staatsidee Alexander Hamiltons in ihrer Entstehung und Entwicklung. München, R. Oldenbourg, 1927. 186 p. port. (Beiheft 12 der Historischen Zeitschrift)   JC211.B4

"Literatur-Verzeichnis": p. [182]–186.

BERNSTEIN, LEONARD H.   Alexander Hamilton and political factions in New York to 1787. 1970. ([321] p.)
Micro AC–1, no. 71–2263

Thesis (Ph.D.)—New York University.
Abstracted in *Dissertation Abstracts International*, v. 31A, Feb. 1971, p. 4076.

BOBBÉ, DOROTHIE.   The boyhood of Alexander Hamilton. American heritage, v. 6, June 1955: 4–9, 96–99. illus. (part col.), map, port.   E171.A43, v. 6

BRAMBLE, MAX E.   Alexander Hamilton and nineteenth-century American historians; a study of selected interpretations of Hamilton. 1968. ([209] p.)
Micro AC–1, no. 69–5844

Thesis (Ph.D.)—Michigan State University.
Abstracted in *Dissertation Abstracts*, v. 29A, Apr. 1969, p. 3553.

CANTOR, MILTON, *comp.*   Hamilton. Englewood Cliffs, N.J., Prentice-Hall [1971] vii, 184 p. (Great lives observed.)   E302.6.H2C3

Bibliography: p. 180–182.

Includes excerpts from the writings of Hamilton and his contemporaries as well as appraisals of Hamilton by four historians.

COOKE, JACOB E., *comp.*   Alexander Hamilton: a profile. New York, Hill and Wang [1967] xxvi, 259 p. (American profiles)   E302.6.H2C73

Bibliography: p. 257–259.

Includes writings by Claude G. Bowers, Richard B. Morris, Broadus Mitchell, Jacob E. Cooke, Dumas Malone, Felix Gilbert, Samuel J. Konefsky, Vernon L. Parrington,

John C. Miller, Clinton Rossiter, Cecelia M. Kenyon, Adrienne Koch, Douglass Adair, and Marvin Harvey.

DAVISSON, ORA B.   The early pamphlets of Alexander Hamilton. Quarterly journal of speech, v. 30, Apr. 1944: 168–173.   PN4071.Q3, v. 30

DIETZE, GOTTFRIED.   Hamilton's concept of free government. *In* New York State Historical Association. New York history, v. 38, Oct. 1957: 351–367.
F116.N865, v. 38

ELLIS, IVAN C.   A study of the influence of Alexander Hamilton on George Washington. 1956. xx, 332 l.
Thesis (Ph.D.)—University of Southern California.

FORD, PAUL L.   Bibliotheca Hamiltoniana; a list of books written by, or relating to Alexander Hamilton. New York, Printed for the author, Knickerbocker Press, 1886. vi, 159 p.   Z8384.F7

Printed on one side of leaf only.
Reprinted in New York by AMS Press (1972).

270 titles in two parts: (1) the writings of Hamilton, other than official, and those relating to him; and (2) the official writings of Hamilton (Treasury reports and circulars).

GOVAN, THOMAS P.   The rich, the well-born, and Alexander Hamilton. Mississippi Valley historical review, v. 36, Mar. 1950: 675–680.   E171.J87, v. 36

HACKER, LOUIS M.   Alexander Hamilton in the American tradition. New York, McGraw-Hill [1957] xi, 273 p.
E302.6.H2H15

Bibliography: p. 264–266.

HAMILTON, JOHN C.   The life of Alexander Hamilton. New York, D. Appleton, 1840. 2 v.
E302.6.H2H261

Volume 1 was first published in New York by Halsted & Voorhies in 1834.

KENYON, CECELIA M.   Alexander Hamilton: Rousseau of the right. Political science quarterly, v. 73, June 1958: 161–178.   H1.P8, v. 73

KOCH, ADRIENNE.   Hamilton, Adams and the pursuit of power. Review of politics, v. 16, Jan. 1954: 37–66.
JA1.R4, v. 16

——— Hamilton and power. Yale review, v. 47, summer 1958: 537–551.   AP2.Y2, v. 47

KROUT, JOHN A.   Alexander Hamilton's place in the founding of the nation. *In* American Philosophical Society, *Philadelphia*. Proceedings, v. 102, Apr. 1958: 124–128.   Q11.P5, v. 102

LARSON, HAROLD.   Alexander Hamilton: the fact and fiction of his early years. William and Mary quarterly, 3d ser., v. 9, Apr. 1952: 139–151.
F221.W71, 3d s., v. 9

LODGE, HENRY CABOT. Alexander Hamilton. Boston, Houghton Mifflin, 1898. xii, 317 p. facsim., plate, ports. (American statesmen, v. 7)　　E302.6.H2L84
E176.A54, v.7

First published in 1882.
Reprinted in New York by AMS Press (1972).

LOOZE, HELENE J. Alexander Hamilton and the British orientation of American foreign policy, 1783–1803. The Hague, Mouton, 1969. 132 p. (Studies in American history, 8)　　E313.L86
Bibliography: p [130]–132.

LOTH, DAVID G. Alexander Hamilton; portrait of a prodigy. New York, Carrick & Evans [c1939] 320 p. plates, ports.　　E302.6.H2L89
Bibliography: p. 311–314.

LYCAN, GILBERT L. Alexander Hamilton & American foreign policy; a design for greatness. Norman, University of Oklahoma Press [1970] xviii, 459 p. illus., map, ports.　　E302.6.H2L95
Bibliography: p. 433–444.

MILLER, JOHN C. Alexander Hamilton: portrait in paradox. New York, Harper [1959] xii, 659 p. illus., plate.　　E302.6.H2M58
Bibliography: p. 623–639.

MITCHELL, BROADUS. Alexander Hamilton. New York, Macmillan, 1957–62. 2 v. illus., facsim.
E302.6.H2M6
Contents: [1] Youth to maturity, 1755–1788.—[2] The national adventure, 1788–1804.

———— and others. Alexander Hamilton bicentennial commemorative issue. Historian, v. 19, Feb. 1957: 125–202.
D1.H22, v. 19
Contents: Alexander Hamilton, his friends and foes, by Broadus Mitchell.—The Report on Manufactures, by Louis M. Hacker.—The papers of Alexander Hamilton, by Harold C. Syrett and Jacob E. Cooke.—Chancellor Kent's "Brief Review of the Public Life and Writings of General Hamilton," by Douglass Adair.

———— Alexander Hamilton in New Jersey. In New Jersey Historical Society. Proceedings, v. 76, Apr. 1958: 84–111.　　F131.N58, v. 76

———— Alexander Hamilton: the Revolutionary years. New York, Crowell [c1970] viii, 386 p. illus., maps, ports. (Leaders of the American Revolution series)
E302.6.H2M62
Bibliography: p. 373–380.

———— Hamilton's quarrel with Washington, 1781. William and Mary quarterly, 3d ser., v. 12, Apr. 1955: 199–216.
F221.W71, 3d s., v. 12

———— Heritage from Hamilton. New York, Columbia University Press, 1957. viii, 160 p. facsims., port.
E302.6.H2M63

"The man in his own words; [letters]": p. [95]–160.
A summary treatment presented as the Gino Speranza Lectures at Columbia University.

———— "If Hamilton were here today": some unanswered questions. South Atlantic quarterly, v. 62, spring 1963: 288–296.　　AP2.S75, v. 62

MITCHELL, LOUISE P. Alexander Hamilton as a lieutenant of Robert Morris. In Mount Holyoke College. "Those having torches . . ." Economic essays in honor of Alzada Comstock, presented by her former students. Edited by Lucile Tomlinson Wessmann. South Hadley, Mass., 1954. p. [77]–86.　　HB34.M66

MORSE, ANSON D. Alexander Hamilton. Political science quarterly, v. 5, Mar. 1890: 1–23.　　H1.P8, v. 5

MORSE, JOHN T. The life of Alexander Hamilton. Boston, Little, Brown, 1876. 2 v.　　E302.6.H2M8

OTTENBERG, LOUIS. Alexander Hamilton's first court case: Elizabeth Rutgers v. Joshua Waddington in the Mayor's Court of New York City, 1784. In New York Historical Society. Quarterly, v. 41, Oct. 1957: 423–439. ports.　　F116.N638, v. 41

PADOVER, SAUL K. The "singular" Mr. Hamilton. Social research, v. 24, summer 1957: 157–190.
H1.S53, v. 24

ROCHE, JOHN F. Alexander Hamilton, by John F. Roche and the editors of Silver Burdett. Morristown, N.J., Silver Burdett Co. [1967] 240 p. illus. (part col.), map, ports. (part col.) (Illustrious Americans)
E302.6.H2R6
Bibliography: p. 232–234.

ROSSITER, CLINTON L. Alexander Hamilton and the Constitution. New York, Harcourt, Brace & World [1964] x, 372 p.　　KF363.H3R6
Bibliographic references included in "Notes" (p. 259–348).

SCHACHNER, NATHAN. Alexander Hamilton. New York, London, D. Appleton-Century Co. [1946] vi, 488 p.　　E302.6.H2S25
Bibliography: p. 473–481.
Reprinted in New York by T. Yoseloff (1957).

———— Alexander Hamilton viewed by his friends: the narratives of Robert Troup and Hercules Mulligan. William and Mary quarterly, 3d ser., v. 4, Apr. 1947: 203–225.　　F221.W71, 3d s., v. 4

STOURZH, GERALD. Alexander Hamilton and the idea of republican government. Stanford, Stanford University Press, 1970. viii, 278 p.　　E302.6.H2S8
Bibliography: p. [207]–268.

SUMNER, WILLIAM G. Alexander Hamilton. New York, Dodd, Mead [1890] x, 281 p. (Makers of America)
E302.6.H2S9
E176.M23
"List of authorities": p. [261]–267.

SYRETT, HAROLD C. Alexander Hamilton: history by stereotype. *In* New York Historical Society. Quarterly, v. 43, Jan. 1959: 38–50. illus., port.
F116.N638, v. 43

TUGWELL, REXFORD G., *and* JOSEPH DORFMAN. Alexander Hamilton: nationmaker. Columbia University quarterly, v. 29, Dec. 1937: 209–226; v. 30, Mar. 1938: 59–72.
LH1.C7Q2, v. 29–30

Also published in their *Early American Policy: Six Columbia Contributors* (New York, Columbia University Press, 1960. HB119.A3D6), p. [7]–42.

WRIGHT, ESMOND. Alexander Hamilton, founding father. History today, v. 7, Mar. 1957: 182–189. plates, port.
D1.H818, v. 7

13524

HAMILTON, ALEXANDER (*d.* 1799)
Scotland; Maryland. Merchant.

——— The letterbooks of Alexander Hamilton, Piscataway factor [1774–76] Maryland historical magazine, v. 61, June, Dec. 1966: 146–166, 305–328; v. 62, June 1967: 135–169.
F176.M18, v. 61–62

Introduction and notes by Richard K. MacMaster and David C. Skaggs.

——— Post-Revolutionary letters of Alexander Hamilton, Piscataway merchant [Jan.–Oct. 1784] Maryland historical magazine, v. 63, Mar. 1968: 22–54; v. 65, spring 1970: 18–35.
F176.M18, v. 63, 65

Introduction and notes by David C. Skaggs and Richard K. MacMaster.

13525

HAMILTON, HENRY (*d.* 1796)
Old Northwest; Canada. British officer in America, governor.

——— Narrative of Gov. Henry Hamilton [1779]; loose notes of the proceedings and sufferings of Henry Hamilton Esq., Governor of Le Detroit with the party that accompanied him from that post to their imprisonment in rebel goal [sic] at Williamsburg, Virginia. Magazine of American history, with notes and queries, v. 1, Mar. 1877: 186–193.
E171.M18, v. 1

——— A new diary of Lieutenant-Governor Henry Hamilton [Oct.7–Dec. 17, 1778] Edited by John D. Barnhart. *In* Missouri Historical Society, *St. Louis.* Bulletin, v. 12, Oct. 1955: 10–24.
F461.M6226, v. 12

BARNHART, JOHN D., *ed.* Henry Hamilton and George Rogers Clark in the American Revolution, with the unpublished journal of Henry Hamilton. Crawfordsville, Ind., R. E. Banta, 1951. 244 p. group port.
E234.H2B3

Bibliography: p. 206–214.

HAFFNER, GERALD O. Colonel Henry Hamilton; a famous P.O.W. of the American Revolution "visits" Louisville. Filson Club history quarterly, v. 29, Oct. 1955: 339–348.
F446.F484, v. 29

JAEBKER, ORVILLE J. Henry Hamilton: British soldier and colonial governor. 1954. ([458] p.)
Micro AC–1, no. 7533

Thesis (Ph.D.)—University of Indiana.
Abstracted in *Dissertation Abstracts*, v. 14, no. 4, 1954, p. 665.

13526

HAMILTON, JAMES (1750–1833)
Pennsylvania; South Carolina. Revolutionary officer.

CLARK, MARTHA B. Major James Hamilton: of the Pennsylvania Line. Lancaster, Pa., Reprinted from the New Era, 1906. [71]–92 p. port. (Lancaster County Historical Society. Papers, v. 10, Mar. 1906)
F157.L2L5, v. 10

13527

HAMILTON, WILLIAM
Pennsylvania. Botanist.

——— Some letters from William Hamilton, of the Woodlands, to his private secretary. Pennsylvania magazine of history and biography, v. 29, Jan.–July 1905: 70–78, 143–159, 257–267.
F146.P65, v. 29

Introduction and notes by Benjamin H. Smith.

13528

HAMMON, JOHN (1760–1868)
Virginia; Kentucky. Revolutionary soldier, settler.

HAMMON, STRATTON O. John Hammon, Revolutionary soldier and Kentucky pioneer. Filson Club history quarterly, v. 23, July 1949: 202–223.
F446.F484, v. 23

13529

HAMMON, JUPITER (1711–*ca.* 1800)*
New York. Poet.

——— An address to the Negroes in the state of New-York. By Jupiter Hammon, servant of John Lloyd, Jun. Esq. of the manor of Queen's Village, Long-Island. New York, printed; Philadelphia, re-printed by Daniel Humphreys, in Spruce-Street, near the Drawbridge, 1787. [Tarrytown, N.Y., Reprinted, W. Abbatt, 1925] [35]–51 p. (The Magazine of history, with notes and queries. Extra number, no. 114, [pt. 3])
E173.M24, no. 114

First published in New York in 1787.

——— America's first Negro poet; the complete works of Jupiter Hammon of Long Island. Edited with an introduction by Stanley Austin Ransom, Jr. Biographical sketch of Jupiter Hammon by Oscar Wegelin. Critical analysis of the works of Jupiter Hammon by Vernon Loggins. Port Washington, N.Y., I. J. Friedman Divi-

sion, Kennikat Press [1970] 122 p. illus., facsims. (Empire State historical publications series, no. 82)
PS767.H15 1970

"Bibliography of the works of Jupiter Hammon": p. 119–122.

VERTANES, CHARLES A. Jupiter Hammon, early Negro poet of L[ong] I[sland] Nassau County historical journal, v. 18, winter 1957: 1–17. F127.N2N3, v. 18

WEGELIN, OSCAR. Jupiter Hammon, American Negro poet; selections from his writings and a bibliography. Miami, Fla., Mnemosyne Pub. Co. [1969] 51 p. facsims. PS767.H15Z8 1969

Bibliography: p. 47–51.
Reprint of 1915 edition.

13530

HAMOND, *Sir* ANDREW SNAPE, *Bart.* (1738–1828)†
England. British naval officer in America.

Guide to the naval papers of Sir Andrew Snape Hamond, Bart., 1766–1783, and Sir Graham Eden Hamond, Bart., 1799–1825. Paul P. Hoffman, editor; Mary F. Crouch, assistant editor; John L. Molyneaux, assistant editor. Charlottesville, University of Virginia Library, 1966. 41 p. V65.H26A2 1966 Guide Mss

MOOMAW, WILLIAM H. The naval career of Captain Hamond, 1775–1779. 1955. ([486] p.)
Micro AC–1, no. 13,844

Thesis (Ph.D.)—University of Virginia.
Abstracted in *Dissertation Abstracts*, v. 16, no. 3, 1956, p. 525.

13531

HANCOCK, DOROTHY QUINCY (1747–1830)
Massachusetts. Wife of John Hancock (1737–1793)

HIGGINS, LUCY P. "Dorothy Q.," who became Dorothy H. Americana, v. 14, Oct. 1920: 408–419. port.
E171.A53, v. 14

WOODBURY, ELLEN C. D. Dorothy Quincy, wife of John Hancock, with events of her time. Washington, Neale Pub. Co., 1901. 259 p. plates, ports.
E302.6.H23W8

"References": p. [247]–259.

13532

HANCOCK, EBENEZER (1741–1819)
Massachusetts. Merchant.

BAXTER, WILLIAM T. A colonial bankrupt: Ebenezer Hancock, 1741–1819. *In* Business History Society. Bulletin, v. 25, June 1951: 115–124.
HF5001.B8262, v. 25

13533

HANCOCK, JOHN (1737–1793)*
Massachusetts. Merchant, assemblyman, delegate to the Continental Congress, Revolutionary officer, governor.

——— Letters of John Hancock, 1776. *In* Massachusetts Historical Society, *Boston*. Proceedings. v. 60; 1926/27. Boston, 1927. p. 98–116. F61.M38, v. 60

Notes by Worthington C. Ford.

——— Some letters, etc., of John Hancock and Thomas Cushing. *In* American Antiquarian Society, *Worcester, Mass*. Proceedings, new ser., v. 15, Apr. 1903: 324–340.
E172.A35, n.s., v. 15

Introduction and notes by Allen C. Thomas.

ADAMS, JAMES T. Portrait of an empty barrel. Harper's magazine, v. 161, Sept. 1930: 425–434.
AP2.H3, v. 161

ALLAN, HERBERT S. John Hancock, patriot in purple. New York, Macmillan Co., 1948. xvi, 422 p. illus., ports. E302.6.H23A4

Bibliography: p. 399–405.

BAXTER, WILLIAM T. The house of Hancock; business in Boston, 1724–1775. Cambridge, Mass., Harvard University Press, 1945. xxvii, 321 p. illus., facsims., plan, plates, ports. (Harvard studies in business history, 10).
HF3163.B6B35

Bibliographic footnotes.
Reprinted in New York by Russell & Russell (1965).

BROWN, ABRAM E. John Hancock, his book. Boston, Lee and Shepard, 1898. xii, 286 p. illus., facsims., plates, ports. E306.6.H23B8

A biographical summary with extensive quotes from Hancock's correspondence.

DICKERSON, OLIVER M. John Hancock: notorious smuggler or near victim of British revenue racketeers? Mississippi Valley historical review, v. 32, Mar. 1946: 517–540. E171.J87, v. 32

Finds that no other American had been singled out for so much personal abuse by British customs officials; Hancock triumphed by keeping his head and insisting upon his legal rights.

SEARS, LORENZO. John Hancock, the picturesque patriot. Boston, Little, Brown, 1912. x, 351 p. port.
E302.6.H23S4

Reprinted, with a new introduction and preface by George A. Billias, in Boston by Gregg Press (1972).

WAGNER, FREDERICK. Patriot's choice; the story of John Hancock. New York, Dodd, Mead [1964] xi, 179 p. illus., map, ports. E302.6.H23W3

Bibliography: p. 165–173.

13534

HAND, EDWARD (1744–1802)*

Ireland; Pennsylvania. Physician, Revolutionary general, delegate to the Continental Congress, assemblyman.

—— Correspondence of General Edward Hand, of the Continental Line, 1779–1781. Pennsylvania magazine of history and biography, v. 33, July 1909: 353–360.
F146.P65, v. 33

FITZPATRICK, PAUL J. General Edward Hand and Rock Ford. Social science, v. 44, Jan. 1969: 3–11.
H1.S55, v. 44

HEATHCOTE, CHARLES W. General Edward Hand—a capable Pennsylvania military officer and colleague of Washington. Picket post, no. 69, July 1960: 14–22. illus., port.
E234.P5, no. 69

ORRILL, LAWRENCE A. General Edward Hand. Western Pennsylvania historical magazine, v. 25, Sept./Dec. 1942: 99–112.
F146.W52, v. 25

13535

HANFORD, LEVI (1759–1854)

Connecticut. Revolutionary soldier.

BUSHNELL, CHARLES I. A narrative of the life and adventures of Levi Hanford, a soldier of the Revolution. New York, Priv. print., 1863. 80 p. ports. [Crumbs for antiquarians, v. 1, no. 5]
E203.B97

A portion of the narrative (p. 13–33) is given in the first person, as related by Hanford.

13536

HANSON, JOHN (1721?–1783)*

Maryland. Assemblyman, delegate to the Continental Congress.

JOHNSON, AMANDUS. John Hanson: first President of the United States under the Articles of Confederation [Philadelphia, Swedish Colonial Society, 1966] 24 p. ports.
E302.6.H27J6

Bibliographic footnotes.

An article with the same title was first published in the *Swedish-American Historical Bulletin*, v. 5, June 1932, p. 31–49.

KREMER, J. BRUCE. John Hanson of Mulberry Grove. New York, A. & C. Boni, 1938. 188 p. facsims, geneal. table, maps, ports.
E302.6.H27K7.

"Bibliography, acknowledgments and sources": p. [183]–188.

NELSON, JACOB A. John Hanson and the inseparable union; an authentic biography of a Revolutionary leader, patriot and statesman. Boston, Meador Pub. Co., 1939. 146 p. illus., facsims., plate, ports.
E302.6.H27N4

SMITH, SEYMOUR W. John Hanson, our first president. New York, Brewer, Warren & Putnam, 1932. x, 140 p. facsims., port.
E302.6.H27S6

13537

HANWAY, JONAS (1712–1786)†

England. Philanthropist, reformer.

—— The seaman's Christian friend; containing moral and religious advice to seamen. London, Dodsley, 1779. liv, [6], 292 p. front.
BV4590.H3

—— The soldier's faithful friend: being moral and religious advice to soldiers: with an historical abridgment of the events of the [l]ast war. To which are prefixed, reflections on the defection of the colonists. Printed on occasion of the benefaction for the relief of soldiers widows, &c., in America. London, 1776. *11, viii, [10], 199 p. front.
U110.H3 1776

First published in London in 1766 with title: *The Soldier's Faithful Friend: Being Prudential, Moral, and Religious Advice to Private Men in the Army and Militia.*

HUTCHINS, JOHN H. Jonas Hanway, 1712–1786. London, Society for Promoting Christian Knowledge; New York, Macmillan Co., 1940. xxii, 197 p. plates, ports.
HV247.H3H8 1940

Thesis (Ph.D.)—Columbia University, 1940. Bibliography: p. 188–194.

13538

HARADEN, JONATHAN (1745–1803)*

Massachusetts. Revolutionary naval officer.

GARDNER, FRANK A. Captain Jonathan Haraden. Massachusetts magazine, v. 2, Oct. 1909: 191–199.
F61.M48, v. 2

13539

HARDING, SETH (1734–1814)*

Massachusetts; Connecticut; New York. Seaman, Revolutionary naval officer.

HOWARD, JAMES L. Seth Harding, mariner; a naval picture of the Revolution. New Haven, Yale University Press, 1930. xv, 301 p. facsims., maps, col. port.
E271.H72

"Private journal on board the *Confederacy* frigate kept by Captain Joseph Hardy in command of marines": p. [213]–277.

Bibliography: p. [280]–283.

13540

HARDY, ELIAS (1744–1798)

England; New York; New Brunswick. Lawyer.

RAYMOND, WILLIAM O. Elias Hardy, councillor-at-law. *In* New Brunswick Historical Society. Collections. [v. 4], no. 10. Saint John, N.B., 1919. p. 57–66.
F1041.N53, v. 4, no. 10

——— A radical and a Loyalist; a biographical sketch of Elias Hardy, barrister-at-law at Saint John, N.B., 1784–1799. *In* Royal Society of Canada. Transactions, 3d ser., v. 13, June/Sept. 1919: 91–101.
AS42.R6, 3d s., v. 13

13541

HARE, ROBERT (*fl.* 1774)
England; Pennsylvania.

——— Memoranda of tour through part of North America in 1774. *In* Pennsylvania. Historical Society. Collections, v. 1, Nov. 1853: 363–376. F146.P34, v. 1

On his journey from Philadelphia to Montreal and back to Boston.

13542

HARLAN, SILAS (1753–1782)
West Virginia; Kentucky. Frontiersman, Revolutionary officer.

GREENE, JAMES S. Major Silas Harlan; his life and times [Cleveland? 1964] 83 p. F454.H28G7
Bibliography: p. [81]–83.

13543

HARMAR, JOSIAH (1753–1813)*
Pennsylvania. Revolutionary officer, Indian fighter.

——— Outpost on the Wabash, 1787–1791; letters of Brigadier General Josiah Harmar and Major John Francis Hamtramck, and other letters and documents selected from the Harmar papers in the William L. Clements Library. Edited by Gayle Thornbrough. Indianapolis, Indiana Historical Society, 1957. 305 p. facsim., fold. map. (Indiana Historical Society. Publications, v. 19)
F521.I41, v. 19
F534.V7H3

Bibliographic footnotes.

PECKHAM, HOWARD H. The papers of General Josiah Harmar. A collection dealing with the earliest days of the Northwest Territory now in the William L. Clements Library. Michigan alumnus quarterly review, v. 43, winter 1937: 428–432. port. AP2.M53, v. 43

SMITH, DWIGHT L. Josiah Harmar, diplomatic courier [1784] Pennsylvania magazine of history and biography, v. 87, Oct. 1963: 420–430. F146.P65, v. 87

13544

HARNETT, CORNELIUS (1723–1781)*
North Carolina. Assemblyman, delegate to the Continental Congress.

CONNOR, ROBERT D. W. Cornelius Harnett; an essay in North Carolina history. Raleigh, Edwards & Broughton Print. Co., 1909. 209 p. E263.N8H3
Reprinted in Freeport, N.Y., by Books for Libraries Press (1971).

——— Cornelius Harnett, the pride of Cape Fear. North Carolina booklet, v. 5, Jan. 1906: 171–201. plate.
F251.N86, v. 5

MORGAN, DAVID T. Cornelius Harnett, Revolutionary leader and delegate to the Continental Congress. North Carolina historical review, v. 49, summer 1972: 229–241. illus., facsims. F251.N892, v. 49

13545

HARRIS, GEORGE HARRIS, *1st Baron* (1746–1829)†
England. British officer in America.

LUSHINGTON, STEPHEN R. The life and services of General Lord Harris, G.C.B., during his campaigns in America, the West Indies, and India. London, J. W. Parker, 1840. xv, 551 p. plan, port. DA67.1.H2L8

13546

HARRIS, JAMES (1709–1780)†
England. Writer, scholar, Member of Parliament.

——— The works of James Harris, Esq., with an account of his life and character. By his son, the Earl of Malmesbury. Oxford, T. Tegg, 1841. xviii, 584 p.
AC7.H35

13547

HARRISON, PETER (1716–1775)*
England; Rhode Island; Connecticut. Architect.

BALDWIN, SIMEON E. The three earliest New Haven architects. *In* New Haven Colony Historical Society, *New Haven.* v. 10. New Haven, 1951. p. 226–239.
F98.N5, v. 10

Concerned with the careers of Peter Harrison, David Hoadley, and Ithiel Town.

BRIDENBAUGH, CARL. Peter Harrison, first American architect. Chapel Hill, University of North Carolina Press, 1949. xvi, 195 p. illus., maps, ports.
NA737.H3B7

"Published for the Institute of Early American History and Culture at Williamsburg, Virginia."
Bibliographic footnotes.

KIMBALL, FISKE. The colonial amateurs and their models: Peter Harrison. Architecture, v. 54, June–July 1926: 155–160, 185–190, 209. illus., plans.
NA1.A77, v. 54

13548

HARRISON, ROBERT HANSON (1745–1790)
Maryland. Lawyer, Revolutionary officer, judge.

NESS, GEORGE T. A lost man of Maryland. Maryland historical magazine, v. 35, Dec. 1940: 315–336. plate.
F176.M18, v. 35

13549

HARROD, JAMES (*ca.* 1744–*ca.* 1793)*

Virginia; Kentucky. Frontiersman, assemblyman.

MASON, KATHRYN H. James Harrod of Kentucky. Baton Rouge, Louisiana State University Press [1951] xxii, 266 p. illus., facsims., maps, port. (Southern biography series)   F454.H3M3

Bibliography: p. [245]–254.

13550

HARROWER, JOHN (1733 *or* 4–1777)

England; Virginia. Clerk, bookkeeper.

——The journal of John Harrower, an indentured servant in the colony of Virginia, 1773–1776. Edited, with an introduction, by Edward Miles Riley. Illustrated by Fritz Kreder. Williamsburg, Va., Colonial Williamsburg; distributed by Holt, Rinehart and Winston, New York [1963] xxi, 202 p. illus., facsims., maps. (Williamsburg eyewitness to history series)   F229.H323 1963

Bibliographical references included in "Notes" (p. 171–191).

A portion of the diary was published in the *American Historical Review*, v. 6, Oct. 1900, p. 65–107.

13551

HART, JOHN (*ca.* 1711–1779)*

New Jersey. Farmer, assemblyman, delegate to the Continental Congress.

BROOKS, ESTELLE A. John Hart, signer of the Declaration of Independence, July 4, 1776. Quarterly review, v. 13, Apr./June 1953: 47–58. illus., port.   BX6201.Q3, v. 13

13552

HART, NANCY MORGAN (*b. ca.* 1735)

Georgia. Settler.

COULTER, ELLIS MERTON. Nancy Hart, Georgia heroine of the Revolution; the story of the growth of a tradition. Georgia historical quarterly, v. 39, June 1955: 118–151. plate.   F281.G2975, v. 39

An undocumented version of the article appeared in the *Georgia Review*, v. 8, fall-winter 1954, p. 261–279, 413–421.

13553

HART, OLIVER (1723–1795)

Pennsylvania; South Carolina. Baptist clergyman.

—— Extracts from the diary of Rev. Oliver Hart, from A.D. 1740 to A.D. 1780. *In* Charleston, *S.C.* Year book. 1896. Charleston. p. 375–401.   JS13.C33, 1896

Contributed by William G. Whilden.

13554

HART, THOMAS (1729 *or* 30–1808)

North Carolina. Planter, merchant, assemblyman, Revolutionary officer.

STOKES, DURWARD T. Thomas Hart in North Carolina. North Carolina historical review, v. 41, summer 1964: 324–337.   F251.N892, v. 41

13555

HARTLEY, DAVID (*ca.* 1730–1813)†

England. Member of Parliament, political writer.

—— Collection of 29 printed pieces. London & York 1775–83. 25 pamphlets in case.   E211.H3 Rare Bk. Coll.

A collection of speeches and papers (five of which are duplicates).

Partial contents: [no. 1] An address to the Committee of association of the county of York. [1781]—[no. 3] Committee upon the American trade bill. [1783]—[no. 4] Considerations on the proposed renewal of the bank charter. 1781.—[no. 6] Draught of a proposed bill for conciliation with America. [1780]—[no. 7] Foreign troops. [1776]—[no. 8] In the Committee of supply for voting the foreign troops for one whole year. [1783]—[no. 9] Lord North's prohibitory bill. [1775]—[no. 10] Lord North's proposition. [1775]—[no. 11] Mr. D. Hartley's speech, December 5. [1777?]—[no. 12] Mr. Hartley's speech, April 9, 1778. [1778]—[no. 13] Motions, December 7, 1775. [1775]—[no. 14] Motions made in the House of Commons, on Monday, the 27th of March, 1775. [1775]—[no. 15] On Lord North's restraining bill. [1775]—[no. 16] On the preliminaries of peace. [1783]—[no. 18] Speech and motions made in the House of Commons, on Monday, the 27th of March, 1775, 2d ed. 1775.—[no. 19] Substance of a speech in Parliament upon the state of the nation and the present civil war with America. 1776—[no. 20] To the Right Honourable the Lord-Mayor of London. [1781]—[no. 21] Two letters from D. Hartley, addressed to the Committee of the county of York. 1780.—[no. 22–24] [Three speeches printed without title or date]—[no. 25] Motions respecting the treaty proposed by Winchcombe Henry Hartley. [1783]

GUTTRIDGE, GEORGE H. David Hartley, M.P., an advocate of conciliation, 1774–1783. Berkeley, Calif., University of California Press, 1926. [233]–340 p. ports. (University of California publications in history, v. 14, no. 3)   E173.C15, v. 14
    DA522.H3G8

Bibliography: p. 333–336.

HARTLEY, JOSEPH W. David Hartley and the American colonies; England's signer of the definitive treaty of peace. Magazine of American history, with notes and queries, v. 24, Dec. 1890: 426–444. E171.M18, v. 24

13556

HARTWICK, JOHN CHRISTOPHER (1714–1796)*

Germany; New York. Itinerant Lutheran clergyman.

ARNDT, KARL J. R. John Christopher Hartwick, German pioneer of central New York. *In* New York State Historical Association. New York history, v. 18, July 1937: 293–303.   F116.N865, v. 18

13557

HARVEY, ALEXANDER (1747–1809)
   Scotland; Vermont.

—— Journal of Colonel Alexander Harvey of Scotland and Barnet, Vermont [1774–75] *In* Vermont Historical Society. Proceedings. 1921/23. Montpelier; 1924. p. 199–262.   F46.V55, 1921/23
   Details of his migration with a company of farmers from Scotland to Vermont, survey of the town's lands, and early development of the community.

13558

HARVEY, JOHN (*ca.* 1725–1775)
   North Carolina. Assemblyman.

CONNOR, ROBERT D. W. John Harvey. North Carolina booklet, v. 8, July 1908: 3–42.   F251.N86, v. 8

13559

HASENCLEVER, PETER (1716–1793)*
   Prussia; New Jersey; New York. Iron manufacturer.

HASENCLEVER, ADOLF. Peter Hasenclever aus Remschied-Ehringhausen, ein deutscher Kaufmann im 18. Jahrhundert (1716–1793). *In* Deutsch-amerikanische Geschichtsblätter. v. 20/21; 1920/21. Chicago, University of Chicago Press, 1922. p. 314–337.
                    F550.G3D4, v. 20/21
   Contents: 1. Jugend und Aufenthalt in Spanien. 1716–1763.—2. Peter Hasenclever als Unternehmer in den englischen Kolonien Nordamerikas. 1764–1773.—3. Der Lebensabend in Landshut in Schlesien. 1776–1793.

SPIELER, GERHARD. Peter Hasenclever, industrialist. *In* New Jersey Historical Society. Proceedings, v. 59, Oct. 1941: 231–256.   F131.N58, v. 59

TORREY, RAYMOND H. Peter Hasenclever, a pre-Revolutionary ironmaster. *In* New York State Historical Association. New York history, v. 17, July 1936: 306–315.
                    F116.N865, v. 17

13560

HASLET, JOHN (1727–1777)
   Ireland; Delaware. Clergyman, physician, assemblyman, Revolutionary officer.

MOYNE, ERNEST J. Who was Colonel John Haslet of Delaware? Delaware history, v. 13, Oct. 1969: 283–300.
                    F161.D37, v. 13

13561

HASLEWOOD, JOHN
   British officer in America.

—— Journal of a British officer during the American Revolution [April 1775 to April 1779] Mississippi Valley historical review, v. 7, June 1920: 51–58.
                    E171.J87, v 7
   Sheds light on the movements of the 63rd British infantry regiment, involved in the Battle of Bunker Hill, the siege of Boston, the campaign of the Hudson, and the operations around Philadelphia. Introduction and notes by Louise P. Kellogg.

13562

HASWELL, ANTHONY (1756–1815)*
   England; Massachusetts; Vermont. Ballad writer, printer, Revolutionary soldier, newspaper publisher.

SPARGO, JOHN. Anthony Haswell, printer-patriot-ballader; a biographical study with a selection of his ballads and an annotated bibliographical list of his imprints. Rutland, Vt., Tuttle Co., 1925. xv, 293 p. 35 facsim.   Z232.H35S7
   Bibliography: p. [241]–293.

13563

HATFIELD, JOHN (1745–1813)
   Pennsylvania. Farmer, Revolutionary soldier.

CLARK, WILLIAM B. John Hatfield, husband and husbandman. Pennsylvania magazine of history and biography, v. 57, Oct. 1933: 299–315.
                    F146.P65, v. 57

13564

HAWKINS, BENJAMIN (1754–1816)*
   North Carolina. Delegate to the Continental Congress, Indian agent.

POUND, MERRITT B. Benjamin Hawkins, Indian agent. Athens, University of Georgia Press [1951] ix, 270 p. map (on lining paper), port.   E93.H34P6
   Bibliography: p. 251–260.
   The author's thesis (Ph.D.), *The Public Career of Benjamin Hawkins,* was submitted to the University of North Carolina in 1939.

—— Benjamin Hawkins, Indian agent. Georgia historical quarterly, v. 13, Dec. 1929: 392–409.
                    F281.G2975, v. 13

—— Colonel Benjamin Hawkins—North Carolinian—benefactor of the southern Indians. North Carolina historical review, v. 19, Jan.–Apr. 1942: 1–21, 168–186.   F251.N892, v. 19

WEEKS, STEPHEN B. Benjamin Hawkins. *In* Georgia Historical Society. Collections. v. 9. Savannah, 1916. p. 5–12.   F281.G35, v. 9

13565

HAWKINS, CHRISTOPHER (1764–1837)
   Rhode Island. Revolutionary seaman, farmer.

—— The adventures of Christopher Hawkins, containing details of his captivity, a first and second time on the high seas, in the Revolutionary War, by the British, and his consequent sufferings, and escape from the Jersey prison ship. Written by himself. With an introduction and notes by Charles I. Bushnell. New York, Priv. print., 1864. x, 316 p. plan, plates, ports. E281.H39
Reprinted in New York by the New York Times (1968).

13566
HAWLEY, JOSEPH (1723–1788)*
Massachusetts. Lawyer, assemblyman.

BROWN, ERNEST FRANCIS. Joseph Hawley, colonial radical. New York, Columbia University Press, 1931. ix, 213 p. E263.M4H362
Thesis (Ph.D.)—Columbia University, 1931.
Bibliography: p. [193]–207.

—— The law career of Major Joseph Hawley. New England quarterly, v. 4, July 1931: 482–508.
F1.N62, v. 4

[HAWLEY, ELIAS S.] Historical sketch of Major Joseph Hawley of Northampton, Mass., 1723–1788. A reprint from the "Hawley record," 1300–1890. Buffalo, N.Y., Press of E. H. Hutchinson, 1890. 48 p. illus.
E263.M4H385

STARKEY, MARION L. Joseph Hawley, forgotten patriot. New-England galaxy, v. 2, spring 1961: 3–16. facsim., ports. F1.N39, v. 2

13567
HAY, HENRY (*fl.* 1789–1790)
Old Northwest.

—— A narrative of life on the old frontier; Henry Hay's journal from Detroit to the Miami River [1789–90] *In* Wisconsin. State Historical Society. Proceedings. 1914. Madison, 1915. p. 208–261. F576.W75, 1914
Edited with introduction and notes by Milo M. Quaife. Also published in the Indiana Historical Society's *Publications*, v. 7 (Indianapolis, 1923), p. 295–361.

13568
HAY, JEHU (*d.* 1785)
Pennsylvania; Old Northwest. Indian fighter and negotiator, British officer in America.

QUAIFE, MILO M. Detroit biographies: Jehu Hay. Burton historical collection leaflet, v. 8, Sept. 1929: 1–16.
F561.B9, v. 8

13569
HAYNES, LEMUEL (1753–1833)
Connecticut; Vermont. Revolutionary soldier, farmer, Congregational clergyman.

COOLEY, TIMOTHY M. Sketches of the life and character of the Rev. Lemuel Haynes, A.M., for many years pastor of a church in Rutland, Vt., and late in Granville, New-York, Harper, 1837. 345 p. port.
BX7260.H315C6 1837

MORSE, W. H. Lemuel Haynes. Journal of Negro history, v. 4, Jan. 1919: 22–32. E185.J86, v. 4

13570
HAYS, JUDAH (1703?–1764)
New York. Merchant.

KORN, HAROLD. Receipt book of Judah and Moses M. Hays, commencing January 12, 1763, and ending July 18, 1776. *In* American Jewish Historical Society. Publications. no. 28. New York, 1922. p. 223–229.
E184.J5A5, no. 28
Describes the contents of the book, containing 296 receipts, in the possession of the Virginia Historical Society.

13571
HAZARD, EBENEZER (1744–1817)*
Pennsylvania; New York. Publisher, historian.

—— Ebenezer Hazard's diary: New Jersey during the Revolution. New Jersey history, v. 90, autumn 1972: 169–180. illus., map. F131.N58, v. 90
Entries from a 10-day trip from Philadelphia to Elizabeth and Newark in August 1777. Edited by Fred Shelley.

—— Ebenezer Hazard's travels through Maryland in 1777. Edited by Fred Shelley. Maryland historical magazine, v. 46, Mar. 1951: 44–54. F176.M18, v. 46

—— The journal of Ebenezer Hazard in North Carolina, 1777 and 1778. Edited by Hugh Buckner Johnston. North Carolina historical review, v. 36, July 1959: 358–381. F251.N892, v. 36

—— The journal of Ebenezer Hazard in Virginia, 1777. Edited by Fred Shelley. Virginia magazine of history and biography, v. 62, Oct. 1954: 400–423.
F221.V91, v. 62

—— A view of coastal South Carolina in 1778: the journal of Ebenezer Hazard. South Carolina historical magazine, v. 73, Oct. 1972: 177–193. F266.S55, v. 73
Introduction and notes by H. Roy Merrens.

BLODGETT, RALPH E. Ebenezer Hazard: the Post Office, the Insurance Company of North America, and the editing of historical documents. 1971. ([241] p.)
Micro AC-1, no. 72–17,243
Thesis (Ph.D.)—University of Colorado.
Abstracted in *Dissertation Abstract International,* v. 32A, June 1972, p. 6880.

SHELLEY, FRED. Ebenezer Hazard, America's first historical editor. William and Mary quarterly, 3d ser., v. 12, Jan. 1955: 44–73. F221.W71, 3d s., v. 12

VERMILYE, ASHBEL G.   The early New York Post-Office: Ebenezer Hazard, postmaster and postmaster-general. Magazine of American history, with notes and queries, v. 13, Feb. 1885: 113–130.   E171.M18, v. 13

Established in 1775.

13572

HAZARD, THOMAS (1720–1798)*

Rhode Island. Abolitionist.

HAZARD, CAROLINE.   Thomas Hazard son of Rob[t], call'd College Tom. A study of life in Narragansett in the XVIIIth century, by his grandson's granddaughter. Boston, Houghton, Mifflin, 1893. viii, 324 p. facsims., map.   F82.H4

13573

HAZARD, THOMAS BENJAMIN (1756–1845)

——— Nailer Tom's diary; otherwise, The journal of Thomas B. Hazard of Kingstown, Rhode Island, 1778 to 1840, which includes observations on the weather, records of births, marriages and deaths, transactions by barter and money of varying value, preaching Friends and neighborhood gossip. Printed as written and introduced by Caroline Hazard. Boston, Merrymount Press, 1930. xxiv, 808 p.   F83.H42 Rare Bk. Coll.

13574

HAZELTINE, JOHN (1702–1777)

Massachusetts; Vermont. Military officer, landowner.

CHENOWETH, CAROLINE VAN D.   An undistinguished citizen. *In* Worcester Historical Society, *Worcester, Mass.* Proceedings, v. 17, Jan. 1900: 14–31.   W74.W9W85, v. 17

13575

HAZELWOOD, JOHN (*ca.* 1726–1800)*

England; Pennsylvania. Mariner, Revolutionary naval officer.

LEACH, JOSIAH G.   Commodore John Hazlewood (sic), commander of the Pennsylvania Navy in the Revolution. Pennsylvania magazine of history and biography, v. 26, Apr. 1902: 1–6.   F146.P65, v. 26

13576

HAZLITT, JOHN (1767–1837)

England; Massachusetts. Portrait artist. Son of William Hazlitt (1737–1820).

MOYNE, ERNEST J.   John Hazlitt, miniaturist and portrait painter in America, 1783–1787. *In* Winterthur portfolio. v. 6. Winterthur, Del., 1970. p. 33–40. illus.   N9.W52, v. 6

13577

HAZLITT, MARGARET (1770–1841)

England. Daughter of William Hazlitt (1737–1820).

——— The journal of Margaret Hazlitt; recollections of England, Ireland, and America. Edited and annotated by Ernest J. Moyne. Lawrence, University of Kansas Press, 1967. x, 195 p. geneal. table, ports.   PR4769.H9Z5

Bibliographic references included in "Notes" (p. [127]–167).

"The Hazlitts in America" [1783–87]: p. 48–99.

13578

HAZLITT, WILLIAM (1737–1820)

Ireland; America; England. Clergyman.

MOYNE, ERNEST J.   The Reverend William Hazlitt: a friend of liberty in Ireland during the American Revolution. William and Mary quarterly, 3d ser., v. 21, Apr. 1964: 288–297.   F221.W71, 3d s., v. 21

——— The Reverend William Hazlitt and Dickinson College [1783–86] Pennsylvania magazine of history and biography, v. 85, July 1961: 289–302.   F146.P65, v. 85

13579

HEARNE, SAMUEL (1745–1792)†

England; Canada. Explorer.

——— Journal of Samuel Hearne and Philip Turnor [1774–92] Edited with introduction and notes by J. B. Tyrrell. Toronto, Champlain Society, 1934. xviii, 611 p. fold. facsim., maps (part fold.), fold. plan. (Champlain Society, Toronto. Publications, [21])   F1060.7.H38 Rare Bk. Coll.

Includes the *Journal of a Journey With the Chepawyans . . . in 1791 & 2*, by Peter Fidler, and parts of the journals of Malchom Ross and several other employees of the Hudson's Bay Company.

Reprinted in New York by Greenwood Press (1968).

——— A journey from Prince of Wales's Fort, in Hudson's Bay, to the Northern Ocean. Undertaken by order of the Hudson's Bay Company, for the discovery of copper mines, a northwest passage, &c., in the years 1769, 1770, 1771, & 1772. London, A. Strahan and T. Cadell, 1795. xliv, 458 p. fold. maps, plates (part fold.)   F1060.7.H41 Rare Bk. Coll.

A new edition, with introduction, notes, and illustrations by Joseph B. Tyrrell, was published in Toronto by the Champlain Society (1911. 437 p. F1060.7.H44) and reprinted in New York by Greenwood Press (1968).

Another edition, edited by Richard Glover, has been published in Toronto by Macmillan Co. (1958. 301 p. F1060.7.H42 1958).

SPECK, GORDON. Samuel Hearne and the Northwest Passage. Caldwell, Idaho, Caxton Printers, 1963. xxii, 337 p. illus., maps, port. F1060.7.H498
Bibliographic footnotes.

13580
HEART, JONATHAN (1748–1791)
Connecticut; New Jersey; Ohio. Revolutionary officer, frontiersman, Indian fighter.

——— Journal of Capt. Jonathan Heart on the march with his company from Connecticut to Fort Pitt, in Pittsburgh, Pennsylvania, from the seventh of September, to the twelfth of October, 1785, inclusive; to which is added the Dickinson-Harmar correspondence of 1784–5; the whole illustrated with notes and preceded by a biographical sketch of Captain Heart by Consul Willshire Butterfield. Albany, N.Y., J. Munsell's Sons, 1885. xv, 94 p. F517.H42

13581
HEATH, WILLIAM (1737–1814)*
Massachusetts. Farmer, Revolutionary general.

——— The Heath papers. pt. 2–3. Boston, Published by the Society, 1904–5. 2 v. fold. plan, port. (Massachusetts Historical Society, Boston. Collections, 7th ser., v. 4–5) F61.M41, 7th s., v. 4–5
Contents: pt. 2. Papers, 1775–1779.—pt. 3. Papers, 1780–1797. Appendix: Extracts from General Heath's orderly book relating to the trial of General McDougall.

The Heath Papers, pt. 1, consists entirely of letters from George Washington and is listed among his other writings in this bibliography.

——— Memoirs of Major-General Heath. Containing anecdotes, details of skirmishes, battles, and other military events, during the American war. Boston, Printed by I. Thomas and E. T. Andrews, 1798. 388 p. E230.H43 Rare Bk. Coll.
The 1904 edition, with an introduction and notes by Rufus R. Wilson (New York, A. Wessels Co. 435 p.), has been reprinted in New York by the New York Times and in Freeport, N.Y., by Books for Libraries Press (1970).

CRAFTS, WILLIAM A. A general of the Revolution. New England magazine, new ser., v. 3, Dec. 1890: 513–519. AP2.N4, n.s., v. 3

DOLAN, GRAHAM P. Major General William Heath and the first years of the American Revolution. 1966. ([375] p.) Micro AC–1, no. 66–11,309
Thesis (Ph.D.)—Boston University.
Abstracted in Dissertation Abstracts, v. 27A, Nov. 1966, p. 1316–1317.

HEATHCOTE, CHARLES W. General William Heath—an earnest patriot and friend of Washington. Picket post, no. 78, Oct. 1962: 4–9. port. E234.P5, no. 78

NICHOLS, FESSENDEN A. The life and public services of General William Heath. In Roxbury Historical Society, Roxbury, Mass. Year-book. 1920. Roxbury. p. 12–24. F74.R9R95, 1920

13582
HECKEWELDER, JOHN GOTTLIEB ERNESTUS (1743–1823)*
England; Pennsylvania; Ohio. Missionary to the Indians.

——— A canoe journey from the Big Beaver to the Tuscarawas in 1773: a travel diary of John Heckewaelder. Translated and edited by August C. Mahr. Ohio archaeological and historical quarterly, v. 61, July 1952: 283–298. map. F486.O51, v. 61

——— Thirty thousand miles with John Heckewelder. Edited by Paul A. W. Wallace. [Pittsburgh] University of Pittsburgh Press [1958] xvii, 474 p. illus., fold. maps, ports. E163.H4
Heckewelder's travel journals, gathered from various repositories, and selections from his published reminiscences woven into a connected story.

RICE WILLIAM H. The Rev. John Heckewelder, born at Bedford, Eng., March 12, 1743; died at Bethlehem, Pa., January 21, 1823. In Ohio State Archaeological and Historical Society. Publications. v. 7. Columbus, 1899. p. 314–348. illus. F486.O51, v. 7

RONDTHALER, EDWARD. Life of John Heckewelder. Edited by B. H. Coates. Philadelphia, T. Ward, 1847. 159 p. port. E77.H44

WALLACE, PAUL A. W. The John Heckewelder papers. Pennsylvania history, v. 27, July 1960: 249–262. port. F146.P597, v. 27

——— John Heckewelder's Indians and the Fenimore Cooper tradition. In American Philosophical Society, Philadelphia. Proceedings, v. 96, Aug. 1952: 496–504. port. Q11.P5, v. 96
Also published in the Society's Library Bulletin for 1952, p. 496–504.

——— John Heckewelder's travels. Now and then, v. 10, Apr. 1952: 105–119. illus. F159.M95N6, v. 10

13583
HEDGES, SILAS (1736–1811)
Virginia. Frontiersman, Revolutionary officer.

GOODWYN, DORA H. Colonel Silas Hedges, pioneer of western Virginia. Daughters of the American Revolution magazine, v. 54, Jan. 1920: 34–39. E202.5.A12, v. 54

13584
HEER, BARTHOLOMAEUS VON
Prussia; Pennsylvania. Revolutionary officer.

Steuben Society of America. Major Bartholomew von Heer . . . commander of George Washington's mounted body guard. [n.p., 1934?] 20 p.

E207.H44S7

13585

HELFFRICH, JOHN HENRY (1739–1810)

Germany; Pennsylvania. German Reformed clergyman and missionary.

——— Diary of the Rev. John Henry Helffrich, September 6, 1771–January 14, 1772. Pennsylvania magazine of history and biography, v. 38, Jan. 1914: 65–82.

F146.P65, v. 38

On his sea voyage from Amsterdam to New York and his ministerial work in Pennsylvania. Translated from the German by William J. Hinke.

13586

HELM, LEONARD (ca. 1720–1782)

Virginia; Kentucky. Frontiersman, Revolutionary officer.

CONKWRIGHT, BESSIE T. Captain Leonard Helm. Indiana history bulletin, v. 10, Mar. 1933: 407–434.

F521.I367, v. 10

13587

HENDERSON, RICHARD (1735–1785)*

North Carolina. Land developer, colonizer.

HENDERSON, ARCHIBALD. The creative forces in westward expansion: Henderson and Boone. American historical review, v. 20, Oct. 1914: 86–107.

E171.A57, v. 20

——— Richard Henderson and the occupation of Kentucky, 1775. Mississippi Valley historical review, v. 1, Dec. 1914: 341–363.

E171.J87, v. 1

——— ———Offprint. [Cedar Rapids, Ia., 1914?] p. [341]–363.

F454.H49

——— Richard Henderson: the authorship of the Cumberland Compact and the founding of Nashville. Tennessee historical magazine, v. 2, Sept. 1916: 155–174. facsims.

F431.T28, v. 2

——— ——— Offprint. [Nashville?] 1916. [20] p. facsims.

F436.H49

13588

HENDERSON, SAMUEL (1746–1816)

North Carolina; Kentucky. Frontiersman, Revolutionary officer, landowner.

BATE, RICHARD ALEXANDER. Colonel Callaway's preparedness, by Dr. R. Alexander Bate. The career of Colonel Samuel Henderson . . . by Archibald Henderson. [Henderson? Ky.] Society of Transylvanians [1941] 42 p. coat of arms, plate, port.

F454.C2B3

13589

HENDERSON, WILLIAM (1748–1788)

South Carolina. Planter, Revolutionary officer, assemblyman.

TAYLOR, BENJAMIN F. General William Henderson. South Carolina historical and genealogical magazine, v. 28, Apr. 1927: 108–111.

F266.S55, v. 28

13590

HENLEY, DAVID (1749–1823)

Massachusetts; Virginia. Revolutionary officer.

WILLIAMS, SAMUEL C. Colonel David Henley. *In* East Tennessee Historical Society, *Knoxville*. Publications. no. 18; 1946. Knoxville, Tenn. p. 3–24.

F442.1.E14, no. 18

13591

HENLEY, SAMUEL (1744–1815)†

England; Virginia. Anglican clergyman, professor.

CHAMBERLAIN, MELLEN. Sketch of the life of the Rev. Samuel Henley, D.D., Professor of Moral Philosophy in William and Mary College, Virginia, 1770–1775. *In* Massachusetts Historical Society, *Boston*. Proceedings. v. 15; 1876/77. Boston, 1878. p. 230–241.

F61.M38, v. 15

GILPIN, WILLIAM. The letters of William Gilpin to Samuel Henley [1768–69] Huntington Library quarterly, v. 35, Feb. 1972: 159–169.

Z733.S24Q, v. 35

Introduction and notes by Fraser Neiman.

HINER, RAY. Samuel Henley and Thomas Gwatkin: partners in protest. Historical magazine of the Protestant Episcopal church, v. 37, Mar. 1968: 39–50.

BX5800.H5, v. 37

13592

HENRY, ALEXANDER (1739–1824)*

New Jersey; Old Northwest. Fur trader, traveler.

——— Travels and adventures in Canada and the Indian territories between the years 1760 and 1776. In two parts. New-York, Printed and published by I. Riley, 1809. vi, 330 p.

F1013.H52 Rare Bk. Coll.

Reprinted in facsimile in Ann Arbor, Mich., by University Microfilms (1966).

A new edition, with notes by James Bain, was published in Toronto by G. N. Morang (1901. 347 p.) and has been reprinted in Rutland, Vt., by C. E. Tuttle Co. (1969), in New York by B. Franklin (1969), and in St. Clair Shores, Mich., by Scholarly Press (1972). Milo M. Quaife also prepared an edition of Henry's *Travels* that was published in Chicago by R. R. Donnelly (1921. 340 p. F1013.H525).

Part 1 of the *Travels*, edited by David A. Armour, has been published under the title *Massacre at Mackinac; Alexander Henry's Travels and Adventures in Canada and the Indian Territories Between the Years 1760 and 1764* (Mackinack Island, Mich., Mackinac Island State Park Commission [1966] 119 p. F551.H42 1966).

QUIMBY, GEORGE I. Alexander Henry in central Michigan, 1763–64. Michigan history, v. 46, Sept. 1962: 193–200. F561.M57, v. 46

13593

HENRY, JOHN (1750–1798)*

Maryland. Lawyer, assemblyman, delegate to the Continental Congress.

——— Letters and papers of Governor John Henry of Maryland, member of Continental Congress 1777–1788, member of United States Senate 1789–1797, governor of Maryland, 1797–1798. With some account of his life, genealogy and descendants, as shown by extracts from records and papers in the Maryland Historical Society, and original letters and memoranda in the hands of the compiler, one of his great-grandsons, J. Winfield Henry. Baltimore, G. W. King Print Co., 1904. 133 p. illus., plates, ports. E302.6.H4H5

13594

HENRY, PATRICK (1736–1799)*

Virginia. Lawyer, assemblyman, orator, delegate to the Continental Congress, Revolutionary officer, governor.

ANGER, CHARLES L. Patrick Henry: practical politician. 1939. viii, 210 l.

Thesis (Ph.D.)—University of Virginia.

AXELRAD, JACOB. Patrick Henry, the voice of freedom. New York, Random House [1947] vii, 318 p. illus., maps (on lining-papers) E302.6.H5A9

Bibliography: p. 301–312.

BOWMAN, ELDON G. Patrick Henry's political philosophy. 1962. ([356] p.) Micro AC–1, no. 62–1228

Thesis (Ph.D.)—Claremont Graduate School and University Center.

Abstracted in *Dissertation Abstracts*, v. 23, July 1962, p. 285.

HALL, VIRGINIUS C. Notes on Patrick Henry portraiture. Virginia magazine of history and biography, v. 71, Apr. 1963: 168–184. ports. F221.V91, v. 71

Discusses portraits from life, posthumous portraits, and lost portraits, providing 12 pages of illustrations.

HENRY, WILLIAM W. Patrick Henry; life, correspondence and speeches. New York, C. Scribner's Sons, 1891. 3 v. port. E302.6.H5H5

Reprinted in New York by B. Franklin (1969).

JEFFERSON, THOMAS. Jefferson's recollections of Patrick Henry. Pennsylvania magazine of history and biography, v. 34, Oct. 1910: 385–418. F146.P65, v. 34

Taken from letters dated 1805 to 1816. Contributed by Stan V. Henkels.

MALLORY, LOUIS A. Patrick Henry, orator of the American Revolution. 1939.

Thesis (Ph.D.)—University of Wisconsin.

MAYO, BERNARD. The enigma of Patrick Henry. Virginia quarterly review, v. 35, spring 1959: 176–195. AP2.V76, v. 35

MEADE, ROBERT D. Judge Edmund Winston's memoir of Patrick Henry. Virginia magazine of history and biography, v. 69, Jan. 1961: 28–41. port. F221.V91, v. 69

——— Patrick Henry. Philadelphia, Lippincott [1957–69] 2 v. illus., facsims., ports. E302.6.H5M4

Includes bibliographies.

Contents: [1] Patriot in the making.—[2] Practical revolutionary.

MORGAN, GEORGE. The true Patrick Henry. Philadelphia, J. B. Lippincott Co., 1907. xi, 492 p. facsims., plates, ports. E302.6.H5M8

TYLER, MOSES COIT. Patrick Henry. Boston, Houghton, Mifflin, 1898. xiv, 454 p. facsim., plate, ports. (American statesmen, v. 3) E302.6.H5T92
E176.A54, v. 3

First published in 1887.

"List of printed documents cited in this book . . .": p. [424]–429.

Reprinted in New York by F. Ungar Pub. Co. (1966) and B. Franklin (1970).

WILLISON, GEORGE F. Patrick Henry and his world. Garden City, N.Y., Doubleday, 1969. xii, 498 p. port. E302.6.H5W67

Bibliographic footnotes.

WIRT, WILLIAM. Sketches of the life and character of Patrick Henry. 15th ed., corr. by the author. New York, Derby & Jackson, 1859. 468 p. port. E302.6.H5W789

First published in 1817. The 9th ed. (1836) has been reprinted in Freeport, N.Y., by Books for Libraries Press (1970).

13595

HENRY, WILLIAM (1729–1786)*

Pennsylvania. Gunsmith, inventor, assemblyman, delegate to the Continental Congress.

——— William Henry memoirs: 1748–1786. *In* Lancaster County (Pa.) Historical Society. Journal, v. 76, spring 1972: 58–68. port. F157.L2L5, v. 76

BECK, HERBERT H. William Henry, progenitor of the steamboat, riflemaker, patriot. *In* Lancaster County (Pa.) Historical Society. Papers, v. 54, no. 4, 1950: 65–88. illus., port. F157.L2L5, v. 54

The author's article, "William Henry, Patriot, Master Gunsmith, Progenitor of the Steamboat," appeared in the

Transactions of the Moravian Historical Society, v. 16, pt. 2 (Nazareth, Pa., 1955), p. 69–95.

JORDAN, FRANCIS. The life of William Henry, of Lancaster, Pennsylvania, 1729–1786, patriot, military officer, inventor of the steamboat; a contribution to Revolutionary history. Lancaster, Pa., Press of the New Era Print. Co., 1910. vii, 185 p. plates, ports.

E207.H55J8

JORDAN, JOHN W. William Henry. *In* Lancaster County (Pa.) Historical Society. Papers, v. 11, Nov. 1907: 303–327.

F157.L2L5, v. 11

Letters to William Henry, of Lancaster, Pennsylvania, 1777–1783. Pennsylvania magazine of history and biography, v. 22, Apr. 1898: 106–113.

F146.P65, v. 22

13596

HERVEY, *Hon.* WILLIAM (1732–1815)

England. Military officer, Member of Parliament.

——— Journals of the Hon. William Hervey, in North America and Europe, from 1755 to 1814. With memoir and notes. Bury St. Edmunds, Paul & Mathew, 1906. lxxvi, 548 p. illus., fold. map, plates, ports. (Suffolk green books, no. 14)

DA506.H5A2

"Introduction" signed: S. H. A. H. [i.e. Sydenham Henry Augustus Hervey]

13597

HESSELIUS, JOHN (1728–1778)*

Pennsylvania; Maryland. Portrait artist.

DOUD, RICHARD K. John Hesselius, Maryland limner. *In* Winterthur portfolio. v. 5. [Winterthur, Del., 1969] p. 129–153. ports.

N9.W52, v. 5

Includes a catalog of Maryland subjects painted by Hesselius.

13598

HEWES, JOSEPH (1730–1779)*

New Jersey; North Carolina. Merchant, shipowner, assemblyman, delegate to the Continental Congress.

JENKINS, CHARLES F. Joseph Hewes, the Quaker signer. *In* Children of light, in honor of Rufus M. Jones. Edited by Howard H. Brinton. New York, Macmillan Co., 1938. p. [211]–239.

BX7615.C53

——— The two Quaker signers [of the Declaration of Independence] *In* Friends' Historical Association. Bulletin, v. 18, spring 1929: 1–32.

BX7635.A1F6, v. 18

Although the sketch mentions Stephen Hopkins of Rhode Island, it is largely devoted to Hewes.

McCURRY, ALLAN J. Joseph Hewes and independence: a suggestion. North Carolina historical review, v. 40, autumn 1963: 455–464. port.

F251.N892, v. 40

SIKES, WALTER. Joseph Hewes. North Carolina booklet, v. 4, Sept. 1904: 25–36. port.

F251.N86, v. 4

13599

HEYNE, JOHANN CHRISTOPH (1715–1781)

Germany; Pennsylvania. Pewterer, Moravian preacher.

JONGE, ERIC DE. Johann Christoph Heyne, pewterer, minister, teacher. *In* Winterthur portfolio. v. 4. Winterthur, Del., 1968. p. 169–184. illus.

N9.W52, v. 4

13600

HICKS, ELIAS (1748–1830)*

New York. Farmer, Quaker minister.

——— Journal of the life and religious labours of Elias Hicks. Written by himself. New-York, I. T. Hopper, 1832. 451 p.

BX7795.H3A3 1832

Reprinted in New York by Arno Press (1969).

FORBUSH, BLISS. Elias Hicks—prophet of an era. *In* Friends' Historical Association. Bulletin, v. 38, spring 1949: 11–19.

BX7635.A1F6, v. 38

——— Elias Hicks, Quaker liberal. With a foreword by Frederick B. Tolles. New York, Columbia University Press, 1956. xxii, 355 p. illus., facsim., geneal. table, maps, ports.

BX7795.H5F6

Bibliographic references included in "Notes" (p. [297]–337).

WILBUR, HENRY W. The life and labors of Elias Hicks. Philadelphia, Friends' General Conference Advancement Committee, 1910. 242 p. facsims., plates, ports.

BX7795.H5W5

"Sources of information": p. 236–237.

13601

HIESTER, JOSEPH (1752–1832)*

Pennsylvania. Revolutionary officer, storeowner, assemblyman.

RICHARDS, HENRY M. M. Governor Joseph Hiester; a historical sketch. Part XVII. of a narrative and critical history prepared at the request of the Pennsylvania-German Society. *In* Pennsylvania-German Society. Proceedings and addresses. v. 16; 1905. [Lancaster, Pa.] 1907. 51 p. (3d group) port.

F146.P23, v. 16

VAUX, RICHARD. Sketch of the life of Joseph Hiester, governor of Pennsylvania. [Philadelphia, Printed by Allen, Lane & Scott, 1887?] 23 p.

F153.H63

13602

HIGGINSON, STEPHEN (1743–1828)*

Massachusetts. Merchant, Revolutionary privateer, assemblyman, delegate to the Continental Congress.

——— Letters of Stephen Higginson, 1783–1804. *In* American Historical Association. Annual report. 1896. v. 1. Washington, 1897. p. 704–841.

E172.A60, 1896, v. 1

Part of the report of the Historical Manuscript Commission, 1896.

————— The writings of Laco, as published in the *Massachusetts Centinel*, in the months of February and March, 1789—with the addition of no. VII, which was omitted. Printed at Boston, 1789. 39 p.

AC901.M5, v. 782 Rare Bk. Coll.

Also published under the title *Ten Chapters in the Life of John Hancock* (New York, 1857. 68 p. E302.6.H23H6).

HIGGINSON, THOMAS W. Life and times of Stephen Higginson, member of the Continental Congress (1783) and author of the "Laco" letters, relating to John Hancock (1789). Boston, Houghton, Mifflin, 1907. vii, 305 p. facsims., plates, ports.   F69.H63

13603

HILL, WILLIAM (1740 *or* 41–1816)*

South Carolina. Iron manufacturer, munitioner, Revolutionary officer.

————— Col. William Hill's memoirs of the Revolution. Edited by A. S. Salley, Jr. Columbia, S.C., Printed for the Historical Commission of South Carolina by the State Co., 1921. 36 p.   E263.S7H64

13604

HILLDRUP, THOMAS (1740–1795)

Connecticut. Watchmaker, postmaster.

KIHN, PHYLLIS. Thomas Hilldrup, 1740–1795. *In* Connecticut Historical Society, *Hartford*. Bulletin, v. 37, July 1972: 76–85. illus., map.   F91.C67, v. 37

13605

HILLEGAS, MICHAEL (1729–1804)*

Pennsylvania. Merchant, assemblyman, treasurer.

Michael Hillegas, the nation's first treasurer. Magazine of history, with notes and queries, v. 6, Oct. 1907: 221–224.   E171.M23, v. 6

MINNICH, MICHAEL R. A memoir of the first treasurer of the United States, with chronological data. Philadelphia, Published for the author and compiler, 1905. 87 p. col. plate, port.   [E302.6.H6M6] Micro 22654 E

————— Michael Hillegas. Pennsylvania-German, v. 2, Oct. 1901: 147–155. port.   F146.P224, v. 2

13606

HILLHOUSE, JAMES (1754–1832)*

Connecticut. Lawyer, Revolutionary officer, assemblyman.

BACON, LEONARD. Sketch of the life and public services of Hon. James Hillhouse of New Haven. New Haven, 1860. 46, [557]–572 p. port.   E302.6.H63B13

13607

HILTZHEIMER, JACOB (1729?–1798)

Germany; Pennsylvania. Farmer, Revolutionary soldier.

————— Extracts from the diary of Jacob Hiltzheimer, of Philadelphia. 1765–1798. Edited by his great-grandson, Jacob Cox Parsons. Philadelphia, Press of W. F. Fell, 1893, viii, 270 p.   F158.44.H65

Selections from the extracts were published in the *Pennsylvania Magazine of History and Biography*, v. 16, Apr.–July 1892, Jan. 1893, p. 93–102, 160–177, 412–422.

HENSEL, WILLIAM U. An old time worthy. *In* Lancaster County (Pa.) Historical Society. Papers, v. 11, Nov. 1907: 328–354.   F157.L2L5, v. 11

13608

HINDMAN, WILLIAM (1743–1822)*

Maryland. Lawyer, assemblyman, delegate to the Continental Congress.

HARRISON, SAMUEL A. A memoir of the Hon. William Hindman, Baltimore [Printed by J. Murphy] 1880. 59 p. (Maryland Historical Society. Fund-publication, no. 14)   F176.M37, no. 14

13609

HITCHCOCK, ENOS (1745–1803)*

Massachusetts; Rhode Island. Congregational clergyman, Revolutionary chaplain.

————— Diary of Enos Hitchcock, a chaplain in the Revolutionary Army [Apr. 8, 1777–Nov. 5, 1780] With a memoir. Edited by William B. Weeden. *In* Rhode Island Historical Society. Publications, v. 7, July 1899–Jan. 1900: 87–134, 147–194, 207–231. port.   F76.R51, v. 7

STAPLES, CARLTON A. A chaplain of the Revolution. Unitarian review, v. 35, Apr. 1891: 267–278.   BX8901.U7, v. 35

————— ————— [Boston, Office of the Unitarian Review, 1891] 12 p.   E207.H6S7

HOBART, JOHN

See BUCKINGHAMSHIRE, JOHN HOBART, *2d Earl of*

13610

HODGKINS, JOSEPH (1743–1829)

Massachusetts. Cobbler, Revolutionary officer.

WADE, HERBERT T., *and* ROBERT A. LIVELY. This glorious cause; the adventures of two company officers in Washington's army. Princeton, N.J., Princeton University Press, 1958. x, 254 p. illus., maps.

E275.W16

"The Hodgkins letters, May 7, 1775, to January 1, 1779": p. [165]–245.

Bibliographic footnotes.

Also treats Nathaniel Wade (1750–1826).

13611

HOLLAND, HENRY FOX, *Baron* (1705–1774)†

England. Member of Parliament, minister.

—— Letters to Henry Fox Lord Holland, with a few addressed to his brother Stephen, Earl of Ilchester, [1743–70] Edited by the Earl of Ilchester. London, Priv. print. for presentation to the members of the Roxburghe Club, 1915. xvi, 299 p.

PR1105.R7 1915a Rare Bk. Coll.

ILCHESTER, GILES STEPHEN HOLLAND FOX-STRANGWAYS, *6th Earl of.* Henry Fox, first Lord Holland, his family and relations. London, J. Murray, 1920. 2 v. plates, ports. DA483.H7I3

RIKER, THAD W. Henry Fox, first Lord Holland; a study of the career of an eighteenth century politician. Oxford, Clarendon Press, 1911. 2 v. DA483.H7R5

"Bibliography of the materials for a study of Henry Fox": v. 2, p. 382–386.

SUTHERLAND, LUCY S., *and* JOHN E. D. BINNEY. Henry Fox as Paymaster-General of the Forces. English historical review, v. 70, Apr. 1955: 229–256.

DA20.E58, v. 70

13612

HOLLAND, PARK (*b. ca.* 1752)

Massachusetts. Revolutionary soldier.

—— A Massachusetts soldier in the Revolution. Edited by H. G. Mitchell. New England magazine, new ser., v. 20, May 1899: 315–324. AP2.N4, n.s., v. 20

13613

HOLLAND, SAMUEL (1728–1801)

England; Canada. Surveyor, British officer in America.

—— Holland's description of Cape Breton Island and other documents. Compiled with an introduction by D. C. Harvey, archivist. Published by authority of the Board of Trustees of the Public Archives of Nova Scotia. Halifax, N.S., 1935. 168 p. (Nova Scotia. Public Archives. Publications of the Public Archives of Nova Scotia, no. 2) F1039.C2H6

CHIPMAN, WILLIS. The life and times of Major Samuel Holland, Surveyor-General, 1764–1801. *In* Ontario Historical Society. Papers and records. v. 21. Toronto, 1924. p. 11–90. plates. F1056.O58, v. 21

13614

HOLLAND, STEPHEN (*b. ca.* 1733)

Ireland; New Hampshire; England. Military officer, tavernkeeper, assemblyman, Loyalist.

SCOTT, KENNETH. Colonel Stephen Holland of Londonderry. Historical New Hampshire, Mar. 1947: 15–27. ports. F31.H57, 1947

13615

HOLLENBACK, MATTHIAS (1752–1829)

Pennsylvania. Trader, Revolutionary officer.

WELLES, EDWARD. Sketch of Col. Matthias Hollenback. Pennsylvania-German, v. 10, Feb.–Mar. 1909: 53–57, 97–103. illus., port. F146.P224, v. 10

13616

HOLLIS, THOMAS (1720–1774)†

England. Political writer, philanthropist.

—— A letter from Thomas Hollis [1766] *In* Cambridge Historical Society, *Cambridge, Mass.* Publications. v. 9. Proceedings. 1914. Cambridge, 1915. p. 38–46. F74.C1C469, v. 9

To Edmund Quincy, Jr., concerning the death of Jonathan Mayhew. Introduction and notes by Archibald M. Howe.

—— Thomas Hollis and Jonathan Mayhew: their correspondence, 1759–1766. Edited by Bernhard Knollenberg. *In* Massachusetts Historical Society, *Boston.* Proceedings. v. 69; 1947/50. Boston, 1956. p. 102–193. F61.M38, v. 69

[BLACKBURNE, FRANCIS] Memoirs of Thomas Hollis. London, 1780. 2 v. illus., coat of arms, plates, ports. CT788.H74B6

[Vol. 2] has title: *Appendix to the Memoirs of Thomas Hollis.*

ROBBINS, CAROLINE. Library of liberty—assembled for Harvard College by Thomas Hollis of Lincoln's Inn. Harvard Library bulletin, v. 5, winter-spring 1951: 5–23, 181–196. Z881.H3403, v. 5

—— The strenuous Whig: Thomas Hollis of Lincoln's Inn. William and Mary quarterly, 3d ser., v. 7, July 1950: 406–453. F221.W71, 3d s., v. 7

SOMMER, FRANK H. Thomas Hollis and the arts of dissent. *In* Winterthur Conference on Museum Operation and Connoisseurship, *16th, 1970.* Prints in and of America to 1850. Edited by John D. Morse. Charlottesville, University Press of Virginia [1970] p. [111]–159. NE505.W55 1970

13617

HOLLISTER, ISAAC (*b.* 1750?)

—— A brief narration of the captivity of Isaac Hollister, who was taken by the Indians, anno Domini, 1763. Written by himself. Printed and Sold at the Printing-Office in New-London [Conn., 1767?] 8 p. E87.H74 Rare Bk. Coll.

13618

HOLLISTER, JOSIAH (1754–1832)

Connecticut; New York. Revolutionary soldier, farmer.

——— The journal of Josiah Hollister, a soldier of the American Revolution and a prisoner of war in Canada. Copied from the original and published by Romanzo Norton Bunn, historian of the Illinois Society of the Sons of the Revolution. [Chicago? ᶜ1928] 43 p. facsims.
E275.H74

13619

HOLLYDAY, JAMES (1722–1786)

Maryland. Lawyer, assemblyman.

HOLLYDAY, GEORGE T. Biographical memoir of James Hollyday. Pennsylvania magazine of history and biography, v. 7, Dec. 1883: 426–447. F146.P65, v. 7

13620

HOLMAN, JONATHAN (1732–1814)

Massachusetts. Revolutionary officer.

CRANE, JOHN C. Jonathan Holman, a Revolutionary colonel. In Worcester Historical Society, *Worcester, Mass.* Collections. v. 13. Proceedings. no. 41; 1893. Worcester, 1894. p. 487–501. port. F74.W9W85, v. 13

——— ——— Offprint. Worcester, Mass., Press of F. P. Rice 1894. E263.M4C8

A pay abstract in Holman's handwriting, dated January 20, 1777, appears in v. 14 of the *Collections* (Proceedings, no. 45; 1894. Worcester, 1895), p. 179–180.

13621

HOLT, JOHN (1721–1784)*

Virginia; New York. Printer, journalist.

MURPHY, LAYTON B. John Holt, patriot, printer and publisher. 1965. ([449] p.)
Micro AC–1, no. 65–11,004

Thesis (Ph.D.)—University of Michigan.
Abstracted in *Dissertation Abstracts*, v. 26, Nov. 1965, p. 2766.

PALTSITS, VICTOR H. John Holt, printer and postmaster; some facts and documents relating to his career. In New York (City). Public Library. Bulletin, v. 24, Sept. 1920: 483–499. Z881.N6B, v. 24

——— ——— Offprint. New York, Public Library, 1920. 19 p. Z232.H75P

VAIL, ROBERT W. G. A patriotic pair of peripatetic printers: the up-state imprints of John Holt and Samuel Loudon, 1776–1783. In Essays honoring Lawrence C. Wroth. Portland, Me., 1951. p. 391–422.
Z1009.Z3W7

Lists and locates copies of about a hundred items.

13622

HOLTEN, SAMUEL (1738–1816)*

Massachusetts. Physician, assemblyman, delegate to the Continental Congress.

——— Journal of Samuel Holten, M.D., while in the Continental Congress, May, 1778, to August, 1780. In Essex Institute, *Salem, Mass.* Historical collections, v. 55, July–Oct. 1919: 161–176, 249–256; v. 56, Jan.–Apr. 1920: 24–32, 88–97. F72.E7E81, v. 55–56

Also published in the *Historical Collections* of the Danvers Historical Society, v. 7 (Danvers, Mass., 1919), p. 59–67, and v. 8 (Danvers, Mass., 1920), p. 97–130.

——— Samuel Holten correspondence [1780–94] In Danvers Historical Society, *Danvers, Mass.* Historical collections. v. 20. Danvers, 1932. p. 43–57.
F74.D2D42, v. 20

Additional Holten correspondence from the 1780's appears in v. 24 (Danvers, 1936), p. 63–64; v. 26 (Danvers, 1938), p. 92–94; and v. 30 (Danvers, 1942), p. 30–31.

TAPLEY, HARRIET S. Some personal characteristics of Doctor Samuel Holten, as revealed by his letters and journals and the testimony of contemporaries. In Danvers Historical Society, *Danvers, Mass.* Historical collections. v. 10. Danvers, 1922. p. 49–68. facsim., port. F74.D2D42, v. 10

13623

HOLYOKE, MARY VIAL (1737–1802)

Massachusetts.

——— Diary of Mrs. Mary (Vial) Holyoke, 1760–1800. In Dow, George F., *ed.* The Holyoke diaries, 1709–1856. Salem, Mass., Essex Institute, 1911. p. 47–138. plates, ports. F74.S1D7

13624

HONEYMAN, JOHN (*fl.* 1775–1779)

New Jersey. Weaver, spy.

FALKNER, LEONARD. A spy for Washington. American heritage, v. 8, Aug. 1957: 58–64. illus. (part col.)
E171.A43, v. 8

HONYMAN, ROBERT W. John Honeyman—fact or fancy? In Historical Society of Montgomery County (*Pennsylvania*). Bulletin, v. 15, spring 1967: 5–21.
F157.M7H45, v. 15

O'DEA, ANNA, *and* SAMUEL A. PLEASANTS. The case of John Honeyman: mute evidence. In New Jersey Historical Society. Proceedings, v. 84, July 1966: 174–181.
F131.N58, v. 84

13625

HONYMAN, ROBERT (1747–1824)

Scotland; Virginia. Physician.

——— Colonial panorama, 1775; Dr. Robert Honyman's journal for March and April. Edited by Philip Padelford. San Marino, Calif., Huntington Library, 1939. xiii, 86 p. 2 fold. maps (in pocket)   E163.H76

Reprinted in Freeport, N.Y., by Books for Libraries Press (1971).

Record of a journey from Virginia to Rhode Island and back.

13626

HOOD, SAMUEL HOOD, *Viscount* (1724–1816)†

England. British admiral in America.

—— Extracts from the papers of Samuel, first Viscount Hood. *In* The Naval miscellany. v. 1. [London] Printed for the Navy Records Society, 1902. (Publications of the Navy Records Society, v. 20) p. [221]–258.
DA70.A1, v. 20

—— Letters from Sir Samuel Hood, 1780–1782. Mariner's mirror, v. 19, Jan 1933: 75–87.   VK1.M4, v. 19

Introduction and notes by J. H. Owen.

—— Letters written by Sir Samuel Hood (Viscount Hood) in 1781–2–3, illustrated by extracts from logs and public records. Edited by David Hannay. [London] Printed for the Navy Records Society, 1895, xlvii, 170 p. port. (Publications of the Navy Records Society, v. 3)   DA70.A1, v. 3

BAUGH, DANIEL A.   Sir Samuel Hood: superior subordinate. *In* Billias, George A., ed. George Washington's opponents: British generals and admirals in the American Revolution. New York, Morrow, 1969. p. 291–326. port.   E267.B56

Bibliography: p. 325–326.

HOOD, *Hon.* DOROTHY.   The Admirals Hood. London, Hutchinson [1942] 255 p. col. front., plates, ports.
DA87.1.A1H6

13627

HOOD, ZACHARIAH (*fl.* 1765–1784)

Maryland; England. Merchant, Loyalist.

LAND, AUBREY C.   The subsequent career of Zachariah Hood. Maryland historical magazine, v. 51, Sept. 1956: 237–242.   F176.M18, v. 51

13628

HOOKER, ZIBEON (1752–1840)

Massachusetts. Drummer, Revolutionary officer.

WISWALL, CLARENCE A., *comp.*   An account of the life and military services of Zibeon Hooker, a lieutenant in the army of Washington. [Reading, Mass.?] 1918. 35 p. facsim., plates, ports.   E275.H78

13629

HOOPER, ROBERT LETTIS (1730?–1797)

New Jersey; Pennsylvania. Deputy Quartermaster General, provisioner.

HART, CHARLES H.   Colonel Robert Lettis Hooper, deputy quartermaster general in the Continental Army and vice president of New Jersey. Pennsylvania magazine of history and biography, v. 36, Jan. 1912: 60–91.
F146.P65, v. 36

—— —— Offprint. Philadelphia, 1912. 32 p.
E207.H68H3

13630

HOOPER, WILLIAM (1742–1790)*

Massachusetts; North Carolina. Lawyer, assemblyman, delegate to the Continental Congress.

—— Unpublished letters [1777] by William Hooper. Historical magazine, 2d ser., v. 4, Aug. 1868: 87–90.
E171.H64, 2d s., v. 4

ALDERMAN, EDWIN A.   Address by Edwin A. Alderman . . . on the life of William Hooper, "the prophet of American independence." Chapel Hill, N.C., University Press [1894] 73 p. illus., port.   E302.6.H7A3

13631

HOPKINS, ESEK (1718–1802)*

Rhode Island. Seaman, Revolutionary naval commander.

—— The correspondence of Esek Hopkins, Commander-in-Chief of the United States Navy; transcribed from the original manuscripts in the library of the Rhode Island Historical Society. Edited and annotated by Alverda S. Beck, A.M., and with an introduction by William Davis Miller. Providence, Printed for the Rhode Island Historical Society, 1933. 101 p. facsim.
E271.H662

A companion volume to the *Letter Book of Esek Hopkins.*

—— The letter book of Esek Hopkins, Commander-in-Chief of the United States Navy, 1775–1777. Transcribed from the original letter book in the library of the Rhode Island Historical Society, with an introduction and notes by Alverda S. Beck, A.M. Providence, Printed for the Rhode Island Historical Society, 1932. 151 p. port.   E271.H66

Thesis (M.A.)—Brown University.

COYLE, JOHN G.   The suspension of Esek Hopkins, commander of the Revolutionary navy. *In* American Irish Historical Society. Journal. v. 21; 1922. New York. p. 193–235.   E184.I6A5, v. 21

Documents on Hopkins' suspension from command and his censure by the Continental Congress in 1777.

FIELD, EDWARD.   Esek Hopkins, commander-in-chief of the Continental Navy during the American Revolution, 1775 to 1778, master mariner, politician, brigadier general, naval officer and philanthropist. Providence, Preston & Rounds Co., 1898. ix 280 p. illus., facsim., maps, plates, ports.   E207.H7F4

GRIEVE, ROBERT. Esek Hopkins, first admiral of the American navy. New England magazine, new ser., v. 17, Nov. 1897: 346–362. illus., ports.

AP2.N4, n.s., v. 17

MILLER, CHARLES H. Admiral number one, some incidents in the life of Esek Hopkins, 1718–1802, first admiral of the Continental Navy. New York, William-Frederick Press, 1962. 74 p. illus., plates, ports.

E207.H7M5

PREBLE, GEORGE H. Esek Hopkins, the first "Commander-in-Chief" of the American navy, 1775. United service, v. 12, Feb.–Mar. 1885: 137–146, 300–317. port.

U1.U4, v. 12

13632
HOPKINS, RICHARD (1762–1832)
Maryland. Physician.

A Maryland medical student and his friends. Maryland historical magazine, v. 23, Sept. 1928: 279–292; v. 24, Mar. 1929: 23–30.　　F176.M18, v. 23–24

Correspondence (1783–87) "from the remains of the letter book of Dr. Richard Hopkins," son of Johns Hopkins, Sr.

13633
HOPKINS, SAMUEL (1721–1803)*
Connecticut; Rhode Island. Congregational clergyman, theologian.

——— Sketches of the life of the late, Rev. Samuel Hopkins, D.D., pastor of the First Congregational Church in Newport, written by himself; interspersed with marginal notes extracted from his private diary . . . With an introduction to the whole, by the editor. Published by Stephen West, D.D., pastor of the church in Stockbridge. Published according to act of Congress. Hartford, Printed by Hudson and Goodwin, 1805. 240 p. port.　　BX7260.H6A3

ELSBREE, OLIVER W. Samuel Hopkins and his doctrine of benevolence. New England quarterly, v. 8, Dec. 1935: 534–550.　　F1.N62, v. 8

KNAPP, HUGH H. Samuel Hopkins and the New Divinity. 1971. ([294] p.)　　Micro AC-1, no. 71-28,344
Thesis (Ph.D.)—University of Wisconsin.
Abstracted in Dissertation Abstracts International, v. 32A, Dec. 1971, p. 3211.

LOVEJOY, DAVID S. Samuel Hopkins: religion, slavery, and the Revolution. New England quarterly, v. 40, June 1967: 227–243.　　F1.N62, v. 40

SCHULTZ, STANLEY K. The making of a reformer: the Reverend Samuel Hopkins as an eighteenth-century abolitionist. In American Philosophical Society, Philadelphia. Proceedings, v. 115, Oct. 1971: 350–365.

Q11.P5, v. 115

SILCOX, CLARIS E. Rev. Dr. Samuel Hopkins. In Newport Historical Society. Early religious leaders of Newport. Newport, R.I., 1918. p. [51]–76.

BR560.N37A5

SWIFT, DAVID E. Samuel Hopkins: Calvinist social concern in eighteenth century New England. Journal of Presbyterian history, v. 47, Mar. 1969: 31–54.

BX8905.P7A4, v. 47

VAN HALSEMA, DICK L. Samuel Hopkins (1721–1803), New England Calvinist. 1956.
Thesis (Ph.D.)—Union Theological Seminary.

13634
HOPKINS, STEPHEN (1707–1785)*
Rhode Island. Assemblyman, judge, governor, delegate to the Continental Congress.

FOSTER, WILLIAM E. Stephen Hopkins, a Rhode Island statesman. A study in the political history of the eighteenth century. Providence, S. S. Rider, 1884. 2 v. facsim., geneal. table. (Rhode Island historical tracts, 1st ser., no. 19)　　F76.R52

E302.6.H78F7

13635
HOPKINSON, FRANCIS (1737–1791)*
Pennsylvania; New Jersey. Lawyer, poet, composer, councilor, delegate to the Continental Congress, judge.

——— The miscellaneous essays and occasional writings of Francis Hopkinson, Esq. Philadelphia, Printed by T. Dodson, at the Stone-House, n° 41, Second Street, 1792. 3 v. fold. plates.　　PS775.A1 1792

Contents: v. 1. Miscellaneous essays.—v. 2. Orations, written for, and at the request of young gentlemen of the university, and delivered by them at public commencements in the college hall. Essays.—v. 3. Judgements in the Admiralty of Pennsylvania. Poems.

——— The old farm and the new farm: a political allegory. With an introduction and historical notes, by Benson J. Lossing. 2d ed. New York, A. D. F. Randolph, 1864. 76 p. illus.　　E296.H79

Originally published under the title A Pretty Story; Written in the Year of Our Lord 1774, by Peter Grievous, Esq. (Philadelphia, Printed and sold by J. Dunlap, 1774).

HASTINGS, GEORGE E. Francis Hopkinson and the American flag. Americana, v. 33, July 1939: 293–309. facsims.　　E171.A53, v. 33

——— Francis Hopkinson and the Anti-Federalists. American literature, v. 1, Jan. 1930: 405–418.

PS1.A6, v. 1

——— The life and works of Francis Hopkinson. Chicago, Ill., University of Chicago Press [ᶜ1926] xi, 516 p. facsims., ports., plates.　　PS776.H3

"A revision of a doctoral thesis written at Harvard University in 1917–18."—Preface.
Bibliography: p. 481–496.
Reprinted in New York by Russell & Russell (1968).

HILDEBURN, CHARLES S. R. Francis Hopkinson. Pennsylvania magazine of history and biography, v. 2, no. 3, 1878: 314–324. F146.P65, v. 2

LEARY, LEWIS G. Francis Hopkinson, Jonathan Odell, and "The Temple of Cloacina": 1782. American literature, v. 15, May 1943: 183–191. PS1.A6, v. 15

MARBLE, ANNIE R. Francis Hopkinson: man of affairs and letters. New England magazine, new ser., v. 27, Nov. 1902: 289–302. illus., facsim., port. AP2.N4, n.s., v. 27

SONNECK, OSCAR G. T. The first American composer: Hopkinson or Lyon? Musical America, v. 37, Feb. 1923: 9, 40. facsim. ML1.M384, v. 37

———— ———— Detached copy. ML410.H81S58

———— Francis Hopkinson, the first American poet-composer (1737–1791), and James Lyon, patriot, preacher, psalmodist (1735–1794); two studies in early American music. Washington, D.C., Printed for the author by H. L. McQueen, 1905. ix, 213 p. illus., facsims., port. ML410.H81

The essay on Francis Hopkinson was published in part in *Sammel-bände der Internationalen Musikgesellschaft*, 1903/4.
The appendix (p. 199–209) consists of music composed by Hopkinson and Lyon.
Reprinted in New York, with a new introduction by Richard A. Crawford, by Da Capo Press (1967. ML410.H81S62 1905a).

WECTER, DIXON. Francis Hopkinson and Benjamin Franklin. American literature, v. 12, May 1940: 200–217. PS1.A6, v. 12

Includes four letters from Hopkinson to Franklin and a Hopkinson satire not previously published in full.

WILKINSON, NORMAN B. Francis Hopkinson: humor propagandist of the American Revolution. Historian, v. 4, autumn 1941: 5–33. D1.H22, v. 4

13636

HORSMANDEN, DANIEL (1694–1778)*
England; New York. Lawyer, councilor, judge.

McMANUS, MARY P., *Sister*. Daniel Horsmanden, eighteenth century New Yorker. 1960.
Thesis (Ph.D.)—Fordham University.

13637

HOUDETOT, ÉLISABETH FRANÇOIS SOPHIE (DE LA LIVE DE BELLEGARDE) *comtesse* D' (1730–1813)

CHINARD, GILBERT. Les amitiés américaines de Madame d'Houdetot, d'après sa correspondance inédite avec

Benjamin Franklin et Thomas Jefferson. Paris.É. Champion, 1924. viii, 62 p. (Bibliothèque de la Revue de littérature comparée, t. 8) E249.3.C53

13638

HOUSTON, JOHN (1723–1798)
New Hampshire. Presbyterian clergyman, Loyalist.

SCOTT, KENNETH. John Houston, Tory minister of Bedford. *In* Presbyterian Historical Society. Journal, v. 22, Dec. 1944: 172–197. BX8905.P7A4, v. 22

13639

HOUSTON, WILLIAM CHURCHILL (1746–1788)*
New Jersey. Professor, Revolutionary officer, assemblyman, delegate to the Continental Congress, lawyer, delegate to the Constitutional Convention.

GLENN, THOMAS A. William Churchill Houston, 1746–1788. Norristown, Pa., Priv. print., 1903. 96 p. facsim. F138.H84

13640

HOW, DAVID (1758–1842)
Massachusetts. Revolutionary soldier.

———— Diary of David How, a private in Colonel Paul Dudley Sargent's Regiment of the Massachusetts Line, in the army of the American Revolution. From the original manuscript. With a biographical sketch of the author by George Wingate Chase, and illustrative notes by Henry B. Dawson. Morrisania, N.Y. [Cambridge, Mass., Printed by H. O. Houghton] 1865. xv, 51 p. (Gleanings from the harvest field of American history, by Henry B. Dawson, pt. 4) E275.H83

13641

HOWARD, JOHN EAGER (1752–1827)*
Maryland. Revolutionary officer, delegate to the Continental Congress, landowner, governor.

HOWARD, CARY. John Eager Howard, patriot and public servant. Maryland historical magazine, v. 62, Sept. 1967: 300–317. F176.M18, v. 62

READ, ELIZABETH. John Eager Howard, Colonel of Second Maryland Regiment—Continental Line. Magazine of American history, with notes and queries, v. 7, Oct. 1881: 276–282. E171.M18, v. 7

13642

HOWARD, MARTIN (*ca.* 1730–1781)
Rhode Island; North Carolina. Lawyer, councilor, judge, Loyalist.

EDES, HENRY H. Chief-Justice Martin Howard. *In* Colonial Society of Massachusetts, *Boston*. Publications. v. 6. Transactions, 1899/1900. Boston, 1904. p. 384–402. port. F61.C71, v. 6

13643

HOWE, BEZALEEL (1750–1825)

Massachusetts; New Hampshire. Revolutionary officer.

HOWE, HERBERT B.   Major Bezaleel Howe, 1750–1825, an officer in the Continental and in the regular armies; a biography and genealogy. [n.p.] 1950. 66 p. illus., ports.   E275.H84H6

Bibliography: p. 58–60.

13644

HOWE, RICHARD HOWE, *Earl* (1726–1799)†

England. British admiral in America.

BARROW, SIR JOHN, BART.   The life of Richard, Earl Howe, K. G., admiral of the fleet, and general of marines. London, J. Murray, 1838. xvi, 432 p. fold. facsims., port.   DA87.1.H8B2

GRUBER, IRA D.   Richard Lord Howe: admiral as peace-maker. *In* Billias, George A., *ed.* George Washington's opponents: British generals and admirals in the American Revolution. New York, Morrow, 1969. p. 233–259. port.   E267.B56

Bibliography: p. 258–259.

MAHAN, ALFRED T.   Admiral Earl Howe. Atlantic monthly, v. 73, Jan. 1894: 20–37.   AP2.A8, v. 73

13645

HOWE, ROBERT (1732–1785 *or* 6)*

North Carolina. Planter, judge, assemblyman, Revolutionary general.

BELLAMY, JOHN D.   General Robert Howe. North Carolina booklet, v. 7, Jan. 1908: 165–192.   F251.N86, v. 7

HEATHCOTE, CHARLES W.   General Robert Howe—a very capable military officer and dedicated to the leadership of Washington. Picket post, no. 81, July 1963: 10–14, 20 port.   E234.P5, no. 81

13646

HOWE, WILLIAM HOWE, *5th Viscount* (1729–1814)†

England. British general in America.

ADAMS, CHARLES F., comp.   Contemporary opinion on the Howes. *In* Massachusetts Historical Society, *Boston.* Proceedings. v. 44; 1910/11. Boston, 1911. p. 94–120.   F61.M38, v. 44

Extracts from pamphlets.

CULLEN, JOSEPH P.   General William Howe. American history illustrated, v. 7, Dec. 1972: 24–32. illus., facsims., ports.   E171.A574, v. 7

FLEMING, THOMAS J.   The enigma of General Howe. American heritage, v. 15, Feb. 1964: 6–11, 96–103. illus. (part col.), col. port.   E171.A43, v. 15

HARGREAVES, REGINALD.   "Good-natured Billy." Army quarterly and defense journal, v. 93, Jan. 1967: 177–190.   U1.A85, v. 93

JONES, MALDWYN A.   Sir William Howe: conventional strategist. *In* Billias, George A., *ed.* George Washington's opponents: British generals and admirals in the American Revolution. New York, Morrow, 1969. p. 39–72. port.   E267.B56

Bibliography: p. 71–72.

13647

HOWLAND, JOHN (1757–1854)

Rhode Island. Revolutionary soldier, historian.

STONE, EDWIN M.   The life and recollections of John Howland, late president of the Rhode Island Historical Society. Providence, G. H. Whitney, 1857. 348 p. facsim., plates, port.   [F83.H865] Micro 18706 F

13648

HOYT, SAMUEL (1744–1826)

Connecticut. Ship captain, Revolutionary soldier.

——— Adventures of an early American sea-captain. Connecticut magazine, v. 10, Oct./Dec. 1906: 631–646.   F91.C8, v. 10

Hoyt's seafaring experiences were related in a journal which he began as a cabin boy in 1762. A second installment, entitled "Experiences of a Sea Captain the First Days of the American Republic [1765–1800]," appeared in v. 11, summer 1907, p. 275–284. Contributed by Julius W. Pease.

13649

HUBBELL, ISAAC (1755–1842)

Connecticut; New York. Frontiersman, Revolutionary soldier.

PRIEST, JOSIAH.   The Fort Stanwix captive, or New England volunteer, being the extraordinary life and adventures of Isaac Hubbell among the Indians of Canada and the West, in the War of the Revolution, and the story of his marriage with the Indian princess. Albany, Printed by J. Munsell, 1841. 64 columns. illus.   E275.H87

13650

HUBLEY, ADAM (*ca.* 1744–1793)

Pennsylvania. Revolutionary officer.

——— Adm Hubley, Jr., Lt. Colo. Comdt 11th Penna Regt, his journal, commencing at Wyoming, July 30th, 1779. Pennsylvania magazine of history and biography, v. 33, Apr.–Oct. 1909: 129–146, 279–302, 409–422. maps, ports.   F146.P65, v. 33

Introduction by John W. Jordan.

13651

HUGHES, HUGH (*d.* 1804)

New York. Revolutionary officer.

—— The memorial and documents in the case of Colonel Hugh Hughes, deputy quarter master general, during the War for American Independence. Respectfully submitted to Congress, by the memorialist. Washington City, January 1802. 44 p.   E255.H89 Rare Bk. Coll.

13652

HUGHES, THOMAS (1759 *or* 60–1790)

England. British officer in America.

—— A journal by Thos. Hughes for his amusement, & designed only for his perusal by the time he attains the age of 50 if he lives so long. (1778–1789) With an introduction by E. A. Benians. Cambridge [Eng.] University Press, 1947. xiv, 187 p. facsim., fold. map.

E267.H9

Printed from the original manuscript in the possession of the author's family and edited by R. W. David.

Reprinted in Port Washington, N.Y., by Kennikat Press (1970).

A portion of the journal was published under the title "Journal of Ensign Thomas Hughes, Prisoner of War at Lancaster, May 1779 to November 1780" in the Lancaster County Historical Society's *Papers*, v. 58, no. 1, 1954, p. 1–25.

13653

HULBERT, JOHN (*fl.* 1775–1807)

New York. Revolutionary officer.

PENNYPACKER, MORTON.   Capt. John Hulbert and his flag. *In* New York State Historical Association. New York history, v. 14, Oct. 1933: 356–369.

F116.N865, v. 14

13654

HULL, WILLIAM (1753–1825)*

Connecticut; Massachusetts. Lawyer, Revolutionary officer.

CAMPBELL, MARIA H.   Revolutionary services and civil life of General William Hull; prepared from his manuscripts, by his daughter. New York, D. Appleton, 1848. 482 p.   E353.1.H9C18
E356.D4C2

CLARK, SAMUEL C.   William Hull. New-England historical and genealogical register, v. 47, Apr.–July 1893: 141–153, 305–314. port.   F1.N56, v. 47

13655

HULTON, ANN (*d.* 1779)

Massachusetts. Loyalist.

—— An eighteenth-century lady and her impressions [1763–68] Gentleman's magazine, v. 297, Aug. 1904: 195–202.   AP4.G3, v. 297

Introduction and notes by E. Rhys Jones.

—— Letters of a Loyalist lady, being the letters of Ann Hulton, sister of Henry Hulton, Commissioner of Customs at Boston, 1767–1776. Cambridge, Harvard University Press, 1927. xi, 106 p. facsim., plates.

E277.H91

Reprinted in New York by the New York Times (1971).

13656

HULTON, HENRY (1732–1791)

Massachusetts; England. British customs officer.

—— An Englishman views the American Revolution: the letters of Henry Hulton, 1769–1776. Huntington Library quarterly, v. 36, Nov. 1972–Feb. 1973: 1–26, 139–151. facsims.   Z733.S24Q, v. 36

Introduction and notes by Wallace Brown.

13657

HUME, DAVID (1711–1776)†

Scotland; England. Historian, philosopher.

—— David Hume: philosophical historian. Edited, with introductory essays, by David Fate Norton and Richard H. Popkin. [Indianapolis] Bobbs-Merrill [ᶜ1965] lvii, 438 p. (The Library of liberal arts, 215)

D13.H85

Bibliography: p. li–lv.

—— Essays and treatises on several subjects. A new ed. Edinburgh, Printed for Bell & Bradfute, 1817. 2 v.

B1455.A5 1817

Contents: v. 1. Essays, moral, political, and literary.— v. 2. An inquiry concerning human understanding. A dissertation on the passions. An inquiry concerning the principles of morals. The natural history of religion.

—— Essays moral, political, and literary. Edited, with preliminary dissertation and notes, by T. H. Green and T. H. Grose. London, Longmans, Green, 1875. 2 v. (The philosophical works of David Hume, v. 3–4)

B1475 1875

Autobiography of author, dated April 18, 1776: v. 1, p. [1]–8.

"History of the editions": v. 1, p. [15]–84. "List of editions": v. 1, p. 85–86.

—— The history of England. London, Printed for A. Millar, 1754–62. 6 v.   DA30.H9 1754

Vol. 5 printed by Hamilton, Balfour, and Neill, Edinburgh.

Contents: v. 1–2. The history of England from the invasion of Julius Caesar to the accession of Henry VII. 1762.—v. [3–4] The history of England under the house of Tudor. 1759. v. 1–2.—v. [5–6] The history of Great Britain: v. 1. Containing the reigns of James I and Charles I. 1754. v. 2. Containing the commonwealth, and the reigns of Charles II and James II. 1757.

—— The letters of David Hume. Edited by J. Y. T. Greig. Oxford, Clarendon Press, 1932. 2 v. fold. facsims., ports.   B1497.A25

"Previous incomplete editions of Hume's letters": v. 1, p. xxvii–xxxi. "Principal sources": v. 1, p. xxxi.

See also the *New Letters of David Hume* (Oxford, Clarendon Press, 1954. 253 p. B1497.A4 1954), edited by Raymond Klibansky and Ernest C. Mossner, which includes 98 letters in the Greig edition and 29 that are not.

——— Letters of David Hume to William Strahan; now first edited with notes, index, etc., by G. Birkbeck Hill. Oxford, Clarendon Press, 1888. xlvi, 386 p. fold. facsim.   B1497.A32

——— The life of David Hume, Esq., the philosopher and historian, written by himself. To which are added, the Travels of a philosopher, containing observations on the manners and arts of various nations, in Africa and Asia. From the French of M. Le Poivre. Philadelphia, Printed and sold by R. Bell, 1778. 62 p.
B1497.A2 Rare Bk. Coll.

——— The philosophical works of David Hume. Edinburgh, Printed for A. Black and W. Tait, 1826. 4 v.
B1453.A2 1826

——— Private correspondence of David Hume with several distinguished persons, between the years 1761 and 1776. Now first published from the originals. London, H. Colburn, 1820. xix, 285 p.   B1497.A3

ABBOTT, WILBUR C. David Hume, philosopher-historian. *In his* Adventures in reputation; with an essay on some "new" history and historians. Cambridge, Mass., Harvard University Press, 1935. p. [118]–146. plate, port.   DA28.4.A28

BRALY, EARL B. The reputation of David Hume in America. 1956. (viii, 322 l.)   Micro AC–1, no. 15,665
Thesis (Ph.D.)—University of Texas.
Abstracted in *Dissertation Abstracts*, v. 16, Aug. 1956, p. 333–334.

BURTON, JOHN H. Life and correspondence of David Hume. Edinburgh, W. Tait, 1846. 2 v. fold. facsims., ports.   B1497.B8
Reprinted in Aalen by Scientia-Verlag (1969).

GREENE, MARJORIE. Hume; sceptic and Tory? Journal of the history of ideas, v. 4, June 1943: 333–348.
B1.J75, v. 4

HALL, ROLAND. A Hume bibliography, from 1930. York, 1971. 80 p.   Z8427.3.H35

HENDEL, CHARLES W. Studies in the philosophy of David Hume. Indianapolis, Bobbs-Merrill [1963] li, 516 p. (The Library of liberal arts)   B1498.H4 1963
Bibliographic footnotes.

JESSOP, THOMAS E. A bibliography of David Hume and of Scottish philosophy from Francis Hutcheson to Lord Balfour. London, A. Brown, 1938. xiv, 201 p.
Z8427.3.J58
Reprinted in New York by Russell & Russell (1966).

KILCUP, RODNEY W. Hume and Burke: theories of ethics, politics, and history. 1969.
Thesis (Ph.D.)—Harvard University.

MOSSNER, ERNEST C. The life of David Hume. Austin, University of Texas Press, 1954. xx, 683 p. illus., facsims., ports. (part col.)   B1497.M65 1954
Bibliography: p. 625–640.
Reprinted in Oxford by the Clarendon Press (1970).

——— Was Hume a Tory historian? Facts and reconsiderations. Journal of the history of ideas, v. 2, Apr. 1941: 225–236.   B1.J75, v. 2

SABINE, GEORGE H. Hume's contribution to the historical method. Philosophical review, v. 15, Jan. 1906: 17–38.   B1.P5, v. 15

SMITH, NORMAN K. The philosophy of David Hume; a critical study of its origins and central doctrines. London, Macmillan, 1941, xxiv, 568 p.   B1498.S5
Bibliographic footnotes.

STEWART, JOHN B. The moral and political philosophy of David Hume. New York, Columbia University Press, 1963. viii, 422 p.   B1498.S8
Bibliographic references included in "Notes" (p. [341]–404). "Hume's principal works: editions published during his lifetime": p. [405]–408.

WERNER, JOHN M. David Hume and America. Journal of the history of ideas, v. 33, July/Sept. 1972: 439–456.
B1.J75, v. 33

13658

HUMPHREYS, DAVID (1752–1818)*
Connecticut. Poet, Revolutionary officer, assemblyman, diplomat.

——— An essay on the life of the Honorable Major-General Israel Putnam: addressed to the state Society of the Cincinnati in Connecticut. Hartford, Printed by Hudson and Goodwin, 1788. 187 p.
E207.P9H9 Rare Bk. Coll.

See also John Fellows' *The Veil Removed; or, Reflections on David Humphrey's Essay on the Life of Israel Putnam; Also, Notices of Oliver W. B. Peabody's Life of the Same, S. Swett's Sketch of Bunker Hill Battle, etc., etc.* (New York, J. D. Lockwood, 1843. 231 p. E207.P9H99).

——— The miscellaneous works of David Humphreys, late minister plenipotentiary . . . to the court of Madrid. New York, Printed by T. and J. Swords, no. 160 Pearl-Street, 1804. xv, 394, [14] p. port. plates.
PS778.H5 1804 Rare Bk. Coll.

Contents: Poems.—Remarks on the war between the United States and Tripoli.—Thoughts on the necessity of maintaining a navy.—Poems.—Life of Putnam.—Political situation of the United States in 1789.—Dissertation on the merino breed of sheep.—Considerations on the means of improving the public defense.—Proceedings for securing the funds of the Cincinnati, in the state of Connecticut.—

Appendix: Letter 1–5. From General Washington to Colonel Humphreys. French tribute to the memory of General Washington. American tribute of respect to Colonel Humphreys.—Subscribers' names.

Reprinted, with an introduction by William K. Bottorff, in Gainesville, Fla., by Scholars' Facsimiles & Reprints (1968).

First published in 1790.

CLANCY, JOHN J. David Humphreys: a forgotten American. 1970. ([330] p.)   Micro AC–1, no. 70–25,598

Thesis (Ph.D.)—St. John's University.

Abstracted in *Dissertation Abstracts International,* v. 31A, Feb. 1971, p. 4066.

HUMPHREYS, FRANCIS L. Life and times of David Humphreys, soldier—statesman—poet, "belov'd of Washington." New York, G. P. Putnam's Sons, 1917. 2 v. facsims., map, plates, port.   E302.6.H89H9

"Bibliography of the works of David Humphreys": v. 2, p. 459–469.

Reprinted in St. Clair Shores, Mich., by Scholarly Press (1971).

MARBLE, ANNIE R. David Humphreys: his services to American freedom and industry. New England magazine, new ser., v. 29, Feb. 1904: 690–704. illus., facsim., ports.   AP2.N4, n.s., v. 29

MASON, JULIAN D. David Humphreys' lost ode to George Washington, 1776. *In* U.S. *Library of Congress.* Quarterly journal, v. 28, Jan 1971: 28–37. facsims., ports.   Z881.U49A3, v. 28

13659
HUNT, JOHN (1740?–1824)
New Jersey. Quaker minister.

——— John Hunt's diary [July 1770–May 1800] *In* New Jersey Historical Society. Proceedings, v. 52, July–Oct. 1934: 177–193, 223–239; v. 53, Jan.–Oct. 1953: 26–43, 111–128, 194–209, 251–262.
F131.N58, v. 52–53

Introduction and notes by Edward Fuhlbruegge.

13660
HUNTER, JAMES (1740–1820)
North Carolina. Planter, Regulator, Revolutionary officer.

MOREHEAD, JOSEPH M. Address of Joseph M. Morehead, Esq., of Guilford, on the life and times of James Hunter, "general" of the Regulators, at Guilford battle ground, Saturday, July 3, 1897. 2d corr. and enl. ed. Greensboro, N.C., C. F. Thomas, Printer, 1898. 73 p.
F257.H94

13661
HUNTER, JAMES (1746–1788)
Virginia. Merchant.

COAKLEY, ROBERT WALTER. The two James Hunters of Fredericksburg: patriots among the Virginia Scotch merchants. Virginia magazine of history and biography, v. 56, Jan. 1948: 3–21.   F221.V91, v. 56

13662
HUNTER, ROBERT (1764–1843)
England. Traveler.

——— Quebec to Carolina in 1785–1786, being the travel diary and observations of Robert Hunter, Jr., a young merchant of London. Edited by Louis B. Wright and Marion Tinling. San Marino, Calif., Huntington Library, 1943. ix, 393 p. map (on lining papers) (Huntington Library publications)   E164.H93

Bibliographic references included in "Notes" (p. 311–376).

13663
HUNTER, SAMUEL (*fl.* 1759–1783)
Pennsylvania. Revolutionary recruiter.

——— Eighteen colonial and Revolutionary documents of Colonel Samuel Hunter, 1759–1783. *In* Northumberland County (Pa.) Historical Society. Proceedings. v. 11. Sunbury, 1939. p. [203]–241. plate.
F157.N8N7, v. 11

13664
HUNTINGTON, BENJAMIN (1736–1800)
Connecticut. Lawyer, delegate to the Continental Congress.

McCRACKAN, WILLIAM D., *ed.* The Huntington letters, in the possession of Julia Chester Wells. Printed for private distribution. New York, Appleton Press, 1897. 220 p.   E302.6.H9M13

Contents: First period (1761–1792), mainly letters which passed between Benjamin Huntington and his wife Anne.—Second period (1796–1798), mainly letters written by Rachel Huntington to her sisters, Lucy and Anne.—Miscellaneous letters and documents.

13665
HUNTINGTON, EBENEZER (1754–1834)
Connecticut. Revolutionary officer.

——— Letters of Ebenezer Huntington, 1774–1781. American historical review, v. 5, July 1900: 702–729.
E171.A57, v. 5

——— Letters written by Ebenezer Huntington during the American Revolution. New York, Printed for C. F. Heartman [1915] 110 p. facsim., port. (Heartman's historical series, no. 2)   E275.H94

13666
HUNTINGTON, JEDEDIAH (1743–1818)*
Connecticut. Merchant, Revolutionary general.

———— Letters of Lieut. Jedediah Huntington [1775–76] *In* Massachusetts Historical Society, *Boston*. Collections. 5th ser., v. 9. Boston, 1885. p. 491–518.
F61.M41, 5th s., v. 9

HEATHCOTE, CHARLES W. General Jedediah Huntingdon rendered patriotic service for his country. Picket post, no. 52, May 1956: 12–18. port.
E234.P5, no.52

13667

HUNTINGTON, JOSHUA (1751–1821)
Connecticut. Revolutionary officer.

———— Huntington papers; correspondence of the brothers Joshua and Jedediah Huntington, during the period of the American Revolution. Hartford, Connecticut Historical Society, 1923. 2 v. in 1. (Connecticut Historical Society. Collections, v. 20)
F91.C7, v. 20

13668

HUNTINGTON, SAMUEL (1731–1796)*
Connecticut. Lawyer, assemblyman, judge, delegate to the Continental Congress, governor.

HUNTINGTON, SUSAN D. Samuel Huntington. Connecticut magazine, v. 6, May/June 1900: 247–253. port.
F91.C8, v. 6

———— ———— Detached copy.
F69.H95

VAN DUSEN, ALBERT E. Samuel Huntington: a leader of Revolutionary Connecticut. *In* Connecticut Historical Society, *Hartford*. Bulletin, v. 19, Apr. 1954: 38–62. illus., port.
F91.C67, v. 19

WAUGH, ALBERT E. Samuel Huntington and his family. Stonington, Conn., Pequot Press [1968] 43 p. illus., port.
F104.N93H98
Sponsored by the Society of the Founders of Norwich, Connecticut.

13669

HURD, NATHANIEL (1730–1777)*
Massachusetts. Silversmith, engraver.

FRENCH, HOLLIS. Jacob Hurd and his sons Nathaniel and Benjamin, silversmiths, 1702–1781. With a foreword by Kathryn C. Buhler. [Cambridge, Mass.] Printed by the Riverside Press for the Walpole Society, 1939, xvi, 147 p. illus., facsims., plates, ports. (part col.)
NK7198.H8F7
"List of references": p. 147–[148].
Reprinted in New York by Da Capo Press (1972).

13670

HUSBAND, HERMAN (1724–1795)*
North Carolina. Farmer, landowner, Regulator.

LAZENBY, MARY E. Herman Husband, a story of his life. Book 1. In Maryland. Book 2. In North Carolina. Book 3. In Pennsylvania. Washington, D.C., Old Neighborhoods Press, 1940. viii, 180 p. facsim., map, plate.
E302.6.H93L3

"Sources": 1 leaf at end.

13671

HUTCHINS, LEVI (1761–1855)
Massachusetts. Revolutionary fifer and soldier, clockmaker, farmer.

———— The autobiography of Levi Hutchins: with a preface, notes, and addenda, by his youngest son. (Private ed.) Cambridge [Mass.] Riverside Press, 1865. 188 p. port.
CS71.H974 1865

Edited by Samuel Hutchins.
Supplementary notes by Charles L. Hutchins, dated September 1918, were added, together with more illustrations, as p. 189–197 to some unbound copies of this edition for distribution (1865 [1918] 197 p. CS71.H974 1865A).

13672

HUTCHINS, THOMAS (1730–1789)*
New Jersey; Pennsylvania. Soldier, engineer, explorer, mapmaker, geographer.

———— The courses of the Ohio River taken by Lt. T. Hutchins, anno 1766, and two accompanying maps. Edited by Beverly W. Bond, Jr. Cincinnati, Historical and Philosophical Society of Ohio, 1942. 85 p. maps (part fold.) (Historical and Philosophical Society of Ohio. Publications, 1942)
F486.H663 1942
VK995.O4H8

Hutchins' *Courses of the Ohio River* and his map are reproduced from the originals in the Huntington Library, and Gordon's map of the Ohio River, from the original in the Library of Congress.
Contents: Introduction.—Courses of the Ohio River, 1766 by Thomas Hutchins.—Map of the Ohio River, 1766, by Captain Harry Gordon.—Table of distances from Fort Pitt to the mouth of the Ohio, 1766, by Captain Harry Gordon.—Map of a tour from Fort Cumberland north westward, etc., 1762, by Thomas Hutchins.—Explanations and table from Hutchins' map, 1762.—Itinerary of a tour from Fort Cumberland north westward, etc., 1762, by Thomas Hutchins.

———— An historical narrative and topographical description of Louisiana and West-Florida, comprehending the river Mississippi with its principal branches and settlements, and the rivers Pearl, Pascagoula . . . &c . . . with directions for sailing into all the bays, lakes, harbours and rivers on the north side of the Gulf of Mexico. Philadelphia, Printed for the author, 1784. 94 p.
AC901.H3, v. 36 Rare Bk. Coll.
E163.H96 Rare Bk. Coll.
Reprinted in Gainesville by the University of Florida Press (1968) with an introduction and index by Joseph G. Tregle (F373.H97 1784a).

——— A topographical description of Virginia, Pennsylvania, Maryland and North Carolina, comprehending the rivers Ohio, Kenhawa, Sioto, Cherokee, Wabash, Illinois, Mississippi, &c. . . . With a plan of the rapids of the Ohio, a plan of the several villages in the Illinois Country, a table of the distances between Fort Pitt and the mouth of the Ohio, all engraved upon copper. And an appendix, containing Mr. Patrick Kennedy's Journal up the Illinois River, and a correct list of the different nations and tribes of Indians, with the number of fighting men, &c. London, Printed for the author, and sold by J. Almon, 1778. 67 p. fold. plans

E163.H97 Rare Bk. Coll.
AC901.H3, v. 53 Rare Bk. Coll.

Second impression, with corrections.
"The map, which the following sheets are intended to explain, comprehends almost the whole of the country lying between the 34th and 44th degrees of latitude, and the 79th and 93d degrees of longitude."—Preface.
The map was issued separately.
The reprint by the Burrows Bros. Co. (Cleveland, 1904. 143 p.), edited by Frederick C. Hicks, includes a biographical sketch of Hutchins, p. 7–51.

ANDERSON, NILES, *and* EDWARD G. WILLIAMS. The Venango Path as Thomas Hutchins knew it. Western Pennsylvania historical magazine, v. 49, Jan.–Apr. 1966: 1–18, 141–151. maps. F146.W52, v. 49

Based on Hutchins' manuscript "The Rout by Land From Fort Pitt to Venango—and From Thence to LeBeauf and Presqu' Isle."

QUATTROCCHI, ANNA M. Thomas Hutchins in western Pennsylvania. Pennsylvania history, v. 16, Jan. 1949: 31–38. F146.P597

——— Thomas Hutchins, provincial soldier and Indian agent in the Ohio Valley, 1758–1761. Western Pennsylvania historical magazine, v. 45, Sept. 1962: 193–207. F146.W52, v. 45

——— Thomas Hutchins, 1730–1789. 1944.

Thesis (Ph.D.)—University of Pittsburgh.

TREGLE, JOSEPH G. British spy along the Mississippi: Thomas Hutchins and the defenses of New Orleans, 1773. Louisiana history, v. 8, fall 1967: 313–327. F366.L6238, v. 8

Sent by General Gage to study Spanish fortifications.

13673

HUTCHINSON, ABIJAH (1756–1843)

Connecticut. Revolutionary soldier and seaman.

HUTCHINSON, K. M. A memoir of Abijah Hutchinson, a soldier of the Revolution. Rochester [N.Y.] W. Alling, Printer, 1843. 22 p. illus., port. E275.H945H8

13674

HUTCHINSON, JAMES (1752–1793)*

Pennsylvania. Revolutionary surgeon.

BELL, WHITFIELD. James Hutchinson (1752–1793): letters from an American student in London. *In* College of Physicians of Philadelphia. Transactions & studies, 4th ser., v. 34, July 1966: 20–25. port.

R15.P5, 4th s., v. 34

Includes three letters to Israel Pemberton written in 1775–76.

13675

HUTCHINSON, THOMAS (1711–1780)*†

Massachusetts; England. Merchant, assemblyman, councilor, judge, royal governor, historian, Loyalist.

——— Correspondence relative to "The History of Massachusetts Bay," between its author, Gov. Thomas Hutchinson, and Rev. Ezra Stiles [1764–67] New-England historical and genealogical register, v. 26, Apr.–July 1872: 159–164, 230–233. F1.N56, v. 26

Communicated by William A. Saunders.

——— The diary and letters of His Excellency Thomas Hutchinson . . . captain-general and governor-in-chief of . . . Massachusetts Bay. Compiled from the original documents still remaining in the possession of his descendants. By Peter Orlando Hutchinson. London, S. Low, Marston, Searle & Rivington, 1883–86. 2 v. illus., col. plates, facsim. [F67.H94]
Micro 8659F

"Pedigree of Hutchinson of Lincolnshire": v. 2, p. 456–478.
Reprinted in New York by B. Franklin (1971).

——— The Hutchinson papers. Albany, Printed for the Society by J. Munsell, 1865. 2 v. (Prince Society, Boston. Publications, [v. 2–3]) E186.P85, v. 2–3

Edited by W. H. Whitmore and W. S. Appleton.
Includes reproduction of title page of original edition: *A Collection of Original Papers Relative to the History of the Colony of Massachusetts-Bay*. Boston, New-England, Printed by Thomas and John Fleet, 1769.
"Intended to support and elucidate the principal facts related in the first part of the History [of Massachusetts-Bay] and may serve as an appendix to it."—Preface.
Reprinted in New York by B. Franklin (1967).

——— Hutchinson papers [used in the preparation of his *History*] *In* Massachusetts Historical Society, *Boston*. Collections. 2d ser., v. 10; 3d ser., v. 1. Boston, 1823–25. p. 181–188; p. 1–152.

F61.M41, 2d s., v. 10; 3d s., v. 1

ELLIS, GEORGE E. Governor Thomas Hutchinson. Atlantic monthly, v. 53, May 1884: 662–676.

AP2.A8, v. 53

FREIBERG, MALCOLM. How to become a colonial governor: Thomas Hutchinson of Massachusetts. Review of politics, v. 21, Oct. 1959: 646–656.

JA1.R4, v. 21

——— Prelude to purgatory; Thomas Hutchinson in provincial Massachusetts politics, 1760–1770. 1951.

Thesis (Ph.D.)—Brown University.

—— Thomas Hutchinson and the province currency. New England quarterly, v. 30, June 1957: 190–208.
F1.N62, v. 30

—— Thomas Hutchinson: the first fifty years (1711–1761). William and Mary quarterly, 3d ser., v. 15, Jan. 1958: 35–55.　　　F221.W71, 3d s., v. 15

HOSMER, JAMES K.　The life of Thomas Hutchinson, royal governor of the province of Massachusetts Bay. Boston, Houghton, Mifflin, 1896. xxviii, 453 p. fold. facsim., plates, port.　　　[F67.H935]
Micro 18510 F

Controversy between the governor and the legislature, 1773: p. 363–428; the letters and the resolves concerning them: p. 429–442.
Reprinted in New York by Da Capo Press (1972).

LEVERMORE, CHARLES H.　Thomas Hutchinson, Tory governor of Massachusetts. New England magazine, new ser., v. 21, Feb. 1900: 646–667. illus., facsims., ports.　　　AP2.N4, n.s., v. 21

MAYO, LAWRENCE S.　Thomas Hutchinson and his *History of Massachusetts-Bay*. *In* American Antiquarian Society, *Worcester, Mass.* Proceedings, new ser., v. 41, Oct. 1931: 321–339.　　　E172.A35, n.s., v. 41

TUELL, HARRIET E.　Thomas Hutchinson, the last colonial governor of Massachusetts. New England historical and genealogical register, v. 51, Oct. 1897: 473–488.
F1.N56, v. 51

13676
HUTSON, RICHARD (1748–1795)*
South Carolina. Lawyer, Revolutionary soldier, assemblyman, delegate to the Continental Congress.

—— Letters of the Hon. Rich'd Hutson. *In* Charleston, S.C. Year book. 1895. Charleston. p. 313–325.
JS13.C33, 1895

Includes eight letters dated October 30, 1765, and May 7–June 30, 1776.

13677
IMLAY, GILBERT (1754?–1828?)*†
New Jersey; Kentucky. Revolutionary officer, land speculator.

RUSK, RALPH L.　The adventures of Gilbert Imlay. [Bloomington, Ind., 1923] 26 p. (Indiana University studies. v. 10, Mar. 1923. Study no. 57)
AS36.14, v. 10, no. 57

Bibliographic footnotes.

13678
INGERSOLL, DAVID (1742–1796)
Massachusetts; England. Lawyer, judge, assemblyman, Loyalist.

TAYLOR, CHARLES J.　David Ingersoll, Jr., Esquire, a Great Barrington Loyalist of the Revolution. *In* Berkshire Historical and Scientific Society, *Pittsfield, Mass.* Collections, v. 3, no. 1; 1899. Pittsfield, Mass. p. [51]–72.　　　F72.B5B6, v. 3

13679
INGERSOLL, JARED (1722–1781)*
Connecticut; Pennsylvania. Lawyer, colonial agent, Loyalist, judge.

—— A selection from the correspondence and miscellaneous papers of Jared Ingersoll [1743–81] *In* New Haven Colony Historical Society, *New Haven.* Papers. v. 9. New Haven, 1918. p. 201–472. port.
F98.N5, v. 9

Edited by Franklin B. Dexter.
An offprint with the abbreviated title *Jared Ingersoll Papers* (New Haven, 1918. [201]–472 p. port. E302.6.I6I6) was also issued.

GIPSON, LAWRENCE H.　Jared Ingersoll; a study of American Loyalism in relation to British colonial government. New Haven, Yale University Press, 1920. 432 p. (Yale historical publications, Miscellany, 8)
E302.6.I6G44

"Bibliographical note": p. [377]–384.
Reprinted in New York by Russell & Russell (1969).
A new edition entitled *American Loyalist: Jared Ingersoll* (New Haven, Yale University Press, 1971. xxvi, 432 p.) includes a bibliographic review of the past half century of Loyalist scholarship.
The author's thesis (Ph.D.), *Jared Ingersoll: A Study of British Colonial Government*, was submitted to Yale University in 1918.

LINES, EDWIN S.　Jared Ingersoll, stamp master, and the Stamp Act. *In* New Haven Colony Historical Society, *New Haven.* Papers. v. 9. New Haven, 1918. p. 174–200.　　　F98.N5, v. 9

13680
INGHAM, JONAS (*b.* 1746)
Pennsylvania. Miller, Revolutionary soldier.

INGHAM, JOSEPH F.　Early days of the Ingham family in Bucks County. *In* Old York Road Historical Society, *Jenkintown, Pa.* Bulletin. v. 6; 1942. Jenkintown, p. 45–64.　　　F146.O58, v. 6

Based on the memoir of Jonas Ingham written in the early 19th century.

13681
INGLIS, CHARLES, *Bp. of Nova Scotia* (1734–1816)*†
Ireland; Pennsylvania; New York; Canada. Anglican clergyman and missionary, Loyalist, Bishop.

—— [A calendar of the] correspondence and journals of Bishop Inglis of Halifax, Nova Scotia, 1775–1814. *In*

Canada. *Public Archives*. Report. 1912. Ottawa, 1913. p. 215–288. F1001.C13, 1912

Forms Appendix M of the *Report*. A second installment appeared as Appendix I (p. 227–283) in the 1913 *Report*, under the title "Completion of the Correspondence and Journals of the Right Reverend Charles and John Inglis, first and third bishops of Nova Scotia." The dates covered in the second part are 1788–1849.

———— A memorial concerning the Iroquois or five confederate nations of Indians in the province of New-York: in which their present state, numbers and situation are set forth; arguments why government should interpose for their conversion to Christianity and reduction to a civilised state are adduced; a plan for their conversion is laid down; circumstances which promise success to such an attempt at this time are pointed out, and some objections to the design are obviated. Humbly addressed to the Right Honorable the Earl of Hillsborough [1771] *In* The Documentary history of the state of New-York. By E. B. O'Callaghan. v. 4. Albany, C. Van Benthuysen, Public Printer, 1851. p. [1089]–1117. fold. map. F122.D63, v. 4

———— ———— Detached copy. E99.I7I5

———— State of the Anglo-American church, in 1776. With notes by the editor. *In* The Documentary history of the state of New-York. By E. B. O'Callaghan. v. 3. Albany, Weed, Parsons, Public Printers, 1850. p. [1047]–1066. F122.D63, v. 3

BATCHELDER, ROBERT C. Charles Inglis, first British colonial bishop. Historical magazine of the Protestant Episcopal church, v. 32, Mar. 1963: 17–25. BX5800.H5, v. 32

EATON, ARTHUR W. H. Bishop Charles Inglis and his descendants. Acadiensis, v. 8, July 1908: 183–202. port. F1036.A16, v. 8

FINGARD, JUDITH. Charles Inglis and his "primitive bishoprick" in Nova Scotia. Canadian historical review, v. 49, Sept. 1968: 247–266. F1001.C27, v. 49

HARRIS, REGINALD V. Charles Inglis, missionary, Loyalist, bishop (1734–1816). Toronto, General Board of Religious Education [1937] 186 p. illus., facsims., plates, ports. BX5620.I5H3

"Sources and bibliography": p. 182–186.

LYDEKKER, JOHN W. The life and letters of Charles Inglis, his ministry in America and consecration as first colonial bishop, from 1759 to 1787. Published for the Church Historical Society. London, Society for Promoting Christian Knowledge [1936] xv, 272 p. fold. map, plates, ports. BX5995.I6L9

Bibliography: p. 266.

RAYSON, ROBERT S. Charles Inglis, a chapter in beginnings. Queen's quarterly, v. 33, Oct./Dec. 1925: 163–177. AP5.Q3, v. 33

VROOM, FENWICK W. Charles Inglis—an appreciation. *In* Nova Scotia Historical Society, *Halifax*. Collections. v. 22. Halifax, 1933. p. 25–42. port. F1036.N93, v. 22

YOUNG, ARCHIBALD H. Dr. Charles Inglis in New York, 1766–1783. *In* Canadian Historical Association. Report. 1932. Ottawa. p. 87–96. F1001.C26, 1932

13682

INMAN, GEORGE (1755–1789)*

Massachusetts; England. Loyalist, British officer in America.

———— George Inman's narrative of the American Revolution. Pennsylvania magazine of history and biography, v. 7, Sept. 1883: 237–248. F146.P65, v. 7

GOZZALDI, MARY ISABELLA JAMES DE. Lieutenant George Inman. *In* Cambridge Historical Society, *Cambridge, Mass*. Publications. v. 19. Proceedings. 1926. Cambridge, 1927. p. 46–79. F74.C1C469, v. 19

Includes a journal kept during his exile in England, Ireland and Grenada (1782–89).

13683

INNES, JAMES (1754–1798)*

Virginia. Revolutionary officer, lawyer, assemblyman, orator.

CARSON, JANE. The fat major of the F.H.C. *In* Rutman, Darrett B., *ed*. The Old Dominion; essays for Thomas Perkins Abernethy. Charlottesville, University Press of Virginia [1964] p. 79–95. F226.R8

———— James Innes and his brothers of the F.H.C. Williamsburg, Va., Colonial Williamsburg; distributed by the University Press of Virginia, Charlottesville [ᶜ1965] ix, 171 p. front. (Williamsburg research studies) F234.W7C345

Bibliographic footnotes.

13684

IREDELL, JAMES (1751–1799)*

England; North Carolina. Customs officer, lawyer.

CONNOR, HENRY G. James Iredell, 1751–1799. North Carolina booklet, v. 11, Apr. 1912: 201–250. F251.N86, v. 11

An offprint, with an extended title, was published in Raleigh by Edwards & Broughton Print. Co. (1912. 52 p. E302.6.I7C7)

HERNDON, NETTIE S. James Iredell. 1944.

Thesis (Ph.D.)—Duke University.

HIGGINBOTHAM, DON. James Iredell's efforts to preserve the first British Empire. North Carolina historical review, v. 49, spring 1972: 126–145. illus., ports. F251.N892, v. 49

McRee, Griffith J. Life and correspondence of James Iredell, one of the associate justices of the Supreme Court of the United States. New York, Appleton, 1857–58. 2 v. facsim., port. E302.6.I7M17

————— Index, compiled by Helen Dortch Harrison. Chapel Hill, N.C., North Carolina Collection, University of North Carolina Library, 1955. 151 l. E302.6.I7M17i

13685

IRVINE, WILLIAM (1741–1804)*†

Ireland; Pennsylvania. Surgeon, Revolutionary general, delegate to the Continental Congress.

————— Extracts from the papers of General William Irvine [1781] Pennsylvania magazine of history and biography, v. 5, no. 3, 1881: 259–275. F146.P65, v. 5

————— Letters of Gen. Irvine to his family [June 14–August 11, 1780] Historical magazine, v. 7, Mar. 1863: 81–83. E171.H64, v. 7

Heathcote, Charles W. General William Irvine—a trusted Pennsylvania officer and friend of Washington. Picket post, no. 67, Feb. 1960: 6–14. illus., port. E234.P5, no. 67

13686

ISAACS, RALPH (1741–1799)

Connecticut. Merchant, Loyalist.

Osterweis, Rollin G. The three houses of Ralph Isaacs, Jr., colonial merchant of New Haven. *In* New Haven Colony Historical Society, *New Haven.* Journal, v. 14, June 1965: 29–36. F91.N4, v. 14

13687

IZARD, ALICE DE LANCEY (1744 *or* 5–1832)

South Carolina. Wife of Ralph Izard (1742–1804).

————— Letters from Mrs. Ralph Izard to Mrs. William Lee [1781–83] Virginia magazine of history and biography, v. 8, July 1900: 16–28. F221.V91, v. 8

Lynah, Mary-Elizabeth. Ralph Izard and Alice De Lancey, famous Huguenot belle, his wife. Americana, v. 28, Oct. 1934: 486–497. ports. E171.A53, v. 28

13688

IZARD, RALPH (1742–1804)*

South Carolina. Planter, diplomat, delegate to the Continental Congress.

————— An account of a journey to Niagara, Montreal and Quebec, in 1765; or, " 'Tis eighty years since." New-York, Printed by W. Osborn, 1846. 30 p. F122.I98 Rare Bk. Coll.

————— Correspondence of Mr. Ralph Izard, of South Carolina, from the year 1774 to 1804; with a short memoir. v. 1. New-York, C. S. Francis, 1844. xiv, 389 p. port. E249.I98

No more published.

Includes Izard's correspondence from 1774 to 1777, during his residence in Europe as commissioner to the court of Tuscany.

————— Izard-Laurens correspondence [1775–1781] South Carolina historical and genealogical magazine, v. 22, Jan.–July 1921: 1–11, 39–52, 73–88. F266.S55, v. 22

————— Letters of Ralph Izard [1784–89] South Carolina historical and genealogical magazine, v. 2, July 1901: 194–204. F266.S55, v. 2

Manigault, G. E. Ralph Izard, the South Carolina statesman. Magazine of American history, with notes and queries, v. 23, Jan. 1890: 60–73. E171.M18, v. 23

13689

JACKSON, HALL (1739–1797)*

New Hampshire. Physician, Revolutionary surgeon.

Jackson, Russell L. Dr. Hall Jackson of Portsmouth. Annals of medical history, new ser., v. 5, Mar. 1933: 103–128. port. R11.A85, n.s., v. 5

13690

JACKSON, JAMES (1757–1806)*

England; Georgia. Revolutionary officer, lawyer.

————— Miscellaneous papers of James Jackson, 1781–1798. Edited by Lilla M. Hawes. Georgia historical quarterly, v. 37, Mar.–June 1953: 54–80, 147–160. F281.G2975, v. 37

General Jackson's letter book, 1788–96, appeared in the September and December issues for 1953. Both the miscellaneous papers and the letter book were reprinted, with an index, as v. 11 of the *Collections* of the Georgia Historical Society (Savannah, 1955. 110 p. F281.G35).

Charlton, Thomas U. P. The life of Major General James Jackson. pt. 1. Augusta, Ga., Printed by G. F. Randolph, 1809. [Atlanta, Reprinted, 1897] ix, 215 p. plates, ports., tables. E207.J13C4

No more published.

In addition to the reprint of Charlton's *Life of Jackson* (p. 1–69) there are included biographical notices of General Jackson from other sources and a selection from his correspondence.

Foster, William O. James Jackson, duelist and militant statesman, 1757–1806. Athens, University of Georgia Press [1960] viii, 220 p. E207.J13F6

Bibliography: p. 202–212.

The author's thesis (Ph.D.), *James Jackson, Militant Georgia Statesman, 1757–1806,* was submitted to the University of North Carolina in 1950.

————— James Jackson in the American Revolution. Georgia historical quarterly, v. 31, Dec. 1947: 249–281. F281.G2975, v. 31

LAWRENCE, ALEXANDER A. James Jackson: passionate patriot. Georgia historical quarterly, v. 34, June 1950: 78–86.   F281.G2975, v. 34

13691
JACKSON, JONATHAN (1743–1810)
    Massachusetts. Merchant, assemblyman, delegate to the Continental Congress.

PORTER, KENNETH W. *ed.* The Jacksons and the Lees; two generations of Massachusetts merchants, 1765–1844. Cambridge, Mass., Harvard University Press, 1937. 2 v. (xx, 1623 p.) facsim., geneal. tables, plates, ports. (Harvard studies in business history, 3)
                    HF3161.M4P6
    "List of manuscripts reproduced": v. 2, p. [1537]–1573.
    "List of manuscript collections": v. 2, p. [1575]–1585.
    Reprinted in New York by Russell & Russell (1969).
    The first volume consists largely of a general introduction, "The Sedentary Merchant in Massachusetts, 1765–1844" (p. 3–150), and the correspondence of Jackson and Joseph Lee (1744–1831).

13692
JACKSON, WILLIAM (1759–1828)*
    South Carolina. Revolutionary officer, secretary.

LITTELL, CHARLES W. Major William Jackson, secretary of the Federal Convention. Pennsylvania magazine of history and biography, v. 2, no. 4, 1878: 353–369.
                    F146.P65, v. 2

13693
JACOB, JOHN JEREMIAH (1758?–1839)
    Maryland; Virginia. Frontiersman, clergyman.

HOLMES, MARJORIE. Jacob and Cresap. West Virginia history, v. 3, Apr. 1942: 213–227.   F236.W52, v. 3

SHERWOOD, LAWRENCE. John Jeremiah Jacob, patriot and preacher. West Virginia history, v. 17, Jan. 1956: 117–137.   F236.W52, v. 17

13694
JACOBS, BARNARD (*d. ca.* 1790)
    Pennsylvania. Merchant.

STERN, MALCOLM H. Two Jewish functionaries in colonial Pennsylvania. American Jewish historical quarterly, v. 57, Sept. 1967: 24–51.   E184.J5A5, v. 57
    Contents: Barnard Jacobs, ritual circumciser.—Mordecai Moses Mordecai (1727–1809).

13695
JAMES, BARTHOLOMEW (1752–1828)†
    British naval officer in America.

——— Journal of Rear-Admiral Bartholomew James, 1752–1828. Edited by John Knox Laughton, with the assis-

tance of James Young F. Sullivan, Commander R.N., James's great-grandson. [London] Printed for the Navy Records Society, 1896. xxvi, 402 p. plates, port. (Navy Records Society, Publications, v. 6)   DA70.A1, v. 6

13696
JARRATT, DEVEREUX (1733–1801)*
    Virginia. Anglican clergyman.

——— The life of the Reverend Devereux Jarratt, rector of Bath Parish, Dinwiddie County, Virginia. Written by himself, in a series of letters addressed to the Rev. John Coleman, one of the ministers of the Protestant Episcopal church, in Maryland. Baltimore, Printed by Warner & Hanna, 1806. 223 p.
                    BX5995.J27A3 Rare Bk. Coll.
    Reprinted in New York by Arno Press (1969).
    The earliest section of Jarratt's autobiography is reprinted in its entirety, with an introduction and notes by Douglass Adair, in the *William and Mary Quarterly*, 3d ser., v. 9, July 1952, p. 346–393.

CHORLEY, EDWARD CLOWES. The Reverend Devereux Jarratt. Historical magazine of the Protestant Episcopal church, v. 5, Mar. 1936: 47–64.   BX5800.H5, v. 5

RABE, HARRY G. The Reverend Devereux Jarratt and the Virginia social order. Historical magazine of the Protestant Episcopal church, v. 33, Dec. 1964: 299–336.
                    BX5800.H5, v. 33

SMITH, JOHN W. Devereux Jarratt and the beginnings of Methodism in Virginia. *In* John P. Branch historical papers of Randolph-Macon College. [v. 1] no. 1; 1901. Ashland, Va. p. 3–21.   F221.J65, v. 1

13697
JARVIS, STEPHEN (1756–1840)
    Connecticut; Canada. Farmer, Loyalist officer.

——— An American's experience in the British Army: manuscript of Colonel Stephen Jarvis . . . revealing the life of the Loyalists. Journal of American history, v. 1, July/Sept.–Oct./Dec. 1907: 441–464, 727–740.
                    E171.J86, v. 1
    Also appeared in v. 11 of the *Connecticut Magazine* for the summer and autumn of 1907, p. 191–215, 477–490. Another version, with different wording, appeared under the title "Reminiscences of a Loyalist," in the *Canadian Magazine of Politics, Science, Art and Literature*, v. 26, Jan.–Apr. 1906, p. 227–233, 366–373, 450–457, 529–536.

13698
JASPER, WILLIAM (1750–1779)*
    South Carolina. Revolutionary soldier, scout.

JONES, CHARLES C. Sergeant William Jasper. [Albany, J. Munsell, Printer] 1876. 36 p.   E263.S7J7
    Reprinted in the *Magazine of History, With Notes and Queries*, v. 8, Nov.–Dec. 1908, p. 262–268, 351–356; v. 9, Mar.–Apr. 1909, p. 153–158, 216–220.

13699

JAY, JOHN (1745–1829)*

New York. Lawyer, delegate to the Continental Congress, diplomat.

―――― Anti-slavery papers of John Jay. Journal of Negro history, v. 17, Oct. 1932: 481–496.   E185.J86, v. 17

Introduction and notes by Frank Monaghan.

―――― The correspondence and public papers of John Jay. Edited by Henry P. Johnston. New York, G. P. Putnam's Sons [1890–93] 4 v.   E302.J42

Contents: v. 1. 1763–1781.―v. 2. 1781–1782.―v. 3. 1782–1793.―v. 4. 1794–1826.

Reprinted in New York by B. Franklin (1970).

―――― The Jay papers. Edited and annotated by Richard B. Morris. American heritage, v. 19, Feb. 1968: 8–11, 85–96; v. 20, Dec. 1968: 24–28, 89–100. illus. (part col.), ports (part col.)   E171.A43, v. 19–20

Contents: 1. Mission to Spain [1779–82]—2. Forging the nation [1784–89]

An illustrative portfolio, mostly in color, entitled "The Jays in Spain," accompanies pt. 1 (p. 12–20).

―――― Letters, being the whole of the correspondence between the Hon. John Jay, Esq; and Mr. Lewis Littlepage: a young man, whom Mr. Jay, when in Spain, patronized and took into his family. A new and correct ed. To which is added an appendix. New-York, Printed and sold by F. Childs, 1786. 102 p.   E302.J4J41 Rare Bk. Coll.

―――― Some conversations of Dr. Franklin and Mr. Jay; being the first publication of a manuscript written by John Jay in Paris during 1783–1784. With an introductory essay on Dr. Franklin & Mr. Jay by Frank Monaghan. New Haven, Conn., Three Monks Press, 1936. 17 p.   E302.J43
E302.6.F8J38

BECKER, CARL L.   John Jay and Peter Van Schaak. In New York State Historical Association. Quarterly journal, v. 1, Oct. 1919: 1–12.   F116.N865, v. 1

Concerned with the influences that prompted Jay to embrace the patriot cause and Van Schaak to become a Loyalist.

DEWEY, DONALD J.   John Jay and Joseph Galloway: a case study in conservatism. Mid-America, v. 29, Oct. 1947: 245-265.   BX1415.I3M5, v. 29

On conditions that pushed two conservatives in opposite directions over the question of separation.

DORFMAN, JOSEPH, and REXFORD G. TUGWELL.   John Jay: revolutionary conservative. In their Early American policy: six Columbia contributors. New York, Columbia University Press, 1960. p. [43]–98.   HB119.A3D6

JAY, WILLIAM.   The life of John Jay: with selections from his correspondence and miscellaneous papers. New York, J. & J. Harper, 1833. 2 v.   E302.6.J4J42

Contents: v. 1. The life of John Jay.—v. 2. Miscellaneous and official correspondence.

Reprinted in Freeport, N.Y., by Books for Libraries Press (1972).

JOHNSON, HERBERT A.   John Jay: colonial lawyer. 1965. ([306] p.)   Micro AC–1, no. 65–11,089

Thesis (Ph.D.)—Columbia University.

Abstracted in Dissertation Abstracts, v. 26, Oct. 1965, p. 2151.

―――― John Jay, 1745–1829. Albany, Office of State History, 1970. 53 p. illus., port.   E302.6.J4J6

Bibliography: p. 53.

MONAGHAN, FRANK.   John Jay, defender of liberty against kings & peoples, author of the Constitution & governor of New York, president of the Continental Congress, co-author of The Federalist, negotiator of the peace of 1783 & the Jay Treaty of 1794, first Chief Justice of the United States. New York, Bobbs-Merrill Co., 1935. 497 p. facsims., plates, ports.   E302.6.J4M6

"The sources": p. [465]–474.

The author's thesis (Ph.D.), John Jay, Defender of Liberty, was submitted to Yale University in 1936.

―――― Samuel Kissam and John Jay. Columbia University quarterly, v. 25, June 1933: 127–133.   LH1.C7Q2, v. 25

Includes letters of Samuel Kissam, Benjamin Kissam, and John Jay, 1769–83.

MORRIS, RICHARD B.   John Jay and the New England connection. In Massachusetts Historical Society, Boston. Proceedings. v. 80; 1968. Boston, 1969. p. 16–37.   F61.M38, v. 80

―――― John Jay, the Nation, and the Court. Boston, Boston University Press, 1967. xi, 114 p. (The Gaspar G. Bacon lecture on the Constitution of the United States, 1965)   KF8745.J3M6

Bibliographic references included in "Notes" (p. 103–113).

PELLEW, GEORGE.   John Jay. Boston, Houghton, Mifflin, 1889. ix, 354 p. fold. facsim., ports. (American statesmen, v. 9)   E202.6.J4P32
E176.A54, v. 9

Reprinted in New York by AMS Press (1972).

SMITH, DONALD L.   John Jay; founder of a state and nation. New York, Teachers College Press, Columbia University [1968] xiv, 138 p. (Social studies sources)   E302.6.J4S6

Bibliography: p. 135–138.

WELLS, LAURA J.   The Jay family of La Rochelle and New York province and state; a chronicle of family tradition. [New York, Printed for the Order of Colonial Lords of Manors in America by the J. B. Watkins Co., 1938]

63 p. illus., ports. (Publications of the Order of Colonial Lords of Manors in America, no. 28)

E186.99.O6, no. 28
CS71.J437 1938

WHITELOCK, WILLIAM. The life and times of John Jay, Secretary of Foreign Affairs under the Confederation and first Chief Justice of the United States, with a sketch of public events from the opening of the Revolution to the election of Jefferson. New York, Dodd, Mead, 1887. vi, 370 p. port. E302.6.J4W5

13700

JAY, SARAH LIVINGSTON (1756–1802)

New Jersey; New York. Daughter of William Livingston (1723–1790); wife of John Jay (1745–1829).

—— Mrs. John Jay to Mrs. Robert Morris [1780–83] *In* Miscellaneous Americana. A collection of history, biography and genealogy. Published by William F. Boogher, Washington, D.C. Philadelphia, Press of Dando Print. and Pub. Co. [1895] p. 26–44. port.

E171.B73

First published serially in v. 1 of *Boogher's Repository* (1883).

13701

JEFFERSON, THOMAS (1743–1826)*

Virginia. Lawyer, assemblyman, writer, delegate to the Continental Congress, governor, educator, scientist, architect, diplomat.

—— Autobiography of Thomas Jefferson, 1743–1790, together with a summary of the chief events in Jefferson's life, an introduction and notes by Paul Leicester Ford, and a foreword by George Haven Putnam. New York, G. P. Putnam's Sons, 1914. xlii, 162 p. port.

E332.J44

Prepared in 1821. Apparently first published in the *Memoir, Correspondence, and Miscellanies.*

—— Basic writings of Thomas Jefferson. Edited by Philip S. Foner. New York, Willey Book Co. [1944] xviii, 816 p. illus., facsims. E302.J442

—— Calendar of the correspondence of Thomas Jefferson. Washington, Dept. of State, 1894–1903. 3 v. (U.S. Bureau of Rolls and Library. Bulletin, no. 6, 8, 10)

CD3031.A3, no. 6, 8, 10
E302.J452

Issued also in the congressional series.
Reprinted in New York by B. Franklin (1970).

—— The commonplace book of Thomas Jefferson, a repertory of his ideas on government. With an introduction and notes by Gilbert Chinard. Baltimore, Md., John [sic] Hopkins Press, 1926. 403 p. (The John [sic] Hopkins studies in Romance literatures and languages, extra volume, 2) [E302.J454]

Micro 37784 E

Jefferson's interpretive notes on law, political science, and religion taken during his early years.

—— The complete Jefferson, containing his major writings, published and unpublished, except his letters. Assembled and arranged by Saul K. Padover, with illustrations and analytic index. New York, Distributed by Duell, Sloan & Pearce [1943] xxix, 1322 p. illus., facsims., port. E302.J4564

"Selected bibliography": p. 1301–1302.
Reprinted in Freeport, N.Y., by Books for Libraries Press (1969).

—— The family letters of Thomas Jefferson. Edited by Edwin Morris Betts and James Adam Bear, Jr. Columbia, Mo., University of Missouri Press [1966] 506 p. illus., geneal. table, maps, ports. E332.86 1966

—— Jefferson himself, the personal narrative of a many-sided American. Edited by Bernard Mayo. Boston, Houghton Mifflin Co., 1942. xv, 384 p. illus., facsim., plan, plates, ports. E332.J464

"Notes and sources": p. [347]–365.
Reprinted in Charlottesville by the University Press of Virginia (1970).

—— A Jefferson profile as revealed in his letters. Selected and arranged with an introduction by Saul K. Padover. New York, J. Day Co. [1956] xxiv, 359 p.

E332.J466

Bibliography: p. 349–350.

—— The Jeffersonian cyclopedia; a comprehensive collection of the views of Thomas Jefferson classified and arranged in alphabetical order under nine thousand titles relating to government, politics, law, education, political economy, finance, science, art, literature, religious freedom, morals, etc. Edited by John P. Foley. New York, Funk & Wagnalls Co., 1900. xxii, 1009 p. plates, ports. JK113.J4 1900

Reprinted in New York by Russell & Russell (1967).

—— The life and selected writings of Thomas Jefferson. Edited, and with an introduction, by Adrienne Koch & William Peden. New York, Modern Library [1944] xliv, 730 p. facsim. (The Modern library of the world's best books) E332.J47

—— The manuscript of Jefferson's unpublished errata list for Abbé Morellet's translation of the *Notes on Virginia. In* Virginia. University. *Bibliographical Society.* Papers. v. 1; 1948/49. Charlottesville, 1948. p. 3–24.

Z1008.V55, v. 1

Introduction and notes by Joseph M. Carrière.

—— Memoir, correspondence, and miscellanies, from the papers of Thomas Jefferson. Edited by Thomas Jefferson Randolph. Charlottesville [Va.] F. Carr, 1829. 4 v. facsims. (part fold.), port. E302.J458

Another edition was published the same year in London.

—— Papers. Julian P. Boyd, editor; Lyman H. Butterfield and [others] associate editors. Princeton, Princeton University Press, 1950+ illus., facsims., maps, ports. E302.J463

Partial contents: v. 1. 1760–1766.—v. 2. 1777 to 18 June 1779.—v. 3. 18 June 1779 to 30 September 1780.—v. 4. 1 October 1780 to 24 February 1781.—v. 5. 25 February 1781 to 20 May 1781.—v. 6. 21 May 1781 to 1 March 1784.—v. 7. 2 March 1784 to 25 February 1785.—v. 8. 25 February to 31 October 1785.—v. 9. 1 November 1785 to 22 June 1786.—v. 10. 22 June to 31 December 1786.—v. 11. 1 January to 6 August 1787.—v. 12. 7 August 1787 to 31 March 1788.—v. 13. March to 7 October 1788.—v. 14. 8 October 1788 to 26 March 1789.—v. 15. 27 March 1789 to 30 November 1789.—v. 16. 30 November 1789 to 4 July 1790.

———— ———— Index, v. 1+ Compiled by Elizabeth J. Sherwood and Ida T. Hopper. Princeton, Princeton University Press, 1954+   E302.J463 Index
Vol. 2 compiled by E. J. Sherwood.

———— Thomas Jefferson, architect; original designs in the collection of Thomas Jefferson Coolidge, Junior, with an essay and notes by Fiske Kimball. Boston, Printed for private distribution at the Riverside Press, Cambridge, 1916. vii, 205, xi p. 233 facsims. on 50 l.
                                E332.J48 Rare Bk. Coll.
                                NA737.J4A3 Rare Bk. Coll.
"The Jefferson papers, by Worthington Chauncey Ford": p. [1]–9.
"The architectural books owned by Thomas Jefferson": p. 90–101.
"Known drawings among Jefferson papers outside the Coolidge collection": p. 200–205.
Reprinted in New York by Da Capo Press (1968. E332.J48 1968).

———— The Thomas Jefferson papers. New York, Dodd, Mead [1963] ix, 304 p. facsims., ports. (The Papers of the Founding Fathers)   E302.J4632

———— Thomas Jefferson's Farm book, with commentary and relevant extracts from other writings. Edited by Edwin Morris Betts. [Princeton] Published for the American Philosophical Society by Princeton University Press, 1953. xxii p., facsim: 178 (i.e. 168) p., 552 p. illus., maps, port. (Memoirs of the American Philosophical Society, v. 35)   S451.V8J4
Bibliography: p. 529–531.

———— Thomas Jefferson's Garden book, 1766–1824, with relevant extracts from his other writings. Annotated by Edwin Morris Betts. Philadelphia, American Philosophical Society, 1944. xiv, 704 p. facsims., plans, plates, ports. (Memoirs of the American Philosophical Society, v. 22)   SB479.J4
"Books and pamphlets on agriculture, gardening, and botany in the library of Thomas Jefferson": p. 655–662. Bibliography: p. 663–666.

———— Thomas Jefferson's thoughts on the Negro. Journal of Negro history, v. 3, Jan. 1918: 55–89.
                                E185.J86, v. 3
Excerpts from the Ford edition of Jefferson's *Writings* with comments and notes by Carter G. Woodson.

———— Unpublished correspondence of Jefferson and Adams to [Philip] Mazzei [1782–1815] Virginia maga-

zine of history and biography, v. 51, Apr. 1943: 113–133.   F221.V91, v. 51

———— The writings of Thomas Jefferson. Collected and edited by Paul Leicester Ford. New York, G. P. Putnam's Sons, 1892–99. 10 v.   E302.J466
Contents: v. 1. 1760–1775.—v. 2. 1776–1781.—v. 3. 1781–1784.—v. 4. 1784–1787.—v. 5. 1788–1792.—v. 6. 1792–1794.—v. 7. 1795–1801.—v. 8. 1801–1806.—v. 9. 1807–1815.—v. 10. 1816–1826.

———— The writing of Thomas Jefferson. Library ed., containing his Autobiography, Notes on Virginia, parliamentary manual, official papers, messages and addresses, and other writings, official and private, now collected and published in their entirety for the first time, including all the original manuscripts, deposited in the Department of State and published in 1853 by order of the Joint Committee of Congress; with numerous illustrations and a comprehensive analytical index. Andrew A. Lipscomb, editor-in-chief. Albert Ellery Bergh, managing editor. Washington, D.C., Issued under the auspices of the Thomas Jefferson Memorial Association of the United States, 1903–4. 20 v. facsims. (part fold.), fold. map, plates, ports.
                                E302.J4685
"A contribution to a bibliography of Thomas Jefferson, compiled by Richard Holland Johnston": v. 20 (iv, 73 p.)
Facsimile reprint of the "Jefferson Bible" appended to v. 20.

———— The writings of Thomas Jefferson: being his autobiography, correspondence, reports, messages, addresses, and other writings, official and private. Published by the order of the Joint Committee of Congress on the Library. From the original manuscripts, deposited in the Department of State. With explanatory notes . . . by the editor, H. A. Washington. Philadelphia, J. B. Lippincott, 1869–71. 9 v. port.   E302.J465
Earlier edition, 1853–54.
Contents: 1. Autobiography, with appendix. Correspondence.—2–6. Correspondence.—7. Correspondence. Reports and opinions while secretary of state.—8. Inaugural addresses and messages. Replies to public addresses. Indian addresses. Miscellaneous: Notes on Virginia. Biographical sketches of distinguished men. The batture at New Orleans.—9. Jefferson's manual. The Anas. Miscellaneous papers.

ADAMS, HERBERT B. Thomas Jefferson and the University of Virginia. With authorized sketches of Hampden-Sidney, Randolph-Macon, Emory-Henry, Roanoke, and Richmond colleges, Washington and Lee University, and Virginia Military Institute. Washington, Govt. Print. Off., 1888. 308 p. illus., port. (U.S. Bureau of Education. Circular of information, 1888, no. 1. Contributions to American educational history, no. 2)   LD5678.3.A18
Includes bibliographies.

ADAMS, JAMES T. The living Jefferson. New York, C. Scribner's Sons, 1936. vii, 403 p.   E332.A24

American Philosophical Society, *Philadelphia.* Thomas Jefferson. Papers read before the American Philosophical Society in celebration of the bicentennial of Thomas Jefferson, third president of the society. Philadelphia, American Philosophical Society, 1943. 199–289 p. facsims., ports. [*Its* Proceedings, v. 87, July 1943]
Q11.P5, v. 87

Bibliographic footnotes.

Contents: Introduction to the Jefferson bicentennial program, by E. G. Conklin.—What is still living in the political philosophy of Thomas Jefferson? by Carl Becker.—Jefferson as a lawyer, by R. B. Morris.—Thomas Jefferson—farmer, by M. L. Wilson.—Thomas Jefferson and the classics, by L. B. Wright.—Notes on Thomas Jefferson as a natural philosopher, by Harlow Shapley.—Jefferson and the arts, by Fiske Kimball.—The old political philosophy and the new, by John Dickinson.—Jefferson and the American Philosophical Society, by Gilbert Chinard.—The beginnings of the American Philosophical Society, by Carl Van Doren.

ANDREWS, STUART. Thomas Jefferson, American encyclopaedist. History today, v. 17, Aug. 1967: 501–509. illus., ports. D1.H818, v. 17

BEAR, JAMES A. Thomas Jefferson and the ladies. Augusta historical bulletin, v. 6, fall 1970: 4–19. port.
F232.A9A94, v. 6

BEDINI, SILVIO A. Thomas Jefferson, clock designer. *In* American Philosophical Society, *Philadelphia.* Proceedings, v. 108, June 1964: 163–180. illus., facsims.
Q11.P5, v. 108

BELLOT, HUGH HALE. Thomas Jefferson in American historiography. *In* Royal Historical Society, *London.* Transactions. 5th ser., v. 4; 1954. London. p. 135–155.
DA20.R9, 5th s., v. 4

BENSON, C. RANDOLPH. Thomas Jefferson as social scientist. Rutherford, Fairleigh Dickinson University Press [1971] 333 p. E332.2.B4

Bibliography: p. 313–323.

BERMAN, ELEANOR D. Thomas Jefferson among the arts; an essay in early American esthetics. New York, Philosophical Library [1947] xviii, 305 p. illus., facsims., ports. E332.B47

Bibliography: p. 273–281.

BERMAN, ELEANOR D. *and* E. C. McCLINTOCK. Thomas Jefferson and rhetoric. Quarterly journal of speech, v. 33, Feb. 1947: 1–8. PN4071.Q3, v. 33

BINGER, CARL A. L. Thomas Jefferson, a well-tempered mind. New York [1970] 209 p. col. port.
E332.2.B55 1970

Bibliography: p. [197]–198.

BOEHM, DWIGHT, *and* EDWARD SCHWARTZ. Jefferson and the theory of degeneracy. American quarterly, v. 9, winter 1957: 448–453. AP2.A3985, v. 9

On Jefferson's rebuttal, in his *Notes on the State of Virginia*, of Buffon's and Raynal's theory that the American climate caused living organisms to degenerate.

BOWERS, CLAUDE G. The young Jefferson, 1743–1789. Boston, Houghton Mifflin Co., 1945. xxx, 544 p. illus., facsim., plates, ports. E332.B78

Bibliography: p. 525–530.

BOYD, JULIAN P. The chasm that separated Thomas Jefferson and John Marshall. *In* Dietze, Gottfried, *ed.* Essays on the American Constitution; a commemorative volume in honor of Alpheus T. Mason. Englewood Cliffs, N.J., Prentice-Hall [1964] p. 3–20.
KF4550.A2D5

——— Thomas Jefferson's "Empire of Liberty." Virginia quarterly review, v. 24, autumn 1948: 538–554.
AP2.V76, v. 24

BRODIE, FAWN M. The great Jefferson taboo. American heritage, v. 23, June 1972: 48–57, 97–100. facsim., port.
E171.A43, v. 23

On Jefferson's relationship with Sally Hemings.

BROWN, RALPH H. Jefferson's *Notes on Virginia.* Geographical review, v. 33, July 1943: 467–473.
G1.G35, v. 33

Questions Jefferson's skill as a geographer.

BROWN, STUART G. The mind of Thomas Jefferson. Ethics, v. 73, Jan. 1963: 79–99. BJ1.I6, v. 73

BROWNE, CHARLES A. Thomas Jefferson and the scientific trends of his time. Waltham, Mass., Chronica Botanica Co., 1943. 63 p. illus., facsims., maps, plans. (Chronica botanica reprints, no. 1) E332.B9

"References": p. [60]–63.

Also published in *Chronica Botanica*, v. 8, summer 1944, p. 361–423.

CHINARD, GILBERT. Jefferson's influence abroad. Mississippi Valley historical review, v. 30, Sept. 1943: 171–186. E171.J87, v. 30

Contends that Jefferson's liberal principles and writings denied him the reputation enjoyed by either Franklin or Washington in the autocratic nations of Europe.

——— Thomas Jefferson, the apostle of Americanism. 2d ed., rev. Boston, Little, Brown, 1939. xviii, 548 p. illus., facsims., plates, ports. E332.C536 1939

First edition published in 1929.

COHEN, WILLIAM. Thomas Jefferson and the problem of slavery. Journal of American history, v. 56, Dec. 1969: 503–526. E171.J87, v. 56

Argues that Jefferson's wealth, status, and political position were dependent upon the system of slavery, and while he abhorred the institution he never actively opposed it.

COLBOURN, HAROLD TREVOR. The Saxon heritage: Thomas Jefferson looks at English history. 1953.

Thesis (Ph.D.)—Johns Hopkins University.

—— Thomas Jefferson's use of the past. William and Mary quarterly, 3d ser., v. 15, Jan. 1958: 56–70.
F221.W71, 3d s., v. 15

CONANT, JAMES B. Thomas Jefferson and the development of American public education. Berkeley, University of California Press, 1962. x, 164 p. (Jefferson memorial lectures) LB695.J4C6

"Bibliographic notes": p. 65.

CRAGAN, THOMAS M. Thomas Jefferson's early attitudes toward manufacturing, agriculture, and commerce. ([331] p.) Micro AC–1, no. 65–10,112

Thesis (Ph.D.)—University of Tennessee.
Abstracted in *Dissertation Abstracts*, v. 26, Oct. 1965, p. 2158.

CRIPE, HELEN L. P. Thomas Jefferson and music. 1972. ([294] p.) Micro AC–1, no. 72–26,802

Thesis (Ph.D.)—University of Notre Dame.
Abstracted in *Dissertation Abstracts International*, v. 33A, Oct. 1972, p. 1632.

DAVIS, DAVID B. Was Thomas Jefferson an authentic enemy of slavery? An inaugural lecture delivered before the University of Oxford on 18 February 1970. Oxford, At the Clarendon Press, 1970. 29 p. E332.2.D38

DAVIS, RICHARD B. Jefferson as collector of Virginiana. *In* Virginia. University. *Bibliographical Society.* Studies in bibliography; papers. v. 14. Charlottesville, 1961. p. 117–144. Z1008.V55, v. 14

DORFMAN, JOSEPH. The economic philosophy of Thomas Jefferson. Political science quarterly, v. 55, Mar. 1940: 98–121. H1.P8, v. 55

DUMBAULD, EDWARD. A manuscript from Monticello: Jefferson's library in legal history. American Bar Association journal, v. 38, May 1952: 389–392, 446–447.
K1.M385, v. 38

On his preservation of early colonial laws.

—— Thomas Jefferson, American tourist, being an account of his journeys in the United States of America, England, France, Italy, the Low countries, and Germany. Norman, University of Oklahoma Press, 1946. xv, 266 p. facsims., plates, ports. E332.D8

Bibliography: p. 241–260.

FLEMING, THOMAS J. The man from Monticello; an intimate life of Thomas Jefferson. New York, Morrow, 1969. 409 p. illus., ports. E332.F6

Bibliography: p. 391–393.

FOOTE, HENRY W. Thomas Jefferson, champion of religious freedom, advocate of Christian morals. Boston, Beacon Press, 1947. ix, 70 p. port. E332.F65

Reissued in 1960 under the title *The Religion of Thomas Jefferson.*

FORD, PAUL L. Thomas Jefferson in undress. Scribner's magazine, v. 12, Oct. 1892: 509–516. AP2.S4, v. 12

Based on Jefferson's note and expense books, 1771–90.

FRARY, IHNA T. Thomas Jefferson, architect and builder; with an introduction by Fiske Kimball. [3d ed.] Richmond, Garrett and Massie [1950] xiii, 154 p. facsim., plans, plates. E332.F84 1950
NA737.J4F7 1950

Bibliography: p. 151.
The first edition was published in 1931.

GALBREATH, CHARLES B. Thomas Jefferson's views on slavery. Ohio archaeological and historical quarterly, v. 34, Apr. 1925: 184–202. F486.O51, v. 34

GOFF, FREDERICK R. Jefferson the book collector. *In* U.S. *Library of Congress.* Quarterly journal, v. 29, Jan. 1972: 32–47. illus., facsims. Z881.U49A3, v. 29

A discussion of Jefferson's second or "Great Library," which was sold to the Library of Congress in 1815.

GOULD, WILLIAM D. The religious opinions of Thomas Jefferson. Mississippi Valley historical review, v. 20, Sept. 1933: 191–208. E171.J87, v. 20

Contemporary pamphleteers misrepresented his religious opinions and promoted the widespread belief that he was non-Christian; Gould finds that Jefferson believed in God, immortality, and the individual's responsibility for the care of his own soul.

GRAY, GILES W. Thomas Jefferson's interest in parliamentary practice. Speech monographs, v. 27, Nov. 1960: 315–322. PN4077.S6, v. 27

GRISWOLD, ALFRED WHITNEY. The agrarian democracy of Thomas Jefferson. American political science review, v. 40, Aug. 1946: 657–681. JA1.A6, v. 40

HARROLD, FRANCIS L. The upper house in Jeffersonian political theory. Virginia magazine of history and biography, v. 78, July 1970: 281–294.
F221.V91, v. 78

HELLMAN, CLARISSE DORIS. Jefferson's efforts towards the decimalization of United States weights and measures [1783–1817] Isis, v. 16, Nov. 1931: 266–314.
Q1.I7, v. 16

HENLINE, RUTH. A study of *Notes on the State of Virginia* as an evidence of Jefferson's reaction against the theories of the French naturalists. Virginia magazine of history and biography, v. 55, July 1947: 233–246.
F221.V91, v. 55

HESLEP, ROBERT D. Thomas Jefferson & education. New York, Random House [1969] 131 p. (Studies in the Western educational tradition) LA206.H47

Includes bibliographic references.

HONEYWELL, ROY J. The educational work of Thomas Jefferson. Cambridge, Harvard University Press, 1931. xvi, 295 p. plates, port. (Harvard studies in education, v. 16) E332.H77

Bibliography: p. 289–295.
Reprinted in New York by Russell & Russell (1964).

JOHNSTON, RICHARD H. A contribution to a bibliography of Thomas Jefferson. Washington, D.C., 1905. 73 p. Z8452.J75

Printed for the author from the Jefferson memorial edition of *The Writings of Thomas Jefferson.*

KAPLAN, LAWRENCE S. Jefferson and France; an essay on politics and political ideas. New Haven, Yale University Press, 1967. ix, 175 p. (Yale historical publications. The Wallace Notestein essays, 5) E332.45.K3

"Bibliographical note": p. [153]–168.
The author's thesis (Ph.D.), with the same title, was submitted to Yale University in 1951.

KIMBALL, MARIE G. Jefferson, the road to glory, 1743 to 1776. New York, Coward-McCann [1943] ix, 358 p. illus., facsims., map (on lining papers), plates, ports. E332.K5

Bibliographic references included in "Notes" (p. 307–335).

—— Jefferson; the scene of Europe, 1784 to 1789. New York, Coward-McCann [1950] ix, 357 p. illus., map (on lining papers), ports. E332.K513 1950

Bibliographic references included in "Notes" (p. 311–342).

—— Jefferson, war and peace, 1776 to 1784. New York, Coward-McCann [1947] ix, 398 p. map (on lining papers), plate, ports. E332.K52

Bibliographic references included in "Notes" (p. 363–390).

KIMBALL, SIDNEY FISKE. The life portraits of Jefferson and their replicas. *In* American Philosophical Society, *Philadelphia.* Proceedings, v. 88, Dec. 1944: 497–534. plates, ports. Q11.P5, v. 88

KNOLES, GEORGE E. The religious ideas of Thomas Jefferson. Mississippi Valley historical review, v. 30, Sept. 1943: 187–204. E171.J87, v. 30

KOCH, ADRIENNE, *comp.* Jefferson. Englewood Cliffs, N.J., Prentice-Hall [1971] viii, 180 p. (Great lives observed) E332.2.K62

Includes bibliographic references.

Includes contemporary writings by and about Jefferson as well as opinions by five Jefferson scholars.

—— Jefferson and Madison; the great collaboration. New York, Knopf, 1950. xv, 294, xiv p. E332.K58 1950

Bibliographic footnotes.

—— The philosophy of Thomas Jefferson. New York, Columbia University Press, 1943. xiv, 208 p. (Columbia studies in American culture, no. 14) E332.K6

Issued also as thesis (Ph.D.)—Columbia University, 1943.
Bibliography: p. [191]–199.

—— Power and morals and the Founding Fathers: Jefferson. Review of politics, v. 15, Oct. 1953: 470–490. JA1.R4, v. 15

LAMBETH, WILLIAM A., *and* WARREN H. MANNING. Thomas Jefferson as an architect and a designer of landscapes. Boston, Houghton Mifflin Co., 1913. xi, 121 p. facsims., plans, plates. E332.L22 NA737.J4L3

LANCASTER, CLAY. Jefferson's architectural indebtedness to Robert Morris. *In* Society of Architectural Historians. Journal, v. 10, Mar. 1951: 3–10. illus. NA1.A327, v. 10

LEHMANN, KARL. Thomas Jefferson, American humanist. New York, Macmillan, 1947. xiii, 273 p. illus., port. E332.2.L4

Bibliographic references included in "Notes" (p. 211–260).
Reprinted in Chicago by the University of Chicago Press (1965).

LEVY, LEONARD W. Jefferson & civil liberties; the darker side. Cambridge, Belknap Press of Harvard University Press, 1963. xv, 225 p. (A publication of the Center for the Study of the History of Liberty in America, Harvard University) JC599.U5L45

Bibliography: p. 179–186.

LEWIS, ANTHONY M. Jefferson and the American Union, 1769–1781. 1946.

Thesis (Ph.D.)—University of Michigan.

—— Jefferson's *Summary View* as a chart of political union. William and Mary quarterly, 3d ser., v. 5, Jan. 1948: 34–51. F221.W71, 3d s., v. 5

Argues that Jefferson saw more clearly than any of his contemporaries the desirability of a division of sovereign powers between local and central authorities, thus anticipating the American confederacy and the development of a British commonwealth.

LYMAN, JANE L. Jefferson and Negro slavery. Journal of Negro education, v. 16, winter 1947: 10–27. LC2701.J6, v. 16

MALONE, DUMAS. Jefferson and his time. Boston, Little, Brown, 1948+ illus., maps, ports. E332.M25

"Select critical bibliography": v. 1, p. [457]–470; v. 2, p. [494]–504; v. 3, p. [513]–530; v. 4, p. [509]–524.
Contents: v. 1. Jefferson the Virginian. 1948.—v. 2. Jefferson and the rights of man. 1952.—v. 3. Jefferson and the ordeal of liberty. 1962.—v. 4. Jefferson the President: first term, 1801–1805.

MARTIN, EDWIN T. Thomas Jefferson: scientist. New York, H. Schuman [1952] x, 289 p. illus., ports. E332.M33

"References": p. 261–283.

MERRIAM, CHARLES E. The political theory of Jefferson. Political science quarterly, v. 17, Mar. 1902: 24–45. H1.P8, v. 17

MILLER, AUGUST C.   Jefferson as an agriculturist. Agricultural history, v. 16, Apr. 1942: 65–78.
S1.A16, v. 16

MORSE, JOHN T.   Thomas Jefferson. Boston, Houghton, Mifflin, 1883. vi, 351 p. (American statesmen, [v. 11])
E176.A53, v. 11
E332.M88

Reprinted in New Rochelle, N.Y., by Arlington House (1970).

MOTT, ROYDEN J.   Sources of Jefferson's ecclesiastical views. Church history, v. 3, Dec. 1934: 267–284.
BR140.A45, v. 3

O'NEAL, WILLIAM B.   A checklist of writings on Thomas Jefferson as an architect. [Charlottesville? 1959] 18 p. (American Association of Architectural Bibliographers. Publication no. 15)
Z8452.O5

PADOVER, SAUL K.   Jefferson. New York, Harcourt, Brace [1942] 459 p. illus., geneal. table, plates, ports.
E332.P12

Bibliography: p. 435–447.

PALMER, ROBERT R.   The dubious democrat: Thomas Jefferson in Bourbon France. Political science quarterly, v. 72, Sept. 1957: 388–404.
H1.P8, v. 72

PARKS, EDD W.   Jefferson as a man of letters. Georgia review, v. 6, winter 1952: 450–459.   AP2.G375, v. 6

PARTON, JAMES.   Life of Thomas Jefferson, third President of the United States. Boston, J. R. Osgood, 1874. vi, 764 p. port.   E332.P27

Reprinted in New York by Da Capo Press (1971).

—— [Thomas Jefferson] Atlantic monthly, v. 29, Jan.–June 1872: 16–33, 179–197, 312–331, 395–412, 517–534, 676–694; v. 30, July–Nov. 1872: 32–49, 174–192, 273–288, 405–424, 547–565.   AP2.A8, v. 29–30

Contents: College days of Thomas Jefferson.—Jefferson a student of law.—Thomas Jefferson a Virginia lawyer.—Jefferson in the House of Burgesses of Virginia.—Jefferson in the service of Revolutionary Virginia.—Jefferson in the Continental Congress.—Jefferson a reformer of old Virginia.—Jefferson governor of Virginia.—Thomas Jefferson as a sore-head.—Jefferson American minister in France.—Jefferson's return from France in 1789.

PATTERSON, CALEB PERRY.   The constitutional principles of Thomas Jefferson. Austin, University of Texas Press, 1953. xi, 211 p.   E332.P32

Bibliography: p. 191–199.
Reprinted in Gloucester, Mass., by P. Smith (1967) and in Freeport, N.Y., by Books for Libraries Press (1971).

—— Jefferson, the lawyer. University of Pittsburgh law review, v. 11, spring 1950: 369–396.   K25.N7, v. 11

PETERSON, MERRILL D.   The Jefferson image in the American mind. New York, Oxford University Press, 1960. x, 548 p.   E332.2.P4

"Guide to sources": p. [459]–522.

—— comp..   Thomas Jefferson; a profile. New York, Hill and Wang [1967] xx, 262 p. (American profiles)
E332.76.P4

Bibliography: p. 261–262.
Includes writings by Dixon Wecter, Carl Becker, John Dos Passos, Robert R. Palmer, Merrill D. Peterson, William D. Grampp, Dumas Malone, Julian P. Boyd, Louis B. Wright, Horace M. Kallen, and George Harmon Knoles.

—— Thomas Jefferson and commercial policy, 1783–1793. William and Mary quarterly, 3d ser., v. 22, Oct. 1965: 584–610.   F221.W71, 3d s., v. 22

—— Thomas Jefferson and the new Nation; a biography. New York, Oxford University Press, 1970. ix, 1072 p. illus., ports.   E332.P45

Bibliography: p. [1011]–1047.

PLEASANTS, SAMUEL A.   Thomas Jefferson—educational philosopher. In American Philosophical Society, Philadelphia. Proceedings, v. 111, Feb. 1967: 1–4.
Q11.P5, v. 111

PULLEY, JUDITH P.   An agent of nature's republic abroad: Thomas Jefferson in pre-revolutionary France. In Essays in history. v. 11; 1965/66. Charlottesville, Va. [1966?] p. 5–26.   D2.E75, v. 11

—— The bittersweet friendship of Thomas Jefferson and Abigail Adams. In Essex Institute, Salem, Mass. Historical collections, v. 108, July 1972: 193–216.
E72.E7E81, v. 108

RADBILL, SAMUEL X.   Thomas Jefferson and the doctors. In College of Physicians of Philadelphia. Transactions & studies, 4th ser., v. 37, Oct. 1969: 106–114.
R15.P5, 4th s., v. 37

RANDALL, HENRY S.   The life of Thomas Jefferson. New York, Derby & Jackson, 1858. 3 v. illus., facsims. (part fold.), ports.   E332.R18

Reprinted in Freeport, N.Y., by Books for Libraries Press (1970) and in New York by Da Capo Press (1972).

RANDOLPH, SARAH N.   The domestic life of Thomas Jefferson. Compiled from family letters and reminiscences, by his great-granddaughter. New York, Harper, 1871. 432 p. illus., facsims., plan, plates, ports.
E332.25.R2 1871

Reprinted in New York by Ungar (1958) with an introduction by Dumas Malone.

—— —— 3d ed. Cambridge, Mass., University Press, 1939. xiii, 383 p. illus., facsims., plan, plates, port.   E332.25.R2 1939

SCHACHNER, NATHAN.   Thomas Jefferson, a biography. New York, Appleton-Century-Crofts [1951] 2 v. (xiii, 1070 p.) illus., ports.   E332.S32

Bibliography: p. 1049–1060.
Reprinted in New York by T. Yoseloff (1957).

SENSABAUGH, GEORGE F.   Jefferson's use of Milton in the ecclesiastical controversies of 1776. American literature, v. 26, Jan. 1955: 552–559.   PS1.A6, v. 26

SHENKIR, WILLIAM G., GLENN A. WELSCH, *and* JAMES A. BEAR. Thomas Jefferson: management accountant. Journal of accountancy, v. 133, Apr. 1972: 33–47. facsims.　　　　　　　　　　　　　　HF5601.J7, v. 133

SHEPHERD, HENRY E. Thomas Jefferson as a philologist. American journal of philology, v. 3, no. 10, 1882: 211–214.　　　　　　　　　　　　　　P1.A5, v. 3

A supplementary article by H. C. Montgomery, entitled "Thomas Jefferson as a Philologist (II)," appears in v. 55, Oct. 1944, p. 367–371.

THURLOW, CONSTANCE E., *and* FRANCIS L. BERKELEY. The Jefferson papers of the University of Virginia, a calendar. With an appended essay by Helen D. Bullock on the papers of Thomas Jefferson. Charlottesville, Published by the University of Virginia Library, with assistance from the Research Council of the Richmond Area University Center, 1950. xii, 343 p. (University of Virginia bibliographical series, no. 8)　　Z1009.V57, no. 8

Republished, with a supplementary calendar compiled by John Casteen and Anne Freudenberg of manuscripts acquired from 1950 to 1970, in Charlottesville by the University Press of Virginia for the University of Virginia Library ([1973] 495 p. Z6616.J4T45 1973).

TOMPKINS, HAMILTON B. Bibliotheca Jeffersoniana; a list of books written by or relating to Thomas Jefferson. New York, G. P. Putnam's Sons, 1887. 187 p.
　　　　　　　　　　　　　　Z8452.T65

Printed on one side of leaf only.
Lists 301 titles.

TUCKER, GEORGE. The life of Thomas Jefferson, third president of the United States. With parts of his correspondence never before published, and notices of his opinions on questions of civil government, national policy, and constitutional law. Philadelphia, Carey, Lea & Blanchard, 1837. 2 v. illus.　　E332.T89

U. S. *Library of Congress. Jefferson Collection.* Catalogue of the Library of Thomas Jefferson. Compiled with annotations by E. Millicent Sowerby. Washington, Library of Congress, 1952–59. 5 v. illus., facsims., map (on lining papers)　　　　　Z881.U5 1952j
　　　　　　　　　　　　　　Z663.4.C4

See also the compiler's "Thomas Jefferson and His Library," in the *Papers* of the Bibliographical Society of America, v. 50, 3d quarter 1956, p. 213–228.

VAN PELT, CHARLES B. Thomas Jefferson and Maria Cosway. American heritage, v. 22, Aug. 1971: 22–29, 102–103. illus., facsim., ports. (part col.)
　　　　　　　　　　　　　　E171.A43, v. 22

VERNER, COOLIE. The maps and plates appearing with the several editions of Mr. Jefferson's *Notes on the State of Virginia.* Virginia magazine of history and biography, v. 59, Jan. 1951: 21–23.　　　　F221.V91, v. 59

—— Mr. Jefferson distributes his *Notes*; a preliminary checklist of the first edition. *In* New York (City). Public Library. Bulletin, v. 56, Apr. 1952: 159–186.
　　　　　　　　　　　　　　Z881.N6B, v. 56

—— —— Offprint. New York, New York Public Library, 1952. 31 p.　　　　Z8452.V42

—— Mr. Jefferson makes a map. *In* Imago mundi; a review of early cartography. v. 14; 1959. 's-Gravenhage. p. 96–108. fold. map.　　GA1.I6, v. 14

Discusses Jefferson's map of Virginia, 1786.

VOSSLER, OTTO. Die amerikanischen Revolutionsideale in ihrem Verhältnis zu den europäischen; untersucht an Thomas Jefferson. München, R. Oldenbourg, 1929. 197 p. (Beiheft 17 der Historischen Zeitschrift)
　　　　　　　　　　　　　　E210.V97

"Literaturverzeichnis": p. [193]–197.

For a presentation of Vossler's thesis, see Robert R. Palmer's article, "A Neglected Work: Otto Vossler on Jefferson and the Revolutionary Era," in the *William and Mary Quarterly*, 3d ser., v. 12, July 1955, p. 462–471.

WICKS, ELLIOT K. Thomas Jefferson—a religious man with a passion for religious freedom. Historical magazine of the Protestant Episcopal church, v. 36, Sept. 1967: 271–283.　　　　　BX5800.H5, v. 36

WILSTACH, PAUL. Jefferson and Monticello. With a foreword by Edwin Anderson Alderman. 3d ed., rev. Garden City, N.Y., Doubleday, Doran, 1931. xv, 262 p. illus., facsim., plans, plates, ports.　　E332.W754

WILTSE, CHARLES M. Thomas Jefferson on the law of nations. American journal of international law, v. 29, Jan. 1935: 66–81.　　　　JX1.A6, v. 29

WISE, W. HARVEY, *Jr., and* JOHN W. CRONIN. A bibliography of Thomas Jefferson. Washington, D.C., Riverford Co., 1935. 72 p. (Presidential bibliographical series, no. 3)　　　　　Z8452.W81

Lists 1,248 titles, including multiple editions, government documents, and periodical literature.

WOODFIN, MAUDE H. Contemporary opinion in Virginia of Thomas Jefferson. *In* Essays in honor of William E. Dodd, by his former students at the University of Chicago. Edited by Avery Craven. Chicago, University of Chicago Press [1935] p. 30–85.　　E173.E785

WOOLERY, WILLIAM K. The relation of Thomas Jefferson to American foreign policy, 1783–1793. Baltimore, Johns Hopkins Press, 1927. ix, 128 p. (Johns Hopkins University studies in historical and political science, ser. 45, no. 2)　　　　H31.J6, 45th s., no. 2
　　　　　　　　　　　　　　E332.W92

Published also as thesis (Ph.D.)—Johns Hopkins University, 1926.

Bibliography: p. 123–125.

13702

JEFFERYS, THOMAS (*d.* 1771)†
England. Map engraver, geographer.

HARLEY, JOHN BRIAN. The bankruptcy of Thomas Jefferys: an episode in the economic history of eighteenth century map-making. *In* Imago mundi; a review of early cartography. v. 20; 1966. Amsterdam. p. 27–48. facsims., maps. GA1.I6, v. 20

13703

JEFFRIES, JOHN (1743?–1819)*
Massachusetts; England. Physician, Loyalist surgeon, balloonist, scientist.

—— First aerial voyage across the English Channel. Diary of Dr. John Jeffries, the aeronaut. Magazine of American history, with notes and queries, v. 13, Jan. 1885: 66–88. ports. E171.M18, v. 13

—— A narrative of the two aerial voyages of Doctor Jeffries with Mons. Blanchard; with meteorological observations and remarks. The first voyage, on the thirtieth of November, 1784, from London into Kent; the second, on the seventh of January, 1785, from England into France. London, Printed for the author and sold by J. Robson, 1786. 60 p. plate, port.
TL620.B6J4 1786 Rare Bk. Coll.
"Presented to the Royal Society, April 14, 1785; and read before them, January 1786."
Reprinted in New York by Arno Press (1971. 60 p. TL620.B6J4 1971).

NORTON, MARY BETH. America's first aeronaut: Dr. John Jeffries. History today, v. 18, Oct. 1968: 722–730.
DI.H818, v. 18

13704

JEMISON, MARY (1743–1833)*
Pennsylvania; New York. Landowner.

AYRAULT, ISABEL. The true story of Mary Jemison, the white woman of the Genesee. *In* Rochester Historical Society, *Rochester N.Y.* Publications. v. 8. Rochester, 1929. p. 193–218. plate. F129.F7R58, v. 8

SEAVER, JAMES E. A narrative of the life of Mrs. Mary Jemison, who was taken by the Indians, in the year 1755, when only about twelve years of age, and has continued to reside amongst them to the present time. Containing an account of the murder of her father and his family; her sufferings; her marriage to two Indians; her troubles with her children; barbarities of the Indians in the French and Revolutionary wars; the life of her last husband, &c.; and many historical facts never before published. Carefully taken from her own words, Nov. 29th, 1823. To which is added, an appendix, containing an account of the tragedy at the Devil's Hole, in 1763, and of Sullivan's expedition; the traditions, manners, customs, &c., of the Indians, as believed and practised at the present day, and since Mrs. Jemison's captivity; together with some anecdotes, and other entertaining matter. Canandaigua [N.Y.] Printed by J. D. Bemis, 1824. xv, 189 p. E87.J46 Rare Bk. Coll.
Reprinted in Ann Arbor, Mich., by Allegany Press (1967).

—— —— Ed. of 1942, presenting the first ed. literally restored, together with chapters added to later editions by Ebenezer Mix, Lewis Henry Morgan, William Clement Bryant and William Pryor Letchworth. Enl. with historical and archaeological memoranda and critical notes by modern authorities. New York, American Scenic & Historic Preservation Society, 1942. 459 p. illus., facsims., maps, plates, ports. E87.J529
Bibliography of *The Life of Mary Jemison*, by C. D. Vail, revised by Elmer Adler for the 1925 edition and by E. H. Hall for the 1932 edition: p. 274–298. "Tabulation of editions of 'The Life of Mary Jemison' ": fold. table mounted on p. [299].

13705

JENKINS, JAMES (1764–*ca.* 1845)
South Carolina. Revolutionary soldier, Methodist clergyman.

—— Some events of the American Revolution in South Carolina as recorded by the Rev. James Jenkins. *In* South Carolina Historical Association. Proceedings. 1945. Columbia, S.C. p. 23–34. F266.S58, 1945
Introduction and notes by George F. Scheer.

13706

JENKINS, JOHN (1728–1785)*
Connecticut; Pennsylvania. Settler, surveyor, assemblyman, judge.

WILCOX, WILLIAM J. John Jenkins, the judge and the colonel. *In* Wyoming Commemorative Association, *Wilkes-Barre, Pa.* Proceedings. 1949. Wilkes-Barre, Pa. p. 7–19. E241.W9W85, 1949
Gives equal attention to the careers of Judge John Jenkins (1728–1785) and his namesake (1751–1827).

13707

JENNINGS, JOHN (*ca.* 1738–1802)*
Pennsylvania. Revolutionary soldier, frontiersman.

—— John Jennings' journal at Fort Chartres, and trip to New Orleans, 1768. Pennsylvania magazine of history and biography, v. 31, July 1907: 304–310.
F146.P65, v. 31

—— John Jennings "Journal from Fort Pitt to Fort Chartres in the Illinois country," March–April, 1766. Pennsylvania magazine of history and biography, v. 31, Apr. 1907: 145–156. F146.P65, v. 31

13708

JENNISON, WILLIAM (1757–1843)
Massachusetts. Revolutionary officer.

—— Extracts from the journal of William Jennison, Jr., lieutenant of marines in the Continental Navy [1777–80] Pennsylvania magazine of history and biography, v. 15, Apr. 1891: 101–108. F146.P65, v. 15
Introduction and notes by Richard S. Collum.

13709

JENYNS, SOAME (1704–1787)†

England. Poet, writer.

—— The works of Soame Jenyns, Esq. . . . including several pieces never before published. To which are prefixed, short sketches of the history of the author's family, and also of his life, by Charles Nalson Cole, Esq. 2d ed. London, T. Cadell, 1793. 4 v. port.

AC7.J445 1793

Contents: 1. Sketches of the life of Soame Jenyns, Esq. with a short account of his family. Poems.—2. On the immorality of the soul. Pieces, religious, moral, metaphysical, and political.—3. A free inquiry into the nature and origin of evil. Disquisitions on several subjects.—4. A view of the internal evidence of the Christian religion.

13710

JERVIS, JOHN (1735–1823)†

England. British naval officer.

—— Letters of Captain Sir John Jervis to Sir Henry Clinton, 1774–1782. Edited by Marie Martel Hatch. American Neptune, v. 7, Apr. 1947: 87–106.

V1.A4, v. 7

13711

JETT, THOMAS (*d. ca.* 1792)

Virginia. Merchant.

—— Letter book of Thomas Jett [1769–74] William and Mary College quarterly historical magazine, v. 17, July 1908: 20–26; v. 21, Oct. 1912: 84–90.

F221.W71, v. 17, 21

13712

JEWELL, BRADBURY (1752–1828)

New Hampshire. Surveyor, farmer, Revolutionary officer.

—— The fishbasket papers: the diaries, 1768–1823, of Bradbury Jewell, Esquire, of Tamworth, Durham, and Sandwich, New Hampshire. Edited by Marjory Gane Harkness. Peterborough, N.H., R. R. Smith [1963] xii, 236 p. illus., facsims., maps (on lining papers)

F44.T15J4 1963

13713

JOHNSON, GUY (1740–1788)*†

Ireland; New York; Quebec; England. Indian agent, assemblyman, Loyalist.

—— Guy Johnson on the North American Indians: his reply to Dr. Robertson's inquiries, in May 1775. Magazine of American history, with notes and queries, v. 28, Nov. 1892: 372–380. E171.M18, v. 28

Contributed by William L. Stone.

—— Guy Johnson's opinions on the American Indian. Pennsylvania magazine of history and biography, v. 77, July 1953: 311–327. F146.P65, v. 77

Introduction by Milton W. Hamilton.

—— —— Offprint. Philadelphia, 1953. 311–327 p.

E99.I7J75

GIBB, HARLEY L. Colonel Guy Johnson, Superintendent General of Indian Affairs, 1774–82. *In* Michigan Academy of Science, Arts and Letters. Papers. v. 27; 1941. Ann Arbor, 1942. p. 595–613.

Q11.M56, v. 27

13714

JOHNSON, JACOB (1713–1797)

Connecticut; Pennsylvania. Clergyman, missionary, Indian negotiator.

JOHNSON, FREDERICK C. Reminiscences of Rev. Jacob Johnson, M.A., first pastor, First Presbyterian Church, Wilkes-Barre, 1772–1790. *In* Wyoming Historical and Geological Society, *Wilkes-Barre, Pa.* Proceedings and collections. v. 11; 1910. Wilkes-Barre, p. 103–200. F157.W9W94, v. 11

Reprinted, with an expanded title, in Wilkes-Barre by the Wilkes-Barre Record Print (1911. 100 p. F157.W9J4).

—— Rev. Jacob Johnson of Wallingford, (Conn.) and Wilkes-Barre, (Pa.). [Wilkes-Barre?] 1904. 32 p.

CS71.J7 1904

13715

JOHNSON, *Sir* JOHN, *Bart.* (1742–1830)*

New York; Canada. Military officer, landowner, Indian negotiator, Loyalist.

BRYCE, PETER H. Sir John Johnson, Baronet, Superintendent-General of Indian Affairs, 1743–1830. *In* New York State Historical Association. Quarterly journal, v. 9, July 1928: 233–271. port. F116.N865, v. 9

DE PEYSTER, JOHN WATTS. Sir John Johnson, the first American-born baronet. [New York, 1880] 12, xxxvi p.

E278.J6D4

"Proofs considered, in connection with the vindication of Sir John Johnson, Bart." (appendixes 1 and 2): p. [i]–xxxvi.

FRASER, DUNCAN. Sir John Johnson's rent roll of the Kingsborough patent. Ontario history, v. 52, Sept. 1960: 176–189. F1056.O58, v. 52

HAMILTON, MILTON W. An American knight in Britain: Sir John Johnson's tour, 1765–1767. *In* New York State Historical Association. New York history, v. 42, Apr. 1961: 119–144. port. F116.N865, v. 42

—— John Mare's portrait of Sir John Johnson. *In* New York Historical Society. Quarterly, v. 43, Oct. 1959: 440–451. F116.N638, v. 43

MYERS, THEODORUS B. The Tories or Loyalists in America; being slight historical tracings, from the footprints of Sir John Johnson and his contemporaries in the Revolution. Albany, Press of J. Munsell's Sons, 1882. 123 p. facsims., plates, ports. E277.M99

WALKER, MABEL G. Sir John Johnson, Loyalist. Mississippi Valley historical review, v. 3, Dec. 1916: 318–346.
E171.J87, v. 3

13716
JOHNSON, *Lady* MARY WATTS (1753–1815)
New York. Wife of Sir John Johnson (1742–1830).

[JOHNSON, SUSAN G. C.] Adventures of a lady in the War of Independence in America. Workington [Eng.] P. D. Lambe, Printer, "Solway Pilot" Off., 1874. facsim: cover, 9, 4–57 l. E278.J61J65 Rare Bk. Coll.

Photostat (negative) from the original in the Boston Public Library.

Five of the six leaves inserted following the cover contain information in manuscript regarding the author and subject of the book.

13717
JOHNSON, ROBERT (1745–1815)
Virginia; Kentucky. Assemblyman, settler.

GUTHRIE, BEN. Big Crossing Station, built by Robert Johnson. Recorded in John D. Shane's interview with pioneer Ben Guthrie. Filson Club history quarterly, v. 5, Jan. 1931: 1–15. F446.F484, v. 5

Introduction and notes by Mrs. William H. Coffman.

13718
JOHNSON, SAMUEL (1696–1772)*
Connecticut; New York. Anglican clergyman, educator, writer.

——— Samuel Johnson, president of King's college: his career and writings. Edited by Herbert and Carol Schneider; with a foreword by Nicholas Murray Butler. New York, Columbia University Press, 1929. 4 v. facsims., plates, ports. LD1245 1754a

"Bibliography and chronological index": v. 4, p. [283]–361.

Contents: v. 1. Autobiography and letters.—v. 2. The philosopher.—v. 3. The churchman.—v. 4. Founding King's College.

BEARDSLEY, EBEN EDWARDS. Life and correspondence of Samuel Johnson, D.D., missionary of the Church of England in Connecticut, and first president of King's College, New York. New York, Hurd & Houghton, 1874, xii, 380 p. port. LD1245 1754b

DEMILLE, GEORGE E. One man seminary. Historical magazine of the Protestant Episcopal church, v. 38, Dec. 1969: 373–379. BX5800.H5, v. 38

ELLIS, JOSEPH J. The Puritan mind in transition: the American Samuel Johnson (1696–1772). 1969.

Thesis (Ph.D.)—Yale University.

HORNBERGER, THEODORE. Samuel Johnson of Yale and King's College. A note on the relation of science and

religion in provincial America. New England quarterly, v. 8, Sept. 1935: 378–397. F1.N62, v. 8

PENNINGTON, EDGAR L. The Reverend Samuel Johnson, his life and ministry. Hartford, Conn., Church Missions Pub. Co., 1938. 31 p. (Soldier and servant, [no. 192]) BX5995.J59P4

Bibliographic footnotes.

SMITH, P. KINGSLEY. Samuel Johnson of Connecticut. Anglican theological review, v. 39, July 1957: 217–229.
BR1.A5, v. 39

13719
JOHNSON, SAMUEL (1709–1784)†
England. Writer.

——— Letters of Samuel Johnson, LL.D. Collected and edited by George Birkbeck Hill. Oxford, Clarendon Press, 1892. 2 v. fold. facsim. PR3533.A2 1892

Contents: 1. Oct. 30, 1731–Dec. 21, 1776.—2. Jan. 15, 1777–Dec. 18, 1784.

——— The works of Samuel Johnson. Oxford, Printed for W. Pickering, London; and Talboys and Wheeler, Oxford, 1825. 11 v. port. (Oxford English classics) PR3520.E25

Vols. 6–7 and 10–11 have imprint: London, Published by W. Pickering and Talboys and Wheeler, Oxford.

Edited by F. P. Walesby.

Contents: v. 1. Essay on the life and genius of Dr. Johnson [by Arthur Murphy] Poems, and tales.—v. 2–3. The Rambler.—v. 4. The Adventurer and Idler.—v. 5. Miscellaneous pieces.—v. 6. Reviews, political tracts, and Lives of eminent persons.—v. 7–8. Lives of the poets.—v. 9. Journey to the Hebrides. Tales of the imagination. Prayers and sermons.—v. 10–11. Parliamentary debates.

Reprinted in New York under the title *Dr. Johnson's Works* by AMS Press (1970).

BOSWELL, JAMES. Life of Johnson, together with Journal of a tour to the Hebrides and Johnson's Diary of a journey into North Wales. Edited by George Birkbeck Hill. Rev. and enl. ed. by L. F. Powell. Oxford, Clarendon Press, 1934–64. 6 v. illus., facsims., fold. map, ports. PR3533.B6 1934

Vols. 5–6, with revisions by L. F. Powell, first published in 1950; republished in 1964 as second edition, with further revisions.

Contents: v. 1–4. The life.—v. 5. The tour to the Hebrides, and The journey into North Wales. 2d ed.—v. 6. Index, table of anonymous persons, bibliography, errata. 2d ed.

CLIFFORD, JAMES L., and DONALD J. GREENE. Samuel Johnson; a survey and bibliography of critical studies. Minneapolis, University of Minnesota Press [1970] xvi, 333 p. Z8455.8.C62

GREENE, DONALD J. The politics of Samuel Johnson. New Haven, Yale University Press, 1960. xix, 354 p.
PR3537.P6G7

Bibliographic references included in "Notes" (p. 285–324).

The author's thesis (Ph.D.), with the same title, was submitted to Columbia University in 1954 (Micro AC–1, no. 8672).

———— Samuel Johnson. New York, Twayne Publishers [1970] 245 p. (Twayne's English authors series, TEAS 95) PR3533.G73

Bibliography: p. 235–239.

HIBBERT, CHRISTOPHER. The personal history of Samuel Johnson. New York, Harper & Row [c1971] xiv, 364 p. illus. (A Cass Canfield book) PR3533.H38 1971b

Bibliography: p. 339–343.

IRWIN, GEORGE. Samuel Johnson: a personality in conflict. [Auckland] Auckland University Press, 1971. xiv, 168 p. PR3533.I7

Includes bibliographic references.

KRUTCH, JOSEPH W. Samuel Johnson. New York, H. Holt, [1944] xiv, 599 p. facsims, plates, ports. PR3533.K7

"References": p. 555–569.

LANG, DANIEL R. Dr. Samuel Johnson in America; a study of his reputation: 1750–1812. Urbana, Ill., 1939. 20 p. PR3534.L3 1939

Abstract of thesis (Ph.D.)—University of Illinois.

McADAM, EDWARD L. Dr. Johnson and the English law. [Syracuse, N.Y.] Syracuse University Press [1951] xi, 209 p. Law

McCAMIC, CHARLES. Doctor Samuel Johnson and the American colonies. Cleveland, Rowfant Club, 1925. 50 p. (Rowfantia, an occasional publication of the Rowfant Club, no. 10, April 1925) PR3537.A6M3

"Prepared for publication and privately printed for the Rowfant Club, by the Arthur H. Clark Co."

McNAIR, ARNOLD DUNCAN McNAIR, *Baron.* Dr. Johnson and the law. Cambridge [Eng.] University Press, 1948. xi, 114 p. PR3537.L3M3

"Legal bibliography": p. x.

MIDDENDORF, JOHN H. Dr. Johnson and mercantilism. Journal of the history of ideas, v. 21, Jan./Mar. 1960: 66–83. B1.J75, v. 21

O'FLAHERTY, PATRICK. Johnson as rhetorician: the political pamphlets of the 1770's. Studies in Burke and his time, v. 11, spring 1970: 1571–1584. DA506.B9B86, x. 11

See Donald J. Greene's comment on O'Flaherty's article on p. 1585–1588 and O'Flaherty's reply on p. 1589–1591.

[TOWERS, JOSEPH] An essay on the life, character, and writings, of Dr. Samuel Johnson. London, C. Dilly, 1786. 124 p. [PR3533.T6] Micro 34556 PR

WINANS, ROBERT B. Works by and about Samuel Johnson in eighteenth-century America. *In* Bibliographical Society of America. Papers, v. 62, 4th quarter 1968: 537–546. Z1008.B51P, v. 62

13720

JOHNSON, STEPHEN (1724–1786)

Connecticut. Clergyman, Revolutionary chaplain.

SILL, EDWARD E. A forgotten Connecticut patriot. [New Haven, Conn., Tuttle, Morehouse & Taylor Co., 1901] 45 p. (Publications of the Connecticut Society of the Order of the Founders and Patriots of America, no. 4) E186.6.C75, no. 4
E263.C5S5

13721

JOHNSON, THOMAS (1732–1819)*

Maryland. Lawyer, delegate to the Continental Congress, governor.

DELAPLAINE, EDWARD S. The life of Thomas Johnson, member of the Continental Congress, first governor of the state of Maryland, and associate justice of the United States Supreme Court. New York, F.H. Hitchcock, 1927. xi, 517 p. illus., facsims., plates, ports. E302.6.J65D3
KF8745.J6D4

First published in the *Maryland Historical Magazine*, v. 14–21, passim.

13722

JOHNSON, THOMAS (1742–1819)

Vermont. Revolutionary officer.

———— Colonel Thomas Johnson's papers. *In* Vermont Historical Society. Proceedings. 1923/25. Bellows Falls, Vt. 1926. p. 87–140. F46.V55, 1923/25

KEYES, FRANCIS P. The story of Colonel Thomas Johnson. Granite monthly, v. 52, Aug.–Sept. 1920: 316–324, 355–367. illus. F31.G75, v. 52

13723

JOHNSON, *Sir* WILLIAM, *Bart.* (1715–1774)*†

Ireland; New York. Trader, landowner, militia officer, Indian agent.

———— Manuscripts of Sir William Johnson [1754–74. From the originals on file in the Secretary of State's Dep't, Albany] *In* The Documentary history of the state of New-York. By E. B. O'Callaghan. v. 2. Albany, Weed, Parsons, Public Printers, 1849. p. [543]–1009. fold. maps, plans, port. F122.D63, v. 2

The original manuscripts of these Johnson papers were deposited in the secretary of state's office in 1801. The entire collection is printed here with the exception of a few papers and letters that disappeared before 1849. The manuscripts were later rearranged in other collections and transferred to the State Library. They must, however, be distinguished from the collection of Sir William Johnson manuscripts in 26 volumes acquired by the State Library between 1850 and 1863, even though a number of the papers printed here found their way later to that collection. All the Johnson papers in the State Library are listed in the *Calendar of the Sir William Johnson Manuscripts in the New York State Library* (Albany, 1909), compiled by Richard E. Day.

———— The papers of Sir William Johnson [1738–74] Prepared for publication by the Division of Archives and History. Albany, University of the State of New York, 1921–62. 13 v. facsims., fold. charts, maps (part fold.), plans (part fold.), plates (part fold.), ports.

E195.J62

Partial contents: v. 4–8. Post-war period, 1763–1774 [personal correspondence]—v. 10. The Indian uprising, 1763.—v. 11. The Indian uprising, 1764–1765.—v. 12. Indian affairs, 1766–1774.—v. 13. Miscellaneous documents, 1738–1774. Chronological list of documents.

BRADLEY, ARTHUR G. Johnson of the Mohawk. Army quarterly, v. 26, Apr. 1933: 59–70. U1.A85, v. 26

BUELL, AUGUSTUS C. Sir William Johnson. New York, D. Appleton, 1903. vii, 281 p. map, plates, ports. (Appletons' historic lives series) E195.J67

DAILEY, WILLIAM N. P. Sir William Johnson, Baronet. Chronicles of Oklahoma, v. 22, summer 1944: 164–175. F691.C55, v. 22

FLEXNER, JAMES T. Mohawk baronet: Sir William Johnson of New York. New York, Harper [1959] ix, 400 p. maps, col. plates, col. ports. E195.J659

"Sources": p. 359–368.

GRIFFIS, WILLIAM E. Sir William Johnson and the Six Nations. New York, Dodd, Mead [1891] xii, 227 p. ("Makers of America") E195.J68
E176.M23

HAMILTON, MILTON W. The library of Sir William Johnson. *In* New-York Historical Society. Quarterly, v. 40, July 1956: 209–251. illus., facsims., port.

F116.N638, v. 40

———— Myths and legends of Sir William Johnson. *In* New York State Historical Association. New York history, v. 34, Jan. 1953: 3–26. F116.N865, v. 34

———— A new portrait of Sir William Johnson. *In* New York Historical Society. Quarterly, v. 42, Oct. 1958: 316–327. ports. F116.N638, v. 42

Attributed to Matthew Pratt, who may have painted it about 1772 or 1773.

———— Sir William Johnson and Pennsylvania. Pennsylvania history, v. 19, Jan. 1952: 52–74. port.

F146.P597, v. 19

———— Sir William Johnson and the Indians of New York. [Albany?] University of the State of New York, State Education Dept., Office of State History [1967] vii, 47 p. illus., ports. E195.J663

Bibliography: p. 46–47.

———— Sir William Johnson, interpreter of the Iroquois. Ethnohistory, v. 10, summer 1963: 270–286.

E51.E8, v. 10

———— Sir William Johnson of Johnson Hall. American heritage, new ser., v. 3, spring 1952: 20–25. illus. (part col.), col. ports. E171.A43, n.s., v. 3

———— Sir William Johnson's wives. *In* New York State Historical Association. New York history, v. 38, Jan. 1957: 18–28. F116.N865, v. 38

KLINGBERG, FRANK J. Sir William Johnson and the Society for the Propagation of the Gospel (1749–1774). Historical magazine of the Protestant Episcopal church, v. 8, Mar. 1939: 4–37. BX5800.H5, v. 8

LINCOLN, CHARLES H. *comp.* A calendar of the manuscripts of Sir William Johnson in the library of the Society. *In* American Antiquarian Society, *Worcester, Mass.* Proceedings, new ser., v. 18, Oct. 1907: 367–401. E172.A35, n.s., v. 18

MISHOFF, WILLARD O. The Indian policy of Sir William Johnson. 1933.

Thesis (Ph.D.)—State University of Iowa.

New York (State). State Library, *Albany.* Calendar of the Sir William Johnson manuscripts in the New York State Library. Compiled by Richard E. Day. Albany, University of the State of New York, 1909. 683 p. (*Its* History bulletin no. 8) Z881.N61BH, no. 8
E195.J673

POUND, ARTHUR. Johnson of the Mohawks; a biography of Sir William Johnson, Irish immigrant, Mohawk war chief, American soldier, empire builder. In collaboration with Richard E. Day. New ed. with supplementary chapter. New York, Macmillan Co., 1930. xvii, 568 p. coats of arms, facsims., maps, plates, ports.

E195.J676

Bibliography: p. 549–550.
The first edition, also dated 1930, has been reprinted by Books for Libraries Press (Freeport, N.Y., 1971).

SEYMOUR, FLORA W. S. Lords of the valley, Sir William Johnson and his Mohawk brothers. London, New York, Longmans, Green, 1930. ix, 278 p. map, plates, ports. E195.J682

"Bibliographical notes": p. 274–278.

STONE, WILLIAM L. The life and times of Sir William Johnson, Bart. Albany, J. Munsell, 1865. 2 v. illus., port. E195.J685

The material for this work was collected and the first seven chapters were written by William L. Stone, father of the author.

13724

JOHNSON, WILLIAM SAMUEL (1727–1819)*

Connecticut. Lawyer, assemblyman, colonial agent, delegate to the Continental Congress, delegate to the Constitutional Convention.

———— Letters of William Samuel Johnson to the governors of Connecticut [1766–71] *In* Massachusetts Historical Society, *Boston*. Collections. 5th ser., v. 9. Boston, 1885. p. 211–490.   F61.M41, 5th s., v. 9

BEARDSLEY, EBEN EDWARDS. Life and times of William Samuel Johnson, LL.D., first senator in Congress from Connecticut, and president of Columbia College, New York. New York, Hurd and Houghton, 1876. xii, 218 p. port.   E302.6.J7B3
          Micro 8528E

Reprinted in Freeport, N.Y. by Books for Libraries Press (1972).

CURLEY, THOMAS M. William Samuel Johnson, an American at Twickenham, 1768. *In* Connecticut Historical Society, *Hartford*. Bulletin, v. 30, Apr. 1965: 45–49.   F91.C67, v. 30

GREENE, EVARTS B. William Samuel Johnson and the American Revolution. Columbia University quarterly, v. 22, June 1930: 157–178. port.   LH1.C7Q2, v. 22

GROCE, GEORGE C. William Samuel Johnson; a maker of the Constitution. New York, Columbia University Press, 1937. x, 227 p. double plan, port.   E302.6.J7G8

Bibliography: p. [199]–218.
The author's thesis (Ph.D.), with the same title, was submitted to Columbia University in 1937.

13725

JOHNSTON, ELIZABETH LICHTENSTEIN (1764–1848)

Georgia; Scotland. Loyalist.

———— Recollections of a Georgia Loyalist. Written in 1836. Edited by Rev. Arthur Wentworth Eaton. New York, M. F. Mansfield, 1901. 224 p. ports.   E278.J7J72

Reprinted in Spartanburg, S.C., by the Reprint Co. (1972).

13726

JOHNSTON, JAMES (1738–1808)

Scotland; Georgia. Printer, publisher.

LAWRENCE, ALEXANDER A. James Johnston, Georgia's first printer. With decorations & remarks on Johnston's work by Ray Dilley. Savannah, Pigeonhole Press, 1956. 54 p. illus., facsims.   Z232.J7L3

Bibliographic references included in "Notes" (p. [45]–54).

McMURTRIE, DOUGLAS C. James Johnston, first printer in the royal colony of Georgia. Library, 4th ser., v. 10, June 1929: 73–84.   Z671.L69, 4th s., v. 10

————————— Offprint. London, Bibliographical Society, 1929. [73]–80 p.   Z232.J7M2

———— The pioneer printer of Georgia. Chicago, Eyncourt Press, 1930. 11 p.   Z232.J7M3

13727

JOHNSTON, JONAS (ca. 1740–1779)

North Carolina. Assemblyman, Revolutionary officer.

BATTLE, KEMP D. Life and services of Colonel Jonas Johnston. North Carolina booklet, v. 18, Apr. 1919: 178–187.   F251.N86, v. 18

JOHNSTON, HUGH B. Colonel Jonas Johnston, a North Carolina patriot. Daughters of the American Revolution magazine, v. 91, May 1957: 606–610, 698.   E202.5.A12, v. 91

13728

JOHNSTON, SAMUEL (1733–1816)*†

North Carolina. Lawyer, assemblyman, delegate to the Continental Congress, governor.

ALLEN, T. MURRAY. Samuel Johnston in Revolutionary times. *In* Duke University, Durham, N.C. Trinity College Historical Society. Historical papers. ser. 5; 1905. Durham. p. 39–49.   [F251.D83, ser. 5]
          Micro 9370F

CONNOR, ROBERT D. W. Governor Samuel Johnston of North Carolina. North Carolina booklet, v. 11, Apr. 1912: 259–285.   F251.N86, v. 11

13729

JOHNSTON, WILLIAM (1732–1772)

Connecticut. Portrait artist.

CONNELL, NEVILLE. William Johnston, American painter, 1732–1772. *In* Barbadoes Museum and Historical Society. Journal, v. 24, Aug. 1958: 152–160.   F2041.B217, v. 24

LYMAN, LILA P. William Johnston (1732–1772); a forgotten portrait painter of New England. *In* New York Historical Society. Quarterly, v. 39, Jan. 1955: 62–78. facsim., ports.   F116.N638, v. 39

SAWITZKY, SUSAN. The portraits of William Johnston; a preliminary checklist [1760–64] *In* New York Historical Society. Quarterly, v. 39, Jan. 1955: 79–89. ports.   F116.N638, v. 39

13730

JONES, DAVID (1736–1820)*

Delaware; New Jersey. Baptist clergyman, missionary, Revolutionary chaplain.

—— A journal of two visits made to some nations of Indians on the west side of the river Ohio, in the years 1772 and 1773. With a biographical notice of the author, by Horatio Gates Jones. New York, Reprinted for J. Sabin, 1865. xi, ix, 127 p. (Sabin's reprints, no. 2)

F517.J6

Micro 01291, reel 160, no. 5E

From the original edition published at Burlington, N.J., 1774.

The 1774 edition has also been reprinted in New York by Arno Press (1971).

13731

JONES, HORATIO (1763–1836)

New York. Settler.

HARRIS, GEORGE H. The life of Horatio Jones: the true story of Hoc-sago-wah, prisoner, pioneer, and interpreter. *In* Buffalo Historical Society. Publications. v. 6. Buffalo, 1903. p. 383–514. F129.B8B88, v. 6

13732

JONES, JOHN (1729–1791)*

New York; Pennsylvania. Surgeon, physician.

—— John Jones' introductory lecture to his course in surgery (1769), King's College, printed from the author's manuscript. With an outline of the succeeding lectures and of his notes on the lectures of William Hewson. *In* College of Physicians of Philadelphia. Transactions & studies, 4th ser., v. 8, Dec. 1940: 180–190. R15.P5, 4th s., v. 8

Introduction by W. B. McDaniel.

—— Plain concise practical remarks, on the treatment of wounds and fractures; to which is added, an appendix, on camp and military hospitals; principally designed, for the use of young military and naval surgeons, in North-America. [2d ed.] Philadelphia, Printed, and sold, by Robert Bell, in Third Street, 1776. 114 p.

RD30.J6 1776 Rare Bk. Coll.

Micro 01291, reel 186, no. 2E

First edition published in 1775.

Published in 1795 under title: *The Surgical Works of the Late John Jones.*

Reprinted in New York by the New York Times (1971).

CHARLES, STEVEN T. John Jones, American surgeon and conservative patriot. Bulletin of the history of medicine, v. 39, Sept./Oct. 1965: 435–449. facsim., port. R11.B93, v. 39

HUME, EDGAR E. Surgeon John Jones, U.S. Army, father of American surgery and author of America's first medical book. Bulletin of the history of medicine, v. 13, Jan. 1943: 10–32. facsims., port. R11.B93, v. 13

13733

JONES, JOHN PAUL (1747–1792)*†

Scotland; Virginia. Revolutionary naval commander.

—— Letters of John Paul Jones, printed from the unpublished originals in Mr. W. K. Bixby's collection. With introductory remarks by General Horace Porter and Franklin B. Sanborn. Boston, Printed exclusively for members of the Bibliophile Society [New York, De Vinne Press] 1905. 123 p. facsims., port.

E271.J778 Rare Bk. Coll.

Recovery of the body of John Paul Jones, by General Horace Porter: p. 57–123.

—— Life and correspondence of John Paul Jones, including his narrative of the campaign of the Liman. From original letters and manuscripts in the possession of Miss Janette Taylor. New York [D. Fanshaw, Printer] 1830. 555 p. port. E207.J7J63

Edited by Robert Charles Sands.

Extract of a journal of the campaign in the Liman, in 1788: p. 407–472.

—— Memoirs of Rear-Admiral Paul Jones . . . Now first compiled from his original journals and correspondence; including an account of his services under Prince Potemkin, prepared for publication by himself. Edinburgh, Oliver & Boyd, 1830. 2 v. E207.J7J65

Micro 01291, reel 246, no. 7E

Reprinted in one volume in New York by Da Capo Press (1972. E207.J7A3 1972).

An edition entitled *Life of Rear-Admiral John Paul Jones* was published in Philadelphia by Walker & Gillis in 1845 (399 p. E207.J7J68) and reprinted in New York by the J. W. Lovell Co. (1883. E207.J7J7).

BELKNAP, GEORGE E. The life and character of John Paul Jones. In New Hampshire Historical Society. Proceedings. v. 3; 1897/99. Concord, 1902. p. 414–435.

F31.N52, v. 3

BONNEL, ULANE. John Paul Jones et Paris. Neptunia, no. 87, 3rd trimester 1967: 23–29. illus., ports.

V2.N4, no. 87

BRADY, CYRUS T. Commodore Paul Jones. New York, D. Appleton, 1900. xv, 480 p. maps, plan, port. (Great commanders) E207.J7B8

BUELL, AUGUSTUS C. Paul Jones, founder of the American Navy; a history. New York, C. Scribner's Sons, 1900. 2 v. double facsim., map, plan, ports.

E207.J7B92

Reprinted in Freeport, N.Y. by Books for Libraries Press (1971).

COTTEN, ELIZABETH H. The John Paul Jones-Willie Jones tradition; a defense of the North Carolina position. Chapel Hill, N.C., 1966. viii, 118 p. ports.

E207.J7C6

Bibliographic footnotes.

CULLEN, JOSEPH P. John Paul Jones: a personality profile. American history illustrated, v. 1, Apr. 1966: 12–19. illus., ports. E171.A574, v. 1

A note entitled "How Jones's Body Was Discovered" appears on p. 20–21.

DE KOVEN, ANNA F.   The life and letters of John Paul Jones. New York, C. Scribner's Sons, 1913. 2 v. illus., facsims., maps. plates, ports.   E207.J7D29

"Sources of information": v. 2, p. 485–490.

FISKE, JOHN.   Paul Jones and the Armed Neutrality. Atlantic monthly, v. 60, Dec. 1887: 786–804.   AP2.A8, v. 60

JOHNSON, AMANDUS.   John Paul Jones and the Swedes. *In* American Swedish Historical Foundation, *Philadelphia*. Yearbook. 1959. Philadelphia. p. 40–46.   E184.S23A685, 1959

JOHNSON, G. A.   John Paul Jones—strategist and tactician. *In* United States Naval Institute. Proceedings, v. 54, July 1928: 539–545. port.   V1.U8, v. 54

See also L. H. Bolander's notes on Jones' birthplace and his qualifications as a naval officer on p. 546–549.

LORENZ, LINCOLN.   John Paul Jones, fighter for freedom and glory. Annapolis, Md., United States Naval Institute, 1943. xxii, 846 p. illus., facsims., maps, plates, ports.   E207.J7L8

Bibliography: p. [783]–794.

MACKENZIE, ALEXANDER S.   The life of Paul Jones. By Edward Hamilton [pseud.] Aberdeen, G. Clark, 1848. 304 p.   E207.J7M16

Reprinted in Freeport, N.Y., by Books for Libraries Press (1971). First published in Boston by Hilliard, Gray (1841).

MAHAN, ALFRED T.   John Paul Jones in the Revolution. Scribner's magazine, v. 24, July–Aug. 1898: 22–36, 204–219. illus., map, port.   AP2.S4, v. 24

MORISON, SAMUEL E.   John Paul Jones, a sailor's biography. With charts and diagrams by Erwin Raisz and with photographs. Boston, Little, Brown [1959] 453 p. illus., maps, ports.   E207.J7M6

Bibliography: p. [431]–443.

——— The Willie Jones-John Paul Jones tradition. William and Mary quarterly, 3d ser., v. 16, Apr. 1959: 198–206.   F221.W71, 3d s., v. 16

Casts doubt on the legend that John Paul added "Jones" to his name out of gratitude to his alleged benefactor, Willie Jones of North Carolina.

SALISBURY, WILLIAM.   John Paul Jones and his ships: the need for more research. American neptune, v. 28, July 1968: 195–205.   V1.A4, v. 28

SHERBURNE, JOHN H.   The life and character of John Paul Jones, a captain in the United States Navy. During the Revolutionary War. 2d ed. New York, Adriance, Sherman, 1851. xvi, 408 p. fold. facsim., port.   E207.J7S6

First edition published in Washington in 1825.

STEWART, CHARLES W., *comp*.   John Paul Jones commemoration at Annapolis, April 24, 1906. Washington, Govt. Print. Off., 1907. 210 p. illus., ports. (part col.)   E207.J7S83 1907

"Compiled in the office of Library and Naval War Records, Navy Department, under authorization of the Joint Committee on Printing."

Includes bibliographies.

Contents: Introduction.—Addresses at Annapolis.—Papers and reports. Discovery, identification, and transfer of remains of John Paul Jones.—Letters of John Paul Jones.—Chronology.—Appendix.

Reissued in 1966.

STILES, W. C. I.   Paul Jones and Arnold. *In* United States Naval Institute. Proceedings, v. 61, Mar. 1935: 337–344.   V1.U8, v. 61

TAYLOR, JANETTE.   New light upon the career of John Paul Jones. *In* United States Naval Institute. Proceedings, v. 33, June 1907: 683–710.   V1.U8, v. 33

A letter written by Jones' niece to James Fenimore Cooper in 1843. See also "The Sword Presented by Louis XVI to John Paul Jones," by Charles H. Hart, on p. 712–715.

THOMSON, VALENTINE.   Knight of the seas; the adventurous life of John Paul Jones. New York, Liveright Pub. Co. [ᶜ1939] viii, 608 p. facsim., plates, ports.   E207.J7T53

"Sources and bibliography": p. [589]–603.

U.S. *Library of Congress. Manuscript Division.*   A calendar of John Paul Jones manuscripts in the Library of Congress. Compiled under the direction of Charles Henry Lincoln, of the Division of Manuscripts. Washington, Govt. Print. Off., 1903. 316 p. port.   Z6621.U58J6
Z663.34.J6

"The manuscripts calendared [883 entries] are a part of the Peter Force collection purchased by the National Government in 1867."

WARNER, JAMES H.   John Paul Jones: fighting sentimentalist. South Atlantic quarterly, v. 47, Jan. 1948: 35–44.   AP2.S75, v. 47

WARNER, OLIVER.   Paul Jones in battle. History today, v. 15, Sept. 1965: 613–618. illus.   D1.H818, v. 15

13734

JONES, JOSEPH (1727–1805)*

Virginia. Lawyer, assemblyman, delegate to the Continental Congress, judge.

——— Letters of Joseph Jones, of Virginia. 1777–1787. Washington, Dept. of State, 1889. xiv, 157 p.   F230.J77

Edited by Worthington C. Ford.

The letters are addressed to Madison, Washington and Jefferson, and a few addressed by Washington and Madison to Jones are included. "The interest of Judge Jones' letters lies mainly in the careful picture he gives of the condition of

Virginia politics subsequent to the treaty of peace with Great Britain."—Prefatory note.

Reprinted in New York by the New York Times (1971).

13735

JONES, NOBLE WYMBERLEY (*ca.* 1724–1805)*

England; Georgia. Physician, assemblyman, delegate to the Continental Congress.

COULTER, ELLIS MERTON. Wormsloe; two centuries of a Georgia family. Athens, University of Georgia Press [1955] xv, 322 p. illus., maps, ports. (Wormsloe Foundation. Publications, no. 1)　　　F289.J69C6

Bibliography: p. 289–302.

GRIMES, JOHN. Eulogy on the life and character of Dr. Noble Wymberley Jones. Georgia historical quarterly, v. 4, Mar., Dec. 1920: 17–32, 141–158.
　　　F281.G2975, v. 4

Delivered by Grimes in 1805.

13736

JONES, SAMUEL (1734–1819)*

New York. Lawyer, assemblyman.

MERRITT, JESSE. Samuel Jones. *In* Long Island Historical Society. Quarterly, v. 1, Jan. 1939: 5–11.
　　　F116.L875, v. 1

SEABURY, SAMUEL. Samuel Jones, New York's first comptroller. *In* New York State Historical Association. New York history, v. 28, Oct. 1947: 397–403. port.　　　F116.N865, v. 28

13737

JONES, SOLOMON (1756–1822)

New Jersey; Canada. Loyalist surgeon.

PIERCE, LORNE A. Doctor Solomon Jones, United Empire Loyalist. Queen's quarterly, v. 36, summer 1929: 437–448.　　　AP5.Q3, v. 36

Settler in Upper Canada in 1783.

13738

JONES, STEPHEN (1739–*ca.* 1826)

Maine. Soldier, farmer, merchant.

———— Autobiography of Stephen Jones. Sprague's journal of Maine history, v. 3, Apr. 1916: 199–218.
　　　F16.S76, v. 3

A brief biographical sketch, entitled "Stephen Jones, the First Justice of Peace East of the Penobscot," appeared in v. 1, Jan. 1914, p. 187–191.

13739

JONES, THOMAS AP THOMAS (*d.* 1800)

Virginia. Revolutionary officer, landowner.

JONES, LEWIS H. Major Thomas ap Thomas Jones, of Bathurst, a Revolutionary soldier. *In* Kentucky Historical Society. Register, v. 22, May 1924: 208–213. facsims.　　　F446.K43, v. 22

13740

JONES, *Sir* WILLIAM (1746–1794)†

England. Lawyer, Oriental scholar.

———— The works of Sir William Jones. London, G. G. and J. Robinson, 1799. 6 v. facsims., geneal. tables, plates, port.　　　AC7.J6

CANNON, GARLAND H. Freedom of the press and Sir William Jones. Journalism quarterly, v. 33, spring 1956: 179–188.　　　PN4700.J7, v. 33

On the seditious libel trial arising from the publication of his *Principles of Government* in 1782.

13741

JONES, WILLIE (1741–1805)*

North Carolina. Planter, delegate to the Continental Congress, assemblyman.

ROBINSON, BLACKWELL P. Willie Jones of Halifax. North Carolina historical review, v. 18, Jan.–Apr. 1941: 1–26, 133–170.　　　F251.N892, v. 18

13742

JOSIAH, JAMES (1751–1820)

Pennsylvania. Seaman, Revolutionary naval officer.

CLARK, WILLIAM B. James Josiah, master mariner. Pennsylvania magazine of history and biography, v. 79, Oct. 1955: 452–484. port.　　　F146.P65, v. 79

13743

JOSLIN, JOSEPH (*b.* 1759)

Connecticut. Revolutionary soldier.

———— Journal of Joseph Joslin, Jr., of South Killingly, a teamster in the Continental Service, March 1777–August 1778. *In* Connecticut Historical Society, *Hartford*. Collections. v. 7. Hartford, 1899. p. [297]–369.
　　　F91.C7, v. 7

13744

JOYNES, LEVIN (1753–1794)

Virginia. Planter, Revolutionary officer.

———— Letters from Colonel Levin Joynes to Ann, his wife, February 9, 1780–December 28, 1790. Virginia magazine of history and biography, v. 56, Apr. 1948: 142–153.　　　F221.V91, v. 56

13745

JUNCKEN, HENRY (*d. ca.* 1803)

Pennsylvania; England. Farmer, shopkeeper, Loyalist.

REED, JOHN F.   The papers of Henry Juncken, Tory, and his wife, of Springfield Township. *In* Historical Society of Montgomery County (*Pennsylvania*). Bulletin, v. 14, spring 1965: 315–330.   F157.M7H45, v. 14

13746

JUNIUS, *pseud., author of the "Letters."*

England. Signature attached to a series of letters that appeared in the *Public Advertiser*, 1769–71. The identity of Junius has never been definitely established.

——— Junius: including letters by the same writer, under other signatures, (now first collected.) To which are added, his confidential correspondence with Mr. Wilkes, and his private letters addressed to Mr. H. S. Woodfall. London, Printed by G. Woodfall, for F. C. and J. Rivington, 1812. 3 v. fold. facsims., plates.
DA508.A2 1812

Edited by John Mason Good.

——— Junius. Stat nominis umbra. London, Printed for H. S. Woodfall [1773?] 2 v.   DA508.A2 1773

Reprinted in New York by Research Reprints (1970) and Argosy-Antiquarian (1970).

——— The letters of Junius. Complete in one volume, with a copious index. Philadelphia, Printed and sold by Prichard & Hall, in Market Street between Front and Second Streets. 1791. 283 p.   DA508.A2 1791

The first American edition.

——— The letters of Junius. Edited with an introduction by C. W. Everett. London, Faber & Gwyer [1927] lviii, 410 p. illus., ports.   DA508.A2 1927

"This edition is an exact reprint of the Henry Sampson Woodfall edition of 1772."—Editor's preface.

——— The letters of Junius. With notes and illustrations, historical, political, biographical, and critical, by Robert Heron. Philadelphia, Published by Samuel F. Bradford, no. 4, South Third-Street; H. Maxwell, Printer, 1804. 2 v. ports.   DA508.A2 1804

Attributes authorship to John Dunning, first Baron Ashburton.

——— The letters of Junius complete: interspersed with the letters and articles to which he replied, and with notes, biographical and explanatory; also a prefatory enquiry respecting the real author, by John Almon. [London] Printed for R. Phillips, by J. Adlard, 1806. 2 v. fold. facsim., ports.   DA508.A2 1806

Attributes authorship to Hugh Boyd.

——— The posthumous works of Junius. To which is prefixed An inquiry respecting the author, also A sketch of the life of John Horne Tooke. New York, G. & C. & H. Carville, 1829. xii, 428 p. facsims., port.
DA508.T6J8 1829a

Preface signed J. F. (i.e., John Fellows).
The "Sketch of the Life of John Horne Tooke" is from the *Memoirs* of Alexander Stephens.

BARKER, EDMUND H.   The claims of Sir Philip Francis, K.B., to the authorship of Junius's letters, disproved: II. Some enquiry into the claims of the late Charles Lloyd, Esq., to the composition of them: III. Observations on the conduct, character, and style of the writings, of the late Right Hon. Edmund Burke: IV. Extracts from the writings of several eminent philologists, on the laconic and Asiatic, the Attic and Rhodian styles of eloquence. London, J. Bohn, 1828. lxxii, 504 p.
DA508.A6B3

BLAKEWAY, JOHN B.   An attempt to ascertain the author of the letters published under the signature of Junius. Shrewsbury [Eng.] Printed and sold by W. Eddowes, 1813. 72 p.   DA508.T6B5

The author ascribes the letters to John Horne, afterwards John Horne Tooke. See also Blakeway's second pamphlet, *The Sequel of An Attempt To Ascertain the Author of the Letters Published Under the Signature of Junius, in Which That Hitherto Impenetrable Secret Is, It Is Presumed, Fully Disclosed* (London, Longman, Hurst, Rees, Orme, and Brown, 1815. 29 p. DA508.T6B5).

BOYD, HUGH.   Miscellaneous works of Hugh Boyd, the author of the letters of Junius. With an account of his life and writings by Lawrence Dundas Campbell. London, T. Cadell and W. Davies, 1800. 2 v.
PR3326.B26 1800

Contents: v. 1. Life. Political essays: The freeholder, a series of letters addressed to the electors of the county of Antrim. Democraticus, a series of letters, originally printed in the *Publick Advertiser*, 1779. The Whig, a series of letters published in the *London Courant*, 1779–80. Genuine abstracts from two speeches of the late Earl of Chatham. Miscellaneous poems.—v. 2. Embassy to Candy. The Indian observer, 1793–94.

BRITTON, JOHN.   The authorship of the letters of Junius elucidated: including a biographical memoir of Lieutenant-Colonel Isaac Barré, M.P. London, Printed for the author, and sold by J. R. Smith, 1848. xlviii, 96 p. port.   DA508.B3B7

[BURR, WILLIAM H.]   Thomas Paine: Was he Junius? [2d ed. Washington, D.C., 1892?] 31 p.
DA508.P3B8 1892

BUSBY, THOMAS.   Arguments and facts demonstrating that the letters of Junius were written by John Lewis De Lolme . . . Accompanied with memoirs of that "most ingenious foreigner." London, Printed for Sherwood, Neely and Jones, 1816. 228 p. fold. facsim.
DA508.D4B8

CHALMERS, GEORGE.   The author of Junius ascertained: from direct proofs, and a concatenation of circumstances; amounting to moral demonstration. A new ed. with a postscript, evincing that Boyd wrote Junius, and not Francis. London, Printed for T. Egerton, 1819. vi, 148 p.   DA508.B6C55

CORDASCO, FRANCESCO.   A Junius bibliography, with a preliminary essay on the political background, text and identity; a contribution to 18th century constitutional and literary history. With eight appendices. New York, B. Franklin, 1949. 125 p. port (Burt Franklin bibliographical series, no. 2) Z8459.C6

Contends that Laughlin MacLeane (1727–1777), a Scotch adventurer and regimental surgeon, was Junius. See Cordasco's addenda to his bibliography in the *Bulletin of Bibliography*, v. 21, Sept./Dec. 1953, p. 48; v. 22, Sept./Dec. 1957, p. 96; v. 26, Apr./June 1969, p. 41. See also the compilation by Tony H. Bowyer, *A Bibliographical Examination of the Earliest Editions of the Letters of Junius* (Charlottesville, University of Virginia Press, 1957. 147 p.).

———— Thomas Paine and the history of "Junius": a forgotten *cause célèbre*. Journal of English and Germanic philology, v. 52, Apr. 1953: 226–228. PD1.J7, v. 52

COVENTRY, GEORGE. A critical enquiry regarding the real author of the letters of Junius, proving them to have been written by Lord Viscount Sackville. London, W. Phillips, 1825. xxii, 382 p. facsims., plates, port.
DA508.S3C7

EDMANDS, JOHN. A Junius bibliography. *In* Philadelphia. Mercantile Library Company. Bulletin, v. 2, July 1890–Jan. 1892: 48–52, 64–68, 85–88, 105–108, 121–124, 142–144. Z881.P543B, v. 2

———— ———— Detached copy. Z8459.E4

Lists editions of the letters of Junius published in England and America and indicates various publications on the history and authorship of the letters.

ELLEGÅRD, ALVAR. A statistical method for determining authorship: the Junius letters, 1769–1772. [Göteborg, 1962] 115 p. illus. (Acta Universitatis Gothoburgensis. Gothenburg studies in English, 13) DA508.A6E4

Includes bibliographic references.

See also the author's companion volume, *Who Was Junius?* (Stockholm, Almqvist & Wiksell [1962] 159 p. DA508.A6E42), in which he concludes that the stylistic similarities in the writings of Junius and Sir Philip Francis prove indisputably that they were one and the same.

MACLEAN, JAMES N. M. Grant of Blairfindy, Junius, and Francis. *In* London. University. *Institute of Historical Research*. Bulletin, v. 41, May 1968: 73–85.
D1.L65, v. 41

———— Reward is secondary; the life of a political adventurer and an inquiry into the mystery of 'Junius.' [London] Hodder and Stoughton [1963] xix, 558 p. illus., ports.
DA506.M3M3

Bibliography: p. 454–463.

MONAGHAN, FRANK. A new document on the identity of "Junius." Journal of modern history, v. 4, Mar. 1932: 68–71. D1.J6, v. 4

Gives the background for a 1774 report prepared for the Comte de Muy by Grant de Blairfindy who contends that double-agent Thomas Mante is Junius and states that Blairfindy himself saw Mante pen the famous letter to the King. In "Some Notes on Thomas Mante (Alias "Junius"?)," June 1932, p. 232–234, Helen B. Bates supplies additional biographical information.

[MOODY, JOEL] Junius unmasked; or, Thomas Paine the author of the letters of Junius, and the Declaration of Independence. Washington, D.C., J. Gray, 1872. 335 p. DA508.P3M5

The appendix (p. 323–335) was issued separately, and contains an examination of the claim that Sir Philip Francis was Junius.

PETERSON, F. H. The mystery of Junius. American law review, v. 55, Mar. 1921: 251–261. LL

Also published in the *Canadian Law Times*, v. 41, Aug. 1921, p. 527–536.

ROCHE, JOHN. An inquiry concerning the author of the letters of Junius; in which it is proved, by internal, as well as by direct and satisfactory evidence, that they were written by the late Right Hon. Edmund Burke. London, Printed by Whittingham and Rowland, for J. Carpenter, 1813. 294 p. DA508.B8R7

SEDGWICK, ROMNEY. The letters of Junius. Under the penname of Junius, Sir Philip Francis "threw his firebrands" at King and government during the years 1769–72. History today, v. 19, June 1969: 397–404. illus., ports. D1.H818, v. 19

SERRES, OLIVIA W. The life of the author of the letters of Junius, the Rev. James Wilmot. London, Sold by E. Williams, 1813. xcvii, 224 p. fold. facsims., plates, port.
DA508.A6S4

"The writing of Dr. Wilmot": three facsimiles at end.

SUTHERLAND, LUCY S., W. DOYLE, and J. M. J. ROGISTER. Junius and Philip Francis: new evidence. *In* London. University. *Institute of Historical Research*. Bulletin, v. 52, Nov. 1969: 158–172. D1.L65, v. 52

SYMONS, JELINGER C. William Burke the author of Junius; an essay on his era. London, Smith, Elder, 1859. 144 p. DA508.B9S8

[TAYLOR, JOHN] A discovery of the author of the letters of Junius, founded on such evidence and illustrations as explain all the mysterious circumstances and apparent contradictions which have contributed to the concealment of this "most important secret of our times." London, Printed for Taylor and Hessey, 1813. 139 p.
DA508.F8T2

An attempt "to prove that Dr. Francis, and his son . . . Sir Philip Francis, were the authors of the letters of Junius."—p. 11.

13747

KALB, JEAN, *baron* DE (1721–1780)* Originally Johann Kalb.
Germany. Revolutionary general.

———— *La Caroline méridionale*; some French sources of South Carolina Revolutionary history, with two unpublished letters of Baron de Kalb [1777] Edited by

Paul G. Sifton. South Carolina historical magazine, v. 66, Apr. 1965: 102–108.　　F266.S55, v. 66

Also lists the location of manuscript sources, in French repositories, for South Carolina history.

AEGIDI, LUDWIG K. J.　Der amerikanische General Johann Kalb. Historische Zeitschrift, 11. Bd. [2. Heft] 1864: 373–390.　　D1H6, v. 11

A review of Friedrich Kapp's biography.

COLLEVILLE, LUDOVIC, comte DE.　Les missions secrètes du général-major baron de Kalb, et son rôle dans la guerre de l'indépendance américaine. Paris, É. Perrin, 1885. 161 p.　　E207.K14C6

GREENE, GEORGE W.　General John de Kalb. Atlantic monthly, v. 36, Oct. 1875: 476–492.　AP2.A8, v. 36

HEATHCOTE, CHARLES W.　General Baron John DeKalb, who rendered loyal and devoted service for the achievement of American independence. Picket post, no. 61, July 1958: 4–9, 35. port.　　E234.P5, no. 61

KAPP, FRIEDRICH.　The life of John Kalb, major-general in the Revolutionary army. New York, H. Holt, 1884. ix, 337 p. port.　　E207.K14K2

Translated from the German.

SMITH, JOHN S.　Memoir of the Baron de Kalb. Baltimore, Printed by J. D. Toy, 1858. 36 p.　E207.K14S6

"List of Continental officers killed, captivated, wounded, and missing, in the action of the 16th and 18th August, 1780": p. [31]–32.

ZUCKER, ADOLF E.　General de Kalb, Lafayette's mentor. Chapel Hill, University of North Carolina Press [1966] ix, 251 p. port. (University of North Carolina. Studies in the Germanic languages and literatures, no. 53)　　PD25.N6, no. 53

Bibliography: p. 234–239.

13748

KALM, PEHR (1716–1779)

Sweden. Botanist, traveler.

———— The America of 1750; Peter Kalm's travels in North America; the English version of 1770, revised from the original Swedish and edited by Adolph B. Benson . . . With a translation of new material from Kalm's diary notes. New York, Wilson-Erickson, 1937. 2 v. (xvii, 797 p.) facsims., maps (part fold.), plates.　　E162.K165

Includes reproductions of the title pages of the original English, Swedish, and Dutch editions.

"The present version is the first exclusively American edition . . . in English . . . and the first one dealing with the part on United States and Canada to appear in this country . . . The part on Norway and England had been omitted . . . The hitherto untranslated portion . . . has been done into English by Miss Edith M. L. Carlborg . . . and the present

editor. The remainder . . . is based on Forster's translation."—p. xv.
"A bibliography of Peter Kalm's writings on America": v. 2, p. 770–776.
Reprinted in New York by Dover Publications (1966).

———— Travels into North America. Translated into English by John Reinhold Forster. Introduction by Ralph M. Sargent. Barre, Mass., Imprint Society, 1972. xxvi, 514 p. illus.　　E162.K173

Translation of En resa til Norra America.
Forster's translation was first published in London (1770–71. 3 v.).

BENSON, ADOLPH B.　Pehr Kalm's writings on America: a bibliographical review. Scandinavian studies and notes, v. 12, May 1933: 89–98.　　PD1505.S6, v. 12

GOWINIUS, SVEN.　Peter Kalm's America: the benefits which England could derive from her colonies in North America. Sven Gowinius, respondent, 20 June 1763, Peter Kalm, preceptor. Translated and edited by Esther Louise Larsen. Pennsylvania history, v. 22, July 1955: 216–228.　　F146.P597, v. 22

A thesis prepared by Sven Gowinius, one of Kalm's students, reflects Kalm's attitudes toward America and predicts the possibility of the separation of the English colonies from the mother country.

KERKKONEN, MARTTI.　Peter Kalm's North America journey; its ideological background and results. Helsinki, 1959. 260 p. facsims., port. (Studia historica, 1)　　E162.K22

Bibliography: p. [246]–251.

13749

KARZHAVIN, FEDOR VASIL'EVICH (1745–1812)

Russia; Virginia. Professor, translator, merchant.

DVOICHENKO-MARKOVA, EUFROSINA M.　A Russian traveler to eighteenth-century America. In American Philosophical Society, Philadelphia. Proceedings, v. 97, Sept. 1953: 350–355.　　Q11.P5, v. 97

13750

KEARSLEY, JOHN (1684–1772)*

Pennsylvania. Physician, educator.

MIDDLETON, WILLIAM S.　The John Kearsleys. Annals of medical history, v. 3, Dec. 1921: 391–402. illus., ports.　　R11.A85, v. 3

Also refers to his nephew, John Kearsley (d. 1777) a Loyalist physician.

13751

KEARSLEY, JOHN (d. 1777)

England; Pennsylvania. Physician, Loyalist.

KLEIN, RANDOLPH S. Dr. John Kearsley, Jr., the mad Tory doctor. *In* College of Physicians of Philadelphia. Transactions & studies, 4th ser., v. 36, Jan. 1969: 158–166. R15.P5, 4th s., v. 36

13752
KEITH, GEORGE KEITH ELPHINSTONE, *Viscount* (1746–1823)†

Scotland. British naval officer in America, Member of Parliament.

———— The Keith papers, selected from the letters and papers of Admiral Viscount Keith, and edited by W. G. Perrin. [London] Printed for the Navy Records Society, 1927–55. 3 v. facsim., maps (part fold.), ports. (Publications of the Navy Records Society, v. 62, 90, 96) DA70.A1, v. 62, 90, 96

Vols. 2–3 edited by Christopher Lloyd.

ALLARDYCE, ALEXANDER. Memoir of the Honourable George Keith Elphinstone, K.B., Viscount Keith, Admiral of the Red. Edinburgh, W. Blackwood, 1882. vi, 432 p. illus., maps (part fold., part col.), ports. DA87.1.K2A4

13753
KELLY, JOHN (1744–1832)

Pennsylvania. Settler, Revolutionary officer, assemblyman.

THEISS, LEWIS E. Colonel John Kelly. *In* Northumberland County (Pa.) Historical Society. Proceedings. v. 9. Sunbury, 1937. p. 119–132. facsims. F157.N8N7, v. 9

13754
KEMBLE, STEPHEN (1740–1822)

New Jersey. British officer in America.

———— The Kemble papers. [New York, Printed for the Society, 1884–85] 2 v. fold. map, port. (New York Historical Society. Collections, 1883. Publication fund series [v. 16–17]) F116.N63, 1883

Contents: v. 1. Journals of Lieut. Col. Stephen Kemble, 1773–1779, 1784–1789. General orders by Major General William Howe, Nov. 15, 1775–June 29, 1776, Oct. 6, 1776–Jan. 28, 1777, June 20–Nov. 19, 1777, Feb. 23–May 23, 1778. Gen. Sir Henry Clinton's orders, May 24–July 5, 1779. Orders by Maj.-Gen. Daniel Jones, commanding His Majesty's troops on New York island and posts depending, May 2–June 2, 1778.—v. 2. Journals of . . . Kemble, brigadier-general in command of the expedition to Nicaragua, 1780–1781. Orders of Brigadier-General Stephen Kemble, 1780–1781. Documents and correspondence, expedition to the Spanish Main and Nicaragua, 1779–1781. Index.

Volume 1 has been reprinted, with a fuller title and a new introduction and preface by George A. Billias, in Boston by Gregg Press (1972. E267.K44 1972).

FLANAGAN, VINCENT, *and* GERALD KURLAND. Stephen Kemble, New Jersey Loyalist. New Jersey history, v. 90, spring 1972: 5–26. F131.N58, v. 90

13755
KEMPE, JOHN TABOR (*fl.* 1759–1782)

New York. Lawyer, landowner, Loyalist.

CRARY, CATHERINE S. The American dream: John Tabor Kempe's rise from poverty to riches. William and Mary quarterly, 3d ser., v. 14, Apr. 1957: 176–195. F221.W71, 3d s., v. 14

13756
KEMPER, JEPTHA (*fl.* 1785)

Virginia; Kentucky. Settler.

———— John D. Shane's notes on an interview with Jeptha Kemper of Montgomery County. Filson Club history quarterly, v. 12, July 1938: 151–161. F446.F484, v. 12

Introduction and notes by Lucien Beckner.

13757
KENT, DAN (1758–1835)

Vermont. Revolutionary soldier, clergyman.

———— Action in Vermont during the Revolutionary War: Dan Kent's narrative. Vermont history, v. 39, spring 1971: 107–112. F46.V55, v. 39

Statement made to local officials in a pension application.

13758
KENT, JAMES (1763–1847)*

New York. Lawyer.

———— An American law student of a hundred years ago. American law school review, v. 2, spring 1911: 547–553. LL

In a letter to Thomas Washington in 1828, Kent described his early life and training. The letter appeared earlier in the *Southern Law Review*, v. 1, July 1872, p. 381–391, under the title "Autobiographical Sketch of Chancellor Kent."

COXE, MACGRANE. Chancellor Kent at Yale, 1777–1781. New York, Priv. print., 1909. 53 p. facsim., plates, col. port. F123.K37

HORTON, JOHN T. James Kent, a study in conservatism, 1763–1847. New York, D. Appleton-Century Co. [ᶜ1939] xi, 354 p. port. KF368.K4H6 1939

Bibliography: p. 327–341

Reprinted in New York by Da Capo Press (1969).

The author's thesis (Ph.D.), *The Life of James Kent, Chief Justice and Chancellor of New York*, was submitted to Harvard University in 1935.

13759

KENTON, SIMON (1755–1836)*
Virginia; Kentucky. Frontiersman, scout,

CLARK, THOMAS D. Simon Kenton, Kentucky scout. New York, Toronto, Farrar & Rinehart [1943] x, 275 p. illus., map. F517.K35
Bibliography: p. 273–275.

ECKERT, ALLAN W. The frontiersmen, a narrative. Boston, Little, Brown [1967] xii, 626 p. maps. F517.K362
Bibliographic references included in "Chapter Notes" (p. [589]–607).

JAHNS, PATRICIA. The violent years; Simon Kenton and the Ohio-Kentucky frontier. New York, Hastings House [1962] ix, 309 p. F517.K367
Bibliography: p. 293–299.

KENTON, EDNA. Simon Kenton; his life and period, 1755–1836. Garden City, N.Y., Doubleday, Doran [ᶜ1930] xxiii, 352 p. illus., map (on back lining paper), ports. F517.K37

Bibliography: p. 337–340.
Reprinted in New York by Arno Press (1971).

McFARLAND, ROBERT W. Simon Kenton. Ohio archaeological and historical quarterly, v. 13, Jan. 1904: 1–39. illus. F486.O51, v. 13
A supplementary note on Kenton appears in the April issue, p. 281.

13760

KEPPEL, AUGUSTUS KEPPEL, *Viscount* (1725–1786)†
England. British naval officer.

KEPPEL, THOMAS R. The life of Augustus, Viscount Keppel, Admiral of the White, and first Lord of the Admiralty in 1782–3. London, H. Colburn, 1842. 2 v. port. DA87.1.K3K3

Bibliographic footnotes.

KERMORVAN, *chevalier* DE
See BARAZER DE KERMORVAN, GILLES JEAN MARIE ROLLAND

13761

KILBY, JOHN (1758–1826)
Maryland; Virginia. Revolutionary seaman.

—— Narrative of John Kilby, quarter-gunner of the U.S. ship "Bon Homme Richard," under Paul Jones. With introduction and notes by Augustus C. Buell. Scribner's magazine, v. 38, July 1905: 23–41. port. AP2.S4, v. 38
An improved version of Kilby's narrative, edited by Durward T. Stokes, appeared in the *Maryland Historical Magazine*, v. 67, spring 1972, p. 21–53.

13762

KIMBALL, JACOB (1761–1826)
Massachusetts. Revolutionary fifer, schoolteacher, musician.

WILCOX, GLENN C. Jacob Kimball, a pioneer American musician. *In* Essex Institute, *Salem, Mass.* Historical collections, v. 94, Oct. 1958: 356–378. F72.E7E81, v. 94

13763

KING, BOSTON (1760?–1802)
South Carolina; Nova Scotia. Carpenter.

BLAKELEY, PHYLLIS R. Boston King: a Negro Loyalist who sought refuge in Nova Scotia. Dalhousie review, v. 48, autumn 1968: 347–356. AP5.D3, v. 48

13764

KING, EDWARD (1735?–1807)†
England. Lawyer, writer.

—— An essay on the English constitution and government. London, Printed for B. White, 1767. viii, 184 p. JN216.K5
AC901.M5, v. 403 Rare Bk. Coll.

13765

KING, ROBERT (1747–1826)
Ireland; Pennsylvania. Revolutionary officer, frontiersman.

SIEBENECK, HENRY K. The life and times of Robert King, Revolutionary patriot. Western Pennsylvania historical magazine, v. 5, Apr. 1922: 145–173. F146.W52, v. 5

13766

KING, RUFUS (1755–1827)*
Maine; Massachusetts. Lawyer, assemblyman, orator, delegate to the Continental Congress, delegate to the Constitutional Convention.

—— Letters of Rufus King [1784–86] *In* Massachusetts Historical Society, *Boston*. Proceedings. v. 49; 1915/16. Boston, 1916. p. 81–89. F61.M38, v. 49

—— The life and correspondence of Rufus King; comprising his letters, private and official, his public documents, and his speeches. Edited by his grandson Charles R. King. New York, G. P. Putnam's Sons, 1894–1900. 6 v. ports. E302.K54
Reprinted in New York by Da Capo Press (1971). Volume 1 covers the period 1755–94.

ARBENA, JOSEPH L. Politics or principle? Rufus King and the opposition to slavery, 1785–1825. *In* Essex Institute, *Salem, Mass.* Historical collections, v. 101, Jan. 1965: 56–77. F72.E7E81, v. 101

BRUSH, EDWARD H. Rufus King and his times. New York, N. L. Brown, 1926. 159 p. plates, ports.
E302.6.K5B8

ERNST, ROBERT. Rufus King, American federalist. Chapel Hill, Published for the Institute of Early American History and Culture at Williamsburg, Va., by University of North Carolina Press [1968] ix, 446 p. ports.
E302.6.K5E7

Bibliographic footnotes.

WELCH, RICHARD E. Rufus King of Newburyport: the formative years (1767–1788). *In* Essex Institute, *Salem, Mass.* Historical collections, v. 96, Oct. 1960: 241–276.
F72.E7E81, v. 96

13767
KINLOCH, FRANCIS (1755–1826)

South Carolina. Revolutionary officer, planter, assemblyman, delegate to the Continental Congress.

————Letters of Francis Kinloch to Thomas Boone, 1782–1788. Edited by Felix Gilbert. Journal of southern history, v. 8, Feb. 1942: 87–105.   F206.J68, v. 8

13768
KINNERSLEY, EBENEZER (1711–1778)*

England; Pennsylvania. Scientist, professor.

LEMAY, JOSEPH A. LEO. Ebenezer Kinnersley, Franklin's friend. Philadelphia, University of Pennsylvania Press [1964] 143 p. illus., facsim.   CT788.K494L4

"This study . . . in an earlier form [was] presented as a Master's thesis at the University of Maryland." Bibliography: p. 123–136.

13769
KIRBY, EPHRAIM (1757–1804)*

Connecticut. Revolutionary officer, lawyer.

BRICELAND, ALAN V. Ephraim Kirby: pioneer of American law reporting, 1789. American journal of legal history, v. 16, Oct. 1972: 297–319.   LL

13770
KIRKLAND, SAMUEL (1741–1808)*

Connecticut; New York. Clergyman, missionary to the Indians.

———— The journal of Samuel Kirkland, November 1764–February 1765. Clinton, N.Y., Alexander Hamilton Private Press, 1966. 20 p. port.   E99.S3K5

An excerpt from the original manuscript in the Hamilton College Library.

LENNOX, HERBERT J. Samuel Kirkland's mission to the Iroquois. 1932. ix, 275 l. map.   E99.I7L46 1932

Thesis (Ph.D.)—University of Chicago. Bibliography: leaves 260–275.

13771
KIRKWOOD, ROBERT (1756–1791)

Delaware; Ohio. Revolutionary officer, farmer.

————The journal and order book of Captain Robert Kirkwood of the Delaware Regiment of the Continental Line. Edited by Rev. Joseph Brown Turner. Wilmington, Historical Society of Delaware, 1910. 277 p. (Historical Society of Delaware. Papers, 56)
F161.D35, no. 56

Contents.—pt. 1. A journal of the southern campaign, 1780–1782.—pt. 2. An order book of the campaign of New Jersey, 1777.

Reprinted in Port Washington, N.Y., by Kennikat Press (1970. E263.D3K59 1970).

13772
KNOWLTON, THOMAS (1740–1776)*

Massachusetts; Connecticut. Revolutionary officer.

COHEN, SHELDON S. The death of Colonel Thomas Knowlton. *In* Connecticut Historical Society, *Hartford.* Bulletin, v. 30, Apr. 1965: 50–57. illus., map.
F91.C67, v. 30

Killed at the Battle of Harlem Heights.

PERLEY, SIDNEY. Colonel Thomas Knowlton. *In* Essex Institute, *Salem, Mass.* Historical collections, v. 58, Apr. 1922: 89–100. plates.   F72.E7E81, v. 58

WOODWARD, ASHBEL. Col. Thomas Knowlton. New England historical and genealogical register, v. 15, Jan. 1861: 1–12.   F1.N56, v. 15

An offprint, entitled *Memoir of Col. Thomas Knowlton, of Ashford, Connecticut,* was issued in 1861 (Boston, Printed by H. W. Dutton. 16 p. E207.K7W8).

13773
KNOX, HENRY (1750–1806)*

Massachusetts. Revolutionary general.

———— The Henry Knox letters [1776–86] from the Ely collection. *In* New Jersey Historical Society. Proceedings, v. 61, Jan. 1943: 23–31.   F131.N58, v. 61

BROOKS, NOAH. Henry Knox, a soldier of the Revolution; major-general in the Continental Army, Washington's chief of artillery, first secretary of war under the Constitution, founder of the Society of the Cincinnati; 1750–1806. New York, G. P. Putnam's Sons, 1900. 286 p. facsim., plates, ports. (American men of energy)   E207.K74B8

CALLAHAN, NORTH. Henry Knox: American artillerist. *In* Billias, George A., *ed.* George Washington's generals. New York, W. Morrow, 1964. p. 239–259. port.
E206.B5

Bibliography: p. 258–259.

———— Henry Knox, General Washington's general. *In* New York Historical Society. Quarterly, v. 44, Apr. 1960: 150–165. illus., port.   F116.N638, v. 44

———— Henry Knox, General Washington's general. New York, Rinehart [1958] x, 404 p. illus., port.
E207.K74C18
"Bibliographical note ": p. 386–393.
The author's thesis (Ph.D.), *Henry Knox—His Part in the American Revolution, 1775 to 1784*, was submitted to New York University in 1956 (Micro AC–1, no. 59–6695).

DRAKE, FRANCIS S.   Life and correspondence of Henry Knox, major-general in the American Revolutionary army. Boston, S. G. Drake, 1873. 160 p. illus., port.
E207.K74D7
Also published in the *Memorials of the Society of the Cincinnati of Massachusetts* (Boston, 1873), p. [89]–205. E202.1.M38

DYER, WESTON A.   The influence of Henry Knox on the formation of American Indian policy in the northern department, 1786–1795. 1970. ([193] p.)
Micro AC–1, no. 71–9049
Thesis (Ph.D.)—Ball State University.
Abstracted in *Dissertation Abstracts International*, v. 31A, Apr. 1971, p. 5315.

FORD, WORTHINGTON C.   Henry Knox and the London Book-Store in Boston, 1771–1774. *In* Massachusetts Historical Society, *Boston.* Proceedings. v. 61; 1927/28. Boston, 1928. p. 225–303.   F61.M38, v. 61

HEATHCOTE, CHARLES W.   General Henry Knox—great artillerist and intimate friend of Washington. Picket post, no. 53, July 1956: 11–18.   E234.P5, no. 53

Historical Records Survey. *Massachusetts.*   A calendar of the General Henry Knox papers, Chamberlain Collection, Boston Public Library. Boston, Mass., Historical Records Survey, 1939. 19 p.   Z6621.B74K55
Reproduced from typescript.

Index to the Henry Knox papers owned by the New England Historic Genealogical Society and deposited in the Massachusetts Historical Society.   Boston, 1960. 1 v. (unpaged)   Z6616.K555N44 Mss

WILLIAMSON, JOSEPH.   General Henry Knox. *In* Maine Historical Society. Collections and proceedings. 2d ser., v. 1. Portland, 1890. p. 1–27. port.
F16.M33, 2d s., v. 1
"Bibliographical Memoranda Relating to General Knox": p. 23–27.

13774
KNOX, HUGH (1727–1790)
Ireland; New Jersey; West Indies. Clergyman, tutor.

MITCHELL, BROADUS.   The man who discovered Hamilton. *In* New Jersey Historical Society. Proceedings, v. 69, Apr. 1951: 88–114.   F131.N58, v. 69

13775
KNOX, LUCY FLUCKER (1757?–1824)
Massachusetts. Wife of Henry Knox (1750–1806).

ROBERTSON, DIANA F.   "Lady" Knox. American heritage, v. 17, Apr. 1966: 46–47, 74–79. illus., col. ports.
E171.A43, v. 17

13776
KNOX, WILLIAM (1732–1810)†
Ireland; England. Writer, colonial agent.

BELLOT, LELAND J.   Mr. Secretary Knox: a biographical study of an eighteenth-century civil servant. 1967. ([236] p.)   Micro AC–1, no. 67–14,798
Thesis (Ph.D.)—University of Texas.
Abstracted in *Dissertation Abstracts*, v. 28A, Nov. 1967, p. 1753.

Gt. Brit. *Historical Manuscripts Commission.*   The manuscripts of Captain H. V. Knox. *In its* Report on manuscripts in various collections. v. 6. Dublin, Printed for H.M. Stationery Off. by J. Falconer, 1909. p. [xiv]–xxviii, [81]–296, [440]–449.   DA25.M2V2, v. 6
Parliament. Papers by command. Cd. 4832.
A report, prepared by Mrs. S. C. Lomas, on the correspondence of William Knox, relating mainly to American affairs, 1757–1808, and to Ireland, 1767–84. The supplementary report contains a calendar of letters from Dr. Philip Skelton to William Knox, 1765–80.
Reprinted, with a new introduction and preface by George A. Billias, in Boston by Gregg Press (1972. E195.G67 1972).

13777
KNYPHAUSEN, WILHELM, *freiherr* VON (1716–1800)
Germany. Hessian officer in America.

Wilhelm, Baron Innhausen and Knyphausen. Pennsylvania magazine of history and biography, v. 16, July 1892: 239–245.   F146.P65, v. 16

13778
KOLLOCK, SHEPARD (1750?–1839)*
Delaware; New Jersey. Printer, Revolutionary officer, publisher.

HUTCHINSON, ELMER T.   A pioneer New Jersey printer. *In* New Jersey Historical Society. Proceedings, v. 55, Apr. 1937: 133–148.   F131.N58, v. 55

13779
KOLLOCK, SIMON (1737–1817)
Delaware. Landowner, Revolutionary officer, assemblyman.

HILL, J. BENNETT. The Simon Kollocks of Sussex in the eighteenth century. Delaware history, v. 9, Apr. 1960: 51–65.   F161.D37, v. 9

13780

KOŚCIUSZKO, TADEUSZ ANDRZEJ BONAWENTURA (1746–1817)*
Poland. Revolutionary officer.

BUSHNELL, GEORGE H. Kościuszko, a short biography of the Polish patriot. St. Andrews [Scot.] Published for the Society by W. C. Henderson, 1943. 54 p. ports. (Scottish-Polish Society publications, no. 4)
DK434.8.K8B8

EVANS, ANTHONY W. W. Memoir of Thaddeus Kosciuszko, Poland's hero and patriot, an officer in the American Army of the Revolution and member of the Society of the Cincinnati. New York, 1883. New York, Reprinted, W. Abbatt, 1915. 43, 23 p. (The Magazine of history with notes and queries. Extra number, no. 36)
E173.M24, no. 36

GARDNER, MONICA M. Kościuszko, a biography. Rev. 2d ed. Edited by Mary Corbridge. London, G. Allen & Unwin [1942] 148 p. port.   DK434.8.K8G3 1942
First edition published in 1920.
"Chief works consulted": p. 143.

GRIFFIN, MARTIN I. J. General Thaddeus Kosciuszko. American Catholic historical researches, new ser., v. 6, Apr. 1910: 129–216. illus., port.
E184.C3A5, n.s., v. 6

HAIMAN, MIECISLAUS. Kosciuszko in the American Revolution. New York City, Polish Institute of Arts and Sciences in America, 1943. vii, 198 p. facsims., plans, ports. (Polish Institute series, no. 4)   E207.K8H3
Bibliography: p. 168–179.
Reprinted, with a new introduction and preface by George A. Billias, in Boston by Gregg Press (1972).

―――― Kosciuszko, leader and exile. New York, Polish Institute of Arts and Sciences in America, 1946. vii, 183 p. facsims., plates, ports. (Polish Institute series, no. 9)   E207.K8H32
Bibliography: p. 157–167.
The second and last part of Haiman's biography.

HONEYMAN, ABRAHAM VAN DOREN. The great patriot, Kosciuszko, including his New Brunswick visit. Somerset county historical quarterly, v. 7, Jan. 1918: 1–16. port.   F142.S6S6, v. 7

13781

KOVÁTS, MIHÁLY, FABRICY (1724–1779)
Hungary. Revolutionary officer.

PÓKA-PIVNY, ALADÁR. A Hungarian under Washington. Hungarian quarterly, v. 7, autumn 1941: 366–373.
DB901.H83, v. 7

13782

KUHN, ADAM (1741–1817)*
Pennsylvania. Physician, professor.

BELL, WHITFIELD J. Physicians and politics in the Revolution: the case of Adam Kuhn, with a note on Philip Turpin. In College of Physicians of Philadelphia. Transactions & studies, 4th ser., v. 22, June 1954: 25–31.   R15.P5, 4th s., v. 22

BROWN, MARION E. Adam Kuhn: eighteenth century physician and teacher. Journal of the history of medicine and allied sciences, v. 5, spring 1950: 163–177.
R131.A1J6, v. 5

13783

KUNZE, JOHANN CHRISTOPH (1744–1807)*
Germany; Pennsylvania. Lutheran clergyman, educator.

OAKLEY, HENRIETTA M. Rev. John C. Kunze, D.D. Pennsylvania-German, v. 3, July 1902: 99–108. illus., port.   F146.P224, v. 3

13784

LA BROSSE, JEAN BAPTISTE DE (1724–1782)
Canada. Clergyman, missionary

CHAMBRE, ALEXANDRE. Un grand apôtre du Canada, originaire de l'Angoumois, le R.P. J.-B. de la Brosse, né à Jualdes (Charentes), mort à Tadoussac (Saguenay). Jauldes, par Coulgens, En vente chez l'auteur [1904] xix, 363 p.   F1032.C45

13785

LACEY, JOHN (1755–1814)*
Pennsylvania. Revolutionary general, assemblyman.

―――― Memoirs of Brigadier-General John Lacey, of Pennsylvania. Pennsylvania magazine of history and biography, v. 25, Apr. 1901–Jan. 1902: 1–13, 191–207, 341–354, 498–515; v. 26, Apr.–July 1902: 101–111, 265–270.   F146.P65, v. 25–26

DAVIS, WILLIAM W. H. General John Lacey—our Quaker general. In Bucks County Historical Society, Doylestown, Pa. Collection of papers. v. 3. Doylestown, 1909. p. 32–41.   F157.B8B84, v. 3

―――― Sketch of the life and character of John Lacey, a brigadier general in the Revolutionary Army. Printed privately. [Doylestown? Pa.] 1868. 118, 6 p.
E207.L14D2

13786

LADD, JOSEPH BROWN (1764–1786)*
Rhode Island; South Carolina. Physician, poet.

―――― The literary remains of Joseph Brown Ladd, M.D. Collected by his sister, Mrs. Elizabeth Haskins, of

Rhode Island. To which is prefixed, A sketch of the author's life, by W. B. Chittenden. New York, H. C. Sleight, 1832. xxiv, 228 p.   PS791.L15 1832

Verse and prose.

Reprinted, with a new foreword by Lewis Leary, in New York by Garrett Press (1970).

LEARY, LEWIS G. A forgotten Charleston poet: Joseph Brown Ladd, 1764–1786. Americana, v. 36, Oct. 1942: 571–588.   E171.A53, v. 36

———— The writings of Joseph Brown Ladd (1764–1786). Bulletin of bibliography, v. 18, Jan./Apr. 1945: 131–133.   Z1007.B94, v. 18

13787

LAFAYETTE, MARIE JOSEPH PAUL YVES ROCH GILBERT DU MOTIER, *marquis* DE (1757–1834)*
France. Revolutionary general, diplomat.

———— Correspondance inédite de La Fayette: lettres écrites au comte d'Estaing pendant la campagne du vice-amiral De La Delaware [sic] á Boston du 14 juillet au 20 octobre 1778. Revue d'histoire diplomatique, 6. année, no. 3, 1892: 395–448.   JX3.R3, v. 6

Edited by Henri Doniol.

———— Lafayette as commercial expert. American historical review, v. 36, Apr. 1931: 561–570.   E171.A57, v. 36

Lafayette's 1783 memoir to the Ministry of Foreign Affairs making specific recommendations for the improvement of Franco-American trade. Introduction and notes by Louis R. Gottschalk.

———— Lafayette in Virginia. Unpublished letters from the original manuscripts in the Virginia State Library and the Library of Congress. Baltimore, Johns Hopkins Press, 1928. xi, 64 p. fold. facsim. (Institut francais de Washington. Historical documents, cahier 2)   E237.L16

Forty-five hitherto unpublished letters, written by Lafayette, February 21–October 31, 1781, to Thomas Jefferson, General Wayne, Colonel Davis, and Governor T. Nelson; also a letter to Jefferson on October 11, 1784, when the latter was appointed to succeed Benjamin Franklin at Paris, and a letter to Governor Patrick Henry, on March 16, 1785.

Compiled by Gilbert Chinard.

———— Letters from Lafayette to Luzerne, 1780–1782. American historical review, v. 20, Jan.–Apr. 1915: 341–376, 577–612.   E171.A57, v. 20

Introduction and notes by Waldo G. Leland.
———— ———— Offprint. [New York, 1915] 341–376, 577–612 p.   E265.L16

———— Letters from the Marquis de Lafayette to Hon. Henry Laurens, 1777–1780. South Carolina historical and genealogical magazine, v. 7, Jan.–Oct. 1906: 3–11, 53–68, 115–129, 179–193; v. 8, Jan.–Oct. 1907: 3–18, 57–68, 123–131, 181–188; v. 9, Jan.–Oct. 1908: 3–8, 59–66, 109–144, 173–180.   F266.S55, v. 7–9

———— The letters of Lafayette and Jefferson. With an introduction and notes by Gilbert Chinard. Baltimore, Md., Johns Hopkins Press, 1929. xiv, 443 p. facsims, map, port. (The Johns Hopkins studies in international thought)   E207.L2L18

———— The letters of Lafayette to Washington, 1777–1799. Edited by Louis Gottschalk. New York, Priv. print. by H. F. Hubbard, 1944. xxxvi, 417 p.   E207.L2L185

Bibliographic footnotes.

———— Memoirs, correspondence, and manuscripts of General Lafayette. Published by his family. London, Saunders and Otley, 1837. 3 v. port.   DC146.L2A3

Also published in Brussels, by the Société belge de librairie (1837–39).

A brief selection from the *Memoirs*, entitled *Lafayette in the American Revolution*, was published in Boston by the Directors of the Old South Works (1898. 24 p. E173.O44, v. 4) as Old South leaflet no. 97.

ADAMS, JOHN QUINCY. Life of General Lafayette. By John Quincy Adams. To which is added The life of General Kosciusko. New York, Nafis & Cornish, 1847. 255 p. plates (part col.)   E207.L2A24

The life of General Lafayette is a reprint of Adams' *Oration on the Life and Character of Gilbert Motier de Lafayette, Delivered at the Request of Both Houses of the Congress . . . 31st December, 1834* (Washington, Printed by D. Green, 1835).

BILL, SHIRLEY A., *and* LOUIS R. GOTTSCHALK. Silas Deane's "worthless" agreement with Lafayette. Prologue, v. 4, winter 1972: 219–223. facsim.   CD3020.P75, v. 4

On the document signed on December 7, 1776, by Deane, the American commissioner in France, making Lafayette a major general in the American army.

FITZPATRICK, JOHN C. A liberty loan of the Revolution. Daughters of the American Revolution magazine, v. 52, June 1918: 327–331. facsim., port.   E202.5.A12, v. 52

On the advancement of £1550 sterling to the Marquis de Lafayette by 18 citizens of Baltimore in 1781.

GOTTSCHALK, LOUIS R. Franklin and Lafayette. *In* Institut français de Washington, *Washington, D.C.* Bulletin, no. 12, Dec. 1939: 7–24.   E183.8.F8I8, no. 12

———— Lafayette. Journal of modern history, v. 2, June 1930: 281–287.   D1.J6, v. 2

A review of 19th- and early 20th-century literature on Lafayette.

———— Lafayette and the close of the American Revolution. Chicago, Ill., University of Chicago Press [1942] xiii, 458 p. fold. maps.   E207.L2G68

"Bibliographical notes" at end of each chapter. Bibliographic footnotes.

—— Lafayette between the American and the French Revolution (1783–1789). Chicago, University of Chicago Press [1950] xi, 461 p.　　DC146.L2G59

Includes bibliographic notes.

—— Lafayette comes to America. Chicago, Ill., University of Chicago [1935] xiii, 184 p.　　DC146.L2G6

Bibliography at end of each chapter.

—— Lafayette joins the American Army. Chicago, Ill. University of Chicago Press [1937] xv, 364 p. maps.　　E207.L2G7

"Bibliographical notes" at end of each chapter.

HUME, EDGAR E.　LaFayette and the Society of the Cincinnati. Baltimore, Johns Hopkins Press, 1934. 63 p. plates, ports. (Institut français de Washington. Historical documents)　　E207.L2H86

JACKSON, STUART W.　La Fayette, a bibliography. With a foreword by Brand Whitlock. New York, W. E. Rudge, 1930. xxiii, 226 p. illus.　　Z8470.J18

"A chronological conspectus of the career of General La Fayette": p. 3–27.

KIRK, GRAYSON L.　The Marquis de Lafayette. *In* New York Historical Society. Quarterly, v. 42, Jan. 1958: 5–19. illus., facsims., port.　　F116.N638, v. 42

MONTBAS, HUGUES, *vicomte* DE.　Avec Lafayette chez les Iroquois. Paris, Firmin-Didot, 1929. 131 p. plates, ports. (Histoires de France)　　E207.L2M7

Barbé-Marbois was a member of the expedition to the Iroquois, 1784, and much of this account has been taken from his writings.

NOLAN, JAMES BENNETT.　Lafayette in America, day by day. Baltimore, Johns Hopkins Press, 1934. x, 324 p. plates, ports. (Institut français de Washington. Historical documents, cahier 7)　　E207.L2N74 Rare Bk. Coll.

Bibliography: p. 307–316.

NUSSBAUM, FREDERICK L.　The revolutionary Vergennes and Lafayette versus the Farmers General. Journal of modern history, v. 3, Dec. 1931: 592–604.　　D1.J6, v. 3

Concerned with the efforts of Vergennes and Lafayette to circumscribe or abolish the tobacco monopoly of the Farmers General in the hope of encouraging free commerce between France and the United States, 1783–87. See also Nussbaum's appendix, "Lafayette's Attack Upon the Tobacco Farm in the American Committee of 1786," p. 605–613, which is reproduced exactly from the original.

PECKHAM, HOWARD H.　Marquis de Lafayette: eager warrior. *In* Billias, George A., *ed.* George Washington's generals. New York, W. Morrow, 1964. p. 212–238. port.　　E206.B5

Bibliography: p. 237–238.

SEDGWICK, HENRY D.　La Fayette. Indianapolis, Bobbs-Merrill Co. [c1928] 433 p. map., plates, ports.　　DC146.L2S4

"Authorities": p. 421–424.

SELLERS, JOHN R.　Lafayette papers at the Library of Congress. *In* U.S. *Library of Congress.* Quarterly journal, v. 29, Apr. 1972: 138–154. illus., facsims., port.　　Z881.U49A3, v. 29

See also, in the same issue, "Adrienne and Lafayette at La Grange," by René de Chambrun, p. 81–94, and "The Lafayette Collection at Cornell," by Mary F. Daniels, p. 95–137.

STEVENS, JOHN A.　Visit of Lafayette to the United States, 1784. Magazine of American history, v. 2, Dec. 1878: 724–733.　　E171.M18, v. 2

TOWER, CHARLEMAGNE.　The Marquis de La Fayette in the American Revolution. With some account of the attitude of France toward the War of Independence. Philadelphia, J. B. Lippincott Co., 1895. 2 v. illus., facsim., maps, plan, ports.　　E207.L2T65

Reprinted in New York by Da Capo Press (1970) and in Freeport, N.Y., by Books for Libraries Press (1971).

TUCKERMAN, BAYARD.　Life of General Lafayette, with a critical estimate of his character and public acts. New York, Dodd, Mead, 1889. 2 v. plates.　　DC146.L2T8

WALN, ROBERT.　Life of the Marquis de La Fayette; major-general in the service of the United States of America, in the War of the Revolution. Philadelphia, Published by J. P. Ayres, 1825. 505 p. port.　　DC146.L2W3 1825
E207.L2W13

WHITLOCK, BRAND.　La Fayette. New York, D. Appleton, 1929. 2 v. facsims., (part fold.), plates, ports.　　DC146.L2W5

"Works read or consulted": v. 2, p. 419–426.

WHITRIDGE, ARNOLD.　La Fayette goes to America. History today, v. 20, Aug. 1970: 527–533. illus., ports.　　D1.H818, v. 20

WOODWARD, WILLIAM E.　Lafayette. New York, Farrar & Rinehart, [1938] xii, 472 p. facsim., plates, ports.　　DC146.L2W6

Bibliography: p. 452–453.

13788

LA LUZERNE, ANNE CÉSAR DE (1741–1791)
France. Diplomat.

O'DONNELL, WILLIAM E.　The Chevalier de La Luzerne, French minister to the United States, 1779–1784. Bruges, Desclée de Brouwer, 1938. 286 p. facsim., port. (Université de Louvain. Recueil de travaux, publiés par les membres des Conférences d'histoire et de philologie, 2. sér., 46. fasc.)　　E249.L39

Bibliography: p. [259]–266.

WALSH, JAMES J. The Chevalier de La Luzerne. *In* American Catholic Historical Society of Philadelphia. Records, v. 16, June 1905: 162–186. E184.C3A4, v. 16

13789

LAMB, JOHN (1735–1800)*

New York. Instrument maker, merchant, Revolutionary officer, assemblyman.

LEAKE, ISAAC Q. Memoir of the life and times of General John Lamb, an officer of the Revolution, who commanded the post at West Point at the time of Arnold's defection, and his correspondence with Washington, Clinton, Patrick Henry, and other distinguished men of his time. Albany, J. Munsell, 1850. x, 431 p. plans, port. E207.L22L3

Reprinted in New York by Da Capo Press (1971). The 1857 edition (Albany, J. Munsell) has been reprinted in Glendale, N.Y., by the Benchmark Pub. Co. (1970).

13790

LAMB, JOHN (*fl.* 1786)

Connecticut. Sea captain, diplomat.

ROSS, FRANK E. The mission of John Lamb to Algiers 1785–1786. Americana, v. 28, July 1934: 287–294. E171.A53, v. 28

13791

LAMB, ROGER (1756–1830)

Ireland. British soldier in America, schoolteacher.

——— Memoir of his own life. Dublin, Printed by J. Jones, 1811. 296 p. E275.L21

——— An original and authentic journal of occurrences during the late American War, from its commencement to the year 1783. By R. Lamb, late serjeant in the Royal Welch Fuzileers. Dublin, Printed by Wilkinson & Courtney, 1809. xxiv, 438 p. E208.L21

"A summary and impartial view of . . . the rise, progress and consummation of the late American war."
Reprinted in New York by the New York Times (1968).

13792

LAND, ROBERT (1736?–1818)

Pennsylvania; Canada. Farmer, Loyalist soldier.

COLEMAN, JOHN M. Robert Land and some frontier skirmishes. Ontario history, v. 48, spring 1956: 47–62. F1056.O58, v. 48

13793

LANDAIS, PIERRE (1731?–1820)*

France; New York. Seaman, Revolutionary naval officer.

Charges and proofs respecting the conduct of Peter Landais. New-York, Printed by Francis Childs [1787] 18 p. illus. AC901.M5, v. 26 Rare Bk. Coll.

MORRIS, RICHARD B. The Revolution's Caine Mutiny. American heritage, v. 11, Apr. 1960: 10–13, 88–91. illus. (part col.), ports. E171.A43, v. 11

On Landais' tour as master of the *Alliance*.

PAULLIN, CHARLES O. Admiral Pierre Landais. Catholic historical review, v. 17, Oct. 1931: 296–307. BX1404.C3, v. 17

SMITH, HORATIO D. Captain Pierre de Landais, commander Continental frigate "Alliance." United service, 3d ser., v. 8, Sept. 1905: 214–228. U1.U4, 3d s., v. 8

13794

LANE, JOEL (1740–1795)

North Carolina. Pioneer, assemblyman, landowner.

HAYWOOD, MARSHALL D. Joel Lane, pioneer and patriot. A biographical sketch, including notes about the Lane family and the colonial and Revolutionary history of Wake County, North Carolina. Raleigh, N.C., Alford, Bynum & Christophers, 1900. 23 p. F258.L26

A third edition was published in Raleigh, N.C., by the Wake County Committee of the Colonial Dames of America in 1952.

——— Joel Lane, a pioneer and patriot of Wake County, North Carolina. North Carolina booklet, v. 20, Oct. 1920/Apr. 1921: 191–206. F251.N86, v. 20

13795

LANE, SAMUEL (1718–1806)

New Hampshire. Farmer.

——— A journal for the years 1739–1803. Edited by Charles Lane Hanson. Concord, N.H., New Hampshire Historical Society, 1937. vi, 115 p. facsim., plans, plates. F38.L23

13796

LANE, TIDENCE (1724–1806)*

Maryland; North Carolina; Tennessee. Baptist clergyman.

WILLIAMS, SAMUEL C. Tidence Lane—Tennessee's first pastor. Tennessee historical magazine, 2d ser., v. 1, Oct. 1930: 40–48. F431.T28, 2d s., v. 1

13797

LANGBORNE, WILLIAM (*d.* 1814)

Virginia. Revolutionary officer.

CURTIS, CARROLL D. The curious Colonel Langborn, wanderer and enigma from the Revolutionary period.

Virginia magazine of history and biography, v. 64, Oct. 1956: 402–432. port.   F221.V91, v. 64

The author provides a further note on Langborne in v. 66, Jan. 1958, p. 88–89.

13798

LANGDON, JOHN (1741–1819)*

New Hampshire. Merchant, assemblyman, Revolutionary officer, delegate to the Continental Congress, governor, delegate to the Constitutional Convention.

—— Letters by Washington, Adams, Jefferson, and others, written during and after the Revolution, to John Langdon, New Hampshire. Philadelphia, Press of H. B. Ashmead, 1880. 131 p.
E302.1.L35 Rare Bk. Coll.

The letters were edited by Alfred Langdon Elwyn.

CORNING, CHARLES R.   John Langdon. Concord, Rumford Print. Co., 1903. 31 p.   E302.6.L26C8

ELWYN, JOHN L.   Some account of John Langdon. In New Hampshire. Early state papers of New Hampshire. v. 20. Concord, 1891. p. 850–880.   F31.N42, v. 20

LACY, HARRIET S.   The Langdon papers, 1716–1841. Historical New Hampshire, v. 22, autumn 1967: 55–65.
F31.H57, v. 22

The majority of the manuscripts described and listed relate to the Atlantic trading voyages of the brothers, John and Woodbury, from 1762 to 1775.

MAYO, LAWRENCE S.   John Langdon of New Hampshire. Concord, N.H., Rumford Press, 1937. xiv, 303 p. plate, ports.   E302.6.L26M3

Reprinted in Port Washington, N.Y., by Kennikat Press (1970).

—— John Langdon's speech; a New Hampshire tradition. In Colonial Society of Massachusetts, Boston. Publications, v. 26. Transactions, 1924/26. Boston, 1927. p. 270–275.   F61.C71, v. 26

Concerning a speech supposedly made by Langdon offering to finance Stark's expedition in July 1777.

13799

LANGDON, SAMUEL (1723–1797)*

Massachusetts; New Hampshire. Clergyman, educator.

SANBORN, FRANKLIN B.   Samuel Langdon, S.T.D., scholar, patriot, and president of Harvard University. In Massachusetts Historical Society, Boston. Proceedings. 2d ser., v. 18; 1903/4. Boston, 1905. p. 192–232.
F61.M38, 2d s., v. 18

13800

LANGLADE, CHARLES MICHEL DE (1729–1800)*

Canada; Wisconsin. Soldier, trader, Indian negotiator.

GRIGNON, AUGUSTIN.   Augustin Grignon's recollections [of the life of Charles Michel de Langlade] In Wisconsin. State Historical Society. Report and collections. v. 3; 1856. Madison, 1857. p. [195]–295.
F576.W81, v. 3

Corrections to this and other accounts are presented by Reuben G. Thwaites in v. 18 (Madison, 1908), p. 130–132.

Langlade papers, 1737–1800.   In Wisconsin. State Historical Society. Report and collections. v. 8; 1877/79. Madison, 1879. p. [209]–223.   F576.W81, v. 8

Introduction and notes by Morgan L. Martin.

McINTOSH, MONTGOMERY E.   Charles Langlade—first settler of Wisconsin. [Milwaukee, Wis., 1896] [205]–223 p. (Parkman Club publications, no. 8)
F576.P24, no. 8

TASSÉ, JOSEPH.   Memoir of Charles de Langlade. [Translated from the French, by Mrs. Sarah Fairchild Dean] In Wisconsin. State Historical Society. Report and collections. v. 7; 1873/76. Madison, 1876. p. [123]–187.
F576.W81, v. 7

The author also provided the Society with letters from British Major Arent Schuyler de Peyster to Sir Guy Carleton which appear on p. 405–408 under the title "Langlade's Movements in 1777."

13801

LANGWORTHY, EDWARD (ca. 1738–1802)*

Georgia; Maryland. Schoolteacher, delegate to the Continental Congress.

BURNETT, EDMUND C.   Edward Langworthy in the Continental Congress. Georgia historical quarterly, v. 12, Sept. 1928: 211–235.   F281.G2975, v. 12

KONKLE, BURTON A.   Edward Langworthy. Georgia historical quarterly, v. 11, June 1927: 166–170.
F281.G2975, v. 11

MACKALL, LEONARD L.   Edward Langworthy and the first attempt to write a separate history of Georgia, with selections from the long-lost Langworthy papers. Georgia historical quarterly, v. 7, Mar. 1923: 1–17.
F281.G2975, v. 7

LANDSDOWNE, WILLIAM PETTY, 1st Marquis of See SHELBURNE, WILLIAM PETTY, 2d Earl of

13802

LA ROUËRIE, CHARLES ARMAND TUFFIN, marquis DE (1750–1793)

France. Revolutionary general.

—— Letters of Col. Armand (marquis de la Rouerie). 1777–1791. In New York Historical Society. Collections. 1878. Publication fund series, [v. 11] New York, 1879. p. [287]–396.   F116.N63, 1878

BATCHELLER, TRYPHOSA BATES. Le Marquis de la Rouërie. Daughters of the American Revolution magazine, v. 82, Sept. 1948: 671–676. port.
E202.5.A12, v. 82

HAARMANN, ALBERT W. General Armand and his partisan corps. 1777–1783. Military collector & historian, v. 12, winter 1960: 97–102. port. UC463.M54, v. 12

KITE, ELIZABETH S. Charles-Armand Tufin, Marquis de la Rouërie. Légion d'honneur magazine, v. 10, Apr. 1940: 451–462. port.
CR5061.U6A3, v. 10

STUTESMAN, JOHN H. Colonel Armand and Washington's cavalry. In New York Historical Society. Quarterly, v. 45, Jan 1961: 5–42. illus., map, ports.
F116.N638, v. 45

WARD, TOWNSEND. Charles Armand Tufin, marquis de La Rouerie, brigadier-general in the Continental Army of the American Revolution. Pennsylvania magazine of history and biography, v. 2, no. 1, 1878: 1–34. port.
F146.P65, v. 2

WHITRIDGE, ARNOLD. The Marquis de La Rouërie, Brigadier General in the Continental Army. In Massachusetts Historical Society, Boston. Proceedings. v. 79; 1967. Boston, 1968. p. 47–63. F61.M38, v. 79

13803
LATHROP, JOSEPH (1731–1820)
Connecticut; Massachusetts. Clergyman.

—— A miscellaneous collection of original pieces: political, moral, and entertaining, in one volume . . . Springfield (Massachusetts), Printed by John Russell, At his Office near the Great Ferry, MDCLXXXVI [i.e. 1786] 180 p. PS530.L3 Rare Bk. Coll.
Dedication signed: John Russell.

13804
LAURENS, HENRY (1724–1792)*
South Carolina. Merchant, delegate to the Continental Congress, diplomat.

—— Correspondence of Henry Laurens, of South Carolina. [New York, Printed for the Zenger Club, 1861] 240 p. port. (Materials for history, 1st ser.)
E203.L38

—— Letters from Henry Laurens to William Bell of Philadelphia [1785] South Carolina historical and genealogical magazine, v. 24, Jan. 1923: 2–16.
F266.S55, v. 24

—— Letters from Hon. Henry Laurens to his son John, 1773–1776. South Carolina historical and genealogical magazine, v. 3, Apr.–Oct. 1902: 86–96, 139–149, 207–215; v. 4, Jan.–Oct. 1903: 26–35, 99–107, 215–220, 263–277; v. 5, Jan.–July 1904: 3–14, 69–81, 125–143.
F266.S55, v. 3–5

Additional correspondence between Laurens and his son for the years 1777–80 appeared in volume 6, Jan.–Oct. 1905, p. 3–12, 47–52, 103–110, and 137–160.

—— Mr. Lauren's true state of the case. By which his candor to Mr. Edmund Jenings is manifested, and the tricks of Mr. Jenings are detected. [London?] 1783. 77 p.
E302.6.L3L3
AC901.M5, v. 26 Rare Bk. Coll.

—— A narrative of the capture of Henry Laurens, of his confinement in the Tower of London, &c., 1780, 1781, 1782. In South Carolina Historical Society. v. 1. Charleston, 1857. p. 18–83.
F266.S71, v. 1
Also published under the same title in the Firelands Pioneer, new ser., v. 16, May 1907, p. 1258–1302.

—— The papers of Henry Laurens. Philip M. Hamer, editor. Columbia, Published for the South Carolina Historical Society by the University of South Carolina Press [1968]+ col. port.
E302.L3
Contents: v. 1. Sept. 11, 1746–Oct. 31, 1755.—v. 2. Nov. 1, 1755–Dec. 31, 1758.—v. 3. Jan. 1, 1759–Aug. 31, 1763.

—— A South Carolina protest against slavery: being a letter from Henry Laurens, second president of the Continental Congress, to his son, Colonel John Laurens; dated Charleston, S.C., August 14th, 1776. Now first published from the original. New York, G. P. Putnam, 1861.
E446.L38
Privately (re)printed for Columbia University Libraries in New York (1964) with a foreword by Alfred C. Berol and an introduction by Richard E. Morris.

FORCE, PETER. Henry Laurens in England. Historical magazine, 2d ser., v. 1, Mar. 1867: 129–135.
E171.H64, 2d s., v. 1

FRECH, LAURA P. The career of Henry Laurens in the Continental Congress, 1777–1779. 1972. ([529] p.)
Micro AC–1, no. 72–24,788
Thesis (Ph.D.)—University of North Carolina at Chapel Hill.
Abstracted in Dissertation Abstracts International, v. 33A, Oct. 1972, p. 1637.

HAMER, PHILIP M. Henry Laurens of South Carolina—the man and his papers. In Massachusetts Historical Society, Boston. Proceedings. v. 77; 1965. Boston, 1966. p. 3–14.
F61.M38, v. 77

JENINGS, EDMUND. A full manifestation of what Mr. Henry Laurens falsely denominates candor in himself, and tricks in Mr. Edmund Jenings. London, 1783. 80 p.
E302.6.L3J5
AC901.M5, v. 26 Rare Bk. Coll.

LAMB, MARTHA J. R. N. Henry Laurens in the London Tower [1780–81] Magazine of American history, with notes and queries, v. 18, July 1887: 1–12.
E171.M18, v. 18

WALLACE, DAVID D.   The life of Henry Laurens, with a sketch of the life of Lieutenant-Colonel John Laurens. New York, G. P. Putnam's Sons, 1915. xi, 539 p. fold. geneal. tables, ports.   E302.6.L3W2

Bibliography: p. 511–515.

Reprinted in New York by Russell & Russell (1967).

13805
LAURENS, JOHN (1754–1782)*

South Carolina. Revolutionary officer, diplomat. Son of Henry Laurens (1724–1792).

—— The army correspondence of Colonel John Laurens in the years 1777–8, now first printed from original letters to his father, Henry Laurens, President of Congress. With a memoir by Wm. Gilmore Simms. New York, 1867. 250 p. port. (Bradford Club series, no. 7)   E275.L38

Reprinted in New York by the New York Times (1969). Also printed from the same plates under the title *A Succinct Memoir of the Life and Public Services of Colonel John Laurens* (Williamstadt [Albany] 1867). An extra-illustrated copy, in the Library's Rare Book Collection (E275.L39), contains 33 additional portraits.

Additional letters intended to supplement this volume appeared under the title "Army Correspondence of Col. John Laurens [July 1777–Sept. 1780]" in the *South Carolina Historical and Genealogical Magazine*, v. 2, Oct. 1901, p. 268–272, and v. 3, Jan. 1902, p. 16–23.

—— Letters from John Laurens to his father, Hon. Henry Laurens, 1774–1776. South Carolina historical and genealogical magazine, v. 5, Oct. 1904: 197–208.   F266.S55, v. 5

LYNAH, MARY-ELIZABETH.   John Laurens—Carolina's romantic contribution to the Revolutionary ranks. Americana, v. 30, Apr. 1936: 341–367. ports.   E171.A53, v. 30

REED, JOHN F.   "Lest we forget." Picket post, Oct. 1970: 12–19.   E234.P5, 1970

A brief record of Laurens' service during the war.

TOWNSEND, SARA B.   An American soldier; the life of John Laurens drawn largely from correspondence between his father and himself. Raleigh, N.C., Edwards & Broughton Co. [ᶜ1958] xiii, 266 p. illus., facsims., map (on lining papers), ports.   E207.L28T6

Bibliography: p. 265–266.

13806
LAUZUN, ARMAND LOUIS GONTAUT, *duc* DE (1747–1793) Later duc de Biron.

France. French officer in America.

—— Memoirs of the duc de Lauzun (Armand Louis de Gontaut, duc de Biron) 1747–1783. Translated from the French by E. Jules Méras. New York, Sturgis & Walton Co., 1912. xi, 364 p. plates, ports. (The court series of French memoirs)   DC137.5.B6A24

Another translation, with an appendix, by Charles K. Scott-Moncrieff, an introduction by Richard Aldington, and notes by Miss G. Rutherford, was published in London by G. Routledge (1928. DC137.5.B6M7) and reprinted in New York by the New York Times (1969. DC137.5.B6A24 1969).

MAUGRAS, GASTON.   The duc de Lauzun and the court of Marie Antoinette. London, Osgood, McIlvaine, 1896. xi, 523 p.   DC137.5.B6M6

STEVENS, JOHN A.   The Duke de Lauzun in France and America. American historical magazine, v. 2, Sept. 1907: 343–375.   E171.A53, v. 2

13807
LAW, ANDREW (1749–1821)*

Connecticut. Presbyterian clergyman, musician, hymnal compiler.

CRAWFORD, RICHARD.   Andrew Law, American psalmodist. Evanston, Northwestern University Press, 1968. xix, 424 p. facsims., music. (Pi Kappa Lambda Studies in American music)   ML423.L26C7

Bibliography: p. 400–411.

CRAWFORD, RICHARD, *and* HUGH WILEY HITCHCOCK. The papers of Andrew Law in the William L. Clements Library. Ann Arbor, 1961. 13 p. (Bulletin [of the Clements Library] 68)   E172.M53, no. 68
ML429.L32C7

LOWENS, IRVING.   Andrew Law and the pirates. *In his* Music and musicians in early America. New York, W. W. Norton [1964] p. 58–88.   ML200.L7

On Law's appeal to the Connecticut General Assembly in 1781 for copyright protection of his *Select Harmony.*

MANGLER, JOYCE E.   Andrew Law, class of 1775; the contributions of a musical reformer. *In* Books at Brown. v. 18, no. 2; 1957. Providence. p. 61–77. facsims.   Z733.P958B6, v. 18

13808
LEACOCK, JOHN (1729–1802)

Pennsylvania. Craftsman, playwright.

—— The fall of British tyranny; or, American liberty triumphant. The first campaign. A tragi-comedy of five acts, as lately planned at the Royal Theatrum Pandemonium, at St. James's. The principal place of action in America. Published according to act of Parliament. Philadelphia, Printed by Styner and Cist, in Second-Street, near Arch-Street, 1776. viii, 66 p.
E295.L43 Rare Bk. Coll.
AC901.H3, v. 42 Rare Bk. Coll.

Dedication signed: Dick Rifle.

DALLETT, FRANCIS J.   John Leacock and *The Fall of British Tyranny*. Pennsylvania magazine of history and biography, v. 78, Oct. 1754: 456–475.

F146.P65, v. 78

13809

LEAMING, JEREMIAH (1717–1804)*

Connecticut. Anglican clergyman, Loyalist.

———— Letters of the Reverend Doctor Jeremiah Leaming to the Reverend Doctor Samuel Peters, Loyalist refugee in London, and one time bishop elect of Vermont [1782–1793] Historical magazine of the Protestant Episcopal church, v. 1, Sept./Dec. 1932: 116–142, 179–203.

BX5800.H5, v. 1

Introduction and notes by E. Clowes Chorley.

13810

LEARNED, EBENEZER (1728–1801)*

Massachusetts. Revolutionary general.

HEATHCOTE, CHARLES W.   General Ebenezer Learned—a courageous patriot and friend of Washington. Picket post, v. 59, Feb. 1958: 4–7, 34–36.   E234.P5, no. 59

13811

LE DESPENCER, FRANCIS DASHWOOD, *Baron* (1708–1781)†

England. Member of Parliament.

KEMP, BETTY.   Sir Francis Dashwood: an eighteenth century independent. London, Macmillan; New York, St. Martin's Press, 1967. ix, 210 p. facsims., plan, plates, ports.   DA483.L4K4 1967

13812

LEDYARD, JOHN (1751–1789)*†

Connecticut. Mariner, explorer.

———— A journal of Captain Cook's last voyage to the Pacific Ocean, and in quest of a north-west passage, between Asia & America; performed in the years 1776, 1777, 1778, and 1779. Illustrated with a chart, shewing the tracts of the ships employed in this expedition. Faithfully narrated from the original ms. of Mr. John Ledyard. Hartford, Printed and sold by Nathaniel Patten, a few rods north of the court-house, 1783. 208 p. fold. map.   G420.C72L3 Rare Bk. Coll.

AC901.W7, v. 13 Rare Bk. Coll.

A reprint, edited by James Kenneth Munford, with an introduction by Sinclair H. Hitchings, notes on plants by Helen M. Gilkey, and notes on animals by Robert M. Storm, was published in Corvallis, Oregon, by the State University Press (1964, ᶜ1963).

AUGUR, HELEN.   Passage to glory; John Ledyard's America. Garden City, N.Y., Doubleday, 1946. 310 p. map (on lining papers), plates, ports.   G226.L5A8

Bibliography: p. 295–300.

BEDERMAN, SANFORD H.   The ethnological contributions of John Ledyard. Atlanta, Georgia State College, 1964. 29 l. (Georgia. State College, Atlanta. School of Arts and Sciences. Research papers, no. 4)

AS36.G378A3, no. 4

Bibliography: leaves 26–27.

DAVIE, DONALD.   John Ledyard: the American traveler and his sentimental journeys. Eighteenth-century studies, v. 4, fall 1970: 57–70.   NX452.E54, v. 4

SPARKS, JARED.   The life of John Ledyard, the American traveller; comprising selections from his journals and correspondence. Cambridge [Mass.] Hilliard and Brown, 1828. xii, 325 p.   G226.L5S7

Reissued in 1847 as volume 14 in the second series of Sparks' Library of American Biography (Boston, C. C. Little and J. Brown. 419 p.).

13813

LEE, ANN (1736–1784)*†

England; New York. Religious sect leader.

BLINN, HENRY C.   The life and gospel experience of Mother Ann Lee. East Canterbury, N.H., The Shakers [pref. 1901] 264 p.   BX9793.L4B6 1901

EVANS, FREDERICK W.   Shakers. Compendium of the origin, history, principles, rules and regulations, government, and doctrines of the United Society of Believers in Christ's Second Appearing. With biographies of Ann Lee, William Lee, Jas. Whittaker, J. Hocknell, J. Meacham, and Lucy Wright. New York, D. Appleton, 1859. 189 p.   BX9771.E85 1859

SHAKERS.   Testimonies concerning the character and ministry of Mother Ann Lee and the first witness of the gospel of Christ's second appearing; given by some of the aged brethren and sisters of the United Society, including a few sketches of their own religious experience: approved by the church. Albany, Printed by Packard & Van Benthuysen, 1827. 178 p.

BX9793.L4A5 1827

"To the reader" signed: Seth Y. Wells.

13814

LEE, ARTHUR (1740–1792)*

Virginia. Lawyer, political writer, diplomat, delegate to the Continental Congress.

GIDDENS, PAUL H.   Arthur Lee, first United States envoy to Spain. Virginia magazine of history and biography, v. 40, Jan. 1932: 3–13.   F221.V91, v. 40

Guide to the microfilm edition of the Lee family papers, 1742–1795. Paul P. Hoffman, editor; John L. Molyneaux, assistant editor. Charlottesville, University of Virginia Library, 1966. 51 p. Z5315.L4H6 Mss

Harvard University. *Library.*   Calendar of the Arthur Lee manuscripts in the library of Harvard University. Reprinted from the Harvard University *Bulletin.* [no. 8–

23, 1878–82] Cambridge, Mass., University Press; J. Wilson, 1882. 43 p. (*Its* Bibliographical contributions, no. 8)   Z1009.H33
                                                             Z6621.H33L4

HENDRICK, BURTON J.   Arthur Lee, that volunteer diplomat. Atlantic monthly, v. 156, Sept. 1935: 316–323.
                                                             AP2.A8, v. 156

LEE, MARGUERITE DU PONT, *ed.*   Arthur Lee, M.D., LL.D., F.R.S., 1740–1792. [Richmond, Va., William Byrd Press, ᶜ1936] 293 p. plates, ports.
                                                             E207.L45L4 Rare Bk. Coll.

Cover-title: *Arthur Lee, Diplomat, 1740–1792.*

"Letters written by Arthur Lee, and to him . . . An effort has been made to assemble everything possible touching upon personal, social, and family life."—p. 39.

LEE, RICHARD H.   Life of Arthur Lee, LL.D., joint commissioner of the United States to the court of France, and sole commissioner to the courts of Spain and Prussia, during the Revolutionary War. With his political and literary correspondence and his papers on diplomatic and political subjects, and the affairs of the United States during the same period. Boston, Wells and Lilly, 1829. 2 v.   E249.L49

The "Life of Arthur Lee" occupies p. [11]–183 of v. 1. Reprinted in Freeport, N.Y., by Books for Libraries Press (1969).

MACMASTER, RICHARD K.   Arthur Lee's "Address on Slavery": an aspect of Virginia's struggle to end the slave trade, 1765–1774. Virginia magazine of history and biography, v. 80, Apr. 1972: 141–157.
                                                             F221.V91, v. 80

MONTAGUE, LUDWELL L.   Arthur Lee. *In* Northern Neck historical magazine. v. 17; 1967. Montross, Va. p. 1658–1666.   F232.N86N6, v. 17

POTTS, LOUIS W.   Arthur Lee—American revolutionary. 1970. ([483] p.)   Micro AC–1, no. 71–10,413

Thesis (Ph.D)—Duke University.
Abstracted in *Dissertation Abstracts International,* v. 31A, May 1971, p. 5994.

RIGGS, ALVIN R.   Arthur Lee, a radical Virginian in London, 1768–1776. Virginia magazine of history and biography, v. 78, July 1970: 268–280. port.
                                                             F221.V91, v. 78

———— Arthur Lee and the radical Whigs, 1768–1776. 1967. ([267] p.)   Micro AC–1, no. 68–13,192

Thesis (Ph.D.)—Yale University.
Abstracted in *Dissertation Abstracts,* v. 29A, Sept. 1968, p. 857–858.

SMITH, GLENN C.   Dr. Arthur Lee: political pamphletteer of pre-Revolutionary Virginia. Madison quarterly, v. 3, May 1943: 130–137.   LH1.M23Q3, v. 3

TYLER, LYON G.   Arthur Lee—a forgotten statesman. Tyler's quarterly historical and genealogical magazine, v. 14, Oct. 1932–Apr. 1933: 65–77, 129–138, 197–216.   F221.T95, v. 14

13815
LEE, CHARLES (1731–1782)*†
England; Virginia. Planter, Revolutionary general.

———— Conflicting opinions in 1775; Charles Lee, major-general in the provincial army, *versus* General Burgoyne, of His Majesty's forces in Boston. United service magazine, new ser., v. 55, Aug. 1917: 357–368.
                                                             U1.U6, n.s., v. 55

An exchange of correspondence between Lee and Burgoyne, under whom Lee served during the Seven Years' War, on the merits of their respective positions. Introduction by Katharine F. Doughty.

———— The Lee papers . . . 1754–[1811. New York, Printed for the Society, 1872–75] 4 v. (New York Historical Society. Collections, 1871–74. Publication fund series, [v. 4–7])
                                                             F116.N63, 1871–74

"The basis of the whole collection has been the mass of original papers left by General Lee to William Goddard, and still preserved in his family."—Final note.
Contents: 1. [Correspondence] 1754–1776. Strictures on a pamphlet, entitled, a *Friendly Address to All Reasonable Americans, on the Subject of Our Political Confusions.* 1774.—2. [Correspondence of Lee and others] 1776–1778.—3. Proceedings of a general court martial . . . for the trial of Major General Lee. July 4th, 1778. [Correspondence, etc.] 1778–1782.—4. The Lee papers, 1782–1811. Memoir of Major General Charles Lee, by Edward Langworthy. 1792. Memoir of Charles Lee, by Sir Henry Bunbury. Reprinted from the *Life and Correspondence of Sir Thomas Hanmer.* London, 1838. Life of Charles Lee, by Jared Sparks. 1846. "Mr. Lee's plan—March 29, 1777." The treason of Charles Lee, by George H. Moore. 1860. Indexes.

———— Memoirs of the life of the late Charles Lee, Esq., second in command in the service of the United States of America during the Revolution: to which are added his political and military essays. Also, letters to, and from many distinguished characters, both in Europe and America. London, Printed for J. S. Jordan, 1792. xii, 439 p.   E207.L47L4

The memoir (p. [1]–70) is by Edward Langworthy.

ALDEN, JOHN R.   General Charles Lee, traitor or patriot? Baton Rouge, Louisiana State University Press [1951] ix, 369 p. illus., maps (part fold.), port.
                                                             E207.L47A5

Bibliographic references included in "Notes" (p. [312]–355).

FLEMING, THOMAS J.   The "military crimes" of Charles Lee. American heritage, v. 19, Apr. 1968: 12–15, 83–89.
                                                             E171.A43, v. 19

HEATHCOTE, CHARLES W.   General Charles Lee in the American Revolution. Picket post, no. 65, July 1959: 7–13. port.   E234.P5, no. 65

MOORE, GEORGE H.   "Mr. Lee's plan—March 29, 1777." The treason of Charles Lee, major general, second in command in the American Army of the Revolution.

New-York, C. Scribner, 1860. xii, 115 p. fold. facsims., ports.   E207.L47M8

Reprinted in Port Washington, N.Y., by Kennikat Press (1970).

PATTERSON, SAMUEL W.   Knight errant of liberty; the triumph and tragedy of General Charles Lee. New York, Lantern Press [1958] 287 p. illus., map, plates, ports.   E207.L47P35

Bibliography: p. 281–282.

ROBINS, EDWARD.   Charles Lee—stormy petrel of the Revolution. Pennsylvania magazine of history and biography, v. 45, Jan. 1921: 66–97.   F146.P65, v. 45

SHY, JOHN W.   Charles Lee: the soldier as radical. *In* Billias, George A., *ed.* George Washington's generals. New York, W. Morrow, 1964. p. 22–53. port.   E206.B5

Bibliography: p. 52–53.

13816

LEE, HENRY (1756–1818)*
Virginia. Revolutionary officer, assemblyman, delegate to the Continental Congress.

——— Memoirs of the war in the Southern Department of the United States. Philadelphia, Published by Bradford and Inskeep; and Inskeep and Bradford, New York, Fry and Kammerer, Printers, 1812. 2 v. ports.
                        E230.5.S7L47 Rare Bk. Coll.

Reprinted in New York by B. Franklin (1970).

A new edition, with revisions and a biography of the author by Robert E. Lee, was published in New York by the University Pub. Co. (1869. 620 p.). It has been reprinted in New York by the New York Times (1969).

BOYD, THOMAS A.   Light-horse Harry Lee. New York, C. Scribner's Sons, 1931. 359 p. port.   E207.L5B78

"Manuscript sources": p. [345]
Bibliography: p. 347–350.

GERSON, NOEL B.   Light-Horse Harry; a biography of Washington's great cavalryman, General Henry Lee. Garden City, N.Y., Doubleday, 1966. 257 p. port.
                                        E207.L5G4

Bibliography: p. [245]–248.

13817

LEE, JESSE (1758–1816)*
Maryland. Itinerant Methodist preacher.

——— Memoir of the Rev. Jesse Lee. With extracts from his journals. By Minton Thrift. New York, Published by N. Bangs and T. Mason, for the Methodist Episcopal Church, 1823. viii, 360 p.   BX8495.L4A3
Reprinted in New York by Arno Press (1969).

——— A short account of the life and death of the Rev. John Lee, a Methodist minister in the United States of Amer-

ica. Baltimore, Printed by John West Butler, 1805. 179 p.   BX8495.L43L4

DUREN, WILLIAM L.   The top sergeant of the pioneers; the story of a lifelong battle for an ideal. Emory University, Ga., Banner Press, 1930. 191 p. facsim., plates, port.   BX8495.L4D8

A biography of Jesse Lee.

LEE, LEROY M.   The life and times of the Rev. Jesse Lee. Richmond, Va., J. Early, for the Methodist Episcopal Church, South, 1848. 517 p.   BX8495.L4L4

13818

LEE, RICHARD (1747–1823)
Massachusetts. Pewterer, farmer, preacher.

——— Narrative of Richard Lee (1747–1823). *In* Vermont Historical Society. Proceedings, new ser., v. 11, June–Sept. 1943: 76–94, 174–182. facsim.
                                        F46.V55, n.s., v. 11

13819

LEE, RICHARD HENRY (1732–1794)*
Virginia. Assemblyman, shipper, delegate to the Continental Congress.

——— Letters from Richard Henry Lee to Patrick Henry [1776–79] Virginia historical register and literary advertiser, v. 1, no. 4, 1848: 171–185.   F221.V81, v. 1

——— The letters of Richard Henry Lee. Collected and edited by James Curtis Ballagh. New York, Macmillan Co., 1911–14. 2 v. port.   E302.L47
"Published under the auspices of the National Society of the Colonial Dames of America."
Contents: v. 1. 1762–1778.—v. 2. 1779–1794.
Reprinted in New York by Da Capo Press (1970).

American Philosophical Society, *Philadelphia. Library.* Calendar of the correspondence of Richard Henry Lee and Arthur Lee. In the Library of the American Philosophical Society. Prepared under the direction of the Committee on Historical Manuscripts. *In its* Proceedings, v. 38, Jan. 1899: 114–131.   Q11.P5, v. 38

Also published in a volume with two other calendars (see no. 708).

BOWERS, PAUL C.   Richard Henry Lee and the Continental Congress: 1774–1779. 1965. ([373] p.)
                        Micro AC–1, no. 66–82

Thesis (Ph.D.)—Duke University.
Abstracted in *Dissertation Abstracts*, v. 26, Mar. 1966, p. 5394–5395.

CHITWOOD, OLIVER P.   Richard Henry Lee, statesman of the Revolution. Morgantown, West Virginia University Library, 1967. xiv, 310 p. illus., ports.
                                        E302.6.L4C5

Bibliography: p. 286–300.

COOK, FRANK G.   Richard Henry Lee. Atlantic monthly, v. 66, July 1890: 23–35.   AP2.A8, v. 66

HENDRICK, BURTON J.   The Lees of Virginia; biography of a family. Boston, Little, Brown, 1935. xii, 455 p. illus., ports.   E467.1.L4H35

Concerned particularly with the Revolutionary generation.

LEE, CAZENOVE G.   Lee chronicle, studies of the early generations of the Lees of Virginia. Compiled and edited by Dorothy Mills Parker. New York, New York University Press, 1957. xx, 411 p. illus., maps, ports.   CS71.L48 1957

Includes bibliographic references.

LEE, RICHARD H.   Memoir of the life of Richard Henry Lee, and his correspondence with the most distinguished men in America and Europe, illustrative of their characters, and of the events of the American Revolution. By his grandson. Philadelphia, H. C. Carey and I. Lea, 1825. 2 v. port.   E302.6.L4L4

MATTHEWS, JOHN C.   Richard Henry Lee and the American Revolution. 1939. 402 l.

Thesis (Ph.D.)—University of Virginia.

SMITHER, ETHEL L.   Richard Henry Lee. *In* Richmond College historical papers. v. 1, no. 1; 1915. Richmond. p. [38]–56.   F221.R53, v. 1

13820
LEE, THOMAS SIM (1745–1819)*
Maryland. Governor, delegate to the Continental Congress.

———— Revolutionary mail bag: Governor Thomas Sim Lee's correspondence, 1779–1782. Edited by Helen Lee Peabody. Maryland historical magazine, v. 49, Mar.–Dec. 1954: 1–20, 122–142, 223–237, 314–331; v. 50, Mar.–June 1955: 34–46, 93–108. illus.   F176.M18, v. 49–50

———— ———— Offprint. [Baltimore? 1956?] [108] p. illus.   F185.L437 1956

13821
LEE, WILLIAM (1739–1795)*
Virginia; Europe. Agent of Congress, diplomat.

———— Four unpublished letters of William Lee: 1779–1780. Virginia magazine of history and biography, v. 50, Jan. 1942: 38–46.   F221.V91, v. 50

Introduction and notes by Milton Rubincam.

———— Letters of William Lee, sheriff and alderman of London; commercial agent of the Continental Congress in France; and minister to the courts of Vienna and Berlin. 1766–1783. Collected and edited by Worthington Chauncey Ford. Brooklyn, N.Y., Historical Print. Club, 1891 (xvi, 987 p.) 3 v. port.   E249.L5

Includes bibliographic references.

Reprinted in New York by B. Franklin (1969) and the New York Times (1971).

———— Reply of William Lee to the charges of Silas Deane. 1779. Edited by Worthington Chauncey Ford. Brooklyn, N.Y., Historical Print. Club, 1891. 60 p.   E249.L51

13822
LEE, WILLIAM (b. 1744?)

———— The true and interesting travels of William Lee, born at Hadfield, near Doncaster: where his parents were farmers, who apprenticed him to a flaxdresser at Doncaster, with whom he served seven years, and afterwards in 1768 went with a venture to America, where he travelled through the back settlements, and endured numerous hardships and vicissitudes of furtune in the war between Great Britain and her Colonies, till he finally settled at Richmond, the county town of Georgia, where he became a justice of the peace. Copied verbatim from Mr. Lee's original mss. written at the express request of his aged mother. London, Printed for T. and R. Hughes [1808] 40 p. port.   E163.L47 Rare Bk. Coll.

13823
LEE, WILLIAM RAYMOND (1745–1824)
Massachusetts. Merchant, Revolutionary officer.

LEE, THOMAS A.   Colonel William Raymond Lee of the Revolution. Salem, Mass., Essex Institute, 1917. 29 p. plate, ports.   E263.M4L45

"Reprinted from the Essex Institute Historical Collections, vol. 53; with additions."

13824
LEEDS, FRANCIS GODOLPHIN OSBORNE, 5th Duke of (1751–1799)†
England. Diplomat.

———— The political memoranda of Francis, fifth Duke of Leeds, now first printed from the originals in the British Museum. Edited, together with other papers, and with notes, introduction, and appendix, by Oscar Browning. [London] Printed for the Camden Society, 1884. xiv, 266 p. (Publications of the Camden Society, new ser., v. 35)   DA20.C17, n.s., v. 35

13825
LEES, JOHN (fl. 1764)
Quebec. Merchant.

———— Journal of J.L., of Quebec, merchant. Published by the Society of Colonial Wars of the State of Michigan. Detroit [Speaker-Hines Press] 1911. 55 p. fold. maps.   E163.L48

Records a journey from London to Boston and travels through Rhode Island and New York on the way to Quebec from April to October 1768.

13826

LEETH, JOHN (1755–1832)

Pennsylvania; Ohio. Farmer, fur trader.

—— A short biography of John Leeth, with an account of his life among the Indians; reprinted from the original edition of 1831. With introduction by Reuben Gold Thwaites. Cleveland, Burrows Bros. Co., 1904. 70 p. (Narratives of captivities)   E87.L49

Reprinted in New York by B. Blom (1972).

Another edition, with illustrative notes by Consul W. Butterfield, was issued in Cincinnati by R. Clarke (1883).

13827

LEGGE, FRANCIS (1719–1783)

England; Nova Scotia. Governor.

BARNES, VIOLA F.   Francis Legge, governor of Loyalist Nova Scotia, 1773–1776. New England quarterly, v. 4, July 1931: 420–447.   F1.N62, v. 4

13828

LEGGETT, ABRAHAM (1755–1842)

New York. Revolutionary officer.

—— The narrative of Major Abraham Leggett, of the army of the Revolution, now first printed from the original manuscript. With an introduction and notes, by Charles I. Bushnell. New York, Priv. print., 1865. 72 p. plates, port. [Crumbs for antiquarians, v. 2, no. 1]   E203.B97

Reprinted in Tarrytown, N.Y., by W. Abbatt (1924. [37]–57 p. E173.M24, no. 101) as extra number, no. 101, of *The Magazine of History, With Notes and Queries,* and in New York by the New York Times (1971. 72 p. E275.L5 1971).

13829

LEHMAN, BENJAMIN (1760–1839)

Pennsylvania. Joiner-craftsman.

GILLINGHAM, HARROLD E.   Benjamin Lehman, a Germantown cabinetmaker. Pennsylvania magazine of history and biography, v. 54, Oct. 1930: 289–306. facsims.   F146.P65, v. 54

Lehman's 1786 "price list" for furniture that he made and sold appears on p. 290–304.

13830

LEIGH, *Sir* EGERTON, *Bart.* (1733–1788?)

England; South Carolina. Lawyer, assemblyman, councilor, judge, Loyalist.

BELLOT, HUGH HALE.   The Leighs in South Carolina. *In* Royal Historical Society, *London.* Transactions. 5th ser., v. 6; 1956. London. p. 161–187.   DA20.R9, 5th s., v. 6

CALHOON, ROBERT M., *and* ROBERT M. WEIR.   "The Scandalous History of Sir Egerton Leigh." William and Mary quarterly, 3d ser., v. 26, Jan. 1969: 47–74.   F221.W71, 3d s., v. 26

13831

LEIPER, THOMAS (1745–1825)*

Scotland; Maryland; Pennsylvania. Merchant, Revolutionary officer.

SMYTH, SAMUEL G.   Thomas Leiper, lieutenant of light horse, patriot and financier in the Revolution, and pioneer in the development of industries and inland commerce in Pennsylvania. Conshohocken, Pa., Record Print, 1900. 17 p. illus.   F153.L48

13832

LELAND, JOHN (1754–1841)*

Massachusetts; Virginia. Baptist clergyman.

—— The writings of John Leland. Edited by L. F. Greene. New York, Arno Press, 1969. 744 p. port. (Religion in America)   BX6495.L43A2 1969

Reprint of the 1845 ed.

BUTTERFIELD, LYMAN H.   Elder John Leland, Jeffersonian itinerant. *In* American Antiquarian Society, *Worcester, Mass.* Proceedings, new ser., v. 62, Oct. 1952: 155–242. illus.   E172.A35, n.s., v. 62

PETITCLER, *Mrs.* F. F.   Recollections of Elder Leland. *In* Berkshire Historical and Scientific Society, *Pittsfield, Mass.* Papers. v. 1; 1891. Pittsfield, Mass. p. [269]–290.   F72.B5B6, v. 1

SMITH, JOSIAH TORREY.   Life and times of the Rev. John Leland. Baptist quarterly, v. 5, Apr. 1871: 230–256.   BX6021.B5, v. 5

13833

L'ENFANT, PIERRE CHARLES (1754–1825)*

France; New York. Revolutionary officer and engineer, architect.

CAEMMERER, HANS P.   The life of Pierre Charles L'Enfant, planner of the city beautiful, the city of Washington. Washington, National Republic Pub. Co., 1950. xxvi, 480 p. illus., maps, ports.   F195.L53

Bibliography: p. 472–473.

13834

LENNOX, CHARLOTTE RAMSAY (1720–1804)*†

New York; England. Poet, novelist.

MAYNADIER, GUSTAVUS H.   The first American novelist? Cambridge, Mass., Harvard University Press, 1940. 79 p. plate, port.   PR3541.L27M3

Reprinted in Freeport, N.Y., by Books for Libraries Press (1971).

SÉJOURNÉ, PHILIPPE. The mystery of Charlotte Lennox, first novelist of colonial America (1727?–1804). [Gap] Editions Ophrys, 1967. 182 p. plates (Publications des Annales de la Faculté des lettres, Aix-en-Provence. Nouvelle sér., 62) PR3541.L27S4
Bibliography: p. 163–177.

SMALL, MIRIAM R. Charlotte Ramsey Lennox, an eighteenth century lady of letters. New Haven, Yale University Press, 1935. 268 p. facsims., plates, port. [Yale studies in English, v. 85] PR3541.L27S6 1925 PR13.Y3, v. 85
Thesis (Ph.D)—Yale University, 1925.
Bibliography: p. 248–264.
Reprinted in Hamden, Conn., by Archon Books (1969).

13835
LEONARD, DANIEL (1740–1829)*
Massachusetts; England. Lawyer, assemblyman, councilor, Loyalist.

JACKMAN, SYDNEY W. Daniel Leonard, 1740–1829. Bermuda historical quarterly, v. 13, autumn 1956: 136–145. F1636.B55, v. 13

13836
LETTSOM, JOHN COAKLEY (1744–1815)†
England. Physician.

JACOBSEN, VICTOR C. John Coakley Lettsom and his relations with Jonathan Carver, explorer of the Middle West. Annals of medical history, new ser., v. 2, Mar. 1930: 208–216. facsim., port. R11.A85, n.s., v. 2

THOMSON, Sir ST. CLAIR. The strenuous life of a physician in the 18th century. Annals of medical history, new ser., v. 1, Jan. 1929: 1–13. illus., facsims., map, ports. R11.A85, n.s., v. 1

TRENT, JOSIAH C. John Coakley Lettsom. Bulletin of the history of medicine, v. 22, Sept./Oct. 1948: 528–542. R11.B93, v. 22

13837
LEVY, AARON (ca. 1742–1815)
Pennsylvania. Revolutionary soldier, land speculator.

FISH, SIDNEY M. Aaron Levy, founder of Aaronsburg; with a foreword by Lee M. Friedman. New York, American Jewish Historical Society, 1951. ix, 81 p. illus., ports. (Studies in American Jewish history, no. 1) F153.L5F5
Bibliographic footnotes.

13838
LEWIS, FRANCIS (1713–1802 or 3)*
Wales; New York. Merchant, delegate to the Continental Congress.

BURLINGHAM, CHARLES C. Francis Lewis, one of the New York signers of the Declaration of Independence. [New York? 1926] 14 p. E302.6.L6B9

DELAFIELD, JULIA L. Biographies of Francis Lewis and Morgan Lewis. New York, A. D. F. Randolph, 1877. 2 v. E302.6.L6D3

13839
LEWIS, JOSEPH (fl. 1783–1795)
New Jersey. Farmer.

—— Diary or memorandum book kept by Joseph Lewis of Morristown, from the first of November 1783 to November 26, 1795. In New Jersey Historical Society. Proceedings, v. 59, July–Oct. 1941: 155–173, 263–282; v. 60, Jan.–Oct. 1942: 58–66, 124–137, 199–209, 254–269; v. 61, Jan.–July 1943: 47–56, 115–129, 194–200; v. 62, Jan.–Oct. 1944: 35–53, 106–117, 167–180, 217–236. F131.N58, v. 59–62

13840
LEWIS, STEPHEN CHRISTOPHER (d. 1790)
Massachusetts. Anglican clergyman.

MERRITT, EDWARD PERCIVAL. Sketch of the Rev. Stephen Christopher Lewis. In Colonial Society of Massachusetts, Boston. Publications. v. 25. Transactions, 1922/24. Boston, 1924. p. 362–381. facsim. F61.C71, v. 25
Reprinted in Cambridge, with a fuller title, by J. Wilson (1924. [362]–381 p. BX5995.L4M4).

13841
LEWIS, WILLIAM (1751–1819)*
Pennsylvania. Lawyer, assemblyman.

PRIMROSE, WILLIAM. Biography of William Lewis, by William Primrose, Philadelphia, 1820. Pennsylvania magazine of history and biography, v. 20, Apr. 1896: 30–40. port. F146.P65, v. 20
Contributed by George C. Lewis.

13842
L'HOMMEDIEU, EZRA (1734–1811)*
New York. Assemblyman, Revolutionary provisioner, delegate to the Continental Congress.

L'HOMMEDIEU, WILLIAM A. Ezra L'Hommedieu—intimate of Washington. Americana, v. 27, July 1933: 290–299. port. E171.A53, v. 27

13843
LIDNER, BENGT (1757–1793)

ELOVSON, HARALD. Bengt Lidners Greifswalder Dissertation "De iure revolutionis americanorum." Jena, Frommann, 1928. 26 p. E249.3.E48

13844

LIELE, GEORGE (*b. ca.* 1751)

Virginia; West Indies. Clergyman.

DAVIS, JOHN W.   George Liele and Andrew Bryan, pioneer Negro Baptist preachers. Journal of Negro history, v. 3, Apr. 1918: 119–127.   E185.J86, v. 3

13845

LIGHTFOOT, BENJAMIN (*b. ca.* 1726)

Pennsylvania. Merchant, surveyor.

LIGHTFOOT, THOMAS MONTGOMERY, *ed.*   Benjamin Lightfoot and his account of an expedition to "Tankhannink" in the year 1770. [Muncy? Pa., 1937?] 22 p. plate.   F152.L64

First published in the *Proceedings* of the Northumberland County (Pa.) Historical Society, v. 9 (Sunbury, 1937), p. 171–188, the journal covers Lightfoot's expedition to inspect large timber for masts.

13846

LILLINGTON, JOHN ALEXANDER (1725–1786)

North Carolina. Planter, Revolutionary officer, assemblyman.

BELLAMY, JOHN D.   Address by John D. Bellamy on the life and services of General Alexander Lillington. Washington, D. C., Press of Judd & Detweiler, 1905. 16 p.   F262.H3B5

13847

LINCOLN, BENJAMIN (1733–1810)*

Massachusetts. Farmer, assemblyman, Revolutionary general.

Guide to the microfilm edition of the Benjamin Lincoln papers.   Frederick S. Allis, Jr., editor; Wayne A. Frederick, associate editor. Boston, Massachusetts Historical Society, 1967. 70 p.   Z6616.L6A46 Mss

HEATHCOTE, CHARLES W.   General Benjamin Lincoln—a dedicated military officer and intimate friend of General Washington. Picket post, no. 75, Feb. 1962: 14–20. port.   E234.P5, no. 75

Notices of the life of Major General Benjamin Lincoln.   *In* Massachusetts Historical Society, *Boston.* Collections. 2d ser., v. 3. Boston, 1815. p. 233–255.   F61.M41, 2d s., v. 3

Article signed P. C.

SHIPTON, CLIFFORD K.   Benjamin Lincoln: old reliable. *In* Billias, George A., *ed.* George Washington's generals. New York, W. Morrow, 1964. p. 193–211. port.   E206.B5

Bibliography: p. 211.

13848

LINCOLN, RUFUS (1751–1838)

Massachusetts. Revolutionary officer.

——— The papers of Captain Rufus Lincoln, of Wareham, Mass. Compiled from the original records by James Minor Lincoln. [Cambridge, Mass., Riverside Press] 1904. 272 p. facsim.   E275.L73

Reprinted in New York by the New York Times (1971).

13849

LINCTOT, DANIEL MAURICE GODFREY DE (*ca.* 1730–*ca.* 1781)

Canada; Illinois. Military officer, fur trader, Indian agent.

BRENNAN, GEORGE A.   De Linctot, guardian of the frontier *In* Illinois State Historical Society. Journal, v. 10, Oct. 1917: 323–366.   F536.I18, v. 10

13850

LINN, BENJAMIN (1750–1814)

Pennsylvania; Kentucky. Hunter, Revolutionary scout and officer, Baptist clergyman.

BEATTIE, GEORGE W., *and* HELEN P. BEATTIE.   Pioneer Linns of Kentucky. Filson Club history quarterly, v. 20, Jan.–July 1946: 18–36, 137–161, 220–250.   F446.F484, v. 20

Contents: pt. 1. Pioneer Linns of Kentucky.—pt. 2. Benjamin Linn—hunter, explorer, preacher.—pt. 3. Colonel William Linn—soldier, Indian fighter.

13851

LISTER, JEREMY (1752–1836)

British officer in America.

——— Concord fight, being so much of the narrative of Ensign Jeremy Lister of the 10th Regiment of Foot as pertains to his services on the 19th of April, 1775, and to his experiences in Boston during the early months of the siege. Cambridge, Mass., Printed at the Harvard University Press, 1931. 55 p.   E267.L82

"The brief narrative of Jeremy Lister [was] written late in 1782 . . . Extracts from his narrative first appeared in the *London Telegraph* in December, 1928."—Introduction.

Three letters written by Lister during 1774–75 to his father, and one letter written by Lieutenant-Colonel Val Jones, are included in the appendix (p. 47–[56]).

——— Jeremy Lister, 10th Regiment, 1770–1783. *In* Society for Army Historical Research, *London.* Journal, v. 41, Mar.–June 1963: 31–41, 59–73.   DA49.S6, v. 41

Letters to his father, brother, and cousin. Introduction and notes by R. A. Innes.

13852

LITCHFIELD, ISRAEL (1753–1840)

Massachusetts. Revolutionary soldier, assemblyman.

———— Diary of Israel Litchfield [Nov. 4, 1774–Aug. 25, 1775] *In* Litchfield, Wilford J., comp. The Litchfield family in America. pt. 1, no. 5 [Southbridge, Mass.] 1906. p. 312–351.   CS71.L776 1901/1906

13853

LITTELL, ELIAKIM (1742–1805)

New Jersey. Revolutionary officer.

LITTELL, S.   Memoir of Captain Eliakim Littell. *In* New Jersey Historical Society. Proceedings, 2d ser., v. 7, no. 2, 1882: 83–101.   F131.N58, 2d s., v. 7

13854

LITTLE, LUTHER (1756–*ca.* 1841)

Massachusetts. Revolutionary seaman.

———— An American sea captain in the Revolution: the personal narrative of Captain Luther Little before, during, and after the Revolutionary War. Journal of American history, v. 11, July/Sept. 1917: 409–420; v. 13, Apr./June 1919: 217–252. facsims., ports.   E171.J86, v. 11, 13

13855

LITTLEPAGE, LEWIS (1762–1802)*

Virginia; Europe. Soldier, diplomat.

———— An American courtier in Europe: Lewis Littlepage's "Private Political Memoir" (Hamburg, 1795). Translated and edited by Curtis C. Davis. *In* American Philosophical Society, *Philadelphia*. Proceedings, v. 101, June 1957: 255–269.   Q11.P5, v. 101

The memoir covers the period from about March 1787 through November 1794.

———— Answer to a pamphlet, containing the correspondence between the Honorable John Jay, secretary for foreign affairs; and Lewis Littlepage, Esquire, of Virginia; at present chamberlain and secretary of the cabinet of His Majesty the King of Poland. Philadelphia, Printed and sold by E. Story, corner of Walnut & Second Streets [1786] 35 p.   E302.J4L7 Rare Bk. Coll.

BOAND, NELL H.   Lewis Littlepage. Richmond, Va., Whittet & Shepperson, 1970. x, 290 p. ports.   E302.6.L65B6

DAVIS, CURTIS C.   The king's chevalier; a biography of Lewis Littlepage. New York, Bobbs-Merrill [1961] 442 p. illus., plates, ports.   E302.6.L65D3

Bibliography: p. 395–402.

13856

LIVERMORE, DANIEL (1749–1798)

Massachusetts; New Hampshire. Revolutionary officer, farmer.

WALKER, JOSEPH B.   Major Daniel Livermore, a citizen soldier of the Revolution. *In* New Hampshire Historical Society. Proceedings. v. 3, pt. 1; 1895/97. Concord, 1897. p. 63–75.   F31.N52, v. 3

13857

LIVERPOOL, CHARLES JENKINSON, *1st Earl of* (1727–1808)†

England. Secretary at War.

———— The Jenkinson papers, 1760–1766. Edited with an introduction by Ninetta S. Jucker. London, Macmillan, 1949. xxix, 451 p. (Studies in modern history)   DA506.L65A4

JOHNSTON, CHARLES M.   Charles Jenkinson, Lord Hawkesbury, at the Committee for Trade, 1784–1792. 1954. ([190] p.)   Micro AC–1, no. 7790

Thesis (Ph.D.)—University of Pennsylvania.
Abstracted in *Dissertation Abstracts*, v. 14, no. 6, 1954, p. 969–970.

13858

LIVINGSTON, ANNE HOME SHIPPEN (1763–1841)

Pennsylvania.

———— Nancy Shippen, her journal book; the international romance of a young lady of fashion of colonial Philadelphia, with letters to her and about her. Compiled and edited by Ethel Armes. Philadelphia, J. B. Lippincott Co., 1935. 348 p. illus., facsims., fold. geneal. table, plans (on lining papers), plates, ports.   E302.6.L67L6

Bibliography: p. 317–[321].
Reprinted in New York by B. Blom (1968).

13859

LIVINGSTON, HENRY (1714–1799)

New York. Surveyor, assemblyman.

POUCHER, JOHN WILSON.   Dutchess County men of the Revolutionary period: Henry Livingston. *In* Dutchess County Historical Society. Year book. v. 23; 1938. Poughkeepsie. p. 39–51. illus., plates.   F127.D8D93, v. 23

13860

LIVINGSTON, PHILIP (1716–1778)*

New York. Merchant, assemblyman, delegate to the Continental Congress.

GORDON, PATRICIA J.   The Livingstons of New York, 1675–1860: kinship and class. 1959. ([350] p.)   Micro AC–1, no. 60–13

Thesis (Ph.D.)—Columbia University.

Abstracted in *Dissertation Abstracts*, v. 20, Mar. 1960, p. 3877.

Studies six generations of the Livingston family to determine how class and status affected their behavior.

LIVINGSTON, EDWIN B. The Declaration of Independence and the Livingstons. American historical register, v. 1, Oct. 1894: 123–141.   E171.A56, v. 1

———— The Livingstons of Livingston manor. [New York, Knickerbocker Press] 1910. xxxiii, 590 p. illus., fold. geneal. tables, plates (part col.), ports.

          CS71.L787 1910

Treats all members of the Livingston families, most notably Philip, William, and their cousin, Robert R. The Livingstons' involvement in the Revolution is considered on p. 150–328. See also the author's article, "A List of Livingstons Who Held Commissions in the American Army and Navy During the War of Independence, 1775–1783," in the *New York Genealogical and Biographical Record*, v. 41, July-Oct. 1910, p. 192–199, 299–308.

13861
LIVINGSTON, ROBERT R. (1746–1813)*

New York. Lawyer, delegate to the Continental Congress, diplomat, judge.

CLARKSON, THOMAS S. A biographical history of Clermont, or Livingston Manor, before and during the War for Independence, with a sketch of the first steam navigation of Fulton and Livingston. Clermont, N.Y., 1869. 319 p. illus.   F129.C6C6

DANGERFIELD, GEORGE. Chancellor Robert R. Livingston of New York, 1746–1813. New York, Harcourt, Brace [1960] viii, 532 p. geneal. table, port.

          E302.6.L72D3

"A bibliographical note": p. 441–450.

DELAFIELD, JOSEPH L. Chancellor Robert R. Livingston of New York and his family. *In* American Scenic and Historic Preservation Society. Annual report. 16th; 1911. Albany. p. 311–356.   E151.A51, v. 16

McANEAR, BEVERLY. Mr. Robert R. Livingston's reasons against a land tax. Journal of political economy, v. 48, Feb. 1940: 63–90.   HB1.J7, v. 48

POUCHER, JOHN WILSON. Dutchess County men of the Revolutionary period: Judge Robert R. Livingston, his sons and sons-in-law. *In* Dutchess County Historical Society. Year book. v. 30; 1945. p. 54–74.

          F127.D8D93, v. 30

13862
LIVINGSTON, WILLIAM (1723–1790)*

New York; New Jersey. Lawyer, political writer, delegate to the Continental Congress, Revolutionary officer, governor, delegate to the Constitutional Convention.

———— Unpublished correspondence of William Livingston and John Jay [1777–90] *In* New Jersey Historical Society. Proceedings, v. 52, July 1934: 141–162.

          F131.N58, v. 52

Introduction and notes by Frank Monaghan.

———— ———— Offprint. Newark, N.J., New Jersey Historical Society, 1934. 24 p.   E302.6.L75L7

KLEIN, MILTON M. The American Whig: William Livingston of New York. 1954. ([799] p.)

          Micro AC–1, no. 8699

Thesis (Ph.D.)—Columbia University.

Abstracted in *Dissertation Abstracts*, v. 14, no. 9, 1954, p. 1377–1378.

———— The rise of the New York bar: the legal career of William Livingston. William and Mary quarterly, 3d ser., v. 15, July 1958: 334–358.

          F221.W71, 3d s., v. 15

SEDGWICK, THEODORE. A memoir of the life of William Livingston, member of Congress in 1774, 1775, and 1776; delegate to the federal convention in 1787, and governor of the state of New-Jersey from 1776 to 1790. With extracts from his correspondence, and notices of various members of his family. New-York, J. & J. Harper, 1833. 449 p. port.   E302.6.L79S4

"List of Governor Livingston's works": p. 448.

THATCHER, HAROLD W. The political ideas of New Jersey's first governor. *In* New Jersey Historical Society. Proceedings, v. 60, Apr.–July 1942: 81–98, 184–199.   F131.N58, v. 60

———— The social and economic ideas of New Jersey's first governor. *In* New Jersey Historical Society. Proceedings, v. 60, Oct. 1942: 225–238; v. 61, Jan. 1943: 31–46.

          F131.N58, v. 60–61

———— The social philosophy of William Livingston. 1935. 317 l.

Thesis (Ph.D.)—University of Chicago.

13863
LIVIUS, PETER (1727–1795)

England; New Hampshire; Canada. Councilor, Loyalist, judge.

BURT, ALFRED L. The tragedy of Chief Justice Livius. Canadian historical review, v. 5, Sept. 1924: 196–212.

          F1001.C27, v. 5

MAYO, LAWRENCE S. Peter Livius, the trouble-maker. *In* Colonial Society of Massachusetts, *Boston*. Publications. v. 25. Transactions, 1922/24. Boston, 1924. p. 125–129.   F61.C71, v. 25

13864
LLOYD, EDWARD (1744–1796)*

Maryland. Planter, assemblyman, delegate to the Continental Congress.

BEIRNE, ROSAMOND R. The Chase house in Annapolis. Maryland historical magazine, v. 49, Sept. 1954: 177–195. illus., plates, ports.   F176.M18, v. 49

On the completion of its construction during the 1770's by Lloyd, its second owner.

13865
LLOYD, JOHN (1745–1792)
New York. Farmer, Revolutionary provisioner.

[BARCK, DOROTHY C.] ed. Papers of the Lloyd family of the manor of Queens Village, Lloyd's Neck, Long Island, New York, 1654–1826. New York, Printed for the Society, 1927. 2 v. (xii, 981 p.) maps. (New York Historical Society. Collections, 1926–27. The John Watts De Peyster publication fund series, [v. 59–60])   F116.N63, 1926–27

"The letters are principally the correspondence of the two men most closely associated with Lloyd's Neck, Henry Lloyd I (1685–1763) . . . John Lloyd II (1745–1792) . . ."—Introduction.

Contents: v. 1. 1654–1752.—v. 2. 1752–1826, with genealogical appendix.

13866
LOGAN, BENJAMIN (1743–1802)*
Virginia; Kentucky. Revolutionary officer, settler, assemblyman.

CONKWRIGHT, BESSIE T. A sketch of the life and times of General Benjamin Logan. In Kentucky Historical Society. Register, v. 14, May 1916: 19–35; Sept. 19–33.   F446.K43, v. 14

TALBERT, CHARLES G. Benjamin Logan, Kentucky frontiersman. [Lexington] University of Kentucky Press [1962] ix, 322 p.   F454.L78T3

Includes bibliographic references.

The author's thesis (Ph.D.), *The Life and Times of Benjamin Logan*, was submitted to the University of Kentucky in 1952 (Micro AC–1, no. 60–710).

13867
LOGAN, DEBORAH NORRIS (1761–1839)*
Pennsylvania. Wife of George Logan (1753–1821).

SWEENEY, JOHN A. H., *ed.* The Norris-Fisher correspondence: a circle of friends, 1779–82. Delaware history, v. 6, Mar. 1955: 187–232.   F161.D37, v. 6

13868
LOGAN, GEORGE (1753–1821)*
Pennsylvania. Physician, farmer, assemblyman.

LOGAN, DEBORAH N. Memoir of Dr. George Logan of Stenton, by his widow Deborah Norris Logan, with selections from his correspondence. Edited by their great-granddaughter, Frances A. Logan. With an introduction by Charles J. Stillé. Illustrations from photographs by C. S. Bradford. Philadelphia, Historical Society of Pennsylvania, 1899. 207 p. facsim., plates, ports.   E302.6.L8L8

TOLLES, FREDERICK B. George Logan and the agricultural revolution. In American Philosophical Society, Philadelphia. Proceedings, v. 95, Dec. 1951: 589–596.   Q11.P5, v. 95

———— George Logan of Philadelphia. New York, Oxford University Press, 1953. xix, 362 p. illus., ports.   E302.6.L8T6

Bibliographic references included in "Notes" (p. 320–350).

Reprinted in New York by Arno Press (1972).

13869
LOGAN, JAMES, *Mingo chief* (d. 1780)*

JONES, HOWARD, comp. Tah-jah-jute, or Logan, the Mingo chief; with material pertaining to his "speech" and the times taken from Thomas Jefferson's "Notes on Virginia," printed in the year 1800. Circleville, O., 1937. 47 p. map, plates.   E99.M64L855

"A copy of appendix no. 4, of 'Jefferson's Notes on the State of Virginia,' printed in 1800. Also the letter of General George Rogers Clark to Doctor Brown for the use of Mr. Jefferson": p. 7–47.

Logan—the Mingo chief. 1710–1780. Ohio archaeological and historical quarterly, v. 20, Jan. 1911: 137–175.   F486.O51, v. 20

"The following biography of Logan, probably as authentic as can now be obtained, is from the Draper Manuscripts—Border Forays, 2 D., Chapter 12—in the Library of the Wisconsin Historical Society. The notes also herewith published were made by a recent student of the manuscripts."

"References": p. 168–175.

MAYER, BRANTZ. Tah-gah-jute; or, Logan and Cresap, an historical essay. Albany, J. Munsell, 1867. x, 204 p. illus. (Munsell's series of local American history, v. 2)   F517.M48 Rare Bk. Coll.

SANDEFUR, RAY H. Logan's oration [1774]—how authentic? Quarterly journal of speech, v. 46, Oct. 1960: 289–296.   PN4071.Q3, v. 46

SAWVEL, FRANKLIN B. Logan the Mingo. Boston, R. G. Badger [c1921] 110 p. plates, port.   E99.M64L86

Bibliography: p. 109–110.

13870
LOGAN, *Capt.* JOHN, *Cayuga chief* (1718–1820)
Pennsylvania. Revolutionary scout. Brother of James Logan, *Mingo chief* (d. 1780).

SHOEMAKER, HENRY W. Captain Logan, Blair Country's Indian chief; a biography. Altoona, Pa., Altoona Tribune Pub., 1915. 40 p. plates, ports.   E90.L82S55

13871

LOGAN, JOHN (1747–1807)

Virginia; Kentucky. Settler, Revolutionary officer, assemblyman.

TALBERT, CHARLES G. John Logan, 1747–1807. Filson Club history quarterly, v. 36, Apr. 1962: 128–150.
F446.F484, v. 36

13872

LOGAN, WILLIAM (1718–1776?)

Pennsylvania. Merchant, councilor.

Town house and country house: inventories from the estate of William Logan, 1776. Pennsylvania magazine of history and biography, v. 82, Oct. 1958: 397–410. facsims. F146.P65, v. 82

Introduction by Frederick B. Tolles.

13873

LOLME, JEAN LOUIS DE (1740–1806)

Switzerland; England. Lawyer, historical writer.

RUFF, EDITH. Jean Louis de Lolme und sein Werk über die Verfassung Englands. Berlin, Verlag Dr. E. Ebering, 1934. 108 p. (Historische Studien, Heft 240)
JN117.L75R8

Inaug. Diss.—Heidelberg.
"Quellen- und Literaturverzeichnis": p. [103]–108.

13874

LONG, JOHN, *Indian trader*

—— John Long's journal, 1768–1782. Cleveland, Ohio, A. H. Clark Co., 1904. 329 p. fold. map. (Thwaites, Reuben G., ed. Early western travels, 1748–1846, a series of annotated reprints, v. 2) F592.T54, v. 2

—— John Long's voyages and travels in the years 1768–1788. Edited with historical introduction and notes by Milo Milton Quaife. Chicago, R. R. Donnelley, 1922. xxx, 238 p. fold. map. (The Lakeside classics)
E77.L843 Rare Bk. Coll.

—— Voyages and travels of an Indian interpreter and trader, describing the manners and customs of the North American Indians; with an account of the posts situated on the river St. Laurence, Lake Ontario, &c. To which is added a vocabulary of the Chippeway language . . . a list of words in the Iroquois, Mohegan, Shawanee, and Esquimeaux tongues, and a table, shewing the analogy between the Algonkin and Chippeway languages. London, Printed for the author, sold by Robson, 1791. x, 295 p. fold. map.
E77.L84 Rare Bk. Coll.
Micro 01291, reel 190, no. 6 E

Reprinted in Toronto by Coles Pub. Co. (1971).

13875

LOPEZ, AARON (1731–1782)*

Portugal; Rhode Island. Merchant.

—— Aaron Lopez's family affairs from "The Commerce of Rhode Island." In American Jewish Historical Society. Publications. no. 35. New York, 1939. p. 295–304.
E184.J5A5, no. 35

Mostly letters to and from Lopez relating to the business conduct of his son-in-law, Abraham Pereira Mendes, selected from the *Collections* of the Massachusetts Historical Society (entry 9809).

BIGELOW, BRUCE M. Aaron Lopez, colonial merchant of Newport. New England quarterly, v. 4, Oct. 1931: 757–776. F1.N62, v. 4

Reprinted in *Rhode Island Jewish Historical Notes*, v. 2, June 1956, p. 4–17.

CHYET, STANLEY F. Aaron Lopez: a study in buenafama. American Jewish historical quarterly, v. 52, June 1963: 295–309. E184.J5A5, v. 52

—— Lopez of Newport; colonial American merchant prince. Detroit, Wayne State University Press, 1970. 246 p. illus., ports. F82.L66C5 1970

Bibliography: p. [226]–230.

FRIEDMAN, LEE M. Aaron Lopez' long deferred "Hope." In American Jewish Historical Society. Publications. no. 37. New York, 1947. p. 103–113.
E184.J5A5, no. 37

On the protracted litigation, 1778–82, over the capture of Lopez' schooner by American privateers.

—— Some further sidelights on Aaron Lopez. Jewish quarterly review, v. 45, Apr. 1955: 562–567. facsim.
DS101.J5, v. 45

GUTSTEIN, MORRIS A. Descriptive index of Aaron Lopez material at the Newport Historical Society. In American Jewish Historical Society. Publications. no. 37. New York, 1947. p. 153–162. E184.J5A5, no. 37

PLATT, VIRGINIA B. Tar, staves, and New England rum: the trade of Aaron Lopez of Newport, Rhode Island, with colonial North Carolina. North Carolina historical review, v. 48, winter 1970: 1–22.
F251.N892, v. 48

Lopez dispatched at least 37 voyages to North Carolina between 1761 and 1775.

13876

LOPEZ, MOSES (1706–1767)

Portugal; Rhode Island. Merchant.

LOPEZ, MOSES. Charles Town in 1764. Edited by Thomas J. Tobias. South Carolina historical magazine, v. 67, Apr. 1966: 63–74. F266.S55, v. 67

Letters to his brother, Aaron, in Newport, Rhode Island.

13877

LORING, JOSHUA (1716–1781)*

Massachusetts; England. Naval officer, councilor, Loyalist.

BOYD, EVA P.　Jamaica Plain by way of London. *In* Society for the Preservation of New England Antiquities, *Boston.* Old-time New England, v. 49, Apr./June 1959: 85–103. illus., port.　F1.S68, v. 49

Contains information on the careers of Loring and his son, Joshua (1744–1789).

13878

LOTBINIÉRE, LOUIS EUSTACHE (1741–1786)

Canada. Roman Catholic priest, Revolutionary chaplain.

GRIFFIN, MARTIN I. J.　A Canadian patriot priest of the eighteenth century. *In* American Catholic Historical Society of Philadelphia. Records, v. 15, Mar. 1904: 69–82.　E184.C3A4, v. 15

13879

LOTT, ABRAHAM (*ca.* 1726–1794)

New York. Loyalist.

—— A journal of a voyage to Albany, etc., made by Abraham Lott, treasurer of the colony of New York, 1774. Historical magazine, 2d ser., v. 8, Aug. 1870: 65–74.　E171.H64, 2d s., v. 8

13880

LOUDON, SAMUEL (1727?–1813)*

New York. Merchant, printer, publisher.

WALL, ALEXANDER J.　Samuel Loudon (1727–1813), (merchant, printer and patriot) with some of his letters. *In* New York Historical Society. Quarterly bulletin, v. 6, Oct. 1922: 75–92. facsims.　F116.N638, v. 6

—— —— Offprint. [New York, 1922] 75–92 p. facsims.　Z232.L8W2

13881

LOUIS XVI, *King of France* (1754–1793)

FAŸ, BERNARD.　Louis XVI; or, The end of a world. Translated by Patrick O'Brian from the French. Chicago, H. Regnery Co. [1968, c1967] 414 p. illus., geneal. table, ports.　DC136.F313 1968b

Translation of *Louis XVI; ou, la Fin d'un monde.*

PADOVER, SAUL K.　The life and death of Louis XVI. New York, D. Appleton-Century Co., 1939. xiv, 373 p. illus., facsims., plan (on lining papers), plates, ports.　DC137.P12

Reissued in New York by the Taplinger Pub. Co. (1963).

13882

LOVE, DAVID (*fl.* 1764–1779)

Maryland. Anglican clergyman.

—— Letters from the Reverend David Love to Horatio Sharpe, 1774–1779. Historical magazine of the Protestant Episcopal Church, v. 19, Dec. 1950: 355–368.　BX5800.H5, v. 19

Introduction and notes by James High.

13883

LOVELL, JAMES (1737–1814)*

Massachusetts. Schoolteacher, delegate to the Continental Congress.

JONES, HELEN F.　James Lovell in the Continental Congress, 1777–1782. 1968. ([645] p.)　Micro AC–1, no. 69–12,977

Thesis (Ph.D.)—Columbia University.

Abstracted in *Dissertation Abstracts International,* v. 30A, Aug. 1969, p. 639.

13884

LOVELL, SOLOMON (1732–1801)

Massachusetts. Farmer, assemblyman, Revolutionary general.

NASH, GILBERT.　Sketch of Gen. Solomon Lovell. *In* Weymouth Historical Society, *Weymouth, Mass.* [Publications] no. 1. Weymouth, 1881. p. 19–92. illus., map, plates.　F74.W77W7, no. 1

13885

LOWELL, JOHN (1743–1802)*

Massachusetts. Lawyer, Revolutionary officer, assemblyman, delegate to the Continental Congress, judge.

DEANE, CHARLES.　Judge Lowell and the Massachusetts declaration of rights. *In* Massachusetts Historical Society, *Boston.* Proceedings. v. 13–14; 1873/76. Boston, 1875–76. p. 299–304; p. 108–109.　F61.M38, v. 13–14

GREENSLET, FERRIS.　The Lowells and their seven worlds. Boston, Houghton Mifflin Co., 1946. xi, 442 p. plates, ports.　CS71.L915 1946

"Revolution": p. [41]–84.

13886

LUDINGTON, HENRY (1739–1817)

Connecticut; New York. Landowner, Revolutionary officer.

JOHNSON, WILLIS F.　Colonel Henry Ludington, a memoir. New York, Printed by his grandchildren L. E. Ludington and C. H. Ludington, 1907. ix, 235 p. illus., facsims., maps, plates, ports.　E263.N6L9

PATRICK, LEWIS S. Secret service of the American Revolution. Connecticut magazine, v. 11, summer 1907: 265–274. F91.C8, v. 11

A biographical sketch of Ludington which also appeared in the *Journal of American History*, v. 1, 1907, p. 497–508.

POUCHER, JOHN WILSON, *and* BARBARA CORLISS. Dutchess County men of the Revolutionary period—Colonel Henry Ludington and his daughter Sybil. *In* Dutchess County Historical Society. Year book. v. 30; 1945. Poughkeepsie. p. 75–82. F127.D8D93, v. 30

13887
LUDWICK, CHRISTOPHER (1720–1801)*
Germany; Pennsylvania. Baker, Revolutionary officer.

—— Baker-General in the Army of the United States during the Revolutionary War. Pennsylvania magazine of history and biography, v. 16, Oct. 1892: 343–348. F146.P65, v. 16

CONDIT, WILLIAM W. Christopher Ludwick, patriotic gingerbread baker. Pennsylvania magazine of history and biography, v. 81, Oct. 1957: 365–390. F146.P65, v. 81

RUSH, BENJAMIN. An account of the life and character of Christopher Ludwick. First published in the year 1801. Rev. and republished by direction of the Philadelphia Society for the Establishment and Support of Charity Schools. To which is added, an account of the origin, progress, and present condition of that institution. Philadelphia, Printed for the Society by Garden and Thompson, 1831. 61 p. CT275.L835R7

13888
LYDEKKER, GERRIT (1729–1794)
New Jersey; New York; England. Dutch Reformed clergyman, Loyalist.

LYDEKKER, JOHN W. The Rev. Gerrit (Gerard) Lydekker, 1729–1794. Historical magazine of the Protestant Episcopal church, v. 13, Dec. 1944: 303–314. port. BX5800.H5, v. 13

13889
LYNAH, JAMES (1735?–1809)
Ireland; South Carolina. Revolutionary surgeon.

—— Dr. James Lynah, a surgeon of the Revolution. South Carolina historical and genealogical magazine, v. 40, July 1939: 87–90. F66.S55, v. 40

Notes by Alexander S. Salley.

13890
LYNCH, THOMAS (1749–1779)*
South Carolina. Planter, assemblyman, delegate to the Continental Congress, Revolutionary officer.

FIELDS, JOSEPH E. A signer and his signatures; or, The library of Thomas Lynch, Jr. Harvard Library bulletin, v. 14, spring 1960: 210–252. facsims. Z881.H3403, v. 14

13891
LYNDE, BENJAMIN (1700–1781)*
Massachusetts. Assemblyman, councilor, judge, Loyalist.

—— The diaries of Benjamin Lynde [1690–1742] and of Benjamin Lynde, Jr. [1721–80], with an appendix. Boston, Priv. print. [Cambridge, Riverside Press] 1880. xvi, 251 p. facsim., geneal. table, ports. [F67.L98] Micro 71644

Edited by Fitch Edward Oliver.

13892
LYON, MATTHEW (1749–1822)*
Ireland; Vermont. Settler, Revolutionary officer.

AUSTIN, ALEINE. Matthew Lyon, "new man" of the democratic revolution: his early career, 1749–1801. 1970 ([337] p.) Micro AC–1, no. 73–16,181

Thesis (Ph.D.)—Columbia University.
Abstracted in *Dissertation Abstracts International*, v. 34A, July 1973, p. 238–239.

BLACKWELL, ROBERT L. Matthew Lyon, a forgotten patiot recalled. Filson Club history quarterly, v. 46, July 1972: 219–240. F446.F484, v. 46

CAMPBELL, TOM W. Two fighters and two fines; sketches of the lives of Matthew Lyon and Andrew Jackson. Little Rock, Ark., Pioneer Pub. Co., 1941. 557 p. E302.6.L9C3

Bibliography: p. 540–542.

McLAUGHLIN, JAMES F. Matthew Lyon, the Hampden of Congress, a biography. New York, Wynkoop Hallenbeck Crawford Co., 1900. xi, 531 p. plate, ports. E302.6.L9M16

WHITE, PLINY H. The life & services of Matthew Lyon. Burlington, Times Job Office Print, 1858. 26 p. E302.6.L9W5

13893
LYTLE, WILLIAM (1770–1831)
Kentucky. Frontiersman.

—— Personal narrative of William Lytle. Cincinnati [University of Cincinnati Press, 1906] 3–30 p. (Historical and Philosophical Society of Ohio. Quarterly publication, v. 1, Jan./Mar. 1906) F486.H676, v. 1

An account of pioneer experiences and Indian troubles in Kentucky, 1780–1788.

13894

LYTTELTON, GEORGE LYTTLETON, *Baron* (1709–1773)†

England. Member of Parliament.

——— The works of George Lord Lyttelton. Published by George Edward Ayscough, Esq. 2d ed. London, Printed for J. Dodsley, 1775. vii, 742 p. port.
PR3542.L8 1775

DAVIS, ROSE M. The good Lord Lyttelton; a study in eighteenth century politics and culture. Bethlehem, Penna., Times Pub. Co., 1939. ix, 443 p. port.
DA501.L9D3 1940

Thesis (Ph.D.)—Columbia University, 1940.
Bibliography: p. 416–432.

13895

LYTTELTON, THOMAS LYTTELTON, *Baron* (1744–1779)†

England. Member of Parliament.

FROST, THOMAS. The life of Thomas, Lord Lyttelton. London, Tinsley Bros., 1876. xxiv, 367 p.
DA512.L9F9

13896

LYTTELTON, WILLIAM HENRY LYTTELTON, *Baron* (1724–1808)*†

England; South Carolina; Jamaica. Lawyer, Member of Parliament, governor, diplomat.

ATTIG, CLARENCE J. William Henry Lyttelton: a study in colonial administration. 1958. ([332] p.)
Micro AC–1, no. 58–1552

Thesis (Ph.D.)—University of Nebraska.
Abstracted in *Dissertation Abstracts*, v. 18, May 1958, p. 1775–1776.

Investigates Lyttelton's governorships of South Carolina, 1756–60, and Jamaica, 1762–66.

13897

MABANE, ADAM (*ca.* 1734–1792)

Scotland; Quebec. Physician, councilor, judge.

NEATBY, HILDA M. The political career of Adam Mabane. Canadian historical review, v. 16, June 1935: 137–150.
F1001.C27, v. 16

WARREN, *Mrs.* F. C., *and* E. FABRE SURVEYER. From surgeon's mate to Chief Justice; Adam Mabane (1734–1792). *In* Royal Society of Canada. Proceedings and transactions. 3d ser., v. 24, section 2; 1930. Ottawa. p. 189–210.
AS42.R6, 3d s., v. 24

13898

McADAM, JOHN LOUDON (1756–1836)†

Scotland; New York. Merchant, Loyalist.

SPIRO, ROBERT H. John Loudon McAdam in revolutionary New York. *In* New York Historical Society. Quarterly, v. 40, Jan. 1956: 28–54. illus., map, port.
F116.N638, v. 40

13899

McAFEE, JAMES (1736–1811)

Ireland; Kentucky. Settler.

——— Journals of James and Robert McAfee, kept in May-August, 1773. *In* Woods, Neander M. The Woods-McAfee memorial, containing an account of John Woods and James McAfee of Ireland and their descendants in America. Louisville, Ky., Courier-Journal Job Print. Co., 1905. p. [425]–437.
CS71.W875 1905

13900

McAFEE, ROBERT (1745–1795)

Virginia; Kentucky. Settler, Revolutionary officer.

——— The life and times of Robert B. McAfee and his family and connections. *In* Kentucky Historical Society. Register, v. 25, Jan.–Sept. 1927: 5–37, 111–143, 215–237. port.
F446.K43, v. 25

13901

McALPINE, JOHN

Scotland. British soldier in America.

——— Genuine narratives, and concise memoirs of some of the most interesting exploits, and singular adventures, of J. McAlpine, a native Highlander, from the time of his emigration from Scotland, to America, 1773; during the long period of his faithful attachment to and hazardous attendance on the British army's under the command of the generals, Carleton and Burgoyne, in their several operations that he was concerned in; till December 1779. To complain of his neglected services; and humbly to request government for reparations of his losses in the royal cause . . . To which is added, a description of Botany Bay, Nova-Scotia, and Canada. [n.p.] Printed in the year 1788. 72 p.
E278.M13M13 Rare Bk. Coll.

An earlier edition was published at Greenock, Scotland, in 1780.

13902

MACARTNEY, GEORGE MACARTNEY, *Earl* (1737–1806)†

Ireland. Diplomat, Member of the Irish Parliament.

U.S. *Library of Congress. Manuscript Division.* Lord Macartney's letter books, West Indies, Grenada, February 1777–June 1779. Calendared from the original letter books in the Division of Manuscripts of the Library of Congress, by Ruth Anna Fisher. Washington, Library of Congress, 1947. 1 v. (various pagings)
F2131.M12

Typescript.

13903
MACAULAY, ALEXANDER (1754–1798)
Scotland; Virginia. Merchant.

—— Journal of Alexander Macaulay. William and Mary College quarterly historical magazine, v. 11, Jan. 1903: 180–191.   F221.W71, v. 11

A letter and a fragmentary journal both dated 1783.

13904
MACAULAY, CATHARINE SAWBRIDGE (1731–1791)†
England. Historian, writer.

BECKWITH, MILDRED C.   Catharine Macaulay, eighteenth century rebel. *In* South Carolina Historical Association. Proceedings. 1958. Columbia, S.C., 1959. p. 12–29.   F266.S58, 1958

—— Catharine Macaulay, eighteenth century English rebel: a sketch of her life and some reflections on her place among the historians and political reformers of her time. 1953. ([297] p.)   Micro AC–1, no. 58–755

Thesis (Ph.D.)—Ohio State University.
Abstracted in *Dissertation Abstracts*, v. 18, April 1958, p. 1221–1223.

DONNELLY, LUCY M.   The celebrated Mrs. Macaulay. William and Mary quarterly, 3d ser., v. 6, Apr. 1949: 173–207. plates.   F221.W71, 3d s., v. 6

"Bibliographical note": p. 204–207.
Includes a section of 10 plates entitled "Catharine Macaulay and her famous *History*: a pictorial record."

FOX, CLAIRE G.   Catharine Macaulay, an eighteenth-century Clio. *In* Winterthur portfolio. v. 4. Winterthur, Del., 1968. p. 129–142. illus., facsims.
                          N9.W52, v. 4

GUTTMACHER, MANFRED S.   Catharine Macaulay and Patience Wright: patronesses of the American Revolution. Johns Hopkins alumni magazine, v. 24, 1936: 309–326.   LH1.J7J7, v. 24

HILL, BRIDGET, *and* CHRISTOPHER HILL.   Catharine Macaulay and the seventeenth century. Welsh history review, v. 3, Dec. 1967: 381–402.
                          DA700.W468, v. 3

13905
McCALL, ARCHIBALD (d. 1814)
Virginia. Merchant.

—— The correspondence of Archibald McCall and George McCall, 1777–1783. Edited by Joseph S. Ewing. Virginia magazine of history and biography, v. 73, July–Oct. 1965: 312–353, 425–454.
                          F221.V91, v. 73

13906
McCAULEY, MARY LUDWIG HAYS (1754–1832)*
Pennsylvania.

LANDIS, JOHN B.   Investigation into American tradition of woman known as "Molly Pitcher." Journal of American history, v. 5, Jan./Mar. 1911: 83–96. ports.
                          E171.J86, v. 5

13907
McCLURE, DAVID (1748–1820)
Rhode Island; Connecticut. Clergyman, schoolmaster.

—— Diary of David McClure, Doctor of Divinity, 1748–1820, with notes by Franklin B. Dexter. Priv. print. New York, Knickerbocker Press, 1899. vi, 219 p. port.
                          F516.M165

13908
McCLURE, JAMES (1750–1791)
New Hampshire. Seaman, Revolutionary officer.

PAGE, ELWIN L.   Two sea captains of Exeter. Historical New Hampshire, June, 1945: 7–28. illus., facsims., ports.   F31.H57, 1945

13909
McCOMB, ELEAZER (d. 1798)
Delaware. Revolutionary officer, councilor, delegate to the Continental Congress.

—— Eleazer McComb letters [1774] Edited by George V. Massey. Delaware history, v. 2, Mar. 1947: 41–55. port.   F161.D37, v. 2

13910
M'CULLOCH, JOHN (1754?–1824)
Pennsylvania. Textbook compiler.

SPIESEKE, ALICE W.   The first textbooks in American history and their compiler, John M'Culloch. New York City, Teachers College, Columbia University, 1938. vi, 135 p. facsims., maps.   E175.85.S72

Thesis (Ph.D)—Columbia University, 1938.
Published also as Columbia University Teachers College, Contributions to Education, no. 744.
"Books printed by John M'Culloch, alone or with others": p. [107]–116. "Almanacs printed by John M'Culloch, alone or with others": p. [117]–121. Bibliography: p. [122]–131.

13911
McCULLOH, HENRY (d. 1778)
England. Merchant, land speculator, colonial agent.

CANNON, JOHN A.   Henry McCulloch and Henry McCulloh. William and Mary quarterly, 3d ser., v. 15, Jan. 1958: 71–73.   F221.W71, 3d s., v. 15

Because they are often confused by historians, the author distinguishes between Henry McCulloch, an insignificant civil servant who died in 1755, and Henry McCulloh, the London merchant who speculated in North Carolina lands and authored the scheme for a stamp duty.

HIGH, JAMES H. Henry McCulloh: progenitor of the Stamp Act. North Carolina historical review, v. 29, Jan. 1952: 24–38.   F251.N892, v. 29

SELLERS, CHARLES G. Private profits and British colonial policy: the speculations of Henry McCulloh. William and Mary quarterly, 3d ser., v. 8, Oct. 1951: 535–551.   F221.W71, 3d s., v. 8

13912
McDONALD, ALEXANDER (*fl.* 1769–1779)
Canada. Loyalist officer.

——— Letter-book of Captain Alexander McDonald, of the Royal Highland Emigrants, 1775–1779. *In* New York Historical Society. Collections. 1882. Publication fund series, [v. 15] New York, 1883. p. [203]–498.   F116.N63, 1882

13913
MACDONALD, FLORA MACDONALD (1722–1790)†
Scotland; North Carolina. Loyalist.

MACGREGOR, ALEXANDER. The life of Flora Macdonald. Stirling, E. Mackay, 1901. xx, 152 p. plates, port.   DA814.M14M2

First edition published in 1882.

MACLEAN, JOHN P. Flora Macdonald in America, with a brief sketch of her life and adventures. Lumberton, N.C., A. W. McLean, 1909. 84 p. illus., plates, ports.   E263.N8M16

QUYNN, DOROTHY M. Flora Macdonald in history. North Carolina historical review, v. 28, July 1941: 236–258.   F251.N892, v. 28

13914
McDONALD, HUGH (*b.* 1762)
North Carolina. Revolutionary soldier.

——— A teen-ager in the Revolution. American history illustrated, v. 1, May-June 1966: 25–34, 38–47. illus.   E171.A574, v. 1

A transcription of McDonald's journal, covering the years 1776–78, first appeared in the *North Carolina University Magazine* for 1854–55.

13915
McDOUGALL, ALEXANDER (1732–1786)*
Scotland; New York. Mariner, merchant, Revolutionary general, delegate to the Continental Congress.

SHANNON, ANNA M., *Sister.* General Alexander McDougall: citizen and soldier, 1732–1786. 1957.

Thesis (Ph.D.)—Fordham University.

13916
McGILLIVRAY, ALEXANDER (*ca.* 1759–1793)*
Georgia. Creek Indian leader, Loyalist.

CAUGHEY, JOHN W. McGillivray of the Creeks. Norman, University of Oklahoma Press, 1938. xvi, 385 p. facsims., map (on lining papers) (Civilization of the American Indian)   E99.C9C3

Bibliography: p. 365–369.

McGillivray's correspondence and related papers—214 items, 1783–94—with an introductory essay on his career.

FOREMAN, CAROLYN T. Alexander McGillivray, emperor of the Creeks. Chronicles of Oklahoma, v. 7, Mar. 1929: 106–120.   F691.C55, v. 7

O'DONNELL, JAMES H. Alexander McGillivray: training for leadership, 1777–1783. Georgia historical quarterly, v. 49, June 1965: 172–186.   F281.G2975, v. 49

PUTNAM, ALBIGENCE W. Alexander McGillivray, the Creek chief. American historical magazine, v. 4, Oct. 1899: 304–315.   [F431.A53, v. 4]
                                          Micro 38843

WHITAKER, ARTHUR P. Alexander McGillivray, 1783–1789. North Carolina historical review, v. 5, Apr.–July 1928: 181–203, 289–309.   F251.N892, v. 5

13917
McHENRY, JAMES (1753–1816)*
Ireland; Maryland. Physician, Revolutionary officer, delegate to the Continental Congress, delegate to the Constitutional Convention.

——— Dr. James McHenry's speech before the Maryland House of Delegates in November, 1787. Maryland historical magazine, v. 4, Dec. 1909: 336–344.   F176.M18, v. 4

Introduction and notes by Bernard C. Steiner.

——— James McHenry, a minor poet. *In* Rutgers University, *New Brunswick, N.J. Library.* Journal, v. 8, June 1945: 33–64. port.   Z733.R955F

Includes over a dozen of McHenry's previously unpublished poems. Introduction and notes by Oral S. Coad.

——— Journal of a march, a battle, and a waterfall, being the version elaborated by James McHenry from his diary of the year 1778, begun at Valley Forge, & containing accounts of the British, the Indians, and the Battle of Monmouth. [Greenwich? Conn.] Priv. print., 1945. vii, 11 p.   E275.M2

BROWN, FREDERICK J. A sketch of the life of Dr. James McHenry. Baltimore [Printed by J. Murphy] 1877. 44 p. (Maryland Historical Society. Fund-publication, no. 10)   F176.M37, no. 10

Some Revolutionary correspondence of Dr. James McHenry. Pennsylvania magazine of history and biography, v. 29, Jan. 1905: 53–64. F146.P65, v. 29

Communicated by Bernard C. Steiner.
Includes letters from Benjamin Rush, John Cochran, John Beatty, and Robert Troupe.

STEINER, BERNARD C. The life and correspondence of James McHenry, Secretary of War under Washington and Adams. Cleveland, Burrows Bros. Co., 1907. x, 640 p. ports. (part col.). E302.6.M12S8

13918

McILWORTH, THOMAS (*fl.* 1758–1769)
New York. Portrait artist.

SAWITZKY, SUSAN. Thomas McIlworth. *In* New York Historical Society. Quarterly, v. 35, Apr. 1951: 117–139. ports. F116.N638, v. 35

13919

McINTIRE, SAMUEL (1757–1811)*
Massachusetts. Woodcarver, architect.

COUSINS, FRANK, *and* PHIL M. RILEY. The wood-carver of Salem: Samuel McIntire, his life and work. Boston, Little, Brown, 1916. xx, 168 p., 64 l. facsims., plans, plates. NA737.M25C6

Reprinted in New York by AMS Press (1970).

KIMBALL, SIDNEY F. Mr. Samuel McIntire, carver, the architect of Salem. Portland, Me., Southworth-Anthoensen Press, Published for the Essex Institute of Salem, Mass., 1940. xiii, 157 p. map, plans, plates, port. NA737.M25K5

Reprinted in Gloucester, Mass., by P. Smith (1966).

Samuel McIntire: a bicentennial symposium, 1757–1957. Contributors: Abbott Lowell Cummings [and others] Benjamin W. Labaree, editor. Salem, Mass., Essex Institute, 1957. vii, 113–230 p. illus., facsims., plates, ports. (Essex Institute, Salem, Mass. Historical collections, v. 93, Apr./July 1957) F72.E7E81, v. 93

Partial contents: Samuel McIntire, by Fiske Kimball.—Samuel McIntire and his sources, by Abbott L. Cummings.—The furniture of McIntire, by Dean A. Fales, Jr.—Carved figures by Samuel McIntire and his contemporaries, by Nina F. Little.—A factual estimate of Samuel McIntire, by Mabel M. Swan.—Samuel McIntire and the arts of post-colonial America, by Oliver W. Larkin.—McIntire in print—a selected bibliography, by Benjamin W. Labaree.

13920

McINTOSH, GEORGE (1737?–1793?)
Georgia. Surveyor, assemblyman.

[HARDEN, WILLIAM] The case of George McIntosh. Georgia historical quarterly, v. 3, Sept. 1919: 131–145. F281.G2975, v. 3

13921

McINTOSH, LACHLAN (1725–1806)*
Scotland; Georgia. Revolutionary general.

———— Lachlan McIntosh papers in the University of Georgia libraries. Edited, with an introduction, by Lilla Mills Hawes. Athens, University of Georgia Press, 1968. vii, 141 p. port. (University of Georgia libraries miscellanea publications, no. 7) E207.M13A3

———— The papers of Lachlan McIntosh, 1774–1799. Edited by Lilla M. Hawes. Georgia historical quarterly, v. 38, June–Dec. 1954: 148–169, 253–267, 356–368; v. 39, Mar.–Dec. 1955: 52–68, 172–186, 253–268, 356–375; v. 40, Mar.–June 1956: 65–88, 152–174. map. F281.G2975, v. 38–40

Also published separately as v. 12 of the *Collections* of the Georgia Historical Society (Savannah, 1957. 167 p. F281.G35, v. 12).

HEATHCOTE, CHARLES W. General Lachlan McIntosh, loyal American and friend of Washington. Picket post, no. 55, Feb. 1957: 9–16. port. E234.P5, no. 55

LAWRENCE, ALEXANDER A. General Lachlan McIntosh and his suspension from Continental command during the Revolution. Georgia historical quarterly, v. 38, June 1954: 101–141. F281.G2975, v. 38

13922

McJUNKIN, JOSEPH (1755–1846)
South Carolina. Revolutionary officer.

SAYE, JAMES H. Memoirs of Major Joseph McJunkin, Revolutionary patriot. [Greenwood? 1925?] 42 p. F273.M3S3

Reprinted from the Greenwood, S.C., *Index-Journal.*

13923

MACKAY, JAMES (*d.* 1785)
Georgia. Military officer, planter, councilor.

HARDEN, WILLIAM. James Mackay, of Strathy Hall, comrade in arms of George Washington. Georgia historical quarterly, v. 1, June 1917: 77–98. plates. F281.G2975, v. 1

13924

McKEAN, THOMAS (1734–1817)*
Pennsylvania; Delaware. Lawyer, assemblyman, delegate to the Continental Congress, judge.

BUCHANAN, ROBERDEAU. Life of the Hon. Thomas McKean. Lancaster, Pa., Inquirer Print. Co., 1890. 136 p. facsims. (part fold.), port. E302.6.M13B9

"List of books containing biographies of Thomas McKean, and other works": p. 125–128.

COLEMAN, JOHN M. Thomas McKean and the origin of an independent judiciary. Pennsylvania history, v. 34, Apr. 1967: 111–130. port. F146.P597, v. 34

PEELING, JAMES H. The public life of Thomas McKean, 1734–1817. Chicago, 1929. viii, 336 l. E302.6.M13P43

Thesis (Ph.D.)—University of Chicago.
Bibliography: leaves 324–336.

ROWE, GAIL S. Power, politics, and public service: the life of Thomas McKean, 1734–1817. 1969. ([443] p.)
Micro AC–1, no. 70–10,516

Thesis (Ph.D.)—Stanford University.
Abstracted in *Dissertation Abstracts International*, v. 30A, June 1970, p. 5394.

——— Thomas McKean and the coming of the Revolution. Pennsylvania magazine of history and biography, v. 96, Jan. 1972: 3–47. F146.P65, v. 96

——— A valuable acquisition in Congress: Thomas McKean, delegate from Delaware to the Continental Congress, 1774–1783. Pennsylvania history, v. 38, July 1971: 225–264. F146.P597, v. 38

13925

McKEE, ALEXANDER (d. 1799)
Pennsylvania; Canada. Loyalist, British Indian agent.

HOBERG, WALTER R. Early history of Colonel Alexander McKee. Pennsylvania magazine of history and biography, v. 58, Jan. 1934: 26–36. F146.P65, v. 58

——— A Tory in the Northwest. Pennsylvania magazine of history and biography, v. 59, Jan. 1935: 32–41. F146.P65, v. 59

13926

MACKENZIE, *Sir* ALEXANDER (1763 or 4–1820)†
Scotland; New York; Canada. Fur trader, explorer.

——— The journals and letters of Sir Alexander Mackenzie. Edited by W. Kaye Lamb. Cambridge [Eng.] Published for the Hakluyt Society at the University Press, 1970. viii, 551 p. facsims., maps, port. (Hakluyt Society. [Works] Extra series, no. 41) F1060.7.M13
Bibliography: p. 531–538.

——— Voyages from Montreal, on the river St. Laurence, through the continent of North America, to the Frozen and Pacific oceans, in the years 1789 and 1793. With a preliminary account of the rise, progress, and present state of the fur trade of that country. London, T. Cadell and W. Davies, 1801. viii, cxxxii, 412 p. fold. maps, port. F1060.7.M16 Rare Bk. Coll.
Compiled by William Combe from Mackenzie's notes. Reprinted in Ann Arbor, Mich., by University Microfilms (1966).

WADE, MARK S. Mackenzie of Canada; the life and adventures of Alexander Mackenzie, discoverer. Edinburgh, W. Blackwood, 1927. xii, 332 p. illus., geneal. table, maps, plates, ports. F1060.7.M27
"Authorities consulted": p. [321]–322.

13927

MACKENZIE, FREDERICK (d. 1824)
Ireland. British officer in America.

——— Diary of Frederick Mackenzie, giving a daily narrative of his military service as an officer of the regiment of Royal Welch Fusiliers during the years 1775–1781 in Massachusetts, Rhode Island and New York. Cambridge, Mass., Harvard University Press, 1930. 2 v. (vii, 737 p.) facsims., maps (part. fold.), plan, port. E267.M17
Reprinted in New York by the New York Times (1968).
The part of the diary describing the engagements at Concord and Lexington was published in 1926 under the title *A British Fusilier in Revolutionary Boston*.

13928

MACKINTOSH, EBENEZER (1737–1816)
Massachusetts. Shoemaker, fireman.

ANDERSON, GEORGE P. Ebenezer Mackintosh: Stamp Act rioter and patriot. *In* Colonial Society of Massachusetts, *Boston*. Publications. v. 26. Transactions, 1924/26. Boston, 1927. p. 15–64. facsims. F61.C71, v. 26

——— ——— Offprint. Cambridge, J. Wilson, 1924. [15]–64 p. facsims. E215.2.M15

——— A note on Ebenezer Mackintosh. *In* Colonial Society of Massachusetts, *Boston*. Publications. v. 26. Transactions, 1924/26. Boston, 1927. p. 348–361. F61.C71, v. 26

13929

McLANE, ALLAN (1746–1829)*
Pennsylvania; Delaware. Revolutionary officer, assemblyman.

COOK, FRED J. Allan McLane, unknown hero of the Revolution. American heritage, v. 7, Oct. 1956: 74–77, 118–119. illus. (part col.) E171.A43, v. 7

13930

MACLAY, WILLIAM (1737–1804)
Pennsylvania. Surveyor, assemblyman.

GEARHART, HEBER G. William Maclay, the surveyor. *In* Northumberland County (Pa.) Historical Society. Proceedings. v. 9. Sunbury, 1937. p. 20–43. map, plate. F157.N8N7, v. 9

HAMILTON, ADAM BOYD. William Maclay, city planner. *In* Northumberland County (Pa.) Historical Society. Proceedings. v. 9. Sunbury, 1937. p. [5]–19. map. F157.N8N7, v. 9

13931

McMICHAEL, JAMES
Pennsylvania. Revolutionary officer.

——— Diary of Lieutenant James McMichael, of the Pennsylvania Line, 1776–1778. Pennsylvania magazine of history and biography, v. 16, July 1892: 129–159. F146.P65, v. 16

Contributed by William P. Michael.

Also printed in *Pennsylvania Archives*, 2d ser., v. 15 (Harrisburg, 1890), p. 193–218.

13932

McMILLAN, JOHN (1752–1833)

Pennsylvania. Clergyman, missionary, educator.

BENNETT, DANIEL M.   Concerning the life and work of the Rev. John McMillan, D.D. *In* Presbyterian Historical Society. Journal, v. 15, Sept./Dec. 1932: 133–158, 208–216; Mar. 1933: 217–248.   BX8905.P7A4, v. 15

The last installment includes, on p. 222–238, McMillan's diary from October 26, 1774, to August 6, 1776.

———— *comp.* Life and work of Rev. John McMillan, D.D., pioneer, preacher, educator, patriot, of western Pennsylvania. Bridgeville, Pa., 1935. xvi, 525 p. illus., facsim., map, ports.   BX9225.M28B4
CS71.M1675 1935

GUTHRIE, DWIGHT R.   John McMillan. *In* Presbyterian Historical Society. Journal, v. 33, June 1955: 63–85.   BX8905.P7A4, v. 33

———— John McMillan, the apostle of Presbyterianism in the West, 1752–1833. [Pittsburgh] University of Pittsburgh Press [1952] x, 296 p. illus., maps, port.   BX9225.M28G85

Bibliography: p. 227–287.

MACARTNEY, CLARENCE E.   John McMillan, the apostle of the gospel and Presbyterianism in western Pennsylvania. *In* Presbyterian Historical Society. Journal, v. 15, Sept. 1932: 121–132.   BX8905.P7A4, v. 15

13933

McNEILL, HECTOR (1728–1785)*

Ireland; Massachusetts. Mariner, Revolutionary naval officer.

ALLEN, GARDNER W.   Captain Hector McNeill, Continental Navy. *In* Massachusetts Historical Society, *Boston.* Proceedings. v. 55; 1921/22. Boston, 1923. p. 46–152. facsims.   F61.M38, v. 55

An offprint with a slightly different title was published in Boston (1922. 108 p. E207.M15A4).

Includes NcNeill's *Autobiographical Sketch*, selections from his correspondence and journal, and an alphabetical list of officers and men aboard the ship *Boston* in 1777.

MORGAN, WILLIAM J.   The stormy career of Captain McNeill, Continental Navy. Military affairs, v. 16, fall 1952: 119–122.   E181.M55, v. 16

13934

McNUTT, ALEXANDER (*ca.* 1725–1811)*

Virginia; Nova Scotia. Military officer, land speculator.

EATON, ARTHUR W.   Alexander McNutt, the colonizer. Americana, v. 8, Dec. 1913: 1065–1106.   E171.A53, v. 8

13935

MACON, NATHANIEL (1757–1837)*

North Carolina. Revolutionary soldier, assemblyman.

COTTEN, EDWARD R.   Life of the Hon. Nathaniel Macon, of North Carolina; in which there is displayed striking instances of virtue, enterprise, courage, generosity and patriotism. His public life. Baltimore, Printed by Lucas & Deaver, 1840. 272 p.   E302.6.M17C8 Rare Bk. Coll.

DODD, WILLIAM E.   The life of Nathaniel Macon. Raleigh, N.C., Edwards & Broughton, Printers, 1903. xvi, 443 p.   E302.6.M17D6

"Sources of information": p. xvi.

Reprinted in New York by B. Franklin (1970).

———— The place of Nathaniel Macon in southern history. American historical review, v. 7, July 1902: 663–675.   E171.A57, v. 7

HELMS, JAMES M.   The early career of Nathaniel Macon: a study in "pure republicanism." 1962. ([518] p.)   Micro AC–1, no. 62–5922

Thesis (Ph.D.)—University of Virginia.

Abstracted in *Dissertation Abstracts*, v. 23, Feb. 1963, p. 2883–2884.

13936

MACPHERSON, CHARLES (*fl.* 1773–1790)

———— Memoirs of the life and travels of the late Charles Macpherson, Esq., in Asia, Africa, and America. Illustrative of manners, customs, and character; with a particular investigation of the nature, treatment, and possible improvement, of the Negro in the British and French West India Islands. Edinburgh, A. Constable, 1800. xv, 258 p.   F2066.M17

This volume, the only one published, relates chiefly to the West Indies. The manuscript was purportedly written between 1773 and 1790.

13937

McPHERSON, CHRISTOPHER (*d.* 1817?)

Virginia. Entrepreneur, educator.

BERKELEY, EDMUND.   Prophet without honor; Christopher McPherson, free person of color. Virginia magazine of history and biography, v. 77, Apr. 1969: 180–190.   F221.V91, v. 77

13938

MacPHERSON, JOHN (1754?–1775)

Pennsylvania. Revolutionary officer.

—— Extracts from the letters of John MacPherson, Jr., to William Patterson, 1766–1773. Pennsylvania magazine of history and biography, v. 23, Apr. 1899: 51–59. port., facsim. F146.P65, v. 23

Contributed by William M. Hornor.

13939
McQUEEN, JOHN (1751–1807)

South Carolina; Georgia. Revolutionary naval officer, land speculator.

—— The letters of Don Juan McQueen to his family, written from Spanish East Florida, 1791–1807. With a biographical sketch and notes by Walter Charlton Hartridge. Columbia, S.C., Published for the Georgia Society of the Colonial Dames of America by Bostick & Thornley, 1943. xxxiv, 89 p. F314.M24

Includes 12 letters written to McQueen, 1779–86.

13940
McROBERT, ARCHIBALD (d. 1807)

Scotland; Virginia. Clergyman, landowner.

EGGLESTON, JOSEPH D. Prince Edward County, Virginia; Archibald McRobert, patriot, scholar, man of God. [Farmville, Va., 1928] 15 p. illus. F232.P83E3

Reprinted from the Farmville *Herald*, April 20, 1928.

13941
M'ROBERT, PATRICK

Scotland. Traveler.

—— Tour through part of the north provinces of America: being a series of letters wrote on the spot, in the years 1774, & 1775. To which are annex'd, tables, shewing the roads, the value of coins, rates of stages, &c. Edinburgh, Printed for the author, 1776. 64 p. E163.M17 Rare Bk. Coll.

Carl Bridenbaugh's edition of M'Robert's journal, which appeared in the *Pennsylvania Magazine of History and Biography*, v. 59, Apr. 1935, p. 134–180, has since been reprinted by the New York Times (New York, 1968. x, 47 p.).

13942
MACWHORTER, ALEXANDER (1734–1807)*

New Jersey. Presbyterian clergyman, Revolutionary chaplain, educator.

MARTING, ELIZABETH. Alexander MacWhorter's southern adversities. *In* Presbyterian Historical Society. Journal, v. 26, Mar. 1948: 11–18. BX8905.P7A4, v. 26

13943
MADISON, JAMES, Bp. (1749–1812)*

Virginia. Anglican clergyman, professor, Revolutionary officer, scientist, educator.

—— Letters of Rev. James Madison, president of the College of William and Mary, to Thomas Jefferson [1778–1811] William and Mary College quarterly historical magazine, 2d ser., v. 5, Apr.–July 1925: 77–95, 145–158. F221.W71, 2d s., v. 5

CROWE, CHARLES. Bishop James Madison and the republic of virtue. Journal of southern history, v. 30, Feb. 1964: 58–70. F206.J68, v. 30

—— The Reverend James Madison in Williamsburg and London, 1768–1771. West Virginia history, v. 25, July 1964: 270–278. F236.W52, v. 25

13944
MADISON, JAMES (1751–1836)*

Virginia. Assemblyman, councilor, delegate to the Continental Congress, delegate to the Constitutional Convention.

—— Calendar of the correspondence of James Madison. Washington, Dept. of State, 1894. 739 p. (U.S. Bureau of Rolls and Library. Bulletin no. 4) CD3031, no. 4 E302.M155

—— —— Index. Washington, Dept. of State, 1895. 70 p. (U.S. Bureau of Rolls and Library. Bulletin no. 4, suppl.) CD3031, no.4 E302.M155

Bound with the *Calendar*.
Reprinted in New York by B. Franklin (1970).
The Madison papers are now in the Library of Congress.

—— The complete Madison; his basic writings. Edited and with an introduction by Saul K. Padover. New York, Harper [1953] xi, 361 p. port. E302.M17

—— James Madison's autobiography. Edited by Douglass Adair. William and Mary quarterly, 3d ser., v. 2, Apr. 1945: 191–209. F221.W71, 3d s., v. 2

Madison's summary of his life, written in 1832 for his intended biographer, James Kirke Paulding.

—— James Madison's essay on "Symmetry of Nature." Princeton University Library chronicle, v. 23, spring 1962: 109–114. Z733.P93C5, v. 23

The original five-page manuscript, hitherto unpublished, is in the Madison papers of the Library of Congress. Introduction by Stewart M. Robinson and Anne Payne Robinson.

—— Letters and other writings of James Madison. Published by order of Congress. Philadelphia, J. B. Lippincott, 1865. 4 v. port. E302.M18

Edited by Philip R. Fendall.
Contents: v. 1. 1769–1793.—v. 2. 1794–1815.—v. 3. 1816–1828.—v. 4. 1829–1836.

—— Madison's "detached memoranda." Edited by Elizabeth Fleet. William and Mary quarterly, 3d ser., v. 3, Oct. 1946: 534–568. F221.W71, 3d s., v. 3

Includes Madison's reflections upon Franklin, Washington, and the writing of *The Federalist*.

———— Papers. Edited by William T. Hutchinson and William M. E. Rachal. Editorial staff: Jean Schneider [and others. Chicago] University of Chicago Press [1962]+ illus., maps, ports.   E302.M19

Bibliographic footnotes.
Contents: v. 1. 16 March 1751–16 December 1779. —v. 2. 20 March 1780–23 February 1781.—v. 3. 3 March 1781–31 December 1781.—v. 4. 1 January 1782–31 July 1782.—v. 5. 1 August 1782–31 December 1782.—v. 6. 1 January 1783–30 April 1783.—v. 7. 3 May 1783–20 February 1784.

———— The papers of James Madison, purchased by order of Congress; being his correspondence and reports of debates during the Congress of the Confederation, and his reports of debates in the Federal Convention; now published from the original manuscripts, deposited in the Department of State, by direction of the Joint Library Committee of Congress, under the superintendence of Henry D. Gilpin. Washington, Langtree & O'Sullivan, 1840. 3 v. facsims.   JK111.M2

Contents: v. 1. Prefatory note. The debates in 1776 on the Declaration of Independence, and on a few of the Articles of Confederation, preserved by Thomas Jefferson. Letters of Mr. Madison preceding the debates of 1783. Debates in the Congress of the Confederation, from November 4, 1782, to June 21, 1783. Letters contemporary with, and subsequent to, the debates of 1783.—v. 2. Debates in the Congress of the Confederation, from February 19th, 1787, to April 25th, 1787. Correspondence during and subsequent to the debates in the Congress of the Confederation from February 15, 1787, to November 2d, 1788. Debates in the Federal Convention, from Monday, May 14th, 1787, to Monday, August 6th, 1787.—v. 3. Debates in the Federal Convention, from Tuesday, August 7th, 1787, until its final adjournment, Monday, September 17th, 1787. Appendix to the debates. References. Index.

———— The writings of James Madison, comprising his public papers and his private correspondence, including numerous letters and documents now for the first time printed. Edited by Gaillard Hunt. New York, G. P. Putnam's Sons, 1900–10. 9 v. illus., facsims. (part fold.), port.   E302.M22

Contents: v. 1. 1769–1783.—v. 2. 1783–1787.—v. 3–4. 1787. The journal of the Constitutional Convention.—v. 5. 1787–1790.—v. 6. 1790–1802.—v. 7. 1803–1807.—v. 8. 1808–1819.—v. 9. 1819–1836.

BOLTON, THEODORE. The life portraits of James Madison. William and Mary quarterly, 3d ser., v. 8, Jan. 1951: 25–47. plates, ports.   F221.W71, 3d s., v. 8

BRANT, IRVING. James Madison. Indianapolis, Bobbs-Merrill [1941–61] 6 v. facsims., plates, ports.
E342.B7

Includes bibliographies.
Contents: [1] The Virginia revolutionist.—[2] The nationalist, 1780–1787.—[3] Father of the Constitution,

1787–1800.—[4] Secretary of State, 1800–1809.—[5] The President, 1809–1812.—[6] Commander in Chief, 1812–1836.

Brant's condensation of his six-volume biography appeared under the title *The Fourth President; a Life of James Madison* (Indianapolis, Bobbs-Merrill [1970] 681 p.).

———— James Madison and his times. American historical review, v. 57, July 1952: 853–870.   E171.A57, v. 57

———— Madison: on the separation of church and state. William and Mary quarterly, 3d ser , v. 8, Jan. 1951: 3–24.   F221.W71, 3d s., v. 8

———— Madison, the "North American," on Federal power. American historical review, v. 60, Oct. 1954: 45–54.
E171.A57, v. 60

Discusses Madison's authorship of two letters which appeared in the *Pennsylvania Journal and Weekly Advertiser* on September 17 and October 8, 1783.

BURNS, EDWARD M. James Madison, philosopher of the Constitution. New Brunswick, Rutgers University Press, 1938. x, 212 p. (Rutgers University studies in history, v. 1)   E342.B87

Bibliography: p. 201–206.
Reprinted with a new preface and a new chapter by the author in New York by Octagon Books (1968).

CRONIN, JOHN W., *and* W. HARVEY WISE, *Jr.* A bibliography of James Madison and James Monroe. Washington, D.C., Riverford Pub. Co., 1935. 48 p. (Presidential bibliographical series, no. 4)
Z8540.C91

Includes 489 titles.

FORNOFF, CHARLES W. The political ideas of James Madison. 1926.

Thesis (Ph.D.)—University of Illinois.

GAY, SYDNEY H. James Madison. Boston, Houghton, Mifflin, 1884. vi, 342 p. (American statesmen, [v. 12])
E176.A53, v. 12
E342.G28

Reprinted in New Rochelle, N.Y., by Arlington House (1970).

HUNT, GAILLARD. The life of James Madison. New York, Doubleday, Page, 1902. viii, 402 p. port.
E342.H943

Reprinted in New York by Russell & Russell (1968).

INGERSOLL, DAVID E. Machiavelli and Madison: perspectives on political stability. Political science quarterly, v. 85, June 1970: 259–280.   H1.P8, v. 85

James Madison bicentennial celebration. New York University law review, v. 27, Apr. 1952: 248–298.   LL

Contents: James Madison as founder of the Constitution, by Irving Brant.—Madison and the pursuit of happiness, by Edmond N. Cahn.—James Madison: layman publicist, and exegete, by Edward S. Corwin.

KETCHAM, RALPH L.   James Madison; a biography. New York, N.Y., Macmillan [1971] xiv, 753 p. map (on lining papers), plates, ports.   E342.K46 1971

Bibliography: p. 673–678.

——— James Madison and religion—a new hypothesis. *In* Presbyterian Historical Society. Journal, v. 38, June 1960: 65–90.   BX8905.P7A4, v. 38

——— James Madison and the nature of man. Journal of the history of ideas, v. 19, Jan. 1958: 62–76.   B1.J75, v. 19

——— James Madison at Princeton. Princeton University Library chronicle, v. 28, autumn 1966: 24–54. facsims.   Z733.P93C5, v. 28

——— The mind of James Madison. 1956. ([233] p.)   Micro AC-1, no. 18,023

Thesis (Ph.D.)—Syracuse University.
Abstracted in *Dissertation Abstracts*, v. 16, no. 10, 1956, p. 1892.

KOCH, ADRIENNE.   James Madison and the workshop of liberty. Review of politics, v. 16, Apr. 1954: 175–193.   JA1.R4, v. 16

——— Madison's "Advice to my country." Princeton, N.J., Princeton University Press, 1966. xx, 210 p. (The Whig-Clio bicentennial lectures)   E342.K6

Bibliography: p. 193–195.

LUTZ, DONALD S.   James Madison as a conflict theorist: the Madisonian model extended. 1969. ([214] p.)   Micro AC-1, no. 70-12,404

Thesis (Ph. D.)—University of Indiana.
Abstracted in *Dissertation Abstracts International*, v. 31A, July 1970, p. 440.

MOORE, WILBUR E.   James Madison, the speaker. Quarterly journal of speech, v. 31, Apr. 1945: 155–162.   PN4071.Q3, v. 31

PADOVER, SAUL K.   Madison as a political thinker. Social research, v. 20, spring 1953: 32–54.   H1.S53, v. 20

RIEMER, NEAL.   James Madison. New York, Washington Square Press [1968] 238 p. (The Great American thinkers series)   JC211.M35R52

"Bibliographical essay": p. 200–208.

——— James Madison's theory of the self-destructive features of republican government. Ethics, v. 65, Oct. 1954: 34–43.   BJ1.I6, v. 65

——— Political theory as a guide to action: Madison and the prudential component in politics. Social science, v. 35, Jan. 1960: 17–25.   H1.S55, v. 35

——— The republicanism of James Madison. Political science quarterly, v. 69, Mar. 1954: 45–64.   H1.P8, v. 69

RIVES, WILLIAM C.   History of the life and times of James Madison. Boston, Little, Brown, 1859–68. 3 v. port.   E342.R62

Reprinted in New York by Books for Libraries Press (1970).

SCHULTZ, HAROLD S.   James Madison. New York, Twayne Publishers [c1970] 241 p. (Twayne's rulers and statesmen of the world series, TROW 13)   E342.S38

Bibliography: p. 229–235.

SMITH, ABBOT E.   James Madison: builder; a new estimate of a memorable career. New York, Wilson-Erickson, 1937. vii, 366 p. illus., plates, ports.   E342.S55

"Bibliographical note": p. 351–352.

SMYLIE, JAMES H.   Madison and Witherspoon: theological roots of American political thought. Princeton University Library chronicle, v. 22, spring 1961: 118–132.   Z733.P93C5, v. 22

U.S. *Library of Congress. Manuscript Division.*   Index to the James Madison papers. Washington [For sale by the Supt. of Docs., U.S. Govt. Print. Off.] 1965. xii, 61 p. (*Its* Presidents' papers index series)   Z6616.M2U63
           Z663.34.M25

VANDEROEF, JOHN S.   The political thought of James Madison. 1968. ([431] p.)   Micro AC–1, no. 69–02788

Thesis (Ph.D.)—Princeton University.
Abstracted in *Dissertation Abstracts*, v. 29A, Feb. 1969, p. 2772.

13945

MAGAW, ROBERT (1738–1790)
Pennsylvania. Revolutionary officer.

HIMES, CHARLES F.   Col. Robert Magaw, the defender of Fort Washington, major in Colonel William Thompson's "Battalion of Pennsylvania Riflemen" . . . colonel of the Fifth Pennsylvania Regiment. [Carlisle] Hamilton Library Association, 1915. 60 p.   E207.M18H6

13946

MAGILL, JOHN (1759–1842)
Virginia; Kentucky. Revolutionary soldier, frontiersman.

JILLSON, WILLARD R.   A chronology of John Magill, Kentucky pioneer and historian, 1759–1842. Louisville, Ky., Standard Print. Co., 1938. 22 p. front.   F454.M25

"Bibliography of source material": p. 20–22.

13947

MALCOLM, JOHN (1723–1788)
Massachusetts; England. Shipmaster, customs officer, Loyalist.

HERSEY, FRANK W. C.   Tar and feathers; the adventures of Captain John Malcolm. *In* Colonial Society of Massachusetts, *Boston*. Publications. v. 34. Transactions, 1937/42. Boston, 1943. p. 429–473. plates.

F61.C71, v. 34

13948

MANIGAULT, ANN ASHBY (*d.* 1782)

South Carolina. Wife of Gabriel Manigault (1704–1781).

—— Extracts from the journal of Mrs. Ann Manigault, 1754–1781. South Carolina historical and genealogical magazine, v. 20, Jan.–Oct. 1919: 57–63, 128–141, 204–212, 256–259; v. 21, Jan.–July 1920: 10–23, 59–72, 112–120. F266.S55, v. 20–21

Notes by Mabel L. Webber.

13949

MANIGAULT, GABRIEL (1704–1781)*

South Carolina. Merchant, planter, assemblyman.

CROUSE, MAURICE A. Gabriel Manigault, Charleston merchant. South Carolina historical magazine, v. 68, Oct. 1967: 220–231. F266.S55, v. 68

13950

MANIGAULT, GABRIEL (1758–1809)

South Carolina. Architect. Grandson of Gabriel Manigault (1704–1781).

—— Papers of Gabriel Manigault, 1771–1784. Edited by Maurice A. Crouse. South Carolina historical magazine, v. 64, Jan. 1963: 1–12. F266.S55, v. 64

13951

MANIGAULT, PETER (1731–1773)*

South Carolina. Lawyer, assemblyman, estate manager. Son of Gabriel Manigault (1704–1781).

—— The letterbook of Peter Manigault, 1763–1773. Edited by Maurice A. Crouse. South Carolina historical magazine, v. 70, Apr.–July 1969: 79–96, 177–195.

F266.S55, v. 70

—— Letters concerning Peter Manigault, 1773. South Carolina historical and genealogical magazine, v. 21, Apr. 1920: 39–49. F266.S55, v. 21

CROUSE, MAURICE A. The Manigault family of South Carolina, 1685–1783. 1964. ([469] p.)

Micro AC–1, no. 64–12,266

Thesis (Ph.D.)—Northwestern University.

Abstracted in *Dissertation Abstracts*, v. 25, Jan. 1965, p. 4102–4103.

13952

MANLEY, JOHN (*ca.* 1734–1793)*

Massachusetts. Mariner, Revolutionary naval officer, privateersman.

DOW, H. E. Captain John Manley of the Continental Navy. *In* United States Naval Institute. Proceedings, v. 52, Aug. 1926: 1554–1561. V1.U8, v. 52

GREENWOOD, ISAAC J. Captain John Manley, second in rank in the United States Navy, 1776–1783. Boston, C. E. Goodspeed, 1915. xxx, 174 p. facsims., plates (part col.). E271.M27

PEABODY, ROBERT E. The naval career of Captain John Manley of Marblehead. *In* Essex Institute, *Salem, Mass.* Historical collections, v. 45, Jan. 1909: 1–27.

F72.E7E81, v. 45

—— —— Offprint. Salem, Mass., Essex Institute, 1909. 27 p. facsim. E271.P35

13953

MANNING, JAMES (1738–1791)*

New Jersey; Rhode Island. Baptist clergyman, educator, delegate to the Continental Congress.

BACKUS, ISAAC. A brief account of the life of James Manning, D.D., president of Rhode Island College. Edited by William G. McLoughlin, Jr. *In* Books at Brown. v. 22; 1968. Providence. p. 155–160.

Z733.P958B6, v. 22

13954

MANNING, WILLIAM (1747–1814)

Massachusetts. Farmer, Revolutionary soldier.

—— The key of libberty, shewing the causes why a free government has always failed, and a remidy against it; written in the year 1798. With notes and a foreword by Samuel Eliot Morison. Billerica, Mass., Manning Association, 1922. xv, 71 p. JK171.M25

Printed from manuscript copy.

Reprinted with slight changes in the foreword, in the *William and Mary Quarterly*, 3d ser., v. 13, Apr. 1956, p. 202–254.

Includes observations on the Society of the Cincinnati, the constitution of Massachusetts, the Federal Constitution, and Shays' Rebellion. In "A Sidelight on Eighteenth Century American English," which appeared in the *Queen's Quarterly*, v. 31, Oct./Dec. 1923, p. 173–181, Henry Alexander studied the curious spelling in Manning's *Key of Libberty* for clues about eighteenth-century New England speech patterns.

13955

MANSFIELD, WILLIAM MURRAY, *1st Earl of* (1705–1793)†

England. Lawyer, Member of Parliament, judge.

HOLLIDAY, JOHN. The life of William, late earl of Mansfield. London, Printed for P. Elmsly, 1797. xi, 515 p. ports. LL

13956

MANSKER, KASPER (*ca.* 1750–1820)

Tennessee. Hunter, settler.

DURHAM, WALTER T. Kasper Mansker, Cumberland frontiersman. Tennessee historical quarterly, v. 30, summer 1971: 154–177.　　　　F431.T285, v. 30

13957

MARCHANT, HENRY (1741–1796)*

Massachusetts; Rhode Island. Lawyer, delegate to the Continental Congress, assemblyman.

BRAYTON, SUSAN S. The library of an eighteenth-century gentleman of Rhode Island. New England quarterly, v. 8, June 1935: 277–283.　　　　F1.N62, v. 8

LOVEJOY, DAVID S. Henry Marchant and the *Mistress of the World*. William and Mary quarterly, 3d ser., v. 12, July 1955: 375–398.　　　F221.W71, 3d s., v. 12

About Marchant's journey to London in 1771–72.

13958

MARE, JOHN (1739–1802)

New York; North Carolina. Merchant, portrait painter, councilor.

SMITH, HELEN B., *and* ELIZABETH V. MOORE. John Mare, a composite portrait. North Carolina historical review, v. 44, winter 1967: 18–52. facsims., ports.　　　　F251.N892, v. 44

SMITH, HELEN B. John Mare (1739–c. 1795) New York portrait painter, with notes on the two William Williams'. *In* New York Historical Society. Quarterly, v. 35, Oct. 1951: 355–399. facsims., ports.　　　　F116.N638, v. 35

13959

MARION, FRANCIS (1732–1795)*

South Carolina. Planter, assemblyman, Revolutionary general.

———— Letters of General Francis Marion. *In* Charleston, S.C. Year book. 1895. p. 326–332.　JS13.C33, 1895

Includes five letters dated January 26–March 11, 1780, and a muster roll of Marion's regiment.

———— Marion-Gadsden correspondence [November 1782] South Carolina historical and genealogical magazine, v. 41, Apr. 1940: 48–60.　　　　F266.S55, v. 41

BASS, ROBERT D. Swamp Fox; the life and campaigns of General Francis Marion. [New York] Holt [1959] x, 275 p. illus., map, ports.　　　　E207.M3B3

"Sources and notes": p. 247–261.

DEAN, SIDNEY W. Knight of the revolution. With illustrations by Manning de V. Lee. Philadelphia, Macrae-Smith-Co. [*c*1941] 312 p. illus., map, plates.　　　　E207.M3D4

Bibliography: p. [307]–312.

JAMES, WILLIAM D. A sketch of the life of Brig. Gen. Francis Marion, and a history of his brigade, from its rise in June, 1780, until disbanded in December, 1782; with descriptions of characters and scenes, not heretofore published. Containing also, an appendix, with copies of letters which passed between several of the leading characters of that day; principally from Gen. Greene to Gen. Marion. Charleston, S.C., Printed by Gould and Riley, 1821. 182, 39 p.　　　　E263.S7J2 Rare Bk. Coll.

Reprinted in Marietta, Ga., by the Continental Book Co. (1948).

SCHEER, GEORGE F. The elusive Swamp Fox. American heritage, v. 9, Apr. 1958: 40–47, 111. illus. (part col.), col. map.　　　　E171.A43, v. 9

SIMMS, WILLIAM GILMORE. The life of Francis Marion. New York, H. G. Langley, 1844. 347 p. plates.　　　　E207.M3S5

Reprinted in Freeport, N.Y., by Books for Libraries Press (1971).

13960

MARKLAND, JOHN (1755–1837)

Pennsylvania. Revolutionary officer.

NORTH, CALEB, *and others.* Revolutionary services of Captain John Markland. Pennsylvania magazine of history and biography, v. 9, Apr. 1885: 102–112.　　　　F146.P65, v. 9

A campaign sketch written in 1826 by four of Markland's political supporters.

13961

MARKOE, PETER (1752?–1792)*

Danish West Indies; Pennsylvania. Revolutionary officer, poet.

———— The Algerine spy in Pennsylvania; or, Letters written by a native of Algiers on the affairs of the United States in America, from the close of the year 1783 to the meeting of the Convention. Philadelphia, Printed and sold by Prichard & Hall, in Market between Front and Second Streets, 1787. 129 p.　　　　F153.M34 Rare Bk. Coll.

Translator's letter to the publisher, in which the letters are ascribed to "Mehemet," is signed S. T. P.

DIEBELS, MARY C., *Sister.* Peter Markoe (1752?–1792). A Philadelphia writer. Washington, D.C., Catholic University of America Press, 1944. x, 116 p.　　　　PS801.M7Z57

Thesis (Ph.D.)—Catholic University of America, 1944. Bibliography: p. 102–113.

13962

MARRANT, JOHN (*b.* 1755)

——— A narrative of the Lord's wonderful dealings with John Marrant, a black, (now going to preach the gospel in Nova-Scotia) born in New-York, in North-America. Taken down from his relation, arranged, corrected, and published by the Rev. Mr. Aldridge. 2d ed. London, Printed by Gilbert and Plummer, 1785. 38 p.

E99.C5M34 Rare Bk. Coll.

Also published under the title *A Narrative of the Life of John Marrant* (Leeds, Printed by Davies, 1810. 24 p. E99.C5M35 Rare Bk. Coll.).

13963

MARRETT, JOHN (1741–1813)

Massachusetts. Clergyman.

——— Rev. John Marrett's diary [1769–1812] *In* Dunster, Samuel. Henry Dunster and his descendants. Central Falls, R.I., E. L. Freeman, Printers, 1876. p. 81–94.

CS71.D926 1876

13964

MARSHALL, BENJAMIN

Pennsylvania.

——— Extracts from the letter-book of Benjamin Marshall, 1763–1766. Pennsylvania magazine of history and biography, v. 20, July 1896: 204–212.

F146.P65, v. 20

The extracts relate in part to the Presbyterian-Quaker political rivalry in Philadelphia and the effect of the Stamp Act on trade.

13965

MARSHALL, CHRISTOPHER (1709–1797)*

England; Pennsylvania. Pharmacist.

——— Extracts from the diary of Christopher Marshall, kept in Philadelphia and Lancaster, during the American Revolution, 1774–1781. Edited by William Duane. Albany, J. Munsell, 1877. 330 p. E275.M36

Reprinted in New York by the New York Times (1969).

The first edition, covering only the years 1774–76, was published in 1839 under the title *Passages From the Remembrances of Christopher Marshall* (Philadelphia, Printed by J. Crissy. 124, xvi p.). An edition published in 1849 under the title *Passages From the Diary of Christopher Marshall* (Philadelphia, Hazard & Mitchell. 174, xix p.), included the years 1774–77. Portions of the diary also appeared in *Potter's American Monthly*, v. 4, Apr. 1875, p. 252–256.

13966

MARSHALL, EDWARD (*ca.* 1713–1789)

Pennsylvania. Frontiersman, farmer.

BUCK, WILLIAM J. History of the Indian Walk, performed for the proprietaries of Pennsylvania in 1737, to which is appended a life of Edward Marshall [Philadelphia] 1886. 269 p. F152.B92

13967

MARSHALL, HUMPHREY (1760–1841)*

Virginia; Kentucky. Revolutionary officer, surveyor, lawyer.

QUISENBERRY, ANDERSON C. The life and times of Hon. Humphrey Marshall, sometime an officer in the Revolutionary War . . . Senator in Congress from 1795 to 1801. Winchester, Ky., Sun Pub. Co., 1892. 142 p. port. E302.6.M35Q8 Rare Bk. Coll.

13968

MARSHALL, HUMPHRY (1722–1801)*

Pennsylvania. Botanist.

BELDEN, LOUISE C. Humphry Marshall's trade in plants of the New World for gardens and forests of the Old World. *In* Winterthur portfolio. v. 2; 1965. Winterthur, Del. p. 107–126. illus. N9.W52, v. 2

HARSHBERGER, JOHN W. Additional letters of Humphry Marshall, botanist and nurseryman. Pennsylvania magazine of history and biography, v. 53, July 1929: 269–282. facsims. F146.P65, v. 53

PLEASANTS, HENRY. Humphry Marshall, 1722–1801. *In his* Three scientists of Chester County. [West Chester, Pa., Printed by H. F. Temple, 1936] p. 9–20.

QK26.P55

13969

MARSHALL, JOHN (1755–1835)*

Virginia. Revolutionary officer, lawyer, assemblyman.

BEVERIDGE, ALBERT J. The life of John Marshall. Boston, Houghton Mifflin Co., 1916–19. 4 v. facsims., plates, ports. E302.6.M4B57

"Works cited" at end of each volume.

Contents: 1. Frontiersman, soldier, lawmaker, 1755–1788.—2. Politician, diplomatist, statesman, 1789–1801.—3. Conflict and construction, 1800–1815.—4. The building of the nation, 1815–1835.

FORAN, WILLIAM A. John Marshall as a historian. American historical review, v. 43, Oct. 1937: 51–64.

E171.A57, v. 43

In writing his *Life of Washington*, Marshall borrowed heavily from the *Annual Register*, Belsham, Gordon, Ramsay, and Stedman.

KUTLER, STANLEY O., *comp.* John Marshall. Englewood Cliffs, N.J., Prentice-Hall [1972] xi, 179 p. (Great lives observed) KF8745.M3K85

A Spectrum book.

Bibliography: p. 174–176.

LOTH, DAVID G. Chief Justice; John Marshall and the growth of the Republic. New York, W. W. Norton [1949] 395 p. port. KF8745.M3L6 1949

Bibliography: p. 383–388.

Reprinted in New York by Greenwood Press (1970?).

MAGRUDER, ALLAN B. John Marshall. Boston, Houghton, Mifflin, 1885. viii, 290 p. (American statesmen, [v. 10]) E176.A53, v. 10 E302.6.M4M2

The 1898 edition has been reprinted in New York by AMS Press (1972. KF8745.M3M33 1972).

MAYS, DAVID J. Political questions in the Virginia of Marshall's youth. In Jones, William M., ed. Chief Justice John Marshall; a reappraisal. Ithaca, N.Y., Published for College of William and Mary [by] Cornell University Press [1956] p. 13–23. KF8745.M3J64

PADOVER, SAUL K. The political ideas of John Marshall. Social research, v. 26, spring 1959: 47–70. H1.S53, v. 26

RHODES, IRWIN S. John Marshall and the western country, early days. In Historical and Philosophical Society of Ohio. Bulletin, v. 18, Apr. 1960: 117–136. illus., facsim., port. F486.H653, v. 18

——— The papers of John Marshall, a descriptive calendar. Norman, University of Oklahoma Press [1969] 2 v. col. ports. KF213.M3R5

Documents for the years 1755–89 are listed in v. 1, p. [3]–91.

RICHARDS, GALE L. Alexander Hamilton's influence on John Marshall's judiciary speech in the 1788 Virginia federal ratifying convention. Quarterly journal of speech, v. 44, Feb. 1958: 31–39. PN4071.Q3, v. 44

SWINDLER, WILLIAM F. John Marshall: preparation for the bar—some observations on his law notes. American journal of legal history, v. 11, Apr. 1967: 207–213. LL

THAYER, JAMES B. John Marshall. Atlantic monthly, v. 87, Mar. 1901: 328–341. AP2.A8, v. 87

13970

MARSTON, BENJAMIN (1730–1792)

Massachusetts; Nova Scotia. Merchant, Loyalist, mariner.

RAYMOND, WILLIAM O. Benjamin Marston of Marblehead, Loyalist, his trials and tribulations during the American Revolution. In New Brunswick Historical Society. Collections. [v. 3], no. 7. Saint John, N.B., 1907. p. 79–112. F1041.N53, v. 3, no. 7

——— The founding of Shelburne. Benjamin Marston at Halifax, Shelburne and Miramichi. In New Brunswick Historical Society. Collections. [v. 3], no. 8. Saint John, N.B., 1909. p. 204–297. illus., fold. plan. F1041.N53, v. 3, no. 8

Includes numerous extracts from Marston's journal, 1782–84. Excerpts from his diary from June 1785 to July 1786 appear in [v. 2], no. 4 (Saint John, N.B., 1899), p. 95–109.

VESEY, MAUD M. Benjamin Marston, Loyalist. New England quarterly, v. 15, Dec. 1942: 622–651. F1.N62, v. 15

13971

MARTIN, ALEXANDER (1740–1807)*

New Jersey; North Carolina. Merchant, assemblyman, Revolutionary officer, governor, delegate to the Constitutional Convention.

NASH, FRANCIS. Presentation of portrait of Governor Alexander Martin to the state of North Carolina, in the hall of the House of Representatives, at Raleigh, November 16, 1908, by the North Carolina Society of the Sons of the Revolution. [n.p., 1908] 19 p. E263.N8N2

13972

MARTIN, EPHRAIM (1733–1806)

New Jersey. Revolutionary officer, councilor.

JAMES, EDMUND J. Some additional information concerning Ephraim Martin, Esquire, colonel of the Fourth New Jersey Regiment of the Continental Line. Pennsylvania magazine of history and biography, v. 36, Apr. 1912: 143–161. F146.P65, v. 36

13973

MARTIN, JOHN (b. 1750)

Ireland; Massachusetts. Clergyman.

MURDOCK, HAROLD. The remarkable story of the Rev. John Martin. In Massachusetts Historical Society, Boston. Proceedings. v. 58; 1924/25. Boston, 1925. p. 201–214. F61.M38, v. 58

13974

MARTIN, JOSEPH (1740–1809)

Virginia; North Carolina. Frontiersman, Indian agent, Revolutionary officer, assemblyman.

——— Gen. Joseph Martin and the Cherokees. In Southern History Association. Publications, v. 8, Nov. 1904: 443–450; v. 9, Jan 1905: 27–41. F206.S73, v. 8–9

Martin's correspondence on Cherokee affairs, principally 1778–88.

MARTIN, WILLIAM. A biographical sketch of General Joseph Martin. Virginia magazine of history and biography, v. 8, Apr. 1901: 347–359. F221.V91, v. 8

PUSEY, WILLIAM A. General Joseph Martin of Virginia, an unsung hero of the Virginia frontier. Filson Club history quarterly, v. 10, Apr. 1936: 57–81. F446.F484, v. 10

REDD, JOHN. General Joseph Martin. With accompanying documents. *In* Southern History Association. Publications, v. 7, Jan.–July 1903: 1–6, 73–78, 193–199, 257–268. F206.S73, v. 7

WEEKS, STEPHEN B. General Joseph Martin and the War of the Revolution in the West. *In* American Historical Association. Annual report. 1893. Washington, 1894. p. 401–477. E172.A60, 1893

13975

MARTIN, JOSEPH PLUMB (1760–1850)

Massachusetts; Maine. Revolutionary soldier, farmer.

——— Private Yankee Doodle; being a narrative of some of the adventures, dangers, and sufferings of a Revolutionary soldier. Edited by George F. Scheer. Boston, Little, Brown [1962] 305 p. maps. E275.M38 1962

Reprinted in New York by the New York Times (1968). Originally published anonymously under the title *A Narrative of Some of the Adventures, Dangers and Sufferings of a Revolutionary Soldier* (Hallowell [Me.] Glazier, Masters, 1830. 213 p. E275.M38 Rare Bk. Coll.).

Portions of the Scheer edition, with connective summaries, have appeared in *American Heritage*, v. 13, Apr. 1962, p. 33–48. Those sections relating to Montgomery County, Pennsylvania, appeared under the title "Private Yankee Doodle in Montgomery County" in the *Bulletin* of the Historical Society of Montgomery County, v. 14, fall 1963, p. 23–41.

13976

MARTIN, LUTHER (*ca.* 1748–1826)*

New Jersey; Maryland. Lawyer, delegate to the Constitutional Convention.

——— The "autobiography" of Luther Martin. Maryland historical magazine, v. 50, June–Sept. 1955: 152–171, 269–270. F176.M18, v. 50

Excerpts from his *Modern Gratitude* ([Baltimore, 1801?] 54 p. F185.K24), in which Martin describes his studies at Princeton, early legal practice, and political activities in Maryland, 1761–77.

CLARKSON, PAUL S., *and* SAMUEL JETT. Luther Martin of Maryland. Baltimore, Johns Hopkins Press [1970] ix, 336 p. port. KF368.M3C5

Bibliography: p. 319–329.

GODDARD, HENRY P. Luther Martin: the "Federal Bull-Dog." *In* Maryland Historical Society. Fund-publication. no. 24. Baltimore, 1887. p. 9–42. F176.M37, no. 24

SOUTHARD, ERWIN N. Reprobate genius, Luther Martin, attorney-at-law; a biography. 1941. x, 341 l. maps, port.

Thesis (Ph.D.)—Ohio State University.

13977

MASERES, FRANCIS (1731–1824)†

England; Canada. Lawyer, judge, mathematician.

——— The Maseres letters, 1766–1768. Edited with an introduction, notes and appendices, by W. Stewart Wallace. Toronto, University of Toronto Library, Oxford University Press, Canadian branch, 1919. 135 p. (University of Toronto studies. History and economics, [v. 3, no. 2]) H31.T6, v. 3, no. 2
F1032.M413

13978

MASON, CHARLES (1728–1786)†

England; Pennsylvania. Astronomer, surveyor.

——— Field notes and astronomical observations of Charles Mason and Jeremiah Dixon. Made by them in their surveys of the boundary lines between the provinces of Pennsylvania, Delaware, and Maryland, 1763–68. Transcribed from the original autograph manuscript of Mason and Dixon, now in the possession of the Historical Society of Pennsylvania. *In* Pennsylvania. *Dept. of Internal Affairs*. Report of the Secretary. Harrisburg, E. K. Meyers, State Printer, 1887. p. [59]–281. F157.B7P3 G&M

——— The journal of Charles Mason and Jeremiah Dixon. Transcribed from the original in the United States National Archives. With an introduction by A. Hughlett Mason. Philadelphia, American Philosophical Society, 1969. 231 p. illus., facsims., map. (Memoirs of the American Philosophical Society, v. 76) F157.B7M27
Q11.P612, v. 76

Bibliography: p. 27.

COPE, THOMAS D., *and* H. W. ROBINSON. The astronomical manuscripts which Charles Mason gave to Provost John Ewing during October 1786. *In* American Philosophical Society, *Philadelphia*. Proceedings, v. 96, Aug. 1952: 417–423. Q11.P5, v. 96

Also published in the Society's *Library Bulletin* for 1952, p. 417–423.

COPE, THOMAS D. Charles Mason and Jeremiah Dixon. Scientific monthly, v. 62, June 1946: 541–554. illus., map. Z1.S817, v. 62

ROBINSON, H. W. A note on Charles Mason's ancestry and his family. *In* American Philosophical Society, *Philadelphia*. Proceedings, v. 93, May 1949: 134–136. map. Q11.P5, v. 93

Also published in the Society's *Library Bulletin* for 1949, p. 134–136.

13979

MASON, GEORGE (1725–1792)*

Virginia. Planter, assemblyman, delegate to the Constitutional Convention.

—— Last will and testament of George Mason of Gunston Hall. *In* Historical Society of Fairfax County, Virginia. Yearbook. v. 6; 1958/59. Vienna, 1959. p. 1–14.

F232.F2H5, v. 6

—— Letters of George Mason [1775–81] Virginia historical register and literary advertiser, v. 2, no. 1, 1849: 21–34. F221.V81, v. 2

—— The papers of George Mason, 1725–1792. Robert A. Rutland, editor. Chapel Hill, University of North Carolina Press, 1970. 3 v. (cxxvii, 1312 p.) illus., map, ports. E302.M38 1970

Includes bibliographic references.

Contents: v. 1. 1749–1778.—v. 2. 1779–1786.—v. 3. 1787–1792.

BAILEY, KENNETH P. George Mason, westerner. William and Mary College quarterly historical magazine, 2d ser., v. 23, Oct. 1943: 409–417.

F221.W71, 2d s., v. 23

COLEMAN, ELIZABETH D. George Mason, spokesman for human rights. Virginia cavalcade, v. 1, summer 1951: 4–8. illus., map, ports. F221.V74, v. 1

See also Hilda N. Schroetter's "Georgian Gem: George Mason's Gunston Hall," on p. 9–13.

GANTER, HERBERT L. The machiavellianism of George Mason. William and Mary College quarterly historical magazine, 2d ser., v. 17, Apr. 1937: 239–264.

F221.W71, 2d s., v. 17

MILLER, HELEN D. HILL. George Mason and the Virginia bill of rights. American heritage, new ser., v. 3, winter 1952: 38–47. illus. (part col.), facsims., map, col. port.

E171.A43, n.s., v. 3

—— George Mason, constitutionalist. Cambridge, Mass., Harvard University Press, 1938. xxii, 300 p. facsim., map, plates, ports. E302.6.M45M5

"Sources": p. [259]–262. "Notes": p. [263]–290.

Reprinted in Gloucester, Mass., by P. Smith (1966).

A condensation of the author's study was published under the title *George Mason of Gunston Hall* (Lorton, Va., Board of Regents of Gunston Hall [1958] 68 p.).

MOORE, ROBERT WALTON. George Mason, the statesman. William and Mary College historical quarterly magazine, 2d ser., v. 13, Jan. 1933: 10–17.

F221.W71, 2d s., v. 13

PITTMAN, ROBERT CARTER. George Mason and the rights of man. Georgia bar journal, v. 13, May 1951: 406–418.

LL

—— George Mason of Gunston Hall (1725–1792): father of the American Bill of Rights. Alabama lawyer, v. 15, Apr. 1954: 196–207. LL

—— George Mason, the architect of American liberty. Georgia bar journal, v. 18, Nov. 1955: 143–152. LL

RIELY, HENRY C. George Mason. Virginia magazine of history and biography, v. 42, Jan. 1934: 1–17.

F221.V91, v. 42

ROWLAND, KATE M. The life of George Mason, 1725–1792. Including his speeches, public papers, and correspondence. With an introduction by General Fitzhugh Lee. New York, G. P. Putnam's Sons, 1892. 2 v. facsims., port. E302.6.M45R8

Bibliography: v. 1, p. xvii.

Reprinted in New York by Russell & Russell (1964).

RUTLAND, ROBERT A. George Mason, reluctant statesman. Foreword by Dumas Malone. Williamsburg, Va., Colonial Williamsburg; distributed by Holt, Rinehart and Winston, New York [1961] 123 p. illus. (Williamsburg in America series, 4) F234.W7W7, v. 4

Bibliography: p. 115–116.

13980

MASSIE, NATHANIEL (1763–1813)

Virginia; Kentucky. Revolutionary soldier, frontiersman.

MASSIE, DAVID M. Nathaniel Massie, a pioneer of Ohio. A sketch of his life and selections from his correspondence [1786–1813] Cincinnati, R. Clarke Co., 1896. 285 p. fold. map, port. F483.M41

13981

MATCH-E-KE-WIS, *Chippewa chief (ca. 1736–ca. 1805)*

DRAPER, LYMAN C. Notice of Match-e-ke-wis. The captor of Mackinaw, 1763. *In* Wisconsin. State Historical Society. Report and collections. v. 7; 1873/76. Madison, 1876. p. [188]–194. F576.W81, v. 7

13982

MATHER, SAMUEL (1706–1785)*

Massachusetts. Congregational clergyman.

—— The dying legacy of an aged minister of the everlasting gospel, to the United States of North-America. Boston, Printed by Benjamin Edes and Sons, in Cornhill, 1783. 29 p. E303.M42 Rare Bk. Coll.

MATTHEWS, ALBERT. Samuel Mather (H. C. 1723), his honorary degrees and works. *In* Colonial Society of Massachusetts, *Boston*. Publications. v. 18. Transactions. 1915/16. Boston, 1917. p. 206–228.

F61.C71, v. 18

13983

MATHEWS, DAVID (*ca.* 1746–1811)

Vermont; New York. Revolutionary soldier, farmer.

SPARGO, JOHN. The true story of Capt. David Mathews and his state line house, being the vindication of the memory of a Revolutionary patriot & the exposure of fantastic legends concerning the house he built. Rutland, Vt., Tory press, 1930. 12 p. plates. (Bennington Historical Museum publications, no. 1)

F59.B4B6, no. 1
E263.N6S7

13984

MATHEWS, GEORGE (1739–1812)*

Virginia; Georgia. Revolutionary officer, governor.

HERNDON, GEORGE MELVIN. George Mathews, frontier patriot. Virginia magazine of history and biography, v. 77, July 1969: 307–328. F221.V91, v. 77

13985

MATLACK, TIMOTHY (*ca.* 1736–1829)*

Pennsylvania. Merchant, Revolutionary officer, delegate to the Continental Congress.

STACKHOUSE, ASA M. Col. Timothy Matlack, patriot and soldier. [n.p.] Priv. print., 1910. 105 p. fold. facsim., port. E263.P4M3

An oration delivered March 16, 1780, before the American Philosophical Society by Timothy Matlack: p. [29]–58.

13986

MATTHEWMAN, LUKE (*fl.* 1776–1787)

Revolutionary naval officer.

—— Narrative of Lieut. Luke Matthewman of the Revolutionary navy. Magazine of American history, with notes and queries, v. 2, Mar. 1878: 175–185.
E171.M18, v. 2

13987

MATTHEWS, JOHN (*b.* 1765)

Massachusetts. Schoolteacher, surveyor.

—— A journal &c [of John Matthews, 1786–87] *In* Hulbert, Archer B., *ed.* Ohio in the time of the Confederation. Marietta, Ohio, Marietta Historical Commission, 1918. (Marietta College historical collections, v. 3) p. [187]–214. F495.H92

13988

MATTOON, EBENEZER (1755–1843)

Massachusetts. Revolutionary officer, farmer.

WALKER, ALICE M. Mary Mattoon and her hero of the Revolution [General Ebenezer Mattoon] Amherst, Mass. [Press of Carpenter & Morehouse] 1902. 83 p. plates, ports. F74.A5M44

13989

MAUDUIT, ISRAEL (1708–1787)†

England. Merchant, colonial agent, political writer.

FORD, WORTHINGTON C. The Mauduit pamphlets. *In* Massachusetts Historical Society, *Boston*. Proceedings. v. 44; 1910/11. Boston, 1911. p. 144–175.
F61.M38, v. 44

TAYLOR, ROBERT J. Israel Mauduit. New England quarterly, v. 24, June 1951: 208–230. F1.N62, v. 24

13990

[MAUSSION DE LA BASTIE, GASTON MARIE LÉONARD]

RADZIWILL, CATHERINE, *Princess*. They knew the Washingtons; letters from a French soldier with Lafayette and from his family in Virginia. Indianapolis, Bobbs-Merrill Co. [c1926] 255 p. E265.R14

Letters, of doubtful authenticity, signed by Gaston de Maussion, or De Maussion (i.e., Gaston Marie Léonard Maussion de la Bastie) and by members of his family. The editors of *The American Campaigns of Rochambeau's Army* (entry 7195) regard the letters as fictitious (see v. 1, p. 342–343).

13991

MAXWELL, HUGH (1733–1799)

Massachusetts. Revolutionary officer.

—— The Christian patriot: some recollections of the late Col. Hugh Maxwell, of Massachusetts. Collected and preserved by a daughter. 2d ed. New York, S. W. Benedict, 1833. [Hartford? Conn., 1936] 146 p.
E275.M4 1936

GUILD, EDWARD P. Hugh Maxwell, patriot and soldier of the Revolution. New-England historical and genealogical register, v. 45, Jan. 1891: 38–41.
F1.N56, v. 45

13992

MAXWELL, THOMPSON (1742–1835)

Massachusetts. Revolutionary officer.

—— The narrative of Major Thompson Maxwell. *In* Essex Institute, *Salem, Mass.* Historical collections, v. 7, June 1865: 97–113. F72.E7E81, v. 7

Introduction by E. F. Miller.

—— Thompson Maxwell's narrative, 1760–1763. *In* Wisconsin. State Historical Society. Collections. v. 11. Madison, 1888. p. [213]–217. F576.W81, v. 11

Narrative of an expedition to take possession of Detroit, Mackinaw, and other western posts surrendered to the British by the capitulation of Montreal.

[GLEASON, BENJAMIN] A remarkable military life. New-England historical and genealogical register, v. 45, Oct. 1891: 271–278. F1.N56, v. 45

An offprint, entitled *Narrative of the Military Life of Major Thompson Maxwell, of Massachusetts*, was issued in 1891 ([Boston, D. Clapp, Printers] 8 p. E181.G56).

13993

MAXWELL, WILLIAM (*ca.* 1733–1796)*

Ireland; New Jersey. Revolutionary general, assemblyman.

GRIFFITH, J. H. William Maxwell of New Jersey, Brigadier General in the Revolution. *In* New Jersey Historical Society. Proceedings, 2d ser., v. 13, no. 2, 1894: 111–123.　　　　F131.N58, 2d s., v. 13

HEATHCOTE, CHARLES W. General William Maxwell—earnest patriot. Picket post, no. 47, Feb. 1955: 13–18.
E234.P5, no. 47

13994

MAY, JOHN (1748–1812)

Massachusetts; Ohio. Merchant, Revolutionary officer.

——— Side lights on the Ohio Company of Associates, from the John May papers. Edited by Elbert Jay Benton, with an introduction. *In* Western Reserve Historical Society, *Cleveland.* Tracts. no. 97. Cleveland, 1917. p. [63]–231. maps (part fold.)
F486.W58, no. 97

——— The western journals of John May [1788–89], Ohio Company agent and business adventurer. Edited with an introduction by Dwight L. Smith. [Cincinnati] Historical and Philosophical Society of Ohio [1961] xii, 176 p. port.　　　　　　F495.M39

Bibliography: p. 167–169.

In an extended introduction, Smith describes the textual inaccuracies in the editions of May's journals edited by Richard S. Edes and published as the *Journals and Letters of Col. John May, of Boston, Relative to Two Journeys to the Ohio Country in 1788 and '89* (Cincinnati, R. Clarke for the Historical and Philosophical Society of Ohio, 1873. 160 p. F517.M46); the "Letters and Journal of Col. John May, of Boston," in the *New-England Historical and Genealogical Register*, v. 27, Jan. 1873, p. 14–24; and the "Journal of Col. John May, of Boston, Relative to a Journey to the Ohio Country, 1789," in the *Pennsylvania Magazine of History and Biography*, v. 45, Apr. 1921, p. 101–179.

13995

MAYHEW, JONATHAN (1720–1766)*

Massachusetts. Clergyman, religious and political writer.

AKERS, CHARLES W. Called unto liberty; a life of Jonathan Mayhew, 1720–1766. Cambridge, Harvard University Press, 1964. xii, 285 p. illus., facsims., ports.
BX9869.M45A7

"Bibliography of Jonathan Mayhew, with short titles used in the Notes": p. [238]–241. Bibliographic references included in "Notes" (p. [243]–272).

The author's thesis (Ph.D.), *The Life of Jonathan Mayhew, 1720–1766*, was submitted to Boston University in 1952.

——— The making of a religious liberal: Jonathan Mayhew and the Great Awakening. New England social studies bulletin, v. 11, Mar. 1954: 18–25.　　H1.N4, v. 11

BRADFORD, ALDEN. Memoir of the life and writings of Rev. Jonathan Mayhew, D.D., pastor of the West Church and Society in Boston, from June, 1747, to July, 1766. Boston, C. C. Little, 1838. iv, 484 p. port.
BX9869.M45B8

LEWIS, EARL E. The theology and politics of Jonathan Mayhew. 1966. ([295] p.)
Micro AC–1, no. 66–12,219

Thesis (Ph.D.)—University of Minnesota.

Abstracted in *Dissertation Abstracts*, v. 27A, Dec. 1966, p. 1735–1736.

RICHEY, McMURRAY S. Jonathan Mayhew: American Christian rationalist. *In* Henry, Stuart C., *ed.* A miscellany of American Christianity; essays in honor of H. Shelton Smith. Durham, N.C., Duke University Press, 1963. p. [292]–327.　　　　BR515.H46

ROSSITER, CLINTON. The life and mind of Jonathan Mayhew. William and Mary quarterly, 3d ser., v. 7, Oct. 1950: 531–558.　　　　F221.W71, 3d s., v. 7

13996

MAZZEI, FILIPPO (1730–1816)*

Italy; England; Virginia. Merchant, horticulturist, agent.

——— Mazzei's correspondence with the Grand Duke of Tuscany during his American mission. William and Mary College quarterly historical magazine, 2d ser., v. 22, July–Oct. 1942: 275–301, 361–380.
F221.W71, 2d s., v. 22

Introduction by Howard R. Marraro.

——— ——— Offprint. [Williamsburg, Va., 1942?] 47 p.　　　　　　E203.M4

——— Mazzei's narrative. American historical record, v. 1, Feb.–Apr. 1872: 70–74, 106–109, 148–152.
[E171.P86, v. 1]
Micro 39031

Having been commissioned in 1779 by the state of Virginia to solicit a loan or to obtain supplies on the states' credit in Italy, Mazzei submitted to the governor and council upon his return to Virginia a statement of his movements from the time of his appointment until he relinquished his mission. See also the explanatory footnote to Mazzei's letter of April 21, 1780, to Maj. Gen. William Heath which was included in the January issue, p. 33–35.

——— Memoirs of the life and peregrinations of the Florentine, Philip Mazzei, 1730–1816. Translated by Howard R. Marraro. New York, Columbia University Press, 1942. xvi, 447 p. facsim., plate.　　E203.M472

Bibliography: p. [419]–429.

First published in Lugano, Switzerland, 1845–46.

——— Memoirs of the life and voyages of Doctor Philip Mazzei. Translated by Dr. E. C. Branchi. William and

Mary College quarterly historical magazine, 2d ser., v. 9, July–Oct. 1929: 161–174, 247–264; v. 10, Jan. 1930: 1–18.   F221.W71, 2d s., v. 9–10

Refers only to Mazzei's activities in Virginia after 1773.

―――― Philip Mazzei on American political, social, and economic problems [1774–85] Edited and translated by Howard R. Marraro. Journal of southern history, v. 15, Aug. 1949: 354–378.   F206.J68, v. 15

―――― Philip Mazzei, Virginia's agent in Europe; the story of his mission as related in his own dispatches and other documents. Edited by Howard R. Marraro. *In* New York (City). Public Library. Bulletin, v. 38, Mar.–Apr., June–July 1934: 155–175, 247–274, 447–474, 541–562. facsim., port.   Z881.N6B, v. 38

―――― ―――― Offprint. New York, New York Public Library, 1935. 106 p. facsim., port.   E263.V8M38

―――― Recherches historiques et politiques sur les États-Unis de l'Amérique Septentrionale, où l'on traite des éstablissemens des treize colonies, de leurs rapports & de leurs dissentions avec la Grande-Bretagne, de leurs gouvernemens avant & après la révolution, &c. A Colle, et se trouve a Paris, chez Froullé, 1788. 4 v.
E303.M47 Rare Bk. Coll.
JK136.M2 Rare Bk. Coll.
Micro 01291, reel 278, no. 3 E

The second and third volumes are occupied with criticisms of the works of Mably and Raynal.

―――― Unpublished Mazzei correspondence during his American mission to Europe, 1780–1783. William and Mary College quarterly historical magazine, 2d ser., v. 23, July–Oct. 1943: 309–327, 418–434.
F221.W71, 2d s., v. 23

Introduction and notes by Howard R. Marraro.

GARLICK, RICHARD C. Philip Mazzei, friend of Jefferson: his life and letters. Baltimore, Md., Johns Hopkins Press, 1933. 179 p. port. (The Johns Hopkins studies in Romance literatures and languages, extra v. 7)
D285.8.M35G3
PC13.J6, v. 7

Thesis (Ph.D.)—University of Virginia, 1931.
"Mazzei's published writings": p. 167. Bibliography: p. 169–171.

ZIMMERN, HELEN. Story of Mazzei. New England magazine, new ser., v. 27, Oct. 1902: 198–211.
AP2.N4, n.s., v. 27

13997
MEADE, GEORGE (1741–1808)*
Pennsylvania. Merchant.

MEADE, R. W. George Meade, a patriot of the Revolutionary era. *In* American Catholic Historical Society of Philadelphia. Records. v. 3; 1888/91. Philadelphia, 1891. p. 193–220. port.   E184.C3A4, v. 3

13998
MEASON, ISAAC (1742–1818)*
Virginia; Pennsylvania. Settler, Revolutionary officer, assemblyman.

ABRAHAM, EVELYN. Isaac Meason, the first ironmaster west of the Alleghenies. Western Pennsylvania historical magazine, v. 20, Mar. 1937: 41–49.
F146.W52, v. 20

13999
MECOM, BENJAMIN (*b.* 1732)*
Massachusetts. Printer, bookseller.

EAMES, WILBERFORCE. The Antigua press and Benjamin Mecom, 1748–1765. *In* American Antiquarian Society, *Worcester, Mass.* Proceedings, new ser., v. 38, Oct. 1928: 303–348.   E172.A35, n.s., v. 38

14000
MECOM, JANE FRANKLIN (1712–1794)
Massachusetts. Sister of Benjamin Franklin (1706–1790).

VAN DOREN, CARL C. Jane Mecom, the favorite sister of Benjamin Franklin: her life here first fully narrated from their entire surviving correspondence. New York, Viking Press, 1950. vii, 255 p. illus., map, ports.
CT275.M46553V3

14001
MEIGS, RETURN JONATHAN (1740–1823)*
Connecticut. Revolutionary officer.

JOHNSTON, HENRY P. Return Jonathan Meigs, Colonel of the Connecticut Line of the Continental Army. Magazine of American history, with notes and queries, v. 4, Apr. 1880: 282–292.   E171.M18, v. 4

14002
MEIN, JOHN (*fl.* 1755–1775)
Massachusetts. Printer, publisher.

ALDEN, JOHN E. John Mein, publisher: an essay in bibliographic detection. *In* Bibliographical Society of America. Papers, v. 36, 3d quarter 1942: 199–214.
Z1008.B51P, v. 36

―――― ―――― Offprint. [n.p.] Bibliographical Society of America, ᶜ1942. 16 p.   Z473.M4A4

―――― John Mein, scourge of patriots. *In* Colonial Society of Massachusetts, *Boston.* Publications. v. 34. Transactions, 1937/42. Boston, 1943. p. 571–599.
F61.C71, v. 34

14003
MELSHEIMER, FREDERICK VALENTINE (1749–1814)*
Germany; Pennsylvania. Clergyman, Hessian chaplain in America, entomologist.

——— Tagebuch von der Reise der braunschweigischen auxiliär Truppen von Wolfenbüttel nach Quebec. Frankfurt, 1776. 40 p.   E268.M52

——— ——— Erste Fortsetzung. Frankfurt, 1776. 32 p.   E268.M52

Bound with his *Tagebuch*.

A translated version of the journal was published in the *Transactions* of the Literary and Historical Society of Quebec, no. 20, 1889/91 (Quebec, 1891), p. 133–178.

PROWELL, GEORGE R.   Frederick Valentine Melsheimer, a pioneer entomologist, and a noted clergyman and author. [York, Pa., 1903] 17–26 p. [Historical Society of York County. Proceedings and collections, v. 1, no. 2]   F157.Y6H6, v. 1

14004

MELVILLE, HENRY DUNDAS, *1st Viscount* (1742–1811)†

Scotland. Member of Parliament.

FURBER, HOLDEN.   Henry Dundas, first viscount Melville, 1742–1811, political manager of Scotland, statesman, administrator of British India. London, Oxford University Press, H. Milford, 1931. maps, port.   DA506.M5F8 1929

Thesis (Ph.D.)—Harvard University, 1929. "Authorities": p. [314]–324.

LOVAT-FRASER, JAMES A.   Henry Dundas, viscount Melville. Cambridge [Eng.] University Press, 1916. x, 146 p. port.   DA522.M5L6

"List of the principal authorities used by the author": p. [142]–143.

MATHESON, CYRIL.   The life of Henry Dundas, first viscount Melville, 1742–1811. London, Constable, 1933. x, 432 p. facsim., plates, ports.   DA506.M5M3

"Authorities": p. 411–415.

14005

MERCER, GEORGE (1733–1784)

Virginia; England. Surveyor, assemblyman, planter, agent.

——— Colonel George Mercer's papers [1763–66] Virginia magazine of history and biography, v. 60, July 1952: 405–420.   F221.V91, v. 60

On his role as Stamp agent. Introduction and notes by J. E. Tyler.

JAMES, ALFRED P.   George Mercer of the Ohio Company; a study in frustration. [Pittsburgh] University of Pittsburgh Press [1963] 96 p.   F229.M5J3

Bibliographic references included in "Notes" (p. 85–90).

Also published in the *Western Pennsylvania Historical Magazine*, v. 46, Jan.–Apr. 1963, p. 1–43, 141–183.

Pittsburgh. University. *Library. Darlington Memorial Library.*   George Mercer papers relating to the Ohio Company of Virginia [in the Darlington Memorial Library] Compiled and edited by Lois Mulkearn. [Pittsburgh] University of Pittsburgh Press, 1954. xxxviii, 731 p. facsims., fold. maps.   F517.P57

Bibliography: p. 675–703.

14006

MERCER, HUGH (*ca.* 1725–1777)*†

Scotland; Pennsylvania; Virginia. Physician, Revolutionary general.

EGBERT, DONALD D.   General Mercer at the Battle of Princeton as painted by James Peale, Charles Willson Peale, and William Mercer. Princeton University Library chronicle, v. 13, summer 1952: 171–194. illus., map, plates.   Z733.P93C5, v. 13

Includes excerpts from the correspondence of Charles Willson Peale and George Weedon, 1783–86. See v. 14, autumn 1952, p. 41–43, for a comment by Thomas Jefferson Wertenbaker and a reply by the author.

GOOLRICK, JOHN T.   The life of General Hugh Mercer; with brief sketches of General George Washington, John Paul Jones, General George Weedon, James Monroe and Mrs. Mary Ball Washington, who were friends and associates of General Mercer at Fredericksburg. New York, Neale Pub. Co., 1906. 140 p. plates, ports.   E207.M5G6

HEATHCOTE, CHARLES W.   General Hugh Mercer—a courageous Revolutionary officer and friend of Washington. Picket post, no. 72, May 1961: 4–10. port.   E234.P5, no. 72

KEENE, JAMES S.   Hugh Mercer. *In* John P. Branch historical papers of Randolph-Macon College. v. 2, no. 3/4; 1908. Ashland, Va. p. 198–213.   F221.J65, v. 2

WATERMAN, JOSEPH M.   With sword and lancet; the life of General Hugh Mercer. Richmond, Va., Garrett and Massie [ᶜ1941] xi, 177 p. plates, ports.   E207.M5W3

Bibliography: p. 167–170.

14007

MERCER, JAMES (1736–1793)*

Virginia. Lawyer, assemblyman, delegate to the Continental Congress, judge.

——— Letters of James Mercer to John Francis Mercer [1783] Edited by John Melville Jennings. Virginia magazine of history and biography, v. 59, Jan.–Apr. 1951: 89–102, 184–194. port.   F221.V91, v. 59

GARNETT, JAMES M.   James Mercer. William and Mary College quarterly historical magazine, v. 17, Oct. 1908–Jan. 1909: 85–99, 204–223.   F221.W71, v. 17

14008

MERCER, JOHN (1704–1768)

Ireland; Virginia. Lawyer, planter.

STETSON, SARAH P. John Mercer's notes on plants. Virginia magazine of history and biography. v. 61, Jan. 1953: 34–44. facsim.   F221.V91, v. 61

14009

MESPLET, FLEURY (*ca.* 1735–1794)
France; Canada. Printer.

FAUTEUX, AEGIDIUS. Fleury Mesplet: une étude sur les commencements de l'imprimerie dans la ville de Montréal [1773–93] *In* Bibliographical Society of America. Papers, v. 28, pt. 2, 1934: 164–193.
Z1008.B51P, v. 28

JACKES, LYMAN B. The strange adventures of Fleury Mesplet. Canadian magazine of politics, science, art and literature, v. 51, July 1918: 177–185.   AP5.C2, v. 51

MCLACHLAN, ROBERT W. Fleury Mesplet, the first printer at Montreal. *In* Royal Society of Canada. Proceedings and transactions. 2d ser., v. 12, section 2; 1906. Ottawa. p. 197–309.   AS42.R6, 2d s., v. 12

———— ———— Offprint. Ottawa, J. Hope, 1906. 197–309 p.   Z232.M58M

Consists primarily of 80 documents relating to Mesplet's career.

———— Some unpublished documents relating to Fleury Mesplet. *In* Royal Society of Canada. Proceedings and transactions. 3d ser., v. 14, section 2; 1920. Ottawa. p. 85–95.   AS42.R6, 3d s., v. 14

14010

MEYER, JACOB (*b. ca.* 1720) Also called Jacob Philadelphia
Pennsylvania; Europe. Scientist, lecturer.

SACHSE, JULIUS F. Jacob Philadelphia, mystic and physicist. *In* American Jewish Historical Society. Publications. no. 16. New York, 1907. p. [73]–83.
E184.J5A5, no. 16

His role in encouraging European trade relations with the United States is revealed in documents on p. 85–94 that appear under the title "Jacob Philadelphia and Frederick the Great."

14011

MEYERS, JOHN WALDEN (1745–1821)
New York; Canada. Farmer, Loyalist officer.

CRUIKSHANK, ERNEST A. Captain John Walden Meyers, Loyalist pioneer. *In* Ontario Historical Society. Papers and records. v. 31. Toronto, 1936. p. [11]–55.
F1056.O58, v. 31

14012

MICHAUX, ANDRÉ (1746–1803)*
France; New Jersey. Botanist.

CHINARD, GILBERT. André and François-André Michaux and their predecessors. An essay on early botanical exchanges between America and France. *In* American Philosophical Society, *Philadelphia.* Proceedings, v. 101, Aug. 1957: 344–361.   Q11.P5, v. 101

ROBINS, WILLIAM J., *and* MARY C. HOWSON. Andre Michaux's New Jersey garden and Pierre Paul Saunier, journeyman gardener. *In* American Philosophical Society, *Philadelphia.* Proceedings, v. 102, Aug. 1958: 351–370. illus., maps.   Q11.P5, v. 102

14013

MIDDLETON, ARTHUR (1742–1787)*
South Carolina. Assemblyman, delegate to the Continental Congress, Revolutionary soldier, planter.

———— Correspondence of Hon. Arthur Middleton, signer of the Declaration of Independence [1763–1783] South Carolina historical and genealogical magazine, v. 26, Oct. 1925: 183–213; v. 27, Jan.–July 1926: 1–29, 51–80, 107–155.   F266.S55, v. 26–27

Introduction and notes by Joseph W. Barnwell.

14014

MIFFLIN, BENJAMIN (*b.* 1718)
Pennsylvania. Merchant.

———— Journal of a journey from Philad[elphi]a to the Cedar Swamps & back, 1764. Pennsylvania magazine of history and biography, v. 52, Apr. 1928: 130–140.
F146.P65, v. 52

———— Journal of Benjamin Mifflin on a tour from Philadelphia to Delaware and Maryland, July 26 to August 14, 1762. Edited by Victor Hugo Paltsits. *In* New York (City). Public Library. Bulletin, v. 39, June 1935: 423–438.   Z881.N6B, v. 39

An offprint with a slightly different title was published in New York by the New York Public Library (1935. 18 p. E162.M59).

14015

MIFFLIN, THOMAS (1744–1800)*
Pennsylvania. Merchant, assemblyman, delegate to the Continental Congress, Revolutionary general, delegate to the Constitutional Convention.

HEATHCOTE, CHARLES W. General Thomas Mifflin—colleague of Washington and Pennsylvania leader. Picket post, no. 62, Nov. 1958: 7–12. port.
E234.P65, no. 62

RAWLE, WILLIAM. Sketch of the life of Thomas Mifflin. *In* Pennsylvania. Historical Society. Memoirs. v. 2; pt. 2. Philadelphia, 1830. p. [105]–126.   F146.P36, v. 2

ROSSMAN, KENNETH R. Thomas Mifflin and the politics of the American Revolution. [Chapel Hill] University of North Carolina Press [1952] 344 p. illus., ports.
E207.M6R6

"Bibliographical note": p. [326]–330.

The author's thesis (Ph.D.), *Thomas Mifflin: the Revolutionary Patriot from Pennsylvania*, was submitted to the State University of Iowa in 1940.

——— Thomas Mifflin—Revolutionary patriot. Pennsylvania history. v. 15, Jan. 1948: 9–23.   F146.P597, v. 15

14016

MILES, SAMUEL (1740–1805)

Pennsylvania. Merchant, Revolutionary officer, assemblyman, judge.

——— Auto-biographical sketch of Col. Samuel Miles. American historical record, v. 2, Feb.–Mar. 1873: 49–53, 114–118.   [E171.P86, v. 2] Micro 39031

14017

MILFORT, LOUIS (*ca.* 1750–1817)

France; Louisiana; Georgia. Creek Indian leader.

——— Memoir; or, A cursory glance at my different travels & my sojourn in the Creek Nation. Translated by Geraldine de Courcy. Edited by John Francis McDermott. Chicago, R. R. Donnelley, 1956. lvi, 257 p. facsim., maps. (The Lakeside classics, no. 54)   E99.C9M513

Bibliography: p. 231–237.

Another edition, translated and edited by Ben C. McCary, was published in Kennesaw, Ga., by the Continental Book Co. (1959. 230 p.) and again in Savannah, Ga., by the Beehive Press ([1972, ᶜ1959] 145 p.).

14018

MILLER, HENRY (1751–1824)

Pennsylvania. Lawyer, Revolutionary officer.

WATTS, HENRY M.   A memoir of General Henry Miller. Pennsylvania magazine of history and biography, v. 11, Oct. 1887: 341–345; v. 12, Jan. 1889: 425–431.   F146.P65, v. 11–12

14019

MILLER, JOHN HENRY (1702–1782)*

Germany; Pennsylvania. Printer, newspaper editor.

DAPP, CHARLES F.   The evolution of an American patriot, being an intimate study of the patriotic activities of John Henry Miller, German printer, publisher, and editor of the American Revolution. Philadelphia, 1924. 68 p. facsim., plates.   Z232.M64D2

Thesis (Ph.D.)—University of Pennsylvania, 1913.
Bibliography: p. 66–68.

First published as pt. 32 of Pennsylvania: the German Influence in its Settlement and Development in the *Proceedings and Addresses*, v. 32, 1921 (F146.P23, v. 32), of the Pennsylvania-German Society.

14020

MILLS, NATHANIEL (*fl.* 1773–1784)

Massachusetts: Nova Scotia. Newspaper editor, Loyalist.

——— The letter-book of Mills & Hicks (Nathaniel Mills and John Hicks), August 13th, 1781, to August 22nd, 1784, at Charles Town (South Carolina), Saint Augustine (East Florida), New York (New York), and Granville (Nova Scotia). Edited by Robert E. Moody and Charles C. Crittenden. North Carolina historical review, v. 14, Jan 1937: 39–83.   F251.N892, v. 14

14021

MINTZER, MARK (1709–1781)

Switzerland; Pennsylvania. Carter and hauler.

HOUGH, JAMES E.   Mark Mintzer, Revolutionary War patriot (1709–1781). *In* Historical Society of Montgomery County (*Pennsylvania*). Bulletin, v. 13, spring 1962: 71–80.   F157.M7H45, v. 13

See also the author's "Genealogy of Mark Mintzer" on p. 81–119.

14022

MIRALLES, JUAN DE (*d.* 1780)

Spain; Pennsylvania. Diplomat.

GRIFFIN, MARTIN I. J.   Requiem for Don Juan de Miralles. American Catholic historical researches, v. 6, Apr. 1889: 60–72.   E184.C3A5, v. 6

14023

MIRANDA, FRANCISCO DE (1750–1816)

Venezuela; Europe. Spanish military officer in America.

——— The diary of Francisco de Miranda, tour of the United States, 1783–1784; the Spanish text edited, with introduction and notes, by William Spence Robertson. New York [Hispanic Society of America] 1928. xxxvi, 206 p. facsims., maps, plates, ports.   E164.M67

Bibliography: p. [173]–178.

A new edition of the diary, translated by Judson P. Wood and edited by John S. Ezell, was published as *The New Democracy in America; Travels of Francisco de Miranda in the United States, 1783–84* (Norman, University of Oklahoma Press [1963] 217 p.), no. 40 in The American Exploration and Travel Series.

——— The sojourn of Francisco de Miranda in Massachusetts and New Hampshire, September 16th to December 20th, 1784, as recorded in his diary. *In* Society for the Preservation of New England Antiquities, *Boston*. Old-time New England, v. 26, July-Oct. 1935: 3–17, 41–54. illus., facsim., port.   F1.S68, v. 26

Translated from the Spanish by Dr. Rudolf Schuller and communicated by George Francis Dow.

PETERSON, ROY M. A South American's impressions of New England after Yorktown. New England quarterly, v. 4, Oct. 1931: 713–734. F1.N62, v. 4

RIPPY, JAMES FRED. A view of the Carolinas in 1783. North Carolina historical review, v. 6, Oct. 1929: 362–370. F251.N892, v. 6

An account based on Miranda's *Diary.*

14024

MITCHELL, JOHN (1711–1768)*†

Virginia; England. Physician, botanist, scientist, mapmaker.

BERKELEY, EDMUND. Dr. John Mitchell: the first Virginia-born scientist. Fredericksburg, E. Lee Trinkle Library, Mary Washington College, 1972. 26 p. ([Mary Washington College, Fredericksburg, Va. Library] Occasional papers, no. 5) Z881.F84O25, no. 5

Bibliography: p. [27]

CARRIER, LYMAN. Dr. John Mitchell, naturalist, cartographer, and historian. *In* American Historical Association. Annual report. 1918. Washington, 1921. p. 199–219. E172.A60, 1918

DORMAN, JOHN F., *and* JAMES F. LEWIS. Dr. John Mitchell, F.R.S., and native Virginian. Virginia magazine of history and biography, v. 76, Oct. 1968: 437–440. F221.V91, v. 76

HORNBERGER, THEODORE. The scientific ideas of John Mitchell. Huntington Library quarterly, v. 10, May 1947: 277–296. Z733.S24Q, v. 10

JONES, GORDON W. Doctor John Mitchell of Virginia. Virginia cavalcade, v. 12, spring 1963: 32–39. illus., facsim., port. F221.V74, v. 12

THATCHER, HERBERT. Dr. John Mitchell, M.D., F.R.S., of Virginia. Virginia magazine of history and biography, v. 39, Apr.–July 1931: 126–135, 206–220; v. 40, Jan.–Oct. 1932: 48–62, 97–110, 268–279, 335–346; v. 41, Jan.–Apr. 1933: 59–70, 144–156. plates, ports. F221.V91, v. 39–41

14025

MONROE, JAMES (1758–1831)*

Virginia. Revolutionary officer, assemblyman, delegate to the Continental Congress.

———— Autobiography. Edited, and with an introduction, by Gerry Brown, with the assistance of Donald G. Baker. [Syracuse] Syracuse University Press [1959] xi, 236 p. illus., facsims., ports. E372.A3

———— Calendar of the correspondence of James Monroe. New ed., with corrections and additions. Washington, Dept. of State, 1893 [repr. 1902] 371 p. (U.S. Bureau of Rolls and Library. Bulletin no. 2) E302.M75

U.S. 57th Congress, 1st session. House. Doc. no. 620. Covers the years 1783–1831.

———— The writings of James Monroe, including a collection of his public and private papers and correspondence now for the first time printed. Edited by Stanislaus Murray Hamilton. New York, G. P. Putnam's Sons, 1898–1903. 7 v. E302.M74

Contents: 1. 1778–1794.—2. 1794–1796.—3. 1796–1802.—4. 1803–1806.—5. 1807–1816.—6. 1817–1823.—7. 1824–1831.

AMMON, HARRY. James Monroe: the quest for national identity. New York, McGraw-Hill [1971] xi, 706 p. E372.A65

Bibliography: p. 676–687.

CRESSON, WILLIAM P. James Monroe. Chapel Hill, University of North Carolina Press [1946] xiv, 577 p. facsim., plates, ports. E372.C7

"List of references": p. 549–559.

Reprinted in Hamden, Conn., by Archon Books (1971).

DICKSON, CHARLES E. Politics in a new nation: the early career of James Monroe [1782–94] 1971. ([221] p.) Micro AC–1, no. 72–15,198

Thesis (Ph.D.)—Ohio State University.

Abstracted in *Dissertation Abstracts International,* v. 32A, May 1972, p. 6334–6335.

GILMAN, DANIEL C. James Monroe in his relations to the public service during half a century, 1776 to 1826. Boston, Houghton Mifflin, 1883. xiii, 287 p. (American statesman, [v. 14]) E176.A53, v. 14

"Bibliography of Monroe, and the Monroe doctrine . . . by J. F. Jameson": p. 253–280.

Guide to the microfilm edition of James Monroe papers in Virginia repositories. Curtis W. Garrison, editor; David L. Thomas, assistant editor. [Charlottesville] University of Virginia Library, 1969. 86 p. Z6616.M69G352 Mss

HEMPHILL, WILLIAM EDWIN. His course fixed for life? Virginia cavalcade, v. 7, spring 1958: 40–47. illus., facsims., ports. F221.V74, v. 7

On his early career.

HOES, LAURENCE G. The military career of James Monroe. Daughters of the American Revolution magazine, v. 87, Aug. 1953: 993–996. E202.5.A12, v. 87

HOES, ROSE G. James Monroe, soldier; his part in the war of the American Revolution. Daughters of the American Revolution magazine, v. 57, Dec. 1923: 721–727. illus., facsim., port. E202.5.A12, v. 57

MORGAN, GEORGE. The life of James Monroe. Boston, Small, Maynard [ᶜ1921] xvi, 484 p. plates, ports. E372.M84

Reprinted in New York by AMS Press (1969).

STYRON, ARTHUR. The last of the cocked hats; James Monroe & the Virginia dynasty. Norman, University of Oklahoma Press, 1945. xiii, 480 p. plates, ports.
E372.S75

Bibliography: p. 456–474.

U.S. *Library of Congress. Manuscript Division.* Index to the James Monroe papers. Washington [U.S. Govt. Print. Off.] 1963. xiii, 25 p. (*Its* Presidents' papers index series)
Z6616.M69U5
Z663.34.M58

Bibliography: p. xi.

U.S. *Library of Congress. Manuscript Division.* Papers of James Monroe, listed in chronological order from the original manuscripts in the Library of Congress. Compiled under the direction of Worthington Chauncey Ford, chief, Division of Manuscripts. Washington, Govt. Print. Off., 1904. 114 p. illus., facsims.
Z6621.U58M6
Z663.34.M6

Intended to complement the alphabetical *Calendar of the Correspondence of James Monroe* issued as *Bulletin* of the Bureau of Rolls and Library of the Department of State, no. 2, November 1893.

MONTAGU, JOHN
See SANDWICH, JOHN MONTAGU, *4th Earl of*

14026
MONTESQUIEU, CHARLES LOUIS DE SECONDAT, *baron* DE LA BRÈDE ET DE (1689–1755)
France. Social philosopher, writer.

FLETCHER, FRANK T. H. Montesquieu and English politics (1750–1800). London, E. Arnold [1939] 286 p.
JCC179.M8F5

LEVIN, LAWRENCE M. The political doctrine of Montesquieu's *Esprit des lois*: its classical background. New York, Columbia University [^1936] xii, 359 p. (Publications of the Institute of French studies)
JC179.M8L45 1936a

Issued also as thesis (Ph.D.)—Columbia University.
Bibliography: p. 331–359.

MERRY, HENRY J. Montesquieu's system of natural government. West Lafayette, Ind., Purdue University Studies, 1970. xvi, 414 p.
JC179.M8M4

Bibliography: p. 386–389.

SHACKLETON, ROBERT. Montesquieu; a critical biography. [London] Oxford University Press, 1961. xiv, 432 p. illus., port.
JC179.M8S35 1961

"Bibliography of Montesquieu": p. [400]–418.

SPURLIN, PAUL M. Montesquieu in America, 1760–1801. University, La., Louisiana State University Press, 1940. xi, 302 p. ([Louisiana State University] Romance languages series, no. 4)
PC13.L64, no. 4
JC179.M8S65

Issued also as thesis (Ph.D.)—Johns Hopkins University.
Bibliography: p. 263–282.
Reprinted in New York by Octagon Books (1969).
See the author's resumé of his work, under the title "Montesquieu et l'opinion américaine au dix-huitième siècle," in the *French American Review*, v. 2, Jan./Mar. 1949, p. 12–21.

14027
MONTESQUIEU, CHARLES LOUIS DE SECONDAT, *baron* DE LA BRÈDE ET DE (1749–1824)
France. French officer in America.

——— Un petit-fils de Montesquieu, soldat de l'independance américaine (d'après des documents inédits) [1780–82] Revue historique de la révolution française et de l'empire, v. 5, Apr./June 1914: 233–263.
DC139.R5, v. 5

Introduction and notes by Octave Beuve.

——— Quelques lettres du baron de Montesquieu sur la guerre de l'indépendance américaine [1780–81] Franco-American review, v. 2, winter 1938: 192–204.
E183.8.F8F88, v. 2

Introduction and notes by Emmanuel de Lévis Mirepoix.

CÉLESTE, RAYMOND. Charles-Louis de Montesquieu à l'Armée (1772 à 1782). Revue philomathique de Bordeaux et du sud-ouest, v. 6, Nov. 1903: 504–524.
AP20.R63, v. 6

——— Un petit-fils de Montesquieu en Amérique (1780–1783). Revue philomathique de Bordeaux et du sud-ouest, v. 5, Dec. 1902: 529–556. port.
AP20.R63, V 5

——— ——— Offprint. Bordeaux, Impr. G. Gounouilhou, 1902. 30 p. port.
E265.C39

14028
MONTGOMERY, JANET LIVINGSTON (1743–1828)
New York. Wife of Richard Montgomery (1738–1775).

——— Reminiscences written by Janet Livingston, widow of General Richard Montgomery. With an introduction and editorial notes by John Ross Delafield. *In* Dutchess County Historical Society. Year book. v. 15; 1930. Poughkeepsie. p. 45–76.
F127.D8D93, v. 15

14029
MONTGOMERY, JOHN (1727–1808)
Ireland; Pennsylvania. Merchant, Revolutionary officer, assemblyman, delegate to the Continental Congress.

BELL, WHITFIELD J. The other man on Bingham's porch. *In* Dickinson College, *Carlisle, Pa.* "John and Mary's College." [Westwood N.J.] Revell [1956] (The Boyd Lee Spahr lectures in Americana, 1951–1956) p. 33–59.
LD1663.A53

On the efforts of Benjamin Rush and John Montgomery to establish Dickinson's College.

14030

MONTGOMERY, JOHN (1738?–1794)

Kentucky; Illinois. Hunter, Revolutionary officer, settler.

GOODPASTURE, ALBERT V. Colonel John Montgomery. Tennessee historical magazine, v. 5, Oct. 1919: 145–150. F431.T28, v. 5

MESE, WILLIAM A. Colonel John Montgomery, an "Irishman full of fight," commander-in-chief of the Virginia troops in the county of Illinois. Illinois Catholic historical review, v. 5, July 1922: 51–58.
BX1415.I3M5, v. 5

14031

MONTGOMERY, RICHARD (1738–1775)*†

Ireland; New York. British military officer, farmer, Revolutionary general.

CULLUM, GEORGE W. Major-General Richard Montgomery. Magazine of American history, with notes and queries, v. 11, Apr. 1884: 273–299. illus., maps.
E171.M18, v. 11

FAUCHER DE SAINT-MAURICE, NARCISSE H. E. Quelques notes sur le général Richard Montgomery. *In* Royal Society of Canada. Proceedings and transactions. v. 9, section 1; 1891. Montreal, 1892. p. 3–22.
AS42.R6, v. 9

Also published separately under the title *Notes pour servir à l'histoire du général Richard Montgomery* (Montréal, E. Senécal, imprimeurs, 1893. 97 p. E231.F25), with the addition of illustrative material.

[HUNT, LOUISE L.] Biographical notes concerning General Richard Montgomery, together with hitherto unpublished letters. [Poughkeepsie, "News" Book and Job Print. House] 1876. 31 p. E207.M7H9

Notes written by Mrs. Montgomery to be used for a memoir of her husband: p. 4–8.

Major General Richard Montgomery: a contribution toward a biography from the Clements Library. Ann Arbor [Published for the Clements Library Associates by] University of Michigan, 1970. 23 p. port.
E207.M7M3

Includes letters by Richard and Janet Montgomery (p. 12–23).

O'REILLY, VINCENT F. Major-General Richard Montgomery. *In* American Irish Historical Society. Journal. v. 25. New York, 1926. p. 179–194.
E184.I6A5, v. 25

ROBINSON, THOMAS P. Some notes on Major-General Richard Montgomery. *In* New York State Historical Association. New York history, v. 37, Oct. 1956: 388–398. F116.N865, v. 37

Mainly on his invasion of Canada and death at Quebec.

14032

MONTGOMERY, SAMUEL (*fl.* 1785)

Pennsylvania; Ohio. Indian agent.

——— A journey through the Indian country beyond the Ohio, 1785. Mississippi Valley historical review, v. 2, Sept. 1915: 261–273. E171.J87, v. 2

Journal of a government agent sent to negotiate a treaty with the Shawnee to supplement the Treaty of Fort McIntosh.

14033

MONTOUR, ANDREW (*d.* 1772)

Pennsylvania; New York; Virginia. Indian agent, interpreter.

LEWIN, HOWARD. A frontier diplomat: Andrew Montour. Pennsylvania history, v. 33, Apr. 1966: 153–186.
F146.P597, v. 33

14034

MONTRÉSOR, JOHN (1736–1799)*†

Gibraltar; England. British military engineer in America.

GOODRICH, FRANCIS L. D. John Montresor, 1736–1799, engineer and cartographer. Michigan alumnus quarterly review, v. 64, winter 1958: 124–129.
AP2.M53, v. 64

MONTRÉSOR, FRANK M. Captain John Montrésor in Canada. Canadian historical review, v. 5, Dec. 1924: 336–340. F1001.C27, v. 5

SCULL, GIDEON D., *ed.* The Montresor journals. [New York, Printed for the Society, 1882] xiv, 578 p. illus., maps (part fold.), ports. (New York Historical Society. Collections, 1881. Publication fund series, [v. 14])
F116.N63, 1881

Contents: Family of Montresor.—Journals of Col. James Montresor. 1757–1759.—Journals of Capt. John Montresor. 1757–1778.—Appendix.

WEBSTER, JOHN C. Life of John Montrésor. *In* Royal Society of Canada. Proceedings and transactions. 3d ser., v. 22, section 2; 1928. Ottawa, p. 1–31. maps.
AS42.R6, 3d s., v. 22

——— ——— Offprint. Ottawa, 1928. 31 p. maps.
E199.M81

The journal of Montresor's expedition to Detroit in 1763 in relief of Major Gladwin appears on p. 10–29.

14035

MOODY, JAMES (1744–1809)*

New Jersey; Nova Scotia. Farmer, Loyalist.

———— Lieut. James Moody's narrative of his exertions and sufferings in the cause of government, since the year 1776; authenticated by proper certificates. 2d ed. London, Printed by Richardson and Urquhart, 1783. 57, [7] p.   E278.M8M82 Rare Bk. Coll.

Reprinted in New York by the New York Times (1968). Also issued as v. 2, no. 1 (New York, 1866. E203.B97, v. 2) of Bushnell's *Crumbs for Antiquarians*.

SAUSSER, MALCOLM G.   An American Loyalist—Moody of New Jersey. Magazine of history, with notes and queries, v. 12, Sept.–Oct. 1910: 164–168, 220–230.   E171.M23, v. 12

14036
MOORE, ALFRED (1755–1810)*
North Carolina. Lawyer, Revolutionary officer, planter.

DAVIS, JUNIUS.   Alfred Moore and James Iredell, Revolutionary patriots, and Associate Justices of the Supreme Court of the United States. [Raleigh, Published by the Society] 1899. 37 p.   F258.M82

14037
MOORE, JAMES (1730–1802)
Pennsylvania. Lawyer, councilor, assemblyman, judge.

LONG, W. S.   Judge James Moore and Major James Moore, of Chester County, Pennsylvania. Pennsylvania magazine of history and biography, v. 12, Oct. 1888–Jan. 1889: 304–309, 465–474.   F146.P65, v. 12

14038
MOORE, JAMES (1756 *or* 7–1813)
Pennsylvania. Revolutionary officer.

NORRIS, G. HEIDE.   A history of Col. James Moore of the Revolutionary army, together with an account of his ancestors and descendants and the distribution of his estate. [Philadelphia, Times Print. House] 1893. 57 p.   E263.P4M8

14039
MOORE, JAMES (ca. 1770–1848)
Virginia. Frontiersman.

QUAIFE, MILO M.   Two captives of old Detroit. Burton historical collection leaflet, v. 5, May 1927: 65–80.   F561.B9, v. 5

14040
MOORE, JOHN (1745–*ca.* 1820)
New York. Merchant, Loyalist.

———— Memoirs of an American official in service of the King: posthumous manuscript of a Loyalist in America during the American Revolution. Journal of American history, v. 4, Jan./Mar. 1910: 29–47.   E171.J86, v. 4

14041
MOORE, PLINY (1759–1822)
Massachusetts; New York. Revolutionary officer, settler.

The first years of the Revolution. Letters to Pliny Moore, 1774–1776. Moorsfield antiquarian, v. 1, Nov. 1937: 163–178.   E171.M66, v. 1

Pliny Moore papers. [1]–4.   Champlain, Priv. print. at the Moorsfield Press, 1928–29. 4 v.   E302.6.M56P6

Contents: 1. Captain Job Wright's Company, Colonel Marinus Willett's levies at Ballston, New-York, 1782, edited by Hugh McLellan.—2. Judge Pliny Moore (1759–1822); obituary notice from the *Plattsburgh Republican* . . . with selections fron [sic] his papers and historical notes by Hugh McLellan.—3. A letter, Lieut. Moore to his father, Fort Rensselaer, March 23, 1783.—4. "Journal of drink," 1774 . . . with a foreword by Hugh McLellan.

14042
MOORE, STEPHEN (1734–1799)
New York; North Carolina. Merchant, Revolutionary officer.

MILLER, AGNES.   Owner of West Point. *In* New York State Historical Association. New York history, v. 33, July 1952: 303–312.   F116.N865, v. 33

14043
MORÉ DE PONTGIBAUD, CHARLES ALBERT DE (1758–1837)
France. Revolutionary officer.

———— A French volunteer of the War of Independence (the chevalier de Pontgibaud). Translated and edited by Robert B. Douglas. New York, J. W. Bouton, 1897. xi, 209 p. port.   E265.M827

A translation of *Mèmoires du comte de Moré* (Paris, 1827).

Reprinted in New York by B. Blom (1972).

DOLLOT, RENÉ.   A companion of La Fayette, Count de Moré, 1758–1837. Légion d'honneur magazine, v. 10, Apr. 1940: 463–468.   CR5061.U6A3, v. 10

14044
MOREY, ISRAEL (1735–1809)
New Hampshire. Settler, judge, Revolutionary officer.

WELLS, FREDERIC P.   Colonel Israel Morey. *In* New Hampshire Historical Society. Proceedings. v. 5, pt. 1; 1905/7. Concord, 1908. p. 59–72.   F31.N52, v. 5

Reprinted in *Granite Monthly*, v. 44, Feb. 1912, p. 53–60.

14045
MORGAN, DANIEL (1736?–1802)*
Virginia. Revolutionary general, planter.

CALLAHAN, NORTH. Daniel Morgan, ranger of the Revolution. New York, Holt, Rinehart and Winston [1961] x, 342 p. illus., maps, plates, ports.

E207.M8C3

"Bibliographical notes": p. 303–330.

EDWARDS, WILLIAM W. Morgan and his riflemen. William and Mary College historical quarterly magazine, v. 23, Oct. 1914: 73–106. illus., maps, plates.

F221.W71, v. 23

GRAHAM, JAMES. The life of General Daniel Morgan, of the Virginia Line of the Army of the United States, with portions of his correspondence. Comp. from authentic sources. New York, Derby & Jackson, 1856. 475 p. plates, port.

E207.M8G7

HEATHCOTE, CHARLES W. General Daniel Morgan's service for his country. Picket post, no. 41, July 1953: 4–8, 10. port.

E234.P5, no. 41

HIGGINBOTHAM, DON. Daniel Morgan: guerilla fighter. *In* Billias, George A., *ed.* George Washington's generals. New York, W. Morrow, 1964. p. 291–316. port.

E206.B5

Bibliography: p. 215–216.

———— Daniel Morgan, Revolutionary rifleman. Chapel Hill, Published for the Institute of Early American History and Culture at Williamsburg, Va., by the University of North Carolina Press [1961] xi, 239 p. illus., maps, port.

E207.M8H5

"Bibliographical essay": p. [217]–223.

The author's thesis (Ph.D.), *Daniel Morgan: Revolutionary Soldier*, was submitted to Duke University in 1959 (Micro AC–1, no. 63–870).

M'CONKEY, REBECCA. The hero of Cowpens; a Revolutionary sketch. Rev. ed. New York, Funk & Wagnalls, 1885. xiv, 295 p. maps, plan. (Standard library, no. 136)

E207.M8M13

First edition, 1881, published anonymously.

14046

MORGAN, GEORGE (1743–1810)*

Pennsylvania. Merchant, Indian trader and agent, Revolutionary officer, farmer.

———— Morgan's journey down the Mississippi in 1767. *In* International Geographic Congress, *8th, Washington, 1904.* Report. Washington, 1905. p. 952–955.

G56.I58, 1904

———— ———— Offprint. [Washington?1905] 952–955 p.

F352.M84

Introduction by James M. Morgan.

DOWNES, RANDOLPH C. George Morgan, Indian agent extraordinary, 1776–1779. Pennsylvania history, v. 1, Oct. 1934: 202–216.

F146.P597, v. 1

FEE, WALTER R. Colonel George Morgan at Fort Pitt. Western Pennsylvania historical magazine, v. 11, Oct. 1928: 217–224.

F146.W52, v. 11

Guide to the microfilm of the Baynton, Wharton, and Morgan papers in the Pennsylvania state archives manuscript group 19. Donald H. Kent, project director; Martha L. Simonetti, assistant project director; George R. Beyer, editor of microfilm. Harrisburg, Pennsylvania Historical and Museum Commission, 1967. 29 p.

HF3025.B38

SAVELLE, MAX. George Morgan, colony builder. New York, Columbia University Press, 1932. xiv, 266 p. facsim., fold geneal. table, map, plates, port.

E302.6.M6S3

Bibliography: p. [241]–250.

The author's thesis (Ph.D.), with the same title, was submitted to Columbia University in 1932.

14047

MORGAN, JOHN (1735–1789)*

Pennsylvania. Physician, professor, Revolutionary officer.

———— A discourse upon the institution of medical schools in America; delivered at a public anniversary commencement, held in the College of Philadelphia, May 30 and 31, 1765. With a preface containing, amongst other things, the author's apology for attempting to introduce the regular mode of practising physic in Philadelphia. Philadelphia, W. Bradford, 1765. vii, xxvi, 63 p.

R745.M7 Rare Bk. Coll.

Reprinted, with an introduction by Abraham Flexner, in Baltimore by the Johns Hopkins Press (1937) and in Philadelphia by the University of Pennsylvania Print. Off. (1965).

———— John Morgan's medical thesis, 'Pus Production', Edinburgh, 1763. Translated by Maria Wilkins Smith, with an historical introduction by Whitfield J. Bell, Jr. *In* College of Physicians of Philadelphia. Transactions & studies, 4th ser., v. 32, Jan. 1965: 123–147. facsim., port.

R15.P5, 4th s., v. 32

———— The journal of Dr. John Morgan of Philadelphia, from the city of Rome to the city of London, 1764, together with a fragment of a journal written at Rome, 1764, and a biographical sketch [by Julia Morgan Harding] Philadelphia, Printed for private circulation by J. B. Lippincott Co., 1907. 258 p. facsims., plates, ports.

DG424.M83

———— A recommendation of inoculation, according to Baron Dimsdale's method. Boston, Printed by J. Gill, in Queen-Street, 1776. 18 p.

RM786.M86 Rare Bk. Coll.

———— Two letters from John Morgan's Italian travels [1764] Isis, v. 54, Dec. 1963: 475–479. Q1.I7, v. 54

Introduction and notes by Antonio Pace.

———— A vindication of his public character in the station of director-general of the military hospitals, and physician in chief of the American Army; anno, 1776. Boston, Printed by Powars and Willis, 1777. lxiii (i.e. xliii), 158 p.

RD202.M8

BELL, WHITFIELD J. John Morgan. Bulletin of the history of medicine, v. 22, Sept./Oct. 1948: 543–561.
R11.B93, v. 22

——— John Morgan, Continental doctor. Philadelphia, University of Pennsylvania Press [1965] 301 p. illus., facsims., ports. R154.M74B4 1965

Bibliographical references included in "Notes" (p. 267–291).

——— John Morgan, founder of the medical school: adventures on the trail of his biography. General magazine and historical chronicle, v. 53, summer 1951: 213–223.
LH1.P3A4, v. 53

MIDDLETON, WILLIAM S. John Morgan, father of medical education in North America. Annals of medical history, v. 9, Mar. 1927: 13–26. facsims., port.
R11.A85, v. 9

PACE, ANTONIO. Notes on Dr. John Morgan and his relations with Italian men and women of science. Bulletin of the history of medicine, v. 18, Nov. 1945: 445–453. R11.B93, v. 18

ROGERS, FRED B. John Morgan's outlines of a general history of physic (1765). Medical history in 18th century academic medical teaching. Journal of the history of medicine and allied sciences, v. 14, Oct. 1959: 440–445. R131.A1J6, v. 14

WILBERT, MARTIN I. John Morgan, the founder of the first medical school and the originator of pharmacy in America. American journal of pharmacy, v. 76, Jan. 1904: 1–15. facsim., port. RS1.A45, v. 76

14048
MORGAN, LEWIS (1767–1821)
New Jersey. Physician, Loyalist surgeon.

FREEMAN, WALTER. Lewis Morgan, the notebooks of a Tory medical student. Annals of medical history, new ser., v. 2, Nov. 1930: 602–613. illus., port.
R11.A85, n.s., v. 2

14049
MORISON, DANIEL
Old Northwest. Surgeon's mate.

——— The doctor's secret journal [1769–72] Edited by George S. May. Mackinac Island [Mich.] Fort Mackinac Division Press, 1960. 47 p. illus., facsims. (on lining papers) F574.M17M6

14050
MORRIS, ASA (1740–ca. 1825)
New Jersey.

MORRIS, WILLIAM A. Asa Morris of Woodbridge, New Jersey. In New Jersey Historical Society. Proceedings, v. 59, Jan. 1941: 24–37. F131.N58, v. 59

14051
MORRIS, CADWALADER (1741–1795)*
Pennsylvania. Importer, Revolutionary soldier, banker, delegate to the Continental Congress.

——— Shipwrecked in the West Indies, 1764. Pennsylvania magazine of history and biography, v. 76, Jan. 1952: 30–38. F146.P65, v. 76

Introduction and notes by William W. Comfort.

14052
MORRIS, GOUVERNEUR (1752–1816)*
New York. Lawyer, delegate to the Continental Congress, diplomat, delegate to the Constitutional Convention.

——— The diary and letters of Gouverneur Morris, minister of the United States to France . . . etc. Edited by Anne Cary Morris. New York, C. Scribner's Sons, 1888. 2 v. ports. E302.6.M7M8 Rare Bk. Coll.

Reprinted in New York by Da Capo Press (1970).

KLINE, MARY-JO. Gouverneur Morris and the new Nation, 1775–1788. 1970. ([359] p.)
Micro AC–1, no. 71–6204

Thesis (Ph.D.)—Columbia University.
Abstracted in Dissertation Abstracts International, v. 31A, Mar. 1971, p. 4680.

LODGE, HENRY C. Gouverneur Morris. Atlantic monthly, v. 57, Apr. 1886: 433–448. AP2.A8, v. 57

MINTZ, MAX M. Gouverneur Morris and the American Revolution. Norman, University of Oklahoma Press [1970] xiii, 284 p. illus., ports. E302.6.M7M5

Bibliography: p. 241–262.
The author's thesis (Ph.D.), Gouverneur Morris, 1752–1779: The Emergence of a Nationalist, was submitted to New York University in 1957 (Micro AC–1, no. 60–513).

ROOSEVELT, THEODORE. Gouverneur Morris. Boston, Houghton, Mifflin, 1898. 341 p. facsim., ports. (American statesmen, v. 8) E302.6.M7R73
E176.A54, v. 8

First published in 1888.
Reprinted in St. Clair Shores, Mich., by Scholarly Press (1970) and in New Rochelle, N.Y., by Arlington House (1970).

SPARKS, JARED. The life of Gouverneur Morris, with selections from his correspondence and miscellaneous papers; detailing events in the American Revolution, the French Revolution, and in the political history of the United States. Boston, Gray & Bowen, 1832. 3 v. port. E302.6.M7S7

SWIGGETT, HOWARD. The extraordinary Mr. Morris. Garden City, N.Y., Doubleday, 1952. xix, 483 p. illus., facsims., ports. E302.6.M7S9

Bibliography: p. [463]–472.

WALTHER, DANIEL. Gouverneur Morris, witness of two revolutions. Translated by Elinore Denniston. New York, Funk & Wagnalls Co., 1934. xi, 314 p. plates, ports.   E302.6.M7W32

Bibliography: p. 295–314.

14053

MORRIS, JAMES (1752–1820)
Connecticut. Schoolmaster, Revolutionary officer.

———— Memoirs of a Connecticut patriot. Connecticut magazine, v. 11, autumn 1907: 449–455.
    F91.C8, v. 11

Contributed by Mrs. Washington Choate.

14054

MORRIS, LEWIS (1752–1824)
New York. Revolutionary officer.

———— Letters from Col. Lewis Morris to Miss Ann Elliott [1782–88] South Carolina historical and genealogical magazine, v. 40, Oct. 1939: 122–136; v. 41, Jan. 1940: 1–14.   F266.S55, v. 40–41

Contributed by Morris Rutherfurd.

———— Letters to General Lewis Morris [1775–82] In New York Historical Society. Collections. 1875. Publication fund series, [v. 8] New York, 1876. p. [431]–512.
    F116.N63, 1875

Of the 50 letters given here, most are from Lt. Col. Lewis Morris, Jr.

14055

MORRIS, MARGARET HILL (1737–1816)
New Jersey. Physician.

———— Margaret Morris, her journal. With biographical sketch and notes by John W. Jackson. Philadelphia, G. S. MacManus Co., 1949. 132 p. illus., ports.
    E263.N5M84

Bibliography: p. [115]–120.

———— Private journal, kept during a portion of the Revolutionary War, for the amusement of a sister. Philadelphia, Priv. print., 1836. 31 p.   E263.N5M8

Reprinted in New York by the New York Times (1969).

The journal extends from December 6, 1776, to June 14, 1777.

———— The Revolutionary journal of Margaret Morris, of Burlington, N.J., December 6, 1776, to June 11, 1778. In Friends' Historical Association. Bulletin, v. 9, May 1919–May 1920: 2–14, 65–75, 103–114.
    BX7635.A1F6, v. 9

14056

MORRIS, MARY PHILIPSE (1731?–1825)
New York; England. Landowner, Loyalist.

DESMOND, ALICE C. Mary Philipse, heiress. In New York State Historical Association. New York history, v. 28, Jan. 1947: 22–32.   F116.N865, v. 28

14057

MORRIS, MARY WHITE (1749–1827)
Maryland; Pennsylvania. Wife of Robert Morris (1734–1806).

HART, CHARLES H. Mary White—Mrs. Robert Morris. Pennsylvania magazine of history and biography, v. 2, no. 2, 1878: 157–184.   F146.P65, v. 2

14058

MORRIS, ROBERT (1734–1806)*
England; Pennsylvania. Financier, delegate to the Continental Congress, assemblyman, delegate to the Constitutional Convention.

———— The confidential correspondence of Robert Morris, the great financier of the Revolution and signer of the Declaration of Independence, embracing letters of the most vital historical importance from signers of the Declaration of Independence (many of them written in 1776), members of the Continental Congress, generals, commodores, other officers and patriots in the Revolution . . . to be sold Tuesday afternoon and evening, Jan. 16th, 1917. Phila[delphia] Pa., S. V. Henkels [1917?] xvi, 208 p. facsims.   Z999.H505, no. 1183
    Z1238.M87

———— Items from the Morris family collection of Robert Morris papers [1777–94] Pennsylvania magazine of history and biography, v. 70, Apr. 1946: 185–208.
    F146.P65, v. 70

Introduction and notes by Hubertis Cummings.

———— [Letters from Robert Morris to John Hancock, 1776] Philadelphia, 1845. [19] p. (Pennsylvania. Historical Society. Bulletin, v. 1, no. 4)   F146.P83, v. 1

———— Letters of Chief Justice Morris, 1777–79. In New Jersey Historical Society. Proceedings, new ser., v. 5, July 1920: 168–178.   F131.N58, n.s., v. 5

Describes the Battle of Monmouth and a Tory engagement near Shrewsbury.

BRANDON, J. CAMPBELL. In defense of Robert Morris. Picket post, no. 52, May 1956: 4–7, 37–41. port.
    E234.P5, no. 52

COOK, FRANK G. Robert Morris. Atlantic monthly, v. 66, Nov. 1890: 607–618.   AP2.A8, v. 66

CUMMINGS, HUBERTIS M. Robert Morris and the episode of the polacre Victorious [1779] Pennsylvania magazine of history and biography, v. 70, July 1946: 239–257.
    F146.P65, v. 70

The circumstances surrounding the purchase and resale of the ship's cargo to Continental agents left Morris open to the charge of making personal profit at public expense.

DOS PASSOS, JOHN R. Robert Morris and the "art magick." American heritage, v. 7, Oct. 1956: 86–89, 113–115. illus., port. E171.A43, v. 7

On his financial manipulations.

GOULD, DAVID. Life of Robert Morris, an eminent merchant of Philadelphia, a signer of the Declaration of American Independence, and Superintendent of Finance for the United States, from 1781 to 1784. With extracts from his speeches, illustrating his biography, and the early history of finance, banking, and commerce in the United States. Boston, L. W. Kimball, 1834. 126 p. E302.6.M8G6

HART, ARMINE N. Robert Morris. Pennsylvania magazine of history and biography, v. 1, no. 3, 1877: 333–343. F146.P65, v. 1

HEIGES, GEORGE L. Robert Morris in Manheim. In Lancaster County (Pa.) Historical Society. Papers, v. 34, June 1930: 121–134. illus., port. F157.L2L5, v. 34

Letters to Robert Morris, 1775–1782. In New York Historical Society. Collections. 1878. Publication fund series, [v. 11] New York, 1879. p. 397–488. F116.N63, 1878

A series of letters addressed to Morris by John Jay, Benjamin Harrison, John Hancock, Thomas Paine, and others.

OBERHOLTZER, ELLIS P. Robert Morris, patriot and financier. New York, Macmillan Co., 1903. xi, 372 p. facsim., plates, ports. E302.6.M8O12

Bibliography: p. 359–361.
Reprinted in New York by B. Franklin (1968).

SUMNER, WILLIAM G. Robert Morris. New York, Dodd, Mead, 1892. 172 p. port. ("Makers of America") E302.6.M8S9

VER STEEG, CLARENCE L. Robert Morris: Revolutionary financier. With an analysis of his earlier career. Philadelphia, University of Pennsylvania Press, 1954. 276 p. E302.6.M8V4 1954

Bibliography: p. [255]–269.
Reprinted in New York by Octagon Books (1954).
The author's thesis (Ph.D.), Robert Morris, Revolutionary Financier, With Some Account of His Earlier Career, was submitted to Columbia University in 1950 (Micro AC-1, no. 2559).

VIVIAN, JAMES F. A note on the Maryland land holdings of Robert Morris. Maryland historical magazine, v. 61, Dec. 1966: 348–353. F176.M18, v. 61

YOUNG, ELEANOR M. Forgotten patriot: Robert Morris. New York, Macmillan, 1950. xii, 280 p. ports. E302.6.M8Y6

Bibliography: p. 268–271.

14059
MORRIS, THOMAS (b. 1732?)
Old Northwest. British officer.

———— Journal of Captain Thomas Morris of His Majesty's 17th Regiment of Infantry; Detroit, September 25, 1764. Reprint from the author's Miscellanies in Prose and Verse (London, 1791), p. 1–39. In Thwaites, Reuben G., ed. Early western travels, 1748–1846, a series of annotated reprints. v. 1. Cleveland, A. H. Clark Co., 1904. p. [293]–328. F592.T54, v. 1

Also reprinted in Tarrytown, N.Y., by W. Abbatt (1922. 5–29 p. E173.M24, no. 76) as extra number, no. 76, of The Magazine of History, With Notes and Queries. University Microfilms has recently published a facsimile reproduction of the original (Ann Arbor [Mich.] 1966. 39 p. E83.76.M6 1791a).

VAN SCHAACK, HENRY C. Captain Thomas Morris in the country of the Illinois. Magazine of American history, with notes and queries, v. 8, July 1882: 470–479. E171.M18, v. 8

14060
MORRIS, VALENTINE (1727–1789)
West Indies; Wales. Planter, governor.

———— A narrative of the official conduct of Valentine Morris, late captain general, governor in chief &c. &c. of the island of St. Vincent and its dependencies. London, Printed by J. Walter and sold by S. Hooper, 1787. xvii, 467 p. F2106.M87

WATERS, IVOR. The unfortunate Valentine Morris. Chepstow [Wales] Chepstow Society [1964] xii, 96 p. maps, plates, port. F2106.W3

Bibliography: p. 87–90.

14061
MORSE, JEDIDIAH (1761–1826)*
Connecticut. Congregational clergyman, geographer, textbook writer.

———— Geography made easy. Being a short, but comprehensive system of that very useful and agreeable science. New Haven, Meigs, Bowen & Dana, 1784. 214 p. G125.M85 1784 Rare Bk. Coll.

———— Letters of a young geographer [1782–86] New England quarterly, v. 14, Dec. 1941: 696–704. F1.N62, v. 14

Submitted by Leonard Twinem.

MORSE, JAMES K. Jedidiah Morse, a champion of New England orthodoxy. New York, Columbia University Press, 1939. ix, 179 p. (Columbia studies in American culture, no. 2) BX7260.M57M37 1939

Issued also as thesis (Ph.D.) Columbia University. Bibliography: p. 163–[172]

SPRAGUE, WILLIAM B. The life of Jedidiah Morse, D.D. New York, A. D. F. Randolph [1874] viii, 333 p. port. BX7260.M57S7

14062

MORTON, SARAH WENTWORTH APTHORP (1759–1846)*

Massachusetts. Poet.

PENDLETON, EMILY, *and* HAROLD MILTON ELLIS. Philenia; the life and works of Sarah Wentworth Morton, 1759–1846. Orono, Me., Printed at the University Press, 1931. 122 p. plates, ports. (University of Maine studies. Second ser., no. 20) PS808.M7Z8 1931
Bibliography: p. [113]–115.

14063

MOSLEY, JOSEPH (1731–1787)

England; Maryland. Roman Catholic priest.

———— Letters of Father Joseph Mosley, S.J., and some extracts from his diary (1757–1786). Compiled with notes by Edward I. Devitt. *In* American Catholic Historical Society of Philadelphia. Records, v. 17, June–Sept. 1906: 180–210, 289–311. E184.C3A4, v. 17

14064

MOSS, WILLIAM (*fl.* 1772–1787)

England; Georgia. Merchant.

ROBERTS, WILLIAM I. The losses of a Loyalist merchant in Georgia during the Revolution. Georgia historical quarterly, v. 52, Sept. 1968: 270–276.
F281.G2975, v. 52

14065

MOULTRIE, JOHN (1729–1798)*

South Carolina; East Florida. Physician. Brother of William Moultrie (1730–1805).

TOWNSHEND, ELEANOR W. John Moultrie, Junior, M.D., 1729–1798, royal lieutenant-governor of East Florida [1764–74] Annals of medical history, 3d ser., v. 2, Mar. 1940: 98–109. facsims., port.
R11.A85, 3d s., v. 2

14066

MOULTRIE, WILLIAM (1730–1805)*

South Carolina. Planter, assemblyman, Revolutionary general, governor.

———— The correspondence of Lord Montague with General Moultrie. 1781. [New-York, Press of T. L. De Vinne, 1885] 19 p. port. E207.M85M8
Originally published in Moultrie's *Memoirs*; also published in the historical appendix of the Charleston *Year Book* for 1884.

———— The journal of William Moultrie while a commissioner on the North and South Carolina boundary survey, 1772. Edited by Charles S. Davis. Journal of southern history, v. 8, Nov. 1942: 549–555.
F206.J68, v. 8

14067

MOWAT, HENRY (1734–1798)

Scotland. British naval officer in America.

BAXTER, JAMES P. A lost manuscript. *In* Maine Historical Society. Collections and proceedings. 2d ser., v. 2. Portland, 1891. p. 345–375. F16.M33, 2d ser., v. 2
Discusses "A Relation of the Services in Which Captain Henry Mowat of the Royal Navy was Engaged in America, From 1759 to the end of the American War in 1783," which appears on p. 356–375.

14068

MOYLAN, STEPHEN (1737–1811)*

Ireland; Pennsylvania. Merchant, Revolutionary general.

GRIFFIN, MARTIN I. J. Stephen Moylan, muster-master general, secretary and aide-de-camp to Washington, quartermaster-general, colonel of Fourth Pennsylvania Light Dragoons and brigadier-general of the War for American Independence, the first and the last president of the Friendly Sons of St. Patrick of Philadelphia. Philadelphia, 1909. 142 p. col. front. E207.M9G8

HEATHCOTE, CHARLES W. General Stephen Moylan—a trusted officer of the Revolution. Picket post, no. 51, Feb. 1956: 23–28. E234.P5, no. 51

MONAGHAN, FRANK. Stephen Moylan in the American Revolution. Studies, v. 19, Sept. 1930: 481–486.
AP4.S78, v. 19

Selections from the correspondence of Col. Stephen Moylan, of the Continental cavalry [1776–97] Pennsylvania magazine of history and biography, v. 37, July 1913: 341–360. F146.P65, v. 37

14069

MUHLENBERG, FREDERICK AUGUSTUS CONRAD (1750–1801)*

Pennsylvania. Lutheran clergyman, assemblyman.

———— Diary of F. A. Muhlenberg. From the day of his ordination, October 25, 1770, until August, 1774. Translated by Rev. J. W. Early. Lutheran church review, v. 24, Jan.–Oct. 1905: 127–137, 388–390, 562–571, 682–694; v. 25, Jan.–Apr. 1906: 134–147, 345–356.
BX8001.L2, v. 24–25
The diary extends only to August 8, 1773.

———— F. A. C. Muhlenberg's report of his first trip to Shamokin [Port Trevorton and Selinsgrove, Pa., 1771], sent to his father. Lutheran church review, v. 25, July 1906: 535–544. BX8001.L2, v. 25

———— The journal of Frederick A. C. Mulenberg on his trip to the Shamokin region in 1771. Edited by Charles F. Snyder. *In* Northumberland County (Pa.) Historical Society. Proceedings. v. 9. Sunbury, 1937. p. 208–226. plate. F157.N8N7, v. 9

RICHARDS, HENRY M. M. Frederick Augustus Conrad Muhlenberg. Pennsylvania-German, v. 3, Apr. 1902: 51–60. illus. F146.P224, v. 3

14070

MUHLENBERG, HENRY MELCHIOR (1711–1787)*

Germany; Pennsylvania. Lutheran clergyman. Father of Frederick Augustus Conrad Muhlenberg (1750–1801) and John Peter Gabriel Muhlenberg (1746–1807).

———— Henry Muhlenberg's Georgia correspondence [1777–84] Georgia historical quarterly, v. 49, Dec. 1965: 424–455. F281.G2975, v. 49

Introduction and notes by Andrew W. Lewis.

———— The journals of Henry Melchior Muhlenberg. Translated by Theodore G. Tappert and John W. Doberstein. Philadelphia, Evangelical Lutheran Ministerium of Pennsylvania and Adjacent States, 1942–58. 3 v. port. BX8080.M9A4

Tappert and Doberstein also edited *The Notebook of a Colonial Clergyman, Condensed from the Journals of Henry Melchior Muhlenberg* (Philadelphia, Muhlenberg Press, 1959. 250 p. BX8080.M9A43).

FRICK, WILLIAM K. Henry Melchior Muhlenberg, "patriarch of the Lutheran Church in America." Philadelphia, Lutheran Publication Society [1902] 200 p. port. (Lutheran handbook series) BX8080.M9F8

HOOVER, MARGARET H. The Trappe neighbors of Henry Melchior Muhlenberg as mentioned in his *Journals*, vol. III, 1777–1787. *In* Historical Society of Montgomery County (*Pennsylvania*). Bulletin, v. 16, fall 1968: 139–160. F157.M7H45, v. 16

MANN, WILLIAM J. The conservatism of Henry Melchior Mühlenberg. Lutheran church review, v. 7, Jan. 1888: 18–46. BX8001.L2, v. 7

———— Life and times of Henry Melchior Mühlenberg. Philadelphia, G. W. Frederick, 1887. xvi, 547 p. port. BX8080.M9M3

RIFORGIATO, LEONARD R. Missionary of moderation: Henry Melchior Muhlenberg and the Lutheran Church in English America. 1971. ([276] p.) Micro AC–1, no. 72–19,368

Thesis (Ph.D.)—Pennsylvania State University.
Abstracted in *Dissertation Abstracts International*, v. 33A, Sept. 1972, p. 1126.

TAPPERT, THEODORE G. Henry Melchior Muhlenberg and the American Revolution. Church history, v. 11, Dec. 1942: 284–301. BR140.A45, v. 11

WALLACE, PAUL A. W. The Muhlenbergs and the Revolutionary underground [1777–78] *In* American Philosophical Society, *Philadelphia*. Proceedings, v. 93, May 1949: 119–126. Q11.P5, v. 93

Also published in the Society's *Library Bulletin* for 1949, p. 119–126.

———— The Muhlenbergs of Pennsylvania. Philadelphia, University of Pennsylvania Press, 1950. ix, 358 p. illus., ports. CS71.M95 1950

Bibliographic references included in "Notes" (p. 321–342).
Reprinted in Freeport, N.Y., by Books for Libraries Press (1970).

14071

MUHLENBERG, JOHN PETER GABRIEL (1746–1807)*

Pennsylvania. Clergyman, assemblyman, Revolutionary general.

————Journal of Rev. Peter Muhlenberg, in London, 1772. Lutheran church review, v. 4, Oct. 1885: 294–300. BX8001.L2, v. 4

Introduction by Jacob Fry.

Gen. John Peter G. Muhlenberg. Pennsylvania-German, v. 3, Jan. 1902: 3–18. illus. F146.P224, v. 3

GERMANN, WILHELM. The crisis in the early life of General Peter Mühlenberg. Pennsylvania magazine of history and biography, v. 37, July–Oct. 1913: 298–329, 450–470. F146.P65, v. 37

HEATHCOTE, CHARLES W. General John Peter Gabriel Muhlenberg. Picket post, no. 42, Oct. 1953: 4–10. port. E234.P5, no. 42

HOCKER, EDWARD W. The fighting parson of the American Revolution; a biography of General Peter Muhlenberg, Lutheran clergyman, military chieftain, and political leader. Philadelphia, Pa., Published by the author, 1936. 191 p. plates, port. E207.M96H6

"Authorities": p. [184]–186.

MUHLENBERG, HENRY A. The life of Major-General Peter Muhlenberg, of the Revolutionary army. Philadelphia, Carey and Hart, 1849. xii, 456 p. port. E207.M96M9

RIGHTMYER, THOMAS N. The holy orders of Peter Muhlenberg. Historical magazine of the Protestant Episcopal church, v. 30, Sept. 1961: 183–197. BX5800.H5, v. 30

14072

MULLIGAN, HERCULES (1740–1825)

Ireland; New York. Merchant, intelligence agent.

O'BRIEN, MICHAEL J. Hercules Mulligan, confidential correspondent of General Washington. New York, P. J. Kenedy [ᶜ1937] 190 p. facsims. E302.6.M8803

14073

MUNFORD, ROBERT (*ca.* 1737–1783)*

Virginia. Planter, assemblyman, Revolutionary officer, poet, dramatist.

———— A collection of plays and poems, by the late Col. Robert Munford, of Mecklenburg County in the state of Virginia. Now first published together. Petersburg, Printed by W. Prentis, 1798. 206 (i.e. 188) p.

PS808.M75 1798 Rare Bk. Coll.

Preface by the author's son, William Munford.

Contents: The candidates; or, The humours of a Virginia election.—The patriots.—The book of Ovid's Metamorphoses, translated.—Miscellaneous poems, consisting of: The ram, a comic poem; Letters from the Devil to his son; Answer to "The winter piece"; Colin and Celia, a pastoral poem; A dream; and A patriotic song.

BAINE, RODNEY M. Robert Munford; America's first comic dramatist. Athens, University of Georgia Press [1967] ix, 132 p. PS808.M75Z57

Bibliography: p. 115–123.

CANBY, COURTLAND. Robert Munford's *The Patriots*. William and Mary quarterly, 3d ser., v. 6, July 1949: 437–447. F221.W71, 3d s., v. 6

Munford's play focuses upon the economic and social tensions that developed among contending segments of Virginia society—Whig planters, lesser gentry, Loyalists, Scotch merchants, local military leaders—during the early years of the war. The text of *The Patriots, a Comedy in Five Acts* appears on p. 448–503.

HUBBELL, JAY B., *and* DOUGLASS G. ADAIR. Robert Munford's *The Candidates*. William and Mary quarterly, 3d ser., v. 5, Apr. 1948: 217–225.

F221.W71, 3d s., v. 5

An analysis of Virginia political culture in 1770 as seen in the pages of Munford's play. The text of the comedy, *The Candidates: or, The Humours of a Virginia Election*, follows, on p. 227–257.

14074

MURPHY, TIMOTHY (1751–1818)

New Jersey; Pennsylvania. Revolutionary soldier and rifleman.

MOWERY, DANIEL F. Timothy Murphy. *In* Northumberland County (Pa.) Historical Society. Proceedings. v. 9. Sunbury, 1937. p. 83–91. F157.N8N7, v. 9

O'BRIEN, MICHAEL J. Timothy Murphy, hero of the American Revolution. New York, Eire Pub. Co. [c1941] vi, 216 p. plates, port. E275.M94

Bibliography: p. 210–212.

[SIGSBY,   ] Life and adventures of Timothy Murphy, the benefactor of Schoharie, including his history from the commencement of the Revolution, his recontres with the Indians. Schoharie C[ourt] H[ouse] N.Y., Printed by W. H. Gallup, 1839. 32 p.

E275.M97 1839 Rare Bk. Coll.

Reprinted in Tarrytown, N.Y., by W. Abbatt (1926. [3]–32 p. E173.M24, no. 118) as extra number, no. 118, of *The Magazine of History, With Notes and Queries*.

14075

MURRAY, JAMES (1713–1781)

Scotland; North Carolina; Massachusetts; Nova Scotia. Planter, councilor, merchant, Loyalist.

———— Letters of James Murray, Loyalist. Edited by Nina Moore Tiffany, assisted by Susan I. Lesley. Boston, Printed; not published, 1901. ix, 324 p. facsims., plates, ports. E278.M98M9

Reprinted, with a new introduction and preface by George A. Billias, in Boston by Gregg Press (1972 E278.M98A4 1972).

STUART, CHARLES. Charles Stuart and James Murray letters, 1766–1772. *In* Massachusetts Historical Society, *Boston*. Proceedings. v. 43; 1909/10. Boston, 1910. p. 449–458. F61.M38, v. 43

Notes by Worthington C. Ford.

14076

MURRAY, JAMES (*ca.* 1721–1794)†

Scotland; Canada; Minorca. British military officer, governor.

———— [Calendar of the] correspondence of General James Murray, 1759–1791. *In* Canada. *Public Archives*. Report. 1912. Ottawa, 1913. p. 84–123.

F1001.C13, 1912

———— *defendant*. The sentence of the court-martial . . . for the trial of the Hon. Lieut. Gen. James Murray, late governor of Minorca, on the twenty-nine articles exhibited against him by Sir William Draper. With His Majesty's order thereon. To which are added, the whole of the evidence on the two articles of which the general was found guilty; and likewise upon the four articles of complaint of personal wrong and grievance. Taken in short-hand by Joseph Gurney. With an appendix, containing Gen. Murray's defence . . . all the correspondence between Gen. Murray and Sir William Draper,—the several councils of war,—and the subsequent proceedings of the court-martial relative to the private dispute between Gen. Murray and Sir William Draper. London, Sold by M. Gurney, 1783. 100 p.

DA67.1.M8A3

MAHON, REGINALD H. Life of General the Hon. James Murray, a builder of Canada. London, J. Murray, 1921. ix, 457 p. facsim., maps, plates, port.

F1030.9.M93

14077

MURRAY, JAMES (1732–1782)†

Scotland; England. Clergyman.

———— Sermons to asses. [n.p.] 1768. 135 p.

BX5202.M83 1768 Rare Bk. Coll.

A satirical work dedicated to "the very excellent and reverend Mess. G**rg* Wh*tf**ld, J*hn W*sl*y, W*ll**m R*m**n & M. M*dd*n" (i.e., George Whitfield, John Wesley, William Romain, and Martin Madan).

First American edition? Manuscript note on title page: "Mein & Fleming, Boston."

—— Sermons to ministers of state. By the author of, *Sermons to Asses*. Dedicated to Lord North, prime minister of England, for the use of the religious, political, and philosophical rationalists, in Europe and America. Philadelphia, Printed and sold by R. Bell, in Third Street, 1783. 79 p.

> BX5202.M85 1783 Rare Bk. Coll.
> AC901.D8, v. 15 Rare Bk. Coll.

Dedication signed: James Murray, New-Castle, upon Tyne, October 19th, 1781.

Ten "Sermons," followed (p. [76]–79) by the "laughable composition, which hath been handed about in manuscript at Philadelphia" . . . reported to be written by the Rev. J.W.-th-sp-n, D.D., one of the members of the American Congress: The humble confession, declaration, recantation and apology of Benjamin Towne, printer in Philadelphia."

14078

MURRAY, JOHN (1720–1794)

Ireland; Massachusetts; England. Landowner, assemblyman, military officer, Loyalist, councilor.

COFFIN, EDWARD P.   Some historical notes about "Tory" John Murray and his family. *In* Worcester Historical Society, *Worcester, Mass.* Publications. new ser., v. 2, no. 5; 1940. Worcester. p. 233–246.

> F74.W9W858, n.s., v. 2

POTTER, BURTON W.   Col. John Murray and his family. *In* Worcester Historical Society, *Worcester, Mass.* Proceedings, v. 24, no. 1, 1908: 15–34.

> F74.W9W85, v. 24

14079

MURRAY, JOHN (1742–1793)

Ireland; Pennsylvania; Maine. Presbyterian clergyman.

VERMILYE, ASHBEL G.   Memoir of the Rev. John Murray, first minister of the church in Boothbay. *In* Maine Historical Society. Collections. v. 6. Portland, 1859. p. 153–170.   F16.M33, v. 6

14080

MURRAY, WILLIAM (*fl.* 1764–1786)

Illinois. Indian trader.

MARKS, ANNA E.   William Murray, trader and land speculator in the Illinois country. *In* Illinois State Historical Society. Transactions; 1919. Springfield, 1920. (Illinois State Historical Library. Publication, no. 26) p. 188–212.   F536.I34, 1919

14081

MURRAY-PULTENEY, *Sir* JAMES, *Bart.* (*ca.* 1751–1811)†

England; Scotland. British officer in America.

—— Letters from America, 1773 to 1780; being the letters of a Scots officer, Sir James Murray, to his home during the War of American Independence. Edited by Eric Robson. New York, Barnes & Noble [1953] xxvi, 90 p. illus.   E203.M8 1953

Bibliography: p. 77–85.

14082

MYERS, MYER (1723–1795)

New York. Goldsmith.

ROSENBAUM, JEANETTE W.   Myer Myers, goldsmith, 1723–1795. Philadelphia, Jewish Publication Society of America, 1954. 141 p. illus., facsims., map, plates, port. (The Jacob R. Schiff library of Jewish contributions to American democracy)   NK7198.M9R6

Contents: Foreword, by S. G. C. Ensko.—Craftsman and patriot.—Contemporary newspaper notices concerning Myer Myers.—Colonial court records, by H. A. Fogel, Esq.—Genealogy.—Technical notes, by K. C. Buhler.—Bibliography (p. 139–141).

14083

NAPIER, *Lady* SARAH LENNOX (1745–1826)

England.

—— The life and letters of Lady Sarah Lennox, 1745–1826, daughter of Charles, 2nd duke of Richmond, and successively the wife of Sir Thomas Charles Bunbury, Bart., and of the Hon: George Napier; also a short political sketch of the years 1760 to 1763, by Henry Fox, 1st lord Holland. Edited by the Countess of Ilchester and Lord Stavordale. London, J. Murray, 1901. 2 v. plates, ports.   DA506.N2A2

Partial contents: 1. Introduction. Lord Holland's memoir. Mr. Henry Napier's memoir. Letters of Lady Sarah Lennox.—2. Letters of Lady Sarah Lennox.

CURTIS, EDITH R.   Lady Sarah Lennox, an irrepressible Stuart, 1745–1826. New York, G. P. Putnam's Sons [1946] viii, 346 p.   DA506.N2C8

Bibliography: p. 336–340.

14084

NASH, FRANCIS (*ca.* 1742–1777)*

Virginia; North Carolina. Merchant, assemblyman, judge, Revolutionary general.

REED, JOHN F.   Tragic sword: a biography of Brigadier General Francis Nash of North Carolina, 1742–1777. *In* Historical Society of Montgomery County (*Pennsylvania*). Bulletin, v. 18, fall 1972: 227–297. maps.   F157.M7H45, v. 18

WADDELL, ALFRED M.   Gen. Francis Nash. Greensboro, N.C., Guilford Battle Ground Co. [1906] 19 p.   E207.N2W2

Later reprinted in the *North Carolina Booklet*, v. 14, Oct. 1914, p. 74–90.

WILLIAMS, SAMUEL C. Generals Francis Nash and William Lee Davidson. Tennessee historical quarterly, v. 1, Sept. 1942: 250–268.   F431.T285, v. 1

14085

NEALE, SAMUEL (1729–1792)

Ireland. Quaker minister.

―――― Some account of the life and religious labours of Samuel Neale, who died at Cork, in Ireland, in the year 1792. Written by himself; together with letters addressed to his friends. *In* Friends' library. v. 11. Philadelphia, 1847. p. 1–72.   BX7615.F8, v. 11

Neale traveled throughout the American colonies in 1771–72.

14086

NEIL, DANIEL (*d.* 1777)

New Jersey. Revolutionary officer.

HOPSON, EDWIN N. Captain Daniel Neil (a short biography). [Paterson, N.J., Braen-Heusser Print. Co.] 1927. 29 p. illus. (Captain Abraham Godwin Chapter, New Jersey Society, Sons of the American Revolution. Monograph no. 1)   E302.6.N4H8

14087

NEILSON, JOHN (1745–1833)*

New Jersey. Merchant, Revolutionary officer.

THOMPSON, ROBERT T. Colonel Neilson, salt merchant. *In* Rutgers University, *New Brunswick, N.J. Library.* Journal, v. 1, Dec. 1937: 11–16. port.   Z733.R955F, v. 1

14088

NEISSER, GEORG (1715–1784)

Europe; Pennsylvania. Moravian clergyman.

―――― Incidents in the history of York, Pennsylvania, 1778, extracted from the diary of Rev. George Neisser, Moravian minister. Pennsylvania magazine of history and biography, v. 16, Jan. 1893: 433–438.
F146.P65, v. 16

―――― Items of history of York, Penna., during the Revolution [1775–82] Pennsylvania magazine of history and biography, v. 44, Oct. 1920: 309–324.
F146.P65, v. 44

14089

NELSON, THOMAS (1738–1789)*

Virginia. Councilor, planter, assemblyman, delegate to the Continental Congress, Revolutionary general, governor.

EVANS, EMORY G. The Nelsons: a biographical study of a Virginia family in the eighteenth century. 1957. ([393] p.)   Micro AC–1, no. 22,891

Thesis (Ph.D.)—University of Virginia. Abstracted in *Dissertation Abstracts*, v. 17, no. 11, 1957, p. 2385.

―――― The rise and decline of the Virginia aristocracy in the eighteenth century: the Nelsons. *In* Rutman, Darrett B., *ed.* The Old Dominion; essays for Thomas Perkins Abernethy. Charlottesville, University Press of Virginia [1964] p. 62–78.   F226.R8

GAINES, WILLIAM H. Thomas Nelson, Jr.—governor-at-arms. Virginia cavalcade, v. 1, autumn 1951: 40–43. illus., facsim., ports.   F221.V74, v. 1

14090

NESBITT, SAMUEL (*ca.* 1746–1811)

England; Connecticut. Physician, Episcopal clergyman.

STOOKEY, BYRON P. Samuel Nesbitt, M.D., a founder of the Medical Society of New Haven County. Bulletin of the history of medicine, v. 40, May/June 1966: 264–276.   R11.B93, v. 40

14091

NEVILLE, PRESLEY (1755–1818)

Virginia; Pennsylvania. Revolutionary officer, settler.

HOGG, J. BERNARD. Presley Neville. Western Pennsylvania historical magazine, v. 19, Mar. 1936: 17–26.
F146.W52, v. 19

14092

NEWELL, THOMAS (*b.* 1749)

Massachusetts.

―――― Diary for 1773 to the end of 1774, of Mr. Thomas Newell, Boston. *In* Massachusetts Historical Society, *Boston.* Proceedings. v. 15; 1876/77. Boston, 1878. p. 335–363.   F61.M38, v. 15

Extracts relating to the Boston Tea Party appeared earlier in v. 4, the *Proceedings* for 1858/60 (Boston, 1860), p. 216–224.

14093

NICHOLAS, JOHN (1756?–1819)*

Virginia. Lawyer, Revolutionary officer, assemblyman.

―――― The statement and substance of a memorial, &c., of John Nicholas; presented to the Virginia legislature, 1819–20. Richmond, Printed by J. Warrock, 1820. 30 p.   E275.N59 Rare Bk. Coll.

A narrative of the author's military service during the Revolutionary War.

14094

NICHOLAS, SAMUEL (1744–1790)

Pennsylvania. Innkeeper, Revolutionary marine officer.

FAGAN, LOUIS E. Samuel Nicholas, first officer of American marines. Marine Corps gazette, v. 18, Nov. 1933: 5–15. illus. VE7.M4, v. 18

STEVENS, HAROLD R. Samuel Nicholas, innkeeper-Marine. Marine Corps gazette, v. 37, Nov. 1953: 12–15. illus. VE7.M4, v. 37

14095

NICHOLLS, JOHN (1745?–1832)

——— Recollections and reflections, personal and political, as connected with public affairs, during the reign of George III. London, Printed for Longman, Hurst, Rees, Orme, and Brown, 1822. 2 v. DA506.N61

Vol. 1: second edition.

14096

NICHOLS, JOSEPH (ca. 1730–1770)

Delaware; Maryland. Religious sect leader.

CARROLL, KENNETH L. The influence of John Woolman on Joseph Nichols and the Nicholites. In Brinton, Anna C., ed. Then and now; Quaker essays, historical and contemporary, by friends of Henry Joel Cadbury. Philadelphia, University of Pennsylvania Press [1960] p. 168–179. BX7615.B7

——— Joseph Nichols and the Nicholites; a look at the "New Quakers" of Maryland, Delaware, North and South Carolina. Easton, Md., Easton Pub. Co. [1962] 116 p. BX7775.N5C3

"Selected bibliography": p. 101–104.

——— Joseph Nichols of Delaware: an eighteenth century religious leader. Delaware history, v. 7, Mar. 1956: 37–48. F161.D37, v. 7

14097

NICHOLSON, JOHN (1757–1800)*

Wales; Pennsylvania. Financier.

——— Address to the people of Pennsylvania; containing a narrative of the proceedings against John Nicholson, comptroller-general of the said commonwealth. Philadelphia, Printed by F. Bailey, 1790. 67 p. HJ669.N4 Rare Bk. Coll.

ARBUCKLE, ROBERT D. John Nicholson, 1757–1800, a case study of an early American land speculator, financier and entrepreneur. 1972. ([591] p.) Micro AC–1, no. 72–33,146

Thesis (Ph.D)—Pennsylvania State University.

Abstracted in Dissertation Abstracts International, v. 33A, Jan. 1973, p. 3506.

Guide to the microfilm of the John Nicholson papers in the Pennsylvania state archives (manuscript group 96). Donald H. Kent, project director; Martha L. Simonetti, assistant project director; George R. Beyer, editor of microfilm. Harrisburg, Pennsylvania Historical and Museum Commission, 1967. v, 52 p. Z6616.N58K43

[HOGAN, EDMUND] ed. The Pennsylvania state trials: containing the impeachment, trial, and acquittal of Francis Hopkinson, and John Nicholson, esquires. The former being judge of the Court of Admiralty, and the latter, the comptroller-general of the commonwealth of Pennsylvania. v. 1. Philadelphia, Printed by Bailey, at Yorick's Head, no. 116, High-Street, for Edmund Hogan, 1794. xii, 776 p. JK3682.H6 Rare Bk. Coll.

No more published.

14098

NICHOLSON, THOMAS (1715–1780)

North Carolina. Quaker minister.

——— The journal of Thomas Nicholson. A journal of part of the life, travails and labours of that faithful servant, and minister of the gospel, Thomas Nicholson. In Southern Historical Association. Publications, v. 4, May–Sept. 1900: 172–186, 233–247, 301–315. F206.S73, v. 4

"The journal is not a complete record of the life of the author. Its historical parts are those relating to the trip to Cape Fear in 1746, the visit to England in 1749–51, and the visit to the North Carolina Assembly in 1771. These are presented herewith in their entirety."—Introduction.

14099

NILES, ELISHA (1764–1845)

Connecticut. Revolutionary soldier, schoolmaster, farmer.

——— Living and working in central Connecticut, 1764–1845. The journal of Elisha Niles. In Connecticut Historical Society, Hartford. Bulletin, v. 35, Oct. 1970: 114–121. F91.C67, v. 35

Introduction and summaries of some passages by Doris E. Cook.

14100

NISBET, CHARLES (1736–1804)*†

Scotland; Pennsylvania. Presbyterian clergyman, professor.

——— Scottish emigration to America: a letter of Dr. Charles Nisbet to Dr. John Witherspoon, 1784. William and Mary quarterly, 3d ser., v. 11, Apr. 1954: 276–289. F221.W71, 3d s., v. 11

Introduction and notes by Whitfield J. Bell.

MILLER, SAMUEL. Memoir of the Rev. Charles Nisbet, D.D., late president of Dickinson College, Carlisle. New York, R. Carter, 1840. 357 p. port. LD1662.7.1785.M5

[PARKINSON, SARAH W.] Charles Nisbet, first president of Dickinson College; his book, 1736–1804. [n.p., 1908] 14 p. LD1662.7.1785.P3

SPAHR, BOYD L. Charles Nisbet, portrait in miniature. *In* Dickinson College, *Carlisle, Pa.* Bulwark of liberty; early years at Dickinson. [New York] Revell [1950] (The Boyd Lee Spahr lectures in Americana, v. 1, 1947–1950) p. 55–73. plate. LD1663.A5

THOMSON, HERBERT F., *and* WILLARD G. BLOODGOOD. A classical economist on the frontier. Pennsylvania history, v. 26, July 1959: 195–212. port. F146.P597, v. 26

14101

NIXON, JOHN (1727–1815)*

Massachusetts. Revolutionary general.

MERRIAM, JOHN M. The military record of Brigadier General John Nixon of Massachusetts. *In* American Antiquarian Society, *Worcester, Mass.* Proceedings, new ser., v. 36, Apr. 1926: 38–70. E172.A35, n.s., v. 36

14102

NIXON, JOHN (1733–1808)*

Pennsylvania. Merchant, Revolutionary officer.

HART, CHARLES H. Colonel John Nixon. Pennsylvania magazine of history and biography, v. 1, no. 2, 1877: 188–202. F146.P65, v. 1

An offprint, entitled *Memoir of the Life and Services of Colonel John Nixon*, was published in Philadelphia by Collins, Printer (1877. [19] p. E263.P4N7).

HENNESSY, MICHAEL. Col. John Nixon. Historical magazine, and notes and queries, v. 4, Dec. 1860: 371–373; v. 5, Jan. 1861: 25–26. [E171.H64, v. 4–5] Micro LAC 31018–19

14103

NOAILLES, LOUIS MARIE, *vicomte* DE (1756–1804)*
France. French officer in America.

WOOD, ANNA W. S. The Robinson family and their correspondence with the Vicomte and Vicomtesse de Noailles [1781–93] Newport, R.I., 1922. 39 p. (Bulletin of the Newport Historical Society, no. 42) F89.N5N615, no. 42

14104

NOBLE, NATHAN (1723–1777)
Connecticut; Massachusetts. Farmer, Revolutionary soldier.

GOOLD, NATHAN. A soldier of three wars: Nathan Noble of New Boston, now Gray, Maine. *In* Maine Historical Society. Collections and proceedings. 2d ser., v. 9. Portland, 1898. p. 172–196. F16.M33, 2d s., v. 9

Also published in Portland, Me., by Thurston Print (1898. 25 p. E275.N75).

14105

NORMAN, JOHN (1748?–1817)*
Pennsylvania; Massachusetts. Engraver, publisher.

WEISS, HARRY B. John Norman, engraver, publisher, bookseller; John Walters, miniaturist, publisher, bookseller; and the "World Turned Upside-Down" controversy. *In* New York (City). Public Library. Bulletin, v. 38, Jan. 1934: 2–14. Z881.N6B, v. 38

14106

NORRIS, ISAAC (1701–1766)*
Pennsylvania. Merchant, assemblyman.

NORRIS, GEORGE W. Isaac Norris. Pennsylvania magazine of history and biography, v. 1, no. 4, 1877: 449–454. F146.P65, v. 1

PARSONS, WILLIAM T. Isaac Norris II, the Speaker. 1955. ([336] p.) Micro AC–1, no. 13,416
Thesis (Ph.D.)—University of Pennsylvania.
Abstracted in *Dissertation Abstracts*, v. 16, no. 1, 1956, p. 11.

——— Wills and contested wills: experiences of Isaac Norris II. *In* Historical Society of Montgomery County (*Pennsylvania*). Bulletin, v. 16, fall 1967: 16–39. F157.M7H45, v. 16

14107

NORTH, FREDERICK NORTH, *Baron* (1732–1792)†
England. Member of Parliament, First Lord of Treasury.

——— Lord North's correspondence, 1766–83. English historical review, v. 62, Apr. 1947: 218–238. DA20.E58, v. 62
Introduction and notes by Edward Hughes.

BUTTERFIELD, HERBERT. Lord North and Mr. Robinson, 1779. *In* Cambridge historical journal. v. 5, no. 3. Cambridge [Eng.] 1937. p. 255–279. D1.C25, v. 5

CANNON, JOHN A. Lord North; the noble Lord in the blue ribbon. London, Historical Association, 1970. 29 p. port. (Historical Association, London. General ser., no. 74) DA506.N7C34
Includes bibliographic references.

LUCAS, REGINALD J. Lord North, second Earl of Guilford, K.G., 1732–1792. London, A. L. Humphreys, 1913. 2 v. geneal. table, ports. DA506.N7L8

PEMBERTON, WILLIAM BARING. Lord North. London, New York, Longmans, Green [1938] xii, 445 p. plates, ports. DA506.N7P4
Bibliography: p. 418–422.

ROBSON, ERIC. Lord North. History today, v. 2, Aug. 1952: 532–538. D1.H818, v. 2

SMITH, CHARLES D. Lord North, a reluctant debater: the making of a cabinet minister, 1754–1767. Quarterly journal of speech, v. 53, Feb. 1967: 17–27.
PN4071.Q3, v. 53

—— Lord North's posture of defense. Quarterly journal of speech, v. 45, Feb. 1959: 29–38.
PN4071.Q3, v. 45

On North's leadership as a factor in maintaining the stability of government in the face of vehement opposition.

VALENTINE, ALAN C. Lord North. Norman, University of Oklahoma Press [1967] 2 v. ports. DA506.N7V3

Bibliography: v. 2, p. 481–502.

WHITE, JAMES B. Lord North—1778: a character and personality analysis. Social studies, v. 51, Feb. 1960: 53–60. D16.3.S65, v. 51

14108

NORTH, J. MERVIN (1737–1825)

England. British military surgeon in America.

—— Letters relating to the American Revolutionary war [1776–1782] In Royal Society of Canada. Proceedings and transactions. v. 11, section 2; 1893. Ottawa, 1894. p. 69–76. AS42.R6, v. 11

Communicated by William Kingsford.

14109

NORTHUMBERLAND, HUGH PERCY, *2d Duke of* (1742–1817)†

England. British officer in America, Member of Parliament.

—— Letters of Hugh, Earl Percy, from Boston and New York, 1774–1776. Edited by Charles Knowles Bolton. Boston, C. E. Goodspeed, 1902. 88 p. port.
E275.N87

Reprinted, with a new introduction and preface by George A. Billias, in Boston by Gregg Press (1972).

—— Original letters of Hugh, Earl Percy and afterwards Duke of Northumberland, between April 17, 1774, and July 11, 1778. In Boston. Public Library Bulletin, v. 10, Jan. 1892: 317–327. Z881.B75B, v. 10

14110

NORTON, ELIZABETH CRANCH (*b.* 1743)

Massachusetts.

—— The journal of Elizabeth Cranch [October 1785–March 1786] With an introductory note by Lizzie Norton Mason and James Duncan Phillips. In Essex Institute, *Salem, Mass.* Historical collections, v. 80, Jan. 1944: 1–36. ports. F72.E7E81, v. 80

Concerned with social life in Haverhill.

14111

NORTON, GEORGE (*b.* 1739)

Massachusetts. Boatmaker, Revolutionary soldier.

—— Revolutionary diary kept by George Norton of Ipswich, 1777–1778. In Essex Institute, *Salem, Mass.* Historical collections. v. 74, Oct. 1938: 337–349.
F72.E7E81, v. 74

14112

NOURSE, JAMES

England; Virginia. Land speculator.

—— Journey to Kentucky in 1775; diary of James Nourse, describing his trip from Virginia to Kentucky. Journal of American history, v. 19, Apr./June–Oct./Dec. 1925: 121–138, 251–260, 351–364.
E171.J86, v. 19

14113

NOYES, JOHN (1740–1784)

Massachusetts. Revolutionary officer.

—— Letters written during the Revolution by Capt. John Noyes of Newbury [1775–78] In Essex Institute, *Salem, Mass.* Historical collections, v. 45, Jan. 1909: 77–86. F72.E7E81, v. 45

14114

NOYES, NATHANIEL (1743–1823)

Massachusetts. Apothecary, Revolutionary officer, assemblyman.

—— Letters of Nathaniel Noyes to William Henshaw, 1774–1775. New-England historical and genealogical register, v. 43, Apr. 1889: 140–149. F1.N56, v. 43

—— —— Offprint. [Boston, Press of D. Clapp, 1889?] 11 p. E211.N95

14115

NUTTING, JOHN (1739?–1800)

Massachusetts; Canada. Carpenter, Loyalist.

BATCHELDER, SAMUEL F. Adventures of John Nutting, Cambridge Loyalist. In Cambridge Historical Society, *Cambridge, Mass.* Publications. v. 5. Proceedings. 1910. Cambridge, 1911. p. 55–98. F74.C1C469, v. 5

An offprint, with an expanded title, was published in Cambridge, Mass. (1912. [55]–98 p. E207.N9B3). Also published in his *Bits of Cambridge History* (Cambridge, Harvard University Press, 1930), p. [282]–349.

14116

O'BRIEN, JEREMIAH (1744–1818)*

Maine. Lumberman, privateersman.

SHERMAN, ANDREW M. Life of Captain Jeremiah O'Brien, Machias, Maine, commander of the first American naval flying squadron of the War of the

Revolution. [Morristown, N.J.] G. W. Sherman, 1902.
xvii, 247 p. facsims., plates.   E207.O13S5

14117

OCCOM, SAMSON (1723–1792)*

Connecticut. Presbyterian clergyman and missionary.

BLODGETT, HAROLD W. Samson Occom. Hanover,
N.H., Dartmouth College Publications, 1935. 230 p.
port. (Dartmouth College manuscript series, no. 3)
                                         E98.M6O13
Bibliography: p. 219–221.

LOVE, WILLIAM DE LOSS. Samson Occom, and the Christian Indians of New England. Boston, Pilgrim Press
[c1899] xiii, 379 p. illus., facsim., map, ports.
                                         E98.M6O15

14118

ODELL, JONATHAN (1737–1818)*

New Jersey. Physician, Anglican clergyman, Loyalist
chaplain, satirist, secret agent.

———— The American times: a satire. In three parts. In which
are delineated the characters of the leaders of the American rebellion. Amongst the principal are, Franklin,
Laurens, Adams, Hancock, Jay, Duer, Duane, Wilson,
Pulaski, Witherspoon, Read, M'Kean, Washington,
Roberdeau, Morris, Chase, &c. By Camillo Querno,
poet-laureat to the Congress. London, Printed for the
author and sold by W. Richardson, 1780. 40 p.
                                  E295.O23 Rare Bk. Coll.
Ascribed also to George Cockings.

REDE, KENNETH. A note on the author of *The Times*.
American literature, v. 2, Mar. 1930: 79–82.
                                         PS1.A6, v. 2

———— ———— Offprint. [Baltimore?] 1930. [79]–82 p.
                                         E295.O27
Suggests that Daniel Batwell may have been the long
disguised writer of the satire.

ROGERS, FRED B. Dr. Jonathan Odell—Tory satirist. *In*
College of Physicians of Philadelphia. Transactions &
studies, 4th ser., v. 24, Aug. 1956: 70–75.
                                    R15.P5, 4th s., v. 24

14119

O'FALLON, JAMES (1749–1794?)*

Ireland; North Carolina; Kentucky. Revolutionary
surgeon.

PARISH, JOHN C. The intrigues of Doctor James O'Fallon. Mississippi Valley historical review, v. 17, Sept.
1930: 230–263.   E171.J87, v. 17

———— ———— Reprint. [Cedar Rapids, Iowa, The
Torch press, 1930] p. 230–263.   CT99.O313P3
A sketch of O'Fallon's varied career, centering principally on his colonizing activities in East Florida and Kentucky during the period 1788–93.

14120

OGDEN, AARON (1756–1839)*

New Jersey. Revolutionary officer, lawyer.

———— Autobiography of Col. Aaron Ogden, of Elizabethtown. An original document written by Col.
Aaron Ogden for his children. Paterson, N.J., Press
Print. and Pub. Co., 1893. 33 p.   E263.N503
Includes unpublished autograph letters that did not
appear with the autobiography published in the *Proceedings*
of the New Jersey Historical Society, 2d ser., v. 12, no. 1,
1892, p. 15–31.

14121

OGDEN, DAVID (*b.* 1764)

PRIEST, JOSIAH. A true narrative of the capture of David
Ogden, among the Indians, in the time of the Revolution, and of the slavery and sufferings he endured, with
an account of his almost miraculous escape after several
years' bondage; with eight other highly interesting stories of the Revolution, and tales of hunters. Lansingburgh [N.Y.] Printed by W. B. Harkness, 1841. 32 p.
illus.   E275.P95 Rare Bk. Coll.

14122

OGLE, JOSEPH (1738–1821)

Maryland; Virginia; Illinois. Revolutionary officer,
farmer.

HIBBARD, FRANCIS H. Captain Joseph Ogle of Virginia
and Illinois in the defense of the Upper Ohio. West
Virginia history, v. 9, Apr. 1948: 224–239.
                                         F236.W52, v. 9

14123

OGLETHORPE, JAMES EDWARD (1696–1785)*†

England; Georgia. Member of Parliament, colonizer.

COOPER, HARRIET C. James Oglethorpe, the founder of
Georgia. New York, D. Appleton, 1904. xi, 217 p.
plates, ports. (Appletons' historic lives series)
                                         E289.O31
"Authorities consulted": p. 210–211.

ETTINGER, AMOS A. James Edward Oglethorpe, imperial
idealist. Oxford, Clarendon Press, 1936. xi, 348 p. fold.
map, plates, ports.   F289.O33
Bibliographic footnotes.
Reprinted in Hamden, Conn., by Archon Books
(1968).

WRIGHT, ROBERT. A memoir of General James Oglethorpe, one of the earliest reformers of prison discipline
in England, and the founder of Georgia, in America.
London, Chapman and Hall, 1867. xvi, 414 p. map.
                                         F289.O37

14124

O'HARA, CHARLES (1740?–1802)†

England. British officer in America.

———— Letters of Charles O'Hara to the Duke of Grafton [1780–81] Edited by George C. Rogers, Jr. South Carolina historical magazine, v. 65, July 1964: 158–180.

F266.S55, v. 65

14125

OLIVER, PETER (1713–1791)*

Massachusetts; England. Judge, councilor, Loyalist.

WESTON, THOMAS. Peter Oliver, the last chief justice of the superior court of judicature of the province of Massachusetts Bay. New England historical and genealogical register, v. 40, July–Oct. 1886: 241–252, 349–359. port.

F1.N56, v. 40

Reprinted in Boston by Cupples, Upham (1886. 36 p. F67.O49).

14126

OLIVER, ROBERT (1757?–1834)

Ireland; Maryland. Merchant, importer-exporter.

BRUCHEY, STUART W. Robert Oliver, merchant of Baltimore, 1783–1819. Baltimore, Johns Hopkins Press, 1956. 411 p. port. (The Johns Hopkins University studies in historical and political science, ser. 74, no. 1)

HF3163.B2O42

Bibliography: p. 399–405.

14127

OLIVER, THOMAS (1734–1815)†

Massachusetts; England. Councilor, Loyalist.

ELTON, OLIVER. Lieutenant Governor Thomas Oliver, 1734–1815. In Colonial Society of Massachusetts, Boston. Publications. v. 28. Transactions, 1930/33. Boston, 1935. p. 37–66, 305–306. port. F61.C71, v. 28

14128

OLIVER, THOMAS FITCH (1757–1797)

Massachusetts. Clergyman.

HODGKINSON, HAROLD D. A clergyman's comments on the life of young America, 1787–1791. In Essex Institute, Salem, Mass. Historical collections, v. 102, Jan. 1966: 74–85. F72.E7E81, v. 102

Based on the letters of the Rev. Thomas Fitch Oliver, rector of St. Michael's Church, Marblehead.

14129

OLMSTED, GIDEON (1750?–1845)*

Connecticut; Pennsylvania. Seaman, privateersman.

FOWLER, WILLIAM M. A Connecticut captain in a Pennsylvania court. In Connecticut Historical Society, Hartford. Bulletin, v. 37, Apr. 1972: 59–63.

F91.C67, v. 63

MIDDLEBROOK, LOUIS F. Captain Gideon Olmsted, Connecticut privateersman, Revolutionary War. Salem, Mass., Newcomb & Gauss Co., 1933. ix, 172 p. facsims., map, plates, port.

E207.O5M63 Rare Bk. Coll.

"Consulted sources": p. 171–172.

14130

O'REILLY, ALEXANDER (ca. 1725–1794)*†

Ireland; Spain; Louisiana. Spanish officer, governor.

———— An account of Governor Alejandro O'Reilly's voyage from Havana to New Orleans in July 1769. Translated and edited by David Ker Texada and Fernando Faraldo. Louisiana history, v. 10, fall 1969: 370–375.

F366.L6238, v. 10

CASADO, VINCENTE R. O'Reilly en la Luisiana. Revista de Indias, v. 2, no. 3, 1941: 115–138.

F1401.R442, v. 3

General O'Reilly's arrival at New Orleans. Mid-America, v. 39, Apr. 1957: 96–111. BX1415.I3M5, v. 39

An anonymous document, in Spanish and English, describing O'Reilly's activities on his arrival in Louisiana in 1769. Introduction and notes by Donald G. Castanien.

TEXADA, DAVID K. Alejandro O'Reilly and the New Orleans rebels. Lafayette, University of Southwestern Louisiana, ᶜ1970. 134 p. (USL history series no. 2)

F372.O7T49

Bibliography: p. 126–130.

14131

ORMSBY, JOHN (1720–1805)

Ireland; Virginia; Pennsylvania. Land speculator.

KAMPRAD, WALTER T. John Ormsby, Pittsburgh's original citizen. Western Pennsylvania historical magazine, v. 23, Dec. 1940: 203–222. F146.W52, v. 23

14132

ORR, LUCINDA LEE (fl. 1787)

Virginia.

————Journal of a young lady of Virginia. 1782. Baltimore, J. Murphy, 1871. 56 p. F230.O75

Personal and literary allusions, and days of the week and month referred to in the journal, indicate that it was dated 1787, not 1782. Reprinted in the Northern Neck Historical Magazine, v. 17, (Montross, Va., 1967), p. 1591–1610.

14133

OSGOOD, SAMUEL (1748–1813)*

Massachusetts; New York. Revolutionary officer, delegate to the Continental Congress.

——— Sketch of the life of Samuel Osgood, first Postmaster-General of the United States, written by himself. Magazine of American history, with notes and queries, v. 21, Apr. 1889: 324–328.   E171.M18, v. 21

14134

OSWALD, ELEAZER (1755–1795)

England; Maryland; Pennsylvania. Revolutionary officer, printer, editor.

STUMPF, VERNON O.   Colonel Eleazer Oswald: politician and editor. 1968. ([369] p.)
     Micro AC–1, no. 69–3896

Thesis (Ph.D.)—Duke University.
Abstracted in *Dissertation Abstracts*, v. 29A, Mar. 1969, p. 3085–3086.

14135

OTIS, JAMES (1725–1783)*

Massachusetts. Lawyer, pamphleteer, assemblyman.

——— Letters of James Otis, 1764, 1765. *In* Massachusetts Historical Society, *Boston*. Proceedings. v. 43; 1909/10. Boston, 1910. p. 202–207.   F61.M38, v. 43

——— Some political writings of James Otis. Collected with an introduction by Charles F. Mullett. Columbia, University of Missouri, 1929. 2 v. (176 p.) facsims. ([Missouri. University] The University of Missouri studies; a quarterly of research, v. 4, July–Oct. 1929)
     E211.O885
     AS36.M82, v. 4

Contains reproductions of title pages of original editions.

Contents: 1. A vindication of the conduct of the House of Representatives of the Province of Massachusetts-Bay (1762). The rights of the British colonies asserted and proved (1764)—2. Considerations on behalf of the colonists in a letter to a noble lord (1765). A vindication of the British colonies (1765). Brief remarks on the defence of the Halifax libel on the British-American colonies (1765).

BELL, HUGH F.   James Otis of Massachusetts—the first forty years, 1725–1765. 1970. ([473] p.)
     Micro AC–1, no. 71–7349

Thesis (Ph.D.)—Cornell University.
Abstracted in *Dissertation Abstracts International*, v. 31A, June 1971, p. 6507.

——— "A melancholy affair"—James Otis and the pirates. American Neptune, v. 31, Jan. 1971: 19–37.
     V1.A4, v. 31

BRENNAN, ELLEN E.   James Otis, recreant and patriot. New England quarterly, v. 12, Dec. 1939: 691–725.
     F1.N62, v. 12

ELLIS, J. H.   James Otis. American law review, v. 3, July 1869: 641–665.   LL

GRINNELL, FRANK W.   James Otis and his influence as a constructive thinker. *In* Bostonian Society, *Boston*. Proceedings. v. 55; 1936. Boston. p. 31–50. ports.
     F73.1.B86, v. 55

RIDPATH, JOHN C.   James Otis, the pre-revolutionist, by John Clark Ridpath. The character of James Otis by Charles K. Edmunds, Ph.D., with an essay on the patriot by G. Mercer Adam . . . together with anecdotes, characteristics, and chronology. Milwaukee, H. G. Campbell Pub. Co., 1903. 184 p. illus., ports. (Great Americans of history)   E302.6.O8R54
     Micro 19072 E

Original copyright 1898.
Bibliography: p. 184.

SHIPTON, CLIFFORD K.   James Otis and the Writs of Assistance. *In* Bostonian Society, *Boston*. Proceedings. v. 80; 1961. Boston. p. 17–25.   F73.1.B86, v. 80

An overall assessment of Otis' place in the Revolutionary pantheon.

STARRETT, VINCENT.   Otis at Bunker Hill; a mystery of the Revolutionary War. American book collector, v. 6, Apr. 1935: 148–154.   Z1007.A47, v. 6

TUDOR, WILLIAM.   The life of James Otis, of Massachusetts: containing also, notices of some contemporary characters and events, from the year 1760 to 1775. Boston, Wells and Lilly, 1823. xx, 508 p. illus., facsim., plate, port.   E302.6.O8T9

Reprinted in New York by Da Capo Press (1970).

VERING, ALICE.   James Otis. 1954. ([320] p.)
     Micro AC–1, no. 11,231

Thesis (Ph.D)—University of Nebraska.
Abstracted in *Dissertation Abstracts*, v. 15, no. 5, 1955, p. 812.

WATERS, JOHN J.   The Otis family, in provincial and Revolutionary Massachusetts. Chapel Hill, Published for the Institute of Early American History and Culture at Williamsburg, Va., by the University of North Carolina Press [1968] xi, 221 p. illus., maps, ports.
     CS71.O88 1968

"Notes on sources": p. [209]–212.
The author's thesis (Ph.D.), with the same title, was submitted to Columbia University in 1965 (Micro AC–1, no. 69–575).

14136

OTTO, BODO (1711–1787)*

Germany; Pennsylvania. Revolutionary surgeon and medical administrator.

GIBSON, JAMES E.   Bodo Otto, senior hospital physician and surgeon of Valley Forge. Historical review of Berks County, v. 2, Oct. 1936: 10–15. illus., facsim., port.
     F157.B3H48, v. 2

—— Dr. Bodo Otto and the medical background of the American Revolution. Springfield, Ill., C. C. Thomas [ᶜ1937] ix, 345 p. plates, ports. E283.O87

STOLTZ, PAUL K. Dr. Bodo Otto, senior surgeon of the Valley Forge encampment. Historical review of Berks County, v. 27, winter 1961/62: 6–12. illus., port. F157.B3H48, v. 27

14137
OTTO, BODO (1748–1782)
Germany; Pennsylvania; New Jersey. Physician, judge, assemblyman, Revolutionary officer.

GIBSON, JAMES E. Bodo Otto, Junior. *In* New Jersey Historical Society. Proceedings, v. 66, Oct. 1948: 171–183. F131.N58, v. 66

14138
OWEN, WILLIAM (1738?–1778)
British naval officer.

—— The journal of Captain William Owen, R.N., during his residence on Campobello in 1770–71, together with other documents and notes upon the history of the island. Edited by William F. Ganong. *In* New Brunswick Historical Society. Collections. v. 1, no. 2; [v. 2], no. 4. Saint John, N.B., 1896, 1899. p. 193–220; p. 8–27. illus., map, plates, ports.
[F1041.N53, v. 1, no. 2; v. 2. no. 4]
Micro 04070

—— Narrative of American voyages and travels of Captain William Owen, R.N., and the settlement of the island of Campobello in the Bay of Fundy, 1766–1771. Edited by Victor Hugo Paltsits. *In* New York (City). Public Library. Bulletin, v. 35, Feb.–Mar., May, Sept.–Oct. 1931: 71–98, 139–162, 263–300, 659–685, 705–758. facsims., maps (part fold.), plans, plates, port. Z881.N6B, v. 35

An offprint with a slightly different title was published in New York by the New York Public Library (1942. 169 p. F1013.Q9).

14139
OXNARD, EDWARD (1747?–1803)
Massachusetts; Maine; England. Merchant, Loyalist.

—— Extracts from journal of Edward Oxnard [1775–85] New-England historical and genealogical register, v. 26, Jan.–July 1872: 3–10, 115–121, 254–259. plate. F1.N56, v. 26

On his 10-year exile in England. Introduction and notes by Edward S. Moseley.

14140
PACA, WILLIAM (1740–1799)*
Maryland. Lawyer, assemblyman, delegate to the Continental Congress, judge, governor.

SILVERMAN, ALBERT. William Paca, signer, governor, jurist. Maryland historical magazine, v. 37, Mar. 1942: 1–25. port. F176.M18, v. 37

14141
PAGAN, ROBERT (1750–1821)
Scotland; Maine; New Brunswick. Merchant, shipbuilder, Loyalist.

JACK, DAVID R. Robert and Miriam Pagan. Acadiensis, v. 2, Oct. 1902: 279–287. ports. F1036.A16, v. 2

See also the memorial of Robert and Thomas Pagan to the governor of Nova Scotia, October 16, 1783, in v. 6, Oct. 1906, p. 262.

14142
PAINE, ROBERT TREAT (1731–1814)*
Massachusetts. Lawyer, assemblyman, delegate to the Continental Congress.

—— Diary of Robert Treat Paine.—Extracts [1768–76] *In* Paine, Sarah C. Paine ancestry. The family of Robert Treat Paine, signer of the Declaration of Independence. Edited by Charles Henry Pope. Boston, Printed for the family [Press of D. Clapp] 1912. p. 31–40. CS71.P146 1912a

DAVOL, RALPH. Two men of Taunton, in the course of human events, 1731–1829. Taunton, Mass., Davol Pub. Co., 1912. xiii, 406 p. facsims., plan, plates, port. E302.6.P14D2

Biographies of Robert Treat Paine and Daniel Leonard.

RILEY, STEPHEN T. Robert Treat Paine and his papers. 1953. ([369] p.) Micro AC–1, no. 5849
Thesis (Ph.D.)—Clark University.
Abstracted in *Dissertation Abstracts*, v. 13, no. 5, 1953, p. 785.

14143
PAINE, THOMAS (1737–1809)*†
England; Pennsylvania. Journalist, pamphleteer.

—— The complete writings of Thomas Paine. Collected and edited by Philip S. Foner. With a biographical essay, and notes and introductions presenting the historical background of Paine's writings. New York, Citadel Press [1945] 2 v. port. JC177.A3 1945

—— Life and writings of Thomas Paine; containing a biography by Thomas Clio Rickman and appreciations by Leslie Stephen, Lord Erskine, Paul Desjardins, Robert G. Ingersoll, Elbert Hubbard and Marilla M. Ricker. Edited and annotated by Daniel Edwin Wheeler. New York, V. Parke [ᶜ1908] 10 v. facsims., plates (part col.), ports. JC177.A3 1908

Contents: v. 1. Life and appreciations.—v. 2. Common sense; Miscellany.—v. 3. The crisis.—v. 4. The rights of man. v. 1.—v. 5. The rights of man. v. 2. Miscellany.—v. 6. The age of reason. v. 1.—v. 7. The age of reason. v. 2.

Miscellany.—v. 8–9. Essays, letters, addresses.—v. 10. Essays, letters, poems.

———— Thomas Paine, French propagandist in the United States. *In* American Catholic Historical Society. Records, v. 57, Mar. 1946: 1–21.   E184.C3A4, v. 57
Introduction and notes by John J. Meng.

Includes four essays published by Paine in the *Pennsylvania Packet* on December 1, 5, 10, and 12, 1778, entitled "A Serious Address to the People of Pennsylvania on the Present Situation of Their Affairs," and intended as a contribution to the debate over the advisability of amending or rewriting the state constitution that had been adopted in 1776.

———— Thomas Paine; representative selections. With introduction, bibliography, and notes, by Harry Hayden Clark. Rev. ed. New York, Hill and Wang [1916] clxiii, 436 p. (American century writers, ACW43)
                                    JC177.A5 1961
Bibliography: cxxv–clxiii.
First edition published in 1948.

———— Writings; collected and edited by Moncure Daniel Conway. New York, Putnam, 1894–96. 4 v.
                                    JC177.A3 1894
Reprinted in New York by AMS Press (1967).

———— The writings, of Thomas Paine, secretary for foreign affairs to the Congress of the United States of America, in the late war. Containing, 1. Rights of man. 2. Common sense. 3. The crisis. 4. Public good. 5. Letter to Abbe Raynal. 6. Letter to the Earl of Shelburne. 7. Letter to Sir Guy Carlton. 8. Letter to the authors of the Republican. 9. Letter to Abbe Syeyes. Albany—State of New-York, Printed by Charles R. & George Webster [1792?] [615] p.   JC177.A3 1792e Rare Bk. Coll.

ABEL, DARREL.   The significance of the letter to the Abbé Raynal in the progress of Thomas Paine's thought. Pennsylvania magazine of history and biography, v. 66, Apr. 1942: 176–190.   F146.P65, v. 66

ALDRIDGE, ALFRED O.   Man of reason, the life of Thomas Paine. Philadelphia, Lippincott [1959] 348 p. illus., port.   JC178.V2A8
Bibliographic references included in "Notes" (p. 325–341).

———— The poetry of Thomas Paine. Pennsylvania magazine of history and biography, v. 79, Jan. 1955: 81–99.
                                    F146.P65, v. 79

———— Some writings of Thomas Paine in Pennsylvania newspapers. American historical review, v. 56, July 1951: 832–838.   E171.A57, v. 56
Contemporary Pennsylvania newspapers contain two papers in the *Crisis* series, three letters on the Bank of North America, and an explanation in an advertisement of Paine's publishing arrangements for *Common Sense* that have not appeared in previous collections of Paine's works.

———— Thomas Paine and Comus. Pennsylvania magazine of history and biography, v. 85, Jan. 1961: 70–75.
                                    F146.P65, v. 85
One of Paine's pseudonyms.

———— Thomas Paine and the classics. Eighteenth-century studies, v. 1, June 1968: 370–380.   NX452.E54, v. 1

———— Why did Thomas Paine write on the Bank? *In* American Philosophical Society, *Philadelphia*. Proceedings, v. 93, Sept. 1949: 309–315.   Q11.P5, v. 93
On Paine's defense of the Bank of North America, 1785–86.

BRUNEL, ADRIAN H.   The repercussions of Thomas Paine (with particular reference to his work in America). History today, v. 2, Mar. 1952: 191–197.
                                    D1.H818, v. 2

CLARK, HARRY H.   An historical interpretation of Thomas Paine's religion. University of California chronicle, v. 35, Jan. 1933: 56–87.   LD739, v. 35

———— Thomas Paine's theories of rhetoric. *In* Wisconsin Academy of Sciences, Arts and Letters. Transactions. v. 28. Madison, 1933. p. [307]–339. AS36.W7, v. 28

———— Toward a reinterpretation of Thomas Paine. American literature, v. 5, May 1933: 133–145.
                                    PS1.A6, v. 5

CONWAY, MONCURE D.   The life of Thomas Paine; with a history of his literary, political, and religious career in America, France, and England. To which is added a sketch of Paine by William Cobbett (hitherto unpublished). New York, G. P. Putnam's Sons, 1892. 2 v. ports.   JC178.V2C7
The sketch by Cobbett, who, from hating Paine, had become his ardent admirer, is based on manuscript notes prepared by Madame de Bonneville.
"The Hall manuscripts": v. 2, p. 460–472 (extracts from the journals of John Hall, a mechanic who emigrated from England to Philadelphia in 1785, recording his daily intercourse with Paine).
A one-volume edition of 1909 was reprinted, with a new introduction, in New York by B. Blom (1969).

DORFMAN, JOSEPH.   The economic philosophy of Thomas Paine. Political science quarterly, v. 53, Sept. 1938: 372–386.   H1.P8, v. 53

ELDER, DOMINIC, *Brother*.   The common man philosophy of Thomas Paine; a study of the political ideas of Paine. Notre Dame, Ind., Dept. of Political Science, 1951. xii, 146 p.   JC177.A4E55
Thesis (Ph.D.)—University of Notre Dame.
Bibliography: p. [135]–144.

FALK, ROBERT P.   Thomas Paine and the attitude of the Quakers to the American Revolution. Pennsylvania magazine of history and biography, v. 63, July 1939: 302–310.   F146.P65, v. 63

—— Thomas Paine: Deist or Quaker? Pennsylvania magazine of history and biography, v. 62, Jan. 1938: 52–63. F146.P65, v. 62

GIBBENS, V. E. Tom Paine and the idea of progress. Pennsylvania magazine of history and biography, v. 66, Apr. 1942: 191–204. F146.P65, v. 66

GIMBEL, RICHARD. Thomas Paine: a bibliographical check list of *Common Sense*, with an account of its publication. New Haven, Yale University Press, 1956. 124 p. facsims. Z8654.G5

—— Thomas Paine fights for freedom in three worlds, the new, the old, the next. Catalogue of an exhibition commemorating the one hundredth anniversary of his death. Yale University Library, October 1959. *In* American Antiquarian Society, *Worcester, Mass.* Proceedings, new ser., v. 70, Oct. 1960: 397–492. illus., facsims., ports. E172.A35, n.s., v. 70

An annotated guide to the letters, manuscripts, pamphlets, collected works, portraits, engravings, caricatures, and tokens in the exhibition. Gimbel's opening lecture, "The Resurgence of Thomas Paine," appeared in v. 69, Oct. 1959, p. 97–111.

GINSBERG, ELAINE K. The rhetoric of revolution: an analysis of Thomas Paine's *Common Sense*. 1971. ([187] p.) Micro AC–1, no. 72–3393
Thesis (Ph.D.)—University of Oklahoma.
Abstracted in *Dissertation Abstracts International*, v. 32A, Jan. 1972, p. 3950.

GUMMERE, RICHARD M. Thomas Paine: was he really anticlassical? *In* American Antiquarian Society, *Worcester, Mass.* Proceedings, v. 75, Oct. 1965: 253–269. E172.A35, v. 75

HINZ, EVELYN J. The "reasonable" style of Tom Paine. Queen's quarterly, v. 79, summer 1972: 231–241. AP5.Q3, v. 79

KENYON, CECILIA M. Where Paine went wrong. American political science review, v. 45, Dec. 1951: 1086–1099. JA1.A6, v. 45

KING, ARNOLD K. Thomas Paine in America, 1774–87. 1951. 409 l.
Thesis (Ph.D.)—University of Chicago.

LEFFMANN, HENRY. The real Thomas Paine, patriot and publicist, a philosopher misunderstood. Pennsylvania magazine of history and biography, v. 46, Apr. 1922: 81–99. F146.P65, v. 46

—— —— Offprint. [Philadelphia? 1922] [81]–99 p. JC 178.V2L4

MENG, JOHN J. The constitutional theories of Thomas Paine. Review of politics, v. 8, July 1946: 283–306. JA1.R4, v. 8

METZGAR, JOSEPH V. Thomas Paine: a study in social and intellectual history. 1965. ([202] p.) Micro AC–1, no. 66–4447

Thesis (Ph.D.)—University of New Mexico.
Abstracted in *Dissertation Abstracts*, v. 26, Apr. 1966, p. 6001–6002.

PALMER, ROBERT R. Tom Paine, victim of the rights of man. Pennsylvania magazine of history and biography, v. 66, Apr. 1942: 161–175. F146.P65, v. 66

PEARSON, HESKETH. Tom Paine, friend of mankind. New York, Harper, 1937. vii, 293 p. facsim, plates, ports. JC178.V2P4

PENNIMAN, HOWARD R. Thomas Paine—democrat. American political science review, v. 37, Apr. 1943: 244–262. JA1.A6, v. 37

SEDGWICK, ELLERY. Thomas Paine. Boston, Small, Maynard, 1899. xv, 150 p. port. (The Beacon biographies of eminent Americans) JC178.V2S4
Bibliography: p. 148–150.

SHELDON, FREDERICK. Tom Paine's first appearance in America. Atlantic monthly, v. 4, Nov. 1859: 565–575. AP2.A8, v. 4

SMITH, FRANK. New light on Paine's first year in America, 1775. American literature, v. 1, Jan. 1930: 347–371. PS1.A6, v. 1

—— Thomas Paine, liberator. New York, F. A. Stokes Co., 1938. 338 p. port. JC178.V2S65

WECTER, DIXON. Hero in reverse. Virginia quarterly review, v. 18, spring 1942: 243–259. AP2.V76, v. 18

—— Thomas Paine and the Franklins. American literature, v. 12, Nov. 1940: 306–317. PS1.A6, v. 12

Includes three letters from Paine to Benjamin Franklin and one to Benjamin Franklin Bache.

WILSON, JEROME D. Thomas Paine in the twentieth century: his reputation in America, 1900–1970, and an annotated bibliography, 1900–1970. 1972. ([271] p.) Micro AC–1, no. 73–8259

Thesis (Ph.D.)—Auburn University.
Abstracted in *Dissertation Abstracts International*, v. 33A, Apr. 1973, p. 5697.

WOODWARD, WILLIAM E. Tom Paine: America's godfather, 1737–1809. New York, E. P. Dutton, 1945. 359 p. facsims., plates, ports. JC178.V2W64
Bibliography: p. 342–343.
Reprinted in Westport, Conn., by Greenwood Press (1972).

14144
PAINE, WILLIAM (1750–1833)
Massachusetts; New Brunswick. Physician, Loyalist.

FRANCIS, GEORGE E. William Paine. *In* American Antiquarian Society, *Worcester, Mass.* Proceedings, new ser., v. 13, Apr. 1900: 394–408.
E172.A35, n.s., v. 13

SHIPTON, CLIFFORD K. Harvard Loyalists in New Brunswick. Fredericton, N.B., University of New Brunswick, 1964. 1 v. (unpaged) ([New Brunswick. University] Founders' Day address, 1964)   E278.P34S56

14145

PAINTER, THOMAS (1760–1847)

Connecticut. Revolutionary soldier and seaman.

——— Autobiography of Thomas Painter, relating his experiences during the War of the Revolution. Printed for private circulation. [Washington? D.C., 1910] 106 p. plates, port, geneal. table.   E275.P14

A portion of the autobiography, edited by Henry Howe, appeared earlier under the title, "Personal Reminiscences of the Revolutionary War, by the late Thomas Painter, of West Haven," in the *Papers* of the New Haven Colony Historical Society, v. 4 (New Haven, 1888), p. 231–252.

14146

PALLISER, *Sir* HUGH, *Bart.* (1723–1796)†

England. British naval officer.

HUNT, ROBERT M. The life of Sir Hugh Palliser, Bart., Admiral of the White, and governor of Greenwich Hospital. London, Chapman and Hall, 1844. xvi, 463 p. port., geneal. table.   DA87.1.P2H9

14147

PALMER, JOSEPH (1716–1788)*

England; Massachusetts. Manufacturer, Revolutionary general.

[PALMER, CHARLES S.] Biographical sketch of Gen. Joseph Palmer. New Englander, v. 3, Jan. 1845: 1–23. port.   AP2.N5, v. 3

——— ——— Detached copy.   E207.P1P1

Includes Palmer's correspondence from 1774–78.

14148

PALMER, TIMOTHY (1751–1821)

Massachusetts. Architect.

PEASE, GEORGE B. Timothy Palmer, bridge-builder of the eighteenth century. *In* Essex Institute, *Salem, Mass.* Historical collections, v. 83, Apr. 1947: 97–111. illus. (part fold.), facsims., plate, ports.   F72.E7E81 v. 83

14149

PALMERSTON, HENRY TEMPLE, *2d Viscount* (1739–1802)†

England. Member of Parliament.

——— Portrait of a golden age; intimate papers of the second Viscount Palmerston, courtier under George III. Compiled and edited by Brian Connell. Boston,

Houghton Mifflin, 1958 [c1957] 488 p. illus., plates, ports.   DA506.P28A3

"List of sources and bibliography": p. 466–475.

14150

PANTON, WILLIAM (1742?–1801)*

Scotland; Florida. Indian trader, Loyalist.

GREENSLADE, MARIE T. William Panton. Florida Historical Society quarterly, v. 14, Oct. 1935: 107–129.   F306.F65, v. 14

WATSON, THOMAS D. Merchant adventurer in the Old Southwest: William Panton, the Spanish years, 1783–1801. 1972. ([343] p.)   Micro AC–1, no. 73–4082

Thesis (Ph.D.)—Texas Tech University.

Abstracted in *Dissertation Abstracts International*, v. 33A, Feb. 1973, p. 4323.

14151

PAOLI, PASQUALE (1725–1807)†

Corsica; England. Corsican officer.

ANDERSON, GEORGE P. Pascal Paoli, an inspiration to the Sons of Liberty. *In* Colonial Society of Massachusetts, *Boston.* Publications. v. 26. Transactions, 1924/26. Boston, 1927. p. 180–210.   F61.C71, v. 26

14152

PARADISE, JOHN (1743–1795)†

England; Virginia. Linguist, scholar.

SHEPPERSON, ARCHIBALD B. John Paradise and Lucy Ludwell of London and Williamsburg. Richmond, Va., Dietz Press, 1942. 501 p. facsim., geneal. tables, map, plates, ports.   DA506.P3S4

"Selective bibliography": p. [461]–465.

STRUVE, GLEB. John Paradise—friend of Doctor Johnson, American citizen and Russian "agent." Virginia magazine of history and biography, v. 57, Oct. 1949: 355–375.   F221.V91, v. 57

14153

PARKE, THOMAS (1749–1835)

Pennsylvania. Physician.

BELL, WHITFIELD J. Thomas Parke, M.B., physician and Friend. William and Mary quarterly, 3d ser., v. 6, Oct. 1949: 569–595.   F221.W71, 3d s., v. 6

——— Thomas Parke's student life in England and Scotland, 1771–1773. Pennsylvania magazine of history and biography, v. 75, July 1951: 237–259.   F146.P65, v. 75

14154

PARKER, JAMES (1714–1770)*

New Jersey; New York; Connecticut. Printer, publisher, judge.

—— Letters from James Parker to Benjamin Franklin [1764–70] *In* Massachusetts Historical Society, *Boston.* Proceedings. 2d ser., v. 16; 1902. Boston, 1903. p. 186–232.   F61.M38, 2d s., v. 16

Introduction and notes by Worthington C. Ford.

BENEDICT, WILLIAM H. James Parker, the printer, of Woodbridge. *In* New Jersey Historical Society. Proceedings, new ser., v. 8, July 1923: 194–199.
F131.N58, n.s., v. 8

McANEAR, BEVERLY. James Parker versus John Holt. *In* New Jersey Historical Society. Proceedings, v. 59, Apr.–July 1941: 77–95, 198–212.   F131.N58, v. 59

—— James Parker versus William Weyman. *In* New Jersey Historical Society. Proceedings, v. 59, Jan. 1941: 1–23.   F131.N58, v. 59

REDWAY, VIRGINIA L. James Parker and the "Dutch Church." Musical quarterly, v. 24, Oct. 1938: 481–500. facsims.   ML1.M725, v. 24

14155

PARKER, JAMES (1725–1797)

New Jersey. Estate manager, councilor, Loyalist.

PARKER, CHARLES W. Shipley: the country seat of a Jersey Loyalist. In New Jersey Historical Society. Proceedings, 4th ser., v. 16, Apr. 1931: 117–138. facsim., map.   F131.N58, 4th s., v. 16

14156

PARKER, JAMES (1744–1830)

Massachusetts. Farmer, Revolutionary soldier.

—— Extracts from the diary of James Parker of Shirley, Mass. [1770–1829] New England historical and genealogical register, v. 69, Jan.–Oct. 1915: 8–17, 117–127, 211–224, 294–308; v. 70, Jan.–Oct. 1916: 9–24, 137–146, 210–220, 294–308.   F1.N56, v. 69–70

14157

PARKER, JOSIAH (1751–1810)*

Virginia. Revolutionary officer, assemblyman.

—— Revolutionary correspondence of Col. Josiah Parker, of Isle of Wight County, Va. [1780–81] Virginia magazine of history and biography, v. 22, July 1914: 257–266.   F221.V91, v. 22

14158

PARKER, SAMUEL (1744–1804)

New Hampshire; Massachusetts. Schoolteacher, Anglican clergyman.

LACY, HARRIET S. An eighteenth-century diarist identified: Samuel Parker's journals for 1771. Historical New Hampshire, v. 25, summer 1970: 3–12. map.
F31.H57, v. 25

The text of Parker's diary and a list identifying the persons mentioned in it appears on p. 13–44.

14159

PARKMAN, EBENEZER (1703–1782)

Massachusetts. Clergyman.

—— The diary of Rev. Ebenezer Parkman, of Westborough, Mass., for the months of February, March, April, October, and November 1737, November and December of 1778, and the years of 1779 and 1780. Edited by Harriette M. Forbes. [Westborough, Mass.] Westborough Historical Society, 1899. 327 p. illus., plates, ports.   F74.W5P2

For the location of other manuscript diaries of Parkman, see the *Proceedings* of the American Antiquarian Society, October 1907.

14160

PARRY, EDWARD (*fl.* 1775–1777)

New Hampshire; England. Merchant, Loyalist.

MAGUIRE, JAMES H. A critical editon of *Edward Parry's Journal, March 28, 1775 to August 23, 1777.* 1970. ([406] p.)   Micro AC–1, no. 71–6875

Thesis (Ph.D.)—Indiana University.

Abstracted in *Dissertation Abstracts International,* v. 31A, Mar. 1971, p. 4724.

—— "Elisium and the wilds": a Loyalist's account of experiences in America at the beginning of the American Revolution. Historical New Hampshire, v. 26, winter 1971: 31–44. facsims.   F31.H57, v. 26

14161

PARSONS, SAMUEL HOLDEN (1737–1789)*

Connecticut. Lawyer, assemblyman, Revolutionary general.

HALL, CHARLES S. Life and letters of Samuel Holden Parsons, major-general in the Continental Army and chief judge of the Northwestern Territory, 1737–1789. Binghamton, N.Y., Otseningo Pub. Co., 1905. xiii, 601 p. plan.   E207.P2H17

LORING, GEORGE B. Vindication of General Samuel Holden Parsons. Magazine of American history, with notes and queries, v. 20, Oct. 1888: 286–303.
E171.M18, v. 20

14162

PARSONS, THEOPHILUS (1750–1813)*

Massachusetts. Lawyer.

PARSONS, THEOPHILUS. Memoir of Theophilus Parsons, chief justice of the supreme judicial court of Massachusetts; with notices of some of his contemporaries. By his son. Boston, Ticknor and Fields, 1859. viii, 476 p. port.   F69.P26

Reprinted in New York by Da Capo Press (1970. KF368.P36P3 1970).

14163

PATERSON, CORNELIA BELL (1755–1783)

New Jersey. Wife of William Paterson (1745–1806).

—— The Cornelia (Bell) Paterson letters [1777–84] *In* New Jersey Historical Society. Proceedings, 4th ser., v. 15, Oct. 1930: 508–517; v. 16, Jan.–Apr. 1931: 56–67, 186–201.   F131.N58, 4th s., v. 15–16

14164

PATERSON, JOHN (1744–1808)*

Connecticut; Massachusetts. Lawyer, Revolutionary general.

BOOTH, BULKELEY. General John Paterson, a soldier of the Revolution. New England magazine, new ser., v. 11, Sept. 1894: 42–51. illus.   AP2.N4, n.s., v. 11

EGLESTON, THOMAS. The life of John Paterson, major-general in the Revolutionary army. 2d ed., rev. and enl. New York, G. P. Putnam's Sons, 1898. xiii, 488 p. geneal. table, maps, plans (part fold.), plates, port.   E207.P3E31

Appendix: The Paterson families.
"List of books and manuscripts from which information has been obtained": p. 448–450.
First edition published in 1894.

HEATHCOTE, CHARLES W. General John Paterson—ardent patriot who loyally supported Washington. Picket post, no. 58, Nov. 1957: 20–26. illus.   E234.P5, no. 58

LEE, WILLIAM H. An address on the life and character of Major-General John Paterson, of the Revolutionary Army. New York genealogical and biographical record, v. 21, July 1890: 99–112. port.   F116.N28, v. 21

14165

PATERSON, WILLIAM (1745–1806)

New Jersey. Lawyer, delegate to the Constitutional Convention.

—— Glimpses of colonial society and the life at Princeton College, 1766–1773, by one of the class of 1763. Edited by W. Jay Mills. Philadelphia, J. B. Lippincott Co., 1903. 182 p. facsim., plates, ports.   E163.P29
Reprinted in Detroit by Grand River Books (1971).

—— Political essays of William Paterson. *In* Rutgers University, *New Brunswick, N.J. Library.* Journal. v. 18, June 1955: 38–49.   Z733.R955F, v. 18

Introduction and notes by Richard P. McCormick.

HASKETT, RICHARD C. Village clerk and country lawyer: William Paterson's legal experience, 1763–1772. *In* New Jersey Historical Society. Proceedings, v. 66, Oct. 1948: 155–171.   F131.N58, v. 66

—— William Paterson, Attorney General of New Jersey: public office and private profit in the American Revolution. William and Mary quarterly, 3d ser., v. 7, Jan. 1950: 26–38.   F221.W71, 3d s., v. 7

—— William Paterson, counsellor at law. 1952. Thesis (Ph.D.)—Princeton University.

PATERSON, WILLIAM. William Paterson, United States senator, governor of New Jersey, justice U.S. Supreme Court. New York genealogical and biographical record, v. 23, Apr. 1892: 81–91.   F116.N28, v. 23

ROSENBERG, LEONARD B. William Paterson: New Jersey's nation-maker. New Jersey history, v. 85, spring 1967: 7–40.   F131.N58, v. 85

SHRINER, CHARLES A. William Paterson. [Paterson, N.J.] Paterson Industrial Commission, 1940. 96 p. port.   E302.6.P3S5

WOOD, GERTRUDE S. William Paterson of New Jersey, 1745–1806. [Fair Lawn, N.J., Fair Lawn Press, ᶜ1933] 217 p. port.   E302.6.P3W7

Bibliography: p. [201]–211.
The author's thesis (Ph.D.), with the same title, was submitted to Columbia University in 1933.

14166

PATTEN, MATTHEW (1719–1795)

New Hampshire. Judge, farmer.

—— The diary of Matthew Patten of Bedford, N.H. From seventeen hundred fifty-four to seventeen hundred eighty-eight. Published by the town. Concord, N.H., Rumford Print. Co., 1903. 545 p. front.   F44.B3P3

SCOTT, KENNETH. Matthew Patten of Bedford, New Hampshire. *In* Presbyterian Historical Society. Journal, v. 28, Sept. 1950: 129–145. BX8905.P4A4, v. 28

14167

PATTERSON, JOHN (1748 *or* 9–1808)

Scotland; Nova Scotia. Landowner, merchant, trader.

PATTERSON, FRANK H. John Patterson, the founder of Pictou Town, by his great-grandson. Truro, N.S., Truro Print. & Pub. Co., 1955. 110 p. illus.   F1039.5.P5P3

Bibliography: p. 110.

14168

PATTILLO, HENRY (1726–1801)*

Scotland; North Carolina. Presbyterian clergyman, teacher.

STOKES, DURWARD T. Henry Pattillo in North Carolina. North Carolina historical review, v. 44, autumn 1967: 373–391. F251.N892, v. 44

14169
PATTISON, JAMES (1724–1805)
England; New York. British officer in America.

—— A New York diary of the Revolutionary War [June 17, 1778, to December 28, 1779] Edited, with an introduction, by Carson I. A. Ritchie. *In* New York Historical Society. Quarterly, v. 50, July 1966: 221–280, 401–446. illus., maps, ports. F116.N638, v. 50

—— Official letters of Major General James Pattison, commandant of artillery. *In* New York Historical Society. Collections. 1875. Publication fund series, [v. 8] New York, 1876. p. [1]–430. F116.N63, 1875

Contents: pt. 1. As commandant of the Royal Artillery in North America.—pt. 2. As commandant of the City of New York.

14170
PAULINT, ANTOINE (1737–1813)
Canada. Revolutionary officer.

REED, ADELA P. Memoirs of Antoine Paulint, veteran of the old French war, 1755 to 1760; captain in Hazen's Second Canadian, "Congress' Own" Regiment, 1775 to 1783; brevet major at the close of the Revolutionary War. Los Angeles, D. M. Peltier, 1940. 61 p. facsim., plates, port. E263.C2P3

14171
PAXTON, CHARLES (1704–1788)
Massachusetts; England. Customs agent, Loyalist.

—— Letters of Charles Paxton [1768–69] *In* Massachusetts Historical Society, *Boston.* Proceedings. v. 56; 1922/23. Boston, 1923. p. 343–352. port. F61.M38, v. 56

Introduction and notes by George G. Wolkins.

14172
PEAK, JOHN (1761–1842)
New Hampshire. Baptist clergyman.

—— Memoir of Elder John Peak. Boston, Printed by J. Howe, Merchants Row, 1832. 203 p. port. F8.P35

14173
PEALE, CHARLES WILLSON (1741–1827)*
Maryland; Pennsylvania. Portrait painter, Revolutionary officer, assemblyman.

JENSEN, OLIVER O. The Peales. American heritage, v. 6, Apr. 1955: 40–51, 97–101. illus. (part col.), ports. (part col.) E171.A43, v. 6

PEALE, ALBERT C. Charles Willson Peale and his public services during the American Revolution. [Washington? 1897?] 31 p. ports. E207.P4P3

Also published in the *American Monthly Magazine,* v. 14, Feb.–Mar. 1899, p. 197–208, 371–391.

RICHMAN, IRWIN. Charles Willson Peale and the Philadelphia Museum. Pennsylvania history, v. 29, July 1962: 257–277. illus. F146.P597, v. 29

SELLERS, CHARLES C. Charles Willson Peale. Philadelphia, 1947. 2 v. illus., facsims., ports. (Memoirs of the American Philosophical Society, v. 23, pt. 1–2) ND237.P27S43
Q11.P612, v. 23

Vol. 1 published in 1939 under title: *The Artist of the Revolution; the Early Life of Charles Willson Peale.*
Bibliography: v. 2, p. 424–440.
Contents: v. 1. Early life (1741–1790)—v. 2. Later life (1790–1827).
A revision of the author's two-volume biography was published with the same title in New York by Scribner (1969. 510 p. ND237.P27S44).

—— Charles Willson Peale and the American Philosophical Society. *In* American Philosophical Society, *Philadelphia. Library.* Library bulletin. 1944. Philadelphia, 1945. p. 18–25. facsim. Z881.P49, 1944

—— Charles Willson Peale's career as a painter. *In* American Philosophical Society, *Philadelphia.* Proceedings, v. 92, May 1948: 105–106. Q11.P5, v. 92

Also published in the Society's *Library Bulletin* for 1948, p. 105–106.

—— Portraits and miniatures by Charles Willson Peale. Philadelphia, American Philosophical Society, 1952. 369 p. illus. (part col.), ports. (part col.) (Transactions of the American Philosophical Society, new ser., v. 42, pt. 1) Q11.P6, n.s., v. 42
Bibliography: p. 272–274.

—— Charles Willson Peale with patron and populace; a supplement to *Portraits and Miniatures by Charles Willson Peale*, with a survey of his work in other genres. Philadelphia, American Philosophical Society, 1969. 146 p. illus., facsims., ports. (Transactions of the American Philosophical Society, new ser., v. 59, pt. 3) Q11.P6, n. s., v. 59

SELLERS, HORACE W. Charles Willson Peale, artist-soldier. Pennsylvania magazine of history and biography, v. 38, July 1914: 257–286. port. F146.P65, v. 38

Includes Peale's military journal covering the period December 4, 1776–January 20, 1777.

—— Engravings by Charles Willson Peale, limner. Pennsylvania magazine of history and biography, v. 57, Apr. 1933: 153–174. plate, ports. F146.P65, v. 57

14174

PEERY, WILLIAM (1743–1800)

Delaware. Revolutionary officer, assemblyman, delegate to the Continental Congress, lawyer, judge.

PERRY, LYNN. Some letters of and concerning Major William Peery. Strasburg, Va., Shenandoah Pub. House, 1935. xi, 43 p. port. E207.P44P4

14175

PEMBERTON, ISRAEL (1715–1779)*

Pennsylvania. Merchant, assemblyman.

DiStefano, Judy M. A concept of the family in colonial America: the Pembertons of Philadelphia. 1970. ([371] p.) Micro AC–1, no. 71–7434

Thesis (Ph.D.)—Ohio State University.

Abstracted in *Dissertation Abstracts International*, v. 31A, Mar. 1971, p. 4667.

Thayer, Theodore G. Israel Pemberton, king of the Quakers. Philadelphia, Historical Society of Pennsylvania, 1943. v, 260 p. F152.P275T5 1943a

Bibliography: p. 234–250.

The author's thesis (Ph.D.), with the same title, was submitted to the University of Pennsylvania in 1941.

14176

PEMBERTON, JOHN (1727–1795)*

Pennsylvania. Quaker minister and missionary.

——— The diary of John Pemberton, for the years 1777 and 1778. Edited from the mss. in the possession of the Society, by Eli K. Price. Philadelphia, H. B. Ashmead, Printer, 1867. 14 p. E275.P39

The *Diary* (p. [3]–5) is taken from manuscript notes, made in *Poor Will's Pocket Almanack* in 1777 and 1778. The remainder of the work treats of Pemberton's ancestry, and of the banishment of Friends from Pennsylvania during the Revolution.

——— The life and travels of John Pemberton, a minister of the Gospel of Christ. *In* Friends' library. v. 6. Philadelphia, 1842. p. 267–380. BX7615.F8, v. 6

14177

PEMBROKE, HENRY HERBERT, *10th Earl of* (1734–1794)†

England. Military officer.

——— Henry, Elizabeth, and George (1734–80). Letters and diaries of Henry, tenth Earl of Pembroke, and his circle. Edited by Lord Herbert. London, J. Cape [1939] 576 p. fold. geneal. table, plates, ports. DA506.P37A4

A continuation has been published under the title *Pembroke Papers (1780–1794); Letters and Diaries of Henry, Tenth Earl of Pembroke and His Circle* (London, Cape [1950] 509 p. DA506.P37A42).

14178

PENDLETON, EDMUND (1721–1803)*

Virginia. Lawyer, assemblyman, delegate to the Continental Congress, judge.

——— The letters and papers of Edmund Pendleton, 1734–1803. Collected and edited by David John Mays. Charlottesville, Published for the Virginia Historical Society [by] University Press of Virginia, 1967. 2 v. (xxvii, 753 p.) facsim., port. (Virginia Historical Society. Documents, v. 7–8) F230.P385

Bibliography: p. [719]–723.

——— Unpublished letters of Edmund Pendleton [1765–82] *In* Massachusetts Historical Society, *Boston*. Proceedings. 2d ser., v. 19; 1905. Boston, 1906. p. 107–167. F61.M38, 2d s., v. 19

Hilldrup, Robert L. The life and times of Edmund Pendleton. Chapel Hill, University of North Carolina Press, 1939. xi, 363 p. plates, ports. F230.P42

Bibliography: p. [341]–350.

Mays, David J. Edmund Pendleton, 1721–1803. *In* Virginia State Bar Association. Annual report. v. 37; 1925. Richmond. p. 392–401. LL

An offprint, with an expanded title, was published in Richmond by the Richmond Press, Printers (1926. 9 p. LL).

——— Edmund Pendleton, 1721–1803; a biography. Cambridge, Harvard University Press, 1952. 2 v. illus., maps, ports. F230.P425

Bibliography: v. 2, p. [407]–429.

14179

PENN, JOHN (1741–1788)*

Virginia; North Carolina. Lawyer, delegate to the Continental Congress.

Pittman, Thomas M. John Penn. North Carolina booklet, v. 4, Sept. 1904: 5–23. F251.N86, v. 4

14180

PENN, JOHN (1760–1834)†

England. Writer.

——— John Penn's journal of a visit to Reading, Harrisburg, Carlisle, and Lancaster, in 1788. Pennsylvania magazine of history and biography, v. 3, no. 3, 1879: 284–295. F146.P65, v. 3

14181

PERKINS, JOSEPH (1749–1789)

Rhode Island. Silversmith, gunsmith, merchant.

Miller, William D. Joseph Perkins, silversmith. *In* Rhode Island Historical Society. Collections, v. 21, July 1928: 77–84. illus. F76.R47, v. 21

14182

PERKINS, NATHAN (1748–1838)

Connecticut. Clergyman.

—— A narrative of a tour through the state of Vermont from April 27 to June 12, 1789. Woodstock, Vt., Elm Tree Press, 1920. 31 p. ports. F52.P44

Reprinted, with an introduction and appendix by Charles V. S. Borst, in Rutland, Vt., by C. E. Tuttle Co. (1964).

Extracts from the Narrative were published in the *Vermont Quarterly*, new ser., v. 19, Jan. 1951, p. 43–52.

14183

PERKINS, SIMEON (1735–1812)

Connecticut; Nova Scotia. Merchant, assemblyman, judge.

—— Diary. Toronto, Champlain Society, 1948–67. 4 v. illus., maps (part fold.), port. (The publications of the Champlain Society, 29, 36, 39, 43) F1038.P48A3

Contents: [1] 1766–1780, edited by H. A. Innis.—[2] 1780–1789, edited by D. C. Harvey, with notes by C. B. Fergusson.—[3] 1790–1796, edited by C. B. Fergusson.—[4] 1797–1803, edited by C. B. Fergusson.

Volumes 1–2 have been reprinted in New York by Greenwood Press (1969).

14184

PERKINS, WILLIAM LEE (1737–1797)

Massachusetts; Nova Scotia; England. Physician, Loyalist.

MATTHEWS, ALBERT. Dr. William Lee Perkins (1737–1797). *In* Colonial Society of Massachusetts, *Boston.* Publications. v. 20. Transactions, 1917/19. Boston, 1920. p. 10–18. F61.C71, v. 20

14185

PERRAULT, JEAN BAPTISTE (1761–1844)

Canada; Old Northwest. Fur trader.

—— Narrative of the travels and adventures of a merchant voyageur in the savage territories of Northwest America leaving Montreal the 28th of May 1783 (to 1820). Edited with introduction and notes by John Sharpless Fox. *In* Michigan. *Historical Commission.* Historical collections and researches. v. 37. Lansing, 1910 p. 508–619. F561.M47, v. 37

14186

PERRAULT, JOSEPH FRANÇOIS (1753–1844)

Canada; Old Northwest. Fur trader.

BENDER, LOUIS P. Old and new Canada. 1753–1844. Historic scenes and social pictures; or, The life of Joseph-François Perrault. Montreal, Dawson Bros., 1882. xv, 291 p. F1032.B45

LELAND, MARINE E. Joseph-François Perrault, années de jeunesse, 1753–1783. *In* Quebec (City). Université Laval. Revue, v. 13, Oct.–Nov. 1958, Jan.–May 1959: 107–115, 212–225, 417–428, 529–534, 630–639, 689–699, 804–820. AP21. Q4, v. 13

14187

PERRY, DAVID (*b.* 1741)

New England. Revolutionary officer.

—— Recollections of an old soldier. The life of Captain David Perry, a soldier of the French and Revolutionary wars. Containing many extraordinary occurrences relating to his own private history, and an account of some interesting events in the history of the times in which he lived. Written by himself. Windsor, Vt., Printed at the Republican & Yeoman Print. Off., 1822. 55 p. E199.P46 Rare Bk. Coll.

Reprinted at Tarrytown, N.Y., by W. Abbatt (1928. 37 p. E173.M24, no. 137) as extra number, no. 137, of *The Magazine of History, With Notes and Queries.*

14188

PERRY, ICHABOD JEREMIAH (1758–1839)

Connecticut. Revolutionary soldier and seaman.

—— Reminiscences of the Revolution. Lima, N.Y., Ska-hase-ga-o Chapter, Daughters of the American Revolution, 1915. 63 p. E275.P46

14189

PERSON, THOMAS (1733–1800) *

North Carolina. Surveyor, landowner, assemblyman.

WEEKS, STEPHEN B. Thomas Person. North Carolina booklet, v. 9, July 1909: 16–35. F251.N86, v. 9

14190

PETERS, RICHARD (1704–1776)*

England; Pennsylvania. Anglican clergyman, lawyer, councilor, Indian agent.

CUMMINGS, HUBERTIS M. Richard Peters, provincial secretary and cleric, 1704–1776. Philadelphia, University of Pennsylvania Press—1944. viii, 347 p. port. (Pennsylvania lives) F152.P45C8

"Bibliographical note": p. 330–333.

FAIRBANKS, JOSEPH H. Richard Peters (c. 1704–1776): provincial secretary of Pennsylvania. 1972. ([269] p.) Micro AC–1, no. 72–31,843

Thesis (Ph.D.)—University of Arizona.

Abstracted in *Dissertation Abstracts International,* v. 33A, Dec. 1972, p. 2840–2841.

14191

PETERS, RICHARD (1744–1828)*

Pennsylvania. Lawyer, Revolutionary officer, delegate to the Continental Congress.

—— Memoranda of Judge Richard Peters relating to events that occurred during the Revolutionary War. American historical record, v. 2, May 1873: 220–225.
[E171.P86, v. 2]
Micro 39031

STINSON, JOSEPH W. Opinions of Richard Peters (1781–1817). University of Pennsylvania law review and American law register, v. 70, Mar. 1922: 185–197.
K25.N69, v. 70

14192

PETERS, SAMUEL (1735–1826)*
Connecticut; England. Anglican clergyman, Loyalist.

—— The works of Samuel Peters of Hebron, Connecticut, New England historian, satirist, folklorist, antipatriot, and Anglican clergyman, 1735–1826, with historical indexes. Edited by Kenneth Walter Cameron. Hartford [Conn.] Transcendental Books [1967] 184 l. map, port. F97.P42 1967

Comprises facsimile reproductions of the author's works, including original title pages.
Bibliography included in preface (leaf [4]).

COHEN, SHELDON S. The correspondence of Samuel Peters and Benjamin Trumbull. *In* Connecticut Historical Society, *Hartford.* Bulletin, v. 32, July 1967: 83–93. ports. F91.C67, v. 32

—— Samuel Peters, Connecticut's eccentric historian. New-England galaxy, v. 13, spring 1972: 3–14. illus., facsim., ports. F1.N39, v. 13

MAMPOTENG, CHARLES. The Reverend Samuel Peters, M.A., missionary at Hebron, Connecticut, 1760–1774. Historical magazine of the Protestant Episcopal church, v. 5, June 1936: 73–91. BX5800.H5, v. 5

MIDDLEBROOK, SAMUEL. Samuel Peters: a Yankee Munchausen. New England quarterly, v. 20, Mar. 1947: 75–87. F1.N62, v. 20

O'NEIL, MAUD. Samuel Andrew Peters: Connecticut Loyalist. 1947.
Thesis (Ph.D.)—University of California, Los Angeles.

TRUMBULL, JAMES HAMMOND. The Rev. Samuel Peters, his defenders and apologists, with a reply to *The Churchman's* review of "*The True-Blue Laws of Connecticut,*" &c. Hartford, 1877. 26 p. F97.P45
Reprinted from the *Hartford Daily Courant.*
Chiefly a review of Samuel J. McCormick's edition of Peters' *General History of Connecticut* (New York, D. Appleton, 1877). In the title Trumbull refers to his own publication, *The True-Blue Laws of Connecticut and New Haven and the False Blue-Laws Invented by the Rev. Samuel Peters* (Hartford, Conn., American Pub. Co., 1876. 360 p. LL).

14193

PETTIGREW, CHARLES (1744–1807)*
Pennsylvania; North Carolina. Anglican clergyman.

LEMMON, SARAH M. Parson Pettigrew of the "Old Church," 1744–1807. Chapel Hill, University of North Carolina Press, 1970. 168 p. (The James Sprunt studies in history and political science, v. 52)
F251.J28, v. 52

Bibliography: p. [149]–155.

The Pettigrew papers. v. 1. 1685–1818. Edited by Sarah McCulloh Lemmon. Raleigh [N.C.] State Dept. of Archives and History, 1971. xl, 699 p. illus.
F254.P48

Selected papers of the Pettigrew family in the Southern Historical Collection, Library of the University of North Carolina at Chapel Hill, and the North Carolina State Dept. of Archives and History.
Includes bibliographic references.

WALL, BENNETT H. Charles Pettigrew, first bishop-elect of the North Carolina Episcopal church. North Carolina historical magazine, v. 28, Jan. 1951: 15–46.
F251.N892, v. 28

14194

PEYTON, JOHN ROWZÉE (1752–1798)
Virginia. Planter

PEYTON, JOHN L. The adventures of my grandfather. With extracts from his letters, and other family documents, prepared for the press with notes and biographical sketches of himself and his son John Howe Peyton, Esq. London, J. Wilson, 1867. x, 249 p.
F229.P51

Narrative of the circumstances connected with the settlement of M. Jean Louis or John Lewis and his family in Virginia: p. 215–224.

14195

PHELPS, CHARLES (1717–1789)
Connecticut; Vermont. Lawyer, judge, theologian.

HUNTINGTON, JAMES L. The Honorable Charles Phelps. *In* Colonial Society of Massachusetts, *Boston.* Publications. v. 32. Transactions, 1933/37. Boston, 1937. p. 440–455. F61.C71, v. 32
A comment on Huntington's paper, by George P. Anderson, appears on p. 455–460.

14196

PHELPS, MATTHEW (d. 1817)
New England. Traveler.

—— Memoirs and adventures of Captain Matthew Phelps; formerly of Harwington in Connecticut, now resident in Newhaven in Vermont. Particularly in two voyages, from Connecticut to the river Mississippi, from December 1773 to October 1780 . . . Compiled from the original journal and minutes kept by Mr. Phelps, during his voyages and adventures, and revised and corrected according to his present recollection. By

Anthony Haswell. Bennington, Vt., from the Press of Anthony Haswell, 1802. 210, 63, xii p.
F341.P54 Rare Bk. Coll.

14197

PHELPS, OLIVER (1749–1809)*

Connecticut; Massachusetts. Merchant, assemblyman, councilor, land speculator.

WANDELL, SAMUEL H.   Oliver Phelps. *In* New York State Historical Association. New York history, v. 23, July 1942: 275–282.   F116.N865, v. 23

PHILADELPHIA, JACOB
See MEYER, JACOB

PHILIPSE, MARY
See MORRIS, MARY PHILIPSE

14198

PHILLIPS, SAMUEL (1752–1802)*

Massachusetts. Revolutionary munitioner, judge, philanthropist.

TAYLOR, JOHN L.   A memoir of His Honor Samuel Phillips, LL.D. Boston, Congregational Board of Publication, 1856. xi, 391 p. fold. facsim., plates, ports.
F69.P57

14199

PICKENS, ANDREW (1739–1817)*

Pennsylvania; South Carolina. Settler, Revolutionary general, assemblyman.

FERGUSON, CLYDE R.   General Andrew Pickens. 1960. ([708] p.)   Micro AC–1, no. 65–14,143
Thesis (Ph.D.)—Duke University.
Abstracted in *Dissertation Abstracts*, v. 26, Dec. 1965, p. 3278–3279.

PICKENS, ANDREW L.   Skyagunsta, the border wizard owl, Major-General Andrew Pickens (1739–1817). Greenville, S.C., Observer Print. Co., ᶜ1934. 161 p.
E207.P63P642
"Sources and acknowledgments": p. 160–161.
A revision of *The Wizard Owl of the Southern Highlands, a Life of General Pickens of the Revolution Thru the Battle of Cowpens*, published in 1933.

TURNER, DOUGLAS K.   General Andrew Pickens. *In* Bucks County Historical Society, *Doylestown, Pa.* Collection of papers. v. 3. Doylestown, 1909. p. 657–669.   F157.B8B84, v. 3

WARING, ALICE N.   The fighting elder: Andrew Pickens, 1739–1817. Columbia, University of South Carolina Press, 1962. vi, 252 p. illus., maps, plates, ports.
E207.P63W3
"Notes and references": p. 210–239.

14200

PICKERING, TIMOTHY (1745–1829)*

Massachusetts; Pennsylvania. Lawyer, assemblyman, Revolutionary general, merchant.

Guide to the microfilm edition of the Timothy Pickering papers. Frederick S. Allis, Jr., editor; Roy Bartolomei, associate editor. Boston, Massachusetts Historical Society, 1966. 46 p.   Z6616.P52A4 Mss

PHILLIPS, EDWARD H.   The public career of Timothy Pickering, Federalist, 1745–1802. 1950.
Thesis (Ph.D.)—Harvard University.

PICKERING, OCTAVIUS.   The life of Timothy Pickering. Boston, Little, Brown, 1867–73. 4 v. ports.
E302.6.P5P5
Vols. 2–4 by Charles Wentworth Upham.

SWETT, SAMUEL.   Defence of Col. Timothy Pickering, against Bancroft's history. Boston, Crocker and Brewster, 1859. 12 p.   E302.6.P5S9
At the time of the Battle of Lexington, Pickering was colonel of the 1st Essex County Regiment, and criticism was directed against him for delay in attacking the British on their retreat.

14201

PIERSON, ABRAHAM (1756–*ca.* 1822)

Connecticut. Schoolmaster, Revolutionary soldier.

——— Abraham Pierson's journal [1776–86] *In* Connecticut Historical Society, *Hartford.* Bulletin, v. 15, July–Oct. 1950: 18–24, 31–32; v. 16, Jan. 1951: 6–7.
F91.C67, v. 15–16
A brief autobiography appeared in volume 15, July 1950, p. 17–18.

14202

PILMORE, JOSEPH (1739–1825)*

England; Pennsylvania. Clergyman.

——— The journal of Joseph Pilmore, Methodist itinerant, for the years August 1, 1769, to January 2, 1774. With a biographical sketch of Joseph Pilmore by Frank B. Stanger. Editors: Frederick E. Maser [and] Howard T. Maag. Philadelphia, Printed by Message Pub. Co. for the Historical Society of the Philadelphia Annual Conference of the United Methodist Church, 1969. 262 p. illus., facsim., ports.   BX8495.P548A3

RIGHTMYER, NELSON W.   Joseph Pilmore, Anglican evangelical. Historical magazine of the Protestant Episcopal church, v. 16, June 1947: 181–198.
BX5800.H5, v. 16

14203

PINCKNEY, CHARLES COTESWORTH (1746–1825)*

South Carolina. Lawyer, assemblyman, Revolutionary general, delegate to the Constitutional Convention.

ZAHNISER, MARVIN R. Charles Cotesworth Pinckney, founding father. Chapel Hill, Published for the Institute of Early American History and Culture, Williamsburg, Va., by the University of North Carolina Press [1967] ix, 295 p. port. E302.6.P55Z3

Bibliographic footnotes.

The author's thesis (Ph.D.), *The Public Career of Charles Cotesworth Pinckney*, was submitted to the University of California, Santa Barbara, in 1963 (Micro AC–1, no. 66–5969).

14204

PINCKNEY, ELIZA LUCAS (1723?–1793)*

South Carolina. Planter. Mother of Charles Cotesworth (1746–1825) and Thomas Pinckney (1750–1828).

——— The letterbook of Eliza Lucas Pinckney, 1739–1762. Edited by Elise Pinckney, with the editorial assistance of Marvin R. Zahniser, and an introduction by Walter Muir Whitehill. Chapel Hill, University of North Carolina Press [1972] xxix, 195 p. illus. F272.P6416

BASKETT, SAM S. Eliza Lucas Pinckney; portrait of an eighteenth-century American. South Carolina historical magazine, v. 72, Oct. 1971: 207–219. F266.S55, v. 72

RAVENEL, HARRIOTT H. R. Eliza Pinckney. New York, C. Scribner's Sons, 1896. xi, 331 p. fold. facsim. (Women of colonial and Revolutionary times) F272.P65

Reprinted in Spartanburg, S.C., by the Reprint Co. (1967. F266.S53, no. 10).

14205

PINCKNEY, THOMAS (1750–1828)*

South Carolina. Lawyer, Revolutionary officer, assemblyman, governor.

——— Letters of Thomas Pinckney, 1775–1780. Edited by Jack L. Cross. South Carolina historical magazine, v. 58, Jan.–Oct. 1957: 19–33, 67–83, 145–162, 224–242. F266.S55, v. 58

PINCKNEY, CHARLES COTESWORTH. Life of General Thomas Pinckney. Boston, Houghton, Mifflin, 1895. 237 p. port. E302.6.P57P6

14206

PINDELL, RICHARD (1755–1833)

Maryland. Revolutionary surgeon.

——— A militant surgeon of the Revolution: some letters of Richard Pindell, M.D. Maryland historical magazine, v. 18, Dec. 1923: 309–323. F176.M18, v. 18

WROTH, PEREGRINE. Dr. Richard Pindell, one-man army. Daughters of the American Revolution magazine, v. 87, July 1953: 897–902. E202.5.A12, v. 87

14207

PINKNEY, WILLIAM (1764–1822)*

Maryland. Lawyer.

FLANDERS, HENRY. William Pinkney; lawyer, statesman, diplomat. [n.p., 1906?] 14 p. E302.6.P6F5

PINKNEY, WILLIAM, *Bp.* The life of William Pinkney, by his nephew, the Rev. William Pinkney. New York, D. Appleton, 1853. 407 p. port. E302.6.P6P6

Contains some of Pinkney's correspondence and speeches.

Reprinted in New York by Da Capo Press (1969).

14208

PINNEY, JOHN (*ca.* 1740–1818)

England; Nevis. Planter, assemblyman, councilor.

PARES, RICHARD. A West-India fortune. London, New York, Longmans, Green [1950] viii, 374 p. maps, plates, ports. HD9114. W44P56

Bibliographic references included in "Notes" (p. 340–367).

Reprinted in Hamden, Conn., by Archon Books (1968).

14209

PINTO, ISAAC DE (1715–1787)

Netherlands. Economist, financier.

HÜHNER, LEON. Isaac de Pinto. A noted European publicist and defender of Great Britain's policy during the American Revolution. *In* American Jewish Historical Society. Publications. no. 13. New York, 1905. p. 113–126. E184.J5A5, no. 13

14210

PIPE, *Captain, Delaware chief* (*d.* 1794)

BARNHOLTH, WILLIAM I. Hopocan (Capt. Pipe) the Delaware chieftain. [Rev. and enl.] Akron, Ohio, Summit County Historical Society, 1966, 19 l. E99.D2B3 1966

Bibliography: leaf 1.

14211

PITCAIRN, JOHN (1722–1775)*

Scotland. British officer in America.

HUDSON, CHARLES. The life and character of Major Pitcairn. *In* Massachusetts Historical Society, *Boston.* Proceedings. v. 17; 1879–80. Boston, 1880. p. 315–326. F61.M38, v. 17

——— ——— Offprint. [Boston, 1880] [315]–326 p. E207.P68H8

14212

PITT, WILLIAM, *1st Earl of Chatham* (1708–1778)†

England. Member of Parliament, orator, Secretary of State.

―――― Correspondence of William Pitt, Earl of Chatham. Edited by the executors of his son, John, Earl of Chatham, and published from the original manuscripts in their possession. London, John Murray, 1838–40. 4 v. facsim.　　　　DA483.P6A2

Vols. 2–4 "Edited by William Stanhope Taylor, Esq., and Captain John Henry Pringle."

[ALMON, JOHN]　Anecdotes of the life of the Right Hon. William Pitt, Earl of Chatham, and of the principal events of his time. With his speeches in Parliament, from the year 1736 to the year 1778. 6th ed., corr. London, Printed for L. B. Seeley, 1797. 3 v.
DA483.P6A5

BUTLER, HENRY M.　Lord Chatham as an orator. Oxford, Clarendon Press, 1912. 40 p. (The Romanes lecture, 1912)　　　　DA483.P6B8

[GODWIN, WILLIAM]　The history of the life of William Pitt, Earl of Chatham. London, Printed for the author, and sold by G. Kearsley, 1783. xv, 302 p.
DA483.P6G6 Rare Bk. Coll.

GREEN, WALFORD D.　William Pitt, Earl of Chatham, and the growth and division of the British Empire, 1708–1778. New York, G. P. Putnam's Sons, 1901. xiii, 391 p. fold. map, plates, plan, ports. (Heroes of the nations, [v. 32])　　　　DA483.P6G8

HARRISON, FREDERIC.　Chatham. New York. Macmillan Co., 1905. vi, 239 p.　　　　DA483.P6H3

LONG, JOHN C.　Mr. Pitt and America's birthright; a biography of William Pitt, the Earl of Chatham, 1708–1778. New York, F. A. Stokes Co., 1940. xiii, 576 p. illus., facsims., maps, plates, ports.　　　DA483.P6L6

Bibliography: p. 557–564.

MACAULAY, THOMAS BABINGTON MACAULAY, *1st Baron*.　The Earl of Chatham. New York, Harper, 1878. 204 p. (Harper's half-hour series, [v. 38])
AC1.H2, v. 38

An essay from the *Edinburgh Review* of January 1834, on "Francis Thackeray's History of the Right Honorable William Pitt, Earl of Chatham, 1827."

―――― Macaulay's second essay on the Earl of Chatham; with notes and a sketch of Macaulay's life by D. H. M. Boston, Ginn, 1891. v, 91 p. (Annotated English classics)　　　　DA483.P6M17

First published in the *Edinburgh Review* for October 1844.

PLUMB, JOHN H.　Chatham. London, Collins [1953] 159 p. illus., maps, plate. (Brief lives, no. 7)
DA483.P6P5

―――― The Earl of Chatham. History today, v. 2, Mar. 1952: 175–180.　　　　D1.H818, v. 2

REA, ROBERT R.　The Earl of Chatham and the London press, 1775. Journalism quarterly, v. 31, spring 1954: 186–192.　　　　PN4700.J7, v. 31

ROBERTSON, *Sir* CHARLES G.　Chatham and the British Empire. London, Published by Hodder & Stoughton for the English Universities Press [1946] xii, 200 p. map, port. (Teach yourself history library)　　DA483.P6R65

"Books on Chatham": p. 197–198.

ROSEBERY, ARCHIBALD PHILIP PRIMROSE, *5th Earl of*.　Lord Chatham, his early life and connections. New York, Harper, 1910. xi, 480 p.　　DA483.P6R7

RUVILLE, ALBERT VON.　William Pitt, Earl of Chatham. Translated by H. J. Chaytor, assisted by Mary Morison, with an introduction by Professor Hugh E. Egerton. London, W. Heinemann; New York, G. P. Putnam's Sons, 1907. 3 v. ports.　　　DA483.P6R93

Appendixes: 1. Authorities (v. 3, p. 349–358). 2. Documents (v. 3, p. 359–394).

Translation of Ruville's *William Pitt, Graf von Chatham* (Stuttgart, J. G. Cotta, 1905).

SHERRARD, OWEN A.　Lord Chatham; a war minister in the making. [London] Bodley Head [1952] 323 p. plates, ports.　　　　DA483.P6S5

Bibliography: p. 311–313.

―――― Lord Chatham and America. London, Bodley Head [1958] 395 p.　　　　DA483.P6S52

Bibliography: p. 381–384.

This third volume of the author's life of Lord Chatham explores Pitt's activities from his resignation as Secretary of State in 1761 to his death in 1778.

THACKERAY, FRANCIS.　A history of the Right Honourable William Pitt, Earl of Chatham: containing his speeches in Parliament; a considerable portion of his correspondence, when secretary of state, upon French, Spanish, and American affairs, never before published. London, Printed for C. and J. Rivington, 1827. 2 v. geneal. table.　　　　DA483.P6T3

TUNSTALL, WILLIAM C.　William Pitt, Earl of Chatham. London, Hodder and Stoughton [1938] 556 p. illus., geneal. tables, maps, ports.　　　DA483.P6T8 1938

Bibliography: p. 479–489.

WILLIAMS, BASIL.　The life of William Pitt, Earl of Chatham. London, New York, Longmans, Green, 1913. 2 v. fold. maps, port.　　DA483.P6W5

"List of speeches delivered by William Pitt, Earl of Chatham, with a note on the authenticity of Pitt's speeches": v. 2, p. 335–351.

Bibliography: v. 2, 352–368.

Reprinted in New York by Octagon Books (1966).

14213
PITT, WILLIAM (1759–1806)†
England. Lawyer, Member of Parliament, First Lord of Treasury. Son of William Pitt (1708–1778).

———— The speeches of the Right Honourable William Pitt, in the House of Commons. London, Longman, Hurst, Rees and Orme, 1806. 4 v.   DA522.P45 1806
Edited by W. S. Hathaway.

DERRY, JOHN W.   William Pitt. London, Batsford [1962] 160 p. illus., ports. [Makers of Britain]
          DA522.P6D4
"A note on further reading": p. 153–154.

EHRMAN, JOHN.   The younger Pitt. v. 1. The years of acclaim [1759–89] New York, Dutton [1969] xv, 710 p. illus., ports. (part col.)   DA522.P6E36, v. 1
"Notes on sources": p. 669–695.

GIFFORD, JOHN.   A history of the political life of the Right Honourable William Pitt; including some account of the times in which he lived. London, Printed for T. Cadell and W. Davies, 1809. 6 v. ports.
          DA522.P6G4

ROSE, JOHN HOLLAND.   William Pitt and national revival. London, G. Bell, 1911. xii, 655 p. ports.
          DA522.P6R7
"Abbreviations of the titles of the chief works referred to": p. xi–xii.

ROSEBERY, ARCHIBALD PHILIP PRIMROSE, *5th Earl of*.   Pitt. London and New York, Macmillan, 1892. viii, 298 p. (Twelve English statesmen) DA522.P6R8
Reprinted in New York by Haskell House (1968) and AMS Press (1969).

STANHOPE, PHILIP HENRY STANHOPE, *5th Earl*.   Life of the Right Honourable William Pitt. London, J. Murray, 1861–62. 4 v. facsims., ports.   DA522.P6S7
The 1867 edition has been reprinted in New York by AMS Press (1970).

TOMLINE, *Sir* GEORGE PRETYMAN, *Bart., Bp. of Winchester*.   Memoirs of the life of the Right Honorable William Pitt. 2d ed. London, J. Murray, 1821. 3 v.
          DA522.P6T6

Closes with 1793.

14214
PITTS, JAMES (1712–1776)
Massachusetts. Merchant.

GOODWIN, DANIEL.   Memorial of the lives and services of James Pitts and his sons, John, Samuel and Lendall, during the American Revolution, 1760–1780. Chicago, Culver, Page, Hoyne, 1882. 63 p.   CS71.P691 1882
          E263.M4G59

14215
PLEASANTS, ROBERT (*b.* 1722)
Virginia. Planter, merchant.

PLEASANTS, ROBERT.   Letters of Robert Pleasants, of Curles [1771–74] William and Mary College quarterly historical magazine, 2d ser., v. 1, Apr. 1921: 107–113; v. 2, Oct. 1922: 257–275.   F221.W71, 2d s., v. 1–2

14216
PLUMER, WILLIAM (1759–1850)*
Massachusetts; New Hampshire. Lawyer, assemblyman.

———— Letters of William Plumer, 1786–1787. *In* Colonial Society of Massachusetts, *Boston*. Publications. v. 11. Transactions, 1906/7. Boston, 1910. p. 383–403. port.
          F61.C71, v. 11

HOYT, ALBERT H.   William Plumer, senior. New England historical and genealogical register, v. 25, Jan. 1871: 1–10. port.   F1.N56, v. 25

PLUMER, WILLIAM.   Life of William Plumer, by his son, William Plumer, Junior. Edited with a sketch of the author's life, by A. P. Peabody. Boston, Philips, Sampson, 1857. xvi, 543 p. ports.
          E302.6.P73P7 Rare Bk. Coll.
Reprinted in New York by Da Capo Press (1969).

TURNER, LYNN W.   William Plumer of New Hampshire, 1759–1850. Chapel Hill, Published for the Institute of Early American History and Culture, Williamsburg, Va., by University of North Carolina Press [1962] 366 p. illus., port.   E302.6.P73T8
Based on thesis, Harvard University.
"Note on the sources": p. 349–354.

WAIT, ALBERT S.   The life, character, and public services of Governor William Plumer. *In* New Hampshire Historical Society. Proceedings. v. 3; 1895/99. Concord, 1902. p. 119–142.   F31.N52, v. 3

14217
POINTE DE SABLE, JEAN BAPTISTE (1745?–1818)
Illinois. Trader, trapper, farmer.

MEEHAN, THOMAS A.   Jean Baptiste Point du Saible, the first Chicagoan. Mid-America, v. 19, Apr. 1937: 83–92.   BX1415.I3M5, v. 19

SIMON, ELIZABETH M., *and* HUBERT V. SIMON. Chicago's first citizen—Jean Baptiste Pointe de Sable; a historical sketch of a distinguished pioneer. Chicago, E. Matlock-Simon and H. V. Simon Co. [ᶜ1933] 27 p.   F548.4.P747
Bibliography: p. 26

14218

POLK, EZEKIEL (1747–1824)

North Carolina. Frontiersman, Revolutionary officer.

Democratic Party. *Tennessee.* Vindication of the Revolutionary character and services of the late Col. Ezekiel Polk, of Mecklenburg, N.C. Published and prepared by order of the Tenn. State Central Committee. [Nashville, Printed by J. P. Heiss, 1844] 16 p. E275.P72

SELLERS, CHARLES G. Colonel Ezekiel Polk, pioneer and patriarch. William and Mary quarterly, 3d ser., v. 10, Jan. 1953: 80–98. F221.W71, 3d s., v. 10

14219

POLLOCK, OLIVER (1737–1823)*

Ireland; Pennsylvania; Louisiana. Merchant, trader, planter, Revolutionary munitioner and supplier.

DOWNING, MARGARET B. Oliver Pollock, patriot and financier. Illinois Catholic historical review, v. 2, Oct. 1919: 196–207. BX1415.I3M5, v. 2

JAMES, JAMES A. Oliver Pollock and the free navigation of the Mississippi River. Mississippi Valley historical review, v. 19, Dec. 1932: 331–347. E171.J87, v. 19

———— Oliver Pollock and the winning of the Illinois country. *In* Illinois State Historical Society. Transactions; 1934. Springfield. (Illinois State Historical Library. Publication, no. 41) p. 35–59. F536.I34, 1934

———— Oliver Pollock, financier of the Revolution in the West. Mississippi Valley historical review, v. 16, June 1929: 67–80. E171.J87, v. 16

———— Oliver Pollock; the life and times of an unknown patriot. New York, D. Appleton-Century Co., 1937. xiii, 376 p. facsim., map, plates. E302.6.P84J3

Bibliography: p. 360–368.

Reprinted in Freeport, N.Y., by Books for Libraries Press (1970).

MULLANEY, WILLIAM F. Oliver Pollock, Catholic patriot and financier of the American Revolution. *In* United States Catholic Historical Society. Historical records and studies. v. 28. New York, 1937. p. 164–236. E184.C3U5, v. 28

14220

POMEROY, SETH (1706–1777)*

Massachusetts. Gunsmith, Revolutionary general.

———— The journals and papers of Seth Pomeroy, sometime general in the colonial service. Published by the Society of Colonial Wars in the State of New York, and, at the request of its Committee on Historical Documents, edited by Louis Effingham de Forest. [New York] 1926. vi, 180 p. [Society of Colonial Wars in the State of New York. Publication, no. 38] E186.3.N64, no. 38

14221

POND, PETER (1740–1807?)*

Connecticut; Old Northwest. Fur trader, explorer, mapmaker.

———— The narrative of Peter Pond. *In* Gates, Charles M., ed. Five fur traders of the Northwest. [Minneapolis] Published for the Minnesota Society of the Colonial Dames of America [by] the University of Minnesota Press, 1933. p. 11–59. F483.G25

"Introductory note": p. 11–16.

———— Remarkable experiences in early wars of New World. Connecticut magazine, v. 10, no. 2, 1906: 239–259. illus. F91.C8, v. 10

Reprinted under the title "1740–75: Journal of Peter Pond" in the *Collections* of the Wisconsin Historical Society, v. 18 (Madison, 1908), p. 314–354.

INNIS, HAROLD A. Peter Pond and the influence of Capt. James Cook on exploration in the interior of North America. *In* Royal Society of Canada. Proceedings and transactions. 3d ser., v. 22, section 2; 1928. Ottawa. p. 131–141. AS42.R6, 3d s., v. 22

———— ———— Offprint. Ottawa, 1928. 131–141 p. F1060.7.P79

———— Peter Pond, fur trader and adventurer. Toronto, Irwin & Gordon, 1930. xi, 153 p. fold. map. F1060.7.P793

Includes extracts from Pond's journal. Bibliography: p. 144–153.

WAGNER, HENRY R. Peter Pond, fur trader & explorer. [New Haven] Yale University Library, 1955. 103 p. fold. maps. (Yale University. Library. Western historical series, no. 2) F1060.7.P794

Maps, in separate folder, and text volume issued together in case.

14222

POOR, ENOCH (1736–1780)*

Massachusetts; New Hampshire. Trader, shipbuilder, Revolutionary general.

BAKER, HENRY M. Oration upon the unveiling of the statue of Gen. Enoch Poor at Hackensack, N.J., October 7, 1904. *In* Bergen County Historical Society, *Hackensack, N.J.* Papers and proceedings. no. 1; 1902/5. Hackensack, 1905. p. 37–52. F142.B4B4, no. 1

BEANE, S. C. General Enoch Poor. *In* New Hampshire Historical Society. Proceedings. v. 3; 1897/99. Concord, 1902. p. 435–473. F31.N52, v. 3

HEATHCOTE, CHARLES W. General Enoch Poor—loyal patriot and devoted friend of Washington. Picket post, no. 56, May 1957: 4–10. illus. E234.P5, no. 56

REED, JOHN F. The mystery of Enoch Poor. Picket post, Apr. 1972: 24–26. port. E234.P5, 1972

On the nature of Poor's death.

14223

POPP, STEPHAN (1755–1820)

Hessian soldier.

———— Popp's journal, 1777–1783. Pennsylvania magazine of history and biography, v. 26, Apr.–July 1902: 25–41, 245–254. maps, facsims.   F146.P65, v. 26

Translated with introduction and notes, by Joseph G. Rosengarten.

———— ———— Offprint. Philadelphia, 1902. 29 p. maps.   E268.P83

A new translation by Reinhart J. Pope was printed privately under the title *A Hessian Soldier in the American Revolution; the Diary of Stephan Popp* ([Racine? Wis.] 1953. 39 p. E268.P83 1953).

14224

PORTEOUS, JOHN (*d.* 1799)

Scotland; Canada. Indian trader, merchant.

———— Schenectady to Michilimackinac, 1765 & 1766. Journal of John Porteous. *In* Ontario Historical Society. Papers and records. v. 33. Toronto, 1939. p. 75–98.   F1056.O58, v. 33

Introduction and notes by Fred C. Hamil.

14225

PORTER, ANDREW (1743–1813)*

Pennsylvania. Schoolmaster, mathematician, Revolutionary munitioner and officer, farmer.

PORTER, WILLIAM A.   A sketch of the life of General Andrew Porter. Pennsylvania magazine of history and biography, v. 4, no. 3, 1880: 261–301. port.   F146.P65, v. 4

Porter's journal of his travels as one of the Pennsylvania commissioners to fix the western boundary of the state, 1785–86, appears on p. 268–285.

14226

PORTER, SAMUEL (*d.* 1798)

Massachusetts; England. Lawyer, Loyalist.

———— Salem Loyalists—unpublished letters [1777–88] New-England historical and genealogical register, v. 26, July 1872: 243–248.   F1.N56, v. 26

Communicated by John J. Latting.

14227

POTTER, ISRAEL RALPH (1744–1826?)

Rhode Island. Farmer, Revolutionary soldier.

———— Life and remarkable adventures of Israel R. Potter (a native of Cranston, Rhode-Island), who was a soldier in the American Revolution . . . after which he was taken prisoner by the British, conveyed to England, where for 30 years he obtained a livelihood . . . by crying "Old chairs to mend.'' Providence [R.I.] Printed by J. Howard, for I. R. Potter, 1824. 108 p. front.   E281.P86 Rare Bk. Coll.

Potter served in Captain Edmund Johnson's company, 1st Rhode Island Regiment at Bunker Hill, later being transferred to the brigantine *Washington*. The vessel was captured and the crew taken to England where Potter escaped from his captors.

Reprinted, with an introduction by Leonard Kriegel, in New York by Corinth Books (1962).

14228

POTTER, JAMES (1729–1789)*

Ireland; Pennsylvania. Farmer, Revolutionary general.

HEATHCOTE, CHARLES W.   General James Potter—a resolute Pennsylvania military officer and friend of Washington. Picket post, no. 68, May 1960: 13–18.   E234.P5, no. 68

LINN, MARY H.   General James Potter: his life and his times. *In* Northumberland County (Pa.) Historical Society. Proceedings. v. 12. Sunbury, 1942. p. [5]–26.   F157.N8N7, v. 12

14229

POTTER, JARED (1742–1810)

Connecticut. Physician, professor, Revolutionary surgeon.

THOMS, HERBERT.   Jared Potter. *In his* The Doctors Jared of Connecticut: Jared Eliot, Jared Potter, Jared Kirtland. Hamden, Conn., Shoe String Press, 1958. p. [32]–51. (Dept. of the History of Medicine, Yale University School of Medicine. Publication no. 35).   R153.T35

14230

POTTS, JAMES (1752–1822)

Pennsylvania. Blacksmith, Revolutionary officer, farmer.

POTTS, THOMAS M.   A short biographical sketch of Major James Potts, born 1752, died 1822, to which is appended copies of the most important papers relating to him, and two ancestral charts. [Canonsburg, Pa.] Print. priv. by the author, 1877. 85 p.   F157.P56P9

14231

POTTS, JONATHAN (1745–1781)*

Pennsylvania. Physician, Revolutionary medical officer.

NEILL, EDWARD D.   Biographical sketch of Doctor Jonathan Potts. New England historical and genealogical register, v. 18, Jan. 1864: 21–36.   F1.N56, v. 18

———— ———— Offprint. Albany, J. Munsell, 1863. 18 p.   E283.P87

Includes the texts of several letters written to Potts during the war.

———— A contribution to the medical history of the American Army during the War for Independence. *In* Macalester College, *St. Paul, Minn. Department of History, Literature, and Political Science.* Contributions. 2d ser., no. 10. St. Paul, Pioneer Press Pub. Co., 1892. p. [223]–254. E173.M12, 2d s., no. 10

Mostly letters written to Dr. Potts during the war taken from manuscripts at the Pennsylvania Historical Society.

SMITH, HELEN B. Surgeon Jonathan Potts planned inoculations at the winter camp [Valley Forge] Picket post, no. 17, Apr. 1947: 16–21. illus. E234.P5, no. 17

14232

POWEL, SAMUEL (1739–1793)

Pennsylvania. Judge.

———— Powel-Roberts correspondence, 1761–1765. Pennsylvania magazine of history and biography, v. 18, Apr. 1894: 35–42. F146.P65, v. 18

14233

POWELL, ANN (*b.* 1769)

Canada.

———— Letters from Miss Ann Powell combined in a journal during a tour to Niagara and Detroit, 1789. *In* Essex Institute, Salem, Mass. Historical collections, v. 86, Oct. 1950: 331–349. F72.E7E81, v. 86

14234

POWELL, LEVEN (1737–1810)

Virginia. Planter, Revolutionary officer.

———— Letters from Colonel Leven Powell to his wife. *In* John P. Branch historical papers of Randolph-Macon College. [v. 1] no. 1; 1901. Ashland, Va. p. 24–38. F221.J65, v. 1

The Leven Powell correspondence—1775–1787. *In* John P. Branch historical papers of Randolph-Macon College. [v. 1] no. 2; 1902. Ashland, Va. p. 111–138. F221.J65, v. 1

Letters from the period 1786–1829 appear in no. 3 for 1903, p. 217–256.

POWELL, ROBERT C., *ed.* A biographical sketch of Col. Leven Powell, including his correspondence during the Revolutionary War. Alexandria, Va., G. H. Ramey, 1877. 104 p. E263.V8P8

"Letters from Col. George Johnston, Jr.": p. [35]–62.
"Letters from Rev. David Griffith, M.D.": p. [63]–80.

14235

POWELL, WILLIAM DUMMER (1755–1834)

Massachusetts; Canada. Lawyer, Loyalist, judge.

QUAIFE, MILO M. Detroit biographies: William Dummer Powell. Burton historical collection leaflet, v. 9, Mar. 1931: 51–64. F561.B9, v. 9

RIDDELL, WILLIAM R. The life of William Dummer Powell, first judge at Detroit and fifth chief justice of Upper Canada. Lansing, Michigan Historical Commission, 1924. 305 p. plates, ports. F1032.P88

———— Two incidents of Revolutionary times. Journal of criminal law and criminology, v. 12, Aug. 1921: 223–237. HV6001.J63, v. 12

Concerns Powell's legal involvement with prisoners taken during the British and Indian expedition from Detroit against the settlements in Ohio and Kentucky in 1780.

14236

POWNALL, THOMAS. (1722–1805)*†

England; New Jersey; Massachusetts. Governor, Member of Parliament.

FOWLER, ROBERT L. Governor Thomas Pownall, colonial statesman. Magazine of American history, with notes and queries, v. 16, Nov. 1886: 409–432. illus. E171.M18, v. 16

MULKEARN, LOIS. The biography of a forgotten book— Pownall's *Topographical Description of . . . North America. In* Bibliographical Society of America. Papers, v. 43, 1st quarter 1949: 63–74. Z1008.B51P, v. 43

POWNALL, CHARLES A. W. Thomas Pownall, M.P., F.R.S., governor of Massachusetts Bay, author of *The Letters of Junius;* with a supplement comparing the colonies of Kings George III and Edward VII. London, H. Stevens, Son & Stiles; [Binghamton, N.Y., Printed by the Binghamton Book Mfg. Co.] ᶜ1908. 488 p. F67.P88

ROBBINS, CAROLINE. An active and intelligent antiquary, Governor Thomas Pownall. Pennsylvania history, v. 26, Jan. 1959: 1–20. illus., port. F146.P597, v. 26

SCHUTZ, JOHN A. Thomas Pownall and his Negro commonwealth. Journal of Negro history, v. 30, Oct. 1945: 400–404. E185.J86, v. 30

———— Thomas Pownall, British defender of American liberty; a study of Anglo-American relations in the eighteenth century. Glendale, Calif., A. H. Clark Co., 1951. 340 p. illus., facsim., map, port. (Old Northwest historical series, 5) F67.P893

Bibliography: p. [291]–309.
The author's thesis (Ph.D.), *Thomas Pownall: Eighteenth Century Imperialist*, was submitted to the University of California, Los Angeles, in 1945.

———— Thomas Pownall's proposed Atlantic federation. Hispanic American historical review, v. 27, May 1946: 263–268. F1401.H66, v. 27

14237

PRATT, MATTHEW (1734–1805)*

Pennsylvania. Portrait artist, sign painter.

——— Autobiographical notes of Matthew Pratt, painter. Pennsylvania magazine of history and biography, v. 19, Jan. 1896: 460–467. F146.P65, v. 19

Contributed by Charles H. Hart.

SAWITZKY, WILLIAM. Matthew Pratt, 1734–1805, a study of his work. New York, New-York Historical Society in co-operation with the Carnegie Corporation of New York, 1942. x, 103 p. port. (*His* Studies in early American portraiture, 1) ND237.P83S3

14238

PRATT, SAMUEL JACKSON (1747–1814)†

England. Novelist, poet.

HAYRE, CHARLOTTE R. W. Samuel Jackson Pratt, novelist and poet, 1747–1814. 1949. ([200] p.) Micro AC–1, no. 4364

Thesis (Ph.D.)—University of Pennsylvania.
Abstracted in *Dissertation Abstracts*, v. 13, no. 2, 1953, p. 228–229.

In two works, *Pupil of Pleasure* (1776) and *Emma Corbett* (1780), Pratt became the first English author to employ the American Revolution as a fictional theme.

14239

PREBLE, EDWARD (1761–1807)*

Maine; Massachusetts. Seaman, Revolutionary naval officer.

MCKEE, CHRISTOPHER. Edward Preble; a naval biography, 1761–1807. Annapolis, Naval Institute Press, 1972. x, 394 p. illus. E335.P78M32

Includes bibliographic references.

14240

PREBLE, JEDIDIAH (1704–1784)

Maine. Farmer, landowner, councilor, military officer, merchant, judge.

PREBLE, GEORGE H. Brigadier General Jedidiah Preble. *In his* Genealogical sketch of the first three generations of Prebles in America. Boston, Printed for family circulation, D. Clapp, 1868. p. [61]–128.
[CS71.P922 1868
Micro 8684 CS

Included in the biographical sketch are diary fragments and letters written by Preble, 1775–82.

14241

PRESTON, SAMUEL (*fl.* 1787)

Pennsylvania. Surveyor.

——— Extracts from the journal of Samuel Preston, surveyor, 1787. Pennsylvania magazine of history and biography, v. 22, Oct. 1898: 350–365.
F146.P65, v. 22

14242

PRESTON, WILLIAM (1729–1783)

Ireland; Virginia; Kentucky. Surveyor, assemblyman, frontiersman, Revolutionary officer.

——— The Preston papers relating to western Virginia [1774–83] Virginia magazine of history and biography, v. 26, Oct. 1918: 363–379; v. 27, Jan.–July/Oct. 1919: 42–49, 157–166, 309–325; v. 28, Apr.–July 1920: 109–116, 241–246, 346–353; v. 29, Jan. 1921: 29–35.
F221.V91, v. 26–29

——— Preston papers [1774–83] *In* John P. Branch historical papers of Randolph-Macon College. v. 4, no. 3; 1915. Ashland, Va. p. 289–346. F221.J65, v. 4

MARSTON, RUMSEY B. Colonel William Preston. *In* John P. Branch historical papers of Randolph-Macon College. v. 4, no. 3; 1915. Ashland, Va. p. 257–288.
F221.J65, v. 4

14243

PRÉVOST, AUGUSTINE (1744–1821)

Switzerland; Pennsylvania. British officer in America.

——— Turmoil at Pittsburgh; diary of Augustine Prevost, 1774. Pennsylvania magazine of history and biography, v. 85, Apr. 1961: 111–162. F146.P65, v. 85

Introduction and notes by Nicholas B. Wainwright.

14244

PRICE, EZEKIEL (1728–1802)

Massachusetts. Insurance writer.

——— Diary of Ezekiel Price, 1775–6. *In* Massachusetts Historical Society, *Boston.* Proceedings. v. 7; 1863/64. Boston, 1864. p. 185–262. F61.M38, v. 7

In addition to personal affairs, the diary includes detailed notes on the Siege of Boston.

——— Items from an interleaved Boston almanac for 1778, being a diary of Ezekiel Price. New England historical and genealogical register, v. 19, Oct. 1865: 329–338.
F1.N56, v. 19

14245

PRICE, RICHARD (1723–1791)†

Wales; England. Clergyman, pamphleteer, reformer.

——— Letters to and from Richard Price [1767–90] *In* Massachusetts Historical Society, *Boston.* Proceedings. 2d ser., v. 17; 1903. Boston. p. 262–378.
F61.M38, 2d s., v. 17

Introduction and notes by Charles E. Norton.
An offprint with a slightly different title was published in Cambridge by J. Wilson (1903. 119 p. E203.P94).

AGNEW, JOHN P. Richard Price and the American Revolution. 1949. 249 l.

Thesis (Ph.D.)—University of Illinois.

BARNES, WINSTON H. F. Richard Price: a neglected eighteenth-century moralist. Philosophy, v. 17, Apr. 1942: 159–173. B1.P55, v. 17

CONE, CARL B. Torchbearer of freedom; the influence of Richard Price on eighteenth century thought. Lexington, University of Kentucky Press [1952] 209 p. illus., ports. JC176.P73C6

"Bibliographical note": p. [201]–202.

HOLLAND, J. D. An eighteenth-century pioneer: Richard Price, D.D., F.R.S. (1723–1791). In Royal Society of London. Notes and records, v. 23, June 1968: 43–64. port. Q41.L835, v. 23

LANE, NICHOLAS. Life insurance and the War of Independence. History today, v. 9, Aug. 1959: 560–564. port. D1.H818, v. 9

On Price's extraordinary diversity of interests—from an investigation of actuarial principles to an espousal of revolutionary doctrines.

14246
PRIESTLEY, JOSEPH (1733–1804)*†

England; Pennsylvania. Clergyman, teacher, scientist.

——— Joseph Priestley, selections from his writings. Edited by Ira V. Brown. University Park, Pennsylvania State University Press, 1962. 343 p. port. AC7.P68

——— Memoirs of Dr. Joseph Priestley, to the year 1795, written by himself, with a continuation to the time of his decease, by his son, Joseph Priestley, and observations on his writings, by Thomas Cooper . . . and the Rev. William Christie. Northumberland [Pa.] Printed by J. Binns, 1806. 2 v. (v, 824, x p.) QD22.P8

An abridgement, edited by John T. Boyer, was published under the title The Memoirs of Dr. Joseph Priestley, Eighteenth Century Religious Liberal (Washington, Barcroft Press [1964] 173 p. QD22.P8A33 1964).

——— The theological and miscellaneous works of Joseph Priestley. Edited, with notes, by John Towill Rutt. [London, Printed by G. Smallfield, 1817–32] 25 v. in 26. BX9815.P68

——— Writings on philosophy, science, and politics. Edited, with an introduction by John A. Passmore. New York, Collier Books [1965] 352 p. AC7.P69 1965

Bibliography: p. 341–343.

BROWNE, CHARLES A. Joseph Priestley and the American "fathers." American scholar, v. 4, spring 1935: 133–146. port. AP2.A4572, v. 4

FULTON, JOHN F. and CHARLOTTE H. PETERS. An introduction to a bibliography of the educational and scientific works of Joseph Priestley. In Bibliographic

Society of America. Papers. v. 30; 1936. Chicago [1938] p. 150–167. Z1008.B51P, v. 30

HOLT, ANNE. A life of Joseph Priestley. With an introduction by Francis W. Hirst. London, Oxford University Press, H. Milford, 1931. xviii, 221 p. port. BX9869.P8H6

"Bibliography and manuscript sources": p. [xv]–xviii.

RUTT, JOHN T. Life and correspondence of Joseph Priestley. London, R. Hunter, 1831–32. 2 v. port. QD22.P8R8

"Works of Joseph Priestley in the order of their publication": v. 2, p. 535–544.

THORPE, Sir THOMAS E. Joseph Priestley. London, J. M. Dent; New York, E. P. Dutton, 1906. viii, 228 p. illus., plate, port. (English men of science) QD22.P8T5

WALKER, W. CAMERON. The beginnings of the scientific career of Joseph Priestley. Isis, v. 21, Apr. 1934: 81–97. facsims., ports. Q1.I7, v. 21

14247
PRIME, BENJAMIN YOUNG (1733–1791)*

New York. Physician, poet.

WHEELOCK, CHARLES WEBSTER. Dr. Benjamin Young Prime (1733–1791), American poet [with] Volume II: a facsimile edition of the published verse. 1967. ([488] p.) Micro AC–1, no. 68–9670

Thesis (Ph.D.)—Princeton University.
Abstracted in Dissertation Abstracts, v. 29A, no. 1, July 1968, p. 242.

——— The poet Benjamin Prime (1733–1791). American literature, v. 40, Jan. 1969: 459–471. PS1.A6, v. 40

14248
PRINGLE, ROBERT (1702–1776)

Scotland; South Carolina. Merchant.

——— Letters and will of Robert Pringle (1702–1776). Edited by Mary Pringle Fenhagan. South Carolina historical and genealogical magazine, v. 50, Apr.–July 1949: 91–100, 144–155. F226.S55, v. 50

14249
PROCTOR, THOMAS (1739–1806)

Ireland; Pennsylvania. Carpenter, Revolutionary officer.

NEAD, BENJAMIN M. A sketch of General Thomas Procter, with some account of the First Pennsylvania Artillery in the Revoltion. Pennsylvania magazine of history and biography, v. 4, no. 4, 1880: 454–470. F146.P65, v. 4

14250
PROUD, ROBERT (1728–1813)*

England; Pennsylvania. Teacher, Loyalist, historian.

—— Letters of Robert Proud [1777–78] Pennsylvania magazine of history and biography, v. 34, Jan. 1910: 62–73. F146.P65, v. 34

NEUENSCHWANDER, JOHN A. Robert Proud: a chronicle of scholarly failure. Pennsylvania magazine of history and biography, v. 92, Oct. 1968: 494–506. F146.P65, v. 92

POWELL, JOHN H. Robert Proud, Pennsylvania's first historian. Pennsylvania history, v. 13, Apr. 1946: 85–112. F146.P597, v. 13

THOMSON, CHARLES W. Notices of the life and character of Robert Proud, author of *The History of Pennsylvania*. *In* Pennsylvania. Historical Society. Memoirs. v. 1; pt. 2. Philadelphia, 1826. p. [389]–408. F146.P36, v. 1

14251

PROVOOST, SAMUEL, *Bp.* (1743–1815)*

New York. Protestant Episcopal clergyman and bishop.

CHORLEY, EDWARD CLOWES. Samuel Provoost, first bishop of New York. Historical magazine of the Protestant Episcopal Church, v. 2, June 1933: 1–25; Sept.: 1–16. BX5800.H5, v. 2

MAMPOTENG, CHARLES. Samuel Provoost, King's College 1758, Bishop of New York and Trustee of Columbia College. Columbia University quarterly, v. 29, Sept. 1937: 148–163. LH1.C7Q2, v. 29

NORTON, JOHN N. Life of Bishop Provoost, of New York. New York, General Protestant Episcopal S. School Union, and Church Book Society, 1859. 183 p. port. BX5995.P7N6

WILSON, JAMES G. Samuel Provoost, first bishop of New York. New York genealogical and biographical record, v. 18, Jan. 1887: 1–13. F116.N28, v. 18

14252

PULASKI, KAZIMIERZ (1747–1779)*

Poland; America. Revolutionary general.

—— Correspondance du général Casimir Pulaski avec Claude de Rulhière, 1774–1778. [Préface de François Pulaski] Paris, 1948. xvi, 41 p. DK434.8.P8A4 1948

ABODAHER, DAVID J. Freedom fighter: Casimir Pulaski. New York, J. Messner [1969] 190 p. E207.P8A57

Bibliography: p. 183.

[GIRARDIN, LOUIS HUE] Pulaski vindicated from an unsupported charge inconsiderately or malignantly introduced in Judge Johnson's *Sketches of the Life and Correspondence of Major Gen. Nathaniel Greene.* By Paul Bentalou. Baltimore, Printed by John D. Toy, 1824. New York, Reprinted, W. Abbatt, 1909. 39 p. (The Magazine of history, with notes and queries. Extra number, no. 8, [pt. 2]) E173.M24, v. 2

First published anonymously. The authorship was claimed by both Girardin and Bentalou. In a letter to Thomas Jefferson, dated October 27, 1824, Girardin said, "I lately wrote this pamphlet to gratify my . . . friend Colonel Bentalow . . . He furnished me with notes and I wrote the vindication." See Edith Philips' *Louis Hue Girardin and Nicholas Gouin Dufief, and Their Relations with Thomas Jefferson* (Baltimore, Johns Hopkins Press, 1926), p. 54.

GORDON, WILLIAM W. Count Casimir Pulaski. Georgia historical quarterly, v. 13, Sept. 1929: 167–227. illus., map, ports. F281.G2975, v. 13

GRIFFIN, MARTIN I. J. General Count Casimir Pulaski, "the father of the American cavalry." American Catholic historical researches, new ser., v. 6, Jan. 1910: 1–128. illus., facsim., port. E184.C3A5, n.s., v. 6

HEATHCOTE, CHARLES W. General Count Casimir Pulaski fought earnestly for the liberty of the United States and cooperated with Washington. Picket post, no. 64, May 1959: 8–15. illus., map. E234.P5, no. 64

JONES, GILBERT S. Pulaski campaigned Valley Forge area; opposed going into winter camp here; gave life on battlefield for liberty. Picket post, no. 20, Jan. 1948: 50–56. E234.P5, no. 20

LEWIS, JOHN F. Casimir Pulaski. Pennsylvania magazine of history and biography, v. 55, Jan. 1931: 1–23. plates, ports. F146.P65, v. 55

LYNAH, MARY-ELIZABETH. Casimir Pulaski. Americana, v. 26, Oct. 1932: 474–488. E171.A53, v. 26

MANNING, CLARENCE A. Casimir Pulaski, a soldier of liberty. *In* Polish Institute of Arts and Sciences in America, *New York.* Bulletin, v. 2, Jan. 1944: 445–458. AS36.P84, v. 2

—— Soldier of liberty, Casimir Pulaski. New York, Philosophical Library [1945] 304 p. port. DK434.8.P8M3

14253

PUTNAM, ISRAEL (1718–1790)*

Massachusetts; Connecticut. Farmer, assemblyman, Revolutionary general.

—— The two Putnams, Israel and Rufus, in the Havana Expedition, 1762, and in the Mississippi River exploration, 1772–73, with some account of the Company of Military Adventurers. Hartford, Connecticut Historical Society, 1931. x, 279 p. facsims., ports. F1781.P94

The shorter journal was "printed in "The Memoirs of Rufus Putnam," issued in 1903 by the National Society of the Colonial Dames of America in the State of Ohio."— Preface.

Preface signed: Albert C. Bates.

Contents: Historical introduction.—Israel Putnam's company at Havana.—Orderly book of Havana expedition.—Israel Putnam's journal.—Rufus Putnam's journal (the longer journal).—Rufus Putnam's journal (the shorter journal).

CUTTER, WILLIAM. The life of Israel Putnam, major-general in the army of the American Revolution. New York, G. F. Cooledge, 1847. 383 p. maps, plates, port. E207.P9C89

Bibliography: p. [vii]–viii.
The fourth edition (1850), has been reprinted in Port Washington, N.Y., by Kennikat Press (1970).

HEATHCOTE, CHARLES W. General Israel Putnam—a devoted patriot and colleague of Washington. Picket post, no. 79, Feb. 1963: 4–9. port. E234.P5, no. 79

HILL, GEORGE C. Gen. Israel Putnam: "Old Put"; a biography. Boston, E. O. Libby, 1858. 270 p. plates. (American biography) E207.P9H5

A later edition was published in New York by the A. L. Burt Co. (1903).

LIVINGSTON, WILLIAM F. The homes and haunts of Israel Putnam. New England magazine, new ser., v. 17, Oct. 1897: 193–212. illus., ports. AP2.N4, n.s., v. 17

—— Israel Putnam, pioneer, ranger, and major-general, 1718–1790. New York, G. P. Putnam's Sons, 1901. xviii, 442 p. facsims., plates, ports. (American men of energy) E207.P9L78

Bibliography: p. xi–xviii.

LUTHER, F. S. General Israel Putnam. In Worcester Historical Society, Worcester, Mass. Proceedings, v. 20, no. 4, 1904: 204–218. F74.W9W85, v. 20

PUTNAM, ALFRED P. A sketch of Gen. Israel Putnam. Putnam's monthly historical magazine, v. 1, May-June 1892: 3–18, 45–57. F1.P98, v. 1

TARBOX, INCREASE N. Life of Israel Putnam ("Old Put"), major-general in the Continental Army. Boston, Lockwood, Brooks, 1876. 389 p. map, plates, port. E207.P9T2

Reprinted in Port Washington, N.Y., by Kennikat Press (1970).

14254

PUTNAM, RUFUS (1738–1824)*
Massachusetts. Farmer, surveyor, Revolutionary officer.

—— Letter of Gen. Rufus Putnam, regarding the northeastern boundary [1784] Genealogical magazine, [4th] ser., v. 4, Mar. 1917: 77–82. F1.P98, [4th] s., v. 4

—— The memoirs of Rufus Putnam and certain official papers and correspondence, published by the National Society of the Colonial Dames of America in the state of Ohio. Compiled and annotated by Miss Rowena Buell. Boston, Houghton, Mifflin, 1903. xxxvi, 460 p. maps, plans, plates, port. F483.P94

CONE, MARY. Life of Rufus Putnam, with extracts from his journal and an account of the first settlement in Ohio. Cleveland, W. W. Williams, 1886. 142 p. (Historical publications, no. 1) F483.P96

CRAWFORD, SIDNEY. Rufus Putnam and his pioneer life in the Northwest. In American Antiquarian Society, Worcester, Mass. Proceedings, new ser., v. 12, Oct. 1898: 431–454. E172.A35, n.s., v. 12

—— —— Offprint. Worcester, Mass., Press of C. Hamilton, 1899. 26 p. F476.C89

14255

PYNCHON, WILLIAM (1723–1789)
Massachusetts. Lawyer.

—— The diary of William Pynchon of Salem. A picture of Salem life, social and political, a century ago. Edited by Fitch Edward Oliver. Boston, Houghton, Mifflin, 1890. ix, 349 p. F74.S1P95

The diary extends from 1776 to 1789.

14256

QUESNAY DE BEAUREPAIRE, ALEXANDRE MARIE (1755–1820)*
France; Virginia. Revolutionary officer, educator.

—— Mémoire, statuts et prospectus, concernant l'Académie des sciences et beaux arts des États-Unis de l'Amérique, établie à Richemond, capitale de la Virginie. Paris, De l'impr. de Cailleaa, 1788. 114 p. AS36.R5 Rare Bk. Coll.

A translation by Rosewell Page was published in Richmond by D. Bottom, Superintendent of Public Printing, in 1922 (50 p. AS36.R52) as part of the report of the Virginia State Library for 1920/21.

GAINES, RICHARD H. Richmond's first academy, projected by M. Quesnay de Beaurepaire in 1786. In Virginia Historical Society, Richmond. Collections. new ser., v. 11; 1892. Richmond. p. [165]–175. F221.V82, n.s., v. 11

ROBERTS, JOHN G., ed. An exchange of letters between Jefferson and Quesnay de Beaurepaire [1787–89] Virginia magazine of history and biography, v. 50, Apr. 1942: 134–142. F221.V91, v. 50

—— François Quesnay's heir. Virginia magazine of history and biography, v. 50, Apr. 1942: 143–150. F221.V91, v. 50

14257

QUICK, THOMAS (1734–1796)
Pennsylvania. Frontiersman, Indian fighter.

CRUMB, FREDERICK W. Tom Quick, early American. Narrowsburg, N.Y., Delaware Valley Press, 1936. 85 p. plates, port. F106.Q75

"Reference material and items of Americana which contain references to Tom Quick": 1 leaf at end.

[QUINLAN, JAMES E.]   Tom Quick, the Indian slayer: and the pioneers of Minisink and Wawarsink. Monticello, N.Y., De Voe & Quinlan, 1851. 264 p.
E87.Q6 Rare Bk. Coll.

A later edition was published under the title *The Original Life and Adventures of Tom Quick, the Indian Slayer* (Deposit, N.Y., Deposit Journal, 1894. 123 p. [E87.Q62] Micro 8059 E).

QUINCY, DOROTHY
See HANCOCK, DOROTHY QUINCY

14258
QUINCY, JOSIAH (1744–1775)*
Massachusetts. Lawyer, agent.

——— Journal of Josiah Quincy, Jun., during his voyage and residence in England from September 28th, 1774, to March 3d, 1775. *In* Massachusetts Historical Society, *Boston*. Proceedings. v. 50; 1916/17. Boston, 1917. p. 433–470.   F61.M38, v. 50

Notes by Mark A. D. Howe.

——— Journal of Josiah Quincy, Junior, 1773. *In* Massachusetts Historical Society, *Boston*. Proceedings. v. 49; 1915/16. Boston, 1916. p. 424–481.
F61.M38, v. 49

On his journey to South Carolina, Pennsylvania, and New York. Introduction and notes by Mark A. D. Howe.

Letters to Josiah Quincy, Jr. [1774–75] *In* Massachusetts Historical Society, *Boston*. Proceedings. v. 50, 1916/17. Boston, 1917. p. 471–496.   F61.M38, v. 50

NASH, GEORGE H.   From radicalism to revolution: the political career of Josiah Quincy, Jr. *In* American Antiquarian Society, *Worcester, Mass.* Proceedings, v. 79, Oct. 1969: 253–290.   E172.A35, v. 79

QUINCY, JOSIAH.   Memoir of the life of Josiah Quincy, Jun., of Massachusetts. Boston, Cummings, Hilliard, 1825. viii, 498 p. facsims.   E263.M4Q7

Observations on the Act of Parliament Commonly Called the Boston Port-Bill (Boston, 1774), by Josiah Quincy, Jr.: p. [355]–469.
Reprinted in New York by Da Capo Press (1971).

14259
QUINCY, SAMUEL (1735–1789)
Massachusetts; Antigua. Lawyer, Loyalist.

——— Diary of Samuel Quincy [London, 1776–77] *In* Massachusetts Historical Society, *Boston*. Proceedings. v. 19; 1881/82. Boston, 1882. p. 211–223.
F61.M38, v. 19

14260
QUYNN, WILLIAM (ca. 1763–1784)
Maryland. Physician.

——— Letters of a Maryland medical student in Philadelphia and Edinburgh (1782–1784). Maryland historical magazine, v. 31, Sept. 1936: 181–215.
F176.M18, v. 31

Introduction and notes by Dorothy M. and William R. Quynn.

14261
RAMAGE, JOHN (ca. 1748–1802)*
Ireland; New York. Portrait artist, Loyalist officer.

MORGAN, JOHN H.   John Ramage. *In* New York Historical Society. Quarterly bulletin, v. 13, Jan. 1930: 127–148; v. 14, Apr. 1930: 13–32. illus., facsims., ports.
F116.N638, v. 13–14

Reprinted under the title *A Sketch of the Life of John Ramage, Miniature Painter* (New York, New-York Historical Society, 1930. vi, 55 p. ND1337.U6R3) as no. 8 in the John Divine Jones fund series of histories and memoirs.

SHERMAN, FREDERIC F.   American miniatures of the Revolutionary period. Art in America, v. 21, June 1933: 101–105. ports.   N1.A43, v. 21

14262
RAMSAY, ALLAN (1713–1784)†
Scotland; England. Portrait artist, pamphleteer.

WILLIAMSON, CHILTON.   The artist in politics: Allan Ramsay and the Revolution In Pennsylvania. Pennsylvania magazine of history and biography, v. 77, Oct. 1953: 452–456.   F146.P65, v. 77

14263
RAMSAY, DAVID (1749–1815)*
Pennsylvania; South Carolina. Physician, assemblyman, delegate to the Continental Congress, historian.

——— A review of the improvements, progress and state of medicine in the XVIIIth century. Charleston, Printed by W. P. Young, Franklin's Head, no. 43, Broad-street [1801] 47 p.   R148.R3 1801 Rare Bk. Coll.

——— Selections from his writings. Edited with introduction and notes by Robert L. Brunhouse. Philadelphia, American Philosophical Society, 1965. 250 p. illus., facsim., ports. (Transactions of the American Philosophical Society, new ser., v. 55, pt. 4)
Q11.P6, n.s., v. 55
F273.R15

Includes bibliographies.

BRUNHOUSE, ROBERT L.   David Ramsay's publication problems, 1784–1808. *In* Bibliographical Society of America. Papers, v. 39, 1st quarter 1945: 51–67.
Z1008.B51P, v. 39

WEEKS, CARNES.   David Ramsay, physician, patriot, and historian. Annals of medical history, new ser., v. 1, Sept. 1929: 600–607. illus., map, port.
R11.A85, n.s., v. 1

14264

RAMSAY, DAVID (*fl.* 1763–1792)

Scotland; New York. Indian trader.

———— The story of David Ramsay, trapper, smuggler, and Indian slayer on the shores of Lake Erie and the Niagara. *In* Buffalo Historical Society. Publications. v. 7. Buffalo, 1904. p. 437–451.   F129.B8B88, v. 7

Narrative reprinted from Patrick Campbell's *Travels in the Interior Inhabited Parts of North America* (Edinburgh, 1793).

14265

RAMSAY, JAMES (1733–1789)†

England; West Indies. Anglican clergyman, abolitionist.

SCHUTZ, JOHN A.   James Ramsay, essayist, aggressive humanitarian. *In* McCulloch, Samuel C., *ed.* British humanitarianism; essays honoring Frank J. Klingberg. Philadelphia, Church Historical Society [1950] (Church Historical Society (U.S.) Publication 32) p. 145–165.   HN15.M2

14266

RAMSAY, MARTHA LAURENS (1759–1811)

South Carolina. Daughter of Henry Laurens (1724–1792). Wife of David Ramsay (1749–1815).

———— Memoirs of the life of Martha Laurens Ramsay, who died in Charleston, S.C., on the tenth of June, 1811 . . . With an appendix, containing extracts from her diary, letters, and other private papers, and also from letters written to her, by her father, Henry Laurens, 1771–1776. By David Ramsay. Philadelphia, James Maxwell, Printer, 1811. 308 p.   F273.R16 Rare Bk. Coll.

A revised edition was published in Philadelphia by the American Sunday-School Union (1845. 262 p.)

14267

RAMSAY, NATHANIEL (1741–1817)*

Maryland. Lawyer, Revolutionary officer, delegate to the Continental Congress. Brother of David Ramsay (1749–1815).

BRAND, WILLIAM F.   A sketch of the life and character of Nathaniel Ramsay, Lieut.-Col. Commandant of the Third Regiment of the Maryland Line. *In* Maryland Historical Society. Fund-publication. no. 24. Baltimore, 1887. p. 45–60.   F176.M37, no. 24

14268

RANDOLPH, EDMUND (1753–1813)*

Virginia. Lawyer, Revolutionary officer, delegate to the Continental Congress, governor, delegate to the Constitutional Convention.

CONWAY, MONCURE D.   Omitted chapters of history disclosed in the life and papers of Edmund Randolph, Governor of Virginia; first Attorney-General United States, Secretary of State. New York, G. P. Putnam's Sons, 1888. vi, 401 p. plate, port.   E302.6.R18C7

Reprinted in New York by Da Capo Press (1971).

HOBSON, CHARLES F.   The early career of Edmund Randolph, 1753–1789. 1971. ([474] p.)
Micro AC–1, no. 72–15,454

Thesis (Ph.D.)—Emory University.
Abstracted in *Dissertation Abstracts International*, v. 32A, May 1972, p. 6342.

THOMAS, EMORY M.   Edmund Randolph, his own man. Virginia cavalcade, v. 18, spring 1969: 4–12. illus., ports.   F221.V74, v. 18

14269

RANDOLPH, JOHN (1727?–1784)*

Virginia; England. Lawyer, Loyalist.

———— John Randolph's "Plan of Accomodations." William and Mary quarterly, 3d ser., v. 28, Jan. 1971: 103–120.   F221.W71, 3d s., v. 28

Submitted to Lord George Germain in 1780. Introduction and notes by Mary Beth Norton.

———— A letter from the Virginia Loyalist John Randolph to Thomas Jefferson, written in London in 1779. *In* American Antiquarian Society, *Worcester, Mass.* Proceedings, new ser., v. 30, Apr. 1920: 17–31.   E172.A35, n.s., v. 30

Introduction and notes by Leonard L. Mackall.

DANIELS, JONATHAN.   The Randolphs of Virginia. Garden City, N.Y., Doubleday, 1972. viii, 362 p. illus.   CS71.R193 1972

Bibliography: p. 335–345.

ECKENRODE, HAMILTON J.   The Randolphs; the story of a Virginia family. Indianapolis, Bobbs-Merrill Co. [1946] 310 p. plates, ports.   CS71.R193 1946

14270

RAY, JAMES (*ca.* 1761–1835)

North Carolina; Kentucky. Frontiersman, Revolutionary officer.

MASON, KATHRYN H.   The career of General James Ray, Kentucky pioneer. Filson Club history quarterly, v. 19, Apr. 1945: 86–114.   F446.F484, v. 19

14271

READ, CHARLES (1715–1774)*

Pennsylvania; New Jersey. Lawyer, judge, assemblyman, councilor, land speculator, iron manufacturer.

WOODWARD, CARL R.   Ploughs and politicks; Charles Read of New Jersey and his *Notes on Agriculture*, 1715–1774. New Brunswick, Rutgers University Press, 1941.

xxvi, 468 p. illus., facsims., maps, plates (Rutgers University studies in history, no. 2)   F137.R3W6

"Read's Notes on Agriculture": p. [227]–403. Bibliography: p. 413–442.

14272

READ, GEORGE (1733–1798)*

Maryland; Delaware. Lawyer, assemblyman, delegate to the Continental Congress, councilor, delegate to the Constitutional Convention.

BOUGHNER, DANIEL T.   George Read and the founding of the Delaware State, 1781–1798. 1970. ([218] p.)
Micro AC–1, no. 70–19,214

Thesis (Ph.D.)—Catholic University of America.
Abstracted in *Dissertation Abstracts International*, v. 31A, Oct. 1970, p. 1719.

HEANEY, HOWELL J.   A signer of the Declaration of Independence orders books from London: two documents of George Read of Delaware. American journal of legal history, v. 2, Apr. 1958: 172–185.   LL

On 93 law books ordered by Read in 1762.

READ, WILLIAM T.   Life and correspondence of George Read, a signer of the Declaration of Independence; with notices of some of his contemporaries. Philadelphia, J. B. Lippincott, 1870. 575 p. port.   E302.6.R27R2

14273

READ, JAMES (1718–1793)

Pennsylvania. Lawyer, clerk, assemblyman, councilor.

GERTNEY, KENNETH.   James Read—obscure public servant. Historical review of Berks County, v. 35, autumn 1970: 6–10, 33. illus., facsims.   F157.B3H48, v. 35

14274

RECORDS, SPENCER (1762–1851)

Kentucky. Frontiersman.

——— Spencer Records' memoir of the Ohio Valley frontier, 1766–1795. Indiana magazine of history, v. 55, Dec. 1959: 323–377.   F521.I52, v. 55

Contributed by Naomi Mullendore Hougham. Edited by Donald F. Carmony.

——— Spencer Records, pioneer experiences in Pennsylvania, Kentucky, Ohio and Indiana, 1766–1836, a memoir. Indiana magazine of history, v. 15, Sept. 1919: 201–232.   F521.I52, v. 15

14275

RED JACKET, *Seneca chief* (*ca.* 1751–1830)*

New York.

HUBBARD, JOHN NILES.   An account of Sa-go-ye-wat-ha, or Red Jacket and his people, 1750–1830. Albany, J.

Munsell's Sons, 1886. xiv, 356 p. plates, port. (Munsell's historical series, no. 13)   E99.S3R3

Reprinted in New York by B. Franklin (1971).

STONE, WILLIAM L.   Life and time of Red-Jacket, or Sa-go-ye-wat-ha; being the sequel to the history of the Six Nations. New York, Wiley and Putnam, 1841. x, 484 p. plates, ports.   E99.S3R4

Includes bibliographic references.
Reprinted in St. Clair Shores, Mich., by Scholarly Press (1970).

14276

REDD, JOHN (1755–1850)

Virginia. Frontiersman, settler.

——— Reminiscences of western Virginia, 1770–1790. Virginia magazine of history and biography, v. 6, Apr. 1899: 337–346; v. 7, July 1899–Apr. 1900: 1–16, 113–128, 242–253, 401–405.   F221.V91, v. 6–7

The author's responses in his later years to questions about men and events along the frontier during the Revolutionary period.

14277

REDDING, DAVID (*d.* 1778)

Loyalist.

SPARGO, JOHN.   David Redding, Queen's Ranger, who was hanged in Bennington, Vermont, June 11, 1778; a study in historical reconstruction. Bennington, Vt., Bennington Historical Museum and Art Gallery, 1945. 68 p. facsim., port.   F52.R457

Bibliographic references included in "Notes" (p. 67–68).

14278

REDMAN, JOHN (1722–1808)*

Pennsylvania. Physician, educator.

BELL, WHITFIELD J.   John Redman, medical preceptor, 1722–1808. Pennsylvania magazine of history and biography, v. 81, Apr. 1957: 157–169.
F146.P65, v. 81

Also published under the title "John Redman (1722–1808): Medical Preceptor of Philadelphia" in the *Transactions & Studies* of the College of Physicians of Philadelphia, 4th ser., v. 25, Aug. 1957, p. 103–111.

MIDDLETON, WILLIAM S.   John Redman. Annals of medical history, v. 8, Sept. 1926: 213–223. facsims., ports.   R11.A85, v. 8

14279

REDWOOD, ABRAHAM (1709?–1788)*

Rhode Island. Planter, philanthropist.

BOLHOUSE, GLADYS E.   Abraham Redwood, philanthropist, botanist. Newport history, v. 45, spring 1972: 17–35. illus., port.   F89.N5N615, v. 45

14280
REED, ESTHER DE BERDT (1747–1780)
England; Pennsylvania. Relief organizer. Daughter of Dennys De Berdt (1694?–1770). Wife of Joseph Reed (1741–1785).

REED, WILLIAM B.   The life of Esther De Berdt, afterwards Esther Reed, of Pennsylvania. Priv. print. Philadelphia, C. Sherman, Printer, 1853. 336 p.
                                        E302.6.R3R3
Reprinted in New York by the New York Times (1971).

14281
REED, JACOB (1730–1820)
Pennsylvania. Farmer, Revolutionary officer.

REED, WILLOUGHBY H.   Lieutenent Colonel Jacob Reed. In Reed, Willoughby H., comp. Lieut. Col. Jacob Reed; proceedings at the dedication of the monument erected to his memory in Franconia Township, Pennsylvania. Norristown, Pa., 1905. p. [9]–72. illus.
                                        F159.F8R3

14282
REED, JAMES (1723–1807)*
Massachusetts; New Hampshire. Revolutionary general.

BLAKE, AMOS J.   Gen. James Reed. Sketch of his life and character. In New Hampshire Historical Society. Proceedings. v. 1, pt. 3; 1876/84. Concord, 1885. p. [109]–115.   F31.N52, v. 1
——— ——— Detached copy.   E207.R32B6

GARFIELD, JAMES F. D.   General James Reed. In Fitchburg Historical Society, Fitchburg, Mass. Proceedings. v. 4. 1900/1906. Fitchburg, 1908. p. 113–124. port.
                                        F74.F5F6, v. 4
——— ——— Fitchburg, Sentinel Print. Co., Printers, 1908. 14 p. port.   E207.R3G2

14283
REED, JOHN (fl. 1774–1785)
Pennsylvania; Louisiana. Merchant-trader.

WHITAKER, ARTHUR P.   [John] Reed and [Standish] Forde: merchant adventurers of Philadelphia; their trade with Spanish New Orleans. Pennsylvania magazine of history and biography, v. 61, July 1937: 237–262.   F146.P65, v. 61

14284
REED, JOSEPH (1741–1785)*
New Jersey; Pennsylvania. Lawyer, delegate to the Continental Congress, Revolutionary officer, councilor.

——— Letters of Gen. Joseph Reed to Gen. Irvine. Historical magazine, v. 8, Apr. 1864: 129–138.
                                        E171.H64, v. 8

BANCROFT, GEORGE.   Joseph Reed; a historical essay. New York, W. J. Widdleton, 1867. 64 p.
                                        E302.6.R3B2 Rare Bk. Coll.

ELIOT, ELLSWORTH.   The patriotism of Joseph Reed. New Haven, Yale University Library, 1943. 42 p. facsim., port. (Yale University Library miscellanies, 3)
                                        E302.6.R3E4
"Newspapers, pamphlets, and books dealing with the question of Joseph Reed's alleged apostasy": p. 35–38. "Books cited": p. 39–42.

HEATHCOTE, CHARLES W.   General Joseph Reed—a devoted patriot and loyal supporter of General Washington. Picket post, no. 73, July 1961: 12–18. port.
                                        E234.P5, no. 73

REED, JOHN F.   The Joseph Reed controversy. Picket post, Jan. 1972: 12–19, 37; Apr: 12–21. ports.
                                        E234.P5, 1972
Over Reed's actions and reported statements at the time of the Battle of Trenton in December 1776.

REED, WILLIAM B.   Life and correspondence of Joseph Reed, military secretary of Washington, at Cambridge; adjutant-general of the Continental Army; member of the Congress of the United States; and president of the Executive Council of the State of Pennsylvania. Philadelphia, Lindsay and Blakiston, 1847. 2 v. port.
                                        E302.6.R3R297
                    Micro 01291, reel 247, no. 3E

——— President Reed of Pennsylvania. A reply to Mr. George Bancroft and others. Philadelphia, H. Challen [1867] 132 p.   E302.6.R3R36

ROCHE, JOHN F.   Joseph Reed, a moderate in the American Revolution. New York, Columbia University Press, 1957 [c1954] x, 298 p. port. (Columbia studies in the social sciences, no. 595)   H31.C7, no. 595
Bibliography: p. [271]–285.
Reprinted in New York by AMS Press (1968. E302.6.R3R6 1968).
The author's thesis (Ph.D.), The Zealous Patriot: A Life of Joseph Reed, 1741–1785, was submitted to Columbia University in 1954 (Micro AC–1, no. 8769).

——— Was Joseph Reed disloyal? William and Mary quarterly, 3d ser., v. 8, July 1951: 406–417.
                                        F221.W71, 3d s., v. 8
Finds unswerving loyalty.

14285
REEVES, ENOS (d. 1807)
Pennsylvania. Revolutionary officer.

——— Extracts from the letter-books of Lieutenant Enos Reeves, of the Pennsylvania Line [Sept. 1780–Apr. 1782] Pennsylvania magazine of history and biography,

v. 20, Oct. 1896, Jan. 1897: 302–314, 456–472; v. 21, Apr.–Oct. 1897, Jan. 1898: 72–85, 235–256, 376–391, 466–476.　　　　　　　F146.P65, v. 20–21

Contributed by John B. Reeves.

14286

REID, JAMES (*fl.* 1768–1769)
Scotland; Virginia. Poet, satirist.

DAVIS, RICHARD B. James Reid, colonial Virginia poet and moral and religious essayist. Virginia magazine of history and biography, v. 79, Jan. 1971: 3–19.
F221.V91, v. 79

14287

REMICK, CHRISTIAN (*b.* 1726)
Massachusetts. Portrait artist.

CUNNINGHAM, HENRY W. Christian Remick, an early Boston artist. Boston, Club of Odd Volumes, 1904. 28 p.　　　　　ND1839.R4C8 Rare Bk. Coll.

14288

REVEL, GABRIEL JOACHIM DU PERRON, *comte* DE (1756–1814)
French officer in America, mapmaker.

——— Journal particulier d'une campagne aux Indes occidentales (1781–1782). Paris, H. Charles-Lavauzelle [1898?] 287 p. maps, plans.　　　E263.W5R4

14289

REVERE, PAUL (1735–1818)*
Massachusetts. Silversmith, engraver.

FORBES, ESTHER. Paul Revere & the world he lived in. Boston, Houghton Mifflin Co., 1942. xiii, 510 p. illus., facsims., maps (on lining-papers), plates (part col.), ports.　　　　　　　　　　F69.R4175
Bibliography: p. [491]–496.

GETTEMY, CHARLES F. The true story of Paul Revere, his midnight ride, his arrest and court-martial, his useful public services. Boston, Little, Brown, 1905. xxix, 294 p. facsim., plates, port.　　　E207.R4G3

GOSS, ELBRIDGE H. The life of Colonel Paul Revere. Boston, J. G. Cupples, 1891. 2 v. illus., facsims., plates, ports.　　　　　　　　　　　F69.R42
Reprinted in Freeport, N.Y., by Books for Libraries Press (1971), and in Boston, with a new introduction and preface by George A. Billias, by Gregg Press (1972).

HAYWARD, WALTER S. Paul Revere and the American Revolution, 1765–1783. 1933.
Thesis (Ph.D.)—Harvard University.

TAYLOR, EMERSON G. Paul Revere. [New York] E. V. Mitchell and Dodd, Mead, 1930. ix, 237 p. plates, ports.　　　　　　　　　　　F69.R446

14290

REYNELL, JOHN (1708–1784)
England; Pennsylvania. Merchant, insurance broker.

ROMANEK, CARL L. John Reynell, Quaker merchant of colonial Philadelphia. 1969. ([223] p.)
Micro AC–1, no. 70–7244
Thesis (Ph.D.)—Pennsylvania State University.
Abstracted in *Dissertation Abstracts International*, v. 30A, May 1970, p. 4924.

14291

RHOADS, SAMUEL (1711–1784)
Pennsylvania. Builder, assemblyman, delegate to the Continental Congress.

BIDDLE, HENRY D. Colonial mayors of Philadelphia: Samuel Rhoads, 1774. Pennsylvania magazine of history and biography, v. 19, Apr. 1895: 64–71.
F146.P65, v. 19

14292

RHODE, LONNON (*d.* 1777)
Maine. Revolutionary soldier.

DOLE, SAMUEL T. Windham's colored patriot. *In* Maine Historical Society. Collections and proceedings. 3d ser., v. 1 Portland, 1904. p. 316–321.
F16.M33, 3d s., v. 1

14293

RICE, DAVID (1733–1816)*
Virginia; Kentucky. Presbyterian clergyman.

BISHOP, ROBERT H. Memoir of David Rice. *In his* An outline of the history of the church in the state of Kentucky, during a period of forty years. Lexington, T. T. Skillman, 1824. p. [13]–116.
BR555.K4B6 Rare Bk. Coll.

MARTIN, VERNON P. Father Rice, the preacher who followed the frontier. Filson Club history quarterly, v. 29, Oct. 1955: 324–330.　　　F446.F484, v. 29

14294

RICHARDS, SAMUEL (1753?–1841)
Connecticut. Revolutionary officer.

——— Personal narrative of an officer in the Revolutionary War. United service, 3d ser., v. 4, Sept.–Oct. 1903: 235–261, 352–376.　　　　U1.U4, 3d s., v. 4
A different version was published under the title, *Diary of Samuel Richards, Captain of Connecticut Line, War of the Revolution, 1775–1781* (Philadelphia, Pa. [Press of Leeds & Biddle Co.] 1909. 117 p. E275.R5).

14295

RICHARDSON, WILLIAM (1743–1786)

South Carolina. Merchant, planter, Revolutionary officer.

—— Letters of William Richardson, 1765–1784. Edited by Emma B. Richardson. South Carolina historical and genealogical magazine, v. 47, Jan. 1946: 1–20. F266.S55, v. 47

14296

RICHE, THOMAS

Pennsylvania. Merchant.

SOLTOW, JAMES H. Thomas Riche's "adventure" in French Guiana, 1764–1766. Pennsylvania magazine of history and biography, v. 83, Oct. 1959: 409–419. F146.P65, v. 83

14297

RICHMOND AND LENNOX, CHARLES LENNOX, 3d *Duke of* (1735–1806)†

England. British officer, Secretary of State.

MURPHY, ARTHUR J. The Duke of Richmond and the Rockingham Whigs, 1765–1783. 1954.

Thesis (Ph.D.)—Fordham University.

OLSON, ALISON G. The radical duke: career and correspondence of Charles Lennox, third Duke of Richmond. [London] Oxford University Press, 1961. 262 p. (Oxford historical series, 2d ser.) DA506.R5055

Bibliography: p. [237]-247.

14298

RIDGELY, CHARLES (1733–1790)

Maryland. Merchant, assemblyman, ironmaster.

HOYT, WILLIAM D. Captain Ridgely's London commerce, 1757 to 1774. Americana, v. 37, Apr. 1943: 326–370. E171.A53, v. 37

WAGSTAFFE, THOMAS. A London shopkeeper's struggle to recover a colonial debt, 1763–1769. Maryland historical magazine, v. 45, June 1950: 126–133. F176.M18, v. 45

A series of letters to Captain Charles Ridgely, edited and with commentary by William D. Hoyt, Jr.

14299

RIDGELY, FREDERICK (1757–1824)

Maryland. Revolutionary surgeon.

—— A soldier writes home—1776: letters from the Revolutionary War. Filson Club history quarterly, v. 41, Oct. 1967: 297–303. F446.F484, v. 41

Introduction and notes by Joan Titley.

14300

RIDOUT, THOMAS (1754–1829)

England; Maryland; Canada. Merchant.

—— An account of my capture by the Shawanese Indians [1788] Western Pennsylvania historical magazine, v. 12, Jan. 1929: 3–31. F146.W52, v. 12

—— Reminiscences of Thomas Ridout. Maryland historical magazine, v. 20, Sept. 1925: 215–235. F176.M18, v. 20

14301

RIEDESEL, FRIEDERIKE CHARLOTTE LUISE VON MASSOW, *Freifrau* VON (1746–1808)

Germany. Hessian nurse in America. Wife of Friedrich Adolf Riedesel (1738–1800).

—— Baroness von Riedesel and the American Revolution; journal and correspondence of a tour of duty, 1776–1783. A rev. translation, with introduction and notes, by Marvin L. Brown, Jr., with the assistance of Marta Huth. Chapel Hill, Published for the Institute of Early American History and Culture at Williamsburg, Virginia at the University of North Carolina Press [1965] xlvii, 222 p. illus., facsims., maps, ports. E268.R523

A new translation which includes letters from General Riedesel to his wife, 27 letters never before published, and portions of letters omitted from other editions.

The first German edition for general circulation was published under the title *Die Berufs-Reise nach America* (Berlin, Haude und Spener, 1800. 352 p. E268.R52 Rare Bk. Coll.). A privately printed edition was also published in Berlin the same year under the title *Auszüge aus den Briefen und Papieren des Generals Freyherrn von Riedesel und seiner Gemalinn* (386 p. E275.R538 Rare Bk. Coll.).

The translation by William L. Stone, published as *Letters and Journals Relating to the War of the American Revolution, and the Capture of the German Troops at Saratoga* (Albany, J. Munsell, 1867. 235 p. E268.R555), has been reprinted in New York by the New York Times (1968).

SINNICKSON, LINA. Frederika, Baroness Riedesel. Pennsylvania magazine of history and biography, v. 30, Oct. 1906: 385–408. illus., plates. F146.P65, v. 30

—— ——Offprint. Philadelphia, 1906. 385–408 p. illus., plates, ports. E275.R57

THARP, LOUISE H. The baroness and the general. Boston, Little, Brown [1962] xii, 458 p. maps, plates. E268.R58T5

14302

RIEDESEL, FRIEDRICH ADOLF, *Freiherr* VON (1738–1800)

Germany. Hessian officer in America.

EELKING, MAX VON. Memoirs, and letters and journals, of Major General Riedesel, during his residence in America. Translated from the original German of Max von Eelking by William L. Stone. Albany, J. Munsell,

1868. 2 v. ports, plates. [Munsell's series of local American history, v. 8–9]   E268.E264

A translation of volume 2 and part of volume 3 of the author's *Leben und Wirken des herzoglich braunschweig'schen General-Lieutenants Friedrich Adolph Riedesel* (Leipzig, 1856).

Reprinted in New York by the New York Times (1969).

FAIRCHILD, FRANCES I.   With Von Bernstorff's ancestors in America. Queen's quarterly, v. 33, July 1925: 21–33.
                                                            AP5.Q3, v. 33

14303
RITTENHOUSE, DAVID (1732–1796)*
Pennsylvania. Astronomer, scientist, surveyor, munitioner, assemblyman, professor.

BABB, MAURICE J.   David Rittenhouse. Pennsylvania magazine of history and biography, v. 56, July 1932: 193–224. illus.   F146.P65, v. 56

BARTON, WILLIAM.   Memoirs of the life of David Rittenhouse, LL.D. F.R.S., late president of the American Philosophical Society, &c. interspersed with various notices of many distinguished men: with an appendix, containing sundry philosophical and other papers, most of which have not hitherto been published. Philadelphia, E. Parker, 1813. 614 p. fold. facsim., port.
                                                            QB36.R4B3

COPE, THOMAS D.   David Rittenhouse—physicist. *In* Franklin Institute, *Philadelphia*. Journal, v. 215, Mar. 1933: 287–297.   T1F8, v. 215

———— The Rittenhouse diffraction grating. *In* Franklin Institute, *Philadelphia*. Journal, v. 214, July 1932: 99–104.   T1.F8, v. 214

FORD, EDWARD.   David Rittenhouse, astronomer-patriot, 1732–1796. Philadelphia, University of Pennsylvania Press, 1946. viii, 226 p. port. (Pennsylvania lives)
                                                            QB36.R4F6
"Bibliographical note": p. 213–217.

HINDLE, BROOKE.   David Rittenhouse. Princeton, N.J., Princeton University Press, 1964. ix, 394 p. illus., maps, port.   QB36.R4H5
"Bibliographical note": p. 367–375.

HINDLE, BROOKE, *and* HELEN M. HINDLE.   David Rittenhouse and the illusion of reversible relief. Isis, v. 50, June 1959: 135–140.   Q1.I7, v. 50

LOVE, J. BARRY.   The miniature solar systems of David Rittenhouse. Smithsonian journal of history, v. 3, winter 1968/69: 1–16. plates.   CB3.S55, v. 3

RUBINCAM, MILTON.   David Rittenhouse, LL.D., F.R.S.; a study from contemporary sources. *In* Historical Society of Montgomery County (*Pennsylvania*). Bulletin, v. 2, Oct. 1939: 8–30.   F157.M7H45, v. 2

RUFUS, WILL CARL.   David Rittenhouse as a mathematical disciple of Newton. Scripta mathematica, v. 8, Dec. 1941: 228–231.   QA1.S35, v. 8

14304
RIVINGTON, JAMES (1724–1802)*†
England; Pennsylvania; New York. Printer, bookseller, newspaper publisher, Loyalist.

CRARY, CATHERINE S.   The Tory and the spy: the double life of James Rivington. William and Mary quarterly, 3d ser., v. 16, Jan. 1959: 61–72. F221.W71, 3d s., v. 16

DAVIDSON, ALEXANDER.   James Rivington and Silas Deane. *In* Bibliographical Society of America. Papers, v. 52, 3d quarter 1958: 173–178.   Z1008.B51P, v. 52
On Rivington's publication in 1781 of Deane's pro-British correspondence.

HEWLETT, LEROY.   James Rivington, Loyalist printer, publisher, and bookseller of the American Revolution, 1724–1802; a biographical-bibliographical study. 1958. ([532] p.)   Micro AC-1, no. 58–7727
Thesis (Ph.D.)—University of Michigan.
Abstracted in *Dissertation Abstracts*, v. 19, Dec. 1958, p. 1393–1394.

LAWSON, JOHN L.   The "remarkable mystery" of James Rivington, "spy." Journalism quarterly, v. 35, summer 1958: 317–323.   PN4700.J7, v. 35
Based on thesis (M.A.)—University of California.
On the evidence adduced to support the assertion that Rivington, Loyalist editor of a New York newspaper, served as a spy for George Washington, 1781–83.

SARGENT, GEORGE H.   James Rivington, the Tory printer; a study of the Loyalist pamphlets of the Revolution. American collector, v. 2, June 1926: 336–341.
                                                            Z1007.A475, v. 2
The author's "A Bibliography of the Imprints of James Rivington" appeared in the July 1926 issue, p. 369–377.

14305
ROBB, ROBERT (1727–1814)
Pennsylvania. Soldier, farmer, settler.

MEGINNESS, JOHN F.   Life and times of Robert Robb, Esq. Muncy Township, Lycoming County, Pa. Muncy, Luminary Press, 1899. 53 p.   E263.P4M4
Cover-title: *History of a Remarkable Character of Revolutionary Times; Robert Robb and His Trouble With the Committee of Safety, 1778.*

14306
ROBERDEAU, DANIEL (1727–1795)*
West Indies; Pennsylvania. Merchant, Revolutionary general, delegate to the Continental Congress.

BUCHANAN, ROBERDEAU.   Genealogy of the Roberdeau family, including a biography of General Daniel Roberdeau, of the Revolutionary Army, and the Continental Congress; and signer of the Articles of Confederation.

Printed for private distribution. Washington, J. L. Pearson, Printer, 1876. 196 p. geneal. table, plates.
CS71.R639 1876

PATTEN, WILLIAM. A Huguenot leader for American independence: General Daniel Roberdeau. Légion d'honneur, v. 7, July 1936: 15–23. CR5061.U6A3, v. 7

14307
ROBERTS, EPHRAIM (1756–1835)
New Hampshire. Farmer, Revolutionary soldier.

——— Ephraim Roberts—memorandum book, 1771–1776. Historical New Hampshire, v. 24, fall 1969: 20–33.
F31.H57, v. 24

14308
ROBERTS, GEORGE (1755–1829)
New Hampshire. Revolutionary seaman, farmer.

ROBERTS, CHARLES H. A sketch of the life of George Roberts. Granite monthly, v. 33, Aug. 1902: 91–97.
F31.G75, v. 33

An offprint with corrections, additional memoranda, and a slightly different title was published in 1905 ([Concord? N.H.] 8 p. facsim. E275.R638).

14309
ROBERTS, HUGH
Pennsylvania.

——— Selections from the correspondence between Hugh Roberts and Benjamin Franklin [1758–80] Pennsylvania magazine of history and biography, v. 38, July 1914: 287–301. F146.P65, v. 38

14310
ROBERTS, JOHN (1712?–1772)†
England. Member of Parliament.

TYLER, J. E. John Roberts, M.P., and the first Rockingham administration. English historical review, v. 67, Oct. 1952: 547–560. DA20.E58, v. 67

14311
ROBERTS, LEMUEL (b. 1751)
Revolutionary soldier.

——— Memoirs of Captain Lemuel Roberts. Containing adventures in youth, vicissitudes experienced as a Continental soldier, his sufferings as a prisoner, and escapes from captivity. With suitable reflections on the changes of life. Written by himself. Bennington, Vermont, Printed by Anthony Haswell, for the author, 1809. 96 p. E275.R64 Rare Bk. Coll.
Reprinted in New York by the New York Times (1969).

14312
ROBERTSON, ARCHIBALD (ca. 1745–1813)
Scotland. British officer in America.

——— Archibald Robertson, Lieutenant-General Royal Engineers, his diaries and sketches in America, 1762–1780. Edited with an introduction by Harry Miller Lydenberg. New York, New York Public Library, 1930. x, 300 p. illus., facsims., maps, plans, plates, ports. E275.R66

Also published in the Library's *Bulletin*, v. 37, Jan.–Apr., June–Nov. 1933, p. 7–37, 113–143, 181–199, 277–290, 479–503, 577–608, 660–692, 775–795, 865–901, 953–969, and reissued in 1971 under the title *Archibald Robertson; his Diaries and Sketches in America*.

14313
ROBERTSON, JAMES (1742–1814)*
Virginia; North Carolina. Frontiersman, Indian negotiator, assemblyman.

——— The correspondence of Gen. James Robertson [1784–89] American historical magazine, v. 1, Jan. 1896: 71–91. F431.A53, v. 1

Mainly letters addressed to Robertson, with a few written by him.
Reproduced from the originals preserved in the University of Nashville Library.

MATTHEWS, THOMAS E. General James Robertson, father of Tennessee. Nashville, Tenn., Parthenon Press [c1934] 588 p. illus., facsim., plates, port. F436.R67
"Sources": p. 7–11; "Authorities cited": p. 582–588.

14314
ROBIN abbé (fl. 1781)
France. French chaplain in America.

——— Nouveau voyage dans l'Amérique septentrionale, en l'année 1781; et campagne de l'armée de m. le comte de Rochambeau. A Philadelphia, et se trouve à Paris, Chez Moutard, Imprimeur-Libraire de la Reine, de madame, & de madame comtesse d'Artois, rue des Mathurins, Hôtel de Cluni, 1782. ix, 222 p.
E163.R65 Rare Bk. Coll.

The translation by Philip Freneau, *New Travels Through North-America* (Philadelphia, Printed and sold by Robert Bell, 1783. 112 p. E163.R67 Rare Bk. Coll.), has been reprinted in New York by the New York Times (1969).

14315
ROBIN, CHARLES (b. 1742 or 3)
Island of Jersey; Canada. Indian trader, merchant.

LEGROS, ARTHUR G. Charles Robin on the Gaspe coast, 1766–[87] Revue d'histoire de la Gaspésie, v. 2, Jan./Mar.–July/Sept. 1964: 33–43, 93–102, 141–151; v. 3, Jan./Mar.–July/Sept. 1965: 39–45, 77–84, 148–155;

v. 4, Jan./Mar. 1966–Oct./Dec. 1966: 10–16, 87–93, 150–158, 195–204. illus., facsim., maps.

F1054.G2R4, v. 2–4

Based on Robin's diary.

SAUNDERS, ARTHUR C. Charles Robin, pioneer of the Gaspé fisheries. *In his* Jersey in the 18th and 19th centuries, containing an historical record of commercial enterprise. Privateering activities of the islanders. Charles Robin, pioneer of the Gaspé fisheries, and an account of the Newfoundland fisheries. Jersey, Channel Islands, J. T. Bigwood, 1930. p. [193]–212.

DA670.J5S3

14316

ROBINSON, JOHN (1704–1766)*
Virginia. Assemblyman, planter.

DABNEY, WILLIAM M. John Robinson and the fall of the conservative Virginia oligarchy. *In* Dabney, William M., *and* Josiah C. Russell, *eds.* Dargan historical essays; historical studies presented to Marion Dargan by his colleagues and former students, University of New Mexico. Albuquerque, University of New Mexico Press, 1952. (University of New Mexico publications in history, no. 4) p. 55–64. AC5.D25

14317

ROBINSON, JOHN (1727–1802)†
England. Lawyer, Member of Parliament, Treasury secretary.

―――― Parliamentary papers of John Robinson, 1774–1784. Edited for the Royal Historical Society by William Thomas Laprade. London, Offices of the Society, 1922. xx, 198 p. [Royal Historical Society. Publications. Camden 3d ser., v. 33] DA20.R91, s. 3, v. 33

CHRISTIE, IAN R. The political allegiance of John Robinson, 1770–1784. In London. University. *Institute of Historical Research*. Bulletin, v. 29, May 1965: 108–122. D1.L65, v. 29

14318

ROBINSON, THOMAS (1729–1786)
Delaware; Nova Scotia. Merchant, Loyalist.

HANCOCK, HAROLD B. Thomas Robinson: Delaware's most prominent Loyalist. Delaware history, v. 4, Mar. 1950: 1–36. port. F161.D37, v. 4

14319

ROCHAMBEAU, JEAN BAPTISTE DONATIEN DE VIMEUR, *comte* DE (1725–1807)*
France. French general in America.

―――― Memoirs of the Marshal Count de Rochambeau, relative to the War of Independence of the United States. Extracted and translated from the French by M. W. E. Wright, Esq. Paris, At the French, English,

and American Library [Printed by Belin] 1838. 114 p. ports. E265.R6

From v. 1. of Rochambeau's *Mémoires militaires, historiques et politiques* (Paris, 1809), p. 237–329.

Reprinted in New York by the New York Times (1971). Portions of the *Memoirs* also appeared in the *North American Review*, v. 205, May–June 1917, p. 788–802, 978–992, and v. 206, July 1917, p. 161–176.

―――― Rochambeau's *Mémoire de la guerre en Amérique*. Edited by Claude C. Sturgill. Virginia magazine of history and biography, v. 78, Jan. 1970: 34–64.

F221.V91, v. 78

Since there are at least three major versions of Rochambeau's official report on the French expedition, the editor provides a translation of the 1781 dispatch, which he believes to be the original.

CONTENSON, LUDOVIC GUY MARIE DU BESSEY DE, *baron.* Le maréchal de Rochambeau et la société des Cincinnati. Revue d'histoire diplomatique, 45. année, oct./déc. 1931: 385–393. JX3.R3, v. 45

GUILLON, ÉDOUARD L. M. Le maréchal de Rochambeau (1725–1807). Nouvelle revue, 4th ser., v. 32, Dec. 15, 1917: 323–340. AP20.N8, 4th s., v. 32

RENARD, MAURICE C. Rochambeau, libérateur de l'Amérique. Paris, Fasquelle, 1951. 219 p.

E265.R677

Bibliography: p. 217.

ROSENGARTEN, JOSEPH G. The Château de Rochambeau. *In* American Philosophical Society, *Philadelphia*. Proceedings, v. 33, Jan. 1895: 353–361. Q11.P5, v. 33

―――― ―――― Offprint. [Philadelphia] 1895. 353–361 p. port. E265.R81

THOMPSON, MARSHALL P. Rochambeau. Magazine of history, with notes and queries, v. 22, June 1916: 220–229; v. 23, July-Aug. 1916: 31–40, 61–79.

E171.M23, v. 22–23

WEELEN, JEAN E. Rochambeau, father and son; a life of the Maréchal de Rochambeau, by Jean-Edmond Weelen, and the Journal of the Vicomte de Rochambeau (hitherto unpublished), translated by Lawrence Lee with a preface by Gilbert Chinard. New York, H. Holt [c1936] xvii, 285 p. illus., facsim., maps, plates, ports. E265.R686

"The war in America; an unpublished journal (1780–1783), by the Vicomte de Rochambeau": p. [191]–285. "Sources": p. 187–189.

―――― Rochambeau; préface de Gabriel Hanotaux. Paris, Plon [1934] viii, 278 p. map, plates, ports.

DC146.R65W4

"Sources": p. [276]–278.

WHITRIDGE, ARNOLD. Rochambeau. New York, Macmillan [1965] 340 p. illus., maps, ports. E265.R69

Includes bibliographic references.

———— Rochambeau and the American Revolution. History today, v. 12, May 1962: 312–320. illus., ports.
D1.H818, v. 12

14320

ROCHEBLAVE, PHILLIPPE FRANÇOIS DE RAS-TEL, *chevalier* DE (1727–1802)

France; Canada; Illinois. Trader, British officer.

———— Rocheblave papers [1776–78] *In* Chicago Historical Society. Collections. v. 4. Chicago, 1890. p. 382–419.
F548.1.C4, v. 4

Reprinted on p. 253–290 of *Early Illinois* (Chicago, Fergus Print. Co., 1890. 386 p. Fergus' historical series, no. 31–34. F536.F35, no. 31–34), edited by Edward G. Mason.

Concerning his tenure as British commandant of Illinois. Notes by Edward G. Mason.

MASON, EDWARD G. British Illinois: Phillippe François de Rastel, Chevalier de Rocheblave. *In* Chicago Historical Society. Collections. v. 4. Chicago, 1890. p. 360–381.
F548.1.C4, v. 4

Reprinted on p. 231–252 of *Early Illinois* (Chicago, Fergus Print. Co., 1890. 386 p. Fergus' historical series, no. 31–34. F536.F35, no. 31–34), edited by Edward G. Mason.

ROCHEFONTAINE, STEPHEN
See BÉCHET, ÉTIENNE NICOLAS MARIE, *SIEUR DE ROCHEFONTAINE*

14321

ROCHESTER, NATHANIEL (1752–1831)*

Virginia; North Carolina; Maryland. Revolutionary officer, assemblyman, merchant.

STOKES, DURWARD T. Nathaniel Rochester in North Carolina. North Carolina historical review, v. 38, Oct. 1961: 467–481.
F251.N892, v. 38

14322

ROCKINGHAM, CHARLES WATSON-WENT-WORTH, *2d Marquis of* (1730–1782)†

England. First Lord of Treasury.

ALBEMARLE, GEORGE THOMAS KEPPEL, *6th Earl of*. Memoirs of the Marquis of Rockingham and his contemporaries. With original letters and documents now first published. London, R. Bentley, 1852. 2 v. port.
DA512.R6A3

GUTTRIDGE, GEORGE H. The early career of Lord Rockingham, 1730–1765. Berkeley, University of California Press, 1952. vi, 54 p. (University of California publications in history, v. 44)
E173.C15, v. 44
DA512.R6G87

Bibliographic footnotes.

HOFFMAN, ROSS J.S. Lord Rockingham: the inheritance. Studies in Burke and his time, v. 13, fall 1971: 1963–1985.
DA506.B9B86, v. 13

14323

RODGERS, JOHN (1727–1811)*

Pennsylvania; Delaware; New York. Presbyterian clergyman, Revolutionary chaplain.

———— Letters of John Rodgers, preacher and patriot. Introduction by Charles A. Anderson. *In* Presbyterian Historical Society. Journal, v. 27, Dec. 1949: 195–205.
BX8905.P7A4, v. 27

HANDY, ROBERT T. John Rodgers, 1727–1811: "A life of usefulness on earth." *In* Presbyterian Historical Society. Journal, v. 34, June 1956: 69–82.
BX8905.P7A4, v. 34

14324

RODNEY, CAESAR (1728–1784)*

Delaware. Assemblyman, delegate to the Continental Congress, Revolutionary general, judge, governor.

———— Letters to and from Caesar Rodney, 1756–1784; member of the Stamp Act Congress and the First and Second Continental Congresses; speaker of the Delaware colonial assembly; president of the Delaware State; major general of the Delaware militia; signer of the Declaration of Independence. Edited by George Herbert Ryden. Philadelphia, Published for the Historical Society of Delaware by the University of Pennsylvania Press, 1933. vi, 482 p. ports.
E207.R6R65

"Bibliographical note" at end of "Caesar Rodney, a biographical sketch" (p. 17); "Sources of material": p. [449]–452.

Reprinted in New York by Da Capo Press (1970).

———— Letters to and from Caesar Rodney [1765–81] Edited by Harold B. Hancock. Delaware history, v. 12, Apr.–Oct. 1966: 54–76, 147–168.
F161.D37, v. 12

———— Rodney letters [1754–81] Edited by Leon de Valinger. Delaware history, v. 1, July 1946: 99–110, v. 3, Sept. 1948: 105–115.
F161.D37, v. 1, 3

Supplementing the Ryden edition.

14325

RODNEY, GEORGE BRYDGES RODNEY, *Baron* (1719–1792)†

England. British admiral, Member of Parliament.

———— Letter-books and order-book of George, Lord Rodney, Admiral of the White Squadron, 1780–1782. New York, Printed for the Naval History Society by the New York Historical Society, 1932. 2 v. (Publications of the Naval History Society, v. 12–13)
E271.R76

Contents: 1. Letter-books, July 6, 1780–February 4, 1781, December 10, 1781–September 21, 1782.—2. Order-book, July, 1781, November 27, 1781–September 21, 1782. Index.

Also published by the New York Historical Society in its Collections, 1932–33, as v. 65–66 of the John Watts De Peyster Publication Fund Series (F116.N63, 1932–33).

———— Letters from Sir George Brydges now Lord Rodney, to His Majesty's ministers, &c., &c., relative to the capture of St. Eustatius, and its dependencies; and shewing the state of the war in the West Indies, at that period. Together with a continuation of His Lordship's correspondence with the governors and admirals in the West-Indies and America, during the year 1781, and until the time of his leaving the command and sailing for England. London, Printed by A. Grant, and sold by J. Robson & W. Clarke, 1789. 180 p.   F2097.R69

Reprinted, with an introduction and index by K. G. Davies, in Shannon by the Irish University Press (1972).

HANNAY, DAVID.   Rodney. London and New York, Macmillan, 1891. xi, 222 p. port. (English men of action)
DA87.1.R6H2

Reprinted, with a new introduction and preface by George A. Billias, in Boston by Gregg Press (1972).

LLOYD, CHRISTOPHER.   Sir George Rodney: lucky admiral. *In* Billias, George A., *ed.* George Washington's opponents: British generals and admirals in the American Revolution. New York, Morrow, 1969. p. 327–354. port.   E267.B56

Bibliography: p. 353–354.

MACINTYRE, DONALD G. F. W.   Admiral Rodney. New York, Norton [1963, ᶜ1962] 280 p. illus., port.
DA87.1.R6M3 1963

Bibliography: p. 272.

MUNDY, GODFREY B.   The life and correspondence of the late Admiral Lord Rodney. London, J. Murray, 1830. 2 v. port.   DA87.1.R6M9

Reprinted, with a new introduction and preface by George A. Billias, in Boston by Gregg Press (1972).

SPINNEY, DAVID.   Rodney. London, Allen & Unwin [1969] 484 p. illus., facsims., geneal. tables, maps, plans, plates, ports.   DA87.1.R6S6

"Sources": p. 447–468.

TUNSTALL, WILLIAM C. Brian.   Rodney. *In his* Flights of naval genius. London, P. Allan [1930] p. [35]–127.
DA87.1.A1T8

14326

RODNEY, THOMAS (1744–1811)*

Delaware. Farmer, lawyer, assemblyman, Revolutionary officer, judge, delegate to the Continental Congress.

———— Anglo-American law on the frontier: Thomas Rodney & his territorial cases. [Edited by] William Baskerville Hamilton. Durham, N.C., Duke University Press, 1953. x, 498 p.   KF363.R6A32

A biography of Rodney appears on p. 3–90.

———— Thomas Rodney [letters, 1770–1802] Pennsylvania magazine of history and biography, v. 43, Jan. 1919: 1–23.   F146.P65, v. 43

Introduction and notes by Simon Gratz.

14327

ROGERS, JOHN (1723–1789)

Maryland. Lawyer, delegate to the Continental Congress, judge.

KLINGELHOFER, HERBERT E.   The non-signer of the Declaration of Independence: John Rogers of Maryland. Manuscripts, v. 8, summer 1956: 225–232. facsim.
Z41.A2A925, v. 8

14328

ROGERS, JOSIAS (1755–1795)†

England. British naval officer in America.

GILPIN, WILLIAM.   Memoirs of Josias Rogers, Esq., Commander of His Majesty's ship *Quebec.* London, Printed for T. Cadell and W. Davies, 1808. 184 p. front.
DA87.R7G4

Rogers' naval service in the American Revolution: p. 1–61.

14329

ROGERS, ROBERT (1731–1795)*

Massachusetts; New Hampshire; Old Northwest. Frontiersman, Indian fighter, British officer.

———— A concise account of North America: containing a description of the several British colonies on that Continent, including the islands of Newfoundland, Cape Breton, &c. . . . Also of the interior, or westerly parts of the country, upon the rivers St. Laurence, the Mississippi, Christino, and the Great Lakes. To which is subjoined, an account of the several nations and tribes of Indians residing in those parts, as to their customs, manners, government, numbers, &c. London, Printed for the author, and sold by J. Millan, 1765. vii, 264 p.
E162.R69 Rare Bk. Coll.

———— Journals of Major Robert Rogers: containing an account of the several excursions he made under the generals who commanded upon the continent of North America during the late war; from which may be collected the most material circumstances of every campaign upon that continent, from the commencement to the conclusion of the war. With an introduction and notes, and an appendix containing numerous documents and papers relating to the doings of Major Rogers while commanding at Michilimackinack, in 1767; and his conduct in the early part of the Revolutionary War. By Franklin B. Hough. Albany, J. Munsell's Sons, 1883. 297 p. fold. map.   E199.R726

The first edition (London, Printed for the author, and sold by J. Millan, 1765. 236 p. E199.R72 Rare Bk. Coll.) has been reprinted, with an introduction by Howard H. Peckham, in New York by Corinth Books (1961. 171 p. E199.R727) and reproduced in facsimile by University Microfilms (Ann Arbor, 1966. 236 p. E199.R722 1966).

——— Reminiscences of the French war; containing Rogers' expeditions with the New-England rangers under his command, as published in London in 1765; with notes and illustrations. To which is added an account of the life and military services of Maj. Gen. John Stark; with notices and anecdotes of other officers distinguished in the French and Revolutionary wars. Concord, N.H., L. Roby, 1831. 275 p. port.   E199.R73

Edited by Caleb Stark.

——— Roger's Michillimackinac journal. *In* American Antiquarian Society, *Worcester, Mass.* Proceedings, new ser., v. 28, Oct. 1918: 224–273. map, plan.
E172.A35, n.s., v. 28

Introduction and notes by William L. Clements.
Previously unpublished, the journal covers the period from September 1766 to July 1767. An offprint was issued under the title *Journal of Major Robert Rogers* (Worcester, Mass., The Society, 1918. 52 p. F572.M16R7

——— *defendent.* Treason? At Michilimackinac: the proceedings of a general court martial held at Montreal in October 1768 for the trial of Major Robert Rogers. Edited by David A. Armour. Mackinac Island, Mich., Mackinac Island State Park Commission, 1967. v, 103 p. illus., facsims., map (on lining papers), ports.
E199.R735

CUNEO, JOHN R. Robert Rogers of the rangers. New York, Oxford University Press, 1959. xii, 308 p. illus., facsims., maps, plates, ports.   E199.R74

"Sources and textual notes": p. [285]–299.

[Hall, Edward H.] Major Robert Rogers; sketch of the picturesque career of a famous scout, Indian fighter and partisan commander. *In* American Scenic and Historic Preservation Society. Annual report. 10th; 1905. Albany. p. [215]–247.   E151.A51, v. 10

QUAIFE, MILO M. Detroit biographies: Robert Rogers. Burton historical collection leaflet, v. 7, Sept. 1928: 1–16.   F561.B9, v. 7

Reprinted in *Michigan History*, v. 35, June 1951, p. 139–150.

ROBERTS, KENNETH L. Northwest passage. Garden City, N.Y., Doubleday, Doran, 1937. 2 v. maps (on lining papers), port.   PS3535.O176N6 1937

Vol. 2: Appendix, containing the courtmartial of Major Robert Rogers, the courtmartial of Lt. Samuel Stephens, and other new material, with notes by Kenneth Robert.
"Book I of this novel appeared serially under the title of *Rogers' Rangers.*"
Bibliography: v. 2, p. [3]–8.

14330
ROGERS, WILLIAM (1751–1824)
Rhode Island; Pennsylvania. Revolutionary chaplain, clergyman.

——— Journal of my visit to the eastward commencing in August, 1781. *In* Rhode Island Historical Society. Collections, v. 33, Apr.–July 1940: 39–44, 65–72.
F76.R47, v. 33

——— A journal of my visits to Rhode Island, April 17, 1776[–June 4, 1776] *In* Rhode Island Historical Society. Collections, v. 32, Oct. 1939: 117–128; v. 33, Jan. 1940: 14–17.   F76.R47, v. 32–33

14331
ROLLE, DENYS (1730–1797)
England; Florida. Colonizer, Member of Parliament.

CORSE, CARITA D. Denys Rolle and Rollestown, a pioneer for Utopia. Florida Historical Society quarterly, v. 7, Oct. 1928: 115–122.   F306.F65, v. 7

See also Carl Bohnenberger's article, "The Settlement of Charlotia (Rolles Town), 1765," in v. 4, July 1925, p. 43–49.

MOWAT, CHARLES L. The tribulations of Denys Rolle. Florida historical quarterly, v. 23, July 1944: 1–14.
F306.F65, v. 23

14332
ROMANS, BERNARD (*ca.* 1720–*ca.* 1784)*†
Netherlands; East Florida; New York; Pennsylvania. Engineer, surveyor, mapmaker, writer, Revolutionary officer.

BROWN, HORACE. Capt. Bernard Romans and his map of Vermont [1778] *In* Vermont Historical Society. Proceedings, new ser., v. 11, June 1943: 95–98. map.
F46.V55, n.s., v. 11

PHILLIPS, PHILIP LEE. Notes on the life and works of Bernard Romans. Deland, Fla., Florida State Historical Society, 1924. 128 p. facsim. and atlas of 2 maps in 13 folded sections. (Publications of the Florida State Historical Society, no. 2)   F306.F75, no. 2
Atlas in G & M

Atlas lettered on cover: Bernard Romans Map of Florida 1774.
Bibliography: p. 74–99.
The description of West Florida written by Romans on the earliest of his maps (1772) is reproduced in an appendix (p. [119]–128).

14333
ROMEYN, DIRCK (1744–1804)
New York; New Jersey. Dutch Reformed clergyman, educator.

BLODGETT, HAROLD W. Union College and Dirck Romeyn. *In* New York State Historical Association. New York history, v. 26, July 1945: 332–342.
F116.N865, v. 26

14334

ROOSEVELT, NICHOLAS (1715–1769)
New York. Goldsmith.

SMITH, HELEN B. Nicholas Roosevelt, goldsmith. *In* New York Historical Society. Quarterly, v. 34, Oct. 1950: 301–314. illus. F116.N638, v. 34

14335

ROSBRUGH, JOHN (1714–1777)
Scotland; New Jersey. Revolutionary chaplain.

CLYDE, JOHN C. Rosbrugh, a tale of the Revolution; or, Life, labors and death of Rev. John Rosbrugh . . . chaplain in the Continental Army; clerical martyr of the Revolution, killed by Hessians, in the battle of Assumpink, at Trenton, New Jersey, Jan. 2d, 1777. Easton [Pa.] 1880. 101 p. facsim., maps. E263.P4R72

14336

ROSE, GEORGE (1744–1818)†
England. Member of Parliament.

—— The diaries and correspondence of the Right Hon. George Rose: containing original letters of the most distinguished statesmen of his day. Edited by the Rev. Leveson Vernon Harcourt. London, R. Bentley, 1860. 2 v. port. DA506.R7A2

McQUISTON, JULIAN R. George Rose and William Eden; a study in the relation of party management to national economics. 1954. ([257] p.) Micro AC–1, no. 8726
Thesis (Ph.D.)——Columbia University.
Abstracted in *Dissertation Abstracts*, v. 14, no. 9, 1954, p. 1382.

14337

ROSS, BETSY GRISCOM (1752–1836)*
Pennsylvania. Seamstress, upholsterer.

HANFORD, FRANKLIN. Did Betsy Ross design the flag of the United States of America? Scottsville, N.Y., I. Van Hooser, Printer, 1917. 21 p. (Publications of the Scottsville Literary Society, no. 7) CR113.H3
Bibliography: p. 20–21.

MILLER, WILLIAM C. The Betsy Ross legend. Social studies, v. 37, Nov. 1946: 317–323.
D16.3.S65, v. 37
Surveying the available sources, the author finds no convincing evidence that Betsy Ross made the first American flag.

PARRY, EDWIN S. Betsy Ross, Quaker rebel, being true story of the romantic life of the maker of the first American flag. Illustrations by J. L. G. Ferris and Edwin John Prittie. Philadelphia, John C. Winston Co. [ᶜ1930] xix, 252 p. illus., facsims., plates (part col.)
E302.6.R77P3 1930

THOMPSON, RAY. Betsy Ross: last of Philadelphia's Free Quakers. [Fort Washington, Pa., Bicentennial Press, 1972] 112 p. illus. E302.6.R77T45
Bibliography: p. 109–110.

14338

ROSS, ROBERT
England; Louisiana. Merchant.

HOLMES, JACK D. L. Robert Ross' plan for an English invasion of Louisiana in 1782. Louisiana history, v. 5, spring 1964: 161–177. F366.L6238, v. 5

14339

ROTCH, WILLIAM (1734–1828)*
Massachusetts. Whaling merchant, shipowner.

—— An autobiographical memoir of William Rotch [1775–94] written in the eightieth year of his age. New-England historical and genealogical register, v. 31, July 1877: 262–264; v. 32, Jan.–Oct. 1878: 36–42, 151–155, 271–274, 389–394. F1.N56, v. 31–32
Communicated by Frederick C. Sanford.

—— Memorandum written by William Rotch in the eightieth year of his age. Boston, Houghton Mifflin Co., 1916 xi, 88 p. plates, ports. F72.N2R84

HINCHMAN, LYDIA S. William Rotch and the neutrality of Nantucket during the Revolutionary War. *In* Friends' Historical Society of Philadelphia. Bulletin, v. 1, Feb. 1906: 49–55. BX7635.A1F6, v. 1

JONES, AUGUSTINE. William Rotch of Nantucket. Philadelphia, American Friend Pub. Co., 1901. 30 p. ports. F72.N2J6

MELENDY, ROBERT G. William Rotch. *In* Nantucket Historical Association. Proceedings. v. 36; 1930. Nantucket, Mass. p. 26–38. F72.N2N16, v. 38

STACKPOLE, EDOUARD A. William Rotch (1734–1828) of Nantucket, America's pioneer in international industry. New York, Newcomen Society in North America, 1950. 36 p. illus. HC102.5.R6S8

14340

ROTH, JOHANNES (1726?–1791)
Prussia; Pennsylvania. Moravian missionary.

—— Diary of a Moravian Indian mission migration across Pennsylvania in 1772. Translated and edited by August C. Mahr. Ohio state archaeological and historical quarterly, v. 62, July 1953: 247–270.
F486.O51, v. 62

14341

ROUBAUD, PIERRE JOSEPH ANDRÉ (1730–1791)

—— Histoire générale de l'Asie, de l'Afrique et de l'Amérique. A Paris, Chez Des Ventes de la Doué, 1770–75. 15 v. fold. maps. D22.R85

Partial contents: t. 13. Histoire ancienne de l'Amérique.—t. 14–15. Suite de l'histoire moderne de l'Amérique.

For an analysis of the last three volumes, see Durand Echeverría's "Roubaud and the Theory of American Degeneration," in the *French American Review*, v. 3, Jan./Mar. 1950, p. 24–33.

ROUËRIE, CHARLES ARMAND TUFFIN, *marquis* DE LA

See LA ROUËRIE, CHARLES ARMAND TUFFIN, *marquis* DE

14342

ROUSSEAU, JEAN JACQUES (1712–1778)
Switzerland; France. Writer, political theorist.

CROCKER, LESTER G. Rousseau's *Social Contract*; an interpretive essay. Cleveland, Press of Case Western Reserve University, 1968. xi, 198 p. JC179.R9C7
Bibliography: p. [192]–198.

JOST, FRANÇOIS. La fortune de Rousseaux aux Etats-Unis: esquisse d' une étude. *In* International Congress on the Enlightenment, *1st, Geneva*. Transactions. v. 2. Geneve, Institut et Musée Voltaire, 1963. (Studies on Voltaire and the eighteenth century, v. 24) p. 899–959. PQ2105.A2S8, v. 24

MASTERS, ROGER D. The political philosophy of Rousseau. Princeton, N.J., Princeton University Press, 1968. xxiii, 464 p. JC179.R9M35
Bibliography: p. 445–457.

OSBORN, ANNIE M. Rousseau and Burke; a study of the idea of liberty in eighteenth-century political thought. London, New York, Oxford University Press, 1940. xi, 272 p. JC179.R9O76
Bibliography: p. 263–268.
Issued also as thesis (Ph.D.)—Columbia University.
Reprinted in New York by Russell & Russell (1964).

SHKLAR, JUDITH N. Men and citizens: a study of Rousseau's social theory. Cambridge [Eng.] University Press, 1969. viii, 245 p. (Cambridge studies in the history and theory of politics) JC179.R9S55
Bibliographic footnotes.

SPURLIN, PAUL M. Rousseau in America, 1760–1809. University, University of Alabama Press [1969] 175 p. port. JC179.R9S67
Bibliography: p. [141]–161.
See the author's article of the same title in the *French American Review*, v. 1, Jan./Mar. 1948, p. 8–16.

WARNER, JAMES H. The reaction in eighteenth-century England to Rousseau's two *Discours*. *In* Modern Language Association. Publications, v. 48, June 1933: 471–487. PB6.M6, v. 48
Warner also published "A Bibliography of Eighteenth-Century English Editions of J.-J. Rousseau, With Notes on the Early Diffusion of his Writings," in the *Philological Quarterly*, v. 13, July 1934, p. 225–247, with an addendum that appeared in v. 19, July 1940, p. 237–243.

Richard B. Sewall confirms Warner's conclusions regarding the unfavorable reception accorded Rousseau's writings in England in three separate articles. "Rousseau's First *Discourse* in England," appeared in the *Publications* of the Modern Language Association, v. 52, Sept. 1937, p. 908–911, while "Rousseau's Second *Discourse* in England from 1755 to 1762" and "Rousseau's Second *Discourse* in England and Scotland From 1762 to 1772" were published in the *Philological Quarterly*, v. 17, Apr. 1938, p. 97–114, and v. 18, July 1939, p. 227–242.

14343

ROWE, JOHN (1715–1787)
Massachusetts. Merchant.

——— Extracts from the diary of John Rowe, a Boston merchant, covering the period from 1764 to 1779. *In* Massachusetts Historical Society, *Boston*. Proceedings. 2d ser., v. 10; 1895/96. Boston, 1896. p. 11–108. F61.M38, 2d s., v. 10
An offprint with a slightly different title was published in Cambridge by J. Wilson (1895. [11]–108 p. F73.4.P61).
In his introductory remarks, Edward L. Pierce provides a biographical sketch of Rowe and an analysis of his diary (p. 11–60).

——— Letters and diary of John Rowe, Boston merchant, 1759–1762, 1764–1779; edited by Anne Rowe Cunningham, with extracts from a paper written for the Massachusetts Historical Society, by Edward Lillie Pierce. Boston, W. B. Clarke Co., 1903. 453 p. plates, ports. F73.44.R87
Reprinted in New York by the New York Times (1969).

14344

RUDULPH, MICHAEL (*b*. 1758)
Maryland; Georgia. Revolutionary officer.

RUDULPH, MARILOU A. Michael Rudulph, "Lion of the Legion." Georgia historical quarterly, v. 45, Sept. 1961: 201–222. F281.G2975, v. 45
In a subsequent article, "The Legend of Michael Rudulph," v. 45, Dec. 1961, p. 309–328, the author examines the 19th-century legend that Rudulph, who disappeared in 1793, altered his identity and became Napoleon's famous marshal, Michel Ney.

14345

RUGGLES, TIMOTHY (1711–1795)*
Massachusetts; Nova Scotia. Lawyer, assemblyman, military officer, judge, Loyalist.

RUGGLES, HENRY S. General Timothy Ruggles, 1711–1795. [Wakefield? Mass.] Priv. print., 1897. 40 p. coat of arms. F67.R93
"Some papers bearing the signature of General Ruggles": p. [25]–30.
"Letter from General Peck": p. [31]–40.

14346

RUMFORD, *Sir* BENJAMIN THOMPSON, *Count* (1753–1814)*†
Massachusetts; England. Scientist, Loyalist officer.

—— The channel fleet in 1779; letters of Benjamin Thompson to Lord George Germain. *In* The Naval miscellany. v. 3. [London] Printed for the Navy Records Society, 1928. (Publications of the Navy Records Society, v. 63) p. [121]–154.   DA70.A1, v. 63

BAKER, HENRY M. Why did Benjamin Thompson, now known as Count Rumford, become a Tory? Magazine of history, with notes and queries, v. 8, Sept.–Oct. 1908: 136–142, 196–204.   E171.M23, v. 8

BRADLEY, DUANE. Count Rumford. Princeton, N.J., Van Nostrand [1967] vii, 176 p. illus., ports.   Q143.R8B68

BROWN, SANBORN C., AND ELBRIDGE W. STEIN. Benjamin Thompson and the first secret-ink letter of the American Revolution. Journal of criminal law and criminology, v. 40, Jan./Feb. 1950: 627–636. facsims.   HV6001.J63, v. 40

BROWN, SANBORN C. Benjamin Thompson, Count Rumford. Historical New Hampshire, v. 18, Oct. 1963: 18–35. illus., facsims.   F31.H57, v. 18

—— Count Rumford: a bicentennial review. American scientist, v. 42, Jan. 1954: 113–127. illus.   LJ85.S502, v. 42

BROWN, SANBORN C., AND KENNETH SCOTT. Count Rumford, international informer. New England quarterly, v. 21, Mar. 1948: 34–49.   F1.N62, v. 21

BROWN, SANBORN C. Scientific drawings of Count Rumford at Harvard. Harvard Library bulletin, v. 9, autumn 1955: 350–364. plates.   Z881.H3403, v. 9

DWIGHT, C. HARRISON. Count Rumford: His Majesty's colonel in Carolina. South Carolina historical magazine, v. 57, Jan. 1956: 23–27. port.   F266.S55, v. 57

ELLIS, GEORGE E. Memoir of Sir Benjamin Thompson, Count Rumford, with notices of his daughter. Published in connection with an edition of Rumford's complete works, by the American Academy of Arts and Sciences, Boston. Philadelphia, For the Academy by Claxton, Remsen, and Haffelfinger [1871] xvi, 680 p. illus., facsim., plates, ports.   Q143.R8E4

Reprinted in Boston, with a new introduction and preface by George Athan Billias, by Gregg Press (1972).

HALE, RICHARD W. Some account of Benjamin Thompson, Count Rumford. New England quarterly, v. 1, October 1928: 505–531.   F1.N62, v. 1

JONES, HENRY B. The Royal Institution: its founder and its first professors. London, Longmans, Green, 1871. 431 p.   Q41.R88J7

The early chapters are, in effect, a biography of Rumford.

LEHRBURGER, EGON. An American in Europe; the life of Benjamin Thompson, Count Rumford, by Egon Larsen [pseud.] London, New York, Rider [1953] 224 p. illus., ports.   Q143.R8L4 1953

"Extracts from Rumford's essays": p. 175–215. Bibliography: p. 217–218.

LOWRY, LUCIA M., C. D. LOWRY, *and* JOHN R. MINER. The graveyard fort; a disputed incident in the life of Count Rumford. Isis, v. 27, Aug. 1937: 268–285.   Q1.I7, v. 27

In discussing Thompson's activities as commander of a regiment of British cavalry during the war, the authors question in particular the wisdom of his building a fort for his troops on the site of a Huntington, Long Island, graveyard in 1782.

MAECHLING, CHARLES. Count Rumford: scientific adventurer. History today, v. 22, Apr. 1972: 245–254. illus., ports.   D1.H818, v. 22

POWELL, E. ALEXANDER. The remarkable American count. American heritage, v. 8, Dec. 1956: 74–77, 98–100. illus. (part col.), col. port.   E171.A43, v. 8

SPARROW, W. J. Benjamin Thompson and Lord George Germain. *In* Birmingham, Eng. University. Historical journal. v. 5, no. 2; 1956. Birmingham. p. 138–146.   D1.B37, v. 5

—— Knight of the White Eagle, Sir Benjamin Thompson, Count Rumford of Woburn, Mass. New York, T. Y. Crowell Co. [1965, ᶜ1964] 301 p. illus., facsims., ports.   Q143.R8S65 1965

Bibliography: p. 285–[289]

THOMPSON, EVERETT A. Count Rumford and his early life. *In* Connecticut Valley Historical Society, *Springfield, Mass.* Papers and proceedings. v. 1; 1876/81. Springfield, Mass., 1881. p. 133–151.   F72.C7C7, v. 1

THOMPSON, JAMES A. Count Rumford of Massachusetts. New York, Farrar & Rinehart [ᶜ1935] xvi, 275 p. front., plates, ports.   Q143.R8T45

Bibliography: p. 271–275.

THORNBROUGH, GAYLE. The Count in the kitchen. American heritage, v. 4, summer 1953: 6–9. illus.   E171.A43, v. 4

On Rumford as "the originator of the modern kitchen."

WALKER, JOSEPH B. Benjamin Thompson—Count Rumford—in New Hampshire. Historical New Hampshire, Feb. 1948: 3–19, illus., facsims.   F31.H57, 1948

14347

RUMSEY, JAMES (1743?–1792)*
Maryland. Inventor.

—— Letters of James Rumsey [1784–89] Edited by James A. Padgett. Maryland historical magazine, v. 32, Mar.–Sept. 1937: 10–28, 136–155, 271–285.   F176.M18, v. 32

—— A short treatise on the application of steam, whereby is clearly shewn, from actual experiments, that steam may be applied to propel boats or vessles of any burthen against rapid currents with great velocity. The same principles are also introduced with effect, by a machine of a simple and cheap construction, for the purpose of raising water sufficient for the working of grist-mills, saw-mills, &c., and for watering meadows and other purposes of agriculture. Philadelphia, Printed by Joseph James, Chestnut-Street, 1788. 26 p.

T7.T25, v. 7 Rare Bk. Coll.

Reprinted in Tarrytown, N.Y., by W. Abbatt (1924. [5]–35 p. E173.M24, no. 100) as extra number, no. 100, of *The Magazine of History With Notes and Queries.*

BELTZHOOVER, GEORGE M. James Rumsey, the inventor of the steamboat. The West Virginia Historicel [sic] and Antiquarian Society's publication. [Charleston? W. Va., Press of Butler Print. Co.] 1900. 28 p.

VM140.R8B4

Bibliography: p. 28.

GOSNELL, HARPUR A. The first American steamboat [1785–88]; James Rumsey its inventor, not John Fitch. Virginia magazine of history and biography, v. 40, Jan.–Apr. 1932: 14–22, 124–132. plates.

F221.V91, v. 40

HUNTER, THOMAS MARSHALL. James Rumsey. Virginia cavalcade, v. 14, autumn 1964: 33–40. illus., facsim., ports. F221.V74, v. 14

TURNER, ELLA M. James Rumsey, pioneer in steam naviagation. Scottdale, Pa., Mennonite Pub. House, 1930. x, 245 p. facsims., plates, ports. VM140.R8T8

Bibliography: p. [231]–238.

14348
RUSH, BENJAMIN (1745–1813)*
Pennsylvania. Physician, delegate to the Continental Congress, reformer.

—— An account of the manners of the German inhabitants of Pennsylvania. With an introduction and annotations by Theodore E. Schmauk, and with the notes of I. D. Rupp revised. *In* Pennsylvania-German Society. Proceedings and addresses. v. 19; 1908. [Lancaster, Pa.] 1910. 128 p. (2d group) illus., facsims., plates, port. F146.P23, v. 19

Part XXI of Pennsylvania: the German Influence in its Settlement and Development.
The notes of I. D. Rupp originally appeared in an edition of Rush's account published in Philadelphia by S. P. Town (1875. 72 p. F160.G3R8).

—— The autobiography of Benjamin Rush; his *Travels Through Life* together with his commonplace book for 1789–1813. Edited with introduction and notes by George W. Corner. [Princeton] Published for the American Philosophical Society by Princeton Universi-

ty Press, 1948. 399 p. illus., facsims., ports. (Memoirs of the American Philosophical Society, v. 25)

E302.6.R85R8
Q11.P612, v. 25

"Works frequently cited in the notes": p. [19]–20.
Reprinted in Westport, Conn., Greenwood Press (1970).

—— Benjamin Rush's medical thesis, "On the Digestion of Food in the Stomach", Edinburgh, 1768. Translated and with an historical introduction by David F. Musto. *In* College of Physicians of Philadelphia. Transactions & studies, 4th ser., v. 33, Oct. 1965: 121–138.

R15.P5, 4th s., v. 33

—— The correspondence of Benjamin Rush and Granville Sharp, 1773–1809. Edited by John A. Woods. Journal of American studies, v. 1, Apr. 1967: 1–38.

E151.J6, v. 1

Letters mainly from 1773 to 1786 that touch upon many matters, but especially the evils of the slave trade.

—— A discourse delivered before the College of Physicians of Philadelphia, Feb. 6, 1787, on the objects of their institution. *In* College of Physicians of Philadelphia. Transactions. 4th ser., v. 4, suppl. Philadelphia, 1937. p. 5–10. R15.P5, 4th s., v. 4, suppl.

—— Dissertatio physica inauguralis, de coctione ciborum in ventriculo. Edinburgi, Apud Balfour, Auld, et Smellie, 1768. 30 p. QP141.R9

Thesis (M.D.)—University of Edinburgh.

—— Dr. Benjamin Rush's journal of a trip to Carlisle in 1784. Pennsylvania magazine of history and biography, v. 74, Oct. 1950: 443–456. F146.P65, v. 74

Introduction and notes by Lyman H. Butterfield.

—— Essays, literary, moral and philosophical. 2d ed., with additions. Philadelphia, Printed by T. and W. Bradford, no. 8, South Front Street, 1806. 364 p.

AC7.R85

—— Further letters of Benjamin Rush [1765–1812] Pennsylvania magazine of history and biography, v. 77, Jan. 1954: 3–44. F146.P65, v. 74

—— Historical notes of Dr. Benjamin Rush, 1777. Pennsylvania magazine of history and biography, v. 27, Apr. 1903: 129–150. F146.P65, v. 27

—— —— Detached copy. E216.R95
Taken from notebooks kept while he was in Congress.

——Letters. Edited by L. H. Butterfield [Princeton] Published for the American Philosophical Society by Princeton University Press, 1951. 2 v. (lxxxvii, 1295 p.) illus., fold. map, ports. (Memoirs of the American Philosophical Society, v. 30, pts. 1–2) F154.R9A4
Q11.P612, v. 30

Bibliography: p. 1219–1229.
Contents: v. 1. 1761–1792.—v. 2. 1793–1813.

———— Medical inquiries and observations. Philadelphia, Printed by T. Dobson, at the Stone-House, n° 41, South Second-Street, 1794–98. 5 v.

R117.R95 1794 Rare Bk. Coll.

Generally regarded as the first complete edition of Rush's works.

———— A plan for the punishment of crime; two essays. Edited by Negley K. Teeters. Philadelphia, Pennsylvania Prison Society [1954] 24 p. facsims., plate, ports.

HV8671.R82

The essays were originally published under the titles *An Enquiry Into the Effects of Public Punishments Upon Criminals and Upon Society* (1787) and *Considerations on the Injustice and Impolicy of Punishing Murder by Death* (1792).

————The selected writings of Benjamin Rush. Edited by Dagobert D. Runes. New York, Philosophical Library [1947] xii, 433 p. facsim., port. AC7.R88

"List of the writings of Benjamin Rush published during his lifetime": p. 419–422. "Selected bibliography": p. 423–424.

———— A survey of Benjamin Rush papers [1759–1813] Pennsylvania magazine of history and biography, v. 70, Jan. 1946: 78–111. F146.P65, v. 70

Introduction (p. 78–85) and notes by Lyman H. Butterfield.

———— Thoughts upon female education, accommodated to the present state of society, manners, and government, in the United States of America. Philadelphia, Printed by Prichard & Hall, in Market Street, Between Front and Second Streets, 1787. 32 p. LC1752.R8

———— Two essays on the mind: an enquiry into the influence of physical causes upon the moral faculty, and on the influence of physical causes in promoting an increase of the strength and activity of the intellectual faculties of man. Introduction by Eric T. Carlson. New York, Brunner/Mazel, 1972. R128.7.R94 1972

xv, 40, 90–120 p. port.

The essays were previously published as *An Oration, Delivered Before the American Philosophical Society, Held in Philadelphia on the 27th of February, 1786* (1786) and as lecture IV of the *Six Introductory Lectures, to Courses of Lectures, Upon the Institutes and Practice of Medicine, Delivered in the University of Pennsylvania* (1801) respectively. Includes bibliographic references.

BINGER, CARL A. L. The dreams of Benjamin Rush. American journal of psychiatry, v. 125, June 1969: 1653–1659. RC321.A52, v. 125

———— Revolutionary doctor: Benjamin Rush, 1746–1813. New York, Norton [1966] 326 p. port. R154.R9B5

Bibliography: p. 303–306.

BLAIN, DANIEL. Benjamin Rush, M.D.—1970. *In* College of Physicians of Philadelphia. Transactions & studies, 4th ser., v. 38, Oct. 1970: 61–98.

R15.P5, 4th s., v. 38

BUTTERFIELD, LYMAN H. The American interests of the firm of E. and C. Dilly, with their letters to Benjamin Rush, 1770–1795. *In* Bibliographical Society of America. Papers, v. 45, 4th quarter 1951: 283–332.

Z1008.B51P, v. 45

"The Dilly letters": p. 302–332.

———— Benjamin Rush: a physician as seen in his letters. Bulletin of the history of medicine, v. 20, July 1946: 138–156. R11.B93, v. 20

———— Benjamin Rush and the beginnings of "John and Mary's College" over Susquehanna. *In* Dickinson College, *Carlisle, Pa.* Bulwark of liberty; early years at Dickinson. [New York] Revell [1950] (The Boyd Lee Spahr lectures in Americana, v. 1, 1947–1950) p. 29–54. plates. LD1663.A5

First published in the *Journal of the History of Medicine and Allied Sciences*, v. 3, summer 1948, p. 427–442.

———— Benjamin Rush as a promoter of useful knowledge. *In* American Philosophical Society, *Philadelphia.* Proceedings, v. 92, Mar. 1948: 26–36. facsims.

Q11.P5, v. 92

———— Dr. Rush to Governor Henry on the Declaration of Independence and the Virginia Constitution. *In* American Philosophical Society, *Philadelphia.* Proceedings, v. 95, June 1951: 250–253. Q11.P5, v. 95

Also published in the Society's *Library Bulletin* for 1951, p. 250–253.

———— Love and valor; or, Benjamin Rush and the Leslies of Edinburgh. Princeton University Library chronicle, v. 9, Nov. 1947: 1–12. plate. Z733.P93C5, v. 9

———— The milliner's mission in 1775; or, The British seize a treasonable letter from Dr. Benjamin Rush. William and Mary quarterly, 3d ser., v. 8, Apr. 1951: 192–203.

F221.W71, 3d s., v. 8

Extracts from the letter, containing a handsome tribute to George Washington, were published in the London *Morning Post* for January 16, 1775.

———— The reputation of Benjamin Rush. Pennsylvania history, v. 17, Jan. 1950: 3–22. port. F146.P597, v. 17

CARLSON, ERIC T., *and* MERIBETH M. SIMPSON. Benjamin Rush's medical use of the moral faculty. Bulletin of the history of medicine, v. 39, Jan./Feb. 1965: 22–33. R11.B93, v. 39

D'ELIA, DONALD J. Benjamin Rush: an intellectual biography. 1965. ([252] p.)

Micro AC–1, no. 65–9800

Thesis (Ph.D.)—Pennsylvania State University. Abstracted in *Dissertation Abstracts*, v. 26, Dec. 1965, p. 3263.

———— Benjamin Rush, David Hartley, and the revolutionary uses of psychology. *In* American Philosophical Society, *Philadelphia.* Proceedings, v. 114, Apr. 1970: 109–118. Q11.P5, v. 114

On Rush's preoccupation with Hartley's Christian system of physiological psychology first developed in his *Observations on Man* (1749).

—— Dr. Benjamin Rush and the American medical revolution. *In* American Philosophical Society, *Philadelphia*. Proceedings, v. 110, Aug. 1966: 227–234. Q11.P5, v. 110

—— Dr. Benjamin Rush and the Negro. Journal of the history of ideas, v. 30, July/Sept. 1969: 413–422. B1.J75, v. 30

—— The republican theology of Benjamin Rush. Pennsylvania history, v. 33, Apr. 1966: 187–203. F146.P597, v. 33

DIETZE, GOTTFRIED. Benjamin Rush and the American Revolution. *In* Dickinson College, *Carlisle, Pa. Library*. Early Dickinsoniana. Carlisle, Pa., 1961 [c1965] (The Boyd Lee Spahr lectures in Americana, 1957–1961) p. 75–90. LD1662.A53

GOOD, HARRY G. Benjamin Rush and his services to American education. Berne, Ind., Witness Press [c1918] x, 283 p. R154.R9G6
Bibliography: p. [259]–275.

GOODMAN, NATHAN G. Benjamin Rush, physician and citizen, 1746–1813. Philadelphia, University of Pennsylvania Press, 1934. 421 p. facsim., plates, ports. R154.R9G65
Bibliography: p. [377]–406.

HAWKE, DAVID F. Benjamin Rush, revolutionary gadfly. Indianapolis, Bobbs-Merrill [1971] x, 490 p. port E302.6.R85H3
Bibliography: p. [399]–454.

KAHN, EUGEN. Benjamin Rush, the founder of modern psychiatry. Confinia psychiatrica, v. 10, no. 2, 1967: 61–76. RC321.C64, v. 10

KIEFFER, JOHN E. A physician philanthropist of the eighteenth century: Benjamin Rush, 1746–1813. Social service review, v. 2, June 1928: 274–304. HV1.S6, v. 2

KUNITZ, STEPHEN J. Benjamin Rush on savagism and progress. Ethnohistory, v. 17, winter/spring 1970: 31–42. E51.E8, v. 17
Views of the Indian character.

KURITZ, HYMAN. Benjamin Rush: his theory of republican education. History of education quarterly, v. 7, winter 1967: 432–451. L11.H67, v. 7

LAMBERT, PAUL F. Benjamin Rush and American independence. Pennsylvania history, v. 39, Oct. 1972: 443–454. F146.P597, v. 39

LLOYD, JAMES H. Benjamin Rush and his critics. Annals of medical history, new ser., v. 2, Sept. 1930: 470–475. R11.A85, n.s., v. 2

MACKLER, BERNARD, *and* KAY HAMILTON. Benjamin Rush: a political and historical study of the "father of American psychiatry." Psychological reports, v. 20, June 1967: 1287–1306. (Contributions to the history of psychology, 7) BF21.P843, v. 20

MIDDLETON, WILLIAM S. Gleanings from *Medical Inquiries and Observations* of Benjamin Rush. *In* College of Physicians of Philadelphia. Transactions & studies, 4th ser., v. 36, July 1968: 55–60. R15.P5, 4th s., v. 36

MILES, WYNDHAM D. Joseph Black, Benjamin Rush and the teaching of chemistry at the University of Pennsylvania. Library chronicle, v. 22, winter 1956: 9–18. Z733.P418, v. 22

RADBILL, SAMUEL X. The iconography of Benjamin Rush. *In* College of Physicians of Philadelphia. Transactions & studies, 4th ser., v. 16, June 1948: 73–79. R15.P5, 4th s., v. 16

RUCKER, MARVIN PIERCE. Benjamin Rush, obstetrician. Annals of medical history, 3d ser., v. 3, Nov. 1941: 487–500. R11.A85, 3d s., v. 3

SHRYOCK, RICHARD H. Benjamin Rush from the perspective of the twentieth century. *In* College of Physicians of Philadelphia. Transactions & studies, 4th ser., v. 14, Dec. 1946: 113–120. R15.P5, 4th s., v. 14

—— The medical reputation of Benjamin Rush: contrasts over two centuries. Bulletin of the history of medicine, v. 45, Nov./Dec. 1971: 507–552. R11.B93, v. 45

SMITHCORS, J. F. The contributions of Benjamin Rush to veterinary medicine. Journal of the history of medicine and allied sciences, v. 12, Jan. 1957: 13–20. R131.A1J6, v. 12

STRAUB, JEAN S. Benjamin Rush's views on women's education. Pennsylvania history, v. 34, Apr. 1967: 147–157. F146.P597, v. 34

14349

RUSH, JACOB (1746?–1820)
Pennsylvania. Lawyer, assemblyman, judge.

RICHARDS, LOUIS. Hon. Jacob Rush, of the Pennsylvania judiciary. Pennsylvania magazine of history and biography, v. 39, Jan. 1915: 53–68. F146.P65, v. 39

14350

RUSSELL, ELIZABETH HENRY CAMPBELL (1749–1825)
Virginia. Settler.

PRESTON, THOMAS L. A sketch of Mrs. Elizabeth Russell, wife of General William Campbell, and sister of Patrick Henry. Nashville, Pub. House of the M.E. Church, South, 1888. 44 p. plates, ports. E207.C19P9

14351

RUSSELL, PETER (1733–1808)
Ireland; Virginia; Canada. British officer in America.

—— The early life and letters of the Honourable Peter Russell [1755–92] *In* Ontario Historical Society. Papers and records. v. 29. Toronto, 1933. p. 121–140.

F1056.O58, v. 29

Introduction and notes by Ernest A. Cruikshank.

14352

RUTLEDGE, JOHN (1739–1800)*

South Carolina. Lawyer, assemblyman, delegate to the Continental Congress, governor, delegate to the Constitutional Convention, judge.

—— Letters of John Rutledge [1780–82] South Carolina historical and genealogical magazine, v. 17, Oct. 1916: 131–146; v. 18, Jan.–Oct. 1917: 42–49, 59–69, 131–142, 155–167.

F266.S55, v. 17–18

Annotated by Joseph W. Barnwell.

BARNWELL, ROBERT W. Rutledge "the dictator." Journal of southern history, v. 7, May 1941: 215–224.

F206.J68, v. 7

BARRY, RICHARD H. Mr. Rutledge of South Carolina. New York, Duell, Sloan and Pearce [1942] ix, 430 p. facsims., port.

E302.6.R89B3

Bibliography: p. 401–411.
Reprinted in Freeport, N.Y., by Books for Libraries Press (1971).

14353

SACKVILLE, GEORGE SACKVILLE GERMAIN, *1st Viscount* (1716–1785)†

England. British military officer, Member of Parliament, Secretary of State, President of the Board of Trade.

ADAMS, RANDOLPH G. The papers of Lord George Germain; a brief description of the Stopford-Sackville papers now in the William L. Clements Library. Ann Arbor, William L. Clements Library, 1928. 46 p. illus., facsims., port. (William L. Clements Library—University of Michigan. Bulletin no. 18).

E172.M53, no. 18
E203.S117

CUMBERLAND, RICHARD. Character of the late Lord Viscount Sackville. London, C. Dilly, 1785. 24 p.

DA67.1.S2C9
AC901.M5 Rare Bk. Coll.

Gt. Brit. *Historical Manuscripts Commission.* Report on the manuscripts of Mrs. Stopford-Sackville, of Drayton House, Northamptonshire. London, Printed for H.M. Stationery Off., by Mackie, 1904–10. 2 v. [*Its* Report. unnumbered series]

DA25.M2S7

Parliament. Papers by command. Cd. 1892, 5038.
Vol. 2 printed by Hereford Times Co.
Edited by W. O. Hewlett; revised by Mrs. S. C. Lomas.
Revised and enlarged edition of its 9th *Report*, pt. 3, 1884, Cd. 3773–II.

Reprinted, with a new introduction and preface by George A. Billias, in Boston by Gregg Press (1972. DA483.S2G7).

Composed chiefly of letters, reports, and other official documents to and from Germain.

ROBSON, ERIC. Lord George Germain and the American colonies. History today, v. 3, Feb. 1953: 115–121.

D1.H818, v. 3

VALENTINE, ALAN C. Lord George Germain. Oxford [Eng.] Clarendon Press, 1962. x, 534 p. port.

DA483.S2V3

Bibliography: p. [506]–515.

[WILKINSON, LOUIS U.] Sackville of Drayton (Lord George Sackville till 1770, Lord George Germain, 1770–1782, Viscount Sackville from 1782). By Louis Marlow [*pseud.*] London, Home & Van Thal [1948] 300 p. plate, ports.

DA483.S2W5

Bibliography: p. 290–295.

14354

SAILLY, PETER (1754–1826)

New York. Settler.

BIXBY, GEORGE S. Peter Sailly (1754–1826), a pioneer of the Champlain Valley, with extracts from his diary and letters. Albany, University of the State of New York, 1919. 94 p. facsim., port. (New York (State). State Library, Albany. History bulletin no. 12)

Z881.N61BH, no. 12
E302.6.S13B6

14355

ST. CLAIR, ARTHUR (1736–1818)*

Scotland; Pennsylvania. Landowner, judge, Revolutionary general, delegate to the Continental Congress.

BEALS, ELLIS. Arthur St. Clair, western Pennsylvania's leading citizen, 1764–1818. Western Pennsylvania historical magazine, v. 12, Apr.–July 1929: 75–96, 175–196.

F146.W52, v. 12

HEATHCOTE, CHARLES W. General Arthur St. Clair—a patriotic Pennsylvania military officer and colleague of Washington. Picket post, no. 74, Nov. 1961: 4–10. port.

E234.P5, no. 74

SMITH, WILLIAM H. The St. Clair papers. The life and public services of Arthur St. Clair, soldier of the Revolutionary War; president of the Continental Congress; the governor of the North-western Territory; with his correspondence and other papers. Cincinnati, R. Clarke, 1882 [c1881] 2 v. fold. map, ports.

F483.S15

Reprinted in Freeport, N.Y., by Books for Libraries Press (1970) and in New York by Da Capo Press (1971).

WILSON, FRAZER E. Arthur St. Clair, rugged ruler of the old Northwest; an epic of the American frontier. Richmond, Garrett and Massie [1944] xiii, 253 p. illus., facsims., maps, plates, ports. F483.S19

Bibliography: p. 247.

14356

SAINT-EXUPÉRY, GEORGES ALEXANDRE CÉSAR, *comte* DE (1757–1825)

France. French officer in America.

——— Journal d'un officier du régiment de la Sarre-Infanterie pendant la guerre d'Amérique (1780–1782). Carnet de la sabretache, v. 12, Mar.–June 1904: 169–185, 240–255, 305–319, 361–383. port. DC44.C3, v. 12

Introduction and notes by S. Churchill.

14357

SAINT-SIMON-MONTBLÉRU, CLAUDE ANNE DE ROUVROY, *marquis* DE (1743–1819)

French officer in America.

LARRABEE, HAROLD A. Henri de Saint-Simon at Yorktown; a French prophet of modern industrialism in America. Franco-American review, v. 2, autumn 1937: 96–109. E183.8.F8F88, v. 2

——— A neglected French collaborator in the victory of Yorktown: Claude-Anne, Marquis de Saint-Simon (1740–1819). *In* Société des américanistes de Paris. Journal, nouv. sér., t. 24, fasc. 2, 1932: 245–257. E151.S68, n.s., v. 24

14358

SALISBURY, SAMUEL (1739–1818)

Massachusetts. Merchant, importer.

NICHOLS, CHARLES L. Samuel Salisbury—a Boston merchant in the Revolution. *In* American Antiquarian Society, *Worcester, Mass.* Proceedings, new ser., v. 35, Apr. 1925: 46–63. E172.A35, n.s., v. 35

——— ——— Offprint. Worcester, Mass., The Society, 1926. 20 p. F73.44.S16

14359

SALOMON, HAYM (1740–1785)*

Poland; New York; Pennsylvania. Merchant, broker.

FAST, HOWARD M. Haym Salomon, son of liberty, Illustrated by Eric M. Simon. New York, J. Messner [ᶜ1941] 243 p. illus., plates. E302.6.S17F3

GRINSTEIN, HYMAN B. A Haym Salomon letter to Rabbi David Tevele Schiff, London, 1784. *In* American Jewish Historical Society. Publications. no. 34. New York, 1937. p. 107–122. E184.J5A5, no. 34

An essay on the historical significance of the letter.

KOHLER, MAX J. Haym Salomon, the patriot broker of the Revolution; his real achievements and their exag-

geration. An open letter to Congressman Celler, by Max Kohler. [n.p.] 1931. 22 p. E302.6.S17K6

RUSSELL, CHARLES E. Haym Salomon and the Revolution. New York, Cosmopolitan Book Corp., 1930. xv, 317 p. facsim., plates, ports. E302.6.S17R8

Reprinted in Freeport, N.Y., by Books for Libraries Press (1970).

[SALOMON, HAYM M.] A sketch of Haym Salomon. From an unpublished ms. in the papers of Jared Sparks. Contributed by Herbert B. Adams. *In* American Jewish Historical Society. Publications. v. 2; 1893. [Baltimore] 1894. p. 5–19. E184.J5A5, v. 2

See also "Some Further References Relating to Haym Salomon," by Jacob H. Hollander, in v. 3, 1894 (Baltimore, 1895), p. 7–11.

14360

SALTONSTALL, RICHARD (1732–1785)

Massachusetts; England. Military officer, Loyalist.

MOODY, ROBERT E., *comp.* The Saltonstall papers, 1607–1815. Selected and edited with biographies of ten members of the Saltonstall family in six generations. v. 1. 1607–1789. Boston, Massachusetts Historical Society, 1972. xx, 574 p. illus., ports., map. (Massachusetts Historical Society, Boston. Collections, v. 80) F61.M41, v. 80

Bibliography: p. [558]–574.

14361

SALVADORE, JOSEPH (1716–1786) Also known as Joseph Jessurun Rodrigues

England; South Carolina. Financier, scientist, landowner.

——— A description of America, 1785. American Jewish archives, v. 17, Apr. 1965: 27–33. E184.J5A37, v. 17

Introduction and notes by Cecil Roth.

14362

SANDERSON, ELIJAH (1751–1825)

Massachusetts. Woodworker.

SWAN, MABEL M. Elijah and Jacob Sanderson, early Salem cabinetmakers; a Salem eighteenth-century furniture trust company. *In* Essex Institute, *Salem, Mass.* Historical collections, v. 70, Oct. 1934: 323–364. facsims., plates. F72.E7E81, v. 70

An offprint, entitled *Samuel McIntire, Carver, and the Sandersons; Early Salem Cabinet Makers*, was published in Salem, Mass., by the Essex Institute (1934. 44 p. NK2439.M3S8).

14363

SANDWICH, JOHN MONTAGU, *4th Earl of* (1718–1792)†

England, British naval officer, First Lord of Admiralty.

—— The private papers of John, Earl of Sandwich, first Lord of the Admiralty, 1771–1782. Edited by G. R. Barnes and J. H. Owen. [London] Printed for the Navy Records Society, 1932–38. 4 v. ports. (Publications of the Navy Records Society, v. 69, 71, 75, 78)
DA70.A1, v. 69, 71, 75, 78

"List of authorities cited": v. 1, p. [xxvii]–xxviii.

HAAS, JAMES M. The pursuit of political success in eighteenth-century England: Sandwich, 1740–71. In London. University. *Institute of Historical Research.* Bulletin, v. 53, May 1970: 56–77. D1.L65, v. 53

MARTELLI, GEORGE. Jemmy Twitcher: a life of the Fourth Earl of Sandwich, 1718–1792. London, J. Cape [1962] 292 p. illus., maps, ports. DA506.S3M3

Includes bibliographic footnotes.

SPENCER, FRANK, *comp.* The fourth Earl of Sandwich: diplomatic correspondence, 1763–1765. Edited, with an introduction by Frank Spencer. [Manchester, Eng.] Manchester University Press [c1961] vii, 334 p.
DA506.S3S63 1961

Includes bibliographic references.

The introduction (p. 1–66) provides an overview of European diplomatic history in the mid-1760's and sheds light on the functioning of the Secretary of State's offices.

14364

SANGMEISTER, EZECHIEL (1723 or 4–1784)
Germany; Pennsylvania.

REICHMANN, FELIX. Ezechiel Sangmeister's diary. Pennsylvania magazine of history and biography, v. 68, July 1944: 292–313. F146.P65, v. 78

Evaluates Sangmeister's diary, published under the title *Das Leben und Wandel des in Gott ruhenten und seligen Br. Ezechiel Sangmeisters* (Ephrata, J. Bauman, 1825–26. 3 v. in 1. BX7843.S3A3 Rare Bk. Coll.), as a source of information about the 18th-century history of the Ephrata Community and the life and contributions of its spiritual leader, Conrad Beissel.

14365

SARGEANT, NATHANIEL PEASLEE (1731–1791)
Massachusetts. Lawyer, judge.

ABBOTT, IRA A. Life and times of the Hon. Nathaniel Peaslee Sargeant, chief justice of the Supreme Judicial Court of Massachusetts. *In* Essex Institute, *Salem, Mass.* Historical collections, v. 86, July–Oct. 1950: 211–246, 350–379. plates, ports. F72.E7E81, v. 86

14366

SARGENT, PAUL DUDLEY (1745–1827 or 8)
Massachusetts; Maine. Revolutionary officer, judge.

SARGENT, IGNATIUS. Colonel Paul Dudley Sargent of Sullivan, Maine, and family. Bangor historical magazine, v. 2, Jan. 1887: 125–131. F16.M21, v. 2

[SARGENT, WINTHROP] Colonel Paul Dudley Sargent. 1745–1827. [Philadelphia? 1920] 46 p. illus., facsims., ports. E207.S24S242

Printed for private circulation.

Contents: Colonel Paul Dudley Sargent of Sullivan, Maine.—Concerning Col. Paul Dudley Sargent and his daughter, Mrs. Julia Sargent Johnson.—Sanders' ancestry [from notes by Dr. Samuel Worcester]—The Sargent family of Gloucester, by Charles Sprague Sargent.

14367

SARGENT, WINTHROP (1753–1820)*
Massachusetts; Ohio. Revolutionary officer, settler.

Guide to the microfilm edition of the Winthrop Sargent papers. Frederick S. Allis, Jr., editor; Roy Bartolomei, associate editor. Boston, Massachusetts Historical Society, 1965. 55 p. Z6616.S175A5 Mss

PERSHING, BENJAMIN H. A surveyor on the Seven Ranges. Ohio state archaeological and historical quarterly, v. 46, July 1937: 257–270.
F486.O51, v. 46

—— Winthrop Sargent. Ohio archaeological and historical quarterly, v. 35, Oct. 1926: 583–602. ports.
F486.O51, v. 35

—— Withrop Sargent: a builder in the old Northwest. 1927. 208 l. E302.S2P4

Thesis (Ph.D.)—University of Chicago.
Typescript (carbon copy).
Bibliography: leaves [189]–208.

PLEASANTS, HENRY. Winthrop Sargent, patriot and pioneer. [Philadelphia?] Printed by order of the Society [1944] 31 p. (Historical publications of the Society of Colonial Wars in the Commonwealth of Pennsylvania, v. 6, no. 5) E186.3.P41, v. 6

14368

SASH, MOSES (*b.* 1752)
Massachusetts. Farmer, Revolutionary soldier.

KAPLAN, SIDNEY. A Negro veteran in Shays' Rebellion. Journal of Negro history, v. 33, Apr. 1948: 123–129.
E185.J86, v. 33

SAUER, CHRISTOPHER
See SOWER, CHRISTOPHER

14369

SAUGRAIN DE VIGNI, ANTOINE FRANÇOIS (1763–1820)*
France; Ohio. Physician, scientist, explorer.

—— Dr. Saugrain's note-books, 1788. *In* America Antiquarian Society, *Worcester, Mass.* Proceedings, new ser., v. 19, Oct. 1908: 221–238.

E172.A35, n.s., v. 19

—— —— Offprint. Worcester, Mass., Davis Press, 1909. 21 p.   F516.S25

Introduction and notes by Eugene F. Bliss.

Contents: 1. Stay opposite Louisville,—2. Observations upon Post Vincennes.—3. Diary of journal from Louisville to Philadelphia.

—— Dr. Saugrain's relation of his voyage down the Ohio River from Pittsburgh to the falls in 1788. *In* American Antiquarian Society, *Worcester, Mass.* Proceedings, new ser., v. 11, Apr. 1897: 369–380.

E172.A35, n.s., v. 11

—— —— Offprint. Worcester, Mass., Press of C. Hamilton, 1897. 14 p.   F516.S26

Translated with notes by Eugene F. Bliss.

—— L'odyssée américaine d'une famille française [par] le docteur Antoine Saugrain; étude suivie de manuscrits inédits et de la correspondance de Sophie Michau Robinson, par H. Fouré Selter. Baltimore, Johns Hopkins Press, 1936. ix, 123 p. facsims., maps, plates, ports.

F516.S27

At head of title: Institut français de Washington.

—— Translation of Dr. Saugrain's narrative of his capture by the Indians, his subsequent escape, adventures in the woods, arrival at Louisville, sickness, etc.; time from March 19th to May 11th, 1788. [n.p., 194–?] 9, 10 p.

F517.S3

Reproduced from typescript.

"Notes and comments on the travels of Dr. Saugrain, by John M. Newton": 10 p. at end.

BYARS, WILLIAM V.   The first scientist of the Mississippi Valley; a memoir of the life and work of Doctor Antoine François Saugrain. St. Louis, B. Von Phul [190–] 18 p. illus., facsim., ports.   R154.S26B9

CHINARD, GILBERT.   Gallipolis and Dr. Saugrain. Franco-American review, v. 1, winter 1937: 201–207.

E183.8.F8F88, v. 1

DANDRIDGE, NATHANIEL P.   Antoine Francois Saugrain (de Vigni). "The first scientist of the Mississippi Valley." Ohio archaeological and historical quarterly, v. 15, Apr. 1906: 192–206. port.   F486.O51, v. 15

First published in the *Journal* of the American Medical Association, v. 63, Dec. 31, 1904, p. 2007–2011. An offprint was issued in Chicago by the Press of the American Medical Association (1905. 15 p. CT99.S255D3).

14370

SAVAGE, NATHANIEL LITTLETON

Virginia. Planter, merchant.

AMES, SUSIE M.   A typical Virginia business man of the Revolutionary era: Nathaniel Littleton Savage and his

account book. Journal of economic and business history, v. 3, May 1931: 407–423.   HC10.J6, v. 3

14371

SAVAGE, SAMUEL PHILLIPS (1718–1797)

Massachusetts. Merchant.

—— Savage papers, 1703–1779. *In* Massachusetts Historical Society, *Boston.* Proceedings. v. 44; 1910/11. Boston, 1911. p. 84–86, 683–702.   F61.M38, v. 44

Mostly letters dealing with events in Boston, 1776–79.

14372

SAVERY, WILLIAM (1750–1804)*

Pennsylvania. Tanner, Quaker minister and missionary.

—— A journal of the life, travels, and religious labours, of William Savery, late of Philadelphia, a minister of the gospel of Christ, in the Society of Friends. Compiled from his original memoranda, by Jonathan Evans. London, C. Gilpin, 1844. vii, 316 p.   BX7795.S15A3

TAYLOR, FRANCIS R.   Life of William Savery of Philadelphia, 1750–1804. New York, Macmillan Co., 1925. x, 474 p. plates, ports.   BX7795.S15T3

14373

SAVILE, *Sir* GEORGE, *Bart.* (1726–1784)†

England. Member of Parliament.

GRAY, FRANCIS J.   The parliamentary career of Sir George Savile, Bart., 1759–1783. 1958.

Thesis (Ph.D.)—Fordham University.

14374

SAYRE, STEPHEN (1736–1818)*

New York; England. Merchant, banker, diplomat.

BOYD, JULIAN P.   The remarkable adventures of Stephen Sayre. Princeton University Library chronicle, v. 2, Feb. 1941: 51–64. ports.   Z733.P93C5, v. 2

14375

SCAMMELL, ALEXANDER (1747–1781)*

Massachusetts; New Hampshire. Schoolteacher, surveyor, Revolutionary officer.

—— Colonel Alexander Scamell and his letters, from 1768 to 1781, including his "love letters" to Miss Nabby Bishop. Historical magazine, 2d ser., v. 8, Sept. 1870: 129–146.   E171.H64, 2d s., v. 8

CLOUGH, WILLIAM O.   Colonel Alexander Scammell. Granite monthly, v. 14, Sept. 1892: 262–275. port.

F31.G75, v. 14

14376

SCATTERGOOD, THOMAS (1748–1814)*

New Jersey; Pennsylvania. Tanner, itinerant Quaker minister.

—— Memoirs of the life and religious labours of Thomas Scattergood, a minister of the Gospel in the Society of Friends. *In* Friends' library. v. 8. Philadelphia, 1844. p. 1–225. BX7615.F8, v. 8

14377

SCHAUKIRK, EWALD GUSTAV (1725–1805)

Germany; New York. Moravian clergyman.

—— Occupation of New York City by the British. Pennsylvania magazine of history and biography, v. 10, Jan. 1887: 418–445. F146.P65, v. 10

Reprinted in New York by the New York Times (1969. F128.44.S3 1969).

Extracts from Schaukirk's diary, 1775–83, kept while he was pastor of the Moravian congregation, New York City.

14378

SCHAW, JANET (*ca.* 1731–*ca.* 1801)

Scotland. Traveler.

—— Journal of a lady of quality; being the narrative of a journey from Scotland to the West Indies, North Carolina, and Portugal, in the years 1774 to 1776. Edited by Evangeline Walker Andrews, in collaboration with Charles McLean Andrews. [2d ed., with additional notes and illus.] New Haven, Yale University Press, 1934. 349 p. facsim., maps (on lining papers), plates, port. F257.S35

"The manuscript from which the present text is printed is known as Egerton 2423, and is . . . in the British Museum."—p. [1]

Reprinted in Spartanburg, S.C., by the Reprint Co. (1971). The first edition was published in 1921.

14379

SCHERMERHORN, FREDERICK (1762 *or* 3–1847)

New York.

PRIEST, JOSIAH. The Low Dutch prisoner: being an account of the capture of Frederick Schermerhorn. When a lad of seventeen years old, by a party of Mohawks, in the time of the Revolution. Who took him near the famous Mountain House in the state of New-York, and of his sufferings through the wilderness with the Indians. Also, the story of the hermit, found in a cave of the Allegany Mountains. And of the miners of the Minisink: with some other curious matters, which the reader may consider useful as well as interesting. Albany, 1839. 32 p. illus. E275.P94 Rare Bk. Coll.

14380

SCHLATTER, MICHAEL (1716–1790)*

Switzerland; Pennsylvania. German Reformed clergyman and missionary.

HARBAUGH, HENRY. The life of Rev. Michael Schlatter; with a full account of his travels and labors among the Germans in Pennsylvania, New Jersey, Maryland and Virginia; including his services as chaplain in the French and Indian War, and in the War of the Revolution, 1716 to 1790. Philadelphia, Lindsay & Blakiston, 1857. xxxi, 375 p. front. F152.S33

A True History of the Real Condition of the Destitute Congregations in Pennsylvania, by Michael Schlatter (a translation of *Getrouw verhaal van den waren toestant der meest herderloze gemeentens in Pennsylvanien* (Amsterdam, 1751): p. 87–234.

HINKE, WILLIAM J. Michael Schlatter, the organizer of the Reformed Church in the United States. Pennsylvania-German, v. 1, Oct. 1900: 3–21. illus.

F146.P224, v. 1

14381

SCHLÖZER, AUGUST LUDWIG (1735–1809)

Germany. Professor, magazine publisher.

FORD, GUY S. Two German publicists on the American Revolution. Journal of English and Germanic philology, v. 8, Apr. 1909: 145–176. PD1.J7, v. 8

On Schlözer, who published *Briefwechsel meist historischen und politischen Inhalts,* and Christian Friedrich Daniel Schubart, editor of *Die Deutsche Chronik.*

FÜRST, FRIEDERIKE. August Ludwig von Schlözer, ein deutscher Aufklärer im 18. Jahrhundert. Heidelberg, C. Winter, 1928. 206 p. (Heidelberger Abhandlungen zur mittleren und neueren Geschichte, Hft. 56)

D15.S5F8

ZELGER, RENATE F. Der historisch-politische Briefwechsel und die Staatsanzeigen August Ludwig v. Schlözers als Zeitschrift und Zeitbild. München, 1953. 179, [14] l. illus., map. PN5220.S8Z4

Typescript (carbon copy).
Inaug.-Diss.—Munich.
Bibliography: leaves [180]–[183]

14382

SCHÖPF, JOHANN DAVID (1752–1800)*

Germany. Hessian surgeon in America, traveler.

—— Beyträge zur mineralogischen Kenntniss des östlichen Theils von Nordamerika und seiner Geburge. Erlangen, J. J. Palm, 1787. 194 p. E164.S36

—— The climate and diseases of America. Translated by James Read Chadwick. Boston, H. O. Houghton, 1875. 31 p. RA804.S43

—— The diseases of America, by Dr. Johann David Schoepff, surgeon of the Anspach-Bayreuth troops in America. Translated and edited by James R. Chadwick. Boston medical and surgical journal, v. 92, June 17–24, 1875: 715–724, 733–737; v. 93, July 1, 1875: 6–11.
R11.B7, v. 92–93

Letters taken from a pamphlet published in 1781 in Erlangen, Bavaria.

—— Materia medica americana potissimvm regni vegetabilis. Erlangae, Svmtibvs I.I. Palmii, 1787. xviii, 170 p. [With Linné, Carl von Amoenitates. Erlangae, 1790. v. 10]   RS169.S36 1787 Rare Bk. Coll.

Reprinted in Cincinnati by J. V. & C. G. Lloyd (1903) as Bulletin no. 6 of the Lloyd Library of Botany, Pharmacy and Materia Medica.

—— Reise durch Einige der mittlern und südlichen Vereinigten Nordamerikanischen Staaten nach Ost-Florida und den Bahama-Inseln unternommen in den Jahren 1783 und 1784. Erlangen, J. J. Palm, 1788. 2 v. fold. map.   E164.S67

Translated and edited by Alfred J. Morison, Schöpf's work was published in the United States as Travels in the Confederation, 1783–1784 (Philadelphia, W. J. Campbell, 1911. 2 v.). Vol. 1 contains the author's impressions of New Jersey, Pennsylvania, Maryland, and Virginia, while v. 2 covers Pennsylvania, Maryland, Virginia, the Carolinas, East Florida, and the Bahamas. Both volumes were reprinted in New York by Bergman (1968) and B. Franklin (1968).

MORRISON, ALFRED J.   Doctor Johann David Schoepf. German American annals, new ser., v. 8, Sept./Dec. 1910: 255–264.   E184.G3G3, n.s., v. 8

14383

SCHUYLER, CATHERINE VAN RENSSELAER (1734?–1803)
New York. Wife of Philip John Schuyler.

HUMPHREYS, MARY G.   Catherine Schuyler. New York, C. Scribner's Sons, 1897. xi, 251 p. port. (Women of colonial and Revolutionary times)   E207.S31H9

Reprinted in Spartanburg, S.C., by the Reprint Co. (1968).

14384

SCHUYLER, PHILIP JOHN (1733–1804)*
New York. Landowner, assemblyman, delegate to the Continental Congress, Revolutionary general.

BUSH, MARTIN H.   Revolutionary enigma; a re-appraisal of General Philip Schuyler of New York. Port Washington, N.Y., I. J. Friedman, 1969. xiv, 295 p. map, ports (Empire State historical publications series, no. 80)   E207.S3B8

Bibliography: p. 187–198.
The author's thesis (Ph.D.), Philip Schuyler; the Revolutionary War Years, was submitted to Syracuse University in 1966 (Micro AC–1, no. 67–7061).

GERLACH, DON R.   After Saratoga: the general, his lady, and "Gentleman Johnny" Burgoyne. In New York State Historical Association. New York history, v. 52, Jan. 1971: 5–30. ports.   F116.N865, v. 52

—— Philip Schuyler and the American Revolution in New York, 1733–1777. Lincoln, University of Nebraska Press, 1964. xxi, 358 p. illus., map, ports.   E207.S3G4

Bibliography: p. 332–344.
The author's thesis (Ph.D.), Philip Schuyler: the Origins of a Conservative Patriot, 1733–1777; a Study in Provincial Politics and the American Revolution in New York, was submitted to the University of Nebraska in 1961 (Micro AC–1, no. 61–5374).

—— Philip Schuyler and the growth of New York, 1733–1804. Albany, Office of State History, 1968. 48 p. illus.   E207.S3G42

Bibliography: p. 48–[49]

—— Philip Schuyler and the New York frontier in 1781. In New York Historical Society. Quarterly, v. 53, Apr. 1969: 148–181. illus., map, port.   F116.N638, v. 53

—— Philip Schuyler and "the road to glory": a question of loyalty and competence. In New York Historical Society. Quarterly, v. 49, Oct. 1965: 341–386. illus., map, ports.   F116.N638, v. 49

HEATHCOTE, CHARLES W.   General Philip Schuyler—an ardent patriot and sincere friend of General Washington. Picket post, no. 77, July 1962: 8–12, 42. port.   E234.P5, no. 77

LOSSING, BENSON J.   The life and times of Philip Schuyler. New York, Sheldon [1872]–73. 2 v. ports.   E207.S3L82

Vol. 1 first published in New York by Mason Bros. (1860).

PELL, JOHN.   Philip Schuyler: the general as aristocrat. In Billias, George A., ed. George Washington's generals. New York, W. Morrow, 1964. p. 54–78. port.   E206.B5

Bibliography: p. 78.

TUCKERMAN, BAYARD.   Life of General Philip Schuyler, 1733–1804. New York, Dodd, Mead, 1905. 277 p. map, plates, port.   E207.S3T8

Reprinted in Freeport, N.Y., by Books for Libraries Press (1969).

14385

SCOTT, CHARLES (ca. 1739–1813)*
Virginia; Kentucky. Revolutionary general, settler.

HEATHCOTE, CHARLES W.   General Charles Scott—an able officer on whom Washington depended. Picket post, no. 57, July 1957: 4–11. port.   E234.P5, no. 57

14386

SCOTT, JOB (1751–1793)*

Rhode Island. Schoolmaster, Quaker minister.

———— Journal of the life, travels and gospel labours of that faithful servant and minister of Christ, Job Scott. 4th ed. New-York, Printed and sold by Isaac Collins, no. 189, Pearl-Street, 1798. xii, 360 p.
BX7795.S4A5 1798

First edition published in 1797.

WILBUR, HENRY W. Job Scott, an eighteenth century Friend. Philadelphia, Friends' General Conference Advancement Committee, 1911. 112 p.
BX7795.S4W5

14387

SCOTT, JOHN MORIN (1730–1784)*

New York. Lawyer, political writer, Revolutionary general, delegate to the Continental Congress.

DUNKAK, HENRY M. John Morin Scott and Whig politics in New York (1752–1769). 1968. ([349] p.)
Micro AC–1, no. 69–4122

Thesis (Ph.D.)—St. John's University.

Abstracted in *Dissertation Abstracts*, v. 29A, Mar. 1969, p. 3069–3070.

14388

SCOTT, JONATHAN (1744–1819)

Massachusetts; Nova Scotia. Fisherman, Congregational clergyman.

———— The life of Jonathan Scott. Edited with an introduction and notes by Charles Bruce Fergusson. Halifax, N.S., 1960. (Nova Scotia. Public Archives. Bulletin, no. 15)
CD3645.N82, no. 15

Written in the form of a journal, *The Life* covers the years 1744 to 1777.

14389

SCOTT, WILLIAM (1744–1815)

Ireland; New Hampshire; New York. Revolutionary officer, farmer.

SMITH, JONATHAN. Two William Scotts of Peterborough, N.H. *In* Massachusetts Historical Society, *Boston*. Proceedings. v. 44; 1910/11. Boston, 1911. p. 495–502.
F61.M38, v. 44

14390

SEABURY, SAMUEL, *Bp.* (1729–1796)*

Connecticut; New York. Physician, Anglican clergyman and missionary, pamphleteer, Loyalist chaplain, bishop.

————Letters of a Westchester farmer (1774–1775) by the Reverend Samuel Seabury (1729–1796). Edited with an introductory essay by Clarence H. Vance. White Plains,

N.Y., Published for Westchester County by the Westchester County Historical Society, 1930. ix, 162 p. facsims., port. (Publications of the Westchester County Historical Society, v. 8)
F127.W5W7, v. 8

Includes facsimiles of the original title pages of the pamphlets.

"That . . . Seabury was the author of the . . . [three] pamphlets signed A. W. Farmer, there is no longer any doubt; but, through an error of judgment . . . their authorship has been attributed to some of his contemporaries, notably, to Isaac Wilkins."—p. 19.

Reprinted in New York by Da Capo Press (1970).

BEARDSLEY, EBEN EDWARDS. Life and correspondence of the Right Reverend Samuel Seabury, D.D., first bishop of Connecticut, and of the Episcopal Church in the United States of America. Boston, Houghton, Mifflin, 1881. xvii, 497 p. port.
BX5995.S3B4

BEARDSLEY, WILLIAM A. Samuel Seabury, the man and the bishop. Hartford, Conn., Church Missions Pub. Co., 1935. 18 p. (Soldier and servant series, no. 178)
BX5995.S3B43

LINSLEY, GEORGE T. Bishop Seabury. American Church monthly, v. 33, Mar.–Apr. 1933: 193–202, 254–262.
BX5800.A6, v. 33

A reprint of the article (Hartford, Conn., Church Missions Pub. Co. [1933] [29] p. BX5995.S3L5) includes unpublished letters by Bishop Samuel Seabury and Bishop John Skinner of Aberdeen. See also Edward R. Hardy's "The Significance of Seabury" in v. 37, Jan. 1935, p. 26–40.

MAMPOTENG, CHARLES. Samuel Seabury, presbyter. Historical magazine of the Protestant Episcopal church, v. 3, Sept. 1934: 133–145.
BX5800.H5, v. 3

PERRY, WILLIAM S., *Bp.* Bishop Seabury and Bishop Provoost: an historical fragment [n.p.] Priv. print., 1862. 20 p.
BX5995.S3P4

SEABURY, WILLIAM J. Memoir of Bishop Seabury. New York, E. S. Gorham, 1908. vii, 453 p. port.
BX5995.S3S4

STEINER, BRUCE E. Samuel Seabury, 1729–1796; a study in the High Church tradition. [Athens] Ohio University Press [1972, c1971] xiii, 508 p. illus.
BX5995.S3S73

Bibliography: p. 464–482.

The author's thesis (Ph.D.), *Samuel Seabury and the Forging of the High Church Tradition: a Study in the Evolution of New England Churchmanship, 1722–1796*, v. 1–3, was submitted to the University of Virginia in 1962. (Micro AC–1, no. 62–5950).

THOMS, HERBERT. Samuel Seabury; priest and physician, Bishop of Connecticut. Hamden, Conn., Shoe String Press, 1963 [c1962] 166 p. illus., facsim., ports.
BX5995.S3T5 1963

Bibliography: p. [160]–161.

14391
SEARLE, JAMES (1733–1797)*

New York; Pennsylvania. Merchant, Revolutionary officer, delegate to the Continental Congress.

LOMBARD, MILDRED E.   James Searle: radical businessman of the Revolution. Pennsylvania magazine of history and biography, v. 59, July 1935: 284–294.
F146.P65, v. 59

14392
SEARS, ISAAC (1730–1786)*

Massachusetts; New York. Privateer commander, assemblyman.

CHRISTEN, ROBERT J.   King Sears: politician and patriot in a decade of Revolution. 1968. ([363] p.)
Micro AC–1, no. 69–398

Thesis (Ph.D)—Columbia University.
Abstracted in Dissertation Abstracts, v. 29A, Feb. 1969, p. 2635.

14393
SEBASTIAN, BENJAMIN (1745–1834)*

Virginia; Kentucky. Clergyman, lawyer.

WARREN, ELIZABETH.   Benjamin Sebastian and the Spanish conspiracy in Kentucky. Filson Club history quarterly, v. 20, Apr. 1946: 107–130.
F446.F484, v. 20

14394
SEDGWICK, THEODORE (1746–1813)*

Connecticut; Massachusetts. Lawyer, Revolutionary supplier, assemblyman, delegate to the Continental Congress.

WELCH, RICHARD E.   Theodore Sedgwick, Federalist; a political portrait. Middletown, Conn., Wesleyan University Press [1965] viii, 276 p. port.   E302.6.S4W4

Bibliography: p. 255–268.
The author's thesis (Ph.D.), Theodore Sedgwick, 1746–1813: Federalist, was submitted to Harvard University in 1952.

14395
SEELY, SYLVANUS (b. 1740)

Pennsylvania; New Jersey. Farmer, settler.

THAYER, THEODORE G.   An eighteenth-century farmer and pioneer: Sylvanus Seely's early life in Pennsylvania. Pennsylvania history, v. 35, Jan. 1968: 45–63.
F146.P597, v. 35

14396
SEGAR, NATHANIEL (1755–1847)

Massachusetts. Revolutionary officer.

———— A brief narrative of the captivity and sufferings of Lt. Nathan'l. Segar, who was taken prisoner by the Indians and carried to Canada, during the Revolutionary War. Paris (Me.), Printed at the Observer Office, and published at the Oxford Bookstore, 1825. 36 p.
E87.S4 Rare Bk. Coll.

William B. Lapham, writing in his History of Bethel (Augusta, Me., Press of the Maine Farmer, 1891), p. 46, states that the narrative was dictated by Segar and taken down by the Reverend Daniel Gould.
"The destruction at Pejypscot Falls": p. [33]–36.

14397
SÉGUR, LOUIS PHILIPPE, comte DE (1753–1830)

France. French officer in America, diplomat.

———— Memoirs and recollections of Count Ségur. London, H. Colburn, 1825–27. 3 v. facsim., fold. map, port.
DC146.S37A42

Reprinted in one volume in New York by Arno Press (1970. DC146.S37A423 1970).

APT, LEON.   Louis-Philippe de Ségur. An intellectual in a revolutionary age. The Hague, M. Nijhoff, 1969. xv, 161 p. (Archives internationales d'histoire des idées, 25)
DC146.S37A65 1969

Bibliography: p. [148]–158.

14398
SEIXAS, GERSHOM MENDES (1745 or 6–1816)*

New York. Rabbi, professor.

KESSNER, THOMAS.   Gershom Mendes Seixas: his religious "calling," outlook and competence. American Jewish historical quarterly, v. 58, June 1969: 444–471.
E184.J5A5, v. 58

MARCUS, JACOB R.   The handsome young priest in the black gown: the personal world of Gershom Seixas. In Hebrew Union College annual. v. 40/41. Cincinnati, 1970. p. 409–467.   BM11.H4, v. 40/41

14399
SELBY, WILLIAM (1738 or 9–1798)*

Massachusetts. Organist, composer.

McKAY, DAVID.   William Selby, musical émigré in colonial Boston. Musical quarterly, v. 57, Oct. 1971: 609–627.   ML1.M725, v. 57

14400
SELLERS, NATHAN

Pennsylvania. Revolutionary soldier.

———— Extracts from the [military] diary of Nathan Sellers, 1776–1778. Pennsylvania magazine of history and biography, v. 16, July 1892: 191–196.
F146.P65, v. 16

Contributed by Horace W. Sellers.

14401

SELWYN, GEORGE AUGUSTUS (1719–1791)†
England. Member of Parliament.

——— George Selwyn; his letters and his life. Edited by E. S. Roscoe and Helen Clergue. London, T. F. Unwin, 1899. xiv, 302 p. ports. DA512.S4A2

JESSE, JOHN HENEAGE. George Selwyn and his contemporaries; with memoirs and notes. London, R. Bentley, 1843. 4 v. ports. DA512.S4J5

See also Lady Louisa Stuart's *Notes by Lady Louisa Stuart on George Selwyn and His Contemporaries by John Heneage Jesse* (New York, Oxford University Press, 1928. 65 p. DA512.S4S7), edited from the original manuscript by W. S. Lewis.

14402

SEMPLE, JAMES GEORGE, *called* SEMPLE-LISLE (*b.* 1759)†
British officer in America.

——— The life of Major J. G. Semple Lisle; containing a faithful narrative of his alternate vicissitudes of splendor and misfortune. Written by himself. The whole interspersed with interesting anecdotes, and authentic accounts of important public transactions. London, For W. Stewart, 1799. xxii, 382 p. port. CT788.S45A3 1799

14403

SENHOUSE, WILLIAM (*b.* 1741)
England; West Indies. Seaman, customs agent, planter.

——— The autobiographical manuscript of William Senhouse, Surveyor-General of His Majesty's customs—Barbados and the Windward and Leeward Islands—from 1770 until 1787. *In* Barbados Museum and Historical Society, *Bridgetown.* Journal, v. 2, Feb.–Aug. 1935: 61–79, 115–134, 191–209; v. 3, Nov. 1935: 3–19. F2041.B217, v. 2–3

14404

SERLE, AMBROSE (1742–1812)†
England. Secretary, religious writer.

——— The American journal of Ambrose Serle, secretary to Lord Howe, 1776–1778. Edited with an introduction by Edward H. Tatum, Jr. San Marino, Calif., Huntington Library, 1940. xxx, 369 p. illus., maps. (Huntington library publications) E267.S47
"Lists of works cited": p. 347–353.
Reprinted in New York by the New York Times (1969).

TATUM, EDWARD H. Ambrose Serle, secretary to Lord Howe, 1776–1778. Huntington Library quarterly, v. 2, Apr. 1939: 265–284. Z733.S24Q, v. 2

14405

SEUME, JOHANN GOTTFRIED (1763–1810)
Germany. Hessian soldier in America.

——— Memoir's [sic] of a Hessian conscript: J. G. Seumes reluctant voyage to America. William and Mary quarterly, 3d ser., v. 5, Oct. 1948: 553–570. F221.W71, 3d s., v. 5
Translated, with introduction and notes, by Margaret Woelfel.

14406

SEVIER, JOHN (1745–1815)*
Virginia; North Carolina. Frontiersman, Revolutionary officer, land speculator.

DRIVER, CARL S. John Sevier, pioneer of the old Southwest. Chapel Hill, University of North Carolina Press, 1932. viii, 240 p. port. E302.6.S45D8
Bibliography: p. [219]–225.

GILMORE, JAMES R. John Sevier as a commonwealth-builder. A sequel to *The Rear-Guard of the Revolution*. New York, D. Appleton, 1887. xvi, 321 p. fold. map. E302.6.S45G4

TURNER, FRANCIS M. Life of General John Sevier. New York, Neale Pub. Co., 1910. 226 p. port. E302.6.S45T9

14407

SEWALL, HENRY (1752–1845 *or* 6)
Maine; Massachusetts. Farmer, Revolutionary officer.

——— The diary of Henry Sewall [June 1776–July 1777] *In* Fort Ticonderoga, N.Y. Museum. Bulletin, v. 11, Sept. 1963: 75–92. E199.F75, v. 11

——— Fourteen letters [1780] written by General Henry Sewall to his parents while a soldier in the Revolutionary War, 1775–1783. *In* Sewall, William. Diary of William Sewall, 1797–1846. [Lincoln, Ill., Printed by Gordon & Feldman] 1930. Appendix 1. 19 p. (2d group) CT275.S4345A3

14408

SEWALL, JONATHAN (1728–1796)*
Massachusetts; England. Lawyer, Loyalist.

——— A cure for the spleen; or, Amusement for a winter's evening; being the substance of a conversation on the times, over a friendly tankard and pipe. Between Sharp, a country parson; Bumper, a country justice; Fillpot, an inn-keeper; Graveairs, a deacon; Trim, a barber; Brim, a Quaker; Puff, a late representative. Taken in short hand by Sir Roger de Coverly (Jonathan Sewall). America, Printed and sold in the year 1775. Tarrytown, N.Y., Reprinted, W. Abbatt, 1922. 43 p. (The Magazine of history, with notes and queries. Extra number, no. 79) E173.M24, no. 79

BERKIN, CAROL R. Jonathan Sewall: odyssey of an Anglo-American conservative. 1972.
Thesis (Ph.D.)—Columbia University.

ZOBEL, HILLER B. Jonathan Sewall: a lawyer in conflict. *In* Cambridge Historical Society, *Cambridge, Mass.* Publications. v. 40; 1964/66. Cambridge, 1967. p. 123–136.   F74.C1C469, v. 40

14409

SEYMOUR, JAMES (*d.* 1784)

Georgia. Anglican clergyman, Loyalist.

PENNINGTON, EDGAR L. The Reverend James Seymour, S.P.G. missionary in Florida. Florida Historical Society quarterly, v. 5, Apr. 1927: 196–201.

     F306.F65, v. 5

14410

SEYMOUR, WILLIAM

Delaware. Revolutionary soldier.

——— A journal of the southern expedition, 1780–1783. By William Seymour, sergeant-major of the Delaware Regiment. Wilmington, Historical Society of Delaware, 1896. 42 p. (Historical Society of Delaware. Papers, 15)   F161.D35, no. 15

     E237.S48

Also published in the *Pennsylvania Magazine of History and Biography*, v. 7, Sept.–Dec. 1883, p. 286–298, 377–394.

14411

SHANNON, WILLIAM (*ca.* 1752–1794)

Pennsylvania; Kentucky. Revolutionary officer, frontiersman.

SHANNON, EDGAR F. A Revolutionary frontiersman. South Atlantic quarterly, v. 40, Oct. 1941: 379–396.

     AP2.S75, v. 40

14412

SHARP, GRANVILLE (1735–1813)†

England. Clerk, reformer, writer.

——— The legal means of political reformation, proposed in two small tracts, viz. the first on "equitable representation," and the legal means of obtaining it. (1777.) The second on "annual parliaments, the ancient and most salutary "right of the people." (1774.) To which are added, a letter to a member of the Surry committee, in defence of the right of the people to elect representatives for every session of Parliament; viz. not only "every year once," but also "more often if need be." (1780.) And a circular letter to the several petitioning counties, cities, and towns, to warn them against the late proposition for triennial elections. (1780.) 7th ed. [London, 179–?] 95 p.   JN539.1780.S5

LASCELLES, EDWARD C. P. Granville Sharp and the freedom of slaves in England. London, Oxford University Press, H. Milford, 1928. viii, 151 p. ports.

     DA506.S6L3

"Authorities consulted": p. [147]–148.

Reprinted in New York by Negro Universities Press (1969).

14413

SHARPE, HORATIO (1718–1790)*

England; Maryland. Royal governor.

——— Correspondence of Governor Sharpe [1763–68] Maryland historical magazine, v. 12, Dec. 1917: 370–383.   F176.M18, v. 12

——— The familiar letters of Governor Horatio Sharpe [1758–84] Maryland historical magazine, v. 61, Sept. 1966: 189–209.   F176.M18, v. 61

Introduction and notes by Aubrey C. Land.

EDGAR, MATILDA R., *Lady*. A colonial governor in Maryland, Horatio Sharpe and his times, 1753–1773. London, New York, Longmans, Green, 1912. xvi, 311 p. facsims. (part fold.), plates, ports.   F184.S53

GIDDENS, PAUL H. Governor Horatio Sharpe retires [1769] Maryland historical magazine, v. 31, Sept. 1936: 215–225.   F176.M18, v. 31

——— The public career of Horatio Sharpe, governor of Maryland, 1753–1769. 1930.

Thesis (Ph.D.)—State University of Iowa.

HIGH, JAMES H. Reluctant Loyalist, Governor Horatio Sharpe of Maryland, 1753–1769. 1951.

Thesis (Ph.D.)—University of California, Los Angeles.

——— Testing an eighteenth-century personality. Social studies, v. 49, Feb. 1958: 55–59.   D16.3.S65, v. 49

Applies modern psychological test to the recorded facts about Sharpe.

14414

SHARPLES, JAMES (1750?–1811)*†

England. Portrait artist, inventor.

KNOX, KATHARINE M. The Sharples: their portraits of George Washington and his contemporaries; a diary and an account of the life and work of James Sharples and his family in England and America. New Haven, Yale University Press, 1930. xvi, 133 p. illus., facsims., ports.   ND497.S445K6

Reprinted in New York by Kennedy Graphics (1972).

14415

SHAW, JOHN ROBERT (*b.* 1761)

England; Pennsylvania. British soldier in America, Revolutionary soldier.

——— A narrative of the life & travels of John Robert Shaw, the well-digger, now resident in Lexington, Kentucky. Lexington, Printed by D. Bradford, 1807. 180 p. illus., plates.   E275.S53 1807 Rare Bk. Coll.

Another edition was published in Louisville, Ky., by G. Fowler (1930. 242 p. E275.S53 1930).

14416

SHAW, NATHANIEL (*ca.* 1735–1782)*

Connecticut. Merchant, naval agent.

ROGERS, ERNEST E., *ed.* Connecticut's Naval Office at New London during the War of the American Revolution, including the mercantile letter book of Nathaniel Shaw, Jr. [1765–83] New London, Conn., 1933. xvii, 358 p. facsims., maps, plates, ports. (Collections of the New London County Historical Society, v. 2)

F102.N7N8, v. 2
E271.R79

Bibliography: p. [338]

14417

SHAW, SAMUEL (1754–1794)*

Massachusetts. Revolutionary officer, merchant, diplomat.

——— Captain Samuel Shaw's Revolutionary War letters to Captain Winthrop Sargent [1779–81] Pennsylvania magazine of history and biography, v. 70, July 1946: 281–324. F146.P65, v. 70

——— The journals of Major Samuel Shaw, the first American consul at Canton. With a life of the author, by Josiah Quincy. Boston, W. Crosby and H. P. Nichols, 1847. xiii, 360 p. port. DS708.S53

14418

SHEFTALL, LEVI (1739–1809)

Georgia. Recorder.

STERN, MALCOLM H. The Sheftall diaries: vital records of Savannah Jewry (1733–1808). American Jewish historical quarterly, v. 54, Mar. 1965: 243–277. plates, ports. E184.J5A5, v. 54

14419

SHELBURNE, WILLIAM PETTY, *2d Earl of* (1737–1805)†

England. Secretary of State, First Lord of Treasury.

——— Calendar of Shelburne correspondence [relating to Canada, 1763–83] *In* Canada. *Public Archives.* Report. 1921. Ottawa, 1922. p. 229–281. F1001.C13, 1921

Some documents date from an earlier period.

FITZMAURICE, EDMOND GEORGE PETTY-FITZMAURICE, *1st Baron.* Life of William, Earl of Shelburne, afterwards first Marquess of Lansdowne, with extracts from his papers and correspondence. 2d and rev. ed. London, Macmillan, 1912. 2 v. maps (part fold.), plates, ports. DA512.L3F5 1912

Contents: 1. 1737–1776.—2. 1776–1805.
First edition published in three volumes (London, 1875–76).

MERWIN, MILES M. Lord Shelburne and America, 1760–1783: personality for failure. 1971. ([511] p.)
Micro AC–1, no. 72–10,751

Thesis (Ph.D.)—University of North Carolina.
Abstracted in *Dissertation Abstracts International,* v. 32A, Mar. 1972, p. 5157.

NORRIS, JOHN M. Shelburne and reform. London, Macmillan; New York, St. Martin's Press, 1963. xiii, 325 p. port. DA512.L3N6

"Manuscript bibliography": p. 308–309.
The author's thesis (Ph.D.), *Lord Shelburne and the Genesis of Liberal Reform,* was submitted to Northwestern University in 1955 (Micro AC–1, no. 13,122).

SIMPSON, WILLIAM O. Lord Shelburne and North America. History, today, v. 10, Jan. 1960: 52–63. D1.H818, v. 10

14420

SHELBY, ISAAC (1750–1826)*

Maryland; Virginia; Kentucky. Revolutionary officer, assemblyman.

BEASLEY, PAUL W. The life and times of Isaac Shelby, 1750–1826. 1968. ([305]) p.)
Micro AC–1, no. 69–15,455

Thesis (Ph.D.)—University of Kentucky.
Abstracted in *Dissertation Abstracts International,* v. 30A, Oct. 1969, p. 1480.

HENDERSON, ARCHIBALD. Isaac Shelby, Revolutionary patriot and border hero. North Carolina booklet, v. 16, Jan. 1917: 109–144; v. 18, July 1918: 3–56. plate, port. F251.N86, v. 16, 18

14421

SHELBY, JAMES (1752–1783)

Maryland; Kentucky. Revolutionary officer, landowner.

WILLIAMS, SAMUEL C. The military career of Captain James Shelby, brother of Governor Isaac Shelby of Kentucky. Filson Club history quarterly, v. 15, Oct. 1941: 227–237. F446.F484, v. 15

14422

SHERBURNE, ANDREW (1765–1831)

New Hampshire; New York. Revolutionary seaman, Baptist clergyman.

——— Memoirs of Andrew Sherburne: a pensioner of the navy of the Revolution. Utica, Williams, 1828. 262 p.
E271.S53
Micro 02191, reel 247, no. 6E

Reprinted in Freeport, N.Y., by Books for Libraries Press (1970).
A second, enlarged edition was published in Province by H. H. Brown (1831. 312 p. E271.S535).

14423

SHERIDAN, RICHARD BRINSLEY BUTLER (1751–1816)†

England. Dramatist, Member of Parliament.

—— The speeches of the Right Honourable Richard Brinsley Sheridan. With a sketch of his life. Edited by a constitutional friend. [2d ed.] London, H. G. Bohn, 1842. 3 v.   DA522.S4A4

Reprinted in New York by Russell & Russell (1969). First published in five volumes (London, P. Martin, 1816).

14424

SHERMAN, ROGER (1721–1793)*

Massachusetts; Connecticut. Cobbler, surveyor, land-owner, lawyer, assemblyman, judge, merchant, delegate to the Continental Congress, delegate to the Constitutional Convention.

BOARDMAN, ROGER S. Roger Sherman, signer and statesman. Philadelphia, University of Pennsylvania Press, 1938. vii, 396 p. facsims., ports.   E302.6.S6B6

Bibliography: p. 361–373.
Reprinted in New York by Da Capo Press (1971).

BOUTELL, LEWIS H. The life of Roger Sherman. Chicago, A. C. McClurg, 1896. 361 p. port.   E302.6.S5B7

BOYD, JULIAN P. Roger Sherman, portrait of a cordwainer statesman. New England quarterly, v. 5, Apr. 1932: 221–236.   F1.N62, v. 5

COLLIER, CHRISTOPHER. Roger Sherman and Silas Deane; the politics of personalities in the American Revolution. New-England galaxy, v. 4, winter 1963: 11–20. facsim., ports.   F1.N39, v. 4

—— Roger Sherman and the New Hampshire Grants. Vermont history, v. 30, July 1962: 211–219.
                                    F46.V55, v. 30

—— Roger Sherman's Connecticut; Yankee politics and the American Revolution. Middletown, Conn., Wesleyan University Press [1971] xiv, 409 p. map, ports.
                                    E302.6.S5C6

Bibliography: p. [366]–385.
The author's thesis (Ph.D.), *Roger Sherman and the Founding of a Nation: A Political Biography*, was submitted to Columbia University in 1964 (Micro AC–1, no. 65–7501).

PALTSITS, VICTOR H. The almanacs of Roger Sherman, 1750–1761. *In* American Antiquarian Society, *Worcester, Mass.* Proceedings, new ser., v. 18, Apr. 1907: 213–258.   E172.A35, v. 18

PHYFE, R. ESTON. Roger Sherman—a Connecticut man—a maker of the nation. Connecticut magazine, v. 7, no. 3/4, 1901: 234–248. illus., facsim., ports.
                                    F91.C8, v. 7

14425

SHERWOOD, JUSTUS (1747–1798)

Connecticut; Vermont; Canada. Loyalist officer.

—— Journal, Millers Bay, 26th Octr. 1780, by Captain Justus Sherwood (1747–1798), Queens Loyal Rangers. Vermont history, new ser., v. 24, Apr.–July 1956: 101–109, 211–220. plate.   F46.V55, n.s., v. 24

Notes by Jerome A. Johnson.

GALE, ROY L. A Vermonter's tribute to a Loyalist. *In* Vermont Historical Society. News and notes, v. 7, Dec. 1955: 26–31.   F46.V5, v. 7

NOBLE, HENRY H. A Loyalist of the St. Lawrence. *In* Ontario Historical Society. Papers and records. v. 16. Toronto, 1918. p. 29–36.   F1056.O58, v. 16

14426

SHIPLEY, THOMAS (1718–1789)

England; Pennsylvania; Delaware. Merchant, miller.

FAIRBANKS, JONATHAN L. The house of Thomas Shipley "miller at the tide" on the Brandywine Creek. *In* Winterthur portfolio. v. 2; 1965. Winterthur, Del. p. 142–159. illus.   N9.W52, v. 2

14427

SHIPPEN, EDWARD (1703–1781)

Massachusetts; Pennsylvania. Merchant, father of Edward Shippen (1729–1806).

—— Some Shippen letters [1755–80] *In* Lancaster County (Pa.) Historical Society. Papers, v. 11, Jan. 1907: 3–23. ports.   F157.L2L5, v. 11

Edited by Frank R. Diffenderffer.

KLEIN, RANDOLPH S. The Shippen family: a generational study in colonial and Revolutionary Pennsylvania. 1972. ([451] p.)   Micro AC–1, no. 72–17,848

Thesis (Ph.D.)—Rutgers University.
Abstracted in *Dissertation Abstracts International*, v. 32A, June 1972, p. 6896.

14428

SHIPPEN, EDWARD (1729–1806)*

Pennsylvania. Lawyer, Loyalist, judge.

LEWIS, LAWRENCE. Edward Shippen, chief-justice of Pennsylvania. Pennsylvania magazine of history and biography, v. 7, Apr. 1883: 11–34.   F146.P65, v. 7

SHIPPEN, MARGARET
    See ARNOLD, MARGARET SHIPPEN

SHIPPEN, NANCY
    See LIVINGSTON, ANNE HOME SHIPPEN

14429

SHIPPEN, WILLIAM (1736–1808)*

Pennsylvania. Physician, Revolutionary officer.

CORNER, BETSY C. Day book of an education: William Shippen's student days in London (1759–1760) and his subsequent career. *In* American Philosophical Society, *Philadelphia.* Proceedings, v. 94, Apr. 1950: 132–136.
Q11.P5, v. 94

———— William Shippen, Jr., pioneer in American medical education; a biographical essay. With notes, and the original text of Shippen's student diary, London, 1759–1760; together with a translation of his Edinburgh dissertation, 1761. Philadelphia, American Philosophical Society, 1951. xiii, 161 p. illus., map (on lining papers), ports. (Memoirs of the American Philosophical Society, v. 28) Q11.P612, v. 28
R154.S465C6

Includes bibliographic references.

MIDDLETON, WILLIAM S. William Shippen, Junior. Annals of medical history, new ser., v. 4, Sept.–Nov. 1932: 440–452, 538–549. illus., facsims., ports.
R11.A85, n.s., v. 4

14430

SHORT, WILLIAM (1759–1849)*

Virginia; France. Councilor, secretary, diplomat.

BIZARDEL, YVON, *and* HOWARD C. RICE. "Poor in love Mr. Short." William and Mary quarterly, 3d ser., v. 21, Oct. 1964: 516–533. F221.W71, 3d s., v. 21

SHACKELFORD, GEORGE G. William Short: diplomat in Revolutionary France, 1785–1793. *In* American Philosophical Society, *Philadelphia.* Proceedings, v. 102, Dec. 1958: 596–612. ports. Q11.P5, v. 102

Also published in the Society's *Library Bulletin* for 1958, p. 596–612.

———— William Short, Jefferson's adopted son, 1758–1849. 1955. ([584] p.) Micro AC–1, no. 13,851

Thesis (Ph.D.)—University of Virginia.
Abstracted in *Dissertation Abstracts*, v. 16, Mar. 1956, p. 526–527.

14431

SHREVE, ISRAEL (1739–1799)

New Jersey. Farmer, Revolutionary officer.

———— Journal from Jersey to the Monongahala [sic], August 11, 1788. Pennsylvania magazine of history and biography, v. 52, July 1928: 193–204.
F146.P65, v. 52

14432

SHUTE, DANIEL (1756–1829)

Massachusetts. Revolutionary surgeon.

———— The journal of Dr. Daniel Shute, surgeon in the Revolution, 1781–1782. New England historical and genealogical register, v. 84, Oct. 1930: 383–389.
F1.N56, v. 84

Communicated by Mrs. Elno A. Carter.

14433

SIEGFRIED, JOHN (1745–1793)

Pennsylvania. Tavern and ferry keeper, Revolutionary officer.

STOUDT, JOHN B. The life and times of Col. John Siegfried. Northhampton, Pa., Cement News Print., 1914. 62 p. illus., plates, ports. F157.N7S6

14434

SIMCOE, JOHN GRAVES (1752–1806)†

England. British officer in America.

———— Remarks on the travels of the Marquis de Chastellux in North America. London, G. and T. Wilkie, 1787. 80 p. E265.C48 Rare Bk. Coll.

Reprinted in Tarrytown, N.Y., by W. Abbatt (1931. [5]–49 p. E173.M24, no. 172) as extra number, no. 172, of *The Magazine of History, With Notes and Queries.*

BOYLEN, JOHN C. Simcoe's romantic years. Canadian magazine, v. 82, Oct. 1934: 13–35. AP5.C2, v. 82

CALDWELL, E. L. John Graves Simcoe: the first lieutenant-governor of Ontario. Canadian defence quarterly, v. 13, Apr. 1936: 327–345. U1.C3, v. 13

DANGLADE, JAMES K. John Graves Simcoe and the United States: a study in Anglo-American frontier diplomacy. 1972. ([194] p.)
Micro AC–1, no. 72–30,145

Thesis (Ph.D.)—Ball State University.
Abstracted in *Dissertation Abstracts International*, v. 33A, Dec. 1972, p. 2854.

READ, DAVID B. The life and times of Gen. John Graves Simcoe, commander of the "Queen's Rangers" during the Revolutionary War, and first governor of Upper Canada, together with some account of Major André and Capt. Brant. Toronto, G. Virtue, 1890. xv, 305 p. plates, ports. F1058.S57

RIDDELL, WILLIAM R. The life of John Graves Simcoe, first lieutenant-governor of the province of Upper Canada, 1792–96. Toronto, McClelland & Stewart [ᶜ1926] 492 p. illus., plates, ports. F1058.S574

"Notes" at end of each chapter.

SCOTT, DUNCAN C. John Graves Simcoe. London and Toronto, Oxford University Press, 1926. xii, 247 p. plates, ports. (The makers of Canada series, [v. 4])
F1026.M342, v. 4

First edition published in 1905.

14435
SIMPSON, JOHN (1748–1825)
New Hampshire. Revolutionary officer.

SMITH, CHELLIS V.   Major John Simpson. The man who fired the first shot at Bunker Hill. Granite state magazine, v. 2, July 1906: 14–19. plates.   F31.G76, v. 2

14436
SINCLAIR, PATRICK (1736–1820)
Scotland; Old Northwest. British officer in America.

JENKS, WILLIAM L.   Patrick Sinclair. Lansing, Mich., Wynkoop Hallenbeck Crawford Co., State Printers, 1914. 41 p. illus., plans, plates, port.   F572.M16J53

At head of title: Michigan Historical Commission. A state department of History and Archives.
"Advance pages. Proceedings of the Michigan Pioneer and Historical Society."

14437
SKENE, PHILIP (1725–1810)
England; New York. Military officer, landowner, Loyalist.

MORTON, DORIS B.   Philip Skene of Skenesborough. Bicentennial issue. Granville, N.Y., Grastorf Press, 1959. 84 p. illus., facsim., maps, ports.   F129.W73M6

Bibliography: p. 79–80.

PELL, JOHN.   Philip Skene of Skenesborough. In New York State Historical Association. Quarterly journal, v. 9, Jan. 1928: 27–44. map, plates, port.   F116.N865, v. 9

14438
SKINNER, FRANCIS (1709–1785)
Massachusetts; Rhode Island. Bookbinder.

SPAWN, WILLMAN, and CAROL M. SPAWN.   Francis Skinner, bookbinder of Newport: an eighteenth-century craftsman identified by his tools. In Winterthur portfolio. v. 2; 1965. Winterthur, Del. p. 47–61. illus., facsim.   N9.W52, v. 2

14439
SLOCUM, JOSHUA (ca. 1760–ca. 1816)
Massachusetts. Revolutionary soldier.

——— An authentic narrative of the life of Joshua Slocum: containing a succinct account of his Revolutionary services, together with other interesting reminisences [sic] and thrilling incidents in his eventful life. Carefully compiled by his eldest son, John Slocum. Hartford, Printed for the author, 1844. 105 p. plates.
E275.S63

14440
SMALL, WILLIAM (1734–1775)
Scotland; Virginia; England. Professor, physician.

GANTER, HERBERT L.   William Small, Jefferson's beloved teacher. William and Mary quarterly, 3d ser., v. 4, Oct. 1947: 505–511. plate.   F221.W71. 3d s., v. 4

14441
SMILIE, JOHN (1741–1812 *or* 13)
Ireland; Pennsylvania. Revolutionary soldier, assemblyman.

EVERETT, EDWARD.   John Smilie, forgotten champion of early western Pennsylvania. Western Pennsylvania historical magazine, v. 33, Sept./Dec. 1950: 77–89.
F146.W52, v. 33

14442
SMITH, ABIGAIL ADAMS (1765–1813)
Massachusetts. Daughter of John and Abigail Adams. Wife of William Stephens Smith (1755–1816).

——— Journal and correspondence of Miss Adams, daughter of John Adams, second President of the United States. Written in France and England, in 1785. Edited by her daughter. New York, Wiley and Putnam, 1841–42. 2 v.   E322.1.S64

Vol. 2 has title: *Correspondence of Miss Adams.*

MAYO, LIDA.   Miss Adams in love. American heritage, v. 16, Feb. 1965: 36–39, 80–89. illus., col. ports.   E171.A43, v. 16

On John Adams' ministry to England, 1785–86, and the infatuation of his daughter with Col. William Stephens Smith, her father's secretary of legation. A portfolio of predominantly color illustrations, "The Adams Family's London," appears on pages 40–49.

14443
SMITH, ADAM (1723–1790)†
Scotland. Political economist.

——— Adam Smith on the American Revolution: an unpublished memorial. American historical review, v. 38, July 1933: 714–720.   E171.A57, v. 38

Sent in 1778 to Alexander Wedderburn, solicitor-general in Lord North's administration. Introduction by George H. Guttridge.

——— Essays on philosophical subjects. To which is prefixed, an Account of the life and writings of the author. By Dugald Stewart. London, T. Cadell Jun. and W. Davies, 1795. xcv, 244 p.   AC7.S58 Rare Bk. Coll.

Reprinted in New York by Garland Pub.(1971).

——— An inquiry into the nature and causes of the wealth of nations. London, W. Strahan and T. Cadell, 1776. 2 v.   HB161.S6 1776 Rare Bk. Coll.

—— The works of Adam Smith. With an account of his life and writings by Dugald Stewart. London, Printed for T. Cadell, 1811–12. 5 v.　　　　AC7.S6

Contents: v. 1. The theory of moral sentiments.—v. 2–4. The nature and causes of the wealth of nations.—v. 5. Considerations concerning the formation of languages. Essays on philosophical subjects. Account of the life and writings of Dr. Smith.

BENIANS, ERNEST A.　Adam Smith's project of an empire. *In* Cambridge historical journal. v. 1, no. 3. Cambridge [Eng.] 1925. p. 249–283.　　　　D1.C25, v. 1

CLARK, JOHN M.　Adam Smith and the spirit of '76. *In* The Spirit of '76, and other essays. Washington, Robert Brookings Graduate School of Economics and Government, 1927. p. [59]–98.　　　　E203.S76 1927

Examines Smith's writings as part of the 18th-century libertarian tradition.

DUNN, WILLIAM C.　Adam Smith and Edmund Burke: complementary contemporaries. Southern economic journal, v. 7, Jan. 1941: 330–346.
　　　　HC107.A13A67, v. 7

ELIOT, THOMAS D.　The relations between Adam Smith and Benjamin Franklin before 1776. Political science quarterly, v. 39, Mar. 1924: 67–96.　　H1.P8, v. 39

FARRER, JAMES A.　Adam Smith (1723–1790). New York, G. P. Putnam's Sons, 1881. 201 p. (English philosophers)　　　　B1545.Z7F3

FORBES, DUNCAN.　"Scientific" whiggism: Adam Smith and John Millar. Cambridge journal, v. 7, Aug. 1954: 643–670.　　　　AP4.C193, v. 7

RAE, JOHN.　Life of Adam Smith. With an introduction: "Guide to John Rae's Life of Adam Smith" by Jacob Viner. New York, A. M. Kelley, 1965. 145, xv, 449 p. (Reprints of economic classics)　HB103.S6R2 1965

Bibliographic footnotes.
Rae's *Life* was first published in 1895.

SPENGLER, JOSEPH J.　Adam Smith's theory of economic growth. Southern economic journal, v. 25, Apr. 1959: 397–415; v. 26, July 1959: 1–12.
　　　　HC107.A13A67, v. 25–26

14444
SMITH, BENJAMIN (1754–1833)
New York; Pennsylvania. Revolutionary soldier.

—— Benjamin Smith, of Exeter, Luzerne County, Pa. A soldier of the Revolution. *In* Wyoming Historical and Geological Society, *Wilkes-Barre, Pa.* Proceedings and collections. v. 12; 1911/12. Wilkes-Barre, 1912. p. 114–153.　　　　F157.W9W94, v. 12

A reprinting of Smith's *Sketch of the Life of Benjamin Smith, a Native of New York, During the American Revolution, by Land and Sea, in the Years 1776, 1777, 1778, 1779, 1780, and 1781* (Wilkes-Barre, Pa., Printed for B. Smith, 1820), with an introduction by Horace E. Hayden.

14445
SMITH, DANIEL (1748–1818)*
Virginia; Tennessee. Surveyor, Revolutionary officer, mapmaker.

—— The journal of General Daniel Smith, one of the commissioners to extend the boundary line between the commonwealths of Virginia and North Carolina, August, 1779, to July, 1780. Tennessee historical magazine, v. 1, Mar. 1915: 40–65. fold. map.
　　　　F431.T28, v. 1
Introduction and notes by St. George L. Sioussat.
—— —— Offprint. [Nashville, 1915] [41]–66 p. fold. map.　　　　F232.B7S64

14446
SMITH, DAVID (1753–1835)
North Carolina; Tennessee. Farmer, landowner, Revolutionary soldier.

McBEE, MAY W.　The life and times of David Smith; patriot, pioneer, and Indian fighter. [Kansas City? Mo., 1959] 84 p.　　　　F396.M22

Bibliography: p. 73–79.

14447
SMITH, DEVEREUX (1735–1799)
England; Pennsylvania. Settler, merchant.

BOTHWELL, MARGARET P.　Devereux Smith, fearless pioneer. Western Pennsylvania historical magazine, v. 40, winter 1957: 277–291.　　F146.W52, v. 40

14448
SMITH, HEZEKIAH (1737–1805)*
New Jersey; Massachusetts. Baptist clergyman, Revolutionary chaplain.

GUILD, REUBEN A.　Chaplain Smith and the Baptists; or, Life, journals, letters, and addresses of the Rev. Hezekiah Smith, D. D., of Haverhill, Massachusetts. 1737–1805. Philadelphia, American Baptist Publication Society [1885] 429 p.　　　　BX6495.S54G8

14449
SMITH, ISAAC (1736–1807)
New Jersey. Physician, Revolutionary officer, judge.

SMITH, E. KIRBY.　Trent-Town's unknown hero of 1776. [Ann Arbor? Mich., °1963] vi, 24 p. port.
　　　　F144.T7.S6

14450
SMITH, JACOB (1756–1844)
Delaware; Pennsylvania. Loyalist soldier.

—— Diary of Jacob Smith—American born. Edited by Charles William Heathcote. Pennsylvania magazine of history and biography, v. 56, July 1932: 260–264.

F146.P65, v. 56

14451

SMITH, JAMES (*ca.* 1719–1806)*

Ireland; Pennsylvania. Lawyer, delegate to the Continental Congress, assemblyman, judge.

—— Letters of James Smith [1757?–1803] *In* Historical Society of York County, *York, Pa.* Yearbook, 1939. York, p. 15–23. F157.Y6H7, 1939

The letters are continued in the *Yearbook* for 1940, p. 30–42.

14452

SMITH, JAMES (1737–1812)*

Pennsylvania; Kentucky. Frontiersman, Revolutionary officer, assemblyman.

—— An account of the remarkable occurrences in the life and travels of Colonel James Smith . . . during his captivity with the Indians, in the years 1755, '56, '57, '58 & '59, in which the customs, manners, traditions, theological sentiments, mode of warfare, military tactics, discipline and encampments, treatment of prisoners, &c. are better explained, and more minutely related, than has been heretofore done, by any author on that subject. Together with a description of the soil, timber and waters, where he travelled with the Indians during his captivity. To which is added, a brief account of some very uncommon occurrences, which transpired after his return from captivity; as well as of the different campaigns carried on against the Indians to the westward of Fort Pitt, since the year 1755, to the present date, 1799. Philadelphia, J. Grigg, 1831. 162 p.

E87.S638 Rare Bk. Coll.

The first edition (Lexington, Printed by J. Bradford, 1799) was reprinted, with an appendix of illustrative notes by William M. Darlington, in Cincinnati by R. Clarke (1870. 190 p. E87.S65).

JILLSON, WILLARD R. A bibliography of the life and writings of Col James Smith of Bourbon County, Kentucky, 1737–1812. With annotations. Frankfort, Kentucky Historical Society, 1947 [i.e. 1948] 51 p. facsims., port. Z8820.89.J5

"Life sketch": p. 13–26.

NYE, WILBUR S. James Smith: early Cumberland Valley patriot. Carlisle, Pa., Cumberland County Historical Society, 1969. 34 p. facsim., fold. map. E195.S746

Includes bibliographic references.

SWANSON, NEIL H. The first rebel; being a lost chapter of our history and a true narrative of America's first uprising against English military authority and an account of the first fighting between armed colonists and British regulars, together with a biography of Colonel James Smith who . . . led the Pennsylvania rebellion . . . re-

counted from contemporary documents. New York, Farrar & Rinehart [°1937] xix, 393 p. facsims., maps (on lining papers), plates. E195.S75

14453

SMITH, JAMES (1757–1800)

Virginia; Ohio. Methodist clergyman, landowner.

—— Tours into Kentucky and the Northwest Territory. Three journals by the Rev. James Smith of Powhatan County, Va., 1783–1795–1797. Sketch of Rev. James Smith by Josiah Morrow. Ohio archaeological and historical quarterly, v. 16, July 1907: 348–401. illus.

F486.O51, v. 16

—— —— Detached copy. F516.S65

14454

SMITH, JOHN (1722–1771)

Pennsylvania. Merchant, assemblyman.

TOLLES, FREDERICK B. A literary Quaker: John Smith of Burlington and Philadelphia. Pennsylvania magazine of history and biography, v. 65, July 1941: 300–333.

F146.P65, v. 65

14455

SMITH, JOHN BLAIR (1756–1799) *

Pennsylvania; Virginia. Presbyterian clergyman, educator.

SELLERS, CHARLES G. John Blair Smith. *In* Presbyterian Historical Society. Journal, v. 34, Dec. 1956: 201–225.

BX8905.P7A4, v. 34

14456

SMITH, MATTHEW (1734–1794)

Pennsylvania. Revolutionary officer.

GODCHARLES, FREDERIC A. Colonel Matthew Smith, soldier and statesman. *In* Northumberland County (Pa.) Historical Society. Proceedings. v. 12. Sunbury, 1942. p. [35]–54. F157.N8N7, v. 12

14457

SMITH, MELANCTHON (1744–1798)*

New York. Revolutionary officer, judge, merchant, delegate to the Continental Congress.

BROOKS, ROBIN. Melancton Smith: New York Anti-Federalist, 1744–1798. 1964. ([333] p.)

Micro AC–1, no. 64–12,433

Thesis (Ph.D.)—University of Rochester.
Abstracted in *Dissertation Abstracts*, v. 25, Nov. 1964, p. 2940–2941.

POUCHER, JOHN WILSON. Dutchess County men of the Revolutionary period: Melanchthon Smith. *In* Dutchess County Historical Society. Year book. v. 10; 1925. Poughkeepsie. p. 39–48. F127.D8D93, v. 10

14458

SMITH, RESOLVE (*fl.* 1777–1781)

New Jersey; St. Vincent. Secretary.

WATTS, ARTHUR P. Mr. Resolve Smith—traitor or patriot? Historian, v. 15, spring 1953: 129–147.

D1.H22, v. 15

On his ambiguous activities in England, Jamaica, and the United States, 1777–81.

14459

SMITH, RICHARD (1735–1803)*

New Jersey; New York. Lawyer, delegate to the Continental Congress.

—— Diary of Richard Smith in the Continental Congress, 1775–1776. American historical review, v. 1, Jan.–Apr. 1896: 288–310, 493–516.   E171.A57, v. 1

—— A tour of four great rivers: the Hudson, Mohawk, Susquehanna and Delaware in 1769; being the journal of Richard Smith of Burlington, New Jersey. Edited, with a short history of the pioneer settlements, by Francis W. Halsey, New York, C. Scribner's Sons, 1906. lxxiii, 102 p. facsim., maps, plates, ports.   F122.S63

Reprinted in Port Washington, N.Y., by I. J. Friedman (1964).

14460

SMITH, ROBERT (1723–1793)

Ireland; Pennsylvania. Presbyterian clergyman, educator. Father of Samuel Stanhope Smith (1750–1819).

BEAM, JACOB N. Dr. Robert Smith's academy at Pequea, Pennsylvania. *In* Presbyterian Historical Society. Journal, v. 8, Dec. 1951: 145–161.   BX8905.P7A4, v. 8

14461

SMITH, ROBERT (1732–1801)*

England; South Carolina. Anglican clergyman, Revolutionary chaplain, educator.

THOMAS, ALBERT S. Robert Smith—first bishop of South Carolina. Historical magazine of the Protestant Episcopal church, v. 15, Mar. 1946: 15–29. port.

BX5800.H5, v. 15

14462

SMITH, SAMUEL (1752–1839)*

Pennsylvania; Maryland. Revolutionary officer, merchant, land speculator.

CASSELL, FRANK A. Merchant congressman in the young Republic: Samuel Smith of Maryland, 1752–1839. Madison, University of Wisconsin Press [1971] xiii, 283 p. illus.   E302.6.S575C3

Bibliography: p. 267–271.

The author's thesis (Ph.D.), *Samuel Smith, Merchant Politician, 1792–1812*, was submitted to Northwestern University in 1968 (Micro AC–1, no. 69–1813).

PANCAKE, JOHN S. Samuel Smith and the politics of business: 1752–1839. University, University of Alabama Press [1972] 248 p. illus.   E302.6.S575P36

Bibliography: p. [230]–237.

The author's thesis (Ph.D.), *The General From Baltimore: A Biography of Samuel Smith*, was submitted to the University of Virginia in 1949.

14463

SMITH, SAMUEL (1759–1854)

Rhode Island; Massachusetts. Revolutionary soldier.

—— Memoirs of the life of Samuel Smith: being an extract from a journal written by himself, from 1776 to 1786. Middleborough, Mass., 1853. 24 p.

E275.S65 Rare Bk. Coll.

Also issued as v. 1, no. 2 (New York, 1864. E203.B97, v. 1) of Bushnell's *Crumbs for Antiquarians.*

14464

SMITH, SAMUEL STANHOPE (1750–1819)*

Pennsylvania; New Jersey. Presbyterian clergyman, educator.

—— Charles Nisbet and Samuel Stanhope Smith—two eighteenth century educators. Princeton University Library chronicle, v. 6, Nov. 1944: 17–36.

Z733.P93C5, v. 6

Two letters from Smith, 1784–85, explaining American conditions to Nisbet who would soon arrive from Scotland to take up his position as first president of Dickinson College. Introduction and comments by Michael Kraus.

BOWERS, DAVID F. The Smith-Blair correspondence, 1786–1791. Princeton University Library chronicle, v. 4, June 1943: 123–134. port.   Z733.P93C5, v. 4

BRADBURY, MILES L. Samuel Stanhope Smith: Princeton's accommodation to reason. Journal of Presbyterian history, v. 48, fall 1970: 189–202.   BX8905.P7A4, v. 48

HUDNUT, WILLIAM H. Samuel Stanhope Smith: enlightened conservative. Journal of the history of ideas, v. 17, Oct. 1956: 540–552.   B1.J75, v. 17

14465

SMITH, THOMAS (1702–1795)

Massachusetts; Maine. Clergyman.

—— Journals of the Rev. Thomas Smith, and the Rev. Samuel Deane, pastors of the First Church in Portland: with notes and biographical notices: and A summary history of Portland, by Wm. Willis. [2d ed.] Portland, J. S. Bailey, 1849. 483 p. ports.   F29.P9S61

The first edition, *Extracts from the Journals Kept by the Rev. Thomas Smith, Late Pastor of the First Church of Christ in Falmouth, in the County of York (Now Cumberland), From the Year 1720 to the Year 1788, With an Appendix Containing a Variety of Other Matters*, selected by Samuel Freeman, was published in Portland by Thomas Todd (1821. 164, 154 p. F29.P9S6).

14466

SMITH, THOMAS (1745–1809)

Scotland; Pennsylvania. Lawyer, Revolutionary officer, assemblyman, delegate to the Continental Congress.

KONKLE, BURTON A.   The life and times of Thomas Smith, 1745–1809, a Pennsylvania member of the Continental Congress. Philadelphia, Campion, 1904. 303 p. facsims., maps, plates, ports.   F153.K82

14467

SMITH, WILLIAM (1727–1803)*

Scotland; Pennsylvania. Anglican clergyman, educator, political writer.

———— A general idea of the college of Mirania; with a sketch of the method of teaching science and religion, in the several classes: and some account of its rise, establishment and buildings. Address'd more immediately to the consideration of the trustees nominated, by the legislature, to receive proposals, &c. relating to the establishment of a college in the province of New-York. New-York, Printed by J. Parker and W. Weyman, 1753. 86 p.   LD1249.S6 Rare Bk. Coll.
                                                AC901.H3, v. 22 Rare Bk. Coll.

Signed: W. Smith.
Reprinted, with a new introduction by Edward M. Griffin, in New York by Johnson Reprint Corp. (1969).

———— The works of William Smith, D.D., late provost of the College and Academy of Philadelphia. Philadelphia, Published by Hugh Maxwell and William Fry, no. 25, North Second-Street, 1803. 2 v. port.
                                                BX5937.S585W6

BYRNES, DON R.   The pre-Revolutionary career of Provost William Smith, 1751–1780. 1969. ([280] p.)
                                                Micro AC–1, no. 70–6384

Thesis (Ph.D.)—Tulane University.
Abstracted in *Dissertation Abstracts International*, v. 30A, Apr. 1970, p. 4361–4362.

FOX, BERTHA S.   Provost William Smith and his land investments in Pennsylvania. Pennsylvania history, v. 8, July 1941: 189–209.   F146.P597, v. 8

———— Provost Smith and the quest for funds. Pennsylvania history, v. 2, Oct. 1935: 225–238.   F146.P597, v. 2

GEGENHEIMER, ALBERT F.   William Smith, educator and churchman, 1727–1803. Philadelphia, University of Pennsylvania Press, 1943. vii, 233 p. port. (Pennsylvania lives)   LD4525.1755.G4

"Bibliographical note": p. 228–230.

JONES, THOMAS F.   A pair of lawn sleeves; a biography of William Smith (1727–1803). Philadelphia, Chilton Book Co. [1972] 210 p. illus., plates, ports.
                                                LD4525.1755.J6

Bibliography: p. [202]–205.
———— ———— Another copy. With the author's ms. footnote reference numbers added. Accompanied by "Notes" (28 l. Carbon copy of typescript).
                                                LD4525.1755.J62

LIVELY, BRUCE R.   William Smith, the College and Academy of Philadelphia, and Pennsylvania politics, 1753–1758. Historical magazine of the Protestant Episcopal church, v. 38, Sept. 1969: 237–258.
                                                BX5800.H5, v. 38

PETERS, WILLIAM R.   The contribution of William Smith, 1727–1803, to the development of higher education in the United States. 1968. ([291] p.)
                                                Micro AC–1, no. 69–2368

Thesis (Ph.D.)—University of Michigan.
Abstracted in *Dissertation Abstracts*, v. 29A, Mar. 1969, p. 2974–2975.

SMITH, HORACE W.   Life and correspondence of the Rev. William Smith, D.D., first provost of the College and Academy of Philadelphia. First president of Washington College, Maryland. With copious extracts from his writings. By his great grandson, Horace Wemyss Smith. Philadelphia, Ferguson Bros., 1880. 2 v. ports.
                                                LD4525.1755.S6

The 1878 edition has been reprinted in New York by Arno Press (1972. LD4525.1755.S62).

STILLÉ, CHARLES J.   A memoir of the Rev. William Smith, D.D., provost of the College Academy and Charitable School of Philadelphia. Philadelphia [Moore, Printers] 1869. 63 p.   LD4525.1755.S8 Rare Bk. Coll.

14468

SMITH, WILLIAM (1728–1793)*

New York; Quebec. Lawyer, councilor, historian, Loyalist, judge.

———— Diary and selected papers, 1784–1793. Edited by L. F. S. Upton. Toronto, Champlain Society, 1963–65. 2 v. illus., port. (The Publications of the Champlain Society, 41–42)   LL

Includes bibliographies.
Contents: v. 1. The diary, January 24, 1784—October 5, 1785.—v. 2. The diary, October 6, 1785, to May 18, 1787 [and selected papers to December 6, 1793]

———— Historical memoirs of William Smith, historian of the province of New York, member of the governor's council and last chief justice of that province under the crown, chief justice of Quebec. Edited, with an introduction, biography, and notes by William H. W. Sabine, from the previously unpublished ms. in the New York Public Library. New York, 1956–58. 2 v. facsims., maps, ports.   F122.S638

Includes bibliographies.

Contents: [1] From 16 March 1763 to 9 July 1776.—[2] From 12 July 1776 to 25 July 1778.

Reprinted in New York by the New York Times (1969).

———— Information to emigrants, being the copy of a letter from a gentleman in North-America: containing a full and particular account of the terms on which settlers may procure lands in North-America, particularly in the provinces of New-York and Pennsylvania. As also, the encouragement labourers, mechanics, and tradesmen of every kind may find by going there to settle. To which is added, observations on the causes of emigration. Glasgow, Printed for, and sold by Morrison and M'Allum [1773] 16 p.
AC901.H3, v. 103 Rare Bk. Coll.

"Proposals, informations and directions drawn up, and signed by the Hon. Mr. Smith of New-York, June 11th, 1773."

———— Some account of the charitable corporation, lately erected for the relief of the widows and children of clergymen, in the communion of the Church of England in America; with a copy of their charters, and fundamental rules. Philadelphia, Printed by D. Hall and W. Sellers, 1769. 48 p.
BX5965.5.C63S5 1769 Rare Bk. Coll.
AC901.H3, v. 22 Rare Bk. Coll.

———— William Smith's "Observations on America" [1785] In New York State Historical Association. New York history, v. 23, July 1942: 328–340. F116.N865, v. 23

Introduction and notes by Oscar Zeichner.

ACTON, ARTHUR J. The diary of William Smith, August 26, 1778 to December 31, 1779. 1970. ([535] p.)
Micro AC–1, no. 71–4551

Thesis (Ph.D.)—University of Michigan.

Abstracted in *Dissertation Abstracts International*, v. 31A, Feb. 1971, p. 4074.

BUTTERFIELD, LYMAN H. New light on the North Atlantic triangle in the 1780's; a review article. William and Mary quarterly, 3d ser., v. 21, Oct. 1964: 596–606.
F221.W71, 3d s., v. 21

Based upon Smith's *Diary and Selected Papers,* edited by Leslie F. S. Upton.

DELAFIELD, MATURIN L. William Smith—the historian; chief justice of New York and of Canada. Magazine of American history, with notes and queries, v. 6, June 1881: 418–439. port. E171.M18, v. 6

NEATBY, HILDA M. Chief Justice William Smith: an eighteenth-century Whig imperialist. Canadian historical review, v. 28, Mar. 1947: 44–67.
F1001.C27, v. 28

RICHARDSON, A. J. H. Chief Justice William Smith and the Haldimand negotiations. In Vermont Historical Society. Proceedings, new ser., v. 9, June 1941: 84–114.
F46.V55, n.s., v. 9

SABINE, WILLIAM H.W. William Smith and the imperial "compact." Manuscripts, v. 8, fall 1956: 315–318. facsim.
Z41.A2A925, v. 8

UPTON, LESLIE F. S. The loyal Whig: William Smith of New York & Quebec. [Toronto] University of Toronto Press [1969] ix, 250 p.
F122.S66U6

Bibliography: p. 225–237.

The author's thesis (Ph.D.), *William Smith, Chief Justice of New York and Quebec, 1728–1793*, was submitted to the University of Minnesota in 1957 (Micro AC–1, no. 22,479).

14469

SMITH, WILLIAM LOUGHTON (*ca.* 1758–1812)*
South Carolina. Lawyer, assemblyman.

ROGERS, GEORGE C. Evolution of a Federalist: William Loughton Smith of Charleston (1758–1812). Columbia, University of South Carolina Press, 1962. xiv, 439 p. illus., port. E302.6.S58R6

Bibliography: p. 407–412.

14470

SMITH, WILLIAM STEPHENS (1755–1816)*
New York. Revolutionary officer, diplomat.

RAYMOND, MARCIUS D. Colonel William Stephens Smith. New York genealogical and biographical record, v. 25, Oct. 1894: 154–160. port. F116.N28, v. 25

ROOF, KATHARINE M. Colonel William Smith and lady; the romance of Washington's aide and young Abigail Adams. Boston, Houghton Mifflin Co., 1929. xiv, 347 p. facsims., plates, ports. E302.6.S59R7

14471

SMYTH, JOHN FERDINAND DALZIEL (*ca.* 1748–1814)†
Scotland; Maryland; Virginia. Loyalist officer and physician.

———— The memorial of John Ferdinand Dalziel Smyth, Esq., late captain commandant of the Royal Hunters, and of the Queen's American Rangers. With affidavits, and an account of expenditures properly proved and certified before the mayor of New York . . . a schedule of his property; an account of personal effects lost or carried away during the rebellion; and copies of certificates, extracts of letters, and testimonials, in support of, and ascertaining his pretensions, annexed. [London? 1784] [8] p., 8 l. E278.S6S6 Rare Bk. Coll.

Manuscript annotations.

———— Narrative or journal of Capt. John Ferdinand Dalziel Smyth, of the Queen's Rangers [1775–77] Pennsylvania magazine of history and biography, v. 39, Apr. 1915: 143–169. F146.P65, v. 39

———— Tour in the United States of America; containing an account of the present situation of that country; the population, agriculture, commerce, customs, and manners of the inhabitants; anecdotes of several members of the Congress, and general officers of the American Army . . . With a description of the Indian nations. Likewise improvements in husbandry that may be adopted with great advantage in Europe. London, For G. Robinson, 1784. 2 v.   E164.S66

Reprinted in New York by the New York Times (1968).

HANCOCK, HAROLD B.   John Ferdinand Dalziel Smyth, Loyalist. Maryland historical magazine, v. 55, Dec. 1960: 346–358.   F176.M18, v. 55

14472

SNIDER, CHRISTOPHER (1759?–1770)

Massachusetts. Student.

BAENSCH, EMIL.   A Boston boy, the first martyr to American liberty. Manitowoce, Wis., [c1924] 44 p. plate.   F73.4.B13

Accidentally shot on February 22d by Ebenezer Richardson, during a dispute over nonimportation.

14473

SNOWDEN, GILBERT TENNENT (1766–1797)

New Jersey. College student.

———— The journal of Gilbert Tennent Snowden [1783–85] Edited by J. Albert Robbins. Princeton University Library chronicle, v. 14, winter 1953: 72–90.   Z733.P93C5, v. 14

14474

SOWER, CHRISTOPHER, *Bp.* (1721–1784)*

Germany; Pennsylvania. Clergyman, printer. Father of Christopher Sower (1754–1799).

BRUMBAUGH, MARTIN G.   Christopher Sower, Jr. Pennsylvania-German, v. 2, Apr. 1901: 51–65. illus.   F146.P224, v. 2

14475

SOWER, CHRISTOPHER (1754–1799)*

Pennsylvania; New Brunswick. Printer, newspaper publisher, Loyalist.

HARPER, J. RUSSELL.   Christopher Sower, King's printer and Loyalist. *In* New Brunswick Historical Society. Collections. no. 14. Saint John, N.B., 1955. p. 67–109.   F1041.N53, no. 14

KNAUSS, JAMES O.   Christopher Saur the third. *In* American Antiquarian Society, *Worcester, Mass.* Proceedings, new ser., v. 41, Apr. 1931: 235–253.   E172.A35, n.s., v. 41

14476

SOWERS, THOMAS (1735–1774)

British military officer.

BARCK, DOROTHY C.   Captain Thomas Sowers, engineer, and the silver salver, presented to him by Gov. Tryon and the General Assembly of New York. *In* New York Historical Society. Quarterly bulletin, v. 12, July 1928: 59–64. illus.   F116.N638, v. 12

14477

SPAIGHT, RICHARD DOBBS (1758–1802)*

North Carolina. Assemblyman, Revolutionary soldier, delegate to the Continental Congress, delegate to the Constitutional Convention.

ANDREWS, ALEXANDER B.   Richard Dobbs Spaight. North Carolina historical review, v. 1, Apr. 1924: 95–120.   F251.N892, v. 1

WHEELER, JOHN H.   Sketch of the life of Richard Dobbs Spaight of North Carolina. Baltimore, W. K. Boyle, Printer, 1880. 29 p. front.   E302.6.S7W5

14478

SPANGENBERG, CYRIACUS (*d.* 1795)

Netherlands; Pennsylvania. Hessian soldier in America, clergyman.

ROTH, GEORGE L.   Cyriacus Spangenberg. Pennsylvania history, v. 11, Oct. 1944: 284–289.   F146.P597, v. 11

14479

SPAULDING, REUBEN (1758–*ca.* 1844)

Massachusetts; Vermont. Settler, Revolutionary soldier.

———— The retrospect of a pioneer in the New Hampshire Grants. *In* Vermont Historical Society. Proceedings, new ser., v. 8, Sept. 1940: 263–281.   F46.V55, n.s., v. 8

Notes by Dorothy C. Walter.

14480

SPEAR, DAVID (*b.* 1764)

Massachusetts. Clerk.

———— The forgotten courtship of David and Marcy Spear, 1785–1787. *In* Society for the Preservation of New England Antiquities, *Boston.* Old-time New England, v. 52, Jan./Mar. 1962: 61–74. port.   F1.S68, v. 52

A series of letters arranged and edited by Robert B. Haas.

14481

SPENCER, JOSEPH (1714–1789)*

Connecticut. Assemblyman, judge, Revolutionary general, delegate to the Continental Congress.

HEATHCOTE, CHARLES W.   General Joseph Spencer of New England and an associate of Washington. Picket post, no. 80, May 1963: 4–8.   E234.P5, no. 80

WHITTELSEY, CHARLES B., *comp*. Historical sketch of Joseph Spencer, major-general of the Continental troops, member of the council of safety, congressman, judge, deputy, deacon, and farmer. [Hartford, 1904] 11 p.   E302.6.S74W6

14482

SPENCER, THOMAS SHARP (*d*. 1794)

North Carolina; Tennessee. Frontiersman.

DURHAM, WALTER T. Thomas Sharp Spencer, man or legend. Tennessee historical quarterly, v. 31, fall 1972: 240–255.   F431.T285, v. 31

14483

STACEY, RICHARD (1732–1792)

Massachusetts. Mariner, merchant, assemblyman.

TAPLEY, HARRIET S. Captain Richard Stacey of Marblehead, master mariner and merchant of the Revolution. *In* Essex Institute, *Salem, Mass.* Historical collections, v. 56, Apr. 1920: 81–87. port.   F72.E7E81, v. 56

14484

STANSBURY, JOSEPH (1750–1809)*

England; Pennsylvania; New York. Merchant, satirist, Loyalist secret agent.

——— The loyal verses of Joseph Stansbury and Doctor Jonathan Odell; relating to the American Revolution. Now first edited by Winthrop Sargent. Albany, J. Munsell, 1860. xxi, 199 p. [Munsell's historical series, no. 6]   E295.S79

CAFFERTY, PASTORA S. Loyalist rhapsodies: the poetry of [Joseph] Stansbury and [Jonathan] Odell. 1971. ([285] p.)   Micro AC–1, no. 71–27,975

Thesis (Ph.D.)—George Washington University.
Abstracted in *Dissertation Abstracts International*, v. 32A, Dec. 1971, p. 3295.

14485

STARK, JOHN (1728–1822)*

New Hampshire. Frontiersman, settler, Revolutionary general.

GOULD, SYLVESTER C., *comp*. Bibliography on Major-General John Stark. *In* Manchester Historic Association, *Manchester, N.H.* Collections. v. 1, pt. 2; 1898. Manchester. p. 205–211.   F44.M2M3, v. 1

A one-page addenda appeared in v. 1, pt. 3, 1899 (Manchester, 1900), p. 295.

MOORE, HOWARD P. A life of General John Stark of New Hampshire. [New York, 1949] 539 p. illus., maps, ports.   E207.S79M6

"Source material": p. 529.
"Bibliography": p. 530–533.

SANBORN, FRANKLIN B. General John Stark: his genius and achievements as factors in the accomplishment of American independence. *In* New Hampshire Historical Society. Proceedings. v. 3; 1897/99. Concord, 1902. p. 391–414.   F31.N52, v. 3

STARK, CALEB. Memoir and official correspondence of Gen. John Stark, with notices of several other officers of the Revolution. Also, a biography of Capt. Phinehas Stevens and of Col. Robert Rogers, with an account of his services in America during the "Seven Years' War." Concord, G. P. Lyon, 1860. vii, 495 p. port.
E207.S79S7

Contents: Memoir of General John Stark.—Correspondence (p. [107]–317)—General Jacob Bailey.—General Joseph Cilley.—Colonel Marinus Willet.—Major Caleb Stark.—Captain Phinehas Stevens.—Colonel Robert Rogers.—Thomas Burnside.
Reprinted, with a new introduction and preface by George A. Billias, in Boston by Gregg Press (1972).

TARRANT, ISABEL H. John Stark, man of granite. Daughters of the American Revolution magazine, v. 104, Jan. 1970: 16–24. ports.   E202.5.A12, v. 104

14486

STEARNS, SAMUEL (1741–1809)

Massachusetts; Vermont. Physician.

CLARK, JOHN C. L. "The famous Doctor Stearns": a biographical sketch of Dr. Samuel Stearns, with a bibliography. *In* American Antiquarian Society, *Worcester, Mass.* Proceedings, new ser, v. 45, Oct. 1935: 317–424.   F172.A35, n.s., v. 45

14487

STEBBINS, JOSEPH (1749–1816)

Massachusetts. Revolutionary officer.

SHELDON, GEORGE. Joseph Stebbins, a pioneer in the outbreak of the Revolution. Massachusetts magazine, v. 9, Apr. 1916: 59–72. facsim., plate.
E61.M48, v. 9

——— ——— Offprint. Salem, Mass., Salem Press Co., 1916. 15 p. facsim., plate.   E263.M4S8

14488

STEDINGK, CURT BOGISLAUS LUDVIG KRISTOFFER VON, *grefve* (1746–1837)

Sweden; France. Diplomat, French officer in America.

——— Mémoires posthumes du feldmaréchal comte de Stedingk, rédigés sur des lettres, dépèches et autres pièces authentiques laissées à sa famille. Par le général comte de Björnstjerna. Paris, A. Bertrand, 1844–47. 3 v.
DL750.S8

Count Stedingk. Putnam's monthly, v. 4, Oct.–Nov. 1854: 345–356, 492–503.   AP2.P97, v. 4

14489

STEEL, ELIZABETH MAXWELL (1733–1790)

North Carolina. Tavern keeper.

HENDERSON, ARCHIBALD. Elizabeth Maxwell Steel: patriot. North Carolina booklet, v. 12, Oct. 1912: 67–103. plates, ports. F251.N86, v. 12

14490

STEELE, ZADOCK (1758–1845)

Connecticut; Vermont. Revolutionary soldier.

—— The Indian captive; or, A narrative of the captivity and sufferings of Zadock Steele. Related by himself. To which is prefixed an account of the burning of Royalton [1780] Montpelier, Vt., Published by the author; E. P. Walton, Printer, 1818. 142 p. E87.S81 Rare Bk. Coll.

Published in the Indian Captivities Series by H. R. Huntting Co. (Springfield, Mass., 1908), whose edition was reprinted in New York by B. Blom (1971).

14491

STEUBEN, FRIEDRICH WILHELM LUDOLF GERHARD AUGUSTIN, baron VON (1730–1794)*

Germany; New York. Revolutionary general.

BILL, ALFRED H. Drill master at Valley Forge. American heritage, v. 6, June 1955: 36–39, 100. illus. (part col.), port. E171.A43, v. 6

DOYLE, JOSEPH B. Frederick William von Steuben and the American Revolution, aide to Washington and inspector general of the army. With account of posthumous honors at various places. Steubenville, Ohio, H. C. Cook Co., 1913. xviii, 399 p. maps, plates, ports. E207.S8D75

Reprinted in New York by B. Franklin (1970).

DU PONCEAU, PETER STEPHEN. Baron von Steuben's appeal to President Washington for justice. In Deutsch-amerikanische Geschichtsblätter. v. 29; 1929. Chicago, University of Chicago Press. p. 168–187. F550.G3D4, v. 29

Du Ponceau, von Steuben's secretary, details the extent of his employer's Revolutionary service in a letter to George Washington which eventually resulted in a Congressional annuity of $2,500 for life.

Festschrift zur Feier des zweihundertjährigen Geburtstags von Baron Friedrich Wilhelm von Steuben. In Deutsch-amerikanische Geschichtsblätter. v. 30; 1930. Chicago, University of Chicago Press, 1930. p. 4–181. F550.G3D4, v. 30

Partial contents: Steuben, by Richard Barthold.—Steuben as a military statesman, by John M. Palmer.—Baron von Steuben, father of the American Army, by C. J. Hexamer.—Nachrichten von den Lebensumständen des Baron von Steuben, by Christoph David Ebeling.—Memorials of Baron von Steuben. Unpublished and forgotten papers.—Biographisches.

HAMMES, DORIS D. The road to glory and great possessions. Virginia cavalcade, v. 19, autumn 1969: 12–19. illus., ports. F221.V74, v. 19

HEATHCOTE, CHARLES W. General Steuben's services for American independence. Picket post, no. 36, Apr. 1952: 10–16. port. E234.P5, no. 36

KAPP, FRIEDRICH. The life of Frederick William von Steuben, major general in the Revolutionary army. With an introduction by George Bancroft. 2d ed. New York, Mason Bros., 1859. 735 p. port. E207.S8K34

Also published in German (Berlin, 1858).

LINN, WILLIAM A. Baron Steuben's estate at New Bridge, Bergen County, New Jersey; with some account of his European experience and services to the American army. In Bergen County Historical Society, Hackensack, N.J. Papers and proceedings. no. 1; 1902/5. Hackensack, 1905. p. 20–33. F142.B4B4, no. 1

LUVAAS, JAY. "Baron" von Steuben: Washington's drillmaster. American history illustrated, v. 2, Apr. 1967: 4–11, 55–58. illus., ports. E171.A574, v. 2

NORTH, WILLIAM. Memoir of the Baron Steuben. In Deutsch-amerikanische Geschichtsblätter. v. 29; 1929. Chicago, University of Chicago Press. p. 188–206. F550.G3D4, v. 29

PALMER, JOHN M. General von Steuben. New Haven, Yale University Press, 1937. x, 434 p. maps (part fold.), port. E207.S8P3

"Authorities": p. [419]–423.

Reprinted in Port Washington, N.Y., by Kennikat Press (1966).

WITTKE, CARL F. Washington and Steuben. Open court, v. 46, Jan. 1932: 93–106. AP2.O495, v. 46

14492

STEVENS, DANIEL (1746–1835)

Massachusetts; South Carolina. Merchant, Revolutionary officer, assemblyman.

—— Autobiography of Daniel Stevens, 1746–1835. South Carolina historical magazine, v. 58, Jan. 1957: 1–18. F266.S55, v. 58

14493

STEVENS, EBENEZER (1751–1823)

Massachusetts; New York. Revolutionary officer, merchant.

STEVENS, JOHN A. Ebenezer Stevens, Lieut.-Col. of Artillery in the Continental Army. Magazine of American history, with notes and queries, v. 1, Oct. 1877: 588–610. E171.M18, v. 1

14494

STEVENS, ENOS (1739–1808)

New Hampshire; Vermont. Loyalist officer.

—— A fragment of the diary of Lieutenant Enos Stevens, Tory, 1777–1778. New England quarterly, v. 11, June 1938: 374–388.   F1.N62, v. 11

14495

STEVENS, JAMES (*fl.* 1770–1787)
Virginia. Merchant.

—— Stevens' diary [1786–87] Virginia magazine of history and biography, v. 29, Oct. 1921: 385–400.
    F221.V91, v. 29
On his purchasing trip from Norfolk to Glasgow, Scotland.

14496

STEVENS, JOHN (1715–1792)
New Jersey. Merchant, assemblyman, landowner, councilor, delegate to the Continental Congress. Father of John Stevens (1749–1838).

STEVENS, RICHARD F.   Sketch of Hon. John Stevens, of Perth Amboy, of New York City, and of Hunterdon County, N.J. New York genealogical and biographical record, v. 15, Oct. 1884: 145–150.   F116.N28, v. 15

14497

STEVENS, JOHN (1749–1838)*
New York; New Jersey. Lawyer, Revolutionary officer, landowner.

GREGG, DOROTHY.   John Stevens, general entrepreneur, 1749–1838. *In* Miller, William, *ed.* Men in business; essays in the history of entrepreneurship. Cambridge, Harvard University Press, 1952. p. 120–152.
    HF3023.A2M5
Bibliographic references included in "Notes" (p. 321–324).

New Jersey Historical Society.   Guide to the microfilm edition of the Stevens family papers. Edited by Miriam V. Studley, Charles F. Cummings and Thaddeus J. Krom. Newark, N.J., 1968. 32 p.
    CD3029.5.S73A46 Mss

TURNBULL, ARCHIBALD D.   John Stevens, an American record. New York, Century Co. [ᶜ1928] xvii, 545 p. illus., facsims., plates (part fold.), ports.
    VM140.S7T8

14498

STEVENS, ROGER (1743?–1793)
Vermont; Canada. Miller, Loyalist officer.

CRUIKSHANK, ERNEST A.   The adventures of Roger Stevens, a forgotten Loyalist pioneer in Upper Canada. *In* Ontario Historical Society. Papers and records. v. 33. Toronto, 1939. p. 11–38.   F1056.O58, v. 33

14499

STIEGEL, HENRY WILLIAM (1729–1785)*
Germany; Pennsylvania. Ironmaster, glass manufacturer.

BRENDLE, ABRAHAM S.   Henry William Stiegel. [Lebanon, Pa., 1912] [59]–76 p. illus. ([Lebanon County Historical Society. Historical papers and addresses], v. 6, Aug. 1912)   F157.L4L5, v. 6

BYRNE, JACOB H.   Henry William Stiegel's land holdings. *In* Lancaster County (Pa.) Historical Society. Papers, v. 39, no. 1, 1939: 9–20. plate.   F157.L2L5, v. 39

HEIGES, GEORGE L.   Henry William Stiegel and his associates; a story of early American industry. [Manheim? Pa., 1948] 227 p. illus., facsims., ports.
    TP853.P4H39
See also the author's earlier essay, *Henry William Stiegel; the Life Story of a Famous American Glass-Maker* (Manheim, Pa., 1937. 80 p. TP853.P4H4).

HUNTER, F. W.   Baron Stiegel and American glass. *In* New York. Metropolitan Museum of Art. Bulletin, v. 8, Dec. 1913: 258–261. illus.   N610.A4, v. 8

SIELING, J. H.   Baron Henry William Stiegel. *In* Lancaster County (Pa.) Historical Society. Papers, v. 1, Sept. 1896: 44–65. illus.   F157.L2L5, v. 1

14500

STILES, EZRA (1727–1795)*
Connecticut; Rhode Island. Lawyer, Congregational clergyman, scientist, librarian, educator.

—— Extracts from the itineraries and other miscellanies of Ezra Stiles, D.D., L.L.D., 1755–1794, with a selection from his correspondence. Edited under the authority of the corporation of Yale University, by Franklin Bowditch Dexter. New Haven, Conn., Yale University Press, 1916. vi, 620 p. illus.   F7.S85
"In making these selections for publication, one of the chief aims has been to include extracts illustrative of the history of New England, especially of Connecticut, and also of the personal history of Yale graduates."—Preface.

—— Ezra Stiles and the Jews; selected passages from his Literary Diary concerning Jews and Judaism. With critical and explanatory notes by George Alexander Kohut. New York, P. Cowen, 1902. 155 p. illus.
    E184.J5S8
Reprinted from the *American Hebrew*, November 1901 to June 1902.
"Bibliographical": p. 77–78.

—— Letters & papers of Ezra Stiles, president of Yale College, 1778–1795. Edited by Isabel M. Calder. New Haven, Yale University Library, 1933. x, 123 p. illus., plans.   LD6330.1778.A3

—— The literary diary of Ezra Stiles. Edited under the authority of the corporation of Yale University by

Franklin Bowditch Dexter. New York, C. Scribner's Sons, 1901. 3 v. illus., port.　　BX7260.S8A3

—— The news of the evacuation of Boston and the Declaration of Independence. Leaves from the journal of Dr. Ezra Stiles, edited by Amelia L. Hill. New England magazine, new ser., v. 14, May 1896: 317–322.
AP2.N4, n.s., v. 14

—— Plan of a university. A proposal addressed to the Corporation of Yale College 3 December 1777 and now first published by the Fellows of Pierson College as a tribute to Gordon S. Haight, Master of the College. New Haven, 1953. xiv, 21 p.
LD6316.S75 Rare Bk. Coll.

BIRDSALL, RICHARD D.　Ezra Stiles versus the New Divinity men. American quarterly, v. 17, summer 1965: 248–258.　　AP2.S3985, v. 17

CHIEL, ARTHUR A.　Ezra Stiles—the education of an "Hebrician." American Jewish historical quarterly, v. 60, Mar. 1971: 235–241.　　E184.J5A5, v. 60

—— The rabbis and Ezra Stiles. American Jewish historical quarterly, v. 61, June 1972: 294–312.
E184.J5A5, v. 61

CLARK, CHARLES H.　The 18th century diary of Ezra Stiles. North American review, v. 208, Sept. 1918: 410–422.　　AP2.N7, v. 208

EGGLESTON, PERCY C.　Yale and her president, 1777–1795. New England magazine, new ser., v. 40: 137–147.
AP2.N4, n.s., v. 40

HOLMES, ABIEL.　The life of Ezra Stiles . . . president of Yale College. Published according to act of Congress. Boston, Printed by Thomas & Andrews, Faust's Statue, no. 45, Newbury Street, May, 1798. 403 p. port.
LD6330.1778.H7 Rare Bk. Coll.

JASTROW, MORRIS.　References to Jews in the diary of Ezra Stiles. In American Jewish Historical Society. Publications. v. 10; 1902. [Baltimore] p. 5–36.
E184.J5A5, v. 10
Based on an evaluation of Stiles' Literary Diary (New York, C. Scribner's Sons, 1901. 3 v.).

MORGAN, EDMUND S.　Ezra Stiles: the education of a Yale man, 1742–1746. Huntington Library quarterly, v. 17, May 1954: 251–268.　　Z733.S24Q, v. 17

—— The gentle Puritan; a life of Ezra Stiles, 1727–1795. Published for the Institute of Early American History and Culture, Williamsburg, Va. New Haven, Yale University Press, 1962. ix, 490 p. maps, plates, ports.
LD6330.1778.M6
Bibliographic footnotes.

PARSONS, FRANCIS.　Ezra Stiles of Yale. New England quarterly, v. 9, June 1936: 286–316.　　F1.N62, v.9

TERRY, RODERICK.　Rev. Dr. Ezra Stiles. In Newport Historical Society. Early religious leaders of Newport. Newport, R.I., 1918. p. [149]–184.　　BR560.N37A5

14501

STIRKE, HENRY
　England. British officer in America.

—— A British officer's Revolutionary War journal, 1776–1778. Edited by S. Sydney Bradford. Maryland historical magazine, v. 56, June 1961: 150–175.
F176.M18, v. 56
Fought in most major engagements from the Battle of Long Island to the Battle of Germantown.

STIRLING, WILLIAM ALEXANDER, 6th Earl of
See ALEXANDER, WILLIAM

14502

STOCKTON, ANNIS BOUDINOT (1736–1801)
　New Jersey. Poet. Wife of Richard Stockton (1730–1781). Sister of Elias Boudinot (1740–1821).

—— Annis and the General: Mrs. Stockton's poetic eulogies of George Washington. Princeton University Library chronicle, v. 7, Nov. 1945: 19–39. facsims.
Z733.P93C5, v. 7
Poems and letters, 1780–89. Introduction and notes by Lyman H. Butterfield.

14503

STOCKTON, RICHARD (1730–1781)*
　New Jersey. Lawyer, councilor, landowner, delegate to the Continental Congress.

BILL, ALFRED H.　A house called Morven, its role in American history, 1701–1954, by Alfred Hoyt Bill, in collaboration with Walter E. Edge. With an essay on the architecture by George B. Tatum. Princeton, N.J., Princeton University Press, 1954. xi, 206 p. illus., plans, ports.　　F144.P9B5
Bibliography: p. 191–194.

14504

STODDERT, BENJAMIN (1751–1813)*
　Maryland. Revolutionary officer, merchant.

CARRIGG, JOHN J.　Benjamin Stoddert and the foundation of the American Navy. 1953.
Thesis (Ph.D.)—Georgetown University.

TURNER, HARRIOT S.　Memoirs of Benjamin Stoddert, first secretary of the United States Navy. In Columbia Historical Society, Washington, D.C. Records. v. 20. Washington, 1917. p. 141–166. plates.
F191.C72, v. 20

14505

STOEVER, JOHANN CASPAR (1707–1779)
　Germany; Pennsylvania. Lutheran clergyman.

WINTERS, ROY L. John Caspar Stoever, colonial pastor and founder of churches. Norristown, Pennsylvania German Society, 1948. 171 p. map, plates. (Pennsylvania German Society. Proceedings and addresses, v. 53, pt. 3)   F146.P23, v. 53

"References": p. 159–171.

14506

STOKES, ANTHONY (1736–1799)

England; Georgia. Lawyer, judge, councilor, Loyalist.

——— A narrative of the official conduct of Anthony Stokes, of the Inner Temple London . . . His Majesty's Chief Justice, and one of his Council of Georgia; and of the dangers and distresses he underwent in the cause of government: some copies of which are printed for the information of his friends. [London, 1784] 112 p.
                                    E263.G3S8 Rare Bk. Coll.

Apparently written by Stokes, although the third person is used.

LAWRENCE, ALEXANDER A. Anthony Stokes. *In* Montgomery, Horace, *ed.* Georgians in profile; historical essays in honor of Ellis Merton Coulter. Athens, University of Georgia Press [1958] p. 61–88.   F285.M73

14507

STONE, JOEL (1749–1833)

Connecticut; New York; Canada. Merchant, Loyalist.

McDONALD, HERBERT S. Memoir of Colonel Joel Stone, a United Empire Loyalist and the founder of Gananoque. *In* Ontario Historical Society. Papers and records. v. 18. Toronto, 1920. p. 59–90.
                                    F1056.O58, v. 18

14508

STORK, WILLIAM

——— An account of East-Florida, with A Journal kept by John Bartram of Philadelphia, botanist to His Majesty for the Floridas; upon a journey from St. Augustine up the river St. John's. London, Sold by W. Nicoll and G. Woodfall [1766] 90, viii, 70 p.
                                    F134.S88 1766a Rare Bk. Coll.

14509

STORRS, EXPERIENCE (1734–1801)

Connecticut. Farmer, assemblyman, Revolutionary officer.

BROWN, RALPH A. Colonel Experience Storrs, Connecticut farmer and patriot. *In* Connecticut Historical Society, *Hartford.* Bulletin, v. 19, Oct. 1954: 118–121.
                                    F91.C67, v. 19

14510

STRAHAN, WILLIAM (1715–1785)†

Scotland; England. Printer, Member of Parliament.

——— Correspondence between William Strahan and David Hall, 1763–1777. Pennsylvania magazine of history and biography, v. 10, Apr. 1886–Jan. 1887: 86–99, 217–232, 322–333, 461–473; v. 11, Apr. 1887–Jan. 1888: 98–111, 223–234, 346–357, 482–490; v. 12, Apr.–July 1888: 116–122, 240–251.   F146.P65, v. 10–12

——— Some further letters of William Strahan, printer. Pennsylvania magazine of history and biography, v. 60, Oct. 1936: 455–489.   F146.P65, v. 60

Letters written from 1750 to 1778 that deal primarily with British-American issues. Introduction and notes by John E. Pomfret.

——— William Strahan to David Hall [1770] *In* Miscellaneous Americana. A collection of history, biography and genealogy. Published by William F. Boogher, Washington, D.C. Philadelphia, Press of Dando Print. and Pub. Co. [1895] p. 117–128.   E171.B73

First published serially in v. 1 of *Boogher's Repository* (1883). Introduction and notes by Charles H. Hart.

COCHRANE, JAMES A. Dr. Johnson's printer; the life of William Strahan. Cambridge, Harvard University Press, 1964. xiii, 225 p. illus., facsims., geneal. table, port.   Z232.S887C6

Bibliographic footnotes.

HARLAN, ROBERT D. William Strahan's American book trade, 1744–76. Library quarterly, v. 31, July 1961: 235–244.   Z671.L713, v. 31

HERNLUND, PATRICIA. William Strahan's ledgers: standard charges for printing, 1738–1795. *In* Virginia. University. *Bibliographical Society.* Studies in bibliography; papers. v. 20. Charlottesville, 1967. p. 89–111.
                                    Z1008.V55, v. 20

See also "William Strahan's Ledgers, II, Charges for Papers, 1738–1785," in v. 22 of the *Papers* (Charlottesville, 1969), p. 179–195.

NOLAN, JAMES BENNETT. Printer Strahan's book account; a colonial controversy. Reading, Pa., The Bar of Berks County, 1939. ix, 143 p. illus., facsims., port.
                                    F152.R28

14511

STRAWBRIDGE, ROBERT (*d.* 1781)*

Ireland; Maryland. Itinerant Methodist preacher.

MASER, FREDERICK E. Robert Strawbridge, founder of Methodism in Maryland. Methodist history, v. 4, Jan. 1966: 3–21.   BX8235.M44, v. 4

14512

STRETCH, PETER

Pennsylvania. Merchant.

——— Early Revolutionary letters of Peter Stretch, a Philadelphia Whig merchant [1774–75] Pennsylvania magazine of history and biography, v. 36, July 1912: 324–328. F146.P65, v. 36

Introduction by Francis B. Lee.

14513
STRICKER, JOHN (1759–1825)
Maryland. Revolutionary officer, merchant.

STRICKER, JOHN, *Jr.* General John Stricker. Maryland historical magazine, v. 9, Sept. 1914: 209–218. F176.M18, v. 9

14514
STRONG, CALEB (1745–1819)*
Massachusetts. Lawyer, assemblyman, councilor, delegate to the Constitutional Convention.

LODGE, HENRY CABOT. Memoir of Hon. Caleb Strong, LL.D. *In* Massachusetts Historical Society, *Boston.* Proceedings. v. 1; 1791/1835. Boston, 1879. p. 290–316. port. F61.M38, v. 1

———— ———— Offprint. Cambridge, Press of J. Wilson, 1879. 29 p. F69.S92

14515
STUART, *Sir* CHARLES (1753–1801)†
England. British officer in America, Member of Parliament.

———— New records of the American Revolution; the letters, manuscripts and documents sent by Lieut.-General Sir Charles Stuart, to his father, the Earl of Bute, 1775–79; also the letters of General Howe, General Clinton, and other officers to Sir Charles Stuart, during the Revolution, 1779–81. [n.p.] Priv. print. [193–] xxxiv, 115 p. E203.S93

BROWN, J. S. Lieutenant-General Sir Charles Stuart, K.C.B., 1753–1801. Canadian defence quarterly, v. 3, Jan. 1926: 181–189. U1.C3, v. 3

STUART-WORTLEY, *Hon.* VIOLET H. G. M., *ed.* A prime minister and his son, from the correspondence of the 3rd Earl of Bute and of Lt.-General the Hon. Sir Charles Stuart, K.B. With an introduction by the Rt. Hon. Sir Rennell Rodd. London, J. Murray, 1925. ix, 357 p. plates, ports. DA506.B95A3

14516
STUART, ELEANOR CALVERT CUSTIS (*ca.* 1756–1811)
Maryland; Virginia. Daughter-in-law of Martha Washington (1731–1802).

TORBERT, ALICE C. Eleanor Calvert and her circle. New York, William-Frederick Press, 1950. 150 p. geneal. table. F230.S88T6

"Published under the auspices of the National Society of the Colonial Dames of America in the District of Columbia."
Bibliography: p. 129–130.

14517
STUART, GILBERT (1755–1828)*†
Rhode Island; England; Pennsylvania. Portrait artist.

MASON, GEORGE C. The life and works of Gilbert Stuart, with selections from Stuart's portraits. New York, C. Scribner's Sons, 1879. x, 286 p. ports. ND237.S8M4

MORGAN, JOHN H. Gilbert Stuart and his pupils, by John Hill Morgan; together with the complete notes on painting by Matthew Harris Jouett from conversations with Gilbert Stuart in 1816. New York, New-York Historical Society, 1939. 102 p. illus., ports. (The New-York Historical Society. The John Divine Jones fund series of histories and memoirs, 11) ND237.S8M6

Reprinted in New York by the Kennedy Galleries (1969).

———— What was Gilbert Stuart's name? *In* Rhode Island Historical Society. Collections. v. 34, Apr. 1941: 33–44. illus. F76.R47, v. 34

MOUNT, CHARLES M. Gilbert Stuart, a biography. New York, W. W. Norton [1964] 384 p. illus., ports. NK237.S8M65

"The works of Gilbert Stuart": p. [357]–379.
Bibliographic references included in "Notes" (p. [333]–356).

PARK, LAWRENCE. Gilbert Stuart; an illustrated descriptive list of his works. With an account of his life by John Hill Morgan, and an appreciation by Royal Cortissoz. New York, U. E. Rudge, 1926. 4 v. illus., facsims., plates, ports. ND237.S8P3

Work concluded after the death of the author by William Sawitzky, Mrs. E. Hadley Galbreath, John Hill Morgan, and Theodore Bolton.
Contents: v. 1. Lawrence Park. A sketch of the life of Gilbert Stuart. Gilbert Stuart, the artist. Technical note on the painting of Gilbert Stuart. Descriptive list of the portraits by Gilbert Stuart.—v. 2. Descriptive list of the portraits by Gilbert Stuart.—v. 3–4. Portraits.

WHITLEY, WILLIAM T. Gilbert Stuart. Cambridge, Mass., Harvard University Press, 1932. xiv, 240 p. ports. ND237.S8W5

Bibliography: p. [225]–228.
Reprinted in New York by the Kennedy Galleries (1969) and by AMS Press (1971).

14518
STUART, JAMES (*d.* 1781)
England. British officer in America.

———— Letters from America, 1780 and 1781. *In* Society for Army Historical Research, *London.* Journal, v. 20, autumn 1941: 130–135. DA49.S6, v. 20

Introduction and notes by Kenneth C. Corsar.

14519

STUART, JAMES (d. 1805)

Virginia; South Carolina; England. Clergyman, Loyalist.

——— A note on James Stuart, Loyalist clergyman in South Carolina. Edited by Henry D. Bull. Journal of southern history, v. 12, Nov. 1946: 570–575.

F206.J68, v. 12

Stuart's appeal for compensation of losses suffered when he fled South Carolina.

14520

STUART, JOHN (1740–1811)

Pennsylvania; New York; Canada. Anglican clergyman and missionary, Loyalist.

LYDEKKER, JOHN W. The Reverend John Stuart, D.D. (1740–1811), missionary to the Mohawks. Historical magazine of the Protestant Episcopal church, v. 11, Mar. 1942: 18–64. BX5800.H5, v. 11

14521

STUART, JOHN (1749–1823)

Virginia. Revolutionary officer.

——— Memoir of Indian wars, and other occurrences; by the late Colonel Stuart, of Greenbrier. *In* Virginia Historical Society, *Richmond*. Collections. v. 1. Richmond, 1833. p. 35–66. F221.V82, v. 1.

Reprinted in New York by the New York Times (1971) and, with an introduction by Otis K. Rice, in Parsons, W. Va., by McClain Print Co. (1971).

14522

SUDDUTH, WILLIAM (1765–1845)

Virginia; Kentucky. Settler.

——— A sketch of the early adventures of William Sudduth in Kentucky. History quarterly, v. 2, Jan. 1928: 43–70. F446.F484, v. 2

"Copied by Lucien Beckner for publication."

14523

SUFFREN ST. TROPEZ, PIERRE ANDRÉ DE, *called le bailli de Suffren* (1729–1788)

France. French naval officer in America.

——— La campagne des Indes; lettres inédites du bailli de Suffren, publiées par Régine Pernoud. Mantes, Impr. du "Petit Mantais" [1941] 86 p. facsims., fold. map. (Cahiers d'histoire et de bibliographie, cahier no. 2) DC137.5.S8A4

"Bibliographie": p. [85]–86.

——— Relation détaillée de la campagne de M. le Commandeur de Suffren, dans l'Inde du 1er Juin 1782 au 29 Septembre suivant. Port-Louis, 1783. [London, Cornmarket Press, 1970] 32 p. DC137.5.S8A3 1783a

BOUTET DE MONVEL, ROGER. La vie martiale du bailli de Suffren. Paris, Plon [1929] 244 p. (Le roman des grandes existences, 29) DC137.5.S8B6

CUNAT, CHARLES M. Histoire du bailli de Suffren. Rennes, Impr. de A. Marteville et Lefas, 1852. vii, 415 p. fold. maps, port. DC137.5.S8C8

"Liste des vaisseaux des puissances belligérantes, pris, détruits, coulés bas, brûlés, ou naufragés durant la dernière guerre": 7 p. at end.

Reprinted in two volumes in Paris by the Librarie commerciale et artistique (1968).

HENNEQUIN, JOSEPH F. G. Essai historique sur la vie et les campagnes du bailli de Suffren. Paris, Peytieux, 1824. viii, 248 p. fold. facsim., port. DC137.5.S8H4

"Correspondance du bailli de Suffren": p. [191]–235.

LA VARENDE, JEAN DE. Suffren et ses ennemis. Paris, Éditions de Paris, c1948. 336 p. illus., facsim., maps, port. (Les Grands marins) DC137.5.S8L3

Republished in Paris by Flammarion (1967. 315 p.).

MORAN, CHARLES. Suffren, the apostle of action. *In* United States Naval Institute. Proceedings, v. 64, Mar. 1938: 313–325. plates. V1.U8, v. 64

UNIENVILLE, RAYMOND D'. Hier Suffren. Port Louis, Mauritius Print. Cy., 1972. 191 p. illus., facsims., maps, ports. DC137.5.S8U5

Bibliography: p. [189]–191.

14524

SULLIVAN, JAMES (1744–1808)*

Maine; Massachusetts. Lawyer, judge, assemblyman. Brother of John Sullivan (1740–1795).

AMORY, THOMAS C. Life of James Sullivan, with selections from his writings. Boston, Phillips, Sampson, 1859. 2 v. port. F69.S94

BURBANK, HORACE H. James Sullivan. *In* Maine Historical Society. Collections. 3d ser., v. 1. Portland, 1904. p. 322–338. F16.M33, 3d s., v. 1

SPRAGUE, JOHN F. James Sullivan. *In his* Three men from Maine. Dover-Foxcroft, Me., Sprague's Journal of Maine History, 1924. p. [43]–63. port. F23.S76

——— James Sullivan. Sprague's journal of Maine history, v. 7, Feb./Apr. 1920: 171–187. illus., ports.

F16.S76, v. 7

14525

SULLIVAN, JOHN (1740–1795)*

New Hampshire. Lawyer, delegate to the Continental Congress, Revolutionary general, assemblyman, governor.

——— Letters and papers of Major-General John Sullivan, Continental Army. Edited by Otis G. Hammond. Concord, N.H., New Hampshire Historical Society, 1930–39. 3 v. illus., facsim., ports. (part col.). (Collections of the New Hampshire Historical Society, v. 13–15)   F31.N54, v. 13–15

Contents: v. 1. 1771–1777.—v. 2. 1778–1779.—v. 3. 1779–1795.

AMORY, THOMAS C.   The memory of General John Sullivan, of New Hampshire, vindicated from historical misrepresentations. *In* Massachusetts Historical Society, *Boston.* Proceedings. v. 9; 1866/67. Boston, 1867. p. 380–436.   F61.M38, v. 9

Attempts to correct "errors" of interpretation made by George Bancroft in the ninth volume of his *History of the United States.*

————— The military services and public life of Major-General John Sullivan, of the American Revolutionary Army. Boston, Wiggin and Lunt, 1868. 320 p. port.   E207.S9A55

Reprinted in Port Washington, N.Y., by Kennikat Press (1968).

FULLER, ARTHUR O.   General Sullivan as a lawyer and a judge. *In* New Hampshire Bar Association. Proceedings. 1902. Concord. p. 601–614.   LL

HEATHCOTE, CHARLES W.   General John Sullivan—earnest patriot. Picket post, no. 46, Oct. 1954: 5–10. port.   E234.P5, no. 46

SCALES, JOHN.   Master John Sullivan of Somersworth and Berwick and his family. *In* New Hampshire Historical Society. Proceedings. v. 4; 1899/1905. Concord, 1906. p. 180–201.   F31.N52, v. 4

SCOTT, KENNETH.   Major General Sullivan and Colonel Stephen Holland. New England quarterly, v. 18, Sept. 1945: 303–324.   F1N62, v. 18

WHITTEMORE, CHARLES P.   A general of the Revolution, John Sullivan of New Hampshire. New York, Columbia University Press, 1961. 317 p. maps, port.   E207.S9W5 1961

Bibliography: p. [293]–305. Bibliographic references included in "Notes" (p. [231]–290).
The author's thesis (Ph.D.), *New Hampshire's John Sullivan,* was submitted to Columbia University in 1957 (Micro AC–1, no. 58–1367).

————— John Sullivan: luckless Irishman. *In* Billias, George A., ed. George Washington's generals. New York, W. Morrow, 1964. p. 137–162. port.   E206.B5

Bibliography: p. 161–162.

14526
SUMNER, INCREASE (1746–1799)*
Massachusetts. Lawyer, assemblyman, judge.

SUMNER, W. H.   Memoir of Governor Increase Sumner. New England historical and genealogical register, v. 8, Apr. 1854: 105–128c. port.   F1.N56, v. 8

14527
SUMNER, JETHRO (1733–1785)*
Virginia; North Carolina. Planter, Revolutionary general.

BATTLE, KEMP P.   Career of Brigadier-General Jethro Sumner, one of North Carolina's Revolutionary officers. Magazine of American history, with notes and queries, v. 26, Dec. 1891: 415–433.
                    E171.M18, v. 26

————— The life and services of Brigadier General Jethro Sumner. North Carolina booklet, v. 8, Oct. 1908: 111–140.   F251.N86, v. 8

14528
SUMTER, THOMAS (1734–1832)*
Virginia; South Carolina. Revolutionary general, landowner.

————— Official correspondence between Brigadier-General Thomas Sumter and Major-General Nathaniel Greene, from A.D. 1780 to 1783. *In* Charleston, *S.C.* Year book. 1899. Charleston. Appendix, p. [3]–70.
                    JS13.C33, 1899

BASS, ROBERT D.   Gamecock; the life and campaigns of General Thomas Sumter. New York, Holt, Rinehart and Winston [1961] x, 289 p. illus., maps, plates, ports.   E207.S95B3

"Sources and notes": p. 257–275.

GREGORIE, ANNE K.   Thomas Sumter. Columbia, S.C., R. L. Bryan Co., 1931. 313 p. illus., maps (part fold.), plan, plates, ports.   E207.S95G8
Bibliography: p. 283–296.

SMITH, HENRY A. M.   General Thomas Sumter. Magazine of history, with notes and queries, v. 8, Sept.–Dec. 1908: 160–167, 219–224, 277–284, 336–340; v. 9, Jan.–Mar. 1909: 17–22, 80–85, 165–170.
                    E171.M23, v. 8–9

14529
SUTPHIN, SAMUEL (*b. ca.* 1747)
New Jersey. Revolutionary soldier.

HONEYMAN, ABRAHAM VAN DOREN.   Revolutionary war record of a Somerset County slave. Somerset County historical quarterly, v. 3, July 1914: 184–190.
                    F142.S6S6, v. 3

14530
SWANSON, EDWARD (1759–1840)
Tennessee. Settler.

McRAVEN, WILLIAM H.   Life and times of Edward Swanson, one of the original pioneers who with General James Robertson founded Nashville, Tennessee, 1779; first recorded settler of Williamson County, Tennessee,

March, 1780. Nashville, Tenn., 1937. xxiii, 240 p. map
(on lining papers), plates, port.   F436.S95
Bibliography: p. 237–240.

14531

SYMMES, JOHN CLEVES (1742–1814)*

New York; New Jersey; Ohio. Surveyor, Revolutionary officer, judge, delegate to the Continental Congress,
colonizer.

———— The correspondence of John Cleves Symmes, founder of the Miami purchase, chiefly from the collection of
Peter G. Thomson. Edited by Beverley W. Bond, Jr.
New York, Published for the Historical and Philosophical Society of Ohio by the Macmillan Co., 1926.
xii, 312 p. facsims., ports.   F495.S94

"Letters from Jonathan Dayton to John Cleves Symmes": p. 197–277.
Supplemented by *The Intimate Letters of John Cleves
Symmes and His Family* (Cincinnati, Historical and Philosophical Society of Ohio, 1956. 174 p. F495.S95), also edited
by Beverley W. Bond, Jr.

———— To the respectable public. [Trenton, Printed by Isaac
Collins, 1787] 30 p.   F495.S96 Rare Bk. Coll.

The first publication relating to the Miami purchase in
Ohio. Its object was to secure immediate purchasers for the
lands in order to raise the amount due as a first payment to
the government of the United States.

WINFIELD, CHARLES H.   Life and public services of John
Cleves Symmes. *In* New Jersey Historical Society. Pro-
ceedings, 2d ser., v. 5, no. 1, 1877: 21–43.
F131.N58, 2d s., v. 5
———— ———— Offprint. [Newark, 1877] 23–43 p.
E302.6.598W7

14532

TALBOT, SILAS (1751–1813)*

Massachusetts. Mariner, merchant, Revolutionary naval officer.

An Historical sketch, to the end of the Revolutionary War,
of the life of Silas Talbot, Esq., of the State of Rhode-
Island, lately commander of the United States frigate,
the Constitution, and of an American squadron in the
West-Indies.   New-York, Printed by G. & R. Waite,
for H. Caritat, 1803. 147 p.
E207.T13H6 Rare Bk. Coll.

"The Prison-Ship" [by Philip Freneau]: p. 111–125.

Pennsylvania. *Court of Admiralty.* Judgements in the
Admiralty of Pennsylvania in four suits, brought as for
maritime hypothecations. Also, the case of Silas Talbot,
against the brigs *Achilles, Patty,* and *Hibernia,* and of
the owners of the *Hibernia* against their captain, John
Angus. With an appendix, containing the testimony
exhibited in the Admiralty in those causes. The Hon.
Francis Hopkinson, judge. Philadelphia, Printed by T.
Dobson and T. Lang, in Second Street, 1789. 131 p.
LL

Pennsylvania. *High Court of Errors and Appeals.*   The resolution of the High Court of Errors and Appeals, for
the state of Pennsylvania; in the cause of Silas Talbot,
quitam, &c. against the commanders and owners of the
brigs, *Achilles, Patty,* and *Hibernia*: January 14th,
1785. Philadelphia, Printed by T. Bradford, in Front-
Street, 1785. 8, 16 p.   LL

TUCKERMAN, HENRY T.   The life of Silas Talbot, a commodore in the Navy of the United States. New-York,
J. C. Riker, 1850. xii, 137 p.   E207.T13T7

Reprinted in Tarrytown, N.Y., by W. Abbatt (1926.
63 p. E173.M24, no. 120) as extra number, no. 120, of *The
Magazine of History, With Notes and Queries.*

14533

TALLMADGE, BENJAMIN (1754–1835)*

New York; Connecticut. Educator, Revolutionary
officer, merchant.

———— Memoir of Col. Benjamin Tallmadge, prepared by
himself, at the request of his children. New York, T.
Holman, Book and Job Printer, 1858. 70 p. port.
E275.T14

Reprinted in New York by the New York Times (1968).
The *Memoir,* edited by Henry P. Johnston, was pub-
lished in New York by the Gillis Press as volume 1 of the
Publications of the Sons of the Revolution in the State of
New York (1904. 167 p. E275.T15).

HALL, CHARLES S.   Benjamin Tallmadge, Revolutionary
soldier and American businessman. New York, Columbia University Press, 1943. x, 375 p. ports.
E302.6.T2H3

Bibliography: p. [333]–349.
The author's thesis (Ph.D.), with the same title, was
submitted to Columbia University in 1942.

14534

TALLMAN, PELEG (1764–1841)

Rhode Island; Maine. Revolutionary seaman, merchant.

EMERY, WILLIAM M.   Honorable Peleg Tallman, 1764–
1841, his ancestors and descendants. [Boston, Mass., T.
Todd Co., Printers] 1935. 260 p. illus., facsims., plates,
ports.   CS71.T15 1935

"Authorities": p. 84–85, 107.

STURTEVANT, WALTER H.   Peleg Tallman, sailor of the
Revolution, master mariner, and member of Congress.
In Maine Historical Society. Collections and proceed-
ings. 2d ser., v. 10. Portland, 1899. p. 430–446.
F16.M33, 2d s., v. 10

14535

TAPPEN, ELIZABETH CRANNELL (1748–1829)

New York.

VER NOOY, AMY. Elizabeth Crannell, wife of Dr. Peter Tappen. *In* Dutchess County Historical Society. Year book. v. 37; 1952. Poughkeepsie. p. 58–81. port.
F127.D8D93, v. 37

14536
TARDIVEAU, BARTHÉLEMI (*ca.* 1750–1801)
France; Kentucky. Trader, frontiersman.

——— News from the Ohio Valley as reported by Barthélemi Tardiveau in 1783. *In* Historical and Philosophical Society of Ohio. Bulletin, v. 16, Oct. 1958: 267–292. facsims.
F486.H653, v. 16
Introduction and notes by Howard C. Rice.

RICE, HOWARD C. Barthélemi Tardiveau, a French trader in the West; biographical sketch, including letters from B. Tardiveau to St. John de Crèvecoeur (1788–1789). Baltimore, Johns Hopkins Press, 1938. xi, 90 p. facsims. (part fold.), fold. map, plates. (Institut français de Washington. Historical documents, cahier 11)
F352.T36

14537
TARLETON, *Sir* BANASTRE, *Bart.* (1754–1833)†
England. British officer in America.

——— New war letters of Banastre Tarleton [1776–81] Edited by Richard M. Ketchum. *In* New York Historical Society. Quarterly, v. 51, Jan 1967: 61–81. illus., maps, port.
F116.N638, v. 51

BASS, ROBERT D. The green dragoon; the lives of Banastre Tarleton and Mary Robinson. New York, Holt [1957] viii, 489 p. illus., maps, ports.
DA506.T3B3
Bibliography: p. 455–469.

CARTER, WILLIAM H. A British dragoon in the American Revolution. Cavalry journal, v. 32, Oct. 1923: 400–411.
UE1C33, v. 32

14538
TATHAM, WILLIAM (1752–1819)*†
England; Tennessee; North Carolina. Clerk, frontiersman, Revolutionary soldier, lawyer, assemblyman.

HERNDON, GEORGE MELVIN. William Tatham and the culture of tobacco. Including a facsim. reprint of *An Historical and Practical Essay on the Culture and Commerce of Tobacco*, by William Tatham. Coral Gables, Fla., University of Miami Press [1969] xv, 506 p. illus.
SB273.H47
Bibliography: p. [480]–488.

WILLIAMS, SAMUEL C. William Tatham, Wataugan. 2d, rev. and limited ed. Johnson City, Tenn., Watauga Press, 1947. 109 p. facsim.
F436.T21 1947

——— William Tatham, Wataugan. Tennessee historical magazine, v. 7, Oct. 1921: 154–179. F431.T28, v. 7

"Tatham's characters among the North American Indians": p. 174–179.

14539
TAYLOR, AMOS (*b.* 1748)
Massachusetts; Vermont. Farmer, Revolutionary soldier, schoolteacher.

McCORISON, MARCUS A. Amos Taylor, a sketch and bibliography. *In* American Antiquarian Society, *Worcester, Mass.* Proceedings, new ser., v. 69, Apr. 1959: 37–55.
E172.A35, n.s., v. 69

14540
TAYLOR, GEORGE (1736–1781)*
Ireland; Pennsylvania. Ironmaster, assemblyman, delegate to the Continental Congress.

ELY, WARREN S. George Taylor, signer of the Declaration of Independence. *In* Bucks County Historical Society, *Doylestown, Pa.* Collection of papers. v. 5. Doylestown, 1926. p. [101]–112. port.
F157.B8B84, v. 5

FACKENTHAL, BENJAMIN F. The homes of George Taylor, signer of the Declaration of Independence. *In* Bucks County Historical Society, *Doylestown, Pa.* Collection of papers. v. 5. Doylestown, 1926. p. 113–133. illus., facsims. (part fold.), port.
F157.B8B84, v. 5

——— ——— Offprint. [Easton? 1922] 29 p. illus., facsims. (part fold.), port.
E207.T2F13

TREXLER, MILDRED R. George Taylor, Esquire. *In* Lehigh County Historical Society, *Allentown, Pa.* Proceedings. v. 27; 1968. Allentown. p. [1]–63.
F157.L5L52, v. 27

Includes on p. 65–73 a brief analysis by John K. Heyl of the construction of Taylor's mansion at Chawton Manor, now Catasauqua, Pennsylvania.

14541
TAYLOR, GEORGE (*fl.* 1768–1769)
England. Trader.

——— A voyage to North America, perform'd by G. Taylor, of Sheffield, in the years 1768 and 1769; with an account of his tedious passage . . . manner of trading with the Indians . . . his setting sail from Philadelphia to New Orleans . . . and other matters worthy of notice. Nottingham, Printed by S. Creswell for the author, 1771. 248 p.
E163.T24 Rare Bk. Coll.

ARMYTAGE, W. H. G. Taylor's American voyage, 1768–1769. Mid-America, v. 35, Oct. 1953: 195–222.
BX1415.I3M5, v. 35

See also the author's article, "A Sheffielder Visits North America, 1768–69," in the *Dalhousie Review*, v. 31, winter 1952, p. 305–310.

14542

TAYLOR, JOHN (1751–1801)
New Jersey. Teacher, Revolutionary officer.

PRIEST, LORING B. College tutor and Revolutionary colonel. *In* Rutgers University, *New Brunswick, N.J. Library.* Journal, v. 7, June 1944: 48–55. port.
Z733.R955F, v. 7

14543

TAYLOR, JOHN (1752–1835)*
Virginia; Kentucky. Baptist clergyman, farmer.

THOMPSON, DOROTHY B. John Taylor of the ten churches. *In* Kentucky Historical Society. Register, v. 46, July 1948: 541–572. F446.K43, v. 46

14544

TAYLOR, JOHN (1753–1824)*
Virginia. Lawyer, Revolutionary officer, planter, assemblyman.

—— Letters of John Taylor of Caroline [1777–1806] Virginia magazine of history and biography. v. 52, Jan. 1944: 1–14. F221.V91, v. 52
Contributed by Hans Hammond.

SIMMS, HENRY H. Life of John Taylor; the story of a brilliant leader in the early Virginia state rights school. Richmond, Va., William Byrd Press, 1932. viii, 234 p. port. E302.6.T23S5
Bibliography: p. 215–221.

MUDGE, EUGENE T. The social philosophy of John Taylor of Caroline; a study in Jeffersonian democracy. New York, Columbia University Press, 1939. xii, 227 p. (Columbia studies in American culture, no. 4) E302.6.T23M8
Bibliography: p. 209–217.

14545

TAYLOR, THOMAS (1743–1833)
Virginia; South Carolina. Planter, Revolutionary officer.

TAYLOR, BENJAMIN F. Col. Thomas Taylor. South Carolina historical and genealogical magazine, v. 27, Oct. 1926: 204–211. F266.S55, v. 27

14546

TELFAIR, EDWARD (1735–1807)*
Scotland; Georgia. Assemblyman, merchant, planter, delegate to the Continental Congress, judge, governor.

COULTER, ELLIS MERTON. Edward Telfair. Georgia historical quarterly, v. 20, June 1936: 99–124.
F281.G2975, v. 20

14547

TEMPLE, RICHARD TEMPLE GRENVILLE-TEMPLE, *Earl* (1711–1779)†
England. Member of Parliament.

—— The Grenville papers: being the correspondence of Richard Grenville, earl Temple, K.G., and the Right Hon: George Grenville, their friends and contemporaries. Edited with notes, by William James Smith. London, J. Murray, 1852–53. 4 v. facsims.
[DA501.T3A2]
Micro 18428 DA
Reprinted in New York by AMS Press (1970. DA501.T3A22).

14548

TEN BROECK, ABRAHAM (1734–1810)*
New York. Merchant, assemblyman, Revolutionary general.

—— A diary of 1776. Americana, v. 18, Apr. 1924: 169–173. facsims. E171.A43, v. 18
Introduction and comments by J. Neilson Barry.

[JACKSON, GEORGE E. B.] General Abraham Ten Broeck. [Portland, Me., S. Berry, Printer, 1886] 12 p. port.
CS71.T289 1886

14549

TENNENT, WILLIAM (1705–1777)*
Ireland; New Jersey. Presbyterian clergyman, educator. Father of William Tennent (1740–1777).

[BOUDINOT, ELIAS] Memoirs to the life of the Rev. William Tennent, formerly pastor of the Presbyterian church at Freehold, in New Jersey: in which is contained . . . an account of his being three days in a trance, and apparently lifeless: extracted from the "Evangelical Intelligencer" for the year 1806. York, Printed and published by W. Alexander, 1882. 125 p.
BX9225.T4B6 1822a

14550

TENNENT, WILLIAM (1740–1777)
South Carolina. Clergyman.

—— Fragment of a journal kept by the Rev. William Tennent describing his journey, in 1775, to upper South Carolina at the request of the Council of Safety to induce the Tories to sign an Association to support the cause of the colonists. *In* Charleston, *S.C.* Year book. 1894. Charleston. p. 295–312. JS13.C33, 1894

—— Writings of the Reverend William Tennent, 1740–1777. South Carolina historical magazine, v. 61, July–Oct. 1960: 129–145, 189–209. F266.S55, v. 61

14551

TERNAY, CHARLES HENRY LOUIS D'ARSAC, *chevalier* DE (1723–1780)

France. French naval officer in America.

EVERETT, SIDNEY. The Chevalier de Ternay. New-England historical and genealogical register, v. 27, Oct. 1873: 404–418.   F1.N56, v. 27

LINŸER DE LA BARBÉE, MAURICE. Le chevalier de Ternay; vie de Charles Henry Louis d'Arsac de Ternay, chef d'escadre des armées navales, 1723–1780. Grenoble, Editions des 4 Seigneurs, 1972. 2 v. (670 p.) plates.   DC135.T39L56

14552

THACHER, JAMES (1754–1844)*

Massachusetts. Revolutionary surgeon, physician.

—— A military journal during the American Revolutionary War, from 1775 to 1783, describing interesting events and transactions of this period, with numerous historical facts and anecdotes, from the original manuscript. To which is added an appendix, containing biographical sketches of several general officers. Boston, Richardson & Lord, 1823. 603 p.
    E275.T35 Rare Bk. Coll.
    Micro 01291, reel 195, no. 12E

A second, revised and corrected, edition was published in Boston by Cottons & Barnard (1827. 487 p. E275.T354 Rare Bk. Coll.). A new edition of Thacher's *Journal*, with the addition of a life of Washington, his Farewell Address, the Declaration of Independence, and the Constitution, published in Hartford, Conn., by Hurlbut, Williams (1862. 618 [i.e. 538] p. E275.T364 Rare Bk. Coll.), has been reprinted in New York by the New York Times (1969. E275.T3642).

BELL, WHITFIELD J. Lives in medicine: biographical dictionaries of Thacher, Williams, and Gross. Bulletin of the history of medicine, v. 42, Jan./Feb. 1968: 101–120. facsims.   R11.B93, v. 42

STEINER, WALTER R. Dr. James Thacher of Plymouth, Massachusetts, an erudite physician of Revolutionary and post-Revolutionary fame. Bulletin of the Institute of the history of medicine, v. 1, June 1933: 157–173. port.   R11.B93, v. 1

14553

THAYER, JOHN (1758–1815)*

Massachusetts. Clergyman.

MERRITT, EDWARD PERCIVAL. Bibliographical notes on *An Account of the Conversion of the Rev. John Thayer. In* Colonial Society of Massachusetts, *Boston.* Publications. v. 25. Transactions, 1922/24. Boston, 1924. p. 129–140. facsims.   F61.C71, v. 25
—— —— Offprint. Cambridge, J. Wilson, 1923. [129]–140 p. facsims.   Z8869.15.M47

The full title of Thayer's pamphlet is *An Account of the Conversion of the Reverend Mr. John Thayer, Lately a Protestant Minister, at Boston in North-America, Who Embraced the Roman Catholic Religion at Rome, on the 25th of May, 1783; Written by Himself, to Which Are Annexed Several Extracts From a Letter Written to His Brother, in Answer to Some Objections. Also, a Letter From a Young Lady Lately Received by Him Into the Church, Written After Making Her First Communion.* The first American edition, based on the fifth London edition, was printed in Baltimore in 1788.

—— Sketches of the three earliest Roman Catholic priests in Boston. III. John Thayer. *In* Colonial Society of Massachusetts, *Boston.* Publications. v. 25. Transactions, 1922/24. Boston, 1924. p. 211–229.   F61.C71, v. 25

Also reprinted as part of the fuller article in Cambridge [Mass.] by J. Wilson (1923. [173]–229 p. BX1418.B7M4).

14554

THEUS, JEREMIAH (*ca.* 1719–1774)*

South Carolina. Portrait artist.

MIDDLETON, MARGARET S. Jeremiah Theus, colonial artist of Charles Town. Columbia, University of South Carolina Press, 1953. xviii, 218 p. ports.   ND237.T53M5

Bibliography: p. 187–189.

14555

THOMAS, ELIZABETH POAGE (1764–1851)

Virginia; Kentucky. Settler.

—— A Kentucky pioneer tells her story of early Boonesborough and Harrodsburg. History quarterly of the Filson Club, v. 3, Oct. 1929: 223–236. facsim.
    F446.F484, v. 3
Introduction and notes by Louise Phelps Kellogg.

14556

THOMAS, ISAIAH (1749–1831)*

Massachusetts. Printer, Revolutionary soldier, publisher.

—— Extracts from the diaries and accounts of Isaiah Thomas from the year 1782 to 1804 and his diary for 1808. Edited by Charles L. Nichols. *In* American Antiquarian Society, *Worcester, Mass.* Proceedings, new ser., v. 26, Apr. 1916: 58–79.   E172.A35, n.s., v. 26

BATCHELDER, FRANK R. Isaiah Thomas, the patriot printer. New England magazine, new ser., v. 25, Nov. 1901: 284–305. illus., facsims., port.
    AP2.N4, n.s., v. 25

McMURTRIE, DOUGLAS C. A project for printing in Bermuda, 1772. Chicago, Priv. print., 1928. 6 p.
    Z213.B5M2

A letter of Isaiah Thomas to his father-in-law Joseph Dill, proposing that Thomas move his printing office to Bermuda.

MARBLE, ANNIE R. From 'prentice to patron; the life story of Isaiah Thomas. New York, D. Appleton-Century Co., 1935. xii, 326 p. facsims., ports.
Z232.T4M3

"Selective bibliography": p. 313–315.

NICHOLS, CHARLES L. Isaiah Thomas, printer, writer & collector. Boston, Printed for the Club of Odd Volumes, 1912. 144 p. Z232.T4N53 Rare Bk. Coll.

"Bibliography. A list of books, pamphlets, newspapers & broadsides printed by Isaiah Thomas": p. [37]–144, [1] Reprinted in New York by B. Franklin (1971).

——— Some notes on Isaiah Thomas and his Worcester imprints. *In* American Antiquarian Society, *Worcester, Mass.* Proceedings, new ser., v. 13, Apr. 1900: 429–447.
E172.A35, n.s., v. 13

SHIPTON, CLIFFORD K. Isaiah Thomas. American heritage, new ser., v. 3, summer 1952: 48–51. illus. (part col.), facsims., col. port. E171.A43, n.s., v. 3

——— Isaiah Thomas, printer, patriot and philanthropist, 1749–1831. Rochester, N.Y., Print. House of Leo Hart, 1948. xii, 94 p. illus., facsims., port. (The Printers' Valhalla) Z232.T4S5

THOMAS, BENJAMIN F. Memoir of Isaiah Thomas. Boston [Albany, Munsell, Printer] 1874. 73 p. port.
F69.T45

14557

THOMAS, JOHN (1724–1776)*
Massachusetts. Physician, Revolutionary general.

COFFIN, CHARLES. The life and services of Major General John Thomas. New-York, Printed by Egbert, Hovey & King, 1844. 33 p. E207.T45C6

HAMILTON, EDWARD P. General John Thomas. *In* Massachusetts Historical Society, *Boston.* Proceedings. v. 84; 1972. Boston, 1973. p. 44–52. F61.M38, v. 84

LORD, ARTHUR. Major-General John Thomas. *In* Massachusetts Historical Society, *Boston.* Proceedings. 2d ser., v. 18; 1903/4. Boston, 1905. p. 419–432.
F61.M38, 2d s., v. 18

——— A soldier of the Revolution, General John Thomas. *In* Bostonian Society, *Boston.* Publications. v. 12. Boston, 1915. p. [7]–35. F73.1.B88, v. 12

14558

THOMAS, JOHN (1733–1807)
Georgia. Baptist clergyman, landowner.

JOHNSTON, HUGH B. The Reverend John Thomas, Jr., distinguished early citizen of Hancock County, Georgia. Georgia historical quarterly, v. 37, June 1953: 137–141. F281.G2975, v. 37

14559

THOMAS, JOHN (d. 1776)
Mississippi Valley. British officer in America, Indian negotiator.

REA, ROBERT R. Redcoats and redskins on the Lower Mississippi, 1763–1776: the career of Lt. John Thomas. Louisiana history, v. 11, winter 1970: 5–35.
F366.L6238, v. 11

14560

THOMAS, NICHOLAS (1737–1783)
Maryland. Lawyer, assemblyman, judge.

SPENCER, RICHARD H. Hon. Nicholas Thomas. Maryland historical magazine, v. 6, June 1911: 145–163.
F176.M18, v. 6

THOMPSON, BENJAMIN
See RUMFORD, *Sir* BENJAMIN THOMPSON, *Count*

14561

THOMPSON, SAMUEL (1735–1798)
Maine; Massachusetts. Revolutionary general, assemblyman, landowner.

GOOLD, NATHAN. General Samuel Thompson of Brunswick and Topsham, Maine. *In* Maine Historical Society. Collections. 3d ser., v. 1. Portland, 1904. p. 423–458. F16.M33, 3d s., v. 1

——— ——— Offprint. [n.p., 1904?] 36 p.
CT275.T576G5

14562

THOMPSON, WILLIAM (1736–1781)*
Ireland; Pennsylvania. Revolutionary general.

HEATHCOTE, CHARLES W. General William Thompson—an earnest Pennsylvania military officer and supporter of Washington. Picket post, no. 71, Feb. 1961: 4–10. illus. E234.P5, no. 71

14563

THOMSON, CHARLES (1729–1824)*
Ireland; Pennsylvania. Schoolmaster, merchant, secretary to the Continental Congress.

——— The Thomson papers, 1765–1816. *In* New York Historical Society. Collections. 1878. Publication fund series, [v. 11] New York, 1879. p. [1]–286.
F116.N63, 1878

Contents: Correspondence, 1765–1782.—Debates in the Congress of the Confereration, July 22–September 20, 1782.—Correspondence, 1783–1817.—*Joseph Reed's Narrative* [of the beginning of the Revolution in Pennsylvania]—Charles Thomson's *Observations*, etc. [on the same subject]—Note.

EDMUNDS, ALBERT J. Charles Thomson's New Testament: a description of three mss. in the Library of the Historical Society of Pennsylvania. Pennsylvania magazine of history and biography, v. 15, Oct. 1891: 327–335.   F146.P65, v. 15

HEATHCOTE, CHARLES W. Charles Thomson. General magazine and historical chronicle, v. 47, autumn 1944: 46–55.   LH1.P3A4, v. 47

HARLEY, LEWIS R. The life of Charles Thomson, Secretary of the Continental Congress and translator of the Bible from the Greek. Philadelphia, G. W. Jacobs [c1900] 244 p. port.   E302.6.T48H2

Bibliography: p. [213]–235.

HENDRICKS, JAMES EDWIN. Charles Thomson and the American Enlightenment. 1961. ([299] p.)
    Micro AC–1, no. 61–4546

Thesis (Ph.D.)—University of Virginia.
Abstracted in *Dissertation Abstracts*, v. 22, Nov. 1961, p. 1600.

SMITH, PAUL H. Charles Thomson on unity in the American Revolution. *In* U.S. *Library of Congress.* Quarterly journal, v. 28, July 1971: 158–172. facsims., ports.   Z881.U49A3, v. 28

ZIMMERMAN, JOHN J. Charles Thomson, "the Sam Adams of Philadelphia." Mississippi Valley historical review, v. 45, Dec. 1958: 464–480.   E171.J87, v. 45

14564

THOMSON, HANNAH HARRISON (*ca.* 1728–1807)
Pennsylvania. Wife of Charles Thomson (1729–1824).

——— Letters of Hannah Thomson, 1785–1788. Pennsylvania magazine of history and biography, v. 14, Apr. 1890: 28–40.   F146.P65, v. 14

14565

THOMSON, JOHN (1730–1778)
Pennsylvania. Farmer.

THOMPSON, JOHN B. John Thomson and family. Williamsport, Pa., Gazette and Bulletin Print. House, 1889. 29 p. illus., facsims., fold. map.
    CS71.T47 1889

14566

THOMSON, WILLIAM (1727–1796)*
South Carolina. Planter, assemblyman, Revolutionary officer.

SALLEY, ALEXANDER S. Col. Moses Thomson and some of his descendants. South Carolina historical and genealogical magazine, v. 3, Apr. 1902: 97–113. port.
    F266.S55, v. 3

14567

THORNDIKE, ISRAEL (1755–1832)*
Massachusetts. Revolutionary naval commander, merchant-trader, assemblyman.

FORBES, JOHN D. Israel Thorndike, Federalist financier. New York, Published for the Beverly Historical Society by Exposition Press [1953] 160 p. illus., ports.
    HC102.5.T45F6

"Bibliographical note": p. [159]–160.

GLIDDEN, SOPHIA H. Silks, velvets and spices. *In* Business Historical Society. Bulletin, v. 2, Jan. 1928: 8–12.
    HF5001.B8262, v. 2

14568

THORNTON, MATTHEW (1714?–1803)*
Ireland; New Hampshire. Physician, assemblyman, judge, delegate to the Continental Congress.

ADAMS, CHARLES T. Matthew Thornton of New Hampshire, a patriot of the American Revolution. Philadelphia, Penna., Dando Print. and Pub. Co., 1903. 61 p. plates, port.   E263.N4A2

BAILEY, WILLIAM H. Matthew Thornton. Granite monthly, v. 14, Mar. 1892: 77–88.   F31.G75, v. 14

WOODBURY, CHARLES H. [Biographical sketch of Matthew Thornton] *In* New Hampshire Historical Society. Proceedings. v. 3, pt. 1; 1895/97. Concord, 1897. p. 77–109.   F31.N52, v. 3

14569

THURLOW, EDWARD THURLOW, *Baron* (1731–1806)†
England. Lawyer, Member of Parliament, Lord Chancellor.

GORE-BROWNE, ROBERT. Chancellor Thurlow; the life and times of an XVIIIth century lawyer. London, Hamilton [1953] 383 p. illus., plates, ports.   LL

"List of books and manuscripts consulted": p. 364–368.

14570

THURMAN, JOHN (1732–1809)
New York. Merchant.

——— Extracts from the letter books of John Thurman, Junior [1760–88] Historical magazine, 2d ser., v. 4, Dec. 1868: 283–297.   E171.H64, 2d s., v. 4

Communicated by Benjamin H. Hall.

14571

TICE, GILBERT (*d. ca.* 1792)
New York; Canada. Loyalist, British officer in America.

GREEN, ERNEST. Gilbert Tice, U.E. *In* Ontario Historical Society. Papers and records. v. 21, Toronto, 1924. p. 186–197.   F1056.O58, v. 21

14572

TICHENOR, ISAAC (1754–1838)*

New Jersey; Vermont. Lawyer, assemblyman.

Court martial of Isaac Tichenor, sometime governor of Vermont [1780] *In* Vermont Historical Society. Proceedings, v. 11, Sept. 1943: 183–211.   F46.V55, v. 11

14573

TILGHMAN, MARY

Maryland. Sister of Tench Tilghman (1744–1786).

——— Letters of Molly and Hetty Tilghman: eighteenth century gossip of two Maryland girls [ca. 1783–90] Maryland historical magazine, v. 21, Mar.–Sept. 1926: 20–39, 123–149, 219–241.   F176.M18, v. 21

14574

TILGHMAN, TENCH (1744–1786)*

Maryland. Merchant, Revolutionary officer.

BAST, HOMER.   Tench Tilghman—Maryland patriot. Maryland historical magazine, v. 42, June 1947: 71–94.   F176.M18, v. 42

[HARRISON, SAMUEL A.]   Memoir of Lieut. Col. Tench Tilghman, secretary and aid to Washington, together with an appendix, containing Revolutionary journals and letters, hitherto unpublished. Albany, J. Munsell, 1876. 176 p. port.   E207.T57H3

Contents: Memoir of Lieut. Col. Tench Tilghman by S. A. Harrison.—Appendix compiled by Oswald Tilghman: Journal of Tench Tilghman, secretary of the Indian commissioners, appointed by Congress to treat with the Six Nations at German Flats, New York. Col. Tilghman's diary of the siege of Yorktown. Correspondence.

Reprinted in New York by the New York Times (1971).

14575

TILTON, JAMES (1745–1822)*

Delaware. Revolutionary surgeon, delegate to the Continental Congress.

——— The biographical his[tory] of Dionysius, tyrant of Delaware, addressed to the people of the United States of America. By Timoleon [pseud.] Philadelphia, Printed in the year 1788. 100 p.   F168.R28 Rare Bk. Coll.

A hostile attack on the career of George Read of Delaware with observations on local and national politics, 1776–88. Reprinted, with an introduction by John A. Munroe and appended notes by Thomas Rodney, in *Delaware Notes*, v. 31 (Newark, 1958), p. 65–146.

14576

TIMBERLAKE, HENRY (1730–1765)*†

Virginia. Military officer.

——— The memoirs of Lieut. Henry Timberlake (who accompanied the three Cherokee Indians to England in the year 1762), containing whatever he observed remarkable, or worthy of public notice, during his travels to and from that nation; wherein the country, government, genius, and customs of the inhabitants, are authentically described. Also the principal occurrences during their residence in London. Illustrated with an accurate map of their Over-hill settlement, and a curious secret journal, taken by the Indians out of the pocket of a Frenchman they had killed. London, Printed for the author, 1765. viii, 160 p. illus. (part fold.), fold. map.   E99.C5T6 Rare Bk. Coll.

Reprinted in Johnson City, Tenn. by the Watauga Press (1927) under the title *Lieut. Henry Timberlake's Memoirs, 1756–1765*; this edition, which includes annotation, introduction, and index by Samuel C. Williams, has been reprinted in Marietta, Ga., by the Continental Book Co. (1948) and in New York by Arno Press (1971).

RANDOLPH, J. RALPH.   Henry Timberlake and the Cherokees. *In his* British travelers among the southern Indians, 1660–1763. Norman. University of Oklahoma Press [1972, c1973] (The American exploration and travel series, [v. 62]) p. 142–154. illus., facsims., maps, ports.   E78.S65R3

14577

TIMOTHY, PETER (*d.* 1782)

South Carolina. Printer.

——— Four letters from Peter Timothy [to David Hall and Benjamin Franklin], 1755, 1768, 1771. South Carolina historical magazine, v. 50, July 1954: 160–165.   F266.S55, v. 50

——— Letters of Peter Timothy, printer of Charleston, South Carolina, to Benjamin Franklin. Edited with an introduction by Douglas C. McMurtrie. Chicago, Ill., Black Cat Press, 1935. 19 p.

Z232.T58 Rare Bk. Coll.

14578

TODD, JOHN (1750–1782)

Pennsylvania; Virginia; Kentucky. Lawyer, assemblyman, Revolutionary officer.

——— John-Todd papers [1779–80] *In* Chicago Historical Society. Collections. v. 4. Chicago, 1890. p. 317–359.   F548.1.C4, v. 4

Reprinted on p. 187–229 of *Early Illinois* (Chicago, Fergus Print. Co., 1890. 386 p. Fergus' historical series, no. 31–34. F536.F35, no. 31–34), edited by Edward G. Mason.

Concerning his tenure as the first civil governor of Illinois under Virginia law. Notes by Edward G. Mason.

——— John Todd's record-book [1778–88] *In* Chicago Historical Society. Collections. v. 4. Chicago, 1890. p. 289–316.   F548.1.C4, v. 4

Reprinted on p. 159–186 of *Early Illinois* (Chicago, Fergus Print. Co., 1890. 386 p. Fergus' historical series, no. 31–34. F536.F35, no. 31–34), edited by Edward G. Mason. Introduction and notes by Edward G. Mason.

For an earlier description of the record or minute book, see Mason's article, "The Record-Book of Colonel John Todd, First Civil Governor of the Illinois Country," in the *Magazine of American History, With Notes and Queries,* v. 8, Sept. 1882, p. 586–597.

HELM, EMILY T.   Colonel John Todd. Journal of American history, v. 19, July/Sept. 1925: 261–277.
E171.J86, v. 19

14579
TOMLINSON, ROBERT (1733?–1813)
England. Naval officer.

—— The Tomlinson papers, selected from the correspondence and pamphlets of Captain Robert Tomlinson, R.N., & Vice-Admiral Nicholas Tomlinson. Edited by J. G. Bullocke. [London] Printed for the Navy Records Society, 1935. 400 p. illus., maps, port. (Publications of the Navy Records Society, v. 74)
DA70.A1, v. 74

14580
TONDEE, PETER (1723–1775)
Georgia. Carpenter, tavern keeper.

COLQUITT, DOLORES B.   Peter Tondee the carpenter. Georgia historical quarterly, v. 10, Dec. 1926: 302–316.
F281.G2975, v. 10

14581
TONG, WILLIAM (1756–1848)
Maryland. Revolutionary soldier.

—— The autobiography of William Tong, Revolutionary soldier. [Dover, Ohio, Eagle Press, 1946] 18 p. illus., ports.
E275.T6
"Edited by Captain Herald F. Stout."

14582
TOOKE, JOHN HORNE (1736–1812)†
England. Clergyman, political writer.

—— *defendant.* The trial (at large) of John Horne, Esq., upon an information filed ex officio, by his Majesty's Attorney General, for a libel. Before the Right Hon. William Earl of Mansfield, in the Court of King's Bench, Guildhall, on Friday the fourth of July 1777. Published by the defendant, from Mr. Gurney's shorthand notes. London, Sold by G. Kearsly, 1777. 69 p.
KD372.T66 G8

GRAHAM, JOHN A.   Memoirs of John Horne Tooke, together with his valuable speeches and writings: also, containing proofs identifying him as the author of the celebrated letters of Junius. New York, Printed by A. Gould & L. Jacobus, for S. Gould, 1828. viii, 238 p. fold. facsim., port.
DA508.T6G7

REID, WILLIAM HAMILTON.   Memoirs of the public life of John Horne Tooke, Esq., containing a particular account of his connections with the most eminent characters of the reign of George III., his trials for sedition, high treason, &c., with his most celebrated speeches in the House of Commons, on the hustings, letters, &c. London, Printed for Sherwood, Neely & Jones, 1812. xxviii, 192 p.
DA506.T6R3

STEPHENS, ALEXANDER.   Memoirs of John Horne Tooke, interspersed with original documents. London, Printed for J. Johnson, 1813. 2 v.
DA506.T6S8
Reprinted in New York by B. Franklin (1968).

WINSLOW, JOHN.   The Battle of Lexington as looked at in London before Chief-Justice Mansfield and a jury in the trial of John Horne, Esq., for libel on the British government. [New York, 1897] 39 p. (Founders and patriots of America, Order of the.   New York society. Publications. no. 2)
E186.6.N39, no. 2
E241.L6W7

YARBOROUGH, MINNIE C.   John Horne Tooke. New York, Columbia University Press, 1926. xix, 252 p. (Columbia University studies in English and comparative literature)
DA506.T6Y4 1926
Published also as thesis (Ph.D.)—Columbia University, 1926
Bibliography: p. 243–247.

—— John Horne Tooke: champion of the American colonists. South Atlantic quarterly, v. 35, Oct. 1936: 374–392.
AP2.S75, v. 35

14583
TOSCAN, JEAN JOSEPH MARIE (1752–1805)
France; New Hampshire. Diplomat.

—— Through an eighteenth-century looking glass [1789] New England quarterly, v. 27, Dec. 1954: 515–521.
F1.N62, v. 27
Observations on Boston society since his arrival in 1781. Introduction and notes by Constance D. Sherman.

14584
TOWNE, BENJAMIN (d. 1793)*
England; Pennsylvania. Printer, newspaper publisher.

TEETER, DWIGHT L.   Benjamin Towne: the precarious career of a persistent printer. Pennsylvania magazine of history and biography, v. 89, July 1965: 316–330.
F146.P65, v. 89

14585
TOWNSEND, JEREMIAH (1761–1805)
Connecticut. Merchant.

—— The journal of Jeremiah Townsend. *In* New Haven Colony Historical Society, *New Haven.* Journal, v. 16, June–Nov. 1967: 29–37, 57–63, 78–86.
F91.N4, v. 16

An account of a voyage from New Haven to Londonderry, Ireland, from January to April 1784. Edited by Mary Means Huber.

14586

TOWNSEND, ROBERT (1753–1838)
New York. Secret agent.

PENNYPACKER, MORTON. The two spies, Nathan Hale and Robert Townsend. Boston, Houghton Mifflin Co., 1930. vii, 118 p. facsim., plate, ports.
E280.H2P41 Rare Bk. Coll.

See his article by the same title in the *Quarterly Journal* of the New York State Historical Association, v. 12, Apr. 1931, p. 122–128.

14587

TOWNSHEND, CHARLES (1725–1767)†
England. Member of Parliament, Chancellor of the Exchequer.

FITZGERALD, PERCY H. Charles Townshend, wit and statesman. London, R. Bentley, 1866. xv, 360 p. port.
DA501.T7F4

FORSTER, CORNELIUS P. Charles Townshend, a study of his political conduct. 1963. ([197] p.)
Micro AC–1, no. 64–2413

Thesis (Ph.D.)—Fordham University.
Abstracted in *Dissertation Abstracts*, v. 24, May 1964, p. 4647–4648.

NAMIER, Sir LEWIS B., *and* JOHN BROOKE. Charles Townshend. [New York] St. Martin's Press, 1964. vii, 198 p. port. DA501.T7N33 1964

Bibliographic footnotes.
See also Namier's preliminary essay, *Charles Townshend; His Character & Career* (Cambridge, University Press, 1959. 29 p. DA501.T7N3), the Leslie Stephen lecture for 1959. It has been reprinted in his *Crossroads of Power; Essays on Eighteenth-Century England* (New York, Macmillan Co. [1963, ᶜ1962] DA480.N3), p. 194–212.

14588

TRABUE, DANIEL (1760–1840)
Virginia; Kentucky. Revolutionary officer, frontiersman.

HARPER, LILLIE D. V., *ed.* Colonial men and times; containing the journal of Col. Daniel Trabue, some account of his ancestry, life, and travels in Virginia and the present state of Kentucky during the Revolutionary period; the Huguenots, genealogy, with brief sketches of the allied families. Philadelphia, Penna., Innes, 1916. 624 p. col. coats of arms, plates, ports.
CS71.T756 1916

"Lists of works consulted": p. 592–595.
Trabue's journal, appearing on p. 3–156, is a 19th-century reconstruction from "memory and tradition."

14589

TRECOTHICK, BARLOW (*ca.* 1718–1775)
Massachusetts; England. Merchant, colonial agent, Member of Parliament.

JERVEY, THEODORE D. Barlow Trecothick. South Carolina historical and genealogical magazine, v. 32, July 1931: 157–169. F266.S55, v. 32

WATSON, DEREK H. Barlow Trecothick. *In* British Association for American Studies. Bulletin, new ser., no. 1, Sept. 1960: 36–49; no. 2, Mar. 1961: 29–39.
E172.B72, n.s., no. 1–2

14590

TRENT, WILLIAM (1715–1787?)*
Pennsylvania; New Jersey. Military officer, Indian negotiator and trader, land speculator.

——— Journal of Captain William Trent from Logstown to Pickawillany, A.D. 1752. Now published for the first time from a copy in the archives of the Western Reserve Historical Society, Cleveland, Ohio, together with letters of Governor Robert Dinwiddie; an historical notice of the Miami confederacy of Indians; a sketch of the English post at Pickawillany, with a short biography of Captain Trent, and other papers never before printed. Edited by Alfred T. Goodman. Cincinnati, Printed by R. Clarke, for W. Dodge, 1871. 117 p. F517.T79
Micro 01291, reel 77, no. 11 E

Reprinted in New York by Arno Press (1971).

——— William Trent's journal at Fort Pitt, 1763. Mississippi Valley historical review, v. 11, Dec. 1924: 390–413.
E171.J87, v. 11

An Indian trader, Trent headed a militia company supporting the regular soldiers in the defense of Fort Pitt during Pontiac's War. Introduction and notes by Albert T. Volwiler.

LANDIS, CHARLES I. Captain William Trent, an Indian trader. *In* Lancaster County (Pa.) Historical Society. Papers, v. 23, Dec. 1919: 173–183.
F157.L2L5, v. 23

SLICK, SEWELL E. William Trent and the West. Harrisburg, Archives Pub. Co. of Pennsylvania, 1947. vii, 188 p. map (on lining papers) F482.T7S55

"Bibliographical note": p. 177–184.
The author's thesis (Ph.D.), *William Trent, Indian Trader and Land Speculator*, was submitted to the University of Pittsburgh in 1938.

14591

TREUTLEN, JOHN ADAM (1733–*ca.* 1782)
Georgia. Planter, assemblyman, governor.

CANDLER, MARK A. John Adam Treutlen. Magazine of history, with notes and queries, v. 16, Jan. 1913: 3–8.
E171.M23, v. 16

KRETZMANN, KARL. Johann Adam Treutlen, 1733–1782. The first governor of Georgia whom America should remember in this sesquicentennial year of his administration. [Hoboken? N.J., °1927] 8 p. illus. (Concord Society of America. Historical bulletin no. 7)
F290.T82

14592

TREVETT, JOHN (1747–1823)
Rhode Island. Revolutionary marine officer.

——— Journal of John Trevett, U.S.N., 1774–1782. Rhode Island historical magazine, v. 6, July 1885–Apr. 1886: 72–74, 106–110, 194–199, 271–278; v. 7, July 1886–Jan. 1887: 38–45, 151–160, 205–208.   F76.R35, v. 6–7

The journal, which describes voyages and actions from Rhode Island to the West Indies, covers only the period from November 1775 to August 1778. The magazine ceased publication before the remainder of the original, in the Newport Historical Society, could be published.

14593

TROTTER, DANIEL (1747–1800)
Pennsylvania. Cabinetmaker, Quaker overseer.

GOLOVIN, ANNE C. Daniel Trotter: eighteenth-century Philadelphia cabinetmaker. In Winterthur portfolio. v. 6. Winterthur, Del., 1970. p. 151–184. illus.
N9.W52, v. 6

14594

TRUMBULL, BENJAMIN (1735–1820)*
Connecticut. Congregational clergyman, Revolutionary chaplain, historian.

——— Extracts of letters to Rev. Thomas Prince, containing historical notices of sundry towns [1772] In Connecticut Historical Society, Hartford. Collections. v. 3. Hartford, 1895. p. [271]–320.   F91.C7, v. 3

——— A letter to an honourable gentleman of the Council-Board, for the colony of Connecticut, shewing that Yale-College is a very great emolument, and of high importance to the state: consequently, that it is the interest and duty of the commonwealth to afford it publick countenance and support. By a friend of college, the church and his country. New-Haven, Printed by B. Mecom, 1766. 26 p.   LD6309.5.T8

14595

TRUMBULL, JOHN (1750–1831)*
Connecticut. Satirist, lawyer, poet.

——— The poetical works of John Trumbull, LL.D., containing M'Fingal, a modern epic poem, revised and corrected, with copious explanatory notes; The progress of dulness; and a collection of poems on various subjects, written before and during the Revolutionary War. Hartford, Printed for S. G. Goodrich, by Lincoln & Stone, 1820. 2 v. port., plates.
PS852.A1 1820 Rare Bk. Coll.

Contents: v. 1. M'Fingal, Canto 1–4.—v. 2. Progress of dulness, pt. 1–3. Genius of America. Lines to Messrs. Dwight and Barlow. Ode to sleep. To a young lady; a fable. Speech of Proteus; a translation. Prophecy of Balaam. Owl and sparrow; a fable. Prospect of the future glory of America. On the vanity of youthful expectations. Advice to ladies of a certain age. Characters. Elegy, on the death of Mr. St. John. Destruction of Babylon. Elegy on the times.
Reprinted in Grosse Pointe, Mich., by Scholarly Press (1968).

COWIE, ALEXANDER. John Trumbull as a critic of poetry. New England quarterly, v. 11, Dec. 1938: 773–793.
F1.N62, v. 11

——— John Trumbull as revolutionist. American literature, v. 3, Nov. 1931: 287–295.   PS1.A6, v. 3

——— John Trumbull, Connecticut wit. Chapel Hill, University of North Carolina Press, 1936. xi, 230 p. port.
PS853.C6

Bibliography: p. [215]–223.
Reprinted in Westport, Conn., by Greenwood Press (1972).
The author's thesis (Ph.D.), *John Trumbull: a Biographical Study*, was submitted to Yale University in 1930.

——— John Trumbull glances at fiction. American literature, v. 12, Mar. 1940: 69–73.   PS1.A6, v. 12

GRANGER, BRUCE I. John Trumbull and religion. American literature, v. 23, Mar. 1951: 57–79.
PS1.A6, v. 23

GREY, LENNOX B. John Adams and John Trumbull in the "Boston cycle." New England quarterly, v. 4, July 1931: 509–514.   F1.N62, v. 4

Adams' influence in the writing of *M'Fingal*.

SCHULTZ, MAX F. John Trumbull and satirical criticism of literature. Modern language notes, v. 73, Feb. 1958: 85–90.   PB1.M6, v. 73

TRUMBULL, JAMES HAMMOND. The origin of *M'Fingal*. Historical magazine, 2d ser., v. 3, Jan. 1868: 1–10.
E171.H64, 2d s., v. 3

Reissued in a different format in Morrisania, N.Y., in 1868 (40 p. PS852.M4T7).

Contains also a reprint of General Gage's proclamation of June 12, 1775, and Trumbull's rhymed satirical paraphrase, first printed in the *Connecticut Courant*, August 7 and 14, 1775, parts of which were incorporated in *M'Fingal*.

14596

TRUMBULL, JOHN (1756–1843)*
Connecticut. Revolutionary officer, painter and artist. Son of Jonathan Trumbull (1710–1785).

——— The autobiography of Colonel John Trumbull, patriot-artist, 1756–1843. Edited by Theodore Sizer. Containing a supplement to [the editor's] The Works of

Colonel John Trumbull. New Haven, Yale University Press, 1953. xxiii, 404 p. ports. ND237.T8A32

Bibliographic footnotes.

Reprinted in New York by Kennedy Graphics (1970). The *Autobiography* was first published in New York by Wiley and Putnam (1841. 439 p. ND237.T8A3).

—— An early check list of the paintings of John Trumbull. Yale University Library gazette, v. 22, Apr. 1948: 116–123. Z733.Y17G, v. 22

From a record kept by the painter. Introduction and notes by Theodore Sizer.

ABBOTT, SAMUEL. John Trumbull, the painter of the Revolution. *In* Bunker Hill Monument Association. Proceedings. 1911. Boston. p. 53–69. fold. map, plate. E241.B9B9, 1911

—— —— Offprint. [Boston? 1911] 19 p. fold. map, plate. ND237.T8A5

BARTLETT, ELLEN S. John Trumbull, the patriot painter. New England magazine, new ser., v. 13, Jan. 1896: 607–628. illus., ports. AP2.N4, n.s., v. 13

MORGAN, JOHN H. Paintings by John Trumbull at Yale University of historic scenes and personages prominent in the American Revolution. New Haven, Published for the associates in fine arts at Yale University by the Yale University Press, 1926. 90 p. illus., ports. ND237.T8M6

RICHARDSON, EDGAR P. A penetrating characterization of Washington by John Trumbull. *In* Winterthur portfolio. v. 3; 1967. Winterthur, Del. p. 1–23. ports. N9.W52, v. 3

Discusses the background of "Washington at Verplanck's Point [1782]," a portrait that Trumbull painted and gave to Martha Washington in 1790.

SILVERMAN, E. H. Painter of the Revolution. American heritage, v. 9, June 1958: 40–51, 95–97. illus., facsims., ports. E171.A43, v. 9

SIZER, THEODORE. John Trumbull, "patriot-painter," in northern New York. *In* New York State Historical Association. New York history, v. 31, July 1950: 283–293. F116.N865, v. 31

—— Trumbull's "The Battle of Princeton." Princeton University Library chronicle, v. 12, autumn 1950: 1–5. facsims. Z733.P93C5, v. 12

—— The works of Colonel John Trumbull, artist of the American Revolution. By Theodore Sizer, with the assistance of Caroline Rollins. Rev. ed. New Haven, Yale University Press, 1967. xxiii, 181 p. 276 illus., ports. (part col.) ND237.T8S5 1967

Includes bibliographic references.

WEIR, JOHN F. John Trumbull; a brief sketch of his life, to which is added a catalogue of his works. New York, C. Scribner's Sons, 1901. xi, 79 p. facsim., plates, port. ND237.T8W4

14597

TRUMBULL, JONATHAN (1710–1785)*

Connecticut. Merchant, assemblyman, councilor, judge, governor.

—— Letter from his late Excellency Jonathan Trumbull, Esq. to Baron J. D. Vander Capellan, "Seigneur de Pol, membre des nobles de la province d'Overysul, &c." [August 31, 1779] *In* Massachusetts Historical Society, *Boston.* Collections. v. 6; 1794. Boston, 1800. p. 154–185. F61.M41, v. 6

On the state of the American cause.

—— The Trumbull papers. Boston, Published by the Society, 1885–1902. 4 v. (Massachusetts Historical Society, Boston. Collections, 5th ser., v. 9–10; 7th ser., v. 2–3) F61.M41, 5th s., v. 9–10; 7th s., v. 2–3

Contents: pt. 1. Early miscellaneous papers relating to the Narragansett country. Letters of William Samuel Johnson. Letters of Jedediah Huntington.—pt. 2. Correspondence between General Washington and Governor Trumbull and others. Letters of John Hancock, Joseph Warren, Thomas Gage, James Warren, and Governor Trumbull. List of Washington's letters. List of Trumbull's letters to Washington.—pt. 3–4. Letters and documents relating to the Revolution, 1777–83.

ARMSTRONG, ROBERT G. Brother Jonathan. American heritage, new ser., v. 3, winter 1952: 34–37. illus., ports. (part col.) E171.A43, n.s., v. 3

GRIFFIS, WILLIAM E. Brother Jonathan and his home. New England magazine, new ser., v. 17, Sept. 1897: 2–24. illus., facsims, port. AP2.N4, n.s., v. 17

MORGAN, FORREST. Jonathan Trumbull—the evolution of an administrator. Americana, v. 7, Mar. 1912: 227–254. E171.A53, v. 7

ROTH, DAVID M. Jonathan Trumbull, 1710–1785: Connecticut's Puritan patriot. 1971. ([384] p.) Micro AC–1, no. 71–24,740

Thesis (Ph.D.)—Clark University.

Abstracted in *Dissertation Abstracts International,* v. 32A, Sept. 1971, p. 1423.

STUART, ISAAC W. Life of Jonathan Trumbull, Sen., Governor of Connecticut. Boston, Crocker and Brewster, 1859. 700 p. illus., col. plate, ports. (part col.) E263.C5T85

TRUMBULL, JONATHAN. Jonathan Trumbull, governor of Connecticut, 1769–1784. *In* New London County Historical Society, *New London, Conn.* Records and papers. pt. 5, v. 2. New London, 1904. p. 431–447. port. F102.N7N7, v. 2

—— Jonathan Trumbull, Governor of Connecticut, 1769–1784. By his great-great-grandson, Jonathan Trumbull. Boston, Little, Brown, 1919. xiii, 362 p. port. E263.C5T87

Bibliography: p. 341–346.

WEAVER, GLENN. Jonathan Trumbull and the Nantucket trade. Historic Nantucket, v. 7, Jan. 1960: 20–27.
F72.N2H68, v. 7

———— Jonathan Trumbull, Connecticut's merchant magistrate, 1710–1785. Hartford, Connecticut Historical Society, 1956. viii, 182 p. illus., plate.   E263.C5T9

"Bibliographic note": p. 161–174.
The author's thesis (Ph.D.), with the same title, was submitted to Yale University in 1953.

14598
TRUMBULL, JOSEPH (1737–1778)*
Connecticut. Merchant, assemblyman, Revolutionary commissary general. Son of Jonathan Trumbull (1710–1785).

TRUMBULL, JONATHAN. Joseph Trumbull, the first commissary-general of the Continental Army. *In* New London County Historical Society, *New London, Conn.* Records and papers. pt. 2, v. 2. New London, 1897. p. 329–347.   F102.N7N7, v. 2

14599
TRUXTUN, THOMAS (1755–1822)*
New York; Pennsylvania. Revolutionary naval commander, merchant.

FERGUSON, EUGENE S. Truxtun of the *Constellation*; the life of Commodore Thomas Truxtun, U.S. Navy, 1755–1822. Baltimore, Johns Hopkins Press, 1956. xii, 322 p. illus., port.   E182.T7F43

Bibliography: p. 300–307.

ROBISON, SAMUEL S. Commodore Thomas Truxton, U.S. Navy. *In* United States Naval Institute. Proceedings, v. 58, Apr. 1932: 541–554.   V1.U8, v. 58

14600
TRYON, WILLIAM (1729–1788)*†
England; North Carolina; New York. Royal governor.

———— Governor Tryon's house in Fort George. Edited by B. D. Bargar. *In* New York State Historical Association. New York history, v. 35, July 1954: 297–309.
F116.N865, v. 35

An inventory of the contents, which were destroyed by fire on December 29, 1773.

———— Tryon's "Book" on North Carolina [1765] Edited by William S. Powell. North Carolina historical review, v. 34, July 1957: 406–415.   F251.N892, v. 34

HAYWOOD, MARSHALL D. Governor William Tryon, and his administration in the province of North Carolina, 1765–1771; services in a civil capacity and military career as commander-in-chief of colonial forces which suppressed the insurrection of the Regulators. Raleigh, E. M. Uzzell, Printer, 1903. 223 p. map, plates.
F257.H43

Reprinted in Raleigh, N.C., by Edwards & Broughton Co. (1958).

HENNER, SOLOMON. The career of William Tryon as governor of the province of New York, 1771–1780. 1968. ([296] p.)   Micro AC–1, no. 69–7958

Thesis (Ph.D.)—New York University.
Abstracted in *Dissertation Abstracts* v. 29A, May 1969, p. 3949–3950.

14601
TUCKER, DANIEL (1760–1823)
Maine. Revolutionary seaman and privateersman.

———— Capt. Daniel Tucker in the Revolution; an autobiographical sketch. With prefatory remarks by Rev. E. C. Cummings. [Portland? Me., 1896] 30 p.   E241.P8T8

Also published in the Maine Historical Society's *Collections and Proceedings*, 2d ser., v. 8 (Portland, 1897), p. 225–254.

14602
TUCKER, JOSIAH (1712–1799)†
Wales; England. Clergyman, economist, writer.

———— Josiah Tucker; a selection from his economic and political writings. With an introduction by Robert Livingston Schuyler. New York, Columbia University Press, 1931. 576 p. port.   H33.T78

"Bibliography; the books and pamphlets of Josiah Tucker": p. 555–558.
Contents: The elements of commerce and theory of taxes.—Instructions for travellers.—The case of going to war.—A letter from a merchant in London to his nephew in America.—The true interest of Great Britain set forth in regard to the colonies.—A letter to Edmund Burke.—A treatise concerning civil government.

FORD, PAUL L. Josiah Tucker and his writings; an eighteenth century pamphleteer on America. Journal of political economy, v. 2, Mar. 1894: 330–347.
HB1.J7, v. 2

———— ———— Offprint. Chicago, University Press of Chicago [1894] 18 p.   Z8892.F68
Reprinted in New York by B. Franklin (1972).

14603
TUCKER, NATHANIEL (1750–1807)
Bermuda; South Carolina. Poet, physician.

LEARY, LEWIS G. The literary career of Nathaniel Tucker, 1750–1807. Durham, Duke University Press, 1951. ix, 108 p. (Historical papers of the Trinity College Historical Society, ser. 29)   [F251.D83, ser. 29]
Micro 9370 F

"Bibliographical essay": p. [97]–101.
"The writings of Nathaniel Tucker": p. [102]–105.
Reprinted in New York by AMS Press (1970. F251.D832, ser. 29).

14604

TUCKER, ST. GEORGE (1752–1827)*

Bermuda; Virginia. Lawyer, Revolutionary officer, judge.

COLEMAN, MARY H. B. St. George Tucker, citizen of no mean city. Richmond, Va., Dietz Press, 1938. 190 p. plates, ports. F230.T93

CULLEN, CHARLES T. St. George Tucker and law in Virginia, 1772–1804. 1971. ([304] p.)
Micro AC–1, no. 72–7232
Thesis (Ph.D.)—University of Virginia.
Abstracted in *Dissertation Abstracts International*, v. 32A, Feb. 1972, p. 4521.

PRINCE, WILLIAM S. St. George Tucker as a poet of the early republic. 1954.
Thesis (Ph.D.)—Yale University.

The Tucker letters from Williamsburg [1770–92] Bermuda historical quarterly, v. 3, Jan./Mar.–Oct./Dec. 1946: 24–38, 73–87, 143–157, 204–213; v. 4, Jan./Mar.–Oct./Dec. 1947: 15–25, 61–71, 104–115, 154–166; v. 5, Apr./June, Oct./Dec. 1948: 68–94, 170–182; v. 6, Jan./Mar.–July/Sept. 1949: 20–22, 79–91, 135–143; v. 7, Jan./Mar., July/Sept.–Oct./Dec. 1950: 16–23, 106–119, 142–150; v. 8, Oct./Dec. 1951: 143–151; v. 9, Apr./June 1952: 226–240. F1636.B55, v. 3–9

Letters by and to St. George Tucker and various members of his family, taken from the Tucker-Coleman papers, then on deposit in the Research Department at Colonial Williamsburg and now in the collections of the Swem Library, William and Mary College.

14605

TUCKER, SAMUEL (1747–1833)*

Massachusetts. Seaman, Revolutionary naval officer, merchant.

SHEPPARD, JOHN H. Commodore Samuel Tucker. New-England historical and genealogical register, v. 26, Apr. 1872: 105–115. port. F1.N56, v. 26

———— The life of Samuel Tucker, commodore in the American Revolution. Boston, Printed by A. Mudge, 1868. 384 p. E207.T8S7
Commodore Tucker's log-book of a cruise in the United States frigate *Boston*, Feb. 11–Oct. 2, 1778: p. 262–327.
Muster-rolls of the *Boston*, 1778–1779: p. 342–355.

14606

TUDOR, WILLIAM (1750–1819)

Massachusetts. Lawyer, Revolutionary officer.

[TUDOR, WILLIAM, *b.* 1779] Memoir of Hon. William Tudor. *In* Massachusetts Historical Society, *Boston*. 2d ser., v. 8. Boston, 1826. p. 285–325.
F61.M41, 2d s., v. 8

14607

TURGOT, ANNE ROBERT JACQUES, *baron de l'Aulne* (1727–1781)

France. Economist, Controller-General.

DAKIN, DOUGLAS. Turgot and the ancien régime in France. London, Methuen [1939] xi, 361 p. map, port.
DC137.5.T9D3
Bibliography: p. 307–316.
Reprinted in New York by Octagon Books (1965).

14608

TURNBULL, ANDREW (*ca.* 1718–1792)*

Scotland; East Florida. Physician, colonizer.

CORSE, CARITA D. Dr. Andrew Turnbull and the New Smyrna colony of Florida. [Florida, Drew Press, 1919] 212 p. illus., port. F319.N5T9
Bibliography: p. 197–212.
A revised edition has been published in St. Petersburg, Fla., by the Great Outdoors Pub. Co. (1967. 136 p.)

14609

TURNBULL, WILLIAM (1751–1822)

Scotland; Pennsylvania. Merchant, Revolutionary officer and provisioner.

TURNBULL, ARCHIBALD D. William Turnbull, 1751–1822, with some account of those coming after. [Binghamton, N.Y., Printed by the Vail Ballou Press, 1933] vii, 175 p. facsims., plans (part fold.), plates, ports.
F153.T86

14610

TURNER, PHILIP (1740–1815)

Connecticut. Physician, Revolutionary surgeon.

GRAVES, CHARLES B. Dr. Philip Turner of Norwich, Connecticut. Annals of medical history, v. 10, Mar. 1928: 1–24. facsims., port. R11.A85, v. 10

14611

TUTTLE, STEPHEN (*fl.* 1768–1784)

New Jersey; New York; Canada. Loyalist.

———— My services and losses in aid of the King's cause during the American Revolution. Brooklyn, Historical Print. Club, 1890. 24 p. (Winnowings in American history. Revolutionary narratives, no. 2)
E278.T9T96

14612

TYLER, ROYALL (1757–1826)*

Massachusetts. Lawyer, Revolutionary officer, playwright.

———— The prose of Royall Tyler. Collected and edited by Marius B. Péladeau. Montpelier, Vermont Historical Society [1972] 501 p. illus. PS855.T7A16 1972

Bibliography: p. [474]-480.

Tyler's autobiographical *Bay Boy* treats his early years in pre-Revolutionary Boston.

—— The verse of Royall Tyler. Collected and edited by Marius B. Péladeau. Charlottesville, University Press of Virginia [1968] xiv, 269 p. illus., facsims., port. PS855.T7A6 1968

Bibliography: p. [249]-258.

DELL, ROBERT M., *and* CHARLES A. HUGUE-NIN. Vermont's Royall Tyler in New York's John Street Theatre: a theatrical hoax exploded. Vermont history, v. 38, spring 1970: 103-112. F46.V55, v. 38

TANSELLE, GEORGE THOMAS. Royall Tyler. Cambridge, Harvard University Press, 1967. xvi, 281 p. illus., ports. PS855.T7Z86

Includes bibliographic references.

TUPPER, FREDERICK. Royall Tyler, man of law and man of letters. *In* Vermont Historical Society. Proceedings. 1926/28. [Burlington] 1928. p. [63]-101. F46.V55, 1926/28

14613

TYSON, ELISHA (1750-1824)

Pennsylvania; Maryland. Philanthropist, abolitionist.

[TYSON, JOHN S.] Life of Elisha Tyson, the philanthropist. By a citizen of Baltimore. Baltimore, Printed by B. Lundy, 1825. 142 p. E446.T995 Rare Bk. Coll.

14614

ULLOA, ANTONIO DE (1716-1795)*

Spain; Louisiana. Governor, Spanish naval officer.

MOORE, JOHN P. Antonio de Ulloa; a profile of the first Spanish governor of Louisiana. Louisiana history, v. 8, summer 1967: 189-218. F366.L6238, v. 8

WHITAKER, ARTHUR P. Antonio de Ulloa. Hispanic American historical review, v. 15, May 1935: 155-194. F1401.H66, v. 15

14615

VAILL, JOSEPH (1751-1838)

Connecticut. Clergyman.

—— Memoir of the life and character of Rev. Joseph Vaill, late pastor of the Church of Christ in Hadlyme. By Rev. Isaac Parsons. New York, Taylor and Dodd, 1839. 236 p. front. BX7260.V28A3

14616

VALLANDIGHAM, GEORGE (1737 or 8-*ca.* 1810)

Virginia; Maryland. Schoolteacher, settler, lawyer.

VALLANDIGHAM, EDWARD N. Lieutenant Colonel George Vallandigham. Pennsylvania magazine of history and biography, v. 53, Apr. 1929: 159-167. F146.P65, v. 53

14617

VAN CAMPEN, MOSES (1757-1849)

New Jersey; Pennsylvania. Farmer, Revolutionary soldier.

HUBBARD, JOHN N. Sketches of border adventures, in the life and times of Major Moses Van Campen, a surviving soldier of the Revolution. By his grandson. Bath, N.Y., R. L. Underhill, 1842. 310 p. E275.V22 Rare Bk. Coll.

The 1893 edition (Fillmore, N.Y., J. S. Minard. 337 p. E275.V24) adds several chapters by John S. Minard on Van Campen's later years.

14618

VAN CORTLANDT, CATHARINE OGDEN (1746-1828)

New Jersey. Wife of Philip Van Cortlandt (1739-1814).

—— A Loyalist's wife: letters of Mrs. Philip Van Cortlandt, 1776-77. History today, v. 14, Aug. 1964: 574-580. illus., ports. D1.H818, v. 14

Introduction and notes by H. O. H. Vernon-Jackson.

14619

VAN CORTLANDT, PHILIP (1749-1831)*

New York. Surveyor, Revolutionary general, assemblyman.

—— Autobiography of Philip Van Cortlandt, Brigadier-General in the Continental Army. Magazine of American history, with notes and queries, v. 2, May 1878: 278-298. E171.M18, v. 2

PARMELEE, HELEN L. B. Colonel Philip Van Cortlandt and the New York Continentals. New York genealogical and biographical record, v. 5, July 1874: 123-139. F116.N28, v. 5

14620

VAN DER KEMP, FRANCIS ADRIAN (1752-1829)*

Netherlands; New York. Clergyman, military officer.

—— Francis Adrian Van der Kemp, 1752-1829, an autobiography, together with extracts from his correspondence. Edited with an historical sketch, by Helen Lincklaen Fairchild. New York, G. P. Putnam's Sons, 1903. xii, 230 p. illus., facsims., ports. F123.V22

"The writings of Francis Adrian Van der Kemp": p. 213-216.

"List of the principal authorities consulted": p. 217-220.

JACKSON, HARRY F. Scholar in the wilderness: Francis Adrian Van der Kemp. [Syracuse] Syracuse University Press, 1963. xi, 356 p. illus., ports.   F123.V22J3

Bibliographic references included in "Notes" (p. 327–345).

14621

VANDERSLICE, HENRY (1726–1797)

Pennsylvania. Surveyor, Revolutionary soldier.

—— Diary of Henry Vanderslice, wagon-master [1777–78] In Vanderslice, Howard, and Howard N. Monnett, comps. Van der Slice and allied families. [Los Angeles, Printed by the Neuner Corp., c1931] p. 140–161.   CS71.V237 1931

GRAEFF, ARTHUR D. Henry Vanderslice, wagon-master, 1777–1778. Historical review of Berks County, v. 2, Apr. 1937: 67–73. illus.   F157.B3H48, v. 2

14622

VAN GAASBEEK, PETER (1754–1797)

New York. Merchant, Revolutionary officer.

D'INNOCENZO, MICHAEL, and JOHN J. TURNER. The Peter Van Gaasbeek papers: a resource for early New York history, 1771–1797. In New York State Historical Association. New York history, v. 47, Apr. 1966: 153–159.   F116.N865, v. 47

14623

VAN HORNE, WILLIAM (1747–1807)

Pennsylvania. Revolutionary chaplain.

—— Revolutionary War letters of the Reverend William Van Horne [1778–79] Western Pennsylvania historical magazine, v. 53, Apr. 1970: 105–138. port.   F146.W52, v. 53

Introduction and notes by William E. Van Horne.

14624

VAN SCHAACK, PETER (1747–1832)*

New York; England. Lawyer, Loyalist.

HAMLIN, PAUL M. Peter Van Schaack. Columbia University quarterly, v. 24, Mar. 1932: 66–105.   LH1.C7Q2, v. 24

VAN SCHAACK, HENRY C. The life of Peter Van Schaack, LL.D., embracing selections from his correspondence and other writings during the American Revolution, and his exile in England. New York, D. Appleton, 1842. xii, 490 p. port.   E278.V27V2

14625

VARICK, RICHARD (1753–1831)*

New Jersey; New York. Revolutionary officer, assemblyman.

—— defendant. The Varick court of inquiry to investigate the implication of Colonel Varick (Arnold's private secretary) in the Arnold treason. Edited by Albert Bushnell Hart. Boston, Bibliophile Society, 1907. 217 p. illus., fold. facsims., port.   E236.V29

ROMMEL, JOHN G. Richard Varick: New York aristocrat. 1966. ([288] p.)   Micro AC-1, no. 69–565

Thesis (Ph.D.)—Columbia University.

Abstracted in Dissertation Abstracts, v. 29A, Jan. 1969, p. 2195.

14626

VARNUM, JAMES MITCHELL (1748–1789)*

Massachusetts; Rhode Island. Lawyer, Revolutionary general, judge, delegate to the Continental Congress.

DAMON, SAMUEL F. Varnum's "Ministerial Oppression," a Revolutionary drama. In American Antiquarian Society, Worcester, Mass. Proceedings, new ser., v. 55, Oct. 1945: 287–298.   E172.A35, n.s., v. 55

Written between June 1775 and July 1776.

GARDINER, ASA B. General James M. Varnum of the Continental Army. Magazine of American history, with notes and queries, v. 18, Sept. 1887: 185–193.   E171.M18, v. 18

HEATHCOTE, CHARLES W. General James M. Varnum and his services for his country. Picket post, no. 50, Nov. 1955: 4–10. port.   E234.P5, no. 50

VARNUM, JAMES M. A sketch of the life and public services of James Mitchell Varnum of Rhode Island. Boston, D. Clapp, Printers, 1906. 4 p. port.   E302.6.V33V3

Books of reference: p. 41–42.

Reprinted from The Varnums of Dracutt in Massachusetts (Boston, D. Clapp, Printers, 1907. 308 p. CS71.V322 1907), compiled from family papers and official records by John M. Varnum.

14627

VARNUM, JOSEPH BRADLEY (1751–1821)*

Massachusetts. Farmer, Revolutionary general, assemblyman.

—— Autobiography of General Joseph B. Varnum. Magazine of American history, with notes and queries, v. 20, Nov. 1888: 405–414.   E171.M18, v. 20

"From the original manuscript, dictated by General Varnum in 1819, recently discovered and never before published."

Contributed by James M. Varnum.

14628

VASSALL, HENRY (1721–1769)

West Indies; Massachusetts. Planter, assemblyman, militia officer.

BATCHELDER, SAMUEL F. Col. Henry Vassall. *In* Cambridge Historical Society, *Cambridge, Mass.* Publications. v. 10. Proceedings. 1915. Cambridge, 1917. p. 5–85. facsims., port.   F74.C1C469, v. 10

—— Colonel Henry Vassall. *In his* Bits of Cambridge history. Cambridge, Harvard University Press, 1930. p. 114–233. ports.   F74.C1B29

14629

VAUGHAN, BENJAMIN (1751–1835)*†

Jamaica; England. Lawyer, merchant, diplomat.

—— Letters of Benjamin Vaughan to the Earl of Shelburne [1782–83] *In* Massachusetts Historical Society, *Boston.* Proceedings. 2d ser., v. 17; 1903. Boston. p. 406–438.   F61.M38, 2d s., v. 17

Introduction and notes by Charles C. Smith.

GARDINER, ROBERT H. Memoir of Benjamin Vaughan, M.D. and LL.D. *In* Maine Historical Society. Collections. v. 6. Portland, 1859. p. 83–92.   F16.M33, v. 6

ROWELL, GEORGE S. Benjamin Vaughan—patriot, scholar, diplomat. Magazine of history, with notes and queries, v. 22, Mar. 1916: 43–57.   E171.M23, v. 22

14630

VAUGHAN, *Sir* JOHN (*ca.* 1738–1795)†

England. British officer in America, Member of Parliament.

VOSPER, EDNA F. Report on the Sir John Vaughan papers in the William L. Clements Library. Ann Arbor, Mich., William L. Clements Library, 1929. 37 p. facsim., map, port. (William L. Clements Library—University of Michigan. Bulletin no. 19)   F2131.V36   E172.M53, no. 19

"The extent of the Vaughan papers is . . . from November, 1779, to March, 1781."—p. 8.

14631

VAUGHAN, SAMUEL (1720–1802)

England. Merchant, traveler.

—— Samuel A. Vaughan's journal or "Minutes Made by S. V., from Stage to Stage, on a Tour to Fort Pitt" [1787] Edited by Edward G. Williams. Western Pennsylvania historical magazine, v. 44, Mar.–Sept. 1961: 51–65, 159–173, 261–285. illus., map, plate.   F146.W52, v. 44

STETSON, SARAH P. The Philadelphia sojourn of Samuel Vaughan. Pennsylvania magazine of history and biography, v. 78, Oct. 1949: 459–474.   F146.P65, v. 78

14632

VERGENNES, CHARLES GRAVIER, *comte* DE (1719–1787)

France. Diplomat, Foreign Minister.

—— Mémoire historique et politique sur la Louisiane, par M. de Vergennes, ministre de Louis XVI, accompagné d'un précis de la vie de ce'ministre, et suivi d'autres mémoires sur l'Indostan, Saint-Domingue, la Corse et la Guyane. Paris, Lepetit jeune, an X.—1802. 315 p.   F373.V49`

Lettre de M. le chevalier Turgot, à M. le duc Choiseuil, 10 octobre, 1765: p. 273–300.

The *Mémoire* was written about 1777. For a discussion of its authenticity, see the *American Historical Review*, v. 10, Jan. 1905, p. 250.

AIMÉ-AZAM, DENISE. Vergennes: essai de bibliographie historique et critique. Franco-American review, v. 1, autumn 1936: 149–159.   E183.8.F8F88, v. 1

MURPHY, ORVILLE T. Charles Gravier de Vergennes: profile of an old regime diplomat. Political science quarterly, v. 83, Sept. 1968: 400–418.   H1.P8, v. 83

SALOMON, ROBERT. La politique orientale de Vergennes (1780–1784). Paris, Les Presses modernes, 1935. 328 p.   DC131.9.V3S3

Thèse—Université de Paris.
"Bibliographie": p. [5]–7. "Sources": p. [8]–12.

14633

VÉRI, JOSEPH ALPHONSE DE (1724–1799)

France. Clergyman.

—— L'abbé de Véri et son journal. Revue d'histoire diplomatique, 39. année, avril/juin–juil./sept. 1925: 131–167, 263–301.   JX3.R3, v. 39

Introduction and notes by Jehan de Witte.

Fragments relevant to the political activities of the comte de Maurepas during the American Revolution.

14634

VERNON, THOMAS (1718–1784)

Rhode Island. Loyalist.

—— The diary of Thomas Vernon, a Loyalist, banished from Newport by the Rhode Island General Assembly in 1776. With notes by Sidney S. Rider. Providence, R.I., S. S. Rider, 1881. viii, 150 p. (Rhode Island historical tracts, no. 13)   F76.R52, no. 13   E278.V54V5

14635

VERSTILLE, WILLIAM (1757–1803)

Massachusetts; Connecticut. Revolutionary officer, miniature painter.

—— Accounts of William Verstille. *In* Connecticut Historical Society, *Hartford.* Bulletin, v. 25, Jan. 1960: 22–31.   F91.C67, v. 25

14636

VIGO, FRANCIS (1747–1836)*

Italy; Old Northwest. Fur trader, merchant.

CHAMBERLAIN, CECIL H.   Colonel Francis Vigo and George Rogers Clark. Illinois Catholic historical review, v. 10, Oct. 1927: 139–144.
BX1415.I3M5, v. 10

RIKER, DOROTHY L.   Francis Vigo. Indiana magazine of history, v. 26, Mar. 1930: 12–24.   F521.I52, v. 26

ROSELLI, BRUNO.   Vigo: a forgotten builder of the American republic. Boston, Mass., Stratford Co. [c1933] 280 p.   F592.V63

14637
VIOMÉNIL, ANTOINE CHARLES DU HOUX, baron DE (1728–1792)
France. French officer in America.

GOUGH, JOHN F.   A French friend of America. [Jersey City? 1944] 49 p.   DC46.7.G6
Bibliography: p. 39–49.

MONTMORT, ROGER, comte de.   Antoine Charles du Houx, baron de Vioménil, lieutenant-general of the armies of the King, second in command under Rochambeau. Englished by John Francis Gough. Baltimore, Johns Hopkins Press, 1935. 66 p. maps (on lining papers), port.   E265.V56

—— Un compagnon de Rochambeau: Antoine-Charles du Houx, baron de Viomenil, lieutenant général des armées du roi (1728–1792). Revue des questions historiques, v. 123, mai 1935: 63–73.   D1.R5, v. 123

14638
VOLTAIRE, FRANÇOIS MARIE AROUET DE (1694–1778)
France. Philosophe, playwright, historian, writer.

BARR, MARY M. H.   Voltaire in America, 1744–1800. Baltimore, Md., Johns Hopkins Press, 1941. 150 p. port. (The Johns Hopkins studies in Romance literatures and languages, v. 39)   PQ2093.B3 1941
PC13.J6, v. 39
Issued also as thesis (Ph.D.)—Columbia University.
"Bibliographies": p. 121–143.

14639
WACHTMEISTER, HANS FREDERICK (1752?–1807?)
Sweden. British seaman in America.

—— Two Swedes under the Union Jack: a manuscript journal [Aug. 4, 1775–Dec. 21, 1776] from the American War of Independence by Hans Frederick Wachtmeister and Herman Frederick von Walden. Swedish pioneer historical quarterly, v. 7, July 1956: 81–120. facsim., map, ports.   E184.S23S955, v. 7
Originally edited, with introduction and notes, by Wilhelm Odelberg. The journal was translated by Nils W. Olsson and the introduction and notes by Paul A. Varg.

14640
WADDEL, JAMES (1739–1805)*
Ireland; Pennsylvania; Virginia. Presbyterian clergyman, planter.

ALEXANDER, JAMES W.   Memoir of the Rev. James Waddel, D.D. [n.p.] 1880. 44 p.   BX9225.W22A6
Published in the Watchman of the South, a religious paper of Richmond, Virginia, in 1844.

14641
WADDELL, HUGH (1734?–1773)*
Ireland; North Carolina. Military officer, assemblyman, merchant, landowner.

WADDELL, ALFRED M.   A colonial officer and his times. 1754–1773. A biographical sketch of Gen. Hugh Waddell, of North Carolina. With notices of the French and Indian War in the southern colonies; the resistance to the Stamp Act in North Carolina . . . the Regulators' war; and an historical sketch of the former town of Brunswick, on the Cape Fear River. Raleigh, N.C., Edwards & Broughton, 1890. 242 p. plates, port.   F257.W11

14642
WADE, NATHANIEL (1750–1826)
Massachusetts. Carpenter, Revolutionary officer.

WADE, HERBERT T.   [Nathaniel Wade] In Essex Institute, Salem, Mass. Historical collections, v. 89, July–Oct. 1953: 213–252, 357–375; v. 90, Jan.–Apr., Oct. 1954: 84–99, 167–190, 317–349. facsims., maps, plates, ports.   F72.E7E81, v. 89–90
Contents: [1] Nathaniel Wade and his Ipswich minute men.—[2] Colonel Wade and the Massachusetts state troops in Rhode Island—1777–1778.—[3–4] The Massachusetts Brigade on the Hudson, 1780: Nathaniel Wade at West Point.—[5] The Essex Regiment in Shays' Rebellion—1787.

14643
WADSWORTH, JEREMIAH (1743–1804)*
Connecticut. Seaman, Revolutionary officer and provisioner, merchant, delegate to the Continental Congress.

DESTLER, CHESTER M.   The gentleman farmer and the new agriculture: Jeremiah Wadsworth. Agricultural history, v. 46, Jan. 1972: 135–153.   S1.A16, v. 46

PLATT, JOHN D. R.   Jeremiah Wadsworth: Federalist entrepreneur. 1955. ([247] p.)
Micro AC–1, no. 12,464
Thesis (Ph.D.)—Columbia University.
Abstracted in Dissertation Abstracts, v. 15, no. 8, 1955, p. 1383–1384.

14644
WAGG, ABRAHAM (1719–1803)
New York. Merchant.

ROTH, CECIL. A Jewish voice for peace in the War of American Independence; the life and writings of Abraham Wagg, 1719–1803. *In* American Jewish Historical Society. Publications. no. 31. New York, 1928. p. 33–75.   E184.J5A5, no. 31

14645

WAIT, THOMAS BAKER (1762–1830)
Massachusetts; Maine. Newspaper editor, publisher.

MARSH, PHILIP M. Maine's first newspaper editor: Thomas Wait. New England quarterly, v. 28, Dec. 1955: 519–534.   F1.N62, v. 28

14646

WAITE, JOHN (1742–1817)
Rhode Island. Revolutionary officer, silversmith.

MILLER, WILLIAM D. John Waite, silversmith. *In* Rhode Island Historical Society. Collections, v. 21, Jan. 1928: 45–56. illus.   F76.R47, v. 21

14647

WALDECK, PHILIPP
Hessian chaplain in America.

——— Philipp Waldeck's diary of the American Revolution. Printed from the original manuscript with introduction and photographic reproduction of the list of officers, by Marion Dexter Learned. Philadelphia, Americana Germanica Press, 1907. x, 146 p. facsims. (American germanica. New ser., [v. 6])   E267.W15

A revised version of the diary which was first published in the *German American Annals*, v. 5, Feb.–July, Oct., Dec. 1903, p. 97–116, 178–186, 225–232, 275–283, 357–364, 420–428, 577–592, 734–747; v. 6, Jan., Mar.–July, 1904, p. 59–64, 192–198, 252–257, 309–318, 367–378, 435–445.

14648

WALDO, ALBIGENCE (1750–1794)
Connecticut. Physician, Revolutionary surgeon.

———Valley Forge, 1777–1778; diary of surgeon Albigence Waldo, of the Connecticut Line. Pennsylvania magazine of history and biography, v. 21, Oct. 1897: 299–323. map.   F146.P65, v. 21

Published earlier in *The Historical Magazine*, v. 5, May–June 1861, p. 129–134, 169–172.

THOMS, HERBERT. Albigence Waldo, surgeon: his diary written at Valley Forge. Annals of the history of medicine, v. 10, Dec. 1928: 486–497. facsims.
                    R11.A85, v. 10

Also includes entries from his surgical day book, 1782–89.

14649

WALKER, FELIX (1753–1828)
Virginia; North Carolina. Frontiersman, Revolutionary officer.

——— Memoirs of the late the Hon. Felix Walker, of North Carolina . . . From his original manuscript of autobiography. Edited by Sam'l R. Walker. New Orleans, A. Taylor, Printer, 1877. 19 p.   F258.W17

Includes an account of Walker's experiences in Kentucky in 1775.

14650

WALKER, JOHN (1728–1796)
Virginia; North Carolina. Settler, judge, Revolutionary officer. Father of Felix Walker (1753–1828).

GRIFFIN, CLARENCE W. Revolutionary service of Col. John Walker and family, and Memoirs of Hon. Felix Walker. Forest City, N.C., Forest City Courier, 1930. 23 p. coat of arms.   F258.W19

14651

WALKER, THOMAS (1715–1794)*
Virginia. Physician, land speculator, assemblyman, councilor, planter.

DISBROW, NATALIE J. Thomas Walker of Albemarle. *In* Albemarle County Historical Society. Papers. v. 1; 1940/41. Charlottesville, Va., 1941. p. 5–18.
                    F232.A3A5, v. 1

HENDERSON, ARCHIBALD. Dr. Thomas Walker and the Loyal Company of Virginia. *In* American Antiquarian Society, *Worcester, Mass.* Proceedings, new ser., v. 41, Apr. 1931: 77–178.   E172.A35, n.s., v. 41

Includes a section of supporting documents, dated from 1753 to 1797, p. 122–178.

HOPEWELL, JOHN S. Doctor Walker's land title to Castle Hill. *In* Albemarle County Historical Society. Magazine. v. 26; 1967/68. Charlottesville, Va., 1969. p. [81]–85.   F232.A3A5, v. 26

JOHNSTON, JOSIAH S. First explorations of Kentucky: Doctor Thomas Walker's journal of an exploration of Kentucky in 1750, being the first record of a white man's visit to the interior of that territory, now first published entire, with notes and biographical sketch; also Colonel Christopher Gist's journal of a tour through Ohio and Kentucky in 1751, with notes and sketch. Louisville, Ky., J. P. Morton, 1898. xix, 222 p. map, plates, port. (Filson Club publications, no. 13)
                    F454.J73
                    F446.F48, no. 13

NYLAND, KEITH R. Doctor Thomas Walker (1715–1794): explorer, physician, statesman, surveyor, and planter of Virginia and Kentucky. 1971. ([177] p.)
                    Micro AC–1, no. 72–4596

Thesis (Ph.D.)—Ohio State University.

Abstracted in *Dissertation Abstracts International*, v. 32A, Jan. 1972, p. 3896.

14652

WALKER, TIMOTHY (1705–1782)*

Massachusetts; New Hampshire. Congregational clergyman.

———— Diaries of the Rev. Timothy Walker, the first and only minister of Concord, New Hampshire, from his ordination, November 18, 1730, to his death, September 1, 1782. Edited and annotated by Joseph B. Walker. *In* New Hampshire Historical Society. Collections. v. 9. Concord, 1889. p. 123–191. F31.N54, v. 9

———— ———— Offprint. Concord, N.H., I. C. Evans, 1889. 80 p. F44.C7W25

———— Diary of Rev. Timothy Walker of Concord, N.H., for the year 1780. Granite monthly, v. 4, Dec. 1880: 101–108. F31.G75, v. 4

Introduction and notes by Joseph B. Walker.

14653

WALLACE, CALEB (1742–1814)

Virginia; Kentucky. Presbyterian clergyman, assemblyman, judge.

WHITSITT, WILLIAM H. Life and times of Judge Caleb Wallace, some time a justice of the Court of Appeals of the state of Kentucky. Louisville, J. P. Morton, Printers, 1888. 151 p. (Filson Club publications, no. 4) CS71.W22 1888 F446.F48

"Genealogical notices": p. 144–151.

14654

WALPOLE, HORACE *4th Earl of Orford* (1717–1797)†

England. Writer, Member of Parliament.

———— Horace Walpole: memoirs and portraits. Edited by Matthew Hodgart. [Rev. ed.] New York, Macmillan [1963] xxxi, 264 p. illus., ports. [Historical memoirs] DA506.W2A13 1963

Bibliography: p. xxix–xxxi.

Extracts from the memoirs of George II and George III, 1750–71, that focus on the leading personalities of the day.

———— The last journals of Horace Walpole during the reign of George III, from 1771–1783, with notes by Dr. Doran. Edited with an introduction by A. Francis Steuart. London, New York, J. Lane, 1910. 2 v. ports. DA483.W2A7

"The text is printed, except for the removal of a few obvious misprints, exactly as it stood in Dr. Doran's edition of 1858."—Editor's introduction, p. xxiv.

———— The letters of Horace Walpole, earl of Orford. Edited by Peter Cunningham. Now first chronologically arranged. London, R. Bentley, 1857–59. 9 v. ports. DA483.W2A14

———— The letters of Horace Walpole, fourth earl of Orford. Chronologically arranged and edited with notes and indices by Mrs. Paget Toynbee. Oxford, Clarendon Press, 1903–5. 16 v. facsims., ports. DA483.W2A25

"Bibliographical note": v. 1, p. [xxxi]–xxxiii.

Contents: v. 1. 1732–1743.—v. 2. 1743–1750.—v. 3. 1750–1756.—v. 4. 1756–1760.—v. 5. 1760–1764.—v. 6. 1764–1766.—v. 7. 1766–1771.—v. 8. 1771–1774.—v. 9. 1774–1776.—v. 10. 1776–1779.—v. 11. 1779–1781.—v. 12. 1781–1783.—v. 13. 1783–1787.—v. 14. 1787–1791.—v. 15. 1791–1797.—v. 16. Tables and indices. [Addenda et corrigenda. Genealogical tables. List of correspondents. Index of persons. Index of places. Index of subjects]

———— Supplement to The letters of Horace Walpole, fourth earl of Orford. Chronologically arranged and edited with notes and indices by Paget Toynbee. Oxford, Clarendon Press, 1918–25. 3 v. fold. facsims., port. DA483.W2A25 Suppl.

Contents: 1. 1725–1783.—v. 2. 1783–1796.—v. 3. 1744–1797.

———— Memoirs of the reign of King George the Third, first published by Sir Denis Le Marchant, Bart., and now re-edited by G. F. Russell Barker. London, Lawrence and Bullen; New York, G. P. Putnam's Sons, 1894. 4 v. ports. DA506.W2A16

Reprinted in Freeport, N.Y., by Books for Libraries Press (1970) and in New York by AMS Press (1971).

First published in 1845.

The memoirs extend to the year 1771 and are continued in the author's *Journal of the Reign of King George the Third, From the Year 1771 to 1783*, edited by Dr. John Doran (London, R. Bentley, 1859. 2 v. DA506.W2A2).

———— The works of Horatio Walpole, Earl of Orford. London, G. G. and J. Robinson, 1798. 5 v. plans, plates, ports. PR3757.W2 1798

Edited by Mary Berry.

———— The Yale edition of Horace Walpole's correspondence. Edited by W. S. Lewis [New Haven, Yale University Press, 1937+ illus., facsims., ports. DA483.W2A12

Contents: v. 1–2. Correspondence with the Rev. William Cole.—v. 3–8. Correspondence with Madame du Deffand and others.—v. 9–10. Correspondence with George Montagu.—v. 11–12. Correspondence with Mary and Agnes Berry and Barbara Cecilia Seton.—v. 13–14. Correspondence with Thomas Gray, Richard West, and Thomas Ashton. 1 v.—v. 15. Correspondence with Sir David Dalrymple and others.—v. 16. Correspondence with Thomas Chatterton and others.—v. 17–27. Correspondence with Sir Horace Mann.—v. 28–29. Correspondence with William Mason.—v. 30. Correspondence with George Selwyn, and others.—v. 31. Correspondence with Hannah More and others.—v. 32–34. Correspondence with the Countess of Upper Ossory.

BECKER, CARL L. Horace Walpole's Memoirs of the reign of George the Third. American historical review, v. 16, Jan.–Apr. 1911: 255–272, 496–507. E171.A57, v. 16

Analyzes Walpole's journals as an historical source and demonstrates that large sections were either newly written or greatly revised many years after the event when Walpole's opposition to George III had become increasingly bitter.

BINFORD, JOSEPH N.   The politics of Horace Walpole. 1966. ([286] p.)   Micro AC–1, no. 69–18,231
Thesis (Ph.D.)—University of Kentucky.
Abstracted in *Dissertation Abstracts International*, v. 30A, Nov. 1969, p. 1936.

CHRISTIE, IAN R.   Horace Walpole: the gossip as historian. History today, v. 4, May 1954: 291–300. illus., ports.
D1.H818, v. 4

DOBSON, AUSTIN.   Horace Walpole, a memoir, with an appendix of books printed at the Strawberry Hill Press. 4th ed., rev. and enl. by Paget Toynbee. London, H. Milford, Oxford University Press, 1927. xiv, 395 p. illus., plans, plates, ports.   DA483.W2D6 1927
"List of editions of works of Horace Walpole or of works relating to him, published since 1910": p. [ix]–x.
Reprinted in Freeport, N.Y., by Books for Libraries Press (1971) and in New York by Haskell House (1971).

GWYNN, STEPHEN L.   The life of Horace Walpole. London, T. Butterworth [1932] 285 p. plates, ports.
DA483.W2G8
Reprinted in Freeport, N.Y., by Books for Libraries Press (1971) and in Port Washington, N.Y., by Kennikat Press (1972).

HAZEN, ALLEN T.   A catalogue of Horace Walpole's library. New Haven, Yale University Press, 1969. 3 v. illus.   Z997.W24.H38 Rare Bk. Coll.
See also Hazen's *A Bibliography of Horace Walpole* (New Haven, Yale University Press, 1948. 189 p. Z8947.9.H3).

Horace Walpole, writer, politician and connoisseur; essays on the 250th anniversary of Walpole's birth. Edited by Warren Hunting Smith. New Haven, Yale University Press, 1967. xii, 358 p. illus., facsim., port.
DA483.W2H67
Bibliographic footnotes.
Partial contents: Horace Walpole and the politics of the early years of the reign of George III, by J. Brooke.—The only unadulterated Whig, by A. S. Foord.—Walpole, pro-American, by B. Knollenberg.

JUDD, GERRIT P.   Horace Walpole's journal, 1783–1791. 1947.
Thesis (Ph.D.)—Yale University.

—— Horace Walpole's memoirs. New York, Bookman Associates [1959] 119 p.   DA483.W2J8
Bibliographic references included in "Notes" (p. 89–116).

KALLICH, MARTIN.   Horace Walpole against Edmund Burke: a study in antagonism. Studies in Burke and his time, v. 9, winter-spring 1968: 834–863, 927–945.
DA506.B9B86, v. 9

See also James W. Johnson's "Walpole Against Burke: Some Ancillary Speculations" in v. 10, fall 1968, p. 1022–1034.

KETTON-CREMER, ROBERT W.   Horace Walpole, a biography. Ithaca, N.Y., Cornell University Press [1966, ᶜ1964] xv, 317 p. geneal. table, plates, ports.   DA483.W2K4 1966
"Bibliographical note": p. 299–305.
The first edition was published in New York by Longmans, Green (1940. 368 p.)

LEWIS, WILMARTH S.   Horace Walpole. [New York] Pantheon Books [1961] xxvii, 215 p. illus., facsims., ports. (Bollingen series, 35. The A. W. Mellon lectures in the fine arts, 9)   PR3757.W2Z73 1961

—— Horace Walpole, antiquary. *In* Pares, Richard, *and* Alan J. P. Taylor, *eds.* Essays presented to Sir Lewis Namier. London, Macmillan; New York, St. Martin's Press, 1956. p. 178–203.   D6.P28

WHITELEY, EMILY S.   Horace Walpole—early American. Virginia quarterly review, v. 7, Apr. 1931: 212–224.
AP2.V76, v. 7

14655
WALPOLE, THOMAS (1727–1803)
England. Merchant-banker, Member of Parliament.

—— Thomas Walpole's letters to the Duke of Grafton on American affairs, 1776–1778. Huntington Library quarterly, v. 30, Nov. 1966: 17–33.
Z733.S24Q, v. 30
Introduction and notes by Richard W. Van Alstyne.

14656
WALTON, GEORGE (1740–1804)*
Virginia; Georgia. Lawyer, delegate to the Continental Congress, Revolutionary officer, governor, judge.

LAWRENCE, ALEXANDER A., *and* GORDON T. BANKS. Lachlan McIntosh vs. George Walton. Manuscripts, v. 7, summer 1955: 224–228.   Z41.A2A925, v. 7
Appraises Governor Walton's role in the dismissal of Brigadier General McIntosh from the Continental Army, 1777–80.

14657
WALTON, JESSE (*d. ca.* 1792)
North Carolina. Revolutionary officer, assemblyman.

WILLIAMS, SAMUEL C.   The founder of Tennessee's first town: Major Jesse Walton. *In* East Tennessee Historical Society, *Knoxville*. Publications. no. 2; 1930. Knoxville, Tenn. p. 78–80.   F442.1.E14, no.2

—— —— Offprint. [Jonesboro, Banking and Trust Co. of Jonesboro, 1930] 13 p.   F444.J79W72

14658

WANTON, JOSEPH (1705–1780)*

Rhode Island. Mariner, merchant, governor, Loyalist.

BARTLETT, JOHN R. History of the Wanton family of Newport, Rhode Island. Providence, S. S. Rider, 1878. 152 p. (Rhode Island historical tracts, [1st ser.], no. 3)
F76.R52, 1st s., no.3

"Originally appeared in the Providence Journal, in 1871."

MORSE, JARVIS M. The Wanton family and Rhode Island loyalism. *In* Rhode Island Historical Society. Collections, v. 31, Apr. 1938: 33–45. port. F76.R47, v. 31

14659

WARD, ARTEMAS (1727–1800)*

Massachusetts. Judge, assemblyman, councilor, Revolutionary general, delegate to the Continental Congress.

Guide to the microfilm edition of the Artemas Ward papers. Frederick S. Allis, Jr., editor; R. Bruce Pruitt, associate editor. Boston, Massachusetts Historical Society, 1967. 30 p. Z6616.W28A46 Mss

HEATHCOTE, CHARLES W. General Artemas Ward and General Washington in the early days of the American Revolution. Picket post, no. 76, May 1962: 4–10. port.
E234.P5, no. 76

MARTYN, CHARLES. The life of Artemas Ward, the first commander-in-chief of the American Revolution. New York, A. Ward, 1921. xiii, 334 p. facsims., map, plates, port. E207.W2M38

Reprinted in Port Washington, N.Y., by Kennikat Press (1970).

14660

WARD, EDWARD (*ca.* 1730–*ca.* 1793)

Pennsylvania. Settler.

BOTHWELL, MARGARET P. Edward Ward—trail blazing pioneer. Western Pennsylvania historical magazine, v. 43, June 1960: 99–127. F146.W52, v. 43

14661

WARD, JOSEPH (1737–1812)

Massachusetts. Schoolmaster, Revolutionary officer.

BATES, WILLIAM C. Col. Joseph Ward, 1737–1812, teacher, soldier, patriot. *In* Bostonian Society, *Boston.* Publications. v. 4. Boston, 1907. p. [55]–76. port.
F73.1.B88, v. 4

14662

WARD, NANCY (1738–1822)*

Tennessee. Cherokee leader.

McCLARY, BEN H. Nancy Ward: the last beloved woman of the Cherokees. Tennessee historical quarterly, v. 21, Dec. 1962: 352–364. F431.T285, v. 21

14663

WARD, SAMUEL (1725–1776)*

Rhode Island. Farmer, assemblyman, governor, judge, delegate to the Continental Congress.

——— Correspondence of Governor Samuel Ward, May 1775–March 1776, with a biographical introduction, based chiefly on the Ward papers covering the period 1725–1776, edited by Bernhard Knollenberg; and Genealogy of the Ward family: Thomas Ward, son of John, of Newport and some of his descendants, compiled by Clifford P. Monahon. Providence, Rhode Island Historical Society, 1952. ix, 254 p.
E207.W26A4

Bibliography: p. 239–244.

——— Diary of Governor Samuel Ward, delegate from Rhode Island in Continental Congress, 1774–1776. Magazine of American history, with notes and queries, v. 1, July–Sept. 1877: 438–442, 503–506, 549–561.
E171.M18, v. 1

Introduction and supplementary note by John Ward.

GAMMELL, WILLIAM. Samuel Ward, Governor of Rhode Island. *In his* William Gammell; a biographical sketch, with selections from his writings. Edited by James O. Murray. Cambridge [Mass.] Printed at the Riverside Press, 1890. p. [99]–177. E173.G19

Reprinted from Sparks' *American Biography.*

14664

WARD, SAMUEL (1756–1832)*

Rhode Island; New York. Revolutionary officer, merchant. Son of Samuel Ward (1725–1776).

WARD, JOHN. Lieut.-Colonel Samuel Ward of the Revolutionary War. New York genealogical and biographical record, v. 6, July 1875: 113–123. port.
F116.N28, v. 6

14665

WARD, WILLIAM (1736–1829)

Connecticut. Silversmith.

——— A ledger-book (1771–1787) of William Ward, silversmith. *In* Papers in honor of Andrew Keogh, librarian of Yale University. New Haven, Priv. print., 1938. p. [239]–249. Z733.Y18P

Introduction and notes by Emma H. E. Stephenson.

14666

WARDER, ANN (*ca.* 1758–1829)

England; Pennsylvania.

—— Extracts from the diary of Ann Warder [June 1786 to Oct. 1788] Pennsylvania magazine of history and biography, v. 17, Jan. 1894: 444–461; v. 18, Apr. 1894: 51–63.   F146.P65, v. 17–18

On social life in Philadelphia. Contributed by Sarah Cadbury.

14667
WARNER, JONATHAN (1726–1814)
New Hampshire. Merchant, councilor.

WENDELL, WILLIAM G.   Jonathan Warner (1726–1814): merchant & trader, King's councillor, mariner, jurist. Illustrated by Cecile Newbold Barnett. New York, Newcomen Society in North America, 1950. 40 p. illus., port.   F44.P8W4

14668
WARNER, SETH (1743–1784)*
Connecticut; Vermont. Settler, Revolutionary general.

BUTLER, JAMES D., and GEORGE F. HOUGHTON. Addresses on the Battle of Bennington, and the life and services of Col. Seth Warner; delivered before the legislature of Vermont. Burlington, Free Press Office Print, 1849. 99 p.   E241.B4B9

CHIPMAN, DANIEL.   The life of Col. Seth Warner, with an account of the controversy between New York and Vermont, from 1763 to 1775. Burlington, C. Goodrich, 1858. 84 p.   E207.W27C4

First edition (Middlebury, Vt., 1848), published under title, Memoir of Colonel Seth Warner.

FENTON, WALTER S.   Seth Warner. In Vermont Historical Society. Proceedings, new ser., v. 8, Dec. 1940: 325–350.   F46.V55, n.s., v. 8

14669
WARREN, JAMES (1726–1808)*
Massachusetts. Merchant, assemblyman, Revolutionary officer.

—— A study in dissent: the Warren-Gerry correspondence, 1776–1792. Edited with introduction and commentary by C. Harvey Gardiner. Carbondale, Southern Illinois University Press [1968] xxxi, 269 p. illus., facsims., ports.   E203.W26

Massachusetts Historical Society, Boston.   Warren-Adams letters, being chiefly a correspondence among John Adams, Samuel Adams, and James Warren . . . 1743–1814. [Boston] 1917–25. 2 v. facsims., plates, port. (Its Collections, v. 72–73)   F61.M41, v. 72–73

Contents: v. 1. 1743–1777.—v. 2. 1778–1814.
Reprinted in New York by AMS Press (1972).

14670
WARREN, JOHN (1753–1815)*
Massachusetts. Physician, Revolutionary surgeon, professor.

—— Journal of Dr. John Warren [April. 19, 1775–May 11, 1776] In Warren, John C. Genealogy of Warren. Boston, Printed by J. Wilson, 1854. p. 85–98.
CS71.W29 1854

Excerpts from Warren's correspondence from 1774 to 1776 appear on p. 82–84.

WARREN, EDWARD.   The life of John Warren, M.D., surgeon-general during the War of the Revolution; first professor of anatomy and surgery in Harvard College; president of the Massachusetts Medical Society, etc. Boston, Noyes, Holmes, 1874. xv, 568 p. port.
R154.W25W2

14671
WARREN, JOSEPH (1741–1775)*
Massachusetts. Physician, orator, Revolutionary officer.

—— Correspondence of General Joseph Warren [1766–75] In Warren, John C. Genealogy of Warren. Boston, Printed by J. Wilson, 1854. p. 67–81. facsim.
CS71.W29 1854

CARY, JOHN H.   Joseph Warren: physician, politician, patriot. Urbana, University of Illinois Press, 1961. 260 p. port.   E263.M4W234

Bibliography: p. 227–243.
The author's thesis (Ph.D.), with the same title, was submitted to the University of Illinois in 1959 (Micro AC–1, no. 59–4498).

FROTHINGHAM, RICHARD.   Life and times of Joseph Warren. Boston, Little, Brown, 1865. xix, 558 p. facsim., port.   E263.M4W24

Reprinted in New York by Da Capo Press (1971).

TRUAX, RHODA.   The doctors Warren of Boston; first family of surgery. Boston, Houghton Mifflin, 1968. xiii, 369 p. geneal. table (on lining papers)
R154.W274T7

Bibliography: p. [355]–357.

14672
WARREN, MERCY OTIS (1728–1814)*
Massachusetts. Writer, historian.

—— The adulateur; a tragedy, as it is now acted in Upper Servia. Boston, Printed and sold at the New Printing Office, near Concert-Hall, 1773. Tarrytown, N.Y., Reprinted, W. Abbatt, 1918. 35 p. (The Magazine of history, with notes and queries. Extra number, no. 63, [pt. 3])   E173.M24, no. 63

The writing of this play was suggested by the discovery of the Hutchinson and Oliver letters. The characters were designed to represent some of the principal personages of Massachusetts politics at that time.

———— [The Group, as lately acted, and to be re-acted to the wonder of all superior intelligences, nigh head-quarters at Amboyne. Boston, Printed and sold by Edes and Gill, in Queen-Street, 1775] 22 p.
PS858.W8A7 Rare Bk. Coll.

Imperfect; title page wanting. Title of the first edition supplied from Wegelin's *Early American Plays* (no. 233).

The William L. Clements Library has published a facsimile of its first edition (Ann Arbor, University of Michigan, 1953. PS858.W8A7 1775a)

A political satire in two acts in verse, published the day before the Battle of Lexington.

———— Poems, dramatic and miscellaneous. Boston, I. Thomas and E. T. Andrews, 1790. 250 p.
PS858.W8 1790 Rare Bk. Coll.

ANCILLA, JOSEPH, Sister. The political theory of Mercy Otis Warren: a study in American constitutionalism. 1968. ([206] p.) Micro AC–1, no. 69–4123

Thesis (Ph.D.)—St. John's University.

Abstracted in *Dissertation Abstracts*, v. 29A, Mar. 1969, p. 3188.

ANTHONY, KATHARINE S. First lady of the Revolution: the life of Mercy Otis Warren. Garden City, N.Y., Doubleday, 1958. 258 p. PS858.W8A85

Bibliography: p. 249–254.

Reprinted in Port Washington, N.Y., by Kennikat Press (1972).

The Blockheads; or, The affrighted officers. A farce. Boston, Printed in Queen-Street, 1776. 19 p.
PS700.A1B5 Rare Bk. Coll.

"A counter-farce to Burgoyne's Blockade," attributed to Mercy Warren by Paul L. Ford.

BROWN, ALICE. Mercy Warren. New York, C. Scribner's Sons, 1896. xi, 317 p. port. (Women of colonial and Revolutionary times, [v. 5]) PS858.W8B7

Reprinted in Spartanburg, S.C., by the Reprint Co. (1968).

FORD, WORTHINGTON C. Mrs. Warren's "The Group." *In* Massachusetts Historical Society, *Boston*. Proceedings. v. 62; 1928/29. Boston, 1930. p. 15–22.
F61.M38, v. 62

FRITZ, JEAN. Cast for a revolution; some American friends and enemies, 1728–1814. Boston, Houghton Mifflin, 1972. xii, 400 p. illus. PS858.W8F7

Bibliography: p. [365]–380.

HUTCHESON, MAUD M. Mercy Warren: a study of her life and works. 1951.

Thesis (Ph.D.)—American University.

———— Mercy Warren, 1728–1814. William and Mary quarterly, 3d ser., v. 10, July 1953: 378–402.
F221.W71, 3d s., v. 10

MARBLE, ANNIE R. Mistress Mercy Warren; real daughter of the American Revolution. New England magazine, new ser., v. 28, Apr. 1903: 163–180. illus., facsims., ports. AP2.N4, n.s., v. 28

14673

WARREN, WINSLOW (1760–1791)

Massachusetts. Traveler. Son of James Warren (1726–1808) and Mercy Otis Warren (1728–1814).

WARREN, CHARLES. A young American's adventures in England and France during the Revolutionary War. *In* Massachusetts Historical Society, *Boston*. Proceedings. v. 65; 1932/36. Boston, 1940. p. 234–267.
F61.M38, v. 65

14674

WASHINGTON, GEORGE (1732–1799)*

Virginia. Planter, assemblyman, delegate to the Continental Congress, general and commander-in-chief of the Continental Army, delegate to the Constitutional Convention.

———— Diaries, 1748–1799. Edited by John C. Fitzpatrick. Published for the Mount Vernon Ladies' Association of the Union. [Regents ed.] Boston, Houghton Mifflin, 1925. 4 v. facsims., map, port. E312.8 1748–99

Contents: v. 1. 1748–1770.—v. 2. 1771–1785.—v. 3. 1786–1788.—v. 4. 1789–1799.

———— George Washington; a biography in his own words. Edited by Ralph K. Andrist. With an introduction by Donald Jackson. New York, Newsweek; distributed by Harper & Row [c1972] 416 p. illus. (The Founding fathers) E312.W33 1972

"This book is based on *The Papers of George Washington*, edited by Donald Jackson and published by the University Press of Virginia."

Bibliography: p. 408.

———— George Washington and Mount Vernon; a collection of Washington's unpublished agricultural and personal letters. Edited with historical and genealogical introduction by Moncure Daniel Conway. Brooklyn, N.Y., Long Island Historical Society, 1889. xcii, 352 p. illus., ports. (Memoirs of the Long Island Historical Society, v. 4) E312.5.W3
F116.L954, v. 4

See also *The Agricultural Papers of George Washington* (Boston, R. G. Badger [c1919] 145 p. E312.75.A2), edited by Walter E. Brooke.

———— George Washington, colonial traveller, 1732–1775. Indianapolis, Bobbs-Merrill Co. [c1927] xiv, 416 p. illus., map. E312.27.W3

A compilation of extracts from Washington's diary, account books, letters and other papers arranged chronologically with editorial notes.

———— General Washington's correspondence concerning the Society of the Cincinnati. Edited by Lieutenant-

Colonel Edgar Erskine Hume. Baltimore, Johns Hopkins Press, 1941. xliv, 472 p. facsims. (part fold.), port.

E312.75.S6

"Supplement: brief biographies of those with whom General Washington corresponded concerning the Society of the Cincinnati": p. [403]–459.

—— Letters from Washington to [William] Heath. *In* Massachusetts Historical Society, *Boston*. Collections. 5th ser., v. 4. Boston, 1878. p. 1–285.

F61.M41, 5th s., v. 4

Forms pt. 1 of *The Heath Papers*. For pt. 2, see entry 13581.

—— Official letters to the honourable American Congress, written during the war between the United Colonies and Great Britain, by His Excellency George Washington, Commander in Chief of the Continental forces, now President of the United States. Copied, by special permission, from the original papers preserved in the office of the Secretary of State, Philadelphia. Boston, Printed by Manning & Loring, 1795. 2 v.

E203.W29 Rare Bk. Coll.

The letters cover the period from June 24, 1775, to December 31, 1778. Other volumes were projected by the editor, John Carey, but no more were published.

—— Washington and the West; being George Washington's diary of September, 1784, kept during his journey into the Ohio Basin in the interest of a commercial union between the Great Lakes and the Potomac River, and a commentary upon the same by Archer Butler Hulbert. New York, Century Co., 1905. 217 p. illus., maps (part fold.), plan. E312.8 1784

The diary is reproduced from the original manuscript preserved in the Library of Congress.

—— The Washington-Crawford letters. Being the correspondence between George Washington and William Crawford, from 1767 to 1781, concerning western lands. With an appendix, containing later letters of Washington on the same subject; and letters from Valentine Crawford to Washington, written in 1774 and 1775, chronologically arranged and carefully annotated. By C. W. Butterfield. Cincinnati, R. Clarke, 1877. xi, 107 p. E312.75.O37

—— The Washington papers; basic selections from the public and private writings of George Washington. Edited and arr., with an introduction by Saul K. Padover. New York, Harper [1955] 430 p.

E312.72 1955

Bibliography: p. 417–418.
Organized topically in 10 chapters under three major subheadings: personal, political, and maxims, mottoes, and brief opinions.

—— Washington, sa correspondance avec d'Estaing. Paris, Publié par les soins de la Fondation nationale pour la reproduction des manuscrits précieux et pièces rares d'archives [1937] 65 p. fold. facsims.

E312.74 1937

Introduction signed: Ch. de La Roncière.
Each letter by the Comte d'Estaing is followed by an English translation.

—— Washington's "Tour to the Ohio" [1770] and articles of "The Mississippi Company." Ohio archaeological and historical quarterly, v. 17, Oct. 1908: 431–488.

F486.O51, v. 17

Introduction and notes by Archer B. Hulbert.

—— The writings of George Washington; being his correspondence, addresses, messages, and other papers, official and private. Selected and published from the original manuscripts; with a life of the author, notes and illustrations. By Jared Sparks. Boston, American Stationers' Co., 1834–37. 12 v. illus., facsims., maps, plans, ports. E312.7 1834

Contents: v. 1. Life of Washington.—v. 2. Official letters relating to the French war and private letters before the American Revolution: March 1754–May 1775.—v. 3–8. Correspondence and miscellaneous papers relating to the American Revolution: v. 3, June 1775–July 1776. v. 4, July 1776–July 1777. v. 5, July 1777–July 1778. v. 6, July 1778–March 1780. v. 7, March 1780–April 1781. v. 8, April 1781–December 1783.—v. 9. Private letters from the time Washington resigned his commission as Commander-in-Chief of the Army to that of his inauguration as President of the United States: December 1783–April 1789.—v. 10–11. Letters official and private, from the beginning of his presidency to the end of his life: v. 10, May 1789–November 1794. v. 11, November 1794–December 1799.—v. 12. Speeches and messages to Congress, proclamations, and addresses.

—— The writings of George Washington. Collected and edited by Worthington Chauncey Ford. New York, G. P. Putnam's Sons, 1889–[93] 14 v. E312.7 1889

Appendix: "The Washington family" (v. 14, p. 317–431).

Contents: v. 1. 1748–1757.—v. 2. 1758–1775.—v. 3. 1775–1776.—v. 4. 1776.—v. 5. 1776–1777.—v. 6. 1777–1778.—v. 7. 1778–1779.—v. 8. 1779–1780.—v. 9. 1780–1782.—v. 10. 1782–1785.—v. 11. 1785–1790.—v. 12. 1790–1794.—v. 13. 1794–1798.—v. 14. 1798–1799.

—— The writings of George Washington from the original manuscript sources, 1745–1799. Prepared under the direction of the United States George Washington Bicentennial Commission and published by authority of Congress; John C. Fitzpatrick, editor. Washington, U.S. Govt. Print. Off. [1931–44] 39 v. illus., facsims., maps (part fold.), plans. E312.7 1931

"General index by David M. Matteson": v. 38–39.
Reprinted in Westport, Conn., by Greenwood Press (1970).
A selection by Saxe Commins of 242 items from this work was published under the title *Basic Writings of George Washington* (New York, Random House [1948] xvii, 697 p.).

AMBLER, CHARLES H. George Washington and the West. Chapel Hill, University of North Carolina Press, 1936. viii, 270 p. illus., maps, plates, ports.   E312.A62

"Select bibliography": p. 249–259.

Reprinted in New York by Russell & Russell (1971).

American Library Association. Classified Washington bibliography. Compiled by a special committee of the American Library Association. Washington, D.C., United States George Washington Bicentennial Commission, 1931. 76 p. illus., facsims., port.
E312.H77, no. 16
Z8950.A51

BAKER, WILLIAM S. Bibliotheca Washingtoniana: a descriptive list of the biographies and biographical sketches of George Washington. Philadelphia, R. M. Lindsay, 1889. xv, 179 p. illus.   Z8950.B16

Reprinted in Detroit by Gale Research Co. (1967).

——— Washington after the Revolution, MDCCLXXXIV–MDCCXCIX. Philadelphia, J. B. Lippincott Co., 1898. 416 p.   E312.29.B14

A day-by-day calendar that indicates Washington's activities and travels taken from his writings and correspondence and from newspapers.

BALDRIDGE, H. A. Washington's visits *to* colonial Annapolis. *In* United States Naval Institute. Proceedings, v. 54, Feb. 1928: 90–104, 128. map.   V1.U8, v. 54

Identifies 19 visits between 1751 and 1791.

BEALL, MARY S. The military and private secretaries of George Washington. *In* Columbia Historical Society. Records. v. 1. Washington, 1897. p. 89–118.
F191.C72, v. 1

BELLAMY, FRANCIS R. The private life of George Washington. New York, Crowell [1951] v, 409 p.
E312.B45

Bibliography: p. 387–401.

BLANTON, WYNDHAM B. Washington's medical knowledge and its sources. Annals of medical history, new ser., v. 5, Jan. 1933: 52–61.   R11.A85, n.s., v. 5

BOLLER, PAUL F. George Washington & religion. Dallas, Southern Methodist University Press [1963] xii, 235 p.
E312.17.B74

"Selected bibliography": p. 219–227.

——— George Washington and religious liberty. William and Mary quarterly, 3d ser., v. 17, Oct. 1960: 486–506.
F221.W71, 3d s., v. 17

——— George Washington and the Presbyterians. *In* Presbyterian Historical Society. Journal, v. 39, Sept. 1961: 129–146.   BX8905.P7A4, v. 39

——— George Washington and the Quakers. *In* Friends' Historical Association. Bulletin, v. 49, autumn 1960: 67–83.   BX7635.A1F6, v. 49

——— Washington's religious opinions. Southwest review, v. 48, winter 1963: 48–61.   AP2.S883, v. 48

BORDEN, MORTON, *comp*. George Washington. Englewood Cliffs, N.J., Prentice-Hall [1969] vi, 154 p. (Great lives observed)   E312.B6

Bibliographic footnotes.

Presents Washington's views of events from 1753 to 1797 in selections from his diaries, journals, letters, and orders; contemporary appraisals of Washington taken from over 50 documents; and 10 historical assessments from Weems to Flexner.

BOSTON ATHENAEUM. A catalogue of the Washington collection in the Boston Athenaeum. Compiled and annotated by Appleton P. C. Griffin . . . With an appendix, The inventory of Washington's books drawn up by the appraisers of his estate; with notes in regard to the full titles of the several books and the later history and present ownership of those not in the Athenaeum collection, by William Coolidge Lane. [Cambridge, University Press, J. Wilson] 1897. xi, 566 p. illus., facsims., port.   Z8950.B75 Rare Bk. Coll.

"In four parts: 1. Books from the library of General George Washington.—2. Other books from Mount Vernon.—3. The writings of Washington.—4. Washingtoniana."

A considerable portion of the books were left to George C. Washington. They were sold by him to Henry Stevens in 1847 or 1848, and by the latter to the Boston Athenaeum in 1849.

——— ——— Index. By Franklin Osborne Poole. [Cambridge, University Press, J. Wilson] 1900. 85 p.
Z8950.B75 Index

BRADLEY, HAROLD W. The political thinking of George Washington. Journal of southern history, v. 11, Nov. 1945: 469–486.   F206.J68, v. 11

BRIGHAM, WILLIAM T. The private war of George Washington. History today, v. 22, June 1972: 387–393. illus., ports.   D1.H818, v. 22

On the vicissitudes of the tobacco trade.

BRYAN, WILLIAM A. George Washington in American literature, 1775–1865. New York, Columbia University Press, 1952. xii, 280 p. port.   PS169.W3B7

Bibliography: p. [247]–269.

Reprinted in Westport, Conn., by Greenwood Press (1970).

BUTTERFIELD, CONSUL W., *ed*. Washington-Irvine correspondence. The official letters which passed between Washington and Brig.-Gen. William Irvine and between Irvine and others concerning military affairs in the West from 1781 to 1783. Arranged and annotated, with an introduction containing an outline of events occurring previously in the Trans-Alleghany country. Madison, Wis., D. Atwood, 1882. vi, 430 p. fold. map, ports.   E203.B98

CALLAHAN, NORTH. George Washington, soldier and man. New York, Morrow, 1972. xiii, 296 p. illus.
E312.25.C28

Bibliography: p. [281]–284.

CATLIN, GEORGE B. George Washington looks westward. Michigan history magazine, v. 16, spring 1932: 127–142.　　　　　　　　　F561.M57, v. 16

On the development of a Potomac canal route.

CHINARD, GILBERT, *ed. and tr.* George Washington as the French knew him; a collection of texts. Princeton, Princeton University Press, 1940. xviii, 161 p. plates, ports.　　　　　　　　　　　E312.17.C5

Reprinted in New York by Greenwood Press (1969).

COLEMAN, CHRISTOPHER B. George Washington and the west. Indiana magazine of history, v. 28, Sept. 1932: 151–167.　　　　　　　　　F521.I52, v. 28

COOK, ROY B. Washington's western lands. Strasburg, Va., Shenandoah Pub. House, 1930. xv, 176 p. illus., facsims., maps, port.　　　　　　E312.2.C77

Reviews Washington's interest in and connection with the Ohio Valley and the Old Northwest.

CUNLIFFE, MARCUS. George Washington: George Washington's generalship. *In* Billias, George A., *ed.* George Washington's generals. New York, W. Morrow, 1964. p. 3–21. port.　　　E206.B5

Bibliography: p. 20–21.

—— George Washington, man and monument. Boston, Little, Brown [1958] xiv, 234 p. illus.　　E312.C88

"Further reading": p. [217]–233.

DECATUR, STEPHEN. Private affairs of George Washington, from the records and accounts of Tobias Lear, Esquire, his secretary. Boston, Houghton Mifflin Co., 1933. xv, 356 p. facsims., plates, ports.　　　　　　　　　　　　　　E312.29.D32

Bibliography: p. 335–[337].
Reprinted in New York by Da Capo Press (1969).

FAŸ, BERNARD. George Washington, republican aristocrat. Boston, Houghton Mifflin Co., 1931. xvi, 297 p. illus., maps, plates, ports.　　　E312.F32

Published also in French.
"Sources and notes": p. [275]–286.

FITZPATRICK, JOHN C. George Washington and religion. Catholic historical review, v. 15, Apr. 1929: 23–42.　　　　　　　　　　　　BX1404.C3, v. 15

—— George Washington himself; a common-sense biography written from his manuscripts. Indianapolis, Bobbs-Merrill Co. [c1933] 544 p. port.　　E312.F52

—— Washington's election as first president of the United States. Daughters of the American Revolution magazine, v. 58, Feb. 1924: 69–81. facsims., port.　　　　　　　　　　　　E202.5.A12, v. 58

FLEXNER, JAMES T. George Washington and the new Nation, 1783–1793. Boston, Little, Brown [1970] xi, 466 p. illus., facsims., fold. map, plan, ports.　　　　　　　　　　　　E312.29.F55

Bibliography: p. 431–437.

—— George Washington in the American Revolution, 1775–1783. Boston, Little, Brown [1968] xvii, 599 p. illus., facsims., maps, ports.　　E312.25.F69

Bibliography: p. 557–563.

—— George Washington: the forge of experience, 1732–1775. Boston, Little, Brown [1965] x, 390 p. illus., facsim., map (on lining papers), ports.　E312.2.F6

"Source references": p. 361–377.

—— The trumpet sounds again [1783–89] American heritage, v. 20, Apr. 1969: 65–73. facsims., col. port.　　　　　　　　　　　　E171.A43, v. 20

FORD, PAUL L. The true George Washington. Philadelphia, J. B. Lippincott Co., 1896. 319 p. illus., facsims, maps, plates, ports. [The "true" series]　　　　　　　　　　　　　　E312.F6

Reprinted in Port Washington, N.Y., by Kennikat Press (1970) and in Freeport, N.Y., by Books for Libraries Press (1971).

—— Washington, and the theatre. New-York, Dunlap Society, 1899. 68, 14 p. facsims., plates. (Publications of the Dunlap Society. New ser. no. 8)　　　　　　　　　PN2016.D7, n.s., no. 8
　　　　　　　　　E312.17.F67

[FORD, WORTHINGTON C.] *ed.* Washington as an employer and importer of labor. Brooklyn, N.Y., Priv. print., 1889. 78 p.　　　　E312.17.F69

Contents: Introductory note.—Contract agreements, etc.—Importing Palatines, 1774.—Advertisement of runaway servants.—Form of indenture or covenant for servants.

Reprinted in New York by B. Franklin (1971).

FOX, FREDERIC. Pater patriae as pater familias. American heritage, v. 14, Apr. 1963: 32–37, 100–102. illus., ports. (part col.)　　　　　　　E171.A43, v. 14

FREEMAN, DOUGLAS S. George Washington, a biography. New York, C. Scribner's Sons, 1948–[57] 7 v. facsims., maps, ports.　　　　　E312.F82

Includes bibliographies.
Contents: v. 1–2. Young Washington.—v. 3. Planter and patriot.—v. 4. Leader of the Revolution.—v. 5. Victory with the help of France.—v. 6. Patriot and President.—v. 7. First in peace, by J. A. Carroll and M. W. Ashworth.

Selections from the earlier volumes, made by Freeman, were published under the title *Young Washington* (New York, C. Scribner's Sons, 1966. xxviii, 298 p.), while Richard Harwell prepared an abridgment of the entire seven-volume work entitled *Washington* (New York, C. Scribner's Sons, 1968. xvi, 780 p.).

GARRAGHAN, GILBERT J. George Washington and the Catholics. Historical bulletin, v. 20, Mar.–May 1942: 51–52, 62–66, 77–78, 81–82.　　D1.H28, v. 20

—— George Washington, man of character. Mid-America, v. 17, Jan. 1935: 37–59.　　　　　　　　　BX1415.I3M5, v. 17

HAMILTON, STANISLAUS M., *ed.* Letters to Washington, and accompanying papers. Published by the Society of the Colonial Dames of America. Boston, Houghton, Mifflin, 1898–1902. 5 v. facsims.   E312.2.H22

Contents: v. 1. 1752–1756.—v. 2. 1756–1758.—v. 3. 1758–1770.—v. 4. 1770–1774.—v. 5. 1774–1775. General Index.

HAWORTH, PAUL L. George Washington, country gentleman; being an account of his home life and agricultural activities. Indianapolis, Bobbs-Merrill Co. [°1925] 336 p. facsims., plates.   E312.17.H392

Published 1915 under title: *George Washington, Farmer.*

HIXON, ADA H. George Washington, land speculator. *In* Illinois State Historical Society. Journal, v. 11, Jan. 1919: 566–575.   F536.I18, v. 11

Honor to George Washington and reading about George Washington; pamphlets 1 to 16 complete. Washington, D.C., Published under the direction of the United States George Washington Bicentennial Commission [1932] ix, 198 p. illus., facsims., maps, ports.

E312.H771

"Edited by Dr. Albert Bushnell Hart, authorized by the Congress of the United States."

"Selected authorities" at end of each pamphlet.

Contents: 1. Frontier background of Washington's career, by D. M. Matteson.—2. Washington the man of mind, by Dr. A. B. Hart.—3. Tributes to Washington by Dr. A. B. Hart.—4. Washington the farmer, by D. M. Matteson.—5. Washington as a religious man, by Dr. J. C. Fitzpatrick.—6. Washington the colonial and national statesman, by D. M. Matteson.—7. Washington and the Constitution, by D. M. Matteson.—8. Washington as president, by Dr. A. B. Hart.—9. Washington, proprietor of Mount Vernon, by J. H. Penniman.—10. Washington the military man, by Col. S. C. Vestal.—11. Washington the traveler, by Prof. Archibald Henderson.—12. Washington the business man, by Hon. Sol Bloom.—13. Washington as engineer and city builder, by Lieut. Col. U. S. Grant, 3d.—14. Washington's home and fraternal life, by C. H. Claudy.—15. Not in print.—16. Classified Washington bibliography [382 items], by committee of American Library Association.

HOWE, HERBERT B. Colonel George Washington and King's College. Columbia University quarterly, v. 24, June 1932: 137–157.   LH1.C7Q2, v. 24

Includes a mixed selection of letters and diary entries by Washington, Jonathan Boucher, and Myles Cooper, 1768–74, concerning Washington's selection of the college for his stepson, John Parke Custis.

HUGHES, RUPERT. George Washington. New York, W. Morrow, 1926–30. 3 v. illus., facsims., maps, plans, ports.   E312.H924

"Books consulted and quoted": v. 1, p. 565–572; v. 2, p. 675–683; v. 3, p. 796–810.

Contents: [v. 1] The human being & the hero, 1732–1762.—[v. 2] The rebel & the patriot, 1762–1777.—[v. 3] The savior of the states, 1777–1781.

See also the author's "Pitfalls of the Biographer" in the *Pacific Historical Review*, v. 2, Mar. 1933, p. 1–33.

IRVING, WASHINGTON. Life of George Washington. New York, G. P. Putnam, 1855–59. 5 v. illus., facsims., maps, ports.   E312.I6

JACKSON, DONALD D. The papers of George Washington. Manuscripts, v. 22, Winter 1970: 2–11. illus., facsim.   Z41.A2A925, v. 22

JACKSON, JOSEPH. Washington in Philadelphia. Pennsylvania magazine of history and biography, v. 56, Apr. 1932: 110–155.   F146.P65, v. 56

Between 1756 and 1798, Washington made 36 visits to Philadelphia.

JOHNSON, BRADLEY T. General Washington. New York, D. Appleton, 1894. x, 388 p. maps, plans, port. (Great commanders)   E312.J66

JOHNSTON, ELIZABETH B. George Washington day by day. Washington, D.C., 1894. xv, 207 p. plates, port.   E312.15.J73

Brief extracts from Washington's writings and other sources and accounts of events in his life, arranged in the form of a calendar. A later compilation by David M. Matteson, *George Washington Every Day; a Calendar of Events and Principles of His Entire Lifetime*, was published by the United States George Washington Bicentennial Commission (Washington, 1933).

KINNAIRD, CLARK. George Washington, the pictorial biography. New York, Hastings House [1967] vi, 265 p. illus., facsims., maps, plans, ports.

E312.K56

Bibliography: p. 255–256.

KNOLLENBERG, BERNHARD. George Washington, the Virginia period, 1732–1775. Durham, N.C., Duke University Press, 1964. x, 238 p.   E312.2.K56

Bibliography: p. [197]–210.

KNOX, JAMES H. MASON. The medical history of George Washington, his physicians, friends, and advisers. Bulletin of the Institute of the history of medicine, v. 1, June 1933: 174–191.   R11.B93, v. 1

LEWIS, FIELDING O. Washington's last illness. Annals of medical history, new ser., v. 4, May 1932: 245–248.   R11.A85, n.s., v. 4

LIPPINCOTT, HORACE M. George Washington and the University of Pennsylvania. General magazine and historical chronicle, v. 28, Jan. 1926: 153–174.   LH1.P3A4, v. 28

LODGE, HENRY C. George Washington. Boston, Houghton Mifflin, 1891. 2 v. (American statesmen, [v. 4–5])   E312.L82

LOSSING, BENSON J. Life of Washington; a biography, personal, military, and political. New York, Virtue [1860] 3 v. illus., maps, ports.   E312.L88

The work was originally planned by Rufus W. Griswold, who selected the subjects for a greater portion of the illustrations and wrote about 200 pages.

LOWE, DAVID G. A son's tribute. American heritage, v. 17, Feb. 1966: 16–21, 85–87. illus. (part col.), ports (part col.) E171.A43, v. 17

On three long-lost paintings by George Washington Parke Custis of his foster father in action at Germantown, Trenton, and Princeton.

MARSHALL, JOHN, comp. The life of George Washington, Commander in Chief of the American forces, during the war which established the independence of his country, and first President of the United States. Philadelphia, Printed and Published by C. P. Wayne, 1804–7. 5 v. port. E312.M33

Reprinted in New York by AMS Press (1969).
——— Atlas to Marshall' Life of Washington. Philadelphia, Published by J. Crissy [18—] 10 double maps. G1201.S3M3 1807 G&M

MARTIN, LAWRENCE, ed. The George Washington atlas. A collection of eighty-five maps including twenty-eight made by George Washington, seven used and annotated by him, eight made at his direction, or for his use or otherwise associated with him, and forty-two new maps concerning his activities in peace and war and his place in history. Washington, D.C., United States George Washington Bicentennial Commission, 1932. [4] p. 50 plates (40 col.) incl. 85 maps. G1201.S3M34 1932 G&M

Plate 1, front lining paper; plate 50 (continued), back lining paper.

Contains a list of 110 maps and associated drawings made or annotated by George Washington.

MARX, RUDOLPH. A medical profile of George Washington. American heritage, v. 6, Aug. 1955: 42–47, 106–107. illus., facsim., col. port. E171.A43, v. 6

Analyzing Washington's medical history, the author concludes that by today's standards Washington would be considered unfit for military duty.

MAYO, BERNARD. George Washington. Georgia review, v. 13, summer 1959: 135–150. AP2.G375, v. 13

An assessment of Washington's mythic character.

MAZYCK, WALTER H. George Washington and the Negro. Washington, D.C., Associated Publishers [c1932] vii, 180 p. E312.17.M38

MERRIAM, GEORGE E., comp. More precious than fine gold; Washington commonplace book. Collectors' ed. New York, G. P. Putnam's Sons, 1931. ix, 428 p. front., ports. E312.17.M49

Bibliography: p. 419–428.
Extracts from the writings of various authors concerning Washington, and from Washington's own writings.

MEYER, FREEMAN W. George Washington as a popular leader: relations with obscure people. 1951.

Thesis (Ph.D.)—Cornell University.

MOORE, ROBERT WALTON. George Washington as a judge and his attitude toward courts and lawyers. American Bar Association journal, v. 18, Mar. 1932: 151–155. K1.M385, v. 18

On Washington as a justice of the peace for Fairfax County, 1768–74.

MORGAN, JOHN H., and MANTLE FIELDING. The life portraits of Washington and their replicas. Philadelphia, Printed for the subscribers; [Lancaster, Pa., Lancaster Press, c1931] xxiii, 432 p. plates, (part col.), ports. E312.43.M85 Rare Bk. Coll. N7623.W3M6

See also "The Portraits of Washington" in Justin Winsor's *Narrative and Critical History of America*, v. 7 (Boston, Houghton, Mifflin [1888]), p. [563]–582, and Charles H. Hart's *Catalogue of the Engraved Portraits of Washington* (New York, Grolier Club, 1904. 406 p. E312.43.H32 Rare Bk. Coll.).

MORISON, SAMUEL E. The young man Washington. Cambridge, Mass., Harvard University Press, 1932. 43 p. E312.17.M86

Attributes Washington's later success to the discipline and stoic faith acquired in his youth.

MORRIS, RICHARD B. Washington and Hamilton: a great collaboration. *In* American Philosophical Society, *Philadelphia*. Proceedings, v. 102, Apr. 1958: 107–116. Q11.P5, v. 102

NETTELS, CURTIS P. George Washington and American independence. Boston, Little, Brown, 1951. 338 p. maps, ports. E312.25.N4

Bibliography: p. [313]–324.

——— The Washington theme in American history. *In* Massachusetts Historical Society, *Boston*. Proceedings. v. 68; 1944/47. Boston, 1952. p. 171–198. F61.M38, v. 68

O'CONNOR, THOMAS F. Materials on the life of George Washington; a bibliographical guide. Americas, v. 2, Oct. 1945: 220–225. E11.A4, v. 2

An annotated survey of over 50 sources.

PADOVER, SAUL K. George Washington: portrait of a true conservative. Social research, v. 22, summer 1955: 199–222. H1.S53, v. 22

PARKE, JOHN. [Ode to Washington] Virginia: a pastoral drama, on the birth-day of an illustrious personage and the return of peace, February 11th, 1784. Philadelphia, Printed by E. Oswald, at the Coffee-House, 1776 [i.e. 1786] Tarrytown, N.Y., Reprinted, W. Abbatt, 1923. [35]–62 p. (The Magazine of history, with notes and queries. Extra number, no. 91, [pt. 2]) E173.M24, no. 91

An "ode which celebrated the return of Augustus from Spain is made to apply to Washington's victorious return from the Yorktown campaign. It is the earliest-known attempt to celebrate Washington's birthday, which is here given according to the old style, as February 11th."—Editor's preface.

PARTON, ROBERT. The changing images of George Washington from Weems to Freeman. Social studies, v. 56, Feb. 1965: 52–59. D16.3.S65, v. 56

PAULDING, JAMES K. A life of Washington. New-York, Harper, 1835. 2 v. plates, port. (The Family library, no. 75–76) E312.P32

The 1858 edition has been reprinted in Port Washington, N.Y., by Kennikat Press (1970).

PAXSON, FREDERIC L. Washington and the western fronts, 1753–1795. *In* Illinois State Historical Society. Journal, v. 24, Jan. 1932: 589–605. F536.I18, v. 24

PETERSON, RAYMOND G. George Washington, capitalistic farmer: a documentary study of Washington's business activities and the sources of his wealth. 1970. ([204] p.) Micro AC–1, no. 70–26,348

Thesis (Ph.D.)—Ohio State University.
Abstracted in *Dissertation Abstracts International*, v. 31A, Jan. 1971, p. 3449.

PHILLIPS, PHILIP LEE. Washington as surveyor and map-maker. Daughters of the American Revolution magazine, v. 55, Mar. 1921: 115–132. facsims., maps, port. E202.5.A12, v. 55

——— ———Detached copy. E312.17.P54

PICKELL, JOHN. A new chapter in the early life of Washington, in connection with the narrative history of the Potomac Company. New York, D. Appleton, 1856. 178 p. E312.29.P59

Reprinted in New York by B. Franklin (1970).

POWELL, JOHN H. General Washington and the jack ass. South Atlantic quarterly, v. 52, Apr. 1953: 238–252. AP2.S75, v. 52

RAMSAY, DAVID. The life of George Washington, Commander in Chief of the armies of the United States of America, throughout the war which established their independence; and first President of the United States. New-York, Printed by Hopkins & Seymour, 1807. viii, 376 p. port. E312.R13 Rare Bk. Coll.

RICHARDS, GERTRUDE. New letters of George Washington to Benjamin Lincoln. Harvard Library bulletin, v. 10, winter 1956: 39–72. facsims. Z881.H3403, v. 10

Includes a calendar of the 55 pieces in the Galen L. Stone collection and the text of seven letters not published in the Fitzpatrick edition of Washington's letters.

RITTER, HALSTED L. Washington as a business man. With an introduction by Albert Bushnell Hart. New York, Sears Pub. Co. [c1931] 308 p. facsims., plan, port. E312.17.R66

Bibliography: p. 291–295.

SAWYER, JOSEPH D. Washington. New York, Macmillan Co., 1927. 2 v. illus., facsims., ports. E312.S27

Contains over 1,500 illustrations, one-sixth of them portraits.

SEARS, LOUIS M. George Washington. New York, Thomas Y. Crowell Co. [c1932] xiv, 560 p. maps, port. E312.S44

"Bibliographical note": p. 523–525.

SIFTON, PAUL G. The Walker-Washington map [1769] *In* U.S. *Library of Congress.* Quarterly journal, v. 24, Apr. 1967: 90–96. illus., maps. Z881.U49A3, v. 24

A rare map of the "Aligany" region, in Washington's hand, now in the Library's collections.

SMITH, GUY H. Washington's camp sites on the Ohio River [1770] Ohio archaeological and historical quarterly, v. 41, Jan. 1932: 1–19. fold map. F486.O51, v. 41

SMITH, JAMES M., *comp.* George Washington; a profile. New York, Hill and Wang [1969] xxx, 289 p. (American profiles) E312.S64

Bibliography: p. 286–289.
Includes writings by Dixon Wecter, Samuel E. Morison, Curtis P. Nettels, James T. Flexner, Douglas S. Freeman, Harold W. Bradley, Paul F. Boller, Esmond Wright, Leonard D. White, Alexander DeConde, and Daniel J. Boorstin.

SPARKS, JARED, *ed.* Correspondence of the American Revolution, being letters of eminent men to George Washington, from the time of his taking command of the Army to the end of his presidency. Boston, Little, Brown, 1853. 4 v. E203.S73

Reprinted in Freeport, N.Y., by Books for Libraries Press (1970).

Special George Washington bicentennial meeting of the American Historical Association. *In* American Historical Association. Annual report. 1932. Washington, 1934. p. 95–148. E172.A60, 1932

The significance to the historian of the new bicentennial edition of the *Writings* of George Washington, by John C. Fitzpatrick.—Washington and committees at headquarters, by Edmund C. Burnett.—The Potomac environment of George Washington, by Charles Moore.—George Washington, nationalist, by William E. Dodd.

STEPHENSON, NATHANIEL W. The romantics and George Washington. American historical review, v. 39, Jan. 1934: 274–283. E171.A57, v. 39

On literary treatment of the Sally Fairfax affair.

STRYKER-RODDA, KENN. George Washington and Long Island. Journal of Long Island history, v. 1, spring 1961: 8–20. F127.L8J75, v. 1

TONER, JOSEPH M. George Washington as an inventor and promoter of the useful arts. Washington, D.C., Press of Gedney & Roberts Co., 1892. 69, [7] p. E312.17.T66

Reprint from *Proceedings* of the Patent Centennial Congress, held in Washington, D.C. 1891.

——— Some account of George Washington's library and manuscript records and their dispersion from Mount

Vernon, with an excerpt of three months from his diary in 1774 while attending the First Continental Congress, with notes. *In* American Historical Association. Annual report. 1892. Washington, 1893. p. 71–169.
E172.A60, 1892

TROUBETZKOY, ULRICH. Mount Vernon: "heart of America." Virginia cavalcade, v. 11, winter 1961/62: 4–13. illus., ports. F221.V74, v. 11

U.S. *Library of Congress. Manuscript Division.* Calendar of the correspondence of George Washington, Commander in Chief of the Continental Army, with the Continental Congress. Prepared from the original manuscripts in the Library of Congress by John C. Fitzpatrick, Division of Manuscripts. Washington, Govt. Print. Off., 1906. 741 p. illus., facsims. (Washington papers, 1) Z6616.W3U47
Z6621.U58W24
Z663.34.C27

Reprinted in New York by B. Franklin (1970).

—— Calendar of the correspondence of George Washington, Commander in Chief of the Continental Army, with the officers . . . Prepared from the original manuscripts in the Library of Congress by John C. Fitzpatrick, Division of Manuscripts. Washington, Govt. Print. Off., 1915. 4 v. (Washington papers, 2)
Z6616.W3U48
Z6621.U58W25
Z663.34.C28

Contents: 1. June 17, 1775–October 19, 1778.—2. October 19, 1778–December 9, 1780.—3. December 9, 1780–January 4, 1784.—4. Index.

—— Index to the George Washington papers. Washington [For sale by the Supt. of Docs., U.S. Govt. Print. Off.] 1964. xxxi, 294 p. (*Its* Presidents' papers index series) Z8950.U64
Z663.34.W34

The introduction, prepared by Dorothy S. Eaton, was reprinted with minor revisions in the *Quarterly Journal* of the Library of Congress, v. 22, Jan. 1965, p. 3–26.

—— List of the Washington manuscripts from the year 1592 to 1775. Prepared from the original manuscripts in the Library of Congress by John C. Fitzpatrick, assistant chief, Manuscript Division. Washington, Govt. Print. Off., 1919. 137 p. Z6616.W3U7
Z663.34.W35

WHIPPLE, WAYNE. Washington's sense of humor. Century magazine, v. 81, Mar. 1911: 785–790.
AP2.C4, v. 81

WILSON, SAMUEL M. George Washington's contacts with Kentucky. Filson Club history quarterly, v. 6, July 1932: 215–260. F446.F484, v. 6

WOODWARD, WILLIAM E. George Washington, the image and the man. New York, Boni and Liveright, 1926. 460, xiii–xxxv p. facsim., plan, ports. E312.W896
Bibliography: p. xiii–xxvi.
Reissued in 1946 and 1972.

WRIGHT, ESMOND. Washington and the American Revolution. London, English Universities Press [1957] 192 p. maps (on lining papers) (Teach yourself history library) E312.25.W73

—— Washington, the man and the myth. History today, v. 5, Dec. 1955: 825–832. illus., ports.
D1.H818, v. 5

14675

WASHINGTON, MARTHA DANDRIDGE CUSTIS (1731–1802)
Virginia. Wife of George Washington (1732–1799).

KIMBALL, MARIE G. The Martha Washington cook book. New York City, Coward-McCann, 1940. 212 p. illus., facsims., plan (on lining papers), port. TX703.K5

THANE, ELSWYTH. Washington's lady. New York, Dodd, Mead, 1960. xv, 368 p. col. port. E312.19.W95T48
"A bibliographical note": p. 353–356.

WHARTON, ANNE H. Martha Washington. New York, C. Scribner's Sons, 1897. xiv, 306 p. fold. facsim., port. (Women of colonial and Revolutionary times)
E312.19.W95W5

Bibliography: p. ix–x.
Reprinted in Spartanburg, S.C., by Reprint Co. (1967).

14676

WASHINGTON, MARY BALL (1708–1789)
Virginia. Mother of George Washington (1732–1799).

LOSSING, BENSON J. Mary and Martha, the mother and the wife of George Washington. Illustrated by facsimiles of pen-and-ink drawings by H. Rosa. New York, Harper, 1886. xx, 348 p. illus., plates, ports.
E312.19.L89

THOMAS, AUGUSTA D. Mary Ball—the mother of Washington. Picket post, no. 39, Jan. 1953: 4–9, 11. port. E234.P5, no. 39

14677

WASHINGTON, SAMUEL (1734–1781)
Virginia. Planter, Revolutionary officer.

WAYLAND, JOHN W. Colonel Samuel Washington, oldest full brother of General George Washington. Americana, v. 32, Apr. 1938: 305–330. maps, plates.
E171.A53, v. 32

14678

WASHINGTON, WILLIAM (1752–1810)
Virginia; South Carolina. Revolutionary officer.

WASHINGTON, ELLA B. William Washington, Lieut.-Colonel Third Light Dragoons, Continental Army. Magazine of American history, with notes and queries, v. 9, Feb. 1883: 94–106. E171.M18, v. 9

14679

WASMUS, JULIUS FRIEDRICH
Hessian surgeon and barber in America.

NADEAU, GABRIEL. A German military surgeon in Rutland, Massachusetts, during the Revolution: Julius Friedrich Wasmus. Bulletin of the history of medicine, v. 18, Oct. 1945: 243–300.   R11.B93, v. 18

14680

WATERHOUSE, BENJAMIN (1754–1846)*
Rhode Island; Massachusetts. Physician, professor.

TRENT, JOSIAH C. Benjamin Waterhouse (1754–1846). Journal of the history of medicine and allied sciences, v. 1, July 1946: 357–364. port.   R131.A1J6, v. 1

—— The London years of Benjamin Waterhouse. Journal of the history of medicine and allied sciences, v. 1, Jan. 1946: 25–40. facsims., ports.   R131.A1J6, v. 1

14681

WATKINS, JOEL (b. 1758)
Virginia. Revolutionary soldier.

——Joel Watkins' [travel] diary of 1789. Edited by Virginia Smith Herold. In Kentucky Historical Society. Register, v. 34, July 1936: 215–250. F446.K43, v. 34

14682

WATSON, ELKANAH (1758–1842)*
Massachusetts; North Carolina. Merchant, traveler, planter.

—— "The first American flag hoisted in old England." William and Mary quarterly, 3d ser., v. 11, July 1954: 434–439.   F221.W71, 3d s., v. 11

Watson witnessed George III's recognition of the independence of the American states at the opening of Parliament, December 5, 1782. Introduction and notes by Jane Carson.

—— Men and times of the Revolution; or, Memoirs of Elkanah Watson, including his journals of travels in Europe and America, from the year 1777 to 1842, and his correspondence with public men, and reminiscences and incidents of the American Revolution. Edited by his son, Winslow C. Watson. 2d ed., with a portrait of the author, engraved on steel, after the . . . portrait by Copley, and twenty wood engravings. New York, Dana, 1857. 557 p.   E164.W34

DEANE, WILLIAM R. Memoir of Elkanah Watson. New England historical and genealogical register, v. 17, Apr. 1863: 97–105. port.   F1.N56, v. 17

FLICK, HUGH M. Elkanah Watson: gentleman-promotor, 1758–1842. 1947. ([363] p.)
        Micro AC–1, no. 59–732

Thesis (Ph.D.)—Columbia University.
Abstracted in *Dissertation Abstracts*, v. 19, Mar. 1959, p. 2216.

PARRAMORE, THOMAS C. A year in Hertford County with Elkanah Watson [1787–88] North Carolina historical review, v. 41, autumn 1964: 448–463. facsim., map, ports.   F251.N892, v. 41

VAN WAGENEN, JARED. Elkanah Watson—a man of affairs. In New York State Historical Association. New York history, v. 13, Oct. 1932: 404–412.
        F116.N865, v. 13

14683

WATSON, THOMAS (1753–1811)
England; New England. British soldier in America.

BROCK, PETER. The spiritual pilgrimage of Thomas Watson: from British soldier to American Friend. Quaker history, v. 53, autumn 1964: 81–86.
        BX7635.A1F6, v. 53

Derived from Watson's own work, *Some Account of the Life, Convincement, and Religious Experience of Thomas Watson, Late of Bolton, Massachusetts* (New York, 1836), a second edition of which appeared in 1861.

14684

WATTERS, WILLIAM (1751–1827)
Maryland; Virginia. Methodist clergyman.

—— A short account of the Christian experience and ministereal labours, of William Watters. Alexandria [Va.] Printed by S. Snowden [1806?] 142 p.
        BX8495.W325A3 Rare Bk. Coll.

Preface dated Fairfax, May 14, 1806.

WATTERS, DENNIS A. First American itinerant of Methodism, William Watters. Introduction by Bishop Charles C. McCabe. Cincinnati, Printed for the author by Curts & Jennings, 1898. 172 p.
        BX8495.W325W3

14685

WATTS, JOHN (1715–1789)
New York; England. Landowner, assemblyman, councilor, Loyalist.

—— Letter book of John Watts, merchant and councillor of New York, January 1, 1762–December 22, 1765. New York, Printed for the Society, 1928. xvi, 448 p. (New York Historical Society. Collections, 1928. The John Watts De Peyster publication fund series, [v. 61])
        F116.N63, 1928

Transcribed and edited by Dorothy C. Barck.

14686

WAYNE, ANTHONY (1745–1796)*
Pennsylvania. Surveyor, Revolutionary general, assemblyman.

BOYD, THOMAS A. Mad Anthony Wayne. New York, C. Scribner's Sons, 1929. 351 p. maps, port.
E207.W35B78

Bibliography: p. 339–341.

DUNN, FREDERIC S. The classical origins of "Mad Anthony" Wayne's sobriquet. Pennsylvania history, v. 2, July 1935: 172–177.   F146.P597, v. 2

HEATHCOTE, CHARLES W. Anthony Wayne re-appraisal. Picket post, no. 45, July 1954: 4–9. port.
E234.P5, no. 45

PRATT, FLETCHER. Last of the Romans. Infantry journal, v. 45, Sept./Oct. 1938: 433–441. facsim., maps, ports.
UD1.I6, v. 45

PRESTON, JOHN H. A gentleman rebel; the exploits of Anthony Wayne. New York, Farrar & Rinehart, 1930. xi, 370 p. maps, plates, ports.   E207.W35P93

Bibliography: p. 349–359.

RANKIN, HUGH F. Anthony Wayne: military romanticist. In Billias, George A., ed. George Washington's generals. New York, W. Morrow, 1964. p. 260–290. port.   E206.B5

Bibliography: p. 290.

SPEARS, JOHN R. Anthony Wayne, sometimes called "Mad Anthony." New York, D. Appleton, 1903. 249 p. fold. map, plates, port. (Appletons' historic lives)   E207.W35S7

STILLÉ, CHARLES J. Major-General Anthony Wayne and the Pennsylvania Line in the Continental Army. Philadelphia, J. B. Lippincott Co., 1893. x, 441 p. plates, port.   E207.W35S8

Reprinted in Port Washington, N.Y., by Kennikat Press (1968).

WILDES, HARRY E. Anthony Wayne, trouble shooter of the American Revolution. New York, Harcourt, Brace [c1941] 514 p. maps, port.   E207.W35W5

Bibliography: p. 489–501.
Reprinted in Westport, Conn., by Greenwood Press (1970).

14687
WEARE, MESHECH (1713–1786)*
New Hampshire. Farmer, assemblyman, judge, councilor, governor.

BUTTERS, AVERY J. New Hampshire and the public career of Meshech Weare, 1713 to 1786. 1961. ([310] p.)
Micro AC–1, no. 61–1566
Thesis (Ph.D.)—Fordham University.
Abstracted in Dissertation Abstracts, v. 21, May. 1960, p. 3431.

STEARNS, EZRA S. Meshech Weare. Magazine of history, with notes and queries, v. 6, July 1907: 41–54.
E171.M23, v. 6

—— A monograph: Meshech Weare. Priv. print. Concord, N.H., Republican Press Association, 1894. 22 p.
F38.W36

14688
WEBB, GEORGE (1740–1825)
Massachusetts. Revolutionary officer.

PAINE, JOSIAH. A brief sketch of the life of George Webb, a Cape Cod captain in the Revolutionary War. Yarmouthport, Mass., C. W. Swift, 1914. 11 p. (Library of Cape Cod history & genealogy, no. 52)   E275.W37

14689
WEBB, SAMUEL BLACHLEY (1753–1807)
Connecticut; New York. Revolutionary general.

—— Correspondence and journals. Collected and edited by Worthington Chauncey Ford. New York [Lancaster, Pa., Wickersham Press] 1893. 3 v. facsims., maps (part fold.), plates, ports.   E203.W36
Includes letters written and received by Webb, with others which merely relate to his career.
Contents: 1. 1772–1777.—2. 1778–1782.—3. 1783–1806. Biographical sketch of Samuel Blachley Webb.
Reprinted in New York by the New York Times (1969).

STEVENS, JOHN A. Samuel Blatchley Webb, colonel in the Connecticut Line and brevet brigadier general in the Continental Army. Magazine of American history, with notes and queries, v. 4, June 1880: 427–440.
E171.M18, v. 4

WEBB, JAMES W. Reminiscences of Gen'l Samuel B. Webb, of the Revolutionary Army. New York, Globe Stationery and Print. Co., 1882. 402, x p. illus., plates, port.   E207.W36W3

Imperfect copy; p. 46–48 wanting.
A collection of some of the letters and correspondence of General Webb and of Silas Deane, published exclusively for family circulation.
Biographical sketch of General Webb, by J. A. Stevens, reprinted from the Historical Magazine, June, 1880, p. 88–102.

14690
WEBSTER, NOAH (1758–1843)*
Connecticut. Lawyer, teacher, schoolbook writer.

—— Letters. Edited with an introduction by Harry R. Warfel. New York, Library Publishers [1953] xlvi, 562 p.   PE64.W5A4

—— On being American, selected writings, 1783–1828. Edited and with an introduction by Homer D. Babbidge, Jr. New York, Praeger [1967] vii, 184 p. facsims., port.   E169.1.W32

Includes bibliographic references.
Six of the 12 selections were written between 1783 and 1789.

BROMBERGER, BONNIE. Noah Webster's notes on his early political essays in the *Connecticut Courant*. *In* New York (City). Public Library. Bulletin, v. 74, May 1970: 338–342.　　　　　　　　　Z881.N6B, v. 74

FORD, EMILY E. F. *comp*. Notes on the life of Noah Webster. Edited by Emily Ellsworth Ford Skeel. New York, Priv. print., 1912. 2 v. facsim., plates, ports.
　　　　　　　　　PE64.W5F7 Rare Bk. Coll.

"Check list of the writings of Noah Webster": v. 2, p. [523]–540.

"Authorities cited": v. 2, p. [541]–544.

Reprinted in New York by B. Franklin (1971).

ROSEN, GEORGE. Noah Webster—historical epidemiologist. Journal of the history of medicine and allied sciences, v. 20, Apr. 1965: 97–114.
　　　　　　　　　R131.A1J6, v. 20

SKEEL, EMILY E. F. A bibliography of the writings of Noah Webster. Edited by Edwin H. Carpenter, Jr. New York, New York Public Library [1971, ˢ1958] xxxix, 655 p. illus.　　　Z8961.5.S5 1971

WARFEL, HARRY R. Noah Webster, schoolmaster to America. New York, Macmillan Co., 1936. xiii, 460 p. facsims., plates, ports.　　　　　PE64.W5W3

"Sources and bibliography": p. [439]–449.

Reprinted in New York by Octagon Books (1966).

14691

WEBSTER, PELATIAH (1726–1795)*

Connecticut. Clergyman, merchant, essayist.

—— Journal of a voyage to Charlestown in So. Carolina by Pelatiah Webster in 1765. Edited by Prof. T. P. Harrison. *In* Southern History Association. Publications. v. 2. Washington, D.C., 1898. p. [131]–148.
　　　　　　　　　F206.S73, v. 2

—— —— Detached copy.　　　F279.C4W3

—— A plea for the poor soldiers; An essay, to demonstrate that the soldiers and other public creditors, who really and actually supported the burden of the late war, have not been paid! Ought to be paid! Can be paid! And must be paid! By a citizen of Philadelphia. Philadelphia, Printed by Francis Bailey [1790] 39 p.
　　　　　　　　　E255.W38 Rare Bk. Coll.
　　　　　　　　　JA36.P8, v. 96 Rare Bk. Coll.

TAYLOR, HANNIS. The designer of the Constitution of the United States. North American review, v. 185, Aug. 1907: 813–824.　　　　　AP2.N7 v. 185

—— A memorial in behalf of the architect of our Federal Constitution, Pelatiah Webster, of Philadelphia, Pa. [Washington, Govt. Print. Off., 1908] 53 p. ([U.S.] 60th Congress, 1st session. Senate. Doc. 461)
　　　　　　　　　JK148.W4T3 1908

"Pelatiah Webster's invention and the second Federal Constitution of 1787": p. 13–21.

"A dissertation on the political union and constitution of the thirteen United States of North America . . . (first published in Philadelphia 1783)": p. 23–49.

"Notes appended by Pelatiah Webster to the republication made at Philadelphia in 1791": p. 50–53.

See also Gaillard Hunt's *Pelatiah Webster and the Constitution; an Article Prepared by Gaillard Hunt and Published in "The Nation"* of December 28, 1911 (Washington, Govt. Print, Off., 1912. 8 p. [U.S.] 62d Congress, 2d session. Senate. Doc. 402. JK148.W4H8) and Hannis Taylor's rebuttal, *The Real Authorship of the Constitution of the United States Explained; James Madison and Pelatiah Webster Defended by Hannis Taylor Against Attacks . . . by Gaillard Hunt* (Washington [Govt. Print. Off.] 1912. 87 p. [U.S.] 62d Congress, 2d session. Senate. Doc. 787. JK148.W4T33). For a refutation of Taylor's thesis, see Edward S. Corwin's essay, "The Pelatiah Webster Myth," in his work, *The Doctrine of Judicial Review, Its Legal and Historical Basis, and Other Essays* (Princeton, Princeton University Press, 1914. JK1541.C7), p. [109]–126. The essay first appeared in the *Michigan Law Review* for June 1912.

—————Pelatiah Webster's invention of February 16, 1783. *In his* The origin and growth of the American Constitution; an historical treatise in which the documentary evidence as to the making of the entirely new plan of federal government embodied in the existing Constitution of the United States is, for the first time, set forth as a complete and consistent whole. Boston, Houghton Mifflin Co., 1911. p. 139–163.　JK268.T3

14692

WEDDERBURN, DAVID (1740–1772)

Scotland; West Florida. British military officer.

REA, ROBERT R. Outpost of empire: David Wedderburn at Mobile. Alabama review, v. 7, July 1954: 217–232.
　　　　　　　　　F321.A2535, v. 7

14693

WEDGWOOD, JOSIAH (1730–1795)†

England. Potter, manufacturer.

HOWER, RALPH M. The Wedgwoods, ten generations of potters. pt. 1. 1612–1795. Journal of economic and business history, v. 4, Feb. 1932: 281–313.
　　　　　　　　　HC10.J6, v. 4

MCKENDRICK, NEIL. Josiah Wedgwood: an eighteenth-century entrepreneur in salesmanship and marketing techniques. Economic history review, 2d ser., v. 12, Apr. 1960: 408–433.　　HC10.E4, 2d s., v. 12

—— Josiah Wedgwood and cost accounting in the Industrial Revolution. Economic history review, 2d ser., v. 23, Apr. 1970: 45–67.　　HC10.E4, 2d s., v. 23

—— Josiah Wedgwood and factory discipline. Historical journal, v. 4, no. 1, 1961: 30–55.　　D1.H33, v. 4

—— Josiah Wedgwood and Thomas Bentley: an inventor-entrepreneur partnership in the Industrial Revolution. *In* Royal Historical Society, *London*. Transactions. 5th ser., v. 14; 1964. London. p. 1–33.
DA20.R9, 5th s., v. 14

WEDGWOOD, HENSLEIGH C. Josiah Wedgwood, eighteenth-century manager. Explorations in entreprenurial history, 2d ser., v. 2. spring/summer 1965: 205–226.
HB615.E8, 2d s., v. 2

14694

WEEDON, GEORGE (*ca.* 1734–1793)
Virginia. Innkeeper, Revolutionary general.

American Philosophical Society, *Philadelphia. Library.* Calendar of the correspondence of Brigadier-General George Weedon, U.S.A., with celebrated characters of the American Revolution. In the Library of the American Philosophical Society. Prepared under the direction of the Committee on Historical Manuscripts. *In its* Proceedings, v. 38, Jan. 1899: 81–114.
Q11.P5, v. 38

Also published in a volume with two other calendars (see no. 708).

KING, GEORGE H. S. General George Weedon. William and Mary College quarterly historical magazine, 2d ser., v. 20, Apr. 1940: 237–252. illus.
F221.W71, 2d s., v. 20

14695

WEEKS, JOSHUA WINGATE (1738–1806)
Massachusetts; Nova Scotia. Clergyman, Loyalist chaplain.

—— Journal of Rev. Joshua Wingate Weeks, Loyalist rector of St. Michael's Church, Marblehead, 1778–1779. *In* Essex Institute, *Salem, Mass.* Historical collections, v. 52, Jan.–Oct. 1916: 1–16, 161–176, 197–208, 345–356. illus. F72.E7E81, v. 52

14696

WEEKS, WILLIAM (1755–1843)
New Hampshire. Revolutionary officer.

—— Five straws gathered from Revolutionary fields, by Hiram Bingham, J^{un}. Cambridge, Mass. [University Press] 1901. 39 p. E275.W39

Five letters written by William Weeks, 1777–8. The letters relate principally to the Saratoga campaign and experiences at Valley Forge.

14697

WEEMS, MASON LOCKE (1759–1825)*
Maryland; Virginia. Anglican clergyman, itinerant bookseller, biographer.

—— The life of Benjamin Franklin; with many choice anecdotes and admirable sayings of this great man, nev-
er before published by any of his biographers. 5th ed., greatly enl. Baltimore, Printed by J. D. Toy, for the author, 1820. 264 p. port.
E302.6.F8W32 Rare Bk. Coll.

—— The life of General Francis Marion, a celebrated partisan officer, in the Revolutionary War, against the British and Tories in South Carolina and Georgia, by Brig. Gen. P. Horry, of Marion's brigade, and M. L. Weems. Philadelphia, J. B. Lippincott, 1884. 252 p. plates. E207.M3W3 1884

First published in 1809.
"Though bearing Horry's name on the title-page, this was . . . the production of Weems, to whom Horry . . . furnished the materials."—*Cyclopaedia of American Literature*, v. 1 (Philadelphia, T. E. Zell, 1875), by Evert A. Duyckinck and George L. Duyckinck. See also "[Gen. Peter] Horry's [corrective] notes to Weems's *Life of Marion*" in the *South Carolina Historical Magazine*, v. 60, July 1959, p. 119–122.

—— The life of George Washington; with curious anecdotes, equally honourable to himself and exemplary to his young countrymen. 9th ed., greatly improved. Philadelphia, Printed for M. Carey, 1809. 228 p. fold. map, plates, port. E312.W37 Rare Bk. Coll.

A text based on this edition, with introduction and notes by Marcus Cunliffe, was published in Cambridge, Mass., by the Belknap Press of Harvard University Press (1962).

BRYAN, WILLIAM A. The genesis of Weems' "Life of Washington." Americana, v. 36, Apr. 1942: 147–165.
E171.A53, v. 36

MERRITT, ARTHUR H. Did Parson Weems really invent the cherry-tree story? *In* New York Historical Society. Quarterly, v. 40, July 1956: 252–263. illus., port.
F116.N638, v. 40

VAN TASSEL, DAVID D. The legend maker. American heritage, v. 13, Feb. 1962: 58–59, 89–94. illus. (part col.), facsims. E171.A43, v. 13

WROTH, LAWRENCE C. Parson Weems; a biographical and critical study. Baltimore, Md., Eichelberger Book Co., 1911. 104 p. facsim., plates, port.
E302.6.W4W9

14698

WEISSENFELS, FREDERICK (*ca.* 1728–1806)
New York. Revolutionary officer.

POUCHER, JOHN WILSON. Dutchess County men of the Revolutionary period: Colonel Frederick Weissenfels. *In* Dutchess County Historical Society. Year book. v. 27; 1942. Poughkeepsie. p. 74–84.
F127.D8D93, v. 27

14699

WELLES, ROGER (1753–1795)
Connecticut. Revolutionary officer.

—— The Revolutionary war letters of Captain Roger Welles of Wethersfield and Newington, Connecticut, with four such letters from three Newington soldiers. Hartford, Priv. print., 1932. 40 p.   E275.W43

Biographical sketch of Roger Welles, signed by Edwin Stanley Welles: p. [3]–7.

14700

WENTWORTH, BENNING (1696–1770)*

New Hampshire. Royal governor.

LOONEY, JOHN F.   Benning Wentworth's land grant policy: a reappraisal. Historical New Hampshire, v. 23, spring 1968: 3–13.   F31.H57, v. 23

—— The king's representative: Benning Wentworth, colonial governor, 1741–1767. 1961. ([221] p.)
     Micro AC–1, no. 61–3965

Thesis (Ph.D.)—Lehigh University.
Abstracted in *Dissertation Abstracts*, v. 22, Oct. 1961, p. 1144.

14701

WENTWORTH, Sir JOHN, Bart. (1737–1820)*†

New Hampshire; Nova Scotia. Colonial agent, royal governor, Loyalist, merchant.

—— John Wentworth's description of the American colonies in 1765. Historical New Hampshire, v. 27, fall 1972: 141–166.   F31.H57, v. 27

Introduction and notes by Derek H. Watson.

ARCHIBALD, Sir ADAMS.   Life of Sir John Wentworth, governor of Nova Scotia, 1792–1808. *In* Nova Scotia Historical Society, *Halifax*. Collections. v. 20. Halifax, 1921. p. 43–109. port.   F1036.N93, v. 20

LACY, HARRIET S.   The Wentworth papers, 1717–1940. Historical New Hampshire, v. 23, spring 1968: 25–30.
     F31.H57, v. 23

MAYO, LAWRENCE S.   John Wentworth, governor of New Hampshire, 1767–1775. Cambridge, Harvard University Press, 1921. viii, 208 p. map, plates, ports.
     DA506.W4M3

14702

WENTWORTH, JONATHAN (1741–1814)

New Hampshire. Farmer, Revolutionary officer.

SCALES, JOHN.   Col. Jonathan Wentworth. Granite monthly, v. 36, Feb. 1904: 108–114. F31.G75, v. 36

14703

WESLEY, CHARLES (1707–1788)†

England. Methodist clergyman, evangelist.

BAKER, DONALD S.   Charles Wesley and the American Loyalists. *In* Wesley Historical Society. Proceedings, v. 35, Mar. 1965: 5–9.   BX8203.W4A3, v. 35

—— Charles Wesley and the American War of Independence. *In* Wesley Historical Society. Proceedings, v. 34, Sept. 1964: 159–164.   BX8203.W4A3, v. 34

An expanded version of the article, with the same title, appeared in *Methodist History*, v. 5, Oct. 1966, p. 5–37.

JACKSON, THOMAS.   The life of the Rev. Charles Wesley . . . Comprising a review of his poetry; sketches of the rise and progress of Methodism; with notices of contemporary events and characters. London, J. Mason, 1841. 2 v. facsim., port.   BX8495.W4J3

14704

WESLEY, JOHN (1703–1791)†

England. Methodist evangelist and leader.

—— The journal of the Rev. John Wesley . . . enl. from original mss., with notes from unpublished diaries, annotations, maps, and illustrations. Edited by Nehemiah Curnock. London, R. Culley [1909–16] 8 v. facsims. (part fold.), maps (part fold.), plans (part fold.), plates, ports.   BX8495.W5A2 1909

Vols. 2–8 published by C. H. Kelly.

—— Thoughts upon slavery. London, Printed by R. Hawes, 1774. 53 p.   HT871.W4 Rare Bk. Coll.

ANDREWS, STUART.   John Wesley and the Age of Reason. History today, v. 19, Jan. 1969: 25–32. illus., port.
     D1.H818, v. 19

CELL, GEORGE C.   The rediscovery of John Wesley. New York, H. Holt [ᶜ1935] xviii, 420 p. port.
     BX8495.W5C4

"Wesley's published sermons": p. 415–418.

Attempts to demonstrate that the Wesleyan ethic was essentially Calvinistic.

EDWARDS, MALDWYN L.   John Wesley and the eighteenth century; a study of his social and political influence. [Rev. ed.] London, Epworth Press [1955] 207 p.
     BX8495.W5E25 1955

Bibliographic footnotes.
First edition published in 1933.

HAYWOOD, CLARENCE ROBERT.   Was John Wesley a political economist? Church history, v. 33, Sept. 1964: 314–321.   BR140.A45, v. 33

HOLLAND, LYNWOOD M.   John Wesley and the American Revolution. Journal of church and state, v. 5, Nov. 1963: 199–213.   BV630.A1J6, v. 5

KINGDON, ROBERT M.   Laissez-faire or government control: a problem for John Wesley. Church history, v. 26, Dec. 1957: 342–354.   BR140.A45, v. 26

KNIGHT, JOHN A.   Aspects of Wesley's theology after 1770. Methodist history, v. 6, Apr. 1968: 33–42.
     BX8235.M44, v. 6

MADRON, THOMAS W.   John Wesley on race: a Christian view of equality. Methodist history, new ser., v. 2, July 1964: 24–34.   BX8235.M44, n.s., v. 2

SCHOFIELD, ROBERT E.   John Wesley and science in 18th century England. Isis, v. 44, Dec. 1953: 331–340.
Q1.I7, v. 44

SWEET, WILLIAM W.   John Wesley, Tory. Methodist quarterly review, v. 71, Apr. 1922: 255–268.
BX8201.M75, v. 71

WRIGHT, LOUIS B.   John Wesley, scholar and critic. South Atlantic quarterly, v. 29, July 1930: 262–281.
AP2.S75, v. 29

14705

WEST, BENJAMIN (1738–1820)*†
Pennsylvania; England. Historical painter.

CARSON, HAMPTON L.   The life and works of Benjamin West. Pennsylvania magazine of history and biography, v. 45, Oct. 1921: 301–319. facsims., plates, ports.
F146.P65, v. 45

EVANS, GROSE.   Benjamin West and the taste of his times. Carbondale, Southern Illinois University Press, 1959. 144 p. 73 illus., col. plate.   ND237.W45E85
Bibliography: p. 129–138.

FLEXNER, JAMES T.   Benjamin West's American neo-classicism, with documents on West and William Williams. *In* New York Historical Society. Quarterly, v. 36, Jan. 1932: 5–41. plates, ports.   F116.N638

GALT, JOHN.   The life and studies of Benjamin West, Esq., president of the Royal Academy of London, prior to his arrival in England; compiled from materials furnished by himself. Philadelphia, Published by Moses Thomas; J. Maxwell, Printer, 1816. 196 p.   ND237.W45G3

LIPPINCOTT, HORACE M.   Benjamin West, 1757 C. General magazine and historical chronicle, v. 47, autumn 1944: 13–28.   LH1.P3A4, v. 47
On his Quakerism and his parentage.

SAWITZKY, WILLIAM.   The American work of Benjamin West. Pennsylvania magazine of history and biography, v. 62, Oct. 1938: 433–462. plates.   F146.P65, v. 62
Provides full descriptions of 22 of West's paintings, which are reproduced along with several pencil sketches, discusses eight portraits erroneously attributed to him, and considers 15 unlocated paintings traditionally ascribed to the artist.

14706

WEST, BENJAMIN (1746–1817)
Massachusetts; South Carolina. Lawyer, Revolutionary soldier.

——— Life in the South, 1778–1779; the letters of Benjamin West. Edited by James S. Schoff. Ann Arbor [Mich] William L. Clements Library, 1963. 40 p. illus., map.
F273.W4
The six letters comprise the collection in the William L. Clements Library.

14707

WEST, WILLIAM (1733?–1816?)
Rhode Island. Farmer, assemblyman, Revolutionary general.

WEST, GEORGE M.   William West of Scituate, R.I., farmer, soldier, statesman. St. Andrews, Fla., Panama City Pub. Co., 1919. 32 l. plates.   F83.W51

14708

WESTON, HANNAH WATTS (1758–1855)
Massachusetts; Maine.

DRISKO, GEORGE W.   The Revolution; life of Hannah Weston, with a brief history of her ancestry. Also a condensed history of the first settlement of Jonesborough, Machias and other neighboring towns. 2d ed. Machias, Me., G. A. Parlin, 1903. 140 p.
F29.J7D72
First edition published in 1857.

14709

WETHERILL, SAMUEL (1736–1816)*
New Jersey; Pennsylvania. Carpenter, manufacturer.

WETHERILL, *Mrs.* SAMUEL P.   Samuel Wetherill and the early paint industry of Philadelphia. Philadelphia, The Society, 1916. 19 p. illus. (City History Society of Philadelphia. Philadelphia history, v. 2, no. 1)
F158.1.C58, v. 2

14710

WETZEL, LEWIS (1763–1808)*
Pennsylvania; Ohio. Scout, Indian fighter.

ALLMAN, CLARENCE B.   Lewis Wetzel, Indian fighter; the life and times of a frontier hero. New York, Devin-Adair Co., 1961. 237 p. illus.   F517.W512 1961
Originally published under the title, *The Life and Times of Lewis Wetzel.*
Bibliography: p. 227–229.

HARTLEY, CECIL B.   Life and adventures of Lewis Wetzel, the Virginia ranger; to which are added biographical sketches of General Simon Kenton, General Benjamin Logan, Captain Samuel Brady, Governor Isaac Shelby, and other heroes of the West. Philadelphia, G. G. Evans, 1860. 320 p. plates.   F517.W52

14711

WHARTON, THOMAS (1731–1784)
Pennsylvania. Merchant, Loyalist.

——— Selections from the letter-books of Thomas Wharton, of Philadelphia, 1773–1783. Pennsylvania magazine of history and biography, v. 33, July–Oct. 1909: 319–339, 432–453; v. 34, Jan. 1910: 41–61.
F146.P65, v. 33–34

14712

WHARTON, THOMAS (1735–1778)*
Pennsylvania. Merchant, councilor, governor.

WHARTON, ANNE H. Thomas Wharton, Junr., first governor of Pennsylvania under the constitution of '76. Pennsylvania magazine of history and biography, v. 5, no. 4, 1881: 426–439; v. 6, no. 1, 1882: 91–105.
F146.P65, v. 5–6

14713

WHEATLEY, PHILLIS, *afterwards* PHILLIS PETERS (1753?–1784)*
Africa; Massachusetts. Poet.

——— Letters of Phillis Wheatley and Susanna Wheatley [to the Countess of Huntingdon, 1770–73] Journal of Negro history, v. 57, Apr. 1972: 211–215.
E185.J86, v. 57

Introduction and notes by Sara Dunlap Jackson.

——— Letters of Phillis Wheatley [1772–79] *In* Massachusetts Historical Society, *Boston.* Proceedings. v. 7; 1863/64. Boston, 1864. p. 267–278.
F61.M38, v. 7

Introduction and notes by Charles Deane.

——— Life and works of Phillis Wheatley, containing her complete poetical works, numerous letters, and a complete biography of this famous poet of a century and a half ago, by G. Herbert Renfro. Washington, 1916. Miami, Fla., Mnemosyne Pub. Co. [1969] 112 p. port.
PS866.W5 1969c

——— Memoir and poems of Phillis Wheatley, a native African and a slave. Also, Poems by a slave. 3d ed. Boston, I. Knapp, 1838. 155 p. port.
PS866.W5 1838

Memoir (p. [11]–35) by Margaretta M. Odell.
"Poems by a slave [by George M. Horton]": p. [117]–155.
Reprinted in Miami, Fla., by the Mnemosyne Pub. Co. (1969).

——— Poems. Edited with an introduction by Julian D. Mason, Jr. Chapel Hill, University of North Carolina Press, 1966. lviii, 113 p. facsims., port.
PS866.W5 1966

——— Poems and letters. 1st collected ed. Edited by Chas. Fred. Heartman. With an appreciation by Arthur A. Schomburg. New York, C. F. Heartman [1915] 111 p. port. (Heartman's historical series, no. 8)
PS866.W5 1915

Reprinted in Miami by Mnemosyne Pub. Co. (1969).

——— Poems on various subjects, religious and moral. By Phillis Wheatley, Negro servant to Mr. John Wheatley, of Boston, in New England. London, Printed for A. Bell, bookseller, Aldgate; and sold by Messrs. Cox and Berry, King-Street, Boston, 1773. 124 p. port.
PS866.W5 1773 Rare Bk. Coll.

The 1887 edition (Denver, Colo., W. H. Lawrence. 149 p.) includes memoirs by W. H. Jackson and sketches of Phillis Wheatley, Benjamin Banneker, Thomas Fuller, and James Durham (p. 117–149).

——— Some unpublished poems of Phillis Wheatley. New England quarterly, v. 43, June 1970: 287–297.
F1.N62, v. 43

Introduction and notes by Robert C. Kuncio.

HEARTMAN, CHARLES F. Phillis Wheatley (Phillis Peters); a critical attempt and a bibliography of her writings. New York, For the author, 1915. 44 p. facsims. (part fold.), port. (Heartman's historical series, no. 7)
PS866.W5Z6 Rare Bk. Coll.

ROBINSON, WILLIAM H. Phillis Wheatley: colonial quandary. CLA journal, v. 9, Sept. 1965: 25–38.
P1.A1C22, v. 9

SEEBER, EDWARD D. Phillis Wheatley. Journal of Negro history, v. 24, July 1939: 259–262.
E185.J86, v. 24

14714

WHEELER, WILLIAM (1762–1845)
Connecticut. Revolutionary soldier.

——— A journal for the town of Fairfield; or, An exact & impartial account of the most material transactions from the first settlement thereof till the present time [1780–1844] *In* Lathrop, Cornelia P., *ed.* Black Rock, seaport of old Fairfield, Connecticut, 1644–1870. New Haven, Conn., Tuttle, Morehouse & Taylor Co., 1930. p. 21–125. facsim., map, plates.
F104.B52L35

14715

WHEELOCK, ELEAZAR (1711–1779)*
Connecticut; New Hampshire. Congregational clergyman, farmer, educator.

——— Correspondence between Rev. Eleazar Wheelock, of Dartmouth College, and John Phillips, LL.D., of Exeter [1765–87] *In* New Hampshire Historical Society. Collections. v. 9. Concord, 1889. p. 68–122.
F31.N54, v. 7

——— A plain and faithful narrative of the original design, rise, progress and present state of the Indian charity-school at Lebanon, in Connecticut. Boston, Printed by R. and S. Draper, 1763. 55 p.
E97.6.M5W5 Rare Bk. Coll.
AC901.H3, v. 116 Rare Bk. Coll.

Five "continuations" of the author's *Plain and Faithful Narrative* were published in Boston and Hartford between 1765 and 1775. Copies in the Library's Rare Book Collection appear under the call numbers E97.6.M5W53 through E97.6.M5W57. The "continuations" cover the period from November 27, 1762, to February 20, 1775, and are chiefly concerned with the incorporation of Moor's Indian Charity School with Dartmouth College and its removal to Hanover, New Hampshire.

DANIELL, JERE R. Eleazar Wheelock and the Dartmouth College charter. Historical New Hampshire, v. 24, winter 1969: 3–31. ports. F31.H57, v. 24

The text of the charter appears on p. 33–44.

McCALLUM, JAMES D. Eleazar Wheelock, founder of Dartmouth College. Hanover, N.H., Dartmouth College Publications, 1939, ix, 236 p. port. (Dartmouth College manuscript series, no. 4) LD1436.1769.M2

Bibliography: p. 217–219.
Reprinted in New York by Arno Press (1969. LD1436.1769.M212).

——— ed. The letters of Eleazar Wheelock's Indians. Hanover, N.H., Dartmouth College Publications, 1932. 327 p. facsims. (Dartmouth College manuscript series, no. 1) E97.6.M5M2

Bibliography: p. 314–316.

McCLURE, DAVID, and ELIJAH PARISH. Memoirs of the Rev. Eleazar Wheelock, D.D., founder and president of Dartmouth College and Moor's Charity School; with a summary history of the college and school. To which are added, copious extracts from Dr. Wheelock's correspondence. Newburyport, E. Little, 1811. 336 p. LD1436.1769.M3 Rare Bk. Coll.

Reprinted in New York by Arno Press (1972. LD1436.1769.M32).

14716

WHIPPLE, ABRAHAM (1733–1819)*

Rhode Island. Revolutionary naval commander.

MAZET, HORACE S. The Navy's forgotten hero. In United States Naval Institute. Proceedings, v. 63, Mar. 1937: 344–354. plates. V1.U8, v. 63

14717

WHIPPLE, WILLIAM (1730–1785)*

Maine; New Hampshire. Mariner, merchant, delegate to the Continental Congress, Revolutionary general, assemblyman, judge.

———William Whipple's letters [Sept. 15, 1776–Dec. 14, 1778] American pioneer, v. 1, Nov.–Dec. 1842: 396–397, 422–423; v. 2, Jan.–Feb., Apr.–May 1843: 17–19, 72–78, 167–169, 217–219. E516.A53, v. 1–2

——— William Whipple's notes of a journey from Philadelphia to New Hampshire, in the summer of 1777. Pennsylvania magazine of history and biography, v. 10, Jan. 1887: 366–374. F146.P65, v. 10

LITTLE, ARTHUR. William Whipple, signer of the Declaration of Independence, soldier and statesman. In New Hampshire Historical Society. Proceedings. v. 3, pt. 2; 1897/1902. Concord, 1902. p. 318–339.
F31.N52, v. 3

A similar version of the essay appeared in the Magazine of History, With Notes and Queries, v. 9, May 1909, p. 257–268.

SAFFORD, MOSES A. General William Whipple. In Maine Historical Society. Collections and proceedings. 2d ser., v. 6. Portland, 1895. p. 337–357.
F16.M33, 2d s., v. 6

14718

WHITAKER, JOSEPH (1755–1838)

England; Pennsylvania. British soldier in America, woodcutter, weaver.

KURJACK, DENNIS C. Joseph Whitaker of Hopewell Furnace. Historical review of Berks County, v. 14, Jan.–Apr. 1949: 49–53, 66–73, illus., facsims., ports.
F157.B3H48, v. 14

14719

WHITCOMB, ASA (1719–1804)

Massachusetts. Farmer, assemblyman, Revolutionary officer.

WEIS, FREDERICK L. Asa Whitcomb, a sterling patriot. In Massachusetts Historical Society, Boston. Proceedings. v. 67; 1941/44. Boston, 1945. p. 111–127.
F61.M38, v. 67

14720

WHITCOMB, BENJAMIN (1737–1828)

Massachusetts; New Hampshire. Revolutionary officer.

MORRIS, GEORGE F. Major Benjamin Whitcomb, ranger and partisan leader in the Revolution. Historical New Hampshire, v. 11, Oct. 1955: 1–20. ports.
F31.H57, v. 11

PIKE, ROBERT E. The dreaded scout. Vermont life, v. 13, spring 1959: 36–39. illus., port. F46.V54, v. 13

14721

WHITCOMB, JOHN (1712?–1785)

Massachusetts. Farmer, assemblyman, Revolutionary general.

NOURSE, HENRY S. A forgotten patriot. In American Antiquarian Society, Worcester, Mass. Proceedings, new ser., v. 7, Oct. 1890: 94–106.
E172.A35, n.s., v. 7

14722

WHITE, ANTHONY WALTON (1750–1803)

New Jersey. Revolutionary officer.

WOODHULL, ANNA M. W. Memoir of Brig. Gen. Anthony Walton White, of the Continental Army. In New Jersey Historical Society. Proceedings, 2d ser., v. 7, no. 2, 1882: 105–115. port.
F131.N58, 2d s., v. 7

——— Offprint. [n. p., 1882?] 11 p. port.
E207.W58W8

14723

WHITE, GIDEON (1752–1833)

Massachusetts; Nova Scotia. Merchant, farmer, Loyalist.

ELLS, MARGARET, *comp.* A calendar of the White collection of manuscripts in the Public Archives of Nova Scotia. Halifax, N.S., 1940. 130, xi p. (Nova Scotia. Public Archives. Publication no. 5)   CD3645.N88

14724

WHITE, JOSEPH (1755?–1836)

Massachusetts. Revolutionary soldier.

——— An narrative of events, as they occurred from time to time, in the Revolutionary War; with an account of the battles, of Trenton, Trenton-Bridge, and Princeton. Charlestown [1833] 30 p.   E275.W58 Rare Bk. Coll.

Reproduced in *American Heritage*, v. 7, June 1956, p. 74–79.

14725

WHITE, WILLIAM, *Bp.* (1748–1836)*

Pennsylvania. Anglican clergyman.

——— The common sense theology of Bishop White; selected essays from the writings of William White, 1748–1836, first bishop of Pennsylvania and a patriarch of the American church, with an introductory survey of his theological position, by Sydney A. Temple, Jr. New York, King's Crown Press, 1946. x, 169 p. port.
BX5845.W55 1946

Issued also as Sydney A. Temple's thesis (Ph.D.)— Columbia University.

Bibliography: p. [160]–169.

Contents: The source of knowledge.—An argument in favor of divine revelation.—The basis of episcopacy.—The analogy of the understanding and the will.—Of philosophic necessity.—Of baptismal grace.—On the terms: sacrifice, altar, priest.—On certain questions relative to the Eucharist.

——— Memoirs of the Protestant Episcopal Church in the United States of America, from its organization up to the present day: containing, I. A narrative of the early measures of the church; II. Additional statements and remarks; III. An appendix of original papers. 2d ed. New York, Swords, Stanford, 1836. 393 p.
BX5880.W5 1836

Historical magazine of the Protestant Episcopal church. Bishop William White number. [New Brunswick, N.J.] 1937. 186 p. ports. (Historical magazine of the Protestant Episcopal church, v. 6, Mar. 1937)
BX5800.H5, v. 6

Partial contents: Foreword, by Francis M. Taitt.—Ancestry and early life, by William S. Perry.—The presbyter, by Walter H. Stowe.—The bishop, by Louis C. Washburn.—The teacher, by James A. Montgomery.

Historical magazine of the Protestant Episcopal church. The Bishop William White number. [New Brunswick,

N.J.] 1953. 371–506 p. facsims., plates, port. (Historical magazine of the Protestant Episcopal church, v. 22, Dec. 1953)   BX5800.H5, v. 22

Contents: William White, ecclesiastical statesman, by Walter H. Stowe.—The autobiography of Bishop William White, edited by Walter H. Stowe.—William White's "The Case of the Episcopal Churches in the United States Considered" (1782), edited by Richard G. Salomon.

MANROSS, WILLIAM W. William White, ecclesiastical statesman in an age of revolution. With summary by Joseph Gillespie Armstrong. [Philadelphia] 1959. 14 p. port. (Historical publications of the Society of Colonial Wars in the Commonwealth of Pennsylvania, v. 8, no. 3)   E186.3.P41, v. 8

STOWE, WALTER H. The life and letters of Bishop William White. New York, Morehouse Pub. Co. [c1937] xiii, 306 p. mounted illus., plates, ports. (Church Historical Society (U.S.). Publication no. 9)   BX5995.W5S85

Includes bibliographies.

WARD, JULIUS H. The life and times of Bishop White. New York, Dodd, Mead, 1892. 199 p. port. ("Makers of America")   BX5995.W5W3

14726

WHITEFIELD, GEORGE (1714–1770)*†

England. Clergyman, itinerant evangelist.

———A select collection of letters of the late Reverend George Whitefield . . . written to his most intimate friends, and persons of distinction, in England, Scotland, Ireland, and America, from the year 1734, to 1770. Including the whole period of his ministry. With an account of the orphan-house in Georgia, to the time of his death. London, E. and C. Dilly, 1772. 3 v. port.
BX9225.W4A33

BELCHER, JOSEPH, *comp.* George Whitefield: a biography, with special reference to his labors in America. New York, American Tract Society [Pref. 1857] 514 p. plates, port.   BX9225.W4B4

GILLIES, JOHN. Memoirs of the life of the Reverend George Whitefield, M.A., late chaplain to the Right Honourable the Countess of Huntingdon . . . Faithfully selected from his original papers, journals, and letters . . . To which are added, a particular account of his death and funeral; and extracts from the sermons, which were preached on that occasion. London, E. and C. Dilly, 1772. xvi, 357 p. port.   BX9225.W4G45 1772

GLEDSTONE, JAMES P. George Whitefield, M.A., field-preacher. 2d ed. New York, American Tract Society [1901] xii, 359 p. plates, port.   BX9225.W4G6 1901

——— The life and travels of George Whitefield, M.A. London, Longmans, Green, 1871. xii, 533 p.
BX9225.W4G5

PHILIP, ROBERT. The life and times of the Reverend George Whitefield, M.A. London, G. Virtue, 1837. xi, 588 p. port.   BX9225.W4P5

TRESCH, JOHN W. The reception accorded George Whitefield in the southern colonies. Methodist history, v. 6, Jan. 1968: 17–26. BX8235.M44, v. 6

TYERMAN, LUKE. The life of the Rev. George Whitefield. London, Hodder and Stoughton, 1876–77. 2 v. ports. BX9225.W4T9

14727

WHITEFOORD, CALEB (1734–1810)†
Scotland; England. Merchant, diplomat.

—— The Whitefoord papers; being the correspondence and other manuscripts of Colonel Charles Whitefoord and Caleb Whitefoord, from 1739 to 1810. Edited, with introduction and notes, by W. A. S. Hewins. Oxford, At the Clarendon Press, 1898. xxix, 292 p. illus. DA67.1.W5A2

Contains three letters by Benjamin Franklin addressed to Caleb Whitefoord.

14728

WHITEHILL, ROBERT (1735–1813)*
Pennsylvania. Landowner, assemblyman.

CRIST, ROBERT G. Robert Whitehill and the struggle for civil rights. Lemoyne, Pa., Lemoyne Trust Co., 1958. 46 p. illus., maps. F157.C8W5

14729

WHITELAW, JAMES (1748–1829)
Vermont. Land agent.

—— Journal of General James Whitelaw, surveyor-general of Vermont. In Vermont Historical Society. Proceedings. 1905/6. [n.p., 1907] p. 119–157. F46.V55, 1905/6

The journal extends from 1773 to 1793, covering the writer's travels as agent of the Scots-American Company of Farmers of Inchinan, Scotland, and the selection and settlement of Ryegate, Vermont.

GOODWILLIE, THOMAS. Life of General James Whitelaw. In Vermont Historical Society. Proceedings. 1905/6. [n.p., 1907] p. 103–118. F46.V55, 1905/6

14730

WHITING, JOHN (1716–1784)
Massachusetts. Miller.

—— Diary of John Whiting of Dedham, Mass., 1743–1784. New England historical and genealogical register, v. 63, Apr.–July 1909: 185–192, 261–265. F1.N56, v. 63

14731

WHITLEY, WILLIAM (1749–1813)
Virginia; Kentucky. Settler, Indian fighter.

TALBERT, CHARLES G. William Whitley, 1749–1813. Filson Club history quarterly, v. 25, Apr.–Oct. 1951: 101–121, 210–216, 300–316. F446.F484, v. 25

14732

WHITTAKER, JANE STROPE WHITE (ca. 1767–1852)
Pennsylvania. Settler.

—— Narrative of the captivity [1778] of Mrs. Jane Whittaker, daughter of Sebastian Strope, a Revolutionary soldier. In New York State Historical Association. Quarterly journal, v. 11, July 1930: 237–251. F116.N865, v. 11

Contributed by Charlotte T. Luckhurst.

14733

WICKES, LAMBERT (ca. 1735–1777)*
Maryland. Revolutionary naval officer.

BOLANDER, LOUIS H. A forgotten hero of the Revolution. Americana, v. 22, Apr. 1928: 119–128. E171.A53, v. 22

CLARK, WILLIAM B. Lambert Wickes, sea raider and diplomat; the story of a naval captain of the Revolution. New Haven, Yale University Press, 1932. xviii, 466 p. facsims. E207.W63C7

Bibliography: p. [385]–392.

THOM, DECOURCY W. Captain Lambert Wickes, C.N.—a Maryland forerunner of Commodore John Paul Jones, C.N. Maryland historical magazine, v. 27, Mar. 1932: 1–17. F176.M18, v. 27

14734

WIEDERHOLD, ANDREAS (fl. 1776)
Hessian officer in America.

—— Tagebuch des Capt. Wiederholdt, vom 7 October 1776 bis 7 December 1780. [Transcribed and edited] by M. D. Learned and C. Grosse. New York, MacMillan Co. [1901] xvii, 94 p. (Americana Germanica, v. 4, no. 1, 1901) E184.G3G3, v. 4

The introduction includes lengthy excerpts translated from the letters of a Hessian Lt. Henckelmann, 1777–78.

ALTNER, HANNS G. The diary of Captain Wiederhold and the Hessians; a military idyll of the days of 1776. Historical review of Berks County, v. 2, Jan. 1937: 50–54. maps. F157.B3H48, v. 2

14735

WIESENTHAL, CHARLES FREDERICK (1726–1789)
Germany; Maryland. Revolutionary surgeon, physician.

SNYDER, WILLIAM T. Charles Frederick Wiesenthal (1726–1789); an appraisal of the medical pioneer of Baltimore. In Society for the History of the Germans in

Maryland, *Baltimore*. Annual report. 32d; 1966. Baltimore. p. 47–58. F190.G3S6, 32d

14736

WIGG, WILLIAM HAZZARD (1746–1798)
South Carolina. Revolutionary officer.

——A brief memoir of the life, and Revolutionary services, of Major William Hazzard Wigg, of South Carolina, illustrative of the claim, for indemnification, upon the government of the United States for the plunder, and destruction of his property, during the War, by British troops. Prepared by the claimant, for the use of committees of Congress. Washington, C. Alexander, Printer, 1860. 43 p. E275.W65

14737

WIGGLESWORTH, EDWARD (1732–1794)*
Massachusetts. Theologian, demographer, educator.

—— Calculations on American population, with a table for estimating the annual increase of inhabitants in the British colonies. Boston, Printed and sold by John Boyle in Marlboro'–Street, 1775. 24 p.
HB871.W65 Rare Bk. Coll.

VINOVSKIS, MARIS A.   The 1789 life table of Edward Wigglesworth. Journal of economic history, v. 31, Sept. 1971: 570–590. HC10.J64, v. 31

On his attempt to compile actuarial tables as a basis for establishing an annuity fund.

14738

WILD, EBENEZER (1758–1794)
Massachusetts. Revolutionary officer.

—— The journal of Ebenezer Wild (1776–1781) who served as corporal, sergeant, ensign, and lieutenant in the American Army of the Revolution. *In* Massachusetts Historical Society, *Boston*. Proceedings. 2d ser., v. 6; 1890/91. Boston, 1891. p. 78–160.
F61.M38, 2d s., v. 6

14739

WILEY, JENNIE SELLARDS (*d.* 1831)
Kentucky. Settler.

CONNELLEY, WILLIAM E.   Eastern Kentucky papers; the founding of Harman's Station, with an account of the Indian captivity of Mrs. Jennie Wiley and the exploration and settlement of the Big Sandy Valley in the Virginias and Kentucky. New York, Torch Press, 1910. 177 p. illus., maps, plates, ports. E87.W67

Published in 1966, with four additional chapters by Edward R. Hazelett, under the title *The Founding of Harman's Station and the Wiley Captivity* (Paintsville, Ky., Harman Station Publishers. 176 p.).

14740

WILKES, JOHN (1727–1797)†
England. Member of Parliament, Lord mayor.

—— The controversial letters of John Wilkes, Esq., the Rev. John Horne, and their principal adherents; with a supplement, containing material anonymous pieces, &c., &c., &c. London, Printed by T. Sherlock, for J. Williams, 1771. 320 p. DA512.W6A18

—— The correspondence of the late John Wilkes, with his friends, printed from the original manuscripts, in which are introduced memoirs of his life. London, Printed for R. Phillips, by T. Gillet, 1805. 5 v. facsims., port.
DA512.W6A2

Reprinted in New York by B. Franklin (1970).

——English liberty; or, The British lion roused; containiny [sic] the sufferings of John Wilkes, Esq; from the first of his persecution, down to the present time. [London] Printed for T. Marsh [1768?]–69 [70] 2 v. in 1. port. DA512.W6A32 Rare Bk. Coll.

—— John Wilkes and Boston [1768–70] *In* Massachusetts Historical Society, *Boston*. Proceedings. v. 47; 1913/14. Boston, 1914. p. 190–215. F61.M38, v. 47

Letters by Wilkes, the Boston Sons of Liberty, and local politicians, such as William Palfrey, Joseph Warren, Thomas Young, and Benjamin Church, Jr.

—— John Wilkes and William Palfrey [letters, 1769–71] *In* Colonial Society of Massachusetts, *Boston*. Publications. v. 34. Transactions, 1937/42. Boston, 1943. p. 411–428. F61.C71, v. 34

Introduction and notes by George M. Elsey.

——John Wilkes. Patriot. An unfinished autobiography. Harrow, W. F. Taylor, 1888. xxiv, 62, [8] p. port.
DA512.W6A21

Edited by R. des Habits.
Reprinted, with omissions, in London by Lion and Unicorn Press (1955).

—— Letters, from the year 1774 to the year 1796, of John Wilkes, Esq., addressed to his daughter, the late Miss Wilkes: with a collection of his miscellaneous poems. To which is prefixed a memoir of the life of Mr. Wilkes. London, Longman, Hurst, Rees, and Orme, 1804. 4 v. ports. DA512.W6A26

Contents: v. 1. Life of Mr. Wilkes. Poems.—v. 2. Letters, 1774–1783.—v. 3. Letters, 1784–1789.—v. 4. Letters, 1789–1796. Introduction to his History of England.

—— The life and political writings of John Wilkes. Birmingham, Printed for J. Sketchley, 1769. 519 p.
DA512.W6A3

—— The speeches of John Wilkes, one of the knights of the shire for the county of Middlesex, in the Parliament appointed to meet at Westminster the 29.th day of November 1774, to the prorogation the 6.th day of June 1777. With notes by the editor. London, 1777–78. 3 v.
DA512.W6A4 1777

Vol. 3 has title: *The Speeches of Mr. Wilkes in the House of Commons During the Last Session of Parliament.*

BLEACKLEY, HORACE W. Life of John Wilkes. London, John Lane; New York, John Lane Co., 1917. xiii, 464 p. facsim., fold. geneal. table, plates, ports. (part col.) DA512.W6B6

CHENEVIX TRENCH, CHARLES P. Portrait of a patriot; a biography of John Wilkes. Edinburgh, W. Blackwood [1962] 412 p. illus., plates, ports. DA512.W6C5

"Notes on references": p. 381–404.

FITZGERALD, PERCY H. The life and times of John Wilkes, M.P., lord mayor of London, and chamberlain. London, Ward and Downey, 1888. 2 v. plates, ports. [DA512.W6F5] Micro 9214 DA

MCCRACKEN, GEORGE. John Wilkes, humanist. Philological quarterly, v. 11, Apr. 1932: 109–134. P1.P55, v. 11

POSTGATE, RAYMOND W. That devil Wilkes. New York, Vanguard Press [ᶜ1929] 275 p. port. DA512.W6P6

"Sources for the life of John Wilkes": p. 251–253; "References": p. [255]–267.

Revised edition published in London by Dobson (1956. 249 p.).

RUDÉ, GEORGE F. E. Wilkes and liberty. History today, v. 7, Sept. 1957: 571–579. illus., port. D1.H818, v. 7

SHERRARD, OWEN A. A life of John Wilkes. London, G. Allen & Unwin [1930] 319 p. ports. DA512.W6S5

Bibliography: p. [313]–314.

Reprinted in Freeport, N.Y., by Books for Libraries Press (1971) and in New York by B. Blom (1971).

THOMAS, PETER D. G. John Wilkes and the freedom of the press (1771). *In* London. University. *Institute of Historical Research.* Bulletin, v. 33, May 1960: 86–98. D1.L65, v. 33

TRELOAR, *Sir* WILLIAM PURDIE, *Bart.* Wilkes and the City. London, J. Murray, 1917. xxvi, 299 p. facsims., plates, ports. DA512.W6T8

14741

WILKIN, JAMES WHITNEY (1762–1845)

New York. Revolutionary soldier, lawyer.

—— Princeton in 1784: the diary of James W. Wilkin of the Class of 1785. Princeton University Library chronicle, v. 12, winter 1951: 55–66. Z733.P93C5, v. 12

14742

WILKINS, ISAAC (1742–1830)

Jamaica; New York; Nova Scotia. Assemblyman, Loyalist.

—— My services and losses in aid of the King's cause during the American Revolution. Brooklyn, Historical Print. Club, 1890. 23 p. (Winnowings in American history. Revolutionary narratives, no. 3) E278.W6W68

14743

WILKINS, JOHN, (*fl.* 1748–1775)

England; Illinois. British military officer.

STORM, COLTON. The notorious Colonel Wilkins. *In* Illinois State Historical Society. Journal, v. 40, Mar. 1947: 7–22. F536.I18, v. 40

14744

WILKINSON, ANN BIDDLE (*d.* 1807)

Pennsylvania; Kentucky. Sister of Clement Biddle (1740–1814). Wife of James Wilkinson (1757–1825).

—— Letters of Mrs. Ann Biddle Wilkinson from Kentucky, 1788–1789. Pennsylvania magazine of history and biography, v. 56, Jan. 1932: 33–55. port. F146.P65, v. 56

Introduction and notes by Thomas R. Hay.

14745

WILKINSON, ELIZA YONGE

South Carolina.

—— Letters of Eliza Wilkinson during the invasion and possession of Charlestown, S.C., by the British in the Revolutionary War. Arranged from the original manuscripts, by Caroline Gilman. New York, S. Colman, 1839. 108 p. E263.S7W6

Reprinted in New York by the New York Times (1969).

14746

WILKINSON, JAMES (1757–1825)*

Maryland; Pennsylvania; Kentucky. Revolutionary general, assemblyman, trader.

—— Memoirs of my own times. Philadelphia, Printed by Abraham Small, 1816. 3 v. fold. facsims. E353.1.W6W6

—— Diagrams and plans, illustrative of the principal battles and military affairs, treated of in Memoirs of my own times. Philadelphia, Printed by Abraham Small, 1816. 4 l. maps (part fold.), plans. G1201.S3W5 1816 G&M

CHRISTIAN, PERCY W. General James Wilkinson and Kentucky separatism, 1784–1798. 1935.

Thesis (Ph.D.)—Northwestern University.

DREWRY, ELIZABETH B. Episodes in westward expansion as reflected in the writings of General James Wilkinson, 1784–1806. 1933.

Thesis (Ph.D.)—Cornell University.

HAMILTON, RAPHAEL N. General James Wilkinson and his religious affiliations. Mid-America, v. 12, Oct. 1929: 122–132. BX1415.I3M5, v. 12

HAY, THOMAS R., *and* MORRIS R. WERNER. The admirable trumpeter; a biography of General James Wilkinson. Garden City, N.Y., Doubleday, Doran, 1941. x, 383 p. map (on lining-papers), port. E353.1.W6H3

"Bibliographical note": p. 349–352.

HAY, THOMAS R. Some reflections on the career of General James Wilkinson. Mississippi Valley historical review, v. 21, Mar. 1935: 471–494. E171.J87, v. 21

JACOBS, JAMES R. Tarnished warrior, Major-General James Wilkinson. New York, Macmillan Co., 1938. xv, 380 p. illus., facsim., maps (part fold), plates, ports. E353.1.W6J3

Bibliography: p. 341–353.

SHREVE, ROYAL O. The finished scoundrel; General James Wilkinson, sometime commander-in-chief of the army of the United States, who made intrigue a trade and treason a profession. Indianapolis, Bobbs-Merrill Co. ['1933] 319 p. illus., maps (on lining papers), port. E353.1.W6S56

Bibliography: p. [299]–308.

WILKINSON, JAMES. General James Wilkinson; a paper prepared and read by his great-grandson James Wilkinson. Louisiana historical quarterly, v. 1, Sept. 1917: 79–166. F366.L79, v. 1

14747

WILKINSON, JEMIMA (1752–1819)*

Rhode Island; New York. Religious sect leader.

ADAMS, JOHN Q. Jemima Wilkinson, the universal friend. Journal of American history, v. 9, Apr./June 1915: 249–263. E171.J87, v. 9

HUDSON, DAVID. Memoir of Jemima Wilkinson, a preacheress of the eighteenth century; containing an authentic narrative of her life and character, and of the rise, progress, and conclusion of her ministry. Bath, N.Y., R. L. Underhill, 1844. 288 p. port. BR1719.W5H8 1844

Published in 1821 under the title *History of Jemima Wilkinson* (Geneva, N.Y., Printed by S. P. Hull. 208 p.).

ST. JOHN, ROBERT P. Jemima Wilkinson. *In* New York State Historical Association. Quarterly journal, v. 11, Apr. 1930: 158–173. F116.N865, v. 11

WHYTE, J. BRUCE. "The Publick Universal Friend." Rhode Island history, v. 26, Oct. 1967: 103–112; v. 27, Jan. 1968: 18–24. F76.R472, v. 26–27

WISBEY, HERBERT A. Portrait of a prophetess. *In* New York State Historical Association. New York history, v. 38, Oct. 1957: 387–396. port. F116.N865, v. 38

—— A Yankee prophetess. New-England galaxy, v. 3, winter 1962: 2–11. illus., facsims., ports.
F1.N39, v. 3

14748

WILLARD, JOSEPH (1741–1828)

Massachusetts. Clergyman.

CLARKE, GEORGE F. The life and ministry of Rev. Joseph Willard. *In* Worcester Historical Society, *Worcester, Mass.* Collections. v. 14. Proceedings. no. 46; 1895. Worcester, 1896. p. 151–164. F74.W9W85, v. 14

Extracts from Willard's diary, dated 1771–83, appear on p. 161–164.

14749

WILLETT, MARINUS (1740–1830) *

New York. Merchant, Revolutionary officer, assemblyman.

BRONNER, FREDERICK L. Marinus Willett. *In* New York State Historical Association. New York history, v. 17, July 1936: 273–280. F116.N865, v. 17

THOMAS, HOWARD. Marinus Willett, soldier-patriot, 1740–1830. Prospect, N.Y., Prospect Books, 1954. ix, 242 p. map (on lining papers), port. E207.W65T5

Bibliography: p. 235–236.

WAGER, DANIEL E. Col. Marinus Willett. The hero of Mohawk Valley. Utica, N.Y., Printed for the Society, by the Utica Herald Pub. Co., 1891. 50 p. [Oneida Historical Society at Utica. Publications, no. 16] E207.W7W1
F127.O504, no. 16

WILLETT, WILLIAM M. A narrative of the military actions of Colonel Marinus Willett, taken chiefly from his own manuscript. New-York, G. & C. & H. Carvill, 1831. 162 p. plan, port. E207.W65W7

Reprinted in New York by the New York Times (1969).

14750

WILLIAMS, *lieutenant.*

—— Discord and civil wars; being a portion of the journal kept by Lieutenant Williams of His Majesty's Twenty-third Regiment while stationed in British North America during the time of the Revolution. [Buffalo?] Easy Hill Press for the Salisbury Club of Buffalo, 1954. vi, 32 p. illus. facsim. E267.W5

14751

WILLIAMS, DAVID (1754–1831)

New York. Revolutionary soldier, farmer.

RAYMOND, MARCIUS D. David Williams and the capture of Andre. [Tarrytown? N.Y., 1903] [22] p. illus., plates, port. E280.A5R2

14752

WILLIAMS, GEORGE (*b.* 1731)

Massachusetts. Merchant, shipmaster, Revolutionary officer.

———— Revolutionary letters written to Colonel Timothy Pickering by George Williams of Salem [1777–83] *In* Essex Institute, *Salem, Mass.* Historical collections, v. 42, Oct. 1906: 313–330; v. 43, Jan.–July 1907: 7–16, 199–208; v. 44, Oct. 1908: 313–324; v. 45, Apr.–July 1909: 119–129, 286–292.   F72.E7E81, v. 42–45

14753

WILLIAMS, ISRAEL (1709–1788)*

Massachusetts. Merchant, farmer, judge, assemblyman, councilor, Loyalist.

MERRIAM, GEORGE H.   Israel Williams, monarch of Hampshire, 1709–1788. 1961. ([171] p.)
                        Micro AC–1, no. 61–5007

Thesis (Ph.D.)—Clark University.
Abstracted in *Dissertation Abstracts*, v. 22, Mar. 1962, p. 3178.

14754

WILLIAMS, JONATHAN (1750–1815)*

Massachusetts. Merchant.

———— Nantes to Newburyport: letters of Jonathan Williams [1782–83] Edited by Benjamin W. Labaree. *In* Essex Institute, *Salem, Mass.* Historical collections, v. 92, Jan. 1956: 68–81.   F72.E7E81, v. 92

KNOLLENBERG, BERNHARD.   Franklin, Jonathan Williams and William Pitt: a letter of January 21, 1775. Bloomington, 1949. 24 p. (Indiana University Library publications, no. 1)   E211.K7 1949a

Bibliographic references included in "Notes" (p. 22–24).

Reproduces and discusses the letter in which Williams reported to an unnamed correspondent on the debate and rejection by the House of Lords of William Pitt's motion for withdrawal of the British troops from Boston.

14755

WILLIAMS, OTHO HOLLAND (1749–1794)*

Maryland. Clerk, Revolutionary general.

TIFFANY, OSMOND.   A sketch of the life and services of Gen. Otho Holland Williams. Baltimore, Printed by J. Murphy, 1851. 31 p. [Maryland Historical Society. Publications, v. 2, no. 11]   F176.M34, v. 2

14756

WILLIAMS, STEPHEN (1693–1782)

Massachusetts. Congregational clergyman.

MEDLICOTT, ALEXANDER G.   The journals of the Rev. Stephen Williams: 1775–1777. 1962. ([515] p.)
                        Micro AC–1, no. 63–4431

Thesis (Ph.D.)—University of Washington.
Abstracted in *Dissertation Abstracts*, v. 24, July 1963, p. 285.

14757

WILLIAMS, WILLIAM (1727–1791)

England; Pennsylvania. Portrait and landscape artist.

DICKASON, DAVID H.   William Williams: novelist and painter of colonial America, 1727–1791. Bloomington, Indiana University Press [1970] xxi, 269 p. illus., ports. (Indiana University humanities series, no. 67)
                        PS875.W3Z65

Includes bibliographic references.

GERDTS, WILLIAM H.   William Williams: new American discoveries. *In* Winterthur portfolio. v. 4. Winterthur, Del., 1968. p. 159–167. ports.   N9.W52, v. 4

SAWITZKY, WILLIAM.   Further light on the work of William Williams. *In* New York Historical Society. Quarterly bulletin, v. 25, July 1941: 101–112. ports.
                        F116.N638, v. 25

WEST, BENJAMIN.   Benjamin West on William Williams: a previously unpublished letter. *In* Winterthur portfolio. v. 6. Winterthur, Del., 1970. p. 127–133. port.
                        N9.W52, v. 6

A letter to Thomas Eagles dated Oct. 10, 1810. Introduction and notes by David H. Dickason.

14758

WILLIAMSON, HUGH (1735–1819)*

Pennsylvania; North Carolina. Scientist, Indian trader, Revolutionary surgeon, assemblyman, delegate to the Continental Congress, delegate to the Constitutional Convention.

GILPATRICK, DELBERT H.   Contemporary opinion of Hugh Williamson. North Carolina historical review, v. 17, Jan. 1940: 26–36.   F251.N892, v. 17

HOSACK, DAVID.   A biographical memoir of Hugh Williamson. New-York, Printed by C. S. Van Winkle, 1820. 91 p.   E302.6.W6H8 Rare Bk. Coll.

Also published in the *Collections* of the New York Historical Society, v. 3 (New York, 1821), p. [125]–179.

NEAL, JOHN W.   Life and public services of Hugh Williamson. *In* Duke University, Durham, N.C. Trinity College Historical Society. Historical papers. ser. 13; 1919. Durham. p. [62]–111.   [F251.D83, ser.13]
                        Micro 9370F

Two "unpublished letters" of Williamson from 1778 and 1783 are appended on p. 112–115.

14759

WILLING, THOMAS (1731–1821)*

Pennsylvania. Lawyer, merchant, judge, delegate to the Continental Congress.

———— Willing letters and papers. Edited with a biographical essay of Thomas Willing of Philadelphia (1731–1821) by Thomas Willing Balch. Philadelphia, Allen, Lane and Scott, 1922. ix, lxiii, 227 p.   E207.W75W7

BALCH, THOMAS W. Thomas Willing of Philadelphia (1731–1821). Pennsylvania magazine of history and biography, v. 46, Jan. 1922: 1–14. plate, port.
F146.P65, v. 46

SLASKI, EUGENE R. Thomas Willing: moderation during the American Revolution. 1971. ([361] p.)
Micro AC–1, no. 72–281

Thesis (Ph.D.)—Florida State University.
Abstracted in *Dissertation Abstracts International*, v. 32A, Dec. 1971, p. 3227.

14760

WILMER, JAMES JONES (1750–1814)*

Maryland. Clergyman.

———— Memoirs of the Rev. James Jones Wilmer. Edited by J. Hall Pleasants. Maryland historical magazine, v. 19, Sept. 1924: 220–246.   F176.M18, v. 19

14761

WILMOT, JOHN (1750–1815)† Later John Eardley-Wilmot
England. Lawyer, Member of Parliament.

———— Memoirs of the life of the Right Honourable Sir John Eardley Wilmot, knt., late lord chief justice of the Court of Common Pleas, and one of His Majesty's most honourable privy council: with some original letters. By John Wilmot. 2d ed. with additions. London, Printed by J. Nichols, 1811. 241 p. port.
DA506.W75W6

NORTON, MARY BETH. Eardley-Wilmot, Britannia, and the Loyalists: a painting by Benjamin West. *In* Perspectives in American history. v. 6; 1972. [Cambridge] Charles Warren Center for Studies in American History, Harvard University. p. 119–131.
E171.P47, v. 6

14762

WILSON, GEORGE (1729–1777)

Ireland; Pennsylvania. Landowner, Revolutionary officer.

ADAMS, MARCELLIN C. Colonel George Wilson: a genealogical study in western Pennsylvania. Western Pennsylvania historical magazine, v. 26, Sept./Dec. 1943: 89–108.   F146.W52, v. 26

14763

WILSON, JAMES (1742–1798)*

Scotland; Pennsylvania. Lawyer, land speculator, political thinker, delegate to the Continental Congress, delegate to the Constitutional Convention.

———— Selected political essays of James Wilson. Edited with an introductory essay by Randolph G. Adams. New York, A. A. Knopf, 1930. 356 p. (Political science classics)   JK171.W73
"Descriptive bibliography of works of and relating to James Wilson": p. 345–356.

———— The works of the Honourable James Wilson, L.L.D., late one of the associate justices of the Supreme Court of the United States, and professor of law in the College of Philadelphia. Published under the direction of Bird Wilson. Philadelphia, At the Lorenzo Press, Printed for Bronson and Chauncey, 1804. 3 v. port.
JK171.W6 1804
Micro 01291, reel 181, no. 1E
Partial contents: v. 1–2. Lectures on law.—v. 3. Lectures on law (concluded). On the history of property. Considerations on the nature and extent of the legislative authority of the British Parliament. Speech delivered in the convention for the province of Pennsylvania, held at Philadelphia, in January, 1775. Speech delivered on 26th November, 1787, in the convention of Pennsylvania. Oration delivered on the fourth of July 1788, at the procession formed at Philadelphia to celebrate the adoption of the Constitution of the United States. Considerations on the Bank of North America. 1785.
A reprint, edited by Robert G. McCloskey, has been published in Cambridge by the Belknap Press of Harvard University Press (1967. 2 v. [875 p.] KF213.W5 1967).

ALEXANDER, LUCIEN H. James Wilson, nation-builder. Green bag, v. 19, Jan.–Mar., May 1907: 1–9, 98–109, 137–146, 265–276. ports.   LL
———— ———— Offprint. [Boston, 1907] 1–9, 98–109, 137–146, 265–276 p. ports.   E302.6.W64A28

———— James Wilson, patriot, and the Wilson doctrine. North American review, v. 183, Nov. 16, 1906: 971–989.   AP2.N7, v. 183
———— ———— Offprint. [New York, 1906] 19 p.
E306.6.W64A3

DELAHANTY, MARY T. The integralist philosophy of James Wilson. New York, Pageant Press [°1969] 140 p.
JC176.W53D44
Bibliography: p. 138–140.

GUMMERE, RICHARD M. Classical precedents in the writings of James Wilson. *In* Colonial Society of Massachusetts, *Boston*. Publications. v. 32. Transactions, 1933/37. Boston, 1937. p. 525–538.   F61.C71, v. 32

KONKLE, BURTON A. James Wilson and the Constitution. The opening address in the official series of events known as the James Wilson memorial. Delivered before the Law Academy of Philadelphia on November 14,

1906. Published by order of the Law Academy, 1907 [Philadelphia? 1907] 40 p. facsim., plates, port. JK119.K7

LEAVELLE, ARNAUD B. James Wilson and the relation of the Scottish metaphysics to American political thought. Political science quarterly, v. 57, Sept. 1942: 394–410. H1.P8, v. 57

McLAUGHLIN, ANDREW C. James Wilson and the Constitution. Political science quarterly, v. 12, Mar. 1897: 1–20. H1.P8, v. 12

POWELL, FRANCIS D. A Thomistic evaluation of James Wilson and Thomas Reid. Washington, 1951. xii, 371 l. JC176.W53P6

Thesis (Ph.D.)—Georgetown University.
Bibliography: leaves 366–371.

QUATTROCCHI, ANNA M. James Wilson and the establishment of the federal government. Historian, v. 2, winter 1939: 105–117. D1.H22, v. 2

QUERIN, MARY C., Sister. The political theory of James Wilson. 1961. ([292] p.) Micro AC–1, no. 61–6486

Thesis (Ph.D.)—St. Louis University.
Abstracted in Dissertation Abstracts, v. 22, Mar. 1962, p. 3252–3253.

RHYND, JAMES. The thistle in "Old Glory"; James Wilson and the American Constitution. Scots magazine, v. 36, Mar. 1942: 407–418. illus. AP4.S3732, v. 36

ROSENBERGER, HOMER T. James Wilson's theories of punishment. Pennsylvania magazine of history and biography, v. 73, Jan. 1949: 45–63. F146.P65, v. 73

SEED, GEOFFREY. The democratic ideas of James Wilson; a reappraisal. In British Association for American Studies. Bulletin, new ser., no. 10, June 1965: 3–30. E172.B72, n.s., no. 10

SMITH, CHARLES PAGE. James Wilson and the era of the Revolution. In Dickinson College, Carlisle, Pa. "John and Mary's College." [Westwood, N.J.] Revell [1956] (The Boyd Lee Spahr lectures in Americana, 1951–1956) p. 33–59. LD1663.A53

——James Wilson, founding father, 1742–1798. Chapel Hill, N.C., University of North Carolina Press for the Institute of Early American History and Culture [ᶜ1956] xii, 426 p. port. E302.6.W64S6

The author's thesis (Ph.D.), James Wilson, 1787–1798, was submitted to Harvard University in 1951.

YOUNG, GEORGE L. The services of James Wilson in the Continental Congress. 1954. ([362] p.) Micro AC–1, no. 10,343

Thesis (Ph.D.)—Lehigh University.
Abstracted in Dissertation Abstracts, v. 14, no. 12, p. 2183–2184.

14764
WILSON, MATTHEW (1731–1790)
Pennsylvania; Delaware. Clergyman, physician.

CHANCE, ELBERT. Matthew Wilson—professor, preacher, patriot, physician. Delaware history, v. 10, Apr. 1963: 271–284. F161.D37, v. 10

NEILL, EDWARD D. Matthew Wilson, D.D., of Lewes, Delaware. Pennsylvania magazine of history and biography, v. 8, no. 1, 1884: 45–55. facsims. F146.P65, v. 8

——— ——— Detached copy. F174.L6N3

14765
WILSON, RACHEL WILSON (1720–1775)
England. Itinerant Quaker minister.

Rachel Wilson of Kendal, 1722–1776: notes and incidents of her visit to America, 1768–1769. In Friends' Historical Society of Philadelphia. Bulletin, v. 8, Nov. 1917: 25–35. BX7635.A1F6, v. 8

SOMERVELL, JOHN. Isaac and Rachel Wilson, Quakers, of Kendal, 1714–1785. London, Swarthmore Press [1924] 160 p. BX7795.W57S6

14766
WILSON, WILLIAM (d. 1813)
Ireland; Pennsylvania. Revolutionary officer.

LINN, MARY H. General William Wilson. In Northumberland County (Pa.) Historical Society. Proceedings. v. 10. Sunbury, 1938. p. [5]–24. F157.N8N7, v. 10

14767
WINCHESTER, JAMES (1752–1826)*
Maryland; Tennessee. Revolutionary officer, planter, Indian fighter.

DE WITT, JOHN H. General James Winchester. Tennessee historical magazine, v. 1, June–Sept. 1915: 79–105, 183–205. F431.T28, v. 1

HARRELL, DAVID E. James Winchester: patriot. Tennessee historical quarterly, v. 17, Dec. 1958: 301–317. F431.T285, v. 17

14768
WINDS, WILLIAM (1727–1789)
New Jersey. Landowner, assemblyman, Revolutionary general.

TUTTLE, JOSEPH F. Biographical sketch of General William Winds, of Morris Co., New Jersey. In New Jersey Historical Society. Proceedings, v. 7, no. 1, 1853: 13–37. F131.N58, v. 7

14769
WINDSHIP, AMOS (1745–1813)
Massachusetts. Physician, Revolutionary naval surgeon.

ELIOT, EPHRAIM. Dr. Amos Windship (1745–1813; H.C. 1771). *In* Colonial Society of Massachusetts, *Boston*. Publications. v. 25. Transactions, 1922/24. Boston, 1924. p. 141–171. F61.C71, v. 25

A biographical sketch of Windship taken from Eliot's commonplace book. Introduction and notes by Samuel E. Morison.

14770

WINGATE, PAINE (1739–1838)*

Massachusetts; New Hampshire. Congregational clergyman, farmer, delegate to the Continental Congress.

WINGATE, CHARLES E. L. Life and letters of Paine Wingate, one of the fathers of the nation; the story of a New England country gentleman whose life encompassing nearly a hundred years between the reign of George II and the presidency of Van Buren included the duties of clergyman and statesman and illustrated the lives of those who made the union of the United States successful. [Winchester, Mass.] J. D. P. Wingate, 1930. 2 v. facsims., map, plates, port. E302.6.W67W6

14771

WINN, RICHARD (1750–1818)*

Virginia; South Carolina. Landowner, Revolutionary officer, assemblyman.

——— General Richard Winn's notes—1780. Edited by Samuel C. Williams. South Carolina historical and genealogical magazine, v. 43, Oct. 1942: 201–212; v. 44, Jan. 1943: 1–10. F266.S55, v. 43

CURRY, JABEZ L. Richard Winn. *In* Southern History Association. Publications, v. 2, July 1898: 225–229. F206.S73, v. 2

WILLIAMS, SAMUEL C. Major-General Richard Winn, South Carolinian and Tennessean. Tennessee historical quarterly, v. 1, Mar. 1942: 8–20. F341.T285, v. 1

14772

WINSLOW, ANNA GREEN (1759–1779)

Massachusetts. Student.

——— Diary of Anna Green Winslow, a Boston school girl of 1771. Edited by Alice Morse Earle. Boston, Houghton, Mifflin, 1894. xx, 121 p. facsim., plates, ports. F73.4.W78

Reprinted in Detroit by Singing Tree Press (1970).

14773

WINSLOW, EDWARD (1746–1815)

Massachusetts; New Brunswick. Loyalist officer.

DUVAL, L. CARLE. Edward Winslow. *In* New Brunswick Historical Society. Collections. no. 17. Saint John, N.B., 1961. p. 35–40. F1041.N53, no. 17

Letters of a Loyalist family. Edited by Edmund F. Carpenter. New England magazine, new ser., v. 15, Oct. 1896: 150–155. AP2.N4, n.s., v. 15

Includes excerpts of letters by Winslow and other members of his family.

RAYMOND, WILLIAM O., *ed.* Winslow papers, A.D. 1776–1826. Printed under the auspices of the New Brunswick Historical Society. St. John, N.B., Sun Print. Co., 1901. 732 p. illus., facsim., plates, port. F1043.R27

Consists chiefly of letters to Edward Winslow, although other family papers are included.

Reprinted, with a new introduction and preface by George A. Billias, in Boston by Gregg Press (1972).

RIFE, CLARENCE W. Edward Winslow, junior: Loyalist pioneer in the Maritime Provinces. *In* Canadian Historical Association. Report. 1928. Ottawa [1929] p. 101–112. F1001.C26, 1928

14774

WINSLOW, ISAAC (*b.* 1742)

Massachusetts. Merchant, councilor, Loyalist.

WINSLOW, ERVING. A Loyalist in the siege of Boston. New-England historical and genealogical register, v. 56, Jan. 1902: 48–54. F1.N56, v. 56

14775

WINSTON, JOSEPH (1746–1815)*

Virginia; North Carolina. Revolutionary officer, assemblyman.

HENDRICKS, JAMES EDWIN. Joseph Winston: North Carolina Jeffersonian. North Carolina historical review, v. 45, summer 1968: 284–297. illus., port. F251.N892, v. 45

14776

WINTHROP, JOHN (1714–1779)*

Massachusetts. Astronomer, professor.

BRASCH, FREDERICK E. John Winthrop (1714–1779), America's first astronomer, and the science of his period. *In* Astronomical Society of the Pacific, *San Francisco*. Publications, v. 28, Aug./Oct. 1916: 153–170. illus., port. QB1.A4, v. 28

——— Newton's first critical disciple in the American colonies—John Winthrop. *In* History of Science Society. Sir Isaac Newton, 1727–1927, a bicentenary evaluation of his work. Baltimore, Williams & Wilkins Co., 1928. [Special publication no. 1 of the History of Science Society] p. [299]–338. QC16.N7H5

14777

WISNER, HENRY (1720–1790)*

New York. Farmer, assemblyman, delegate to the Continental Congress, Revolutionary officer and munitioner.

BURDGE, FRANKLIN. A memorial of Henry Wisner, the only New Yorker who voted for the Declaration of Independence. [New York? 1878] 14 p.

E302.6.W68B9

—— A second memorial of Henry Wisner. [New York?] 1898. 38 p.   E302.6.W68B92

"Nothing of the Memorial of 1878 is here reprinted except to correct errors and to make new statements intelligible."—p. [3]

14778

WISTER, SARAH (1761–1804)*

Pennsylvania. Student.

—— Sally Wister's journal, a true narrative; being a Quaker maiden's account of her experiences with officers of the Continental Army, 1777–1778. Edited by Albert Cook Myers, with reproductions of portraits, manuscripts, relics and views. Philadelphia, Ferris & Leach [ᶜ1902] 224 p. illus., facsims., plates (part col.), ports.

E263.P4W81

Reprinted in New York by the New York Times (1969). Portions of the *Journal* were published in the *Pennsylvania Magazine of History and Biography*, v. 9, Oct. 1885–Jan. 1886, p. 318–333, 463–478, and v. 10, Apr. 1886, p. 51–60.

14779

WISWALL, JOHN (1731–1821)

Massachusetts; Maine; Nova Scotia. Anglican clergyman, Loyalist.

SAUNDERS, EDWARD M. The life and times of the Rev. John Wiswall, M.A., a Loyalist clergyman in New England and Nova Scotia, 1731–1821. *In* Nova Scotia Historical Society, *Halifax.* Collections. v. 13. Halifax, 1908. p. [1]–73.   [F1036.N93, v. 13]
Micro 03606

Based on his manuscript journal.

14780

WITHERSPOON, JOHN (1723–1794)*†

Scotland; New Jersey. Presbyterian clergyman, educator, delegate to the Continental Congress.

—— Works. Edinburgh, Printed for J. Ogle, 1815. 9 v.

BX8915.W5 1815

Available on microfilm in the American Culture Series (Micro 01291, reels 256–257 E) is another editon in nine volumes, the first six of which were issued by different publishers before 1815.

—— The works of the Rev. John Witherspoon . . . To which is prefixed an account of the author's life, in a sermon occasioned by his death, by the Rev. Dr. John Rodgers. 2d ed., rev. and corr. Philadelphia, Printed and published by William W. Woodward, nᵒ. 52, South Second Street, 1802. 4 v.

BX8915.W5 Rare Bk. Coll.

First published in 1800.

BENSON, LOUIS F. What did Doctor Witherspoon say? *In* Presbyterian Historical Society. Journal, v. 8, June 1916: 241–257.   BX8905.P7A4, v. 8

Examines evidence for the speech allegedly made by Witherspoon during the debate over the adoption of the Declaration of Independence. The author's second essay on the subject, "What Did Doctor Witherspoon Say? A Postscript," appeared in v. 12, Apr. 1927, p. 389–397.

BRADBURY, MILES L. Adventure in persuasion: John Witherspoon, Samuel Stanhope Smith, and Ashbel Green. 1967.

Thesis (Ph.D.)—Harvard University.

BUTTERFIELD, LYMAN H., *ed.* John Witherspoon comes to America; a documentary account based largely on new materials. Princeton University Library, 1953. xiv, 99 p. illus., facsims., ports.   LD4605.1768.B8

Bibliographic references included in "Notes" (p. 87–95).

COLLINS, VARNUM L. President Witherspoon, a biography. Princeton, Princeton University Press, 1925. 2 v. facsims., plates, ports.   E302.6.W7C7

Bibliography: v. 2, p. 273–[275]
Reprinted in New York by Arno Press (1969).

FODY, EDWARD S. John Witherspoon: advisor to the lovelorn. *In* New Jersey Historical Society. Proceedings, v. 84, Oct. 1966: 239–249.   F131.N58, v. 84

GUMMERE, RICHARD M. A Scottish classicist in colonial America. *In* Colonial Society of Massachusetts, *Boston.* Publications. v. 35. Transactions, 1942/46. Boston, 1951. p. 146–161.   F61.C71, v. 35

McALLISTER, JAMES L. John Witherspoon: academic advocate for American freedom. *In* Henry, Stuart C., *ed.* A miscellany of American Christianity; essays in honor of H. Shelton Smith. Durham, N.C., Duke University Press, 1963. p. [183]–224.   BR515.H46

[MONTAGUE, MARY L.] John Witherspoon, signer of the Declaration of Independence; George Washington's close friend and sponsor. [Washington, D.C., Printed by H. L. & J. B. McQueen, 1932] 24 p.

E302.W7M67

NICHOLS, JOHN H. John Witherspoon on church and state. Journal of Presbyterian history, v. 42, Sept. 1964: 166–174.   BX8905.P7A4, v. 42

RICH, GEORGE E. John Witherspoon: his Scottish intellectual background. 1964. ([212] p.)
Micro AC–1, no. 65–3433

Thesis (Ph.D.)—Syracuse University.
Abstracted in *Dissertation Abstracts*, v. 26, Aug. 1965, p. 1010.

ROBINSON, STEWART M. Notes on the Witherspoon pamphlets. Princeton University Library chronicle, v. 27, autumn 1965: 53–59.   Z733.P93C5, v. 27

Discusses the 600 pamphlets collected by Witherspoon and purchased by Princeton College in 1802.

TYLER, MOSES COIT. President Witherspoon in the American Revolution. American historical review, v. 1, July 1896: 671–679.   E171.A57, v. 1

WOODS, DAVID W., *Jr.* John Witherspoon. New York, F. H. Revell Co. [c1906] 295 p. port. E302.6.W7W8

14781

WOLCOTT, OLIVER (1726–1797)*

Connecticut. Judge, delegate to the Continental Congress, Revolutionary general.

BLAND, JAMES E. The Oliver Wolcotts of Connecticut: the national experience, 1775–1800. 1970.

Thesis (Ph.D.)—Harvard University.

14782

WOLTERS, RICHARD (*ca.* 1714–1771)

Netherlands. British agent.

———An eighteenth-century account [1764] of German emigration to the American colonies. Journal of modern history, v. 28, Mar. 1956: 55–59.   D1.J6, v. 28

Introduction and notes by Frank Spencer.

14783

WOOD, JAMES (1750–1813)

Virginia. Assemblyman, Revolutionary officer, councilor.

——— Correspondence of Col. James Wood [1779–82] Tyler's quarterly historical and genealogical magazine, v. 3, July 1921: 28–44.   F221.T95, v. 3

GREENE, KATHERINE G., *and* WILLIAM W. GLASS, *eds.* Brig. General and Governor James Wood, Junior, and the Society of the Cincinnati in the state of Virginia. [Winchester, Va., Printed by Pifer Print. Co., 1946] 62 p. facsims.   E207.W78G7

14784

WOOD, SAMUEL (1724 *or* 5–1816)

New York; Nova Scotia. Cooper, Loyalist.

HOWE, HERBERT B. Samuel Wood—Loyalist. *In* Westchester County Historical Society. Quarterly bulletin, v. 23, Jan./Apr. 1947: 1–17.   F127.W5W594, v. 23

14785

WOODBRIDGE, LUCY BACKUS (1757–1817)

Connecticut; Ohio. Settler.

RAU, LOUISE. Lucy Backus Woodbridge, pioneer mother, January 31, 1757–October 6, 1817. Ohio state archaeological and historical quarterly, v. 44, Oct. 1935: 405–442.   F486.O51, v. 44

14786

WOODFORD, WILLIAM (1734–1780)*

Virginia. Revolutionary general.

——— Unpublished letters of General Woodford, of the Continental Army, 1776–1779. Pennsylvania magazine of history and biography, v. 23, Jan. 1900: 453–463.   F146.P65, v. 23

Contributed by John W. Jordan.

HEATHCOTE, CHARLES W. General William Woodford—a gallant officer who helped Washington. Picket post, no. 60, May 1958: 4–5, 37–41.   E234.P5, no. 60

14787

WOODHULL, NATHANIEL (1722–1776)*

New York. Farmer, Revolutionary general.

SABINE, WILLIAM H. W. Suppressed history of General Nathaniel Woodhull, president of the New York Congress and Convention in 1776. New York [Colburn & Tegg] 1954. 225 p. illus.   E207.W8S3

"Short-title list of sources": p. 212–217.

14788

WOODMASON, CHARLES (*ca.* 1720–*ca.* 1776)

England; South Carolina. Landowner, itinerant Anglican clergyman.

———The Carolina backcountry on the eve of the Revolution; the Journal and other writings of Charles Woodmason, Anglican itinerant. Edited with an introduction by Richard J. Hooker. Chapel Hill, Published for the Institute of Early American History and Culture at Williamsburg, Va., by the University of North Carolina Press, 1953. xxxix, 305 p. map (on lining papers)   F272.W77

Bibliographic footnotes.

14789

WOODS, GEORGE (*fl.* 1755–1800)

Pennsylvania. Surveyor, Revolutionary officer, judge.

KUSSART, S. Colonel George Woods, Pittsburgh's first surveyor. Western Pennsylvania historical magazine, v. 7, Apr. 1924: 73–87.   F146.W52, v. 7

14790

WOOLMAN, JOHN (1720–1772)*†

New Jersey. Itinerant Quaker minister, abolitionist, reformer.

——— The works of John Woolman. In two parts. Philadelphia, Printed by Joseph Crukshank, in Market-Street, between Second and Third streets, 1774. xiv, 436 p.   BX7617.W6 1774 Rare Bk. Coll.

Contents: The testimony of Friends in Yorkshire, at their Quarterly-meeting, held at York the 24th and 25th of the third month, 1773, concerning John Woolman.—A testimony of the Monthly-meeting of Friends, held in Burlington, the first day of the eighth month, in the year of Our Lord, 1774, concerning our esteemed friend John Woolman, deceased.—[pt. 1] A journal of the life, gospel labours, and Christian experiences of that faithful minister of Jesus Christ, John Woolman.—pt. 2. The works of John Woolman: Some considerations on the keeping of Negroes. Considerations on the keeping of Negroes . . . Part the second. Considerations on pure wisdom, and human policy; on labour; on schools; and on the right use of the Lord's outward gifts. Considerations on the true harmony of mankind; and how it is to be maintained. Remarks on sundry subjects. An epistle to the Quarterly and Monthly meetings of Friends.

Reprinted in New York by Garrett Press (1970). The second edition, published in 1775, has been reprinted in Miami, Fla., by Mnemosyne Pub. Co. (1969).

Woolman's journal passed through several editions. The John Greenleaf Whittier edition, with the addition of *A Plea for the Poor* published in 1793, has been reissued with an introduction by Frederick B. Tolles, in New York (Corinth Books [1961] 249 p. BX7795.W7A3 1961) and reprinted in Gloucester, Mass. (P. Smith, 1971). See also *The Journal and Essays of John Woolman, Edited From the Original Manuscripts with a Biographical Introduction by Amelia Mott Gummere* (New York, Macmillan Co., 1922. 643 p. BX7795.W7A3 1922).

ALTMAN, W. FORREST. John Woolman's reading of the mystics. *In* Friends' Historical Association. Bulletin, v. 48, autumn 1959: 103–115.   BX7635.A1F6, v. 48

CADBURY, HENRY J. Sailing to England with John Woolman [1772] Quaker history, v. 55, autumn 1966: 88–103.   BX7635.A1F6, v. 55

Based on the letters of one of Woolman's traveling companions, Samuel Emlen (1730–1799).

HOUSTON, G. DAVID. John Woolman's efforts in behalf of freedom. Journal of Negro history, v. 2, Apr. 1917: 126–138.   E185.J86, v. 2

MOULTON, PHILLIPS P. John Woolman: exemplar of ethics. Quaker history, v. 54, autumn 1965: 81–93.   BX7635.A1F6, v. 54

——— John Woolman's approach to social action—as exemplified in relation to slavery. Church history, v. 35, Dec. 1966: 399–410.   BR140.A45, v. 35

WHITNEY, JANET P. John Woolman, American Quaker. Boston, Little, Brown, 1942. x, 490 p. illus., facsims., map (on lining papers), plates.   BX7795.W7W5
Bibliography: p. [435]–440.

14791
WOOLSEY, MELANCTHON LLOYD (1758–1819)
New York. Revolutionary officer.

——— Woolsey papers; Melancthon Lloyd Woolsey, lieutenant, Continental Army; major, New York levies; brigadier general, Clinton county militia. A memoir, compiled for his descendants, by his great-grandson, Melancthon Lloyd Woolsey. Champlain, Priv. print. at the Moorsfield Press, 1929. 33 p. plates, port.   E199.W92

14792
WOOLSEY, REBECCA LLOYD (1718–1797)
New York; Connecticut.

——— Woolsey papers; letters of Rebecca Woolsey, 1783–1785. Printed for the Rev. M. Lloyd Woolsey for presentation to descendants of the writer. Champlain, Priv. print. at the Moorsfield Press, 1929. 14 p.   E199.W92

14793
WOOSTER, BENJAMIN (1762–*ca.* 1838)
Connecticut. Revolutionary soldier, clergyman.

——— Memoirs: the Reverend Benjamin Wooster. *In* Vermont Historical Society. Proceedings, new ser., v. 4, Dec. 1936: 215–251.   F46.V55, n.s., v. 4

14794
WOOSTER, DAVID (1711–1777)*
Connecticut. Military officer, merchant, Revolutionary general.

DEMING, HENRY C. An oration upon the life and services of Gen. David Wooster. Hartford, Press of Case, Tiffany, 1854. 60 p.   E207.W9D3

REED, JOHN F. Red tape at Valley Forge. Manuscripts, v. 20, spring 1968: 20–27.   Z41.A2A925, v. 20

Concerns the difficulties in collecting back pay for Wooster from the Paymaster Department of the Continental Army.

14795
WRAXALL, *Sir* NATHANIEL WILLIAM, *Bart.* (1751–1831)†
England. Military officer, traveler, Member of Parliament.

——— The historical and the posthumous memoirs of Sir Nathaniel William Wraxall, 1772–1784. Edited, with notes and additional chapters from the author's unpublished ms. by Henry B. Wheatley. London, Bickers, 1884. 5 v. ports.   DA506.W9A2

Reminiscences of royal and noble personages during the last and present centuries: v. 5, p. [341]–396.

The *Historical Memoirs*, first published in 1815 (London, T. Cadell and W. Davies. 2 v. DA506.W9A17), cover the period 1772–84 but deal principally with the author's travels on the continent, 1772–79. The *Posthumous Memoirs* first published in 1836 (London, R. Bentley. 3 v. DA506.W9A3), cover the period 1784–89.

——— Memoirs of the courts of Berlin, Dresden, Warsaw, and Vienna, in the years 1777, 1778, and 1779. 2d ed.

London, Printed by A. Strahan, for T. Cadell Jun. and W. Davies, 1800. 2 v.   D289.W94

First Published in 1779.

———— A short review of the political state of Great-Britain at the commencement of the year one thousand seven hundred and eighty seven. 8th ed., with additions. London, Printed for J. Debrett, 1787. 86 p.
AC901.M5, v. 716 Rare Bk. Coll.

See also *The People's Answer to the Court Pamphlet: Entitled A Short Review of the Political State of Great Britain*, 2d ed. ([London] Printed for J. Debrett, 1787. 50 p. DA507.1787.W85).

———— A tour through some of the northern parts of Europe, particularly Copenhagen, Stockholm, and Petersburgh. In a series of letters. 2d ed., corr. London, T. Cadell, 1775. 411 p. fold. map.   D965.W94

14796

WRIGHT, *Sir* JAMES, *1st Bart.* (1716–1785)†

England; South Carolina; Georgia. Lawyer, Royal governor.

———— Letters from Sir James Wright. *In* Georgia Historical Society. Collections. v. 3. Savannah, 1873. p. [157]–378. fold. map.   F281.G35, v. 3

Letters to the Earl of Dartmouth and Lord George Germain, secretaries of state for America, from December 20, 1773, to February 16, 1782.

Report of September 20, 1773, on the condition of the province of Georgia: p. 158–179.

COLEMAN, KENNETH. James Wright. *In* Montgomery, Horace, *ed.* Georgians in profile; historical essays in honor of Ellis Merton Coulter. Athens, University of Georgia Press [1958] p. 40–60.   F285.M73

HARDEN, WILLIAM. Sir James Wright: governor of Georgia by royal commission, 1760–1782. Georgia historical quarterly, v. 2, Mar. 1918: 22–36.
F281.G2975, v. 2

MITCHELL, ROBERT G. Sir James Wright looks at the American Revolution. Georgia historical quarterly, v. 53, Dec. 1969: 509–517.   F281.G2975, v. 53

14797

WRIGHT, JAMES (*d.* 1781?)

Virginia; Pennsylvania; Kentucky. Military officer, surveyor, settler.

BEATTIE, GEORGE W., *and* HELEN P. BEATTIE. Captain James Wright. *In* Kentucky Historical Society. Register, v. 22, Jan. 1924: 86–92.   F446.K43, v. 22

14798

WRIGHT, PATIENCE LOVELL (1725–1786)*†

New Jersey; England. Sculptress, Revolutionary spy.

LONG, J. C. Patience Wright of Bordentown. *In* New Jersey Historical Society. Proceedings, v. 79, Apr. 1971: 118–123. plates.   F131.N58, v. 79

14799

WRIGHT, ZADOCK (1736–1819)

Massachusetts; Vermont. Loyalist officer.

BASIL, HAMILTON V. Zadock Wright, that "devilish" Tory of Hartland. Vermont history, v. 36, autumn 1968: 186–203.   F46.V55, v. 36

14800

WYLLYS, GEORGE (1710–1796)*

Connecticut. Military officer, secretary.

———— The Wyllys papers; correspondence and documents chiefly of descendants of Gov. George Wyllys of Connecticut, 1590–1796. Hartford, Connecticut Historical Society, 1924. xl, 567 p. facsim. (Collections of the Connecticut Historical Society, v. 21) F91.C7, v. 21
F97.W98

Edited by Albert C. Bates.

14801

WYTHE, GEORGE (1726–1806)*

Virginia. Lawyer, assemblyman, judge, professor, delegate to the Continental Congress, delegate to the Constitutional Convention.

ANDERSON, DICE R. The teacher of Jefferson and Marshall. South Atlantic quarterly, v. 15, Oct. 1916: 329–343.   AP2.S75, v. 15

BOYD, JULIAN P. The murder of George Wythe. William and Mary quarterly, 3d ser., v. 12, Oct. 1955: 513–542. plates.   F221.W71, 3d s., v. 12

Followed by a documentary essay by W. Edwin Hemphill entitled "Examinations of George Wythe Swinney for Forgery and Murder" (p. 543–574).

CLARKIN, WILLIAM. Serene patriot: a life of George Wythe. Albany, Alan Publications, 1970. x, 235 p. port.   KF363.W9C5

Bibliography: p. [222]–230.

HEMPHILL, WILLIAM EDWIN. George Wythe courts the Muses: in which, to the astonishment of everyone, that silent, selfless pedant is found to have had a sense of humor. William and Mary quarterly, 3d ser., v. 9, July 1952: 338–345.   F221.W71, 3d s., v. 9

Wythe sought release from the sectional tensions that gripped Congress in the fall of 1776 by exchanging couplets with his fellow delegate, William Ellery, of Rhode Island.

———— George Wythe, the colonial Briton: a biographical study of the pre-Revolutionary era in Virginia. 1937. Thesis (Ph.D.)—University of Virginia.

HERRINK, LOUIS S. George Wythe. *In* John P. Branch historical papers of Randolph-Macon College. v. 3, no. 4; 1912. Ashland, Va. p. 283–313.

F221.J65, v. 3

14802

YEATES, JASPER (1745–1817)*
Pennsylvania. Lawyer.

LANDIS, CHARLES I. Jasper Yeates and his times. Pennsylvania magazine of history and biography, v. 46, July 1922: 199–231.   F146.P65, v. 46

———— ———— Offprint. [Lancaster? Pa., 1922?] 33 p.
KF363.Y3L3

14803

YOUNG, ARTHUR (1741–1820)†
England. Farmer, agriculturist.

———— The autobiography of Arthur Young, with selections from his correspondence. Edited by M. Betham-Edwards. London, Smith, Elder, 1898. x, 480 p. fold. facsim., plates, ports.   S417.Y6A2

14804

YOUNG, JAMES (*d.* 1789)†
England. British naval officer.

———— Brieven gewisselt tusschen den Engelschen Vice-Admiraal Joung, den Heer Colpoys, kapitein van een Engelsch oorlogsschip, en Zijne Excellentie den Heer Jan de Graaf, gouverneur van St. Eustatius, strekkende ter verantwoordinge en verdediginge van den laatsten, tegen de annklagt der Engelschen. Amsterdam, Bij de erven Houttuyn [1777] 21 p.   F2151.Y73

14805

YOUNG, THOMAS (1732–1777)*
Pennsylvania; Massachusetts. Physician, Revolutionary surgeon.

CALDWELL, RENWICK K. The man who named Vermont. Vermont history, new ser., v. 26, Oct. 1958: 294–300.
F46.V55, n.s., v. 26

EDES, HENRY H. Memoir of Dr. Thomas Young. *In* Colonial Society of Massachusetts, *Boston.* Publications. v. 11. Transactions, 1906/7. Boston, 1910. p. 2–54. map.   F61.C71, v. 11

HAWKE, DAVID F. Dr. Thomas Young, "eternal fisher in troubled waters": notes for a biography. *In* New York Historical Society. Quarterly, v. 54, Jan. 1970: 7–29. illus., facsim., ports.   F116.N638, v. 54

14806

ZANE, EBENEZER (1747–1812)*
Virginia; Ohio. Land speculator, settler.

PATTERSON, JOHN G. Ebenezer Zane, frontiersman. West Virginia history, v. 12, Oct. 1950: 5–45.
F236.W52, v. 12

SMUCKER, ISAAC. The first pioneers on the Ohio. Magazine of western history, v. 2, Aug. 1885: 322–336.
E171.N27, v. 2

14807

ZANE, ISAAC (1743–1795)
Pennsylvania; Virginia. Ironmaster, planter, assemblyman.

MOSS, ROGER W. Isaac Zane, Jr., a "Quaker for the times." Virginia magazine of history and biography, v. 77, July 1969: 291–306. map.   F221.V91, v. 77

14808

ZEISBERGER, DAVID (1721–1808)*
Pennsylvania; Old Northwest. Moravian missionary, Indian negotiator.

———— David Zeisberger's history of northern American Indians. Edited by Archer Butler Hulbert and William Nathaniel Schwarze. [Columbus, Ohio, Press of F. J. Heer, 1910] 189 p. (Ohio archaeological and historical quarterly, v. 19, Jan./Apr. 1910)   E77.Z47
F486.O51, v. 19

[The Moravian records, v. 1]

———— The diaries of Zeisberger relating to the first missions in the Ohio Basin. Edited by Archer Butler Hulbert and William Nathaniel Schwarze. [Columbus, Ohio, Press of F. J. Heer Print. Co., 1912] 125 p. (Ohio archaeological and historical quarterly, v. 19, Jan. 1912)
E98.M6Z45
F486.O51, v. 21

The Moravian records, v. 2.
From the records preserved in the Moravian Library at Bethlehem.
Contents: Introduction: the missions of the Unitas Fratrum, by A. B. Hulbert.—Diary of David Zeisberger's journey to the Ohio, Sept. 20–Nov. 16, 1767.—Report of the journey of John Ettwein, David Zeisberger and Gottlob Senseman to Friedenshuetten, 1768.—Diary of David Zeisberger and Gottlob Senseman: journey to Goschgoschink on the Ohio, May 9, 1768–Jan. 9, 1769.—Notes.

———— Diary of David Zeisberger, a Moravian missionary among the Indians of Ohio. Translated from the original German manuscript and edited by Eugene F. Bliss. Cincinnati, R. Clarke, 1885. 2. v. (Historical and Philosophical Society of Ohio. [Publications], new ser., v. 2–3)   F486.H675, v. 2–3
E98.M6Z37

Reprinted in St. Clair Shores, Mich., by Scholarly Press (1972).
The diary extends from 1781 to 1798.

DE SCHWEINITZ, EDMUND A. The life and times of David Zeisberger, the western pioneer and apostle of the Indians. Philadelphia, J. B. Lippincott, 1870. 747 p.
E98.M6Z4

Reprinted in New York by Johnson Reprint Corp. (1971) and by Arno Press (1971).

14809

ZIEGLER, DAVID (1748–1811)*

Germany; Pennsylvania; Ohio. Revolutionary officer.

KATZENBERGER, GEORGE A. Major David Ziegler. Ohio archaeological and historical quarterly, v. 21, Apr./July 1912: 127–174. illus., facsims., plan, plate, ports.
F486.O51, v. 21

————— ————— Offprint. Columbus, Ohio, F. J. Heer Print. Co., 1912. 50 p. illus., facsims., plan, plate, ports.
F499.C5K19

STEELE, MARY D. The military career of an officer in Harmar's regiment, 1775–1792. Magazine of western history, v. 10, June, Aug. 1889: 247–255, 377–382.
E171.N27, v. 10

14810

ZUBLY, JOHN JOACHIM (1724–1781)*

Switzerland; Georgia. Presbyterian clergyman, delegate to the Continental Congress, Loyalist.

————— Revolutionary tracts. Spartanburg, S.C., Reprint Co. [1972] viii, 30, 26, xx, 41 p.
E297.Z97 1972

Reprint of three sermons by J. J. Zubly: *The Stamp Act Repealed,* first published 1766; *An Humble Enquiry Into the Nature of the Dependency of the American Colonies Upon the Parliament of Great Britain and the Right of Parliament to Lay Taxes on the Said Colonies,* first published 1769; and *The Law of Liberty,* first published 1775.

DANIEL, MARJORIE L. John Joachim Zubly—Georgia pamphleteer of the Revolution. Georgia historical quarterly, v. 19, Mar. 1935: 1–16. F281.G2975, v. 19

PERKINS, EUNICE R. John Joachim Zubly, Georgia's conscientious objector. Georgia historical quarterly, v. 15, Dec. 1931: 313–323.
F281.G2975, v. 15

The Preservation and Publication of Documentary Sources on the American Revolution

Introduction

The character and meaning of the American revolutionary experience have been the subject of debate for nearly two centuries. Changing attitudes, interests, and assumptions and the increasing availability of evidence have led each generation to view the Revolution from its own perspective. In the first 50 years after the Declaration of Independence, men and women of various political and sectional loyalties created a national historical tradition in an effort to tie more firmly the bonds of union. During the middle years of the 19th century Revolutionary historiography passed into the hands of gifted amateur scholars whose faith in the American democratic experiment led them to idealize the accomplishments of the Founding Fathers and to attribute to them great wisdom and virtue. With the development of history as a professional discipline and the growth of America's role in the world, scholars at the turn of the 20th century began to apply "scientific" principles to their study of the Revolution and to view it within the larger context of the Atlantic community. At the same time, the social ferment that accomplished rapid industrialization induced still others to reinterpret the Revolutionary upheaval as a series of internal class struggles for political dominance within each of the new states. After 1945 historians caught up in the psychology of the Cold War began to construe the Revolution as a defense of American liberties against foreign manipulation and subversion. Like all historical movements, the Revolution encompassed so many conflicting strains that it gave rise to and continues to support several pluralistic interpretations.

Beneath this literary record, however, lie the documents that form the permanent record of the past. The most important factors bearing on the historian's ability to interpret complex events are the nature and the availability of evidence. Today, students of the American Revolution are aided in their research by bibliographies and manuscript guides, by large depositories with professionally trained staffs that collect, preserve, and organize historical materials, and by numerous technological innovations of comparatively recent origin. Yet, for more than a century after the Revolution, the greatest challenge lay in rescuing from neglect, decay, and destruction the documentary evidence upon which written history depends. Amateur scholars and antiquaries took the first, halting steps in the early days of the Republic by forming societies for the preservation and publication of documents. Following the War of 1812, their precedent inspired a growing number of collectors, historical societies, state agencies, and the federal government to seek out the records of the Revolutionary generation and to support the publication of selected sources. As beneficial as these efforts were, however, it was not until the end of the 19th century, when the newly organized American Historical Association stimulated professional interest in historical study, that pressure was effectively exerted for improvement in the preservation and organization of archival records, the compilation of calendars and descriptive guides, and the publication of primary sources. By the mid-20th century the cumulative effect of growing professionalism on collectors and scholars transformed Revolutionary historiography. Historians who now study the nation's founders are deeply indebted to those who developed the first archival and historical programs in the United States.

Colonial and Revolutionary Period

During the colonial period little or no effort had been made to preserve or publish government documents or private papers. Since a government's right to the official papers of its servants was not a firmly established principle, colonial officials frequently took their records with them when they left office. Only records that affected everyday life and were essential for social continuity, such as platbooks, deeds, tax rolls, wills, court proceedings, and the acts of legislative bodies were preserved with regularity. The physical conditions under which they were kept varied from colony to colony. Few colonial governments built separate depositories, and even when they did, they were unable to safeguard against the effects of fire, water, vermin, and negligent clerks. And personal papers were not only subject to the same physical dangers as official documents but also to the hazards of frequent changes of residence and the vagaries of inheritance.

Toward the middle of the 18th century a growing interest in history and a desire to emulate European academies and learned institutions led to the incorporation of several literary and philosophical societies, among them the Library Company of Philadelphia (1731), the Library Society of Charleston (1748), and the New York Library Society (1754). More than three dozen public, private, and academic institutions of note had been established by the eve of the Revolution. Yet even among the educated elite who formed such societies, there was little appreciation of the relationship between historical records and the writing of history. Collections were meager by European standards—only Harvard College had more than 3,000 printed works. And many of these collections, such as the priceless library of Thomas Prince, were destroyed during the War for Independence.

The lack of a strong archival tradition, trained clerks, and adequate facilities thus contributed greatly to the loss of documents created by the Revolutionary generation—a fact that provoked concern among contemporaries. In 1791 Thomas Jefferson complained that the War had "done the work of centuries" in despoiling public records stored in state and local offices. John Adams also regretted the fact that many of the secret papers and proceedings of the committees of the Continental Congress were scattered or deliberately destroyed. His concern over the loss of Confederation records was dramatized in 1800 by a fire that devastated the records of the War Department. The survival rate among collections of private papers was equally poor. In a fit of melancholy shortly before his death, James Otis, Jr., consigned to the flames his considerable political correspondence from the years 1760 to 1770. Samuel Adams and William Ellery destroyed many of their personal papers and directed that friends holding letters from them do the same. While the manuscripts of Stephen Hopkins were swept away in a flood, those of Otho Williams were lost at sea, and those of John Rutledge and Joseph Warren were accidentally burned.

Thus, having few organized collections or depositories to draw on, those who wrote the earliest histories of the Revolution were compelled to copy much of their material from the only readily available source on the War—Dodsley's *Annual Register of World Events* (entry 2565). As a result, the works of patriot historians such as the Rev. William Gordon (entry 996), Dr. David Ramsay (entry 1022), and Mercy Otis Warren (entry 1037), and Loyalist writers like Joseph Galloway (entry 3261), George Chalmers (entry 988), and Peter Oliver (entry 1018) have been largely ignored by later generations. Yet, despite the narrow base of their research, these early historians had been participants in a highly dramatic civil war. In preparing their accounts they incorporated their own experiences and used a variety of personal papers to develop sharply etched views of men and events that still merit consideration. Historical reconstruction changed significantly in the next few decades, however, as early national historians benefited from the efforts of those compilers who undertook the first programs of historical preservation.

EARLY ATTEMPTS TO COLLECT AND PUBLISH SOURCES

Considering the magnitude of the problems they faced and the conditions under which they labored, the achievements of the editors who attempted during the early years of the Republic to gather and publish Revolutionary manuscripts appear all the more remarkable. Public interest in documentary publication was not as acute as it would be in another half century when the deeds of the Founding Fathers had receded far enough into the past to attain romantic luster. The practical men of affairs who directed the fledgling nation through its earliest trials were too preoccupied with the business of politics and commerce to reflect nostalgically on a heritage so recently created. Concerned and hopeful antiquaries nonetheless launched several projects that proved beyond their means to complete.

As early as 1774 Ebenezer Hazard of Philadelphia announced that he intended to publish a series of "American State Papers" that would serve as a documentary base for a comprehensive history of colonial development. Encouraged by the promise of a subsidy from the Continental Congress, Hazard solicited copies of papers from officials in every state and transcribed many documents himself during his travels for the postal service from 1775 to 1789. The first two volumes of his *Historical Collections*, published in 1792–94, covered the period from 1492 to 1656. But they sold so poorly that the Revolutionary documents he planned to include in two succeeding volumes remained unpublished, passing through several hands before eventually becoming part of the collections of the Library of Congress. Matthew Carey's *Official Letters [of George Washington] to the Honourable Congress [1775–78]* (entry 14674), transcribed from originals in the Department of State, met with the same reception, causing him to abandon the project. Hezekiah Niles' first editorial effort, the *Political Writings of John Dickinson* (entry 13217), was also spurned by the public, but he remained undaunted, choosing to make the papers of the Revolutionary generation a regular feature of the *Weekly Register* that he launched in 1811 in Baltimore. One of his more noted achievements came in 1822 when he published in his *Principles and Acts of the Revolution in America* (entry 1181) the major speeches, orations, and proceedings from the period 1765 to 1789. Of all the early editorial efforts, however, the most enduring proved to be William Waller Hening's compilation of *The Statutes at Large [of Virginia, 1619–1792]* (entry 2165), based in large part on Thomas Jefferson's invaluable collection of manuscript laws.

Despite the generally poor reception accorded printed documents in the years following the Revolution, they became an important feature in the serial publications issued by the three major historical societies established through the efforts of Jeremy Belknap, a Boston clergyman and historian, John Pintard, a New York merchant and promoter, and Isaiah Thomas, a Worcester printer and antiquary. Based largely upon the European model of the academy as well as the literary and philosophical societies established in the colonies, the Massachusetts Historical Society (1791), the New-York Historical Society (1804), and the American Antiquarian Society (1812) were made up of amateur and semiprofessional scholars whose stated goals were to collect and preserve sources, to publish the more important documents in their transactions, and, in so doing, to promote a general spirit of inquiry. As corresponding secretary of the most productive society, Belknap made known his intention to keep a sharp lookout for worthwhile collections and to pursue them aggressively. In his constant travels through the New England states he solicited compilations of local data and secured either the originals or copies of Revolutionary papers that soon appeared in print in the Society's *Collections*, first issued

in 1792. Over the next 25 years subscribers were provided with a steady flow of local records and history interspersed with selections from the letters, diaries, and journals of noted figures such as Benjamin Church, Richard Henry Lee, Paul Revere, Ezra Stiles, Charles Thomson, and Jonathan Trumbull.

As sources for the study of the Revolution became more plentiful, those who wrote histories during the early years of the Republic began to ignore the old partisan divisions that filled patriot and Loyalist histories and to make the Revolution a symbol of national, or at least party, unity. Local chroniclers like Jeremy Belknap of New Hampshire and Massachusetts (entry 1330), Benjamin Trumbull of Connecticut (entry 4405), and John Daly Burk of Virginia (entry 2169), asserted the importance of their states and the contributions that local political leaders made to the creation of the Union. At the same time, they also emphasized achievements that transcended state and regional boundaries and pointed to the nation's unique origins. Their work served to buttress a growing national conviction that the rebellion against Great Britain was only the first step in a concerted action leading to the drafting and ratification of the Constitution. Indeed, in his *History of America* (entry 1015), Jedidiah Morse skipped entirely the factious interlude of the Confederation period, allowing the Constitution to appear as the direct and necessary outcome of the Revolution. Together with Abiel Holmes (entry 1058), Mason Weems (entry 14697), John Marshall (entry 1066), and other first generation historians, Morse helped to manufacture a new past for America, one in which the Federal Constitution became the symbol and reality of national life. Convinced that the purpose of history was to instruct as well as to explain, they created a historical tradition in which they depicted the American Revolution as the beginning of a world movement to free mankind from the shackles of despotism. The trend toward the creation of a common past was also strongly affected by a shift in public interest which dramatically accelerated the pace of historical and documentary publication during the second quarter of the 19th century, to the point that some scholars have referred to it as the golden age of historical editing.

From the Jubilee of Independence to the Centennial

Few events in the 19th century caused Americans to reflect more intently upon the meaning of their

Revolutionary heritage than the simultaneous deaths on the afternoon of July 4, 1826, of Thomas Jefferson and John Adams. For over 40 years the celebration of the Fourth of July had been a purely political and partisan affair with both Federalists and Democratic-Republicans claiming to be the true conservators of Revolutionary values. But as James Monroe noted in his second inaugural, the nation had entered an "era of good feelings" after the War of 1812. The deaths of Adams and Jefferson laid to rest nearly a half-century of partisanship and marked the nationalization of the holiday. Coming close on the heels of Lafayette's triumphant tour of the United States in 1824 and 1825, the Grand Apotheosis, as one eulogist dubbed it, contributed to a growing national faith that God's hand was guiding the American experiment.

At the same time, publishers of popular and historical magazines became increasingly conscious of the young nation's cultural immaturity and the lack of a substantive body of published historical data on America. New-found pride in the accomplishments of the Founding Fathers, who now loomed larger than life in the public imagination, persuaded them that the study of unvarnished records from the past would lead their readers to a fuller understanding of the nation's origins and heighten civic consciousness by example. With a zeal for minutiae, the editors of such journals as the *North American Review*, the *Historical Magazine*, and the *Virginia Historical Register and Literary Companion* added to their normal fare numerous pages of extracts from private correspondence, official journals and reports, newspapers, and even parish records in a seeming effort to develop overnight a national historical tradition. In a time of rapid expansion and growth, documents from a simpler, bygone era also provided a measure of comfort and intellectual security. By thus appealing to popular interest in the heroic deeds of Revolutionary leaders, publishers helped to create a receptive audience from the impressive historical compilations that came from individual collectors, private societies, state agencies, and the federal government between the Jubilee and the Centennial of independence.

INDIVIDUAL COLLECTORS

At first, the efforts of dedicated and persistent individual collectors overshadowed those of private and public institutions in the preservation of manuscripts. The writing of Revolutionary history, except for purely local studies, would have been far different in the 19th century had it not been for the enterprising feats of such men as Jared Sparks, Peter Force, George

Bancroft, Henry and Benjamin F. Stevens, and Lyman Copeland Draper. Not only did they amass substantive collections of Revolutionary documents from all the states and make them available for research, but they rescued from neglect and destruction materials that otherwise might not have survived.

Following the examples set by Hazard and Belknap, Jared Sparks, a Unitarian minister and editor of the *North American Review*, undertook on the eve of the Jubilee the first major tour of the federal archives in Washington, the state archives from Georgia to New Hampshire, and the more important collections of historical papers in private hands. In his journal he expressed great dismay at finding large gaps in the colonial and state records and commented sarcastically about the apathy and ignorance displayed by the officials responsible for what remained. In a noted article that appeared in the *Review* for October 1826, Sparks called upon gentlemen of "leisure and inquiry" in all the states to establish historical societies whose primary objects would be to collect all relevant manuscripts, pamphlets, assembly journals, and statutes, to publish and disseminate the most important, and to preserve for future historians those of less value. Particularly concerned that the papers of delegates to the Continental Congress, Revolutionary governors, and military officers be preserved, Sparks publicly congratulated Richard Henry Lee for depositing his grandfather's papers in the American Philosophical Society at Philadelphia and those of his great-uncle, Arthur Lee, at Harvard. Having discovered that many essential records for colonial history were "shut up in the office of the Board of Trade in England," Sparks recommended that copies of all papers relating to America be obtained and deposited in the archives at Washington.

Although it would be over a century before his scheme came anywhere near realization, Sparks devoted the remainder of his productive life to editing and writing nearly 70 volumes of documents and biography. Based on the innumerable transcripts and original manuscripts that he borrowed or obtained from foreign archives, state officials, and private collectors, Sparks published within the space of 25 years the *Diplomatic Correspondence of the American Revolution* (entry 8367), multivolume editions of the life and writings of Gouverneur Morris (entry 14052), George Washington (entry 14674), and Benjamin Franklin (entry 13381), and the *Correspondence of the American Revolution; Being Letters of Eminent Men to George Washington* (entry 14674). But more valuable than these works, which suffered from editorial inconsistency and Sparks' tendency to delete from documents passages that detracted from the heroic postures of his subjects, were the 266 volumes and 9 boxes of documents and transcripts that Sparks left to Harvard University. Among them were some of the original papers of Sir Francis Bernard, George Chalmers, and George Washington, copies of letters written to major figures such as Robert Morris, Philip Schuyler, John Sullivan, Anthony Wayne, and George Clinton, and diplomatic correspondence from the Yorke, Stormont, and Grantham papers in the Public Record Office in London and the Gerard and Luzerne papers in the Archives nationales in Paris. Considering the paucity of the Revolutionary material that existed in any one place before, it is not surprising that Sparks' collection served as a major source of research for the remainder of the century.

At the time that Sparks made his celebrated tour of the states, Peter Force, a Washington newspaperman, politician, and publisher launched one of the most ambitious schemes of historical collecting and editing ever undertaken. Relying in part on a congressional subsidy, Force amassed over a 35-year period from virtually all sources and states nearly 23,000 books, 40,000 pamphlets, 250 volumes of colonial and Revolutionary newspapers, 1,200 maps and views, 429 volumes of original manuscripts, and 360 volumes of transcripts that were meant to serve as the basis for his multivolume *American Archives*—a documentary treatment of American history from its beginning to 1789. Only nine folio volumes from the fourth and fifth series covering the years 1774–76 had been published (entry 8688) when Secretary of State William L. Marcy withdrew federal support. Although he found himself in reduced circumstances after lavishing nearly all of his available funds on his library, Force refused several offers from dealers to buy selected portions and continued his practice of allowing historians such as Sparks and George Bancroft free access to his materials. Convinced that Force possessed the finest corpus of Americana ever assembled, the sixth Librarian of Congress, Ainsworth Rand Spofford, proposed to the Joint Committee on the Library in 1867 that Congress purchase the Force collection to ensure its preservation. Congress acted swiftly, accepting the committee's endorsement of Spofford's report and appropriating $100,000 for that purpose. In April of that year the collection was moved to the Library of Congress where it continues to form an impressive proportion of the Library's holdings of Revolutionary maps, pamphlets, and documents.

Since there were no major depositories when he began research for his magisterial *History of the United States* (entry 1043), George Bancroft was compelled, like Sparks and Force, to collect for himself much of the material that he would use. Traveling extensively and spending freely, he purchased original letters of Samuel Adams, Joseph Hawley, and General von Riedesel, among others, and uncovered in his searches the minutes of the Boston Committee of Correspondence for the years 1772–74. Bancroft also obtained from individual collections in the United States transcripts from the papers of such figures as Benjamin Rush, George Mason, Oliver Ellsworth, John Glover, William Samuel Johnson, and John Langdon. While minister to Great Britain from 1846 to 1849, he supplemented the transcripts ordered from London, Paris, and Berlin archives in the mid-1830's with his own researches in European depositories. Bancroft's total cumulation of colonial and Revolutionary records, now in the New York Public Library, eventually reached 416 bound volumes.

Both Sparks and Force had employed a young Yale graduate, Henry Stevens of Vermont, to search local archives in the United States. Little did Sparks realize when he financed Stevens' trip to London in 1845, however, that his young protege would not only supply some states with irreplaceable indexes of their colonial and Revolutionary records in British repositories, but that he would also uncover a large cache of missing Benjamin Franklin papers (now in the Library of Congress) and establish himself as a major London dealer providing rare books and incunabula for the British Museum and many important collectors in America such as John Carter Brown. Stevens also inspired the awesome task undertaken by his younger brother, Benjamin Franklin Stevens, who searched for manuscripts relating to Revolutionary America, 1773–83, in major depositories throughout England, Holland, France, and Spain and compiled a massive 183-volume indexed calendar to 161,000 documents (Stevens' *Catalogue Index of Manuscripts*) that was sold in 1905 to the Library of Congress. Long interested in facsimile reproduction, the younger Stevens produced and sold in 24 folio volumes 2,107 *Facsimiles of Manuscripts in European Archives Relating to America, 1773–1783* (entry 8448).

Historians of the Revolutionary frontier also had their collector in Lyman Copeland Draper, who devoted half a century to acquiring documents and transcripts from the period 1750–1815 and to recording interviews with early settlers and their descendants along the Allegheny frontier from New York to Alabama. Hoping to gain enough data for comprehensive biographies of western heroes whom he greatly admired, Draper traveled thousands of miles during the 1840's, assembling material on the Virginia and Pennsylvania frontiers, the fur trade, the border wars, the western land companies, the settlement of Kentucky and Tennessee, and the Battle of King's Mountain. He also compiled whole series of papers on the lives of major western figures such as Daniel Boone, George Rogers Clark, Joseph Brant, Josiah Harmar, William Irvine, Simon Kenton, Isaac Shelby, George Croghan, William Preston, and Thomas Sumter. Although Draper wrote little himself, his priceless records, totaling 486 volumes, were deposited at his death in the State Historical Society of Wisconsin, of which he had been corresponding secretary and superintendent from 1854 to 1866. Not only did these records provide the backdrop for the provocative thesis advanced by Frederick Jackson Turner, who used the collection before it was opened to the public in 1893, but they also served as the basis for hundreds of monographs and biographies about the settlers of the trans-Appalachian frontier.

In considering the accomplishments of the great 19th-century collectors, it is difficult to ignore the service rendered by those who sought out manuscripts almost entirely for their symbolic value—the autograph collectors. With sufficient wealth to indulge their interests, professional men such as William B. Sprague, an Albany clergyman, Thomas A. Emmett, a New York physician, Simon Gratz, a Philadelphia lawyer, Robert Gilmor, a Baltimore merchant, and Israel K. Tefft, a Savannah merchant, adapted to American conditions the fashionable European hobby of collecting the papers of the nobility by concentrating on the manuscripts of America's "aristocracy"—those who established the independence of the United States and its constitutional form of government. Whether they appreciated the timelessness of historical records, sought vicarious identification with important figures of the past, or tried through their investments to build a collection of economic value, their endeavors saved countless manuscripts from destruction. In the 1820's, when the Reverend Dr. Sprague began to gather his first "Signers" collection by exchanging with Judge Bushrod Washington 1,500 transcripts for original letters signed by George Washinton, the papers of the Revolutionary generation were widely available—so much so, in fact, that by the time of his death in 1876 Dr. Sprague owned some 40,000 autographed letters of colonial and Revolutionary leaders. The disposition of Sprague's vast collection is difficult to trace, but others who followed

him often protected their life's work by donating their holdings to research institutions. The Emmett Collection at the New York Public Library numbers some 10,800 pieces while the Gratz papers at the Pennsylvania Historical Society of Pennsylvania contain nearly 175,000 items. Despite the most diligent efforts, only about 40 Signers' sets have been compiled due to the relative scarcity of letters by Thomas Lynch, Jr., of South Carolina and Button Gwinnett of Georgia.

HISTORICAL SOCIETIES

Although historians are often frustrated over the private ownership of the papers of public figures, it is clear that the energetic activities of autograph collectors contributed immeasurably to the field of documentary preservation and publication in the first half of the 19th century. The same general impulse that guided individual collectors was also responsible for the surge in the number of private historical societies established in the larger cities, state capitals, and university towns of the East. Less than a dozen had been organized before 1820, but nearly 100 were created in the next half century. Reflecting the newly acquired wealth and leisure of the educated, professional classes in New England, statewide societies modeled on that of Massachusetts appeared in rapid succession in Maine (1822), Rhode Island (1822), New Hampshire (1823), and Connecticut (1825). Although the middle states contained half of all the town and country societies formed along the east coast during the period, those with a statewide focus developed more slowly—the Historical Society of Pennsylvania was established in 1826, 20 years after that of New York, and the state societies organized in New Jersey (1845) and Delaware (1864) lagged even farther behind. In contrast, hardly more than a dozen local societies appeared in the southern seaboard states because of a comparative lack of interest, funds, and urban centers to serve as focal points. The Virginia Historical and Philosophical Society of Richmond, organized in 1831, was the first state society to appear in the South. Others followed later in Georgia (1839) and North Carolina and Maryland (1844). The South Carolina Historical Society in Charleston was not formed until 1854.

Established by men of affairs—statesmen, lawyers, merchants, clergymen, physicians—these new ventures were prompted by a mixture of motives. These included a patriotic interest in the preservation of historical materials, desire for the advancement of learning, curiosity about local origins, and concern for state and local prestige. Wounded pride may also have played a role, for a portion of the records of every region had already been lost to the avidity of individual collectors. Almost all of the early societies were supported solely by private funds or endowments. State aid, although requested in many cases, was seldom forthcoming. With financial limitations restricting their activities, the societies were usually dependent for the growth of their collections upon the zeal of individual members. These early organizers tended to limit their acquisitions to local materials—newspapers, artifacts, county, town, church, and school records, and papers of local politicians, educators, churchmen, and businessmen—materials that would meet the needs and reflect the activities of their own regions and people. Moreover, their search was guided by contemporary interest in political and military history, to the detriment of sources reflecting social and economic life. Because they focused almost exclusively on the pre-1789 period, the early societies influenced the course of Revolutionary historiography by the very nature of the sources they preserved and published.

Many of the documents secured by the state societies appeared in the collections, proceedings, memoirs, and transactions that they published between the Jubilee and the Centennial. Rarely, however, did the editors devote an entire issue to a single theme. Most volumes are amalgamations of speeches, addresses, lists, and rosters, intermixed with single or small groups of reprinted manuscripts and sources. They show little foresight or overall planning and are nearly impossible to bring under rigorous bibliographic control, notwithstanding the impressive attempt by A. P. C. Griffin in his *Bibliography of American Historical Societies* (entry 50). Despite the avowed interest of the societies in reprinting the records of the Founding Fathers, the appearance of important selections of Revolutionary material in their publications was sporadic and fortuitous. Over a 35-year period the Massachusetts Historical Society published in its *Collections* papers of Governor Thomas Hutchinson (entry 13675), Timothy Newell's journal of the siege of Boston (entry 5889), and letters of Thomas Cushing from 1767 to 1775 (entry 13153). Of its neighboring societies, the New Hampshire Historical Society included the records of the state's Committee of Safety, 1775–84, in its *Collections* (entry 8880), while the Rhode Island Historical Society printed miscellaneous Revolutionary correspondence, 1775–82 (entry 8978), and Simeon Thayer's journal of the invasion of Canada (entry 5966). The Connecticut Historical Society published the correspondence of Continental Congressman Silas Deane, 1774–76 (entry 13189). In the middle states

the Historical Society of Pennsylvania issued a greater number of documents in the years between 1845 and 1860, printing in its *Bulletin* letters of Robert Morris (entry 14058), the journal of Isaac Senter (entry 5963), the minutes of the Northumberland County Committee of Safety, 1776–77 (entry 9080), and papers relating to the Battle of Brandywine (entry 6167). The journal of Lt. William Feltman (entry 13329) on the southern campaign appeared in its *Collections* for 1853 and the Revolutionary journal of Major Ebenezer Denny (entry 13199) was published in its *Memoirs* for 1860. Scattered through the publications of the New Jersey Historical Society were miscellaneous Revolutionary letters by Governor William Franklin, Richard Stockton, and the Earl of Stirling (entry 12694), but almost nothing of substance from the period was included in the serials of the New York and Delaware societies. Few primary sources appeared in the southern publications as well. The Maryland Historical Society issued the journal of Charles Carroll kept during his visit to Canada in 1776 (entry 13004) and documents touching on wartime events in Baltimore (entry 2147), while the South Carolina Historical Society printed the London papers of Henry Laurens (entry 13804) and the journal of the second Council of Safety (entry 9256). In Georgia the historical society published the letters of Sir James Wright to the Earl of Dartmouth, 1774–82 (entry 14796), and in Virginia the society printed the letters of Governor Thomas Nelson, Jr., for 1781 (entry 9190). Overall, however, a review of the total contents of the serials issued by the privately endowed societies through the mid-19th century reveals little that can be used systematically by present-day scholars and indicates the narrow antiquarian focus of their editors.

State Governments

At the time of the Jubilee the state governments were also caught up in the wave of patriotic enthusiasm that inspired the efforts of individual collectors and the proliferation of historical societies. During his 1826 tour Jared Sparks discovered that no state had provided for the effective concentration of its documents in a separate depository. Since older records had usually been left in the care of the originating office or agency, such indifferent and decentralized control had already resulted in severe losses. Therefore, at the urging of several persons newly attuned to the nation's heritage, some states began in the mid-1820's to take the steps to recover, preserve, and publish their historical records.

Surprisingly, these early efforts focused on

American sources in British and European depositories. In 1827 the North Carolina legislature passed a resolution requesting the governor to obtain from British officials permission for an agent to make transcripts of the state's colonial records in the State Papers Office. Although no copies were actually made at the time, the survey taken resulted in the publication of an *Index to Colonial Documents Relative to North Carolina* in 1843. Thereafter, a significant number of American scholars journeyed abroad to examine the contents of British libraries, museums, and record offices. South Carolina's agent, Henry Granger, spent three years in London copying the state's documents, abstracts of which were later printed in the Historical Society's *Collections* (1857–59). The 22 folio volumes of Georgia records, procured at state expense by the Reverend Charles Wallace Howard in the late 1830's, became the basis of the Georgia Historical Society's collections. Private funds were raised in both Maryland and New Jersey to retain in London the services of Henry Stevens, who provided each state with an analytical index of nearly 2,000 of its documents, the latter of which was published in the *Collections* of the New Jersey Historical Society in 1858. By far the most successful of these foreign copying projects was sponsored by New York, which supported John Romeyn Brodhead four years in English, French, and Dutch archives transcribing 80 volumes of records for which the New York legislature published a full calendar in 1845.

In addition to retrieving material from abroad, attempts were made to improve the conditions under which state documents were stored and to preserve their contents through publication. Despite a lack of facilities and professional expertise, New Hampshire, Massachusetts, New York, Pennsylvania, and South Carolina made substantial gains. In 1836 the New Hampshire legislature authorized the governor to recover the alienated archives of the state and to have the others arranged and bound, and in 1867 New Hampshire issued the first of many volumes of its *Provincial and State Papers*. In 1831 the Massachusetts legislature provided for the construction of fireproof record vaults in the State House and five years later retained the services of the Reverend Joseph Barlow Felt to arrange and bind the state's colonial and Revolutionary archives. Employing his own arbitrary topical classification, which has confounded scholarly critics ever since, Felt salvaged 328 folio volumes of documents that might well have perished. From these, William Lincoln edited the journals of the Massachusetts provincial congresses and the Committee of Safety,

1774–75 (entry 8937). In New York, the legislature generously provided for the publicaton of the journal of the votes and proceedings of the General Assembly, 1766–76 (entry 4416), the journals of the Provincial Congress and Committee of Safety (entry 9023), and the journal of the Legislative Council, 1691–1775 (entry 4414). When it directed in 1847 that all public records be transferred to the State Library in Albany, the legislature supported two projects that were far more comprehensive. Based on the transcripts procured in Europe by Brodhead, Edmund B. O'Callaghan edited *The Documentary History of the State of New York* (entry 1747) and, with Berthold Fernow, *Documents Relative to the Colonial History of the State of New York* (entry 1748). In Pennsylvania a selected committee reported in 1851 on the deplorable condition of the state archives, and a joint memorial from the American Philosophical Society and the Historical Society of Pennsylvania encouraged the legislators to authorize publication of the so-called "Colonial Records of Pennsylvania," which contained the minutes of the Provincial Council from 1683 to 1775 (entry 4502) and the minutes of the Supreme Executive Council from 1777 to 1790 (entry 9097). Samuel Hazard was then employed to edit over 10,000 documents from the years 1664 to 1790 to complement the "Colonial Records." These became the first series of the *Pennsylvania Archives* (entry 1973). To provide a finding aid, Hazard supervised the compilation of a general index to all 28 volumes. The South Carolina legislature, which helped finance the publication of John Drayton's *Memoirs of the American Revolution* (entry 4764) and Robert W. Gibbes' *Documentary History of the American Revolution* (entry 2314), used the disastrous fires in government offices in Columbia in 1843 and 1844 to justify the centralized storage of its records in fireproof vaults in the new State House. The work done by J. S. Green, who was commissioned in 1850 to gather, arrange, and index South Carolina's colonial and Revolutionary records, laid the basis for one of the most comprehensive state archives on the east coast.

Unfortunately, the other states failed to take similar steps, although some made sporadic efforts to bring together and publish scattered sources. North Carolina reprinted the proceedings of its provincial congress of 1775 (entry 9230), Maryland issued the proceedings of the conventions held in Annapolis in 1774–76 (entry 9161), New Jersey published selections from the correspondence of Governor William Livingston, 1776–86 (entry 9065), Connecticut began a series of its colonial records, and Rhode Island employed John R. Bartlett to edit the *Records of the Colony of Rhode Island [1636–1792]* (entry 1641). Yet little interest was shown in preserving the documents themselves. Although Maryland placed some of its colonial and Revolutionary records in the historical society at Baltimore for safekeeping in 1846–47 and again in 1878, they were not organized until after the Civil War when Brantz Mayer provided a rough topical arrangement and had them bound in the so-called "rainbow" books (see entry 740). In Delaware, Virginia, and Georgia nothing at all was done until late in the 19th century. In fact, as a result of frequent fires, Arnold's raid of 1781, and the burning of Richmond in 1865, Virginia arrived at the Centennial with fewer of its Revolutionary records intact than any of the original states. Indeed, the Civil War wreaked havoc on records throughout the South.

Federal Government

The federal archives in Washington suffered similar neglect. Because of Charles Thomson's continuity in office as secretary of the Continental Congress, its official documents had been carefully preserved despite frequent moves. In 1789 Thomson relinquished the Continental and Confederation records in his keeping to the newly created Department of State. When the War and Treasury departments were established soon thereafter, they were entrusted with those portions of the records that pertained to their functions. But a House committee appointed in 1810 to inquire into the condition of the prefederal documents found them to be in great disorder. Its recommendation led to the passage of the first archives act for the systematic preservation and arrangement of the national records. Congress provided fireproof rooms in a building west of the White House that contained the State, War, and Navy departments. Some of the War, Navy, and Treasury papers were destroyed in 1814 when the British captured Washington, and the Treasury records suffered again in 1833. But the documents in the Bureau of Rolls and Library of the Department of State, including the journals of the Continental Congress, the diplomatic correspondence of the Revolutionary and Confederation periods, and the original drafts of important state papers, escaped such perils throughout the 19th century.

Following the passage of the archives act of 1810, the federal government played a surprisingly expansive role in sponsoring the publication of historical documents and preserving the papers of leading statesmen. At first such actions appear to be an anomaly in a period traditionally viewed as one of restrained federal activity in the face of local and private initiative. Yet as the editors of popular magazines, historical serials, and state documents well knew, the public was eager to have historical collections widely available, even if financed by the government. Before the Centennial, Congress supported no fewer than 18 major projects of documentary publication, producing nearly 325 volumes at a cost of well over $7,000,000. Funds were expended in several ways: by assigning government employees to do research, subsidizing editors and publishers, purchasing large editions for free distribution, and procuring through private sale the papers of several of the Founding Fathers. During the 1820's Congress focused on the publication of major official records, issuing the *Journals, Acts and Proceedings of the [Philadelphia] Convention* (entry 9436), the *Secret Journals of the Acts and Proceedings of Congress [1775–89]* (entry 8749), the *Journals of the American Congress from 1774 to 1788* (entry 8748), and Jonathan Elliot's *Debates, Resolutions, and Other Proceedings, in Convention, on the Adoption of the Federal Constitution* (entry 9531). In addition, the government allocated $31,000 for Jared Sparks' *Diplomatic Correspondence of the American Revolution* (entry 8367), which was then supplemented by William A. Weaver's *Diplomatic Correspondence of the United States . . . 1783 to 1789* (entry 8366), and appropriated $228,710 for Peter Force's *American Archives [1774–76]* (entry 8688). Shortly after Sparks' *Writings of George Washington* (entry 14674) appeared, Congress made its first major purchase of statesmen's letters, buying in 1834 200 bound volumes of Washington papers (including 62 volumes of letters by Washington and 119 to him) for $25,000. In 1837 and 1848 the Madison papers were obtained in two installments for $30,000 and $25,000 respectively. The government also acquired in 1848 65 volumes of the Hamilton papers ($25,000), 137 volumes of Jefferson's "public papers," which included 26,000 letters to him and drafts of 16,000 letters by him ($20,000), and the remaining "private" papers of Washington ($20,000). The series was completed the following year with the acquisition of the Monroe papers ($20,000). Thus, in a period of 15 years Congress appropriated $165,000 for the purchase of five major collections to be preserved in the Department of State's Bureau of Rolls and Library. But several of the appropriations included or were supplemented by funds for editing and publishing. The Joint Committee of Congress on the Library sponsored Henry D. Gilpin's edition of the first set of the *Papers of James Madison* (entry 13944), John C. Hamilton's *Works of*

Alexander Hamilton (entry 13523), Henry A. Washington's *Writings of Thomas Jefferson* (entry 13701), and Philip R. Fendall's *Letters and Other Writings of James Madison* (entry 13944), based on the second installment of his papers. When Charles Francis Adams published the *Works of John Adams* (entry 12681), Congress provided $22,500 for the purchase and free distribution of 1,000 sets.

The utility of such beneficence was seldom questioned. In the public mind, the historical collections that received congressional, state, and local support were considered to be monuments to the great men and deeds of the Revolution. Yet the results of all the efforts to gather the minutiae of history between the Jubilee and the Centennial were decidedly mixed. The early editions of documents sponsored by the federal government tended to be limited in scope and unreliable in text. Except for Force's *American Archives* and Elliot's *Debates*, each would be done anew in the late 19th and in the 20th centuries. The records of the states were also uneven. Massachusetts and South Carolina had perhaps the most extensive and best organized holdings. But neither equaled the accomplishments of New York in obtaining copies of its colonial and Revolutionary records in foreign archives or of Pennsylvania in preserving a large proportion of its records through publication. The desperate condition of other archives, such as those of Delaware, would not become public knowledge until early in the 20th century. The 19th-century emphasis upon publication over preservation, moreover, had hidden dangers. For example, the editor of the first series of the Pennsylvania Archives, Samuel Hazard, used many original documents as printer's copy. Moreover, Pennsylvania's failure to provide better storage facilities for the remaining documents that he edited led to further deterioration and loss. Scholars noted long ago that Hazard's editing was uneven in quality and that he had, in some cases, taken great liberties in transcribing originals. As a result, some of the documents in his 12 volumes are known today only in their poorly edited or incomplete printed form.

Among the historical societies, those in the northern states held the largest collections. In a special report prepared in 1876 for the Department of the Interior's Bureau of Education, Henry A. Holmes revealed that the more than 100 reporting societies in the United States held 482,000 books, 568,000 pamphlets, 1,361 bound volumes of documents, and 88,771 portfolios and single manuscripts. Among them, the Massachusetts, New York, and Pennsylvania historical societies held over 20 percent of the books and pamphlets, 70 percent of the bound volumes of documents, and 45 percent of the portfolios and single manuscripts. But the focus of even the largest societies remained local, unscientific, and antiquarian. Their publications were largely accumulations of disjointed fragments to which there were few decent indexes. Considering the relative availability of Revolutionary papers, the pace of their collecting appeared to have been unreasonably slow. In reviewing "Manuscript Sources of United States History" in the eighth volume of his *Narrative and Critical History* (entry 1080), Justin Winsor noted that many of the papers of major Revolutionary figures such as John Sullivan, James and Mercy Warren, Benjamin Lincoln, Philip Schuyler, John Jay, Gouverneur Morris, Charles Thomson, George Read, Caesar Rodney, Charles Carroll, and Patrick Henry were still in private hands. Yet, on balance, the state historical societies and their chief supporters were nearly the sole vehicles for the promotion of historical study in the United States for almost a century after the Revolution.

After the Centennial: The Culmination of the Antiquarian Tradition

By serving as the meeting place and research center for the chroniclers and antiquaries who gathered to celebrate the past or to argue the historical importance of their various communities, the historical societies that were established in profusion after 1825 played a central role in encouraging the compilation of hundreds of state and local histories that appeared before the end of the century. Because the majority of these societies had been established in the urban centers of the Northeast, by far the largest number of histories pertained to that region. In New England, for example, all the states passed statutes between 1860 and 1876 encouraging the publication of such works. Of the more than 1,000 compilations listed in Chapter 2, which reflects the total body of local histories available, fully 45 percent are studies of localities in New England, one-third relate to the middle Atlantic states, and only 22 percent treat the history of the southern seaboard states. The typical author of such a work, normally selected by a publication committee nominated at a town meeting, was a retired clergyman, lawyer, or doctor with a lifelong collecting hobby whose aim was to memorialize the town or region and those who settled it.

Indeed, in treating 19th-century historiography, scholars have perhaps drawn too much attention to the more popular works of the period, such as Robert

Sears' *Pictorial History of the American Revolution* (entry 1072), Lorenzo Sabine's *American Loyalists* (entry 8128), and Benson J. Lossing's *Pictorial Fieldbook of the Revolution* (entry 5734), while neglecting far more typical compilations of local facts, traditions, and anecdotes such as those prepared about the towns of Massachusetts (entry 1444), Connecticut (entry 1668), New York (entry 1753), and New Jersey (entry 1883) by John Warner Barber and Henry Howe. Together with John Thomas Scharf, Israel D. Rupp, and other compilers, Barber and Howe helped to launch a new phenomenon in local history writing that continued far into the 20th century—"memorial" histories of towns, counties, and regions. As the principal editors, men like Scharf and Thomas F. Jewett of Boston hired local antiquaries to write articles about social, economic, political, or military aspects of their regions which were then combined with long historical overviews and sold to the local populace on a subscription basis, sometimes with the aid of a subsidy from a municipal or state government. Once established, the format was further developed and capitalized on by commercial publishers such as the American Historical Company and the Lewis Historical Publishing Company in New York and the American Historical Society and the S. J. Clarke Publishing Company in Chicago. It was Jewett who induced Justin Winsor, librarian of Harvard, to compile and edit two notable examples of the genre, his *Memorial History of Boston* (entry 1482) and his *Narrative and Critical History of America* (entry 1080), both of which focus primarily on the colonial and Revolutionary periods.

The phenomenon that culminated in Winsor's distinguished works, however, had its origins in more fundamental concerns; for the local history movement of the 19th century had a decidedly genealogical orientation. Members of the declining mercantile and professional classes, faced with political and social challenges from the new manufacturing elite and threatened by the influx of German and Irish immigrants, began to wrap themselves in the mantles of their long-dead ancestors. The Civil War and the rapid burst of industrialization that followed only served to heighten the trend. Although slightly more than 100 historical societies had been formed along the east coast before the Centennial, an additional 84 were created in the 15 years after 1876. Located in smaller communities that lay near expanding urban centers, the new societies were mostly "pioneer," "old planters'," "old residents'," or "early settlers'" associations that attempted to protect their sense of common

identity by promoting the study of 17th- and 18th-century history. Many of the documents collected by these societies—rosters of early town officials, ship passenger lists, early census records, muster rolls—were sought for their value in tracing direct lineage to the Founding Fathers and beyond. In Massachusetts, for example, the Essex Institute in Salem, the Society of Mayflower Descendants, the New England Historic and Genealogical Society, and several other societies, town committees, and private persons combined their efforts to publish after 1895 the vital statistics (birth, marriage, and death dates gleaned from town records, newspapers, family Bibles, and cemetery inscriptions) of over 200 Massachusetts towns from the early 17th century to 1850 (see entry 10749).

This renewed interest in early American history was reflected in the documentary publications of the older societies as well. But here the influence of new scholarly techniques made its mark as a number of European-trained historians took up archival and editorial positions. With such leadership the major compilations that appeared after the Centennial assumed a higher quality. The Massachusetts Historical Society began to issue in its *Collections* full-volume editions rather than extracts from the papers of such figures as Jeremy Belknap (entry 12828), Jonathan Trumbull (entry 14597), and James Bowdoin and Sir John Temple (entry 12884), while Connecticut's society produced full texts of the letters of London agent William Samuel Johnson to the governors of Connecticut, 1766–71 (entry 13724) and the orderly books and journals (entry 7931) and muster rolls (entry 7930) kept by Connecticut men during the Revolution. By far the most impressive achievement was the John Watts De Peyster Publication Fund series sponsored by the New-York Historical Society. Among the volumes issued were the papers of General Charles Lee, 1754–1811 (entry 13815); the letters of Major General James Pattison, 1779–80 (entry 14169); the letters to General Lewis Morris, 1775–82 (entry 14054); the letterbooks of Lieutenant Governor Cadwallader Colden, 1760–75 (entry 4420); a volume of Revolutionary and miscellaneous papers that includes the letters of Charles Thomson, 1765–1816 (entry 14563), the Marquis de La Rouërie, 1777–91 (entry 13802), and Robert Morris, 1775–82 (entry 14058); the journal of Captain John Montresor, 1757–78 (entry 14034); the letterbook of Captain Alexander McDonald, 1775–79 (entry 13192); the papers and journals of Lieutenant Colonel Stephen Kemble, 1773–89 (entry 13754); and five volumes of Silas Deane papers, 1774–90 (entry 13189). In 1880 the New Jersey Historical Society, in conjunction with the state archives, began to publish under the half-title *Archives of the State of New Jersey* two series, the early volumes of which focused on the papers of the colonial governors and council. The pioneering *Pennsylvania Magazine of History and Biography,* launched by the state's historical society in 1877, contained in the first 25 volumes hundreds of pages of Revolutionary documents. The society also printed Paul L. Ford's edition of the political writings of John Dickinson, 1764–74, as its *Memoirs* for 1895 (entry 13217). The Delaware society published in its *Papers* between 1887 and 1896 the minutes of the state council, 1776–92 (entry 9144), the diary of Captain Thomas Rodney, 1776–77 (entry 6085), the journal of William Seymour during the southern expedition (entry 14410), and the personal recollections of Captain Enoch Anderson (entry 12720), while the Virginia Historical Society printed the wartime orderly books of the state's First and Third regiments in its *Collections* for 1892 (entries 7085 and 6128).

The wave of historical publishing that followed the Centennial and the entry of the first professional historians into the archives was not, however, confined to the historical societies. G. P. Putnam's Sons attempted to capitalize on the growing academic and public interest in American history by commissioning 11 editors to reproduce in 80 volumes the papers of major Revolutionary statesmen. Based largely on the documents acquired by Congress and deposited in the Department of State, there appeared in steady succession Henry Cabot Lodge's *Works of Alexander Hamilton* (entry 13523), John Bigelow's *Complete Works of Benjamin Franklin* (entry 13381), Worthington C. Ford's *Writings of George Washington* (entry 14674), Henry P. Johnston's *Correspondence and Public Papers of John Jay* (entry 13699), Kate Rowland Mason's *Life [and Correspondence] of George Mason* (entry 13979), Paul L. Ford's *Writings of Thomas Jefferson* (entry 13701), Moncure Conway's *Writings [of Thomas Paine]* (entry 14143), *Charles R. King's Life and Correspondence of Rufus King* (entry 13766), Stanislaus M. Hamilton's *Writings of James Monroe* (entry 14025), Gaillard Hunt's *Writings of James Madison* (entry 13944), and Harry Alonzo Cushing's *Writings of Samuel Adams* (entry 12685), the last major commercial venture in documentary publishing.

The Growth of Professional Standards in Documentary Preservation and Publication

THE AMERICAN HISTORICAL ASSOCIATION

Before the 1870's the writing of American history had fallen solely within the province of semiprofes-

sional scholars or talented amateurs who often transformed their avocations into second careers following successful ventures in business, medicine, or law. The transition from a classical curriculum to an elective system in American colleges and the development of the modern university based on professional training and scholarship, however, signaled the arrival of the teacher-specialist who established by the end of the century new canons of historical methodology and research. In many ways the professionalization of history may have been part of a larger shift in American culture from romanticism to realism, but it also had an impact on the development of reliable sources on the Revolution and their more intensive use; for the empirical approach adopted by professional historians centered on documentary criticism and the steady, patient accumulation of facts. Basing their research upon the haphazard collections of materials gathered by American historical societies, the new historians produced the first wave of local institutional studies that became the hallmark of the seminar systems established by German-trained Ph.D's at The Johns Hopkins University and Columbia University. At the same time historians began to adopt stricter standards in documentary collecting and editing and to develop common centers of professional authority as had their colleagues in law, chemistry, economics, and political science. In their attempt to dominate the field of historical scholarship, promote reform among local historical societies and state archival agencies, and nationalize the study of American history, the new professionals established the American Historical Association in 1884 under the leadership of Herbert Baxter Adams of Johns Hopkins. Adams, as the Association's first corresponding secretary and a member of the Executive Council, succeeded in obtaining in 1889 a federal charter for the AHA and a congressional subsidy for office space in Washington and for publication of the society's *Annual Report.* Nine years later the Association assumed support of the *American Historical Review* which had been established as a private venture in 1895 under the editorship of J. Franklin Jameson. By the turn of the century the *Review* had become the recognized organ of professional historians in the United States, setting national standards through the quality of its articles, documents, and book reviews. The Association's new status and the *Review's* success signaled the beginning of a new era, for they coincided with the creation of large numbers of research institutions (federal and state agencies, college and university libraries, and privately endowed depositories), the compilation of elaborate bibliographies and manuscript guides, the growth of technological services, and the development of new avenues of scholarly publication, communication, and support that combined to transform historical research in the early 20th century.

HISTORICAL MANUSCRIPTS COMMISSION

Those who were most instrumental in creating these new departures exerted pressure through various divisions of the AHA, focusing their attention first at the federal and, later, at the state level. In 1895 the Association established a Historical Manuscripts Commission, based on the British precedent of 1869, and appointed J. Franklin Jameson and four other scholars to draft guidelines for the development of manuscript collections in the United States. Publishing its recommendations in the AHA *Annual Report* for 1896, the commission urged that privately owned documents be deposited in existing agencies, that these agencies extend and upgrade their holdings by including neglected sources for social and economic history, and that the federal and state governments support documentary publication programs. The commission's further resolve that a full listing of available guides to American archives be compiled resulted in the publication of Edmund C. Burnett's *List of Printed Guides to and Descriptions of Archives and Other Repositories of Historical Manuscripts* (entry 609). In the meantime, the commission itself began publishing documentary collections and research guides in an expanded AHA *Annual Report,* beginning with the letters of Stephen Higginson, 1783–1804 (entry 13602), and the correspondence of Phineas Bond, the first British consul to the United States, 1787–94 (entry 12869). Jameson also provided an introduction to the "Colonial Assemblies and Their Legislative Journals" (entry 414) and furnished a "Guide to the Items Relating to American History in the Reports of the English Historical Manuscripts Commission and Their Appendixes" (entry 557).

CARNEGIE INSTITUTION OF WASHINGTON

The work of the Historical Manuscripts Commission was furthered by the AHA Council in 1901 when it appointed Jameson, Charles Francis Adams, and Andrew C. McLaughlin to explore the possibility of establishing an institute for advanced historical studies, a move that nearly coincided with the creation of the Carnegie Institution of Washington, which adopted the AHA panel as an advisory committee and in 1905 appointed Jameson as director of its Department of Historical Research. Until the dissolution of the department in 1928, there followed a period of

immensely creative activity as Jameson launched an effective campaign of propaganda and persuasion in an effort to impress upon public officials and historians alike the critical need to collect, preserve, and organize manuscripts, especially in the federal and state archives. Jameson's personal letters and those he wrote in his capacity as department director (now in the collections of the Library of Congress) attest to the extraordinary range of his activities and influence. Continuing to support projects just begun, such as the *Writings on American History* (entry 63), Edmund C. Burnett's *Letters of the Members of the Continental Congress* (entry 8743), and Charles M. Andrews' survey of manuscripts for American colonial and Revolutionary history in London archives (entries 539 and 540), Jameson commissioned or shouldered the major responsibility for many other undertakings, such as Helen H. Catterall's *Judicial Cases Concerning American Slavery and the Negro* (entry 10264), Elizabeth Donnan's *Documents Illustrative of the History of the Slave Trade to America* (entry 10319), Charles O. Paullin and John K. Wright's *Atlas of Historical Geography of the United States* (entry 907), and, in his capacity as chairman of the American Council of Learned Societies, the compilation of the *Dictionary of American Biography* (entry 12577), which includes over 500 biographical essays on Revolutionary figures. More significant, perhaps, was the publication of the Carnegie guides to American materials in archives in the United States and abroad. Following the publication of Claude H. Van Tyne and Waldo G. Leland's *Guide to the Archives of the Government of the United States in Washington* (entry 764), Jameson oversaw the work of 16 scholars who published between 1907 and 1943 nearly 20 volumes containing their descriptions of relevant collections in British (entries 539, 540, and 562), Spanish (entries 529, 536, and 537), French (entries 525 and 532), Italian (entry 526), German (entry 530), Canadian (entry 591), and West Indian (entry 597 and 603) depositories.

LIBRARY OF CONGRESS

Because of their timely appearance these volumes served as the principal finding and ordering aids used by the Library of Congress as it carried out the extensive foreign copying program begun in 1905 by Herbert Putnam, one of its most innovative and enterprising chiefs. In fact, a very close relationship developed among the major institutions and the professional elite in Washington between 1900 and 1940. The AHA continued to stimulate the growing demand for documentary preservation; the Carnegie Institution published guides to domestic and foreign records; and the Library of Congress assumed the major task of collecting and preserving manuscripts at the national level. Shortly after he became Librarian in 1899, Putnam brought Worthington C. Ford from the Boston Public Library to head the recently created Division of Manuscripts. At that time the division held some 43,000 uncataloged and cataloged documents which came largely from the "Loyalist Papers" transferred from the Smithsonian Institution in 1866, the Force Collection obtained in 1867, the Rochambeau Collection purchased by Congress in 1882, and the Joseph M. Toner Collection donated between 1882 and 1896. In 1903 Theodore Roosevelt ordered that the records of the Continental Congress and the Philadelphia Convention as well as the papers of Franklin, Washington, Jefferson, Hamilton, Madison, and Monroe be transferred from the Department of State to the Library. To embellish this great body of Revolutionary material, Putnam developed an ongoing program of ordering from European depositories handwritten transcripts (later, photostats and microfilm) of colonial and Revolutionary manuscripts by using as a key Steven's *Catalogue Index of Manuscripts in the Archives of England, France, Holland, and Spain Relating to America, 1763–1783* which the Library obtained in 1905. Within a few years, however, the Library was able to rely on the much fuller Carnegie guides. Putnam also proved adept at soliciting gifts and raising funds to purchase additional collections. In 1925 James B. Wilbur gave the Library an endowment of $192,671, the income from which is still used to obtain foreign reproductions. This donation was greatly enhanced in 1927 when John D. Rockefeller, Jr., provided a total of $450,000 over a five-year period to be used for the same purpose. Having obtained 300,000 transcripts and facsimile folios by that date, the Library added nearly 2½ million more pages under the new program. In total, the Library's *Manuscript Sources in the Library of Congress for Research on the American Revolution* (1975), compiled by John R. Sellers, Gerard W. Gawalt, Paul H. Smith and Patricia Molen Van Ee, describes 479 collections of foreign reproductions obtained from 84 European, Canadian, and Mexican depositories. Together with the 1,138 domestic collections in the Manuscript Division, they represent the largest body of Revolutionary sources available for research in the United States. Large sections from both groups, such as the Colonial Office papers from America and the West Indies and the papers of the early presidents, are available on microfilm.

Other programs and collections at the Library have also been vital to the study of the Revolution. While chief of the Division of Manuscripts, Worthington C. Ford began to edit the *Journals of the Continental Congress* (entry 8748). Later, under J. Franklin Jameson's tenure as chief (1928–37), John C. Fitzpatrick, with 30 years of experience in the division, compiled for the Washington Bicentennial Commission the *Writings of George Washington* (entry 14674). Among collections of contemporary printed sources, the newspaper and rare book collections at the Library are second only to those of the American Antiquarian Society in Worcester, Massachusetts. The Library's rare book collection contains more than one-third of the 39,162 books, pamphlets, newspapers, journals, and broadsides listed in Charles Evans' *American Bibliography [1639–1800]* (entry 358). Of these, slightly more than 7,000 fall into the Revolutionary period. The Library's files of 18th-century newspapers contain over 525 titles in nearly 2,200 volumes. By the same token, the Geography and Map Division houses the largest collection of Revolutionary maps and views in the United States—nearly 3,500 plates, charts, atlases, and manuscript maps.

NATIONAL ARCHIVES

The American Historical Association, the Carnegie Institution, and the Library of Congress were thus successful in creating a national focus and a central depository for the study of American history. But professional historians recognized the need for a truly national archival program to preserve the country's documentary heritage. The campaign for a national repository had been long and tedious, originating in post-Civil War demands by federal agencies for a hall of records to store noncurrent material. In his position at the Carnegie Institution, J. Franklin Jameson became the protagonist in the struggle, encouraging the AHA Council to form in 1909 the Conference of Archivists and to petition Congress in 1910 for a national archives modeled on the British Public Record Office. After several interruptions and false starts, the movement culminated in the National Archives Act of 1934 and the appointment of a North Carolina historian, Robert D. W. Connor, as the first Archivist of the United States. Faced with the task of managing nearly 10,000,000 cubic feet of federal records created since 1774, Connor and his staff surveyed the holdings of various departments and agencies in Washington and elsewhere, devised organizational principles and policies, and began the ongoing process of transferring selected record groups to the new Archives building or its outlying branches. Of the 409 record groups acquired by the agency and described in its *Guide to the National Archives of the United States* (1974), 26 contain documents from the Revolutionary period, the most important of which are the records of the Continental and Confederation congresses and the Constitutional Convention (transferred to the Archives from the Library of Congress in 1952). As part of its program of documentary publication on microfilm, the National Archives has made nearly all of these records, with appropriate guides, widely available. More than a little credit for the Archives' accomplishments must go to those members of the American Historical Association whose promotional efforts in Washington made the fate of the nation's records a matter of public and official concern.

The Establishment of State and Local Programs in the 20th Century

PUBLIC ARCHIVES COMMISSION

At the local level members of the AHA also campaigned for the reform of state archives and historical societies. In 1899 the Association created a Public Archives Commission to investigate the condition of state and local manuscript records and to take steps to improve the functions of public depositories. Between 1900 and 1906 the commission's agents surveyed local records in all state and some county and municipal archives along the eastern seaboard, publishing their findings in the AHA's *Annual Report*. The most thorough reviews were made by Herman V. Ames and Albert E. McKinley in Pennsylvania (entries 709–710), John Spencer Bassett in North Carolina (entries 779–780), and Ulrich B. Phillips in Georgia (entry 801). On the whole, the commission's reports showed that the accumulation and care of archival material varied greatly from state to state with the worst conditions being found in Delaware (entry 728). The commission's efforts stimulated local demands for reform and were responsible for the passage of legislation in many of the states relating to the preservation, custody, and administration of noncurrent records. By the end of the First World War five eastern states had created independent historical records commissions as part of the state government, four maintained their archives in state libraries or historical societies, two used the office of the secretary of state as the principal depository, and two others

divided their records among several departments and divisions.

SOUTHERN STATES

The Public Archives Commission's greatest success was achieved in the southern states, which acted almost simultaneously in redressing the regional imbalance in state archival administration that had existed throughout the 19th century. Unlike New England, the South had few well organized historical societies; thus the states were forced to create new governmental agencies for the care of public documents. These agencies usually performed a triple function, serving as collectors, custodians, and publishers. In Virginia, for example, the archives had traditionally been preserved in the State Library by the secretary of the commonwealth. In the 1870's, efforts were made to obtain transcripts of Virginia records in England through the offices of W. Noel Sainsbury. Shortly thereafter, William P. Palmer edited the *Calendar of Virginia State Papers [1652–1869]* (entry 2164), which included land patents, court records, state papers, council proceedings, and public and private correspondence from the Revolutionary period as well as the letters and proceedings of the Committee of Correspondence and Inquiry, 1773–75, and the journal of the Committee of Safety for 1776. Stimulated by the activities of the Public Archives Commission, however, the Virginia legislature empowered the newly established State Library Board to create an Archives Division and a Historical Publications Division to preserve and publish the colonial and Revolutionary records of the state. In steady succession there appeared under the editorship of John P. Kennedy, Henry R. McIlwaine, and others, the *Journals of the House of Burgesses of Virginia [1619–1776]* (entries 4612–4615), the legislative and executive journals of the colonial council, 1680–1775 (entries 4610–4611), the official letters of governors Patrick Henry, Thomas Jefferson, Thomas Nelson, and Benjamin Harrison, 1776–83 (entry 9189), and the *Journals of the Council of State of Virginia [1776–88]* (entry 9184). In its bulletins and annual reports or as separate publications, the State Library also issued a list of Revolutionary soldiers of Virginia (entry 8061), a compilation of justices of the peace, 1757–75 (entry 4676), and the proceedings of the committees of safety of the counties of Cumberland and Isle of Wight (entry 9179), Caroline and Southampton (entry 9178), and Westmoreland and Fincastle (entry 9191).

A similar program was launched in Georgia as a

result of Ulrich B. Phillip's survey of its depositories. In 1902 the legislature directed that transcripts of Georgia material in the Public Record Office in London be obtained and that the state's colonial and Revolutionary records be published. A special Office of Compiler of Records was created for former governor Allen D. Candler who prepared and published in 28 volumes *The Colonial Records of the State of Georgia [1732–82]* (entry 2359), and *The Revolutionary Records of the State of Georgia [1769–85]* (entry 9292). Fourteen volumes in the first series were devoted to the proceedings of the governor and council, 1754–82 (entry 2360), the journals of the upper and lower houses of assembly, 1755–82 (entries 2361 and 4785), and the extant statutes for the years 1754 to 1789 (entry 2362). The *Revolutionary Records* contain such material as the journals of the Provincial Congress, 1775–76, the Council of Safety, 1775–77, and the House of Assembly, 1781–84 (entry 9289); the minutes of the Executive Council, 1778–85 (entry 9283); the records of the sales of confiscated estates, 1769–82; and the journal of the Land Court for 1784. Unfortunately, the failure of the legislature to appropriate additional funds at the time has prevented the publication of an additional 14 volumes of *Colonial Records*.

In North Carolina a single man, William L. Saunders, was largely responsible for publishing the state's historical records. His background as an editor, his political power, and his position as secretary of state from 1879 to 1891 enabled him to obtain legislative sanction for procuring North Carolina documents in foreign archives and publishing the *Colonial Records of North Carolina [1662–1776]* (entry 4686). Saunders' success prompted the legislature to support the efforts of state supreme court justice Walter Clark in publishing a companion series, *The State Records of North Carolina [1777–90]*, issued in 16 volumes between 1895 and 1907 (entry 9232). Saunders had included in the earlier volumes the journals of both the assembly and the council, the correspondence of the royal governors, and a wide variety of other official documents. The later series kept the same overall focus, but also embraced correspondence of prominent public and military figures, colonial and state statutes from 1715 to 1788, and material from the Public Record Office from 1730 to 1776 that Saunders was unable to include in the *Colonial Records*. As a result of these efforts, the Public Archives Commission's report on its archives, and the steps taken in other southern states, the legislature established in 1903 the North Carolina Historical Commission which over-

saw between 1909 and 1914 the publication of a four-volume index to the colonial and state records, compiled and edited by Stephen B. Weeks. The commission (now the Division of Archives and History) has successfully maintained the state's archival preeminence by actively collecting all types of manuscripts, publishing finding aids, and issuing since 1924 one of the leading state historical magazines, the *North Carolina Historical Review*.

Efforts to organize and publish South Carolina's rich archival holdings were aided in 1894 when the general assembly, at the urging of the state's historical society, created a historical commission to complete the task of securing copies of the state's colonial documents in England. It was not until 1905, however, that the assembly empowered the Historical Commission to care for the state's archives, then in the office of the secretary of state, and to publish historical records, which between 1905 and 1949 reached nearly 60 small volumes of primary material. These included documents relating to South Carolina's role in the Revolutionary War (entry 8090), the journals of the general assembly for 1776 (entry 9261), and of the House of Representatives for 1782 (entry 9263), the payment of claims against South Carolina growing out of the Revolution (entry 8094), the journal of the commissioners of the South Carolina navy, 1776–80 (entry 8091), the audited accounts of Revolutionary claims against the state (entry 8093), and the senate journal for 1782 (entry 9264). Yet these represent but a small fraction of the state's records, and it was not until the Archives Act of 1954 that the Historical Commission was abolished and its function transferred to the new Archives Department under the direction of James H. Easterby who developed a plan for extending the series of published colonial records. Thus far Easterby's initiatives have resulted in publication of Indian affairs documents for the period 1750–65 (entry 5557), the journals of the provincial congresses, 1775–76 (entry 9254), the *Journals of the General Assembly and House of Representatives, 1776–1780* (entry 9262), the *Journals of the Privy Council, 1783–1789* (entry 9265), and *The Journal of the Commons House of Assembly* (entry 4759) which will cover the period 1736–76, but has only reached the year 1750.

Among the southern states, Maryland's program has been quite successful. As the de facto archival agency of the state, the Maryland Historical Society, with the support and authority of the state legislature, began to issue in 1883 the *Archives of Maryland* (entry 2120). Under a succession of editors from William

Hand Browne to Aubrey C. Land, the series has reached 70-odd volumes. Among them are the pre-Revolutionary journals of the general assembly and provincial council (entry 4572), the correspondence of Governor Horatio Sharpe, 1753–71 (entry 4573), the proceedings of the council of safety, 1775–77 (entry 9163), and of the state council, 1775–89 (entry 9165), and muster rolls and lists of Maryland soldiers in the Revolution (entry 8037). Moreover, a special commission was created in 1935 to take charge of the newly constructed Hall of Records built in Annapolis on land donated to the state by St. John's College. Among the records placed in its keeping were the "rainbow series," whose content has been carefully described in the *Calendar of Maryland State Papers* (entry 740), composed of the Black Books (miscellaneous colonial and Revolutionary documents to 1785), the Blue Books (Bank Stock Papers dealing with paper money during the Confederation period), the Brown Books (civil and military correspondence focusing on the Revolutionary period), the Red Books (military documents largely from the years 1773–81), and a volume of executive miscellanea.

MIDDLE ATLANTIC STATES

From the middle of the 19th century, Pennsylvania steadfastly supported the publication of its official records. In addition to the first series of *Pennsylvania Archives [1664–1790]* (entry 1960), eight more series totaling 108 volumes were issued between 1874 and 1935 under the successive editorships of John B. Linn, William H. Egle, George E. Reed, Thomas L. Montgomery, Gertrude MacKinney, and Charles F. Hoban (entry 1973). Sources for the Revolution, with a heavy emphasis on military affairs, are concentrated in the second and third series edited by Linn and Egle. Among the scattered groups of miscellaneous documents from the period, there appeared 15 volumes devoted to the minutes of the Board of War (entry 8003), rosters of Pennsylvania's battalions and Continental Line (entry 8004) and associated battalions and militia (entry 7996), documents relating to the Connecticut settlement in the Wyoming Valley (entry 1961), minutes of the Board of Property and other references to land (entry 1962), commissions issued by the province of Pennsylvania with official proclamations, 1733–90 (entry 1967), the wartime accounts of the county lieutenants, 1777–89 (entry 9100), and further muster rolls of the navy, line, militia, and rangers, 1775–83 (entry 7995). The minutes of the council for the Revolutionary period had been published in the *Colonial Records* (entry 4502). The pa-

pers of the Revolutionary governors were part of the fourth series (entry 1968); the election returns of the Pennsylvania counties from 1756 to 1789 formed part of the sixth (entry 1964); and the votes and proceedings of the House of Representatives from 1682 to 1776 (entry 4500) made up the entire eighth series. In response to the Public Archives Commission's surveys in Pennsylvania and the efforts of the AHA, the Division of Public Records was established as part of the State Library in 1903. The first custodian organized the archives in chronological series and preserved them in bound volumes. After seeing through publication the final 40 volumes of the *Pennsylvania Archives,* the division and its records were absorbed by the Pennsylvania Historical and Museum Commission, an independent state agency created in 1945. Four years later the commission issued a guide and finding list to all 138 volumes of the *Archives* and *Colonial Records* (entry 98).

Archival development in New York took a different course. Until they were moved to the State Library in Albany in 1847, New York's records were kept in the office of the secretary of state. Edmund B. O'Callaghan selected many of them for publication in his *Documentary History of the State of New York* (entry 1747) and *Documents Relative to the Colonial History of the State of New York* (entry 1748). In 1884 the State Library and its newly created Manuscripts and History Section were put under the control of the Board of Regents of the University of the State of New York. During this period the state issued *The Colonial Laws of New York From the Year 1644 to the Revolution* (entry 4419) and the journals of Major General John Sullivan's expedition against the Six Nations in 1779 (entry 6499). New York's publication program was considerably enhanced after 1895 with the appointment of Hugh Hastings as state historian, an office separate in function from the State Library. While the library issued a *Calendar of Council Minutes, 1668–1783* in 1902 (entry 1750), the State Historian's office published the *Public Papers of George Clinton, First Governor of New York, 1777–1795, 1801–1804* (entry 9021), the *Military Minutes of the Council of Appointment of the State of New York 1783–1821* (entry 9018), the *Ecclesiastical Records, State of New York* (entry 11163), and the *Minutes of the Commissioners for Detecting and Defeating Conspiracies in the State of New York [1777–81]* (entry 9013). The devastating fire in 1911 that destroyed over two-thirds of the State Library's manuscript holdings, however, led the Board of Regents to create a Division of Archives and History that shared overlapping jurisdiction with the state historian's office and the Manuscript and History Section of the State Library in organizing and publishing what survived. Although the division has printed selected documents on the Sullivan-Clinton campaign in 1779 (entry 6522) and the orderly books of the Second and Fourth New York regiments, 1778–83 (entry 7956), the state's archival program has waned in the past half century.

More than in any other state, the Revolutionary War made a chaos of New Jersey recordkeeping as a result of the depredations of contending armies, the burning of nearly all county courthouses, and the frequent moves of the new state government. In 1872 the state legislature authorized funds to obtain transcripts of colonial documents abroad and to publish the official register of New Jersey officers and men in the Revolution (entry 7979), the minutes of the state's provincial congress and council of safety, 1775–76 (entry 9060), and a reprint of the minutes of the New Jersey ratifying convention of 1787 (entry 9632). More important, at the request of the New Jersey Historical Society, the state began to issue three series known collectively as *Documents Relating to the Colonial, Revolutionary, and Post-Revolutionary History of the State of New Jersey* under the editorship of William Nelson, William A. Whitehead, Abraham V. Honeyman, and others (entry 1882). Given the gaps in available records, however, the editors have been unable to produce a fully rounded series of documents. Of more than 40 volumes published, 36 were devoted to five groups of material. The first 10 focused on the colonial executive, 1631–1776, with the tenth containing the papers of Governor William Franklin, from 1763 to 1776 (entry 4473). Another six volumes were devoted to the journal of the governor and council, 1682–1775 (entry 4472), one to marriage records, 1665–1800 (entry 10803), and nine more to a calendar of New Jersey wills, administrations, etc., 1670–1800 (entry 10805). To achieve some balance in treatment, William Nelson edited 11 volumes of extracts from colonial newspapers published between 1704 and 1775 (entry 4470) that provided outside evidence for many aspects of New Jersey life not covered by official records. A second series of five volumes, issued between 1901 and 1917, extended the coverage to 1792 (entry 9059). Nelson also conducted for the state's Public Record Commission and the AHA's Public Archives Commission full surveys of New Jersey's holdings. After a critical review of the state's archival practices appeared in the AHA's *Annual Report* for 1916 (entry 703), the legislature created the Public Record Office, which merged with the State Library

in 1941 and was changed to the Bureau of Archives and History in 1945. The Bureau completed the first series of *Documents* by extending the coverage of wills and administrations to 1817 and began recently to issue yet a third series. Edited by David A. Bernstein, the first volume to appear is the *Minutes of the Governor's Privy Council, 1777–1789* (1974).

Delaware's archives were devastated to an even greater extent than those of New Jersey. Formed in 1776 from the three lower counties of Pennsylvania, the state stored its records for more than a century in the loft and basement of the capitol at Dover where they were subject to vandalism, theft, and fire. By 1906, Edgar B. Dawson, who investigated the state's holdings for the AHA's Public Archives Commission, found that no state had less material for writing its history than Delaware. Aroused by public appeals, the legislature established a Division of Public Records, changing its name in 1911 to the Public Archives Commission. The first state archivist presided over the publication of the surviving Revolutionary records. The first three volumes of the *Delaware Archives* (entry 8030) contain military and naval records (regimental rolls, militia lists, names of pensioners, memorials, and petitions) and miscellaneous correspondence. The commission has also reprinted the *Proceedings of the [Constitutional] Convention of the Delaware State* (entry 9142) and the *Votes and Proceedings of the Houses of Representatives [1765]* (entry 4554).

New England

In New England there was generally less pressure to alter traditional archival practices or to launch new publishing programs, especially in view of early accomplishments in the field. New Hampshire's records, although small in volume, had been well maintained by the secretary of state in both the state library and the historical society. Over a 76-year period the legislature provided for the publication under several editors of the most important colonial and Revolutionary documents in a series known by its composite title as the *Provincial and State Papers* (entry 1326). Included in the series were papers from the Wentworth administration, 1764–76 (entry 4263); various documents from the period 1776–83 (entry 8877); records of the towns, 1778–84, with an appendix containing the journals of the constitutional conventions of 1778–79 and 1781–83 (entry 8878); miscellaneous documents, 1779–92, including letters of the Committee of Safety, 1779–84 (entry 8876); rolls and documents relating to soldiers in the Revolutionary War (entry 7855); early state papers, 1784–93 (entry 8875); and miscellaneous Revolutionary documents (entry 7852). The state published separately the index to the journals of the House of Representatives, 1711–84 (entry 627) and the colonial and state statutes (entry 1327).

Connecticut was also able to publish a large proportion of its surviving archives. Under the direction of the state librarian, James H. Trumbull and Charles J. Hoadly edited a chronologically arranged series of *Public Records of the Colony of Connecticut [1636–1776]* (entry 4383). A continuation, *The Public Records of the State of Connecticut [1776 +]* (entry 8986), has been edited by Hoadly and Leonard W. Labaree. While the last three volumes of the original series focus on official documents and reports from 1763 to the Revolution, the first six volumes of the state papers contain the journals of the Council of Safety and various state conventions from 1776 to 1789.

In Massachusetts, the strength of the publishing programs of the major historical societies in the Boston area affected the response of the state government. Since the end of the 18th century the state has maintained its archives in the office of the secretary of commonwealth. Just before the Civil War the secretary began issuing *The Acts and Resolves . . . of the Province of Massachusetts Bay [1692–1780]* (entry 4309). These were followed by 17 volumes of *Massachusetts Soldiers and Sailors of the Revolutionary War* (entry 7908). Other projects, such as editing the *Journals of the House of Representatives of Massachusetts* (entry 4307), have been taken up by the Massachusetts Historical Society.

In Rhode Island the *Records of the Colony of Rhode Island and Providence Plantations in New England [1636–1792]* (entry 1641), has served as a staple research source for over a century, but other major series based on the records maintained by the secretary of state have not appeared. Gertrude Kimball's *Correspondence of the Colonial Governors of Rhode Island, 1723–1775* (entry 4372), for example, was sponsored by a private organization, the National Society of Colonial Dames.

The care and maintenance of state archives thus vary widely. Those states that lacked strong archival traditions at the turn of century created independent archival agencies or commissions within the state governments, whereas states with privately-sponsored publication programs tended to leave their records in the care of secretaries of state or divided among several departments or divisions. Much of the credit for the development of new programs can be attributed to

the investigations and influence of the American Historical Association's Public Archives Commission. At the same time, the AHA, in its attempts to take stock of national historical resources, turned its attention to those institutions first responsible for the development of a tradition of preservation—the state and local historical societies.

THE CONFERENCE OF STATE AND LOCAL HISTORICAL SOCIETIES

At the annual meeting of the AHA in Chicago in 1904, the first Conference of State and Local Historical Societies was held to consider the condition and role of the 400 to 500 associations created during the previous century. Benjamin F. Shambaugh, Franklin L. Riley, and Reuben Gold Thwaites were appointed as a committee to circulate questionnaires among the societies and to recommend the best method of organizing state historical work and promoting cooperation. The committee reported the following year in Baltimore that older privately endowed societies, such as those in Massachusetts, New York, and Pennsylvania, had attained a high level of autonomy and usefulness and that elsewhere, especially in the South, state historical organizations had allied with departments of history in the state universities in an effort to strengthen their programs. Locally, town historical societies were the rule in New England, while counties had become the unit of organization in other parts of the country. The committee believed that such decentralization actually hindered the collection and dissemination of historical material and that organization and cooperation were essential, perhaps in the form of a centralized depository in each state for records not purely local in nature. It further recommended that all manuscripts held by state and local societies be systematically cataloged and full inventories widely distributed. One of the immediate results of the committee's efforts was the publication of a guide to those sources already in print, A. P. C. Griffin's "Bibliography of American Historical Societies," as the second part of the AHA's 1905 *Annual Report* (entry 50).

In 1908 a new Committee on the Cooperation of Historical Societies and Departments was appointed to make inquiries into the holdings of local associations and to publish their findings in the *Annual Report*. Unfortunately, fewer than 20 percent of the societies responded, and pleas issued at future meetings of the Conference of State and Local Historical Societies were to little avail. The conference continued to be part of the annual meeting of the

AHA for the next 30 years, but it was superseded in 1940 by the American Association for State and Local History, which assumed the tasks of coordinating the activities of institutions and individuals interested in the promotion of state and local history and serving as a clearinghouse for programs in the field.

Although attempts to organize and focus the activities of local societies were less successful than the AHA anticipated, local institutions continued to proliferate, nearly doubling their number, from 500 to 1,000, by the eve of the Second World War. A major development during this period was the transition in state and local historical publications from irregular and fragmentary collections and proceedings to professionally edited journals such as the *New-York Historical Society Quarterly*, the *Maryland Historical Magazine*, and the *Georgia Historical Quarterly*. Yet, despite the increasing emphasis on scholarship in historical publication, many smaller societies were faced with the need to popularize their activities and to combat spiraling costs by broadening the basis of their support in the local community. The more self-sufficient societies, however, were able to continue documentary publication in some form or another.

NEW ENGLAND

In New England the Massachusetts Historical Society remained a focal point for the other societies in the region, and its *Collections* and *Proceedings* continued to be models for others to emulate. Over 200 volumes had appeared before 1900. Its program continued unabated after the turn of the century with the publication of the diary of John Quincy Adams, 1787–88 (entry 12682), the letters and papers of John Singleton Copley and Henry Pelham, 1739–76 (entry 13112), letters and papers relating to the commerce of Rhode Island, 1726–1800 (entry 9809), the journals of Josiah Quincy, Jr., 1773–75 (entry 14258), and the letters of John and Samuel Adams and James Warren (entry 14669). Other volumes include the letters and papers of the colony's London agent, Jasper Mauduit, 1762–65 (entry 3093), Worthington C. Ford's guide to broadsides and ballads printed in Massachusetts from 1639 to 1800 (entry 478), and commissions of Massachusetts privateers in the Revolution (entry 7373). In addition, the society began in 1919 to publish 36 projected volumes of the *Journals of the House of Representatives of Massachusetts [1715–80]* (entry 4307). Subsequently, funding difficulties led to less expensive means of reproduction, such as two series of rare imprints selected by Worthington C. Ford that were distributed among subscribing libraries, including the

Library of Congress, under the title Photostat Americana. The society also issued photostats of newspapers in its collections, such as *The Boston News-Letter*, 1740–76, *The Georgia Gazette*, 1763–73, and, in collaboration with the Virginia Historical Society, *The Virginia Gazette*, 1736–80. In 1956 the voluminous Adams family papers were deposited in the society's care, and a microfilm edition of the great bulk of the papers was prepared for sale to interested depositories and scholars. Under the general editorship of Lyman H. Butterfield, Harvard University Press began publishing in letterpress selections from the well-known family diaries and correspondence, a program that will reach an estimated 100 volumes in several series. Thus far the focus has been on the 18th century with the appearance of *The Diary and Autobiography of John Adams*, the *Adams Family Correspondence* through 1782, and *The Legal Papers of John Adams* (entry 12681). A new series of the political correspondence of John Adams is now being edited by Robert J. Taylor, who succeeded Butterfield in 1975.

Elsewhere in New England, the New Hampshire Historical Society issued 17 volumes of source material in the 19th century but ended its *Collections* with Otis G. Hammond's edition of the letters and papers of Major General John Sullivan, 1771–95 (entry 14525). It also issued separately in 1937 Samuel Lane's journal of the years 1739–1803 (entry 13795). Thereafter, it directed its publications to more popular works, such as *Historical New Hampshire* which was launched in 1944. The Rhode Island Historical Society included the papers of William Vernon and the Navy Board, 1776–94, in its *Publications* for 1901 (entry 8755) and issued separately Theodore Foster's minutes of the South Kingston convention of March 1790 (entry 9614), the letterbook and correspondence of Esek Hopkins (entry 13631), and the correspondence of Governor Samuel Ward, 1775–76 (entry 14663). Its *Publications* ceased in 1941, to be replaced by *Rhode Island History*, which contains sources relating to Captain James Wallace's patrol of Narragansett Bay in H.M.S. *Rose*, 1774 (entry 3974) and the minutes of the court-martial proceedings relating to the destruction of the *Gaspee* (entry 3977). From its newspaper collection, the society microfilmed and distributed widely a complete file of the *Providence Gazette*, 1762–95. The Connecticut Historical Society had provided its members with 30 volumes of colonial and Revolutionary material in its *Collections* during the 19th century. To those works it added the lists and returns of Connecticut men in the Revolution, 1775–83 (entry 7930), the correspondence and documents of governors Thomas Fitch, 1754–66 (entry 4385), and William Pitkin, 1766–69 (entry 4386), the Revolutionary letters of Joshua and Jedediah Huntington (entry 13667), the correspondence among Silas Deane, his brothers, and their business and political associates, 1771–95 (entry 13189), and the journals of Israel and Rufus Putnam on their exploration of the Mississippi River, 1772–73 (entry 14253). The Connecticut society also adopted in 1934 a more popular format in its quarterly *Bulletin*, in which it has included such items as 1774–75 fragments from the diary of Silas Deane (entries 4148–4149) and an analysis of the correspondence of Samuel Peters and Benjamin Trumbull (entry 14192).

MIDDLE ATLANTIC STATES

Among associations in the Middle Atlantic states, the New-York Historical Society's program of documentary publication continued through the John Watts DePeyster Publication Fund Series. From 1916 it issued the New York muster and pay rolls from the Revolutionary War (entry 6987), the proceedings of the board of general officers of the British Army at New York in 1781 (entry 6810), nine volumes of the letters and papers of Cadwallader Colden, 1711–75 (entry 13088), the minutes of the committee and the first commission for detecting and defeating Loyalist conspiracies in the state of New York, 1776–78 (entry 9014), the minutes of the Council of Appointment for the state of New York, 1778–79 (entry 9019), and the letterbooks and order book of George, Lord Rodney, 1780–82 (entry 14325). A second subseries of the society's *Collections*, the John Divine Jones Fund Series, contained the travel journal of Mrs. L. S. Aikman from Charleston to London (entry 12690), the Loyalist orderly book of Brigadier General Oliver DeLancey, 1776–78 (entry 6839), and a calendar of New York colonial commissions, 1680–1770 (entry 4412). Members of the society also contributed to the intricate task of editing the minutes of the Common Council of the City of New York from 1675 to 1776 (entry 4411), published by the city. In the *Collections* themselves the society included the papers of the Lloyd family of Long Island from 1752 to 1826 (entry 13865), the letterbook of John Watts, 1762–65 (entry 14685), and Philip L. White's edition of the Beekman family mercantile papers, 1746–99 (entry 12827). Although large-scale documentary publications have been curtailed somewhat during the past 40 years, the *New-York Historical Society Quarterly*, which began to appear in 1917, has contained numerous letters and documents, such as a new group of sources on the

Sullivan-Clinton campaign of 1779 (entry 6511) and letters of Governor William Livingston of New Jersey in 1782 (entry 9066).

The historical societies of New Jersey, Pennsylvania, and Delaware have published few single or multivolume document collections in the past 75 years, although the New Jersey Historical Society cooperated with the state archives in completing the 40-odd volume *Archives of the State of New Jersey*, begun in 1880. Its *Proceedings*, dating from 1845, passed through three series before becoming a quarterly journal in 1916. Occasional documents such as Revolutionary pension records (entry 7980) and the letters of Cornelia Bell Paterson (entry 14163) have appeared in its pages. Publication of the Historical Society of Pennsylvania's *Collections* and *Memoirs* ceased in the 19th century. Their place was taken by the pioneering *Pennsylvania Magazine of History and Biography*, launched by Frederick D. Stone. The first general historical quarterly of its type, it established a pattern that is still widely imitated. For over a century the magazine's editors have published, in addition to articles and book reviews, documentary excerpts such as the historical notes of Dr. Benjamin Rush for 1777 (entry 14348), selections from the letterbooks of Thomas Wharton, 1773–83 (entry 14711), letters from William Franklin to William Strahan, 1757–82 (entry 13385), the orderly book of the Second Pennsylvania Continental Line at Valley Forge (entry 7103), letters of Benjamin Rush, 1765–1812, that were not included in Lyman Butterfield's two-volume edition (entry 14348), letters of Gilbert Barkly, a British spy in Philadelphia, 1775–77 (entry 7773), the William Allen– Benjamin Chew correspondence for 1763–64 (entry 12708), and a host of muster rolls, Moravian records from the Revolution, and miscellaneous Revolutionary correspondence. From its large and rich newspaper collection, the society has also issued on microfilm files of the *Pennsylvania Gazette*, 1728–89, *Pennsylvania Journal*, 1742–93, *Pennsylvania Chronicle*, 1767–74, and *Pennsylvania Packet*, 1771–90. Between 1879 and 1922 the neighboring Delaware Historical Society has published 67 volumes of *Papers*, among them the journal and order book of Captain Robert Kirkwood of the Delaware Regiment, Continental Line (entry 13771). A separate edition of letters to and from Caesar Rodney, 1756–84, edited by George H. Ryden, was published in 1933 (entry 14324). Delaware also turned to a more popular format in 1946—its semiannual *Delaware History*—including in its pages minutes of the Council of Safety, 1775–76 (entry 9143) and documents of the Kent County Loyalists (entry 8225).

SOUTHERN STATES

The southern historical agencies have in the 20th century reduced the size and content of their serials and periodicals. The Virginia Historical Society, for example, abandoned its *Collections*, which had reached 11 volumes in 1892, in favor of the quarterly *Virginia Magazine of History and Biography*. Although the early volumes were genealogically oriented, they did include excerpts of legislative documents and papers of the House of Burgesses, 1764–76 (entry 4616), the proceedings of the Virginia Committee of Correspondence, 1759–70 (entry 4617), and the order books of the main army under Washington (entry 6292). The society's interest in documentary publication was revived in the 1960's as a result of statewide programs in Virginia history stimulated by the 350th anniversary of the Jamestown settlement. It has sponsored full editions of the diary of Colonel Landon Carter of Sabine Hall, 1752–78 (entry 13008), the letters and papers of Edmund Pendleton, 1734–1803 (entry 14178), and Edmund Randolph's *History of Virginia* (entry 2186). The society also continues to include such items as the pre-Revolutionary letters of Robert Beverly (entry 12842) and the daybook of Robert Wormeley Carter (entry 13010) in its *Magazine*.

The South Carolina Historical Society also halted publication of its *Collections* and began to issue in 1900 the *South Carolina Historical and Genealogical Magazine*. Select documents have appeared in installments of varying length through the years: the correspondence of Henry Laurens (entry 13804), the order book of the First Regiment, South Carolina Line, 1775–80 (entry 6586), the correspondence of Charles Garth, London agent for the colony, 1766–73 (entry 13418), the letters of Arthur Middleton, 1763–73 (entry 14013), the writings of the Reverend William Tennent, 1740–77 (entry 14550), and the letterbook of Peter Manigault, 1763–73 (entry 13951). In 1968 the society began to sponsor a multivolume edition of the *Papers of Henry Laurens* [1746 +] under the direction of Philip M. Hamer (entry 13804).

Unlike most southern organizations, the Maryland Historical Society found sufficient support to sustain two large-scale projects beginning with its *Fund Publications* in 37 volumes from 1867 to 1901, through the *Archives of Maryland* in 70-plus volumes from 1882 to the present. The society also founded its quarterly *Maryland Historical Magazine* in 1906, using it as a vehicle for the publication of discrete units of material such as the correspondence of Governor Robert Eden, 1769–77 (entry 13275), the Charles Garth Stamp Act papers (entry 3086), the letters of the Reverend Jonathan Boucher (entry 12879), the journals of the committees of observation in the middle and upper districts of Maryland, 1775–76 (entry 9156), extracts from the papers of Charles Carroll, 1750–74 (entry 13004), the familiar letters of Governor Sharpe, 1758–84 (entry 14413), and the letters of Alexander Hamilton, a Piscataway factor, 1774–84 (entry 13524).

The Georgia Historical Society has also managed to maintain a relatively active program. Although few volumes of its *Collections* were published in the 19th century, those that have appeared in the 20th century contain a substantial number of Revolutionary documents. The proceedings of the first provincial congress of Georgia in 1775 (entry 9290), the proceedings of the Georgia Council of Safety from 1775 to 1777 (entry 9282), and a British account of the siege of Savannah in 1779 (entry 6638) were published in 1901, followed by the letterbook of Governor Samuel Elbert, 1785 (entry 9286), the letters of the Honorable James Habersham, 1756–75 (entry 13509), and the letters of Joseph Clay, a Savannah merchant, 1776–93 (entry 13061). The *Georgia Historical Quarterly* began publication in 1917. Among the documents included each quarter have been the official letters of governors John Martin, 1782–83 (entry 9285) and Edward Telfair, 1786–87 (entry 9287), the minutes of the Executive Council for 1777 (entry 9284) not in Candler's *Revolutionary Records*, the proceedings and minutes of the governor and council, 1774–75 and 1779–80 (entry 4786) not in Candler's *Colonial Records*, the letters of the Commons House of Assembly to the Georgia colonial agent, 1762–71 (entry 4787), the minute book of the Savannah Board of Police for 1779 (entry 9293), and Henry Muhlenberg's Georgia correspondence, 1777–84 (entry 14070). The *Quarterly* also includes the texts of documents that have been subsequently reprinted in book form as part of the society's *Collections*, such as the papers of James Jackson, 1781–98 (entry 13690) and the papers of Lachlan McIntosh, 1774–99 (entry 13921).

Thus, a fairly clear pattern emerged in the activities of the major private historical institutions on the east coast. Those with adequate financing from endowments, trusts, and private donations, such as the Massachusetts and New York societies, were able to concentrate on large-scale documentary and bibliographic publication for a longer period of time, although only Massachusetts has been able to maintain its traditional attachment to "proceedings" and "collections." In the other states, rising publication costs and limitations of staff, time, and money have forced all but a few to abandon the publication of whole manuscript collections and to turn to historical interpretation in the form of topically oriented, often illustrated journals and bulletins designed to appeal to a larger audience. If the purpose of most historical societies in the 19th century was to promote a healthy skepticism toward "official" versions of the past by exposing readers to the documentary details of history, then 20th-century institutions have substantially altered that purpose in their attempt to interpret the past broadly and to disseminate historical information among an increasingly greater number of people.

The Rise of Academic, Public, and Private Libraries

One of the more constructive developments in the preservation of historical sources to take place in the 20th century has been the establishment of major research institutions by universities, private collectors, and city governments to complement the work of historical societies and the state and federal governments. The creation of such repositories has not only diversified and strengthened the nation's research resources, but it has also made available to scholars important collections that might have remained in private hands, been obscured in massive public archives, or continued to be virtually inaccessible in foreign institutions.

The emergence of the professional historian as an important part of the college faculty at the turn of the century made the growth of manuscript collections in academic libraries almost inevitable. Few campuses were located near the established centers of research, thus making a strong case for bringing manuscripts, transcripts, or photocopies to the college or university library itself. With the growth of higher education in the 20th century, the size and quality of a library's manuscript holdings became both a status symbol and a means of attracting faculty and students to the institution. Within 75 years hundreds of new depositories were created at such institutions as Dartmouth, Rutgers, William and Mary, and Duke where virtually none had existed before. Three of the oldest universities in the East—Harvard, Princeton, and the University of Virginia—house some of the richest collections of Revolutionary materials. To some degree they illustrate the preservation function of academic establishments.

Benefiting from the generous donations of 18th- and 19th-century alumni like Jared Sparks and the enlightened guidance of such librarians as John L.

Sibley and Justin Winsor, the Harvard Library entered the present century with an outstanding collection of Americana which includes for the Revolution dozens of miscellaneous groupings of diaries, letters, journals, and papers as well as correspondence of Arthur Lee, Paine Wingate, Benjamin Lincoln, Sir Francis Bernard, Thomas Gage, and William Tryon. Many are transcripts or photocopies of the originals found in archives scattered throughout Europe and the United States. The manuscript collection at Princeton University not only includes the Grenville Kane Early Americana Collection but also letters of French officer Louis Alexandre Berthier, Elias Boudinot, Nathaniel Gorham, Richard Stockton, John Witherspoon, Jonathan Dickinson, and several major groups of documents relating to the Revolutionary War in New Jersey. Although Virginia's early collections centered on the Richard Henry Lee papers, a sizable donation from Thomas Jefferson, and a core collection of Landon Carter, William Lee, Dabney Carr, and Wilson Cary Nicholas papers, its 18th-century holdings have been greatly enriched by participation in a project stimulated by the 350th anniversary of the Jamestown settlement. With the full participation of the Virginia State Library and the Virginia Historical Society, the University of Virginia library provided support for a full-time research agent in the various British depositories to seek out and microfilm documents relevant to Virginia colonial and Revolutionary history. The Virginia Colonial Records Project, as it came to be known, is a direct descendant of those visionary programs undertaken in foreign archives in the 19th century by men such as Sparks, Bancroft, and O'Callaghan. With the aid of a small staff, Dr. George Reese, the project's agent, sifted through nearly all of the major record groups in institutions such as the Public Record Office, the British Museum, and Lambeth Palace in London and the Archives nationales and Bibliotheque nationale in Paris. More than a thousand survey reports of one to 40 pages were prepared, each of which described the contents of hundreds of pages of documents that have been microfilmed and sent to the major research depositories in Virginia. An index to the entire series of survey reports is in preparation. By such generous contributions to scholarship, academic libraries have assumed the lead as the prime collectors of American manuscripts.

Important strides were also made early in the century by wealthy private collectors who founded and endowed separate institutions to perpetuate their libraries. Because of the magnitude and quality of their colonial and Revolutionary holdings, the libraries of John Carter Brown in Providence, William L. Clements at Ann Arbor, and Henry E. Huntington in San Marino have attained preeminence among research institutions for the period. Beginning in the mid-19th century, the Providence merchant, John Carter Brown (1808–1874), acquired through a series of discriminating purchases in the United States and Europe an impressive collection of printed Americana from the age of discovery to 1800. To ensure its preservation and scholarly use, his son, John Nicholas Brown, provided for the establishment in 1901 of a separate institution under the aegis of Brown University. The collections have been consistently enriched by a succession of perceptive librarians—Worthington C. Ford, Lawrence C. Wroth, and Thomas R. Adams, the latter of whom has recently published *American Independence* (entry 474), a bibliographic study of the American political pamphlets printed between 1764 and 1776 dealing with the dispute between Great Britain and the colonies. The collections now include over 25,000 rare books and a strong supporting reference library. The Michigan industrialist, William L. Clements (1861–1934), also began to collect printed books from the colonial period, but later, due to his friendship with Worthington C. Ford and University of Michigan historian Claude H. Van Tyne, turned to the acquisition of British manuscripts of the Revolutionary period, among them the papers of General Thomas Gage, the Earl of Shelburne, Sir Henry Clinton, Lord George Germain, William Knox, Frederick Lord North, John Wilkes, and Richard Oswald. In 1922 Clements gave his entire library as well as a separate building to house it to the University of Michigan where it has become the key American depository for research on the British side of the Revolution. In the West, the creation of the Huntington Library by Henry Edwards Huntington (1850–1927), nephew and business representative of the railway magnate Collis P. Huntington, has provided researchers with one of the most decorative and unique refuges for scholarship in the United States. Turning avidly to the collection of Anglo-American portraits, rare books, and manuscripts after his retirement, Huntington often purchased entire libraries as they became available. One prominent example was the noted Robert A. Brock Collection of 17th- and 18th-century Virginiana which required an entire railroad car to transport it from Richmond to California. Among the nearly 1½ million manuscripts and rare books obtained altogether are letters of John Jay, Thomas Jefferson, Robert Morris, and Ebenezer Huntington, and 55 volumes of Revolu-

tionary War orderly books. Huntington chose to maintain his collection in a special library and art gallery built in the middle of the impressive botanical gardens on his ranch near San Marino. Control of the institution passed upon his death to a board of trustees who adopted a policy of inviting prominent scholars of the caliber of Louis B. Wright to become members of the permanent staff, thereby ensuring the development and continued use of the collections. The library not only subsidizes the publication of monographs based in part on its holdings but invites contributions from the outside to its prestigious *Huntington Library Quarterly*.

Not the least of the major research institutions that have developed in the last century are the municipal and county libraries that have acquired manuscripts of a regional character or have been made the repository for collections that are national in scope. Two prime examples are the city libraries of Boston and New York. The Boston Public Library, founded in 1852, contains the personal library of John Adams, donated by the city of Quincy, a large collection of books printed by Benjamin Franklin plus many from his own library, a substantial corpus of early Boston imprints, and the records of the city of Boston. Among the manuscripts that it holds are the correspondence of John Hancock, Henry Knox, and George Thacher, several volumes of Signers' letters, and material on the Burgoyne campaign. But the nation's premier municipal institution for research on the Revolution is the New York Public Library. Established in 1895, its vast research holdings were acquired and are now sustained by private funds, endowment income, and gifts, although the rest of the Library system operates on public funds. In its manuscript division of more than 9,000,000 documents are the large private collections of George Bancroft, George Chalmers, Thomas A. Emmett, and Paul L. and Worthington C. Ford, as well as dozens of miscellaneous manuscript groups. They contain letters by Horatio Gates, Phillip Schuyler, Peter Gansevoort, Henry Laurens, Timothy Pickering, Robert R. and William Livingston, William Smith, Benjamin Lincoln, Jedidiah Morse, Samuel Adams, Oliver Wolcott, George Clymer, and James Duane. The library's collection of 18th-century rare books and newspapers—over 90,000 items—ranks with those of the American Antiquarian Society and the Library of Congress.

It might seem that the voluminous collections gathered by such institutions as the New York Public, Clements, and Princeton libraries would help to simplify research on the American Revolution. But the proliferation of the newer research depositories in competition with historical societies and state and national archives has created overwhelming problems of bibliographic identification and control. Given the heterogeneity of existing manuscript depositories, the peculiarities in their traditions and modes of service, and the variety of their collections, scholars have found it difficult to plan research effectively without adequate calendars, checklists, guides, or indexes. To resolve the problems of access several steps have been taken at the national level in the past 50 years to establish uniform practices for cataloging, describing, and reporting individual books and manuscript collections.

The Search for Control

Early in the century, the eighth Librarian of Congress, Herbert Putnam, recognized the difficulties that would soon confront depositories if a uniform system of cataloging and identifying books and sources were not adopted. Under his leadership the Library took three far-reaching steps by creating systems for distributing its printed catalog cards, compiling a national union catalog of books in other American libraries, and lending books and other sources to libraries for scholarly use. Somewhat later, the staff of the newly opened National Archives united with their colleagues in state and local organizations to create in 1936 the Society of American Archivists. Their goal was to develop uniform practices of archival preservation and administration. As a platform for continuing discussion they began to publish in 1938 the *American Archivist.* Both of these developments not only encouraged a great exchange of information and material, but they also paralleled the first major archival survey undertaken by the federal government— an attempt to describe in uniform manner the holdings of thousands of county, city, and town archives.

THE HISTORICAL RECORDS SURVEY

After publishing reports on over two-thirds of the state archives by the eve of World War I, the American Historical Society's Public Archives Commission lost much of its initial impetus until the early 1930's when it received many proposals for a new survey. Thereupon, the commission, acting at the direction of the AHA Council, published a pamphlet on *The Preservation of Local Archives; a Guide for Public Officials* (1932) and soon presented plans for a nationwide survey of state, local, and private archives. Although the AHA was unable to take action

then, a similar proposal drawn up by Robert C. Binkley, chairman of the Social Science Research Council-American Council of Learned Societies Joint Committee on Materials for Research, was presented to the Roosevelt administration in 1935 by Luther H. Evans. The result was the establishment, under Evan's direction, of the Historical Records Survey of the Works Progress Administration. After careful planning, Evans published in early 1936 a procedural *Manual for the Survey of Historical Records* which became the authoritative writ for over 3,000 unemployed teachers, file clerks, stenographers, and typists who covered every courthouse in the nation as well as hundreds of other depositories in the next three years, preparing by 1942 28 volumes of inventories of state archives, 628 volumes of county archives, 180 volumes of municipal archives, and 107 guides to manuscript collections. Among the more important works touching on the Revolutionary period were a calendar of the manuscripts in the New Jersey State Library (entry 695), a catalog of the Du Simitiere papers in the Library Company of Philadelphia (entry 714), guides to manuscripts in the Historical Society of Pennsylvania (entry 716), the North Carolina Historical Commission (entry 784), and the Southern Historical Collection of the University of North Carolina (entry 786), and surveys of dozens of county and city archives in the original thirteen states. Expansion of the WPA survey to include early American imprints, under Douglas C. McMurtrie, as well as inventories of portraits, the records of early church congregations, and a Historical American Buildings Survey greatly increased public awareness of local documentation for the study of the colonial and Revolutionary periods. Moreover, the very success of the WPA project provoked greater concern for improved care of local archival records. As part of the same general thrust, the Library of Congress, in association with the University of North Carolina, launched a State Records Microfilm Project which reproduced between 1941 and 1950 the equivalent of $2^1/_2$ million pages of legislative proceedings, statutes, executive and administrative records, and court records for the colonial and Revolutionary periods. *A Guide to the Microfilm Collection of Early State Records* was published in 1950 (entry 616). The Historical Records Survey and the State Records Microfilm Project gave researchers unprecedented access to early public records, but unofficial documents and personal papers stored in state and local historical societies or in academic and private libraries presented vast lacunae for which there still were no adequate guides.

THE NATIONAL UNION CATALOG OF MANUSCRIPT COLLECTIONS

Out of the collaboration of Luther H. Evans, Robert C. Binkley, Douglas C. McMurtrie, and others in the late 1930's came proposals that led to the establishment by the American Historical Association of a Committee on Historical Source Materials under the general chairmanship of Herbert A. Kellar of the State Historical Society of Wisconsin. Kellar's committee investigated several means of obtaining better information about the content of existing manuscript collections and recommended that the most efficient way of making such materials known was to create a centralized pool of data that would be continually supplemented and regularly published. The committee's proposal was adopted in 1949 by the Society of American Archivists and the American Association for State and Local History which formed a Joint Committee on Historical Manuscripts. With Lester J. Cappon as chairman, the joint committee took a series of steps that led to an offer by Luther Evans for the Library of Congress to assume responsibility for the creation and maintenance of a national register of historical manuscripts. The Council on Library Resources, a subsidiary of the Ford Foundation, provided a $200,000 grant to establish the project which began operation in 1959 under the direction of Lester K. Born, head of the Manuscripts Section of the Descriptive Cataloging Division. The Library, in consultation with the American Library Association, adopted uniform rules for cataloging manuscripts and agreed to furnish each participating institution with printed cards for its reported collections. Eighteen volumes of the *National Union Catalog of Manuscript Collections* (NUCMC) had been published through 1980 containing reports on 44,225 collections in 1,099 depositories (see entry 615). The cumulative NUCMC indexes include almost 462,200 references to topical subjects and personal, family, corporate, and geographical names. Despite the best intentions, however, many institutions are unable to catalog and report their holdings fully or on a regular basis. Still, NUCMC remains the most important step ever taken in the United States toward providing researchers with the basic information necessary in determining where their source material is most likely to be found.

To increase awareness of manuscript collections that had already been microfilmed, the Council on Library Resources, which initially sponsored NUCMC, also provided a grant of funds in 1957 to the American Historical Association's Committee on Documentary Reproduction, resulting in the publication of Richard W. Hale's *Guide to Photocopied Historical Materials in the United States and Canada* (entry 523), a union list of 11,137 manuscript collections available at local depositories. In the course of his work Hale succeeded in uncovering large masses of local documents that had been unused by scholars previously because they were unknown or relatively inaccessible.

Indeed, the development of relatively inexpensive techniques of photoreproduction within the past 40 years has succeeded in revolutionizing the distribution of historical materials. Libraries, historical societies, and commercial enterprises have begun to publish and sell extensive editions of photocopied materials, thereby reducing travel expenses. In the area of the 18th-century publications, for example, scholars have benefited immeasurably from the widespread availability of *Early American Imprints, 1639–1800* produced cooperatively by the Readex Corporation and the American Antiquarian Society. Using as guides Charles Evans' monumental *American Bibliography* and Roger P. Bristol's *Supplement to Charles Evans' American Bibliography* (see entry 358), the Readex Corporation, under the supervision of Clifford K. Shipton, has produced a microcard edition of the full text of nearly 50,000 books, pamphlets, newspapers, journals, and broadsides published before 1800, 17,925 of them between 1763 and 1789. For periodicals, University Microfilms produced in the 1940's 33 reels of microfilm containing the full runs of 88 18th-century magazines and journals. Although not all 18th-century newspapers have been filmed, the appearance of Clarence C. Brigham's *History and Bibliography of American Newspapers 1690–1820* in 18 installments of the American Antiquarian Society's *Proceedings* from 1913 to 1927 and as a separate and revised two-volume edition in 1947 (entry 452) prompted many depositories to film and distribute entire series of their holdings. In 1948 George A. Schwegmann, Jr., of the Library of Congress, began to report regularly on the inclusive dates of microfilmed issues of newspapers, the frequency of publication, and the location of positive and negative photocopies. The 1973 edition of *Newspapers on Microfilm: United States* (see entry 471) contains 32,640 reports on domestic newspapers by state and city of publication. It is supplemented annually.

The effects of such innovations have been far-reaching. It can easily be argued, given the increase in the number and quality of historical dissertations, monographs, and essays since World War II, that the development of new technical processes in the dissemination of documentary sources and the increasing involvement of professional associations, foundations, and the federal government in new programs of preservation and control have had a profound influence upon Revolutionary historiography. It is also evident that the Depression and an exhausting war had produced by midcentury a greater appreciation for history and the study of the origins of the United States. Nowhere was this better illustrated than in the rebirth of a national program for the publication of the documentary heritage created by the Founding Fathers.

THE NATIONAL HISTORICAL PUBLICATIONS COMMISSION

In the original legislation creating the National Archives, provisions for a National Historical Publications Commission (NHPC) had been made at the insistence of J. Franklin Jameson, who envisaged an active federal historical publications program. During the 1930's, however, Congress failed to act on the commission's proposals, and with the outbreak of the Second World War the commission became inactive. Not until enactment of the Federal Records Act of 1950, therefore, did a renewed commission receive a mandate to encourage preservation and publication of important historical documents. When Julian Boyd, the editor of *The Papers of Thomas Jefferson*, presented the first volume of the series to President Truman in a May 1950 ceremony, the President enthusiastically responded by directing the commission to develop a broad plan for making available the writings of American statesmen. In its final form, *A National Program for the Publication of Historical Documents* (1954) called for the microfilm and letterpress publication of the papers of 361 individuals as well as documentary histories of the Continental Congress, the ratification of the U.S. Constitution and Bill of Rights, and the work of the first federal Congress. The "priority" projects that were to receive first attention were the latter two documentary histories and five projects already underway—the papers of Thomas Jefferson (entry 13701), Benjamin Franklin (entry 13381), the Adams family (entry 12681), Alexander Hamilton (entry 13523), and James Madison (entry 13944).

With the passage of Public Law 88–383 in 1964 providing the commission with an annual appropriation of $500,000 to make matching grants in-aid to other projects identified in its 1954 *Program* and its report of 1963, the NHPC entered a new phase. The Ford Foundation granted the commission an additional $2,000,000 to fund its priority projects over the next decade, and the NHPC soon made matching grants for several new letterpress editions of documents, among them the papers of Henry Laurens (entry 13804), Isaac Backus, Nathanael Greene, John Jay, James Iredell, Jonathan Trumbull, George Washington, the Marquis de Lafayette, John Marshall, and the Susquehanna Company (entry 4392). The commission also inaugurated its program of microfilm publications, issuing grants for the papers of several persons, families, and institutions from the Revolutionary period—Henry Knox (entry 13773), Mercy Otis Warren, Thomas Penn (entry 713), Eleazar Wheelock, Charles Carroll (entry 13004), Edward Dromgoole (entry 782), Thomas Burke (entry 12957), Artemas Ward (entry 14659), Timothy Pickering (entry 14200), John Nicholson (entry 14097), Winthrop Sargent (entry 14367), Benjamin Lincoln (entry 13847), Sir Andrew Snape Hamond (entry 13530), James Monroe (entry 14025), the Carter and Lee families of Virginia, (entries 13008 and 13814), the Lloyd and Calvert families of Maryland, the Forbes family of Massachusetts, the Stevens family of New Jersey, the firm of Baynton, Wharton, and Morgan of Philadelphia (entry 14046), and the minutes of the Provincial Council of Pennsylvania, 1682–1776 (entry 721). Although supported by other funds, a number of projects have been endorsed and assisted by the NHPC, including the journal and letters of Francis Asbury, the papers of Henry Bouquet, Archbishop John Carroll, George Mason, and Robert Morris, and the Program for Loyalist Studies and Publications.

Another major accomplishment of the NHPC was the publication in 1961 of the *Guide to Archives and Manuscripts in the United States* (entry 618). Under the leadership of the executive director, Philip M. Hamer, the commission's staff made independent investigations and solicited reports from depositories throughout the country in an effort to identify institutions holding documents pertinent to commission-sponsored editorial projects. The final compilation indicated that some 1,300 depositories had holdings estimated at more than 27,000 collections varying in size from a dozen to half a million documents. The first such general guide of its kind, it has proven indispensable as a basic reference tool in libraries throughout the country.

The Fruits of the Bicentennial

With the successes of the NHPC, (now reconstituted as the National Historical Publications and

Records Commission), the entrance of commercial firms into the field of documentary publication on microfilm, and the inception of extensive programs for the bibliographic control of manuscripts, materials for the study of the American Revolution have become available on a scale barely imagined just 50 years ago. Moreover, plans for the observance of the Bicentennial accelerated the process. Various commercial firms, such as Arno Press, University Microfilms, and G.K. Hall's Gregg Press, have reproduced whole series of primary and secondary sources on the Revolution that have long been out of print (see, for example, entries 1025, 3251, 3793, 6179, and 6583). The American Historical Association's Committee on the Commemoration of the American Revolution Bicentennial appointed a subcommittee on scholarly publications which has urged the Department of State to reissue Weaver's *Diplomatic Correspondence of the United States ... 1783 to 1789* (entry 8366) and to fund a completely new edition of Wharton's *Revolutionary Diplomatic Correspondence* (entry 8367). At the local level, state historical commissions and Bicentennial agencies have undertaken popular information programs, producing and sponsoring hundreds of monographs, documentary histories, chronologies, pamphlets, and guidebooks about state and regional participation in the Revolution.

Bicentennial programs at the federal level have been equally valuable. At the National Archives a grant from the Ford Foundation has permitted the staff to compile a computerized index to the 204-reel microfilm edition of the *Papers of the Continental Congress*. The Library of Congress commemoration of the American Revolution began in 1969 with the preparation of guides to contemporary source materials in the Library, bibliographies, documentary and facsimile publications, musical programs, symposia, and exhibits. Among the more important publications to date are *English Defenders of American Freedoms, 1774–1778* (1972. entry 3112), reprints of six British pamphlets attacking the coercive policy of the North ministry; *Manuscript Sources in the Library of Congress for Research on the American Revolution* (1975), a guide to 1,138 domestic collections and 479 collections of foreign reproductions in the Manuscript Division; *The American Revolution in Drawings and Prints* (1975), a checklist, with photoreproductions, of 921 graphics from all areas of the Library's collections; and *Maps and Charts of North America and the West Indies, 1750–1789; a Guide to the Collections in the Library of Congress* (1981), an annotated review

of 2,154 contemporary manuscript and printed maps and their derivatives in the collections of the Geography and Map Division. A generous grant from the Ford Foundation has also permitted a new edition of Burnett's *Letters of Members of the Continental Congress* (entry 8743), which will contain more than 15,000 documents, three-fifths of which are not in Burnett, in a projected 25 volumes.

As the Bicentennial era unfolds dozens of bibliographic projects and documentary publications will be completed that will further reduce the difficulty of locating research materials. Together they will continue to make the American Revolution the best-documented era for study by both professional scholars and interested citizens. None of this would have been possible, however, without the enthusiastic dedication of 19th-century collectors, the development of a rigorous methodology for the preservation and publication of documents by the archival and historical professions, the construction of hundreds of libraries, museums, and depositories for the protection of manuscripts and records, and the widespread dissemination of research materials through photoreproduction. If anything, the increased availability of evidence has made scholars appreciate more fully the complexity and diversity of the Revolutionary experience. The sweeping generalizations that satisfied an earlier age have fallen in the 20th century before the accumulated weight of evidence. To reinterpret the Revolution in the light of the sources and writings now available is a challenge that the present generation of writers and historians has readily accepted. The entries in *Revolutionary America* attest to their continued pursuit of fresh viewpoints and a deeper understanding of the nation's origins.

SOURCES

Adams, Charles F. The printing of old manuscripts. *In* Massachusetts Historical Society, *Boston*. Proceedings. v. 20; 1882/83. Boston, 1884. p. 175–182.

Ames, Herman V. Resumé of the archives situations in the several states in 1907. *In* American Historical Association. Annual report. 1907. v. 1. Washington, 1908. p. 163–187.

Ames, Herman V., *and others*. Tenth annual report of the Public Archives Commission. *In* American Historical Association. Annual report. 1909. Washington, 1911. p. 323–490.

Bassett, John S. The middle group of American historians. New York, Macmillan Co., 1917. xii, 324 p.

Beers, Henry P. Historical development of the records disposal policy of the federal government prior to 1934. American archivist, v. 7, July 1944: 181–201.

Bestor, Arthur E. The transformation of American scholarship, 1875–1917. Library quarterly, v. 23, July 1953: 164–179.

Binkley, William C. A historian looks at the *National Union Catalog of Manuscript Collections.* American archivist, v. 28, July 1965: 399–407.

Boyd, Julian P. State and local historical societies in the United States. American historical review, v. 40, Oct. 1934: 10–37.

Brubaker, Robert L. The publication of historical sources: recent projects in the United States. Library quarterly, v. 37, Apr. 1967: 193–225.

Burnette, O. Lawrence. Beneath the footnote; a guide to the use and preservation of American historical sources. Madison, State Historical Society of Wisconsin, 1969. x, 450 p.

Butterfield, Lyman H. Archival and editorial enterprises, 1850 and 1950; some comparisons and contrasts. *In* American Philosophical Society, *Philadelphia.* Proceedings, v. 98, June 1954: 159–170.

———Draper's predecessors and contemporaries. *In* Wisconsin. State Historical Society. The American collector; [four essays commemorating the Draper Centennial] Edited by Donald R. McNeil. [Madison] 1955. p. 1–23.

———Editing American historical documents. *In* Massachusetts Historical Society, *Boston.* Proceedings. v. 78; 1966. Boston, 1967. p. 81–104.

———Historical editing in the United States. I. The recent past. *In* American Antiquarian Society, *Worcester, Mass.* Proceedings, v. 72, Oct. 1962: 283–308.

Callcot, George H. Antiquarianism and documents in the age of literary history. American archivist, v. 21, Jan. 1958: 17–29.

Cappon, Lester J. American historical editors before Jared Sparks: "they will plant a forest . . ." William and Mary quarterly, 3d ser., v. 30, July 1973: 375–400.

———The National Archives and the historical profession. Journal of southern history, v. 35, Nov. 1969: 477–499.

———A rationale for historical editing, past and pres-

ent. William and Mary quarterly, 3d ser., v. 23, Jan. 1966: 56–75.

Carter, Clarence E. The United States and documentary historical publication. Mississippi Valley historical review, v. 25, June 1938: 3–24.

Crittenden, Christopher C. Publication policies for archival and state agencies. American archivist, v. 3, Oct. 1940: 245–250.

Dunlap, Leslie W. American historical societies, 1790–1860. Madison, Wis., Priv. print [Cantwell Print Co., 1944] ix, 238 p.

Eaton, Dorothy S., *and* Vincent L. Eaton. Manuscripts relating to early America. *In* U.S. *Library of Congress.* Quarterly journal of current acquisitions, v. 8, Nov. 1950: 17–28.

Edwards, Clyde S. American eighteenth-century newspapers. *In* U.S. *Library of Congress.* Quarterly journal of current acquisitions, v. 8, Nov. 1950: 40–43.

Eliot, Margaret S. The manuscript program of the Historical Records Survey. American archivist, v. 2, Apr. 1939: 97–105.

Ford, Worthington C. The editorial function in United States history. American historical review, v. 23, Jan. 1918: 263–286.

Goff, Frederick R. Peter Force. *In* Bibliographical Society of America. Papers, v. 44, no. 1, 1950: 1–16.

Goff, Frederick R., *and* Vincent L. Eaton. Early printed books relating to America, 1493–1801. *In* U.S. *Library of Congress.* Quarterly journal of current acquisitions, v. 8, Nov. 1950: 29–39.

Greene, Jack P. The publication of the official records of the southern colonies. William and Mary quarterly, 3d ser., v. 14, Apr. 1957: 268–280.

Hamer, Philip M. The records of southern history. Journal of southern history, v. 5, Feb. 1939: 3–17.

Hamilton, Joseph G. de Roulhac. Three centuries of southern records, 1607–1907. Journal of southern history, v. 10, Feb. 1944: 3–36.

Hesseltine, William B., *and* Donald R. McNeil, *eds.* In support of Clio; essays in memory of Herbert A. Kellar. Madison, State Historical Society of Wisconsin, 1958. x, 214 p.

Partial contents: The W.P.A. Historical Records Survey, by David L. Smiley.—Public archives in the United States, by G. Philip Bauer.—Mechanical aids in historical research, by George L. Anderson.—Foundations and the study of history, by Richard D. Younger.—Historical organizations as aids to history, by David D. Van Tassel and James A. Tinsley.—The historian as editor, by Lester J. Cappon.

Higham, John.   History [by] John Higham, with Leonard Krieger and Felix Gilbert. Englewood Cliffs, N.J., Prentice-Hall [1965] xiv, 402 p. (The Princeton studies: humanistic scholarship in America)

Jameson, John Franklin.   The American Historical Association, 1884–1909. American historical review, v. 15, Oct. 1909: 1–20.

———Early days of the American Historical Association, 1884–1895. American historical review, v. 40, Oct. 1934: 1–9.

———The functions of state and local historical societies with respect to research and publication. In American Historical Association. Annual report. 1897. Washington, 1898. p. 51–59.

———An historian's world; selections from the correspondence of John Franklin Jameson. Edited by Elizabeth Donnan and Leo F. Stock. Philadelphia, American Philosophical Society, 1956. xi, 382 p. (Memoirs of the American Philosophical Society, v. 42)

———The history of historical writing in America. Boston, Houghton, Mifflin, 1891. 160 p.

Jameson, John Franklin, and others.   Report of the Historical Manuscripts Commission of the American Historical Association. In American Historical Association. Annual report. 1896. v. 1. Washington, 1897. p. 463–480.

Jones, Houston G.   For history's sake; the preservation and publication of North Carolina history, 1663–1903. Chapel Hill, University of North Carolina Press [1966] xvi, 319 p.

———The records of a nation; their management, preservation, and use. New York, Atheneum, 1969. xviii, 308 p.

Kraus, Michael.   A history of American history. New York, Farrar & Rinehart [1937] x, 607 p.

Lacy, Dan M.   The Library of Congress: a sesquicentenary review. I. The development of the collections. Library quarterly, v. 20, July 1950: 157–179.

LeGear, Clara E.   Maps of early America. In U.S. Library of Congress. Quarterly journal of current acquisitions, v. 8, Nov. 1950: 44–53.

Leland, Waldo G.   The prehistory and origins of the National Historical Publications Commission. American archivist, v. 27, Apr. 1964: 187–194.

———Proceedings of the sixth annual conference of historical societies. In American Historical As-

sociation. Annual report. 1909. Washington, 1911. p. 279–322.

Lokke, Carl L.   The Continental Congress papers; their history, 1789–1952. In U.S. National Archives. National Archives accessions, no. 51, June 1954: 1–19.

Lord, Clifford L., ed.   Keepers of the past. Chapel Hill, University of North Carolina Press [1965] 241 p.

Partial contents: By way of background, by Clifford L. Lord.—Jeremy Belknap, by Stephen T. Riley.—John Pintard, by James J. Heslin.—Lyman Copeland Draper, by Larry Gara.—John Franklin Jameson, by David D. Van Tassel.—Robert Digges Wimberly Connor, by Hugh T. Lefler.—Henry Edwards Huntington, by John E. Pomfret.—John D. Rockefeller, Jr., by Fairfield Osborn.

Martin, Thomas P.   Early American interest in historical sources and archives. In American Library Association. Committee on Public Documents. Public documents, with archives and libraries. Papers presented at the 1937 conference of the American Library Association. Chicago, American Library Association, 1937. p. 228–232.

Matheson, William.   Seeking the rare, the important, the valuable: the Rare Book Division. In U.S. Library of Congress. Quarterly journal, v. 30, July 1973: 211–227.

Moore, Frederick W.   First report of the Conference of State and Local Historical Societies. In American Historical Association. Annual report. 1904. Washington, 1905. p. 219–234.

Morris, Richard B.   The current statesman's papers publication program: an appraisal from the point of view of the legal historian. American journal of legal history, v. 11, Apr. 1967: 95–106.

Newsome, Albert R.   Unprinted public archives of the post-colonial period: their availability. American historical review, v. 39, July 1934: 682–689.

O'Neill, James E.   European sources for American history in the Library of Congress. In U.S. Library of Congress. Quarterly journal, v. 24, July 1967: 152–157.

Owen, Thomas M.   State departments of archives and history. In American Historical Association. Annual report. 1904. Washington, 1905. p. 235–253.

Paltsits, Victor H.   An historical résumé of the Public Archives Commission from 1899 to 1921. In American Historical Association. Annual report. 1922. v. 1. Washington, 1926. p. 152–163.

Posner, Ernst. American state archives. Chicago, University of Chicago Press [1964] xiv, 397 p.

Putnam, Herbert. The relation of the national library to historical research in the United States. *In* American Historical Association. Annual report. 1901. v. 1. Washington, 1902. p. 113–129.

Ristow, Walter W. Maps of the American Revolution; a preliminary survey. *In* U.S. *Library of Congress.* Quarterly journal, v. 28, July 1971: 196–215.

Rundell, Walter. In pursuit of American history; research and training in the United States. Norman, University of Oklahoma Press [1970] xv, 445 p.

Schellenberg, Theodore R. The management of archives. New York, Columbia University Press, 1965. xvi, 383 p. (Columbia University studies in library service, v. 14)

———Modern archives: principles and techniques. [Chicago] University of Chicago Press [1956] xv, 247 p.

Shelley, Fred. Ebenezer Hazard: America's first historical editor. William and Mary quarterly, 3d ser., v. 12, Jan. 1955: 44–73.

———The interest of J. Franklin Jameson in the National Archives, 1908–1934. American archivist, v. 12, Apr. 1949: 99–130.

———Manuscripts in the Library of Congress, 1800–1900. American archivist, v. 11, Jan. 1948: 3–19.

Sparks, Jared. Materials for American history. North American review, v. 23, Oct. 1826: 275–294.

Stephenson, Richard W. Maps from the Peter Force collection. *In* U.S. *Library of Congress.* Quarterly journal, v. 30, July 1973: 183–204.

Tebbel, John W. A history of book publishing in the United States. New York, R. R. Bowker Co. [1972] +

  Contents: v. 1. The creation of an industry, 1630–1865.—v. 2. The expansion of an industry, 1865–1919.—

Thwaites, Reuben G. Bibliographical activities of historical societies of the United States. *In* Bibliographical Society of America. Papers. v. 1, pt. 2; 1906/7. New York, 1907. p. 140–145.

———Report of the Committee on Methods of Organization and Work on the Part of State and Local Historical Societies. *In* American Historical Association. Annual report. 1905. v. 1. Washington, 1906. p. 281–325.

———State-supported historical societies and their functions. *In* American Historical Association. Annual report. 1897. Washington, 1898. p. 61–71.

Tyler, Moses C. The neglect and destruction of historical materials in this country. *In* American Historical Association. Annual report. v. 2; 1886. New York, 1888. p. 20–22.

U.S. Office of Education. Public libraries in the United States of America; their history, condition, and management. Special report, Department of the Interior, Bureau of Education. pt. 1. Washington, Govt. Print. Off., 1876. xxxv, 1187 p.

Van Tassel, David D. Recording America's past; an interpretation of the development of historical studies in America, 1607–1884. [Chicago] University of Chicago Press [1960] xii, 222 p.

Whitehill, Walter M. Independent historical societies; an enquiry into their research and publication functions and their financial future. [Boston] Boston Athenaeum; distributed by Harvard University Press, 1962. xviii, 593 p.

Winsor, Justin. Manuscript sources of American history; the conspicuous collections extant. *In* American Historical Association. Annual report. v. 3; 1887. New York, 1889. p. 9–27.

Wish, Harvey. The American historian; a social-intellectual history of the writing of the American past. New York, Oxford University Press, 1960. viii, 366 p.

INDEX

THE INDEX CONTAINS nearly 100,000 references and cross references to the 14,810 numbered entries in the text. Entries 1–9306 appear in volume 1, while entries 9307–14810 are in volume 2. Given the time and staff available, it was not possible to compile a full subject index. The index is limited, for the most part, to proper names (authors, editors, compilers, historical figures, corporate bodies, geographic locations, etc.) with descriptive subdivisions. As a convenient guide, however, the headings for more than 700 subject units in the table of contents are integrated, with their inclusive entry numbers, into the alphabetical arrangement. The greatest number of descriptive subdivisions appear under the names of countries, colonies and states, campaigns and battles, and major Revolutionary era figures such as Benjamin Franklin, George III, Thomas Jefferson, William Pitt, and George Washington. Insofar as practical, descriptive subdivisions conform to the terms found in *Library of Congress Subject Headings*, 9th ed. (1980. 2 v.) Certain usages, however, are unique to this bibliography.

Monographs, articles, and sources that primarily treat the colonies under the British Empire are indexed under "Great Britain—colonies" or, whenever possible, under the specific region or colony. Works dealing with the states after 1776, however, are indexed under "United States" or the specific region or state. Entry numbers for works on western lands or territories throughout the period 1763–89 appear under such headings as Mississippi Valley, Ohio Valley, Old Northwest, Old Southwest, The West, or the names of states that were later formed in those areas.

Entry numbers 12673–14810 for Chapter 12, Biographies and Personal Primary Sources, are treated somewhat differently in the index because each entry also contains a biographical headnote. These headnotes include two sets of terms: first, geographic locations in which subjects were born, lived significant parts of their lives, and died; and second, descriptive terms related primarily to the subjects' occupations, the elective or appointive offices they held, and their military or naval service (e.g., lawyers, merchants, planters, assemblymen, judges, Revolutionary offi-

cers). The latter terms treat the subjects' activities through 1789, but not later. To avoid the duplication of hundreds of entries under the names of both colonies and states, *all* headnote index references to figures who lived on the North American mainland from New Hampshire to Georgia are listed under the names of the states. This is intended primarily to keep together under the same subdivisions references to persons who were active throughout the Revolutionary period, even though it causes some anomalies. For example, the Chapter 12 headnote entry number for Cadwallader Colden (1688–1776) appears in subdivisions under New York (State) rather than New York (Colony). Of course, this and other references to Colden throughout the bibliography appear under his name. The adjective "Revolutionary" is used in Chapter 12 headnotes and in subdivisions in the index to refer to service during the war. Descriptive subdivisions such as "Revolutionary officers" or "Revolutionary surgeons" listed in the index under each of the states refer to individuals who served in a Continental, militia, or irregular military unit between 1775 and 1783. No attempt was made to differentiate among the types of service. Terms such as "military officer" or "soldier," however, refer to service in the British or U.S. armies or the colonial or state militias before or after the war. For French participants who served in the Continental Army, listings are to be found under "France—Revolutionary officers" and "Continental Army—French officers." Officers in the French Army who fought in the Revolutionary War, on the other hand, are listed under "France—Armée—officers." Other foreign participants are listed under the names of their countries.

Finally, entry numbers in Chapters 1–11 identify a single main title. In Chapter 12, however, entry numbers represent from one to several hundred titles. Numbers for major figures such as John Adams and George Washington, therefore, are in **boldface** type to remind the user that substantially more bibliographic information about the subject may be found under that entry number than those from other chapters.

Crawford, John G., 4271
Crawford, Mary C., 1474
Crawford, Richard A., 13635, 13807
Crawford, Sidney, 14255
Crawford, Valentine, letters, George
   Washington, 14674
Crawford, Walter F., 9810
Crawford, William
   about, 6529–34, 12894, 13136
   letters, George Washington, 14674
Crawford Co., Pa., about, 2015
Crawford's Indian Campaign (1782),
   6529–34, 12894
Crecraft, Earl W., 6543
Creech, Margaret, 11049
Creecy, John H., ed., 2230
Creek Indians
   about, 4840, 4902, 4912–13, 4972
   and Alexander McGillivray, 4913, 4939,
     13916
   and William Augustus Bowles, 12890
   impending war with Choctaws, 3686
   Moravian missions, 5169
   relations
     Americans, 4918, 5277, 5283, 5287
     British, 3632, 4892, 4912
     Spanish, 5179, 5243
   Rock Island Conference (1789), 5283
   trading routes, 5110
Creigh, Alfred, 2091
Creighton, Donald G., 3404
Cremin, Lawrence A., 11632
Cresap, Michael, 13137
   about, 13869
Cresap, Thomas, about, 4814, 13138,
   13693
Cresson, Anne H., 13374
Cresson, William P., 13163, 14025
Cresswell, Nicholas, 5694, 13139
   about, 11326
Creswell, John, 7436
Creutz, Gustav Philip, greve, 7823
Crèvecoeur, Michel Guillaume St. Jean
   de, called Saint John de Crèvecoeur,
   948, 1563, 5383, 10673, **13140**
   about, 8525, 8533, **13140**
   agrarian myth, 10174
   bibliography, 236
   nature writings, 12234
Cribbs, George A., 5339
Crick, Bernard R., ed., 548
Crime and Penology, 11033–40
Criminal Law, 10463–71
Cripe, Helen L. P., 13701
The Crisis, 2576, 3361
Crispin, Barbara, 2964
Crissey, Theron W., comp., 1719
Crist, Robert G., 5989–90, 13142, 14728
Critical period. *See* Confederation (1783–
   1789)
Crittenden, Charles Christopher, 1203,
   9856–58, 9921–23, 12158, 14020
   ed., 787
Crocker, Lester G., 8500
Crockett, Joseph, about, 13141
Crockett, Walter H., 1401, 5340, 7861,
   12701
   ed., 8913
Croft, Sir Herbert, supposed author, 3227

Crofut, Florence S. M., 1671
Croghan, George, 5482, 13142
   about, 4814, 4837, 4853, 13142
Croghan, William, about, 13143
Croghan Hall, 13142
Cromot Dubourg, Marie François Joseph
   Maxime, baron, 13144
Cronin, John W., 12681, 13701, 13944
Cronstedt, Carl Olof, 7823
Crooked Billet, Pa., Battle of (1778),
   6298, 6305, 6316
Cropper, John, about, 13145
Crosby, A. Morris, ed., 1563
Crosby, Alfred W., 9896
Crosby, Enoch, 13146
   about, 7772, 13146
Crosby, Gerda R., 2401, 2652
Crosby, Nathan, 11790
Crosby, Sylvester S., 282
Crosfield, George, ed., 13368
Cross, Arthur L., 4100
Cross, Francis E., 9897
Cross, Jack L., ed., 14205
Cross, Urieh, 5933
Crosskey, William W., 9462
Crouch, Mary, about, 10717
Crouch, Mary F., ed., 13008, 13530
Crouse, Maurice A., 4020, 13949, 13951
   ed., 13950–51
Crowe, Carol E., 13377
Crowe, Charles, 13943
Crowell, Edwin, 3551
Crowell, Robert, 1516
Crowhurst, R. P., 3532
Crowl, Philip A., 8731, 9171, 9648, 12598
Crowley, James E., 4508
Crowley, John E., 10240
Crowley, Thomas, 3269
Crown Point, N.Y.
   about, 1794
   capture of (1775), 5815, 5820
   fortifications, plans, 880
Crowther, George R., 166
Crowther, Simeon J., 4518, 9985
Crozier, William A., ed., 2238, 8047
Cruden, John, 8315, 9249
Cruger, Henry, 13147
   about, 2651, 13147
   manuscripts, 665
Cruger, John, manuscripts, 665
Cruger, John Harris, about, 6596
Cruickshank, Helen G., ed., 12795
Cruikshank, Ernest A., 575, 3405, 3506,
   6837, 8261, 12901, 12970, 14011,
   14498
   ed., 8262, 14351
Crum Elbow Precinct, N.Y., about, 1786
Crumb, Frederick W., 14257
Crump, Jesse P., 12871
Crump, Stuart F., 12926
Crumrine, Boyd, 10442
   ed., 5341
Cuba
   archives, 603
   slavery, 10304
Cuffe, Paul, about, 7828
Cugnac, Gaspar Jean Marie René, comte
   de, 6736
Cugnet, François Joseph, about, 13148

Cullen, Charles T., 14604
Cullen, Joseph P., 1258, 4185, 5818,
   5989, 6057, 6626, 6916, 13646, 13733
Cullen, Louis M., 2801, 2965
Cullen, Maurice R., 12094
Cullen, William, about, 11816
Cullum, George W., 6198, 7920, 14031
Culp, Ralph B., 12466
Culpeper Co., Va. County Court, 2212
Culper Ring, 7777
Culver, Francis B., 6599, 7580
   ed., 6130
Cumberland, Richard, 13149, 14353
   about, 8561, 13204
Cumberland, Robert W., 8263–64
Cumberland Association, 5052
   about, 5252
   See also Cumberland Compact (1780);
     Cumberland Settlements
Cumberland Compact (1780), 5086, 5610,
   13587
Cumberland Co., Me., about, 7901–2
Cumberland Co., N.J., about, 1887,
   1912, 4475–76
Cumberland Co., Pa., 10149
   about, 1996, 2019–20
   residents, 12898
Cumberland Co., Vt., about, 1406, 8901,
   8907
Cumberland Co., Va.
   Committee of Safety, 9179
   residents, 13001
Cumberland District, Court and
   Government of Notables, Minutes of
   Cumberland Court, 5610
Cumberland River, 5564
Cumberland Settlements, 4941, 5586–87,
   5591
Cumberland Valley, Pa.
   about, 14452
   fortifications, 5376
Cumming, William P., 930–31
Cummings, Abbott L., 13919
   comp., 12061
Cummings, Charles F., ed., 14497
Cummings, Ephraim C., 14601
Cummings, Henry, about, 11507
Cummings, Hubertis M., 1979, 4509,
   6136, 11016, 14058, 14190
Cummings, J. E., 6544
Cummins, D. Duane, 8667
Cunat, Charles M., 14523
Cundall, Frank, 41, 378, 3732, 12821
Cuneo, John R., 6199, 6838, 14329
Cunliffe, Marcus, 1095, 1144, 6957, 14674
   ed., 14697
Cunningham, Anne R., ed., 14343
Cunningham, Charles E., 5195, 13267
Cunningham, George G., 12654
Cunningham, Henry W., 14287
   ed., 5971
Cunningham, John T., 1048
Cunningham, Letitia, 13150
Cunningham, Peter, 2464
   ed., 14654
Cunningham, Timothy, 2493
Cunningham, Wilbur M., ed., 12961
Cunningham, William, 2769
Cunnington, Cecil Willett, 12049–50

George III (continued)
  charges against, in Declaration of
      Independence, 4176, 4195, 4201
  constitution, 2470, 2472, 2481, 2484
  foreign relations, Spain, 8561
  historiography, 2400–2401, 2407, 2409,
     2413, 2417
  in New York press, 4081
  in Pennsylvania press, 4077
  in *Virginia Gazette,* 4628
  ministers, 2482
  political caricature, 2928
  political character, 2664
  political nicknames, 2934
  political opposition, 2662
  political parties, 2688, 2692, 2696, 2708,
     2717–18
  position in British politics, 2404
  proclamations, bibliography, 410
  regency crisis, 2655, 2670
  statue in New York City, 4468
  wife, 13030
George IV, King of Great Britain, 13424
  about, 2587, 13424
George, Elijah, comp., 645
George, John A., 8231
George, Mary Dorothy G., 143, 2857–59,
  2928, 3343
  ed., 2856
George Washington Bicentennial
  Commission, 12456
George Washington University,
  Washington, D.C., 337
Georgetown, Md., about, 2156, 12755
  Catholic college, 11430
  inns, taverns, etc., 12546
  printing, 403
  tobacco trade, 9868
Georgetown Co., S.C., about, 2349
Georgia (Colony)
  about, 1236, 4560, 4764
  Afro-Americans, 10312
  agents, 3092, 4787
    Franklin, Benjamin, 3077, 13381
    Knox, William, 13776
  agriculture, 10214, 10233
  architecture, 12416
  archives, 800–801
  charters, 3769–70, 3778
  church and state, 11190, 11198
  church history, 11198
  Church of England, 11179, 11198,
    11272
  cities and towns, planning, 10655
  clergy, 11202
  Council, 2360, 4785–86
    presidents, 13507, 13509
  courts, 10434
  education, 11672
  expansion, 4797
  General Assembly, Commons House of
    Assembly, 2361, 4787
    about, 4558
    power of appointment, 4798
    procedure, 4794
    publications, bibliography, 414
    speaker, 4790
  general histories, 4791–4800
  German language, 10649

Georgia (Colony) (continued)
  Governor, about, 3886, 4791
  Governor, 1760–1776 (Sir James
    Wright, Bart.), 14796
    about, 4791, 14796
  Governor, 1779–1782 (Sir James
    Wright, Bart.), 9281, 14796
    about, 9297, 14796
  Great Awakening, 11198, 11525
  Indian boundaries, 4854
  Indians, 4898
  islands, 4792
  land grants, 2389–90, 4763, 4792–93
  law, 10507
  Laws, statutes, etc., 2362, 4788–89
  livestock industry, 10215
  medicine, 11938–39
  mercantilism, 4800
  naval stores, 9990
  newspapers, 12166
  pharmacy, 11961
  plantation system, 10232
  politics and government, 4791, 4799,
    9295, 9297, 9300
    sources, 9281–82, 9290, 9292
  printing, 12162
  proposed college, 11809
  racial elements, 10296
  records, 2359
  registers of births, etc., 10868–69
  religious dissenters, 11179
  religious revivals, 11189
  Scotch-Irish immigration, 4797
  silk industry, 9953
  social life and customs, 10647, 10704
  sources, 4785–90
  Stamp Act (1765), 4022, 4035, 4087
  women, 10704
Georgia
  agriculture, 10214
  Anglican clergymen, James Seymour,
    14409
  architecture, 12416
  archives, 800–801
  assemblymen
    Baldwin, Abraham, 12756
    Few, William, 13336
    Gwinnett, Button, 13507
    Habersham, Joseph, 13511
    Jones, Noble Wymberley, 13735
    McIntosh, George, 13920
    Telfair, Edward, 14546
    Treutlen, John Adam, 14591
  Banishment Act (1778), 8247
  Baptist clergymen, John Thomas, 14558
  bibliography, 123–24, 380
  biography, 12646–47
  boundaries, North Carolina, 2272
  British invasion (1778–1779), 6568,
    6578, 6582
  carpenters, Peter Tondee, 14580
  Cherokee Indians, 6423
  church and state, 11198
  clergymen, 2385
  coastal islands, 2387–88
  colonizers, James Oglethorpe, 14123
  confiscated estates, 9292
  Constitution, ratification, 9684–85

Georgia (continued)
  constitution (1777)
    about, 2380, 8846, 9294, 9306
    text, 9292
  constitution (1789), 2380, 9306
  constitutional history, 2379–80
  constitutions, 2382
  Continental Line, 2d Regt. (1776–1780),
    6570
  Convention (1787–1788), 9685
    about, 9684
  Council of Safety (1775–1777), 9282,
    9292
  councilors
    Bryan, Jonathan, 12938
    Habersham, James, 13509
    Mackay, James, 13923
    Stokes, Anthony, 14506
  Creek Indian leaders, Alexander
    McGillivray, 13916
  Creek Indians, 4912, 5287
    trade, 5110
  delegates
    Constitutional Convention (1787)
      Baldwin, Abraham, 12756
      Few, William, 13336
      Pierce, William, 9427, 9434
    Continental Congress, 8756, 9302
      Baldwin, Abraham, 12756
      Bulloch, Archibald, 12948
      Few, William, 13336
      Gwinnett, Button, 13507
      Habersham, John, 13510
      Hall, Lyman, 13519
      Jones, Noble Wymberley, 13735
      Langworthy, Edward, 13801
      Telfair, Edward, 14546
      Walton, George, 14656
      Zulby, John Joachim, 14810
  Dept. of Archives and History, 8097
  description and travel, gazetteers, 849
  dictionary and encyclopedia, 2368
  economic conditions, 9770
  educators, Abraham Baldwin, 12756
  Executive Council (1777–1789), 4786,
    9283–84, 9292
  frontier, 5541
  frontiersmen, Elijah Clarke, 13057
  genealogy, 12646
    bibliography, 171
  general histories, 2366–84, 9294–9306
  geography, 2114
  Governor, 1776–1777 (Archibald
    Bulloch), about, 12948
  Governor, 1777–1778 (John Adam
    Treutlen), about, 14591
  Governor, 1779 (George Walton),
    about, 14656
  Governor, 1782–1783 (John Martin),
    9285
  Governor, 1783–1784 (Lyman Hall),
    about, 13519
  Governor, 1785–1786 (Samuel Elbert),
    9286
    about, 13281
  Governor, 1786–1787 (Edward Telfair),
    9287
    about, 14546

Pennsylvania (continued)

Hand, Edward, 13534
Henry, William, 13595
Irvine, William, 13685
Matlack, Timothy, 13985
Mifflin, Thomas, 14015
Montgomery, John, 14029
Morris, Cadwalader, 14051
Morris, Robert, 14058
Peters, Richard, 14191
Reed, Joseph, 14284
Rhoads, Samuel, 14291
Roberdeau, Daniel, 14306
Rush, Benjamin, 14348
St. Clair, Arthur, 14355
Searle, James, 14391
Smith, James, 14451
Smith, Thomas, 14466
Taylor, George, 14540
Willing, Thomas, 14759
Wilson, James, 14763
description and travel, 5353, 13140,
    13156, 13209, 13285, 13303, 13580,
    13672, 14069, 14180, 14382, 14431,
    14459, 14468, 14631
    maps, 1963
divorce, 10694
donation lands, 1963
economic conditions, 5369
editors, Eleazer Oswald, 14134
education, 11658, 11662–63
educators
    Ewing, John, 13313
    Kearsley, John, 13750
    Kunze, Johann Christoph, 13783
    McMillan, John, 13932
    Redman, John, 14279
    Smith, Robert, 14452
    Smith, William, 14467
election returns, 1964
emigration and immigration, 10250,
    10252, 10813
    Germans, 1994, 10944
    Mennonites, 1993
English settlers, 10912
entomologists, Frederick Valentine
    Melsheimer, 14003
Episcopal bishops, William White,
    14725
Episcopal Church, music, 11565
Episcopal clergymen, John Andrews,
    12726
explorers
    Bartram, William, 12797
    Biddle, Nicholas, 12845
    Hutchins, Thomas, 13672
farmers, 12510
    Bull, John, 12946
    Burrows, John, 12965
    Crawford, William, 13136
    Dock, Christopher, 13222
    Findley, William, 13340
    Flick, Gerlach Paul, 13357
    Gallatin, Albert, 13402
    Hatfield, John, 13563
    Hiltzheimer, Jacob, 13607
    Juncken, Henry, 13745
    Land, Robert, 13792
    Leeth, John, 13826

Pennsylvania (continued)

Logan, George, 13868
Marshall, Edward, 13966
Morgan, George, 14046
Porter, Andrew, 14225
Potter, James, 14228
Potts, James, 14230
Reed, Jacob, 14281
Robb, Robert, 14305
Seely, Sylvanus, 14395
Thomson, John, 14565
Van Campen, Moses, 14617
ferrykeepers, John Siegfried, 14433
financiers
    Morris, Robert, 14058
    Nicholson, John, 14097
French, 11032
frontier, 5385, 5392, 5409
frontier and pioneer life, 5328, 5333,
    5352, 5363, 5382, 5397–98, 5406
frontier economy, 5101
frontier forts, 4967, 5335, 5376, 5384,
    6393
frontier policy, 5339
frontier settlements, 5334, 5357
frontier trade, 5112
frontier warfare, 6411
    Loyalists, 6836
frontiersmen
    Antes, John Henry, 12729
    Cook, Edward, 13105
    Croghan, George, 13142
    Franklin, Roswell, 13384
    Jennings, John, 13707
    King, Robert, 13765
    Marshall, Edward, 13966
    Quick, Thomas, 14257
    Smith, James, 14452
fur traders, John Leeth, 13826
genealogy, sources, 179, 10812
General Assembly, 9094
    about, 9104–5, 9109, 9119, 9121
    Constitution, ratifying convention,
        9633
    journals, bibliography, 9133
    military land grants, 7041
general histories, 1974–2000, 9103–41
geographers, Thomas Hutchins, 13672
geographical names, 919
German agriculture, 10919, 10926
German-language imprints,
    bibliography, 302
German press, 10934, 10942, 12146
German Reformed clergymen
    Helffrich, John Henry, 13585
    Schlatter, Michael, 14380
German settlement, bibliography, 298
Germans, 11492, 14380
glass manufacturers, Henry William
    Stiegel, 14499
government publications, bibliography,
    440
governor
    about, 12630
    papers, 1968
Governor, 1777–1778 (Thomas
    Wharton), about, 14712
Governor, 1782–1785 (John Dickinson),
    about, 9128, 13217

Pennsylvania (continued)

gunsmiths, William Henry, 13595
High Court of Errors and Appeals,
    about, 13038, 14532
higher education, 11733, 11784
historians, Robert Proud, 14250
historic houses, 4967
Historical and Museum Commission,
    97–98, 721–23
    Division of Public Records, 723–24
    Research and Publication Division,
        723
Historical Commission, 99
Historical Society, 716, 923, 9643
    about, 477
    Library, 424
house decoration, 12058
household consumption, 12510
importers
    Bryan, George, 12937
    Conyngham, David Hayfield, 13103
    Morris, Cadwalader, 14051
imprints, bibliography, 383, 395, 398
indentured servants, 10250, 10252
Indian agents
    Morgan, George, 14046
    Peters, Richard, 14190
Indian fighters
    Brady, Samuel, 12898
    Harmar, Josiah, 13543
    Quick, Thomas, 14257
Indian Forts Commission, 5376
Indian missionaries, David Zeisberger,
    14808
Indian negotiators
    Connolly, John, 13099
    Croghan, George, 13142
    Douglass, Ephraim, 13230
    Francis, Turbutt, 13378
    Gibson, John, 13431
    Johnson, Jacob, 13714
    Trent, William, 14590
Indian towns, 4967–68
Indian trade, 5108
Indian traders
    Elliott, Matthew, 13290
    Findley, John, 13339
    Morgan, George, 14046
    Trent, William, 14590
Indian wars, 2178, 4928, 5363, 5382,
    5408
Indians, 4910, 4935, 4953, 4966–67,
    4982, 5112, 5339, 5349, 5363, 5376,
    14808
    scalp bounties, 4987
inflation, 10101–2
innkeepers
    Antes, John Henry, 12729
    Nicholas, Samuel, 14094
inns, taverns, etc., 12545
insurance brokers, John Reynell, 14290
internal improvements, 9744
inventors
    Collin, Nicholas, 13092
    Fitch, John, 13348
    Franklin, Benjamin, 13381
    Gilpin, Thomas, 13438
    Henry, William, 13595
iron industry and trade, 9967–69, 9980

Advisory Committee

Dessiné par le Barbier Peintre du Roi.

REDDITION DE L'ARMÉ